D3

Alan

With love from Joe

November 1987

The Churches and the Third Reich
Volume One

KLAUS SCHOLDER

The Churches and the Third Reich

VOLUME ONE

Preliminary History and the
Time of Illusions
1918-1934

SCM PRESS LTD

Translated by John Bowden from the German
Die Kirchen und das Dritte Reich.
Band 1. Vorgeschichte und Zeit der Illusionen, 1918-1934,
first published 1977 by Verlag Ullstein,
Frankfurt am Main, second edition 1986.

British Library Cataloguing in Publication Data

Scholder, Klaus
    The churches and the Third Reich.
    Vol. 1: Preliminary history and the time
    of illusions, 1918–1934.
    1. Germany—Church history—20th century
    I. Title II. Die Kirchen und das Dritte
    Reich. *English*
    274.3′0822   BR856

    ISBN 0–334–01922–2

First British edition 1987
published in Great Britain by SCM Press Ltd
26-30 Tottenham Road, London N1 4BZ

Phototypeset by Input Typesetting Ltd
and printed in Great Britain by
Richard Clay Ltd, Bungay, Suffolk

Contents

Glossary

Translations of works on this subject and from this period inevitably bring with them some notorious problems of terminology and there is by no means unanimity over their solution. This glossary simply explains some basic terms which have been left in German, or gives reasons for particular renderings.

Evangelischer Bund Independent, anti-Roman Catholic Protestant association

Evangelical   The German 'Evangelische' does not have the same connotations as the English 'Evangelical', and often the best translation for it is 'Protestant'. However, in German there is also an adjective 'Protestantische'; in addition, there are times when to translate 'Evangelische' as 'Protestant' is not quite right: 'Evangelische' is a much more positive word, not least because of its close link with 'Evangelium', 'gospel'

Führer,
Führerprinzip   Leader, leadership principle

Gauleiter   Leader of a region (Gau, plural Gaue), next below the Reichsleiter

Gemeinde   Literally 'community'; at times it can mean 'congregation', at times be equivalent to 'parish', or even 'church'. None of these three renderings can be used throughout. For the sake of consistency it is therefore always rendered 'community'

Gleichschaltung   Co-ordination. The process of bringing the economic, political and social life of Germany under National Socialist control

Kirchenausschuss   Executive committee of the Kirchenbund

Kirchenaustritt   The movement to leave the churches

Kirchenbund   Federal organization of the Protestant Landeskirchen

Kirchenbundesamt   Kirchenbund office

Kirchenbundesrat   Federal committee of the Kirchenbund

Kreisleiter	Leader of a district (Kreis), junior to the Gauleiter (q.v.)
Kulturkampf	Conflict between church and state
Kultusminister (Kultusministerium)	Minister (Ministry) with responsibility for church and school affairs
Land	German state or province
Landeskirche	Church of a Land
Landtag	Parliament of a Land
Oberkirchenrat	Central administrative authority of the Landeskirche
Ortsgruppenleiter	Leader of a local group (a suburb or a few villages), junior to the Kreisleiter (q.v.)
Reichsleiter	Reich leader, the senior members of the National Socialist hierarchy under Hitler
Volk,völkisch	The German word Volk, its adjective, and various compound words in which it is an element, notably Volkskirche, are virtually untranslatable into English. It has overtones of nation and race as well as 'people', and was a key term in the racialist ideology of the Third Reich. It is therefore often left untranslated, particularly in National Socialist contexts. However, to leave it untranslated all the time would give it too much stress in certain passages, e.g. statements by church leaders, so it is also translated quite frequently. In that case the rendering is always 'people', for the sake of clarity.

Foreword

The preliminary work for this book goes back almost ten years. During this time the Deutsche Forschungsgemeinschaft helped me to provide a broad basis of archive sources for the whole complex of questions. So my special thanks must go first of all to this exemplary organization for the advancement of learning.

This work on the archives has left a clear stamp on the book. Here I am thinking less of my discoveries, large and small, which alter the view of things held so far, although as the expert will notice, there are also plenty of these. As I worked on the archives, what seemed to me to be almost more important was the way in which I was penetrating into the world of day-to-day decisions, as these are to be found in the records. Of course only a fraction of these are incorporated directly into the book. But they determine the spirit of the whole work. For this kind of penetration makes it possible to see both the obvious and the unusual aspects of a period through the eyes of those involved.

As can also be seen from the list of the archives, my interests and reflections over these years was still primarily in the history of the Protestant church. Indeed, even now almost all research in this field has a confessional orientation. Contemporary Catholic church history and contemporary Protestant church history have almost no contact with each other.

In the course of working through the history of one territory – 'Baden im Kirchenkampf des Dritten Reiches' (1970) – it became clear to me, however, that the history of the two major churches belong much closer together than we have previously assumed. Germany is a country divided by confessions. This fact is part of the basic consciousness of both churches, and no church can escape it. Furthermore, it is also part of the fabric of German history. Of course it is still necessary to pursue confessionally orientated research into individual questions, and will remain so. But it is my firm conviction that in future anyone who intends to portray major events or circumstances must attempt to understand to a greater degree than before the history of both churches in Germany: where they come together and where they contrast.

It was a critical moment for me when this necessity gradually became clear, for additional study of the sources in the Catholic archives would have meant a further burden – of unforeseeable duration. At this point help arrived in the fact that since the middle of the 1960s a series of volumes of studies had been issued by the Catholic Academy in Bavaria which can scarcely have been equalled in contemporary history for comprehensiveness, wealth of data, and editorial quality. So in essentials, one can describe the source situation by saying that while the Protestant development will be presented in numerous sections based on unpublished material, on the Catholic side published sources are predominant. For Protestantism material had to be assembled; for Catholicism a collection was already available.

Of course the author cannot and should not conceal his own confession in an integrated portrayal of this kind. No one concerned with the church can seriously claim that he or she transcends the confessions. However, the fact that in this book comparatively more space is devoted to the Protestant development than to the Catholic is not to be attributed to the author's confession. The reason is rather that the history of the one Catholic church in Germany can be described in a more compact and therefore a shorter way than that of the twenty-eight Protestant Landeskirchen; and that all in all there was more chaos, confusion and therefore also more new reflection on the Protestant side than on the Catholic, so that here the description necessarily turned out to be more extensive. I hope that the substantive emphasis which I have given to the two churches is largely the same.

One striking result of this new approach is the way in which we are to understand Hitler's church policy. His basic concept, which Protestant and Catholic theologians have previously sought in vain along separate lines, emerges almost automatically as soon as one looks at both churches. It then becomes clear how Catholic Hitler was in his understanding of the church, and how naturally he carried this understanding over to the Protestant church. This was one reason, and perhaps the decisive one, why his Protestant church policy failed and the Protestant church itself disintegrated with it.

Moreover, a joint portrayal allows something which previously was possible only with difficulty: a comparison of the conduct of the two great Volkskirchen in Germany in an extreme situation. Here I would want to issue a warning against over-hasty generalizations and anachronistic approaches. It might seem natural to see the Protestant concentration round the confession as a model to be imitated today. This apparent parallel overlooks the fact that at that time the enemy was not 'pluralism' but rather a closed group with a specific concern to bring about a radical unification of the church. If the history of this era contains a warning for the Protestant church, then it lies above all in guarding against political enthusiasm, which then as now found its enthusiastic followers in Protestant theology and church.

This book certainly does not make edifying reading for either Protestant or Catholic Christians. Nowhere have I spared anything, but have named blindness and lies, arrogance, stupidity and opportunism for what they were – even in clerical garb, and speaking the language of the church. But I hope that no line of the book gives the impression that I wish to distance myself from the church. Truth may be painful for the church, but untruth is even more so. And I see no reason, in retrospect, not to echo what Karl Barth exclaimed to his fellow pastors at the high point of the confusion in the summer of 1933: 'No, one and all, within the church as she has borne us by means of the word, and within the incomparable sphere of our vocation, we must *abide*, or (if we have left it) *turn back* into the church and into the sphere of our vocation...'

A word about the size of the book. Some readers will ask how large the second volume will have to be if the prehistory and the first year take up so many pages. But this one year 1933 is so extraordinary a year that it is only comprehensible if we trace it through month by month, indeed where necessary week by week and day by day. By the end of this year, at all events as far as the churches were concerned, practically all the fundamental decisions had been made. Later developments are already prepared for here.

One cannot work on such a book and over so long a time without being obligated to many people. Librarians and archivists, colleagues and students have contributed much to its making, by advice, help, support, discussion and critique. My warmest thanks go out to all of them.

Tübingen, 10 July 1977   Klaus Scholder

PART ONE

The Churches in the Weimar Period

1

Between Yesterday and Tomorrow
(1918-1919)

The collapse of the Kaiser's empire also threw the two great churches in Germany into a deep crisis. Both had been nationalist, monarchist and loyal to the Kaiser. The flight of the Kaiser, the overthrow of the old ruling houses and the proclamation of the Republic came as an equal shock to both of them. Nevertheless, there was no mistaking the fact that 9 November 1918 meant different things for Protestantism and Catholicism.

First, as far as Protestantism was concerned, the revolution not only meant the end of its traditional legal order; the revolution also robbed it of its political support, endangered its economic foundations and spiritually was nothing less than a catastrophe.

The legal problem was there for all to see: the overthrow of the monarchy robbed German Protestantism of the buttresses of its church constitution. Since the days of the Reformation, for nearly four centuries, the rulers in the Protestant territories of the Reich had simultaneously been those responsible for governing the church. No matter how many changes this form of church government had undergone in the course of its long history, and no matter how formalized it had often become in its latter days, right down to November 1918 no significant decisions whatever relating to personnel or organization were made other than in the name of the ruler concerned. Of course the problems in this connection had been recognized for a long time. There was also agreement in principle throughout the church as to what had to be done with this church government which had suddenly become as it were homeless: it was to return into the hands of the church. But how this was to happen, that is, what agencies of the church should now exercise the authority of the church in practice and how these agencies were to be constituted were questions on which very different views existed among the various trends within German Protestantism. As soon became evident from the negotiations on the new church constitutions which immediately began everywhere, the legal problems alone posed very considerable difficulties.

No less significant was the conflict of basic dispositions which was bound up with this whole issue. The centuries of shared history had led special relationships to develop between many ruling houses and their Landeskirchen, extending far beyond the legal sphere, especially where – as for instance in Prussia – the ruling house traditionally declared itself for the church. The church prayer for the ruler appointed to be said every Sunday in the liturgy was an expression of this special relationship. Thus the Baden liturgy included the prayer: 'In thy grace rule over our Grand Duke and his entire house. Bless our Kaiser and all his household, and be the strong protection and shield of the German Reich and Volk.'[1] There was a similar prayer in Hessen: 'Fill the German Kaiser with thy Spirit, take under thy watchful care the Grand Duke and his house.'[2] But these very prayers now brought out the conflict in which the overthrow of the monarchy involved many ministers and church members. What were they to do now? On the one hand, necessity, common sense and obedience called for the recognition of the new authorities. On the other hand tacit abandonment of the prayer seemed like faithlessness and ingratitude to the authorities which had been overthrown, who now seemed more than ever in need of the intercession. Apparently only the Württemberg Landeskirche gave official orders that the ruler should continue to be remembered in a church prayer. Many pastors, especially in the older Prussian provinces, might have made a personal decision to do the same thing;[3] in other Landeskirchen the prayer was omitted, without this being a denial of their dependence.[4]

Naturally the same problem also existed on the Catholic side. But here the greater detachment of the Latin Mass to some degree toned down the sharpness of the conflict. Thus on 15 November the Archbishop of Munich, Michael von Faulhaber, recommended to the Bavarian bishops that they should 'incorporate uniformly in the Sunday mass another prayer in place of the royal prayer, to avoid making the omission of the old one all too evident.' For this he suggested an excerpt from the litany for All Saints: '*Versiculus: "Salvos fac servos tuos." Responsum: "Deus meus sperantes in te." Oratio: "Deus a quo sancta desideria..."*' However, Bishop Henle of Regensburg protested only two days later and declared that in his diocese the prayer for the king had not yet been abolished, and that he considered such action inopportune 'because after all we do not know how the wheel of time will go on turning'.[5]

Up to the end of 1919 we still find many signs of the old monarchist allegiance in both churches.[6] However, it was obvious that Protestantism had lost ever more. The opening speech at the Dresden Kirchentag is often cited in this connection. In fact it makes the link with the past impressively clear. 'The glory of the German imperial Reich, the dream of our fathers, the pride of every German is gone. With it have gone those lofty figures who supported German power, the ruler and the ruling house, whom we loved and honoured so deeply as standard-bearers of German greatness... We can do nothing else here but bear solemn witness to what rich blessings have issued from the previous close relations between state and church upon both state and church, and through both these upon the people and the fatherland. Moreover, we can do nothing else here but in deep grief bear solemn witness how the churches of our fatherland owe a deep debt of gratitude to the rulers who have been their patrons, together with their families, a debt which in many cases extends over a history of many centuries. This deeply felt gratitude will abide unforgotten among the Protestant people.'[7] However, as was also evident from the Kirchentag itself, this was to be seen less as a political declaration than as an attempt to express loyalty also towards the past in the 'moral conflict of opinion and responsibility'.[8]

In addition to the legal crisis which 9 November 1918 meant for the Protestant church, there was the political crisis. In contrast to German Catholicism

4

which in the Centre Party possessed reliable political representatives with parliamentary experience, Protestantism had no political grouping of its own on which it could depend. There were historical – and even more, theological – reasons for this. In the course of history German Protestantism had never needed its own party as long as the rulers who also governed the church were as a matter of course its political representatives. And where Protestantism had a Lutheran stamp, it would have found it difficult to provide theological justification for the foundation of a Protestant party, because the Lutheran doctrine of the two kingdoms in principle excluded this option. Thus after the overthrow of the monarchies, German Protestantism found itself without political representation, without the means of expressing its wishes and requirements directly in the political field – and this in a situation which made political action more imperative than ever before. For with the revolution those parties had come to control the state power from whose policies many church people expected at best a faithful separation of church and state and at worst a persecution of the church on the Russian pattern. Because it had virtually no contacts with the Social Democrats, the church saw itself as being apparently at the mercy of the political powers. Since in the first weeks after the revolution no more and no less than the existence of the church as an institution seemed to be at stake, it was natural to seek to represent Protestant interests directly, by founding a 'Protestant People's Party' or combining with the Centre Party in a 'Christian People's Party' which transcended confessional divisions. But all attempts of this kind which were made in November and December 1918 and in January 1919 came to grief.[9] German Protestantism had no alternative than to become involved in the existing political parties, though the socialist parties were *a priori* virtually excluded from consideration as a result of decades of mutual animosity. Without doubt this lack of any political representation of its own made the path of German Protestantism into the new era substantially more difficult. By contrast, the Centre Party eased the way for Catholicism.

Little was said about the economic crisis, which was feared in the church. It was nevertheless omnipresent. Julius Kaftan, Professor of Theology in Berlin and member of the Prussian Oberkirchenrat, reported to his brother in the middle of November: 'The Oberkirchenrat is meeting more frequently than ever... The next thing to affect us is of course the uncertainty of the financial situation. The clergy are naturally very anxious as to what is going to happen, and want guarantees which we cannot given them and indeed no one can give them. For even if everything goes as smoothly as can be and the planned National Assembly restores greater security, no one knows who may have taken control tomorrow or the day after and whether the Assembly will ever come into being as intended. It is as well to be prepared for anything...'[10] In fact all the Landeskirchen were financially dependent to a greater or less degree on the state, which provided considerable sums, especially for pastors' salaries and welfare. Thus in 1918 in Prussia this subsidy amounted to about 28 million marks; while this was only 0.22% of the state expenditure, it was more than half the church budget.[11] The separation of church and state in accordance with the principle that 'religion is a private matter', proclaimed immediately after the revolution in many German states and frequently connected with the declaration of an elimination of all government subsidies, could only throw the churches into total uncertainty about their financial future. Even if the radical resolutions were not implemented anywhere, real emergencies arose in a whole series of Landeskirchen because of reductions in state contributions combined with the progressive devaluation of the currency. In Brunswick, which along with Saxony was especially endangered, the quarterly income of a pastor in autumn 1922 did not even reach the level of the weekly wage of an unskilled labourer.[12]

The situation was therefore bad enough legally, politically and economically. But the heaviest burden was the catastrophe among the clergy. During the war the identification of the German cause with the will of God had reached such a height in German Protestantism that a German victory was made to seem virtually the fulfilment of divine righteousness. Consciousness of the superiority of the German spirit, German morality and piety to Western European civilization was so widespread, and the feeling of being involved in a just war of defence so general, that beyond the political and military catastrophe the defeat toppled the whole German Protestant world-view, which previously had scarcely been dented.

Ernst von Dryander, Court Preacher and Vice-President of the Prussian Oberkirchenrat, at that time seventy-one, had based his sermon in Berlin Cathedral at the opening of the famous 4 August 1914 session of the Reichstag on the text of Romans 8.31: 'If God be for us, who can stand against us?' 'Looking to the state which reared us,' he declared, 'to the fatherland, wherein lie the roots of our strength, we know that we are going into battle *for our culture against the uncultured, for German civilization against barbarism, for the free German personality bound to God against the instincts of the undisciplined masses...* And God will be with our just weapons. For German faith and German piety are intimately bound up with German civilization.'[13] The same convictions were to be found on the Catholic side, and deep down into the ranks of German social democracy.[14] But for German Protestantism they had a personal and special significance beyond that common to all Germans. To German Protestants more than all others this war seemed to be their war. Thomas Mann was one of those who had expressed this at the outbreak of war: 'Thus right from the beginning, I think, there was almost unanimous clarity that the spiritual roots of this war, which with all possible justice is called "the German war", lie in the native and historic "Protestantism" of Germany; that this war essentially represented a new outbreak – perhaps the most magnificent or, as some believed, the last – of the age-long German battle against the spirit of the West... as well as the battle of the Roman world against a stubborn Germany.'[15] The 'Spirit of 1914', so often conjured up then and later, was in truth the climax of a theology of history which manifested and expounded the ways of God with the German people.

German Protestantism had entered the war with this awareness, and with this awareness it had urged perseverance to the very end. On 2 October 1918, just three days before the German armistice offer to Wilson, the General Committee of the Evangelischer Bund had resolved on 'a new mobilization' of the Bund and told its three thousand main and subsidiary associations: 'Now the whole people must go to the barricades! The homeland must muster itself and strengthen the Front. Every channel which leads to the life of the people must now be used to save our fatherland from the destructive purpose of the enemy.'[16]

As a result of this stance and this consciousness, however, the collapse became a spiritual and theological problem of the first order. It is certainly no exaggeration to state that the unresolved question of the spiritual meaning of the defeat spelt doom for the Republic. The radical alternative to it could finally be established not least because the Republic was and remained an unsatisfactory answer to this question.

Even during the war and immediately after it a whole series of very pious or very free spirits managed to free themselves from the spell of this question. But for most of those who were and wished to remain German Protestants, the meaning of the whole situation remained dark and unintelligible. Johannes Schneider, the editor of the *Kirchliches Jahrbuch*, described their quite desperate perplexity immediately after the signing of the peace treaty: 'Where is the justice of God? The question torments thousands, including those who long ago recognized and criticized the inner decline of our people, its mammonism, its passion for pleasure, and who seek to find evidence of God's justice in the signs of the times. Are the others any better? Is not mammonism an import from America; and cold-hearted egoism England's dowry? And moral decline bound up with the insatiable virulence of France's vulgar style? Are we not seeing a triumph of lies and a success of vulgarity of a kind that was rare even in the darkest periods of history? Is Schiller's saying really true: "World history is judgment on the world"? In that case is not justice the judge?'[17] The basic mood of desperation which we keep encountering in the Weimar Republic, unmistakably in the years 1920-1923, and then to a diminishing degree, and increasing again from 1928 to the point of hopelessness, has one of its roots in these rhetorical questions, which tormented so many.

In view of this deep crisis, which proved so complex, it is surprising to find that German Protestantism in the first months after the collapse was in no sense without signs of hope and promise. That is true of its relationship to the new powers in the state as well as of discussion within the church.

The first official statements and proclamations after 9 November showed a church which, while above all expressing its anguish over the lost greatness and glory and anxiety for the future, nevertheless not only completely accepted the new circumstances but even called for loyal co-operation. Thus as early as 10 November the Prussian Oberkirchenrat issued a call to its congregations in which, while it spoke of the Kaiser and the Reich, 'who became precious and valuable to us in an incomparable history', and evoked 'bitterness and humiliation', 'poverty, deprivation, hunger and contempt', there was also a declaration that 'Germany is not lost and the gospel is not chained. The kingdom of Jesus Christ contains sustaining and saving power for the life of our people. Its citizens are duty bound and ready to serve in the earthly fatherland – and now to collaborate in fulfilling new tasks where it is necessary to support the established order. In this way our Evangelical Church seeks to stand as a Volkskirche at the centre of life today, even when outside supports might have collapsed.'[18] The Landeskonsistorium of the Evangelical Lutheran Landeskirche of Saxony put it even more clearly: 'According to God's Word it is our duty as Christians to take our stand on the basis of the new relationships, to preserve moderation and calm, to refrain from any rash judgment, and also not to stand aside and grumble, but to continue to co-operate loyally and willingly – as far as anyone can – for the good of our earthly fatherland.'[19] There is certainly no enthusiasm for the new situation in these and other similar statements, but rather a painful coming to terms with the inevitable. Moreover, some of the statements will have been put like this more with an eye to church politics than out of spiritual conviction. And finally, it would be wrong to see the sole aim of those November weeks as being the preservation of law and order, though in retrospect this problem can easily be underestimated.[20] In spite of these objections, it is still remarkable that the Protestant church did not begin the Weimar period with a politics of basic obstructionism, but rather with a summons to, and an offer of, co-operation.

The question whether this offer was only a concern of the church leadership or whether it also spoke at least for some of the pastors and communities, is hard to answer. That the church governments did not in fact stand utterly alone is indicated by a meeting to which the Pastors' Association invited all the pastors of Greater Berlin on 18 November 1918. Two to three hundred pastors came, amounting to about two-thirds of all the Berlin pastors then in office. The meeting elected a 'Pastors' Council' and passed with only three votes against a statement in which the pastors declared 'also to the new government' their readiness 'to co-operate in all social and humanitarian tasks'[21] in the spirit of the gospel of Jesus Christ. In what seems to be a response to this statement, the new Prussian government turned to the Protestant church several times in December 1918 with a request for help in safeguarding provisions, money, aid and jobs.[22]

The theological justification for this attitude on the part of the church lay in what Christians in Germany regarded as the central text on the doctrine of the state, the famous chapter 13 of the Epistle to the Romans: 'Let every person be subject to the governing authorities. For there is no authority except from God, and those that exist have been instituted by God.' In the calls for action, immediate or indirect reference was constantly made to these verses. And a representative of the 'Positive Union' in Prussia was only being consistent when he concluded, in an extremely conservative church journal: 'If formerly we were opponents of the revolution, today we are opponents of the counter-revolution – no matter from what side it may be planned.'[23]

Contrary to the widespread opinion that from the beginning Protestantism reacted to the new circumstances with inexorable hostility, many of the leading figures on the Protestant side argued resolutely for respect for the new situation and positive co-operation with it. In the 'Conclusion' to a volume of essays entitled *Revolution and Church. Towards a Reordering of the Church in Germany*, which appeared in March 1919, and with eighteen contributions by prominent Protestant and Catholic theologians, churchmen and journalists, gave a vivid portrayal of the various trends, one of the editors summarized the situation in this way: 'However, the Protestant church is no more required to celebrate the revolution totally as a liberating action than is the Catholic church. But even someone who holds it to be the most terrible misfortune in German history can, by reason of the circumstances it has created, consider it the God-given form of the development of a new Christian national life. What Karl Muth says from the Catholic side is also true for the Protestant: "Never yet has the church given its blessing to revolution, a violent overthrow which violates existing laws, as a means to social betterment; nor, however, when confronted with a completed revolution, has it approved the co-operation of its representatives in the intrigues of the vanquished to overturn a newly established government. The church is as much the bitter opponent of every counter-revolution as it is of every revolution." The revolutionary people's state may legitimately expect nothing more from the churches than that they recognize the order established by it, without examining its legal title. If there is eventually to be a beneficial co-operation between state and church in the new Germany, to begin with, neither can demand more of the other than justice.'[24]

However, even more than the development of the relationship between church and state, the discussion within the church gave cause for hope. Just as in the state, overnight the liberal wing of the Protestant church (although numerically it was very much smaller) was given the task of developing guidelines for a far-reaching church reform, and at the same time fighting for its implementation.[25] The various plans for reform met up with a widespread discontent with the old church, dominated by the rulers and the authorities, a discontent which in fact had been growing for a long time. Although German Protestantism could scarcely have rid itself of church government by local rulers of its own accord, now that these rulers had been overthrown, the great opportunity for a new beginning was perceived everywhere. That was the case even with many otherwise strongly conservative spirits. There was basic agreement that in future the church must be built 'from the bottom upwards'. However, the course to be adopted was disputed. The representatives of liberal reform argued that the church people themselves should decide the future shape of the church by primary elections, thus bringing the principles of democracy directly into play, even in the church. By contrast the church officials and above all the elected synods argued that they should themselves supervise the transition into the new age. However, we must be careful not to oversimplify at this point. For example, the Prussian church leadership opted for primary elections, while the Prussian provincial synods decisively rejected them.[26] Not all of those who were against primary elections adopted this position for political reasons. Conversely, the liberal advocates of democracy in the church were quite alarmed when, during summer 1919, the first primary elections in Baden and Württemberg resulted in immense conservative majorities.[27] In fact, in one way or another, in the end the conservative forces in the church retained the upper hand.

But to begin with, in the first weeks after the revolution, the future still seemed open, a future dominated by the slogan 'Free Evangelical Volkskirche'.[28] One of its liveliest and most influential representatives was Martin Rade, by then already over sixty, Professor of Theology at Marburg and editor of the *Christliche Welt*, an 'Evangelical community journal for the educated of all classes', which since its foundation in 1886 had been the most important organ of church theological liberalism in Germany. In the issue of 28 November 1918, under the heading 'Announcements', it contained an appeal for the creation of 'Volkskirche councils' along with 'Guidelines' for governing the councils. Point 3 ran: 'The Evangelical Church is founded on the religious equality of all its members (priesthood of all believers including the laity).' Point 5 declared: 'By taking its destiny into its own hands, from now on it will create for itself its own organs (presbyteries, synods, church government, pastors) by free elections.' In conclusion, Point 7 urged the union of all German Protestantism: 'We need as a permanent foundation for our constitutional life one unified national synod, evolving from general, direct and secret elections by registered church members (both men and women who have reached their twenty-first birthday).'[29] As Point 5 makes most clear, this was an attempt radically to change the constitution and order of the Protestant church from being a church controlled by the authorities and governed by local rulers with a bureaucratic church leadership into a Volkskirche in which all offices and positions of leadership should be bestowed by a free vote of the members. 'It is now or never,' wrote Rade, 'for the pastors' church to be turned into a church of the laity, the church of the consistory to be turned into a church of the community.' '*Vexilla regis prodeunt!* The banners of our king go forward. However astonishingly things may develop out there in the world, however much our poor German nation may tremble in every joint, for us it is a time of hope, a time to build, to work: it is a bad year for idle hands.'[30] *Die Christliche Welt* was able before long to publish nearly 100 signatures of prominent figures, including many with a high reputation in theology and the church.

While Rade's idea of church councils aimed at imitating the political revolution within the church, the Volkskirchenbund founded on 18 November 1918 by the Göttingen professor Arthur Titius aimed at mobilizing the voices of Protestant Christians to enlist them against outside pressure and to advance genuine reforms from within, as the name of the alliance indicated. This proved remarkably successful. The Volkskirchenbünde movement, which soon came to exist in many places, penetrated even the social democrats. When the various Volkskirchenbünde had a rally in Berlin on 29 April 1919, their membership had already reached over half a million.[31] However, by this point the movement had already passed its peak. Summing up the situation in March of that year Otto Dibelius could rightly conclude that 'the most important achievement for church life in the first months after the revolution' was not something like 'a new leadership of communities and churches as a result of free volkskirchliche organizations... but on the contrary a revitalization of the organized church, independent of the volkskirchliche movement in its many forms.'[32] That was to say, quite bluntly, that the revolution in the church had not taken place.

It is naturally difficult to evaluate the real balance of power in the Protestant church around the end of 1918. But all things considered, one can perhaps say that the forces which were open to the future and wanted a real renewal of the church were at least as strong as those whose goal was to leave everything the way it was, as far as that was possible. A large number of 'don't knows' were waiting to see how things might develop in the state and in the church. Certain political events in the last weeks of 1918 were of considerable and ultimately decisive importance for their decision.

The transition from the old to the new was both easier and more difficult for German Catholicism. To be sure, Catholic Germany, too, largely felt the loss of the war and the end of the Kaiser's empire to be a catastrophe – and for innumerable faithful Catholics this remained an open wound. But at the same time on the Catholic side there were important forces which were precisely those needed to carry Catholicism over the crisis of the empire. In contrast to the Protestant churches, in its legal status the Catholic Church remained largely undisturbed by the revolution. In Germany the concept of the papacy emerged strengthened from the war. As distinct from Protestantism, Catholic self-awareness had never been quite so closely tied to imperial Germany, so that as a spiritual catastrophe the defeat had less impact on what was distinctively Catholic. And finally, Catholicism in Germany possessed a well-tried political party, with leaders who had introduced a new trend as early as 1917. But there were also problems here. For the Catholic Party suddenly found itself in the circumstances obliged to endorse a cause which Catholicism as a whole neither desired nor was able to approve unequivocally. The tensions and difficulties which arose from this lasted throughout the whole period of the Republic, and in 1933 contributed to the end of political Catholicism in Germany.

When war broke out in August 1914, the deep wounds which the Kulturkampf had left in German Catholicism had just healed. The thoroughly difficult and laborious process 'of the definitive integration of Catholics into national life and the state created by the founding of the Reich',[33] 'reconciliation with the "Reich nation"',[34] had reached a point which not only made possible full and uninhibited support of the war but even encouraged it. At the 1887 Katholikentag for the first time the threefold salute to the Pope was also accompanied with a salute to the Kaiser; and this was more than mere coincidence.[35] No minority can withstand for ever the call of the times, when this call is as strong as was the growing self-awareness of imperial Germany. And the German Catholics, to whom about one-third of the German populace belonged, were no exception. So they gradually became assimilated to the new era and at the same time adapted themselves 'to the mentality and methods of German politics in the age of imperialism'.[36]

However, the final, complete recognition of Catholics in the Reich was still to come. There was still evidence of the old Protestant judgments and prejudices against the 'enemies of the Reich' and 'Ultramontanists', against Catholic hypocrisy and unscientific narrowness. So the German Catholics found the War a deliverance, because it promised to overcome all this and bring relief at last.[37] They felt that the much-praised remark of the Kaiser on 13 July 1914, 'I no longer recognize any parties, only Germans', applied especially to them.[38] Now the time of trial was at hand, in which they could demonstrate that no one could surpass them in loyalty to the Kaiser and the Reich. Bishop Michael von Faulhaber of Speyer, after 1917 Archbishop of Munich and Freising, and thus one of the central figures of the Catholic church in Germany, was doubtless speaking for the great majority of German Catholics when he declared to the departing troops in 1914: 'The beacon of enthusiasm which today shines out from the German mountains was not kindled by hatred of other peoples and rulers but by love of Kaiser and king, of fatherland and homeland, and by faith in our just cause.'[39] So, too, the war sermons of both sides, in their 'hurrah' patriotism, their determine to hold out and their faith in the 'moral justification and significance of the war' were in no way less vigorous in tone.[40] And the annexionist spirit, that fatal conviction of the conqueror's rights, was supported on the Catholic side just as much as on the Protestant.[41] Other no less expansive visions of the future could be associated with the hope of the victory of the Central Powers. The future political community of the victorious powers of Germany and Austria would be able 'with sixty-three million Catholics over

11

against forty-three million Protestants and six million of other faiths, to give post-war Europe a new, Catholic countenance'.[42]

A joint pastoral letter for All Saints Tide 1917, in which all twenty-seven archbishops and bishops of the Reich joined, shows how thoroughly conservative and monarchistic German Catholicism remained, despite everything. The slogan which was to point the way forward for all dioceses in this 'portentous hour' was Jesus' 'majestic command': 'Render unto Caesar the things that are Caesar's; and unto God the things that are God's' (Matt.22.21). The pastoral letter left no doubt as to what this text was to mean in the fourth year of the War: 'With unshaken faithfulness and a readiness for sacrifice, we therefore stand by those who rule us by God's grace: the Kaiser and the rulers of the Länder. In the course of a development lasting down the centuries, God has given the sceptre into their hand... The War has not loosened the ancient holy covenant in Germany between people and ruler, but in shared suffering and fighting has welded it even tighter together.' The Catholic people, the episcopate vowed, would 'reject anything that might result in an attack on our ruling houses and our monarchist state constitution'. At the same time the pastoral letter repeated the old demands of German Catholicism: 'Catholic schools for Catholic children', 'freedom and independence... for Catholic charities', 'more freedom for our Catholic orders!' Finally, there was vigorous rejection of a slogan which just one year later was to dominate the field everywhere: the separation of church and state. 'No greater misfortune could befall us,' went the German bishops' view, 'than to have so longed-for a peace spoiled both by strife between state and church and by a total alienation and separation between them.'[43]

The significance of this last great pastoral letter before the revolution for the political premises and aims of the Catholic church in Germany can scarcely be exaggerated. It formed a landmark by which the episcopate and clergy still took their bearings when the revolution had completely changed political conditions.

That in spite of this close link with the monarchy the revolution was far from inflicting on the Catholic church the disruption which it meant for Protestantism was something for which the church was indebted, among other things, to the papacy. This was for two reasons.

Traditionally, German Catholicism was particularly close to Rome. With good reason Pius X, in August 1914, a few days before his death, had called the German Catholics 'the best Catholics in the world'.[44] And under his successor, Benedict XV, this special tie continued to remain unbroken. By the end of 1916 the collection for Peter's Pence, for which in the middle of the war Matthias Erzberger, a Centre Party delegate, had appealed to Catholic Germany, had produced twelve million marks – more than all other nations together had contributed for the needs of the Curia.[45] In addition, around the world esteem for the Holy See had grown during the war.[46] So after the revolution it was natural that the German Catholics should turn more than ever to Rome, where in the midst of a major revolution they perceived something durable and permanent. When the new Archbishop of Cologne, Karl Joseph Schulte, led the first German pilgrimage to Rome in October 1920, he expressed these feelings eloquently on presenting the Germans to the Pope: 'All eyes in Germany turn in trust to the Vatican, where in contrast to so many vanished dynasties the papacy is maintained unshaken, and has shown itself to be a rock of faith, a centre of unity, a guardian of order, an apostle of peace and love.'[47] This superiority of the Curia, which also considered itself untouched by contemporary revolutions, no doubt strengthened the self-awareness of German Catholics and at the same time the esteem and influence of the Holy See in Germany. Finally, another expression of this special relationship was the action of Benedict XV in summer 1917 of sending to Germany the most gifted young diplomat the Curia then had at its disposal: the forty-one-year old Eugenio Pacelli. At the time, however, no one could yet have had any inkling what importance this decision was to have. In fact, first as Nuncio in Munich and Berlin, then as Cardinal and Secretary of State in Rome, and finally as Pope Pius XII, Pacelli became increasingly the key figure of the German church.[48]

Nor was it just the fact that the papacy was unshaken which helped the German church to emerge from the revolution: specific papal doctrines now also took on new significance. In view of the difficult situation of the Catholic church in republican France, in the encyclical *Diuturnum illud* (1881), Leo XIII had for the first time intimated that democracy also offered 'an ecclesiastically tolerable form of government'.[49] Four years later, the famous encyclical *Immortale Dei* (1885) gave a basic definition of the freedom of the church over against every form of government. The ruling power, so it said, 'was not necessarily bound (*necessario copulatus*) to any form of government'; it could 'assume one form or another so long as this effectively furthered the common well-being and prosperity'.[50] Now the same situation had developed in Germany as in France: hence the teachings of Leo XIII had a surprising relevance for German Catholics. However difficult it might be to work out in detail, in principle a way of co-operation within the republic had been opened up for German Catholicism. In fact, from the very first the Centre Party assumed political co-responsibility for the new direction in which the nation now had to go.[51]

Finally, no less important was the Catholic self-awareness which had developed since the turn of the century. The founding of the journal *Hochland* in 1903 was both a sign of this change and an impetus towards it. Its aim was 'a renewed encounter between culture and church in Germany'[52] and the editor, Karl Muth, in fact came substantially closer to this aim during the first decade of its existence. The war speeded up this development. In the collapse of the spiritual value systems of the old Europe, the door seemed to have been reopened for Catholicism. More than any other writer, the philosopher Max Scheler formulated this 'unique opportunity for a new orientation of the living generations of the earth, and of Europeans'. For some years during and after the war Scheler was certainly by far the most significant interpreter of this mood of change in Catholic Germany.[53] In a study which appeared in 1915 entitled *Sociological Reorientation and the Task of German Catholics after the War*, he summed up the new Catholic self-awareness in a single, long, breathless sentence. No one in Germany since the age of Romanticism had given such a description of the distinctiveness of Catholicism: 'Not the content of our faith – which we may not demand – but the Catholic style of life and culture, the special form of Catholic humanity, its greater generosity, gentleness, softness, peacefulness, let us say quietly also its gentler tempo in response to work and ambition, so often criticized even within our own ranks as "inferiority"; its more devoted joy in the world and its serene harmony; its more concrete realism over against the abstract

13

notions of order and unity; its innocence more rooted in the people, and its more trustful and less complicated way of living resolutely by living traditions; always to love what has grown up more than what has been made, however cleverly – these and other less rationally definable features of the nature of Catholicism cannot be allowed to stand as before, practically invisible, alongside representative Germanhood and its spirit; rather, they must truly be woven into it, so that this may be evident particularly in international relationships and to those who govern neighbouring countries.'[54] Every single comparative in this statement not only implied a restitution of the special value of the Catholic life-style and culture but at the same time contained a criticism of Protestantism, which had more and more conclusively shaped the intellectual and political direction of Germany since the beginning of the nineteenth century.

A communication which Matthias Erzberger sent at the end of 1917 to Archbishop Faulhaber of Munich made it clear that these convictions were by no means limited to a small circle of intellectuals. Erzberger, a Centre Party deputy, then forty-two and of the same generation as Scheler, was the dominant figure in his party and a man of enormous political influence. Clearly Erzberger was also convinced, under the spell of the great Catholic mood of revival, that the end of the terrible World War would be and must be followed by 'a great Catholic renaissance'. For only Catholicism could answer the hunger for a new foundation for law, towards which humanity would stream. Social Democracy was incapable of it; the Conservatives revered 'the most manifest brutality'. Protestantism was 'totally shattered by the War as a power to seize mind and heart'. 'It died,' Erzberger went on with a reference to the 400th anniversary of the Wittenberg Theses (1917), 'in the year of its jubilee.' To accomplish this new task of German Catholicism Erzberger proposed to the Archbishop of Munich nothing less than the creation of a centre 'for culture and the intellect – for literature, theatre and so on, a centre which would influence and direct all the separate organizations and provide intellectual leadership; the centre of the great Catholic renaissance'.[55] In his view the only possible location was Munich. Unrealistic though this proposal was, given the contradictions in Catholicism, it was nevertheless typical of the new Catholic revival and the hopes that were bound up with it.

When Erzberger wrote this letter he had already shifted the direction of Centre Party politics from a peace of victory to a peace of compromise. So the idea of a 'Catholic renaissance' was no longer necessarily tied to German victory but could demonstrate its significance and its strengths even in defeat.

In those November days of 1918, during which a world in Germany went under, Protestantism had little by which it could take its bearings. The revolution made it homeless – in the church, and both intellectually and politically. Only later did renewal in the church and a theological revival begin. Catholicism, by contrast, though also hard hit by events, had an unshaken church with the papacy at its head; it had hopes of a Catholic renaissance; and finally, it had a political party that went to work without hesitation, and also began to represent its interests in the new circumstances.

In fact the Centre Party took its stand on the often-quoted 'foundation of the new circumstances' remarkably quickly. Only now did the significance of the new coalition with the Social Democrats which Erzberger had established in the

14

Reichstag in 1917 become completely clear. For the 1917 decision now showed the Party the way forward. It meant joining with the Social Democrats in taking responsibility for the government in order to exclude the radical forces and emphasize as vigorously as possible the bourgeois and Christian-Catholic dimension. Even if this in fact came about more through political necessity than through conviction,[56] nevertheless there emerged here the beginnings of a stability which then, as the 'Weimar coalition', was in fact to carry the young republic through its first struggles. Thus as early as 10 November two representatives of the Centre Party joined the Social Democrats in forming the new provisional government of the Land of Baden. Shortly afterwards similar steps were taken in Württemberg and in Hessen.[57]

However, the major decisions had to be taken in Berlin. In the Reich as in Prussia, since 9 November power had lain in the hands of socialist governments composed of radical independents and moderate majority socialists. It was therefore extremely important for the Centre to break the socialist majorities as soon as possible by means of general elections and by co-operating with the main-line socialists to bring the Christian, bourgeois and democratic elements into play. At Erzberger's insistence, on 15 November a general secretariat of the Centre Party was set up in Berlin, under the leadership of his long-standing colleague Maximilian Pfeiffer, and for the first time in the history of the party this took in hand centralized preparations for the impending elections.[58]

At the same time a comprehensive and partly controversial debate on the party programme began. It was principally concerned with the questions whether the Centre Party should reconstruct itself as a large, Christian, popular party transcending confessions, and what new political goals the Party should inscribe on its banners.[59] Here, too, there were different groups: left-wing Republicans, a strong conservative wing and a large silent majority still waiting to see what the new era might bring forth; and here, too, much still remained open in these first weeks, before socialist church policy in Prussia was to set the church on a strictly anti-socialist course.

The contradiction between the two faces of the November revolution in Germany – one the USPD concern for dictatorship by councils and the other the way towards a social and democratic people's state sought by the majority socialists – was nowhere more evident than in the staffing of the Prussian Kultusministerium.[60] As is known, the rivalry between the two parties in what for the moment was the supreme body of the revolutionary movement, the executive council of the revolutionary authorities in Berlin, led to a double occupancy of all Prussian ministries. Each department was headed by USPD and MSPD nominees in parallel, of equal rank and acting jointly. Thus on 12 November two men who were fundamentally different in background, character and conviction took over the 'Ministry for Cultural and Educational Affairs'; from 15 November it was called the 'Ministry for Science, Art and Public Education'.[61] The MSPD nominee, Konrad Haenisch, naturally also advocated the basic principles of the SPD in church policy: religion as a private affair, the separation of church and state and no religion in schools. However, during the War he had shown himself to have some understanding of Christianity and in November 1917 had publicly expressed his respect for Christian culture and ethics in the Prussian House of Deputies.[62] By contrast, the appointment of the

USPD representative Adolf Hoffmann could only be seen by the churches as the most forthright declaration of war. Hoffmann, at that time sixty, a man of a marked proletarian stamp, full of Berlin wit and repartee, had been the most popular figure in the Berlin Kirchenaustritt movement at the turn of the century, for whose cause he had agitated at numerous mass rallies. A speech he had given in 1892, on 'The Ten Commandments and the Owner Class', which was regularly reprinted down to the 1920s, in which with great political skill he exposed the Ten Commandments as a tool of the ruling class, had earned him the nickname 'Ten Commandments Hoffmann'. Hoffmann was so critical of the churches that even when he was right he could not fail to arouse opposition among even the most well-disposed Christian audience, and could only confirm the blackest prejudices of those less well-disposed – who were by far the majority.[63] It was this man who, on 12 November, along with Haenisch, took over responsibility for church policy in Prussia. And although he was in office only six weeks – at the beginning of January 1919 he left the government along with the other Independents – this short period was enough to destroy almost all the beginnings of a co-operation between the Social Democrats and the churches, not only in the revolutionary phase itself but even more in later years. Adolf Hoffmann became a symbol of the radical animosity of the left wing towards the church, which contributed substantially to driving Christian voters into the arms of the right wing.

Among the political decisions relating to the church which Hoffmann made during his short time in office, three in particular aroused attention and caused offence far beyond the churches. Hoffmann made these decisions, although the Council of People's Deputies had expressly referred all matters of principle to the future National Assembly that was to provide a constitution. He justified the decisions by revolutionary right, convinced of their necessity and protected by the power of the Berlin Central Council of Workers' and Soldiers' Councils, which he knew to be behind him on such matters.[64]

The first decision dated from 16 November. At a conference of the clergy division of the Ministry, Hoffmann declared that the separation of state and church should be carried through 'by decree without delay'. The state subsidies which had previously been provided for the churches were to be eliminated 'at the latest by 1 April 1919'.[65] Although this declaration was not published, on 19 November the Centre Party paper *Germania* gave an approximate summary. Its effect was devastating. Even Martin Rade saw here the intent 'of an action so terrible that it can only be compared with the inexorable demands of our enemies in the Armistice...'[66] Those very people on the church side who stood for a separation of state and church had to watch everything that they had hoped to accomplish by free agreements between both partners now being shattered by the irresponsible recklessness of this programme.

The 'Law on Facilitating Departure from the Church and Jewish Synagogue Communities', promulgated on 13 December, which made it substantially easier to leave the church, was understandably the occasion for lively church criticism, especially since there had been no previous discussions with the churches.[67]

But by far the greatest protest was unleashed by a decree of 19 November which abolished religious instruction as a regular subject in most of the schools of Prussia and did away with the Christian character of the schools. Given

Hoffmann's personality, the declaration that 'only ill will' could 'misinterpret such a step taken in the name of freedom of religion and conscience as a diminution of freedom of religion',[68] was quite incredible, especially as the statements of the socialist Ministers of Education in Saxony, Bavaria and Württemberg showed 'that in substance they shared Hoffmann's stand for rapid and open action in the matter of church separation'.[69] Claimed by the church as no less than the abolition of religious instruction – which was hardly a mirepresentation of its intent – the November decree began to mobilize Christian parents in a quite unexpected way. Placatory statements by Haenisch had no effect; not even the formal suspension of the decree on 28 December could stem the tide of protest.

The rigid separatist policy of the provisional Socialist governments at first provoked the resistance of the church administrations.[70] This resistance was all the more vigorous since the legal foundation of this policy was in fact questionable. In almost identical terms the Protestant Oberkirchenrat and the Catholic episcopacy protested in Prussia. The Protestants declared: 'In the name of the Evangelical Church of the Old Provinces of Prussia we formally and solemnly protest against such measures. We refuse to accept that circumstances regulated by law can be changed by other than legal enactments; they certainly cannot be changed by the decrees of a provisional government.'[71] A pastoral letter from the Prussian episcopate stated: 'Hence we raise our voices loudly and solemnly before the whole world, and in all our names, in the names of all the Catholics of Prussia, we resist the plan to separate church and state in Prussia.' Whereas the Protestant Oberkirchenrat still spoke of negotiations, the Catholic bishops declared outright: 'We Catholics of Prussia will in no circumstances and at no price surrender and approve the decree.' The Catholic protest was far harsher and more basic. The pastoral letter called the separation 'injustice and outrage against God the Lord', and 'a bitter wrong against the church and believers', referring in this connection to 'a state without God, without religion', and of 'schools without God and without revelation'.[72] The expression 'a state without God', born in the Kulturkampf mood of the first weeks, thereafter became the great reservation that church circles in both communions had about the young republic.

However, not only did the church leaderships react similarly; Catholics and Protestants drew closer to one another on this basis. Even the Evangelischer Bund, always dominated by a resolute, unshakeable enmity towards Catholics, for some weeks forgot its slogans and declared itself ready 'to go a long way with those of other beliefs, especially with our Catholic allies, in defending religious values'.[73] An 'Interconfesional Committee' was founded with the well-known Berlin Protestant New Testament scholar Adolf Deissmann as chairman. His representative in this post, the Catholic Centre Party deputy Martin Fassbender, made the united front evident in an election appeal for his party. It read: 'With hand on heart we may ask: what are all the controversies between the Christian religious communities which come down to us from the time of the Reformation, important though the individual doctrines may be to each of their adherents, in comparison to the abyss which separates us from – Adolf Hoffmann?'[74]

The depth of the outrage, even in Berlin, which seldom got very excited over church affairs, was demonstrated by a rally that took place on New Year's Day

1919 in the Busch Circus and was directed exclusively against the church and educational policy of the Socialists. In spite of the icy cold, at the close of the rally 60,000 made a protest march to the Prussian Kultusministerium. It was probably the first time that such a large crowd had joined together in singing the Catholic Te Deum and Luther's hymn 'Ein feste Burg ist unser Gott'.[75]

The issue of the church and schools in fact played a surprising role in the election struggle over the National Assembly. The Protestant side, which had previously paid little attention to elections, felt compelled to take an unambiguous stand against the Socialist policy of separation, and to recommend the election of non-Socialist parties (which of course meant those on the right wing).[76] However, on the Catholic side, which was in any case committed to the Centre Party, bishops, clergy and press now closed ranks quite emphatically against the election of Social Democrats and supported the Catholic party.[77]

The 19 January 1919 elections brought a first decision. The churches had succeeded in preventing the dreaded Socialist majority. But in the process the store of common interest had been almost exhausted again. For the results of the election seemed to produce very different situations for the two confessions. The votes of German Protestantism were mainly split. Despite all the warnings, a large number of Protestant voters had voted for the SPD, which throughout the Republic continued to draw its firmest support from among the predominantly Protestant voters.[78] Protestantism could have drawn its own conclusions and sought an agreement with the Social Democrats, as was repeatedly recommended during those years.[79] But apparently the mistrust on both sides could not be overcome. So for the most part church leaders took the opposite tack and sought their salvation in strengthening the right wing.[80]

The situation for Catholicism looked quite different. The Centre Party had been able to hold its voters in spite of the revolutionary situation, and with 19.7% of the votes had again become the second strongest party after the SPD – as it already had been in the old imperial Reichstag. However, the role which thus fell to the party was not comparable to that at the time of the Kaiser's Reich. Compelled by the pressures of the day to enter into a coalition with the Social Democrats, the Centre Party depended for its future upon whether the SPD would succeed in convincing itself and the church of the rightness of this decision. But it was here that the inevitable problems arose. How could a Christian Catholic party honourably join forces with another party which the church saw as the incarnation of godlessness and enmity to the church? The Centre Party was unable to resolve this dilemma throughout the Weimar era, and the National Socialists knew what they were doing when later they directed their propaganda at this very point.

Though after the election the cultural-political themes at first disappeared from the headlines, the agitation in no way subsided. Because the National Assembly now had to make a final decision about the future of schools, on 29 January 1919 the Vertrauensrat, the joint committee set up by the Prussian Oberkirchenrat in November 1918, decided to circulate 'a mass petition to the National Assembly for the preservation of the Christian character of schools'. The text read: 'We the undersigned adult members of the Evangelical Church urge that in the future as in the past our youth should receive an education based on the foundation of Christianity which does not run contrary to Christian education and morality.'[81] The petition became a success which surprised those who started it and their opponents alike, and is without parallel in German parliamentary history. When the collection of signatures was officially closed on 14 June, nearly 6.9 million had been obtained, which in the following weeks increased to just on 7 million.[82] So of the approximately 20 million Protestant voters who had cast their votes on 19 January 1919 more than one third had taken a clear stand on this question.[83] The government could easily work out that there were many Social Democratic voters among them.

There is no doubt that these events proved a heavy burden on the relationship of both churches to the Social Democrats – and thus on the power of the young Republic to come to a decision. Neither church recovered from the shock of the Hoffmann era before the end of the Republic.[84] From then on, at every step its effects were evident in church pronouncements. The consequences were incalculable.

In the summer of 1919 the well-known specialist in church law, Karl Rieker of Erlangen, had expressed his opinion *On the Reconstruction of the Constitution of the Protestant Church in Germany*, in the process declaring 'that the separation of church and state need not necessarily mean the de-Christianizing of the government, its departure from Christian principles'. 'For the church is not the only vehicle of Christianity, and a state which has made the care of the lower classes of the nation one of its chief tasks, and is pervaded by the thought that one member suffers all members suffer with it, cannot be described as un-Christian simply because it has separated itself from the church.'[85] In January 1920 Wilhelm von Pechmann, President of the Land synod of Bavaria and later of the German Evangelical Kirchentag, one of the most important laymen in the Protestant church, took up this phrase.[86] 'However, it is not just for that reason,' he thought, 'but all the more for other reasons, above all because the new state has received its beginning, stamp and goal from a political party whose atheistic and anti-clerical bias cannot seriously be doubted or disputed.'[87]

At the same time, too, the same problem led to vigorous disputes in German Catholicism. The battle was sparked off by the principle formulated in Article 1 of the new national constitution: 'The power of government derives from the people.' While the Centre Party vigorously defended this phrase, and indeed the whole constitution, for which the party substantially shared responsibility, the Benedictine Augustin Galen stated that this principle was 'diametrically opposed to Catholic teaching, indeed to Christian teaching generally'. For in truth, he continued, 'the power of government has its source not in the people but in God. Article 1 is therefore misleading and untrue; it robs God of the honour to which he is entitled as the only true authority – such action may rightly be called sacrilegious.'[88] The *Kirchliches Handbuch für das katholische Deutschland*, like the *Kirchliches Jahrbuch* on the Protestant side in conservative hands, attempted a careful assessment of the various attitudes and as a result came to a conclusion that could not and would not reject dissociation from the Republic. Vicar General Rosenberg of Paderborn wrote on the contemporary situation: 'Of course any Catholic who thinks it necessary to condemn the stance of the Centre Party on Article 1 and other articles of the new constitution will not immediately want to condemn the whole work of the Centre Party but, with the bishops, will recognize with gratitude that much of the original draft was

19

improved, and much added which does justice to the principles of the church. That could not have happened without the co-operation of the Centre Party. But the fact remains that in broad circles of German Catholicism there is pain and regret that when confronted with a constitution which, in von Lüninck's words, is "infused through and through with anti-Christian spirit", the members of the Centre Party delegation did not emphasize the Christian standpoint more clearly and decisively.'[89]

In the Republic both churches became formally correct partners of the republican authorities. But at root there remained an ineradicable mistrust of the 'constitution without God' and the 'state without principles', and the fear remained that if only it had the power the left wing might some day finish what Adolf Hoffmann had begun.

2

The New Orientation of the Protestant Landeskirchen (1919-1930)

The church history of the Weimar period shows one clear winner on the Protestant side: the Landeskirchen. While German Protestantism was without question deeply affected by the political collapse and its result, events turned out to the advantage of the Landeskirchen in almost every respect.

This apparent contradiction is explained by the peculiar legal and institutional division of German Protestantism. Granted, in nineteenth-century Germany it had become customary to speak of one Evangelical Church, or also, if the focus was more on the common intellectual and political history, of 'Evangelical Germany' or simply of 'German Protestantism'. Legally and institutionally, however, these concepts corresponded only to a sum of individual, independent churches, the so-called Landeskirchen, which were extraordinarily diverse in origin, size and constitution. The tension between the interests of individual Landeskirchen and the interests of Protestantism as a whole must be seen as one of the basic facts of modern German church history. Without an awareness of this, the developments of the twentieth century remain largely unintelligible.

The origin of the Landeskirchen lies in the early years of the Reformation, when the disintegration of the old church order called urgently for a new church authority. This authority was taken over and established by the local rulers. At a very early stage this was made into a legal title, the *ius reformandi*, which gave these rulers unlimited power to control and order religious affairs within their Länder. Because there was no common Protestant church law to match canon law on the Catholic side, each individual Protestant territory could develop its own church order. In this way an abundance of individual Landeskirchen grew up, i.e. churches whose boundaries coincided with the boundaries of the ruler of their Land. For about two and a half centuries this coincidence of Land government and Landeskirche remained unchallenged in principle within the territories of the Reich, though there were some important exceptions. The rigorous redrawing of the map of Germany at the beginning of the nineteenth century for the first time brought about a major readjustment. In the course of these changes the Landeskirchen emerged in essentially the form in which we find them at the beginning of the twentieth century.

The political restructuring of Germany in the Napoleonic period changed the centuries-old system in three main respects: territorial, legal and confessional.

The thirty-eight sovereign German states which were left at the end of the Congress of Vienna were formed from a profusion of once-independent territories along with their churches. Public interest demanded that the larger among them should integrate the newly acquired territories politically as quickly as possible. This also involved consolidating the various Landeskirchen in new unified Landeskirchen. This was accomplished, though sometimes with long delays and severe difficulties. For example the communities and churches in the provinces of Rhineland and Westphalia, which Prussia had reconstituted from acquisitions at the Congress of Vienna, raised such vigorous opposition to the adoption by their new ruler of the system of control of the church by the territorial authority that after long negotiations they were given their own order, based more on synods: the 1835 Rhineland-Westphalia Church Order, which later was often imitated elsewhere.

Dating from this time there was a Landeskirche in Prussia with a common head, though it had different structures for the eastern and western provinces. Nevertheless the territorial integration was so successful in these decades, and proved to be so enduring, that the territorial churches erected in this period for the most part survived all the storms of the nineteenth and twentieth centuries. Right up to the middle of the present century the map of the division of Germany according to Landeskirchen still in the main reflected territorial arrangements deriving from the Congress of Vienna!

The legal rearrangement of the old system was necessitated by the fact that one of its presuppositions, namely the coincidence of Land government and Landeskirche, no longer obtained within a whole series of new German states. Thus Bavaria, which used to be purely Catholic, acquired Lutheran subjects amounting to around one third of its population when it gained territories in Franconia; conversely, Lutheran Württemberg acquired the same proportion of Catholic citizens in Upper Swabia. This compelled the states to adopt a confessional neutrality and parity if they wished to avoid permanent religious strife – a course which the political thought of the Enlightenment had already indicated. But confessional neutrality and parity were possible only if the close link between church and state was loosened, and the churches were accorded a certain legal and constitutional independence from the state.

This loosening of the relationship between church and state and the independence of the Landeskirchen was in fact a nineteenth-century tendency, a tendency which was expressed very differently in the different German Länder, but which was more or less marked in most of them.

Politically speaking, the tendency found its most important expression in the draft constitution for the Paulskirche of 27 December 1848, which for the first time called for a basic separation of church and state in Germany. Some of the basic principles formulated here were later included word for word in the constitution of the Weimar state.[1]

Although the 1848 revolution collapsed, it was not without effect on the new constitutions. Thus the revised Prussian constitution of 31 January 1850 not only guaranteed in exemplary fashion 'the freedom of religious confessions of faith' and the independence of public and civil rights from confessions, but also specified in Article 15, which was soon to be much cited and often the centre of attention: 'The Evangelical and Roman Catholic Churches, like every other religious society, define and govern their affairs independently...'[2] This did not mean the separation of church and state but rather their clear distinction in law and in fact. Of course there were no longer 'state churches', but the state remained Christian and showed this through a special obligation to care for and supervise all Christian churches in its territory.[3]

The relaxation of the relationship between church and state and the gradual gaining of independence by the Landeskirchen also, of course, called for a change in the church constitutions. This took place on two fronts. First, special authorities were created to govern the church in the name of the local ruler. They were called 'Oberkirchenrat', as from 1850 in Prussia; elsewhere names like 'Landeskonsistorium' or 'Oberkonsistorium' were used. These authorities very quickly developed their own style of government, imitating that of the state authorities – a church bureaucracy of indisputable effectiveness, which to an increasing extent determined the character of the Landeskirchen. It was these authorities which in the critical situation of 1918-1919 maintained control and were able to strengthen the position of the Landeskirchen decisively.

By contrast, while the second decisive change in the constitution, namely the establishment of synods, received incommensurably greater publicity in the church and in politics, it had very little practical effectiveness. In the call for the people of the church to be involved in its leadership by means of synods, theological and political themes were intertwined. Theologically the issue was to bring about a basic Reformation understanding, according to which a church is built from its communities, i.e. from below upwards, and not from above downwards, as in purely episcopal or consistorial churches. Politically, the issue was the establishment of the constitutional principle in the church as well. Subsequently the synods related to the church government of the local ruler and his authorities rather like parliament to a monarchist régime. It has never become quite clear which principle – the theological or the political – was in fact pursued in the establishment of synods during the nineteenth century.[4]

After the Palatinate (1818) and Baden (1821) had pioneered the establishment of synodical bodies, the rules which the 1835 Rhineland-Westphalia Church Order set up for the western provinces of Prussia was particularly important for subsequent development in other Landeskirchen also.[5] Thereafter synods appeared everywhere alongside consistories (i.e. the church authorities) – an arrangement which understandably did not allow much self-awareness to develop in the synods. When the famous church historian Albert Hauck summed up the situation in 1907, he did not find it very attractive: 'We must not deprecate what the synods have achieved for the territorial churches during the years of their existence. Nevertheless we would be hardly wrong in judging that they have only partially fulfilled the high hopes which were set on their introduction. It must be granted that too much was expected of the new church constitution: no constitutional structure can bring a thing to life. But that is not the whole explanation. It seems to me undeniable that our synods are corporations with very little executive competence. Their very limited authority, their infrequent sessions (four, five, at most six times a year), their overly large membership, the cumbersome structures – imitating Parliament – within which they function, and the superfluous formality with which the sessions are surrounded are all impediments. If more effective synods are wanted, they will have to be given greater freedom of movement; they will have to be changed from machineries of control to instruments of church self-government.'[6] Some of this picture changed after 1918; in other respects it applies to the present day.

Finally, mention must also be made of the confessional changes which ensued in the old system of Landeskirchen in the course of the political reconstruction of Germany, and which were the third essential mark of the new era. As is well known, the period of the Reformation provided two very different movements in theology and the church, the Lutherans and the Reformed. Both movements had created churches in Germany, albeit on very different scales, the Reformed chiefly in the west and north-west of the Reich, the Lutherans in central Germany, the north and the east. After more than two centuries during which there had been no church fellowship between the two trends, the eighteenth century relaxed the rigidly opposed positions. Pietism and the Enlightenment pushed the dogmatic differences into the background and the possibility of a union of the two trends within one church came into view. However, it took political changes to set things in motion. Given the necessity of integrating larger or smaller Reformed areas, from 1817 unions of the two trends in into one church were introduced: in Prussia, but also in Nassau, Baden and the Palatinate, all in different ways. The new churches which thus came into being were called 'United Churches' or 'Union Churches'. However, for various reasons it was impossible to establish unions in all parts of Germany. The movement got stuck as it were at the half-way point, with the result that church relations became even more complicated, rather than simpler, as had been planned. For the Union Movement ultimately resulted in a new type or church, the United Church, which came into being alongside the Lutheran and Reformed Churches. This was all the more problematical because during the nineteenth century, contrary to all expectations, the confessional principle vigorously gained new ground as a result of the Neo-Lutheran movement. Consequently the Lutheran churches showed themselves increasingly less ready to enter into closer church fellowship with United churches.

During the nineteenth century the joint effect of these three lines of development – the territorial, the state- and church-constitutional, and the confessional – gave a powerful boost to the autonomy of the Landeskirchen and their self-awareness. The New Church Order of the Prussian Church, necessitated by the 1866 annexations, is impressive evidence of this trend. Whereas the annexed states of Schleswig-Holstein, Hanover, Kurhessen, Nassau and Frankfurt-am-Main were incorporated into the Prussian provincial administration without delay, the Landeskirchen of these territories protested tenaciously and successfully against a parallel incorporation into the Prussian Landeskirche.[7] This was especially true of the Hanover Landeskirche, which displayed all the characteristics of the new age. It had been formed with difficulty after 1814 within the borders of the new kingdom out of a series of independent churches, and in the process had received a decisively Lutheran self-awareness; in literally its last hour it had been given its own synodical-consistorial church constitution.[8] Not least on the basis of the church independence guaranteed in the Prussian charter, which had been given legal expression in the new constitution, the Lutheran Landeskirche of Hanover resolutely opposed amalgamation with the United Landeskirche of Prussia. The only course for the Prussian régime, which in the face of the general upheaval wanted at all costs to avoid violence in this tricky area, was to concede church independence within the Prussian constitution to Hanover – and with it also to Kurhessen, Nassau, Frankfurt-am-Main and Schleswig-Holstein. Accordingly these Landeskirchen were not put under the Protestant Oberkirchenrat in Berlin as provinces of the Prussian church. Rather, as independent provincial churches with their own consistories they were put directly under the supervision of the Kultusministerium. In fact these churches were held together only by the church administrations set up by local rulers and Prussian law relating to the churches; otherwise in status and self-understanding they remained independent Landeskirchen.

It is essential to know all this prehistory in order to understand the reactions prompted by November 1918. For hardly had the government of churches by local rulers been abandoned, and it had become clear that the new governments intended to bring about the separation of church and state, than a concern among the Landeskirchen for autonomy and separation took firm hold. Here the decisive role was played by the church authorities. Where a Landeskirche had a common authority it held together, even if – as in Prussia with its western and eastern provinces – it had to withstand tremendous tensions. At this juncture the Evangelical Oberkirchenrat in Berlin saw to it that the tendencies towards autonomy in the individual church provinces did not predominate. By contrast, wherever there was an independent church authority it became the nucleus of a concern to form a separate Landeskirche, which sought its independence.

Thus in Prussia seven Landeskirchen took shape: the major Church of the Old Prussian Union, a Lutheran and a Reformed Church in Hanover (usually called Hanover Lutheran and Hanover Reformed for short), and the Landeskirchen in Schleswig-Holstein, Hessen-Kassel, Nassau and Frankfurt-am-Main. In Bavaria the Palatinate, which had had its own consistory since 1848, achieved independence. In Oldenburg, alongside Oldenburg itself the former principalities of Oldenburg-Lübeck and Oldenburg-Birkenfeld claimed independence as Landeskirchen.

Thuringia provided the only significant alternative. Here seven Landeskirchen followed up the consolidation of their territory into the 'Volksstaat of Thuringia' by uniting in 1921 as the 'Evangelical Church of Thuringia'. All in all, at the end of 1918 approximately thirty Landeskirchen (which then became twenty-eight) were in very varied stages of consolidation. From the standpoint of the Landeskirche authorities, which were the driving forces everywhere, the main concern was to settle three problems. The first had to do with relations between church and state. It was still quite impossible to predict how those relations would develop in the future, and certain experiences – for example in Prussia, Saxony and Brunswick – seemed good reason for fearing the worst. The other two problems were internal church matters. Would the Volkskirche movement still bring about a revolution within the church and completely revolutionize its traditional order? And in the final analysis would the efforts towards union within German Protestantism prove so strong as to threaten the independence of the Landeskirchen?

A year later all three problems had been settled in principle. By the end of 1919 there was no longer anything in the way of the consolidation of the Landeskirchen. Johannes Schneider could justly note in the 1920 *Kirchliches*

Jahrbuch: 'The storm which swept over our fatherland, which shattered the German Reich and transformed its mighty power into total impotence, was not able to do much to effect the existence of the church.'[9] The two most important steps towards consolidation were the Weimar National Assembly in the summer and the Dresden Kirchentag in the autumn of 1919.

The state's decision as to the future position of the churches was, of course, of decisive importance. Therefore both churches followed the negotiations in the National Assembly over the new legal arrangements between state and church with appropriate concern. At this point the readiness for compromise among the Social Democrats, who had become the most important political force not only statistically but also *de facto*, was the great surprise. While in a statement of principles on 1 April 1919 the SPD deputy Johann Meerfeld left no doubt that the SPD was holding fast to the demands in its programme, namely, 'the declaration that religion is a private concern; further, that no public support would be provided for the churches and that the churches are private associations which manage their affairs independently', he added that the SPD did not want a Kulturkampf, and recognized 'the importance and power of religion even today': 'So we intend no forcible separation but rather an amicable agreement. To this end my party is ready for a wide-ranging understanding.'[10]

Thanks to this readiness for compromise, which certainly also reflected a reaction to the broad wave of protest that had been set in motion by the first radical declarations – and thanks also to an unusually favourable political situation, in which the Centre Party occupied a key position, it was in fact possible to reach a solution to the problem with which all the major interests felt satisfied.[11] This solution proved so workable that the basic stipulations of the Weimar constitution on this point were the only ones to be taken over word for word into the 1949 Basic Law.

Five main points must be mentioned in any attempt to summarize the substantive stipulations of the Weimar Constitution in connection with 'religious agreements'.[12]

First, it is important to note that a national, legal settlement in this question was actually achieved. It was by no means undisputed, since it certainly amounted to intervention in the independence of the Länder in matters of education and culture. But the fear of radical decisions on the church question by the administrations of individual Länder led even the Centre Party to surrender its federalist principles on this point and, together with the bourgeois right-wing parties and the SPD (which, however, had different motives), to call for a basic control of the relationships of state and church by the national government.[13] The shadow of Adolf Hoffmann hung over these negotiations, too. In the end, Article 10 was adopted with a substantial majority vote, empowering the Reich in the course of passing legislation to establish principles for the 'rights and duties of religious associations'.[14]

The use which the Reich made of this authorization can best be described as a 'Yes... but'.

The decisive Article 137 contained a 'Yes' to the separation of state and church and an affirmation of the church's independence, which was essential for the latter. Paragraph 1 ruled: 'There is no state church.' And Paragraph 3 declared: 'Each religious association orders and administers its affairs independently within the limits of the law which is universally valid. It bestows its offices without the interference of government or the civil community.' On this basis the churches in Germany were in principle separate from the state and definitively liberated.[15]

The 'but', which can be found in the same article, in Paragraph 5, from now on accorded the churches the status of corporations with a special legal status. Granted, there was a legal dispute as to whether this term applied to the churches, and it has yet to be resolved.[16] On the other hand its political significance was and is clear. It lay in the recognition that because of their history, their order and their responsibility within the state the churches came into a different class from associations or special interest groups. It represented 'a rejection of the constitutional model of the radical separation of state and church'[17] and the resolve to arrive at a unique settlement of the question in Germany, appropriate to German conditions, a 'distinctive style of separation'.[18] The most important result of the application of corporate law was the right formulated in Paragraph 6 to levy taxes 'in accordance with the laws laid down by the Länder on the basis of the civil tax lists'. The importance of this law, which marked the introduction of the church tax, can hardly be exaggerated. First of all, in subsequent decades it legally gave the churches the financial independence without which their newly-won freedom could hardly have been exploited, as in fact it was.

In order to make clear that this was not again to result in exclusive privileges for the two major churches, the SPD required that in certain conditions other religious associations should also be able to acquire corporate rights, though this decision meant more in principle than in practice. Finally, following the separatist principle, the SPD made a declaration terminating subsidies to the church (Article 138, Para.1); this was another point which soon proved impracticable.

So on the whole the churches had gained disproportionately far more than they lost. They had won freedom from the state along with special status as corporations in their own right. They had lost the status of a state church, but this had largely existed only on paper, and had been more of a burden than a benefit. But for the government too, the results were positive. It had achieved separation and secured its freedom from the church without running the risk of a new Kulturkampf.[19]

The politicans of both churches also saw the situation in precisely these terms. At the first Party Conference of the Prussian Centre Party in December 1920, Felix Porsch, a veteran, recognized 'with gratitude' that it had proved possible to incorporate within the Weimar Constitution provisions for the freedom of the church 'such as have never before existed in our fatherland, and of which no country in the world possesses a fuller measure.'[20] And even the ultra-conservative Johannes Schneider admitted that the church could 'get by' with the Weimar Constitution. As he wrote in the *Kirchliches Jahrbuch*: 'In all justice one may not deny the new political authorities credit for during the course of 1919 having withdrawn a long way from the iconoclastic ideas sparked off by the catastrophe of November 1918.'[21]

The signing of the Weimar Constitution on 11 August 1919 provided the decisive legal foundations for the rebuilding of the church. The state had resolved to leave this rebuilding entirely to the churches themselves. That posed a question for the Protestant church: Who would now take things in hand? Given the

27

historical development, no one could be surprised that this proved to be the authorities in the Landeskirchen. Often immediately after the revolution, working with the executive bodies of the existing Land synods, and sometimes with the help of other people in positions of responsibility, they created as it were emergency church governments which took over the functions of the church governments established by local rulers, now bereft of their heads. These leading groups had neither a clear theological nor a clear political basis. Their goal was above all to protect the interests of the Landeskirchen and the church authorities, a goal which they attempted to attain through negotiations with as many trends and groups as possible. As I have said, two main problems stood in the way of the complete and unlimited satisfaction of these interests: the possibility of a revolution from below by the Volkskirche movement and the move towards a Reich church.

Otto Dibelius, the executive director of that group which had taken over provisional government of the church in Prussia, had already stated in spring 1919 that the Volkskirche movement had not produced any revolution in the church 'but on the contrary had led to a revival in the organized church'.[22] In fact it had succeeded everywhere in integrating the first spontaneous movements into the Landeskirchen and making these movements subservient to church interests. Here, too, Adolf Hoffmann had exerted his influence. But that did not settle the matter. The representatives of the liberal wing now pinned all their hopes on primary elections, from which they hoped for a democratization of the church and some reduction in the power of the church authorities. The call for a German Evangelical Reich church seemed to pose an even greater threat to the independence of the Landeskirchen. The desire for a consolidation of German Protestantism was not new. In the nineteenth century it had been promoted by both liberalism within the churches and by the nationalist wing; but by 1852 it had achieved only a common advisory council of church leaders, the so-called Eisenach Conference, which had neither power nor public support. Since for various reasons the church authorities showed little enthusiasm for closer collaboration, in the nineteenth century the major Protestant associations had taken up the cause. The most important was the Evangelischer Bund, an alliance 'For the Protection of German Protestant Interests', founded in 1886, which with more than half a million members (in 1914) represented by far the largest organization in Protestant Germany. The aims of the Evangelischer Bund, which even in the Weimar period played a role as important as it was disastrous, were formulated by one of its founders as follows: it was to serve 'to rally German Protestantism against the modern expansion of papal power, to arouse evangelical awareness, to overcome the divisions among the Landeskirchen and the crippling conflicts between partisan groups, and to unite all those among us who hold to Christian and Reformation principles with a view to overcoming the dangers posed to our existence as a nation and a church by Romanism'.[23] 'We must,' it was affirmed to great applause at the inaugural meeting, 'grow out of both the petty divisions within the church and the hair-splitting in theology... The Evangelical Church must grow up in the wake of its German nation.'[24]

The anti-Roman and German nationalist tone of these utterances was, of course a special characteristic of the Evangelischer Bund, but it nevertheless showed how decisively the efforts for unity had in general been influenced by political and church-political aims. This explained its popularity, but at the same time represented a weakness: obviously the nature of the church was not the basis of the argument.

Given the mass of deadlocked efforts after the overthrow of the old structures there was a temptation to revive the plans for a consolidation of German Protestantism. As for instance Martin Rade's appeal showed,[25] the progressive group thought in terms of the creation of a unified national synod, to emerge from primary elections involving all registered Protestant church members, and to be equipped with plenary authority for the whole of German Protestantism. This was the plan for a German Evangelical Reich Church, which was revived in 1932/33 by the 'German Christians' with incomparably greater public response.

At this time, around the end of 1918, the response was more restrained.[26] The political need for common representation was, of course, obvious, and there was no doubt that something had to be done about it. All the Landeskirche authorities were fully agreed on that. But they were also agreed that this new representation to be formed should not affect the autonomy of the Landeskirchen, far less limit it, by the creation of an overall authority. In the rejection of all such efforts the concern of the Landeskirchen also combined with the confessional question. Specifically, the Lutheran churches saw themselves in no position to enter into church fellowship with the United and Reformed churches.

Thus a preliminary conference on 27/28 February 1919 in Kassel, at which representatives of the church administrations met to discuss this issue with representatives of all the important Protestant associations and societies, already established future trends. President Giese of the Schwerin Oberkirchenrat, who had undertaken to give the main address, stated clearly on the reconstruction of the church: 'Although there are still different viewpoints about the manner and extent of the new establishment, I hope that we shall achieve unity, for we… want to make the planned Kirchentag a permanent institution, to provide legally constituted representation of all the common interests of our church – as it were regardless of the independence of the separate Landeskirchen, which we representatives of the church governments intend to maintain.'[27]

The final decision on this matter, as on the matter of primary elections, then fell to the Kirchentag, which took place in Dresden from 1-5 September 1919. Among the 341 participants in this first great post-war church meeting were representatives of the church administrations, the synods, the associations, the theological faculties and the teachers of religion, and a group of sixty-nine people nominated by the Kirchenausschuss which included twelve women and ten 'representatives of the working class'[28] – all in all a thoroughly representative cross-section of German Protestantism. The most important items on the agenda were the question of the 'tasks and responsibilities of the German Evangelical Kirchentag as a permanent institution' and a memorandum on 'the synodical constitution and church elections in the Landeskirchen'. Following the lines of the preliminary conference, the decision on the form of the future consolidation was unanimously in favour of a 'Kirchenbund' – which left the independence and confessional position of the Landeskirchen intact.[29] There was a thorough, lively and entirely open discussion on the question of primary elections. The liberal group attempted to put some pressure on the Landeskirchen through the

Kirchentag, with a recommendation 'that the bodies to be formed in the German Landeskirchen should for the most part be made up from their membership by general and direct elections.[30] But this motion was rejected, and instead it was decided by a majority that 'The first German Evangelical Kirchentag leaves the decision on the system of election... to the relevant church offices, especially to the synods of the Landeskirchen.'[31] Whatever else, this was a complete triumph for the Landeskirche principle. All further assessments are difficult. The question whether rule by a democratic majority represents progress in the church is certainly not easy to decide. The opposing position, which views the church from the perspective of the community and considers primary elections valid only at that level has a good theological basis. Furthermore, the experiences of the year 1933 basically confirmed the fear of the opponents of primary elections of an outside take-over of the church. A national church with a unified organization and elections by majority rule according to the progressive model would doubtless have been seized by the NSDAP at one fell swoop. The opposition within the church would hardly have stood a chance.

With the decisions at Weimar and Dresden, the course of the future development of the Protestant church was set out.

In accordance with the Dresden resolutions, the consolidation of German Protestantism in the 'Deutscher Evangelischer Kirchenbund' was completed during the following years. In line with the historical theatricality typical of the times the Kirchenbund was founded on 25 May 1922, Ascension Day, with a ceremony in Wittenberg at the graves of the Reformers. § 1 of the constitution of the Kirchenbund defined as its aims: 'To establish a close and permanent collaboration for the defence and representation of the German Evangelical Landeskirchen, to cultivate the overall awareness of German Protestantism, and to mobilize the combined forces of the German churches of the Reformation on behalf of the religious and moral world-view of the German Reformation – all this with deference to the total independence of the allied churches in confession, constitution and government.'[32] While in practice this whole conception ruled out the creation of a Reichskirche as being one of the purposes of the Kirchenbund, the founding fathers nevertheless protected themselves at the Stuttgart Kirchentag against the definition of the Kirchenbund as a mere interest group like an alliance between states: 'There is an overall awareness of German Protestantism. And this overall awareness is a genuine empirical reality, which has its one root in the German Reformation, and from which a creative impulse goes forth – as has been demonstrated by the establishment of a common German Evangelical church law, numerous church usages and customs of a similar kind, and common interests – but which also finds expression in a unified Evangelical German religious and moral world-view.'[33] The Kirchenbund was given three bodies: the Kirchentag with 210 members, as it were the parliament; the Kirchenbundesrat, in which the twenty-eight Landeskirchen were represented, forming a Länderkammer; and the Kirchenausschuss, half of whose thirty-six members were elected by the Kirchentag and half delegated by the Kirchenbundesrat; this last was the real governing and executive body. The chairmanship of the Kirchenausschuss lay in the hands of the President of the Prussian Oberkirchenrat, by virtue of his office. The Kirchenbundesamt was subordinate to him in authority. This Kirchenausschuss and its President – from 1925

Hermann Kapler – were thus the main representatives of German Protestantism. Here, then, was the centre of the political and church-political policy-making during the decisive months of 1933. The Kirchenbund was not financed by resources of its own but on the levy principle: in other words the expenses actually incurred were apportioned to the individual Landeskirchen (§ 18). This made the Kirchenbund totally dependent on the Landeskirchen for its financing as well. Finally, the independence of the Landeskirchen was further guaranteed by allowing them – according to § 21 – the freedom to leave the Kirchenbund at any time.[34]

The German Evangelischer Kirchenbund did not last even a decade. The year 1933 put an end to its complicated bureaucratic structure. During this period it had been able to win little respect, above all because of its lack of any real authority. To be sure, the Kirchenausschuss and the Kirchenbundesamt got through a good deal of work, for example in the care of German Protestant communities abroad, in the cultivation of ecumenical relations, or in the co-ordination of individual areas and legal problems in the church. But none of this was particularly popular, and scarcely called for major institutional expense.[35] And where the Kirchenbund arranged a public event – the 'Social Kirchentag' in Bethel in 1924, the 'Fatherland Kirchentag' in Königsberg in 1927; and the Kirchentag to commemorate the four hundredth anniversary of the Augsburg Confession in Nuremberg in 1930 – what it said on the urgent problems of the day was so general, so traditional and so predictable that it found no response worth mentioning either in the church or in the political forum. Nowhere did the Kirchenbund become a formative and creative force in the church. Its major work was to collect and disseminate reports. Otherwise it was and remained the voluntary collaboration which its members had wanted.

Constitutional work in the Landeskirchen ran parallel to the formation of the Kirchenbund. Weimar and Dresden had cleared the way so that each separate Landeskirche could in fact work out its own constitution independently and alone. At first there had still been some political difficulties, because some Länder still claimed the right for the church to be governed by the local ruler as a way of influencing work on the church constitution.[36] But these difficulties had at most an indirect influence on the deliberations. In principle the Landeskirchen held rigorously to the right accorded them in the Reich constitution to order and control their affairs independently, and they made full use of this right. Thus twenty-eight Landeskirchen produced twenty-eight different church constitutions.

In most cases the basic structure of the different constitutions was similar. Each had two or three bodies at its head: the synod, representing the church members; the Oberkirchenrat, as the governing body of the church; and frequently a church senate, a collegiate group made up of members of the synod and the Oberkirchenrat which assumed the actual functions of church government, above all in personnel policy. Within this basic structure there were virtually unlimited possibilities for variation: for expansion through additional bodies, subordination, combination and distribution of responsibility. Considerable confusion was bound to be caused simply by the fact that some of the Landeskirchen put a Land bishop at the head of their governing bodies (e.g. Saxony, Nassau, Hanover, both Mecklenburgs and Brunswick), while others had a president in that position (Bavaria, Württemberg, Baden, the Palatinate, Hessen) and some were even led by a rector (Thuringia, Hessen-Kassel). The wealth of different titles for the same or similar bodies and positions was almost beyond comprehension. The synods were also called Landeskirchentag or Landeskirchenversammlung and the leading collegiate bodies were called church government, Landeskirche Committee, Extended Landeskirchenrat or the like. In Prussia the intermediate authorities between the church governments and the communities were called general superintendents and superintendents; in Württemberg they were called prelates and deans; in Bavaria district deans and deans. Even the *Kirchliches Jahrbuch*, which otherwise always vigorously defended the independence of the Landeskirchen, was finally horrified at 'the excessive variety in the terms for church ministries and authorities', which the deliberations on the constitutions of the Landeskirche had produced. Indeed the *Jahrbuch* felt it appropriate to comment in jest that 'one needs a church lexicon to understand all the different terms for ministries and authorities.'[37] The somewhat tortuous jest, however, disguised the real problems raised by this situation.

The almost infinite range of Protestant church constitutions and their complicated nature made them a sphere for experts. No matter how concerned the founding fathers may have been to realize Volkskirche ideals in the constitutions and to guarantee church people broad participation in the church guaranteed by law, in practice in all the Landeskirchen there were only a handful of lawyers and theologians who were familiar with the constitutions and decided things. Granted, the synods everywhere had been given a dominant position guaranteed by the constitution. However, they were hardly ever in a position to make use of it. They lacked the time, the energy and the experience to find their way through the complexities of the constitutions. The increasing parliamentarization of the synods, the function of parties and the adoption of political parliamentary procedures brought no relief, but only increased the difficulties. In practice, the constitutions which legally provided for the participation of all church members resulted in their generally being excluded. The rule of experts among the authorities in the Landeskirchen was almost impregnable – with a few exceptions in the traditional synodical areas like the Rhineland and Westphalia. And because these authorities did their work well, because they were reliable, because they remained committed to non-partisan government and sought to avoid all offence, people in the church became increasingly satisfied with this development.[38]

The triumph of the Landeskirche principle was not only problematical in this sense. The actual conditions which it created were also unfortunate. That applied above all to the scale of the church bodies. By far the largest of all the twenty-eight Landeskirchen was the Evangelical Church of the Old Prussian Union, with nearly nineteen million members. In second place came the church of Saxony, but with four and a half million members it clearly did not have even a quarter as many as the Prussian church. Then came Hanover with about two and a half million, Württemberg (1.7), Bavaria (1.6), Schleswig-Holstein (1.4), and Thuringia (1.4). About four-fifths of all Protestant Germans belonged to these seven Landeskirchen; another twenty-one Landeskirchen contained the remaining fifth, among them some with less than 50,000 members, like Oldenburg-Lübeck, Oldenburg-Birkenfeld and Schaumberg-Lippe.[39]

Numerically, then, the division of Germany into Landeskirchen was anything but balanced. The resultant tensions were accentuated by differences in confessions of faith. Twelve Union churches with just on twenty-four million members confronted fifteen Lutheran churches with just sixteen million and one Reformed church with 230,000 members. The most important Union church was of course the Church of the Old Prussian Union; however, Nassau, Baden, the Palatinate and Anhalt also had Union churches. Hanover, Schleswig-Holstein, Saxony, Bavaria, Hamburg and the two Mecklenburgs in particular had a marked Lutheran character, while Württemberg and Oldenburg were more mildly Lutheran. The one Reformed Landeskirche, though it had no clearly defined territory, was the Evangelical Reformed Landeskirche of the province of Hanover, with headquarters in Aurich. However, a multitude of individual communities belonged to the Reformed confession, especially in the west, and this made the Reformed trend far more important than the numbers alone suggest. The discrepancies in size meant that the smaller and medium-sized churches were in constant fear of being taken over by Prussia – a thought which was quite intolerable for the committed Lutherans in Saxony, Bavaria and Hanover in view of the Prussian Union. This explains why within the Kirchenbund the independence of the Landeskirchen was stressed so much more than what they had in common. Even when lines were drawn up in the Church Struggle, these anxieties played a decisive role.

There were bitter clashes, especially in Prussia, between the Reformed and the Lutherans over one issue of the church constitution, namely the revival of the office of bishop in some Landeskirchen. The Reformed 'Erlangen Guidelines' of 1919 had already decisively rejected a 'Land bishop at the head of the Landeskirche as its head and representative to the outside world', for the church in Bavaria.[40] But the real struggle over this question inevitably began when the question of bishops became acute in Prussia, the area where the Reformed were directly affected. The churches of the province of Rhineland Westphalia in which the presbyter-synodical tradition had a firm foundation and where as a result of centuries of Catholic oppression the title of bishop had bad connotations, put up a bitter resistance. The two movements clashed at the General Synod of December 1925. On a first reading the title 'bishop' was actually adopted for the general superintendents, but in the second reading it was resolved first to charge the church senate with the preparation of an opinion on the matter of future titles for ministries. The spokesman for the Reformed churches here was the Elberfeld pastor Hermann Albert Hesse; his chief opponent was Otto Dibelius. In the *Reformierte Kirchenzeitung*, the most important mouthpiece for Reformed Christians in Germany, Hesse repeatedly put forward the position of his confession and clearly made its continued involvement in the Prussian Union dependent on the question of bishops.[41] In the Prussian General Synod of spring 1927 those for and those against bishops again clashed in almost equal strength. Only in the actual vote was the title bishop finally rejected, by an extraordinarily narrow margin: 109 to 103 with 3 abstentions. So the old designations for ministers were retained; only now was the question settled over which there had been so much heated dispute. Six years later the question of bishops would again become important in a new way; but this time its most important opponent, again Hesse, who had meanwhile become a member of the Committee of Three, was ready for compromise and finally agreed, albeit with misgivings, to the creation of the office of Reich Bishop.[42]

By about the middle of the 1920s work on church constitutions was essentially complete. The constitutions were in force, the new bodies had been constituted, new men had taken over the reins. The first regular Kirchentag of the new Kirchenbund had been held in Bethel in 1924. In Stockholm in 1925 links with the ecumenical movement were also restored. In short, the transition from the phase of construction to the phase of consolidation was unmistakable.

However, all this was still more a matter of adaptation than a real reorientation. What was lacking was an interpretation of events which disclosed their meaning and at the same time gave the Landeskirchen a new position and new tasks, namely some kind of Landeskirche ideology.

This task was performed by one of the most widely read church books of this era, *Das Jahrhundert der Kirche* (The Century of the Church), by Otto Dibelius. At the age of forty-five Dibelius was from 1925 on the youngest general superintendent in the Prussian church and without doubt the ablest. He was a born church statesman, a man full of courage and decisiveness, independent in judgment, and with a keen eye for political effect. His book appeared – in a purple binding – in December 1926. A fifth edition was called for as early as spring 1928. What Dibelius tried to make clear to his readers in urgent, almost breathless language, was the meaning of the November revolution for the church and the new task which followed from it. The November revolution was 'the liberating storm' which gave the church independence at a stroke. 'The independence of the church has come. Not without qualifications! But by and large we may say that it is here. A church has been formed. An independent Evangelical Church!... Work in the church now has an even more secure basis. *Ecclesiam habemus!* We have a church! We face a change which no one could have anticipated. The goal has been achieved. God wanted one Evangelical Church.' And he went on, not least with an eye to Adolf Hoffmann: 'His will had to be served both by those who would build up the church and those who wanted to tear it apart.'[43] Dibelius left no doubt that the church of which he spoke was the Landeskirche, his Landeskirche. 'The Old Prussian church has been chosen as headquarters. Thorough involvement with the other Evangelical Churches of Germany would have confused the picture. The one church, the largest in Germany, may stand for all the others. For in principle developments in all the churches resembled those in the Evangelical Church of the Old Prussian Union.'[44] The objections made by theological critics, 'ecclesiology', which Dibelius put in quotation marks to dissociate himself from it, were insignificant for church politicians: 'We do not have to develop or reorganize an Evangelical Church from the basic principles of the Reformation onwards: we have to receive what it has become, what it has recently become, from God's hands – not in order to contemplate it but in order to act.'[45]

For Dibelius there was no doubt as to the significance of the development, nor did he permit any. The new task which had now befallen the church was at hand, and before it all misgivings had to be stilled. The task was to validate and defend the Christian norms in a state without norms. Because the new religionless state no longer acknowledged moral standards, while a community life without such standards was unthinkable, the Evangelical Church found itself involved in

34

securing these standards: 'Truly it is high time that someone seized the helm with a strong hand, applied the criterion of an absolute morality to the new conditions and restored humanity to an awareness of what is good and what is evil. Who is to instil this new moral judgment? Who can do it if the church does not?'[46] This was true in all fields – the 'cult of the body' and 'the pursuit of eternal youth', family planning and divorce, the meaning of punishment, gambling, luxury. 'Is there a limit to the profit which the producer gets from his goods? What is the relationship between the right of capital and the right of the worker? How do things stand with the claim of the state on the life of its citizens?' This was to be settled in detail by a church which was to be and had to be the 'leader in the shaping of Evangelical life'.[47]

Dibelius's book was a remarkable mixture of modern social and ethical concerns and conservative solutions. But precisely by virtue of this mixture it was appropriate for facilitating the transition from a compulsory adaptation to a reorientation in the Landeskirchen. Dibelius had created a task for the church out of the loss of the Christian state. The Landeskirchen found the significance of their new independence in this task and they consciously accepted and defended this independence to an ever-increasing degree.

Thus towards the end of the 1920s, in spite of all the continuing difficulties and problems in the church governments, looking back on the first decade of the new freedom led to an unmistakeable feeling of satisfaction. Clearly the worst was over; there were increasing signs of a better future. The constitutions were functioning. On the whole the Kirchenaustritt movement was smaller than had been feared after the War.[48] The church press flourished; since 1924 more than 600 independent papers had been refounded; in 1928 their total circulation amounted to about 17 million.[49] The number of theological students, which in 1925 had still been barely 1,900, had risen in the second semester of 1930 to more than 5,500.[50] In short, there was reason for optimism. In 1928 the moderator of the Provincial Synod of the Rhineland, Walther Wolff, wrote of the Protestant churches in a representative volume of essays entitled *Ten Years of German History, 1918-1928*: 'To one who has shared the life of these times with full awareness, it must seem like a miracle that the German Protestant churches have in ten short years by and large vigorously overcome this tremendous threat to their existence. Yet it is a fact.'[51] Johannes Schneider picked up this sentence in the *Kirchliches Jahrbuch* and added: 'The divine "nevertheless" has triumphed. What we call the empirical "church" has held its own, in its resilience as well as its endurance. The church leadership of the last decade was masterly...'[52] In Priebe's *Kirchliches Handbuch*,[53] in Haack's *Evangelische Kirchenkunde Deutschlands*,[54] and in the ceremonial volume *Die Evangelische Kirche der Neuzeit*,[55] this was the predominant tone throughout: 'For if anyone nowadays ventures to assess the result of the ten years of German history since 1918, he may say that during them an unexpected, well-founded consolidation of German Evangelical Church life has taken place.'[56]

This is how the 'practical men' in the church leadership, at the head of the associations and in the church press, saw things. The Landeskirchen had won through, in internal affairs as well as in external affairs.

However, things could now be viewed in an entirely different way. This tone of satisfaction at what had been achieved could seem almost unbearable. Here a new theology was expressing itself, a theology that stood in stark contrast to any kind of satisfaction in the Landeskirchen. We must now go on to investigate it, since it is the most important theological movement of this period.

3

The Revival of Protestant Theology
(1919-1930)

It is not difficult to answer the question what held German Protestantism together, what it considered to be its task, and how it understood its purpose in the first decades of the twentieth century. This is stated clearly and pointedly in a 1921 statement by the Kirchenbund: 'The purpose of the German Evangelische Kirchenbund is... to cultivate the collective consciousness of German Protestantism and to mobilize the concentrated forces of the German churches of the Reformation on behalf of the religious and moral world-view of the German Reformation.'[1]

Mobilization 'on behalf of the religious and moral world-view of the German Reformation' was the task with which nearly all schools of thought in German Protestantism found themselves confronted. The solemnity of this view, which has become alien to us today, should not cause us to overlook the fact that at the time it represented a vital claim – of undoubted truth and seriousness. The connection between religion and morality formed the centre of this common Protestant world-view. The conviction was that the meaning of individual human existence and of humanity as a whole lay in the development of an ever higher, ever more perfect morality; and that the Christian religion was the goal as well as the instrument of this development. Here a special task fell to the Protestant expression of the Christian religion, in that according to Protestant conviction the slogan on its banner was freedom as a moral postulate, in contrast to Catholicism, which was bound by dogma and authoritarian.

Wilhelm Herrmann, one of the most distinguished and influential Protestant theologians around the turn of the century, had convincingly expounded these convictions in his *Ethics*. Morality, that concept decisive for the Protestant world-view, was here defined: 'We understand morality to be a mode of conduct in which human life ought to rise above its natural mode and through its own activities achieve another mode of life.'[2] This definition already demonstrated what marked the Protestant concept of morality, namely the harshness of the 'ought', which was not tempered by any regard whatsoever for weaknesses. Herrmann did not allow the least doubt to enter here: 'What is morally good for us is always only that in which we overcome previous limitations of our personal life. For at each moment the demand of the Unconditional requires us to be other than we already are in feeling and instinct. In what we already find attractive, in that towards which our desires instinctively turn, we are bound up with present circumstances and form part of them. By contrast the moral law always points us to a future which (in terms of what it will bring us) we do not yet understand. Hence from the standpoint of natural life, moral conduct is not to be seen as self-assertion or self-development, but rather as self-denial.'[3]

While according to Herrmann's conviction, moral ideas and moral demand could in principle be thought and experienced even without religion, it was through the Christian religion that they first became human possibilities. What is impossible for human beings to do by their own power, God is able to accomplish through the power of his love. 'As soon as we become certain of God as the personal power of the Good, as soon as the power of the person of Jesus Christ accomplishes this in us and we experience that God forgives us, there is a transformation in which the question how we are able to deny ourselves is resolved... In his religious experience, then, Christ solved the moral problem posed to humanity.[4]

But above all, the religious and moral world-view also called for action and proof of its worth. Wilhelm Herrmann identified the family, cultural life and the state as the three most important fields of Christian activity.[5] What a morality of self-denial with a religious foundation was able to do for society had to be demonstrated here. Although Herrmann clearly had in mind a commonwealth characterized by clear ordinance – authority, the fulfilment of duty and hard work – he was far from that stereotyped appraisal that sees in this whole design nothing but an élitist ideology. Here there are not only remarkable references to the moral justice of the fight for better working conditions, but there is also a statement on the moral limitations of all forms of community. One wishes that similar statements had been written in 1933: 'In a state dominated e.g. by a basic antisemitism, a person who wants to belong to Jesus Christ, or who really has achieved moral earnestness, finds no fatherland.'[6]

The commanding position of the moral idea in German Protestantism before and after the War can scarcely be exaggerated. Although Herrmann was a liberal theologian and found himself in lively controversies with the 'positives', at this point he was saying something that was in fact common to all Protestantism. However much disagreement there was in Protestant theology over the classical questions of theology – the doctrine of God, the understanding of the person and work of Jesus Christ, the concept of the church – there was no doubt whatever about the moral vision and moral effect of Christianity.

The significance of the moral idea for the role of Protestantism in society was ambivalent. It doubtless contributed towards imparting that feeling of security in the Kaiser's Reich which so memorably survived in the memories of this period. Up to 1914, in fact, statistics reveal an unusually low crime rate[7] – an outward sign of a society orientated both socially and legally on the same moral system. However, the moral demand for self-denial also became the centre of a war theology which could appeal for the supreme sacrifice for the Fatherland. What in retrospect looks like blasphemy, when seen against the subsequent background of killing, could in prospect of the possibility of a self-denying offering of one's life for the community be seen as a thoroughly Christian, moral decision.[8]

The ambivalence of the religious and moral idea survived both the collapse and the period that followed. For the great majority of German Protestants this idea became in essence a disqualification of the new state which could not be overcome. Johannes Schneider sounded the keynote, which was then repeated time and again in innumerable declarations, when in the *Kirchliche Zeitlage* of 1919 he wrote that Germany had 'lost infinitely more' than the World War. 'The German people have surrendered their inner honour and dignity, even their self-respect. Complete destruction of all moral precepts has catapulted us into ghastly depths.'[9] The Heidelberg church historian Hans von Schubert appraised the situation in much the same way. With the collapse, 'the new legal order of the war' had dissolved just as much as 'the old legal order of the peace'. 'Chaos leered at us out of this dissolution of militarism and bureaucracy, and out of all this there arose an utterly immoral atmosphere of general mistrust and general lack of authority.'[10] That the new state not only could not, but in principle would not effectively sustain the fundamental principles of Christian and moral community life further marked the point at which broad circles of German Protestantism knew themselves to be profoundly alienated from it. If the state was encouraging chaos, and if selfishness, jealousy, lust and hatred were gaining the upper hand in society, the Protestant church had even more to be 'a school of work, service, reverence and love of the Fatherland'.[11] Anyone who looked at things in this way inevitably moved politically towards the right and also had to hope that the church, too, would move to the right, because the right alone appeared to promise the restitution of the old moral ideals.

However, the domination of the Christian moral idea led not only to an early and decisive dissociation from the new era but also to remarkable beginnings of Protestant self-criticism. In particular the liberals attacked the authoritarian structures of the old morality and set their new moral ideals over against them. For not only preservation was moral but also the concern for criticism and the search for truth. The Göttingen theologian Arthur Titius, who represented the Volkskirche movement at the Dresden Kirchentag, grounded justice and the necessity of criticism 'upon Luther's fundamental Reformation experience': 'Under the burden of God's judgment, with which Luther knows himself to be confronted, and the blessedness of God's grace, which unexpectedly shines on him from the gospel... he is given strength to smash what he had embraced with heartfelt piety, and to build something new.' And by analogy this was also true for the present: 'How could we undertake to solve the terrible problems of the present without the severest criticism of our dearest hopes and our most precious memories!'[12] To the accompaniment of vigorous disturbances Titius explained to the assembly what such a critique would look like in practice. 'We Christians of Germany want to slay all notions of revenge. We want to bury the ideal of military force. For that is what God wants now. We want to give honest support to the League of Nations [objection] by freely choosing as our supreme task what God's rule has forced on us by our history. Who could deny that here, too, the greatest ideal and the highest task beckon us on?'[13]

Although there were nearly unbridgeable differences in German Protestantism between the conservative majority and the liberal minority in understanding what specifically was the religious and moral task of the present, there was no doubt that there was a task. Conservatives and liberals were united in stressing that the present crisis did not alter religious and moral values, and that on the contrary their significance was much more recognizable. While the content of moral and religious standards might be argued over by conservatives, nationalist Protestants and liberals, the principle that religion was the means and object of moral development and renewal remained intact. Only if we keep this in mind as the only absolutely self-evident and undisputed common ground and foundation of German Protestantism will we understand the weight and significance of a theology which fundamentally and radically challenged precisely this premise.

At the end of September 1919, three weeks after the great Dresden Kirchentag which once more made the religious and moral world-view of the German Reformation the focus of attention, a conference took place in the small Thuringian village of Tambach, a summer resort near Gotha, which brought together about one hundred participants. One of those involved wrote in retrospect: 'Those who met in Tambach came together more or less by chance. They belonged to none of the major, influential schools of thought, inclined to no political party, heeded the word of no leader. If they were united in one point it was that they wanted "something else". Because they suspected rather than knew that the social question was the problem of the time, they devoted themselves to questions which arose out of this problem and asked themselves about the position of Christians in church, state and society. Because they had heard of the Religious Socialist Movement in Switzerland, and because the names of Hermann Kutter and Leonhard Ragaz were familiar to them in this context, they invited these leaders to the conference.'[14] So it was something of a 'bunch of church revolutionaries' that met here, and it was certainly no accident that 'no one had even the slightest interest' in the Dresden Kirchentag.[15]

However, the invitations sent to Switzerland did not meet with a very favourable response from the 'fathers of Religious Socialism'.[16] Neither Kutter nor Ragaz was prepared to travel to Germany. So finally a young Swiss pastor, completely unknown in Germany, stepped in. The lecture which the thirty-three-year-old Barth delivered on 25 September 1919 in Tambach belongs with Karl Holl's 1917 speech on Luther and Rudolf Bultmann's 1941 lecture on demythologizing as one of the most important testimonies of twentieth-century Protestant theology. This lecture, produced in 'uninterrupted day and night shifts',[17] was the first expression of that theology which was thereafter to gain an increasing foothold in Germany, and later to become conclusive in the decisive years before and during the Third Reich.

Günther Dehn, later closely linked to Barth in many ways, is surely right in thinking that those who were at Tambach expected something quite specific from Barth, namely 'a sharp rejection of the capitalist economic and social order that was still in control... and an urgent challenge to contribute vigorously to the coming new socialist order'.[18] Barth knew this too, and in a letter to his closest friend and colleague, Eduard Thurneysen, he made it clear that he would in no circumstances say that. 'What could be done to obtain a real hearing, in this mood of religious and social enthusiasm, in which the cry "God for Kaiser and Fatherland" still echoed, for an indication of the *totaliter aliter* of the kingdom of heaven?'[19]

The topic of his lecture was 'The Christian's Place in Society'.[20] With a bold turn of phrase that anticipated his entire theology, Barth interpreted this theme in his own way. '*The Christian*: we must be agreed that we do not mean *the*

Christians, not the multitude of the baptized, nor the chosen few who are Religious Socialists, nor even the cream of the noblest and most devoted Christians we might think of. The Christian is *the Christ*.'[21]

The shift from Christians to Christ: that was the shift of theology away from human beings and towards God, the God revealed in Jesus Christ, and thus to the God of the cross and the resurrection, in the complete, unlimited and undiminished abruptness and strangeness with which he confronts the world. From this point of view all attempts to reclaim Christianity for society prove to be equally misguided – whether they are conservative, liberal or religious-socialist in origin. For, 'the Divine is something whole, complete in itself, a kind of new and different something in contrast to the world. It does not permit of being divided and distributed, for the very reason that it is more than religion. It does not passively permit itself to be used: it overthrows and builds up as it wills. It is complete or it is nothing... Today for the sake of social democracy, of pacifism, or the youth movement, or something of the sort – as yesterday it would have been for the sake of liberal culture or our countries, Switzerland or Germany – we may very well succeed, if the worst comes to the worst, in secularizing Christ. But the thing is hateful to us, is it not? We do not wish to betray him another time.'[22]

Instead of religion, Christianity, morality, instead of Christian experiences and Christian tasks in the world, Barth wanted to speak of God. But for him, speaking of God meant speaking of a movement. It was in this context that the now famous formulation of the 'vertical from above' appeared for the first time. 'By "movement", to be sure, I do not mean either the socialist movement, the religious socialist movement or the general, somewhat problematical movement of so-called Christianity, I mean the movement which as it were runs through all these movements vertically from above... the movement which has neither its origin nor its aim in space, in time, or in the contingency of things, and yet is not a movement apart from others: I mean the movement... whose power and import are revealed in the resurrection of Jesus Christ from the dead.'[23]

It is a human characteristic, and in a real and true sense a human sin, that human beings close their minds by all possible means to this movement 'vertically, from above', and that they do this specifically by means of religion, Christianity and morality. Therefore God's movement attacks this whole world of values and systems, this world which brings humanity into a 'deadly isolation' from God. It attacks 'authority for its own sake', the 'family for its own sake' ('and the family has been in truth not a holy thing but the voracious idol of the erstwhile middle classes'), 'art for its own sake', 'work for its own sake' and not least 'religion for its own sake'.[24]

The total negation of all that exists: that is God's movement. Is this all there is to be said about it? Certainly not. For there is never only one thing to say about God, but always and at the same time something else: his negation is also a position; by destroying, God builds up; by taking away security, God gives a new security. That was the dialectic which gave dialectical theology its name. It was Barth's way of speaking of God: 'The negation which issues from God, and means God, is positive, and all positives which are not built upon God are negative.'[25] Not only was the individual series of arguments set out dialectically like this; so was the whole lecture. After the radical No to all activity in society it produced a Yes to this very activity, and in turn again transcended this Yes in a great No in order to develop another Yes from this No. So Barth was able to urge co-operation with social democracy: 'In this field we must work out the problem of opposition to the old order and discover a parable of the kingdom of God'. But at the same time he could warn against the error of 'expecting that our criticizing, protesting, reforming, organizing, democratizing, socializing and revolutionizing – however fundamental and thoroughgoing these may be – will do justice to the significance of the kingdom of God'.[26]

But in spite of the No and Yes – and given Barth's conviction at the time it had to be that way – the No stood out more strongly in the Tambach lecture than the Yes. 'Tears are closer to us than laughter. We live more deeply in the No than in the Yes, more deeply in criticism and protest than in naiveté, more deeply in longing for the future than in participation in the present.'[27] The particular political problems of this model for the Weimar period lie in this imbalance. At the same time, this was the point from which Barth was soon to develop his theology further.

Impressively as the theological approach of the young Barth was already developed at Tambach, a decisive aspect of this remarkable revolution was little discussed there, undoubtedly because of the theme. This was the question how such talk of God is possible at all in the twentieth century: how it begins and how it legitimates itself if it decisively rejects all religious experience as the basis for such speaking. Karl Barth answered this question six months after Tambach in a lecture which he gave on 17 April 1920 at a student conference in the Swiss town of Aarau, which bore the evocative title 'Biblical Questions, Insights, and Vistas', a title which this time he had formulated himself.[28] With utter clarity Barth explained in it that what he had learned, he had learned from the Bible. He recognized the historical relativity of the Bible as well as every other modern theologian, but this relativity did not trouble him. For he had discovered a remarkable thing in this relativity: the 'biblical object' that would not let him go.[29] In a significant image he depicted what he had encountered there in the Bible. 'We all know the curiosity that comes over us when from a window we see the people in the street suddenly stop and look up – shade their eyes with their hands and look straight up into the sky toward something which is hidden from us by the roof. Our curiosity is superfluous, for what they see is doubtless an aeroplane. But as to the sudden stopping, looking up and tense attention characteristic of the people of the Bible, our wonder will not be so lightly dismissed. To me personally it came first with Paul: this man evidently sees and hears something which is above everything, which is absolutely beyond the range of my observation and the measure of my thought... I seem to see within so transparent a piece of literature a personality who is actually thrown out of his course and out of every ordinary course by seeing and hearing what I for my part do not see and hear...' There are many such witnesses in the Bible, but the image is always the same: 'always the same seeing of the invisible, the same hearing of the inaudible, the same incomprehensible but no less undeniable epidemic of standing still and looking up.'[30] The Bible in fact remained the centre and the guiding star of Barthian theology – not as a book of readings of religious history nor even as a book of Christian doctrine, but rather as a document and witness to an encounter, the origins of which lie beyond all human thought, will, fear and hope: the Word of God itself.

With this approach, Karl Barth succeeded in solving a problem – for himself and, as later transpired, for others – which had paralysed more recent Protestantism since the time of Lessing. That problem was the question how the claim of the Bible to be God's revelation could be reconciled with insight into its undoubted historical origins. This question had split Protestantism into two camps: that of the fundamentalists, who maintained the sanctity of the Bible and its statements regardless of all historical, scientific knowlege, as it were with closed eyes, and that of the liberals, who understood the Bible without any reservations as a purely historical document, and in so doing lost their perception of it as a source of revelation. With this approach stressing the involvment of the biblical witnesses the Bible remained a historical source: this involvement could be recognized equally by the believing and the non-believing historian alike. It allowed a historical-critical treatment of the Bible; indeed it virtually required it. Yet the mystery of revelation was not affected by critical science, because the cause of the involvement – like the plane concealed by the roof – remained hidden and could only be discovered – or better, disclose itself. This not only gave historical criticism its credentials, but also indicated its limits. It created the presuppositions for theology but did not take its place. In the Preface to the first edition of his *Romans* of August 1918, Barth already explained this in the following remarks, later to become famous and often cited: 'The historical-critical method of biblical investigation has its rightful place: it is concerned with the preparation of the intelligence – and this can never be superfluous. But, were I driven to choose between it and the venerable doctrine of inspiration, I should without hesitation adopt the latter, which has a broader, deeper, more important justification. The doctrine of inspiration is concerned with the labour of apprehending, without which no technical equipment, however complete, is of any use whatever. Fortunately, I am not compelled to choose between the two. Nevertheless, my whole energy of interpreting has been expended in an endeavour to see through and beyond history into the spirit of the Bible, which is the eternal Spirit. What was once of grave importance, is so still. What is today of grave importance... stands in direct connexion with that ancient gravity.'[31]

Following on from the identification of the theological starting point, the Aarau lecture drew up that line of battle which especially incensed Barth's fellow theologians and contemporaries in the church – the line against religion. In contrast to the 'biblical line', which always involves radical commitment, religion is a mere substitute: 'She is not satisfied with hinting at the *x* which is over the world and herself. She acts in her lofty ecclesiastical estate as if she were in possession of a gold mine; and in the so-called "religious values" she actually pretends to give out clinking coins... Confidence in God is commended to the astonished world as a completely attainable and quite useful requisite for life... Prayer... becomes a more or less familiar part of bourgeois housekeeping and church-keeping. One speaks, without blushing, of "Christian" morals, families, clubs, and organizations.'[32] Karl Barth never tires of developing, over and over again, the difference between biblical piety and religion.

The one points beyond itself, the other points to itself. The one is God's work, the other is a human idol: psychology, myth, mysticism, custom, culture. The one is worth seeking; the other must be broken up and destroyed.

Here, too, are the roots of the special relationship with the world which is so characteristic of dialectical theology. For Barth is convinced that the polemic of the Bible is 'directed not against the godless world but against the *religious* world, whether it worships under the auspices of Baal or of Jehovah; and against the heathen only in so far as their gods are relativities, powers, and authorities which they have raised into metaphysical absolutes and which are therefore an abomination unto the Lord and abolished in Christ'.[33] In fact there is no note of complaint against or lamentation over the evil world in Barthian theology. Its power, its depth and its passion lie at a completely different point; the attempt to take God seriously. And that means thinking the unthinkable and speaking the unspeakable. Its subject was, as the eighty-two-year old Barth said in retrospect, 'God for the world, God for humanity, heaven for the earth.'[34]

We find a clear line through the history of the development of this theology. Barth began as a liberal theologian in the Marburg tradition. The first theological book that captivated him was Wilhelm Herrmann's *Ethics*. In 1927, in an autobiographical sketch, Barth wrote of his studies in Marburg during 1908/1909: 'I absorbed Herrmann through every pore. I thought I acquired a sound theological foundation by an intensive study of Schleiermacher and Kant. Through my work on the *Christliche Welt* I came into very interesting contact with the theological and church movements of the day.'[35] It was the German Protestant theology of the pre-war period, Neo-Protestantism in its purest expression, which the young university student accepted and advocated. In autumn 1909 he began his pastoral work, first of all in Geneva and then, in 1911, in 'the peasant and artisan congregation of Safenwil' in the canton of Aargau. Here he was brought up against the social question. 'In the class conflict which I saw concretely before me in my congregation, I was touched for the first time by the real problems of real life.' The result was a leaning towards the Social Democratic Party, of which in 1915 he became a member, a sensational step at that time for a young pastor, and a move towards the Religious Socialism represented by Hermann Kutter and Leonhard Ragaz. The outbreak of World War I brought the decisive turn. 'This brought concretely to light two aberrations: first in the teaching of my theological mentors in Germany, who seemed to me to be hopelessly compromised by their submission to the ideology of war, and second in socialism. I had credulously enough expected socialism, more than I had the Christian church, to avoid the ideology of war, but to my horror I saw it doing the very opposite in every land.'[36]

So as it were without any foundation, Barth and his friend Eduard Thurneysen, who in the meantime had also become a pastor in the Aargau, set out to seek a new beginning. It was all the more urgent since both stood under the pressure of having to preach Sunday by Sunday. The way forward was shown by the two Blumhardts, father and son, who in Bad Boll in Württemberg had refounded a quite distinctive piety with a biblical orientation. So one day a development began, the immediate origin of which was described by Barth in the following way: 'On a certain day in 1916, Thurneysen and I were naively agreed to go back to academic theology to clarify the situation... The following morning, surrounded by a stack of commentaries, I found myself before the Romans of the apostle Paul with what seemed to me to be the newly put question of what was really in it.'[37] This work, this amazingly urgent engagement with the Bible, produced the book that made Barth famous, *Der Römerbrief*. When after some difficulty Barth finally had this book published at the end of 1918, no one yet suspected what it had started. The Tambach and Aarau lectures followed, and to Barth's great surprise, on the basis of his Romans commentary, in February 1921 he was called to a newly established honorary chair in Reformed Theology at the University of Göttingen. During this period *Romans* was revised in a way which, as Barth claimed in the Preface to the second edition, left 'no stone of the first standing on another'. In October 1921 the pastor of Safenwil moved to Göttingen, and at the beginning of 1922 the second edition of *Romans* appeared. With it, Barth the theologian and his theology arrived in Germany. And the four editions which the second edition of *Romans* then passed through in rapid succession up to 1926 showed that this arrival had made its mark.[38]

If anything, the second edition of *Romans* intensified what Barth had already developed in the first edition and at Tambach and Aarau, namely the view that thinking in opposed positions, considering opposed possibilities, was the only way to put the will of God into words. Now Barth had abandoned even more decisively all points of contact and all categories of mediation, and concentrated still more strongly and exclusively on biblical thought.

Thus after a period devoted to neo-Protestantism and social politics, the period of Karl Barth the biblical theologian began. And it was as a biblical theologian that he continued to understand himself, all the more so in the middle of the 1920s when he turned increasingly to church dogmatics.

With the shift to biblical theology, Barth's political involvement plainly retreated. The political world in the narrower sense, the world of political ideas and decisions, no longer formed any basic element of his theological thought. And things remained like this, in spite of the popular view of Karl Barth as a political theologian.[39] That does not affect Karl Barth's constant personal political interest, nor the far-reaching political effects of his theology, which will be thoroughly discussed later. It has to do solely with the biblical starting-point which he would not and could not sacrifice to any party, trend or conviction. A long series of statements from different years in his life testifies to this dissociation in principle, which did not exclude, but included, some very specific political speeches and actions on particular issues.

The theological revival began with the Tambach lecture in autumn 1919. Even before he had made his move to Germany, it associated Barth with a series of young German theologians whom similar impressions had led to similar conclusions. The most significant among them was undoubtedly Friedrich Gogarten. The surprising parallels between the two were more evident to those contemporary with this development than to later theologians affected by the rupture of their relationship in 1933.[40]

Gogarten, born in Dortmund in 1887 and thus just a year younger than Barth, was also a pastor – at that time in the small Thuringian village of Stelzendorf. He too had a background in liberal theology, had experienced the war as a spiritual turning point, and had come to the conclusion – on the basis of his study of Luther – that now was a time of judgment upon all the past. In the *Christliche Welt* of 10 June 1920 a resounding clarion call indicating Gogarten's reckoning with the old authorities appeared between an article on 'The Basic Problem of the Cult' and one on 'The Religious Question in Social Journals'. It bore the title 'Between the Times', and was accepted immediately as the standpoint of an entire generation.[41] 'It is the destiny of our generation to stand between the times. We never belonged to the period presently coming to an end; it is doubtful whether we shall ever belong to the period which is to come, and, if through our own efforts we could be a part of the future, whether it would come as soon. So we stand in the middle – in an empty space.' Gogarten confessed to the old authorities: 'Your concepts were strange to us, always strange. When we did think of them and used them, it was if we were tormented by an inner vacuum. When we heard you, we heard the best and truest intentions, but they sounded hollow, hollow to our ears.'[42] In the expressionist style of the time that was certainly also a 'passionate rejection of conventional theology'.[43] But it was very much more. It was a rejection of the world of the nineteenth century altogether, and of all its traditions. It was a proclamation of judgment upon a past that had become dead, empty, meaningless. 'Today we are witnessing the demise of your world. We can be as calm about all that concerns this decline as if we were seeing the extinction of something with whch we had no connection at all... You cannot require us to stem the tide of this decline; for you could be calm about it if we saw something perish to which we had no ties... You must not ask us to halt this downfall. For you have taught us to understand it. And now we are glad for the decline, since no one enjoys living among corpses.'[44]

Gogarten's critique of the past was as radical as it was comprehensive. 'In all the world we see no form of life which is not being dissolved' – dissolved by historicism, rationalism, science; dissolved in the last analysis by the human, which has penetrated 'into the most refined concept of God'.[45] Gogarten was convinced that this 'refined, sage culture' stood like a wall between God and the human beings of his time. Only its complete collapse could create the precondition for a new inquiry into God. Therefore for the moment there was no solution, no recommendation, no immediate remedy other than to persevere between the times and to be open to the word and act of God. 'This hour is not our hour. We have no time now. We stand between the times.'[46]

It had been Gertrud von le Fort, like Gogarten a former student of Troeltsch in Heidelberg, who wrote to him at Steltzendorf in spring 1920: 'I feel filled with pain, as though not only outwardly but deep within me I were a child of two times and two worlds.' In his answer Gogarten had taken this up and said, 'But we all stand between the times.'[47] And now that saying found an echo almost immediately in far-off Safenwil. As early as 16 June Barth already wrote to Thurneysen: 'Have you read Gogarten's "Between the Times" in the *Christliche Welt*? I sent him a greeting at once and called upon him to cry aloud. This is good.'[48] It was the beginning of a fighting partnership that lasted as long as they could feel that they were standing 'between the times', and it ended when a decision had to be made in summer 1933.[49]

A little later, Gogarten too had his 'Tambach'. On 1 October 1920 he spoke at Wartburg to the 'Friends of the *Christliche Welt*'; his subject was 'The Crisis of Our Culture'. Thinking less completely in opposites than the young Barth, but in the one decisive opposition no less radical and unequivocal, Gogarten declared to the astonished gathering: 'We have, then, either a religion which seeks to be the soul of culture... or else we have a religion which is a constant crisis for this and every culture.'[50] In the one case religion is never more than a 'culture religion', even in its purest and deepest understanding, one which will perish along with its culture: 'Until then, this religion can do nothing but work against the downfall with all its powers and present itself as the best medicine for a culture that has become exceedingly weary and pessimistic. This will have to be done with great zeal, for the declining culture will hardly be willing to hear such "agitatory" voices.'[51]

What Gogarten attacked here with bitter irony was obviously precisely the task that the German Evangelischer Kirchenbund had undertaken at that very time: the recruitment of all energies 'on behalf of the religious and moral world view of the German Reformation'. All the speakers at the Dresden Kirchentag had in fact agreed that precisely at this time the powers of religion and the church were quite indispensable for the people and the state, because they meant deliverance and salvation for a world that was falling apart. But for Gogarten these thoughts were only an 'unmistakable indication... that the religion was long since lost, had lost itself, in fact, because it became infected with culture'.[52]

Over against this culture-religion Gogarten set God's own holiness as the goal. 'For God's holiness annihilates, not just for the sake of annihilation, but to save us that we may live. "When God wants to make us alive, he slays us," says Luther... Luther does not say "he plunges us into creative directness".'[53] Therefore deliverance comes only where God finally does the transforming, as the One who acts completely by himself. 'As it turns out, we will remain exactly where we finally found ourselves – in the annihilating, creating act of God. That is, exactly at that point from which Jesus Christ speaks today, just as he spoke two thousand years ago: Repent, for the kingdom of heaven is at hand.'[54]

Although Gogarten placed some emphases differently in comparison with Barth, although he thought antithetically rather than dialectically and was influenced more strongly by cultural criticism, the parallel features of the two approaches are unmistakable.

Barth and Thurneysen also had the same impression. Immediately after the Wartburg lecture, Gogarten travelled to Switzerland, first of all to Thurneysen, who on 11 October wrote to his friend about his visitor: 'I am astonished at the extent of common ground between him and us. He comes from a completely different side from us, has wandered along all the detours and by-ways of mysticism and romanticism, but now stands near us. The study of Luther has become a turning point in the road for him.'[55] In fact Thurneysen had noted a decisive point here. In a special sense Gogarten was and remained throughout his life a Lutheran theologian, though the significance of this did not become evident at that time. On the contrary: on 27 October Barth was able to report a 'highly pleasing' visit from Gogarten and to add: 'Here is a dreadnought for us and our opponents. Who knows, perhaps one day yet he will teach us something! He has quite the manners and also the equipment to be the man who... I have great expectations concerning him.'[56]

So it was not surprising that in autumn 1922 Barth, Thurneysen and Gogarten undertook to provide a literary voice for their common theological venture. Under the editorship of the young theologian Georg Merz from Franconia, the bi-monthly *Zwischen den Zeiten* (Between the Times) appeared, which from then on collected and published what emerged from the new trend. Among the authors of the first two years, 1923 and 1924, we can find almost all the names of those who had literary associations with dialectical theology during the Weimar period: besides Barth, Gogarten, Thurneysen and Merz there were Karl Barth's younger brother Heinrich, lecturer in philosophy in Basel; Emil Brunner, lecturer and after 1924 professor at Zurich, whose great day of reckoning with Schleiermacher was soon to cause a furore:[57] and among the Swiss, Fritz Leib and Alfred de Quervain, also lecturers in Basel from 1924 and 1930 respectively. Among the young German theologians, Günther Dehn was there from a very early stage, and during the 1920s more or less close adherents of the new theology included Rudolf Bultmann (though in the 1940s, alongside Barth and against Barth he became the representative of another theological trend), and also a series of young Württemberg theologians like Paul Schempp and Hermann Diem.

By the middle of the 1920s the new theology was on the march everywhere. And this was not just achieved through literary channels, but equally through the personal influence of Karl Barth, who in these years tirelessly presented his theology on numerous lecture tours, especially in western and eastern Germany. Even if the ironical tone of the reports from the 'battlefields' is unmistakable,[58] it is clear enough that he was really fighting for the establishment of his theology. 'Romans,' he recorded of an assembly of Emden pastors in October 1922, 'was read very diligently there. The discussion began immediately from the essentials. I was vigorous enough to be able to give satisfaction to all around me, on all sides, and so it came about that the opposition was finally crushed and the General Superintendent could solemnly express the confidence of the East Friesian clergy in me.' Thurneysen answered in exactly the same vein: 'Today your battlefront report from the far north... arrived here, and was read with interest and amazement at this breakthrough battle.'[59] Two years later a similar report came from Königsberg: 'A great day of battle of the first magnitude: 50-200 pastors with General Superintendent, superintendents and students all drawn up in a square, to whom I delivered a two-hour lecture and in addition made a half-hour closing speech.'[60] The battle over his theology in Germany was ultimately one of the reasons why Barth did not return to Switzerland at that time, in spite of tempting offers. 'Am I really allowed or commanded to break off the undertaking which has now at last begun on a broad front: (a) in theology generally; (b) among the students; and (c) in Germany?'[61] It was actually almost like a planned campaign, and it is typical of Barth's success that in 1927 he could almost exult over the opposition of the Basel people to Thurneysen: that is, 'that we are evidently not yet accepted by Christendom, that we have not yet been conquered to the point of death, that we have enough trajectory yet to give more offence...'[62]

Nevertheless, by the middle of the 1920s the breakthrough in Germany had undoubtedly succeeded. At least when Paul Schempp wrote his critical and ironical 'Marginal Notes on Barthianism' in 1928 he no longer saw his opponent as traditional theology but in the guise of Barthianism: 'A few defensive precautions and a few readjustments in the mode of thought, and Barth has become fit for church, faculties and society.'[63] And there was certainly more than a grain of truth in Schempp's biting analysis of the phenomenon: 'Barth finds adherents because his theology corresponds more to the contemporary spiritual situation than do other theologies, because the *sacrificium intellectus* satisfies those who have little to sacrifice here, because the paradoxicality seems to be profound, because a critique of the decadent is in itself a considerable achievement of the weak, because he has again made theology interesting, problematical and viable, a refuge for doubters and believers and the whole host of stages of religious belief in between.'[64]

Dialectical theology was certainly the most-discussed theological theme at the end of the 1920s. But one should not confuse this breakthrough with dominance. 'The religious and moral world-view of the German Reformation' was much too deeply rooted in German Protestantism to allow that. Moreover, the group itself was too disunited. Even in the mid-1920s the differences grew between Barth and Gogarten on the one hand, and between Barth and Brunner on the other. What kept them together was increasingly the same opposition and decreasingly a common theology.[65] In spite of these limitations, dialectical theology exercised a profound influence during this period, above all upon the younger generation. Here from the beginning the concept of crisis played a decisive role. Perhaps it was not so clear to the Swiss, who came from the secure order of their country, how far the concept of crisis matched a general way of thinking in Germany which in political terms was undoubtedly extremely problematical.[66] The fact is that the theology of crisis corresponded to a widespread feeling up and down the country that the new age was merely an age of transition, which expected nothing of the present and everything of the future.

Among the Germans, the sense of homelessness in the Republic, the feeling among many of them that it was transitory, a feeling stressed time and again by the conservative revolutionaries, certainly contributed much to Hitler's final victory. However, a theology that lived 'between the times' was hardly likely to counter this sense of homelessness in the present. There is much to be said for the view that, at least for Gogarten in the 1920s, the crisis came first and God's word as the answer came second, and the Yes in the No was not so articulated in every case that it could be both heard and understood. And that could have fateful results. A specific historical moment – with its particular combination of cultural, political and economic combination of factors – was explained, as Gogarten's article 'Between the Times' suggested, as 'God's time'. Marked off from a yesterday forgotten by God, ready for a new tomorrow, the time appeared to be lifted out of the stream of history. The world-political crisis immediately became God's judgment upon cultures and peoples. And whatever was undertaken in the way of reason and good will to overcome the crisis thus became a helpless, miserable attempt to escape this judgment.

And there was a problem generally, that on the periphery of dialectical theology, Christian world-views no longer thrived in terms of providing new, clear and manageable guidance. Doubtless one of the aims of the new theology was to destroy such guidance and to expose its ideologically idolatrous nature. And incorporated in this goal, as was very soon to be demonstrated, was a substantial political potential. But for the moment this theology simply deprived the Republic of important supports.

Adolf von Harnack, the great liberal theologian, who had joined the group of rational Republicans, had met Barth at the Aarau conference. Harnack's daughter and biographer has recorded how much Barth's lecture affected him. 'The effect on Harnack was distressing. Here was not one sentence, not one thought, with which he could identify. He recognized the deep seriousness with which Barth spoke, but this theology frankly made him shudder. "The lecture by Barth," he later wrote to Eberhard Vischer, "loses none of its grievous offence in my memory. On the contrary, it appears to me increasingly more disquieting, indeed in many respects more shocking. The thought that this kind of religion usually does not permit itself to be translated into real life, but rather can appear only as a meteor, albeit an exploding one, over it, does not do much to mitigate the impression as one has to keep asking how a pastor, who should after all care for souls, can have such opinions."'[67]

In fact it was out of the question for a Christian liberalism of the kind represented by Harnack, as by Troeltsch, Deissmann, Titius, Baumgarten and Rade, and indeed by the young Theodor Heuss, a student of Friedrich Naumann, to be found in the environs of dialectical theology. Even though Rade, the tireless mediator, did not break off contact with the 'dialecticians', he confessed personally that he had 'found no point of contact with this theology'.[68] And the circle of his friends reported, no doubt accurately, an 'impression of great irritation with the people around Barth and Gogarten'.[69] Irritation at a theology which gave Christian liberalism no chance could still be detected decades later in Theodor Heuss, when he depicted the 'odd effect of a circle of Swiss theologians', 'who had themselves never experienced such a shock, even to the church establishment', and who now suddenly questioned the achievements of an entire theological generation. 'As far as I can judge,' Heuss asserted in retrospect, in a thoroughly characteristic turn of phrase, the rising generation with its criticism of culture-Protestantism 'with a few exceptions still falls far behind the level of scholarly achievement of that generation'.[70]

What applied to Christian liberalism now also applied to Religious Socialism. Ragaz had reacted, if anything, even more vehemently to the themes of the first edition of *Romans* than did Harnack to the Aarau lecture. 'I felt *Romans*,' he wrote to Thurneysen, 'as a stab in the back. My heart is strong, otherwise this book would have been enough to damage it fatally.'[71] While this reaction referred essentially to Barth's polemic, Ragaz believed that in substance he agreed with Barth. But the Tambach lecture showed that Barth's approach, despite all his personal inclination towards social democracy, actually destroyed the hope of the Religious Socialist for a kingdom of God just as radically as it did the Kulturprotestantismus of the Christian liberals. Thus Paul Tillich, one of the leading thinkers among the young Religious Socialists in Germany, announced his misgivings about dialectical theology at a very early stage. He found 'something complacent and passive' in Barth's attitude, and that it ended up 'in supernaturalism and pietism'.[72] At the conclusion of a long literary confrontation with Tillich at the beginning of 1924, Gogarten again summarized very precisely the difference between dialectical theology on the one side and Christian liberalism and Religious Socialism on the other. 'To summarize the differences, I would say that I – and I believe I may also speak for Barth here – seek the reality of the world and life and knowledge of it in terms of Jesus Christ, or rather, in Jesus Christ. Tillich seeks the understanding of Jesus Christ or, as he says significantly, of the spirit of Christ in the knowledge of the world and of life.'[73]

So while the party of Christian liberalism gained few young adherents in the Weimar period, the Religious Socialists also remained a small group which could not achieve appreciable influence either in theology or in the church. Those among the young theologians and pastors who did concur in a theology of history based on a new, national Lutheranism followed the theological revolution of dialectical theology. The middle ground, like that in the state and society, had little chance to take shape.

No more radical critique of ideology has been developed in the twentieth century than that made by dialectical theology. It had in view, and hit hard, everything that raised an unconditional ideological claim: both bourgeois capitalism and proletarian socialism, militarism and pacifism, nationalism and internationalism, the former decisively and more clearly, but the latter in principle just as much and just as clearly. And it hit home with particular weight and particular harshness when the ideologies made use of Christian, church ties and supports, as did liberal culture-Protestantism, authoritarian nationalist Protestantism, and Religious Socialism. In the Tambach lecture Barth had already criticized 'all those combinations like "Christian-social", "evangelical-social", "religious-social"', and had asked 'whether the hyphens which we draw with such intellectual courage do not really make dangerous short circuits'.[74] This criticism clearly and impressively persisted through all the transformations of Barthian theology. For the Weimar period, this criticism was ambivalent, at least in its political effects. It hit the attempts to establish and to preserve the Republic on the basis of feelings of Christian responsibility just as hard as the designs of the opponents of the Republic. But this was the price to be paid for the presence in the field at the decisive moment of a theology which could establish theologically, and therefore in a way that the entire church could understand, why Christian theology could not now ally itself with National Socialism and why, therefore, the German Evangelical Church did not have to attach itself to the brown battalions.

4

Church, Curia and Concordats
(1919-1929)

While on the Protestant side the growing self-awareness of the Landeskirchen and the awakening of theology determined the way forward, the Catholic Church received its controlling impulses in a reorientation of church politics from Rome. The most important expression of this development was the Vatican concordat policy. For people at the time, however, this was not immediately obvious. The multiform and many-coloured picture presented by German Catholicism in the Weimar period made this line of development at first seem only one of several. The Centre Party, the thriving Catholicism in the church associations, the new theological initiatives and the spiritual renaissance (which many had anticipated, and which actually occurred) appeared far more significant for the church and political life of German Catholics in the 1920s than the matter of the concordat. But the events of the year 1933 showed that this question was in fact the decisive one.

The central position which the Vatican's concordat policy attained after the War was the direct articulation of an understanding of the church which had developed consistently and purposefully from the elevation of papal infallibility to the status of a dogma at the First Vatican Council. It had reached a new, significant zenith with the publication of the *Codex Juris Canonici* at Pentecost 1917. Amidst the turmoil of the war this event had attracted little attention. Nevertheless it not only represented a milestone in the history of canon law but was of quite supreme importance to the entire Catholic Church. In more than ten years of laborious work, a papal commission had sifted, sorted and reformulated the entire enormous volume of material in the canon law tradition. The result was a book of law that included a complete codification – similar in kind to the modern civil law book – of Catholic canon law, valid for the entire church.[1] The essential character of this law book did not lie in new legal definitions. The *Codex* scarcely included any new law.[2] Rather, the decisive point was the intent which was expressed in this work, clearly aimed at further centralization, standardization and legalization of the church. 'Now that infallibility in the areas of faith and morals has been attributed to the Papacy,' wrote the Protestant canon lawyer Ulrich Stutz, at that time highly esteemed by both confessions, 'it has completed the work in the legal sphere and given the church a comprehensive law-book which exhaustively regulates conditions within the church, a *unicus et authenticus fons* for administration, jurisdiction and legal instruction – unlike anything the church has previously possessed in its two-thousand-year existence'.[3]

In fact the *Codex Juris Canonici* describes the Catholic Church as one great legal entity within whose elaborate order all offices and rites have their own fixed and well-defined place, and over which a specific jurisdiction and penal law keep guard. At the head of this church stands the Pope, of whose all-encompassing supremacy Canon 218 says: he has *supremam et plenam potestatem iurisdictionis in universam Ecclesiam tum in rebus quae ad fidem et mores, tum in iis quae ad disciplinam et regimen Ecclesiae per totum orbem diffusae pertinent.*[4] Within the framework of this legal order, culminating in this primacy, the entire life of the church is regulated in 2414 canons: from, for example, the nomination of bishops by the Pope to the duty of the pastor to live near his church in the clergy house; from the exclusive right of the priest to celebrate the sacrifice of the Mass to a long list of impediments to marriage; from the right to ban particular books *ex justa causa* to the precise ordering of the powers and procedures of spiritual jurisdiction, hearings and punishments. None of this, as I have said, was new. Nevertheless the old law gained a new and greater significance through the new concentration and formulation.[5]

The effect of the Codex within the church on the centralization and unification of the world church was undoubtedly substantial; we can see that now from the criticism of it in particular.[6] No less important, however, was the influence that the law book would have in the relationship of the Catholic church to state authorities. To be sure, canon law limits itself entirely to questions within the church, and for good reasons in no way regulates the relationship between church and state. Moreover, any explicit conflict with government law is avoided – for example in the law dealing with marriage.[7] Nevertheless, it was clear that by means of the Codex the Catholic Church was not only pressing towards complete autonomy and unconditional independence from all state action and influence but in addition was necessarily claiming state recognition and protection for canon law. This meant the termination in principle of all arrangements supporting the authority of a state church, and the replacement of those arrangements by concordats – wherever that did not damage the church.

This fixed the main course of church politics for the Curia during the coming decades. The most important goal of the Curia's policies, to which all other goals were subordinated, was the protection, both internally and externally, of the principles of canon law. Internally, this meant unification and centralization – not least, for example, in the abolition of special church rights in the election of bishops. Externally, it meant the full acknowledgment and guarantee of church law by the state, along with the complete independence of the church. The Vatican's concordat policy served this purpose. The Curia felt that the rights and freedoms of the Catholic Church, and with it the very existence of the church and the faith, were best and most perfectly guaranteed, as far as this lay within the capacity of any earthly power, by the contractual approval and protection of the state. The principles of canon law thus became in fact the guideline of Vatican politics and determined its decisions far more, and more persistently, than was realized by most Catholics of the day.

The supreme importance of the new canon law for Vatican policy was also evident in the fact that for more than half a century after 1914 the management of this policy lay in the hands of its two creators. Pietro Gasparri, whom Benedict XV called to be Cardinal Secretary of State in 1914, and who also held this office under Pius XI, was the President of the Papal Commission on Codification and was considered the real author of the Codex. His successor, Eugenio Pacelli, had worked closely with Gasparri as Secretary of the Papal Commission. From 1930 as Cardinal Secretary of State and then from 1939 as Pope Pius XII, Pacelli impressed the stamp of his strong personality upon the Catholic church. Gasparri and Pacelli had worked together decisively for more than a decade on the codification of canon law. Both became representatives of a policy whose goal was the world-wide state recognition and protection of the principles of this law.

There were two reasons why this Vatican policy made itself felt most particularly in Germany, as well as in Italy: the nomination of Pacelli as Apostolic Nuncio in Munich and the German revolution, which, by the overthrow of the old order, cleared the field for the new policy.

The nomination of Pacelli as Nuncio in Munich in May 1917 was one of the most important events of twentieth-century German Catholicism. For from this moment on the young and ambitious diplomat considered the German church his special responsibility, which he did not relinquish when he was recalled to Rome at the end of 1929 to assume leadership of the universal church. We must compare Pacelli with both of his successors in order to evaluate his impact. Neither Vasallo di Torregrossa, who moved into the Munich nunciature in 1925, nor Cesare Orsenigo, who followed him in 1930 in the Berlin nunciature, made any special mark on the German church. The influence of Pacelli was, and remained, all the greater. In fact virtually no one in the first half of the century determined more persistently the ecclesiastical and political destiny of German Catholicism than this authentic Roman who, in May 1916, with unlimited self-confidence and cool determination, entered upon the task of representing the interests of Rome in Germany.

Pacelli's name had been brought up in connection with the Munich nunciature as early as 1914. The description which the Bavarian ambassador to the Holy See, Baron von Ritter, gave at that time of Pacelli, who was not quite forty, was still free of the later widespread tendency to elevate Pacelli's image almost to ethereal heights.[8] Ritter identified Pacelli's strengths and weaknesses very precisely when he pointed out that 'for all his good qualities, Pacelli of course remains an Italian who will never clearly understand our political and religious situation and therefore never fully appreciate its justification and its benefits, nor have the necessary regard for it, as would a German of Frühwirth's type'. Pacelli again had to stand comparison with Frühwirth, the Nuncio in Munich since 1907, when Ritter continued: 'Moreover, with an official like Mgr Pacelli who has made his entire career in the State Secretariat, and so quickly as that, and who in addition belongs to the Holy Office and to the Commission on the Codification of Canon Law, there always remains the fear that despite the best and most conciliatory intentions, which he would certainly have in any employment in the foreign service, he might lapse here and there into doctrinaire rigidity and thus damage his diplomatic mission. Finally, I do not believe that Pacelli would be as free from ambition as a Frühwirth.'[9] The concern that Pacelli had altogether too strong a Roman character, which Ritter clearly expresses here, and in which he probably included the young diplomat's passion for legal questions and solutions,[10] was to prove not unfounded in the future. In the critical years from 1930 to 1934 it was probably also this strong curial stamp which distorted Pacelli's perception of what was actually going on in Germany.

When Pacelli was nominated Nuncio in Munich in May 1917, the situation had changed completely from that in 1914. Now, for the time being, Pacelli the canon lawyer was less needed than Pacelli the diplomat. For Benedict XV had entrusted the Nuncio with the most delicate task that he could assign him: the preparation and negotiation of the planned papal peace campaign. His most important political informant in Germany was the most influential Catholic politician of this period, Matthias Erzberger. On his journey to Munich Pacelli met Erzberger in Switzerland, and from then on Erzberger remained his constant source of information.[11] Not least through the regular reports of the Centre Party deputy, Pacelli was able to establish his subsequent reputation as the best-informed diplomat in Berlin.[12]

Thus the Nuncio, who had established contact with German government circles in July 1917, was undoubtedly prepared for the July crisis which culminated in the resignation of the Chancellor and in the Reichstag's peace resolution. By the same token, Erzberger will already have been informed of the papal peace note in advance.[13] The heart of the negotiations in these weeks in which Germany's fate was being decided was a guarantee by the national government of the restoration of Belgium which had been demanded by the Entente as a precondition for the peace negotiations and transmitted through the Vatican.[14] However, in view of the difficult balance of power in Germany, the government proved incapable of a clear decision on this matter. So both the official German note of 19 September in response to the Pope and the confidential notification to Pacelli by the Chancellor soon afterwards lacked the required guarantee. That also ruined the papal peace campaign. The war ran its course to the bitter end.[15]

While Pacelli's peace mission foundered on the unpropitiousness of the hour, he was able to prepare the way in another field for a decision which affected the immediate interests of the Curia in Germany. It had to do with the establishment of diplomatic representation in Berlin.

The Berlin nunciature was an old problem and, like nearly all old problems between Germany and the Holy See, it was highly complicated and burdened with an abundance of inherited difficulties and sensitive areas. Normal relations as the Vatican understood them existed only between the Holy See and Bavaria. Since 1785 there had been an Apostolic nunciature in the Bavarian capital – Pacelli's new sphere of operation – and since 1803 also a Bavarian legation at the Holy See. Reflecting this mutual recognition was the conclusion, in 1817, of a concordat that ever since had formed the legal basis of relations between church and state in Bavaria.[16]

Things were more difficult in Prussia. To be sure, since 1747 Prussia, too, had had diplomatic representation at the Curia which had boasted such brilliant names as Wilhelm von Humboldt, Niebuhr and Bunsen. But from the time of Frederick the Great reciprocal representation of the Curia in Berlin had always been flatly refused on principle. How equivocal was the refusal is shown, for example, by the instructions of Friedrich Wilhelm III to Wilhelm von Humboldt, then Prussian chargé d'affaires in Rome. They stated that the Roman court was always trying 'to send a papal legate or nuncio here' or to entrust the task of representation to 'some subject with some title or other'. Since the Prussian king would not want to permit this in any circumstances, the ambassador was to give his undivided attention to these attempts, 'in order, if necessary, as it were to cut the thing short at a distance' and to conduct himself 'so that Roman intentions are nipped in the bud'. However, the reason for the vigorous rejection of a papal nuncio in Berlin lay by and large in the rejection of the concordat principle. On this point, too, the instructions left no doubt. 'A concordat between a sovereign and the Pope,' they said, 'presupposes that the sovereign yields in some respect, concedes some advantage to the Pope and thus requires reciprocal advantages for himself. But we, as a Protestant sovereign, and according to the principles of our government, by no means intend to arrive at this point of surrender or concession of advantages. Rather, we will neither yield nor concede advantages.'[17] The Prussian government held firm to this position. The after-effects could still be felt clearly in the 1920s. But since relations between the state and the Catholic Church had to be put in order in Prussia, too, the method of a 'concealed agreement' was arrived at.[18] The results of the negotiations between Prussia and the Holy See were published in the form of a papal announcement, to which the Prussian king gave his 'permission and sanction'. The Bull *De salute animarum* of 1821, which was thus raised to the level of a Prussian state law, and which in combination with the letter *Quod de fidelium* formed the legal basis of the Catholic Church in Prussia for more than a century, in fact amounted to a concordat,[19] even if it legally and studiously avoided mutual recognition.[20]

Finally and additionally, to complete all the obstacles, there was the special history of relations between the German Reich and the Curia. This history included a failed Reich concordat of 1804;[21] the transformation in 1871 of a Prussian legation to the Holy See into a Reich legation; its dissolution in 1872 during the era of the Kulturkampf and the restoration of a Prussian legation – but not a Reich legation – to the Holy See in 1882.[22] In connection with the dissolution of the Reich legation, Bismarck repeated in his famous Canossa speech to the Reichstag the old Prussian reservations against concordats which had been further strengthened by the meetings of the Vatican Coucil. 'I do not believe,' Bismarck declared, 'that after the recently expressed and publicly promulgated dogmas of the Catholic church it is possible for a secular power to arrive at a concordat without that power to some degree or in some manner losing face. This the German Reich cannot accept at all. Do not fear. We are not going to Canossa, either physically or spiritually.'[23]

These, then, were the historical and legal circumstances which the new Munich Nuncio found in Germany. However, they had been considerably altered and moderated by a process which had brought a steady integration of Catholicism into the Kaiser's Reich since the 1880s.

Pacelli likewise discovered during his first briefing in Switzerland on the way to Germany how far the War had also advanced and hastened things in this sector. At the same time, however, he also found out how complicated things were in the Reich nunciature. For in a conversation with the Bavarian minister at the Vatican, Otto von Ritter (who because of Italy's entry into the war had to reside, with all his Prussian colleagues, in Lugano), brought up 'quite frankly' the Bavarian anxieties about the Berlin nunciature. That is to say, for a long time Bavaria had feared for the status, indeed even the existence, of its nunciature. Not only Bavarian interests, Ritter assured Pacelli, but also the general interests 'of the Catholic cause in the German Reich' would be endangered by the establishment of papal representation in Berlin. This was because, he said, this representation would be exposed to completely different political pressure and, in addition, the Centre Party could come under false suspicion, to the detriment of Catholic interests. When Pacelli retorted that he grasped this point of view completely and that the whole question should 'be dropped, at any rate until after the War',[24], that did not mean that he had not already decided on a Reich nunciature.

Matthias Erzberger, the Centre Party representative, whom Pacelli met soon afterwards, and who resolutely defended the plan for a Reich nunciature, may have made a more lasting impression on Pacelli than the harmless and anxious Ritter. Since 1916 Erzberger, always endeavouring to reconcile German and Vatican interests, had constantly stessed the urgency of a Vatican mission in Berlin.[25] While he, too, wanted to avoid a quarrel with Munich in time of war, he nevertheless left no doubt that after the War he would prosecute the matter with vigour.[26] In this he was clear that he represented not only German but also Roman interests. For in the Vatican, too, the need for diplomatic representation in the German Reich had increased. The goal of Vatican politics – the recognition and protection of the principles of canon law throughout Germany – presupposed central diplomatic representation of the Holy See. In other words, anyone who wanted a Reich concordat first of all had to accept a Reich nunciature.

This, roughly, was the state of affairs when the revolution changed the situation totally.

While the Reich was in chaos, and German Catholics were bewildered, having difficulty in finding their bearings in the new era, the Curia did not waste a moment in taking the new facts into account.

A letter written by Benedict XV to Gasparri and published in *L'Osservatore Romano* of 10 November 1917 declared: 'The church, which is the perfect community, has as its only purpose the sanctification of men of all times and all countries. Just as it accommodates itself to different forms of government, so it has no difficulty in accepting lawful territorial and political changes among the nations.'[27] This meant that the Curia was determined above all to represent the interests of the Catholic church, even under the changed conditions. That this not only meant the acceptance of this development but also from the start included new possibilities was shown by the Pope's reaction to the election of Friedrich Ebert as Reich President on 11 February 1918. Benedict XV responded on 2 April to the official announcement of Ebert's election with his congratulations on the high office, all the more so, 'as we see that you will take care that the existing relationships between Our Apostolic See and the German Reich will not only remain unaltered but become still stronger. You may assume,' continued the letter, 'that there will be no lack of co-operation in this matter on our part.'[28] The desire for a Reich nunciature and also perhaps for a concordat with the Reich was unmistakeable.

Otherwise, however, until the summer of 1919 papal policy in Germany had largely to limit itself to the role of an observer. Specific measures could only be considered after the new Reich constitution had been implemented. The legal framework for the new relationship between state and church had first to be marked out before its inherent potentialities could be tested. Thus 11 August 1919, the day on which the constitution was ratified, at the same time marked the point at which Pacelli's political efforts for a concordat with Germany began.

The Nuncio, with his legal training, obviously perceived very quickly that from the perspective of the Curia the Weimar constitution offered unusually favourable opportunities. This was true in several respects. First, Article 137 in principle removed the prerogatives of the state over the church and thus voluntarily also gave the church those rights for which otherwise it would have had to fight in long negotiations. Granted, in terms of constitutional law the question whether the Bavarian concordat of 1817 and the provisions of the 1821 *De salute animarum* which applied to Prussia had automatically been rescinded was still open, and continued to be disputed until the conclusion of the new agreements. But in the long run, as Pacelli was well aware, the guarantees of Article 137 put the church in a superior position. A report from the Prussian minister in Munich, Graf Zech, dated the end of November 1919, showed that Pacelli intended to exploit his position to the full. The Nuncio, so Zech told Berlin, took the view that the legal situation which had held hitherto 'possibly' might be abrogated by the constitution. The question called for negotiations between the Prussian government and the Curia. Here Pacelli considered the position of the church to be very strong for the moment, 'with the most important rights guaranteed to it, and completely without any action on its part'.[29]

In fact the state had planned little more in connection with the church. By the standards of the *Codex Juris Canonici*, basically the church had come off badly only over one major issue: the school question, regulated in Articles 143-149 of the constitution. So this was the point at which the Fulda Bishops' Conference immediately began its criticism, declaring in a motion on the constitution that these articles contained 'various provisions... which on the one hand are incompatible with the rights of the church (cf. the relevant canons of the *Codex Juris Canonici*) and with the rights of those who are entitled to education, especially the parents, and on the other hand give the state excessive powers ...'[30] For Pacelli, too, the school question became the central point in all the negotiations he was to conduct in the future.

By a small alteration of Article 78 the Reich constitution gave the Curia a lever which was no less important, and extraordinarily effective for implementing its purpose. This article regulated the exclusive terms of the Reich's foreign diplomatic representation. In contrast to the original draft, which spoke in very general terms about 'foreign relations', the Bavarian representatives established another wording. Paragraph 1 of the article now ran: 'The maintenance of relations with *foreign states* is exclusively the business of the Reich.' Since the Holy See was regarded as a foreign sovereign but not a foreign state this in principle opened up the possibility that not only the Reich but also individual Länder could maintain diplomatic relations with the Vatican, and could conclude their own concordats.[31] The significance of this alteration for the Vatican's policy in Germany was almost incalculable, It gave the Nuncio the opportunity to begin where the conditions for a concordat were most favourable, and at the same time to play off the Länder and the Reich against each other. Pacelli made the most of this opportunity.

In these circumstances Bavaria had to become the first and most important negotiating partner of the Curia. Bavaria alone already had a tradition of concordats, which it immediately followed. Furthermore, even under the new government the state still felt itself to be, as the former Minister President Graf Hertling had on occasion put it, 'called to be the Catholic pre-eminence in the Reich',[32] thus laying claim to special relations with the Vatican. Finally, these special relations had now become for Bavaria nothing short of 'a matter of life and death', because they were a way of proving its independence, at least in this area, from the centralist tendencies of the Reich constitution.[33] As early as August 1919 Pacelli seems to have begun to sound out the chances of a new Bavarian concordat. At all events, at the beginning of September the Bavarian Bishops' Conference said that 'negotiations should begin with the Nunciature as soon as possible' on the future relations of state and church in Bavaria. At the same time a strict instruction from Gasparri was published, to the effect that he himself would not enter into any negotiations with the government, 'in order not to anticipate the general negotiations for a concordat!'[34] At the end of the year, on 27 December, the official offer of negotiations was presented by the Curia to the Bavarian Minister President. In it the Nuncio announced that the Holy See was ready 'to establish contact with the Bavarian government, to reorder the entire content of relations between state and church, and has authorized me to initiate negotiations for a new treaty'.[35]

Playing the Bavarian card first also commended itself to Pacelli because at the same time his experience with Prussia compelled him to exercise greater discretion. These experiences were connected with the death of the Cardinal Archbishop of Cologne, Felix von Hartmann, on 11 November 1919. Among the most important privileges given to the Catholic church in Prussia by *De salute animarum* was that the cathedral chapter could nominate its own bishops in a free election. But this privilege clearly contradicted the new general law of the *Codex Juris Canonici*, which in canon 329, § 2, reserved the nomination of bishops to the Pope. So it seemed natural to Pacelli, in view of the unsettled legal situation, to attempt immediately to impose canon law on the Cologne cathedral chapter. Accordingly, four days after Hartmann's death he informed the Cologne chapter of an instruction from Gasparri: 'The supreme metropolitan chapter should await instructions on the nomination of an archbishop which the Holy See, will not fail to send.'[36] But the chapter was not inclined to allow its ancient rights to be taken away so easily, and in this attitude it found decisive support from the Prussian government. At the end of December, on the basis of several opinions, a government investigation came to the conclusion 'that the Prussian government and the Vatican are bound to the existing treaties until an alteration of the current legal status – resting on the consent of both parties – is arranged'.[37] During a discussion of the whole question on 29 December in Berlin, Konrad Haenisch, the Kultusminister, confirmed to the Nuncio that the Prussian government was quite determined to maintain this position. On this occasion the Kultusminister presented a memorandum to the Nuncio in which the Prussian government stated that 'in accord with the Reich government' it was proceeding on the assumption that the existing treaties would continue for the time being and that it would be necessary to enter into new negotiations.[38] That Pacelli acknowledged this declaration was without doubt a victory for the Prussian government. For of course it made quite a difference whether one proceeded with future negotiations on the basis of existing treaties, which had only to be adjusted, or whether one accepted a precondition of no treaties – which would necessitate entirely new treaties. At the same time it made a compromise in the Cologne affair possible. Pacelli, who travelled on to Cologne immediately afterwards, told the cathedral chapter that it could elect on the basis of its previous rights, though with the reservation that this was not to anticipate a final settlement.[39] Pacelli accepted this concession the more easily because all those involved – the Curia, the Prussian state and the cathedral chapter – were already agreed upon a candidate: Josef Schulte, Bishop of Paderborn. Thus the election had become more or less a formality. At the same time it is not unreasonable to assume that the determined attitude of the government and the cathedral chapter prepared the way for a partial continuation of the rights of the chapter to elect even in the Prussian concordat of 1929.[40]

Perhaps Pacelli would have been less forthcoming towards Prussia had not the development of relations with the Reich, which were far more interesting to him, at the same time taken a generally favourable turn for the Curia. Thus he could hope to obtain from Prussia indirectly, through the Reich, those concessions which it still withheld.

In fact the foreign relations of the Reich after the Treaty of Versailles were so desperate that even the Social Democrats in the Reich government pressed for entering into full diplomatic relations with the Vatican. In this way the iron curtain of rejection and silence might be pierced at one point, at any rate. The development hardly required any help from Erzberger, who had meanwhile been promoted to Reich Minister, but his hand was in evidence everywhere.

By February 1919, in the Reichstag the Centre Party deputy Peter Spahn had already called for Reich diplomatic representation at the Vatican. The argument that he used, which was very characteristic of the post-war period, was that in view of the small number of neutral nations which had maintained friendly relations with the German Reich this representation was 'an order of duty and wisdom'. 'The eyes of the Christian world,' he declared, 'look with increased expectancy towards Rome. Broad sectors of the population look to the papacy, which in changing times has remained, and will remain, unaltered, for salvation, redemption, freedom and clarity in an age which is so rich in error...'[41] Only a few weeks later, as a first step, on 1 April 1919 Erzberger persuaded the Reich cabinet to restore the Prussian legation to the Holy See. It remained the only diplomatic appointment of that year.[42] The new envoy, Diego von Bergen, was reputed to be a friend of Erzberger's in the Foreign Office, and had already been received by Pacelli during the War.[43] Thus the transformation of the Prussian legation into an embassy of the Reich as had happened once before, in 1871, had probably been envisaged from the start. As a further indication, only a few weeks later, on 27 September, the SPD Foreign Minister Hermann Müller informed the Reichstag Committee on Foreign Affairs that the establishment of a German embassy to the Vatican had been decided on. Prussia had asked the Reich to take over its legation, and the Prussian envoy already had the concurrence of the Curia.[44] That this development was to lead directly and immediately to a Reich concordat was again made clear by Erzberger, when he declared at the celebration banquet which the Reich President and Reich Chancellor gave in Berlin at the end of the year in honour of the Nuncio that the negotiations on the necessary reordering of church-state relations in Germany were 'to be conducted by all Länder in concert, under the leadership of the Reich'.[45]

However, at least by this stage it had become clear that this development, which was basically so encouraging for the Curia, had a serious snag. For as a matter of course all the participants in Berlin proceeded on the assumption that the new Reich embassy to the Vatican would represent the entire Reich and therefore that an independent Bavarian legation would be superfluous. In fact by the beginning of 1920 not only had the agreement for the dissolution of the Bavarian legation been prepared; the Bavarian representatives in Berlin had already been authorized to sign it.[46] But this would have lost the Curia a decisive advantage. The thought of now having to enter into negotiations solely with the traditionally Protestant Reich, rather than with traditionally Catholic Bavaria, could hold little attraction for Pacelli. It was with good reason that immediately before his departure for Berlin he had submitted his official offer for negotiations to the Bavarian government. So he now employed the request of the Bavarian government for an opinion on the matter of the Munich nunciature as an occasion to intervene in German politics in a most unusual way. The Holy See, so he informed the governments in Munich and Berlin, 'would prefer a Reich embassy to the Vatican, with a papal nunciature for German affairs, excluding Bavaria, in Berlin, and a Bavarian legation to the Vatican, with a papal nunciature in Munich, for church affairs.' And probably knowing how concerned the Reich was over diplomatic relations at this time, he added coolly that if the Reich government did not agree, the Holy See would wish 'to maintain the *status quo ante*, i.e. Prussian and Bavarian legations to the Vatican, with a papal nunciature in Munich'. However, in one way or another the Holy See desired 'to maintain the nunciature in Munich'.[47]

Intelligible though it was in terms of curial tactics, this declaration was perhaps a fatal mistake. For while it helped Pacelli to achieve the triumph of the Bavarian concordat which he had hoped for, in the final analysis it closed off to him the path to a Reich concordat and thus created the fatal starting point from which in 1933 Hitler was to force the capitulation of German Catholicism within a few weeks.

In view of the overall situation, the Reich had no choice but to submit to the demands of the Curia. Prussia, which had made the dissolution of the Bavarian legation a condition for the transformation of its own representation into a Reich embassy, dropped this demand in February 1920.[48] At the same time Erzberger, the only person who could still have represented the interests of the Reich, had come to the end of his political career. After the judgment of the court against him in his great litigation with Helfferich, in March he could only resign. Eighteen months later, on 26 August 1921, the controversial man was dead – murdered by men who wished to get at him as the representative of a hated system: a Democrat and not least a Catholic.[49]

Thus the Bavarian embassy to the Vatican continued to exist alongside the newly-established embassy of the German Reich. How much this was the work of Pacelli became evident when the Cardinal Secretary of State, Pietro Gasparri, informed the German ambassador at the beginning of May of the intention of the Holy See now to establish another Nunciature in Berlin and to entrust this

61

to the Nuncio in Munich, Mgr Eugenio Pacelli: for the time being this would be in personal union with the Nunciature in Munich.[50] Thus Pacelli in fact had all the reins in his hands. He could negotiate simultaneously with Bavaria and with the Reich, and in their known rivalry he had a lure and a lever which would have to be used skilfully, particularly in view of the expected difficulties in Bavaria.

Although from the start the Nuncio primarily followed the Bavarian plan, at the same time he strove for a good and impressive improvement in his relations with the Reich. So he made the presentation of his credentials to Reich President Friedrich on 30 June 1920 a solemn and highly political act. As he stressed in his address, he had a charge from the Holy See 'so to order with the proper authorities the relations between church and state in Germany that they correspond to the new situation and to contemporary conditions'. And with almost the same phrase that was to be used for the same matter, i.e. the Reich concordat, in Hitler's famous government declaration of 23 March 1933,[51] he affirmed that he would apply all his energies 'to preserving and strengthening further relations between the Holy See and Germany...' No one thought of Canossa any more when Ebert replied that this was also the Reich's intention, and that the Nuncio 'may be assured at the very outset of the greatest under-standing and co-operation from the German side'.[52]

In spite of these solemn declarations, however, and in spite of the first approach to the Foreign Office which immediately ensued, it was clear that initially Pacelli's main interest was focussed on Bavaria. This emerged not only from the fact that, in spite of repeated pressure from Berlin, for the time being he remained in the Bavarian capital, but also from the swiftness with which he presented his proposals there. Since 4 February 1920 a compact package of Roman demands had lain on the table in Munich which left nothing to be desired in the way of clarity. With his typical disregard for German circumstances and possibilities Pacelli had envisaged in them a position for the Catholic church, above all in the matter of schools, which would have assured it almost unlimited rights of supervision and intervention. But in all the other areas, too, the demands were of such a kind that all rights were granted to the church and all duties allotted to the state.[53] Thus the church naturally had 'free and full right of appointment to all church offices', while for example in the case of teachers of religion the state was to be bound by the proposals of the bishop and even to remove teachers from their posts if he complained about them. It was affirmed that the state was to continue to meet all financial obligations and that there was to be an unrestricted government guarantee of canon law through the promise 'to acknowledge the ordinances of the church administrations within their jurisdiction and, if required, to offer its support in their implementation'.[54]

Even considering the tactical significance of such proposals, the whole package was an affront, and so it was taken to be in Munich. When the official in charge of Vatican affairs in the Foreign Office, Professor Richard Delbrück, an ardent advocate of the idea of a concordat, discussed the matter of a concordat in September 1920 in the Bavarian Kultusministerium, he discovered there that Pacelli had 'aroused ill-feeling by his excessive demands'. 'The most striking thing about Pacelli,' he reported to Berlin, 'is that he seems to have little awareness of what is possible in Germany and that he negotiates as if he were dealing with Italians.' In Pacelli's proposals 'very little account was taken' of

German circumstances and the Reich constitution. The Curia appeared 'to demand an enormous amount in order to gain at least something'.[55] This impression was not confined to the Bavarian ministerial bureaucracy. Even Ritter, certainly a faithful Catholic, himself observed two years later on an already substantially altered proposal that it was not, 'at least in appearance, aimed at *do ut des*. That is the first impression one gets on reading only about the obligations of the state for seven and a half pages and then right at the very end, in barely nineteen lines, discovers to what reciprocal efforts the church is obligated.'[56]

What Delbrück also learned personally from Pacelli showed that the Nuncio was determined to use any means to force through his demands. It was typical of Pacelli's disregard for German constitutional law that he openly declared: 'the Curia certainly wants nothing that might violate the Reich constitution, but hopes for advantages *praeter legem*', i.e. in addition to or beyond the constitution. That here he found himself in a strong position over against the powerless Reich and also exploited it ruthlessly was betrayed by the undisguised threat that otherwise 'a situation without a concordat would be preferable'. But in that case the Curia would not be in a position to call on its contractual obligations towards Germany in the face of possible demands by Germany's neighbours – and now the Nuncio became even clearer – 'for example in the question of the Saar diocese, which could become an acute issue at any time. With deep regret it would have to yield.'[57] Although Pacelli tried to tone down his remarks as far as possible when Delbrück objected, it was nevertheless clear that this was a real threat touching one of the Reich's weakest spots: the Saar. In fact the Nuncio also succeeded early in 1922, on the occasion of a vacancy in see at Trier, in forcing Prussia to capitulate on the school question by using this same argument.[58] However, he was to regret this triumph in the future.

There were good reasons for the vigour with which Pacelli fought for the Bavarian concordat in these years. His entire policy in Germany was directed towards exploiting the unusual advantages of the moment, which resulted from the new constitutional situation, to secure the acceptance of canon law. What the ambitious Nuncio was striving for was nothing less than a model concordat, to show what opportunities for the church had been afforded by the new conditions. Thus he deliberately delayed negotiations with the Reich during summer 1920 because it seemed to him wiser, as he wrote to Cardinal Bertram in Berlin, 'first of all to conclude the concordat with Bavaria, where in the present situation a favourable concordat is more to be hoped for... This Bavarian concordat could then serve as a model and precedent for the other German Länder.'[59] And the following year Ritter was even able to report from Rome that the Vatican also wished to present the Bavarian concordat 'as a model concordat' to those abroad.[60]

Bavaria was in principle in agreement with the role which Pacelli proposed for it. Delbrück learned in Munich that the Land stood 'firm by the separate concordat' and also would in no way give preference to the Reich. On the other hand, the Bavarian bureaucrats in the Kultusministerium were well aware of the purposes pursued by the Curia through its efforts in Munich, and therefore promised to be 'doubly careful'.[61]

In these circumstances, the approval of the Reich Foreign Minister which

Pacelli obtained in Berlin in November 1920 signified a clear victory for the Curia. It was a sign of sheer ignorance of church policy that the Foreign Minister gave the insistent Nuncio a binding, written assurance that the Reich Government had no objection to a Bavarian concordat, and that there was complete agreement 'that the concordat concluded with Bavaria would not be affected by later laws of the Reich'.[62] Thus the Nuncio and the Bavarian government had a free hand for their negotiations. The Reich had blocked its own efforts to take the lead in the negotiations for a concordat. As a consequence any uniform settlement of the school question in the Reich had become nearly impossible. Even later, the Reich was unable successfully to remove its head from this noose which it had itself tied. No wonder that Pacelli was 'very proud'[63] of this result. So in an interview with *Temps* early in December 1920 the Nuncio could now speak openly of his plans to follow up the Bavarian concordat with 'a Reich concordat for the rest of Germany, or a special concordat in Prussia'.[64] Here again he obviously retained for himself the choice of the most favourable occasion.

In the meantime, Prussia, too, began to play its own role in the whole concordat question. The special course adopted by Bavaria naturally also aroused the desire for a separate concordat in Prussia, which at first was doubtless interested in a common settlement throughout the Reich. The Reich, only interested in a treaty with the Vatican for the sake of foreign relations anyway, seemed to the Prussian government all too weak and easy-going a negotiating partner for the Curia.[65] And the first guidelines for a Reich concordat put forward early in January 1921 by the Reich Minister of the Interior, Erich Koch-Weser, could only strengthen Prussia in this suspicion. Compared with the demands which Pacelli had already presented in Bavaria, and which had been similarly formulated for the Reich,[66] these guidelines actually looked restrained. Vigilance seemed all the more necessary for Prussia. As early as the beginning of February the liberal Karl Heinrich Becker, who as Secretary of State and Minister played a decisive role in the Prussian Kultusministerium, dismissed outright the guidelines of the Reich government as 'utterly impossible'.[67] But in summer 1921 the rejection of the Reich initiative almost inevitably led to Prussia's demand to the Reich and the Curia 'like Bavaria, to arrange its own relations with the Holy See'.[68] Pacelli, however, knew that he would have a tougher negotiating partner here, against whom he could seriously play off neither the Reich nor Bavaria. On the other hand, the fact that he called the Prussian ideas a 'minimal concordat'[69] showed what he expected from Bavaria and indeed from the Reich.

To the degree that it was an expression and confirmation of his various possibilities, it was highly gratifying for Pacelli that the Reich government itself in autumn 1921 should initiate large-scale efforts for a Reich concordat.

Throughout this whole affair, a man who was later for a short time to become a key figure in German politics and the German church, Ludwig Kaas, began to familiarize himself with the complicated subject-matter of the concordat. In January 1920 Pacelli had asked the President of the Fulda Bishops' Conference, Cardinal Bertram, to put at his disposal a competent man who could advise him in his negotiations outside Bavaria, above all with Prussia and the Reich. The choice had fallen upon the Trier canon lawyer Ludwig Kaas, who not only had the specialized qualifications, but as a representative of the Centre Party in the Reichstag also had important political connections at his disposal.[70] Thus Kaas became the closest German collaborator with the Nuncio in all questions affecting the Reich concordat and the Prussian concordat and, at the same time, Pacelli's unbounded admirer. But this inevitably reinforced Pacelli's orientation on canon law in Germany. A canon lawyer like the Nuncio, Kaas shared his conviction of the central importance of canon law for all Catholic church policy and the need for it to be protected by concordats. It was indeed difficult to say who was more determined upon a Reich concordat: Pacelli or his collaborator Kaas.

As early as May 1920, when he began the first discussions with the Prussian Ministry of State, Kaas had declared that the Curia wanted a comprehensive Reich concordat 'in order to be better protected against measures on the part of individual Länder characteristic of the Kulturkampf and to avoid as many problems in the discussion as possible'.[71] This remained his conviction, leading him in 1933 into an alliance with the man who offered precisely this assurance: Hitler. Kaas was already by this time practised in the remarkable double role which he was to play as adviser simultaneously to the Reich government and to the Curia. When he sat at the negotiation table in Berlin in November 1921 for preliminary negotiations on a Reich concordat, Kaas was listed in the protocol after the representatives of the Ministry of the Interior and the Foreign Office as 'spokesman of the Reich and the Prussian government and of the Curia'.[72]

The Reich government's efforts on behalf of a Reich concordat began in the summer and autumn of 1921 on the initiative of Joseph Wirth, the second Chancellor the Centre Party had provided for the Weimar Republic. There were several reasons why he was the one who undertook this initiative. Wirth belonged on the left wing of his party, and he encountered mistrust and rejection even in its own ranks. A concordat with the Holy See would no doubt have strengthened his position. This, in turn, was the precondition for the safeguarding of the internal political stability of his government which was urgently necessary. At the same time, in summer 1921 the Reich had got into such a desperate situation in foreign relations because of the reparations issue and Poland's claim to Upper Silesia that even the slightest outside support had to be pursued by the Reich government.[73] Since in other respects, too, Wirth largely took Erzberger's line, it was natural for him also to adopt Erzberger's plans for a concordat, and again to attempt by means of a treaty with the Vatican to gain some of that recognition which the Chancellor and the Reich so urgently required.

Of course it is hard to say whether the conclusion of a Reich concordat would in fact have had the effects for which Wirth hoped. However, it is certain that the negotiations failed above all because of Pacelli's determined preference for a favourable concordat with Bavaria to uncertain negotiations with the Reich. Here neither the situation of the Reich nor a controversial Centre Party Chancellor, whose leftist tendencies seemed to him to be questionable, could deflect him fom his purpose.

Hence the matter was basically finished before it ever began. Wirth's primary aim was somehow or other to win Bavaria over to collaboration with his plans. In a discussion with the Bavarian Prime Minister, Graf Lerchenfeld, which took place on 11 November in Berlin, the Chancellor virtually implored the Bavarian delegation, assuring it that '...the attaining of a Reich concordat is a matter of prime importance to the entire Reich. He is prepared to enter into any arrangement with Bavaria that would permit this goal to be reached.' Lerchenfeld, however, coolly referred to the promise of the Reich dated 13 November 1920, and declared himself not in a position to suspend the Bavarian negotiations. He was neither able nor willing even to mention the topics of the negotiations.[74] This position was certainly in line with the deepest Bavarian convictions. But it was equally evident that these convictions only derived their political effectiveness from Pacelli's decision. Bavaria could have had no objections to the Curia's wish first to conclude a concordat with the Reich. Therefore Wirth acted quite logically when he instructed Ambassador Bergen in the Vatican to work for a change in the Nuncio's position. But this was just as futile as all other attempts to change the Nuncio's mind on this point.

Although Wirth's plans hardly had a chance after the Bavarian rejection, after personal negotiations with Pacelli the Reich Chancellor officially requested from the Nuncio on 14 November an enumeration of those points 'to which the Curia attached special value in concluding a Reich concordat'.[75] In response, the very next day the Nuncio presented the Reich government with the draft of a concordat which he had long since prepared and which in its extent and claims did not fall short of his suggestions for the Bavarian concordat.[76] The decisive point in it was the demand that the school issue should also be included in the negotiations. Yet for Prussia this was the very point that was 'fundamentally unacceptable', as was stated in the first opinion of the Ministry,[77] and Pacelli knew that. However, he was determined no matter what to break the Prussian resistance on this question. During a visit to the Kultusministerium at the end of 1921 he surprised the Minister, Otto Boelitz, and the Secretary of State, Carl Heinrich Becker, with open threats. A rapid reappointment to the episcopal see at Trier, an urgent matter for the Prussians because of the Saar question, would be considered only if the Prussian government would declare 'its basic agreement to discuss the school question in the Reich concordat'. For the Holy See this question was the key issue in a concordat. If the school articles were omitted, the church would no longer have 'any kind of interest' in a settlement. 'The Vatican would then find a situation without a treaty much better. All other issues were indeed secured by the constitution.' However, to his discomfort the Nuncio had to be reminded of that memorandum which he had accepted almost exactly two years before to the day, in which the continued validity of the Prussian treaties was expressly maintained. Pacelli's retort, that he had indeed accepted the declaration, 'but it had not been approved by the Vatican', did not sound exactly convincing. Finally, the German representatives pointed out 'that the German people in its present predicament would hardly understand such strong pressure by means of an ultimatum in which both issues', i.e. the vacancy-in-see at Trier and the school question, 'were fused'. It is hardly surprising that at the end the record gave the general impression that Pacelli on the whole had 'an approach orientated one-sidedly on Bavaria and the church. The great problems of German politics' were 'rather foreign' to him.[78]

However, all Prussia's objections could not alter the fact that for the moment the Nuncio had a good deal of leverage. So in intensive negotiations, on 6 January 1922, in return for a speedy appointment to the see at Trier, he finally wrung from the Prussian government the concession that 'at the request of the Reich' it would enter 'into negotiations on the settlement of the religious aspect of the school issue'.[79]

Pacelli considered this declaration a great success. His negotiations and the tough manner of his methods had, he informed Bertram, 'with God's help not been without success'.[80] But both Bertram and Karl Joseph Schulte, the Archbishop of Cologne, were of a different opinion. Schulte even described the package deal of which Pacelli was so proud as 'a most extraordinary risk', because in the final analysis it amounted to 'support of the French policy in the Saar which is drunk with the lust for conquest', and would be regarded for all time 'as a heavy, hostile blow by the Vatican against Germany'. Furthermore, even a rumour of these negotiations would unleash a national storm in Germany against Rome and Catholicism. Bertram also warned Pacelli at the same time against having too high hopes. State jurisdiction over the schools in Prussia was untouchable, and neither the Prussian Kultusministerium nor the non-Catholic majority in the Reichstag would yield on this point.[81] But this would not be the only time that Pacelli thought himself wiser than the German bishops.

One can find nearly all the characteristics of Pacelli's negotiating style in these years repeated in the 1933 negotiations. The exclusive concentration of church politics on the legal form of the concordat; the tendency to reckless exploitation of a situation apparently favourable to the church; almost complete lack of interest in specifically German problems and difficulties, and, not least, disregard for the German episcopate – all this made Pacelli a decade later a nearly ideal negotiating partner for Hitler.

In the Weimar Republic, however, despite all his forcefulness the Nuncio did not make progress nearly as quickly as he had no doubt hoped. It became apparent that the misgivings of the Prussian bishops were completely justified. Thus, in spite of that forced declaration of 6 January and in spite of all further efforts, the year 1922 brought no tangible progress for the Curia – either in the Reich or in Prussia.

On the part of the Reich, at first interest in the concordat seemed to remain as lively and constant as before. In March 1922 the Ministry of the Interior prepared a catalogue of questions requiring clarification, and as a result the first complete draft of a Reich concordat appeared in April, in collaboration with the Foreign Office. As the indefatigable Vatican official, Richard Delbrück, noted, discussions of this draft with Kaas, Cardinal Schulte of Cologne and Pacelli himself did not raise 'substantial difficulties of any kind'. 'The Nuncio and the Cardinal declared themselves thoroughly satisfied with the draft, and considered it proper that it should now be discussed confidentially and in an informal way with the Curia, which was planned for the beginning of June. However, this surprising concurrence also revealed the bias in the draft. In fact it went a long way towards meeting the Curia, which was hardly a burden to the Reich, and especially in its broad approach to the school question along Catholic lines presumably came very close to the Roman ideal.[82] However, that meant that the first draft was even less suitable as a basis for discussion with Prussia. Naturally Delbrück knew this, too, and had therefore already prepared a political strategy to overcome Prussian opposition. 'After agreement in principle with the Curia', parliamentary majorities were to be created for the Reich concordat: Delbrück hoped for them from the majority socialists through the influence of the Reich President and the Reich Chancellor.[83]

The hope of being able to force Prussia through a collaboration of the Reich government and the Curia to surrender on two fronts, namely by abandoning any idea of a concordat of its own and by adapting the Catholic school proposals was, however, a political delusion. Delbrück discovered this no later than June 1922 when he went to Rome with the draft of the concordat. The German ambassador whom he met there still represented Prussian interests too, as had been agreed, and in this capacity he declared to the Vatican officials in no uncertain terms and without diplomatic circumlocutions that it was 'a hopeless business to coerce Prussia to serve the ends of the Curia'.[84] Accordingly, the embassy also clearly dissociated itself from Delbrück's mission. In these circumstances, success was out of the question. The fact that Delbrück was soon afterwards recalled to Berlin by telephone was only the external expression of an impossible political situation in which Pacelli, through his insistence on the Bavarian concordat and the regulation of the schools in the Reich, had been foremost in pressurizing the Reich government.

This meant that for the time being the plans for a concordat were at an end. Staggering from crisis to crisis after the late summer of 1922, the Reich became increasingly incapable of negotiations. Reparations, the struggle over the Ruhr and inflation thrust aside the theme of the concordat. Even Pacelli understood this and in September declared himself ready to postpone further negotiations with the Reich to a more favourable moment.[85]

During these weeks Prussia, too, declared itself incapable of negotiating over a concordat. And it was perhaps not just 'the spirit of the cultural-political state direction of the Bismarck era' which led Carl Heinrich Becker, the Secretary of State, in a political situation of extreme tension, to refuse to comply directly with the Catholic demand for an abandonment of all government reservations, especially since there could be no serious doubt as to the actual freedom of the Catholic Church in Prussia.[86]

For the Curia, the failure of its plans in the Reich was the signal to devote itself anew, with increased efforts, to the Bavarian concordat – which in any case it had always preferred. The change in the pontificate which had taken place in the meantime did not make the slightest difference. On the contrary, by his unusual recall of Gasparri to be Cardinal Secretary of State Pius XI, who had succeeded Benedict XV on 6 February 1922, had already made it clear that in principle he intended to continue the present line in church politics. And in fact it very soon emerged that the new Pope, too, adhered to the Curia's concordat policy. Indeed he was even more interested, indeed personally interested, in this policy. But in this context the next goal was the Bavarian concordat.

After the College of Cardinals had approved Pacelli's draft in August 1922, at the beginning of September Pius XI asked the Bavarian envoy to the Vatican 'to assert more emphatically' to the Bavarian Minister President his – the Pope's – 'urgent wish' for a prompt conclusion of the treaty. The Pope seemed almost to echo the Munich Nuncio's thinking when he declared: 'The Bavarian concordat would be a suitable model for a concordat to be concluded with the Reich. It could also be of use beyond the borders of Germany. Let your government,' he instructed Ritter, 'be in no doubt that I am personally interested in this question, which I have studied thoroughly, and that I would be very pleased if my wish for the earliest possible conclusion of the concordat were considered and fulfilled by the Bavarian government'.[87]

In spite of this insistent pressure from Rome, and in spite of all Pacelli's efforts in Munich, it took another eighteen months for the Bavarian concordat finally to be ready for signing, in March 1924. This was not because of resistance by the government. As Pacelli had correctly foreseen, Bavaria was ready to accept all the essential demands of the Curia, so long as they could be reconciled with the constitution of the Reich and the Land. What delayed things was, rather, the difficult political situation and the necessity of negotiating a similar church treaty with the Protestant Landeskirche in Bavaria. Furthermore, the parliamentary situation also had to be considered carefully. Hence nearly another year passed before the concordat question was finally settled. At the beginning of January Pacelli and Pius XI reviewed the German text 'word by word' one last time.[88] A few days later the treaty was approved in the Landtag by 73 votes to 52.[89]

As Ritter reported of the Cardinal Secretary of State: as a result the Curia was 'in a most exalted mood'. Now at last, as Gasparri put it, 'this important work is completed, which has occupied almost five years, and it remains to be hoped that it will be a blessing to Bavaria, especially in the settling of the school question. The Cardinal also expects a favourable effect from the Bavarian concordat on the readjustment of the relationship between church and state in the rest of the German Reich.' But above all, as Ritter finally reported, Gasparri praised Pacelli in this context, as being 'one of the best Nuncios, if not the best'.[90]

With the Bavarian concordat Pacelli had in fact attained his major goal. The sixteen articles of the treaty could scarcely have turned out more favourably for the church.[91] The concordat secured the principles of canon law in the nomination of archbishops and bishops and in the appointment of canons and dignitaries. It gave the church, in its comprehensive articles on schools, far-reaching influence over the entire educational system, especially over the elementary schools, and it obligated the state to the perpetual protection, recognition and advancement of the Catholic church and all its organizations and institutions. Over against this, the sole concession of the church appeared more than modest. It was embodied in Article 13, where, 'in view of the expenditure of the Bavarian state on the salaries of the clergy', the church gave an assurance essentially to employ clergy which 'have Bavarian citizenship or citizenship of another German state'. In view of the concordat as a whole and in detail it was quite understandable that years later the Bavarian government was still afraid that individual stipulations of the concordat could be contested on the basis of Reich law.[92]

Even before the Bavarian concordat was fully settled, the Nuncio had already begun to concentrate again on the Reich concordat. If all had gone according to his plans, the Bavarian treaty should have been followed as soon as possible by a corresponding treaty with the Reich, which would have been the consummation of the great Bavarian success. The situation in autumn 1923 seemed far more favourable than three years earlier. Conditions in the Reich had stabilized, but it was still the case that the Reich government had to make efforts towards achieving diplomatic recognition. And in Wilhelm Marx it again had a Chancellor from the Centre Party at its head. So in October 1924 the Nuncio approached the Reich government with a request to resume the consultations over a Reich concordat which had been suspended for the time being. After a discussion in the cabinet, Marx instructed the Ministry of the Interior to prepare a new concordat draft. In the middle of November this new draft was presented, but only to vanish again at once into the files.[93] However, nine years later, in the spring of 1933, the draft was to be included in the documents with which Hitler's agent, von Papen, set out for Rome for negotiations on a concordat. It gave the impression that these negotiations were merely the continuation of a long-standing policy.

Pacelli's hopes of a Reich concordat in autumn 1924 were shattered so quickly as a result of his own policy. For the more the Curia got out of the Bavarian treaty, the more distrustful Prussia inevitably became of a Reich concordat which, according to the declared purpose of the Nuncio, was to impose the same terms on the largest German Land by way of the Reich. Therefore the Prussian government declared categorically on 27 November 1924, in a note to the Reich government, that after the conclusion of the Bavarian concordat Prussia could consider only a concordat of its own. It was utterly unacceptable for Prussia to enter the sphere of church politics 'as a state with inferior rights to other German Länder'.[94] What appeared to be a question of prestige was in reality a political determination to decide the relations between church and state in Prussia: in Berlin and not in Rome. However, this clear negative on the part of Prussia put paid to plans for the Reich. Without the consent of the Prussian government there could be no Reich concordat.[95]

The Nuncio, too, finally had to accept this. So he embarked, against his will, on the only course now possible, namely to enter into negotiations with the Prussian government for a Prussian concordat. Here both sides had distinct interests to protect. The state was concerned to prevent, if possible, the full impact of canon law on the Catholic Church in Prussia, and to guarantee the cathedral chapters at least some of their traditional rights of nomination, and to secure for itself some control over the personnel as well as the re-establishment, definition and organization of the Prussian diocese. For financial, confessional and territorial reasons this particular issue was a political question of the first order. On the other side, apart from removing the rest of the Kulturkampf legislation, the Curia's interest lay in two items: the establishment of a see of Berlin and the widest possible inclusion of the school question.[96]

After the Nuncio had finally moved from Munich to Berlin in 1925, the mutual negotiating positions were first defined – between March and June 1926. Here it very soon became apparent that references to the Bavarian concordat found no echo of any kind in Prussia. It was brought home to Pacelli that in the Prussian Kultusministerium, led by Carl Heinrich Becker, for the first time in Germany he had come up against his equal in negotiations. While he had ultimately achieved his aim fairly easily in Bavaria because of the special situation of the Land, and the Reich government was acting in more or less dilettante fashion on alien ground, in Prussia he was up against officials who were determined to defend the liberal and Protestant legacy of the Land and who were in no way inferior to himself in their qualifications in church law and politics.

In these circumstances a rapid conclusion to the negotiations was inconceivable. They were further complicated by the passionate reactions of the public. On the one hand Catholic voices almost unanimously demanded full rights for the church, including those of confessional schools; on the other hand, certain Protestant circles sharing the views of the Evangelischer Bund, hand in hand with the German Communist Party (KPD), and with a fear of the 'Blacks' bordering on hysteria, saw the Counter-Reformation already on the move. Despite this tense atmosphere it was possible up to summer 1927 – not least through the mediation and conciliation of Kaas, who was constantly involved – to arrive at a preliminary agreement on a long list of questions. But a year later, in summer and autumn 1928, essential problems still remained unsettled: the establishment of the Berlin see, the rules for the nomination of bishops, and the school question.[97] Finally, after the Prussian government had met both of the Curia's first two points, only the school question was still under discussion. Here, however, Prussia could not and would not yield. The Prussian Minister President Otto Braun personally assured the Nuncio 'that no provision of any kind about the schools could be included in the concordat'. The word 'school' might not even appear in the text. The Nuncio, Braun reported later, 'declared in despair that he could not possibly go to the Holy Father in Rome with a draft concordat that did not mention the schools. I retorted that I could not go before parliament with a concordat that did mention the schools without exposing myself to certain defeat.'[98] At the end of the year it was still by no means certain whether the entire negotiations would not founder on this one issue.

But then it proved that the Curia could yield too. In spring 1929 Pacelli succeeded in convincing the Pope and the Cardinal Secretary of State of the need to accept the Prussian conditions in principle. On 14 June 1929 the treaty between the free state of Prussia and the Holy See was signed. Barely four weeks later, the Prussian Landtag approved it by a vote of 243 to 171. This brought Pacelli's second German concordat plan to a conclusion.

The Prussian concordat consisted of fourteen articles.[99] It regulated the boundaries of the new dioceses in Prussia, largely in accordance with the church's wishes, and in this connection also permitted the establishment of an independent diocese of Berlin. In the disputed question of the nomination of bishops, the chapters retained the right to put forward names and the final right of election from three candidates nominated by the Holy See on the basis of the proposals. A political clause guaranteed the Prussian state government the right of veto if need be. A compromise was also arrived at in the appointment of dignitaries and canons. A further article stipulated that the clergy had to be citizens of the German Reich and academically trained; in the case of certain prominent posts prior notification of appointments had to be made to the public authorities. Moreover, in addition to liberal provisions for endowment the treaty included not least a guarantee of the existence of publicly-supported Catholic theological faculties in Breslau, Bonn, Münster and Braunsberg. Finally, nothing was said on the school issue, as the state had made that a precondition.

In retrospect, too, this treaty could be described as a good agreement. Neither state nor church had given anything away, but they had finally followed a line which took the interests of both partners into account. This achieved more towards peace between the two parties than if one side or the other had secured its maximum demands.

However, for the Curia and especially for the ambitious Nuncio, accustomed to success, the Prussian concordat was certainly a disappointment. This was true not only from the perspective of the Bavarian concordat, which had turned out so favourably for the church, but also from that of the Lateran Treaties, which in spring 1929 had demonstrated what extraordinary concessions the young

Fascist Italy was ready to make. Compared with this, the Prussian concordat was really only a compromise.[100]

The Nuncio made it quite plain that the Curia had entered into this compromise only because it had to, and that it would not in any way give up its demands in the school question. In an official note of 5 August he reminded the Prussian Minister President of the promise made under pressure on 6 January 1922, and of the compromise formulae which had already been arrived at in the negotiations. Even if the treaty had nevertheless been concluded, the Nuncio wrote, the Holy See was still unable 'to refrain from declaring formally that its position ought never to be represented as a renunciation of the fundamental principles which led it to demand that, as in the other concordats of recent times, the school question should be included in the solemn agreement with Prussia.'[101]

This meant that Catholic demands over schools had not been abandoned, but only adjourned to a more favourable time. The simultaneous publication in the *Acta Apostolicae Sedis* of this note and the Prussian response along with the treaty confirmed this stand and this resolve.

Despite the disappointing result of the Prussian negotiations, Pacelli was determined resolutely to pursue his concordat policy in Germany. Because successful negotiations for a Reich concordat were unthinkable in present circumstances, he directed his attention to the south-western sector of the Reich: Baden. In Baden the legal relations between state and church were similar to those in Prussia. Here, too, the relationship between church and state was regulated by papal decree – the Bulls *Provida solersque* of 1821 and *Ad dominici gregis custodiam* of 1826,[102] which had been given the rank of state laws by the Grand Dukes. Thus it seemed natural here, too, to undertake negotiations for the revisions of the old relations which were needed. In addition, the political situation in Karlsruhe had improved in the late autumn of 1929, in favour of the Centre Party. Thanks to a considerable gain in votes in the Landtag elections in October, the Party was in a position to form a government in co-operation with the SPD and to include a readiness for concordat negotiations in the conditions for a coalition.[103]

Even before the formation of the new Baden government a preliminary discussion took place in Constance at the suggestion and with the mediation of Ludwig Kaas, in which the two Centre Party Baden politicians, Prelate Schofer and Dr Föhr (later and for many years the Vicar General of Freiburg) joined Pacelli and Kaas.[104] The subject was particulary tricky, in that Archbishop Fritz of Freiburg had clearly dissociated himself from the plans for a concordat.

So it was all the more important that the talks in Constance were able to arrive at a preliminary agreement. Armed with this, on 29 November Pacelli could officially turn to the Baden Ministry of State with the request that negotiations be opened towards the conclusion of a concordat between the Holy See and the Baden government.[105]

But before these negotiations could begin, changes had taken place in Rome that gave Pacelli new responsibilities. Following the successful conclusion of the Lateran Treaties, Gasparri, almost eighty years old, had retired. Pius XI nominated the Nuncio in Berlin as his successor, probably not least with the aim of ensuring the continuity of the papal concordat policy. On 10 December 1929 Pacelli took leave of Berlin.[106] By Christmas he had already been made a cardinal in Rome. His appointment as Cardinal Secretary of State and thus as the new director of world-wide papal policy followed on 7 February 1930.

When in a lecture to the Prussian Academy of Sciences at the end of 1930 Ulrich Stutz, from whose school a whole generation of canon lawyers of both churches had emerged, assessed the legal development of Catholicism following the publication of the *Codex Juris Canonici*, he spoke of 'unprecedently favourable circumstances which no one could have dreamt of in the remotest way, not even its author, even when the law code took effect, far less on its promulgation, or even during its preparation and elaboration'. He then suggested that the transformation of the circumstances, namely 'the reform of the constitution completed under the sign of the separation of church and state', had cleared 'the way unexpectedly for the new church law as well'. 'Examination of the concordats and similar agreements during the last decade' revealed, Stutz concluded, that 'both in them and through them the Codex is on the march'.[107]

Correct as this observation was even for Germany in particular, the crowning achievement here, the Reich concordat, was still lacking. With political conditions the way they were in the Reich, there was no prospect of a concordat in the foreseeable future. So it was with all the more attention that the Curia watched the change in these circumstances over the coming years, a change which began with the National Socialist landslide in the elections of September 1930 and was to present all of German Catholicism, the episcopate, the Centre Party, and not least the Curia, with completely new decisions.

5

The Völkisch Movement, Hitler, and the Beginnings of the NSDAP (1919-1923)

In September 1919, while Protestant Germany was meeting in Dresden, the theological revival was being launched in Tambach, and a new concordat was already being discussed in Munich, Adolf Hitler joined the German Workers' Party in the Bavarian capital. On the course along which Hitler led this party there lay a long series of decisions which directly concerned its relationship with the Christian churches. These decisions were connected with the nature and development of the völkisch movement.

The development of the so-called völkisch movement or völkisch idea must be seen as one of the most important things to happen in Germany in the period during and after the War. Without it, the spread and rule of the National Socialists is inconceivable. In fact the NSDAP was simply a völkisch movement which became a political party in the sense that the Communist parties are Marxism embodied in political parties.

The parallel between the völkisch movement and Marxism is not a haphazard one. Rather this movement represents, after Marxism, the second great comprehensive, totalitarian ideology produced by the nineteenth century. It might seem surprising to say that nowadays. This is because the völkisch idea – albeit with all conceivable justification – was so completely erased from our memories after the collapse of the Third Reich that since then this key word no longer appears even in multi-volume lexicons.[1] But as a result the recollection has also been lost that many of those living in the Weimar period saw Marxism and the völkisch movement as opposed forces, basically of the same kind. 'The Communist,' wrote an observer as early as 1924, 'may despise the Fascists and fight strongly against them; nevertheless Communism and Fascism are so much from the same stem that, as we experience every day, their followers move from one to the other with astonishing ease.'[2]

The völkisch movement was doubtless much inferior to Marxism in systematic theoretical development. It was, however, quite clearly superior to it at that time in its capacity to mobilize. That was one of the points on which Hitler concentrated and with which he achieved success.

Even today we still lack a comprehensive, historical, systematic portrayal of the völkisch movement.[3] That is probably first because of the vagueness of its theory and secondly because of the comparative anonymity of its origin (in contrast to Marxism it had not just one father but many in the nineteenth century). And, not least, it is also because of the diversity associated with it, which makes any portrayal of it extraordinarily difficult.[4] Hence the following account must also restrict itself to indicating a series of philosophical, theological, historical and political lines of development which are indispensable for understanding the period and Hitler's role in it.

The world-view of the völkisch movement was characterized by a marked ethical dualism. Good and evil, light and darkness, idealism and materialism, bravery and cowardice, purity and corruption fought in it for supremacy. But the German Volk – and this was the intrinsic belief of the völkisch – had been called to this end and was capable of deciding this battle for the world in favour of the principle of the good. This was the common basic conviction of the entire völkisch movement. It derived in the first place from Fichte, then in the course of the nineteenth century underwent numerous changes, and after the First World War became an interpretative system for the New Right. No one can understand the power which National Socialism achieved without realizing that behind it stood the claim and the conviction to be fighting on the side of good against evil.

The decisive change which völkisch dualism underwent in the nineteenth century came about through the adoption of the racial dogma of Gobineau and his successors. The good and evil principles were attached to race: the good to the Aryan race and the evil to the Jewish-semitic race. Only then was the völkisch idea bound up with that murderous antisemitism which then increasingly became its real essence. In 1920, Max Robert Gerstenhauer, a well-known völkisch theoretician, aptly expressed the völkisch movement's understanding of the relationship of the old national-völkisch principle to racial dogma in these terms: 'Racial dogma, consequently, has become the scientific biological foundation of the nationalist idea, and the results of the latest biological research completely confirm the traditional, familiar views of the nationalists – that the Volk is an entity created by blood...'[5]

This appeal to the most recent results of racial research contributed much to the persuasive power of the völkisch idea. In contrast to pre-scientific views of the world, it seemed legitimated as objective knowledge.[6]

We cannot go into every detail of the origin and development of the völkisch idea in the nineteenth century here. Indeed - and this can be said almost with certainty – it would never have played a decisive role had not war and defeat driven a deeply distraught nation to search for primordial causes and ways out.[7]

Although the historical explanations of the rise of certain ideas at certain times frequently remain unsatisfying, the decisive role of war and defeat in the case of völkisch antisemitism is clear. Nearly all accounts agree that völkisch antisemitism had no serious political and social significance in the Kaiser's Reich. P.W.Massing, to whom we owe one of the first works on the prehistory of political antisemitism, has described the position in these terms: 'Neither the Christian-social variety of antisemitism in the 1880s nor the völkisch variety in the 1890s could impair the legal position of the Jews in any way. Not a single bill was passed that would have limited the 1869 Law of Emancipation, while there was no lack of oppression directed against Catholics, Socialists and Poles. The völkisch demands for special laws against the Jews never had the slightest chance of being put into practice. When in 1882 at the First International Congress of Antisemitists in Dresden Ernst Henrici moved that all Jews should be expelled from Germany, it was no less a person than Stoecker himself who assured him that if it should ever come to a vote as to who was to be expelled from Germany, Jews or antisemitists, the antisemitists would certainly find themselves at a disadvantage.'[8]

Thus in 1918 the völkisch idea was in fact still nothing but the affair of a handful of agitators, who found growing interest and a hearing only amidst defeat and chaos. Among them, three were especially well known: Theodor Fritsch, almost seventy at that time, with his *Handbook on the Jewish Question*;[9] Artur Dinter and his exceedingly successful 'contemporary novel' *The Sin against the Blood*;[10] and the Munich author Dietrich Eckart and his periodical, *Plain Speaking*.[11] These three names largely cover the ideology of the völkisch movement, but not its organization. They form a kind of triangle of agitation in which, for all the differences in temperaments and objectives, there is a constantly recurring unity of certain basic convictions and arguments.

This applies first and foremost to the radically dualistic racial character of the völkisch world-view. 'The Jewish nature,' Fritsch (for example) wrote repeatedly, 'is the complete inversion of civilized, honourable humankind. The Jew turns all concepts upside down. He makes despicable what to others is holy, and he exalts the immoral and the depraved. The characteristic feature of Judaism is hatred of humanity and hostility to morality.'[12] In a similar vein Dinter declared that the Jewish race is 'physically and spiritually opposed to the German race'. This opposition is 'insurmountable'. 'The Jew is not capable of German ideals, German thought, feeling and desire..., German joy and power and greatness, since his race lacks the spiritual organs to perceive them. He is rich in all the qualities which are also the foundations of German vices, which the Jew is incessantly at work to incite and provoke: avarice and selfishness, sensual lust and godlessness, unfaithfulness and insincerity.'[13] Dietrich Eckart also represented the radical völkisch dualism, according to which on earth 'at least among the cultured nations there are two kinds of human beings: the Jews – and the rest'.[14] But for him it was rather the Jewish-materialistic spirit that made the Jews Jews.[15] The phrase 'the battle with Judaism within us and outside us'[16] which appeared again word for word in Article 24 of the Party programme as a struggle against 'the Jewish materialist spirit within us and outside us' was doubtless Eckart's conviction and makes it clear that Eckart understood völkisch dualism to be more than a spiritual principle.

The whole völkisch movement combined the dualistic principle with belief in a Jewish world conspiracy which had been responsible from the beginning of history for all the evil of mankind and which was now trying in a last, powerful strenuous effort to annihilate Aryan humanity and to help evil on to final victory.[17] 'Over millions of corpses,' wrote Fritsch, 'surrounded by streams of blood, the Universal Jew strides towards the throne of world domination. He dares to commit monstrous crimes, for which he will have to atone with his death.'[18] All revolutions and wars, all upheavals and political breakdowns were therefore a planned, staged work of the Universal Jew – who needed anarchy and decline to assure his domination. In the present, capitalism and socialism above all represented the instruments of which the Jews made use to sow discord and to destroy the social order. The World War, too, was their work, as was the Russian revolution and American capital.[19]

In the face of this world conspiracy and its goals, there could be only one watchword for the völkisch movement: Struggle, *Kampf*.

Alarm, alarm, alarm! Alarm, alarm, alarm!
Ring the bells from tower to tower,
Ring, that sparks to fly begin -
Judas comes the Reich to win.
Ring, that ropes with blood turn red
round burnings, tortures and the dead;
sound the alarm that earth mounts higher
beneath the thunder of saving ire!
Woe to the people still wrapped in dreams,
Germany, awake![20]

These verses by Eckart clearly show the solemn mood of the völkisch struggle. It was no coincidence that 'Germany, awake' became the battle cry of the National Socialist movement.[21]

Dinter also had the hero of his novel, Dr Hermann Kämpfer, deciding to use money inherited from a Jewish commercial counsellor 'for the struggle against Judaism'. 'He had the unshakable confidence that of its own accord the German Volk would find ways and means of ridding itself of this enemy – once it had recognized it in all its frightfulness and insidiousness.' Thus the sum of twelve million marks was to be allocated to a scientific association for the purpose 'of founding an Institute for Racial Hygiene'.[22]

The task which the völkisch movement had set for itself is evident from these voices, namely struggle against Jewry by means of journalistic and scientific enlightenment. It was typical that hardly one of the völkisch journalists and agitators thought things through completely. To be sure, there was unanimity that 'the final solution of the Jewish problem... was to be found only in the complete elimination of all Jews from the life of the Aryan people'.[23] But Fritsch, like Dinter and Eckart, rejected the consequences of this position. 'We do not want to kill the Jews or do them any violence. We simply want to see them eliminated from the life of our Volk... In the free competition between nations, Judah may release his best energies in a fatherland of his own...'[24] The Jewish question was never to be solved 'by physical force', Dinter also declared, but only 'through spiritual power'. To facilitate this solution he called for legislation to protect the Germans from Jewish influences.[25]

Germany's mission was the struggle against the Jewish world-enemy. The aim of the struggle which beckoned was nothing less than 'the redemption of the world': 'Nowhere on earth is there another people that would be more capable, more thorough in bringing about the Third Reich than ours! *Veni creator spiritus!*'[26]

It is not hard to see the fascinations of this world-view in the post-war period. It explained in a simple way the causes of the German defeat and its continuing effects. It identified their author and at the same time pointed the way towards a better future. That this was an utterly ideological proposition, having nothing to do with actual circumstances, hardly mattered. It had all the more to do with

77

the sensitivities and imaginings of many Germans. They were convinced that they had stood for the better cause in this war. They had been braver, more serious, greater and truer than their enemies. In spite of this the war had been lost. There had to be a strange, unknown, sinister reason. The völkisch movement claimed to have known this reason for a long time. And in the unimaginable confusion of the post-war period what in the secure order of the Kaiser's Reich they had dismissed as fantasy suddenly became plausible to certain individuals.[27] The reminiscences of Justizrat Heinrich Class, the leader of the Pan-Germans, are thoroughly typical of this situation. He wrote in retrospect: 'My train of thought was like this. The frightful débacle of November 1918 cannot and should not mean the end of German history – especially as it stood in blatant contradiction to the attitude of our people at the outbreak of the war, and contradicted their tremendous efforts throughout its course. Hence something foreign to the disposition of our Volk must have been introduced from the outside. Out of the whole struggle which I had waged with my friends up to this point I came to realize, as they did, what the foreign element was: simply put, internationally directed forces were active, destroying Bismarck's work.'[28]

This was also the programmatic explanation of the War and the post-war period for the two men who at the beginning of the 1920s were considered to be the political leaders of the völkisch movement.

One of them was Erich Ludendorff, the military chief of German operations in the War and, next to Hindenburg, Germany's most popular army commander – a man of unusual arrogance and narrowness of mind. Himself not a little to blame for the situation, he increasingly foisted responsibility for what had happened upon 'supra-national powers' which had brought about Germany's downfall. As he wrote in his memoirs: 'I had become aware that in my efforts to preserve the life of the people I had come up against something secret and mysterious, and I would have to penetrate deeply into the conditions that had brought about our fearful calamity... Ever more apparent, secret, supra-national powers emerged before me as a fungus which destroyed the unanimity of the people, namely the Jewish race and Rome, along with their tools: the freemasons, the Jesuits, and occult and satanic groups.'[29]

Hitler, the other leader of the völkisch movement, also turned the collapse into a moment of awareness and decision. The scene in which he describes how, temporarily blinded and lying in a military hospital, he learned of the defeat, ends: 'The more I tried to achieve clarity on the monstrous event in this hour, the more the shame of indignation and disgrace burned my brow. What was all the pain in my eyes compared to this misery? There followed terrible days and even worse nights – I knew that all was lost...In these nights hatred grew in me, hatred for those responsible for this deed.' Something had happened which Hitler, according to his own testimony, 'had so often feared but had never been able to believe with my emotions. Kaiser Wilhelm II was the first German Emperor to hold out a conciliatry hand to the leaders of Marxism, without suspecting that scoundrels have no honour. While they still held the imperial hand in theirs, the other hand was reaching for the dagger.' Then follow the two decisive sentences, deliberately formulated so as to be terse and monumental: 'There is no making pacts with Jews; there can only be the hard: either-or.

I, for my part, decided to go into politics.'[30]

The function of antisemitism as the explanation for a defeat which otherwise remained inexplicable is obvious here. The thought of a Jewish world conspiracy against Germany was, of course, absurd. But it did not seem more absurd to many Germans than a beaten army, a scuttled fleet, street battles in Berlin, a government of workers' councils in Munich, a continuing food blockade and a progressive devaluation of the currency. And anyone who had once given way to these thoughts immediately found evidence for them everywhere. Jews in France, in England and America; Jews in Berlin and Munich, on the stock exchange, in the press, and at the universities – was that not proof enough?[31]

For the völkisch ideologist Judah was as ubiquitously at work as the class enemy for the Marxist. And no knowledge, no historical or political education, prevented him from rediscovering in reality the truth of his ideology – by force, if necessary.[32]

Without war and defeat völkisch antisemitism would almost certainly have remained a fringe phenomenon. But they created the conditions for its spread. This can be demonstrated convincingly with reference to the organizational development of the völkisch movement. For example, in 1913 the Reichshammerbund, an organization founded by Fritsch, numbered just nineteen groups in Germany. The wretched existence of the Nuremberg group, with twenty-three members and an annual budget of M94.64 is a typical example of one of them.[33] How unpopular völkisch antisemitism actually was is also demonstrated by the stance of the Alldeutscher Verband. Its leadership, otherwise completely uninhibited in propagating the most extreme nationalistic goals which its name, the Pan-German Alliance, indicated, did not dare to commit the Verband overtly to an antisemitic course in the pre-War period.[34] The decision to expand the work of the Verband to include the Jewish question was first taken at the last session during the War, in October 1918.[35] Then, in February 1919, in the so-called 'Bamberg Declaration', völkisch antisemitism was officially introduced into the Alldeutsch programme,[36] and at the same time it was decided to form a new alliance, which would be dedicated entirely to the antisemitic struggle. From this point a direct line leads to the first great völkisch-antisemitic organization in Germany, the Deutschvölkischer Schutz- und Trutzbund, which in October 1919 took in most of the more important antisemitic groups. For some time, and not by chance, the rise and end of the Bund paralleled the development of the NSDAP, the National Socialist Party. Even after take-overs and mergers, at the beginning of December 1919 the Bund did not comprise more than 25,000 members nationwide, a number which, compared with the mass movements on the left, made it still seem a fringe phenomenon in society as a whole. However, 1920 brought a kind of breakthrough. By the end of the year the membership of the Bund had climbed to well over 100,000. From that point, though, the rapid upward growth slowed down again. By the time the Bund was banned in the summer of 1922, the number of members was between 160,000 and 180,000.[37] Uwe Lohalm attributes the relative stagnation to two main factors. 'First, the Deutschvölkischer Schutz- und Trutzbund had no political programme of any kind beyond antisemitism... Secondly, it was unable to bring the masses together in such a way that solid organization capable of effective political work could emerge.'[38] These were the two very points in which Hitler surpassed the völkisch movement.

The earliest political utterances of Hitler's that we have[39] show him completely under the spell of völkisch ideas. In these utterances there is not a thought, an idea, an argument of any importance that is not repeated frequently in the völkisch literature of the day. There is therefore little point in making a search for Hitler's spiritual forebears. These forebears are – with the exception of Richard Wagner, who probably played a special role[40] – identical with the spiritual forebears of the völkisch movement.[41]

In Hitler's case, too, radical racial-ethical dualism formed the basis of his world-view. The first political document of his that we know is a statement on the Jewish question. It begins with a distinction between antisemitism as 'a mere emotional phenomenon' and genuine political antisemitism, which rests on a 'clear knowledge', the 'knowledge of facts'. Among these facts the thirty-year-old Hitler included the racial character of the Jewish question – Judaism is 'absolutely a race and not a religious association' – and the ineradicable ethical moral differences of the races. 'And from this there follows the fact that among us lives a non-German, foreign race, neither inclined nor in a position to sacrifice its racial characteristics, to deny its own feelings, thought and effort, and which nevertheless politically has all the rights that we do. As the feeling of the Jew is stirred by purely material things, all the more so are his thought and effort. The dance round the golden calf becomes the inexorable stuggle for all those material possessions which, our inner feelings tell us, should not be the highest things, those most worth striving for in the world.' It was Hitler's conviction that the activity of the Jews destroyed all the higher spiritual and moral values of the nations. 'That has the following effect: on purely emotional grounds antisemitism will find its final expression in pogroms. But rational antisemitism must lead to a well-planned and legal struggle against the Jews and removal of their privileges... However, its ultimate goal must inexorably be the removal of the Jews.' This excerpt closes with the political declaration: 'Only a government of national power is capable of both, not a government of national powerlessness.' This, once again, is not a matter of the form of the state, but of the 'rebirth of the moral and spiritual powers of the nation' which is put on course 'through the ruthless action of nationally minded leadership personalities'.[42]

It cannot be said that even the smallest point is left unclear in these utterances. On the contrary, what distinguished them from many völkisch documents of the time was precisely their greater consistency and the firmer political resolve, which from the beginning excluded compromises, doubt and objections.

Barely a year later, the speech of 13 August 1920 showed Hitler on the way towards developing a coherent political programme out of the different elements in the völkisch movement. Here, too, his originality lay not in individual ideas but in the deft and logical way in which he connected basic political questions with the dualistic principle. This particular speech was concerned above all with the association between antisemitism and socialism. Hitler made the connection by means of the concept of work: 'Aryanism means a moral conception of work and therefore that about which we so often talk today: socialism, civic spirit, public advantage before private advantage. Judaism means an egotistical conception of work and therefore mammonism and materialism – the complete opposite of socialism.'[43] In developing this thesis Hitler argued in the same way as the Marxists on the other side. While they saw Fascism as an instrument of the capitalist world conspiracy, Hitler saw Marxism as an instrument of the Jewish world conspiracy. National Socialist racial struggle and Marxist class struggle were given the same ideological and political status extending to specific formulae; 'In order to free our economy from these shackles we need the struggle against this agitation, the politically organized struggle of the masses against their oppressors.'[44] In place of the proletarian masses against their capitalist oppressors, here there were the German masses against their Jewish oppressors. 'Tumultuous applause' rewarded Hitler for this phrase.

The decisive factor, however, was that by this time Hitler had grasped the fundamental connection between programme and action, theory and praxis, and this then became the basis of his rise to power.

We know for sure, he declared, 'that scientific knowledge can only be the preparatory work, and that this knowledge must be followed by organization which one day will turn into action. And that action remains unalterably fixed for us: it is the removal of the Jews from our nation....'[45]

Without doubt in his programme Hitler was and always remained a convinced völkisch ideologist. Thus even in his last word from the rubble of collapsing Berlin he bound 'the leadership of the nation and its followers to scrupulous observation of the racial laws and to pitiless resistance to the universal poisoner of all nations: international Jewry'.[46] But what marked him off from the völkisch movement was the consistency with which he transformed völkisch thought into a political world-view and the insight that programme, organization and action belong indissolubly together. That enabled him to become the consummate leader who, even after the disaster of a failed Putsch, still towered above his rivals.[47]

On the way from völkisch thought to the 'consistent logical synthesis' of the National Socialist world-view,[48] Hitler not only achieved the union of radical antisemitism and Lebensraum imperialism, as Eberhard Jäckel has proved convincingly.[49] He also eliminated the religious elements which he had accepted along with völkisch thought. Little attention has so far been paid to this process. Nevertheless it not only is of great importance for the unity of the movement but also provides the decisive foundations for Hitler's later church policy.

One of the main problems of the völkisch movement was the religious claim bound up with the völkisch idea. This claim was connected with the ethical dualism of the approach and, of course, from the beginning, made relations with Christianity fraught. Obviously a radical antisemitism of the kind represented by the völkisch movement had to define its relationship to Christianity more closely. Yet this definition proved to be extremely difficult. For on the one hand the völkisch movement understood itself to be a religious world-view which thought that it knew something about creation, sanctification and salvation, but on the other hand Christianity undoubtedly originated in Jewish soil and was therefore a Jewish religion.

The most important man to concern himself with this question during the second half of the nineteenth century was the theologian and orientalist Paul de Lagarde. In an essay published in 1873 'On the Relationship of the German State to Theology, Church and Religion. An Attempt to Guide Non-Theologians', he put forward the thesis 'that Christianity, namely Catholicism and Protestantism, is a distortion of the gospel'.[50] The Jew Paul was responsible for this distortion:

'Paul has brought the Old Testament to us in the church, and through its influence the gospel has been ruined – as far as this is possible. Paul has blessed us with Pharisaic exegesis, which proves anything from anything... Paul has brought us the Jewish sacrificial theory and everything connected with it. The whole... Jewish view of history has been foisted on us by him. He did this against the vigorous opposition of the early church which, Jewish though it was, thought less Jewishly than did Paul, who at least did not consider sophisticated Jewishness to be a gospel sent from God.'[51]

Here was the scheme for a solution to the problem, many times repeated and varied in the subsequent period in a flood of trivial religious literature. This split the Christian tradition fundamentally into two mutually opposed traditions. On the one side stood the noble Jesus and his misunderstood gospel; on the other the cunning Jew Paul, the Old Testament, Jewish history and Jewish theology. This theory was not new. As early as the second half of the eighteenth century, in his large-scale Enlightenment work, Hermann Samuel Reimarus had called 'the whole of Christianity by and large Paul's system and enterprise',[52] and a generation later, in his famous lecture on 'The Principles of the Present Age', Johann Gottlieb Fichte had made Paul responsible for the 'degeneration of Christianity' which concealed the truth of Jesus in the present.[53] In Fichte the combination of this theory with völkisch thought is already hinted at. Fichte was convinced that Christianity, Jesus, the truth and the Germans belonged together in the same way as Judaism, Paul and error.[54]

Fichte was undoubtedly the most important impetus to the religious-völkisch idea.[55] Only with Lagarde, however, did it have a theologically qualified chief witness, who also drew the political conclusions for the first time. Since in his view Christianity in all its confessional expressions was in fact a Jewish Paulinism and thus adulterated and corrupt, yet a nation cannot live without religion, Lagarde called upon the state to prepare the way for a German national religion which, by direct recourse to the pure message of Jesus, would provide the German Volk with an appropriate religiousness. To this end Lagarde wanted the state to declare the Christian churches to be sects, close the theological faculties, and in their place establish new chairs which would show what theology ought to be: 'the pathfinder of German religion'.[56]

Here was the keyword by which the völkisch movement would thereafter define its relationship to Christianity: German religion. This meant purifying Christianity of all Jewish overlays and corruptions and returning to its original essence: the pure religion of the saviour.

A wide range of trivial religious literature immediately took on this task. One example was a voluminous book which was published in 1905 and went through several editions; it bore the striking title *Forward to Christ! Away with Paul! German Religion!* Its author, a certain Oskar Michel, made it his task at last to show the German people the real Paul, 'the poisoner of the religious sources and the false teacher', for only when 'this arch-enemy of Jesus, his Volk, and humanity has been removed from the entrance to the kingdom of God' could its doors again open.[57] In this book a large section was also devoted to the 'Pauline poison in the history of the people', and in this context the role of anti-Paulinism in völkisch dualism was also clear. 'The good and evil principles,' wrote the author, 'Christianity and anti-Christianity, noble humanity and its most malicious enemy Paulinism, the principle of perfection and that of destruction, emerged from the same ground' – this meant early Christianity.[58] The writings of Lanz von Liebenfels, who felt himself to be 'a true Christian' in contrast to 'false, judaized Christianity',[59] also belonged to this religious trivial literature. Lanz is also an example of the grotesque constructions to which this approach could lead.

This brief glance at the prehistory makes it clear why in 1919 the atmosphere of the völkisch movement was totally saturated with religious components. Many of the völkisch authors and agitators not only sought political effectiveness but at the same time felt themselves to be men of religious renewal.

For Theodor Fritsch it was certain that 'Christ's entire life... was a struggle against Judaism and its perfidy'. 'He called them "a generation of vipers" and "children of the devil", and he drove the hagglers from the Temple with a whip.'[60] For the convinced racial antisemitist who still did not want to repudiate Christianity utterly, there was only one expedient: to declare Jesus an Aryan. And after Houston Stewart Chamberlain's widely-read *Foundations of the Twentieth Century* the case was ready-made.[61] Fritsch coarsened this argument by a philological artifice which made Galileans Gauls and Gauls Germans and thus demonstrated 'how from Germanic blood could emerge a religious genius whose great idealism appears just as Germanically related to us as the traditional picture of his bodily appearance'. In any case, Fritsch concluded, 'the unfathomable opposition between Christian and Jewish doctrine... precludes any racial kinship'. 'The life-affirming religion of the future' should, Fritsch was convinced, be a purified Christianity that makes 'the divine seriousness of the material world', namely 'the recent insights into the laws or the life of nations and races', the foundation of knowledge and faith.[62]

Even more strongly than Fritsch, Dietrich Eckart felt himself to be at the same time both a defender and a renewer of Christianity. In 1917 he had praised Christianity in an article, 'Christ, Buddha and Nietzsche', as 'the source of the highest culture' and defended it against Nietzsche, 'this crazy despiser of our religious foundations'.[63] 'To be an Aryan,' he maintained, 'and to sense transcendence is one and the same thing.' Whereas the Aryan has an innate feeling for the other-worldly, for immortality, the Jew embodies utter worldliness. For Eckart, völkisch dualism was a struggle between heaven and earth, between God and the devil, and in this struggle the Germans, as true Christians, had a decisive contribution to make.[64]

Whereas Fritsch took up this theme because it necessarily followed from the antisemitic interpretation of the Jewish tradition, and Dietrich Eckart saw himself as issuing a call to battle, Artur Dinter felt himself to be a man of religious renewal. For him – like Eckart, he was a Catholic – what he called a Christian religious renewal was the indispensable precondition of a völkisch rebirth. With his confusion and inconstancy, his exaggerated sense of mission and his sectarian fanaticism, Dinter was the embodiment of a type thoroughly characteristic of the völkisch movement. He named Chamberlain and Lagarde as his mentors. Under their influence and in the light of the spiritual teaching which he invented, there automatically came into being, as he wrote, 'the foundations for the reconstruction of a purely Aryan Christianity, including the elimination of the Jewish Old Testament and all the Jewish-Christian dogmatic business. Out of it came my Geistchristentum...'[65] The slogans of this Geistchristentum were '*Down with the Old Testament! Down with Paul! Back to Christ!*'[66] Dinter's sense of mission led him later to found a sect, the 'Religious Association of Geistchristentum', which caused quite a sensation at the end of the 1920s. But we shall hear more of this later.

Not only did many well-known publicists of the völkisch movement occupy themselves with religious questions, but a great many of the organizations under its wing were simply associations of völkisch-religious sects, from the German Faith Society, the Germanic Order and the Loyal Alliance for Improved Living to the Alliance for a German Church, founded in Berlin at the end of May 1921. This last was a Protestant völkisch organization that represented the völkisch idea in the Protestant church.[67]

Hitler, too, entered this völkisch-religious circle of ideas when in September he joined the German Workers' Party. True, from the very beginning, this party, founded on 5 January 1919 by the locksmith Anton Drexler and the journalist Karl Harrer,[68] was one of the politically orientated groups of the völkisch movement, but it was also still wide open to religious ideas.

An example of this openness was given during the party meeting of 24 February 1920. According to Hitler's reminiscence, his historic role began with this 'first great public meeting' of the young movement.[69] He described the meeting as a dramatic discussion which came to a climax with the first reading and explanation of the Party programme. 'And when I finally submitted the twenty-five theses, point for point, to the masses, and asked them personally to pronounce judgment on them, one after another was accepted with steadily mounting joy, unanimously and again unanimously, and when the last thesis had found its way to the hearts of the masses, there stood before me a hall full of people united by a new conviction, a new faith, a new will.'[70]

It has been known for a long time that in reality the espousing of the Party by the masses, which Hitler described here so impressively, occurred very differently. The main speaker secured for this meeting was a völkisch propagandist well-known in Munich, the physician Dr Johannes Dingfelder,[71] who apparently was completely committed to the religious völkisch wing. At any rate, the police reporter noted on this historic meeting: 'Lecture of Dr Dingfelder on "What we have to do".' And he gave his impression of the lecture as follows: 'The remarks of the speaker were entirely to the point and were often presented in a deeply religious spirit. When the speaker said that God alone is our best ally, he won heavy applause.'[72]

In this meeting, and at the conclusion of the lecture, Hitler then did in fact present the programme of his party, from now on called the National Socialist German Workers Party (NSDAP).[73]

The background and formulation of the Party programme which was so often cited later can no longer be determined exactly. Hitler can hardly have played a decisive part in it.[74] Point 24 showed that the group which adopted this programme wanted to be religious, as Christian-völkisch faith understood the term.

We demand freedom for all religious confessions in the state, in so far as they

84

do not endanger its existence nor offend against the customs and moral feelings of the Germanic race.

The party as such represents the standpoint of a positive Christianity, without binding itself to any particular confession. It fights the spirit of Jewish materialism *within* us and *outside* us, and is convinced that a lasting recovery of our Volk can only take place from *within*, on the basis of the principle that 'public advantage comes before individual advantage.[75]

Regardless of what explanation of this point was given later, in 1920 it was nothing but the most general summary possible of the religious convictions of the völkisch movement. The qualification 'in so far as they do not endanger the existence of the state nor offend against the customs and moral feelings of the Germanic race' was meant not only to prevent the Jewish religion being given equal status but also to point to a renewed German Christianity, freed from Jewish falsifications. In this setting the standpoint of a positive Christianity, which later seemed so misleading to the churches, could only mean a völkisch Christianity, a Christianity that had become conscious of its task to fight against the Jewish-materialistic spirit within and without. When Alfred Rosenberg, himself totally convinced of the mission of the völkisch movement, wrote the first authentic exposition of the Party programme at the end of 1922, he left no doubt that it was concerned not with 'new thoughts' but rather with a 'new thinking', with the victory of the 'völkisch concept of the state and the völkisch philosophy of life'.[76] And this was once again made explicit in the commentary on Point 24: 'The only thought that is capable of uniting all classes and confessions in the German nation is the new, and yet ancient, völkisch world-view... This world-view is today called National Socialism.'[77]

These religious aspects were in no sense alien to the young Hitler. We can leave open the question when he came into contact with them. At all events, from 1919 on he knew and even argued the most important religious theses of the völkisch movement.

Remarkable testimony to Hitler's accord with religious-völkisch ideas is provided by the draft of a basic summary of the völkisch world-view which he sketched out at the age of thirty.[78] The sub-headings in the 'Introduction' were: '1. Bible; 2. The Aryan; 3. His activity; 4. The Jew; 5. His activity.' Evidently the well-known dualistic scheme was to be elaborated with reference to the Bible. For under 'Bible' Hitler noted: 'Monumental History of Mankind', and the two perspectives of 'Idealism – Materialism'. The headings which follow made the role of dualism clear. It explained the riddle of the world: 'Nothing without a cause – history makes men – two types of men – creators and drones – builders and destroyers – the children of God and men.' Then come the words 'muddled and confused' – (Lord Disraeli) racial principle –'. This was a reference to a quotation that apparently had central significance for the völkisch movement. It is found in Fritsch's *Handbook on the Jewish Question* and runs: 'No one may deal indifferently with the racial law, the racial question. It is the key to world history. And the only reason why history is so confused is because it is written by people who were not aware of the racial question...' As a source Fritsch gave 'D'Israeli (Beaconsfield) in his novel *Endymion*'.[79] Sebottendorff used the same quotation in an article 'Keep Your Blood Pure', which was published in the

Münchener Beobachter in autumn 1918.[80] For Hitler this was doubtless a decisive insight, since it formed the basis of *Mein Kampf* and was also repeated there word for word: 'The racial question gives the key not only to world history, but to all human culture.'[81]

However, Hitler did not repeat later the conclusions which he drew from this approach in 1919. They read: 'First consequence. Purification of the Bible – what of it is consistent with our spirit. Second consequence. Critical scrutiny of the remainder.' These headings betray Hitler's familiarity with the völkisch-religious tradition and its solution to the Christian problem. This solution lay in the 'purification of the Bible' from Jewish falsification and in the 'critical scrutiny of the remainder' with reference to the Aryan-Germanic heritage.

A famous speech outlining his principles, which Hitler made on 12 April 1922 in the Bürgerbräukeller in Munich and which was distributed for the first time as a special issue of the *Völkischer Beobachter* under the title 'The "Rabble-rousers" of the Truth', shows how far and in what detail he had adopted the völkisch-religious ideas at the time. Hitler began the relevant passage with the question whether as a Christian one could be antisemitic. In a session of the Landtag, the Minister President of Bavaria, Graf Lerchenfeld, a member of the Bayerischer Volkspartei, had declared his feelings that 'as a human being and a Christian' (so Hitler quoted him) he was restrained from being antisemitic. Hitler went on at this point: '*I say: my Christian feeling points me to my Lord and Saviour as a fighter* (tumultuous, prolonged applause). It points me towards the man who, once lonely and surrounded by only a few followers, recognized these Jews and called for battle against them, and who, as true God, was not only the greatest as a *sufferer* but also the greatest as a *warrior*. In boundless love, as a Christian and a human being, I read the passage which declares to us how the Lord finally rose up and seized the whip to drive the usurers, the brood of serpents and vipers, from the Temple! (tumultuous applause).' He saw the evidence for this assertion, as was usual in the völkisch interpretation of the New Testament, in the crucifixion. 'Today, however, two thousand years later, I am deeply moved to perceive that his tremendous struggle for this world against the Jewish poison was most profoundly marked by the fact that he had to bleed on the cross for it (stirring in the hall).' Thus Hitler felt himself to be involved in the same struggle as Jesus, nor did he shy away from making this comparison: 'Two thousand years ago a man was also denounced by the same race... The man was dragged before the court and it was also said of him, "He stirred up the people". So he too had been a "rabble-rouser"! And against whom? Against "God", they cried. Yes, indeed he roused the rabble against the "God" of the Jews, for this "God" is only gold (tumultuous applause).'[82] This, moreover, was an idea which Hitler maintained right to the end. Even in November 1944 Bormann could note an utterance of Hitler that Jesus had fought 'against the depraved materialism of his time and thus against the Jews', and that it was 'Saul-Paul who had first falsified the Christian idea in a subtle way'.[83]

It is clear that this line leads directly to that famous confession in *Mein Kampf* in which Hitler declared that his struggle was in conformity with the 'work of the Lord': 'Hence today I believe that I am acting in accordance with the will of the almighty Creator: *by defending myself against the Jews, I am fighting for the work of the Lord.*'[84]

This conviction was doubtless part of the 'granite' foundation (to use one of Hitler's favourite expressions) of his world view. The only explanation of his sense of mission is that he thought himself to be in tune with the eternal laws of creation. He shared this conviction with the entire völkisch movement, just as he shared the Aryan understanding of Christianity with it. What differentiated him from it was the insight that the triumph of these ideas could not be attained through the development of a völkisch religion, but only through the organization of a political party.

Hitler's Basic Decision on Church Policy
(1924-1928)

Insight into the special relationship between völkisch religion and political organization was Hitler's own political achievement. He seems only to have become quite clear about this – as also in his thinking about foreign policy[1] when drafting his book. For although in *Mein Kampf* he made his confessional statement about the 'work of the Lord' and still put forward the völkisch understanding of the nature and work of Jesus along the lines of his speech of 12 April 1922,[2] the book at the same time contained such vehement criticism of the 'German-völkisch wandering scholars',[3] the 'völkisch Saint Johns of the twentieth-century',[4] that a firm decision by Hitler is unmistakable here.

Various factors combined to bring about this decision.

The fate of the Schutz- und Trutzbund, which meekly dissolved itself in 1922;[5] of the Thule Gesellschaft, which had been paralysed by disputes since the end of 1919;[6] and of many other völkisch organizations and groups which in this period disappeared as quickly as they had appeared, could not but be a warning to Hitler. The irony with which he speaks in *Mein Kampf* of the absurdity of the 'völkisch comedians', of the 'völkisch sleep-walkers' and of the 'so-called religious reformers on an old-Germanic basis', whose activity simply resulted in the nation 'wasting its strength on inner religious squabbles as senseless as they are disastrous',[7] clearly indicates that Hitler saw the danger which threatened every political organization from this direction.

At the same time, it had become clear to Hitler that the step from a religious world-view to völkisch religion would entangle the Party deeply in the confessional problem. That chiefly affected relations with the Catholic Church. For even if, as we shall see in due course, the völkisch idea could for a while associate itself with Protestantism, no understanding with Catholicism was possible. And in fact the struggle of the founders of German-völkisch religion was frequently directed just as vehemently against 'fundamentalism' as against the Jewish danger.

From his Vienna period, however, Hitler thought that he knew that a struggle directed against the Catholic Church was doomed to failure from the start.[8] He wanted to avoid this mistake at all costs. For that reason, too, he tried to draw a line between the religious and the political spheres. In order not to get involved in a confrontation with the churches, especially with the unusually strong Bavarian Catholic Church, he sacrificed the religious claim of the völkisch idea and decisively rejected for the movement 'any position on questions which either lie outside the frame of its political work or, being not of basic importance, are irrelevant for it'. This is also the context of the later statement, so often cited, that the task of the movement 'is not a religious reformation, but a political reorganization of our people'.[9] If we are clear how strongly the völkisch movement had presented itself under the banner of a religious reformation, of a purification and renewal of Christianity, then it is evident that at this point Hitler in fact dissociated himself in a decisive way. And the years to come were to show that he was also determined to draw the consequences of this dissociation. In any case it became clear enough when he wrote: 'I do not hesitate to declare that I regard the men who today draw the völkisch movement into the crisis of religious quarrels as worse enemies of my people than any international Communist'.[10]

All this, however, belonged within the framework of the basic conception which he had followed from the beginning, according to which the decisive implementation of theory in practice could take place only in the organization. The central importance of organization was stressed clearly in *Mein Kampf*, again and again. The 'transformation of a general, philosophical ideal conception of the highest truth into a definitely delimited, tightly organized political community of faith and struggle, unified in spirit and will, is the most significant achievement, since on its happy solution alone the possibility of the victory of the idea depends'.[11] If this 'alone' were true – and according to Hitler's belief it was true – then anything that disturbed it or might disturb it had to be sacrificed to the unity of the organization. It was only too obvious that the völkisch religious debates, like the confessional issue, represented such inner disturbance. So Hitler made the decision to dissociate himself from völkisch religion and its representatives. Controversial though this decision understandably was in the völkisch movement, Hitler knew exactly why he held to it. With the frankness peculiar to his book, he explicitly justified the choice of the name 'National Socialist German Workers Party' by the split with völkisch-religious ideas. 'The first expression' – here he was referring to 'workers' party' – 'kept away the antiquity enthusiasts, the big-mouths and superficial proverb-makers of the so-called "völkisch idea", and the second freed us from the entire host of knights of the "spiritual sword", all the poor wretches who wield the "spiritual weapon" as a protecting shield to hide their actual cowardice.'[12]

This decision against the völkisch movement and for the political party was, in terms of Hitler's goals, probably his first independent political achievement. He made it, although the sketch of his world-view and his politics had been fully derived from this movement. He had no predecessor for this course. On the contrary, he had to push it through against the convictions of his most important mentors and comrades – against Eckart, Dinter and Ludendorff. It took the rise of the Party after its refounding at the end of the 1920s to show that this decision had been correct. A religious, völkisch group would not have had the slightest chance of becoming the basis for a party of the masses. The NSDAP got its chance because it concentrated with utter determination on the attainment of political goals and not on the further development of a völkisch religion.

How little all this was taken for granted before 1925 is indicated by a work by Hitler's friend and mentor Dietrich Eckart, which was published in Munich in

1924, a few months after Eckart's death. It bore the title *Bolshevism from Moses to Lenin. A Conversation between Adolf Hitler and Me*. Ernst Nolte, who rescued it from oblivion in 1961, believed at the time that it was 'an early source of Hitler's antisemitism', to which should be attributed the highest degree of authenticity.[13] Since then, however, it has been made probable that the work originated with Eckart alone and that the 'he' in the dialogue cannot be identified either directly or indirectly with Hitler.[14]

This work closes with a final comment by the publishers which is of interest in this context. The death of Eckart, it said, 'prevented the completion of this highly significant work showing the Christian approach to the völkisch movement. We may hope that Adolf Hitler, after the conclusion of the trial for high treason now pending against him in Munich, will have the kindness to undertake to finish this work which is almost completed'.[15] Hitler never gave any indication that he recognize himself as a partner in this conversation, let alone that he intended to fulfil his publisher's hopes. On the contrary, eighteen months later, the first volume of *Mein Kampf* was published, containing the sharpest imaginable rejection of völkisch-religious ideas. Hence it seems quite conceivable that in this work Eckart was again making an attempt to dissuade Hitler from his decision for a political party, and to commit him anew to the völkisch-religious point of view, from which he and the NSDAP had increasingly begun to withdraw.

That, at any rate, was the way in which Eckart's work was understood by Artur Dinter, who in the meantime had become Hitler's Gauleiter in Thuringia. He advertised it in 1928 in his periodical *Das Geistchristentum* and explicitly commended it to 'members of the Society for Geistchristentum who come from the political world and have become convinced that the völkisch movement can never achieve its goal by purely political means'. It could be particularly useful to 'the National Socialists among them as a transition to the higher religious level to which they aspire… They will find in it the first attempt to give a comprehensive moral and religious foundation to the National Socialists and to the völkisch movement generally.'[16]

In fact Eckart's work reads like a kind of catechism of völkisch religion. Its fundamental idea is the bane that the Jews have been to world history from Moses to Lenin, a thesis which is evoked with familiar enough arguments. In sharp contrast to this the picture of a völkisch Aryan Christianity, as it had been known in basic outline since Lagarde and Chamberlain, was developed. Here stands Christ, not of course a Jew – 'never otherwise than erect, never otherwise than upright' – 'flashing eyes in the midst of the creeping Jewish rabble… and the words fall like whiplashes: "Your father is the devil…" (John 8.44)'.[17] Here, too, Paul is the Jewish perverter of Chrsitianity.[18] Through his translation of the Old Testament Luther had spread a halo over 'Satan's Bible',[19] but on the other hand in his writing about the Jews he had much more insight than the Christian churches today, which swarm 'with Jewish and half-Jewish clergy'.[20] Had Luther recognized the real danger earlier he would not have attacked Catholicism, 'but behind it the Jew! There would never have been a schism, never the war which, as the Jews wanted, for thirty years shed torrents of Aryan blood.' The front against the Jews is the true Christian front. The accusation that this expresses a concern to leave Christ for Wotan is nonsense. 'In Christ,' says the Hitler of the dialogue, 'the embodiment of all manliness, we find all that we need. And if we occasionally speak of Baldur, our words always contain some joy, some satisfaction that our pagan ancestors were already so Christian as to have intimations of Christ in this ideal figure.'[21] The predilection of both partners in the conversation for Catholicism is unmistakable. 'We are both Catholics,' Hitler confesses, and thinks: 'Our Protestants are now beyond help.'[22]

Eckart's text contained almost all the religious-völkisch arguments and propositions conceivable for creating a virtually solid front against the Party in both Christian confessions. It is out of the question that this was not evident to the author of *Mein Kampf*. Hence Hitler's conspicuous disregard for the last programmatic writing of his only 'fatherly friend'[23] is a sign that he did not consider this course the one to follow. If Eckart wanted to make Hitler yet another völkisch prophet with his book, Hitler had decided not to be a völkisch prophet but rather a political leader.

Eckart died in December 1923. We cannot rule out the probability that the death of Hitler's oldest mentor came at a very opportune time for Hitler. There was now no one left in his immediate vicinity to go on representing the völkisch religion with similar determination and authority. In spite of this the problem had by no means been settled for him.

On 9 November 1923 Hitler's Putsch in Munich had collapsed. On 10 November the NSDAP was banned. From 11 November Hitler found himself in the fortress of Landsberg, where until 20 December 1924 he served out the prison sentence imposed on him.

During this time Ludendorff became the most important man in the völkisch movement.[24] The General had moved from Berlin to Munich in the spring of 1920, after the failed Kapp Putsch, seething with rage 'that the Officer Corps of the Reichswehr had failed him'.[25] Here he had very quickly made contact with the greatest variety of völkisch circles and individuals, but in his arrogance he just as quickly quarrelled with them, and had finally come under the influence of a religious-völkisch prophetess, the neurologist Dr Mathilde von Kemnitz. If the memoirs of a friend of Ludendorff may be trusted, since 1920 Frau von Kemnitz had tried to press her religious-völkisch notions on the NSDAP; but with Hitler, 'to whom her ideas and teaching seemed to be confused delusions', she ran up against a 'brusque rejection'.[26] That made her all the more successful with Ludendorff. It was typical of this man's intellectual level that very soon he found himself fully dependent upon the ideas of a woman who, in her tireless struggle against the judaized Christianity of both confessions, tried to found a new, German 'vision of God'. For Ludendorff, the affirmation of secret, supranational powers was no doubt a way to explain his own failure, while the ambitious and fanatical Mathilde von Kemnitz perceived in the famous army leader a welcome instrument for the realization of her ideas.

The problem which Ludendorff's increasing dependence on these ideas posed to the party first became evident during his defence speech delivered on 29 February 1924 before the People's Court in Munich. There he attributed the collapse and all its aftermath not only to Marxism and Judaism, which corrupted the German Volk 'physically, racially and morally', but equally to Ultramontanism, which, in long, confused explanations, he blamed for the deliberate destruction of Bismarck's Reich.[27]

These attacks unleashed a violent public reaction. Ludendorff was nevertheless so prominent that Gustav Stresemann, the Reich Foreign Minister, felt it necessary to repudiate them 'most emphatically' in an official statement and to express his regrets to the Holy See. Otto Braun, the Prussian Minister President, sent a letter to the Nuncio 'to express how deeply the Prussian government regrets the General's attacks on His Holiness'.[28]

Ludendorff's action also met with criticism in the ranks of the Party. True, the General later denied that he had promised Hitler not to bring up the religious question. But it is certain that even at this time Hitler considered this kind of agitation to be erroneous, indeed fatal. So it is quite credible that there should have been frequent confrontations between the two völkisch leaders on precisely this point. 'Ludendorff,' according to Wilhelm Breucker's report, 'charged Hitler with having expressly based the party on positive Christianity in his programme, and sought to demonstrate to him with biblical quotations that Christianity was and by nature had to be the sharpest opponent of every völkisch movement. Hitler retorted: I think the same way as Your Excellency, but Your Excellency – Hitler always spoke to the general in a submissive, servile voice, and always addressed him in the third person, as he had learned to as a corporal – can afford to announce to his enemies beforehand that he intends to slay them. I, however, need the Catholics of Bavaria just as much as the Protestants of Prussia to build up a great political movement. The other matter can be taken care of later.'[29]

Despite these misgivings, while Hitler was imprisoned in Landsberg in 1924 he could not prevent Ludendorff from becoming the senior figure in the völkisch movement. In spite of vigorous opposition from groups still loyal to Hitler, the General succeeded in mediating between North German and South German völkisch National Socialists and entering the Reichstag in May 1924 with the German-Völkisch Freedom Party. However, the relative success of this party was short-lived. As early as the Reichstag elections in December 1924 it paid the price of its hopeless divisions. It lost more than half its votes and fell back to three per cent of the vote and to fourteen of its previous thirty-two seats.

For chroniclers of the history of the Pope and the Curia after the First World War there was no doubt that this marked the failure of the 'advance of National Socialism against Rome', and that above all by their hostility the völkisch representatives to the Catholic church bore the guilt for this failure.[30]

That Ludendorff was in fact determined to commit the party to the völkisch-religious line of Mathilde von Kemnitz was demonstrated at the Freedom Party conference in Weimar in August 1924. True to his intention 'that the religious basis of the völkisch movement' should also be discussed, the General assigned the main speech of this party conference to Mathilde von Kemnitz. She spoke on 'The Power of the Pure Idea', and in her speech she accused Christianity of every possible sinister intrigue and crime.[31] At the end of the conference Artur Dinter delivered a speech about Ludendorff and 'committed all those present, including himself, to undying faithfulness' to the General.[32]

The 'Action Arm of the National Socialist Freedom Movement of Greater Germany', a type of programme set up in autumn 1924 under Ludendorff's direction for the December elections, also emphasized especially in accordance with his wishes 'that the question of faith would be given first place in the statement of our aims'. Accordingly, the section entitled 'The Völkisch Movement among the Religious', began with the affirmation: 'The National Socialist Freedom Movement, like every great renewal movement, has sprung from religious soil'[33] – a formulation that could only embroil the party directly in the controversies over völkisch religion.

To understand Hitler's reactions after his release from prison, we must keep in mind Ludendorff, Frau Kemnitz and the entire völkisch religious trend.

Imprisoned in Landsberg, Hitler had watched this development throughout 1924 without even lifting a finger towards the consolidation of the movement. On the contrary, he seemed to know that the struggle of each against all would prove conclusively that he was indispensable as leader.[34] At the same time the experience of this collapse must have confirmed his conviction that any kind of discussion of völkisch religious principles was fatal to the organization.

At all events, Hitler's first public utterance after his emergence from a year in prison was devoted substantially to this issue. This discussion came in the leading article which he wrote for the first edition of the *Völkischer Beobachter* after the lifting of the ban. It appeared on 26 February 1925 under the headline 'On the Resurrection of our Movement'. After a short historical survey and the emphatic assurance that 'the struggle of the movement' would go on as planned from the beginning, Hitler wrote: 'At this point I must object especially to the attempt to try to drag religious disputes into the movement, indeed to equate the movement with them. I have always been wary of the collective term "völkisch" because the extraordinarily vague interpretation of this concept itself opens the floodgates to damaging ventures... I regard the attempt made today from various directions to associate the völkisch movement with religious concerns as the beginning of the end. Religious reformations cannot be made by political children. But these gentlemen are seldom concerned with anything else. I am quite clear about the possibility of beginning such a struggle, but I doubt whether the gentlemen active in it are also clear about its probable outcome.' He then went on to repeat an assertion, in which he also demonstrated his anxiety about a new Kulturkampf, that the struggle against the Centre Party would be carried on 'not out of considerations of a religious kind, but solely on the basis of political perceptions'.[35]

This programmatic article about the new beginning showed that at this time Hitler thought the religious issue to have decisive significance for the further development of the party. In practice it meant a split with Ludendorff, who, after his totally unsuccessful candidature for the office of Reich President[36] in spring 1925 began to distance himself increasingly from Hitler, finally – convinced of Hitler's 'Roman captivity' – to become one of his bitterest enemies.

The further history of the house of Ludendorff is only remotely related to our topic. The General divorced his wife and married Mathilde von Kemnitz. Together in the later 1920s they made the Tannenbergbund, founded in 1925 and originally purely nationalistic, into a religious-völkisch sect.[37] In a circular letter in 1927 Hitler announced that Ludendorff was not a member of the NSDAP and had no influence within it, and that NSDAP party members were banned from being simultaneously members of the Tannenbergbund. 'But that does not mean that war may be declared on His Excellency Ludendorff, who is still to be honoured as a general, or on his associations.'[38] Hitler kept to this line even when he came to power, and the Tannenbergbund – which in the meantime had degenerated to nothing but crude sectarianism – was allowed to live a half-banned, half-tolerated existence.[39]

However, the leading article of 26 February was more than a dissociation from Ludendorff. It referred equally to other leading Hitler followers, who came within his closest political entourage. That became clear on the very day of the refounding of the party.

On this day, 27 February 1925, Hitler delivered his famous speech on the 're-establishment' of the Party in the Munich Bürgerbräukeller. 'Overwhelmed,' runs the official report of the meeting, 'by Hitler's words and by the jubilation of the assembly, Herr Streicher, Dr Dinter, Herr Esser, Dr Buttmann, Herr Feder and Dr Frick mounted the speaker's podium and promised Herr Hitler steadfast loyalty, at the same time clasping one another by the hand.'[40] Of these six men who after the re-establishment formed Hitler's most intimate circle, at least two – the Catholics Streicher and Dinter – represented an extreme völkisch-religious position and Dinter, at least, was in no mind to give up this position.

Dr Artur Dinter was born in Alsace in 1876, the son of a Prussian customs official. He was first a science teacher in Strassburg, then an author, dramatist and theatre director in Rostock and Berlin. A prominent member of the Schutz-und Trutzbund, and from the early 1920s living in Thuringia, even before the War he was one of the radical völkisch antisemitists. He had made substantial contributions to the popularizing of völkisch religion in his books, which were printed by the hundred thousand.[41] He had become acquainted with Hitler in Munich in the spring of 1923, and after the failed Putsch he had joined an assocation loyal to Hitler, the Grossdeutsche Volksgemeinschaft, from the leadership of which Esser and Streicher had ousted Rosenberg.[42] He had collected supporters for this successor to the banned NSDAP in Thuringia, where he had a seat in the legislature. By the end of 1924 he had 'reclaimed thirty local groups for the NSDAP'.[43] A Party member with the serial number 5, he was present at the re-establishment, was entrusted with the leadership of the Party in Thuringia, and was vigorously applauded at the general convention in Munich on 23 May 1926.[44] Furthermore, the organization of the first party conference after the re-establishment, held in the National Theatre in Weimar in July 1926, was chiefly Dinter's work. But Dinter was not only important as an organizer. Hitler seems also to have regarded him as something of a spiritual authority. At all events, in a letter of 28 July 1928 he described the 'dear Herr Doktor' as a man 'whom I personally admire and whose whole life-work has contributed so immeasurably to our great völkisch idea' – a form of words that was very unusual for Hitler at this time.[45]

Dinter was without doubt the most determined and the most striking represen-tative of a völkisch religion among the prominent leaders of the NSDAP. His goal was 'the restoration of the pure teaching of the Saviour', the 'completion of the Reformation', and the creation of a German national church, which would overcome the confessional division and proclaim 'an appropriate faith' to the German people.[46] In his belief this religious renewal was the precondition of all politics: 'If the völkisch movement gets stuck in the lowlands of merely political struggle, it will certainly become bogged down again... So the völkisch movement will only reach its goal when it raises itself to the pure moral and spiritual heights which shine upon us from the teaching of the greatest antisemitist and anti-materialist of all time, the Hero of Nazareth. It will only conquer and can only conquer when it lays the axe to the spiritual roots of Judaism, that is, to Judaism in the Christian church.'[47] 'The history of all peoples and ages teaches,' so Dinter found, 'that the religious revolutions always precede the epoch-making political revolutions. It is never the other way round.'[48] This was the exact opposite of the position that Hitler held to be the only correct one. But it took almost three years and required numerous precautions for the controversies over this issue to be concluded – with Dinter's expulsion from the party in October 1928.

Dinter had doubtless intended to impress his religious-völkisch line on the Party, beginning with Thuringia. In this he set his hopes especially on Julius Streicher, later Gauleiter in Franconia, whom he endorsed in June 1928 as being 'one of the very few in the Party who have a natural feeling for religion and a general understanding of the religious question'[49] – undoubtedly a somewhat surprising description of the editor of *Der Stürmer*, the worst antisemitic smear-sheet in the Party.

But Dinter had deceived himself over Hitler's steadfastness and over his friends and comrades in the Party in Thuringia.

That Hitler was determined also to draw conclusions from his declarations of principle on the relationship of politics and religion was shown in a 'Circular Letter to the Official Party Organs of the NSDAP' dated 23 February 1927. In it the Reich leadership in Munich issued 'a warning to the other official Party organs' that the authorization and permission given to a party newspaper 'to carry on its masthead the emblem of the NSDAP (the swastika with wreath and eagle) had been revoked by Hitler'. The reason given was 'the offence of the newspaper against one of the first principles of the NSDAP', according to which 'attacks on religious associations and their institutions are categorically forbidden; arguments on these matters may not be carried into the ranks of the NSDAP'. Herr Hitler would act 'ruthlessly' on this point. 'Articles about which the editors have even the slightest doubt as to whether or not the above mentioned principle is violated should not be published.'[50]

After a considerable period of conflict in Thuringia over Dinter's person, Fritz Sauckel, a rival leader in the organization, officially demanded in June 1927 that Dinter should resign his post as Gauleiter, since 'time and again he had announced his intention of resuming his religious fight...'[51] In fact Dinter was dismissed as Gauleiter of Thuringia on 30 September 1927 on grounds of 'executive stress'. Hitler expressly thanked him and ackowledged 'services rendered to the movement in years of work for the struggle'.[52]

But Dinter in no way gave up. Rather, in November 1927 in Nuremberg he founded the non-partisan 'Geistchristliche Religionsgemeinschaft', which was intended finally to press forward the religious renewal of the völkisch movement.[53] The project had little success, but it understandably annoyed the party, and at any rate it received a certain amount of publicity in völkisch circles through the journal *Geistchristentum*, financed almost exclusively by Dinter. For this reason Martin Bormann, at the time just a minor Party leader in Weimar, officially proposed Dinter's expulsion from the Party in a letter to the national headquarters.[54]

The way in which the matter was further dealt with makes it clear how problematical this expulsion, and with it the final separation from the religious wing of the völkisch movement, still seemed to Hitler at that time.

The case went first, as usual, to the investigations and mediations committee of the Reich leadership, USCHLA (Untersuchungs- und Schlichtungsausschuss der Reichsleitung) for short, presided over since 2 January 1928 by a retired Major Walter Buch,[55] a true devotee of Hitler, from 1929 Martin Bormann's father-in-law, and for many years undoubtedly one of the most influential men in the background. In the Dinter case, USCHLA, which could deal with higher-ranking Party members only with Hitler's permission,[56] decided to pursue a method very unusual for a party based on the Führer principle. On 5 June 1928, Walter Buch sent the following note to seven Gauleiters: 'Some time ago party member Dr Dinter founded the Geistchristliche Religionsgemeinschaft with the aim of "completing the Reformation". In so doing he is turning against the "Jewish-Roman" and the "Jewish-Protestant" church and issuing a call for a Kulturkampf, in order to help the "pure teaching of the Saviour" to victory. The question is whether this step by a party member is or is not helpful to the NSDAP. Herr Hitler does not want to decide the question without the opinion of individual Gauleiters. I therefore ask you for your comments.'[57] When the replies came in, as expected, all but one were negative.[58] Thus for example Hinrich Lohse, Gauleiter of Hamburg, formally proposed Dinter's expulsion, 'emphasizing once again, first, that I myself am a Protestant and, second, that here in Protestant areas the greatest difficulties arise for us'.[59] The Gauleiter of the Ruhr Gau also asserted on 19 June that in his 'humble opinion' Dinter's activity was 'ultimately intolerable'.[60]

Thereupon on 12 July USCHLA passed a resolution to call on Dinter to discontinue his religious battle 'to avoid expulsion'.[61] Hitler himself sent this resolution on to Dinter on 25 July, together with a long letter unparalleled in Hitler's meagre correspondence. In a tone of respect and reverence, he attempted to explain the USCHLA decision to Dinter, saying that it was governed by the absolute priority of political affairs – a priority which he, Hitler, had to defend. 'The fate of our Volk, at least to the extent that it is a race problem, will be decided in less time than the carrying out of a religious reformation would call for. Either our Volk will tear itself away as quickly as possible from the ruin that faces it, especially racially, or it will perish in the process.' The twenty years which were still available to him, Hitler, would suffice for the victory of a political movement, 'if fate does not decide otherwise,' but they would be much too short for a religious reformation. 'Should you,' the letter ended, 'feel the need, dear Doctor, to speak with me personally, I would welcome it very much and would be at your disposal at any time.'[62]

Hitler's next statement was a public one at the Party leaders' conference and general meeting in Weimar at the end of August and beginning of September 1928. One of the chief themes of this conference was the Dinter problem. Dinter himself, in spite of Hitler's telegraphed order, had not appeared. He had, however, tabled a motion that the Party chairman be given an advisory senate. The motion was unanimously rejected, and Hitler repeated his determination to keep the movement free of all religious discussions and struggles 'for all time to come'.[63]

Dinter replied with an article, 'Religion and National Socialism', in which for the first time he attacked even Hitler himself, and accused him of blindness to the fact that 'the Romish Pope's church is just as terrible an enemy of a völkisch Germany, to say nothing of a völkisch Greater Germany, as the Jew'.[64]

After this attack expulsion was inevitable. But surprisingly, even now the Party leadership did not seem quite sure of its case. For on 8 October 1928 Gregor Strasser, the director of the national organization of the Party, sent a letter to a series of leading members in which he pointed out the 'severe test' which the imminent disciplining of Dinter would no doubt represent and therefore requested them to confirm, with their signatures, their agreement with Hitler's decision. In this statement Dinter's position was rejected: it was not 'as if there were a split in the National Socialist movement between Adolf Hitler and the other leaders over his position in the religious struggle, and Adolf Hitler alone opposed Dinter's attempt to involve the movement in religious discussions. We, the undersigned leaders of the National Socialist German Workers Party, Protestants and Catholics, decisively reject this attempt.'[65] The number of statements returned is too small to establish whether the absence of the signatures of Streicher, Esser and Rosenberg was by chance or deliberate. However, no serious objections appear to have been made.[66]

On 11 October 1928 Hitler signed the expulsion order. It referred only to Dinter's article 'Religion and National Socialism', which was termed 'damaging to the Party', and explicitly declared the expulsion to be 'final'.[67]

Thus as far as the party was concerned the Dinter affair was settled. Dinter's subsequent petition for readmission dated 29 April 1933 was rejected, as was a petition for clemency of 15 June 1937. Thereafter, Dinter's writings were proscribed. He was expelled from the Reichschriftumskammer in 1939. According to information in the personnel card index of the national leadership of the Party, after 1937 the 'Reich file card' of former member no.5 bore the annotations 'acceptance impossible', 'never to be readmitted', 'clemency petition to the Führer for readmission rejected on 15 May 1937'.[68]

The expulsion of Dinter was a victory for Hitler and his personal claim to leadership. But it also represented a fundamental decision on the future policy of the Party on church and religion. In expelling Dinter the Party had firmly dissociated itself from the last independent representative of that völkisch tradition from which it had emerged in 1919 and to which it owed its world-view, its fundamental principles and its goals. However, in no sense had it also separated itself from this world-view. In this respect Dinter's accusations were completely unjustified. But what basically distinguished Hitler from all those with völkisch fellow feeling was the conviction that the victory of this world-view was not a matter of theory but of political struggle. With this conviction he defended the absolute validity of the leadership principle and an equally absolute internal cohesion in the organization, but the greatest possible degree of external political flexibility.

When in autumn 1929 Dinter complained that the issue for Hitler today, 'as in the lifetime of Dietrich Eckart, was no longer the victory of a pure, völkisch movement as such, but simply and solely to achieve political power as quickly as possible',[69] he made the same mistake that many of Hitler's critics had already made and would continue to make, namely to confuse Hitler's growing political flexibility with a mere opportunistic grab for power. Rather, among the many things that Hitler had learned from Marxism was the insight that it was ultimately the correct determination of the relationship between theory and practice that determined political success. For that reason Dinter, who stood for the primacy of the pure völkisch world-view, had to go.

What this break meant for Hitler was made clear in a speech in almost triumphant language which he gave in Passau on 27 October 1928, a few weeks after Dinter's expulsion. There, in the crowded Schmeroldkeller-Saal, he declared: 'This movement has gained a remarkable freedom of operation which in the supreme sense of the word allows the rejection of anything which could in any way divide the people. We are a people of different faiths, but we are one. Which faith conquers the other is not the question; the question, rather, is whether Christianity stands or falls!... We tolerate no one in our ranks who offends against the ideas of Christianity, who offers resistance to someone with another disposition, fights against him or acts as the arch-enemy of Christianity. This, our movement, is in fact Christian. We are filled with a desire for Catholics and Protestants to discover one another in the deep distress of our own people. We shall suppress any attempt to put religious issues on the agenda of our movement.'[70]

His success proved Hitler correct. The move towards becoming a party for the masses, which was made in 1930, would certainly never have succeeded had not Hitler secured this 'freedom of operation' for the Party. Power could indeed be won without Christian Germany; but against Christian Germany the party had no chance.

There remained, however, a balancing act that Hitler had constantly to perform. For a section of his young veterans – like Hess, Rosenberg and Streicher, and also some of those who became important later, like Himmler, Bormann and Schirach, came from the völkisch camp and maintained the ideals of the movement's religious mission. Some of them, especially Rosenberg, saw themselves as völkisch reformers in very much the same way that Dinter had once seen himself in this role. But at least after Dinter's expulsion Hitler had things so securely in his grasp that none of them was in a position to shape the Party independently.

It was vital for the important years of the seizure and consolidation of power between 1930 and 1934 that Hitler had succeeded in leading the 1923 party out of its threefold ghetto: out of the ghetto of a party of nothing but rowdyism and Putsch; out of the parochial ghetto of a Bavarian-Austrian splinter group; and out of the religious ghetto of a völkisch sect.

Of these three points, it is important not to underestimate the significance of the last.

7

The Origin of Political Theology and the Jewish Question in German Protestantism (1917-1930)

Hitler's decision to cut loose from the religious wing of the völkisch movement made him and his party in principle eligible for the vote of German Protestantism. This can be read out of the history of the relationship between Protestantism and the völkisch movement, even before Hitler and the NSDAP were topics of discussion. In the debate on this relationship which was carried on between 1924 and 1930, those categories and concepts were developed which were to dominate the field when things became serious: after 14 September 1930.

German Protestantism found itself in a difficult position over against the völkisch movement. On the one hand, it discovered in it certain things which a large number above all of its younger theologians energetically affirmed. On the other hand, the völkisch sector made demands which were utterly out of the question for a Christian church.

The main reason why the völkisch movement could become a problem for German Protestantism at all was the simple fact of its national character. In contrast to the universalism of the Catholic church, which was always maintained in principle, at least theologically, Lutheran Protestantism was of necessity and by conviction nationalist. It had profited from the victory of the national idea in the nineteenth century in Germany, and now also shared in its great crisis. And in so far as the völkisch movement was simply the attempt to overcome this crisis and to re-establish the old national idea in its new, völkisch form, the völkisch movement and Protestantism were clearly natural allies.

On the other hand racial dualism, an Aryan Jesus and Aryan religion were not even a topic for serious Christian theologians, much less a possibility. The discussion on the pros and cons of the völkisch movement which was carried on after 1924 reflected this situation.

It all began with a remarkable shift in the ethical point of reference in theology. Whereas Wilhelm Herrmann had identified the family, the culture and the state as still being the most important fields of human activity,[1] in the course of the War and in the post-war period a series of younger Lutheran theologians had discovered the concept of the Volk. It was a discovery which seems utterly to have overwhelmed a part of this generation. Within it they found something which transcended an individualism of which they had long been weary, because this individualism seemed too narrow, small and unfeeling. What German

Protestantism had treasured as virtues, namely the desire for community and solidarity, for dedication and sacrifice, now flowed directly into the concept of the Volk. The family seemed too limited as a field of Christian activity; the culture of the nineteenth century had been destroyed by the War; the state seemed to have become questionable. The Volk alone seemed to have survived; it now carried the future, and appeared worthy of any sacrifice and any dedication. Thus the Volk became the new ethical point of reference for theology, as previously the throne had been: the embodiment of the civil and social order. The new expression 'God and Volk' replaced the old formula 'throne and altar'. It was, of course, a piece of romantic tradition restored to life. Herder, Arndt, and above all Fichte had sponsored this völkisch concept and, in some respects, it all reminded people of the time of the wars of liberation, in which piety and patriotism had once met in the concept of the Volk.[2] But it made a critical difference whether one spoke of Volk at a time when völkisch thought very quickly came up against the political borders of the German territorial states, or whether one used this concept in circumstances which were like kindling an open fire in a gunpowder store.

Among the theologians who created and taught the link between God and Volk in this new, special way were some of the most significant theological thinkers of their time. They included Paul Althaus, Emanuel Hirsch and Friedrich Gogarten, who belongs to this group, though for a decade, from 1919 to 1929, he appeared to stand in another camp. Of equal, if not greater, influence was the journalist Wilhelm Stapel who, with his monthly *Deutsches Volkstum*, founded in 1919, was also a member of this school.[3]

The changes which began in German Protestantism with the outbreak of the First World War can be observed in a lecture given by Paul Althaus at a general conference of pastors in the Warsaw consistorial district, which took place in Lodz on 8-9 April 1919. At the time he was a twenty-eight-year old university lecturer and army chaplain. It bore the title 'The Place of the Church in the Life of the Volk'. In the divided Land, which was extremely sensitive to nationalist questions, the Protestant church, a provincial church of the Evangelical Church of the Old Prussian Union, of course occupied a difficult position. As early as October 1905 a general synod of pastors of the Protestant clergy in Poland had therefore accepted a resolution which expressly established the 'standpoint of neutrality over the völkisch question'. 'The pastor,' this statement said, 'has to place himself above nationalities. He is not a politician but a pastor of souls. His task is neither Germanization or Polandization, but the faithful proclamation of the gospel, in which he must as far as possible do justice to each nationality.'[4]

By contrast, Althaus, who quoted this resolution, referred in his lecture to the growing German-völkisch movement which had by then made the resolution obsolete. 'The church's indifference to völkisch questions, at a time of valuable stocktaking in present-day German culture', had already 'in many places damaged the relationship between the pastors and the German communities'. Althaus therefore set against the resolution of the 1905 synod the thesis that 'Neutrality of the church over the völkisch question is repugnant to the calling of the church when rightly understood'.[5] Holding fast to Germanhood was a matter of character. It was a matter of faithfulness, of perseverance, of 'moral duty', which called for 'protecting one's own God-given nature'. Althaus saw the affirmation of German Volkstum, even, indeed specifically, in difficult circumstances, as being above all a moral accomplishment: the readiness for solidarity, for devotion and sacrifice. 'Volkisch self-determination,' he therefore maintained, 'is already an awakening from the apathy of day to day life governed purely by material needs; it is already a matter of growing into a world of moral, invisible duties, and can thus certainly become the outer court of the sanctuary of religion.'[6]

The conception which was at the basis of this völkisch appeal to the German Evangelical Church in Poland saw the Volk as a community which existed prior to the individual, from which the individual derived his earthly life, and to which he therefore also owed that life. And since in principle a higher moral worth was attached to the claim of the community upon the individual than to the claim of the individual upon himself, in fact this meant the end of liberal individualism.

Three years later, in 1919, Althaus published a paper in which he strove to portray the church, too, as having a fundamentally communal character, in the light of the community formed by the Volk. This paper is especially interesting because it shows how naturally and with what conviction Althaus was already advocating the völkisch position at this time. At the same time, however, it also demonstrates that he definitely knew how to distinguish the community of the Volk from the community of the church.

'Who would attempt to explain and justify, say, the community of the Volk in terms of the individual?', Althaus asked. 'The Volk comes before the individual, in time and substance. There is, strictly speaking, no individual... What I am and have, I have and am from the sources of my Volk...'[7] This was the insight which in his conviction had generally made itself felt through the experience of the World War. Only in the church – and this was the starting point of the paper – was a religious individualism still subscribed to, ignoring the fact that the relationship of Christians to the church is in this respect subject to the same laws as the relationship of the member of the Volk to that Volk. Another decisive factor here for a correct understanding of the church was that we do not define the church in terms of the religious need of the individual, as did Schleiermacher, but understand that it is there before us, as 'the one great means of God's grace through which he grasps for himself, prepares and hallows the individual'. As this great means of God's grace it serves no alien purpose, but is itself the purpose, namely the founding of community. 'We perceive the community not only as the means, but also as the real goal of grace, indeed as God's goal for the world.' And at this point Althaus now saw a remarkable interweaving of the call to the community of the church with the call to the community of the Volk. It is the community of the church, established by God, that makes us also capable of community in the world. 'The God of all love and sacrifice, whose most personal nature is the will for community, presents us with the capacity for community in self-knowledge, in a new willingness for service, in a new power for patience and sacrifice.'[8] But though it is the community of the church that makes possible the community of the Volk, the community of the church is greater and higher than that of the Volk, namely 'the one people of God in all peoples and churches, the one community scattered throughout generations, nations and confessions, consisting of those whose hearts God has won through his revelation in Jesus Christ'.[9]

It is evident that here the community of the Volk is given a particular dignity of its own. It is in fact part of the divine order. But it is just as clear that Althaus does not intend for a moment to substitute this community of the Volk for that of the church, or even to set it above the church. The difference between the völkisch theologian and the Christian theologian has not been smoothed over. Nevertheless, as I shall demonstrate, a degree of uncertainty remained which was to increase enormously towards 1933.

Emanuel Hirsch put the problem more sharply, and in many ways more consistently than his friend Althaus, who was the same age, but always mild and conciliatory. Hirsch, from 1916 lecturer in church history at Bonn and from 1921 professor in Göttingen (and thus a close colleague of Karl Barth), is beyond question one of the most difficult figures of the recent history of theology to interpret. A polymath, with amazing diligence and stupendous erudition, well into the 1950s he produced a long series of outstanding works, some of which are unsurpassed even today. Hirsch was one of those who rediscovered Kierkegaard, all of whose works he translated into German, and he wrote the only comprehensive history of modern theology that we possess, the five-volume *History of Modern Protestant Theology in the Context of the General Movement of European Thought*. But at the same time he was a passionate political theologian, of an unshakable and stubborn narrow-mindedness on all matters relating to Germany's mission and destiny. He was a supporter of the völkisch movement from the start and an ardent admirer of Hitler, though never a Party member – and assuredly no opportunist, either in 1933 or in 1945. In some respects Hirsch, whose personal fate is surrounded with an aura of tragedy, is almost a symbol of political Protestantism in Germany, in which passion and unawareness, higher moral claims and crass failure, spiritual breadth and political narrowness, are so oddly mingled.

Hirsch took his stand in a book which originated in a series of lectures in the summer of 1920, under the significant title *Germany's Destiny. State, Volk and Humanity in the Light of an Ethical View of History*.[10] This was nothing short of an attempt to interpret the War and the defeat. Hirsch's starting point was that of the entire völkisch movement after 1918, namely the puzzling absurdity of the German collapse.[11] 'We were a world-people, a noble people, perhaps the most flourishing, the best of them all,' wrote Hirsch. It was no coincidence that this and many other expressions brought to mind Fichte's 1806 *Addresses to the German Nation*, with its unintelligible but impressive concept of the German 'Urvolk'. 'We stand in danger,' Hirsch went on to explain, 'of being brought low, of being destroyed as a people, so that only a formless mass of workers is left in the service of foreign interests. This fate is so dreadful, so contradicts what we and no others could accomplish among humanity, that it constantly raises doubts about the meaning and the justice of history.'[12] Given this problem, there were two questions to be answered: what caused the defeat, and what was the solution. Hirsch's answer to the question what caused the defeat followed that of the rest of the völkisch movement: internationalism and pacifism had destroyed the will for victory and had thus caused the defeat. However – and this marked a decisive difference from the radical völkisch partisans – Hirsch did not yet put the blame for this development on the Jews. On the contrary, 'we are the authors of our own fate'.[13]

No Volk without state and no state without power and the will to power. This, reduced to a short formula, was Hirsch's political conviction. And it had already pointed to the solution. The Volk, as the fundamental element of history, must reflect on itself, declare itself for a strong state and through it realize its moral task in the world. Therefore Hirsch issued a call for all intellectual and cultural forces to be used for the education of the Volk. 'Only a Volk that is very proud of its God-given nature, that considers itself indispensable to all humanity, will want to stake so much on its future and its state. So, precisely where the whole world despises us, we must learn pride in being German.'[14] For Hirsch, all this was a question less of politics than of morality and piety. In the final analysis, it was 'ultimately moral conditions that decide our fate'. However, morality is unthinkable without belief in God. The shift in German destiny, the way taken by the Volk to its appointed task, depended on the Germans 'becoming a pious Volk, a Volk among whom the gospel has power over the conscience'.[15]

One of Hirsch's fundamental convictions which was never touched by even the shadow of a doubt was that the great peoples had emerged directly from the creative will of God, each with the task of fulfilling in the world a special task peculiar to itself. This conviction, shared by Hirsch with many of his contemporaries, led him at the moment of decision to feel more closely related to the völkisch movement than to a church which did not hold this conviction, or did not hold it in the same way. This is the same phenomenon as that which brings a Christian convinced of the truth of Marxism to see, in perplexity, the Christian proclamation better adopted and transcended in a Communist Party than in a church that shuts itself off from Marxism. When Hirsch tried to explain the essential aspects of *Deutschlands Schicksal* in a long letter to his Danish friend and colleague Eduard Geismar, who was Professor of Theology in Copenhagen – the Dane naturally had had considerable reservations about this historical and theological imperialism – he explicitly stressed that the most important thing was correct method. But this method was totally controlled by that fundamental conviction. 'In order to judge the acts of a nation and of a state one must put oneself in the midst of the Volk concerned and measure its actions against the particular purpose of this Volk. And here three criteria emerge: 1. Is this Volk true to the purpose which God has entrusted to it? 2. Has this Volk not chosen for itself a fantastic notion that does not correspond to its own strength and significance? 3. Has this Volk in its decision become clear about the ideas (the necessary interests) of the other peoples, and does it believe that in return for the damage that it must perhaps inflict on them... it can give them something greater?'[16]

The task of the theologian was to clarify to the Volk its spiritual and political mission in the name of God. But this decisively altered the approach of liberal theology. Wilhelm Herrmann's point of reference had been the activity of the individual Christian in the family, culture and state. Now individual destiny retreated and 'German's destiny' moved into the foreground. The ethical point of reference in theology changed accordingly. For Althaus and Hirsch and their friends, responsibility for the community of the Volk became the decisive theological task, from which theology and the church were in no circumstances to be allowed to draw back. At this juncture there appeared a new, modern type of theology: political theology.

Of course every theology is political. In modern political theology, however, political ethics becomes the key question in theological understanding and church action. That is its general hallmark and characteristic.

In 1933 Althaus himself gave an apt description of this in terms of the political theology of his time. As he declared in an article on 'The Third Reich and the Kingdom of God': 'To every age the one eternal gospel must be proclaimed. But to every age it has to be proclaimed differently, as an answer to the specific questions of that age... At the time of the Reformation the question of salvation was the question of deliverance from guilt, of peace with God... Today we are an utterly political species. And our quest for 'salvation' comes alive in the political dimension. People of our day are not concerned about peace with God, but with overcoming political calamity in the broadest sense – the mortal distress of a people, the destruction of the national community, the freedom of the Volk for its own life, the fulfilment of its particular mission. If that is the key question for our age, the gospel must be preached to it in terms of its "political" concept: the kingdom of God, the Lordship of God.'[17] In practice, political theology thus had a twofold significance here: the revival of the question of salvation 'in the dimension of the political' and the definition of its content as 'overcoming political need in the broadest sense, the need of a Volk for life'. What theology had to say about this *qua* political theology – including what it had to say critically – had to be within the scope of this question, which could not be done away with as such.

The development of the political theology of völkisch National Socialism in the 1920s occurred in close conjunction with the intellectual and political currents of the period. In his monograph *Anti-Democratic Thought in the Weimar Republic*, which is still a basic work, Kurt Sontheimer is certainly right in counting the concept of Volk as being 'one of the most essential and politically most fertile' among the basic concepts of this way of thinking.[18] Among the names which he mentions especially in this context is at least one which directly represented the union between the intellectual and political ideas of the young conservatives and the political theology of German Protestantism: Wilhelm Stapel.[19] In his monthly *Deutsche Volkstum*, Stapel, who was only a little older than Althaus and Hirsch, from 1919 on presented a conscious völkisch-nationalist and Christian-Lutheran position. According to his own testimony it was Fichte and Luther who had helped him to attain clarity out of the shock of war and defeat.[20] Thus as in the case of Hirsch, Stapel's concept of Volk had marked echoes of Fichte. For him, too, the Volk was an original entity created by God, the real subject of history, prior to and above the individual.

'The German Volk,' he wrote in 1922 in a programmatic article, 'is not an idea of humanity but an idea of God's.' This, in a sentence, was the new recognition and the content of the starting point of political theology. Because the Volk was a living reality and as such followed a specific law of development, it had its destiny – here Stapel and Hirsch employed the same concept. Abstract ideas such as 'Gothicism', 'Reformation', 'World Citizenship' had no destiny. But 'the German Volk, the French Volk', Stapel suggested, 'has a destiny, for as a living entity it is an idea of divine power and discloses its destiny in "Gothicism", "Reformation", "Rationalism"'.[21] Thus according to Stapel's conviction, only nations were the vehicles of historical life. The right of the individual was determined by his position in the Volk. The will of the Volk was determined, not by the majority, but by the 'predetermined' leader. In this context there was a völkisch instinct, a 'völkisch life-process', there were questions of assimilation and the problem of Volk and race. And finally, morality was always the responsibility of the Volk. 'I live not only to myself but in the chain of the generations and in the circle of the Volk. I am morally bound by loyalty towards our ancestors and by concern for our descendants. This morality applies to all political and economic actions.'[22]

In the middle of the 1920s Stapel certainly stood closest in viewpoint and personal interests to the radical völkisch, though he is no doubt not to be included directly among them. But plainly antisemitic tones could be heard from him as early as 1919, though he did not want to see the civil rights of the Jews attacked.[23] And he even let himself be persuaded to stand in the Reichstag elections of May 1924 in Hamburg, as a candidate for the Völkisch-Social Block, an alliance of the Deutschvölkischer Freiheitspartei and the NSDAP.[24] In so doing he was even more politically naive than Hirsch or Althaus. For example, after Hitler's trial, at the beginning of 1924, in *Deutsches Volkstum* he said that Ludendorff of all people was the 'man of destiny for the German Volk'. In 1926 he complained to Harnack that 'Liebknecht-Spartacus, and not Ebert, should have become the first President', so that the German Volk would have experienced an 'inaugural fever',[25] and in the same year in all seriousness he contemplated Germany allying itself with world Bolshevism in order to join Russia in opening a front against England.[26] Such opinions were not, of course, confined to Stapel. It was almost a hallmark of the representatives of political theology that they displayed an overwhelming naivety about the actual conditions and possibilities of German politics. Political theology saw itself as an expression of the direct responsibility of theology for politics. But the crass imbalance between claims and capabilites in fact made it an expression of irresponsibility. It is hard to assess what weight Stapel's opinions up to 1930 actually carried. Between 1930 and 1933, however, he was one of those who, by their errors of judgment, contributed substantially to the dismantling of the barriers between Protestantism and the NSDAP.

Obviously this political theology, with its claim to share in the responsibility for Germany's destiny, harmonized very well with the notions of the German Evangelischer Kirchenbund. Indeed it seemed simply a new way of realizing the 'religious and moral world-view of the German Reformation' referred to in the statutes of the Kirchenbund. The Landeskirchen first noticed that things were not so simple, and that there was a different spirit at work here from that evoked by the Kirchenbund Basis of 1922, when this political theology began to capture pulpits and its representatives began to make a stand against the church leadership, appealing to a higher law.

Clearly though political theology before 1930 might have felt itself to be in agreement with the Kirchenbund, from the beginning it was in irreconcilable conflict with dialectical theology. In 1922 Emanuel Hirsch added an 'Afterword' to the new edition of *Deutschlands Schicksal* which maintained this conflict. The crucial point was the relationship between morality and conscience. For Barth even morality, even conscience belonged on the human side; they were part of human religion and culture and, like religion, were not bridges to God but walls against him. Thus any kind of political theology was already nipped in the bud.

For political theology stands and falls with the conviction that it is possible through taking sides politically to be directly obedient to the will of God; or, as Hirsch put it, to overcome 'the dialectical separation between the eternal and the temporal through an ethical commitment'.[27] Like Wilhelm Herrmann, Karl Holl and the whole German Protestant tradition, Hirsch argued – over against Barth – that Luther's religion was a 'religion of conscience in the most precise sense of the word',[28] that the question of God was to be heard 'in the accusation and the demand of the conscience'. For that reason, for Hirsch 'the holy earnestness which... resides in the relationship between Volk and state' was 'an earnestness of obedience'.[29] The second difference from Barth lay in Hirsch's understanding of God. Where Barth always saw God at work in contradictions, in the Yes and the No, in destruction and construction, Hirsch thought that he could 'read God's real intention for creation out of the formative and creative forces of history'. Hirsch declared himself for God's Yes in history – 'unlike the purely destructive No, in which the philosophy of revolution claims to find the traces of God'.[30] Hirsch concluded by summarizing his position once again: 'There is no other way to inscribe sacrifice for state and nation on the hearts of our Volk than by awakening faith in the Lord of history, who testifies in the conscience that he is alive.'[31] The decisive and fatal error in this statement lay in the confusion of God's revelation with national history. However justified the national demands after 1918 may have been, they were not God's demands, so sacrifice for state and nation was not the fulfilment of obedience to God. Where political decision becomes the criterion of theology – and that happens in every political theology – politics and theology become blind, helpless and corrupt. That is a lesson that emerges from the history of political theology in the twentieth century.

Political theology was the response of German Protestantism to the völkisch movement. It was not the only response, but it was the first and for some time the most important one. Thus in 1924, as the discussion of the attitude of the church to the völkisch movement began, several basic decisions had already been made. The discovery of the Volk as the new ethical point of reference for theology was largely accepted. At the same time this marked a recognition of the direct responsibility of the church for the Volk and Volkstum. Both of these decisions were of fundamental importance in that from the beginning they presented the relationship of the church to the völkisch movement in a positive light. Thereafter the völkisch movement appeared basically to be a good, important, acceptable phenomenon. From 1924 on this was the basic attitude of most contributions on the theme of the völkisch movement and the church.

However, it is important not to conclude from this that German Protestantism already had a general commitment to the völkisch movement. In reality only small groups were interested in the topic at all: the Evangelischer Bund for nationalist reasons and individual pastors and teachers for practical professional reasons, since above all the youth were attached to völkisch ideas. For the overwhelming majority of German Protestant the völkisch issue would not yet have represented a problem – before the elections of September 1930. Certainly it was not yet a crucial issue for the church. The conservative nationalist pastors tended to keep their distance from the völkisch movement,[32] and no one in the circle of dialectical theologians took serious note of the business at all. On the other hand, it is possible to detect an advance in political theology during the 1920s. At the latest from the time of Althaus's lecture on 'Church and Volkstum' at the 1927 Königsberg Kirchentag it was clear that the theme of God and Volk could without contradiction be presented as a völkisch theme at the very heart of German Protestantism.[33]

It is not entirely clear why the church discussion of this whole question began in the year 1924 in particular. Probably it was a consequence of the failed Hitler Putsch of 9 November 1923, which for the first time directed public attention generally to the völkisch movement and its leader.[34] The comparative electoral success of the völkisch candidates in the Reichstag elections of May 1924 would also support this.

These connections are clear at least in the case of the Evangelischer Bund. The Twenty-Eighth General Assembly of the Bund took place in Munich on 31 August and 1 September 1924.[35] Whereas the main assembly kept to the traditional national and anti-Roman programme, with lectures by Bruno Doehring, the former court and cathedral preacher and now the new First President, and the church historian Karl Holl,[36] the topic of 'Protestantism and the Völkisch Movement' was discussed in a special closed section of the Bavarian branch of the Bund. The speaker was Konrad Hoefler, a secondary school teacher who was head of the Nuremberg section of the Evangelischer Kirchenbund.[37] The fourteen theses of his lecture contain nearly all the arguments which were later to be used in support of a decision for Hitler in German Protestantism. 'The völkisch movement,' ran Hoefler's first thesis, 'is a German populist movement on a large scale which not only touches the surface of the German folk but stirs it to the depths. It moves and compels it as a whole to respond with either a Yes or a No. It has emerged out of German distress, provoked from outside by our enemies' desire for our annihilation and their work of destruction, and directed from within instinctively by the urge for self-preservation and intellectually by an awareness of the right and duty of German Volkstum to live.'[38] Only on the basis of the preparatory theological work done by Althaus, Hirsch and Stapel, in which the Volk became the new ethical point of reference in theology, was it possible for a Christian theologian to speak so freely about the right and the duty of German Volkstum to live. For this was beyond question the pivotal point; it was the right and the duty, in the face of which all other rights and duties had to give way. One cannot understand how Christians were ready to accept the flood of hate and vulgarity which völkisch antisemitism spewed forth without realizing that the beginnings of political theology had made the right of the Volk the embodiment of the divine will in creation. For Hoefler, moreover, the move into the völkisch movement was a direct move into a religious movement. 'This German will to live, in part felt instinctively and in part perceived clearly, which many experience as a divine command,' he continued, 'on the one hand gives the völkisch movement its enormous vitality, and on the other hand also accounts for the religious and moral power which is alive in the völkisch movement. It obliges us as Christians to recognize and value the religious ground and centre of the movement.' By way of a warning in an argument that was later to become very significant, Hoefler referred to the encounter with a great völkisch movement that had been missed in the past when German Protestantism neglected 'to enrich Socialism along the lines of the Protestant world-view and view of life'. And he explicitly stressed that Christian charity was not 'a general humane love of mankind', but rather the 'dedication of goods and blood to the fatherland.' From the standpoint of preserving German Volkstum, even antisemitism was morally justified, and it reflected 'obedience to the God-given natural laws'.

However, and here Hoefler presented reservations typical of all remarks of this kind, Protestantism had to reject all 'radicalism', and test 'the attempts to solve the Jewish question' to see whether they 'correspond to and serve the building up and organization of the völkisch state or overshoot the mark'. 'It will also reject all excesses and violations of proper limits, all unscientific treatments of scientific and especially biblical-theological questions... It will especially reject the theological dilettantism of many antisemitic pamphlets. It will reject, refuse and combat the frequently exaggerated, confused and unscientific struggle of individual völkisch authors against the Old Testament and parts of the New Testament, and every fanatical attempt to replace Christianity with a renovated old Germanic religion or a new "German religion"...'[39]

Hoefler ended his comments with the favourite theme of the Evangelischer Bund, the struggle against ultramontanism, in which the völkisch movement and Protestantism were called to work together closely.

Round about the time that Hoefler delivered this lecture, in autumn 1924, Hitler had probably dictated at Landsberg those sections at the end of the first volume of *Mein Kampf* containing his settling of scores with the 'wandering völkisch scholars' and the 'völkisch Saint Johns of the twentieth century' which ushered in the Party's definitive demarcation from the religious wing of the völkisch movement.[40] Although at this time Hoefler in fact represented only a small group in German Protestantism, and although Hitler did not draw the obvious consequences of his words until the split with Dinter in 1928, it is clear that two complementary trends are at work here. Indeed at this early stage we can already see the conditions under which a later convergence of German Protestantism and the NSDAP became possible: Protestantism affirmed the völkisch idea and the political course of the movement, but demanded that the Party withdrew from völkisch religion. The Party effected this withdrawal and in so doing put Protestantism in its debt.

The Munich General Assembly ended with a 'Proclamation to the German People'. It coined a slogan which was to be repeated frequently from then on, and which confirmed the new theological status of the Volk: 'The Evangelischer Bund, which perceives in the gospel the supreme *eternal* value and which as a German Bund perceives in German Volkstum the highest *temporal* value...'[41]

The vigorous support of the Evangelischer Bund for the völkisch movement provoked a series of no less emphatic responses. On 4 September, under the headline '"Evangelischer Bund", Ludendorff and the "Völkisch"', the Catholic *Bayerischer Kurier* devoted its entire front page to this question. It contained a detailed report of the closed meeting, including Hoefler's main points, along with the observation that these comments had been 'enthusiastically approved' and that the discussion that followed could have taken place 'peaceably even in a Hitler meeting'. It was further reported that a 'Völkischer Bund of Protestant Pastors in Bavaria' had been founded, which already numbered eighty members. The *Bayerischer Kurier* rightly concluded from this that the Evangelischer Bund wanted 'to wage its religious-political struggle against Rome with the help of the völkisch party movement, because it is quite firmly convinced of the intrinsic similarity of its own world-view to the world-view of the "Völkisch party" movement'. Both in fact coincided perfectly in the name of Ludendorff.[42] There was vigorous opposition on the Protestant side, too. Thus Otto Baumgarten protested in the *Frankfurter Zeitung*, the Berlin pastor Dietrich Graue in the *Berliner Tagblatt* and Georg Merz in the *Christliche Welt*.

The reaction of the Evangelischer Bund showed just how justified the protests were, and how much it had in fact already committed itself to the völkisch cause and language. In the confidential newsletter of the executive, the First President, Bruno Doehring, declared that it would continue unwaveringly on the course on which it had embarked in Munich. 'Neither the cries of the ultramontanist press nor the harsh protests of its Jewish confederates will get in our way.' And then Doehring spoke emphatically once again of the task of the Bund to free 'the soul of the German Volk', maltreated under 'Jewish and ultramontanist compulsory tutelage', by establishing 'the Reformation concept of life'.[43]

The controversy also brought out the confessional problem, which made it difficult for some circles in German Protestantism to grasp the character of the völkisch movement. Here the Kulturkampf was not forgotten; anti-Catholic resentment outweighed all objections; Ultramontanism and world Jewry appeared as one front. But that was a further reason for Hitler, who wished to avoid a struggle with the Catholic church at all costs, to dissociate himself from the religious Völkists.

The Evangelischer Bund was the first Protestant organization to side with Hitler. For a long time it remained the only one. As late as December 1931 the liberal pastor in Breslau, Ernst Moering, could still censure the Bund for the Munich Conference, in a leading article in the *Vossische Zeitung*. The President of the Bund, Wilhelm Fahrenhorst, in sending a 'German Evangelical greeting', had been able to say nothing in reply except that Moering had become the regrettable victim of 'an old, ultramontanist, journalistic lie...'[44]

A lecture by Wilhelm Stählin, at the time Pastor of St Lorenz in Nuremberg and later Professor of Theology in Münster, after 1945 Bishop of the Oldenburg Landeskirche,[45] showed that one could welcome the völkisch movement in principle and yet remain much more critical than Hoefler. Stählin was one of the young theologians closely associated with the Youth Movement. After the War he too had experienced at first hand the direct penetration of the youth by völkisch ideas. In May 1934, at the age of forty-one, he spoke at the 'Hoheneck Conference on the Church and the Youth Movement', which had become a regular occasion, on 'The Völkisch Movement and Our Responsibility'. Later in the year the lecture appeared in pamphlet form.[46]

Stählin, too, was impressed by the power and the depth of the völkisch movement and called for an understanding of its elemental character. His question was one that was again to confront the church urgently at the beginning of the 1930s. What was to be done when the best representatives of an entire young generation thought in a völkisch way? What could and should the church say about that?

Here Stählin took what seemed to be the only possible and imaginable course, unsatisfying though it still appears today, and presumably already appeared then. He attempted to explore as positively as possible what in his belief was legitimate in the völkisch movement in order at a later stage to be able to present the problems and limitations of the völkisch idea with that much more credibility.

Stählin recognized three main aspects of the völkisch movement: 'the experience of the Volk', the 'consciousness of solidarity among members of the Volk', and the 'will to act'.[47]

He evaluated the experience of the Volk in a positive way, almost without qualifications, because it made clear 'to our rootless and high-handed contemporaries, trapped in the cult of personality or the class struggle', that they were bound 'to a particular place in the world and their lives to a particular hour of history',[48] and because it established a new relationship to the neighbour, namely solidarity. Stählin also welcomed the will to act, because passionate action for a lofty goal had its own value even if 'quiet rationality and clarity of purpose' were lacking.[49] Stählin then, however, just as frankly contrasted these values of the völkisch movement, expressed so movingly and convincingly, with the dangers posed by the movement: the danger of a loss of inwardness when a national activity became an end in itself; the attempt to forget one's own guilt and to reach out for quick and comfortable solutions; and finally the flight into antisemitism, which Stählin called a 'gigantic blunder' and 'a shameful sign of lack of insight and decency even in the multitude that calls itself völkisch'. 'Unmoved by the charge that we are not really völkisch, but rather secret friends of the Jews, we must,' Stählin declared with utter clarity, 'struggle against this incitement of the young, against this unrepentant darkness, against this most difficult obstacle to a real movement and a real change.'[50]

Stählin touched on the heart of political theology when he saw the way in which the völkisch idea was given priority to the Christian community as the 'unbridgeable gap' between Christianity and the völkisch movement. In that case, Christianity was no longer 'the higher authority, the final standard by which the life of an individual and the historical achievement of a people is measured. Rather, Christianity itself becomes one of the historical forces which have to serve the task of the Volk...'[51]

Stählin's lecture was an attempt to exercise political responsibility without falling victim to a political theology. For, convinced though Stählin doubtless was at this time of the value and significance of the völkisch movement,[52] he still saw no reason to give the concept of the Volk a new theological quality which, along with a general responsibility of Christians for political life, would have created a special responsibility for Volk and Volkstum. The decisive consequence of the political theological approach was in fact that at this point it seemed necessary for the Christian church to have special responsibility for a particular manifestation of political life. Other laws had to operate for Volkstum as 'the highest temporal value', as the Evangelischer Bund had put it, than those applying to other 'temporal values' which were inferior to it in rank and importance. In contrast to Hoefler, who was an advocate of this type of political theology, Stählin, though no less oppressed by the question, did not yield here. This made his lecture important as criticism, despite its basically nationalistic tone.

Around the middle of the 1920s the relationship of German Protestantism to the völkisch movement had still by and large to be clarified. Those who on the

110

one hand welcomed its national aspirations, approved its affirmation of law, discipline and order, and were ready to join in the struggle against Marxism and mammonism, were on the other hand repelled by its 'raucous antisemitism', condemned the style of its political campaigning and emphatically disputed its religious claims and ideas. Accordingly, opinions and positions vacillated between approval and rejection. When Stählin spoke on this question, as in the autumn of 1924 to a group of pastors and teachers in Thuringia, the critical dimension predominated. The conviction reached here was that it would be good if there were pastors in the völkisch movement, just as it would be good for other pastors to join the socialist movement, so long as a criticism of all movements 'governed by Christianity' were not lost.[53] When Heinrich Weinel, a nationalist-liberal theologian from Jena, took the floor in autumn 1925 at the conference of the League for Contemporary Christianity in Coburg, the audience was given a typical 'on the one hand, on the other hand...' On the one hand, the 'excesses' were to be resisted: that is, the unjustifiable attacks on the Old Testament, on Paul and Luther; the rejection of the Jewish saviour; the hate-filled antisemitism, the idolatry of race. On the other hand, it was still worthwhile to strengthen an appreciation of völkisch dignity and love of the homeland, responsibility for one's own race, public spirit, heroism and selfless values, and not let one's perception of these things become clouded by the excesses.[54] And when a pastor strongly influenced by the Volksmission, like Karl Themel, later a member of the Reich leadership of the German Christians, expressed his opinion that, for all the reservations, the völkisch movement and Christianity were directly related to each other: 'Not only for the sake of Christianity but for the sake of German culture and its future, the völkisch movement and völkisch thought need redemption in Christ to become their true self.'[55]

In view of these fluctuating statements and opinions on the völkisch movement, often not thought through theologically and in part very subjective, the lecture which Paul Althaus delivered in the summer of 1927 at the Königsberg Kirchentag, and the 'Patriotic Declaration' which was passed in this context, marked a clear break. The very fact that all the representatives of German Protestantism had decided to have a lecture on 'Church and Volkstum' showed that in the meantime the völkisch question had shifted from the periphery of the church to its centre. And the fact that Althaus, who was not yet forty, had been invited to speak, clearly indicated that a fresh theological answer was expected.

Officially the Königsberg Kirchentag was exclusively concerned with 'Ideas about the Fatherland'. It was very soon called the 'Fatherland Kirchentag' and its most important declaration was called the 'Fatherland Declaration'; and to many of its older participants the whole affair may have seemed almost indistinguishable from a kind of contemporary celebration of Sedan.

Nevertheless, Althaus's lecture was in no sense merely the old patriotic-national tradition in new garb. Rather, in carefully guarded formulations, he developed the fundamentals of a new political theology. The fact that those present were largely under the impression that this was just a new version of the old national and conservative theology was a result of Althaus's extremely careful way of saying things, an approach, moreover, which was not tactics but one which was second nature to him. It is significant that even Karl Barth had his doubts on reading this lecture and wrote to Althaus that he found in it everything 'that impresses me about you and is at the same time ominous: your capacity to be open on all sides and to be carried away by your enthusiasm, which, from my point of view, is also the capacity to swallow and approve entirely too much for me to be able always to hear the totally clear sound of your own trumpet'.[56]

Another reason for the confusion lay in the conceptual horizon of the gathering, for which the concepts of Volk and Fatherland still belonged together, although they had long since parted company.

Althaus, however, had known since his early works[57] that the concept of Volkstum was something new and different. He also put this plainly enough at the beginning of his lecture: 'I define Volkstum as that special characteristic of the soul, different from others, which appears to be the common factor in the feelings, values, aspirations and thinking of all fellow-members of the Volk; the womb of a unique spiritual essence of the soul; an overarching reality, originally given for all of us with our life, antecedent to our decision and will.'[58] What he had already emphasized in his earlier works was unmistakable here: the 'givenness' of the Volk, prior to all individual existence. Did Althaus understand this givenness racially and biologically, or spiritually and culturally? Althaus the political theologian had obviously taken over racial thought from völkisch ideology, but Althaus the Christian theologian knew that this was no concept of community that could be vindicated theologically. And so those 'yes and no' expressions which were so typical of this lecture and of hundreds of similar lectures, books, publications and sermons appeared. 'Never,' said Althaus, 'does a Volkstum come into existence without a precondition, e.g. the unity of blood.' But once the Volkstum is there, 'begotten', as Althaus believed, then that which predominates is 'the spirit and not the blood'.[59]

Althaus went on to divide his lecture into two sets of questions: 'Is there a path that leads from the völkisch purpose to the church?', and conversely, 'What is the path from the church to Volkstum?'[60]

In spite of a traditional evaluation of völkisch values, the answer to the first question was given in rather critical terms. Althaus emphatically condemned all approaches to a ' "völkisch religion" as a solution to the search of Volkstum for God'. They represented 'a short-circuit and an impossibility'.[61] The Volkstum does not 'find' itself in its own völkisch religion but in the church's Christian gospel.

The correct answer to the second question was therefore all the more important. And at this point Althaus in fact moved over to political theology. For the church the path to Volkstum meant struggling 'to become or to remain truly a Volkskirche'. But to be a Volkskirche meant three things: 'serving the Volk as Volk, as a total life; and serving it according to its nature, which involves two further things: a truly German proclamation of the gospel, and the entering of the church into the organic forms of life and living customs of Volkstum'.[62]

The central theological assertion that was to support these demands to the church – and at the same time the *proton pseudos*, the basic falsehood of this kind of political theology – ran as follows: '...God wants not only to sanctify the individual but also to struggle for families and peoples as totalities. The peoples as a whole have their calling in divine history. Peoples sin; God judges peoples. Thus the whole Volk is committed to the German churches, not only as the embodiment of individual souls but as Volkstum...'[63] What was involved here, as with Hirsch and Stapel, was Germany's destiny. Here Althaus had given theological legitimation to the foundations of the völkisch movement. The Volk was a distinctive order, specially raised up and singled out by God. For that reason the church was committed to it above all others, to it and to the movement that translated the will of the Volk into political action. After that, it no longer mattered that Althaus went on to attempt to guard this assertion against misunderstandings from all sides; that he pointed out its limits and emphasized that this could not mean 'betraying the kingdom of God to a völkisch purpose', but rather just the opposite, 'truly sanctifying a völkisch purpose to God's kingdom'.[64] The first false step had been taken, and further ones necessarily followed. The church now had to 'have an eye and a word for the Jewish threat to our Volkstum';[65] the value of the Old Testament had now to be defended laboriously: 'a book at war with itself: Semitic and yet at the same time... the most antisemitic book in the world'.[66]

With the theological legitimation of the Volk, derived from the political demands of the hour, Christian credentials had been provided for the key principle of the völkisch movement. But this had at the same time opened up a way to a recognition of Hitler and his movement, and that already had immediate and fatal consequences. On the basis of Althaus's lecture, the triumphal march of the NSDAP had to look like the active fulfilment of God's will. By means of political theology the essence and accidents of the movement were virtually reversed. Its nature, its murderous contempt for the individual, now appeared to be only an unfortunate accident, an excess of something that was good in itself; while what were in truth only accidents – order, community spirit, sense of sacrifice, solidarity – appeared to be its nature. Many people were only able to correct this fundamental error after the collapse of the Third Reich. Indeed, the worst result of political theology was that with its claim to read the signs of the times it in fact became blind to the true signs of the times. There will be more to say about this later.

The Kirchentag ended with a 'Fatherland Declaration' which was considered so important that its immediate distribution was decided on. All the same, its significance did not lie so much in any kind of public effect: as a result declarations of this type interest only a few people. Rather, the declaration was important as a joint statement by German Protestantism which commanded a certain degree of loyalty. In subsequent years it was also perceived as a recognized landmark and it was often referred to as such in church circles.[67]

Moreover the declaration, which was apparently hailed unanimously on the last day, had been reached only after long and vigorous arguments. A group of conservative members of the Kirchentag under the leadership of Baron von Pechmann had stubbornly refused to agree to the statements in the prepared draft which referred to 'obedience to the will of God as we discern it again today in Romans 13'. Moreover, fourteen predominantly conservative members placed on record a comment on the final version which was not, however, for publication and in fact has never been published. In reference to a statement that the church demands that 'everyone, for the sake of the Word of God, be subject to the state order', the fourteen declared that they could not agree to the declaration because they would then have 'to recognize, in certain circumstances, even the orders of

113

a government hostile to the church and Christianity', 'directed specifically against the church and Evangelical Christianity'.[68] This comment was, of course, directed against the Weimar Republic and the left-wing dictatorship that was still feared. But some of the signatories, above all Pechmann himself, did not hesitate also to draw conclusions from this position to the right-wing dictatorship of the Third Reich. Accordingly, Pechmann left the Protestant church in April 1934 because it refused to adopt a position against antisemitism and thus had ceased to be the church.[69]

The declaration itself was a document of almost classic compromise. It combined Christian truths and political theology without giving the slightest indication which Protestantism was to choose in case of doubt. However, this very character of compromise, which left all decisions open, made the declaration beyond question a true reflection of the official church. Each time, the combination of Christian truth and political theology was produced by a 'but'. 'God is the God of all nations, Jesus Christ is the saviour of the whole world. God's cause is not to be identified with the cause of any people.' The practical part of the declaration began with these sentences and with an affirmation of their implications – the 'community of faith and love which unites all who confess Christ beyond all boundaries of Volk and differences of race' – but then immediately opposed it with a 'but': 'But the diversity of the peoples is also ordained by God'. This statement, too, was developed consistently in what followed: the rejection of cosmopolitanism, a defence of the close connection between Christianity and Germanhood. 'Work on the soul of our Volk' was therefore emphatically advocated.

Once again the 'yes' and the 'but' were repeated. 'The church proclaims that above the earthly homeland there is an eternal one. But that does not lead the church to have a low opinion of homeland and fatherland.'

There then followed the statement of a principle which was constantly repeated in subsequent years: 'The church stands above parties'. After this came the demands of the church on the state and its members, who were called to co-responsibility for and commitment to the Volk and the state. 'Such service to the fatherland,' the declaration finally stated, 'is also service to God.'

If we look forward to the years to come, the decisive weakness of this declaration becomes clear – a weakness which was to a large extent the weakness of German Protestantism. It consisted in uncertainty as to how the gospel of 'the saviour of the whole world' related to the God-ordained diversity of peoples. As the declaration had been formulated, a traditional confessional or liberal theology could be as happy with it as a political theology. With this uncertainty, in normal times the church would not have been any use to any one, but it would not have harmed anyone either. However, the uncertainty could only prove fateful at a moment when the church was forced to make a decision on precisely this point.

The 'Fatherland Declaration' was not a document of political theology. But it recognized political theology as a possibility. That was its problem. And it was no coincidence that a pastor from Breslau, who in summer 1930 wrote a three-part article in the *Deutsches Pfarrerblatt* on the topic 'We Pastors and the völkisch Issue', started with the 'Fatherland Declaration' and claimed that it was proof that the church had fully recognized the significance of the völkisch movement.[70]

114

Political theology was the answer of German Protestantism to the völkisch movement. Even if it did not experience its short heyday until between 1930 and 1934, this theology already made it possible for German Protestantism in the Weimar period to make certain decisions which it could hardly have made otherwise, or if it had, would have made with little confidence.

The most important of these decisions was on antisemitism.

There is no doubt that antisemitism also increased in German Protestantism during the Weimar years. This was a result of the continuous propaganda of the völkisch movement, which would have developed even if political theology had not made antisemitism a topic for theological discussion. The fact that it actually made it a respectable topic here, by its assertion of the divine order of Volkstum, meant that the church lost its claim to speak for the simple truth of the Christian command to love. The church could certainly have drawn attention to the injuries and wrongs which doubtless arose in individual cases as a result of mass Jewish immigration. But in no circumstances should it have allowed itself to agree to the principle of antisemitism. Political theology enticed it to exactly the opposite position: to assent to the principle and to oppose certain unjust cases and measures.

As we follow the discussion in the Weimar period we are struck by the gradual loss of the church's claim to speak for the truth. For it was not as if no one spoke for it in this time. In 1926 Otto Baumgarten, who was already almost seventy, wrote a small pamphlet with the title *Cross and Swastika*, which was sent to all Protestant pastors in Germany. It was probably the first work with this title, which later was to become so popular. Significantly, here the swastika did not stand exclusively for Hitler and the NSDAP but as a symbol for the German-völkisch movement as a whole. Baumgarten argued essentially in two directions. First, after an appraisal of the 'ideal goals and motives' of the swastika, he dealt with its contradictions 'with scientific research and within itself', and thus with the antisemitic theories of the völkisch movement.[71] In doing this he brought out the whole profusion of grotesque and banal contradiction and declared: 'The methods by which in recent decades Fritsch and Dinter have with their passionate agitation moved the broad masses to the *odium generis humani* mock every scholarly and civil decency.'[72] He saw an explanation for these things, and found 'the only excuse among respectable people' in 'German-völkisch fanaticism' and, above all, in the 'war psychosis'. Baumgarten exposed the historical fabrications of the antisemitists, set the humane ethics of the Old Testament over against Germanic mythology, and questioned any possibility of a scientific theory of race, since no distinction among the types of humanity was 'as questionable and muddled' as that of the races. Even more important, however, was the last section, which dealt with the 'exclusive opposition of cross and swastika'.[73] What was at issue here was the doctrine of original sin or – following Kant – the radical evil in human nature, which is the same in all human beings and races: the issue of self-denial and pride; and in the end the simple Christian truth itself. 'What compels, and should compel, us disciples of the cross more than anything else to a rejection of the swastika is the Christian commandment to love...' It was the lovelessness of the swastika, as Baumgarten finally demonstrated through I Corinthians 13, that ruled out any association of cross and swastika: 'For those who live under the cross of Christ, the one who died for all without distinction and therefore lives for all without distinction, there can be no swastika that excludes the Jews.'[74]

There were many reasons why this voice of simple bourgeois and Christian truth was heard so little in the church, as little as other similar voices at the same time. The continuing effect of the war psychosis was one, and certainly not the least. But the fact that political theology was also an important factor is evident from the way in which it hardly needed to feel that Baumgarten was getting at it. It seemed that the references were only to Fritsch and Dinter and all the 'raucous antisemitism', not political theology. For political theology was not concerned with antisemitism but rather with the preservation of a God-given order: German Volkstum. As a result, however, as long as it followed this line the church saw itself suddenly placed in a completely new situation over against antisemitism. It now no longer had to struggle against it, but rather to bear a joint responsibility for it. It had to be careful that it did not erupt in emotional hatred, but rather followed orderly, legal paths. It had a moral task in the antisemitic movement and no longer against it.

This kind of argument, like political theology itself, first came fully into play in 1933. But its consequences could already often be traced in the middle of the 1920s. German Protestantism in fact became less and less responsive to simple bourgeois and Christian truth.

This also applied to what was probably the best-known and most impressive church publication against antisemitism in this period, Eduard Lamparter's book *Evangelical Church and Judaism*.[75] It had emerged from articles which the author published in winter 1927-28 in the monthly *Abwehr-Blätter* of the 'Association for Defence against Antisemitism'. Like Baumgartner, Lamparter, a city pastor in Stuttgart, wrote from the standpoint of a humane and liberal Christianity. His book included, in the first three chapters, a critical discussion of antisemitism in the history of Protestantism from Luther to Stoecker, which was admirable, for all its brevity. The fourth chapter then dealt with 'The Present Position of the Protestant Church on Judaism'. Above all it refuted the religious historical theses of the religious Völkists, not least launching a sharp attack on the 'National Socialist leader Dr A.Dinkler'.[76] Finally, it exposed the irreconcilable conflict between antisemitic racial theories and Christian ethics. The book ended, as in fact had Baumgarten's, with a reference to the decisive attitude of the Catholic church, specifically Pope Pius XI,[77] on this matter. 'Should not the Protestant church also feel an obligation, should not it too find the courage, to speak out against the serious antisemitic violations of law, truth and love? What is important is to make up for old injustices and to see to it that no new injustice occurs.'[78]

As a Foreword to Lamparter's treatise, twelve well-known theologians wrote a commendation: 'Without underestimating the idealistic motives which underlie the antisemitic movement here and there, we believe that Protestant clergy, in the pulpit as well as in their parish work, should make it quite clear that they consider the ostracism of a "race" or a religious confession to be a sin against Christ...'[79]

Representatives of completely different trends appeared among the signatories: liberals like Otto Baumgarten, Martin Rade and Dietrich Graue, pastor and DDP deputy in the Prussian Landtag; Christian Geyer and Hermann Schafft, pastors influenced by the Berneuchener renewal movement; Wilhelm Kahl, the conservative canon lawyer and DVP representative in the Reichstag; Karl Barth; Paul Tillich as a representative of Religious Socialism; and Friedrich Siegmund-Schultze, the unswerving champion of the ecumenical movement.

However, even this commendation could not overcome the increasing difficulties over hearing Christian truth.

This does not yet complete a description of German Protestantism in so far as it was under the more or less distant influence of political theology. For German Protestantism not only dissociated itself on the one hand from the bourgeois liberal objections to völkisch antisemitism, but on the other also fought against a group of radical völkisch pastors who pressed for a synthesis of Volk and faith. This small radical group, which never represented a serious danger to the church, nevertheless shifted the spectrum of opinion so far to the right that political theology could in fact perceive itself to be a theological centre position.[80]

One of the fathers of this group was the chief pastor in Flensburg, Friedrich Andersen. Born in 1860, he had come to Flensburg at the age of thirty and for the thirty-eight years until his retirement in 1928 was pastor at the Johanniskirche there. Andersen began as a traditional Lutheran, but under the impact of reading Chamberlain, he underwent a lasting conversion about 1905.[81]

The result of his new insights appeared in 1907 under the title *Anticlericus*.[82] On the authority of Schleiermacher and of Harnack's *Marcion*, Andersen called above all for a reappraisal of the Old Testament: it had no significance for salvation history, but was only a kind of dark background against which the gospel stood out all the more brightly. This brought him a reprimand from the Royal Consistory, followed in 1913 by a 'warning'. It was probably only the outbreak of war that prevented the institution of disciplinary proceedings which, in the circumstances, would perhaps have ended with his dismissal from office.[83] Andersen, however, remained unimpressed, and together with the völkisch literary historian from Weimar, Adolf Bartels, Kirchenrat Ernst Katzer from Dresden and the Bayreuth author Paul von Wolzogen, produced a book entitled *German Christianity on the Foundation of the Pure Gospel*, with the sub-title 'Ninety-five Guidelines for the Feast of the Reformation 1917'.[84] Essentially it contained völkisch variations on the theme of German culture and Christianity; the style was still moderate, but the authors had already made up their minds on the issue. Thus Thesis 6 already talked of the 'ruinous effects of mixing blood'. The abolition of the Old Testament was looked upon throughout as the precondition for a religion that was truly suitable for Germans.

Here too, war and defeat marked the dividing line. What before the War had been the opinion of individuals and hardly taken seriously, rapidly gained significance after the War as a result of the formation of groups and the founding of associations. Thus in 1921 the Berlin schoolmaster Dr Joachim Niedlich founded the 'Alliance for a German Church' along the lines of the Andersen theses. From 1922 it also had a fortnightly journal, *Die Deutschkirche. Sonntagsblatt für das Deutsche Volk*. Andersen became 'Bundeswart' for life, joined the NSDAP at the end of the 1920s, became education director for the Party, and as late as 1936 gave six lectures in defence of Rosenberg's *Myth*.[85]

In 1926 an umbrella organization was founded from the numerous associations of the völkisch-religious groups, entitled 'The German Christian Working Group of Greater Germany', which was to advance the völkisch-religious cause.

However, it was always only the 'German Church' that seemed to be offensive to the church. Its members wanted to remain within the church, and insisted that they were only drawing the basic consequences of the latest findings of historical theology and the claim of the völkisch movement. The demands of the Bund – the abolition of the Old Testament; the removal of all Jewish elements from Christianity, the restoration of the pure image of the Saviour; the acceptance of German stories and sagas as a German form of revelation – [86] were, it is true, widely rejected in German Protestantism. However, they remained as a more or less extreme possibility on the way towards the Völkists who were opposed to the church.

With the growth of the völkisch movement the attitude of Protestantism towards the 'German Church' changed in an almost startling way. Whereas the *Kirchliches Jahrbuch* of 1924 still mocked the 'German Church' as 'a product of fantastic super-nationalism',[87] in 1931 the Kirchenbundesrat thought it necessary and appropriate to spend a whole day discussing its 'attitude towards the German Church'. Ultimately the assembly rejected, by 76 to 12, a resolution to the effect that 'German Church' pastors might not exercise their ministry in contradiction to the confession of faith and ordinances of the church. This happened not because of a lack of theological insight into the heretical character of the German Church, about which the speeches and contributions to the discussions were quite clear, but because of a fear that the public might suspect that 'the church rejected the German idea, indeed fought against it'.[88]

The Alliance for a German Church was quite simply the direct penetration of the church by the völkisch movement. As the decision of the Kirchenbundesrat indicated, the difficulty for the church arose from the fact that it wanted to welcome the völkisch movement and at the same time to keep a good theological conscience.

It was here that the precise function of political theology lay. Since it gave a new decisive status in theology and in the church to the basic concepts of the völkisch movement, it was able all the more emphatically to reject all syntheses and syncretism represented by the 'German Church'. One of the two speakers at the session of the Kirchenbundesrat mentioned above, Bishop Mordhorst of Kiel, made this function quite clear. In his first thesis he expressly started from Althaus's Königsberg lecture and declared that it had made the decisive assertions about church and Volkstum which fulfilled the völkisch concerns for the German church. Moreover, Mordhorst was in some respects theologically even more critical than Althaus, as was demonstrated by a thesis he presented on the subject of confession and order in the church in relation to the German Church.[89]

That the 'attempt so far made by the völkisch movement to achieve a synthesis of Germanhood and Christianity' was to be rejected as 'a failure' was argued by Karl Witte, who as a former head of the Fichte Academy in Hamburg had a close association with the Völkists, when in 1928 he summarized the general opinion in the church. And he hit on the decisive question when he went on to say: 'If the völkisch movement has not so far been successful in combining Christianity and Volkstum in an inner unity, it has at least posed the problem sharply. In the long run the only satisfactory solution is one in which each comes into its own: in which on the one hand "the religious meaning, the revelatory value, for the völkisch determination of our lives is recognized, and on the other its relationship to the perfect revelation of the gospel is clarified".[90] Witte did not expect this clarification either from culture Protestantism or from supranaturalism, or from pietism, and certainly not from dialectical theology. What was needed was a new, 'comprehensive cultural theology'.[91] The aim should be not the synthesis of Christianity and Volkstum but rather their critical integration, which would enable and compel the church to hallow Volkstum.

What Witte called for and described here was quite simply political theology. And his theological sources were the same as for all those who thought in this way: Stapel, Althaus and Hirsch.

If we look back once again from this standpoint at Hitler's decision to dissociate himself from the religious wing of the völkisch movement, it becomes clear that at this juncture two developments meshed as precisely as if they had been planned, though this was certainly not the case. Political theology gave German Protestantism the opportunity of making the völkisch idea its own cause, as long as this völkisch idea did not present its own religious claims. It represented, defended and legitimated völkisch ideas as much to its conservative, liberal and socialist critics as to its fanatical adherents in the German Church. Hitler met this approach head on with his decision. By emphasizing the political character of the movement, dissociating himself from fanatics like Dinter, and committing the Party to a general religious air, he fulfilled all the essential requirements posed by political theology to the future Führer of Germany and his party.

At this point, however, one must be careful not to regard political theology as a kind of Hitler party in the church. It did not seek to be that, nor was it. Rather, the real point of this theology lay precisely in the creation of a critical solidarity with the völkisch movement. Thus it was completely consistent, for example, that for a long time Hirsch voted for the German National Party (DNP),[92] that in 1933 Stapel refused to become a member of the National Socialist Party because he did not want to give up his independence,[93] and that as early as autumn 1933 Althaus came into conflict with the régime when he criticized certain measures.[94] Moreover, in judging political theology one must take into account an obvious point which is nevertheless hardly ever taken seriously: that the political theology of the 1920s still had Hitler to come, while we have him behind us. Still, political theology must be made responsible for the fact that in 1933 German Protestantism was almost coordinated with the Third Reich.

8

The Struggle for the Church
(1929-1931)

During the 1920s, sympathy for the völkisch movement was undoubtedly on the increase in German Protestantism. But just as undoubtedly, in spite of political theology and the Königsberg Kirchentag, the völkisch movement did not offer any serious threat even in 1928. This was made surprisingly clear by a survey sent to all Landeskirchen by the Kirchenbundesamt early in 1928.

In a long letter occasioned by two petitions from the 'German Church' side, the President of the Kirchenausschuss, Hermann Kapler, referred to the increasing ideological claims of the völkisch and patriotic associations on the one hand and the Social Democratic Party on the other. Moreover, specifically in connection with the impending Reichstag election in May 1928 he wanted to know what the Landeskirchen thought of this development and whether special measures were necessary.[1] The answers showed that except for the Berlin Oberkirchenrat, of which Kapler was also President, no Landeskirche attached much significance to the völkisch movement. Some people were disturbed by the aggressive ideological atheism of Social Democracy. As to the völkisch movement, however, Hanover for example reported that 'from what we have observed so far' it had 'no special significance for church life in our area. We think that at present there is no danger of a strong movement for withdrawal from the church on the part of people who are occupied with völkisch issues.'

Darmstadt reported: 'In Hessen we have little to do with a specifically völkisch movement and "Teutonic" religion.' Brunswick reported that 'the issues... raised in the letter in question do not yet have the importance for the Evangelical Lutheran Landeskirche in Brunswick that they may have for other larger Landeskirchen'. And at the end of February Stuttgart even presented a 'Survey of Organizations represented in Württemberg', which came to the conclusion over the NSDAP that 'the Party, like the entire völkisch movement, suffers (political experience apart) from its ideological vagueness, and in the next elections might decrease rather than increase'.

The Reichstag election of 28 May 1928 showed that this prognosis was correct. The NSDAP lost another 0.4% of the vote compared with the poor result of December 1924, and with 2.6% and twelve seats remained an insignificant party. During these years anyone in the church who was not specifically concerned with the völkisch movement would not yet need to take any notice of it. The problem was not a pressing one. On the contrary, it was hidden, and anyone who might want to learn about it first had to search for it.

By contrast, another issue was fairly clearly in the foreground. It had arisen out of the church policy of the post-war period which had defended and secured the status of the church so successfully, and from a theology which rightly raised the question of the theological legitimacy of this development.

This complex of problems can be observed at a whole series of points.

In 1929 the *Diary of a Metropolitan City Pastor* appeared, at first anonymously. This was an account of church life in the 1920s in letters to a friend, which was as intelligent as it was critical and committed. It was not only one of the best but also one of the most-read books of church theology in this period.[2] The author was Gerhard Jacobi, at that time thirty-eight and a pastor in Magdeburg. A few years later he was one of the most resolute representatives of the Confessing Church in Berlin and after the war he was Stählin's successor as Bishop of Magdeburg. Jacobi had been influenced theologically by Karl Barth, at least in his critical attitude to all types of hyphenated Christianity. Thus time and again in his descriptions one finds fervent opposition to the 'Stahlhelm pastors' and to the 'godless war theology'.[3] Nevertheless, even in the writings of this attentive observer one searches in vain for any indication that the church as a whole might perhaps be threatened by a political, völkisch national theology. Although Jacobi's sympathies undoubtedly lay with the left, he criticized the 'SPD pastors' no less than the Stahlhelm people.[4]

Moreover, completely different problems really moved, occupied and upset this city pastor. These were related to the profusion of cares, sorrows, joys, hopes and hopelessness with which he had to deal daily to the point of exhaustion; to the inability of the church and his own inability to find the right word, the Word of God. What was impressive about this book was not only the reality which it described but also the honesty with which the author confessed his weakness and his faith. 'What sort of thing is a sermon? One must speak about things which one knows well: the congregation neither understands nor comprehends them; these things are remote from it. The congregation will go out of church and think: "I can't make anything of that." As a preacher one knows this, and yet one must talk as we do. We must not go by what the congregation understands and what it wants to hear. Rather, we must invoke God's coming.'[5] This was the question which most oppressed Jacobi, namely whether this church with its bourgeois self-satisfaction was still in fact capable of witnessing to God's coming. So he wrote to his friend: 'You know that there is still so much to pull down in bourgeois church-Christianity. That is truly the situation today. The battle for God goes by way of criticism, criticism of church piety and the church, of bourgeois righteousness and of the economy...[6]

Hence the situation in the church at the end of the 1920s could also be viewed in another way. The front did not run between modern political theology on the one hand and traditional church or liberal theology on the other, but between the conservative views of the Landeskirchen and the theology of the Word of God; between the promotion of a Volkskirche and belief in the freedom of the gospel; between satisfaction over what had already been attained and despair at this very satisfaction. Among the young pastors, and also in the communities, a good many people saw things in this way. The success of the *Diary* was proof of that.[7]

What Jacobi raised was the question of the church's mission and service. Two theological publications that appeared at about the same time showed how suddenly it had become a focus of interest. One, with the title *Credo Ecclesiam*, was an attempt by Lutheran theologians to redefine the place of the church in the light of its confession.[8] The other, also a collection of essays, undertook the same task from the standpoint of the Gemeinschaft movement.[9] Common to both works was a conviction that the church question was the question of the day.

However, these and other contributions would not have stirred things up in such a way had not Karl Barth launched an attack with an unusually critical article. For no one else had his acuteness and consistency in exposing the whole problem without regard for the consequences.

Since he had come to Germany in 1921, the Swiss theologian had not been much bothered about political questions, whether outside or inside the church. He had devoted all his energies and passion towards developing his theology.[10] It is extremely significant that in his lively correspondence with Eduard Thurneysen, which kept his friend in Switzerland regularly up to date with all important developments, the name 'Hitler' appears only once between 1921 and 1930. It occurs in the description of lodgings in Königsberg where in November 1924 Barth slept, as he noted ironically, 'in the bed of an ardently nationalist high school student... Round me hung Frederick the Great, Schlageter, Bismarck, Ludendorff, Hitler...'[11] He once reported – and this, too, was characteristic of the way he saw political matters at this time – 'an ethical conversatorium' which he had organized, 'with a very large membership', on the topic of the political autobiographies of the past few years: 'Tirpitz and Liebknecht have already been dealt with, and Michaelis, the Kaiser, Scheidemann, the Crown Prince, Ludendorff, Bethmann Hollweg, Erzberger, Dryander and so on are to follow. So far it has gone very well: exclusion of the purely political, questions about the motives for their behaviour and their relationship with one another.'[12]

The 'exclusion of the purely political' from theological ethics represented a position directly opposed to political theology. It was also a characteristic of Barth's work in the decade between 1920 and 1930. What political theology felt to be an absolute necessity, the demands of the völkisch movement, was not even noted as a theological problem by dialectical theology before 1930. So it was not at all surprising that Karl Barth should have opened up discussions for the fateful 1930s on a front which appeared to be remote from the issues directly pressing on the church.

It was with the short article '*Quousque tandem...?*' that these conflicts began. It appeared at the beginning of 1930 in *Zwischen den Zeiten*, was greeted enthusiastically by Thurneysen as 'at last a word that speaks to the situation',[13] and is one of the sharpest pieces of polemical criticism ever formulated by Barth.[14]

Embittered at the feeling of smugness in the Landeskirchen that was beginning to gain ground at the end of the 1920s,[15] 'in disregard of all professorial formality, consideration and caution', Barth declared: 'It is a scandal crying out to high heaven that the German Evangelical Church constantly talks in this way.' What

Barth found fault with in this talk of mastering the crisis, of preserving the empirical church, and of the 'masterpiece' of church leadership in the previous decade, was that the church that talked in this way 'as blatantly as one can imagine desires only itself, builds up only itself, praises only itself. The only difference between it and others rallied around other flags and banners is that, puffed up by the claim to represent God's cause, the church does so in a much bolder, more cherubic-faced, less restrained manner than all the others. If it is really concerned about God's cause, should it, with the complacency with which one looks back after surviving a bout of influenza, speak of the time, happily now past, when it was "literally threatened with destruction"? Should it speak with this self-satisfied mockery (as though the great apostasy were perhaps only the fault of others!) of those atheists, intellectuals and chatterboxes who are supposed to have erred so completely in those days? Should it speak with this sweeping contentment (as though that were not a wretched phrase) of the "religious ideas" rooted deeply in the soul of the German people?' Barth was convinced that the decisive question in all this was the credibility of the proclamation. If *this* church 'says "Jesus Christ", even if it says it a thousand times, we inevitably have the voice of its own satiation and security. So it should not be surprised if, in tossing its cries of "Jesus Christ" to the winds, it overlooks the real need of real people...'[16]

The reckless sharpness of this article was unusual even in German Protestantism, which was accustomed to controversy. It marked the beginning of a controversy which was inherent in the approach of dialectical theology and which continued down to the 1960s. It was a new form of the old dispute between the freedom of faith and the laws of the institution, between Christian hope and Christian tradition.

The understanding of the church against which Barth fought here was perhaps expressed most clearly in the works of Dibelius. So it was no coincidence that in '*Quousque tandem...?*' Barth, referring to the binding of Dibelius' famous book, had spoken ironically of the 'purple *Century of the Church*'.[17] And Dibelius gave a prompt answer. In the report which he made to the Prussian General Synod on 24 February 1930 in the name of the Church Senate and the Protestant Oberkirchenrat, he resolutely rejected Barth's attack on 'our entire style of working'. Here he remained completely within his own frame of reference when earlier he asserted that 'in a basically Christian state' there was no danger when one criticized the church within the realm of the possible. 'I say again,' Dibelius continued, 'the times have changed completely (Hear, hear.) If a religionless state is not to lead to a national community without religion, then it must have as a correlative the church of flesh and blood, which puts the proclamation of the gospel into effect in its work. Since this is so, we therefore insist that the church be strengthened with joy in its work. We call for gratitude that God has given us the instrument of our church.'[18]

Two conceptions of the church confronted each other here, with absolutely no chance of coming to an understanding. It is true that both sides were talking about the same thing, 'the proclamation of the gospel', but each meant something completely different by it. For Dibelius, for the majority of the Prussian General Synod and undoubtedly also for the majority of the leaders of the Landeskirchen, the proclamation of the gospel by the church was above all a moral task. The important thing was to put 'the proclamation of the gospel into effect', as Wilhelm Herrmann understood this. That meant setting standards for the family, for public life, for Volk and fatherland, by which everyone could take bearings. The Landeskirchen and the Kirchenbund were dominated by the idea that the church had to and could have a moral effect. They spared no pains in carrying this claim of the church to the public by every available means.

In opposition to this, Barth, in the first draft of his *Dogmatics*, had defined the church's proclamation as 'the risk, the venture that the truth for which man assumes the responsibility here, which he declares to be valid for all, speaks for itself; that it will cover him; that it will have and demonstrate the power to find the recognition and acknowledgment from all that is due to the truth'.[19] There was no suggestion here that the church itself might be able to put 'the proclamation of the gospel into effect'; what God did not do could not be replaced by all the church's action. Moreover the proclamation was in no sense addressed to the public at large (although of course it had to be a public proclamation), and was certainly not a public morality. It was aimed solely and exclusively at the individual human being as a member of the church. 'Anyone who does not want to end up with a German theology, a proletarian theology, a youth theology and so on, in short, with a polytheism, will have to be very hard-hearted here. It is not the human being as a member of the public who hears from God. Rather, it is that hidden part of humanity without reference to Volkstum, sex, age, class, culture, etc., the human being *qua* human, the human being *qua* individual and not as a member of one of the many categories...'[20] This marked off the potential and the tasks of the church's proclamation over against all the efforts of the Landeskirchen, however well-meaning, to help to put this proclamation into effect. But it also marked them off from the basic approach of political theology, which insistently considered the church's proclamation to be a proclamation tied to the Volk.

The struggle over the church, set up long beforehand and fanned vigorously by '*Quousque tandem...?*', lasted throughout 1930. In January 1931 Karl Barth again spelt out his viewpoint in a lecture delivered in Berlin, Bremen and Hamburg. It dealt with the twofold distress of the church: the real one which lies in its very nature, that is, the inability to offer a reassuring synthesis; and the false one, which lies in the flight from visibility and the flight into visibility.[21] Again the nature and mission of the church were at issue. 'Does it still know that that involves two things: "Thou hast borne all our sins", and encouragement towards a battle for religious renewal, moral purity, personal freedom, völkisch or social community?' To the indignation of many people, he declared, 'According to my knowledge and insight, what is proclaimed in the average sermon in our church as the gospel of our church is, despite all the appeals to the Bible and despite all the solemnity of Luther, a mysticism mixed with a little morality, or a morality mixed with a little mysticism, and not the Word of the cross as the Reformers understood it.'[22]

The Berlin lecture also demonstrated how much the subject had attracted popular thinking in the meantime. '1400 people,' Barth reported in February to his friends, '...flocked together in the new auditorium in a crush that threatened life and limb, and for two hours I held the floor from a small desk. In the background there was a fresco showing Fichte making an impassioned appeal to the German nation, surrounded by General Scharnhorst, Pastor Schleiermacher and all the rest of the personnel from the war of liberation'. Naturally the irony of the situation did not escape Karl Barth, and he commented on it in a characteristic enough style. 'The situation was certainly dignified, but also rather comic, because the man behind kept talking incessantly, doubtless about something completely different.' The reactions of the listeners showed how controversial the whole business was. 'The reception of the lecture by the audience was very lively. It was often almost like a public meeting, with interruptions for applause and argument. But it all ended happily, and without any of the incidents which are unfortunately possible in Germany today.'[23]

Again Dibelius answered immediately, this time with a lecture from the same place only eight days later, 'The Responsibility of the Church. An Answer to Karl Barth'. He accused Barth, as a theoretician, of not having grasped the practice of the church, namely the activity of practical love. Theological criticism had its own time and place, but not here and now: 'We are forced into a battle more serious than any conducted since the cross of Christ was first carried upon German soil. In this battle, no one sends notes of excuse based on theological scruples.'[24]

Barth accepted this challenge, and now declared of Dibelius's statements that 'it should become clear to every reader that he cannot put himself in a middle ground between Dr Dibelius and myself, however clever, however fashionable, however Christian. The only person who can understand at all is one who joins the *party* and takes up the *fight* without ifs and buts.'[25]

And the fight was in fact often taken up. An unusual number of committed statements appeared[26] in the *Deutsches Pfarrerblatt*, the paper of the German Protestant pastors' association.[27] Here the controversies reached an extent and a vigour which was equalled only in the dispute over National Socialism which began in the same paper in autumn 1930. Johannes Schneider,[28] who was directly attacked in '*Quousque tandem...?*', here took the side of Dibelius, as he did in the *Kirchliches Jahrbuch*, and so did Dibelius's colleague Martin Schian, General Superintendent of Silesia,[29] with a work of his own. The message which the Nuremberg Kirchentag issued in the summer of 1930 on the occasion of the 400th anniversary of the Augsburg Confession also spoke of the 'highest duty and holy responsibility' which accrued to the church 'in the present collapse' and of its task 'to offer, in the power of faith and love, to a torn and divided people a tangible and lively community...'[30] This was precisely the Protestant style of declaration that Barth had had in mind in his criticism.

On the other side, the shift in generations which took place during these years showed how much ground the critique had already gained. This happened most strikingly in the case of the *Kirchliches Jahrbuch*. Johannes Schneider had died in the summer of 1930, at the age of seventy-three, having supervised thirty-seven volumes since 1894. The Berlin pastor Hermann Sasse, who was thirty-five, took over as his successor. The new editor was a determined Lutheran, and as such by no means a whole-hearted supporter of Karl Barth. Nevertheless, in his first report on the contemporary church situation he resolutely took Barth's side on this question. 'Make no mistake,' he wrote about the controversy, 'about the gravity of these attacks. Behind them stands a broad front of theologians, including some who reject dialectical theology and some who do not agree with everything in these polemical documents.' The issue was not, as Dibelius suggested, a confrontation between theory and practice. Rather, in view of a flood of public church statements – '"Save like a Protestant", as we are exhorted in an appeal by one of our largest church associations, distributed in innumerable copies, to join a life insurance scheme' – the very foundations of the church had to be re-examined.

Sasse was quite right to point out in this connection that 'a fatal chasm' had opened up 'between theology and the practical work of the church'. 'The substantive work of rebuilding the church and the profound theological work of the last decade stand side by side, with virtually no connection between them.'[31] Until these controversies, the re-ordering of the Landeskirchen and the theological revival had taken place in virtually separate spheres. That situation was now ended. Church and theology had each other in view again, even if under decidedly critical omens.

A sign of this changed situation was the fact that Karl Barth's second approach to dogmatics in 1932 – the *Christian Dogmatics in Outline* had been published in 1927 – bore the title *Church Dogmatics*. The reason for this change and its implications, at first hardly noted in the tumult of the struggle, dawned upon church and theology in autumn 1933: 'Dogmatics is not a "free" science, but one bound to the sphere of the church, where and where alone it is possible and sensible.'[32]

The struggle over the nature and mission of the Protestant church at first appeared to be a purely theological affair, which had only marginal political significance. However, it was very soon to prove that it was exactly this issue that led to the centre of the political struggle awaiting German Protestantism. For the new theme of the church was now governed by politics.

126

9

Catholicism, Protestantism and National Socialism after the Elections of September 1930

The dramatic change in the political situation which took place in Germany in autumn 1930 also marks a decisive turn in the history of the churches in the Weimar period. In retrospect, it was to seem as though nothing was ever the same again after the September elections: all statements, all discussions, considerations, resolutions and activities from then on had a feverish political flush which began to colour everything increasingly strongly.

It was clear at the latest by autumn 1929 that the good years of the Republic were coming to an end. This was the period of the demand for a plebiscite against the Young Plan, which for the first time brought Hitler together with the German Nationalists.[1] Hirsch later wrote to Althaus, 'For the first time since the shake-up caused by the Young Plan we have in Germany a youthful, national movement of passion and depth. And for the first time since then all the successes of the right, and particularly of its strongest part, the Nazi part, have become possible.'[2] At the same time it was the period of the world economic crisis which entered its acute phase with the spectacular collapses on the New York Stock Exchange at the end of October 1929. The condition of German domestic politics, already difficult, began to become hopeless. The number of unemployed rose from 2.8 million in January 1929 to 3.2 million in January 1930, and did not decrease substantially throughout the year.

The signs that this situation would above all benefit the National Socialists multiplied from the time when Hitler first made common cause with the German Nationalists, in the demand for the plebiscite. Granted, this demand for a plebiscite, with 10.2% of the electorate, barely scraped into the Reichstag – where in November it failed pitifully. Even the plebiscite itself received only a modest response.[3] But when the Landtag in Thuringia was re-elected in November 1929, Hitler's party managed for the first time to surmount the ten per cent barrier. With six representatives instead of the previous two, the NSDAP tripled the number of its seats. The distribution of votes made it possible to continue the civil government only with the help of the NSDAP, and Hitler used the opportunity for the first time to put a National Socialist in a key political position. He demanded and received for the Party the Ministry of the Interior and the Ministry of Education, which were occupied by Dr Wilhelm Frick – later Reich Minister of the Interior.[4] The Landtag elections in Saxony in 1930 confirmed this trend. Here the NSDAP received as much as 14.4% of the votes.[5]

Another danger signal was given by the elections to the General Student Committees (Allgemeine Studentenausschüsse = AStA) of the universities and colleges in the winter semester of 1929-1930. The German students, who were politically volatile and easily excitable, in some cases helped the National Students Union to striking successes. At two universities, Erlangen and Greifswald, the NS students already had an absolute majority.[6]

Even if, in view of these tendencies, a marked increase in the NSDAP had been expected everywhere, the result of the Reichstag election of 14 September 1930 was quite a sensation. By a 'landslide never before experienced in the parliamentary history of Germany',[7] Hitler's radical right wing splinter party at a stroke became the second strongest party in the Reich. In a period of just over two years the NSDAP had raised its share of the vote from 2.6% to 18.3%, and the number of its parliamentary seats from 12 to 107. The other party to gain from the election was the KPD on the left, whose parliamentary group, with 13.1% of the votes, grew from 54 to 77 representatives. Of the other parties, only the Centre Party had been able to some extent to hold its own; the SPD registered a loss in votes of about 5%, while the DNVP and the DVP were almost halved.[8]

The result of the 14 September election meant a complete change in the German political landscape. No one could fail to perceive this – least of all German Protestantism, which to a special degree had been involved in the achievement of the result.

Among the well-known facts (though so far they have hardly been analysed in depth) is that between 1930 and 1933 the NSDAP scored its above-average results in electoral districts with a Protestant majority, while its results in electoral districts with a Catholic majority were usually far below the national average.[9] To explain such manifestly different behaviour on the part of the electorate between the two great confessions, we must take a closer look at the details of the election results.

Because there was still so little mixing of the confessions in Germany at that time, twenty-five of the thirty-five Reichstag electoral districts each had confessional majorities of over 70%. Nineteen had a Protestant majority and six a Catholic.[10] Going through the election results of 1930 in detail, one's eye is caught by the fact that the NSDAP chalked up its above-average results in electoral districts with a Protestant majority. Schleswig-Holstein, Pomerania, South Hanover-Brunswick, Chemnitz-Zwickau, Frankfurt an der Oder and Liegnitz were examples of such Protestant electoral districts in which the movement in part gained considerably more than 20%. Conversely, it remained under 15% in typically Catholic electoral districts such as Oppeln, Cologne-Aachen, Koblenz-Trier, and throughout Lower Bavaria.[11] If we take the result of all nineteen predominantly Protestant electoral districts together, the NSDAP had an average of 20.2%, while in the six predominantly Catholic electoral districts it had only 14%. Now the astounding thing – and here we have a way of understanding this phenomenon – is that these results correspond exactly to those of the SPD. The SPD, too, obtained a comparatively much larger share of the votes in the Protestant electoral districts than in the Catholic districts. Expressed in numbers: with an average of 24.5% in the Reich, it received 29.4% in the nineteen Protestant electoral districts; in the Catholic districts, on the other hand, it received only 12.8%. Differences in social structure play no part here, since agricultural and industrial areas had about the same representation in both groups of electoral districts. The explanation of these parallels lies, of course, in the Centre Party. In fact the Centre Party, with an average of 14.8% in the Reich, gained more than 37% of its votes from the six Catholic electoral districts. But this meant that the Centre Party, as a party with a Catholic ideology, tied up a definite – almost fixed – share of the Catholic vote. By contrast, the Protestant vote did not face a comparable situation. So it divided. A considerable part went to the ideological party of the left, the SPD. This is the only explanation for the relatively much higher Protestant share of the votes for the SPD, as Hermann Mulert already observed.[12] The other part went to the middle-class right-wing parties, the German Nationalists and the Liberals. Yet both these parties were political interest-groups rather than distinct and organized ideological parties. So when the NSDAP emerged with its claim to be a new, national, interdenominational party yet with a positively Christian world-view, it had no difficulty in winning that part of the Protestant vote that had waited only for a chance to attach itself to a genuine ideological party of the right. The desperate economic situation, which seemed to cry out for radical solutions, accelerated this process. The greater success of the NSDAP in Protestant areas is thus explained by the fact that Protestant voters came to it who wanted to commit themselves ideologically but for national or confessional reasons could not do so in the existing ideological parties: the KPD, the SPD and the Centre Party.

The surprising parallel between the SPD and the NSDAP in relation to the Protestant vote is confirmed by contemporary analyses of the election. Thus Adolf Grabowsky, editor of the *Zeitschrift für Politik*, who as a middle-class democrat was certainly not suspected of radical tendencies, attributed Hitler's victory above all to the fact that the SPD had not in the least appreciated the need for a national policy: 'The false psychological attitude of the ruling parties and movements prevailing since the War produced a national vacuum in Germany which demanded to be filled. The people felt itself devastated as a nation in three ways. First, by the ...disregard for, indeed almost the slighting of, its national traditions...; secondly, by the way in which the reparations policy was pursued; and thirdly, by inadequate concern for the lost territories...' These were three points of considerable importance for German Protestantism. Thus Grabowsky's conclusion applied especially to Protestant voters, though he did not make a specific reference to them: 'The National Socialists have simply thrust themselves into the national vacuum which was created. That is the most elementary significance of the election results. Nearly six and a half million eligible voters have voted for the National Socialists, not because they wish to endorse their programme – the National Socialists have neither a political nor even an economic programme worth taking seriously – but only because the area left empty by the other leading parties was occupied by no one so resolutely as by the Hitler people.'[13]

A neo-Marxist analysis of the electoral results by Theodor Geiger arrived at the same conclusion. In his analysis Geiger distinguished between the 'original proletariat of the dependent industrial work force' and the 'new proletariat of salaried employees' which since the nineteenth century had increased from seven to seventeen per cent of all wage earners. He accused the SPD of not having taken account of this 'restratification of the population'; it had 'remained a workers' party, when its concern – socialism – was no longer merely an affair for the work force, for the identification of "work force" with "proletariat" had not been valid for some time'.[14] But the decisive point – and here Grabowsky's analysis coincided with that of Geiger, in the neglect of the national idea. 'The new proletariat, not prepared to renounce its nationalist feelings, was driven into the arms of National Socialism.'[15]

The greater successes of the SPD – as well as those of the NSDAP – in Protestant territories can also easily be seen from this analysis. Tied to no confessional party, the Protestant voters on the left wing had long since had a political home in the SPD. Right-wing voters, on the other hand, doubtless all predominantly belonging to the 'new proletariat', were politically homeless; they fell to Hitler as he appeared with the claim to be a social and national saviour.

Of course the Protestant voters were not identical with the Protestant church. Many of them had just enough to do with it to know that they were not Catholic. But that was sufficient to bring about a marked change in their electoral behaviour in comparison with Catholic voters (for whom, of course, the same was true the other way round) – and to give the NSDAP a clear advantage in the Protestant territories.

The confessional election statistics of the early 1930s have occasionally raised the question 'whether National Socialism would ever have come to power at all in a Catholic Germany'.[16] But this question is pointless: it overlooks the fact that the confessional difference was itself a decisive prerequisite for the political behaviour of both great confessions. One might just as well ask, in the light of the Fascist systems in Italy and Spain on the one hand, and of the democratic governments in England or Scandinavia on the other, whether Hitler would have had a chance in a purely Protestant Germany. It was the confessional division which created a climate of competition, fear and prejudice between the confessions, which burdened all German domestic and foreign politics with an ideological element of incalculable weight and extent. This climate erected an almost insurmountable barrier to the formation of a broad democratic centre. And it favoured the rise of Hitler, since ultimately both churches courted his favour – each fearing that the other would complete the Reformation or the Counter-Reformation through Hitler. To put the question of the political behaviour of one or the other confession separately is to forget a definitive historical prerequisite of its action and reaction, and so the question does not in fact arise.

After 14 September, German Protestantism therefore had a large variety of reasons for occupying itself intensively with National Socialism. Indeed its cause, the national cause, was at stake; and it was in its heartland that the movement had above all gained a foothold; it was its sociological basis that had fallen to it; and it was clearly also its youth that supported it.

Psychologically, too, this was an extremely important point.

The impression that the NSDAP was a young party, that it was carried forward by the youth with passion and enthusiasm, was of considerable importance for the judgment of the church. This impression was nearly universal and therefore clearly almost overwhelming. Thus as early as December 1930, in the *Christliche*

Welt, Martin Rade had already reported the comment of a theological student who belonged to the SA that 'almost all students of theology in his university were National Socialists'. Rade reported above all of the North German universities that 'about 90% of the Protestant theologians appear at lectures with the National Socialist party badge'. The situation in the seminaries was not very different. Rade's article carried the moving title 'Our Sons'. We can see from it how despairing this otherwise confident man was at the turn of events. Was it proper for a theology student to be a member of the NSDAP? On his 'general principles' Rade the liberal was inclined to say yes. He continued: 'But as far as I am concerned it is out of the question that he should participate in and approve what we are now experiencing in Berlin; that he should join the rest in bellowing "To hell with the Jew!", that he should join in singing the coarse songs...; my presupposition is that he keeps to the "ideal core" of the "movement" and abhors the extravagances of his troop. (Can he do that if he is a stormtrooper?)' The title 'Our Sons' represented the effort of the older generation to understand, and at the same time a resigned lack of comprehension. 'Earlier, many a mother was dismayed when her son came home with the first fresh cuts on his face. But today parents must be much more frightened when their sons come home with a hero's fame from such rowdiness.'[17]

The Protestant youth became enthusiastic for the movement not only in the universities but also in the schools. Udo Smidt, who as Reichswart of the German Students' Bible Circle had a good view, wrote in 1931 of the 'cause which at present is most strongly linked with the name of National Socialism and which certainly – on a conservative estimate – is met by 70% of our youth with ardent sympathy, often untroubled by precise knowledge...'[18]

This enthusiasm could not but affect the judgment of those who had regular contact with this youth. In fact this influence made itself felt even in the consistory reports. Thus on 19 January 1931, in reponse to an inquiry by the church authorities, the executive pastor of the Church of the Holy Spirit in Berlin NW 21 reported that the influence of the National Socialists on the Protestant youth was 'extremely strong' and to be welcomed 'from the religious point of view'. 'My best former and present confirmation candidates are all Nazis.' This was also true of the members of the Alliance for Christian Scholars. The conclusion of the report shows how deeply impressed the pastor was by their attitude. 'The self-discipline of the young Nazis is nothing short of exemplary and automatically raises them above the others, involuntarily giving them a position of leadership. From the church's point of view, therefore, I welcome this movement.' 'The Evangelical Church has to be careful,' he concluded, repeating a concern which was typical of German Protestantism at this time, 'to secure for itself the same towering influence in the movement as have the Catholic members' – a reference to Hitler, Goebbels and the entire Bavarian leadership.[19]

We have learned in the meantime that these were not just casual impressions, but that the NSDAP was in fact by far the youngest of the major parties in the nation. The average age of the party members between 1930 and 1933 was estimated at twenty-five to twenty-six years.[20] By contrast, in the SPD in 1930 not even 8% of the members were younger than twenty-five.[21] It is impossible to estimate what this National Socialist reponse among the youth meant wherever the youth were courted, in the associations, groups, unions and not least in the churches. But it goes without saying that processes of assimilation were at work here against which resistance was possible only with difficulty, if one did not wish to risk the existence of one's group.

Before 14 September 1930 the issue of Hitler and the NSDAP in both churches was the concern of just a few who for one reason or another took a special interest in it. Thereafter it was the dominant theme in discussion within the church. Here the two churches reacted in very different ways. Whereas the Catholic church immediately made a clear and authoritative statement on the incompatibility of the church's teaching with National Socialism, in the Protestant church an open discussion began, the scope and animation of which soon overshadowed all other themes in the church.

Up to the end of the Republic the Catholic church, seen as a whole, presented a picture of impressive unanimity on this issue. When Walter Dirks, a young, critical Catholic journalist and convinced Democrat, analysed the relationship between Catholicism and nationalism in *Die Arbeit*, the journal of the German Federation of Trade Unions, in March 1931 he could begin by rightly observing: 'The ideology of the National Socialists as proclaimed at present in fact stands in blatant, explicit contrast to the doctrinal system of the church, and this can easily be demonstrated. The battlefront of the official Catholic organs is also clear: Catholicism is engaged in an open, declared, defensive war against National Socialism.' In connection with the warnings given by the German bishops which we shall consider later, he continued: 'The entire Catholic press without exception has taken up these battle cries, and the Catholic organizations are working on similar lines. In preaching, too, the backlash against the recent National Socialist propaganda plays a major role. The only detectable weak point on this front is the activity of the student bodies in a few universities...' And speaking particularly to his trade-union readers, he asserted that 'a glance at any issue of a Catholic newspaper' was enough 'to show to those who perhaps still believe in a united clerical-Fascist front that this front does not in the least dominate the political foreground. At present it is dominated by quite the opposite: open warfare.'[22]

In fact the impression of a solid front and an implacable antagonism between Catholicism and National Socialism was quite general and dominant among both friend and foe, Of course there were weak spots here, too. But it would be unjust to conceal the earnestness and forthrightness with which German Catholicism carried on the battle against National Socialism in the last years of the Republic. Ernst Deuerlein is right in saying that 'no officials of equal status in the public life of Germany' confronted 'the rising flood with the same determination'.[23] Why they did not achieve more, and in the end capitulated like the others, is a question which this makes all the more urgent.

A much-studied correspondence at the end of September 1930 between the Gauleitung of the NSDAP in Hessen and the diocesan offices in Mainz provided a stimulus towards a clarification of the two fronts. With feigned or real innocence the press office of the Gauleitung had contacted the diocese on 27 September 1930 to ask whether the following points, which the priest at Kirschhausen had made in a sermon, in fact reflected the view of the diocesan authorities: '1. No Catholic may be a card-carrying member of the Hitler Party. 2. No member of the Hitler party may participate in corporate demonstrations at funerals or any other events. 3. So long as a Catholic is a card-carrying member of the Hitler party he may not be admitted to the sacraments.'[24] The diocesan authorities immediately confirmed that it had issued these instructions. In their reply, Dr Meyer, the Vicar-General of Mainz who had signed the letter, referred especially to Article 24 of the Party programme as the justification for this position. According to his letter it was not out of the question that National Socialism might include the Catholic church among those confessions which were a danger to the state. 'The moral sense and moral feeling of the Germanic race' could in no way be a criterion for the church. Rather, racial hatred was fundamentally 'un-Christian and un-Catholic'. Finally, with this 'positive Christianity' the party was evidently aspiring to a German National Church. 'In his book *Mein Kampf*,' wrote the Vicar-General, 'Hitler certainly has written some appreciative words about the Christian religion and Catholic institutions, but that does not disguise the fact that the religious and educational policy of National Socialism is inconsistent with Catholic Christianity.'[25]

The uncompromising nature of this decision, which Mainz had made without the concurrence of the other German bishops, was not, however, without its problems. It certainly corresponded to the attitude of the Catholic church towards left-wing groups after 1921;[26] but now it raised considerable difficulties when applied to the Hitler party. For these were not groups which wanted to avoid the church anyway, groups the declared and open atheism of which made a refusal of the sacraments a matter of course. Here, rather, was a movement which courted the church, which had written 'positive Christianity' into its programme, and 'fight against God-hating Marxism' on its banners.[27] Thus many a bishop could doubt whether the Mainz decision was practicable or wise in this form, even if he was fundamentally in agreement.

And in fact the Mainz action had by no means gone undisputed among the German bishops. Too far-reaching, 'untenable and indeed... quite inopportune', 'tactically imprudent and unworkable in practice', were a few private comments from Bavaria.[28] They explain why the attempt of the President of the German bishops' conference, Cardinal Bertram of Breslau, failed to produce an agreed statement by all the German bishops on National Socialism, following the Mainz thrust. Since Bertram, on the other hand, was clear that 'the universal silence after the Mainz proceedings' gave rise 'to disagreeable interpretations',[29] at the end of 1931 he decided to make a 'public statement at a grave hour'.[30] It contained impressive warnings against political radicalization, racial madness, and a national church. The degree to which the confessional sensitivity of German Catholicism was involved in all this was shown by the Cardinal's allusion to the Reformation. He twice compared the current fight against bishops, Pope and clergy to the sixteenth century, when 'the same incitement of the masses by means of slogans' had predominated.

Bertram's declaration seemed too vague and imprecise to the Bavarian bishops. But the conditions they, too, faced urgently called for a statement. So in February 1931, under the title 'National Socialism and Pastoral Care, Pastoral Instructions for the Clergy',[31] a statement appeared which undoubtedly represented a notable example of ecclesiastical prudence. It avoided both the uncompromising character of Mainz and the generalizations of Bertram, leaving admission to the sacraments to an examination 'depending on circumstances',[32] and limited the rejection of National Socialism in time and substance. The decisive sentence ran: 'So as guardians of the true teaching of faith and morals, the bishops must warn against National Socialism, so long and so far as it proclaims cultural and political opinions which are incompatible with Catholic teaching.' Given the difficult and embattled situation of the church, this statement was certainly prudent. But at the same time it was extremely problematical, for it betrayed the possibility of compromise and a readiness to compromise which two years later, in March 1933, Hitler was instantly able to turn to his advantage.

However, in March 1931 there was still no talk of this. On the contrary, this month produced three more official declarations from the church provinces of Cologne, Padeborn and the upper Rhine, each of which categorically stated the incompatibility of National Socialism with Catholicism and repeated the decisive sentence of the Bavarian letter.[33] In this way the entire German episcopacy had taken a stand against National Socialism.

Contrary to the suggestion of Ludwig Volk that the fragmentary character of the episcopal declarations had not been exactly 'a demonstration of unanimity on the part of the hierarchy',[34] the fact that the statements followed in rapid succession was, if anything, far more impressive than one joint declaration could have been. The impression given by the universal and consistent rejection of National Socialism by the Catholic church was further strengthened by the fact that most Catholic organizations emphatically endorsed the bishops' decision.[35] And finally, the declarations were accompanied by and supported by a profusion of publications, some of which also launched a political attack of unprecedented sharpness on National Socialism.

Here are a few examples. In spring 1931 a book by the Reichstag representative Karl Trossmann was published under the title *Hitler and Rome*. The author, a director of the Bavarian People's Party from Central Franconia, ended by summarizing the result of his detailed analysis of the Hitler movement as follows: 'What remains for us of National Socialism and all its promises, measured by circumstances in Germany? A brutal party rule that would do away with all the rights of the people. The prospect of a new war which, in present conditions, could only end more disastrously than the last. The ruin of Germany and increased misery to follow.'[36] With no less resolution, at the same time Alfons Wild portrayed the völkisch basis of Hitler's ideology and its irreconcilable contradiction to Catholic teaching. This book was also a sign of how intensively the NSDAP had exploited Dinter's expulsion in Catholic circles as well. For Wild thought it necessary to deal explicitly with this question, which was constantly brought up by National Socialist agitators. In doing so, he came to the conclusion that fundamentally Hitler thought in the same way as Dinter, and that his expulsion was therefore to be seen simply as a tactical manoeuvre. 'Hitler's view of the world is not Christianity, but the message of race, a message that does not proclaim peace and justice, but rather violence and hate.'[37] In late summer of the same year two accounts appeared, including the most important texts, which likewise clearly documented the incompatibility of National Socialism and Catholicism.[38]

Among the most determined and uncompromising opponents of Hitler were two Catholic journalists, a Dr Gerlich and the Capuchin father Ingbert Naab, who from 1930 fought against National Socialism in the Munich-based journal

Der Gerade Weg. For them, Hitler was plainly evil incarnate. Gerlich made the following comment on the parliamentary elections in *Der Gerade Weg* dated 21 July 1932, under the heading 'National Socialism is a Plague!': 'National Socialism... means: enmity with neighbouring countries, despotism in internal affairs, civil war, international war. National Socialism means: lies, hatred, fratricide and unbounded misery. Adolf Hitler preaches the law of lies... You, you who have fallen victim to the deceptions of one obsessed with despotism, wake up!... We who speak to you here do not want power; we serve no party; we are speaking for nothing but our conscience... And we say to you: It is the moral duty of every Catholic to vote for those parties that are determined to defend the inextinguishable rights of his church: the Centre Party or the Bavarian People's Party.'[39]

To be sure, things were not thought out and formulated so uncompromisingly everywhere in the Catholic camp. Clearly there were quite considerable differences between the positions of Gerlich and Naab, the more cautious formulations of the German bishops, and the readiness of the Centre Party to go some way with Hitler on constitutional grounds.[40] Nevertheless, German Catholicism before 1933 essentially presented an almost united front against Hitler. Catholic clergy who openly advocated a National Socialist Christianity remained quite unimportant exceptions: like the Benedictine abbot much favoured by the Nazis, Alban Schachleiter;[41] the Augsburg priest, Dr Haeuser, who felt himself to be 'a pioneer in strengthening German Christianity';[42] or the priest from Baden, Wilhelm Maria Senn, who saw in Adolf Hitler 'the instrument of providence in our age'.[43]

The contrast with German Protestantism was unmistakable.

When the left-wing journalist Hans Eberhard Friedrich wrote a detailed analysis of National Socialism for *Die Christliche Welt* in summer 1931, he too noted the difference in the stance of the confessions: 'This much is certain. Catholicism has argued with National Socialism much more energetically and far more clearly than has Protestantism and its church. It was, of course, a good deal easier for that autocratically constructed organism to do this in a logical, as it were unique and final, form. While the Protestant clergy do not ignore National Socialism, they do not arrive at a unified position. Some go along happily with the new movement and think to save Germany's soul through National Socialism. Others, e.g. the Religious Socialists, reject it. Yet others perceive valuable things in it, but object to the way in which it fights. On the whole this produces an inclination rather than a disinclination.'[44]

As a matter of fact Protestantism lacked everything that produced unity on the Catholic front: a foundation in natural law, a political party and an authoritative hierarchy. In it, everything was wide open. Instead of a clear front there was an immense profusion of opinions and voices which meant that each individual, each theological trend, each church group, and even the Landeskirchen had to seek their own guidelines and make a decision. For this reason, from the autumn elections of 1930 onwards, the problem of 'Church and National Socialism' became one of the most discussed and most disputed topics at church meetings and conferences and in the church newspapers.

The openness of the situation was demonstrated by the fact that trouble was constantly taken to give a hearing to different positions in order to contribute towards an authentic direction and decision.

A few excerpts from this discussion, in the random order in which it began to unfold in the first half of 1931, should make clear its great breadth and deep incoherence.

As early as the beginning of November 1930, the *Deutsches Pfarrerblatt*[45] published an article by Dr Friedrich Wieneke on 'The Standpoint of National Socialism on Christianity'. Wieneke was Dean of the cathedral in Soldin, a small country town in the Neumark, and an ardent champion of National Socialism. His article culminated in the declaration: 'The swastika and the cross of Christ are not opposites... To combine both in harmony would be in accord with true German politics.'[46] In December 1930 he was answered by Georg Sinn, a writer from Stolzenau/Weser, who described the 'tension between church and nationalism' as a 'sharp Either/Or', and made the demand: 'We must ask National Socialism in no uncertain terms... how it plans to make the command of Christian brotherly love compatible with the antisemitism and racial strife, with the "To hell with the Jew" with which the majority of National Socialist rallies begin...'[47] These two contributions opened a discussion that extended into the summer of 1931 and in an extraordinarily typical way demonstrated the different positions among the clergy. Although Wieneke claimed that he had received 'a flood of letters' on his article from every part of Germany 'almost all of which expressed vigorous, indeed enthusiastic, approval',[48] and although the editorial staff of the *Pfarrerblatt* openly indicated that it sympathized with the movement,[49] the critical positions clearly predominated in this discussion. It is worth noting that in this confrontation the ideological foundations of the party, i.e. the völkisch ideology, were the chief issue. Obviously, Hitler's völkisch sources were much more clearly evident at this time than after the seizure of power, when they increasingly receded from view under the impact of his political successes. Hence the question whether Dinter's expulsion was a tactical decision, or whether it meant a fundamental change, played a major role. The decisive factor in making a judgment as long as ideology still stood in the foreground was, of course, a person's particular theological position. Almost all the elements of political theology can be demonstrated among those arguing for a close association between the church and National Socialism. Wieneke himself provides an impressive illustration. For him, the essence of the common interest lay in what he felt to be politically and theologically a central statement, that 'the Volk... is not a theory arising out of human conceptualization, but rather an actuality created by God and established right from the very beginning'.[50] The political theology of Althaus, Hirsch and Stapel – simplified, it is true, but still unmistakable – supplied the decisive theological argument for all who insisted upon a mobilization of the church for the German freedom movement or, at least, demanded a benevolent neutrality.

The first large-scale church theological conference in 1931 was the 'Steinach Conference', an open gathering of Protestant clergy at which 140 pastors assembled on 8 January 1931 in Steinach in Franconia. Here, too, discussion of National Socialism was on the agenda. The speaker was Pastor Eduard Putz of Munich, at the time twenty-four, a member of the NSDAP and a Bavarian Lutheran. For Putz, a passionate propagandist for National Socialism, the movement was a judgment on the individualism and liberalism of the nineteenth century and at the same time 'an obedient return to conditions established at the creation (Volk, etc.).' 'Obedience and commitment' were the key words to which Lutheran theology was particularly responsive. In contrast to Wieneke, however, Putz also perceived dangers if it proved impossible to influence National Socialism 'in a Christian way'.[51] Putz was one of that not very unusual type of clergy who wanted to be good National Socialists and good Lutheran theologians. When developments in the church in 1933 crushed this illusion, he took the side of the Bavarian church leadership against the 'German Christians' and from the time of the Barmen Synod was one of the representatives of the Bavarian Lutherans in the Confessing Church.

On 30 January the 'Central Office for Apologetics' in Berlin, an agency of the Inner Mission concerned with regular observation and analysis of the spiritual and political trends of the time, also showed that the question of National Socialism had become urgent. It chose as its theme for the first apologetics course of the new year 'The World-view of National Socialism and Christianity', and invited Wilhelm Stapel as its speaker. When it came to subject matter, the courses in the Johannesstift at Spandau normally proved to be pioneering. This first course acquired a special significance because Stapel developed his lecture and published it in the spring under the title *Six Chapters on Christianity and National Socialism*. The small pamphlet went through five impressions in the course of the year and undoubtedly made an effect. Stapel was more than ever fascinated by the 'elemental' and 'primitive' elements of the movement. He underestimated or excused the Party's attacks on the church and Christianity and accordingly regarded 'the instinctive and intellectual obstacles which confront Christianity in National Socialism' as being not of 'a fundamental, but rather of a subjective and individual nature'.[52] Like Putz, Stapel developed for himself a relationship between National Socialism and Christianity in which the church had the task of bringing the national movement before God so that the nation could fitly realize its historical task: 'The nation... needs this Christianity and this church. For if the nation were the last and highest thing, then it could bear the injustice of the world only in hate and rage, not in faith. It would be arrogant in good fortune and poisoned in misfortune. Its victory would be nothing but exploitation and its defeat nothing but being exploited...'[53] With the 'nomos' of the Volk, the 'divinely ordained natural constitution of a community',[54] the maintenance and development of which had to be the goal of politics, what Stapel presented here was in effect a political theology. And it was a political theology of a Lutheran stamp which, through the emphasis on the difference between the kingdom of God and the kingdom of this world, deliberately sought to distinguish itself from the enthusiastic mixing of the two which was so customary, for example, in the 'German church'.

In March Wilhelm Laible, the editor of the *Allgemeine Evangelisch-Lutherische Kirchenzeitung*, which was considered to be the most important of the leading church papers in Protestant Germany,[55] took up a position in a programmatic article. His 'Three Requests to National Socialists' were remarkably superficial. For the seventy-three year old Laible, National Socialism was a new German rebellion, like the one which took place at the time of the wars of liberation. It was 'the rebellion of a young German Volk that feels deeply the humiliation of the Fatherland, hates and abhors the poisoning of German thought by foreign influences, and has inscribed upon its banner the old virtues of truthfulness, honour and loyalty'. So he 'dares' to put three requests to the movement, 'not as a critic but as a friend': to guarantee the Protestant denominational schools; not to falsify Christianity in a völkisch manner; and not to attack the Bible.[56] Precisely what this was supposed to mean was left open: not even the beginnings of an attempt was made to arrive at a proper understanding of the phenomenon. The whole work was a documentation of hopelessness rather than of narrow-mindedness or even malevolence; obviously Laible had no more at his disposal than the nationalist-Protestant categories from the nineteenth century. The article made it easy for the Party to conceal its considerable difficulties in this area. When at the end of April, in a session of the Bavarian state legislature, the National Socialist representative Dr Buttmann – one of the co-founders of the Party in 1925 – was taking issue with the position of the Catholic bishops, he referred explicity to the *Allgemeine Evangelisch-Lutherische Kirchenzeitung*, which contained an article in which a position was taken 'that I would dearly like to see also being taken by the Bavarian bishops, and by the leadership of the Catholic Church'.[57]

The week after Easter, the traditional time for church conferences, produced two remarkable events. In Riederau am Ammersee, Paul Althaus spoke to Bavarian pastors 'about the basic Christian notions of Volkstum, race and Judaism, about National Socialism as an expression of the völkisch movement which at present was clearly visible, and about the relationship of the church to National Socialism'. According to a report in the *Allgemeine Evangelisch-Lutherische Kirchenzeitung*, the vigorous discussions, in which representatives of the most diverse movements took part, resulted in agreement in affirming the völkisch task, combined with an emphatic warning against racial antisemitism.[58]

At the same time a theological course for religious Socialists took place in Caub am Rhein, which was to help clarify their position. The various groups of this movement had warned against the Fascist danger since the summer of 1930, albeit with differing emphases. At the fifth conference of the 'Union of Religious Socialists of Germany' which took place in Stuttgart in August 1930, Pastor Aurel von Jüchen from Thuringia for the first time had attempted a critical theoretical analysis of Fascism, and the Union had issued a declaration against Fascism.[59] The fundamental problem of the Religious Socialists lay in the fact that they were utterly unable to make clear to non-socialists why the salvation of church and society should come from, of all things, a movement which – as was demonstrated clearly by events in Russia – had made its aim the destruction of the church and the suppression of Christian proclamation. Even the finest political and economic analysis of conditions was unable to resolve this obvious contradiction. As matters then stood, anyone in Germany who subscribed to a political theology attached himself to the nationalist rather than the Marxist movement; and any person who sought a theological theology found it among the dialecticians. Thus the themes that were discussed in Caub mirrored all the problems of the Religious Socialists. First Leonhard Ragaz, one of the Swiss 'fathers', gave a lecture on 'The Theological and Historical Development of the Swiss Religious Socials through Dialectical Theology into Religious Socialists'. Just as Ragaz here made an attempt at a critical delimitation over against dialectical theology, so in the second lecture the Marburg professor Georg Wünsch attempted a critical definition of the relationship between the kingdom of God and Marxism. Finally, as the third lecturer, Pastor Kappes of Karlsruhe spoke on 'National Socialists and Religious Socialists engaged in Combat' – a declaration of war as clear as it was bold, but one which could not remove the fundamental contradiction in the whole approach.[60] How deeply this fundamental contradiction extended into the circle of Religious Socialists was shown by the contrasting reactions of two of their leading representatives. Whereas Pastor Erwin Eckert from Mannheim, after fierce arguments with the church leadership in Baden, in October 1931 joined the Communist Party of Germany, left the church and was expelled from the Union,[61] from 1933 on Georg Wünsch, the editor of the *Zeitschrift für Religion und Sozialismus*, saw the National Socialist revolution as the realization of the aims of the Union.[62]

The group of Religious Socialists which had gathered around Eduard Heimann, the Hamburg political economist, and Paul Tillich, the Frankfurt theologian and philosopher of religion, with more of a theoretical concern than an interest in practical politics, devoted the April issue of its journal *Neue Blätter für den Sozialismus* entirely to the problem of the Hitler movement. In it Walter Hunziger defined the inner relationship between Protestantism and National Socialism as being theologically 'a vital question for the Protestant church', namely 'whether it – the church – says "no" to the divinization of the human being just as passionately in the face of Nationalism as it does in the face of Communism'. Hunziger's declaration at the end of the article sounded almost like an anticipation of the 1934 Barmen Declaration: 'Its existence as Protestant church will depend at least on whether here, as there, it speaks with uncompromising determination the word which is committed to it, the Word of God to whom alone honour is due, even if as a result it had to become a solitary church.'[63] It is certainly no accident that this circle, where it did not emigrate in 1933, produced a relatively large number of later participants in the active resistance against Hitler, including Carlo Mierendorff, Adolf Reichwein and others.

Among the determined opponents of National Socialism in German Protestantism from the beginning of 1931 there also belonged the representatives of the Christlich-soziale Volksdienst, a small Protestant party which had taken part in the Reichstag election for the first time in 1930 and had won 2.5% of the vote and fourteen seats. The Volksdienst drew its support from elements of the pietistic community movement and the Free Churches.[64] The standpoint of this group on National Socialism was formulated by Hermann Strathmann, Professor of Theology in Erlangen.[65] His book, *A National-Socialist World-View?*, completed on 14 April 1931 and published soon afterwards, is one of the best and aptest analyses of the National Socialist ideology from the Protestant camp.[66] As usual, Strathmann first considered some positive elements in the movement and then went straight to the heart of the matter: the 'utterly dominant' principle of 'racial thought'.[67] Somewhat pedantically, but undeterred by all objections, he developed the consequences of this approach. Strathmann was one of the first to understand that the National Socialist ideology had 'of necessity' to produce 'a completely new ethic in private as well as public life',[68] and that this ethic was in no way and in no circumstances compatible with Christian ethics. At the same time he demonstrated that in these matters the overall appearance of the Party was one 'of amazing unity'.[69] The picture which Strathmann sketched came depressingly close to the reality of the Third Reich. If the Volksdienst nevertheless endorsed the involvement of the National Socialists in responsibility for government, it did so because it was deceived, along with many others, above all as to Hitler's determination and ability actually to achieve these goals.[70]

If these were the voices of individuals or of individual groups, then the lecture which Walther Künneth gave in Dresden on 21 April certainly represented the opinion of a large majority in German Protestantism who were trying hard to consider carefully their 'Yes' and 'No' to the movement. Künneth, then thirty, a lecturer at Berlin University and Director of the Central Office for Apologetics, spoke at one of the church gatherings which were characteristic of this period, at which different speakers – only rarely resolute opponents – expressed their views on National Socialism to a large audience. In this case the occasion was the annual 'Association Days for Inner Mission'. The topic was 'What do we, as Protestant Christians, have to say to the call of National Socialism?' As well as Künneth the speakers were Pastor Wilm of the German National Party from Potsdam, and a Reichstag representative from Potsdam, Hans Schemm, a young Bavarian teacher who was considered the Party's spokesman on religious and educational affairs, and who spoke first in the general discussion. Whereas Wilm and Schemm gave unqualified support to National Socialism and in so doing provoked 'storms of enthusiasm' from the majority of listeners and 'emphatic opposition from a minority',[71] Künneth attempted to present the pros and cons. Here he was of the opinion that from the point of view of the gospel one could say 'Yes' to National Socialism at three points: to the völkisch idea, to social reform, and to its intentions towards Christianity. At three other points, however, he felt a definite 'No' was necessary: to Fascism, to National Socialist educational and religious policies, and to the political practices of the movement.[72] But the extent to which this considered view ultimately corresponded exactly to that of the majority was shown in the report on the assembly in the *Allgemeine Evangelisch-Lutherische Kirchenzeitung*, which concluded with the remark that Künneth's lecture had been received with 'unanimous approval'.[73]

Finally, April also saw the first official statement by a leading member of the clergy, Heinrich Rendtorff, the Land bishop of Mecklenburg, who declared, obviously under the influence of Stapel's political theology: 'Thus for the sake of its calling the Evangelical Church must find and gratefully welcome its great aspiration in the National Socialist movement, but at the same time must proclaim the holy will of God over and above this aspiration, which is human aspiration, in other words, imperfect and broken.'[74]

The statement by the Evangelischer Bund was along the same lines, but still more emphatic in its advocacy of the national goals of the German Freedom Movement and critical only of Hitler's supposed blindness to the Roman Catholic danger. A veteran of the Bund, the Rhineland pastor Hermann Kremers, spoke on 5 June at the General Assembly in Magdeburg on 'National Socialism and Protestantism'. In an almost intolerable mixture of sentimentality, resentment and solemnity, he declared it to be 'our German-Protestant duty towards this movement... to protect and preserve it, so that it is not silted up by naturalism... nor, caught by the evil old enemy of Germanhood, withers to the roots under the alien sun of Rome'.[75]

Two weeks later, on 17 June, the Prussian Oberkirchenrat put the topic of 'National Socialism and the Church' on the agenda of a session. The speaker was the director of the Spandau Johannesstift, Dr Helmut Schreiner, who the same year became Professor of Practical Theology in Rostock. Schreiner, who had been concerned with the völkisch quest since the middle of the 1920s, had already prepared a written opinion for the Oberkirchenrat at the beginning of the year on the foundations of National Socialism.[76] Now he presented its main features in Jebenstrasse, Berlin, and was so well received that the assembly 'considered sending this lecture to the Protestant clergy entirely at the church's expense...'[77] The lecture was in fact later published under the title 'National Socialism confronted with the Question of God. Illusion or Gospel?', and was distributed widely. Schreiner's contribution was a thoroughgoing confirmation of the soundness of Hitler's basic decision in church politics. For the decisive objection which the author had to the movement was its inclination towards a 'völkisch substitute religion'.[78] Schreiner made it quite clear that he would go along with National Socialism so long and in so far as it did not preach a blood religion. 'It will be decisive for the future of the National Socialist will to live,' he asserted, 'whether it gives up its trend towards Rosenberg's blood religion or not.'[79] It says much for Hitler's tactical skill that the author saw at this point 'an unbridgeable gulf' yawning between Hitler and Rosenberg.[80] While he promised Hitler 'obedience according to the will of God', he described Rosenberg's faith as 'the demonic attempt, with the help of an illusion, to put human beings in the place of God'.[81] Schreiner's terrible misunderstanding was not, of course, just a success for Hitler's tactics. It was also the consequence of an approach which – influenced by Emmanuel Hirsch – considered solidarity with the national freedom movement to be basically a Christian commandment.

This, above all, differentiated Schreiner's position from that of a lecture given by the young Lutheran pastor Richard Karwehl on 10 July at the conference of Young Protestants in Hanover. This provided a theological analysis of National Socialism which in its clear-sightedness and acuteness clearly stood out from most of the other voices. This conference was a gathering of younger Hanover pastors who took a critical view of the church for its own sake, somewhat along the lines of 'Quousque tandem...?'[82] Karwehl himself was a student of Karl Barth.[83] His lecture, which was published the same year in Zwischen den Zeiten, attracted considerable attention as the first statement from the group of dialectical theologians. Karwehl understood the notion of race as a special type of the glorification of man, and National Socialism as a world view in which man made himself God, in the form of the Aryan race. Over against this he set the church, which in its proclamation did not begin with the human being 'but rather with the contingent revelation in Jesus Christ'. Therefore National Socialism and Christianity were mutually exclusive, not on ethical or moral grounds but rather because in National Socialism God was no longer the Lord. 'To the aspiration of National Socialism "to disentangle the chaos, to restore order to a disjointed world and to operate as a guardian of this order" (Feder), the church can only say in the most determined way possible: "The downfall of the Titans is inevitable."'[84] However, this could not be the church's last word. Rather, it was important to understand National Socialism – and indeed Marxism – better than it understood itself and to struggle for it 'in the solidarity of the sinners for whom

Christ died'.[85] Karwehl developed this position in detail by means of the three fundamental concepts of Christian theology: creation, reconciliation and redemption. Certainly race and Volkstum were concepts which belonged to creation. But we only understood them properly when at the same time we understood the 'solidarity of all created things', of which Christian preaching has to speak. However, in Karwehl's view, the whole contrast completely fell apart when it came to talk of reconciliation. The Nordic heroic ideal – its self-awareness and its self-confidence – are incompatible with the reality of the crucified Jesus. And the secularized eschatology of the völkisch movement and the legitimate eschatology of the church's proclamation were also ultimately incompatible – although even Protestant pastors nowadays confused the two. Here the interpretation of National Socialism turned into a critique of the church. For National Socialism was none other than a '*de facto* messianism'. But the church had ceded leadership to it: 'There, now, is power, passion and religious faith. There are martyrs, albeit secular ones. National Socialism is unrestrainedly eschatological... The church, on the other hand, cultivates an individualistic pie-in-the-sky Christianity combined with a petty-bourgeois ideology and ecclesiastical self-satisfaction.' Granted, there were strong church activities too. But – and this was the determining factor for Karwehl – 'no religious-moral activism is to be set over against secularized theology, but only the legitimate proclamation of the church which can be heard as a clarifying and guiding voice amidst the chaos of the age'.[86]

Along with Karwehl, Hermann Sasse, the new editor of the *Kirchliches Jahrbuch*, also presented an equally sharp and theologically based rejection of the National Socialist world-view. Having in 1931 criticized the use of the church as a political instrument – 'as a means to the end of renewing the Volkstum, saving the nation, producing a classless society, perfecting humanity – and as a very inferior instrument at that, which moreover is cast aside when it cannot be employed as the user desires',[87] in 1932 he categorically declared that Article 24 of the Party programme made 'any discussion with the church impossible'. Here, too, it was not some dubious, or at least debatable, political analysis which led Sasse to this conclusion but rather a careful examination of what was said by the Lutheran confession. In that light the teaching of the Protestant church was 'a deliberate and permanent offence against "the ethical and moral feeling of the Germanic race"' – because the doctrine of original sin left absolutely no possibility open 'that the Germanic or Nordic or any other race is by nature capable of loving God and doing his will; that rather the newborn child of the noblest German descent... has incurred eternal damnation just as much as the half-breed of two decadent races who is heavily tainted by heredity. We have also to confess that the doctrine of the justification of the sinner *sola gratia, sola fide*, marks the end of Germanic morality, as it marks the end of all human morality. Moreover we allow ourselves to assert... that when the Jews nailed Jesus Christ to the cross for the sake of this teaching, which overthrows all morality, they did so at the same time in the name of the German Volk and the Nordic race.' Sasse also attacked the National Socialist doctrine of the state, which asserted 'the rights of the omnipotent state even over the souls of its citizens'. Sasse's conviction was that anyone who fell in with that came within the scope of a prophetic saying by the strict Lutheran, A.F.C. Vilmar, from the year 1861: 'But over the shoulders of these blind people looks the sharp, flashing eye of the murderer and arsonist of the future.'[88]

The discussion of National Socialism continued undiminished throughout 1931 and into 1932. Its course was still as contradictory and disordered as it had been when it began after the 1930 September elections. A two-volume collection of essays, *The Church and the Third Reich. Questions and Demands of German Theologians*, edited by Leopold Klotz in spring and summer 1932, only confirmed this. A recent analysis has identified among the forty-three opinions which were collected here twelve for, twelve undecided and nineteen against – a proportion which may have accurately reflected the actual position.[89]

Any attempt to bring order into this whole discussion will have to distinguish a series of quite different positions among those for as well as those against.

Among those in favour, at least three positions are clearly discernible. First there was the group of old nationalist Protestants who transferred their conservative patriotism to revolutionary National Socialism without having any idea what they were supporting.[90] Typical of this group was Wilhelm Laible and the *Allgemeine Evangelisch-Lutherische Kirchenzeitung*. Secondly, there was the group of modern political theologians who saw God's will for the self-realization of the Volk fulfilled in National Socialism. For them the movement was part of the divine revelation in history, and solidarity with it was therefore obedience to God. Representatives of this line were Althaus, Hirsch and Stapel; the theological core of the German Christians was later recruited from its adherents. Finally, those in favour also included the representatives of the German Church movements and of völkisch religion, a group that extended beyond the borders of the church.

Among those against, three major groups can also be distinguished, identifiable by their line of argument. The left wing of church liberalism, the group around Martin Rade and the *Christliche Welt*, rejected nationalism above all on moral grounds. In their view, what Hitler propagated and did offended so basically against Christian morality that no compromise was possible or permissible in any circumstances. On the other hand the Religious Socialists (and, in a sense, the members of the Volksdienst) used mainly political and ideological arguments. This line suffered from its obvious bias as well as from its lack of alternatives. It gained hardly any adherents because it countered a political and ideological argument on the one side with the same kind of argument on the other without really being able to illuminate its significance for the church and theology. This was precisely what the third group of opponents, who criticized National Socialism theologically, succeeded in doing. Only this group, the group of theologians who were in the broadest sense influenced by Karl Barth, was able to win a growing number of supporters for its position from the great camp of the undecided, because it was able to demonstrate that a fundamental, absolutely decisive question for the church and theology was at stake here.

Just as in the course of the struggle, among those in favour the group of political theologians absorbed other movements, so various groups of their opponents gathered under the banner of dialectical theology. However, the problematical character of this grouping very quickly became evident to both sides – and remained so for a long time.

While this discussion continued, the fronts hardened and the trenches deepened, the situation of the church administrations became increasingly difficult. In view of the opposed positions in their churches, it was impossible for them to join one or the other movement: that would have aggravated the dispute to the point of schism. But to remain silent was just as impossible if they wanted to fulfil their self-appointed task, i.e. to give direction and help to the German Volk. So the only way left to them was to attempt to adopt a position above the parties and to admonish the pastors to understand and exercise their office along these lines.

An immediate occasion for official statements from the church administrations, on which most Landeskirchen resolved in the course of 1931, was the increasing entanglement of churches and religious services in political agitation and propaganda. From autumn 1930, the number of occasions on which national associations attended church in full uniform greatly increased. With banners, pennants and uniforms, weddings were turned into political demonstrations, as were funerals, at which the pastor's 'Amen' was drowned by the 'Sieg Heil' of the brown-uniformed groups. Things were very bad when a pastor sympathetic to the Party was found. Thus the National Socialist *Preussische Zeitung* reported a 'Brownshirt Wedding' which took place in the Schlosskirche in Königsberg at the beginning of July 1931: 'Probably for the first time, a Königsberg church experienced a Brownshirt Wedding when our comrade Gaukommissar Hermann Schoepe... received the church's blessing for his marital union with our party member Elfriede Siebert. At the door of the Schlosskirche, party members and friends greeted the young couple with a vigorous Hitler salute. The participants in the ceremony took their places before the altar, all of them champions for Hitler's idea – the men in uniform. Pastor Trepte based the ceremony on the biblical passage "Be faithful to death and I will give you the crown of life"... In this way he could take as his starting point the loyalty to Hitler's idea which Party member Schoepe had demonstrated over long years of constant and courageous struggle... After receiving the church's blessing, the young couple and congregation left the Schlosskirche to the sounds of the Horst Wessel Song, played on the organ.'[91]

The marked political effect of such ceremonies is self-evident. While the National Socialist participants felt themselves assured of the blessing of the church on their struggle, and waverers were influenced in the direction of the Party, opponents of the movement were made to feel abandoned and betrayed by the church.

A realization of this situation had led the Catholic church to a strict ban on collective participation by political associations in church events.[92] A similarly authoritative position was not possible for the Protestant church administrations. It went not only against the Protestant understanding of worship, for the ordering of which pastor and congregation, rather than the church administration, were primarily responsible, but also against the state of affairs in the Protestant church, which no longer permitted an unequivocal statement. Thus the church administrations limited themselves to issuing general guidelines in which the party-political neutrality of the church was impressed upon pastors, like that of Württemberg on 31 January 1931: 'In the political conditions prevailing at present, anything that could contribute towards carrying the political struggle into the church must be avoided. The church must remain what it is supposed to

144

be: the vehicle of the proclamation of the gospel to all humanity. It is therefore neutral in party politics, however much it must aspire to help the Volk, in all its conditions, in all its troubles at home and abroad, through the testimony of the gospel and the activity of Christian brotherly love.' It followed from this that in the specific question of the participation of political associations there were no objections as long as 'worship retains the character of community worship and cannot be considered to be a political rally'.[93]

Similar guidelines were issued in March 1931 in the Palatinate, in April in Nassau and Oldenburg, in June in Baden, in July in Hessen and in November in Schleswig-Holstein and the major Church of the Old Prussian Union.[94]

The success of these guidelines was modest. Nowhere did they impede the increasing politicization of the church. For as long as the Protestant church held fast to its claim to be a Volkskirche, a church of the entire Protestant Volk, the church administrations had no alternative than to declare that in principle they stood above the parties. A revolution here was achieved only by the rediscovery of the function of the confession as the foundation which truly unified and divided the church.

10

Concordat Policy and the Lateran Treaties
(1930-1933)

The nearly solid ideological front which the Catholic church formed against National Socialism stood firm until the spring of 1933. Between 1930 and 1933, the opposition to Hitler by Catholics faithful to the church ranked – not least for Hitler himself – as one of the most constant factors in German domestic politics. Nevertheless, this was not a complete description of the political situation of German Catholicism. For in Rome people saw things quite differently. And after the September elections even the Centre Party was increasingly compelled to consider whether and how it was to collaborate, or could collaborate, with the second strongest party (which was soon to become the strongest).

Obviously the Curia also shared the deep aversion of Catholicism towards the nationalism and racist ideology of the NSDAP. But in an overall assessment of politial developments in Germany two other questions were at least as important here. The main international concern of the Vatican was the advance of Communism; hence a vital task appeared to be the construction of a dam against it. As far as Germany was concerned, to secure the new canon law for Germany by means of a treaty seemed to be just as important – hence the Reich concordat. Every German administration was judged by Rome above all on two issues: how resolutely it fought against atheistic Communism and how prepared it was to conclude a Reich concordat. In the end, these two factors also became decisive in its assessment of Hitler.

This view of things clearly differed from the appraisal of the situation by many leading Catholics in Germany itself. Here Hitler was correctly considered to be, for the moment, more threatening than a left-wing dictatorship, no matter how anxiously the growth of Communism was watched. And in any case a desire for a Reich concordat arose more from Roman than from German interests, for in Germany, despite the appreciation of the legal protection that it offered, there were also reservations about further strengthening of Curial centralism. The fact that the Vatican standpoint nevertheless played an important role in German politics was not least the consequence of a special combination of personal factors.

In October 1928, the President of the Centre Party, the universally esteemed ex-Reich Chancellor Wilhelm Marx, resigned from office, worn out and depressed. The party conference in Cologne, which had to elect his successor in December, surprisingly chose Ludwig Kaas. Kaas had not sought the office, but after neither Adam Stegerwald, who was a trade union sympathizer, nor his opponent, Josef Joos, had been able to gain a majority, most of the votes fell to the prelate. Since Kaas was undoubtedly politically experienced and gifted as an orator, he was thought to be the person most easily capable of re-unifying the fragmented party.[1]

The election of Kaas was an event of extraordinary political significance. For he was the first clergyman to take over the leadership of the party, a key position in German politics, and at the same time since 1920 he had had an unparalleled acquaintance with all Pacelli's thoughts, reflections and plans, and had continued to do so even after the latter's move to Rome. This had consequences for both sides. The Curia orientated its decisions on the information given by the prelate, who again and again stayed in Rome for weeks at a time, and of whom the Cardinal of Cologne once declared that there he had 'more influence than three cardinals put together'.[2] Conversely – and this was no less important – through the prelate, with his passion for canon law, and the close relationship which existed between him and the recently nominated Cardinal Secretary of State, Roman viewpoints inevitably became involved in the basic decisions of German politics to a greater extent than was the case with other Centre Party politicians. The weaker the Republic became, and the less its parliamentary controls functioned, the more strongly this of course made itself felt. However, the interests of the Curia, as has been said, were directed above all towards the struggle against Communism and the conclusion of a Reich concordat.

There cannot be the slightest doubt about Pius XI's unqualified antipathy to Communism. With the merciless extermination of the Orthodox Church in Russia clearly before him, and confronted with unmistakable threats that all Christian churches were destined for the same fate,[3] it was understandable enough that he should have this attitude. In the cabinets of European governments the GULAG archipelago may have been considered an internal Russian affair, but it was impossible for the Papacy to be neutral about the greatest persecution in the twentieth century. On the other hand, there were problems in the Curia's lack of a capacity to discriminate, which caused it to count everything left of the political centre as totalitarian Communism – or at least its forerunner and pioneer. Because of this conviction, in 1924 the Pope had prevented an approach in Italy of the Catholic People's Party, the Partito Popolare Italiano, to the Socialists. And with the same conviction, he also responded with deep distrust to the coalitions between the Centre Party and the Social Democrats in Germany. Time and again the Bavarian envoy von Ritter had occasion to send on to Munich confidential comments of the Pope to this effect. Thus for example in June 1928 he reported that, as before, the Pope took 'the view that given the basic position of Social Democracy in regard to the church it would seem to him impossible for a Catholic party to unite with it in a programme of government. For at best Social Democracy would simply use the opportunity to undermine the Catholic party and give it the *coup de grâce* once it had been eroded away.'[4] This conviction, which was undoubtedly shared by the entire Curia, was especially problematical for Germany. For at least in Prussia the coalition between the Centre Party and the SPD represented one of the few elements of political stability that the Republic had at its disposal. However, the German leaders of the Centre Party would not be talked into these political decisions. As late as 1931 both the Reich Minister of the Interior, Joseph Wirth, and the Reich Chancellor, Heinrich Brüning, expressly rejected objections by the Pope to this effect.[5] But with Kaas things would be different – at least in atmosphere. And this could not fail to have an effect on the political course taken by the Centre Party president.

Whereas this general political line was represented above all by the Pope, the pursuit of the concordat question lay primarily in the hands of the Cardinal Secretary of State.

In spite of the laborious negotiations over a Prussian concordat, Pacelli had at no point lost sight of his great goal: a Reich concordat. The issue on which he intended to get things moving again after the conclusion of the Prussian negotiations was the organization of the Catholic chaplaincies in the Reichswehr. In retrospect this was certainly rather a marginal question, but at the time the matter was thought to be of considerable importance. In short, what was at issue was whether the Catholic chaplaincies should be under a separate military bishop and thus be canonically independent – exempt – or whether in each case the chaplain should be looked after by the local bishop. The Reichswehr urged the first solution, on principle as well as for practical considerations. The second solution – provisionally practised since 1920 – was understandably defended by the German bishops. For the Curia this was not a matter of principle but merely one of political expediency. Here was an urgent wish of the Reich, the only one still left, and Pacelli hoped to use this wish to achieve his goal of a comprehensive treaty. How much importance the Nuncio attached to this card is shown by a remark by Bishop Caspar Klein of Paderborn, to whom the episcopate entrusted the negotiations. In October 1928 he wrote to the Nuncio that with the question of the exemption he – the Nuncio – had 'an important trump card in his hand to play against the Reich government in the coming negotiations over the Reich concordat'.[6] With the same argument, in autumn 1929 Pacelli emphatically rejected a compromise suggestion made by the Archbishop of Breslau.[7] And hardly was he in Rome, and not yet even nominated Cardinal Secretary of State, than he had already proposed new negotiations on this issue to the German ambassador to the Vatican.

The conversation on this matter that Pacelli had with Bergen on 31 December 1929 was in many respects extraordinarily typical and instructive. In it the future director of Vatican policy clearly not only indicated his interest in the complex of questions but at the same time suggested to the Foreign Office that Ludwig Kaas, with whom he wished to discuss the entire question as soon as possible, should be nominated a special representative. Given the key political position of the Centre Party president, the Foreign Office obviously had no choice but to fulfil this carefully expressed, somewhat unusual wish. So Kaas, who as early as December 1928 had accompanied Pacelli to Rome as a kind of secretary, stayed in the Holy City another three and a half months – from the beginning of March to the middle of June 1930.[8] He again had a double role as spokesman for the Reich and for the Curia, a role which he had had as early as 1921, in the first negotiations over a Reich concordat, and which he was now to play once more in the summer of 1933.

Kaas and Pacelli used the long period in Rome less for the matter of the military chaplaincy, which could doubtless have been settled in a few days, than for a thorough discussion and extension of the plans for a German concordat.

As early as 9 March the Bavarian envoy to the Vatican, always well informed, reported in alarm to Munich that Kaas was in Rome; that Cardinal Pacelli wanted to discuss the question of an army bishop with him; and that if possible 'for this reason' he wanted to enter 'into a concordat relationship with the Reich in order to secure the fulfilment of the modest wishes of the Holy See as a *quid pro quo* from the Reich'. Ritter, moreover, proved himself to be well informed about the content of the concordat as well as about its intent: 'that a Reich concordat could form a kind of re-insurance of the interests of the church should the continued independent existence of the concordat with the Länder be challenged by the development of a centralized state in the Reich'. The Bavarian envoy rightly thought it not surprising that in order to realize these plans Pacelli should 'appeal above all for the help of Prelate Kaas', who had rendered him 'so much effective service already'.[9]

But the Reich, represented in the Vatican by the German ambassador, was in no way ready to engage in negotiations at this level. At about this time Bergen sent a terse telegram to Berlin: 'Cardinal Secretary of State mentions possibility of solving question military chaplaincy in framework Reich concordat. Transfer of matter to this platform rejected.'[10]

Bergen's lengthy concluding report dated 2 June, possibly in fact written by Kaas, showed the pains taken by the prelate, in the light of this difficult situation, to find compromise formulae. Thus the report emphasized Pacelli's 'earlier professed willingness', if the Reich government was co-operative, 'without further ado to anchor the exemption in the concordat'. On the other hand, however, Kaas pointed out 'that in view of the prior conclusion of the Länder concordats and current majorities in parliament, the prospects for an agreement between the Holy See and the Reich could not be considered to be favourable'. So that the Reich government should not be left unclear as to the basic demands of the Curia, the report included a detailed presentation of the marriage-law problem. This was a topic which, of course, had 'technically no connection' with the military chaplaincy. But Prelate Kaas could not have rejected a discussion of it because it had already formed 'the topic of discussion' in the very first negotiations over a concordat. Even if for the moment there was little prospect of a settlement of this question within the framework of a Reich concordat, the prelate – still according to Bergen's report – considered it desirable for an exchange of opinions with the Reich Minister of the Interior 'and perhaps prompting in the cabinet' to take place 'as soon as possible'.[11] So Kaas evidently attempted to meet Pacelli's urgings for a comprehensive Reich concordat, which he considered hopeless, with compromise formulae on individual issues.

During this period Pacelli and Kaas also devoted themselves to negotiations in Baden just as energetically as to these plans. On 8 March Kaas wrote to Ernst Föhr, the Centre Party prelate in Baden, that the Baden government should send two negotiators to Rome as soon as possible: it was impossible for the moment for the Cardinal Secretary of State to make the journey, and the channels through the new Berlin Nuncio, Cesare Orsenigo, were far too slow. A few days later it became clear that Pacelli did not in any circumstances want to see his successor involved in any kind of concordat negotiations in Germany.

This was his affair alone, and it was to remain so. At all events, on 13 March Kaas urged on his Party associate Föhr that the 'channels via the Nunciature in Berlin are not to be pursued further'. Kaas also shed a very significant light on the church's internal problems and the intentions of Rome's concordat policy when in the same connection he warned the people of Baden against 'viewing the Roman pledge to apply the *ius commune* as merely a "warning shot"'. If the Archbishop of Freiburg thought this 'and from such a perspective regarded it as a matter of indifference whether or not the concordat were concluded,' he was making a serious mistake. 'At the Münsterplatz,' Kaas indicated plainly enough, 'there would soon be much more reason to regret not having a concordat than in Rome.'[12] But in Baden, too, the difficulties were far greater than had been expected in Rome, especially since here, too, Pacelli insisted on the school clauses, which ran into vigorous opposition in this traditionally liberal Land.[13]

While Pacelli and Kaas were urging these plans for a concordat in Rome, the domestic political situation in Germany began to change fundamentally. On 27 March 1930 the grand coalition came to an end. With Müller's cabinet, the last parliamentary government of the Republic withdrew. The immediate occasion had been disagreement over a reorganization of unemployment insurance which had come under heavy pressure with the outbreak of the world depression in October 1929. However, the cause lay deeper. It lay in a widespread and deep-rooted distrust of the possibilities and prospects of parliamentary democracy in Germany generally, which even in the so-called good years of the Republic had never completely vanished, and now as a result of the economic catastrophe began to make itself fully felt. Accordingly the authoritarian style of a solution of the crisis by means of a Presidential cabinet – that is, a government that was no longer supported by a parliamentary majority but rather by trust in the Reich President – was completely in accord with popular sentiment. In the circumstances, it was hardly surprising that in Heinrich Brüning, a Chancellor from the Centre Party, again became head of the new government. For thanks to its central position, as before the Catholic party was the only one capable of mediating between the different political trends.[14]

Developments in the ensuing months did not turn out well for Heinrich Brüning. The 'disaster elections'[15] of 14 September, with their landslide in favour of the NSDAP, followed upon the dissolution of the Reichstag forced by parliament in July 1930 and drastically reduced the political possibilities in Germany. Just as discussion of Hitler and National Socialism began in the churches immediately after the elections, so too the politicians had to see whether it was possible to work politically with the leader of what was now the second largest party – and, if so, how. This question of course also arose for the Centre Party. Here the Catholic party was increasingly caught up in a conflict between German Catholicism and Rome. For whereas German Catholicism openly fought against National Socialism and rejected any co-operation with Hitler, in Rome things were assessed in a different way.

As early as the November of this fateful year, the Bavarian envoy could report confidentially that the decision of the Mainz diocesan authorities to excommunicate members of the NSDAP would not be approved in the Vatican.[16] In fact the *Osservatore Romano* followed up its first uncompromising judgment on the Mainz proceedings with a correction only a few weeks later. Whereas in

150

October the newspaper had written that membership of the NSDAP was 'incompatible with the Catholic conscience, just as in general it is completely incompatible with membership of socialist parties of all shades',[17] in January 1931 it reported that the Mainz declaration was not directed against Hitler's followers for political reasons, 'but because of those elements in its programme that are incompatible with Catholic teaching'.[18] This corresponded to the more cautious line of the Bavarian pastoral letter, and in fact in March 1931 Ritter could report with pleasure that the position of the Bavarian bishops had met with the full approval of the Cardinal Secretary of State.[19]

So there could be no question of any sudden inclination of the Curia towards Hitler. And Rome also carefully avoided anything that might seem like public approval of National Socialism. Thus a personal attempt by Göring at the beginning of May 1931 to obtain a change in the official Catholic rejection from the Cardinal Secretary of State failed. By order of the Pope, Göring only reached the outer office: only the Under-Secretary of State, Giuseppe Pizzardo, was permitted to receive his complaints.[20] That the Curia was nevertheless unwilling to reject Hitler utterly was entirely due to the question whether – in certain circumstances and for certain goals – a limited political co-operation with the National Socialists might be desirable and possible. In this connection, and in the first place, the Pope was thinking of the struggle against the impending threat of Communism. However, for Pacelli the plans for a concordat stood in the foreground.

Brüning, the fourth Centre Party Chancellor to be head of the Reich, obviously represented above all a new opportunity for the Cardinal Secretary of State to make another effort at a concordat. Undeterred by the deterioration of the economic and political situation in Germany, in March 1931 Pacelli therefore presented to the German ambassador at the Vatican a memorandum outlining the plans of the Curia. In it, the Vatican demanded three things from the Reich government, in return for the concession of an exempt military bishop: the repeal of the penal provisions in the Personal Status Law – originating in the Kulturkampf – against clergy who conducted a church marriage ceremony prior to the civil ceremony; the previous understanding with the Holy See over the abolition of financial contributions to the church from the state according to Article 138 of the Reich constitution; and finally a guarantee of the rights of Catholics 'in respect of confessional schools and religious instruction'.[21]

However, the very first response from the Centre Party to these suggestions turned out to be extremely disappointing for Pacelli. Notable Centre Party politicians who spent Easter 1931 in Rome, among them Joseph Wirth, Reich Minister of the Interior, and the party's parliamentary expert on cultural policy, Prelate Schreier, assured the Cardinal Secretary of State 'very vigorously' that, as Bergen cabled Berlin, 'fulfilment of the three wishes of the Curia made known there would seem hopeless in the circumstances'.[22] However, Pacelli persisted in his plans.

This visit was just as disappointing for Pius XI. For Wirth openly and vigorously rejected all the Pope's requests to dissolve the coalition with the SPD in Prussia and finally left the audience 'in great agitation'.[23]

The Vatican must have awaited the visit of the Reich Chancellor himself, planned in connection with a state visit to Mussolini for 8 August 1931, with all the greater expectations.

The circumstances in which Brüning undertook this visit were, however, as unfavourable as they could be. After the Austrian Credit-Anstalt in Vienna had had to close its doors in May 1931, the great bank crisis had spread to Germany with the collapse of the famous Darmstadt and National Bank on 13 July. The deflationary policy of the Reich Chancellor thus entered a dramatic phase. A tremendous wave of withdrawals from German banks and savings banks led to a Reich Cabinet emergency decree declaring 14 and 15 July bank holidays. Only on 5 August, shortly before Brüning's departure from Berlin, could normal business be resumed – but with a bank rate of 15% and a deposit rate of no less than 20%. This meant a real interest on credit of 15-20% and more.[24] On top of 4.5 million unemployed and a drastic decline in industrial production, there was thus a crisis in financial policy, which almost precluded new investment for a long period of time and could only aggravate the desperate situation of the Reich still further. Contact with Mussolini, from whom he could hope for support in the struggle against the unreasonable reparations policy that had played a decisive part in the whole disaster, therefore appeared all the more important to Brüning at this time.

In this situation it was understandable that the German Chancellor could hardly consider the conclusion of a Reich concordat a priority. On the contrary, he sought to avoid anything that would lay even the slightest additional burden upon the domestic political situation in Germany. Pacelli, however, could not, or would not, see this. It was his old weakness, which made him even at this point take seriously only his own goal in church politics and not the problems and difficulties of his partner in the discussion.

The conversation between Pacelli and Brüning took place in the Cardinal's private apartments on the morning of 8 August 1931. According to Brüning's memoirs, difficulties already arose over the question of the military bishop.[25] The Reich Chancellor had committed himself to the exemption for some time,[26] and expected agreement and support from Pacelli. It was puzzling why Kaas, who knew better, had not prepared Brüning on this point. At all events, the Chancellor was obviously surprised when Pacelli advanced 'the opposite point of view' and at the same time raised the question of a Reich concordat. This was precisely in accord with the known political line of the Cardinal. Brüning, however, would have nothing to do with such a connection. As he reported on the course of the conversation: 'I told him that it was impossible for me as a Catholic Chancellor, in view of the tension in Germany, even to approach this issue at all. Almost all the significant German Länder already had concordats, and promising negotiations with the rest of them were going on. If I had raised the question of a Reich concordat now, I would have whipped up the *furor protestanticus* on the one side and run into a complete misunderstanding with the left on the other.' This was clearly an accurate assessment. To Pacelli, however, these domestic German difficulties were obviously unimportant. For he thereupon suggested that Brüning 'ought to form a government of the Right simply for the sake of a Reich concordat, and in doing so make it a condition that a concordat should be concluded immediately'.

Surprising as this suggestion appeared, it fitted in perfectly with the Cardinal's

152

policy of establishing canon law in Germany, by all possible means and in any circumstances, through a concordat. For more than a decade he had devoted all his energies towards reaching this goal. Now a new political situation had arisen and Pacelli was determined to take advantage of it – as he had always sought to take advantage of political situations.

With Brüning, however, this could not be done. Rather, the Chancellor replied firmly to the Cardinal 'that he mistook the political situation in Germany and, above all, the true character of the Nazis'.

The conversation became still more heated when the subject of the Protestant church treaties was mentioned.[27] Pacelli thought it impossible, as Brüning noted, 'that a Catholic Chancellor should conclude a Protestant church treaty. I answered sharply that in accordance with the very spirit of the constitution to which I had sworn an oath, I had to protect the interests of religious Protestantism on the basis of full equality. The Cardinal Secretary of State now condemned my whole policy and declared that the position of Kaas, who approved such a policy, was completely destroyed at the Vatican. He would have to ask Kaas to give up his office as President of the Centre Party and accept the vacant post of a rector at the Campo Santo. I replied to him that I could not oppose him here because Kaas was a priest, but that I had to oppose every attempt by the Vatican to exercise influence on my political decisions and on the stance of the Centre Party.'

The break between Brüning and Pacelli could not now be healed. That very same evening the Chancellor declared curtly to the Cardinal Secretary of State that in view of the mistrust he had encountered he had decided 'to drop the question of the army bishop and the concordat altogether' and to leave the solution to his successor. He hoped, he added ironically, 'that the Vatican would have greater success with Hitler and Hugenberg than with the Catholic Brüning'.[28]

Pacelli's plans for a concordat were thus frustrated again. For Brüning this evidently meant little. But Kaas, President of the Centre Party, was now in an extraordinarily difficult situation. His political existence depended on the possibility of combining the interests of the Curia with the interests of the Reich. If this possibility no longer existed, then he was inevitably caught up in a virtually insoluble conflict of loyalties between his status as a priest and co-worker with Pacelli and President of the Centre Party and co-worker with Brüning.[29]

Perhaps this was one of the reasons why from the late autumn of 1931 the prelate put forward with increasing vigour the idea of a joint political movement in which, as he declared on 8 November, even those right-wing and left-wing groups 'which so far have never co-operated' should collaborate 'for a particular purpose over a limited time'.[30] At all events, early in December 1931 Kaas was again in Rome, and it was no coincidence that shortly afterwards the Bavarian envoy heard from the Pope himself the very considerations that Kaas had put forward in Germany. On 20 December Ritter reported to Munich that according to the Pope the National Socialists had committed the gross mistake of 'not coming to terms wth the German bishops when the latter saw themselves forced, because of the many party principles which were hostile to the church, to warn the faithful against it.' This of course complicated any contact. Nevertheless the Pope thought that co-operation, 'perhaps only temporarily and for specific

153

purposes', would make it possible 'to prevent a still greater evil'.[31] 'However,' the envoy aptly added, 'the words of the Pope betrayed more of an opportunistic position on the question which is discussed so much at the present time in Germany, namely how the Centre Party might possibly react to the National Socialist Party if this party should continue to expand and one day should be summoned to form a government.'[32]

At the same time, the possible conflict of loyalties for the President was also discussed openly among the parliamentary leadership of the Centre Party. It was Kaas himself who brought up the question. As the very terse minutes of 15 December recorded, he reported on comments from the Land which had come to him 'relating to his temporary stays in Rome'. On this matter, however, he wanted to reserve for himself 'freedom of decision for the future as well'. 'But if the leadership had misgivings, he was ready to fall in with them.' That what was in fact at stake was the question of political independence was shown by the comment on the statement that in it Brüning had spoken on 'the related political questions'. Nevertheless, the leadership unanimously decided not to accept the prelate's offer of resignation, but rather to adhere 'to the previous practice'.[33] In fact, up to the end of 1931 there was no sign that the chairman of the Centre Party might have been disloyal to his party and the Chancellor which it had provided. As long as Brüning was in office, Kaas openly stood by him. This changed only when it appeared that there was no longer anything to save.

In the meantime the same process was repeated for a third time over the concordat question. Whenever the negotiations with the Reich had come to a standstill, Pacelli had always devoted all his energies to the next attainable concordat with a Land. It had been like this with Bavaria and Prussia, and now it was Baden's turn.

Here chance came to his aid. Carl Fritz, the Archbishop of Freiburg, died on 7 December 1931. Like many of the older generation of German bishops, he had looked rather coolly on the Curia's insistence on a concordat, and Kaas's assumption that on this question little support was to be expected from the Freiburg Münsterplatz during Fritz's lifetime was certainly not unjustified.[34] However, the Archbishop's death not only made the situation easier in this respect, but above all it provided Pacelli with an important lever against the Baden government. For of course the question of the appointment to the episcopal see in Freiburg was one of the essential matters that the new concordat was to control.

Again, the problem here was whether the old treaties from the nineteenth century might or might not still be valid. The Baden government naturally insisted that they were, especially as for its part it had fulfilled all its obligations, and it also communicated this to the Cardinal Secretary of State at the end of December. Prelate Föhr, who in the meantime had become chairman of the Centre Party parliamentary group in the Baden Landtag, and was thus the key parliamentary figure in negotiations on the concordat, explained personally to Pacelli the difficulties of the government coalition in Baden and urgently requested him to recognize the validity of the treaties. In this case, too, however, the Cardinal Secretary of State was not prepared to take even the slightest notice of the German difficulties. In a letter in which one might suppose that he was still seething with rage at Brüning's unapproachability, he forthrightly reprimanded Föhr and the Baden government. 'Unhappily,' he informed the chairman of the Baden Centre Party on 29 December, 'I cannot help but express my displeasure at the attitude and intentions of the government.' With this attitude in the government, 'a happy outcome' was 'not to be expected'. If a satisfactory arrangement of relations between state and church was to be achieved, 'then one may disregard the theoretical question of the legality of the old agreements and instead (after more than twelve years!) proceed as quickly as possible to a new concordat...' If it could be agreed, Pacelli maintained in remarkable ignorance of the situation in Baden, 'to send authorized representatives to Rome, the concordat could be signed in the shortest possible time'.[35] He was even more frank in his official answer to Kultusminister Baumgartner:[36] 'Should... the government not be prepared to comply with the proposal to conclude a concordat as quickly as possible, the Holy See would have no option than to proceed to the appointment of a new rector of the Diocese of Freiburg in accordance with Canon 329 § 2 of the new canon law.'[37]

However, since the negotiations kept dragging on, Pacelli decided – in spite of Baumgartner's urgent pleas not to complicate his situation in the cabinet still further[38] – to deal with the Freiburg appointment in accordance with canon law. In mid-April Föhr learned from Kaas in the Reichstag building that Conrad Gröber, Bishop of Meissen, was to become Carl Fritz's successor. On 7 May Pacelli also officially informed the Baden government; the nomination followed as early as 21 May.

The choice of Gröber was undoubtedly both clever and skilful. For the new Archbishop of Freiburg came from Constance, and he had a good reputation among Baden Catholics. At the same time he enjoyed Pacelli's confidence and was a whole-hearted supporter of the Vatican concordat policy. As early as July, Gröber joined in the concordat negotiations, taking the same line as the Holy See, and in August 1932 he sat at the negotiating table when the Baden concordat was worked out in Rome.[39] Almost exactly a year later, in summer 1933, Gröber was to become Pacelli's agent among the German bishops on the issue of the Reich concordat, and to have a vital part in its conclusion.

Despite the vigorous efforts of Föhr, Baumgartner and Gröber, the concordat initialled in Rome on 12 August was still to have a rough time in Baden. At the end of 1932 the arguments over the treaties led to fierce battles and finally to the break between the government coalition and the Social Democrats which for fourteen years, since November 1918, had guaranteed 'political stability, law and order' to the Land. With a tied vote in the Landtag, the new coalition of the Centre Party, the German People's Party and the Economic Party succeeded in passing the treaties only with the casting vote of the Landtag president.[40]

The entire proceedings were convincing proof of the soundness of Brüning's decision to spare the Reich at least these battles. And at the same time they were an unmistakable indication to Pacelli that a Reich concordat had no chance whatsoever of getting through parliament in Germany in the foreseeable future. For what had been so difficult to achieve in a state like Baden, with a relatively strong Centre Party, was doomed to failure from the start in the Reichstag, with its different majorities.

The Baden concordat of 12 October 1932 was the last concordat with a German Land that Pacelli was to achieve. It was effective from 11 March 1933 – the very day that the National Socialists took over the administration in Karslruhe. In substance roughly half-way between the Bavarian and the Prussian concordats,[41] it still enjoys 'tranquil validity'[42] – a sign less of the political foresight of its creator than of a different relationship between church and state which, after the Second World War, took the heat out of the fiercely contested positions of the 1930s.

During these negotiations, in the chaotic year 1932, another change had taken place at the head of the Reich which between the middle and the end of the year again caused Pacelli to test its readiness for a concordat.

On 30 May 1932 Brüning resigned, ultimately overthrown by those very right-wing forces whose cause he above all had espoused.[43] In his place the Reich President appointed a former Landtag representative of the Prussian Centre Party, hitherto virtually unknown to the public, Franz von Papen. This solution, engineered above all by the leaders of the Reichswehr, was an almost unprecedented affront to Brüning, Kaas and the entire Centre Party. Only the day before, the new Chancellor had assured the Centre Party Chairman that in no circumstances would he take on the task of forming a cabinet. By his sudden change of mind he now not only disowned Brüning: he also excluded the Centre Party from power and thus paved the way for the man who was just waiting to seize total power: Hitler.

No wonder that Kaas spoke of von Papen in the 'role of Ephialtes',[44] that legendary traitor who had led the Persians to attack the Spartans from the rear at Thermopylae. Half sick with rage and indignation, the Centre Party chairman now retreated early in June to his refuge in the south Tirol, from which he returned to Germany only in September. It is possible that this was the point at which Kaas finally regarded parliamentary democracy as lost in Germany. He was certainly not alone in this. But leaving aside the Social Democrats, he was the only one who still controlled a stable party with a reliable democratic substance. Typically, the prelate clothed his verdict on the Weimar judgment in the garb of a work on canon law. In late autumn 1932 he completed a carefully written manuscript on the significance of the Lateran Treaties, a text which at the same time was a testimony to the efficiency and foresight of Italian Fascism and its leader, Mussolini.[45]

In the meantime, developments in Germany under the Papen cabinet could not but justify this kind of pessimism. Hardly was Papen in office than he dissolved the Reichstag and in so doing gave the extremist parties another opportunity to exploit the general mood to their own ends. At the same, by a *coup d'état* he eliminated the Prussian government, which hitherto had been most persistent in opposing all threats from the right. He had to pay the price for all this in the election of 31 July 1932. In their despair over the 5.5 million who had meanwhile become unemployed and a system which was obviously incapable of solving this problem, the Germans voted more than ever before for the radical extremes. The NSDAP was able once again to more than double its representation over that in the September 1930 elections: it now held 230 instead of 110 seats. And the Communists also scored a substantial increase – from their previous 78 seats to 89. So the two parties controlled a kind of negative obstructive majority in the Reichstag, bound to stifle any constructive approach. Among the democratic parties only the SPD and the Centre Party remained stable – the latter even gained six seats. However, a coalition was now inconceivable. As in Prussia, there was no majority in the Reich.

All this made it more difficult than ever before for German Catholicism to get its bearings. And this was true not only of the Catholic voters, who now also decided in large numbers for Hitler, but also precisely of the shaping of opinion within the Catholic leadership groups themselves.

Even after the July elections of 1932 the German bishops maintained their fundamental condemnation of the NSDAP. This decision was expressly repeated and endorsed at the Fulda Bishops' Conference in August. As the minutes recorded: 'All the diocesan authorities have banned membership of this party, first because parts of its official programme contain false doctrine in what they say and the way in which they must be understood, unless they are reinterpreted; secondly, because the declarations of numerous representatives and spokesmen for the party are of a character hostile to the faith, expressing an attitude inimical to the fundamental teachings and claims of the Catholic church... Thirdly, it is the collective judgment of the Catholic clergy and of the loyally Catholic champions of the church's interests in public life that if the party achieves the monopoly of rule in Germany which it so ardently desires, the church interests of the Catholics will prove extremely bleak.'[46] The Bavarian bishops, who convened at the beginning of September, formulated their statement more cautiously. Here, Bishop Buchberger argued in a report that despite everything National Socialism was more likely than Communism to 'make a convergence seem possible'.[47] However, in a pastoral letter to the clergy it was very clearly emphasized that class hatred and racial hatred were both 'un-Christian and calamitous', and that 'a genuine "freedom movement" had nothing in common with the struggle against the Catholic church and its supreme head'.[48]

By contrast, the Roman appraisal of the situation was remarkably different from these statements. Immediately after the July 1932 elections, Pacelli made some surprising remarks to Ritter about it. The Cardinal found the growth of Communism most disquieting. Therefore, the Bavarian envoy commented, describing Pacelli's view, 'it is to be hoped and desired that, like the Centre Party and the Bavarian People's Party, so too the other parties which stand on Christian principles and which now also include the National Socialist party, now the strongest party in the Reichstag, will use every means to hold off the cultural Bolshevizing of Germany, which is on the march behind the Communist Party.' The NSDAP itself had indeed always maintained that it was a Christian party, and many Protestant circles had accepted the claim. But the fact that the Cardinal Secretary of State was now also ready to class it among the Christian parties, at least with an eye to the Communist threat, was a change that made future co-operation appear not only possible but even necessary. As a matter of fact, Pacelli thought that 'a new coalition among the political parties in the Reichstag must come into being' for the purpose of concentrating the forces of defence, and he raised the question whether in the circumstances 'the Centre Party and the Bavarian People's Party might not now do well to take their bearings more from the right and to look there for a coalition which would correspond to their principles'.[49]

However, when in the weeks after the election the Centre Party set out on this very path, it hardly did so because of Pacelli's ideological concepts, but rather because the election result left no other possibility open. The whole situation was absurd beyond measure, and also showed that parliamentary democracy in Germany had come to the end of the line.

Papen had pinned all hopes for his cabinet on collaboration with Hitler, which as a right-wing conservative he hoped to be in a better position than Brüning to gain. However, Hitler categorically rejected this offer. In a conversation with the Reich President on 13 August 1932 he demanded what he had always demanded, namely 'the total leadership of the state for himself and his party'. But in no circumstances would Hindenburg have this. 'Before God, his conscience and his fatherland,' he retorted, 'he could not be responsible for transferring all government authority to one party and, moreover, to a party that would be unilaterally opposed to those of a different opinion.'⁵⁰ For all practical purposes there was now only one constitutional alternative, namely the formation of a parliamentary majority out of the NSDAP and the Centre Party which, together with the Bavarian People's Party, would be able to rely on 327 out of the 608 votes in the Reichstag. The other possibility was a government against parliament, and that meant an open breach in the constitution. So if the Centre Party, which had always understood itself to be a constitutional party, still wished to proceed constitutionally, it had to make the effort to form a government with Hitler.⁵¹ At the same time, this was obviously the only way to restore to the Catholic party the power which Papen had lost for it.

This was the decisive reason for the negotiations on a coalition with Hitler which the Centre Party, to the dismay of many of the faithful Catholic voters, undertook in August and September 1932. A declaration of the party's Reichstag representatives on 29 August therefore put all the emphasis on the principles of 'constitutional politics'. The search for a clear parliamentary majority and thus also for clear responsibility was 'no "tactical game", no "behind-the-scenes ploy" amidst the distress of the German people, *but rather the dutiful action of a party for which the preservation of constitutional conditions means the welfare of the people and forms the content of its political life'.*⁵²

There is hardly any doubt that the Centre Party was serious about these negotiations, even if in retrospect one is reminded, as *Gerade Weg* put it at the time, of 'a fairy tale of wolves and sheep'.⁵³ On the other hand, they would hardly have been a serious matter to Hitler,⁵⁴ who in any case was exempt from the oath of disclosure. For not least in fear of a possible agreement between the unequal partners, on 12 September Papen again resorted to the ploy of dissolving the Reichstag, thus for the time being ending all further conversations. So these negotiations produced no results. But the mere fact that they were held could only blur the lines still further and assist Hitler in his efforts to achieve recognition as a trustworthy negotiating partner.

Independently of all these developments, during these months the Curia undertook a new, last attempt to move forward in the concordat question. Granted, Papen was weak, but as had been shown in the past, this very weakness could be of considerable advantage. That the new Chancellor attached extraordinary importance to good relations with the Curia was shown by the unusual fact that a few days after his accession to power he informed the Cardinal Secretary of State of the new situation and the aims of his policy through the ambassador in a detailed, confidential letter. It also shed significant light on

Papen's attitude after 30 January 1933 that he argued in the letter that the warnings of the German episcopate, which had been meant to be purely religious, should not have led 'to relieving the *political* party of the German Centre of the duty of contributing the valuable powers of this movement to the state'. However, the new Chancellor saw the greatest danger as the threat of a Kulturkampf. As Papen wrote: 'If the political Catholicism of Germany, based on what are supposed to be the religious instructions of its bishops, opposes the national freedom of the Right in a totally negative way, then naturally and of necessity the anti-Roman feelings of this movement must increase. Nothing, however, would more accelerate the ruin of Germany than a renewed development of Kulturkampf ideas, and it appears to me that from the point of view of national policy one of the greatest concerns must be to do everything possible to spare the country such a spiritual struggle.'[55] With this conviction, only a few months later Papen became the ideal go-between for Hitler's concordat plans.

For the moment, however, Papen himself was still in power. And even if Pacelli was undoubtedly kept informed by the chairman of the Centre Party about all the problems of Papen's cabinet, this report still remained an important sign that Papen would basically be far more approachable for negotiations with the Holy See than, for example, Brüning had been.

The starting point for Pacelli's new attempt was provided by a letter from the Reich Defence Minister, Kurt von Schleicher, to the Archbishop of Paderborn, Caspar Klein. In it Schleicher rejected a plan of the bishops for organizing the military chaplaincies and ended by requiring exemption to be given in full. Schleicher asserted that the suspicions of the German bishops were solely to blame for the delay over the whole business.[56] Crudely attacked in such a manner, the Fulda Bishops' Conference, which met soon after, decided to withdraw from the whole controversy and to accept 'without reservation any reform arranged between the supreme church and the supreme secular authorities'.[57] Thus the German bishops, who in any case could only disrupt Pacelli's plans, were out of the game. The Cardinal Secretary of State himself once more held all the important cards in his hand.

Since through Schleicher's letter the Reich government had so emphatically confirmed its urgent wish for the exemption of the military bishop, the obvious thing was to go back to this wish, at the same time presenting the Curia's counter-demands on the lines of Pacelli's old plans. At the end of October 1932 the Reich government in fact again found itself confronted with the familiar points, in a Promemoria of the Holy See. As in 1931, these were: immunity from prosecution for clergy who consecrated a marriage prior to the civil ceremony; the previous arrangement with the Holy See on a possible withdrawal of financial subsidies; and the provision of guarantees for schools. A new fourth point was added. With a specific reference to the declaration of the Reich Foreign Minister of 13 November 1920 – Pacelli cited it, together with the file number – 'binding promises' were demanded 'that any changes in the constitution or the legislation of the Reich will not impair the rights of the church recognized in solemn concordats'. All this, the Promemoria concluded, entirely in Pacelli's style, represented merely 'a minimum of legitimate church claims'.[58]

While this memorandum was still on its way to Berlin, the Cardinal Secretary of State learned that his successor in the Nunciature, Cesare Orsenigo, had paid a visit to the Chancellor as instructed, in which he had established that the latter appeared ready for far-reaching concessions on the questions of immunity from prosecution and the school guarantees. This caused Pacelli immediately to send a copy of the Promemoria direct to Papen, at the same time expressing his 'sincere confidence' that the Reich Chancellor would 'take into account, and show full understanding of, the legitimate desires of the Holy See expressed in it'.[59] Papen answered immediately that he had 'carefully and with the greatest interest taken note of its content and will arrange its consideration by the Reich government as quickly as possible'.[60]

Pacelli had not had such a favourable response to the Vatican wishes since the days of Wirth and Marx. However, it suffered from two decisive defects. The Reich government mentioned in the answer had resigned even before the letter reached its recipient in Rome. And the further treatment of the Vatican's Promemoria in the government departments showed that the substantive resistance to any kind of concession towards the Curia had not lessened at all. The draft of an answer which the Reich Interior Ministry presented at the end of February 1933 – i.e. already after the seizure of power – left not the slightest doubt as to this resistance. No Reich government would be able to undermine the penal clauses of the personal status law, 'since there is no prospect that there would be the majorities needed for a fundamental change in these provisions in either the Reichsrat or the Reichstag, however these bodies might be structured ideologically or politically'. The question of the financial relief was in no way acute; the school guarantees were provided by the Reich Constitution. But a comprehensive guarantee for the existence of the concordat was quite impossible. 'The present ("no!" was written over it in pencil) Reich government was not in a position to give such a promise. Such a promise would overstep the limits of possible action by a ("any!" was written over it in pencil) Reich government.'[61]

This draft – which was not sent off – was so to speak the last word of the Weimar Republic on the concordat question. On 2 May 1933 a comment from the chief of the Vatican department in the Foreign Office terminated the entire proceedings. On this day Legationsrat Fritz Menshausen noted on a further draft answer: 'The situation has changed completely, on the one hand as a result of the Enabling Act of 24 March this year, which makes it possible for the Vatican's demands to be met without involving parliament, and on the other hand in respect of II Vat.129 (secret). A reply to the note of 25 October 1932 from the Cardinal Secretary of State is therefore in abeyance for the time being.'[62]

The failure of this last attempt to reach a concordat with the Weimar state basically only confirmed what had been well known for a long time: as long as this democratic republic existed in Germany a Reich concordat was inconceivable. But the future of the Republic was uncertain after 1930, and it became more and more uncertain. Thus all the important participants had already begun to direct their attention towards a completely different solution to the concordat issue, towards a new type of concordat of an apparently very modern kind: the concordat with Fascist Italy. In fact, all the negotiations over a concordat in the Weimar period play only a negative role in the prehistory of the Reich concordat. The model for Hitler and Pacelli was the Lateran concordat.

160

The Lateran concordat, along with an international treaty and a financial treaty, belonged to a package of agreements, the so-called Lateran Treaties, which were signed in Rome in the Papal Palace on 11 February 1929. These treaties marked a change in the millennia-old, turbulent and eventful relationship between Italy and the Holy See – a relationship which since the middle of the nineteenth century had developed into open conflict. In 1860 Cavour had used in parliament for the first time the key expression *Roma capitale*: Rome as the capital of the new Italy as a united nation. Here, the age-old authority of the Pope in the Papal States stood over against the young, revolutionary authority of the Italian national state. Ten years later, in autumn 1870, Italian troops occupied the Holy City. Since then the so-called Roman question had become one of the unsolved and evidently insoluble problems of Italy, and not just of Italy. Year after year, for example, even the annual conference of German Catholics issued proclamations which affirmed the authority of the Pope in the Papal States. The rupture between the Vatican and the Quirinal was aggravated by the radical laicism and anti-clericalism which dominated Italian church policy and thwarted every reconciliation of the hostile parties. The reluctance and the inability of the liberal state to solve the Roman question was obvious, and remained so. The completely different way in which Mussolini approached the whole problem must therefore have made all the more profound an impression upon the Curia.

Although he personally had no relationship to the church because of his Marxist origins,[63] the leader of the Fascists from the beginning left no doubt that in his conception of a new Italy Catholicism would have a significant role. In contrast to Hitler, however, after the legendary march on Rome in autumn 1922 Mussolini still took almost five years to secure Fascist rule in Italy.[64] Moreover the process of establishing contact and bringing about reconciliation between the papacy and the new state was similarly protracted. Nevertheless, by the middle of the 1920s the main contours were already clearly recognizable.

After a series of declarations of principle by Mussolini on the significance of the church, and a profusion of measures favourable to the church, in 1925 a government commission began on the revision of the church-political legislation from the liberal era. It dealt with the most important problems of state-church law: the freedom of the church in appointing its officers; the restitution of the legal status of the orders; the revision of the law dealing with church property and the old-age pensions of the clergy.[65] In all these points the state largely co-operated with the church without, however, for the time being renouncing its sovereignty over the church. This sovereignty remained as a stake in the negotiations.

Conversely, the Catholic church gradually gave up its partisan political position – and this was just as important. It dissociated itself from the Partito Popolare and finally dropped the party. This was tantamount to a fundamental recognition of Fascist one-party rule. In place of this the Pope, with growing emphasis, argued for the concentration of all Catholic forces in one great movement which would transcend the parties and be purely religious: 'Catholic Action'.[66]

The political consequences of these extraordinarily far-reaching decisions were already clear in the 1920s. In view of the power of Fascism and the powerlessness of the Catholic party, as well as that of parliamentarianism generally, the young canon lawyer Karl Neundörfer, a friend of Romano Guardini, wrote in *Hochland* in 1926 that the only way open to the church authorities in Italy was the one which it had in fact taken in encouraging a more than partisan action. 'It dissociates the impact of the Catholic faith on public life from involvement in a political party, and on the other hand protects it from the menace of an absolutist government.' At the same time Neundörfer had already understood that there was nothing peculiarly Italian here, but rather a basic European model: 'In almost all European countries the Catholic church today is in the same situation as it is in Italy. One only has to point to France and Germany, where the church is also confronted with parties from which it has just as much to hope as it has to fear. Be this as it may, here too the Catholics faithful to the church are politically divided, in that Catholic action has to disengage itself from political action if it does not want to be without the support of many Catholics who are loyal to the church.'[67] In fact, however, this new basic model of church policy at first remained more a possibility than a reality in Germany. For as long as parliamentary democracy stood firm there, so too did the Catholic party with its consciousness of tradition – and with it the profusion of the vigorous organizations which German Catholicism had developed since the middle of the nineteenth century. So only at a late stage, at the Katholikentag in Magdeburg in September 1928, did Pacelli call for the formation of Catholic Action in Germany, too – and received a rather modest response.[68]

However, that made the new basic model for the development of relationships in Italy all the more important. Since both partners had changed their starting positions, the way was finally clear for direct negotiations between the Curia and the Fascist state. Both had their own clearly-defined goals in view. For Mussolini the issue was *conciliazione*, reconciliation between church and state, which was extremely important for domestic political stability as well as for the international reputation of the new Fascist Italy. The Curia, on the other hand, was vitally concerned to secure the principles of canon law in a solemn concordat which was to guarantee this law finally, as sweepingly as possible, in the homeland of the papacy as well. Both goals were achieved in the Lateran Treaties.

In the first of the three agreements, the *Trattato fra la Santa Sede e l'Italia*, the sovereignty of the Holy See was recognized. As a guarantee and an expression of this sovereignty, the autonomous and independent Vatican City was created. This arrangement made it possible for the Holy See, 'for its part,' as the preamble put it, 'to recognize that the "Roman question", which originated... in 1870 as a result of the incorporation of Rome into the Kingdom of Italy, is finally and irrevocably settled'.[69] This solution, a historical compromise in the classical style, has meanwhile proved itself so convincing that people no longer realize just how recent the Vatican City really is. At the same time, the very first article of the *Trattato* contained the decisive concession from the state: recognition and confirmation of the principle 'according to which the Catholic, Apostolic and Roman religion is the sole state religion'.[70]

Article 1 of the third agreement of the Lateran Treaties, the *Concordato fra la Santa Sede e l'Italia* proper, again takes up the thread of this first article of the *Trattato* in a skilful and systematic manner. At root, this concordat simply

162

represented the development and safeguarding of Catholicism as the sole state religion of Italy. In it the new basic model of Vatican policy could be clearly recognized. Extraordinarily far-reaching concessions from the state to the principles of canon law were met on the church side by repeated and explicit renunciation of any direct political claim and any political intervention. In fact the most important feature of the Italian concordat – which, incidentally, is still in force – lay in its strong orientation on Canon Law, which here was afforded a 'scope hardly to be found anywhere else'.[71] This scope was most striking in Article 34, according to which the state recognized the civil validity of marriages performed in church. This recognition of the church's marriage law wiped out an entire century of confrontations. It can certainly be understood how Pius XI professed that 'he would have been ready to lay down his life for this one Article 34'.[72] Moreover, while the church clauses of the Concordat were not completely satisfying, the church could undoubtedly consider them an improvement over the arrangements existing hitherto. Finally, given the Roman understanding of the church, another decisive factor was that with the concordat all the fragmentary laws relating to the church disappeared. The Lateran concordat appeared 'almost a complete expression of the *ius commune* in all those situations in the church … where hitherto, in other states and in Italy itself, exceptions had still existed'.[73]

However, as later in the German concordat, the basic political design of the entire set of agreements included an article which stood at the very end. The first paragraph of this famous Article 43 secured government recognition for Catholic Action in so far as it developed 'its activity outside every political party and in direct dependence upon the church hierarchy for the dissemination and implementation of Catholic principles'. The second paragraph stated that the Holy See 'takes the occasion of the conclusion of this concordat to renew for all clergy, and all those in religious orders in Italy, the prohibition against registering in and being active in any political party'.

For Italy, where the last parliamentary representatives of the Catholic People's Party had lost their seats in 1926, this clause meant no more than the confirmation of an existing state of affairs. Applied to Germany, the same clause could only lead to catastrophe for the Centre Party.

At first, however, in the assessments of the Lateran treaties by churchmen and canon lawyers, there was no discussion that side of the Alps of any possible political effects on Germany. At any rate Pacelli himself, who at this time was in the middle of the unsatisfactory negotiations with Prussia, suggested this when in the foreword to the first German edition of the treaties he expressed the hope that 'perhaps the idea of an honest and frank peace between church and state in other countries and with other peoples too might achieve tangible success'.[74] Otherwise, however, most commentators saw the significance of the Lateran Treaties far more in the solution of the Roman question than in the basic political demarcations of Article 43. Thus for example this article was thought worthy of only a passing mention by Pacelli's colleague Robert Leiber, although his article decribed in detail the extraordinary significance of the treaties for Mussolini's aims.[75] And in the appraisal of the set of agreements by the Protestant canon lawyer Hans Liermann, who considered the treaties 'a model of a mature, intelligent policy on the part of the state as well as the church', the accent lay –

after the 'world-historical content' – above all on the specifically Italian character of the individual clauses.[76]

Nevertheless, the basic political model of the treaties could also become of incalculable significance for Germany. And at least one person grasped this as early as February 1929: Hitler.

At this time, with the expulson of Dinter, Hitler had just concluded the process of reorientating the Party's church policy. But for the moment this had removed only the most important points of friction. His church policy still lacked a positive point of contact which would permit a constructive policy in respect of both church and political Catholicism. And now the Lateran Treaties provided precisely this point of contact. Although it is frequently maintained that Hitler did not have any view of church policy of his own,[77] this is incorrect. He knew from 1929 that he wanted a treaty with the Catholic Church like the one that Mussolini had concluded.

On 22 February 1929, only eleven days after the signing of the Lateran Treaties, the *Völkischer Beobachter* carried the headline, 'A Speech by Hitler on the Solution to the Roman Question'. Hitler had given his detailed opinion on the treaties the day before, during a major evening meeting of the Party in the Matthäserbräu in Munich. Significantly, however, he was in no way concerned with the 'Roman question', but rather with the 'conclusion of peace between Fascism and the Vatican' and its significance for German politics. He saw this significance as lying in both foreign and domestic affairs. In the area of foreign affairs, in the framework of the policy of alliance to which he aspired, he noted with satisfaction the 'contribution to the power of the Italian people' achieved through 'the elimination of the conflict within Italy between the government and the Vatican'. 'Everything that strengthens Italy today,' Hitler maintained, 'benefits us. For that reason we welcome the present arrangement in Italy most warmly.'[78] Still more important, however, were the theoretical aspects of the set of agreements, to which he then turned. 'It is remarkable,' he declared, 'how the Italian statesman deliberately concentrates all the forces of his people and removes all opposition. But the fact that the Curia is now making peace with Fascism proves that the Vatican trusts this political situation, at any rate, more than the old liberal democratic state, with which it was not able to make peace.' This was the point of contact that Hitler had sought. And without hesitation he immediately applied it to the German situation. 'By attempting to declare that democracy is still preferable for Catholics, organs of the Centre Party or in Munich, for example the *Bayerische Kurier*, are putting themselves in flagrant contradiction to the spirit of that treaty which the Roman See has today concluded with the Fascist state.' Hitler went on to draw the bold conclusion: 'For the fact that the church today has come to an understanding with Fascist Italy which would have been unthinkable with the liberal democratic state, proves beyond any doubt that the Fascist world of ideas is more closely related to Christianity than the Jewish liberal or even the atheistic Marxist, to which the so-called Catholic Party of the Centre today feels itself so closely bound – to the detriment of present-day Christianity and our German people.'

These assertions were undoubtedly false in the form in which they were expressed, as was shown by the defensive front which Catholicism put up against National Socialism. Yet here Hitler had grasped a political possibility of which, four years later, he was able to take advantage with surprising speed and decisiveness.

Thus Hitler's conclusion that evening sounded like an anticipation of the National Socialist commentaries on the Reich concordat: 'One thing is certain, and I see it as the great significance of the treaty concluded between the Pope and Mussolini: it is now established, through a historic event, that nationalism in itself is not anti-Christian and anti-church, as the German Centre Party and its organs deceitfully maintain. The nationalist world-view is positively Christian, regardless of whether it is Fascist in Italy or National Socialist in Germany. Every good Catholic, like every convinced Protestant, can be an opponent of the concept of parliament and a supporter of the dictatorship of the national idea.[79]

That Hitler continued to think consistently along these lines was shown by a publication from the Party office written by Johannes Stark and entitled *National Socialism and Catholic Church*. It was produced in December 1930, and tens of thousands of copies were distributed in subsequent years. Its author was a winner of the Nobel Prize for Physics, a man who had no ambitions of his own and no expertise in this field. Thus his statement should be considered an authentic reproduction of Hitler's convictions.

The basic starting point of February 1929 had now become focussed on the idea of a special concordat for Germany. At the same time the significance of Article 43 of the Lateran concordat had dawned on Hitler, evidently in this context.

Although in July 1929 the small NSDAP group in the Prussian Landtag had declared itself still to be against the conclusion of a Prussian concordat, Stark now declared that the National Socialist state would nevertheless desire co-operation with the Christian churches recognized by it as a matter of principle. It was therefore 'ready as a matter of principle for treaties with them'. The political goals which Hitler pursued in this connection could not be formulated more clearly than they were by Stark in the next sentences of his publication. At the same time these sentences betrayed an excellent knowledge of the difficulties with which the Centre Party saw itself confronted in Rome, and of the political opportunities resulting from them for Hitler. 'There is no known official statement by the Vatican in respect of the Centre Party alliance with the Social Democrats. The political circumstances in Germany today are such that perhaps for the present the Vatican does not yet wish to give up the possibility of defending the church by means of the Centre Party. The Vatican's position in respect of the Centre Party will, however, change as soon as it can count on a fundamental change in political circumstances in Germany, or as soon as this change has come about. As soon as Marxism, the declared enemy of the church, is forced out of power and influence in Germany and is crushed, and as soon as its conqueror implements his programme of granting protection and freedom in the religious sphere to the Catholic church, and declares its connection with the German Volk to be a valuable part of German Volkstum, the leaders of the Catholic Church can conclude treaties with the new power in Germany which is friendly to the church and can do without the political support of the Centre Party. Then, as in the concordat with the Fascist state in Italy, in a treaty with the National Socialist state of Germany the Vatican can declare that it will prohibit all clergy and members of religious orders in Germany from joining any political party or being involved in it. That will mean the end of the Centre Party.'[80] Subsequent events show that between 30 January and 20 July 1933 Hitler implemented this church-political conception point by point and sentence by sentence.

At all events, in 1932 this was clearly already the general conviction of the Party. For in a commentary on the 'concordat elections in Baden', Walter Köhler, the leader of the Baden group of the Party in the Landtag, wrote that 'in accordance with the standpoint of the Führer and the whole of the leadership', people in Baden, too, were of course ready 'to regulate relations between state and church in a treaty'. And Köhler went on to explain: 'It goes without saying that a treaty brought about under the guidance of the National Socialist movement would look different from the treaty brewed up by the Black-Red coalition. What we have in mind as the model for such a treaty is not the Prussian or the Bavarian concordat; we see the *Lateran Treaty* and the concordat which it contains... as the model for such a regulation between state and church. And if all that applies to Italy cannot be taken over directly and applied to Germany, the *basic tenor* of this treaty is such that it must be regarded as a *model*.'[81]

The reason why Hitler managed to implement his political plans for the church so quickly and so smoothly lay in the fact that a key figure of political Catholicism in Germany, Ludwig Kaas, the chairman of the Centre Party, had also turned to the Fascist solution of the church question in the course of the chaotic year 1932. At all events, in the middle of November 1932 he completed a study of the Lateran Treaties which was published in spring 1933. The only conclusion to be drawn from it was that the prelate saw this new type of concordat as also being a new and exemplary possibility for Germany. Kaas called the conclusion of the treaties 'a paradigm of secular significance', and the Lateran concordat itself seemed to him to be 'in a quite unique way the most direct expression of the present-day approach of the Holy See to church politics'.[82]

Hence the prelate and the Centre Party chairman certainly had German problems in mind when alongside the general orientation of the clauses of the concordat on canon law they stressed above all the 'central significance' of Article 43. It cannot be denied, Kaas wrote, 'that even if that was not the intention, this article virtually has the effect of moving out of the purely religious sphere into that of the state, in that it makes the formation of political parties within Catholicism for all practical purposes virtually impossible, and as a result secures a protection against opposite political trends for the Fascism ruling the state which goes considerably beyond the norm'. The political nucleus of the concordat became clear, however, when Kaas added that in exchange for this 'indirect strengthening and consolidation of the régime' Fascism had to be able 'without hesitation to support and to extend to other areas the influence of the church in the purely religious sphere'.[83]

In an extremely positive general appraisal, at the end of his article Kaas described the Lateran concordat once again as an exemplary conclusion of peace between the modern totalitarian state and the modern church, stamped with the centralism of the *Codex Juris Canonici*, which opened up new and unexpected opportunities for the state as well as the church. This, he claimed, was the deepest significance of the treaty. 'According to the inner law of his own being, in which the law of life of the Fascist state is the strictest hierarchical concentration and incorporation of the whole under the basically unlimited and discretionary will of the Duce, Mussolini would have contradicted himself had he made himself a defender of petty features of detailed minutiae in the sphere of canon law. To no one would the claim to validity of a comprehensive church law – within the framework of the scope of activity retained by the church – appear so understandable as to the dictator who, in his own sphere, had erected a radically simple, unbroken and hierarchical edifice for Fascism without any competition.' The modern Führer state had accomplished what was impossible for the liberal state in Italy and – one might add – in Germany. As Kaas suggested: 'According to its postulates the authoritarian church ought to understand the "authoritarian state" better than others.'[84]

The point in time at which Kaas wrote down these thoughts – more than three years after the conclusion of the Lateran treaties and in the midst of the agony of the Republic – suggests that at the time he was motivated by more than just interests connected with canon law. In fact the article perfectly explains Kaas's political action from the time Hitler took power. After the March elections this action was aimed at only one goal: the historical conclusion of peace between the church and the Third Reich by means of a Reich concordat.

Whether Kaas's article also appeared with Pacelli's prior knowledge and at his desire must remain an open question. Nor is it particularly important. For the personal link between the Cardinal Secretary of State and the Prelate and their association in matters of substance was so close that Kaas undoubtedly would not have permitted anything to appear in their very own special domain that went against Pacelli's convictions in essential respects. Over and above that, however, the spirit and tendency of the article betrayed on almost every page how deeply Kaas was in fact stamped by Pacelli's personality.

This article, after more than ten years of vain efforts for a Reich concordat, thus built a completely new bridge between Rome and Berlin. Only a few weeks later, the prelate was already to test whether it was in fact sound.

11

The Formation of Fronts in Protestant Theology
and the Protestant Church
(1931-1933)

While on the Catholic side the concordat policy of the Holy See paved the way for future decisions, in German Protestantism the fronts of 1933 began to emerge in a series of intense confrontations in the church and theology.

The discussion of National Socialism which was in progress in the Protestant church after the September elections was understood by many to be a political discussion – like that which Protestantism had conducted over other questions during the past decades. However, in a series of incidents in 1931 and 1932, it became apparent that a victory for National Socialism would bring disturbing problems of a completely new kind. Today these problems have long been known. At the time they were so novel and surprising that theology and the church understood them only slowly and with difficulty.

In the 1920s political theology had advanced the thesis that involvement in the political situation was the prerequisite for a correct understanding of the Word of God in the present. Protestant preaching was possible only in ultimate solidarity with the fate of the German Volk, because the person to whom it was addressed was also a member of this Volk and shared in its destiny. This was a theological problem or, more precisely, a problem of theological hermeneutics. It could be discussed in the way in which liberalism and Marxism were also discussed. As long as the völkisch movement remained one political movement among others, political theology in the 1920s also remained one theological current among others. But that began to change in a frightening and almost sinister way when National Socialism became a political power. For in the view of the advocates of political theology this was not a political but a theological process: God's will was asserting itself at this point, in full view, in history: anyone who rejected solidarity with the völkisch movement was rejecting God himself. At this point it became clear how in political theology, from the beginning, the church's confession was taken up into a political concept. Between the determined political theologian and his opponent there was no longer fellowship in the church.

An incident in the summer of 1931 made this crystal-clear for a moment.

On 2 June the German division of the 'World Alliance for Promoting International Friendship through the Churches' met in Hamburg. This alliance, founded on 1 August 1914, was a branch of the ecumenical movement. On the

168

basis of a Christian humanism, it had set itself the goal of 'nurturing a spirit of friendship between the nations by means of the churches, in order to work against efforts leading to hatred and war'. A considerable number of leading German churchmen and theologians were involved in it.[1] The most important topic of the Hamburg conference was the disarmament question. The resolution on this issue, adopted unanimously, stated: 'The nations of the world are confronted with the decision whether they want to base their security on eternal force or on the justice of their treaties and mutual trust. The German World Alliance expects an unequivocal decision from the churches of the world for a policy of justice and trust.'[2]

The German members of the World Alliance were in no sense a bunch of internationalist fanatics. Rather, like the Germans in the ecumenical movement, they had constantly brought forward emphatically and not without success Germany's national problems, and especially the problems of the Versailles Treaty.[3] But this was not enough for political theology. For it, any ecumenical fellowship with the enemies of Germany was already a betrayal of the national interest of the German Volk.

So on the very day that the Hamburg session opened, Professors Hirsch and Althaus responded by making a joint statement to the press in which with a specific reference to 'the service of the church to the teacher of theology' they presented a radical critique of all the ecumenical efforts of the church. In view of the ongoing 'new, terrible war during peacetime' against Germany they demanded the breaking off of all external church ties. 'In our position, for the moment there is no other sincere service to the community that can be performed than to destroy their misleading pretence...' A 'purely private, personal relationship with individuals from those nations' might still be possible, given that proviso; but Hirsch and Althaus judged that official contacts between 'representatives of German theology or the German church' and corresponding representatives of the other side were ruled out.[4]

This statement, which was printed with a vigorous endorsement, above all from the right-wing press, met with considerable, if not unanimous, criticism within the church.[5] In fact this was the first time that two significant theologians had openly expressed the implications of political theology: relationship to the German Volk was the criterion for Christian fellowship.

In separate replies to criticism, both Hirsch and Althaus emphatically confirmed their point of view – Hirsch more vigorously, Althaus as usual more carefully. In July Hirsch justified the necessity of the declaration by referring to the 'divided conscience' which threatened to develop out of the speeches of Protestant church leaders about reconciliation between the peoples and world peace, and the 'suffering and cares of numerous faithful German Protestant Christians about the fate of their Volk'. The criticism had showed that the rift was already deeper than they had feared; in fact, 'a far-reaching alienation from Protestant Christianity' had already set in 'among nationally-minded, morally earnest people'. Only an unconditional commitment to truth – and that meant, in this case, the truth about Germany's destiny – could prevent 'the complete bankruptcy of the ecumenical movement in the enslaved Germany of today'.[6]

Althaus gave his views six months later in an article in the *Schweizerische Evangelische Pressedienst*, which had accused both professors of theology of being infected with the 'bug of National Socialism'. Althaus's answer at this point was especially interesting, in that it made clear the relationship to National Socialism of a political theology that was in no way mindless, but critical and capable of making distinctions. The Erlangen theologian explained first of all that neither Hirsch nor he were members of the NSDAP. As far as he was concerned this was on the one hand because of political misgivings and on the other – and primarily – because of the 'naturalistic racial ideology in the "world view" of this party'. In fact Althaus never did become a National Socialist. That he nevertheless told 'every other person that he was ready to join the National Socialist movement without further ado' was because this movement would not disappear 'either in its guise as a party or in its ideology'. 'In its innermost essence, National Socialism is based upon the resolute desire of the nation's youth for freedom'. In it 'the injured pride of our great people and also the brutal struggle of the Germans for existence has been given the strongest and most passionate expression'.[7] A political theology which adopted solidarity with the destiny of Germany as the precondition of responsible theological speech had to arrive at this differentiation between 'movement' and 'ideology'. It had to call for solidarity with the movement precisely in order to extract from it criteria for a criticism of the ideology. There should be no question that behind this there stood a respectable decision which was at least worthy of theological consideration; all the more so because the nature of totalitarian ideologies had not yet become clear at this time. Nevertheless, even Althaus should already have been able to realize the problems of this approach, because the consequences of political theology made the possibility of Christian fellowship subject to conditions which Christian theology had at no time recognized to be valid. The 'church of Jews and Gentiles' always recognizes only faith and confession as the prerequisite of Christian community – nothing else. Therefore political theology, which lays down other prerequisites, destroys the church itself.

Hirsch was the one who almost spelt this out when with reference to 'Messrs Niebergall and Rade' – both had objected to the declaration in the *Christliche Welt*[8] – he flatly affirmed: 'I attach no importance at all to having fellowship with them in any sort of national or church question...'[9]

It began to become increasingly clear in the church during 1931 that where discussions about National Socialism were conducted on matters of principle, the issue was no longer just a political difference of opinion, but rather a problem of political theology. The development of the Eckert case made a considerable contribution here.

For a long time the Mannheim pastor Erwin Eckert had caused offence as a leading member of the 'Union of Religious Socialists' and a vigorous agitator for the left wing of the SPD. When the leadership of the church in Baden wanted to impose greater political constraints on him in January 1931 he protested in an open letter which accused the Oberkirchenrat of 'manifest bias and the arbitrary misuse of its official power' because it disciplined Social Democrat pastors but allowed National Socialist pastors to agitate unhindered. This exceedingly vehement 'J'accuse' – which in its reference to bias had some justification – was followed on 4 February 1931 by Eckert's temporary suspension, to which he responded with a complaint to the church's administrative court in Karlsruhe.[10]

In this situation the Kassel pastor Hermann Schafft raised the question in

170

the magazine *Neuwerk* whether one really ought 'to become... tremendously indignant about the collaboration of pastors in the National Socialist movement by referring to the un-Christian nature of this movement, while entertaining the possibility of one's own personal involvement in the socialist movement, though here too substantial antagonistic elements are present'. Schafft did not challenge the right to become involved with left-wing parties so long as this was also readily conceded in connection with right-wing parties in the church. His question dealt, rather, with whether a pastor, for the sake of his office, did not have to renounce all 'passionate involvement in the political struggle'.[11] This critical inquiry was of special significance in that Schafft and the Neuwerk circle represented a marked tendency towards reform in politics and church politics, which was clearly to be included within left-wing Protestantism.[12] Of course the Religious Socialists rejected Schafft's reflections altogether. Georg Wünsch declared that it was unthinkable to pass the same verdict on Religious-Socialist Christianity and National-Socialist Christianity as a politicizing of Christianity. In substance, at this point two different things were involved. 'The group of National Socialist pastors... has not joined forces in their movement in order critically to combat the paganism of power ethics, the military craze and antisemitism, but rather to say an enthusiastic "yes" to them all, and to bestow the Christian halo on their movement as it is.' In contrast to this, the Religious Socialists fought for the freedom of Christian witness in the political party and for the freedom of political-socialist witness in the church.[13]

That seemed to exhaust the different possibilities for the adopting of ecclesiastical and theological positions. Either one committed oneself politically and justified this – on the right as well as on the left – with a political theology, in which case one abandoned the church community for the sake of political goals. Or one advocated the political neutrality of all responsible persons in the church, and thus exposed oneself to the charge of tactical opportunism or pietistic escapism.

In this apparently inextricable dilemma for the church, it became imperative for the new theology now to make a statement. Hermann Schafft, who had certainly never concealed the fact that politically he stood on the left, had not meant his inquiry to be either opportunistic or quietistic. Now, in the summer of 1931, a representative of dialectical theology elucidated for the first time the basic problems in the relations between church and politics.

Günther Dehn, himself a former Religious Socialist, who took part in the Tambach conference and from then on was more and more strongly influenced by Karl Barth, firmly took Schafft's side in the controversy between Schafft and Wünsch. His decisive argument against political theology went like this: 'The church... is concerned with man in his – if one may put it that way – pre-political and pre-national situation. Before one is a proletarian and before one is a German, one stands before God in one's existence as a human being.' According to Dehn, there was no conceivable situation in which social distress could be so great that everything else was to be subordinated to it; that one ought only 'to practise socialism' and nothing else; that everything – even the church, even religion – had to be subsumed 'under ideas of socialist liberation'. And the same was true of the 'völkisch distress', which could never be so great that 'everything had to be sacrificed to the national idea'. Naturally, the message of the gospel deals with the individual human being 'who is always at the same time also a proletarian or also a citizen or also a German'. But through his Word God calls this person not primarily just as a proletarian or as a German, but rather as someone existing as a human being and 'thus, and only thus, along the way of this human being's existence as a human being, real life and the message of the gospel come into contact with each other'. If the church no longer speaks to the human being but – as political theology would have it – 'only to the citizen or to the proletarian or to the German, whose citizenship or membership of the proletariat or Germanhood is from now on seen as an element of his original existence', then the proclamation is without power; then 'the salt of the church has lost its savour'. For the gospel can then 'no longer disturb the bourgeois or proletarian or national attitude, or show them a new direction, but rather basically can only confirm and harden them'. Hence Dehn warned the church emphatically against any 'direct association with political and social elements' and arrived at the sharpest conceivable condemnation of all political theology: 'The political pastors and, of course, also the political church-Christians are the real corrupters of the church. They poison it at the source. They deprive it of its deepest impact.'[14]

While political theology thus made acceptance of a specific political situation a precondition for the correct understanding of the Word of God, by contrast dialectical theology declared acceptance of God's Word to be the precondition for the correct understanding of the political situation.

That this fundamental insight into the relationship of church and politics did not exclude, but rather included, political decisions for the individual pastor and church-Christian; that it thus led neither to a tactical opportunism nor to a pietistic quietism, and also in no sense put peace in the church above everything else, was what Günther Dehn put into practice in his own life, precisely at the time when the article was published.

The so-called 'Dehn Case', which aroused church, university and public to a great fervour in the years 1931 and 1932, had begun in November 1928.[15] At that time Dehn, at the invitation of his friend Gerhard Jacobi, the 'Diary pastor', had given a lecture in Magdeburg on 'The Church and Reconciliation between Nations'. Following Karl Barth's ideas, Dehn here attempted to pave the way for a sober reflection on war. He condemned every glorification of war, such as – in a contemporary phrase – 'the bath of steel for the rejuvenation of a nation', yet he also dismissed as impossible a 'naive pacifism', in the face of 'the disastrous reality of our life', and therefore urged that war should be looked on realistically as a last act of self-defence. The church had to stand up for peace and reconciliation between nations and avoid everything that could give war a romantic or in any way a Christian face. It was in this context that statements appeared which were later to prove so controversial, criticizing the identification, which was customary in the church, of death for the Fatherland with a pure sacrificial death: 'This portrayal, however, ignores the fact that the one who was killed had himself also wanted to kill. Thus the parallel with the Christian supreme sacrifice becomes impossible.' In this connection Dehn presented for further consideration the question whether it was right to erect war memorials in church and whether – for the sake of the genuinely free proclamation of the gospel – the institution of military chaplaincies should not be abolished.[16]

172

The radicalism of this lecture lay at a completely different point from the radicalism of the statement by Hirsch and Althaus. While the two latter unconditionally affirmed the implementation of the national interest, Dehn in principle left this political question open and urged the church instead to orientate itself in every situation – including this one – primarily on the Word and will of God. The church did not have to choose between nationalism and internationalism, capitalism and socialism, unconditional attack and unconditional surrender; rather, it had to proclaim and assert God's word and will in the face of all these political phenomena. Thus it did not escape into indifference, as Dehn proved; rather, it took a positive position, but as a church rather than as a party.

This lecture had a notable consequence. Individual members of the audience, but also, for example, the 'Völkisch Committee of the German National Volkspartei of Magdeburg-Anhalt' protested in public and to Dehn's superiors, the Berlin Consistory, that Dehn had publicly insulted 'our fallen heroes', compared them with 'murderers' and – after the meeting ended – had called the war-guilt lie a 'stupid phrase'. Although Dehn at once put things straight, the Consistory did not dare to protect him, but at the end of July 1929, without going into the substance of the matter at all, informed Dehn in the style of the loftiest church authority that through his bluntness he had regrettably 'caused great agitation in many responsible circles and had damaged church interests generally'; at the same time it expressed 'the specific expectation' that he would restrain himself in the future. The reply to the complaints from Magdeburg was even more problematical.[17]

That settled things for the time being. However, two years later the matter became a 'case'. That the political climate had changed in Germany at this time became particularly evident in the German universities. In many places the National Socialist Students' Union began a vigorous agitation against unpopular professors, which with increasing frequency led to more or less serious incidents.[18] For example, early in October 1930 Otto Baumgarten, a Kiel theologian who had already retired by that time, had delivered the ceremonial sermon at the German Bach festival. He was abused by National Socialist students in a pamphlet as a traitor to the fatherland, a philo-semite, a pacifist and a betrayer of National Socialism. This campaign ended, however, in a defeat for the students. The person responsible, a dentistry student by the name of Pennig, was summarily dismissed by the university senate on 22 October.[19]

The 'Dehn case' developed very differently. In December 1930 the Berlin pastor received a call to the Chair of Practical Theology in the University of Heidelberg. After he had negotiated there, had found himself 'in good standing' with members of the faculty, and had accepted the call,[20] early in 1931 a short article in *Eiserne Blätter* by the editor, Gottfried Traub, called to mind the Magdeburg affair from the point of view of the 'National Circle'. This article was a deliberate denunciation and was indeed intended to be.[21] It was not without effect. The Heidelberg faculty, intimidated by the rioting of right-wing students against a Jewish professor,[22] denied Dehn the declaration of confidence that he sought for the sake of 'the calm and secure progress of academic activity' by a vote of six to one. Only Martin Dibelius, the New Testament professor, declared in a separate opinion that he was unable and unwilling in any circumstances to give way to the attacks of student groups. 'I would have to disavow my theology, my academic honour, and all my life up to this moment if I were to yield on this point.'[23] Immediately after this, Dehn sent a telegram indicating his refusal of the Heidelberg chair.

This refusal was easier for him since at the same time the Prussian Kultus-minister, Adolf Grimme, who was a Religious Socialist sympathizer, secured the call of Dehn to the University of Halle. Yet hardly had Dehn said no to Heidelberg and yes to Halle than the National Socialist Students' Union took the initiative. By 4 February 1931, pamphlets against Dehn were being distributed in the university, stating: 'Herr Pastor Dehn wants to educate German children in the crassest and most cowardly pacifism. Are we supposed to look on as such a person receives a chair at our university?'[24] Open warfare broke out as Dehn began teaching in the winter semester of 1931-32. The scene which took place at his first lecture on 3 November 1931, in a lecture hall filled to bursting, deserves to be recorded. As Dehn later recalled: 'Rector Aubin, a quite splendid man who had always stood by me, tried in vain to get silence. Counter-shouts such as "Stop the noise, we want to hear Professor Dehn", were drowned out. The whole entrance hall of the university building was crammed with students, and the whole square in front of the building was occupied by them... "Dehn out!", "Throw him out!" – at times even "To hell with Dehn" – was shouted out in chorus. In the intervals small groups called out "Hurrah for Dehn", which was of little use. I kept going, and even attempted to write my theses on the board, but I didn't get very far.'[25]

This was the distinctive form of anonymous, political mass terrorism against individuals which developed at the German universities in this period.[26]

The details of the confrontations at Halle need not concern us here. In the middle of November they ended for the time being, though not before Rector, Senate and Faculty had put up vigorous resistance, in a semi-surrender by the university instructors and a questionable 'truce' by the students. Dehn's courage, however, was unbroken. In an epilogue to a documentation of his 'case' which was published in December 1931, he declared unequivocally that he believed these incidents to be a 'battle of modern, demonized political thought not only against the freedom of scholarship but rather – and this appears to me to be much more important – against the freedom of the church, denying its right to say what it is obliged to say in the fear of God, even on the question of war'.[27]

Essentially the 'Dehn case' became particularly significant only as a result of this epilogue, which distinguished it from many similar cases and made it a prelude to what was yet to come. Günther Dehn himself was far from over-rating himself and his person. It was precisely that fact that enabled him to see with almost prophetic acumen what made his 'case' a paradigm. As he wrote in the epilogue: 'Perhaps what happened in Heidelberg and Halle is only a prelude to coming events, where a state, purely orientated on power politics, which knows nothing of its responsibility towards God, will either demand complete obedience from the church or will declare it to be a danger to the state. It is possible that the church of the present stands on the threshhold of the most difficult struggles with modern nationalism, in which case its very existence will be challenged. Should I give these coming confrontations a troubled omen by timidly yielding and evading the attack in the interest of my personal tranquillity?'

174

And here for the first time, indeed with a special emphasis, resistance was mentioned, as Dehn continued: 'Here resistance must be offered'. Even stronger than this prophetic confession, however, was the effect of those sentences in which Dehn destroyed the legend of the 'youthful idealism' of the students. 'One is accustomed most of the time to concede a praiseworthy if misguided idealism to the youth in their present struggles. But I would like to express serious doubts about this. Distorted idealism is demonic. It is simply not true that this fanatical patriotism, with a religious tinge because of me, but in fact quite removed from God, really helps the fatherland. On the contrary, it will lead the fatherland into ruin...'[28]

This epilogue became a welcome occasion for the students to accuse Dehn of breaking the 'truce' and to resume the battle against him. At the same time, his colleagues also began increasingly to dissociate themselves from him. The Magdeburg lecture could still be protected under the banner of academic freedom; the remarks about misguided youth, on the other hand, appeared intolerable to many people, theologians as well as non-theologians.[29]

However, the fundamental theological significance of the confrontations finally became quite clear when Emmanuel Hirsch again took a public stand, this time jointly with his Göttingen colleague Hermann Dörries. After a whole series of statements for and against Dehn had already appeared, Hirsch and Dörries published their own opinion on 31 January 1932 in the German nationalist *Deutsche Allgemeine Zeitung*. In it they demanded two things from 'German theologians speaking on this issue', without prejudice to the freedom to be permitted to think through all problems impartially: 'first, a recognition that the nation and its freedom, for all the questionableness of creaturely life, are also regarded by the Christian as being sanctified by God and demanding total surrender of heart and life; and, following on this recognition, acknowledgment of the passionate will for freedom in our Volk, enslaved and violated by power-hungry and avaricious enemies'.[30]

The political theology which voiced itself here thus demanded that a theologian should show his political solidarity if he wished at this time to teach and to speak as a theologian. This was precisely what Dehn, and all dialectical theology with him, denied. Hence it was only logical that Karl Barth, too, should now enter the fray.

Karl Barth's reactions in the Dehn case were remarkably characteristic of him and his cause. For him political theology was essentially a theological, not a political error.

As early as the spring of 1931, in a confrontation with the director of the Berlin Mission, Siegfried Knak, over the significance of völkisch nationalism, he had evocatively summarized the cardinal point in his criticism of political theology. As he wrote to Knak at that time: 'What concerns me is 1. to avoid temptation and scandal connected with faith in the one God, a faith which is always endangered and often more than endangered where, within the reality of creation, such selective exaggerations are made; 2. to continue in openness to the riches of God's commandment, which even as a creation commandment is already more universal than that exaggeration allows it to be, and moreover cannot be fully understood from the perspective of the creation alone; 3. to continue in openness to the gospel, which *qua* gospel is everywhere threatened or in fact pushed into the background where people think that they are able to interpret the commandment of God independently and unilaterally (this insight has made me dissociate myself from the Religious Socialists! in exactly the same way it forbids me to become a 'religious nationalist'); 4. the freedom of the consciences of all those on whose hearts God, also in the politics of this hour, has written another commandment as urgent and as binding for them as the power of their Volk; and upon whom a yoke is laid other than the yoke of Christ when the church allows that exaggerated notion of Volkstum to be proclaimed.'[31]

On the basis of this position, however, in the Dehn case Barth could not simply adopt a contrary political stand and thus in turn set up a law which was no more the law of Christ than was the *nomos* of Volk and Volkstum. Hence he had to try to make it clear that what was at stake was essentially a theological issue. As late as October 1931 he therefore expressly advised Dehn against publishing a document on his case. 'Would you not rather,' he wrote to him with a typical turn of phrase, 'write a good article on any subject in practical theology for the *Theologische Blätter* or *Zwischen den Zeiten*, in which you would again draw attention to yourself as *de facto* a "valuable" member of the theological working community, whereas such a publication of files with all that old stuff... even at best could evoke only ephemeral impressions.'[32] Correctly and fortunately, Dehn, who could see the fundamental significance of his 'case' much more clearly than Barth, did not let himself be diverted from his documentation by this appeal. This did not make things any easier for Barth. So when Martin Rade and Leopold Cordier urged him finally to make a public statement, he first of all wrote two rude letters back to them – and then that very day, 9 February 1932, sat down at his desk and produced a long article for the *Frankfurter Zeitung*.[33]

This article, which was published on 15 February, was narrowly focussed on the theological problems which Barth felt to be the only important ones for theologians. Of Hirsch and Dörries he wrote: 'Should they not conduct their struggle... on a much wider front, in other words develop the tumultous and, in detail, increasingly sordid struggle against the one man Dehn into a struggle against so-called "dialectical" theology that "somehow" stands behind him? What is and must be at stake is the theology represented by Dehn... the attempt to understand church and gospel, in contrast to the two tendencies of Protestant theology dominant hitherto, from the standpoint of their foundation and substance as documented in Holy Scripture, instead of in the light of the Christian or other piety current in their time.' Referring to the political slogans which were the sole weapons in the battle, he saw a 'rime of barbarism over this whole battlefield', and appealed to the students of Halle and their professorial defenders 'to act in a scholarly way, even if with passion'. And in the same style and intent as his *Theological Existence Today* of June 1933, which later became so famous, he was already arguing: 'Should it not now be possible for all parties to get on with theological work, even while carrying on the Dehn case, so that this progress leads to a settlement?' And turning to his 'colleague Hirsch, clearly particularly hot on this case,' he concluded: 'I fear that he and I will never understand each other either theologically or politically. However, I hope that his and my primary interest lies in theology and not in politics.'[34]

The article suggests that at this time Barth had not yet completely grasped the real significance of political theology and its radical demand. That made the controversy which ensued, in which the opposing positions were once more laid out, all the more important. Thus in his answer of 27 February, which was addressed to Barth, Hirsch repeated the fundamental presupposition of political theology: 'Do you wish to deny that integration into Volk and state and into the historical hour and historical task of Volk and state is so interwoven with my existence as a human being that I could deny it only by being disobedient to the one who has placed me in it, and could fail to make it the fundamental point of that understanding of Volk, state and war which is my task as a theologian only by lapsing into non-existential, i.e. theologically insignificant, chatter?'[35]

Now Karl Barth, too, had understood that, given its approach, political theology could neither recognize nor acknowledge 'a point above or beyond... political agitation'. In a bitter letter to Hirsch he reproached himself for the self-deception of his article of 15 February: 'Did I first have to compel you to explain time and again that human existence, to be seen directly as a divine ordinance in its "interwovenness" with creation and sin, rather than any kind of authority standing clearly and irreversibly over against human existence and all its determination, is to be seen as the "cornerstone" of your theological understanding of Volk, state and war? How could I have wanted to remind you of that which is above and beyond political agitation?... Perhaps a "God", perhaps a "gospel", perhaps a "church" which could lay claim to a passion which was completely independent and superior?... Perhaps a theology which even when faced with politics would not itself become politics but rather would remain theology?'[36]

Nothing substantial was added to these basic positions throughout the *theological* discussion during 1933 except that in this year the demands of the 'historic hour' appeared almost overpowering, and the reference to 'that which is above and beyond political agitation' seemed to be little more than credulity and denial.

In the summer of 1932, in the journal *Zwischen den Zeiten*, Helmut Traub, the young son of the Heidelberg informer, made a careful analysis of the theological positions under discussion under the title 'Demology and Theology in the So-Called Dehn Case', which once again brought out the most important differences. After that things again became quieter.

Dehn himself resigned in autumn 1932 in the face of the continuing conflicts and the growing hostility. He applied for a one-year sabbatical, which was granted. In November he was one of the first to be dismissed under the 'Law for the Reconstruction of the Civil Service'. His career led him logically to a teaching position in the Confessing Church.

The theological faculty of the University of Halle greeted the students at the beginning of the 1933 summer semester with a declaration which stated: 'The Faculty today declares with complete candour that it regards the call of Pastor Dr Dehn under the Grimme system, a call which it never wanted, to be a calamity for faculty and university. Moreover it has known for a long time that it was deceived over the character of Dr Dehn. The Dehn case is over. A stumbling block has been cleared out of the way; a source of misunderstanding has been removed. Fellow students, a new Germany calls us to new work!'[37]

The 'Dehn case' was an academic affair. For the time being, the clarification of fronts which it introduced was restricted to a small circle of theologians. The Berlin church leadership, whose questionable procedure had contributed towards starting the dispute, was not involved, and obviously was happy not to be drawn into the affair officially. And in any case the fate of just one professor of theology did not trouble the communities during this agitated period.

At this point other problems called for an answer. Even before the September 1930 elections the form of political controversies in Germany had steadily intensified. The National Socialists were mainly to blame, increasingly using the SA to command the streets and in so doing provoking bitter resistance, above all from the Communists. Hitler knew that street terror was particuarly effective as propaganda, and he ruthlessly made use of it to draw attention to the Party, to impress the public, and at the same time to propagate a general climate of uncertainty and fear. Thus there were increasingly frequent brawls and more or less bloody incidents which claimed hundreds of deaths on both sides in the last years of the Republic. Especially before the major electoral decisions, a situation resembling civil war prevailed in many places, against which the state appeared increasingly impotent.[38]

At this juncture the church governments were clearly called on to extend the basic principles of morality to public life if they wanted to take their self-appointed task seriously. So in the course of 1931 a series of decrees appeared, directed 'against the degeneration of morals in public life', calling 'for mutual toleration and brotherly understanding', and admonishing the church communities 'to co-operate in the overcoming of such deplorable public abuses'.[39]

On 5 December 1931 no less a figure than the Reich Minister of the Interior, General Groener, wrote a letter to the German Evangelischer Kirchenausschuss, requesting it 'to give effective assistance to the state in preventing acts of violence'. Without making detailed suggestions, the Minister asked the Kirchenausschuss to consider his ideas 'and to produce proposals for steps and measures to be taken by the church'.[40] Kapler passed this request on to all the Landeskirchen and at the same time asked to be told what had already been done by the individual Landeskirchen. On 19 March 1932 he was able to pass nine comments by different Landeskirchen on to the Minister of the Interior and in addition to remark that the Minister might learn from them 'that those in positions of responsibility in the Protestant church are taking up the problem of church and politics with all the vigour that could be desired, giving clarification, admonishing and making demands, and in this way, unaffected by the views of the day, are putting the truth of the gospel at the service of the true community of the Volk in principle and in practice'.[41]

In style and content this answer was very typical. It betrayed how much the church governments understood themselves to be administrative bodies which exercised their executive office in public above all by means of announcements, statements and declarations. Presumably, given the way in which political passions had been aroused, it was clear to those in the consistories that these statements, which were little more than admonitions to see reason, had little chance of being heard. But because of their self-understanding and their composition the consistories were not in a position to say or do anything else.

Moreover, the first completely different reaction from the church to events did not come fom the church leadership but from a group of local clergy. On 17 July 1932, a Sunday two weeks before the Reichstag elections which made the NSDAP the strongest party, the SA of southern Holstein had scheduled a propaganda march through Altona. During the afternoon, as the procession of almost 10,000 SA people neared the old section of the city, which was a well-known Communist bastion, there was a sudden concentration of Communist fire, which immediately turned into an open street battle. Some of the fighting took place directly beneath the walls of the main church of Altona in which the afternoon service was being held.[42] Only in the evening did the police succeed in restoring calm. Seventeen dead and more than a hundred wounded, some of them seriously, were the sad result of this 'Altona Bloody Sunday'.[43]

It would have been in keeping with the church style of the time had the church government in Kiel issued a statement of concern at these events and a general admonition to keep the peace. Instead, something quite extraordinary happened. The pastors of the Altona deanery called for 'emergency church services' on the evening of 21 July, all of which were to follow the same liturgy. In these services a message was read out 'from the Evangelical Lutheran Church in Altona to its members and to all who want to listen'. This message was no official declaration or admonition; rather, it was a solemn confession in the name of the triune God. So it was not addressed just to anyone but expressly to confessing Christians: 'We pastors of the Evangelical Lutheran Church in Altona understand ourselves to be servants of God who are sent, in the great confusion and distress of our days, to proclaim to their communities and to all who wish to hear, that this is God's will: In all moral, economic and political disasters there is only one name in which we can be helped, Jesus Christ. For our deepest distress is that all we, like sheep, have gone astray and each one looks to his own way but does not ask about God, and therefore does not perceive how things are with others.'

Obviously at this point there could be no question of placing oneself above the parties and admonishing those in dispute to peace and reason with well-weighed words. On the contrary, the distress called for a confession of faith, and the confession of faith called for recognition of the solidarity of guilt: 'We who have shared in the experience of the bloodbath on Sunday do not just ask how things could have got to this state or who is guilty. Rather, we confess before God the Holy One that it originates in the fact that we are no longer willing to be sinners together, before God, with all the brothers and sisters of our people, irrespective of social status and party. Each one wants to claim his own righteousness... But we bear witness to our congregations that all that is evil arises out of this self-righteousness.'[44]

In this confession the church no longer spoke as a bureaucracy or a party, but as the church. The Altona pastors and their congregations had left behind them both the theology of the Landeskirchen and political theology. This was a step into new territory, the significance of which was to be demonstrated completely only in the years to come. This step was taken deliberately by the Christians of Altona.[45] For this reason, immediately after the service they appointed a working party of five members to think about the next step. The result was the 'Proclamation and Confession of Faith of the Pastors of Altona', of 11 January 1933, which we shall look at in due course.

Only a few weeks after the 'Altona Bloody Sunday', a different event again led to heated controversies in the church, in the course of which future fronts began to be established.

In the night of 9-10 August five uniformed SA men in the small village of

Potempa, in Upper Silesia, forced their way into the home of a Communist worker, dragged him from his bed and trampled him to death before the eyes of his mother. Also on 9 August, in view of the increasing number of political murders, the Papen government had issued an emergency decree which provided for the death penalty in cases of political murder. The first implementation of this law applied to the Potempa murderers. As early as 22 August a special court in Beuthen condemned all five of them to death.[46] So far this was an extreme but not unusual case as far as the public were concerned. It only became intrinsically significant by virtue of the fact that on 23 August Hitler assured the condemned men in a telegram: 'In view of this most monstrous blood-judgment, I feel committed to you with unbounded loyalty. From this moment on your freedom is a question of our honour. It is our duty to fight a government under which this is possible!'[47]

The *Völkischer Beobachter* was able to report that one of the condemned men had hung Hitler's telegram in his cell with the comment: 'This telegram and his picture will be the small altar before which I shall pray daily.'[48]

Whereas the events in Altona concerned everyone in the church, Hitler's solidarity with the Potempa murderers undoubtedly posed a problem most of all to that group in the church which more or less openly supported National Socialism. In fact, here for the first time there were signs of dissociation; but there were also demonstrations of solidarity, which caused fears for the worst in the future. Granted, the Potempa case nowhere became the subject of official church statements; but the internal discussions connected with it were all the more fervent. Thus three days after Hitler's telegram, President Wurm of the Württemberg churches wrote to Wilhelm Pressel, the student pastor at Tübingen, whom he knew to be a member of the NSDAP, that he, Wurm, also hoped for the victory of the German freedom movement and had every understanding of Hitler's situation. 'But some kind of word of condemnation of such attacks by National Socialists ought not to be left unsaid. I have the impression that a very serious hour has now come upon my colleagues who support National Socialism, in which they can render a great service to both the church and the national movement.' He therefore suggested that the group of National Socialist pastors should make an appropriate statement 'which may perhaps at present be considered politically inopportune and which will bring its signatories a political reprimand from the Brown House, but will certainly have a good effect'.[49] In fact Pressel's criticism went very much further. To a leading figure in the small group of National Socialist pastors, Pastor Wilhelm Rehm of Simmersfeld, he wrote: 'An intolerable glorification of what in spite of everything was a brutal act; a glorification of political murder; a complete distortion of the facts of the case! No trace of condemnation of the act as such; renunciation of any judgment based on moral conscience; declaration of solidarity with the culprits: here and there almost an identification with the deed! Dear Rehm! This is ghastly.' At the same time Pressel induced the National Socialists taking part in a church vacation course to send a clear statement on this issue to the Gauleiter in Stuttgart.[50] There was a prompt reaction. Pressel was summoned to Stuttgart in October 1932 to discuss the matter and subsequently was expelled from the Party by the Gauleiter for 'mutiny'. After urgent representations from the leader of the NS students in March 1933 he was allowed to stay, but finally, not least because of this incident, at the end of 1934 he was expelled for good by the Gau court and in the middle of 1935 by the Party supreme court.[51]

If here the alienation caused by this incident was obvious, on the other hand it demonstrated the degree to which the demand for solidarity made by political theology had already relativized ethical standards. In a Sunday meditation in the Stuttgart *NS Kurier*, entitled 'Sow Righteousness to Yourself and Reap Love (Hosea 10.12)', Pastor Rehm defended the Potempa murderers, who, he said, had committed only one crime: 'to love their Volk and fatherland above all else...'[52] In a letter to Pressel, another member of this group, the city pastor Immanuel Schairer, from the suburb of Hedelfingen in Stuttgart, interpreted Hitler's reaction as an 'elemental cry of blood for blood: inarticulate, indistinct, unstatesmanlike, undiplomatic, but – genuine!' 'Hitler's sharp statement that in German a traitor has no "rights" – is, no doubt, frighteningly strident. It is an upsetting of the whole of "morality". But I cannot bring myself, as a Christian, simply to deny him and to say an absolute "no" to it.' The letter ended, 'In spite of everything and more than ever in deep earnestness: Heil Hitler!'[53]

At this point it became recognizable how the political theology of the time could justify even political murder: the higher authority of 'love of Volk and fatherland' or of the 'blood' allowed the positive law to appear as objective injustice. Even the commentary in the *Allgemeine Evangelisch-Lutherische Kirchenzeitung* pointed in this direction when it applied to the judgment at Beuthen the principle *summa ius, summa injuria* – 'the law carried to its extreme is supreme injustice', and described the call for an immediate repeal of the death sentence as 'a demand of justice, and indeed of national necessity'.[54] The *Christliche Welt*, on the other hand, had a clearer view and declared: 'Those on the right who think they are Christians while blindly glorifying violence, to whom the end justifies ever more dubious means, must be told: your way of thinking is getting further and further removed from Christianity.'[55]

Again, barely four weeks later, an incident in Oldenburg came to public attention which for the first time brought about a direct confrontation between Party and church. If the times had not been so out of joint that outside those directly concerned no one could be sure just what had actually happened, this affair would undoubtedly have caused far more of a sensation than it did. Nevertheless, it showed how sensitively a Landeskirche could react to a civil encroachment on its authority, even on the eve of the seizure of power, and how clearly certain developments were already coming into view without anyone having yet had the chance to ward them off.

In the Landtag elections of 29 May 1932, the NSDAP in Oldenburg – with 48.4% of the vote – had been able for the first time to gain an absolute majority in a German Land parliament.[56] On 16 June Carl Röver, the Gauleiter of Weser-Ems, an uncommonly brutal representative even by National Socialist standards, came to head the new National Socialist government as Minister President of the Land. Under his leadership a policy that was decidedly hostile to the church began immediately in Oldenburg.

The occasion of the open conflict was a lecture tour by the black President of the Ewe Church in Togo, Pastor Robert Kwami, arranged by the North German Mission Society of Bremen. In the course of this tour Kwami was to speak on 20 September at two meetings in the Lambertikirche in Oldenburg, the old main

181

church of the city. Hardly had this been announced than the Gauleitung let it be known through the Oldenburg press that it had requested the Kultusministerium 'to stop immediately such a cultural disgrace and challenge to the National Socialist ministry in Oldenburg'.[57] At the same time the district pastor of Oldenburg, Kirchenrat Hermann Buck, was told on the telephone by the head of the police department 'in the name of the Minister President, on the basis of a "cabinet meeting" (!) that the event would not take place'.

A minute in the records of the Oberkirchenrat involved, dated the same day, recorded the toing and froing that now followed. 'KRat Buck retorted that the Minister was confused about his jurisdiction. Further telephone call... The Minister President had KRat Buck summoned to be told personally what was required. Telephone call from KRat Buck to me, asking what was to be done. I advise against the visit. KRat Buck informs the Ministry that if the Minister President believes he has something to say about this purely church matter it ought to be put in writing. So far no further developments.'[58] In fact the Kultusministerium said that it had no jurisdiction, and handed the matter over to the Oberkirchenrat, which on 15 September 'emphatically' rejected the NSDAP protest. That seemed to end the matter.[59] The meetings involving Kwami took place as planned, with an audience large enough to be reckoned a demonstration. 'Since the splendid and solemn funeral of our Grand Duke last year,' reported the middle-class *Oldenburger Nachrichten*, 'Lambertikirche will not have had so large a congregation as gathered yesterday evening at the lecture by the black pastor from what used to be German Togo.'[60]

But Röver was not the sort of man to put up with this defeat. A further statement by the Gauleitung declared: 'For us, first as National Socialists and secondly as Germans, and thirdly as members of the Evangelical Lutheran Church, there is a quite certain principle, endorsed by a healthy racial instinct, that a Negro may not appear as a preacher in the church in Germany. – If you want to show niggers to the children, there are enough circuses for that, often enough with sideshows.'[61] However, the affair only became an open scandal when Röver himself took up the subject at a campaign rally and declared: 'He had to regard the action of the Oberkirchenrat as either stupidity or triviality, which really ought to have been punished with a prison sentence. A time will come when the National Socialists will tell these gentlemen who have so disgraced the white race what is what. And this would be so terrible, that life for these people would be worth nothing...'[62] There was some dispute as to whether the last sentence actually went like that. However, there was no dispute over what came next: 'The time will come when in Germany people will talk of this hour when the nigger preacher spoke as an hour of deepest shame. The house of God, the loftiest sanctuary, is desecrated by a human being of the lowest race. To be sure, all races are creations of heaven, but it ought not to be concluded from this that all human beings are equal!'[63]

There would be few public utterances from members of National Socialist governments before 1933 in which National Socialist racial teaching, with all its implications, was presented so openly.

In the face of these utterances, evasion by the church was impossible. It reacted without hesitation and with remarkable determination.

The pastor in charge of Lambertikirche publicly called on Röver to withdraw, 'with a clear expression of regret, those words of his which contain a threat to the security and life of a citizen of Oldenburg acting in accordance with his duty' or to publish a correction.[64] Since despite vigorous efforts neither the one nor the other happened, on 7 October the Oberkirchenrat filed a complaint against the Minister President on the grounds of 'serious public defamation'.[65] Although this complaint met with no success, it was still a proper and – in the circumstances – a courageous step.

In the meantime the Oldenburg church also entered the controversy. On 21 September the General Association of Preachers, in a unanimous declaration, 'while endorsing a healthy national movement', warned 'against a race hatred which is incompatible with "positive" Christianity'.[66] Even more important was the fact that in Oldenburg people had recognized the fundamental significance of this issue for the church. As a result the theological committee of the General Association of Preachers was directed to work out a ruling on the race question. When the editorial staff of *Evangelisches Deutschland* published the result in December, it introduced the theses 'as an ecclesiastical epilogue' to the Oldenburg dispute. In fact, however, they were the first in a long series of theses, statements, opinions and declarations in which German Protestantism sought clarity on this question.

A new tone was struck in this series of theses, as it was by the Christians of Altona: 'Standing under the command of God the Creator, the Christian believes and confesses that God has given him his life as one who belongs to a specific Volk.' Strongly influenced by the results of contemporary racial research, these theses emphasized 'the irrevocable diversity of the races'; yet the only conclusion that faith and confession could draw from this was that 'the individual races are called to serve one another'. Problematical though the differentiation between strong and weak races seems to be in the theses, in the face of Röver's statements it was clear that faith and confession ruled out any form of racism for the church.[67] The Oldenburg theses indicated how difficult it was for the church to find its way in this matter. But they were also a sign that even before 1933 there was no lack of attempts to do so.

The last reaction to the Kwami affair, which was literally a last word, was a long article by the President of the Oldenburg Kirchenrat, Heinrich Tilemann, in *Evangelisches Deutschland*. This article was particularly significant in that it showed how a small Landeskirche on the very eve of the Nazi seizure of power – the article appeared on 8 January 1933 – was able to grasp the basic significance of National Socialist rule. In his account Tilemann connected the Kwami affair with other measures by the government (its attempt at politicizing the schools and the dismissal of senior officials) and saw in it a basic 'disdain for personal freedom and legal norms'. 'It was the Protestant church that first saw itself called to draw attention to the serious dangers and to call the state government to order.' The President of the Oberkirchenrat 'made a statement that must find a strong response throughout the Land... that the right of free speech was at present in great danger in Oldenburg, and it was the concern of the church to bring understanding and help to those who had to suffer under terror.' The service due from the church to the state was to ward off pressure on consciences, to protect personal freedom, to oppose contempt for established law, and to remind the state of its limitations. 'No one can render this service to the state in the way the church can.'[68] Striking and courageous as this was, it very soon proved that even in Oldenburg the seizure of power released forces that made even the best of intentions ineffectual.

The events in Oldenburg were revealing in many respects. Among other things they showed that the Landeskirchen were determined to repulse encroachment upon their rights, and that at this point, even in strongly National Socialist areas, they could count on remarkable support from the population. But they also showed – and this was another typical aspect – that the two churches were far removed from seeing this as their common concern. Rather, confessional distrust was far stronger than Christian solidarity.

In principle, Röver's comments concerned the Catholic Church, too, to which about twenty-five per cent of the population in Oldenburg belonged – primarily in the area of Vechta. But the Catholic protest failed to appear. Rather, people recalled a letter of protest from the Oberkirchenrat written in June against the appointment of a Catholic Kultusminister in the new government, and took this as proof that the Catholics were left to their own devices. 'Catholic people know,' wrote the Catholic *Oldenburger Volkszeitung*, 'that they have nothing to expect from National Socialism and, after the experiences of decades, just as little from the circles which stand behind the authors of the letter mentioned above. Here is another serious warning to Catholic people to go on standing together, united and unanimous, over the next months as well, and to create for themselves a position from which they can defend their rights and their freedom with success against all their opponents.'[69]

Anyone who follows the history of German Protestantism in the years 1931 and 1932, the great disorderly discussion in which nevertheless positions gradually began to become clear and fronts to emerge, cannot say that the Protestant church was taken by surprise, ignorant and unprepared, by the Third Reich. Of course no one knew what a Hitler victory would bring and what it would in fact mean. But for all that there is no mistaking the fact that at many points in the church preliminary work was being done on future decisions, and this could be built on when things became serious.

The last and most important piece of this preliminary work was 'The Proclamation and Confession of the Pastors of Altona in the Distress and Confusion of Public Life', dated 11 January 1933.

Immediately after the emergency church service of 21 July 1932 various members of the community had approached the Provost in Altona, Georg Heinrich Sieveking, with a request for further progress along the course that they had chosen.[70] At the same time, the Altona pastors, too, had seen clearly that their 'proclamation' was only a first step, and that they now had to move on from here to specific statements about the task of the church in the given political situation. A committee of five pastors was appointed to start this work. The driving force was Pastor Hans Asmussen, at that time thirty-four. He was an unusually gifted and energetic man, but also difficult, who very quickly was to become one of the most important theologians in the Church Struggle that was now beginning. He formed a personal link between the Altona Declaration and the famous Barmen Declaration of 1934, which he also helped to formulate and to interpret in a compelling way at the Synod of Barmen. Asmussen and his colleague Karl Hasselmann, who was the same age, also brought with them the experiences of a theological study group which had met regularly in Neumünster under their leadership since 1931, and to which the Kiel church historian Kurt Dietrich Schmidt and the Regensburg Landrat Theodor Steltzer belonged. Schmidt later became the most important historian of the Confessing Church and Steltzer became a leading member of the resistance in the Kreisau Circle.[71]

The committee got to work that very July. It prepared a series of sixty-five theses which were at first intended to be the basis for a conversation with the political parties, and later developed into the final 'Declaration and Confession of Faith' in an exceedingly fruitful collaboration of all the Altona pastors. On 19 December 1932, with the signatures of twenty-one pastors, it was delivered officially to Bishop Mordhorst of Holstein.

It is evident from Asmussen's memoirs that the pastors of Altona knew what they were doing. According to them, one of the five, the oldest, had said openly at the beginning of their work: 'The church stumbled into the 1914 war. Now we again face an upheaval like that one, it is our responsibility to be well-prepared when we face what God has imposed on us.'[72]

The central assertion of the Altona Confession was to be found in the first sentence of Article 1: 'We believe, teach and confess that the church is the company called through God's Word, taking place now, in which Christ is truly present.'[73] Thus the church was neither an agency nor an association, but rather *creatura verbi divini*, the creature of the divine Word and will, on each occasion the chosen company of the *Christus praesens*. The long road from the Tambach lecture in September 1919, via countless theological arguments, the road from dispute in the church and about the church to the confession of the church, the road of Karl Barth's theology, here issued in a new perception of itself by the church. Where the Five Articles of the Altona pastors made remarkable and startling assertions, these were all derived from this one, new, basic insight. This was above all true of the relationship between church and politics. Here, too, the church stood above parties, but no longer in the sense of the wisdom of church administrations who were concerned to avoid conflicts, but rather in its commitment to God's word. The church, said Article 1, 'must speak the word freely. It is subject to no man and precisely in this respect it is the servant of all. This is the way in which the Word must be demanded of us.' From this, however, it followed specifically that 'Anyone who expects the proclamation of the pastor to justify or endorse a certain economic reform, war or peace, military service or conscientious objection – anyone who asks the pastor to speak of the highest service of which a human being is capable, the death of a hero for the fatherland, unconditionally as a blessed death, induces him to deny the Lord Christ and his work of salvation.'

The basic function of this new approach to the criticism of ideology – as critical of bourgeois ideologies as of left-wing and right-wing ideologies – is expressed in an equally strong and direct way in Article 2: 'We therefore firmly reject the dream of a coming earthly universal kingdom of righteousness, of peace, and of the general good in all its varieties... Regardless of whether one believes in a coming earthly kingdom of peace and the security of all nations, or in a classless society without hunger, hardship and misfortune, or in a national state of the future with perfect justice and fairness, in all cases one denies the limitation set by God, falsifies political behaviour and teaches contempt for salvation through Christ. Any party which holds out a promise of such goals becomes a religion...'

However, Articles 3,4 and 5, which deal with the state, its tasks and the commandments of God, now made clear the way in which the confession was conditioned by the time. Underlying these articles was clearly an authoritarian understanding of the state which orientated itself almost exclusively on the categories of law, duty and order. Nevertheless, for all that, the confession rediscovered what for a long time had appeared to be entirely lost in Lutheranism: the right to political resistance. 'We are called to show obedience to the authorities, but if a case should arise in which the authorities themselves act against "the best interests of the city", then each must decide, when the moment has come, where one must obey God more than men' (Article 3).

However, it would be incorrect simply to equate the theology of the Altona Confession with the theology of Karl Barth. From Barth came the decisive new beginning, the understanding of the church as *creatura verbi* which has only one task in the world: the proclamation of the word of the cross. This had transcended the culture-Protestant, the German-Christian and the Religious-Socialist understandings of the church. But it was only a beginning, and its development in the Reformed world of the west looked quite different from that in North German Lutheranism. In the latter it was combined with the Lutheran doctrine of the separation of the two realms or swords, and with a way of thinking about order that was far removed from that in Reformed Christianity.

How independently Lutheranism had already accepted and digested Barthian theology in this period was indicated by a book by Hans Asmussen which was written in the summer and autumn of 1932 in parallel with his work on the Altona Confession and was published in February 1933 with the title *Politics and Christianity*. It was not only a sign of Asmussen's independent theological work, but also an interpretation of the Altona Confession, which clearly brought out its main outlines.

Asmussen was convinced that the decisive error of the present and at the same time the reasons for the distresses in it lay in the fact that the state was no longer the state and the church no longer the church. For the state claimed to deal in salvation and redemption, and the church confused civil freedom and divine justice. It was because the church had not spoken the truth to the political parties, the truth 'that no party slogan has the least connection with the righteousness of God', that political life was so poisoned. For every party member thought himself in possession of a portion of righteousness which he denied to the other. No one was any longer in danger 'of being seized with amazement at the fact that, in spite of all his manifest unrighteousness, God still lets him live'. On the contrary, he wishes, rather, 'to become a little saviour, who at any rate does his bit in reducing injustice on earth'.[74] But the injustice did not decrease by means of visionary utopias; rather, it increased to that degree in confusion, perplexity and calamity, as anyone could see at present.

The inference was clear, but not without problems: 'A beneficial relationship between state and church is thus possible only when it becomes clear that the healthy points of contact between the two lie in the sphere of the commandments and the law. If, however, a positive contact is sought within the sphere of salvation, then the state cannot avoid ceasing to be the state, and the church

186

ceasing to be the church.'[75] For that reason, the proclamation of the church must treat the state truly as the state. 'It will at no point hold out any prospect of salvation for this aeon. Rather, it will show human beings their duties in terms of the commandments, because it has an interest in human beings seeing themselves without illusions.'[76] Should a future government – even a possible Hitler government – wish to be Christian in this sense, it would be welcome. But if it were to use Christianity as 'a justifying ideology', as a 'bonus', or as 'a source of power', it was to be decisively rejected.[77]

In Asmussen's interpretation it became clear what the Barthian approach – in its Lutheran version, as expressed in the Altona Confession – could and could not achieve in the year 1933. What it could achieve was a fundamental criticism of National Socialist ideology and its claim to totality. Here could be seen, so to speak, the Archimedean point which lay outside the 'German hour of destiny', and indeed outside every historical hour, and was not involved in movement and change, even if everything else became involved in feverish movement and change. What this approach could not contribute was direct political criticism of the new order. For it derived its powers of persuasion specifically from the fact that the church had to speak as the church and not politically. Nevertheless, from the beginning the Altona confession was a political issue. Its significance could be read from the response which it found everywhere, and which was greater than that which any kind of official church declaration had ever received during the Weimar period.

Provost Sieveking read out the confession at an afternoon service on 11 January 1933, in the main church of Altona, which was packed to the doors. For the first time, too, the seat reserved for the Mayor of Altona, long since disused, was again occupied. There sat the Lord Mayor of Altona, Max Brauer; a few months later he was already in 'protective custody'; later he emigrated; and after the war for many years he was First Bürgomeister of Hamburg.[78] His presence was a sign that this word was being heard politically, even though, indeed precisely because, it was being spoken by the church.

In fact almost all the major German daily papers commented on the Altona Confession.[79] Typically, all the National Socialist papers rejected it outright. The *Hamburger Tageblatt* spoke for them: 'Anyone who is not for us is against us – or, as far as we are concerned, he is dead.' 'Twenty-one Altona pastors have not yet understood our time.' The Communists were also unanimously critical, objecting above all to the article on the limits of the human. According to the headlines of the *Hamburger Volkszeitung* that meant: 'The perpetuation of the misery of the masses, oppression and war... A more than heavy-handed attempt at deception by the church... Now more than ever: mass resignation!' On the other hand, many commentaries from the liberal and indeed from the Catholic side were surprisingly clear and in agreement. Perhaps Hans Beyer in the *Tägliche Rundschau* summarized the significance of the Altona Proclamation most evocatively: 'We see it first of all in the fact that the German will again begin to "listen" to the church because it really speaks to him and does not sing psalms over him. We then see it in a sharpening of the consciousness of political responsibility among the members of the community and in a proclamation of genuine political significance. We see it, however, above all in the fact that a genuine community can again emerge around this confession of faith.'[80]

The echo aroused in the church was also lively and frequently affirmative, and in part it led, above all in North Germany, to further confessions.[81] Thus on 28 January the church leadership and 213 pastors of the Mecklenburg church presented their own confession to their communities with the request: 'Hear the Word, come to terms with it, profess it in word and deed.'[82] On 14 February the church of Lübeck followed – albeit more cautiously.[83] In March the Committee of the Hanover Conference of Young Protestants declared itself 'solidly united with the proclamation of the people of Altona'.[84] Other individual declarations likewise referred to it.[85] Then, however, the discussion was broken off under the impact of the dispute in church politics which was beginning at that time.

The Altona Confession was always overshadowed by the famous Barmen Confession. Thus what the latter owes to the former has been overlooked. It was in no way an 'indistinct prelude',[86] but rather the church's first step in clarifying the fronts. The young Berlin university lecturer was right when, at the conclusion of his course of lectures in the winter semester of 1932-33, he came 'to speak of the Altona Confession with almost unqualified joy'.[87] Indeed, where would the Protestant church have gone had the confession not been made and heard in this way on the threshold of the Third Reich?

12

The German Christians
(1931-1933)

With the conclusion of the Lateran treaties, Hitler had a clear political plan for the Catholic Church. He was Catholic enough to understand the structure of Catholicism and to see the opportunities which the Vatican's concordat policy afforded him.[1] On the Protestant side, however, matters were much more difficult. Here there was no uniform pattern of church politics to relate to and no leader to negotiate with. In general the whole of Protestantism was foreign ground for Hitler. Only in the spring of 1933, therefore, did he outline his own political plan for the Protestant church. This was significantly just a copy of the Catholic concept.

So until 1933 the policy of the NSDAP on the Protestant church to a large extent lay in the hands of individual Party leaders. This explains the confusing image which the Party presented to anyone who wanted to get some idea of its policy on the church. In fact between 1930 and 1933 there were dozens of declarations and opinions worth noting which could have led to completely different assessments of the movement's intentions for the church.

In Thuringia, for example, where early in January 1930, at the express wish of Hitler, Dr Frick had taken over the Ministry of Education along with the Ministry of the Interior,[2] the cultural policies of the National Socialists appeared to indicate that the Party was strongly influenced by the 'German Church' movement and was striving for a non-denominational German Reich Church. At all events, Max Robert Gerstenhauer,[3] the Chairman of the 'German Christian Working Group of Greater Germany',[4] declared at the annual conference of the group (at Weimar in early March 1930) that the hope was 'to be able to achieve perhaps as much in the next six weeks as otherwise would have taken six years'.[5] This hope obviously rested on firm promises from Frick, and it was emphasized by the presence of the Education Minister and one of the most important men in the Munich party leadership, Judge Walter Buch. The specific issue was a revision of the religious curricula along German Christian lines, with recommendations for appropriate new school prayers. In fact, Frick entered into negotiations with the Thuringian school administration and with the teachers in April; however, his decree met with the unanimous opposition of the Thuringian church, with the exception of the small German Christian group. Ultimately, a complaint brought by the Reich Interior Minister to the Staatsgerichtshof against the school prayers led to a partial success: three of the five prayers proposed were declared unconstitutional. As a result, in July 1930 the Thuringian government withdrew the decree.[6]

Even more than Frick's school policy, a publication in February 1930 caused grounds for suspicion that the Party was in fact taking a radical course along the lines of völkisch religion, in spite of Dinter's expulsion. This was the National Socialist book which came second only to Hitler's *Mein Kampf* in terms of distribution: Alfred Rosenberg's *The Myth of the Twentieth Century*.[7] *The Myth* was simply a summary of the ideology of völkisch religion as it had developed in the 1920s – a mixture of Fichte, Gobineau, Lagarde, Chamberlain, Fritsch, Eckart and Dinter. It was a decidedly anti-Christian book, and it spite of its dubious reference to the German mysticism of Meister Eckart it was perceived as such by both churches. What Rosenberg advocated was no longer capable of reconciliation with Christian tradition in any respect. It was 'the religion of blood', 'a new faith: the myth of blood; the belief that with the blood one is also defending the very divinity of human nature. The belief, embodied in the clearest knowledge, that Nordic blood represents this sacred mystery which has overcome and replaced the old sacraments.'[8] While the line of this book was clear and unmistakable, it was difficult for contemporaries to establish its real significance for the Party. To be sure, Rosenberg was editor-in-chief of the central organ of the NSDAP, the *Völkische Beobachter*, and therefore ranked as a leading ideological figure. On the other hand he clearly emphasized in the Foreword that his ideas were 'throughout personal convictions, not points of the programme of the political movement to which I belong'. And, very much in line with Hitler's basic decision, he went on to say that the movement 'has its great and special task, and as an organization must avoid confrontations of a religious, church-political nature and indeed a commitment to a particular philosophy of art or a particular architectural style'. And perhaps it was not just tactics but a real reflection of Rosenberg's firm conviction of the forthcoming victory of his ideas that he assured the churches that his book was directed 'not at human beings who live and work happily and in solidarity within their communities of faith, but at all those who have inwardly withdrawn from these, and have not yet fought their way through to new ideological commitments.'[9]

These sentences could be assessed as transparent tactics. But they could also be read as a challenge to enter into a dialogue with Rosenberg over the future spiritual foundations of the movement. They were understood in this way almost without exception by those groups in the Protestant church which were supporters of National Socialism but opponents of Rosenberg. In this way the effect of *The Myth* was not that of a deterrent but rather almost that of a summons to fight in the NSDAP for a 'German Church' orientation and against a völkisch neo-pagan orientation.

A noteworthy correction indicating the theoretical neutrality of the Party was also made by the new edition of Gottfried Feder's official Party publication *The Programme of the NSDAP and its Ideological Foundations*. Whereas Point 24 of the fifth edition dated February 1929 had read: 'Certainly some day the German Volk, too, will find a form for its knowledge of God, its experience of God, such as its members of Nordic blood demand...', from now on subsequent editions ran: 'All questions, hopes and desires as to whether the German Volk will some day once and for all find a new form for this knowledge of God and its

190

experience of God do not belong here...'[10] And the new Introduction, which was supposed to remove various misunderstandings, contained the stilted assurance that nothing was further from the intentions of the NSDAP 'than to attack the Christian religion and its worthy servants'.[11]

Confronted with these confusing views, the German Evangelischer Kirchenausschuss understandably sought direct information about the Party's intentions. So on 4 March 1931 there was a conversation in the Reichstag between Oberkonsistorialrat Gustav Scholz of the Kirchenbundesamt and Franz Stöhr, an old völkisch supporter who had joined the NSDAP in 1927 and was now a National Socialist representative in the Reichstag. This was the first official contact between a representative of German Protestantism and the Party. To begin with, Stöhr emphasized that the 'character of a Christian party was fundamentally rejected': the movement and the Party were 'secular political institutions'. However, they were 'supported and led by Christian people who seriously intend to implement the ethical principles of Christianity in legislation, and to bring them to bear upon the life of the people'. Of the 107 members of the NSDAP parliamentary group in the Reichstag, about two-thirds were Protestants and a third Catholics. For the sake of its goal of 'creating a united German Volkstum,' Stöhr said, the Party laid aside confessional differences, But in its leadership it was clearly 'shaped by Protestantism', even if 'for certain reasons' the Catholic leaders had not left their church. Stöhr undoubtedly assessed the deep-seated mutual distrust of the confessions correctly when he gave assurances that there was 'no danger that the movement will be pulled into the Catholic stream or be caught up in the Catholic church'. On the contrary, the Party was fighting against the claims of the Catholic hierarchy. A battle against the church itself, however, was far from the Party's intentions, as Dinter's expulsion proved. Stöhr further declared that the Party would support the confessional schools. 'Against the individual human being in liberalism, against the collective human being in Marxism, against the human being dominated by the hierarchy in Catholicism', it fought for the independent human being who emerged from the community and was called to its service. Finally Stöhr declared 'that his remarks could be regarded as official Party statements...'

At that time, without a doubt, all this did not sound too bad to Protestant ears. Nevertheless the Kirchenbundesamt remained distrustful, and Scholz noted: 'Given the present significance of the NS Party and the many obscurities in the movement, a close watch must be kept to see whether the actions of the Party everywhere or in individual districts correspond to the principles laid down here'.[12]

However, this observation hardly produced any greater clarity. For the Party was putting forward only one point, namely its rejection in principle of all direct connections with the churches. All else was left to personal convictions, or even simply to the adroitness or clumsiness of each individual subordinate leader.

How broad was the spectrum of these convictions in the Party was shown by the much-noted and much-quoted speech of the Bavarian Landtag deputy Dr Buttmann, a man from the early days of the Party.[13] On 29 April 1931 he gave a detailed presentation in the Landtag of the 'Position of National Socialism in Respect to Religion and the Church'. This speech was printed in the *Völkischer Beobachter* of 1 May under the headline 'The "Positive Christianity" of the

NSDAP', and thus acquired a kind of semi-official character for the Reich as a whole.[14] Buttmann's intention was to defend the Party against the declarations of the Catholic bishops, especially against the Bavarian pastoral letter.[15] In this connection he emphasized two points. First, he declared that it was impossible that the cultural programme of the NSDAP should contain heresy, 'because we are no more concerned with the internal affairs of the Catholic church than with the internal affairs, the dogmas and the moral teaching of Protestantism'. Hitler, in connection with the Dinter affair, had made it unequivocally clear that this was a basic principle of the Party. 'There is nothing against which we are more on our guard,' Buttmann repeated once more towards the end of his speech, 'than the mixing of the spheres of church and politics, as our Party leader has explained.' This was one point. The other was an assurance that the Party in fact embraced the standpoint of a positive Christianity, and this positive Christianity in Article 24 'as a matter of course' meant Christianity 'as it exists today'. The restrictions in Article 24 were aimed only at new communities of faith which – in contrast to the provisions of Article 137 of the Reich constitution – the National Socialist state would not accept without examination. In no way was, for example, 'the official Catholic church' to be examined. 'For us as a party – the Führer has stated this often enough and that is the criterion for our actions – there is therefore no further search for a new world-view, for a new religion. Rather, positive Christianity is the foundation for us as a party.' At this point the protocol noted: 'Quite so! – for the National Socialists.' The *Völkischer Beobachter* clearly emphasized the central significance of this by printing it in bold type.

For Buttmann, these remarks were certainly not just tactics, but an expression of his firm conviction. His conduct after the seizure of power provided proof of this. From May 1933 ministerial director in the Reich Ministry of the Interior with responsibility for cultural and church matters, he defended the right of the churches to autonomy within the framework of established policy – though ultimately, of course, in vain. In 1933 and 1934 he became the most important point of contact for the Protestant and Catholic bishops. Over the spectrum of convictions among the leading National Socialists, Buttmann certainly represented the standpoint that was most favourably disposed to the church. It will emerge that in this respect he was by no means standing alone in the NSDAP. But regardless of where the individual stood, and what he had thought and hoped for, he had now gone over flesh and blood to the Party, and in principle the Party had to be politically neutral to the churches.

This theoretical principle posed hardly any problems over against the Catholic Church. However, the situation was different on the Protestant side. Parallel to the growth of the Party, Protestant pastors and congregational groups began to consider how they could collaborate in the Party as church groups. And conversely, the Party began to wonder how the Protestant church might be involved in the organization. Both movements led to contacts at different places and in different ways, and to an initial co-operation between Party and church.

The idea of including the pastors in the movement came from Hans Schemm. Schemm, a school teacher in Bayreuth, and after 1928 Gauleiter of Upper Franconia, was the embodiment of the faithful religious National Socialist. Deeply convinced that National Socialism and the Christian religion went together, in countless lectures, dedication speeches and ceremonial addresses he gave his listeners the feeling of participating not only in a political movement but also in a religious revival. For example, he declared: 'Our confession of God is a confession of a doctrine of totality. Anyone who strives for totality strives for the religious, because the ultimate totality always finds itself at the point of the ultimate supreme idea. Thus our doctrine is basically a doctrine of totality. To give ultimate significance to the totalities of race, resistance and personality there is added the supreme totalitarian slogan of our Volk: "Religion and God". God is the greatest totality and extends over all else... A Volk lives and grows through devotion to the Führer, proud profession of race, a will to resist, and a religious quality.'[16] It was precisely the triviality of such phrases which carried conviction, because they appeared to refer to secrets which made the individual transcend himself. Schemm's religious speeches not only met with enthusiastic approval in the Party; they also provoked a lively response in church circles.[17] Hence it was fully in line with his ideas about the nature of National Socialism that he sought also to incorporate the clergy into the National Socialist Teachers Association which he had founded in 1927 and which was officially approved in 1929. So Point 7 of the aims of this Teachers' Association was: 'To gather all German-minded clergy of both confessions in a working group within the NS Teachers' association under the great slogan: The education of our Volk on a Christian religious foundation...'[18]

In contrast to the remarkably successful Teachers Association, the 'Working Group of National Socialist Clergy' did not do very well. This was first because of the small number of Party members among the pastors: of approximately 18,000 Protestant pastors, as late as 1931 there may have been no more than 100 Party members.[19] A second reason for the failure was the Party's principle of neutrality which at root precluded a pastors' association as an independent Party organization. For every Party organization had, of course, to acknowledge Hitler's unconditional leadership; thus an independent NS Pastors' Association would in fact have meant interference in the church. The only possibility was to gather the pastors into a loose 'working group', which had little appeal. And against all tendencies towards independence, the most powerful man in the Party organization, Gregor Strasser, Reich Chief of Organization, clearly emphasized once again at a discussion among leaders in April 1931 that 'no National Socialist Pastors' Association would be allowed'.[20]

So only the beginnings of an organization were there: in Bavaria around Pastor Friedrich Klein in the community of Grafengehaig in Upper Franconia; in Hanover around Pastor Heinrich Meyer in Aurich; in Saxony around Pastor Wilibald Hase in Mochau near Döbeln. How harmless these enterprises were is clear from the way in which people were recruited by advertisements. For example Wilibald Hase advertised in the *Neues Sächsisches Kirchenblatt*: 'All colleagues in Saxony who are willing to join a working group of National Socialist pastors are requested to notify me by 1 April 1931...'[21] On 4 September 1931 the Prussian Kultusministerium informed the Protestant Oberkirchenrat that the Reich administration of the NSDAP had begun 'the formation of a "Working Group of National Socialist Pastors for the Districts of Pomerania and Brandenburg"'; it gave the names of three pastors who were supposed to be in charge and requested 'information on the matter'. The reference proved, however, to be inaccurate and the Oberkirchenrat replied that 'there would be no need for an official intervention against pastors... because of their acceptance of such an undertaking'.[22] This answer showed that the church administration thought the whole affair insignificant, and not without reason: the 'Working Group of National Socialist Pastors' never exercised any kind of tangible influence. It did, though, have some significance for Hans Schemm, who through the mediation of his friends in the Working Group was invited to numerous church events to speak on 'Christianity and National Socialism'.[23] And finally, it offered a few pastors the chance to work for the NSDAP at an early stage and thus to prepare for a later career.

The history of the Working Group indicated the difficulties which stood in the way of an organized connection between Party and church from the Party point of view. And in another way it also showed the various efforts being made on the church side to establish such a connection.

The most important of these early groups started up in Thuringia, through the initiative of two young pastors, Siegfried Leffler and Julius Leutheuser (at that time they were both twenty-eight). The two of them (who incidentally had married two sisters) had changed from the Bavarian to the Thuringian church, where they rightly expected more freedom for their convictions. In 1928 they obtained two neighbouring pastorates in the Wiera valley, not far from Altenburg. There they began, with great success, to establish a völkisch-Christian movement. Using the youth movement from which they came as a model, they practised 'the study of völkisch literature'; organized amateur theatre groups; and recruited members through youth evenings, 'men's discussion evenings' and 'German Volk evenings'.[24] What emerged here in the circle of pastors and teachers of the Wiera valley and to an increasing degree won over the communities was so to speak a model of the völkisch-Christian movement as it was dreamed of by many of its best young minds. There was no longer any distinction between church, cultural and political work, because everything was done in the same spirit and served the same goal: the Christian-völkisch renewal of the German nation. So it was only logical that in February 1930 the two pastors should found the first NSDAP local group in the Wiera valley. Their circle made a substantial contribution to the building up of the party organization in the Altenburg district and shaped its activities. Conversely, the Party organization helped them to promote their völkisch-Christian ideas, which immediately had an effect far beyond the Wiera valley. When elections were held of representatives of the Altenburg communities in November 1931, the circle around the two pastors made its debut as a church-political group under the name which later became so famous: 'German Christians'. Five of the sixteen representatives elected came from its list of nominees, eight from a church list, and three were Religious Socialists. This was primarily a local matter, but it was symbolic, as was demonstrated a year later, in January 1933, when with barely 31% of the votes the German Christians won at least sixteen out of the fifty-one seats in the elections for the Landeskirchentag – the Thuringian synod.[25]

The 'Thuringian movement' within the German Christian movement emerged from the circle around Leffler and Leutheuser. This movement kept its independence even during the period of Berlin leadership in 1933-1934, and after the collapse of German Christian hopes it proved to be the only movement with

194

enough substance to continue an independent existence, indeed even to be able to continue to grow.

To understand this development it is necessarily to take the religious enthusiasm of the Thuringians seriously. Of all the German Christian movements they made the fewest compromises; they appeared to be personally the least opportunistic; and they represented the political theology of the period most resolutely. What the academic proponents of political theology always put forward with qualifications, out of respect for theological tradition, and what their church representatives expressed only with hesitation because of the church-political situation, the Thuringians articulated openly and directly: 'The fact of the matter is that in the pitch-dark night of Christian church history Hitler became, as it were, the wonderful transparency, the window of our age, through which light fell upon the history of Christianity. Through him we were able to see the saviour in the history of the Germans.'[26] In these 1935 statements of Leffler, the political theology of the Thuringians becomes very clear. What distinguished them from the other German Christian movements was above all the consistency with which they elevated this approach to being the only correct and essential epistemological principle for the Christian faith. Leffler himself explicitly called the political events of the period the 'starting point' for Christianity: 'The essential element in the starting point of the German Christians is that God is met in the demand for a practical faith in Germany, giving himself in daily devotion since 1918 to the National Socialist battle for his Volk, and has not abandoned them again... Anyone who passes by this experience heedlessly and without respect, anyone who claims that it could have happened just as well in some other way, will never have any grasp of German Christianity, will never find his way to it.' For Leffler it was a 'delusion' to suppose that one could 'understand everything by means of an acquired knowledge of God'. 'The deepest basis of existence, the background to all that happens, is often contrary to the understanding and incomprehensible to it. At this point one makes progress only with a heart full of awe and faith.'[27]

What fascinated contemporaries in this approach was the apparent recovery of the unity of thinking and doing, of faith and action, of church and politics. German Christianity no longer existed apart from the Volk and its history; the German church was no longer just a 'sect', and the 'tendency to turn away from the world, nature and life'[28] disappeared, because Christian community and political movement had the same goal: faith in the mission of Germany. Leffler did not shy away from calling Germany the 'anti-Volk to the Jews', chosen to 'tear the veil of darkness from the cross and to demonstrate to the world the truly redeeming service to which hitherto no people on earth has found its way'.[29] The Thuringian group, its theology and its significance for church politics, will be discussed in more detail later. It was the first of those spontaneous church movements which provided a direct connection between church and Party, and which owed their emergence to the religious enthusiasm of pastors and communities, not to any political calculation by the Party.

After 1930 the air was evidently full of the idea of being active along these lines, of linking National Socialist pastors and members of the communities together in order to win the church over to the idea of the Third Reich. However, whether anything came of it, and what, still depended entirely on the chance initiative of individuals. In Nassau, for example, it was Gustav Lehr, a superintendent and pastor from Gladenbach in Kreis Biedenkopf, who started things moving with an eye on the imminent church elections in March 1931. In a short time he organized a new church party which appeared in all four electoral districts and in competition with the unified list of the other groups in the church under the name 'Christian-National Confessors Alliance'. This new list of candidates, advertised everywhere before the election as a National Socialist list, secured fourteen of the sixty seats in the synod and thus scored a considerable success. However, this activity, which in comparison to that in Thuringia was from the very beginning associated with church politics, was at the same time an occasion for Munich to disown it. The NSDAP Kreisleiter in Wiesbaden had spread the word in the Party newspaper that every member of the Party was to vote for the Lehr list. This would have meant that very step by the Party into domestic church controversies which Hitler so feared. Once Lehr's opponents pointed this out, the Reich administration of the Party promptly notified 'the Nassau Gauleitung as clearly as can be... that it does not want any intervention in the sphere of church politics'. Thereupon the Party in fact largely withdrew from the election campaign, though its local organizations had at first given vigorous support to the Confessors Alliance, a fact that the church press acknowledged with general satisfaction.[30]

It was certainly no accident that the first National Socialist church parties emerged in Landeskirchen which were considered Religious Socialist strongholds. At all events that was true of Thuringia and also of Baden. Here the process of politicizing the churches had already begun, and the Protestant National Socialists had only to continue it. In fact the right now proceeded in exactly the way that Erwin Eckert had prescribed for the left as early as 1926. 'In order to achieve their tasks,' Eckert had written at the time, 'the Religious Socialists must seize power in the Christian churches. They will conquer the Evangelical Protestant Church through the general, direct and secret voting right of all members of the church who are entitled to vote.'[31] It was bitterly ironical that it should have been in Eckert's Landeskirche, of all places, that the National Socialists first came close to the goal on which the Mannheim pastor and his friends had foundered: the conquest of the church via elections.

The consolidation of the Protestant Nationalist Socialists in Baden followed early in 1932, possibly not without the assistance of the Gauleiter of Baden, Robert Wagner. In the elections to the Land synod on 10 July 1932 they appeared under the name 'Church Association for Positive Christianity and German Volkstum' – a clever reference to the 'positive Christianity' of the NSDAP which in this connection sounded far more 'positive' than was ever intended. The election brought the National Socialists fourteen seats, the Religious Socialists nine, the Liberals twelve and the 'Church-Positive Association', the real coalition party in the Landeskirche, twenty-nine.[32] Through adroit politics, at the first session of the new synod in October 1932 the National Socialists succeeded in forming a coalition with the Church-Positive Association and having just managed to achieve a two-thirds majority of forty-two votes, excluded the Liberals and Religious Socialists from the church government.[33] The whole process, which understandably caused furious indignation among the people directly involved, cast a revealing light on conditions in the church at the end of the Weimar period. The alliance between the majority in the Landeskirche and the National Socialists was just as remarkable as the fact that in the politicized churches the majority now exercised its power so ruthlessly. Until then it had been taken for granted that all groups in the church should be granted a share in the church government. Now only the one who controlled the majority ruled. The rather disreputable role of the Baden church administration in the years ahead was here prefigured quite clearly.

However, none of these events was enough to disturb and upset German Protestantism as a whole. The National Socialist Pastors Association, with its minute membership of less than one per cent of all active pastors, was in fact hardly cause for anxiety. And the proceedings in Thuringia, Nassau and Baden could be attributed with a measure of justice to the special circumstances in those Landeskirchen, which for a long time had been strongly polarized in political terms by the Religious Socialists, quite apart from the fact that in any case no one paid much attention to the problems of the smaller Landeskirchen.

The decisions of German Protestantism were made, like the decisions of the Reich, in Prussia. Here the years 1931 and 1932 brought fundamental and, as soon was to become apparent, momentous changes for all Protestant Germany. The initiator and focus of these changes was the Gauleiter of Brandenburg, the chairman of the National Socialist group in the Prussian Landtag, Wilhelm Kube.

Kube, born in Glogau in 1887, came from the völkisch movement. He had studied some theology as well as history and political science. He was a member of the Christian völkisch 'German Students Association' (Verein Deutscher Studenten = VDS). In 1920 he became the General Secretary of the Berlin Land association of the new German National Volkspartei. In 1923 he joined the 'National Socialist Freedom Movement' and after various detours in 1928 reached the top of both the NS parliamentary group in the Prussian Landtag and the newly created NSDAP Gau of the 'Ostmark', which at that time had a total of sixty-six party members. The conquest of this district in the next five years brought Kube Hitler's enduring gratitude.[34] During this period – probably early in the 1920s – Kube also took part in church affairs. He was a member of the community council of the Gethsemane community in Berlin N 58, and of the synod of the Diocese of Berlin City III.[35] Thus in contrast to most of the other National Socialist leaders, he had a direct knowledge of the Protestant church and its administrative bodies, and was able to appreciate the possibilities that they offered. So it was obvious that he should not only deal with church questions within the parliamentary group but also keep an eye on church developments in Prussia generally on behalf of the Party.

The church-political line that Kube represented became clear when on 1 July 1929 he made a speech on the Prussian concordat in the Prussian Landtag on behalf of his party. Beginning from the völkisch conviction of the unity of Christianity and nationality, he rejected the concordat on the grounds 'that the question of Christian education or the organization of church life is in the final analysis a question of legislation by the state. In accordance with these views, we are unable in any circumstances to accept an equation of the two parties, state and church.' No state, he declared, should tolerate 'any powers whatever, whether in religious or in free ideological associations, becoming so effective as to approach the authority of the state'. This was no contradiction to the 'positive Christianity' of the Party. On the contrary, 'precisely because we affirm it, because we are convinced that Christianity and Germanhood have come together in so infinitely many respects that they cannot be separated... we have confidence in this German state, that its politics are not opposed to Christian interests and Christian sensibilities, but rather that it will look after these interests in all circumstances'.[36] Two years later, on 13 June 1931, when the treaty with the Protestant churches was under discussion, he once again explicitly confirmed this decision. The relationship between state and church was not, he said, a treaty relationship; it would 'be legislated for in the victorious National Socialist state – indeed within the foreseeable future'. It was a 'matter for the state and indeed for the National Socialist state' to order this relationship 'on the principles of Germanhood and Christianity'.[37] Only later did Kube notice that Hitler had revised this conviction, following the Lateran treaties, in favour of the concordat principle.

Kube was no doubt firmly convinced that in adopting this position he could represent the true interests of German Protestantism. Nor did this conviction come out of thin air, in that as late as the end of 1925 a section of the members of the Prussian Synod had actually rejected categorically any concordat resolution 'because it was incompatible with the idea of the sovereignty of the state'. Instead, they expected 'that in the future the state would regulate the state-church relationship by law'.[38] The organized National-Protestant wing in the Evangelischer Bund was particularly resolute in defending this thesis.[39] However, the Prussian church administration had revised its position in the course of the concordat negotiations and had now decided to support the conclusion of a suitable treaty between Prussia and the Protestant Landeskirchen. At first, of course, this was simply a matter of equal treatment; increasingly, however, insight developed into the expediency of contractual arrangements between church and state.[40] When the final treaty was at last laid before the church senate in 1931, it was 'described as a great step forward towards the independence of the church and also state-church relationships'.[41] On the whole this was a result of the changes in the consciousness of the Landeskirchen which had taken place between 1920 and 1930.[42]

For Kube, however, the consent of the Prussian administration to this treaty must have looked like sheer treason. He saw the leading representatives of Prussian Protestantism making common cause with the hated Weimar parties – that is, with the Volk conservatives and the Christian Socialists, whereas it was his conviction that 'the position, dignity and self-respect of the Protestant churches' should prevent them from 'placing themselves under the influence of Marxist-infiltrated governments'.[43] Hence early in 1931 he made the decision to take the Protestant church in Prussia in hand politically. An opportunity for this was offered in the Prussian church elections which lay ahead, in autumn 1932. This decision was the real hour of the birth of the German Christians, who within a short period were to put the Protestant church in a completely new situation.

However, to begin with the way towards the conquest of the church proved difficult and complex. For all attempts to found a National Socialist church party were opposed by Hitler's fundamental decision that the Party might in no circumstances be drawn into church questions. Some expedient had therefore to be sought, and in fact the whole of 1931 was marked by different attempts to conquer the church without proving too much of a burden on the Party. Finally, however, the foundation of a special group proved to be the only promising way.

In January 1931 Kube suggested for the first time to Gregor Strasser, Chief of the Reich Party organization, that they should 'nominate our own lists of National Socialist candidates' for the imminent church elections in Prussia 'in order to gain control of the church'.[44] Whether Kube then discussed this plan with Hitler, as Strasser suggested, cannot be established with any certainty. Clearly, however, known difficulties caused the Party leadership to delay in giving its consent to a direct Party intervention in the church elections. Kube therefore first sought to realize his plans with the help of a new church-political group which had formed in Berlin in 1930: the 'Christian German Movement'.

The 'Christian German Movement' had been founded in 1930 by Werner Wilm, youth pastor for the province of Brandenburg, 'in connection with groups from the patriotic associations, the Stahlhelm and the German nationalists'.[45] The point of all this was a concentration of the right-wing forces in the Protestant church, with the aim of supporting the well-known cultural, ecclesiastical and political demands of national Protestantism. To begin with, National Socialists had not taken part. Among the prominent members of the movement were the former imperial court preacher Bruno Doehring, at that time a pastor at Berlin Cathedral and Professor of Practical Theology, a muddled nationalist, but hardly a follower of Hitler, and Ewald von Kleist-Schmenzin, who had an estate in Pomerania and was a member of its synod, a German nationalist who at least after 1932 was an uncompromising opponent of the National Socialists.[46] At one time or another a series of German nationalist professors also joined, among them Paul Althaus, Emanuel Hirsch and Heinrich Bornkamm. It is hard to establish precisely what other characteristics the group had in 1930, whether it did anything, and if so what. On the other hand, it is certain that the September 1930 election also upset this movement. For the question of its relationship to National Socialism now arose. Wilm himself was determined to bring the Party and the German Christian movement together. The man through whom he attempted to achieve this was Friedrich Wieneke, cathedral pastor in the little Brandenburg country town of Soldin. He had been there since 1929, was leader of the National Socialist group on the town council, and one of the first clergymen in Prussia to join the Party. Wieneke was a genuine National Socialist who argued for its racial doctrine with conviction. The reason why he nevertheless seemed harmless in comparison with his later very robust German-Christian friends was because of his utter political and theological naivety.

So at the end of 1930 Wilm invited Wieneke to speak, under the auspices of the Christian German Movement, on 'Christianity and National Socialism', a subject on which the Soldin pastor had already expressed his opinion several times in Kube's party newspaper, *Der Märkische Adler*, and also in the *Pfarrer-blatt*.[47] The meeting took place, and it was typical of the Christian Germans that two Prussian princes, August Wilhelm and Eitel Friedrich, were involved in the event. Later there was even a conversation with the Crown Prince.[48] The contacts were so satisfactory that in December 1930 Wieneke could recommend in the *Deutsches Pfarrerblatt*, in connection with the 'active desire for an association of pastors with nationalist views', a 'purely church-political group' 'which takes our interests seriously: the Christian-German Movement (which includes a Pastors Group), 2a Duisberger Strasse, Berlin-Wilmersdorf'.[49] Wieneke's book *Christianity and National Socialism* also appeared in the publication series of this movement.

It is unclear precisely how the relationship between German nationalists and National Socialists in the Christian German Movement developed during 1931. However, the formation of the 'Harzburg Front', that great and apparently united front of everyone on the right,[50] on 11 October appears at first to have strengthened Kube in his plans. At all events, late in September 1931 he negotiated with representatives of the 'Christian German Movement' and promised that the NSDAP would support only this group in the next church elections.[51] Soon afterwards he informed Strasser of his plans. 'The Protestant church,' he declared, 'is at present in the hands of our enemies. The consistories consist of unprincipled money-makers who bend over backwards for the present system. The leadership of the Protestant church now offers the opportunity to bring this extraordinarily important instrument under our control through participation in the church elections.' Kube was very much in line with general developments in going on to say that the Party would 'not, of course, put forward lists of National Socialist candidates for the church elections'. A preparatory discussion had taken place among Protestant circles in the Stahlhelm, National Socialists and German nationalists who wished to appear together in the elections as a 'Christian-German Movement'. And finally he asked that 'You, as Chief of Organization, should make a decision now on the form in which the Party can encourage this extraordinarily important work – not officially, but discreetly in the background.'[52]

However, Kube did not succeed in translating this plan into action. For now opposition arose from two sides. First, the 'Alliance for a German Church' complained to the Reich administration in Munich about the one-sided 'church-political commitment of the Protestant members of the NSDAP to a party which,' as the letter actually said, 'quite deliberately takes its stand on Old Testament, i.e. Jewish-völkisch ground'.[53] However, the political hesitations were more important. For while Hitler was not very concerned to have an alliance with the German nationalists in the political sphere, the Party did not want to relinquish its claim to exclusive and total power in the church as well. Consequently, when the representatives 'of all leading patriotic associations' met in Berlin to give the final form to a resolution on a church-political programme, the attempt foundered on the opposition of the Gauleiter of Berlin. This programme, Wieneke reported of the conference, was an attempt to declare 'for a German Volkskirche, which would also go along with demands of a völkisch kind'. One representative after another had given his assent. 'The statement by Dr Goebbels was awaited with suspense. For all the skill in the way in which it was formulated, it was a tangible disappointment to those present.' In fact the Gauleiter of Berlin carefully but firmly rejected any co-operation by the NSDAP with the patriotic associations in the Protestant church. Thus the 'Harzburg Front' of German Protestantism had failed even before it had been properly founded.[54]

From the Party standpoint, this decision was no doubt correct, as the further development of the 'Christian German Movement' proved. For about this time the Bishop of Mecklenburg, Heinrich Rendtorff, took over as its leader, and it was probably already with his co-operation that eight guidelines were established which could hardly have been to the liking of the National Socialists.[55] These guidelines certainly contained fervent declarations in favour of the German freedom movement, but they also included the statement 'that the cross of Christ is the deepest, indeed the only, interpretation of our destiny'. In accordance with Rendtorff's conviction, they associated the future of the German freedom movement with their obedience to God and declared: 'If the German Volk refuses this obedience, then it will stand under the judgment of God and be rejected.' The task of the church, they said, was to proclaim this to the German Volk, and therefore the church should 'just be the "church", free from party-political and economic ties, bearing witness to the reality and will of its Lord in word and deed – but this is what it should be with and for the German Volk.'[56]

While the distance between the 'Christian German Movement' and the NSDAP in the north and east plainly increased during 1932, its South German branch underwent the opposite development. Founded in September 1931 by Otto Lohss, Volk missionary in Stuttgart, it had at first explicitly left open the choice between the major freedom parties, the 'German National People's Party and the National Socialist German Workers Party (NSDAP) [and] the associated German Agricultural Workers Union'.[57] In autumn 1932, however, it increasingly came round to the National Socialist line. Since Lohss was convinced that the struggle was between National Socialism and Bolshevism, support for the German Nationals was no longer possible. Given this alternative, unconditional solidarity with Hitler was called for.[58] Consequently the South German branch of the 'Christian German Movement' was incorporated into the 'German Christians' in spring 1933.

By contrast, further developments in Prussia now took a completely different turn. Kube realized that he had to act independently, and his hatred of the Prussian church administration encouraged him to attempt a great coup. At the end of October 1931, he therefore rejected the complaints of the Deutschkirche in a further letter to Strasser, and declared that the matter was 'a purely internal concern of the Protestant church' in which the Party could in no circumstances intervene. Kube's interests lay in quite a different direction. 'We want to gain control of the Protestant church,' he declared with remarkable frankness, 'because the present administration of the church has concluded an unprecedented church treaty with the Marxist Prussian state and because the consistories and general superintendents are already beginning to persecute National Socialist pastors. Here only a great movement emerging from the church itself, with no party-political ties, can serve our purposes.'[59]

In the meantime a decree of the Prussian Oberkirchenrat goaded on Kube's hatred still further. While in this decree the church administration did not directly forbid closed uniformed political organizations to attend church with their banners, something over which there was controversy, it did warn against the dangers attached to this, and recommended pastors and local church councils to exercise the utmost caution and restraint in the matter.[60] Kube considered this statement to be a direct attack on the Party. He launched a vigorous polemical attack and replied to a request by the *Evangelische Pressedienst* that he at least cite the decree correctly in the arrogant tone that was typical of him: 'You need not have appealed to my loyalty, for I am accustomed to write only about things that I have studied thoroughly, and in this area I need no advice, least of all from the Christian Socialist and Volks-conservative quarters of the Protestant church, who have concluded the church treaty with the Marxists and the Centre Party in Prussia.' The letter ended with the comment that Kube was well aware of the possibilities in the Protestant church and would make use of them.[61]

On 9 December the Gauleiter of Brandenburg approached Munich for the last time over the whole affair. His plans had now taken shape. He asked the Reich Chief of Organization also to approve for Prussia, on the pattern of Thuringia, the preparation of the National Socialists' own lists of candidates for the church elections. These were to carry the name 'Evangelical National Socialists'.[62] On 17 December final approval came from Munich. Strasser wrote: 'I confirm receipt of your letter of 9 December and agree with you that at all events we must attempt to intervene in the Protestant church elections proportionately to the size and strength of the Party.' All essential matters relating to organization had now also been cleared up. 'I have no objections to the designation of the candidates as "Evangelical National Socialists". In order on the one hand to inform the other districts of this and on the other to keep the Party activity here as much in the background as possible, I would suggest that as leader of the Prussian group you inform the other leaders after consultation with me to recommend the procedure discussed above.' Finally, Strasser further recommended enclosing 'with this message to the people an instruction worked out by your own church consultant', telling Party districts 'to carry on further correspondence in this matter with their church consultants. In my opinion this is the way to get what we want without highlighting the Party apparatus to any great degree. Besides, we can always point out that the election work as such, like the preparation of lists of candidates and the name used by them, has arisen spontaneously from the members and that the Reich administration has merely acquiesced passively in this spontaneous expression of concern.'[63]

Thus the way was clear, and Kube began to take action. First he mobilized the public. Early in January 1932 a sensational article by the Gauleiter appeared in the *Völkischer Beobachter* which summoned the National Socialists to conquer the church. In support of his position Kube marshalled all his favourite themes: 'The provocative statements by the well-known Brandenburg General Superintendent Dr Vits against Adolf Hitler... the Prussian concordat... the unprecedented decree of the Protestant Oberkirchenrat against corporate church attendance by nationalist groups...' All this showed 'with frightening clarity', 'how little the situation of our Volk is known and appreciated by the highest-paid officials of the Protestant Landeskirchen'. Together with the – and here came the key words – 'Evangelical National Socialists' one had to see that things could not go on like this. And after this had once again been documented in detail, the decisive passages followed: 'It is time for the Protestant Volk in Germany to devote more attention to its church. The church should not remain a sinecure of the Christian-Social and Volks-conservative general superintendents. We need a Protestant Reich Church covering all Germany, a church which finally puts an end to the fragmentation into a dozen and a half Landeskirchen.' Then the church-political plan was presented quite openly: 'The United Church of the Old Prussian provinces has a self-government of sorts, and here the lever must be applied. In 1932 the elections will take place to the local bodies from which the synods, etc., will later be elected, and which control the election of pastors. Every Protestant Christian is eligible to vote... He only needs to register in the list of church voters in his local church in plenty of time.' The article ended with a stirring appeal: 'National Socialists! Do not let the doors of your church be slammed in your faces!... Take your church and fill it with the living Christian spirit of the awakened German nation! Register now in the voters lists in city and country by the hundred thousands and millions...'[64]

The remarkable thing about this article was that it not only called openly for the political conquest of the Prussian church but at the same time showed that more was at stake than the Old Prussian provinces, namely the entire Reich. Here for the first time, propaganda was made for the only plausible electoral goal which the German Christians were later to offer: the termination of the so-called fragmentation of the church and the establishment of a Reich church. What fundamentally distinguished Kube's initiative from the proceedings in Thuringia, Nassau and Baden was his political approach and the decision now to tackle things on a large scale, starting from Prussia, to create a church organization of National Socialists throughout the Reich, far beyond local and regional level.

After the mobilization of the public, Kube's next step was to brief the Prussian Gauleiter. Here he followed precisely the suggestions that Strasser had made in his letter of 17 December. Together with Pastor Karl Eckert, whom he had named as his church consultant as early as 1931,[65] and who as a result of the Prussian Landtag elections in April 1932 entered the Landtag for the National Socialists, he designed a programme of action which brought together all the points discussed with Strasser and at the same time contained the main features of the later guidelines. After it had been circulated in Silesia in February 1932, 'to all sub-divisions of the NSDAP in the district of Silesia', this programme of action became known as 'Church-political Special Circular no.1'. These internal instructions reached the Evangelischer Oberkirchenrat through various channels, and also came into the possession of the Berlin *Tägliche Rundschau*, which published them verbatim on 25 February.[66]

The circular began: 'In the year 1932 the church elections for the Evangelical Landeskirche of the Old Prussian Union will be held. They are of the utmost importance for the coming Third Reich. The Reich administration has permitted the preparation of a list of candidates to be known as "Evangelical National Socialists". The election campaign should be carried on under the direction of special consultants for church questions, hand in hand with the local Party administrations.' After a short paragraph on matters of organization, seven points followed, listing the most important principles of the new church party. They were understood to be an interpretation of 'positive Christianity', and in detail ran: '1. Rejection of the liberal spirit of the Jewish-Marxist Enlightenment. 2. Overcoming the kind of humanity born of the Jewish-Marxist spirit... 3. Emphasis on a fighting faith... 4. Purification and preservation of the race... 5. Struggle against atheistic and subversive Marxism and its Christian Socialist fellow-travellers of all hues... 6. A new spirit in our official and private posts in the church administration' – and here followed the well known Kube points of attack; '7. Purging of the small Protestant Landeskirchen so that they become a strong Protestant Reichskirche...' The paragraph closed with the instruction: 'Accusations that we want to politicize the church are to be denied. We are not acting as a political party. Rather, as Protestant Christians we are following a call for faith from God which we hear in our Volk movement.' And taking up a phrase from Strasser's letter word for word, it said that the Protestant National Socialists had a legitimate claim to be noted in the church 'in proportion to the size and inner strength of National Socialism'. Finally, the last paragraph of the circular gave instructions on how it was to be implemented. These instructions transferred to the leaders of the local groups responsibility for the registration of church voters in the list and made it the duty of each Party member to take part in the church elections. 'At this point the idea is to work inconspicuously, independently and quickly.'

After the mobilization of the public and the instructions to the Party organization, Kube's third step was to rally and enthuse the National Socialist pastors who were to build up the new church party in the church itself. For as the project had been designed, it stood or fell with the willingness of the pastors to take on the mission of the Party. The group on which Kube decided to rely had only just formed itself in Berlin around a young, thirty-two year old pastor, who over the next eighteen months was to become one of the most important figures in German Protestantism: Joachim Hossenfelder.

Later the national leader of the German Christians, in origin and destiny he was a typical representative of his generation. Born in Cottbus the son of a teacher of commerce, he grew up in Hanau, Frankfurt-am-Main and Lübeck; he enlisted as a volunteer in 1917 and went to the front that same year. The curriculum vitae which Hossenfelder submitted to the consistory in 1922, at the age of twenty-three, when registering for his theological examination, revealed what this meant to him: 'Events at the front were the most overwhelming thing in my experience. The tremendous battles on the Somme and near Verdun showed me that rather than Germany, England and France being in the forefront of the fighting, it was God who was dealing directly with humanity in history, in the process of which he was summoning us to fight for home and conscience. The task which the war had granted us was to become warriors for God and fatherland. On my return from the field I matriculated in November 1918 at the University of Kiel... Because my family had lived as farm-owners in Lower Silesia since the seventeenth century, in the fifth semester I moved to Breslau... I interrupted my period of studies twice: in summer 1919 I went to the Frontier Guard East and in summer 1921 to the Frontier Guard in Upper Silesia. I am an active member of the Association of German Students, whose aim – to become a Volksgemeinschaft on a Christian and national basis – appeared to me to be a most noble task.'[67]

It is astonishing how clearly and naturally at twenty-three Hossenfelder already stated the decisive influences and ideas which precisely a decade later were to help to shape the German Christian movement: experience at the front, faith in God's action in history, God and fatherland, and the Christian and nationalist Volksgemeinschaft. His practical decision also fits the picture: twice in the Frontier Guard; work as a coal-trimmer in the gasworks at Kiel;[68] membership of the Völkisch Association of German Students, the very association to which Kube and Müller, later Reich Bishop, also belonged; and a first community in

Upper Silesia, close to the Polish border. Hossenfelder was not a remarkable man, but he had a set of qualities which fitted him for his new task. He had a good talent for organization, a considerable measure of ruthlessness, and in the decisive period one thing above all: an unshakable conviction that with Hitler the German Christians would be victorious.

Early in 1931, after two country communities in Silesia, the young Pastor Hossenfelder was given the post of chief pastor at Christuskirche in south-west Berlin. A party member since 1 April 1929, he immediately also sought to make political contacts in the national capital. By chance he got in touch with Wieneke, gave his first lecture in Soldin on 'Völkisch Renewal' and at the end of the year began to gather a 'round table of like-minded persons' in his Berlin apartment.[69] After the attempt with the Christian German movement had evidently failed, this circle decided to start an independent action group, and put an advertisement in the *Deutsches Pfarrerblatt*. It was published on 5 January 1932 and showed that the group's plans were still quite vague. 'National Socialist pastors, or pastors who sympathize with National Socialism, from Greater Berlin, the province of Brandenburg and the province of Saxony, and who are willing to join a working party or if necessary found a National Socialist Pastors Association, are requested to give their address to...' There followed the addresses of Hossenfelder, Wieneke and a Pastor Gensichen who had come to Halle straight from the Soldin group. According to Wieneke's report the advertisement attracted a large number of replies. Among the names he mentioned in this connection, almost all later played a more or less significant role among the German Christians.[70] This circle, about which Kube was informed by Wieneke and Eckert, offered the Gauleiter the élite troops for his new church party. So he called a conference of National Socialist pastors for 10-11 February 1932, to be held in the Bettermann tavern in Potsdamer Strasse, Berlin: the so-called 'Bettermann Meeting', at which questions about the organization and substance of participation in the church elections were to be discussed.[71]

Kube did not come to the meeting by himself. He brought with him not only his church consultant, Pastor Eckert, but a man who lived in Berlin, though he was a member of the Party administration in Munich, Ministerialrat Hanno Konopath. As became apparent, Konopath was supposed to take over the future direction of the new organization, since Kube was overburdened – not least because of the imminent Landtag elections. However, this plan proved to be a serious mistake.

Since December 1930 Konopath had been director of the race and culture division of the national Party administration.[72] In this capacity, according to the subsequent view of the Party court, he appeared 'to the public at large to be the very embodiment of the "Christian-German" view of the NSDAP and its moral viewpoint'.[73] It therefore seemed reasonable that he be entrusted with the task which Kube intended for him. To the horror of the pastors assembled at Bettermann's, however, it became apparent that Konopath in no way represented a German Christian line; rather, he was one of those loyal to the völkisch-German line, a school of thought that even the most radical of Kube's group could no longer consider Christian. In fact, up until the autumn of 1931 Konopath had even been leader of the 'Nordic Ring', which considered itself to be an organization fighting against Christianity.

The predicament into which Konopath had plunged the meeting was resolved, at Hossenfelder's suggestion, by appointing a 'clergy adjutant' to Konopath. Hossenfelder himself took up this position. A further surprise was the message to those assembled that the name 'Evangelical National Socialists' had to be changed, since Adolf Hitler wanted '...no occasion for confessional division within the Party'.[74] The new and final name was 'German Christians'.[75] In other respects the result of this inaugural meeting of the German Christians precisely matched the principles which Kube and Eckert had laid down for the Party.

A confidential report which reached the Protestant consistory of the Mark of Brandenburg makes clear the atmosphere and direction of this 'Bettermann Meeting'. According to the report, first the well-known accusations against the church administration were repeated, leading to the demand that the NSDAP must participate in the church elections, 'in order there to help the German character to come into its own'. The report went on: 'While the National Socialist pastors were divided over the form and extent of the participation, on Thursday the command was issued that the National Socialists were to nominate their own list of candidates under the name of German Christians, rejecting all coalitions with any parties or groups.'[76]

In spite of this clear course of events, however, by no means all those who took part seem to have been aware that this was a political matter, prearranged long before. At any rate, even after the war Wieneke could still say that there had been a danger 'that our inner concern could be discredited as a matter of political expediency' and give that as the reason for later adding the term 'Faith Movement'.[77]

After the meeting ended, Konopath and Hossenfelder set to work. Their prime task was to build an organization; to compose 'guidelines' based on the Kube-Eckert principles; and to establish connections with like groups in other Landeskirchen, especially also with the German Church.

Understandably, however, the relationship between Konopath and Hossenfelder seems to have been tense from the beginning. Presumably Kube, who after all knew the Protestant church, had also realized that nothing could be achieved with such a man. Finally, the considerably increased influence with the national Party administration which Kube enjoyed after the electoral victory in Prussia in April is also likely to have strengthened his hand. At all events, on 21 May 1932 he informed Konopath, on Strasser's orders, 'that further church work for the Protestant church elections in Prussia is to be performed by Pastor Hossenfelder... answering directly to Gregor Strasser'.[78] And two days later, in circular No.4, Hossenfelder also instructed the 'church consultants' that on that day executive work on the elections had been transferred exclusively to him.[79] Dated 27 May, the notice appeared in the official gazette of the national leadership.[80] This established the final form of the organization of the German Christians.

Like much that the Party undertook at this time, the form of this organization was improvised but practical. The basic point was that the German Christians were not integrated into the Party apparatus as a sub-division of the Party. Thus Hitler's neutrality rule was observed and there was an opportunity at all times to keep the Party at a distance from its supporters in the church. At the same time, however – and this was no less important – it opened up a broad area for the initiative of Hossenfelder and his collaborators. That within a year the German Christians rose to become the dominant party in the Protestant church was due almost solely to the vitality and the ideas of this first group, which knew how to exploit a favourable opportunity. Hossenfelder's direct subordination to Strasser, on the other hand, not only provided a necessary link but also gave him something of a leader's authority in relation to both the Party and the church bodies, without which he would certainly not have got his way so quickly and without challenge. The carefully balanced relationship between a connection with the Party and dissociation from it was also clearly expressed on Hossenfelder's official stationery. He used the official letterhead of the Reich administration with the imprint 'Reich Organization Leader' and beneath it 'Church Affairs: Pastor Hossenfelder'. Thus on the one hand he commanded the imposing weight of the national administration, while on the other hand it was clear that within it his role was only that of adviser on church affairs. The whole pattern corresponded very closely to the ideas which Strasser and Kube had put forward as early as autumn 1931 and which were then reflected in the February circular letter. And although there was never complete success in implementing this pattern at all levels of Party organization, it cannot be denied that it was extremely effective in the church and in political terms.

With the appointment of Hossenfelder, Konopath's role in the German Christians was exhausted. Soon afterwards the problematical Ministerialrat was deprived of his Party offices too. On 30 June, by the decision of the Party court, he was refused 'the right to hold any office in the Party... for a period of two years' on grounds of immorality.[81] With that he disappears completely from view.

On 6 June 1932 the German Christians made their first public appearance. Konopath and Hossenfelder, still working together, had called a general meeting in Berlin for that day. This meeting now gave the young and ambitious Berlin pastor the opportunity to make a solo appearance as the first leader of the new movement. And Hossenfelder made full use of his opportunity. Directly after Konopath's expulsion he had 'established' guidelines and had had them approved explicitly by Strasser.[82] In this way, he could now not only inform the meeting about the changes in the organization, but also disclose to them the new 'Guidelines for the List of German Christian Candidates' which were to hold for the whole movement in the future.

These 'Guidelines', which later became so famous, in fact amounted to a number of slogans that Hossenfelder had picked up and strung together. His most important models were the guidelines which Kube and Eckert had laid down. Additional sources of ideas were the Berlin Mission[83] and a series of current right-wing slogans from the church and politics. Some sentences had obviously been copied from the programme of the Baden National Socialists.

Point 1 already showed that the 'Guidelines' were more appeal than programme. It ran: 'These guidelines seek to show all faithful German people methods and goals by which they can achieve a reform of the church. These guidelines intend neither to become nor to replace a confession of faith, nor to undermine the confessional principles of the Protestant church. They are the confession of a way of life.'[84] Hossenfelder obviously cherished the hope of escaping all theological arguments with this formula. Consequently a later

'Memorandum for the Sections' also explicitly declared that discussions 'on dogmatic questions' were to be avoided at all costs.[85]

In fact the juxtaposition of 'confession of faith' and 'confession of a way of life' amounted to a theological oath of revelation. Only someone who had never understood the confession of faith could put things like that. On the other hand, this thesis could readily attract all those to whom ideas like 'faithful German people', 'new order' and 'life' in themselves sounded quite promising. In the German Christian commentaries on the guidelines, the 'confession of a way of life' was regularly interpreted as a confession of German Volkstum.[86] In this way they betrayed the influence of political theology, which sought to understand faith through the political 'confession of a way of life'. Certainly none of the major political theologians of the time would have put things in such a primitive way. But Wieneke was a kindred spirit when he wrote on Point 1 that the order of the church 'has to conform to the natural conditions established by God in his creation and still... identifiable even today, which we find in race and Volkstum. On the basis of this fundamental knowlege, we call for the struggle for a truly German church. Only truly German Christians belong in this fellowship. That includes every fellow member of the Volk with German blood... The baptized Jew does not belong to it...[87]

Point 2 of the guidelines not unskilfully put the merger of the twenty-nine Landeskirchen into one Evangelical Reich Church at the head of the list of demands that followed. For this appeared thoroughly plausible and sensible to many people, not just to the German Christians. In fact the Reich Church was the only really popular slogan with which the German Christians gained an audience outside the circle of their immediate followers.

While Point 3 rejected the central idea of a church-political party and called for 'a living Volkskirche', Point 4 represented a clear concession to the German Church tendencies in the Party: 'Our standpoint is one of positive Christianity. We declare ourselves for an affirmative faith in Christ, such as accords with the German spirit of Luther and heroic piety.' This was a markedly völkisch interpretation of the 'positive Christianity' of the Party programme, an interpretation which left the German Christian movement wide open on the right and finally was also to seal its fate.

The next two points repeated Kube's favourite themes almost word for word: 'We want to bring to bear in our church the reawakened German feeling for life and make our church vigorous. In the fateful struggle for German freedom and the future, the leadership of the church has proved to be too weak. So far the church has not called for resolute struggle against atheistic Marxism and the spiritually alien Centre Party. Rather, it has concluded a church treaty with the political parties which represent these forces. In the struggle which decides the very being or non-being of our Volk, we want our church to fight in the front line. It may not stand aside or even withdraw from the struggle for liberation' (Point 5).[88] 'We demand a correction of the political clause of the church treaty and a struggle against atheistic and subversive Marxism and its Christian Socialist fellow-travellers of all hues...' (Point 6).

In Point 7 the demand for maintaining purity of race was justified for foreign missions, while Point 8 on inner mission, though claiming to have some understanding 'of Christian duty and love towards the helpless', obviously considered the 'protection of the Volk from incompetents and inferiors' more important. Point 9 was crucial, because it very quickly led to specific actions. It rejected missionary work among the Jews in Germany 'as long as the Jews have the right of citizenship and therefore the danger of racial camouflage and racial mongrelization exists'. In particular – and here the German Christians virtually anticipated the Nuremberg laws – 'marriage between Germans and Jews is to be forbidden'. Finally, in the last point the 'spirit of Christian world-citizenship' was condemned and there was a proclamation of the overcoming of 'the pernicious spectres arising out of this spirit – such as pacifism, internationalism, freemasonry, etc. – by means of faith in our völkisch mission commanded by God'.

The 'guidelines' were doubtless more a völkisch appeal than a well-thought-out church-political – or even theological – programme. Nevertheless, they cannot be understood apart from the political theology of the time. In his major lecture at the Königsberg Kirchentag Althaus had declared that 'the churches must struggle to become, or to remain, a true Volkskirche'. And he had interpreted this ambiguous concept in the following way. 'A Volkskirche – that means, in the first place: serving the Volk as Volk, as a totality of life; then, serving it according to its nature, which again involves two things: a true German proclamation of the gospel and the entrance of the church into the organic life forms and living customs of the Volk.'[89] Even if with these programmatic formulations Althaus had had something other in mind than what the guidelines now strove for, it is obvious that the guidelines could certainly be understood to be the concrete fulfilment of these demands. Little though they may have reflected or wanted to reflect theologically, the German Christians of the early days were not so far distant from certain theological approaches which at that time were thoroughly approved of in German Protestantism. Inadequate and loaded with slogans as the guidelines indeed appeared, anyone who wanted to could easily think up a theology that justified and supported them. This is the only explanation of why the Prussian Oberkirchenrat raised no technical objections to the 'guidelines' and allowed them to be a church election platform.

Thirteen years later, in the summer of 1945, Hossenfelder, who, after a rapid rise and fall had meanwhile for some time been a pastor in Potsdam, again correctly attached great importance to this fact, as he indicated to the authorities. As he stated at that time in a memorandum addressed to Dibelius: 'The Faith Movement of German Christians was founded in summer 1932 as a church party. It was entered in the Register of Associations... Elected as Chairman, I submitted the guidelines... to Dr Burghart, at that time the clergy Vice-President. There were no objections. They were accepted.'[90] The question why the Prussian church administration did not protest against the 'guidelines' before 1933 has never been answered. The answer has been replaced since 1945 by a general and apparently natural indignation against the activity of the German Christians in destroying the church, in which the question of their theological origins, their method of argument and their goals has largely been lost.

In fact the damage done to the church at this time probably nowhere became more clear than in the discussions which took place in the spring and summer of 1932 in Prussia's church governing bodies on the German Christians, their principles and their goals.

When it was communicated to the Oberkirchenrat at the end of February, the 'Special Circular' had, of course, already triggered off vigorous reactions. A survey of all the consistories revealed that while no such letter was known in any other district, almost everyone had heard of intentions to this effect in the Party.[91] A discussion in Berlin on 10 March 1932 among all the general superintendents showed how this body thought and reacted, above all in terms of church politics. Kapler, who summed up what was said at the discussion, believed that he could identify a certain uniform line: 'Along with valuable elements to be acknowledged and retained, the movement (i.e the NSDAP) also causes strong misgivings, particularly from the church's standpoint. Our task is not to struggle against the movement as such, but rather on the one hand to purge this movement, which is still in turmoil, and further to form a defence against the possible wish of the National Socialists to gain control of our church. Only the gospel may be the foundation and guideline of the church...'[92]

The next few months made it clear that no one from the leading church bodies could or would embark on a theological confrontation with the German Christians. Rather, all the forces of the church administrations were directed towards safeguarding the church against the onslaught from the National Socialists. Therefore Prussia's leading clergyman, Vice-President Burghart (who has been mentioned above), asked the German Christians for a correction in only one point. The 'guidelines' of 6 June had been distributed along with a statement which combined acceptance of candidacy with the simultaneous pledge of the candidates 'in the votes and counting of ballots to follow the directions of the election committee of the "German Christians"'.[93] In a letter to Hossenfelder dated 6 August Burghart quite rightly expressed 'the gravest doubts' about this formula. Hossenfelder and Lörzer, in a discussion with Burghart on 18 August, thereupon gave him to understand that they would change the declaration of commitment. However, the last paragraph of the memorandum in which Burghart recorded the conversation was much more important, because it was characteristic of the whole situation: 'Finally, the debate once again turned, for a moment, to the "Ten Guidelines of the Faith Movement. I stressed once again, quite generally, that I had far-reaching doubts. Since, however, it was explained that nothing else could be changed in these guidelines, I emphasized that, as far as I was concerned, any further debate on them would be pointless.'[94]

Hossenfelder took his time even over changing the declaration of commitment. Only at a further discussion on 9 September did he declare in the presence of Burghart and another member of the Oberkirchenrat that the commitment to which objections had been made was 'finally' withdrawn, and that the signatures provided so far were of 'no value at all' to the election committee.[95] In Circular 10 he conveyed to his co-workers a new formula which removed the stumbling block – albeit only formally. It ran: 'I declare my membership of the Faith Movement of "German Christians", whose programme I know and under whose guidance I place myself. If I become a candidate I will exercise my office in accordance with Article 19, para.2 of the constitutional charter of the Evangelical Church of the Old Prussian Union.'[96]

In this way Hossenfelder had fulfilled the necessary conditions, And however strong the uneasiness over the German Christians and their election campaign was and largely continued to be in the church, officially the Oberkirchenrat stood by its neutrality in church politics, a stance which it assumed towards all church parties and therefore also towards the German Christians.

Once the new church-political movement launched its church election campaign on 6 June, Hossenfelder began on the organizational work. Here he had two problems to solve. Within a few months he had to create an electoral organization for the Old Prussian Church and at the same time set in motion a national organization that was to be represented in all Landeskirchen. At first he achieved only limited success in both matters.

The organization in Prussia involved nine church provinces – East Prussia, Berlin, Brandenburg, the Grenzmark, Pomerania, Silesia, Saxony, Westphalia and the Rhineland – with almost twenty million Protestant Christians. Not until 21 June could Hossenfelder inform his Gau consultants, in Circular Letter 7, of the exact date of the elections: 12, 13, 14 November. Between 21 June and the end of the period of registration in the church voters' lists on 18 September – this registration was necessary for anyone who wanted to vote – the German Christians had barely three months. If they wanted to accomplish anything at all in this short period, the only way open to them was reckless use of the Party apparatus. In fact Hossenfelder declared in the same circular that every 'section consultant' – i.e. the authorized Party representative responsible for church questions at the level of the local group – was 'to supply himself with a sufficient number of forms for written registration in the voters' list and to hand out to every Party member, no matter of what age, twenty forms with specific instructions to return these twenty forms filled out...'[97] However, this procedure apparently met with only modest success. For in a further circular on 31 July Hossenfelder entreated the Gau consultants to forego a holiday this year to secure the co-operation of the district administration, and to carry the canvassing for registration in the voters' list into even the 'smallest country community'. 'Through this canvassing,' Hossenfelder ordered, 'everyone is to be registered who can be registered.' The second task which had to be completed in August was the nomination of candidates. 'Where it is customary in a place to nominate women, we do not want to rule out this practice - but let it be at most in the ratio of 1:10.' Besides, not all candidates needed to be Party members. Especially in country communities an attempt should be made to gain 'the prominent members of the church' for the German Christian list.[98] By the beginning of September, however, a solid organization could hardly have been said to exist. Hossenfelder urgently requested the addresses of the district consultants and the payment to Berlin of the 'fighting contribution' which each candidate was supposed to pay.[99]

Another considerable difficulty for Hossenfelder was that the Gauleiters of individual districts reacted quite differently to Kube's plans. While some tended to disapprove of the whole undertaking, others developed their own projects which interfered considerably with the plans of the Berliners. This was especially true in East Prussia, where Gauleiter Erich Koch, formerly a member of the YMCA, took things in hand personally.[100] On 23 May 1932 an article by Koch appeared in the *Preussische Zeitung*, the 'incorruptible battle-cry for work and bread' of the East Prussian National Socialists, entitled 'Capture the Church'. Its aim was that of Kube, but it was considerably less polemical in its argumentation. Koch was convinced that the most important thing was for the liberal Protestantism of the past to be replaced 'by the völkisch-orientated Protestantism of the near future'. Under Koch's influence, the German Christians in East Prussia acquired their own guidelines, which only distantly resembled Hossenfelder's. They were characterized above all by a much stronger sense of the church. They concluded: 'We commit ourselves, and we demand this commitment not only from the elected representatives of the church, but above all from all Protestant men and women, to: service in our communities! We want to serve: through tireless recruitment to our worship; through chivalrous intervention for the poor and needy; through defence of our faith; ...through true Evangelical witness in public.'[101]

It is impossible to determine precisely to what degree Ludwig Müller, later to become Reich Bishop, but at that time a military chaplain in Königsberg and a close associate of Koch's, assisted in the formulation of these East Prussian guidelines. It is certain that they were attributed to him later and that they helped to create confidence in him within the church.[102]

At all events, at first the East Prussian German Christians went their own way and had only a very loose connection with Berlin.

In Berlin, the focus of the organizational work began to shift after the expiry of the registration period on 18 September. Until then all efforts had been directed towards registering as many Protestant National Socialists as possible in the list of candidates; now it was more urgent to canvass the membership and carry on propaganda. According to Circular 11 of 23 September, after 9 September[103] the new formulation of the pledge was: 'first of all, a declaration of membership of the Faith Movement of German Christians, and only secondarily a so-called affirmation by the candidates'. Care had to be taken 'that as many as possible sign this declaration and thereby join our Faith Movement'. In addition, the register of voters in all church communities was now out and had 'to be transcribed in its entirety, so that afterwards we can canvass every voter with leaflets'.[104] Both the terminology and the procedure showed that Hossenfelder now orientated himself entirely on his major model, the political movement. But that also caused problems. For the Party could not and would not in any circumstances tolerate competition, however modest.

At the same time the circular announced a decision on organization which was important for the Reich movement: the expansion of the Reich administration. As early as the end of July the thirty-nine-year-old Berlin pastor Fritz Lörzer had been named by Gregor Strasser as Hossenfelder's deputy.[105] Lörzer had flown in a fighter squadron during the War with his brother Bruno and with Hermann Goering. Then after his examinations he became a pastor in the Neumark. After 1928 he served in the Advent Community in north-east Berlin, a markedly working-class area in which he became especially active in social concerns. As a short biography put it: the 'man of action' had 'to show to these hate-filled and disinherited people a concern for justice, for humanity, in this life as well... In this way Fritz Lörzer comes quite personally... to Hitler. He sees in National Socialism a practical Christianity.'[106]

This direct social impulse was characteristic of a whole series of German Christian leaders in the early period. For them the concept of the community of the Volk was above all a social concept, the realization of social justice. Certainly it was no accident that the pastors from the working-class districts were the ones who joined the German Christians. This was also the context of a description which was later disputed so fiercely, that of the German Christians as the 'SA of Jesus Christ'. It originated in the *Soziale Botschaft*, where it had other overtones: 'The German Christians are the SA of Jesus Christ in the struggle to eliminate physical, social and spiritual distress.'[107]

Lörzer had thus become Deputy Reich Director in July. Now, in September, Hossenfelder announced the construction of a complete Reich administration composed of twelve departments. Almost all the departmental heads of this first Reich administration later took leading offices. The department of 'Theology and University' was given to Pastor Wieneke of Soldin; 'Religious Instruction and Schools' to the rector of a Berlin elementary school, Kurt Freitag; 'Propaganda and Training' had been taken over by Friedrich Kessel who, after three years of work in the mines, study, service on the front and a church community outside Germany had been pastor at the Nikolaikirche in Spandau from 1927; the press department was directed by Lörzer himself; social questions were the responsibility of the Berlin social pastor Karl Themel;[108] for youth questions Hossenfelder had recruited the pastor of the Eastern Association for Young Working Men, Friedrich Peter, another front-line soldier just forty years old, and like the others a member of the NSDAP.[109] The department of church law was supervised by the lawyer Friedrich Werner, the only one from this early period who held a central post in the German Evangelical Church right through to the end of the war in 1945; missionary matters were under Mission Inspector Weichert; 'Prayer Book and Hymn Books' under Superintendent Johannes Grell from the Neumark; personnel questions under Pastor Siegfried Nobiling; 'Education' under a certain Alfred Bierschwale, and twelfth and last 'National Questions' under the Königsberg chaplain Ludwig Müller, later to become Reich Bishop.

What held this circle of predominantly very young pastors together was not so much a common theology as a common destiny, which they understood in the same way, and a determined commitment to action. Friedrich Peter put this very well in recollecting his first conversation with Hossenfelder: 'The remarkable thing about that moment, indeed about all the times when we worked together, was the principle that the objective has overcome everything subjective. We never thought about whether or not we agreed theologically... The one thing that bound us together inseparably was the goal for which we strove. It gave us a powerful alliance for action.'[110] In that amazingly frenzied time this whole group actually felt itself – as Hossenfelder described it in retrospect with all the solemnity of the 1930s – to be 'a daring band, and perhaps a lost one too... They came without exception from the German Wandervogel, had almost all been front-line soldiers, wandering between two worlds. In their knapsacks they carried the Greek New Testament, Faust and perhaps even Horace.'[111]

The success of this group is almost impossible to understand unless one enters the minds of that generation – that 'daring band' mentality which Hitler could always conjure up, in which the ideology of struggle as the 'father of life'[112] was linked with contempt for bourgeois and Christian convention.

Hossenfelder's next step in the construction of the Reich movement was also of great importance. It was the founding of the German Christians' own Sunday newspaper, which appeared for the first time on 16 October 1932 under the title *Evangelium im Dritten Reich*. The first article was typical of the general trend of the paper. It was a meditation by Hossenfelder on John 10.12-14, the Good Shepherd pericope. It bore the title 'The Saviour and the Leader Idea', and attempted to interpret the mission of the Leader in terms of the figure of Jesus. The Good Shepherd – this was the basic idea – 'knows that he is bound to his flock by the will of God. To the hireling, that is incomprehensible.' The German Volk, however, 'yearns for a Leader who is a shepherd and not a hireling. The hireling will always be hired out to a class or a party. The shepherd, however, is bound most intimately to his Volk. Leader and Volk trust one another because they know that God's call has bound them together.' *Evangelium im Dritten Reich*, which through strenuous promotion soon achieved a fairly high circulation, became the most important propaganda instrument of the German Christians and was frequently their only common basis of information.

There is a kind of enthusiastic commitment to action which is beyond the reach of criticism. During the decisive years this was true of broad sections of the National Socialist Party leadership, but it was also true in 1932 and 1933 of the German Christians. The church election campaign conducted by the new Reich administration met some vigorous opposition from the public. But the leadership group remained completely unaffected by this opposition. On the contrary, it took the struggle to be confirmation of the soundness of the path which it had taken.

One of the first to criticize the 'guidelines' was Hermann Sasse in the *Kirchliches Jahrbuch*. He raised a vast number of questions about the publication of them – questions about confession, church discipline, relations with political parties – all questions which the guidelines left unanswered. Finally, however, he expressed the fear that the authors of the guidelines would not give any reply. 'They have not thought about any of these things, because they are obviously not accustomed to thinking in depth. They do not take Article 24 seriously, any more than they take the confessions seriously. "Feeling is everything"; concepts are sound and fury.' However, Sasse did not want to limit his accusation of theological blindness to the German Christian pastors. 'What a judgment,' he concluded, 'upon German theology, upon theological science and theological education, is represented by the fact that the major political theories have gained such authority over the souls of even the theologians. What failures are manifest here!'[113] The approach of the later Confessing Church as a renewal in theology and the church is already clearly foreshadowed here.

The political opponents of the National Socialists were also far too late in understanding what the German Christians were up to. Early in September, two weeks before the voters' lists were closed, the Social Democrats attempted to start a similar movement. The SPD was, of course, neutral, wrote Bernhard Göring in *Vorwärts*, but the party would 'certainly be of the opinion, along with the Religious Socialists, that all Socialists and Republicans who belong to the Protestant Church in Prussia have an absolute duty to use their vote... Every Protestant man or woman who is more than twenty-four years old must exercise his or her right to vote and be registered in the church voters' list by 17 September.'[114] And a pamphlet of the Union of Religious Socialists proclaimed: 'Comrades, this time we are going to the church election and there we will frustrate the plan of the Fascists!'[115]

Even the conservative right in the church now tried to put up a 'Positive

Fighting List for the Church of the Reformation, Volk and Love of the Fatherland' against the German Christians – under the slogan 'Gospel and Volkstum'. An appeal which was published on 15 September in the Berlin *Tag* was signed by no fewer than eight general superintendents.

Yet all of these attempts were mere afterthoughts, with no hope of success.

An impressive picture of the German Christian election campaign was painted by Agnes von Zahn-Harnack, daughter of Adolf Harnack, at the end of October in the *Vossische Zeitung*. She reported an election rally with Pastor Kessel in her community in a western suburb of Berlin. What did the 'quite numerous' audience hear? 'To say it all in a word: the result was frightening – frightening in its content and almost even more frightening in the demagogic way in which the ideas were presented.' Three things above all struck this intelligent and critical observer. The first was the obscure connection with the NSDAP; then there was the unclarified question of the relationship between the Kingdom of God and the fatherland; and thirdly, 'the almost unfettered antisemitism of the speaker' upset her. It was part of the style of these meetings that discussion was not permitted, and so there was no possibility 'of putting up personal opposition in the meeting'.[116]

We may begin from the fact that in September and October 1932 hundreds of such election rallies took place in the Old Prussian Church. Some of those attending may have been disgusted by the new style which was practised here, but many were certainly impressed.

The result of all these efforts, the church election of 13 November 1932, is hard to judge. There are several reasons for this. First, there were no elections at all in many communities, because there had been agreement in advance on a common list of candidates. Then, comparisons are impossible because the previous elections in 1928 had taken place in completely different conditions. And finally, there is a lack of comprehensive election statistics, about which no one had thought, and which would have run into considerable difficulties.[117]

Thus the number of seats won by the German Christians, about a third of the total, is a mere estimate, though it was generally accepted and recognized. The important question, whether with this third the German Christians had succeeded in penetrating the traditional church electorate, or whether they had above all the mobilization of previous non-voters to thank for their seats, cannot be answered clearly. But numerous reports of a doubling, even quadrupling, of electoral registrations lead one to the conclusion that a large proportion of German Christian voters were in fact taking part in a church election for the first time and in addition had political rather than church motivations.[118]

Moreover, an analysis of the elections by Dibelius just one week afterwards drew attention to the great differences in the individual provinces. In areas with an old synodical tradition, in the Rhineland and in Westphalia, the German Christians in fact secured only about a fifth of the seats; in the east, on the other hand, in the Grenzmark, East Prussia and Pomerania, they sometimes approached fifty per cent. In Brandenburg, Saxony and Silesia the results were without exception more modest. In the city of Berlin the average was under a third; in Berlin-Land it was substantially over a third. Only an exact analysis of individual communities could provide information as to which motives were at work in electoral decisions in each individual case.[119]

How was this trend now to be assessed? Measured against the goal which Kube had set out in January, the election was clearly a defeat. In spite of all the efforts the German Christians were far from having 'captured' the Protestant church. Not even all National Socialists had voted for the German Christians, since their votes were far below the numbers that the results of the political elections would have led one to expect.[120] Moreover, the disappointment among the German Christians was unmistakable. In the first official comment Karl Themel compared the elections to the advance of a reconnaisance party. 'The major attack is launched,' he said in an attempt to encourage supporters, 'when the first thrust has clarified the strengths and the displacements at the front. The church election of 1932 has had this and only this significance. It was a first thrust and not a major advance. That will be launched in 1936, if it is still necessary by then.' In these circumstances the assertion that 'the designated line has been reached' was hardly more than a propaganda phrase.[121] The *Deutsche Nachrichten*, a newspaper of the nationalist opposition, also declared in triumph: 'We see in the "mighty victory of the German Christians" an almost catastrophic defeat for the Nazis.'[122]

However, that was only one aspect of things. Compared with what the elections meant for the church, the results looked very different. The church's Office of Statistics in an internal report correctly stated that 'never before in so short a time after the formation of its programme and organization has a church group secured so high a number of votes'.[123] In fact the election indicated a politicization of the church, the consequences of which could as yet hardly be foreseen.

This was all the more true because the German Christians did not in any way allow themselves to be discouraged by the results of the election. On 8 December Hossenfelder reported in Circular 41 that the elections in Old Prussia had achieved 'complete success'. At the same time he called for increased work in all church provinces and announced 'the first national conference of the Faith Movement of German Christians' in Berlin for February 1933. When this first national conference actually took place, however, from 3-5 April 1933, the situation had already changed completely. And with it the Germans let loose an avalanche which first destroyed the Protestant church and then buried it.

PART TWO

The Churches in the Year of the Seizure of Power: 1933

1

The Seizure of Power and Protestantism
(February-March)

'When Hermann Göring, on leaving the Reich Chancellery, could be the first to say to the people waiting in Wilhelmstrasse, "Adolf Hitler has become Reich Chancellor!", when the jubilation which spontaneously erupted spread out from here and kindled throughout the nation, an entire people felt that on that day the history of a new, genuinely German state had begun.'[1]

What was thus celebrated by National Socialist propaganda and what went down in history as the 'Day of the Seizure of Power' was in fact a process the first phase of which extended over eight weeks, coming to a conclusion only with assent to the Enabling Act. During these weeks it became very clear for the first time that Hitler was not just a band-leader whom a chance political wave had carried to the top, but rather a politician who had a clear vision, an excellent capacity to adapt, and a view of the essentials; who did not let himself be diverted by anything; and who had the ability to create situations in which his opponents had no alternative but to capitulate. In fact, in the course of eight weeks he was successful not only in securing his power politically but also in gradually sweeping along a hesitant nation. It was a sign of success that at the end of this period the two major churches also abandoned their caution. The Catholic bishops did it carefully, expressing in a statement on 28 March their confidence 'that the general prohibitions and warnings need no longer be considered necessary'.[2] The Prussian Oberkirchenrat did so with rejoicing, in an Easter message on 16 April, claiming to be at one with all fellow Protestant believers 'in joy over the awakening of the deepest forces of our nation to awareness of the Fatherland, a genuine sense of the Volk and religious renewal'.[3]

I shall now go on to describe the course of these decisive first eight weeks, Hitler's strategy, and the reactions in both churches.

The expectations which were bound up with Hitler's chancellorship throughout Germany on 30 January and immediately thereafter were quite extraordinarily diverse. The only thing they had in common was that almost without exception they had more to do with experiences, hopes, wishes and fears than with reality. This was just as true of Hitler's supporters as it was of his opponents. Even in retrospect, no criterion can be found which would have reliably conveyed an insight into the true significance of his chancellorship. Within the same confession, the same party, the same ideology; within the same class, the same level of education, the same occupation; within the same province and the same

219

family, the most diverse opinions on the significance of Hitler were possible in February 1933, and all the more so on the question of what might be done or not done in the light of his chancellorship.

One of the most impressive descriptions of the raptures into which Hitler's followers were caught up on 30 January comes from a Hamburg diary. Under the date 6 February 1933 is written:

'Torchlight parade of the National Socialists and the Stahlhelm. A wonderfully uplifting experience for us all. Göring says that the day of the nomination of Hitler and the national cabinet has been like 1914 and this too was something like 1914... We were so to speak drunk with ecstasy, blinded by the light of the torches directly in front of our faces, and always in their smoke like a sweet cloud of incense. And before us men, men, men, brown, multi-coloured, grey, brown, a flood for an hour and twenty minutes. In the flickering light of the torches it seemed as though only a few types kept recurring, but there were 22-25,000 different faces!!!

Next to us a little boy, three years old, kept raising his tiny hand: "Heil Hitler, Heil Hitlerman!"'[4]

Franz Tügel, later German Christian Bishop of Hamburg, reported in a quite similar vein on the 30 January, on which he had 'sat at the radio until long past midnight and listened to the sound of the new event... With pounding heart I experienced the entry of the battalions of men through the Brandenburg Gate and the parade past the aged Reich President and his young Chancellor, amidst the endless jubilation of the masses of people... An indescribable elation, combined with the deepest thanks to the almighty Lord of history, filled my heart – as was surely the case with every other patriotic German.'[5]

What these two, and countless other equally enthusiastic people, saw was in no way a National Socialist dictatorship, but rather the final unification of the right wing and thus the possibility of a new, consistently nationalist policy; not Hitler alone, but rather Hitler and Hindenburg and a cabinet 'of the kind we didn't dare to dream of in July. Hitler, Hugenberg, Seldte, Papen!!!'[6]

Even Theophil Wurm, the Church President of Württemberg, saw things in this way when on 2 February he asked Land Bishop Rendtorff of Mecklenburg whether a political statement by the Kirchenausschuss decided upon in November 1932 was still necessary 'after the latest turn of events'. 'The agreement between Hindenburg, Hitler and Hugenberg has created a different situation. So long as the groups represented by these names and personalities stood against one another, the inner distress of the Protestant voters was especially great; their unification gives at least eighty per cent of professed Protestants a clear solution.'[7]

It was an underestimation of Hitler, a terrible misunderstanding of his goals, as well as of the distribution of political forces in the new government, for him above all to be welcomed as the head of a national cabinet. But this underestimation and misunderstanding were widespread. And in those first eight weeks Hitler did everything possible to keep up this appearance. When in the course of the summer the truth became obvious, for a number of reasons it was too late even to think about resistance.

Significantly, not only Hitler's supporters but many of his opponents succumbed to the wrong perception of this cabinet. For example, for Konrad Adenauer, who on 7 February spoke in Cologne to the Centre Party delegates of the Rhineland, the German nationals were the 'real driving force' in the formation of the government, and the call from the National Catholic Workers' Council urging the election of the Centre Party which appeared on the following day reduced the great misunderstanding of these days to the brief formula: 'Hitler is the name on the door; Hugenberg-Papen is the business.'[8] Further to the left, in the SPD, the party administration also yielded to 'the wave of illusions which after 30 January inundated the whole country. Hopes were pinned on the tensions within the cabinet, on the impossibility of overcoming the economic difficulties and clashes of interest between the unevenly balanced partners, on the rivalry between the SA and the Stahlhelm, on the self-destruction and disintegration of the NSDAP, on the Reichswehr, Herr von Papen, the Reich President and the South German states.'[9] Finally to be noted is the grotesque mistake of the Communists who, true to their thesis of the 'social Fascism' of the SPD,[10] thought Hitler no more than a transitional figure,[11] and until 1934 imperturbably held to the conviction that the SPD was 'the "social mainstay" of German capitalism, the "greatest evil", and the chief enemy of the German Communist Party in its own class'.[12]

The fatal underestimation of Hitler, to be found among his coalition partners on the right as well as among his opponents on the left, was also expressed in the opinion that 30 January would not change things very much. Typical of this view was Karl Barth, who on 1 February wrote a reassuring letter to his mother in Switzerland in which he first of all reported on a bout of common 'flu which he had survived and then continued: 'And while this was going on at home, Hitler took over the helm of the German nation. I don't believe that this will mark the beginning of great novelties in any direction. Both internally and externally Germany is too immobile a body for such surface movements to be able to change anything. And above all, the persons involved are certainly not outstanding enough for that. Moreover at present the German people has too little of that boldness which would be necessary to produce either a Mussolini régime or a counter-revolution.'[13] Nor did he write this just to reassure his mother. Rather, Karl Barth in particular demonstrates just how complex the situation still was during those first eight weeks, and how little even critical observers were able to imagine a dictatorship in Germany. Thus while in conversation with a Scottish theologian six weeks later Barth, then professor in Bonn, thought that 'the political things which we must experience' had meanwhile become 'somewhat disquieting' after all, and felt that it was not out of the question that university professors might be forbidden to be members of the SPD, so that he would have to look round for a new chair abroad. But he urgently requested that absolutely nothing be said about it for the present, 'for I still cannot imagine that events will develop in this way'.[14]

Misunderstandings, errors, illusions among supporters and opponents and, in the end, simple incredulity as to what then came about explain why on 30 January and in subsequent weeks no social group in Germany thought that the hour of unconditional resistance had arrived, in spite of the warning signs.[15] And as long as human beings cannot see the future, neither supporters nor opponents can very well be blamed for basing their decisions on previous experiences and standards, rather than on the figure of a man who in his way was undoubtedly a type that appears once in a century.

Initially, lack of clarity as to the importance and significance of his person was Hitler's most important asset. It made it possible for him, in a cunning game, to create the legal and political preconditions for his absolute rule, and at the same time through an unparalleled campaign of confidence-building to propagate faith in himself and his cause. In this confidence-building campaign, Christianity and the churches played an important role. Never again during his career did Hitler so frequently and so ardently implore God as in these first eight weeks. Never again did he make such use of Christian phrases and adopt Christian images and attributes.

This already began with the 'Appeal of the Reich Government to the German People' which Hitler read over the radio on the evening of 1 February. The very first sentences referred to the blessing of which the Almighty had deprived the people since the days of betrayal, and to the vow which 'we as national leaders make to God, our conscience and our Volk'. Christianity came first among the most important tasks. 'Thus the national government will consider as its supreme and first task that of restoring a unity of spirit and purpose among our Volk. It will preserve and defend the foundations upon which the power of our nation depends. It will take Christianity under its firm protection, as the basis of our entire morality, and the family as the cell in the body of our Volk and state.' At the end of the Appeal Hitler asked the German people to give him four years and ended with a solemn benediction, which no bishop could have made more imposing: 'May Almighty God take our work to his grace, give true form to our will, bless our insight, and endow us with the confidence of our Volk. For we do not mean to fight for ourselves but for Germany!'[16]

This style was typical of subsequent weeks, not only for Hitler himself but also for the language and conduct of many leading Party members. Thus the report of the appointment (at first temporary) of Bernhard Rust, secondary-school master and Gauleiter of Hanover, as the new Prussian Kultusminister, appeared in the *Völkische Beobachter* of 9 February under the headline: 'Our Confession of Christianity'. And Rust, too, gave a pious ending to his first programmatic speech: 'Trusting in God,' he exclaimed to his colleagues in the Prussian Kultusministerium, 'and with faith in our people, we take up our tasks! Can there be anything better?'[17]

But things did not stop at mere formulae like these. The Party forcibly invaded the church buildings themselves, and here, too, Hitler personally gave the signal. During the great torchlight parade on the evening of 30 January, two men were fatally shot in political clashes in Berlin: an SA officer and a city police sergeant, who happened to be a Catholic. When the Luisenstadt community wanted to impose conditions on a large demonstration of mourning that was planned, the new government applied to the cathedral chapter for the victims to lie in state in Berlin Cathedral so that people might be able to pay their respects. While this was rejected (it was a privilege reserved for the former Prussian royal house), a funeral service was permitted. It was thoroughly characteristic of the attitude of the Prussian church in the first weeks that this permission was later vigorously criticized in the Prussian church senate.[18] What the Party made of this permission, however, was no less characteristic: a huge funeral service in the cathedral with Hitler, Göring and the Crown Prince to the fore; with the E minor Prelude and the slow movement of the Eroica; with a sermon by Hossenfelder on John 15.13:

'Greater love has no man than this, that he lay down his life for his friends'; and with a funeral procession to the Invalidenfriedhof which, as the *Völkischer Beobachter* proudly reported, was greeted by hundreds of thousands 'despite the miserable weather'.[19]

Hitler's signal was understood. Now in other places, too, the SA stormtroopers marched into the houses of God, and the *Völkischer Beobachter*, like the smaller Party newspapers in the provinces, never tired of reporting it.[20]

That same week, on 10 February, Hitler opened the campaign for the Reichstag elections with a speech in the Berlin Sports Palace which he made more dramatic by using an unprecedented prayer-like intonation and ended with an 'Amen'. All Germany could hear on the radio Hitler's affirmation 'that now the hour is at hand in which the millions who today hate us will stand behind us and will then welcome the new German Reich that we have jointly created, laboriously fought for and bitterly acquired, a Reich of greatness and honour and power and glory and righteousness. Amen.'[21]

A few days later Hitler used a critical statement by the State President of Württemberg, Dr Eugen Bolz, a prominent Centre Party politician, as the occasion for declaring in a settling of accounts with the hated Catholic Centre Party that his was the true Christian policy rather than that of the Centre Party. In a reference to the long-standing coalition of the Centre Party with the SPD, Hitler declared that 'Christians and not international atheists' had now taken over the leadership of Germany. 'I do not just talk about Christianity,' he continued. 'No, I too declare that I will never join forces with the parties that destroy Christianity. If there are those who now protect a threatened Christianity, where was their Christianity in those fourteen years when they went arm in arm with atheism?'[22] The *NS Kurier* of Stuttgart reported on this statement under the headline, 'Hitler's Affirmation of a Christian State'.[23] Four weeks later, on 16 March, the *Völkischer Beobachter* once again energetically emphasized this slogan in a leading article under the headline: 'The Basis of Adolf Hitler's Government: Christianity'.[24]

But all this was not enough for Hitler. While the attendance at church services by the SA increased and the Party generally requested special servies here and there – e.g. on 12 February in Kassel[25] – Rudolf Hess, as 'Adjutant to the Führer of the NSDAP' informed the Reich Chancellery on 18 February that the Chancellor wished, 'should the occasion arise, to suggest to the government the institution of a "service of intercession for Volk and Fatherland"'. However, this idea was then initially dropped for lack of time, and because people in the Ministry of the Interior, probably rightly, had doubts as to 'whether the arrangements with the two churches would go smoothly'.[26] But the general tenor of the speech at Königsberg and on the Potsdam Day was clearly foreshadowed.

In the meantime, the news of the burning of the Reichstag terrified the German public. Under the impact of this event, which also did not fail to have its effect on the German National members of the cabinet,[27] on 28 February Hitler was successful in getting Hindenburg's signature on the most important special law of the Third Reich: the 'Decree of the Reich President for the Protection of the People and the State'. Together with the decree 'Against Betrayal of the German People and Treasonable Activities', issued the same day, these 'Reichtag Fire

Decrees' created the 'overall framework for co-ordination and permanent terror'.[28]

No less important was the effect of the Reichstag fire on public opinion. As the sign of a supposedly Communist attempt at a Putsch, the incident appeared to prove what Hitler had maintained all along; that the only alternatives were him or a Communist dictatorship. The churches were particularly sensitive on this point. With the extermination of the Orthodox Church in Russia before their eyes, and having been confronted for years with similar Communist propaganda in their own land, they could not be indifferent to this alternative.[29] So the motif of deliverance from Communism played a large and sometimes decisive role for both confessions in the church deliberations over the coming weeks.

Then at the end of this week Hitler spoke in Königsberg. This speech on the evening of 4 March marked the climax and conclusion of the election campaign. Under Goebbels' direction, its transmission over the radio became a profound experience for nationalist Germany. 'From the bleeding eastern frontier, the gospel of awakening Germany is proclaimed, and the entire German people can hear this unique mass event, which is unprecedented in all history',[30] he proclaimed in the *Völkischer Beobachter*. And in fact it proved to be far more effective than all the church intercession services put together, ultimately turning the declaration itself into a kind of service. In his speech Hitler again declared himself for the 'Almighty'. Again he asked, 'Lord God, may we never become vacillating and cowardly, may we never forget the responsibility we have assumed'. And he ended: 'We are all proud that by God's gracious help we have again become true Germans.' Immediately afterwards the radio station broadcast the chorale 'Wir treten zum beten' ('We gather in prayer'), the so-called 'Netherlands Thanksgiving', still familiar to all Germans from the time of the Kaiser:

> We gather in prayer to the God of the righteous,
> His judgment is strict and his will must prevail.
> He will not abandon the good to the wicked,
> All praise to his name, for his power does not fail.
>
> In battle our God was there standing beside us,
> That right should prevail was his purpose divine.
> So close on its opening the combat brought triumph,
> O God, thou wast with us, the victory is thine.[31]

Then the bells of Königsberg Cathedral boomed out, 'and millions of Christians in Germany' – at least that is what the editor of the *Allgemeine Evangelisch-Lutherische Kirchenzeitung* asserted, 'listened to and joined in the hymn "Wir treten zum Beten" and in the very hour that the Königsberg bells rang, prayers ascended to heaven from far and wide, as had certainly never happened before in the history of Germany'.[32]

Of course at that moment no one suspected that the Consistory had forbidden the ringing of the bells, and that chorale and bells were only dubbed in from a record. And the fact that the *Evangelische Gemeindeblatt*, published in Königsberg, called the substitution of a record for the ringing of the cathedral bells 'a high-handed use of radio' and the announcement 'an untruth and an affront to the church' hardly changed the impression that on the eve of the election the Protestant church had virtually blessed Hitler's purposes.[33]

If Hitler had hoped to gain an absolute majority for his party through this tremendous effort, he was disappointed. The NSDAP secured barely 44% of the votes. In spite of this, Hitler could rightly celebrate the result as a success. For together with the 8% of the 'Black-White-Red Battlefront', into which his coalition partners Hugenberg, Papen and Seldte had formed themselves, a clear majority of the voters had placed themselves behind the new government.

Typical of Hitler's dynamism in these first eight weeks was the fact that he never considered the result of the election to be a provisional conclusion. Rather it was just a stimulus to accelerate the tempo towards the total seizure of power.

In this connection he had two important goals: the co-ordination of the Länder and the final emasculation of the Reichstag. He had achieved both goals by the end of March.

Hand in hand with this, Hitler's campaign for confidence continued, now officially directed by one of the most skilful propagandists of his time, Dr Josef Goebbels, who on 13 March had become Reich Minister for Public Enlightenment and Propaganda. More than ever, the foreground was occupied by a union, sworn in God's name, between the glorious old and the revolutionary new, between Hindenburg and Hitler, a union which was to permit every national-minded person, 'regardless of party orientation', to endorse the new state.[34]

The campaign for confidence reached a climax on 21 March with the ceremonial opening of the newly elected Reichstag in the Garrison Church at Potsdam. This event, which was without doubt a masterpiece in the manipulation of propaganda, had been preceded by a series of significant internal negotiations in and with the church administration. After the destruction of the Reichstag building, as early as 2 March, i.e. still before the elections, the government passed a resolution to transfer the proceedings of the new Reichstag to the Garrison Church; this was also a sign that from the beginning Hitler had attached special propaganda value to the election and its result. However, this plan met with vigorous resistance from a great variety of quarters.[35] At a discussion of this question in the Kirchenbundesamt on 3 March, in which the leadership of the Prussian church government took part, it was unanimously thought to be 'the happiest solution to the present difficulties' 'if the Garrison Church could be designated unsuitable for the Reichstag proceedings for technical reasons, and it were made available only for the inaugural service'. At the urging of Dibelius, who as General Superintendent of the Kurmark was responsible for Potsdam, the Potsdam Superintendent Werner Görnandt was given instructions to this effect and authorized to take part in the negotiations at the Garrison Church.[36] The compromise became fact as early as 7 March: the inaugural services took place in the Nicolaikirche and the Catholic parish church; the opening of the Reichstag with a 'state ceremony' in the Garrison Church; and the opening session in the afternoon in Berlin, in the Kroll Opera House, hastily remodelled into a parliamentary chamber.[37] Thus Hitler had what he needed: the best setting imaginable to move and reassure bourgeois Germany. Even the problem of the ringing of bells was now solved: the bells in all the Potsdam churches were rung for a quarter of an hour at the opening of the state ceremony. In this connection Superintendent Görnandt declared (and in so doing highlighted the change in consciousness taking place during those weeks) 'that he rejected the application filed by the National Socialist side over the ringing of bells before the Reichstag election in March of this year, but he had no objections to the ringing of the bells of the Potsdam churches in connection with a ceremony for the opening of the Reichstag, which has become a concern of the whole people. General Superintendent Dibelius also endorsed this point of view.'[38]

With organ music and chorales sung by the congregation, the 'state ceremony' itself, again broadcast by all German stations, almost amounted to a religious service. The pictures of 'Potsdam Day' which Germany saw in numerous special editions during the coming weeks showed the Reich President and the Protestant members of the cabinet at the ceremonial service in the Nikolaikirche; the Reich Chancellor as he outlined his programme from a lectern before the altar of the Garrison Church; uniformed cordons, masses of people and parades, and service after service: a ceremonial service of the Berlin Garrison in the parade ground of the palace; an open-air service for the municipal police; open-air services for the SA.[39]

As it were the conclusion of this campaign for Christian confidence by Hitler, which in retrospect was astoundingly coherent and systematic, was the government policy statement of 23 March. If the church administrations were still more or less distrustful of Hitler's general affirmations and about church bells, chorales and church-going, here was the Reich Chancellor, in clearly stated formulae assuring both churches of their legal inviolability and of the protection and support of the state.

'The national government,' Hitler declared in that part of his speech which dealt with domestic policy, 'perceives in the two Christian confessions most important factors in the preservation of our Volkstum. It will respect the treaties concluded between them and the Länder; their rights shall not be violated. Conversely, however, it expects and hopes that the work on the national and moral elevation of our people which the government has made its task will equally be respected. The national government, in school and education, will grant and guarantee to the Christian confessions the influence that is their due. Its concern is for an honest co-existence between church and state.' In the part of the speech that dealt with foreign policy, Hitler mentioned relations with the Vatican. 'The Reich government, which sees Christianity as the unshakable foundation of the ethical and moral life of our people, likewise sets the greatest store upon further cultivating and developing friendly relations with the Holy See.'

Finally, in the last part, in which he justified the necessity of the Enabling Act, Hitler once again repeated an explicit guarantee to the churches. 'The Länder will not be eliminated. The rights of the churches will not be infringed. Their position in relation to the state will not be changed.'[40]

That very day the parliament – with the exception of the Social Democrats – consented to the Enabling Act. Hitler's way was clear.

The question of the significance of these proceedings takes us to the heart of Hitler's personality. It is too simple to see all this as no more than a National Socialist propaganda show, in which the cynical actors arbitrarily deploy pious groups upon the stage. Rather, there was beyond doubt a real religious dimension in Hitler, a völkisch-religious consciousness of mission, a belief in being called to a great work by 'Providence' or by the 'Almighty' – concepts which Hitler, typically, liked much more than the concept of 'God'. Something of this religious dimension emerged in these weeks in which he so quickly and securely proceeded from victory to victory, and emerged more strongly than ever before or after. Providence itself seemed to be wielding her instrument. The ecstatic ending of the Berlin speech of 10 February is the most obvious sign of this consciousness of a religious mission.

To be distinguished from this are the political and church-political goals which Hitler pursued during these weeks. First of all, he was now able to reap the fruits of his fundamental decision on church policy in 1924 and the years following. The basic rejection of völkisch religion, for himself as a politician and for his party as a political organization, was the precondition for his being able to speak as he now spoke and for his becoming increasingly confident about doing so. And for him confidence was the most important thing in these weeks: confidence not only in his statesmanlike qualities, but at least as much confidence in his trustworthiness when he said that he would not misuse the plenary power granted him, and that he really had only good intentions for the German people. What easier way of obtaining this confidence than by associating himself with the Christian traditions in the most vivid way possible and, so to speak, in spite of everything drawing on their huge resources of confidence in a just and peaceful future? With an adaptability all of his own, Hitler moved within German Protestantism, an alien environment to him, with amazing assurance.

If the question of confidence was the most important explanation of the heightened Christian character of the first weeks, it was certainly not the only one. In addition, there was at least one specific political factor. Hitler's ploy could only succeed if the Reich President stuck to his guns. Hindenburg, however, was a man for whom piety and honesty belonged together. To the eighty-four-year-old President, inexperienced in distinguishing different overtones and undertones, Hitler's profession of divine guidance may in fact have seemed more important and more reliable than the constitutional safeguards which had not been able to prevent the chaotic conditions of the last years of the Republic.

Finally, Hitler also had his eye on the two churches, upon whose great, if somewhat indefinable, influence he counted at all times during his political career.

However, during these first weeks he had specific plans only for the Catholic church. He had to eliminate political Catholicism, and he knew how this was to be done: through a treaty with the Vatican like the one concluded by his great model, Mussolini. The campaign for Christian confidence was also essential for the realization of this plan, because it created a climate in which the defence of the church by the Centre Party could apparently be dispensed with.[41]

Hitler's amazingly single-minded support for Christianity in the first weeks of his term of office (which is more than a matter of retrospect) presented other churches with an enormous challenge. When considering all that happened in the field of church politics over the next weeks and months, we must always keep in mind the impressions of this early period. They had an unbelievably deep and long-lasting effect among personalities and groups in the church right down to the collapse of the Reich. Their importance becomes apparent in the changes that occurred in the attitudes of both churches between January and April 1933.

The situations confronting German Protestantism and German Catholicism were completely different.

From Protestantism Hitler's chancellorship initially did not call for any fundamental decisions. In view of the well-known Protestant sympathies for a right-wing government, the fact that it had finally come about was widely and enthusiastically welcomed. On the other hand, the church administrations saw no occasion for departing from their basic position of being 'above parties'. On the contrary, the more pressing the political demands became, the more emphatically, at first, the political independence of the church was made the centre of attention. At this point the theology of the Altona Confession, which had been published on 11 January 1933, already made itself felt.[42]

When the NSDAP in Kassel requested a special church service in the first week of February, the assembly of all the pastors in Kassel issued a statement typical of the situation in the very first weeks. It referred directly to the first article of the Altona Confession and called for the strict commitment of the church to its fundamental calling in all situations. 'The church exists for all, and its word should be directed to all classes and parties... If the church is called, then it has to proclaim nothing but the gospel, unabridged and not falsified through party-political or other considerations, regardless of the intentions of the call or of the invitation.'[43] A similar statement, which also took up the Altona Confession, was made by the pastors of Frankfurt on 26 February. It affirmed that the church 'is called to serve the entire people, irrespective of parties and ideologies. Certainly every Christian has the task of taking part in the life of the people and of the state and, if necessary, of taking a side. However, the church is independent. The sole criterion of its action is the Word of God.'[44]

That this was not just the opinion of individual groups, but was also an attitude endorsed by a majority in the Protestant church, emerged when the most important body in the Kirchenbund – the Kirchenausschuss – convened in Berlin on 2 and 3 March under its rotation system. Under the chairmanship of President Hermann Kapler, as item 3 on the agenda the representatives of the Landeskirchen and the Kirchentag delegates discussed the 'question of the church's attitude to present political conditions and enterprises' in view of the imminent Reichstag elections. Before the committee was the draft of a resolution which had been discussed the day before by a special commission, drawn up by Theophil Wurm, the Church President of Württemberg. Wurm's remarks were remarkably representative of the church administrations in the first weeks of Hitler's rule. The Church President first praised the movement, which 'with great sacrifice has broken the back of terror' and 'welded together' social classes which had become estranged from one another, and taken up 'the struggle against the influences destructive of our cultural life'. Precisely on the basis of this assessment, however, the Church President of Württemberg also argued for the church's right to state certain demands clearly: '1. Access to the whole people; 2. proclamation of the whole word of God: 3. the claim to complete loyalty from the servants of the church.' Here a threefold resistance was expressed: to growing discrimination against the non-National Socialist part of the nation; to the German Christian and 'German Church' abridgment of the scriptures: and finally to the movement's political grip on those holding office in the church. Wurm's concluding comment shows how much the developments of the Weimar period had changed the Landeskirchen, had awakened their concern for independence and strengthened their self-assurance.[45] 'The most formidable danger at present,' he declared, 'is that we will lose that for which we have fought, a certain liberty of action in reference to nation and state. We must be careful not to lose this freedom again.'[46]

The strength and weakness of the policy of the Landeskirchen which would emerge time and again in the coming years was already startlingly clear in these statements of Wurm's. The strength of this policy lay in its clear-sightedness and keenness of hearing in the face of all attempts at co-ordination which Wurm documented here even before any specific plans along these lines were at all discernible. Its weakness lay in the fact that, through being occupied above all with its own affairs, it did not become aware of issues which we now know that it should have noted.

Nevertheless, these issues were already on the table. Wurm reported 'a petition from a number of ladies' – he specifically named Agnes von Zahn-Harnack, the daughter of Adolf von Harnack – which pointed out 'that to an increasing extent the name of God as well as expressions from the Christian religion and Christian life are being used in the election campaign, or election speeches are concluded with the word "Amen!". In addition there is an identification of religious and political concepts which spiritually and emotionally is deeply confusing. Finally, allied with this is a struggle against our Jewish fellow-countrymen which not only destroys our national community but can also be seen to be a continuing transgression against the highest commandment in Christianity.' The petition therefore requested the Kirchenausschuss to speak out 'in public' against these abuses.[47] The fact that there was no time on the agenda to discuss the petition simply concealed the fact that it would hardly have been possible for the Kirchenbund to arrive at any decision along these lines. That became clear in the subsequent discussion.

A four-hour debate was needed before a clear majority could be arrived at for the commission's draft, For some – Professor Titius, for example – this draft was already too 'feeble' because it lacked any positive reference to the movement. The secular vice-president of the Oberkirchenrat, Ernst Hundt, in fact the only one in the discussion openly to declare himself a National Socialist, demanded an expression of thanks, joy and confidence for the 'gift from God' received in the radical change. He even saw the draft as an '*ex cathedra* condemnation of the German Christians' which he could not approve. On the other hand, Walther Simons, formerly Reich Foreign Minister and now President of the Reich Supreme Court, was one of those who warned against too extensive an offer of co-operation: conceivably there were issues on which the church 'would deviate from the will of the state authority'. The person who expressed himself most resolutely on this side was Baron von Pechmann, the basically conservative president of the Kirchentag – certainly the first among the leading German Protestants to see things in their true light. He spoke of 'the sea of hatred and lies in our days' about which the church had in any event to say something.[48]

So finally, with only slight alterations, the commission's draft was accepted for internal commendation to the Landeskirchen by a clear majority of nineteen to ten. Its basic concern was obviously for the preservation of the independence and freedom of movement of the church. This was specified in three points. The first point, taking up the resolution by the pastors of Kassel, called for all clergy 'to present the message of the Reformation on all occasions'. The second urged the pastors to preserve an attitude of trust, and declared that obligations to a political association ought never to be set above loyalty to the church. The third and final point welcomed the cleansing and renewal of the life of the people and promised the co-operation of the church; but it insisted that the churches be listened to in good time, above all in cultural and political measures, and that their legitimate wishes should be granted.[49]

Surprisingly, at the same time the gathering also agreed to a public declaration the text of which was essentially written by Pechmann. With an eye to the election campaign, three admonitions were addressed to all members of the church, 'irrespective of party': '1. The more hatred there is, the more love there should be! Romans 12.21! 2. The more lies there are, the stricter should truthfulness be! Take the eighth commandment seriously! 3. The more selfishness there is, the more selfless devotion there should be towards one's neighbours' concerns, and to that which stands above everything: the whole people, the whole fatherland![50]

This declaration was published at once. It appeared in the press on the Saturday, the very day on the evening of which Hitler ended his election campaign in Königsberg with the pealing of bells and chorale singing. We may be sure that these pastoral and critical admonitions were not what the Party expected from the Protestant church on the eve of the decisive election. It was also the last time that the whole church expressed itself in such a reserved and detached way on political developments in Germany.

The church administrations, on the other hand, at first still adhered resolutely to the emphasis that the church was independent and above political parties. These key ideas clearly stood at the centre of most declarations and statements by the church during these weeks. A typical example was the message issued by the Landeskirchenamt in Hanover, to be read from the pulpit, in addition to the declaration of the Kirchenbund 'that only a church independent of the parties and groups can now render to our people the unique service of proclaiming the Word of God to all'.[51]

Up to the end of March, only two groups within German Protetantism fundamentally rejected the principle of independence. One of them was the Evangelischer Bund, which added one more to its manifest völkisch-nationalist follies and on 22 February publicly issued an election appeal for the new government: 'Protestant Christians... abandon all suspicions and with your votes join in the struggle for the nationalist, counter-revolutionary movement to achieve victory in a legal way.'[52] However, this election was felt to be so offensive in German Protestantism that as a result a large number of prominent members withdrew from the Bund, including Baron von Pechmann[53] and Hermann Mulert, the editor of *Christliche Welt*.[54]

The other group which vigorously championed Hitler before the election was, of course, the German Christians. The Party made use of them to some degree, for example in having them distribute throughout the Reich the imaginative poster: 'All good Christians, whether Protestant or Catholic, vote this time for the National Socialists. List 1! For the Protestants: Faith Movement of German Christians, signed, Pastor Hossenfelder. For the Catholics: Catholic Alliance for National Politics, signed, Amtsrat Lossau.'[55]

To some extent the German Christians themselves also took the initiative, though only where organized groups existed, and without any uniformity, by publishing bombastic election appeals in the Party newspapers and attempting to win the pastors over to Hitler by means of special circulars. For example, in the Stuttgart *NS Kurier* of 24 February one could read: 'A decisive battle of unprecedented dimensions is being fought in Germany. The battlefronts are clearer than ever before. On the one side stand Free Thought, severed from God, and Muscovite Bolshevism, storming against all that is holy with a hate-filled passion for destruction. The goal of red world-revolution fought for with satanic zeal is, according to its own words: "No marriage, no family, no church, no faith other than faith in Bolshevism alone!..." Christians, do you want to let such a thing happen? If you do not, then come and join the one great German Christian defensive front!...' This appeal was signed by the 'Faith Movement of German Christians, Gau of Württemberg'.[56] However, the effect of Hitler's campaign for Christian confidence became directly visible in a letter to the pastors of Württemberg. 'Every Protestant pastor,' wrote the NS Pastors' Association, 'should be deeply grateful that at last no atheists are at the head of the German people, but rather Christian men.' And in conclusion the letter went so far as to assert that 'Hitler fought fourteen years for Christianity and church, misunderstood and opposed by many Christians. Next to God, the church and Christendom has the National Socialist leader Adolf Hitler to thank for its existence in the face of the attacks of Bolshevism.'[57] On the basis of such convictions, the demand for the unconditional solidarity of the church with the movement was natural. Here the emphasis upon the neutrality of the church no doubt looked like treason, and the declaration by the Kirchenbund like an incomprehensible aloofness on the part of the church which in no circumstances should be allowed to continue. The *NS Kurier* in the middle of March was critical: 'The position which official German Protestantism has adopted over the last fourteen days towards the mighty awakening of the nation is not exactly pleasing. One can hardly avoid the impression that the authorized representatives of German Protestantism seem to have nothing else to do in these great days than in fear and distress to keep watch in case the independence of the church... is attacked. One sees little or no trace of a positive attitude to the great turning point in Germany, and a joyous common struggle in the liberation of the nation.'[58]

The situation of the Protestant church in the first weeks of the Third Reich was basically characterized by the emphasis among a large majority on the independence of the church and an increasing rejection of this position by an aggressive minority. The point at issue in the church, then and for a long time afterwards, was hardly a criticism of the new conditions, let alone any kind of political resistance, but rather quite simply whether the church should remain independent or whether it had to declare its solidarity with the 'awakening of the nation'. Seen in retrospect, this was certainly an unsatisfactory alternative. But it was not in fact quite as unsatisfactory as it appears today. At least where

231

the independence of the church was taken seriously, it soon proved that this attempt intrinsically had considerable explosive potential.

The most important evidence of this state of affairs, and one of the most important political signs generally during these first weeks, was a circular letter which Otto Dibelius, the General Superintendent of the Kurmark, sent on 8 March 1933 to all the pastors of his district. On the same lines as Wurm, but essentially more specifically and more sharply than the Church President of Württemberg, Dibelius here for the first time was to draw a dividing line between the church and the new state, that dividing line over which the struggle began immediately afterwards.

In the letter, four printed pages long and marked confidential, the General Superintendent first dealt with the situation after the election. Completely under the spell of the Nationalist misunderstanding of Hitler, he saw the electoral victory of the right-wing coalition as the final restoration of clear constitutional conditions. He welcomed 'for the first time since the revolution a parliamentary majority with a consciously nationalist attitude'. He also believed that he could expect general approval of the change from his pastors. 'There will only be a few of us,' he thought, 'who do not delight in this change with all their hearts.'

However, the conclusion for the church which Dibelius drew from this was definitely a surprise. The church was now being tested as to whether in this new, tempting situation it was still serious about its independence. 'Now it must be revealed whether the solution that the church is above the parties and independent really arose from truly intrinsic reasons! Now it must emerge whether our church has learned, in the bitter school of almost a decade and a half, to be the church!'

Dibelius elucidated the crucial test in four points which followed closely the discussions and resolutions of the Kirchenausschuss. 'The purity of the proclamation of the gospel is at stake!' was the first point. And the explanation left no doubt as to who and what was meant by this: 'My dear brothers, we may have all sorts of different theological convictions. But we must and will agree that the gospel does not know the independent individual but rather the justified sinner; that it preaches love and not hate; and that it is not Volkstum but the kingdom of God that is the object of Protestant proclamation. We will agree that the gospel contrasts with every human ideology, be it National Socialist or Socialist, liberal or conservative; that the gospel does not confirm the human being in his most selfish desires, but judges... This is the gospel we are to preach! This and no other!'

If the contrast of the gospel to human ideology above all went against the political theology of the German Christians, the second point contained a clear rejection of Hitler's use of Christianity. 'The responsibility of the church for the whole of our people is at stake!' Dibelius explained to his pastors what that meant in concrete terms in the following way. 'Politics may dig trenches; statesmen may speak of annihilation, extermination and suppression; messages of hate at mass rallies may earn applause that does not want to stop. We have received another spirit!... I... will never deviate from the position which the gospel accords us, and I hope that you will act in the same way. Where hatred is preached, and now even hatred against members of our own people, the Spirit of Jesus Christ is not present.' This was said, as the following sentences showed, above all with an eye to the ostracized Social Democrats.

The church now, went the third point, had to remain 'the conscience of the state', and say 'on a large scale and a small scale, bravely and openly, what is right and what is wrong according to God's Word'.

This led to the last admonition, namely to observe church discipline. 'Pastors, supported by a political movement, may not set themselves above the instructions and rules of their church. Pastors may not go through their community wearing political insignia and greeting its members with a Party salute. We may not surrender to the pressure of any political powers whatsoever and allow ourselves to be pressured into measures that are unworthy of the church and one day must wreak their bitter revenge.' This was above all a reference to the 'suggestions', made in increasing number by the Party to the church, that it should put church rooms, bells and pastors at the disposal of the Party. Before Dibelius ended, in this connection he enlightened the pastors as to what had actually happened in Königsberg on the evening of 4 March. 'The bells of Königsberg cathedral were not rung,' he wrote, 'as Dr Goebbels maintained on the radio.' 'A record with the sound of bells was played on the radio and listeners were made to believe that this was Königsberg cathedral. Church discipline in East Prussia has been preserved. We must preserve it too!'[59]

The significance of this circular letter for an insight into the possibilities and limitations of the Protestant church in the first years of the Third Reich can hardly be overestimated. First of all, it makes clear once again the general, catastrophically false appraisal of Hitler's chancellorship. At the same time, however, it shows both surprisingly and convincingly that at the point where the church's cause was maintained seriously and consistently, some truth came to light, to a degree against political misjudgment, in spite of everything. Dibelius merely demanded that the church should also remain the church during the 'awakening of the nation', as the author of *The Century of the Church* had constantly demanded since the middle 1920s. However, by now making this demand specific, he unintentionally moved into opposition to the Third Reich, an opposition which became political precisely because Dibelius rejected the political church.

But this had a further amazing result. Where Protestant Christians held fast to the church's cause with similar determination, this common interest began to an increasing extent to outweigh both the theological and the political differences. An exchange of letters between Otto Dibelius and Karl Barth which followed the circular letter was typical of the development beginning here. Both men, who had appeared in public as opponents as late as the year before in the 'dispute over the church' in Berlin, now discovered that in the face of the new opponent they had been contending for the same thing. Regional church self-awareness and dialectical theology found themselves in agreement that nothing and no one could buy up the church.

On 13 March Dibelius had sent the circular letter to Karl Barth with the comment that he might perhaps be interested 'to have a look at a practical illustration of some of the things that I was saying at that time' – i.e. during a conversation in Berlin in the spring of 1932. Barth answered by return of post. 'I am very grateful to you,' he wrote back, 'for sending me your circular letter

to the pastors in the Kurmark. I am sincerely happy with its decisive content.'
And after expressing some misgivings about certain political and church-political
phrases in the letter, he said that he wanted to take it with him on his forthcoming
trip to Switzerland. 'I know from good sources that the alienation abroad from
some of the voices in the German churches is very great, and I can well imagine
that I shall be glad to refer to a document like your letter as evidence of the fact
that energetic resistance on behalf of the distinctiveness of the church is at any
rate also evident, particularly among the responsible church authorities.'[60]

However, at another point – and this showed how great the differences
between the Prussian general superintendent and the Swiss professor of theology
nevertheless still remained – Dibelius did not live up to Barth's expectations.
This was the matter of the inaugural sermon for the new Reichstag on 21 March
at Potsdam. In his letter Barth reminded Dibelius that he 'would be speaking
this word in a situation... which for many millions of Germans – those who when
the bells ring and the flags wave in Potsdam will stand aside aloof and silent – is
clearly overshadowed by tyranny and oppression. I know that there are also
other perspectives, and I assume that yours is completely different. But I trust
that in the sermon you will also have in your mind's eye all those who are deeply
troubled and angered at what has now happened and what is still to happen.'[61]

If we go on to look at Dibelius's sermon, it is hard to avoid the conclusion that
even he was – at least in part – caught up in the illusory splendour of the Potsdam
Day. Granted, the critical undertones in the sermon could not be ignored.
But they remained undertones, overlaid by the solemn overtone of Prussian
Protestant hopes, already expressed in the unfortunate selection of the text 'If
God be for us, who can be against us?'(Romans 8.31). It was the very text on
which the court preacher Ernst von Dryander had preached at the opening of
the decisive Reichstag session on 4 August 1914. By selecting it, Dibelius
confirmed that he, too, believed in the fraud of Potsdam. And at the same time
he unintentionally came to play an important role in this fraud with his sermon.[62]

More important than this sermon, however, which remained an episode, were
the Party reactions to the circular. The letter, which naturally could not remain
confidential, very quickly fell into National Socialist hands as well. The National
Socialist news service openly called it 'high treason in the church'.[63] However,
at this time the pastors in Brandenburg were still sufficiently united for the
superintendents of Brandenburg, assembled in Berlin on 7 April, resolutely to
reject these charges.[64] The explosion came on 2 April, when the *Märkische
Adler*, Kube's party newspaper, which had followed every action of the German
Christians from the very beginning, printed Dibelius' confidential letter word
for word.[65] This publication, on the eve of the first major national conference of
the German Christians in Berlin, instantly demonstrated that Kube's activities
in church politics were still aimed in the same direction. His concern was for the
replacement of the hated general superintendents and the conquest of the church
for the new system. The connections are so obvious that there can be no doubt
that the circular letter was precisely the statement that Kube had been looking
for as a pretext for finally mobilizing the whole power of the Party against the
old system in the church. In this respect, too, it is a document of historic
significance.

During March some additional statements on the independence of the church appeared. Thus August Kortheuer, Bishop of the Nassau Landeskirche, wrote on 9 March that in no circumstances was it the task of the church 'to advocate ideas of national and economic policy, however correct'; rather, it was merely to 'proclaim God's Word with all loyalty, all seriousness and all devotion – in season and out of season'. Four weeks later he was reprimanded by a pastor in the *Nassauisches Volksblatt*, who complained how deeply regrettable it was that in his appeal there was 'sadly, no trace of an enthusiastic "Yes" to the change in German destiny'.[66] Also on 15 March the Bavarian Church President Friedrich Veit again admonished his pastors 'to be ready to serve all the people of the church, and not to forget that the service of the clergy was to the church and the ministry and not to a party'.[67]

But while these voices were still being heard, there was clearly an increasing readiness in the Protestant church to abandon the caution exercised in the past and now at last also to get caught up in the national enthusiasm. And where inhibitions and reservations may still have existed, they were finally swept away by the Potsdam celebration and the statement of the government programme.

On Laetare Sunday, the Fourth Sunday in Lent, 26 March 1933, official church statements appeared for the first time which supported the new Reich without reservations. They claimed a historical turning point in which God was perceived to be at work, and a government that could be considered a Christian authority.

In Mecklenburg-Schwerin, Heinrich Rendtorff's Landeskirche, the statement ran: 'The Protestant communities of Mecklenburg should know in this hour that their Landeskirche in its faith says a joyful and strong Yes to German Volkstum... to the German nation... to the German Reich.' The bishops of Holstein and Schleswig announced that 'a German freedom movement with a national consciousness has emerged from the distress in Germany... The leaders have acknowledged openly that only on a Christian basis can a healthy state develop. This is a change for which we thank God with all our hearts...'[68] In Saxony, the Lutheran Bishop of the Landeskirche, Ludwig Ihmels, expressed his joy 'that the movement itself already seeks and consciously cultivates a link with God'.[69] And in Baden, too, the church administration saw reason to give thanks 'that he did not let our people founder, but rather saved it from destruction at the eleventh hour'.[70]

To be sure, all these declarations still talked of the independence of the church and of the freedom that it needed for its proclamation, but now this was obviously no longer the first priority. That was, rather, the Yes: solidarity, participation in and enthusiasm for the new era. The Easter message which the Prussian Oberkirchenrat issued on 16 April represented a certain climax and conclusion to this development.

How much the mood had changed, even in the Prussian church, after ten weeks of the new government, and how much it had shifted from a well-meaning reserve to an enthusiastic approval, became clear during a special conference at which twenty-one general superintedents and consistory presidents met with the Prussian Oberkirchenrat in Berlin on 11 April. Almost all the general superintendents who spoke during the long discussion of the attitude of the church to the new state, like General Superintedent Zanker of Breslau, advocated 'that the leaders of the church should publicly demonstrate a positive attitude to the new state'. Zanker added that this demand was to be encountered again and again, 'especially among the younger generation of pastors'. While Dibelius was the only one who warned against the step, Vice-President Burghart announced that the Prussian Oberkirchenrat intended 'to show explicit recognition of the new state in an Easter message'. Burghart's assumption that 'the deliberate choice of the form of an Easter message would take the declaration out of a political context' was, however, a manifest theological miscalculation. Rather, it was precisely this context that made the statement a testimony to the political theology which now began increasingly to penetrate heads and hearts.

The minutes of the session record unanimous consent to this plan for an Easter message, as well as to the suggestion that Hitler's birthday should be commemorated on the second day of the liturgical holiday.[71]So ten thousand copies of the Easter message and an intercession, dated 11 April, went out to all Prussian superintendents with the request: '1. to arrange that the enclosed address be given from the pulpit on the first day of the Easter celebrations; 2. to see that on the second day of the Easter celebrations the impending birthday of the Reich Chancellor is commemorated with an intercession in the service...'[72]

The message of the Prussian church administration which millions of Protestant Christians heard at Easter 1933 was as follows:

This year the Easter message of the risen Christ goes forth in Germany to a people to whom God has spoken by means of a great turning point in history.

We know that we are at one with all Protestant fellow believers in joy at the awakening of the deepest powers of our nation to a patriotic consciousness, to a true community of the Volk, and to a religious renewal.

After a reference to the 'Fatherland Declaration' of the Königsberg Kirchentag in 1927, it went on:

In the conviction that the renewal of Volk and Reich can be achieved and secured only by these powers, the church knows itself bound in gratitude to the leadership of the new Germany. It is joyfully prepared to co-operate in the national and moral renewal of our people.

To perform this service, the church requires complete freedom for the development of its life and its work. It trusts the government which has given us a solemn assurance of this freedom.[73]

If one follows developments from the first church utterances in February, through the still obviously reserved statements at the beginning and in the middle of March, to this Easter message in April, it becomes clear how much the Protestant church, too, was caught up in the dynamic of a development in which maintaining a critical detachment became more and more difficult. As a spiritual process, less concerned with the conquest of positions of political power than with securing the inner conviction of a majority and doing away with the critical detachment of the individual, the seizure of power was essentially completed for the Protestant church by the end of March. This change in church consciousness was a precondition for the rise of the German Christians, which began early in April.

2

The Capitulation of Catholicism
(February-March)

While the winning over of Protestantism presented no special problems to Hitler, things on the Catholic side were much more difficult. Here not only the Centre Party, which had demonstrated its reliability and steadfastness in all the elections of the past, stood in the way of his quest for sole authority, but also the condemnation of National Socialism by the German bishops. Without its reversal the integration of Catholics into the Third Reich was unthinkable. Overcoming this closed Catholic defence was one of the most important tasks that Hitler faced in the first weeks of his rule. In contrast to the political left, which he could attack frontally, here little could be achieved by force. Any such attempt would have conjured up a Kulturkampf, of which for good reasons Hitler was remarkably afraid. Thus he had to develop a plan that checkmated political Catholicism and at the same time put the Catholic bishops in a situation in which they no longer had any choice but to revise their negative stance. Hitler had such a plan, and he was also successful in translating it into reality within a few months.

One fundamental difficulty for German Catholicism lay in the fact that at this time closely connected decisions were made on three different levels without any real co-ordination. On the contrary, each of these three levels was so intent on its own interests that the question of repercussions on the other areas was given hardly any serious consideration. The first level of decision-making, the German hierarchy, was faced with the difficult problem of what should become of the official condemnation of National Socialist ideology, a condemnation that was still in force and had been explicitly confirmed by the Fulda Bishops' Conference as late as August 1932. Though at first the matter seemed not to be an urgent one, the more Hitler established himself in Germany, the more pressing it became. The second level, the Centre Party, was faced with equally serious problems. Robbed of its traditional key role since the March elections, and confronted with the Enabling Act, it was once again called to a decision as inescapable as it was incalculable in its importance to church and state. Finally, the third level, the Vatican, also had to make a decision as to its future relations with the new German governemnt. From the Roman point of view, not only conditions in Germany but the supposed or real interests of the entire church had to be considered at this point.

Hitherto it had been a strength of Catholicism that on individual matters everything was dealt with independently on these three levels within the wider framework of the Catholic world-view and church policy, marked out by natural law and canon law. This now proved to be a fatal weakness. Its result was that the essential decisions increasingly shifted to the Curia, and finally the position and future of Catholicism in the Third Reich was in fact decided almost solely in Rome.

Hitler's most urgent problem in the first weeks was, of course, the Centre Party. In a clever and cunning ploy, when forming his government on 30 January he was so successful in exploiting the Centre Party that it felt deceived more by the German National members of the cabinet than by Hitler himself.[1] Only after the dissolution of the Reichstag, and during the last election campaign beginning immediately afterwards, did the fronts again begin to become clearer. Even if the Centre Party chairman Ludwig Kaas continued to hold fast to the collective thinking[2] which he had so emphatically advocated since autumn 1932, it became increasingly evident that the real issue was a choice between justice and injustice, freedom and dictatorship.

The Catholic party, the Catholic associations and a large part of the Catholic press conducted this last election campaign with admirable courage. Although from the middle of February 'a concentric wave of NS terror' broke on the Centre Party, the banning of meetings, speeches and newspapers multiplied; and everywhere civil servants belonging to the Centre Party were dismissed,[3] an electoral appeal from the Catholic organizations appeared on 17 February in language the clarity of which left nothing to be desired. The appeal, personally signed by the directors of the respective organizations, stated openly in connection with the breaches of law by the new government: 'What will be the fruits of such a government once it knows that it is in possession of lasting power? It will be a civil order in which arbitrariness and partiality will take the place of justice and group interest will be more decisive than the common good. It will be an economic order in which a just assessment of the necessities of life for all social classes will be thrust aside by a one-sided preference for certain social strata...' After criticism of the Christian phrases which were to be heard everywhere, the appeal accused Hitler of nothing short of another form of Bolshevism: 'We know this: that there can also be Bolshevism under a nationalist banner.' Finally, the confession stood for a constitutional state and for a 'strong, organic and creative centre'.[4] The appeal led to a ban on numerous newspapers that printed it. It took the intervention of Göring to lift these bans. A leading article like that published in the *Junge Front* on 10 February also showed that at least a nucleus of Catholic people was determined to fight. 'We will not rest,' the article concluded, 'until we have fought the good fight. We can be outlawed, we can be muzzled, we can be prohibited from opening our mouths; but the truth will cry out all the louder, for it cannot be suppressed...'[5] Despite growing terrorism, the leading Centre Party politicians also kept up the election campaign. Brüning in particular, who headed the party's list of election candidates, harshly attacked the breaches of law by the government in meetings which were packed to the doors. The former Chancellor closed his election campaign in the Berlin Sports Palace on the evening of 3 March. According to his own recollections, those involved in this last free election campaign in Berlin were seized with enormous enthusiasm. 'I was in the frame of mind of someone with nothing to lose, almost cheerful. My words about the constitutional state and the appeal to the Reich President had a powerful effect.' No less typical of the situation was, however, the fact that at the end of the meeting Brüning had to be brought out of a side entrance of the Sports Palace and taken by car 'in a great arc round Berlin' to his 'primary hiding place in east Berlin'.[6]

The German episcopacy was also part of this front, less because of new formulations than simply because it continued its previous policy. Thus Cardinal Faulhaber of Munich, who had already completed his Lenten pastoral letter before 30 January, deliberately refused to make any revisions and dated it 10 February 'in order to show that the principles of the Christian doctrine of the state do not change when governments change'.[7] The pastoral letter itself repeated the principles of basic Catholic teaching on the state by developing the 'fundamentals of the Christian doctrine of the state', the 'responsibilities of the Christian state' and the 'duties of the Christian citizen'.[8]

The Lenten letter of the new Archbishop of Freiburg, Conrad Gröber, also dated 10 February, condemned the radicalizing of the political struggle even more clearly and called on the diocesan bishops 'to take as much care as possible to see that the lies and the slander, the witch-hunting and the hatred, the acts of violence and murder do not continue shamefully to stain the German name'.[9]

How little the bishops were prepared to be diverted from their previous apparently well-tried line was shown above all by the fact that the pastoral message of the Fulda Bishops' Conference for the 5 March election repeated almost unchanged an appeal which the same body had already issued for the Reichstag election of 31 July 1932. In fact the admonition to elect representatives 'whose character and proven attitude gives evidence of their commitment to peace and the social welfare of the people, to the protection of the confessional schools, the Christian religion and the Catholic church' was still sufficiently unequivocal – even if, in the revolutionary situation before the March elections, more vigorous support for the Centre Party could have been devised.[10]

In fact the bishops and the clergy were at one in their loyalty to the Centre Party, as they were in the condemnation of National Socialism. Exceptions were rare, and they met with resolute rejection. For example, when in February 1933 at a meeting of the Catholic Academic Association, Clemens August Graf Galen, at the time pastor of St Lamberti in Münster – and years later to become a leader of the Catholic resistance – demanded that the new political movement should receive at least 'a just and objective appraisal', as Joseph Pieper recalled, this took place 'before a large audience, who clearly disapproved of him and remained icily silent'.[11] And this reaction was undoubtedly typical.

A survey of these first weeks before 5 March clearly reveals that German Catholicism as a whole continued the closed front against National Socialism which it had formed after the September 1930 elections. Although there may have been gradations, doubts about the correctness of this position, errors in judgment about Hitler and his politics, even considerable inroads into the traditional voting strata, seen as a whole Catholicism still represented an ideological block of imposing unanimity.

The election results of 5 March confirmed this impression. The attack on the Centre Party, so often referred to, left it essentially unshaken. With 11.2% of the votes, the party had lost only 0.7% of its voters, and in many places – e.g.

Berlin – had achieved a relative increase. Only the sister Bavarian Volkspartei had suffered really considerable losses; but its structure also remained intact throughout.

Paradoxically, there were two completely different answers to the question of the political significance of this election result.

According to the traditional democratic rules of the game, in spite of its remarkable stability the Centre Party had suffered a severe defeat. Thanks to the majority for the right-wing coalition, it had lost its hitherto key position in the Reichstag and at the same time had also been ousted from its leading position in Bavaria. 'Political Catholicism saw itself wiped out,' commented Rudolf Morsey, summarizing this view of things, 'since there were no further possibilities of influencing the course of events directly... An unusual paralysis seized the Centre Party.'[12]

On the other hand, the result inevitably looked quite different from Hitler's perspective. With a view to his achieving total power, which was to be completed by the Enabling Act, the election result for a short while made the Centre Party a decisive element in his policies. For if he wanted to keep the semblance of legality, which he had so far maintained so successfully, then he needed the votes of this party to get the two-thirds majority necessary for the last law of the parliament. Moreover, Hitler would not have been the völkisch Führer that he was had he not seen the block of almost five and a half million Catholic-controlled votes as an intolerable long-term obstacle to the internal co-ordination of the German people.

Thus the matter of political Catholicism was one of the most important problems that he had to solve after 5 March.

In fact the first post-election cabinet meeting, which took place on the afternoon of 7 March, was basically shaped by this whole complex of questions. Hitler began with an analysis of the election which, in his view, had partly been decided by the mobilization of non-voters. While he saw on the left a general movement towards the right, so that former Communists had voted for the SPD and former Social Democrats for the NSDAP, he made a surprising remark about the manifest stability of the Centre Party: 'As for the voters of the Centre Party and the Bavarian Volkspartei, they will only be conquered by the nationalist parties when the Curia drops both of them.' After touching briefly on the problem of the relationship of the Reich to the Länder, he talked about the necessity of an Enabling Act with a two-thirds majority, and here he expressed his conviction 'that the Reichstag will pass such a law'. After statements by Frick and Hugenberg, Vice-Chancellor von Papen spoke. He reported 'on the foreign policy situation' that the previous day the Chairman of the Centre Party, Prelate Kaas, had visited him: 'He stated that he had come without previous discussion with his party and was now ready to make a clean break with the past. Moreover, he offered the co-operation of the Centre Party.' In Göring's view, too, the Centre Party had an important role in connection with the question of the two-thirds majority. In keeping with his crude nature, his idea was that the party should be threatened with the dismissal of all its officials if it did not agree to the Enabling Act. 'Otherwise the tactics to be employed towards the Centre Party should be politely to ignore it.' The problems posed by Catholicism became the topic of discussion for a last time in this cabinet meeting when the

Minister for Post and Transportation, Baron von Eltz-Rübenach, a National-Conservative Catholic, suggested the publication of an interpretation of Point 24 of the Party programme to satisfy Catholics not bound to the Centre Party who might have hesitations about it. Hitler, who immediately agreed to this suggestion, declared 'that the bishops are entitled to an authentic interpretation of all questions relating to the church. The church will accept the National Socialist Party only when it is forced by circumstances to accept the Party. Besides,' continued Hitler, and this association is worth noting, 'conditions at the German Embassy to the Vatican are very unpleasant. The clergy adviser who has been active there for some years, Prelate Steinmann, frequently plots intrigues against the Ambassador. Here, too, a change will be necessary. A man like Abbot Schachleiter belongs in Steinmann's place.' This was addressed to the Foreign Minister, who immediately pointed out that the post of clergy adviser in the Vatican Embassy had been established only after the War and that there was no need for it. Then the discussion turned to other topics – above all the burning of the Reichstag and the punishment of the perpetrators, for which the Minister of the Interior suggested 'immediate hanging', and added, 'in Königsplatz'.[13]

So we are on firm ground in starting from the assumption that on 7 March Hitler had already considered the idea that the Curia could drop the Catholic parties; that he conceded that the bishops should have an authentic interpretation of all questions concerning the church; that he was informed about conditions in the embassy to the Vatican; and that he had information from his Vice-Chancellor about a peace offer from Kaas. If all this is combined with those ideas which Hitler had expressed as early as 1929 in connection with the Lateran Treaties, it was only one more step to a concrete formulation of the plan that was to determine the policy of the Third Reich towards Catholicism until the summer: the offer of a concordat between the German Reich and the Holy See modelled on the Lateran Concordat. For only with the help of such a concordat could political Catholicism, which was so hated and feared, be safely eliminated. Only in this way could the bishops and the Curia be persuaded to endorse the Third Reich, at the same time making the way free to win Catholic voters to National Socialism.

It cannot be said with certainty whether Hitler's thinking had reached this conclusion by 7 March. But it seems to be out of the question to maintain – as almost all more recent research assumes[14] – that this plan played no role in the major decisions in March and emerged like a *deus ex machina* early in April.

It is certainly true that so far no incontestable proof for March plans for a concordat have been found in either government or church files.[15] But the small circle of persons concerned had such good reasons to treat these plans with the utmost discretion that conversely it would be astonishing if anything at all had been committed to paper before 23 March.

That applies above all to the Centre Party chairman Ludwig Kaas, who probably acted as the key go-between in the whole matter.

For Kaas, the election results of 5 March changed the situation completely. Up to that point he had still fought for the direct political involvement of the Centre Party. The Centre Party had lost this battle because of the majority which Hitler and his coalition partners had obtained. Thus authoritarian government had finally been established, and what mattered most was to adapt to the new circumstances. Kaas's 6 March visit to Papen and his offer of co-operation was the first sign of his new perspective.

When Kaas reviewed the situation at this time with regard to the new government and the expected Enabling Act, two aspects of the situation must have struck him. For the chairman of a constitutional party the Enabling Act contained dangers against which it was important to have as much protection as possible. But the same law also provided a unique opportunity for Kaas as prelate and canon lawyer. A commentary on the Lateran Treaties as early as 1929 had maintained that 'parliamentarianism is not necessary for the treatment and solution of truly major issues'.[16] Kaas had put forward the same view throughout his long study of the new type of concordat, which he had finished only a few weeks earlier. Pacelli's was the school in which he had learned to recognize and make use of auspicious moments in world history. So after 5 March Kaas had to weigh carefully the dangers of an Enabling Act for domestic political development against his chances of concluding a Reich concordat. In fact the prelate may well have made his personal decision for the Enabling Act contingent upon Hitler's promise to use this same law to conclude the Reich concordat which had been frustrated time and again by the parliament of the Republic.

A precondition for this policy was the willingness of Rome to negotiate with Hitler at all. This willingness could not be taken for granted. But at this juncture Hitler's confidence-building campaign and the Pope's anxiety about Communism combined to demolish the existing obstacles.

The German ambassador to the Holy See, Diego von Bergen, had reported as early as 8 February, in connection with the first Roman reactions to the seizure of power, that he had 'reason to assume' that the solemn profession of Christianity in the government appeal of 1 February could not fail to make an effect. The report then continued: 'The resolute declaration of war on Bolshevism, the overcoming of which is one of the greatest concerns of the Holy See, is very welcome.'[17] Four weeks later, on 4 March, Pius XI let his Cardinal Secretary of State know that Hitler was the first and only statesman to speak out openly against Bolshevism.[18] Soon afterwards he repeated this view almost word for word to Cardinal Faulhaber, Archbishop of Munich, who was in Rome for a visit. Faulhaber noted the Pope's opinion of the new Chancellor: 'Hitler. I am pleased; he is the first statesman to have spoken out against Bolshevism.' Faulhaber's note was at the same time a sign that Hitler's confidence-building campaign had also found a response within Catholicism: 'I: He speaks very piously, in Königsberg, about providence and how he prays. He [the Pope] had heard or read all this.'[19] Pius XI expressed similar sentiments in the presence of other diplomats, too.[20]

It was thus totally in accord with his convictions that in an address to the Consistory on 13 March the Pope, speaking indirectly, but clearly enough for those in the know, bestowed praise on the new government in Germany. Another note of Faulhaber's, which he prepared for a situation report to the Bavarian bishops on 20 April 1933, shows how surprising many people found this praise, and how lasting the memory of it remained: 'My journey to Rome confirmed what I might have suspected for a long time. In Rome, National Socialism and Fascism are considered the only deliverance from Communism and Bolshevism.

The Holy Father sees this from a great distance; he does not see the attendant phenomena, but only the grand goal.' As proof, Faulhaber then described the scene on 13 March: 'In the secret consistory on 13 March 1933 people gave a start when the Holy Father said, with special emphasis: "Until recently the voice of the Roman Pope remained the only one to point out the serious dangers threatening Christian culture which has been introduced into almost all nations." Thus, public praise for Hitler.'[21]

The stir in the consistory was not surprising, when we consider that at the same time, to all outward appearance German Catholicism was still presenting a closed front to National Socialism and had just put the hardest election campaign in its history behind it.

However, what the Pope said took on a special political significance only as a result of a notice which was sent the same day by the Papal Secretary of State to the German ambassador to the Vatican. Even before the consistory began, Bergen cabled to Berlin the contents of the decisive sentence from the papal address and added: 'In the State Secretariat it was suggested to me that I should point out that this word was to be construed as an indirect acknowledgment of the action of the Reich Chancellor and the government against Communism.'[22]

However, this produced a highly complicated situation for Catholicism. For while the Vatican thus showed cautious signs of a wish for accommodation, even after 5 March the German bishops still showed no readiness to fall into line. A memorandum on Hitler's view of the church presented in the Vatican by Cardinal Faulhaber on 17 March made it clear that the President of the Freising Bishops' Conference also saw no intrinsic reason for an official revision of the course adopted hitherto. Granted, he praised Hitler's courage in it, 'in confessing the name of God' when the name of God did not appear in the constitution of the German Reich. He also found it praiseworthy that Hitler was fighting against Marxism and Communism. Furthermore, the Cardinal took a positive view of Hitler's desire to overturn capitalism and of the fact that in his speeches as Chancellor he showed restraint. However, the list of those things of which he did not approve turned out to be a good deal longer and more important. The preaching of hatred and violence, the cult of race, the National Socialist claim to be a new religion, and not least the fear that the Protestant groups which were veering *en masse* towards National Socialism could militate against Roman Catholicism, led the Cardinal to a predominantly critical judgment. Of course, if the government by its actions proved these fears unfounded, the bishops would 'gladly give up their mistrust of the Party'.[23]

Certainly the opinions among the bishops were not uniform. Events followed in rapid succession. Unrest at the grass roots grew; even purely Catholic communities were already going over to the Party 'with flags flying',[24] and the episcopal warnings were beginning to turn, as Ludwig Volk put it, from 'a guiding line' into a 'ghetto wall' 'which kept progressive German Catholics from taking part in the "awakening of the nation"'.[25]

Moreover, the theory of the 'social affinity' between Catholicism and National Socialism which Walter Dirks had propounded in 1931 was now beginning to be confirmed among Catholic church people. Both, Dirks had written, were supported 'predominantly by the petty bourgeois', so that with a relaxation of the Catholic ban the social unrest of these classes would 'with some degree of certainty issue in the National Socialist movement'. As Dirks suggested at the time: 'The weak spot of Catholicism is located here. Its democracy is safe against the restoration of the monarchy, against adventurous Putsches, against the dictatorship of the proletariat, against the "old system", against the National Socialism of Rosenberg and of the street. But whether its harassed petty bourgeois, its farmers, its unemployed and intellectuals could protect themselves in an hour of decision against the attraction of an ideologically moderate "Third Reich" – that is a serious question.'[26] In fact, a considerable stir now also developed among Catholic church people: and the bishops could not be indifferent to that.

Nevertheless, when on 18 March Papen sounded out the President of the Fulda Bishops' Conference, Cardinal Bertram, as to the meaning of the accumulating news reports of an imminent change of course, he was still told clearly that the one who had to reverse his position was 'the Führer of the National Socialists' and not the church, which had clearly fixed its position in 1932. In the letter to the members of the conference which contained this news, Bertram at the same time informed the bishops of his conviction that a situation which might call for a general statement to the Catholic people seemed to him 'not yet sufficiently clarified', and that the elimination of the known impediments had 'not yet convincingly taken place'.[27] Until 19 March, then, Catholicism in so far as it was represented by the bishops stood firm in the opinion that there was no occasion for a fundamental change of mind.

This resolute attitude of the German episcopacy could only strengthen Hitler in his concern to make peace with Rome as quickly as possible, and in this concern he had to concur with Kaas, for whom this peace represented the greatest possible goal that might be achieved. However, the price of this peace with an authoritarian state was well known to the author of the study on the Italian concordat: the price was the Centre Party.

In these circumstances, after 5 March the prelate evidently no longer saw any possibility of shaping politics in Germany as President of the Centre Party. Although Kaas knew from the beginning of March that his party had to make a decision with unforeseeable consequences in view of the planned Enabling Act, he kept strangely silent. Instead of probing the situation in conversations inside and outside the party, weighing up the existing chances and dangers, and preparing to form an opinion within the parliamentary group, Kaas did nothing of the kind. Whereas Brüning was still attempting to influence Hindenburg with the help of the German Nationals,[28] nothing is known of any kind of politically significant activity in this period by the man responsible for the leadership of the Centre Party. A protest letter of 15 March to Hitler on a comparatively insignificant matter,[29] and a leading article attributed to the prelate[30] in the Kölnische Volkszeitung of 17 March hardly count as that.

Instead of this, during these weeks Kaas was presumably investigating the possibilities for the church politics of the Curia as a result of an Enabling Act which the Centre Party had helped to pass.[31]

The argument for a connection between the Reich concordat and the Enabling Act was stated and substantiated in detail for the first time by Karl Dietrich Bracher in his opinion on the concordat process in the light of its political context.[32] The publication of Heinrich Brüning's memoirs have made the former

Centre Party Chancellor the key witness for this theory. For Brüning, who doubtless had excellent sources of information at his disposal, in retrospect the setting was quite clear. The crucial paragraph of his memoirs ran as follows: 'Kaas's resistance became weaker as Hitler spoke about a concordat and Papen gave assurances that one was as good as guaranteed. That was the issue which from his point of view naturally and understandably interested Kaas most. Since 1920 he had always hoped to be able to create a national concordat. For him as a prelate, securing relations between the Vatican and the German Reich was a crucial question to which everything else had to be co-ordinated, if not subordinated. Hitler and Papen will have noticed how the growing prospects for a concordat increasingly captivated Kaas. However, he wanted Hitler to commit himself to the conclusion of a concordat in some way.'[33]

If we keep the overall situation in mind, then all the signs are that this is a credible picture, even if all the details cannot be proved. Hitler's basic decision had remained the same since 1929, as had his desire to gain the Catholic votes and eliminate political Catholicism as quickly as possible. If in addition he now also received the consent of the Centre Party to the Enabling Act in exchange for the offer of a concordat, there was no reason why he should hesitate to express his view. Papen's interests in a concordat – part personal and part political – were quite obvious. For more than a decade Kaas had taken part in negotiations over such a treaty. He knew that the Cardinal Secretary of State considered it the most important goal of curial politics *vis à vis* the Reich, and he also recognized the new possibilities for an agreement offered by the Italian concordat. Finally, Pius XI had indicated that he saw Hitler as a possible ally and had therefore considerably mitigated the doubts about Hitler's capacity to keep to a contract. In these circumstances Ludwig Kaas would have been a fool had he not investigated Hitler's willingness to conclude a concordat.

This assumption is supported by a series of assorted statements and remarks. Hitler himself, like Papen, declared that the concordat issue was part of the game from the very beginning. Thus the Reich Chancellor appeared pleasantly surprised in the crucial cabinet meeting on 14 July that 'the goal of an agreement with the Curia which he had constantly sought was reached so much more quickly than he could have imagined possible even on 30 January...'[34] And Papen too maintained again and again that he had put the concordat question to the Chancellor quite early on, 'immediately after 30 January 1933'.[35] That things were settled by March is also indicated by a letter in which immediately after the Centre Party had given its consent, a friend of Papen's, Graf Praschma, expressed his satisfaction with the way things were going. 'However,' Praschma wrote to Papen on 25 March, 'it seems to me that we can be satisfied with the manner and form in which the Centre Party has established contact. I consider it a great success, not to be shrugged off with the comment that it was the only possible thing. It is to be hoped that further developments will preserve us from situations which might again cloud the relationship. I hope, too, that your journey to Rome goes well.'

Obviously, then, Papen had outlined to Praschma, possibly as early as his stay at Praschma's Schloss Falkenstein between 8 and 12 March, certain plans for the Centre Party and the Vatican which were now confirmed by events.[36] This also fits the fact that a zealous National Socialist emissary from Vienna, attempting to convince Papen that the time was ripe for an agreement between Berlin and Rome, found the Vice-Chancellor on 27 March 'already intent on it and authorized to bring it about'.[37]

Generally speaking, the confidence on the National Socialist side that the Centre Party would agree was astonishingly great from the beginning. In the cabinet meeting on 15 March, during which the whole question was discussed, Hitler declared that in his view 'seeing the Enabling Act safely through the Reichstag with a two-thirds majority would come up against no real difficulties'. Frick clarified this by remarking that he had pointed out to the parties in the Reichstag 'that the Reichstag had to pass within three days an Enabling Act with a sufficient majority to amend the constitution. The Centre Party has given no negative response whatever.' Deputy Esser, however, had asked for an interview with Hitler.[38] During the debate Papen made explicit mention of political Catholicism and emphasized that the question of its integration into the new state was 'of special significance'.[39] And on 20 March – the very day on which official negotiations with the Centre Party began – Goebbels recorded in his diary: 'We have news that the Centre Party will also accept it' (i.e. the Enabling Act).'[40] Four years later, in a commemorative article on the conclusion of the concordat, Goebbels' newspaper *Der Angriff* was to maintain openly that in 1933 Kaas had made the Centre Party's approval of the Enabling Act contingent 'upon the willingness of the Reich government to negotiate with the Holy See for a Reich concordat, and to respect the rights of the church.'[41] This tallies with the recollection of Fritz Günther von Tschirschky, a young associate of Papen's in the Vice-Chancellery, who reports negotiations of that kind between Hitler and Kaas immediately before the decisive Reichstag session on 23 March.[42]

Among Centre Party members there were also early suspicions of an arrangement. They are expressed in a record kept by circles in the Centre Party of Cologne of a confrontation between Brüning and Kaas which took place in the days before 20 March. Whereas on this occasion Brüning justified his categorical rejection of the Enabling Act with the remark that the Centre Party, as a 'constitutional party', could in no circumstances participate in this 'material breach of law', no arguments of any kind were produced by Kaas. Rather, in the end he pounded on the table with the words, 'Am I the leader of the party? If not, who is?' This attitude of the leader of the Centre Party, which was not exactly persuasive, induced the writer of the record to ask: 'Had Kaas in his negotiations with Hitler perhaps made promises to the latter so that he *had to* stand firm?'[43]

Still more important than these comments and recollections, which confirmed that things were so to speak in the air, is a reaction from the Protestant side. It provides indirect proof that in fact a Reich concordat was being discussed as early as March.

On 23 March, the day of the Enabling Act, Kapler, the President of the Kirchenbund, was in Eisenach for a short personal holiday. In the morning a call came to him from Berlin which caused him to write a letter to the Reich President the very same day. Referring to the news he had just received from Berlin, he wrote: 'According to reports, the discussions in connection with the negotiations over acceptance of the Enabling Act with representatives of Catholic church interests, political or ecclesiastical, are in the balance over the question of a guarantee of the legal status of the Catholic church in Germany arising out of the Reich constitution, and especially over the question of a Reich concordat to safeguard this legal status.' The purpose of the letter was a request addressed to the Reich President, 'as the chief guardian of the law and of confessional peace' to intervene 'for safeguarding the interests of the Protestant church to an equal degree'.[44] It is inconceivable that Kapler, always correct and careful, should have decided upon such an important step on the basis of an unverifiable rumour. The news which the unknown person passed on to him must have had some foundation. And indeed it was subsequently treated as a fact and, as will emerge in due course, led the leading figure of the Protestant church to extraordinarily far-reaching decisions.[45] The letter itself was answered two days later by Hindenburg's Secretary of State Meissner, with the comment that the Reich President had noted it with interest and 'forwarded it as information to the Reich Minister of the Interior'.[46] In a confidential report on the situation dated 1 April, Kapler officially informed the principal authorities of the Protestant Landeskirchen of this situation. This report stated that it had become known to him, 'confidentially, shortly before the Reichstag deliberations on the Enabling Act, that special negotiations with the Centre Party or the Catholic church had taken place and that further such negotiations were to be expected.' Therefore he had written a personal letter to the Reich President and asked him to protect confessional parity.[47] However, the definitive proof that all this was not a matter of rumour and that such negotiations had actually taken place is provided by the fact that on this 1 April Kapler amazingly met Frick for a conversation in which, without being reassured to the contrary, he expressed the anxieties of the Protestant church over a Reich concordat. Kapler reported this conversation to the Prussian general superintendents on 11 April[48] and to the Kirchenausschuss on 25 April,[49]

Thus if the President was not totally misinformed – and all his actions, conversations and reports, on the contrary, suggest that his initial information was fully confirmed – then the link between the Enabling Act and the Reich concordat was definitely established, at the latest, sometime on 23 March.

Finally, even the most important witness, Kaas himself, in a letter dated 19 November 1935 to the German ambassador to the Vatican, von Bergen, portrayed his role in the acceptance of the Enabling Act in a way that hardly permits any reasonable doubt about the connections. 'Immediately after the passing of the Enabling Act, in the acceptance of which I had played a positive role on the basis of certain guarantees given to me by the Reich Chancellor (guarantees of a general political as well as a cultural political nature), on 24 March I travelled to Rome. Apart from having a holiday, in order to develop the views I put forward in the Reichstag on 23 March I wanted to explain the situation created by the Reich Chancellor's declaration and to investigate the possibilities for a comprehensive understanding between church and state.'[50] It is, of course, possible at a pinch to understand the statements made here to refer to the results of the negotiations of 20 and 22 March, and if necessary also to argue that the 'comprehensive agreement between church and state' need 'not necessarily' refer to a 'Reich concordat',[51] but such interpretations are scarcely very convincing or meaningful.[52]

In the light of this state of affairs, those who dispute a link between the acceptance of the Enabling Act and the conclusion of the Reich concordat definitely seem unconvincing. For example, Josef Joos, a Brüning supporter and one of the leaders of the parliamentary party, declared in retrospect in 1958 that there could 'in fact be no question' of such a link.[53] That was probably true of the official negotiations in the party and the opinion-forming that went on there; but in all probability it was not true of Kaas. Similarly, the firm statement of Fr Robert Leiber, one of Pacelli's closest associates, whom he had followed to Rome in 1929, can be quite true in the literal sense. According to him, Hitler's seizure of power, the consent of the Centre Party to the Enabling Act, and the revision of the bishops' admonitions, had occurred 'without the slightest pressure from the Holy See and Cardinal Secretary of State Pacelli'.[54] Nevertheless, it cannot be denied that the well-known interests and wishes of Rome were present in all the decisions made by Catholicism during those days in the person of Kaas, and that they played an important role.

Much, then, as Kaas had his reasons for working for an endorsement by his party on 23 March, because he had tied the hope of a Reich concordat to this law, these reasons did not coincide with those of the majority in the parliamentary party. If this majority had already 'come to Berlin with a concern to say yes',[55] then with them came a mixture of all the hopes, desires and fears that characterized the state of mind of the German middle-class generally during those stormy weeks. The argument likely to have been most persistent in the parliamentary party was that Hitler was determined to see the plans of the Reich government through even if he did not get a two-thirds majority. There was indeed no doubt about that. And no one could or wanted to predict what would become of the Catholic party if a new Kulturkampf should break out in far harsher circumstances.[56] Hence in the view of the Reichstag representatives, to deny consent would simply have led to unforeseen consequences, while a 'yes' still offered a chance to remind Hitler of his promises and to be able to keep apart of the old influence. This was the exact tone of the speech with which Kaas opened the deliberations of the parliamentary party on 23 March – a few hours before the beginning of the crucial Reichstag session in the Kroll Opera House. In it he first presented the catalogue of demands to be accepted in the government policy statement, and on which the negotiating team had made the consent of the party dependent. After that he pointed out the hopelessness of the situation, in which no alternatives of any kind were, he said, visible. This speech, like the situation as a whole, reflected Hitler's tactical mastery. With its back to the wall, without additional sources of information, in the face of physical terror, and pressed for time, political Catholicism seemed to see grasping at Hitler's promises, uncertain though they might be, as the only possible saving option. Even Brüning's courageous plea to the contrary could not change anything here, but only give a warning; it no longer had any alternative to offer.[57]

This situation must be kept in mind if we are to understand the impression which Hitler's government policy statement at noon on the same day made on the Centre Party representatives and upon all German Catholicism. The Chancellor endorsed – sometimes almost literally – all the demands which the Centre Party had named as prerequisites for its consent to the Enabling Act, point by point. In addition, Hitler behaved throughout the speech in such a

248

statesmanlike, conciliatory, patriotic and Christian way[58] that a refusal could hardly continue to be justified.

So it was that in the meeting of the parliamentary party in the afternoon, despite still vigorous, indeed passionate, opposition from the minority, the majority decision was made as Hitler wanted it. Kaas, who in the morning had still refused to suggest what to decide in this difficult situation, in the afternoon put himself at the head of those who advocated the party's assent. In order not to endanger the unity of the party, the minority finally joined the majority.

It would certainly be wrong to overlook the many and manifest reasons which, in the general setting, moved the majority of representatives to give their consent. But it would be just as wrong to overlook the fact that Kaas played a key role in this decision from the beginning. He was the only one with all the information at his disposal; he had negotiated personally with Hitler and Papen; and everyone knew that in no circumstances would he consent to a decision that infringed the interests of Rome. So for the majority of the parliamentary group, who were looking for their bearings in this unparalleled situation, he became the man whom they could trust. The discipline shown one last time in the loyalty of the minority in the party only served to lend the voice of the chairman special weight.

In this context, two results must be regarded as the real surprises of those days.

A comparison of the demands of the Centre Party with the pledges in Hitler's government policy statement readily demonstrate that Hitler in fact accepted them point by point.[59] Only one crucial sentence in his speech was without a counterpart in the demands submitted by the Centre Party. This was the declaration that the Reich government set 'the highest store' on 'further cultivating and strengthening friendly relations with the Holy See'. Ludwig Volk considers this 'an empty formula within which the later development has a place but in which it was in no way prefigured'.[60] However, from all we know of Hitler's preoccupation with the concordat question since 1929, of the significance which he attached to political Catholicism at this time, and of his determination to solve this problem once and for all, it would be very strange indeed if this sentence of his had meant nothing at all, or nothing special. It would seem much more likely that this sentence also had a prehistory. This supposition is supported by the fact that its formulation, down to the very phraseology, corresponds to the declaration with which Pacelli had announced his concordat plans in 1920 on presenting his credentials as the new Nuncio to the Reich. At that time Pacelli had said, in the presence of the Reich President: 'For my part I will devote my entire strength to cultivating and strengthening the relations between the Holy See and Germany...'[61] The way in which Hitler now seized on this phrase revealed the hand of Ludwig Kaas. In substance, it meant that Hitler was confirming to the President of the Centre Party his willingness, after the consent of the Centre Party to the Enabling Act, to start immediately on a readjustment of relations between Berlin and Rome.

For contemporaries, all these proceedings remained mysterious and enigmatic. In retrospect, however, matters were transparent and obvious. A memorandum dated 5 March 1939 which Cardinal Faulhaber sent to Pacelli – by this time Pope Pius XII – contains the terse sentence: 'But in his first speech, in March 1933,

Adolf Hitler had declared that he would maintain friendly relations with the church and develop them still further by means of a concordat.'[62]

Closely connected with this we have the second surprising event. Barely twenty-four hours after the consent of the Centre Party, Kaas set off for Rome in a hurry, on the afternoon of 24 March, evidently without informing anyone of what he was doing. In his own words he wanted to be there 'to explain the situation created by the Reich Chancellor's statements and to investigate the possibilities for a comprehensive agreement between church and state.'[63] However, neither in the official negotiations nor in the government policy statement can a remark be found upon which such far-reaching purposes could be based, other than that one sentence about the cultivation and strengthening of relations with the Holy See. This sentence can hardly be understood, then, as an 'empty formula'. Rather, we must see it as a quite specific announcement of an imminent initiative by the Reich government in the Reich concordat affair - which then only ten days later, on 2 April, appeared on the official record for the first time.[64]

However, in gaining the consent of the Centre Party to the Enabling Act, Hitler had achieved only one part of his task of eliminating the resistance to the Third Reich within German Catholicism. The second part, which was undoubtedly even more important for Catholicism as a whole, consisted in the reversal of those condemnations with which the German bishops had answered National Socialist ideology since 1930. As has already been indicated, as late as 19 March there was no sign of a rapid change on this matter. In contrast to the Centre Party problem, Hitler himself had virtually no chance of exercising a direct influence on the course of events here. For he could neither negotiate with the bishops nor could he seriously consider the option of publicly abandoning the principles of his ideology in response to Catholic urging. On the other hand, a revision of the episcopal condemnation undoubtedly mattered a great deal to him. For as long as the bishops still hesitated, Hitler had to reckon with a disruptive factor the potential importance of which was difficult to estimate.

But Hitler's extraordinary tactical skill came to his aid even in this difficult situation. It was announced that the Potsdam Day would begin with morning services for both confessions. In order to escape the dilemma of either acknow-ledging the authority of the church by taking part in the Catholic services or of arousing doubts about his piety by staying away, Hitler had had the idea of asking Abbot Schachleiter – who was totally devoted to him – to hold a special service in the palace of the Reich Chancellor. However, this plan was thwarted because shortly beforehand Schachleiter, whose National Socialist agitation in Bavaria had provoked growing offence in the church, had been suspended by a pronouncement of the Religious Congregation in Rome, and was thus prohibited from performing any ecclesiastical act.[65] The expedient which Hitler thereupon very quickly seized on was to prove an extraordinarily effective weapon against the episcopacy. 'The Catholic bishops of Germany,' he declared on 21 March, 'have in a series of recent statements branded leaders and members of the NSDAP as apostates from the church who may not enjoy the benefit of the sacraments, and the Catholic clergy have acted accordingly. Up to the present these statements have not been revoked, and the Catholic clergy still act in accordance with them. The Chancellor therefore found himself, to his great distress, unable to take part in the Catholic service at Potsdam.' Instead of this, the statement went on, together with Reich Minister Dr Goebbels, who was in the same position, at that time he had 'visited the graves of his murdered SA comrades at Luisenstadt cemetery in Berlin', and there laid a wreath with the inscription, 'To my dead comrades'.[66] We will certainly not go far wrong if we see Goebbels' hand in the skilful formulation of this news item. In fact there was hardly a more effective way of embarrassing the bishops than through the half-truth of the accusation combined with Hitler's feigned regret over the situation at the time and the touching loyalty which he maintained to his comrades even beyond the grave. The Rhineland industrialist Fritz Thyssen demonstrated the effect of this trick when he wrote to Cardinal Schulte in Cologne that he and his family 'will naturally follow the example of our Führer and not take part in Catholic church services as long as the unjust treatment of the Führer and members of the NSDAP continues'.[67]

Hitler's statement was part of the war of nerves which he conducted against Catholicism during these weeks. It intensified the pressure under which the bishops already stood. Quite correctly, Archbishop Gröber of Freiburg felt it to be a 'provocation... to which, nevertheless, an answer should be given'.[68] Cardinal Faulhaber was also of the opinion that in consequence the bishops were 'called upon to make a public statement'.[69] As late as 22 March, however, they were still undecided as to how this statement was to be phrased. Whereas some of the bishops recommended a retreat for pastoral or tactical reasons, Cardinal Schulte, supported by the diocesan bishops of Aachen, Limburg, Trier, Münster and Paderborn, openly strove for 'a republication of the decrees against the NS movement.'[70]

Thus manoeuvred into a situation in which they felt that they could no longer put off a statement, yet not knowing what form it should take, the bishops must have seen the government policy statement of 23 March as offering a way out. For while the Party leader Hitler had retracted nothing of what had been the object of the bishops' criticism, Reich Chancellor Hitler had nevertheless given lavish assurances which the German episcopacy could hardly just ignore. And if the bishops were still unsure how they should assess the government policy statement, they could read in their familiar Catholic press the general impression that Hitler's speech had 'stature', and that 'deep down', people could 'go a long way with it'.[71] In *Katholische Korrespondenz*, the Jesuit Friedrich Muckermann, who very soon afterwards, as a refugee, was to become one of the most uncompromising and active opponents of the system, maintained that in his speech Hitler had seen 'the great structures of state and church in their correct relationship'. This inner vision gave the speech 'a touch of classic greatness to raise the spirits'. 'That is far more important for Catholicism,' suggested Muckermann, 'than some binding statement or other.'[72]

So it was quite understandable that the very next day, Friday 24 March, Cardinal Bertram of Breslau, the spokesman for the German hierarchy, sent the draft of a conciliatory statement to the members of the Fulda Bishops' Conference and to Cardinal Faulhaber, and at the same time insisted on prompt replies from the diocesan bishops.[73] What happened next, however, still remains somewhat puzzling. For although this statement was undoubtedly a step of extraordinary

251

significance for the whole of German Catholicism, and although in the circumstances a week here or there made no obvious difference, Bertram fixed the final text that same weekend, and on Monday 27 March sent it with the assertion that the voting in the Fulda Bishops' Conference had 'produced a gratifying agreement'.[74] At this juncture there could be hardly any question of such a vote, because up to that point a whole group of votes had not yet even arrived. On the Tuesday even Cardinal Faulhaber found himself confronted with a *fait accompli*, so that he had no alternative than to send a telegram to Breslau that very day, indicating the agreement of the Bavarians.[75]

Though many explanations could be given for the great urgency of this statement, it is hard to understand the 'almost panic haste' with which Bertram proceeded here. Ludwig Volk, who some years ago devoted a detailed study to this question, was then of the opinion that the spokesman of the German episcopacy had presumably been urged to this haste 'from other quarters'.[76] Meanwhile he has changed his mind, on the basis of a different view of the prehistory of the Reich concordat. However, anyone who examines his earlier arguments will still find them conclusive in their context. According to them it was Papen who that weekend induced the Cardinal to his precipitate step, with a reference to imminent negotiations on the concordat. In fact it is hard to believe that the leading figure of German Protestantism – Kapler – received reliable news about plans for a concordat on 23 March, while the leading figure of German Catholicism should have continued to be ignorant of them. With the idea of a concordat, Volk then deduced – and no new argument of equal weight has surfaced since then – the bishops would have 'a motive, of just the right weight and dimension, to close the considerable gaps in the chain of motives that made the implementation of Bertram's decisions so extraordinarily difficult during the period of discussion'.[77]

The statement itself, which appeared in the press on 29 and 30 March, was most carefully formulated. After a justification of the bishops' previous position and an explicit reference to the 'public and solemn' declarations made by the 'highest representatives of the Reich Government', the crucial sentence ran: 'Without reversing the condemnation of certain religious and moral errors which is contained in our former measures, the episcopate believes that it can be confident that the general prohibitions and warnings issued previously no longer need to be considered necessary.' There followed an admonition 'to loyalty to the lawful authority, and to conscientious fulfilment of civic duties', and then, with a thrice-repeated 'Remains in force...' came the emphatic confirmation that all essential Catholic principles and goals were still valid as before.[78]

However, in spite of the care taken over the formulation and in spite of all Bertram's efforts to prevent misuse of the statement for propaganda purposes,[79] up and down the country it was understood to be a full endorsement by the hierarchy of the Third Reich and its Führer. The effect upon all those both inside and outside the Catholic Church who had so far still opposed the growing demands of the National Socialists was shattering. Konrad Algermissen, the Director of Apologetics in the Volksverein für katholische Deutschland, reported to Bertram on 31 March that the statement had not dispelled the general depression of the previous few weeks, 'but rather has often produced the impression of a retreat on the part of the church'.[80] And the Dominican Father

Stratmann, pastor to students in Berlin, wrote on 10 April to Faulhaber: 'The souls of well-disposed people are in a turmoil as a result of the tyranny of the National Socialists, and I am merely stating a fact when I say that the authority of the bishops among innumerable Catholics and non-Catholics has been shaken by the quasi-approval of the National Socialist movement.'[81]

The fact that both Faulhaber (before the Bavarian bishops on 20 April)[82] and Bertram (before the whole German episcopate at the end of May)[83] felt that they had to offer an explicit justification and defence of the statement indicates the extent and the vehemence of criticism within Catholicism. Here Cardinal Faulhaber was correct when he made a personal note on 20 April that the hierarchy found itself in this tragic situation 'because of the position of Rome'.[84] The pressure from Hitler, Kaas's policy, and the desires and illusions of Rome had put the German bishops in a situation in which in fact they had no alternative but to capitulate. The displeasure of Pacelli, who reproached them by asking why they had obliged the government so quickly and why they could not at least have left their statement for another month, missed the point.[85] With the assurance that Rome stood behind them the bishops would certainly have waited a good deal longer than four weeks.

The bitterness of their defeat, however, was not just confined to the triumphant reports of victory in the National Socialist press. Malicious editorials from the Protestant side also showed them what they had surrendered. For example the *Allgemeine Evangelisch-Lutherische Kirchenzeitung* suggested that this could not be called 'an "honourable" retreat'. But this was precisely the price that Rome had to pay for its inability to learn – 'see Luther and Pope Leo X'. For this Lutheran newspaper the whole affair was little short of a divine judgment: 'Against the *Roma locuta est* the *deus locuta est* has arisen and shattered the mighty word of the bishops'.[86]

Naturally there were also millions of Catholics in Germany who received the statement with relief – indeed with rejoicing – because it finally also cleared the way into the Third Reich for Catholic Christians. It immediately drowned the second thoughts and also the criticism which until 28 March had gone by the attitude of the bishops.

On Laetare Sunday, 26 March, official church acknowledgments of the new Reich and its leadership were read for the first time from Protestant pulpits. On the same day Cardinal Bertram decided on the text of the statement and its immediate publication. This was more than a coincidence. It was an indication that at the end of March, at about the same time, the churches had put behind them the first phase of their history in and with the Third Reich.

Both Catholicism and Protestantism were now faced with new decisions.

3

The Jewish Question
(March-April)

During March 1933 internal and external changes took place at the end of which Protestantism publicly endorsed the nationalist revolution and Catholicism faced a thinly-disguised capitulation. Early in April there were new developments which claimed the churches' full attention. On the Protestant side, with their first Reich Conference the German Christians were preparing to storm the church; on the Catholic side, with organizations doing a U-turn and continued oppressive measures, the hierarchy was having grave difficulty in controlling the church in its new position in the Third Reich. Both these developments will be discussed in the following chapters. In close connection with these events, but as a development that had its own special character, in both churches the decision was taken at that time that no comment would be made on the terrorism of the new system and in particular on the persecution of the Jews that was now beginning in Germany. This decision did not go unchallenged, nor was it made in a day. Rather, it was the result of a development in which political and church-political arguments gained the upper hand over simple Christian responsibility.

From the first day of its existence the Third Reich was a terrorist system. During the time of struggle Hitler had so obviously relied on the power of violence and at the same time had so openly threatened his opponents with extermination – above all the Jews and the Marxists – that after 30 January this prehistory alone was enough to spread a climate of fear and terror among many of those involved. In February, however, things still remained relatively quiet, even though up and down the country political opponents were already constantly threatened and intimidated, and the first incidents gave some inkling of what was to come. After the 5 March election victory, however, a wave of terror broke over Germany which lasted throughout the summer and very quickly engulfed tens of thousands of Germans.[1] The instrument of this wave of terror was Hitler's feared young revolutionary army, the SA. Its victims were Communists, Jews, and other real or supposed opponents of the régime.

An essential precondition for the first major actions had been created by the new Prussian Minister of the Interior, Hermann Göring, who was later to become Minister President. By the middle of February he had appointed numerous SA and SS leaders as chiefs of police, and soon afterwards he ordered the formation of an auxiliary police force comprised of members of the SA, the SS and the Stahlhelm.[2] In a high state of excitement after the Reichstag fire and the alleged attempt at a Putsch by its mortal enemies, the Communists, and drunk with the emotion of its victory and its new position, after the March elections the SA set out on a large-scale hunt for its old opponents. At first the prisoners were sent to the police prisons, but very soon the over-filling of these prisons[3] and the refusal of the police to handle those brought in to them[4] led to the setting up of the SA's own detention and interrogation centres. In the rooms of the SA quarters to which the unfortunate victims were now carried off, and where they were detained for days and even weeks at a time without any contact with the outside world, sadistic tortures and excesses occurred which defy any description.[5] The same was true of the first concentration camps to be established in this context by the SA and SS – e.g. at Oranienburg, Königswusterhausen and Bornim in the Berlin area, and Dachau near Munich.[6]

While these things were going on, largely in secret and known only through individual incidents and rumours, the systematic persecution of the Jews began – and in public. In his first 'Memorandum on the Jews' of September 1919, Hitler had already distinguished between an 'antisemitism for purely emotional reasons', which would find expression in pogroms, and a 'rational antisemitism' which must lead to the 'systematic legal struggle against and removal of the privileges of the Jew', i.e. to 'alien legislation'. 'Its final and irrevocable goal must, however,' wrote the young Hitler at that time, 'be the complete removal of the Jews,'[7] Now, fourteen years later, he began to translate that idea into reality.

Events in Breslau provided an impressive example of the state of affairs.

On 12 March the *Frankfurter Zeitung* published the following report from Breslau. 'At noon today in Breslau a powerful detachment of SA men forcibly entered the Land office and court building. Amid calls of "Jews out!", all the offices and conference rooms were opened and all the Jewish lawyers, judges and state attorneys were forced to leave the building immediately. There were scenes of great agitation in the corridors and chambers. The lawyers' room was cleared in a matter of minutes... After half an hour or so the municipal police appeared in the building and asked the SA to leave. The request was complied with.'[8] On the afternoon of the same day over one hundred judges of the Breslau courts voted to permit a so-called three-day Justitium, i.e. a total suspension of the administration of justice.[9] The major newspapers reported on both 14 and 17 March the compromise negotiated between the National Socialist police chiefs and the judiciary. By it the police would in future ensure the peaceful administration of justice; however, the judiciary should not 'close its eyes to the wish to stem the influence of Jewish elements in the administration of justice'.[10] Subsequently, from among the Jewish lawyers seventeen were selected who were given a special identity card to be shown from then on when entering the court. Two days later, on 19 March, the *Völkische Beobachter* took up the events in Breslau and demanded similar action in Berlin: 'Whereas in Breslau at least the very modest beginnings of a clean-up could be made, in the Berlin courts nothing has yet changed. Anyone entering the lawyers' quarters in the Central Justice Ministry will flee from the gigantic room appalled. Not even in the Cracow ghetto could there be more Jews crawling around.'[11] The new Reich Commissioner for the Prussian Ministry of Justice, Hanns Kerrl, later the first and only Minister of Churches in the Third Reich, and his Secretary of State

Roland Freisler – later the notorious President of the Volksgerichtshof – did not delay in responding to this unambiguous hint. Reshufflings and exclusions of Jewish judges and lawyers from the court building caused the *Völkischer Beobachter* as early as 21 March to speak with satisfaction of the 'iron broom' which was now also beginning to sweep through the Berlin bar.[12] Similar reports from Frankfurt, Stuttgart, Hamburg and Munich showed that there was a uniform strategy for the whole Reich.[13] Nor were Jewish lawyers the only ones who had to fear for their future. Professors and artists, journalists and doctors also saw themselves deprived of all rights almost overnight. This made them the defenceless victims of countless affronts, threats, insults and persecutions.

The actual measures adopted during these first weeks show very little of the human tragedies that resulted. Worse than professional restrictions was the expulsion of the Jews from the legal and moral community of the German Volk which was openly propagated, as well as the degradation, hatred, fear and vileness which from now on separated them from non-Jews in Germany.

The young writer Jochen Klepper, a producer with the Berlin Funkstunde, a Protestant Christian who had recently married a Jewish woman, caught the mood of this first period in his diary. He noted on 8 March 1933: 'What is already demanded of us in the way of antisemitism is terrible. Even Schnabel's Beethoven recitals had quite suddenly to be removed from the programme... at the very time when Oxford University was conferring an honorary degree upon him for his "unequalled interpretation of German art". At the radio station we can understand one another's situation, but the mutual respect is gone. Tired thirty- and forty-year-old compromisers, intimidated by the primitive struggles for existence: from whatever angle we look at it, that's what we are.' On 11 March the entry read: 'It is a dreadful uneasiness, a dreadful pressure, a dreadful isolation – a fearful weakness, a fearful anxiety about existence –.' On 14 March: 'Hanni and the children will go over to the Protestant church. We are quite aware of the reasons...' Finally, on 29 March: 'On the whole Jewish boycott affair I have only one thing to say: I grieve for the Protestant church.'[14]

This was in fact the image of the new era as it impressed itself upon those involved at the time, and as it also looks in retrospect today: a terrorist system had taken power in German and openly and mercilessly exercised this power without regard to life, law, freedom and human dignity. Leonhard Ragaz, the Swiss Religious Socialist,[15] summarized this view of things in a biting commentary on Potsdam Day, 21 March. All this had been a lie, 'this celebration with its false splendour, intoxication and rejoicing against a background of misery, slavery and catastrophe already visible to every dispassionate eye'. The re-emergence of bygone powers was a lie. The apotheosis of this shallow and more than dubious false hero was a lie. 'Ultimately a lie, the apex of lies, *the* lie; the religious display of this whole demonic swindle, this ringing of bells and organ-playing, these chorales, these prayers, these sermons... everything to the tune of "God is with us!" – this last a grave blasphemy. For quite apart from all the lies, amidst this bell-ringing, organ-playing, singing, praying, preaching resound the screams of the sons and daughters of Germany tortured in the barracks of this liberator and restorer of Germany. That is what the inaugural celebration is in the Potsdam Garrison Church... and in the Kroll Opera House, the place of illusion: an edifice of illusion and deceit – crowned by this religious deceit – that will collapse horribly, as a symbol of the downfall of all the forces that came together in it.'[16]

Many of those affected, those who were arrested, beaten, threatened, and the first emigrants, saw things in this or a very similar way. Some of the Western countries saw things this way, as indeed did some of the Germans themselves. But strangely enough another larger and continually growing sector of the Germans saw things quite differently. To them the terror did not look like terror; the hue and cry did not look like hue and cry; the persecution did not look like persecution. Instead they saw in all this only the fully justified measures of a government that had pulled Germany back from the abyss at the eleventh hour. for all the condemnation of individual excesses, they granted that the state had to employ desperate means in a desperate situation, not least in the firm conviction that the Germans would return to law and order as soon as conditions permitted.

This attitude was certainly at first connected with the problems in getting information. Even if everyone could have been informed about the existence of the concentration camps[17] and the first actions against the Jews, and undoubtedly many had heard some rumours about excesses, what was happening in the SA camps and cellars remained utterly unknown and unimaginable. Anyone who knew of specific individual cases remained silent: the victims and possible victims for reasons just as understandable as those of the perpetrators and those responsible. Probably very few were as well informed as Rudolf Diels, the first chief of the Gestapo, who early in 1934 gave Hitler the whole unvarnished truth about the terror of the first year.[18]

But the undoubted difficulty and danger in getting information was only one side of the matter. The other was that, for example, the central authorities of the Protestant church, the Kirchenbundesamt in Berlin, did not want to have any information.

At that time a whole series of attempts was made to gather reliable information about what was going on in Germany. In the Reich Ministry of Justice, Oberregierungsrat Hans von Dohnanyi, Dietrich Bonhoeffer's brother-in-law, had taken on the delicate task of compiling material for a kind of indictment of Hitler,[19] and in Papen's Vice-Chancellery his young associates were building up their own intelligence network, which evidently functioned quite well.[20] Even in the Protestant church there was at least one group concerned with the problem of information. As early as 13 March a certain Elizabeth Rotten of Dresden wrote along these lines to the Berlin theologian Friedrich Siegmund-Schultze. Deeply troubled over the silence and passivity of the 'minority in Germany who think and have remained sober', she asked 'whether in all the larger cities calm and objectively-minded people' might not gather material about the SA brutalities, so that through personal contacts it might be brought to people 'who can give help or indicate where it might be had'.[21] In fact on 6 April Siegmund-Schultze informed the relevant official at the Kirchenbundesamt, Oberkirchenrat Schreiber, that he thought of organizing the July issue of his journal *Die Eiche* 'in such a way as to give our foreign friends, too, certain information about the German situation.' In it there was also to be explicit 'reference to the excesses'. But the Kirchenbundesamt did not want anything to do with it. Instead, on 8 April Schrieber reported to his President, Hermann Kapler, that 'Professor

Siegmund-Schulze was giving no small cause for concern with his inquiries and reports'. This concern was, however, unfounded. Siegmund-Schultze was arrested on 21 June 1933 and deported from Germany 'on the charge of helping Jews in ninety-three cases'.[22]

Important though the problem of information may have been, it was not crucial for the attitude of the majority to the terror. What was decisive was the conviction that at the eleventh hour Hitler had actually saved the state from a Communist attempt at revolution. Only under the impact of the threat of Communist terror was it possible to understand the National Socialist terror not as terror but rather as a necessary and justified counter-measure.

The question whether there really was a danger of a Communist revolution at that time can be left out of account here and is in any case difficult to answer. It is enough to begin from the indisputable fact that, on the basis of the Thomas theorem, countless contemporaries thought the danger real and therefore the consequences were equally real.[23] The question of the reality of the danger thus becomes that of the reasons for this real assessment of the Communist danger. The crucial importance of anti-Communism for the rise of National Socialism in Germany and the seizure of power has been frequently emphasized. However, the connections were presumably far closer than these references suggest. For in Germany the danger of a Communist tyranny would hardly have been thought so real had not the very real Communist tyranny in Russia been evident to all. Not only was National Socialist counter-violence sparked off by the fact that there was a rule of force in Russia with clear terrorist features and an expansionist programme, but the existence of this rule of violence tempted supporters, fellow travellers and outsiders to understand this terrorist counter-violence not as terror but rather as a justified defensive measure. This was true above all for the period of the consolidation of the régime, i.e. specifically for the first weeks and months of the Third Reich. These were the weeks and months that were completely dominated by the burning of the Reichstag and the significance attached to it by propaganda as the sign of a Putsch.

In this atmosphere of civil war the essential difference which was there from the beginning in the case of persecutions got lost. Granted, Communists and Jews came into the same camps and were exposed to the same forms of ill-treatment. But there was a great difference as to whether one suffered as a mortal political enemy or suffered by reason of one's race. This difference emerged most impressively where it became clear that according to National Socialist convictions a Communist could be made a good SA man overnight, something which in fact occurred thousands of times, whereas there was no way in which the Jews could change their skin, in the truest sense of the word. The Communists were misguided and in principle could be re-educated; the Jews were and remained evil by nature. However, since this basic völkisch ideology[24] was accepted by only a small minority in Germany, it was very good policy from the propaganda point of view always to name Jews and Communists together as the authors of a conspiracy against Germany. So it proved effective to represent the long-term programme for a systematic elimination of the Jews from the community of German citizens[25] as a timely measure for the protection of the state and the Volk in a situation of ultimate decisions.

This deception was made easier by the völkisch antisemitism which in an

258

attenuated form had also penetrated the churches, and which there had provoked that insensitivity to the simple Christian truth of the command to love which had already been evident in the 1920s.[26]

Unfortunately, so far we have no investigations of the internal connections between Communist terror and that of National Socialism. Such studies would need to clarify in detail how far Hitler, from the beginning of his political career, had been fascinated by the effect of Communist terror on middle-class attitudes, and also when he decided to beat the Communists at their own game.[27] Furthermore, they would need to clarify how far initially the fear that it would spread to Germany led many Germans not to perceive the terror in their own land as terror – indeed almost to overlook it. Here lies a crucial point, indeed the only one to explain the general behaviour of the broad bourgeois centre in Germany in 1933. Without these presuppositions, despite all the theories it ultimately remains inexplicable why the Germans submitted almost without protest to the yoke of violence.

Where the terrorism of the system was understood to be the state's saving intervention at the decisive hour, an action which, if not altogether legal, was still legitimate, the way was also clear to praise, almost without restraint, the positive side of the revolution. For it was certainly not just a propaganda assertion that the climate in Germany had fundamentally changed after 30 January. No one would have been able to organize the enthusiasm of the masses had not a previously unknown and fresh hope been awakened up and down the country. There was one great goal on which this hope was focussed and towards which all real devotion and self-sacrifice were directed: the concentration of all the forces of the nation in order to surmount by one great effort the economic misery and the political hopelessness of the Weimar period. Who questioned the cost when this goal seemed to be drawing nearer step by step? The *Tägliche Rundschau*, the only major Protestant newspaper, had already stated this point of view in a leading article as early as 14 March. The illusion of a people's state, it said, had been wrong 'because it had preferred to deny the necessity of a higher authority...' Born out of mistrust of political power generally, not out of sacrifice and obedience to the majesty of the Creator hidden in every state order, it had rightly fallen victim to the nationalist revolution. This revolution, according to the newspaper, had created a new and responsible authority which had broken through the restraints of the federal order and 'by means of a unity of political purpose previously unknown in German history had so fundamentally renewed and strengthened the Reich that the fame of this deed alone would almost certainly suffice to bestow on Hitler the full authority to create new law'.[28]

This article made clear the new hope which was associated with Hitler and, at the same time, the Lutheran doctrine of the state, revived at this point, which saw the guiding hand of God at work in every decisive action of the state.

However, all these expectations and hopes were reinforced by the enormously clever way in which the régime presented itself through propaganda which blurred or simply passed over the critical points in advance. It was utterly typical of the surprise which the first months of the Third Reich had in store, particularly for potential critics, when on 20 April Cardinal Faulhaber noted for his situation report to the Bavarian bishops: 'What Hitler has not said or no longer says:

nothing against the Jews; nothing against capital; not even against Poland in Königsberg; a real statesman.'[29]

Thus the picture offered by Germany in the spring and summer of 1933 was marked by a deep split. Never again have such extremely different judgments been made so closely together in Germany. Anyone who – for whatever reasons – had discovered the terrorist character of the régime could only view the future with the gravest concern. Conversely, anyone who could not conceive of the terror as terror could pin the boldest hopes and the most glorious expectations on Hitler and the nationalist revolution. This split, particularly among foreign observers, led to miscalculations which, depending on the choice of informants, portrayed Germany as either one great bloodstained torture chamber or, on the other hand, as a land of exemplary order, resolute strength and a new zest for life.

When the French pastor Henri-Louis Henriod, the new General Secretary of the World Alliance for Promoting International Friendship through the Churches,[30] travelled to Berlin in the middle of April 1933 to get a personal picture of the contradictory situation, he could ultimately only record, with some perplexity, the fundamental oppositions in the assessment of the German situation by the Germans themselves. After numerous conversations with leading churchmen, with pastors and laymen of various trends, and with foreigners living in Berlin, Henriod contrasted the different positions in a confidential circular letter: 'Some are of the opinion that this revolution has so far taken place in an orderly manner and without the shedding of blood. (Nevertheless, they still admit the fact of excesses and atrocities against numerous individuals...) The situation is improving day by day. The era of the Third Reich proclaims itself to be the beginning of a glorious national awakening, of a happy and necessary reaction. The nationalist revolution is said to have become the instrument of salvation for Germany, which was threatened by a terrible and imminent Communist revolution the outbreak of which was prevented at the last moment... According to the opinion of others...the Communist threat was not so serious and immediate... For several of those with whom I talked the revolution has not yet reached its climax. The radical measures adopted against the Communists, they say, will be followed by yet other measures affecting all those who do not comply unequivocally with the orders of the ruling party. There is no longer freedom of the press; criticism is forbidden; the ruling Party has the broadcasting system in its grip; telephone conversations are monitored; the secrecy of the mail is no longer guaranteed. All the rights relating to the freedom of the German citizen contained in the Reich constitution are suspended. Where more than two persons are together there is a strain on the exchange of opinion...'[31]

It was this, two quite opposite views of the political situation, that characterized the state of affairs in Germany in spring and summer 1933. With some differences it was also true for the German churches. This insight into the situation is the necessary precondition for understanding the development which led both churches at the end of April to be silent on the Jewish question.

Of the first great wave of terror, which began after the 5 March elections, little in fact was seen and heard in Germany itself. Moreover, people had very different views when it came to a political appraisal of developments. So many of them were all the more surprised when the foreign press put the terror and antisemitism

260

of the new régime increasingly at the centre of their reporting on Germany. The mood in the Western world changed visibly. German diplomats in the European capitals and in New York reported protest rallies and marches. In the German missions outside the country, and in Germany itself, numerous petitions and letters of protest accumulated from the most diverse groups and personalities, objecting emphatically to the violation of human rights in Germany and, above all, to the persecution of the Jews that was beginning. At the climax of this wave of protest English and American firms even threatened to break off trade relations with Germany and to boycott the importation of German goods.[32]

This wave of protest unleashed an extremely strong counter-reaction in Germany. Most Germans, including many who had definite personal reservations about the Third Reich, were in no way willing simply to put up with the foreign reports, some of which were sensationalized. Here the well-known solidarity effect, which tends to be produced even among divided groups by attacks from the outside, made itself felt. So too did the anti-German feeling outside Germany, which had lasted for decades and since the World War had created a deep-seated mistrust of Germany throughout the Western world. Thus not only did the new political leaders – Hitler himself, Goebbels, Göring and others, declare that the foreign reports were lies; numerous groups and persons also rejected the foreign protests. Economic organizations and politicians overwhelmed their foreign partners with a flood of corrections. Even the German PEN-Club, which at that time had not yet been taken over, sent a telegram to the most important PEN Clubs outside Germany: 'Pen-Club German Group declares atrocity stories circulated throughout foreign lands to be completely false and urgently requests in the interest of truth and reconciliation between nations educative work against this excessive smear campaign.'[33]

Of course the German churches were also entangled in these proceedings. Here Protestantism found itself in an especially difficult situation. On the one hand it was nationalist and by this time had given way more fully to the Third Reich than had Catholicism. On the other hand, the most stubborn protests clearly came from the centres of world Protestantism, i.e. from England, America and Scandinavia, with which the German Protestants were linked by numerous ecumenical relationships. The statements of the leading Protestant representatives show the degree to which foreign political considerations also influenced church decisions. In fact in the history of the churches in the Third Reich, foreign policy plays a major and occasionally – as in summer and autumn 1934 – even a decisive role.

The first news that the ecumenical world was beginning to take a direct interest in German developments reached the Kirchenbundesamt in the middle of March. On 15 March a leading man in the American ecumenical movement, Henry Smith Leiper, had expressed in a letter to the Kirchenbundesamt in Berlin the deep anxiety of American Christians at the developments of the recent period, and at the same time had commented that 'the arbitrary encroachments of the Nazis on American Jews' had 'generally made a very bad impression upon American opinion'. However, he was of course aware how much these things were regretted by his Christian friends in Germany.[34] Even before this letter could be answered, the Federal Council of Churches in America decided on a startling step. On 4 March the Executive Committee of this distinguished

American church federation, sustained by its social commitment, issued a statement condemning the persecution of the Jews in Germany. It was published on 25 March in the *New York Times* and became known in Germany the same day. The German press had already had intimations of this imminent action a few days before.[35]

Thus at the end of the week which, with the Potsdam day, Hitler's government policy statement and the consent of the majority of the Reichstag to the Enabling Act, in the eyes of many Germans represented a first climax on the way to national rebirth, the Protestant church administrations suddenly found themselves confronted with an enquiry from America which was as critical as it was inescapable. The declaration of the Federal Council expressed the conviction that the serious persecutions of the Jews in Germany concerned all Christians; the hope 'that our brothers in the churches of that great land will reject and fight against the prevailing antisemitism within their borders' and the need to protest against all forms of racial and religious intolerance.[36]

In speed and decisiveness the reactions to this declaration in Germany were unprecedented for the churches, which normally worked slowly and carefully. It has sometimes been asserted that the whole campaign was directed, or at least inspired, from the outside.[37] There is no evidence of this. The fact that, for example, the Church President of Baden, Klaus Wurth, in a telegram as early as 24 March requested from the Kirchenbund, in view of the first newspaper reports, 'immediate action and instruction of the churches outside Germany as to Germany's true situation' suggests,[38] rather, that in the course of the general campaign the church bodies decided quite independently on their own steps. At all events, the German Group of the Protestant World Alliance, which in practice was identical with the Evangelischer Bund, was first to resolve to send a protest telegram to the Federal Council in which the German group affirmed 'on its honour and conscience' that no pogroms of any kind had taken place against the Jews, and urgently requested that 'in public declarations, any misleading of public opinion by means of mistaken atrocity stories' might be prevented.[39]

Then on 25 March the planning of an official counter-action began in the Kirchenbundesamt. The official responsible, Oberkirchenrat Schreiber, mobilized all those who had ecumenical contacts in order to get their approval for telegrams to the Federal Council, to the American group of the World Alliance for Promoting International Friendship through the Churches, and to the National Lutheran Council. Seventy-year-old Julius Richter, the doyen of Protestant missions and in no sense a Hitler supporter, had suggested a text which, though rejected, was nevertheless remarkably characteristic of that political view of things which saw terror not as terror but rather as justified defence. 'Jews throughout the world,' ran Richter's suggested text, 'are setting propaganda about atrocities in motion because they feel threatened by Hitler's known antisemitism. The Social Democrats are mobilizing the working classes of the entire world against Germany because the German nationalist movement has inscribed the fight against Marxism on its banners. Warn urgently against giving credence to exaggerated and fabricated reports about terror in Germany.' Only the last sentence of this text, with the signature of Burghart who, as Vice-President of the Prussian Oberkirchenrat, was at the same time Chairman of the

262

German group of the World Alliance, then went to the three above-mentioned American addresses late that same night of 25-26 March.[40]

In his regular Sunday column in the Berlin *Tag* on 26 March, Otto Dibelius raised the fundamental problems in the whole issue. How does an Anglican American bishop in America, asked Dibelius, come 'to set himself up as the protector of the Jews in Germany'? How did the Americans know what was going on in Germany? Upon what did they base their judgment? All ecumenical work would be hopelessly discredited if the churches did not mutually believe one another capable of fulfilling their duty as the conscience of their peoples. A church could and should interfere in the affairs of another country only 'if the church there is prevented by force from speaking freely, or if the church expressly asks the other for help'.[41] The method of argument made it clear that Dibelius's nationalist sensibility was obviously greater than his Christian sensibility. And at this point that was evidently the problem with most of the church administrations.

In the name of the German Evangelischer Kirchenbund, on Monday 27 March Kapler sent a telegram to one of the most influential American clergymen, the Revd Parkes Cadman, asking him to counter the false reports. The Reich government, he said, guaranteed order and security. 'Impartial examinations of conditions here possible and desired at any time.'[42] The deputy chairman of the Lutheran World Federation, Ludwig Ihmels, Bishop of the Landeskirche of Saxony, also protested along the same lines to his New York friend, the American Lutheran Professor John Alfred Morehead.[43] At the same time the national director of the Protestant Young Men's Christian Association, Erich Stange, delivered a protest at a board meeting of the YMCA in Geneva. Shortly afterwards, on 30 March, the German Methodists, represented by their bishop, the American John L. Nuelsen, objected 'to the public meetings and the statements of the press in America and England about alleged persecution of the Jews and atrocities of the nationalist movement in Germany'. All of this was an attempt to revive 'the dreadful atrocity propaganda of the World War', an attempt which Methodists around the world had to combat.[44]

That at least the Kirchenbundesamt realized that all this was a political campaign was shown by the fact that as early as 28 March the Foreign Office, the Reich Ministry of the Interior and the Reich Ministry of Propaganda were informed officially of the various statements.[45]

This mass church denial was not without effect abroad. In Geneva, Paris, London and New York the representatives of the ecumenical groups became uncertain. The Federal Council informed the German Kirchenbund that there was 'full understanding of the signs of a new unity and a new-born hope in the German nation'.[46] From Geneva the American churches were also warned against making any kind of statement without exact knowledge of the state of affairs in Germany.[47] A more careful assessment of events could also be observed in other respects. For a period of weeks, as the *Vossische Zeitung* reported on 28 March from New York, 'reports about acts of violence against Jews' had 'ceased'. A gigantic protest rally in Madison Square Garden against events in Germany had surprisingly taken a moderate course.[48] In fact the German government could be sure that the worst storm against the régime's antisemitism had been weathered for the time being, not least thanks to the broad support from Germany itself.

However, instead of waiting for foreign opinion to calm down further, which would have been natural, given the still unstable condition of his government, Hitler quite surprisingly decided on a major, calculated public provocation. On 28 March he ordered the Party to observe a general boycott of all Jews and Jewish businesses, to begin on 1 April. The significance of this reaction is clear only in retrospect. It was in line with his earlier distinction between an emotive antisemitism and a rational antisemitism. Protected by the misunderstanding that this boycott was only a defensive action against foreign 'atrocity propaganda', in reality he was now taking the first step towards a systematic expulsion of Jews from society. It was no accident that after the boycott not even a week passed before the promulgation of the law 'For the Reconstruction of the Civil Service', with which the legal measures of a comprehensive 'alien legislation' for the Jews in Germany were initiated.

The prehistory of the boycott shows that not even Hitler's closest associates were clear about his basic purpose. In a note on the foreign press campaign, the State Secretary in the Reich Chancellery, Hans Heinrich Lammers, had on 23 March emphasized the ineffectiveness of government counter-measures, and had given the Reich Ministry of Propaganda the task 'of influencing foreign public opinion from Germany by suitable means'. Besides, he suggested, experience taught that such a wave would die down again quite quickly.[49] On the following day, Goebbels noted in his diary, 'The atrocity propaganda abroad is causing us a lot of trouble.' Germany was helplessly exposed to the attacks of its opponents; all counter-propaganda was only 'a drop in the bucket'. Two days later, on 29 March, Hitler informed him at Berchtesgaden that he had decided 'on a large-scale boycott of all Jewish businesses in Germany'.[50]

There was barely a week between this decision of Hitler's, which was made on Sunday 26 March – and which was obviously a surprise even to Goebbels – and the implementation of the boycott on the following Saturday, 1 April. In this week, the week during which the Protestant church was at work everywhere pacifying foreign opinion – the public antisemitic vendetta in German came to its first climax.

As early as Monday the first reports of the imminent action appeared in the press, and the main summons 'to all Party organizations of the NSDAP' for a boycott was already published on Tuesday evening. In retrospect, this summons, which clearly betrays Hitler's hand, becomes one of the most important documents of the Third Reich's Jewish policy. For it was the first major confirmation after Hitler's accession to power that as Reich Chancellor, too, he represented the cause of that völkisch antisemitism for which as party leader he had made propaganda from the start. The hope, frequently expressed, that Chancellor Hitler would not adopt the antisemitic extremism of Party Leader Hitler proved to be an illusion. Instead, the old party slogans now became political slogans for Volk and state. Thus the summons declared that in connection with the 'mad crime' of the Jewish 'atrocity propaganda' 'the National Socialist Party will now take up the defensive battle against this major crime with appropriate means for getting at the guilty ones. For the guilty ones are in our midst. They live among us and day after day abuse the hospitality which the German Volk has granted them... The agitation about the boycott and atrocities must not and will not affect the German Volk, but it will hit the Jews themselves a thousand times harder.' There followed eleven detailed instructions for implementing the boycott. These called for the formation of local action committees which were supposed to assume responsibility for the action and its 'disciplined' development. Individual points covered the protection of foreigners, propaganda and the enlightening of the populace, monitoring the newspapers, a sudden start, a mass call for a limitation of the number of Jews admitted to secondary schools and universities and to the medical and legal professions, an explanation to foreign countries 'by letters, telegrams and telephone calls', and finally, 'calm, discipline and no acts of violence'. Finally, the identity of state, Volk and Party on the question was once again emphatically stressed. 'The government of national revolution does not exist in a vacuum. It represents the creative German Volk. Anyone who attacks it, attacks Germany! Anyone who slanders it, slanders the nation! Anyone who fights it has declared war on sixty-five million!... National Socialists! Saturday. On the stroke of ten o'clock Jewry will discover on whom it has declared war.'[51]

Julius Streicher, the Gauleiter of Nuremberg and an old völkisch antisemitist from the early days of the Party, who had been closely associated with Dinter and represented the latter's approach in its most repulsive form,[52] was appointed chairman of the central committee which was to co-ordinate the whole action. This committee also issued a summons to observe the boycott, which was printed throughout the German press on the Friday and Saturday.[53] The regional boycott committees followed it up with their own declarations, the primitive and vicious style of which has remained characteristic of similar pamphlets down to the present day. For example, *Führer*, the 'Chief Organ of the Baden Gau NSDAP', said: 'Fellow men and women of the German Volk! Avoid the buildings marked with the sign of the boycott. Resist the Jewish atrocity propaganda and boycott vendetta! Boycott all Jewish businesses! Do not buy in Jewish department stores! Do not go to Jewish lawyers! Avoid Jewish doctors! The Jews are our misfortune! Come to the mass meetings!'[54] Goebbels, propaganda director for the campaign, spoke in Berlin on the eve of the boycott and declared that the meaning of the nationalist revolution lay in surmounting liberal individualism and replacing it with a comprehensive völkisch solidarity. 'In this way the year 1789 will be struck from history'. The 'Marxist masses' could only be won over if the 'power of international Jewry' was broken. This was the aim of the boycott, which was to take place in a 'calm, ordered and disciplined fashion'. At the same time Goebbels made known the strategic plan for the boycott, which – though for other reasons than those intended by the Party leadership – in fact immediately led to greater restraint in the public criticism of German affairs. From Sunday evening until Wednesday at ten o'clock, Goebbels indicated, there would be a pause in the boycott. If during that time the atrocity propaganda ceased completely, normal conditions would return in Germany: 'but if not, then the boycott will be taken up again in such a way as to annihilate German Jewry!' The speech concluded with a hymn to these 'wonderful weeks', the 'proud mission' of the movement and a final quotation from Schiller: 'We will trust in the highest God and not be afraid of the power of man.'[55]

Considering this extensive and systematic antisemitic propaganda, the boycott on 1 April did in fact go off relatively calmly. Jewish shops and businesses were marked everywhere. SA posts with placards encouraged the boycott. Passers-by and curious bystanders were informed through handbills and pamphlets. While this frequently gave rise to insults, physical violence and small-scale disturbances against Jews and against Germans who defied the boycott, larger clashes and attacks were largely avoided on strict orders of the Party leadership.[56]

Hence the material losses suffered by the Jews as a result of this action were also small in comparison with its psychological and moral effects. The *Black Book* of 1934 already spoke quite correctly of 'immeasurably great damage' caused by the concentration of hatred of the Jews on one day, by the endorsement of it in orders and speeches by the state leaders, as well as by propaganda that could not be overlooked even by people who were apolitical, had turned away for public life, or were apathetic. 'Eliminate the Jews from the community of the German Volk!' was the way in which the *Black Book* cited an appeal to National Socialist women and continued: 'That was important to the creators of the boycott, and it seems certain that it has been largely achieved.'[57]

It is difficult to say how the German public reacted to this campaign. In spite of the triumphant reports in the National Socialist press, we may proceed on the assumption that the affair was not widely popular and was accepted rather guardedly by the population.[58] In spite of all the official propaganda, in many cases the middle classes remained loyal to Jewish businesses, colleagues and friends.[59] Generally, however, this was done surreptitiously. Only a few risked a demonstration of solidarity, as did Dietrich Bonhoeffer's grandmother, who at ninety-one on 1 April strode through the SA cordons in front of the Jewish Kaufhaus des Westens in Tauentzienstrasse, Berlin.[60] Nowhere was there an organized public protest.

That makes the question of the behaviour of the two churches all the more urgent. For both were affected by the antisemitic propaganda and the boycott in two ways. They were involved as the declared guardians of law and justice, as custodians of the human conscience, who had to insist upon the unconditional authority of the commands of God specifically relating to state and society. And they were involved as the representatives of their baptized Jewish members who, virtually overnight, were made subject to a special law. For Streicher's central committee had expressly declared that religion played 'no role' in the boycott. Item 3 in the guidelines ran: 'For the purposes of this order business people or dissidents of the Jewish race baptized as Catholics or Protestants are also Jews.'[61]

In fact there were now many voices of indignation and protest in both churches in response to these events. They attempted to stir up the church administrations to offer resistance, to criticize, or at least utter a word of solidarity with those affected. Granted, only individuals expressed this concern. But they referred so often to those of like mind that it is obvious that the aversion to antisemitic propaganda extended widely among church people.

One of the most significant and at the same time most resolute of these voices in German Protestantism was that of the long-time President of the German Evangelischer Kirchentag, Wilhelm Baron von Pechmann. Almost seventy-five years old at that time, his career as a Munich banker, politically a German nationalist monarchist and theologically a basically conservative Lutheran, hardly suggested that he was destined for this role.[62] Nevertheless he was one of the first to understand what was at stake here. So at noon on the Thursday of that fateful week before the boycott he called the Kirchenbundesamt in Berlin and told the director, Johannes Hosemann, that 'he had been urgently requested by an influential party in Berlin to urge that the Protestant church, together or in parallel with the Catholic church, should make a grave and decisive statement against the boycott at present being staged against the Jews in Germany'. Hosemann replied that the affair was 'very serious and politically very difficult', especially since the previous day the Chancellor had emphatically stated that the boycott was 'necessary and justified'. Nevertheless he promised to put the matter before President Kapler immediately. In the afternoon Pechmann sent a telegram in which he repeated – 'urgently and with all the innermost conviction at my command' – his statement that he would consider it disastrous 'if our church tried to keep silent at such an hour'.[63] These were the first in an almost unbroken series of statements, declarations and attempts by which Pechmann tried to get the churches to speak out – moreover not only his own church, but also the Catholic church, as is indicated by a letter to Bishop Michael Buchberger of Regensburg dated 5 April.[64] On 14 April Pechmann wrote once again to Kapler that the movement against the Jews had given him 'not a moment's rest for fourteen days'. He protested to the President that this movement had 'caused unspeakable misery for untold families who quite correctly call themselves Christians', and that these church members were waiting anxiously from one day to the next for a word from their church 'which, as they quite correctly assume, owes them protection'. 'But in addition the church cannot and should not pass over in silence what has been done and is still being done to Jewish fellow citizens in violation of Christian justice and love. Here too the church has a mission which it cannot escape without being untrue to itself.'[65]

Theophil Wurm, the Church President of Württemberg, also thought it absolutely necessary for the church to take some steps. In a postscript to a 30 March letter to the Kirchenausschuss he had added that the boycott which had been announced posed a difficult problem to the Protestant church, since this mode of defence met with sharp criticism 'among Protestant church people too'. The very next day he called Berlin and asked Hosemann 'whether something should not be said about the boycott of the Jews. The people of the Württemberg church in no way agree with the boycott movement.' Wurm's suggestion was aimed at convening immediately a special meeting of the Kirchenausschuss to co-ordinate action on the issue. Hosemann's answer revealed how strongly the Berlin church authorities were guided by political factors in their decision. As Hosemann asked the Stuttgart church president, was 'this particular protest to be the first contact between the Kirchenausschuss and the Reich government?' Wurm took the point and conceded that 'it was no longer possible to keep up with the pace of developments' – a confession which Kapler endorsed with 'quite right' written in his own hand on the margin of the note.[66] The next urgent request reached the Kirchenbundesamt from Frankfurt. Kirchenrat Johannes Kübel, also a member of the Kirchenausschuss, wrote on 4 April that the Jewish question was 'causing terrible suffering to virtually all the Landeskirchen. People in Frankfurt can constantly be heard asking "What is the church doing?" and the question is not being asked in the way it has been so often in recent years, that is, in the certainty that the honour of the Christian name and fundamental concepts of Christian ethics are violated even when those who are purely Jewish are defamed. But it is intolerable when families who have belonged to the

Protestant church for three generations are suddenly burdened with the stain of Jewry.' The church made itself an accessory, he said, if it did not enter a protest against this in the name of Christianity. It renounced the duty of the good Samaritan if it did not at least protect its members 'against the resentments of un-Christian fanatics'. 'Even people who are uninvolved, and who are without deep Christian feeling, tell us how deeply they are ashamed of being German and Christian at present when this is happening to the Jews.'[67] During April still other Christians, known and unknown, approached the Kirchenbundesamt along the same lines. For example Gustav Krüger, the liberal church historian at Giessen, already more than seventy years old, asserted that in view of Catholic declarations which will be discussed shortly, 'untold Protestant Christians' had joined him in lamenting the fact that the Protestant church had 'not found itself ready to make a similar declaration'.[68]

However, the protests and complaints at this time did not just penetrate to the highest Protestant church authorities. Rather, there were arguments throughout the Protestant Landeskirchen as to whether anything was to be done in the face of the antisemitic campaigns, and if so, what. For example, Wilhelm Menn, a socialist pastor in the Rhineland, who was closely associated with the Religious Socialists, openly expressed his utter distress to the General Superintendent of Koblenz, Ernst Stoltenhoff, in a characteristic correspondence. More clear-sighted than most, Menn had understood that the boycott movement marked 'the first persecution of the Jews for centuries'. It was apparent, he wrote, 'that one cannot let crowds cry "To hell with the Jews" for years without sometimes indulging in this brutal desire for persecution. And our "Christian people" rejoice.' If no one else dared at this time to express his own opinion, at least the church could and had to speak.[69] This man, as clear-sighted as he was critical, confirms something that is evident from all the testimonies to that time, namely that while 'an overwhelming proportion' of Protestant church people welcomed the nationalist revolution, 'again a very large part... is not, at least not yet, able to share in this experience'.[70] Thus it was not just in the church district of Cologne that assistance for Jewish members of the communities, or for those married to Jews, was considered.[71]

But however much pressure all these voices applied, the church as a whole remained silent. In the decisive days around 1 April no bishop, no church administration, no synod objected publicly to the persecution of the Jews in Germany.

The search for the reasons for this silence leads one to a whole complex of motives. At this point two aspects can clearly be distinguished: the complex of political arguments and decisions and the problem of what was possible and expedient in church politics.

Almost all the political error, misunderstanding and blindness that was compounded here could be found in a speech which Dibelius broadcast to America on short-wave radio on 4 April. It is of special significance because the personality of the General Superintendent of the Kurmark ruled out motives which lay behind so many statements in those days: opportunism and fear. We may proceed on the assumption that Dibelius really saw things as he described them here.

The basic premises of Dibelius's political assessment of the situation were the legality of the seizure of power and the deliverance of Germany from the Bolshevik revolution. In view of this situation he considered the imprisonment of the Communist leaders to be justified. In this connection one piece of information he had to pass on was that along with the American Methodist bishop Dr Nuelsen, he had personally satisfied himself in the prison that the prisoners were being treated correctly. The best known among these Communists, Dibelius reported, 'hitherto the leader of the party, Ernst Thäl-mann, a strong worker with broad shoulders, complained somewhat that the food was not quite adequate for him... The others, however, were all satisfied with the food as well.' Dibelius concluded from this that not a word of 'the hair-raising news reports about cruel and bloody treatment of the Communists in Germany' was true. At that time Dibelius obviously did not suspect how deceptive such visits could be. Rudolf Diels was considerably better informed about such things, and when he visited Thalmann with Göring at about the same time, in order to demonstrate to the Prussian Minister President that the prisoners were being ill-treated, he took the prisoner's coat and shirt forcibly off him. Göring, Diels reported, 'stared at a bloody back studded with welts'.[72]

Dibelius and Nuelsen, the two bishops, saw nothing of this. So Dibelius, with the conviction of one who had made an investigation at first hand, could reject the foreign news reports about the terror in Germany. But this added credibility to the National Socialist thesis of Jewish anti-German agitation, and the boycott was made to seem an act of justified self-defence, especially since, as Dibelius also attested for his diocese, all had been done 'calmly and in order'. The actions against Jewish civil servants only served to restore just conditions, because after the war the Jews had occupied certain positions to a quite disproportionate degree. The church, Dibelius declared, 'cannot and should not hinder the state when it creates order with harsh measures, but it has an urgent wish that before long the hour may strike in which force is no longer necessary, but room is left for love and justice by a new established order in civil life. That will depend on whether or not the agitation against Germany ceases in the world outside.' So finally Dibelius asked his listeners not to believe the sensational news reports but rather to have faith. 'You will see that what is now taking place in Germany will lead to a goal for which anyone who loves and honours the German character can be thankful!'[73]

Next to this widespread error of judgment, which Dibelius presented here with all its typical characteristics, and which utterly barred access to a true understanding of the Jewish question, there were considerations of church policy which seemed no less weighty. A confidential circular letter by Kapler dated 1 April, in which the main church administrations were informed about the situation, showed how much all the efforts in Berlin were focussed on 'taking the correct position over the nationalist awakening, and not endangering the independence of the church and its autonomous action'.[74] Volunteer labour, youth education and schools, questions of finance, the constitutional rights and guarantees of the church, reform of the Reich, the Reich concordat and the development of Catholicism – these were the problems which dominated this circular letter after it had reported on the telegrams against foreign propaganda sent by the President. And especially since the German Christians, with massive state support, had called for a general attack on the old church during their first

Reich Conference in Berlin at the beginning of April, defence against this attack dominated all the thoughts, considerations and decisions of the Prussian church administration. It seemed all the more inconceivable to issue a statement against the persecution of the Jews when a conflict with the state was looming in the sphere of church politics, and in no circumstances did anyone want to be exposed on two fronts at the same time.

When the general superintendents gathered for a discussion with the Prussian Oberkirchenrat in Berlin on 11 April, this line had already emerged quite clearly. In his introductory statement Kapler reported that there were tendencies 'to introduce state classifications into the churches too. Given the basic aim of achieving a totalitarian state, the idea of incorporating the church as a department of state into the totality, i.e. in the National Socialist state, was also being discussed.'[75] At this point Protestantism must have felt a direct threat and challenge, and in fact within a few weeks this development plunged the Protestant church into a maelstrom of events which hardly permitted it to take any stand on the Jewish issue.

But in spite of everything these two things alone, the political error of judgment and the situation in church politics, would not have been enough to account for the silence of the church had it not laid itself open to völkisch antisemitism in the 1920s. The general antisemitic mood which was disseminated in Germany by völkisch ideology had been absorbed and was shared by German Protestantism, too. Out of this antisemitic climate there emerged boycott and persecution. Under its spell even the churches did not see and hear what was going on before their very eyes, on their doorsteps and indeed within their walls. The Evangelischer Bund, Emanuel Hirsch's theology of German destiny, Paul Althaus's ambiguous lecture at the 'Fatherland Kirchentag' of 1927, and the Protestant Christians in Germany who actually thought this correct, conceivable and theologically significant, had prepared and made possible that silence which in retrospect seems to be the major fault at this time.

On the Catholic side the picture resembles that on the Protestant side even down to details. Granted, there were rather fewer German nationalist illusions here, but on the other hand there were even stronger political and church-political interests, In both cases the result was the same: silence.

On 31 March, the day before the boycott, the Director of the Deutsche Bank in Berlin, Oskar Wassermann, who was at the same time President of the Working Group of the Confessions for Peace, called on Cardinal Bertram in Breslau on the recommendation of the senior canon of Berlin Cathedral, Bernhard Lichtenberg, in an effort to induce the bishops to intervene with the Reich President and the Reich government. Because the President of the Fulda Bishops' Conference did not want to act alone in this matter, and also felt that he was personally unable to judge either the reasons for the boycott or its prospects, he promised Wassermann at least to ask the five German archbishops about the 'opportuneness of such a step'. However, in a letter that same day he left no doubt that as far as he was concerned the question was to be answered in the negative. 'My doubts,' he informed the Metropolitans, 'are: 1. that this is an economic struggle in an area of interest which, in church terms, is not directly our concern; 2. that the step seems to be meddling in an affair that has little relevance to the hierarchy's sphere of activity, and the hierarchy has good reason to limit itself to its own sphere of activity; 3. that the step is likely to fail, because the reasons for and against are sufficiently well-known to the authorities concerned even without our views. In addition, 4. the tactical consideration may arise that this step, which cannot remain confidential within a limited group, would certainly receive the worst interpretation in the widest circles throughout Germany. In the exceedingly difficult and sombre situation as a whole, this is by no means unimportant.' And in passing Bertram finally touched on the fact 'that the press, which is overwhelmingly in Jewish hands', had 'kept silence throughout over the persecutions of Catholics in various countries'.[76]

While this letter completely gave away the view of the leading church politicians, and could almost just as well have been composed by the President of the German Evangelischer Kirchenausschuss, the opinion among the archbishops was not quite uniform. Whereas Cardinal Faulhaber sent a telegram, 'Fulfilment of wish hopeless. Would make matters worse. More than that a retreat', Archbishop Gröber of Freiburg declared, 'May fulfilment of wish occur out of regard for innocent and converted.'[77] But Gröber was obviously in the minority. In any case, for Bertram and for the German episcopate as a whole, this action decided the question of official intervention. A joint step on behalf of the persecuted German Jews did not take place, nor was it to take place in the future.

Like others in the Protestant church, many individual Catholic Christians found this decision intolerable. So in April urgent requests to the Catholic bishops kept piling up, that they should stand up for the Jews or at least for the Jewish members of their own church. For example, on 5 April the Bavarian pastor Alois Wurm, editor of the monthly journal *Seele*, addressed to the Cardinal in Munich a complaint 'that in this period when the most extreme hatred is being fomented against Jewish citizens, surely more than ninety-nine per cent of whom are innocent, not a single Catholic paper, as far as I can see, had the courage to proclaim the teaching of the Catholic catechism that one may not hate and persecute any human being, least of all for his race. To very many people that appears to be a Catholic failure.' He pointed out that he himself had written such an article, but that it had been rejected by a large Catholic newspaper.[78] The Cardinal's answer was meant to be sarcastic, but in retrospect it proved to be a singular embarrassment. The article would certainly have been printed, declared the irritated Faulhaber, had the author only signed his full name. He, the Cardinal, assumed that 'a blazing protest' would appear in the next issue of *Seele* under Wurm's name, 'and the courage of the press would increase even more if there were one single person who had the courage to have such a protest printed as a pamphlet with his name on it and to distribute it on the streets'. Every Christian must oppose the persecution of the Jews, he wrote, but 'the main church authorities' had 'far more important present-day problems: schools, the continued existence of the Catholic associations, and sterilization are even more important for Christianity in our homeland...' Finally, it should be realized that the Jews could take care of themselves, so that there was no motive 'for giving the government reason to turn the Jew-baiting into Jesuit-baiting'.[79]

The not unjustified fear that the 'attack on the Jews' might at the same time become an attack on the Catholics was an important reason at this time for

271

Cardinal Faulhaber to restrain himself on the Jewish question.[80] On the other hand, during this period – as on the Protestant side – both well-known and unknown Catholics took their places in the 'procession of petitioners' who, despite all political and ecclesiastical misgivings, attempted to convince the senior church authorities that only through courageous witness to the truth could 'humanity and Christianity' be saved.[81] Among them, the Berlin student chaplain and Dominican Franziskus Stratmann gave perhaps the most resolute expression to the expectations which this group had of the church. 'Authentic Christianity,' wrote Stratmann to Faulhaber, 'comes to grief on opportunism. Only that which is resolute and unswerving today will win respect, a following, and enthusiasm. National Socialism is the best example of this. Only through confessors and martyrs can a languishing Christianity rise again.'[82]

In retrospect this sentence, along with the procession of petitioners in both churches, takes on the overwhelming weight of a compelling Christian truth. But in looking back it can also give one the mistaken notion that this truth must have been obvious even then to every Christian in Germany. Hard though it is for later generations to grasp the fact, truths of this kind are never obvious to every Christian. This should warn all those who make judgments today against uttering any kind of condemnation.

While this whole problem was still being debated in both churches, Hitler had already created new facts. On 7 April the 'Law for the Reconstruction of the Civil Service' was promulgated, which marked the beginning of special National Socialist legislation for the Jews. This law, 'for the reconstruction of a national civil service and for the simplification of the administration', prescribed special treatment for three categories of civil servant. According to § 2, 'Officials who have entered the civil service since 9 November 1918 without the prescribed or customary preparatory training for their career or possessing other qualifications' were to be discharged from the service. According to § 3, the so-called 'Aryan Paragraph', 'Officials who are not of Aryan extraction' were to be forced to retire. Officials were exempted from this provision 'who have already been officials since 1 August 1914 or who... fought at the front for the German Reich in the World War, or whose fathers or sons fell in the World War.' Finally, § 4 contained a general threat, with the aid of which the whole apparatus of the civil service could be manipulated: 'Officials who, in view of their previous political activity, cannot guarantee that they will support the national state at all times and without reservation can be discharged from the service.'[83]

This law was also a masterpiece of propaganda. For the state's apparently legitimate demand for loyalty from the civil service, which here appeared in codified form, to a considerable extent concealed the fact that the Aryan paragraph was concerned with a wholly new type of special legislation. However, in the Reich Ministry of the Interior, which was responsible for the law, there was no doubt about this. For in the Foreword to the first annotated edition at the end of April 1933, Ministerialrat Hanns Seel explained that the particular significance of the law lay in the fact that 'above all in its basic § 3, the so-called "Aryan Paragraph", it creates a completely new law which stands in deliberate contrast to the previous law'. And the co-author of the law could record with satisfaction that the Aryan Paragraph had 'already become the model for a series of other laws, such as the laws on the admission of lawyers and patent lawyers, the decree on admission to banking, and the law against overcrowding in German universities and schools'.[84]

The significance of this law for the policy of the Third Reich and especially for its policy towards the Jews can hardly be overestimated. It marked the first step in special legislation at the end of which stood the extermination of the Jews in Germany and Europe, and it was a clear indication that Hitler was determined to make völkisch ideology the basis of the new state even in law.

The reactions triggered off by the law in the two churches differed considerably. While the Catholic church answered with a series of critical statements, the effects of the law struck much deeper into the Protestant church. Here the attempt to extend the law to the church became the occasion for a fundamental clarification, and finally one of the substantive issues over which opinions divided in summer and autumn 1933. As a single specific example, the declaration of commitment by the Pastors' Emergency League contained the solemn statement 'that the application of the Aryan Paragraph within the sphere of the church of Christ is a violation of the *status confessionis*'.[85]

For the Catholic church things were more involved and more complicated in that the Jewish question was buried under the régime's measures against Centre Party officials. The action against Catholic officials had started intensively as early as March,[86] so that on 6 April, in a detailed letter to the Reich President, Cardinal Bertram saw himself obliged to intervene on behalf of those unjustly threatened and discharged.[87] Only with the publication of the civil service law, however, did the bishop decide on public criticism as well. On the following day, 8 April, the Archbishops of Cologne and Paderborn, Karl-Joseph Schulte and Caspar Klein, and the Bishop of Osnabruck, Wilhelm Berning, already met in Cologne and issued a declaration in which they stated that they perceived 'with deepest distress and concern... how the days of national awakening have at the same time undeservedly become days of the most serious and bitter suffering for many loyal citizens, among them conscientious officials'.[88] On 12 April Cardinal Bertram for the East German Province, and on 15 April Archbishop Gröber for the Upper Rhine Church Province, followed this step.[89] In Bavaria, Bishop Buchberger of Regensburg at the same time prepared the draft of a statement which pointed out in a much more detailed and basic way that the 'Christian principle of justice and love' was the foundation of civil life. True, as was stated in this draft, 'the demands of the common good' were fully recognized, but for all that the government should never 'ignore well-established rights altogether – even when they were the rights of those of another political persuasion or members of another people'. In the final version, which was published on 5 May as a 'Pastoral Letter of the Bavarian Bishops', this section was changed somewhat. It now kept open the hope that the Reich government would not share in these efforts and at the same time stressed that any kind of 'special law', 'any violation of law and legal inequality' was to be rejected in principle.[90]

It is not easy to appraise these episcopal statements. Anyone who wanted to could undoubtedly find support from the Catholic church for the persecuted Jews in them. Not only did Cologne groups of the Centre Party understand things in this way,[91] but so too did such Protestants as Wilhelm von Pechmann, hard-pressed by this issue, who used the statements to stress 'the high priority' of a parallel Protesant declaration,[92] or Gustav Krüger, professor of theology in

Giessen, who asserted that the Catholic bishops, even without any explicit declaration, 'mean to include' the Jewish citizens 'in their admonition'.[93] On the other hand, issues were put in such general terms and combined with so much enthusiastic endorsement of the new state that there was little likelihood of awakening dormant consciences. It was no accident that, for example in the Bavarian hierarchy, there were audible expressions of unease that no one was standing up 'categorically' for the baptized Jews.[94]

While the Catholic church was thus going its way between Christian confession, vacillating judgment and tactical accommodation, in German Protestantism the search began for a fundamental clarification of the whole issue. Probably under the impact of the inquiries from home and abroad which accumulated after the boycott,[95] and impelled by the civil service law, as soon as the law was published Kapler had asked the Central Office for Apologetics in Spandau for an expert opinion on the Jewish issue. At all events, the participants at the major conference in Berlin on 11 April attended by all general superintendents and consistory presidents of the Old Prussian Church were given a paper by Kapler. He called it 'an account written by experts purely for your information',[96] but in fact it largely represented the standpoint of the chief Berlin authoriites. It bore the title 'The Church and the Jewish Question in Germany'. The anonymous author was the head of the Central Office for Apologetics – a young Berlin university lecturer, Walter Künneth.[97]

The basic idea behind this paper was the drawing of a strict distinction between the state and the church aspects of the Jewish question. This basic idea was a Lutheran legacy, and on the basis of Lutheran tradition it was accepted almost throughout German Protestantism. Crucial for the appraisal of the state aspect was the fact that the special legislation was basically perceived to be an act of harsh but necessary justice. The most important argument in this connection was the often-quoted 'percentage discrepancy between the Jewish occupancy of public offices and the proportion of Jews in the population'. This discrepancy, Künneth declared, seemed 'unjust to German civil servants, doctors, etc.' so that the reorganization in principle 'had the character of a protective measure to safeguard the German people'. We may assume that this was in fact the general opinion in German Protestantism. It not only prohibited opposition to the special legislation; it made this legislation seem almost a state necessity. Here, though, there was an almost complete failure to note that this method of argument largely accepted the basic approach of völkisch ideology, i.e. the definition of the Jewish question as a racial problem. Here Künneth's paper took over the official reading without hesitation: 'The concept "of non-Aryan extraction" (§ 3 of the new civil service law) means having one's heredity defined by the Jewish race, in contrast to the smaller Central European races (Nordic, Eastern, Western, Dinaric) out of which the German Volk is formed.' What happened here, and was to be decisive in determining the position of the Protestant church on the Jewish question for a long time to come, was a fateful confusion – based on political theology and supported by the prevailing antisemitism – of government action and völkisch ideology which almost completely prevented Protestantism from understanding the true facts of the case.

In these circumstances the answer to the question how the church was to conduct itself on this issue was all the more important. Künneth was unequivocal on this point, too. The church's position on the Jewish issue was 'not determined by political factors, but rather by the concerns of the Christian community'. It was not 'racial extraction, but rather participation in the sacraments' that was the criterion for membership of the community. 'From this there emerges the obligation on the church to be of service to all members of the community in the same way. Any deviation means the abandonment of the gospel.' From these two starting points, Künneth went on to a practical solution of the problem. On the basis of this approach it consisted essentially in the logical demand that in legislation the state should distinguish between Jews and Jewish Christians; otherwise the significance of the church and the church community for the state would be eliminated. It followed that the conversion of Jews to the Christian church from now on called for especially conscientious examination and pre-paration. The 'outward and inward distress of the Jewish race in Germany' obliged the church generally to show 'unconditional Christian love, independent of the national political situation, above all to suffering Jewish Christians'. As an example, the paper mentioned the possibility of a special collection for the Jewish Christians. Beyond this, the church had to advocate 'that the elimination of the Jews as a foreign body in the life of the Volk should not take place in a manner inconsistent with the Christian ethos', that is, that it should not be achieved by acts of violence.

While in retrospect this paper may seem incomprehensible, inadequate and even scandalous, on the assumptions on which normal government action was based, it was not as wrong as all that. For during the 1920s there had been a plethora of special laws for racial as well as ethnic minorities throughout the civilized world, without the political and church public in all the countries concerned feeling that this was a basic abrogation of the rule of law. It was no accident that on 26 March in his *Sonntagsspiegel* Dibelius had objected to the intervention of the American churches with the argument that after all the German churches were not intervening in the Negro question.[98] In Poland and in Czechoslovakia, for example, there were also special laws for the German minorities. Thus in spring 1933 the Civil Service law could still be perceived in this context basically as an instance of legitimate state action 'for the protection of the German Volk'.

How much this was also true for determined critics of the new régime, and also how far one could nevertheless move beyond it was demonstrated by another Berlin university lecturer who concerned himself with the same issues at the same time: Dietrich Bonhoeffer. His short article entitled 'The Church and the Jewish Question', completed on 15 April and published only in June in an out-of-the-way place, is one of the most illuminating and most significant works produced during these years – politically as well as theologically. Here, with incomparable precision, the theological problems of government action were formulated in a way which is still valid even in the changed conditions of the present.[99]

Like Künneth, Bonhoeffer also started from the idea that the Jewish issue has two aspects – a state-political and a church-theological aspect – and that to begin with these aspects had to be dealt with separately. His first paragraph was on the first aspect: 'Without doubt, the Church of the Reformation has no right to

275

address the state directly in its specifically political actions. It has neither to praise nor to censure the laws of the state, but must rather affirm the state to be God's order of preservation in a godless world; it has to recognize the state's ordinances, good or bad, as they appear from a humanitarian point of view, and to understand that they are based on the sustaining will of God amidst the chaotic godlessness of the world.' Contrary to all the political prophets and pseudo-prophets, Bonhoeffer unequivocally held fast to the idea that 'the action of the state remains free from the church's intervention. There are no piqued or pedantic comments from the church here. History is made not by the church but by the state...' According to Bonhoeffer's conviction this was also true of the Jewish question, which without doubt presented a problem, and in dealing with it the state was doubtless also justified 'in taking new paths'. However necessary moral and humanitarian objections might be as correctives, such objections were not the church's affair. For the church 'recognizes the absolute necessity of the use of force in this world, and also the moral injustice of certain concrete acts of the state which are necessarily bound up with the use of force. The church cannot in the first place exert direct political action, for the church does not pretend to have any knowledge of the necessary courses of history. Thus even today, in the Jewish question, it cannot address the state directly and demand of it some definite action of a different nature.'

These sentences, written directly under the impact of the Civil Service law, make it clear that in spring 1933 Bonhoeffer beyond any doubt still allowed the state the right to solve the Jewish question by special legislation. In this respect, then, he shared the point of view of Künneth and other sectors of the church. This must be said clearly if we are to understand the general historical conditions in which the decisions of that period were made. What distinguished Bonhoeffer from this general point of view was that he did not leave things there but investigated what the further development of the problem might be. In so doing he penetrated into a dimension of which Protestant Christianity as a whole did not even have an inkling in the Germany of that time.

First of all, Bonheoffer established that the right of the state to autonomous political action obviously could not mean that the church 'lets political action slip in a disinterested way'. Instead, 'precisely because it does not moralize in individual instances', it can and should 'continually ask whether its action can be justified as legitimate state action – i.e. as action which leads to law and order and not to lawlessness and disorder'. The crucial next step lay in the question what should happen when the state violates, or even reverses, the task given it by God, which the church knows, and which the state knows through the church: that is, to create law and order. Here Bonhoeffer had two possibilities in view. On the one hand he envisaged insufficient law and order, which would be represented, say, by outlawing the Jews, and on the other hand an excess of law and order, as would be the case in the state suppression of free Christian proclamation.

Here, without being aware of it, Bonhoeffer was describing the two decisive characteristics of the totalitarian ideological state systems of the twentieth century. He was, of course, still unsure whether these characteristics applied to the Third Reich, but at least he felt that sufficiently possible for him to outline a kind of plan of action for the church, just in case. In it there were three possible ways in which the church could act: 'In the first place, it can ask whether its actions are legitimate and in accordance with its character as state, i.e. it can throw the state back on its responsibilities. Secondly, it can aid the victims of state action. The church has an unconditional obligation to the victims of any ordering of society, even if they do not belong to the Christian community.' The church had to make constant use of these two possibilities in respect of every state. The third possibility, however, 'not to bind the victims under the wheel, but rather to put a spoke in the wheel, the direct political action of the church',[100] was left for that last and extreme case when the church in fact saw the state unrestrainedly bring about too much or too little law and order. Bonhoeffer was convinced that this instance in which the church had to abandon its own task and take on that of another was so unique that it could only be resolved by an 'evangelical council'.

Bonhoeffer also made a surprising change of direction in the second part of the article, which dealt with the church aspect. Referring back to the earliest period of Christianity, he made a distinction between Jewish Christians and Gentile Christians, each of which were characterized not by race, but by their relationship to the Law of Moses. Accordingly, a Jewish Christian was someone who made observation of the law of Moses the presupposition for church membership; the Gentile Christian was the one who was free here. So if a group within the Protestant church again made membership of the church dependent on the observation of a divine law, i.e. belonging to a particular race, this group would have to be categorized as a type of Jewish Christianity: the exclusive form of church membership which it practised would thus 'constitute it as Jewish Christian'. Otherwise, the question was not whether church members 'today can still tolerate church fellowship with the Jews. It is rather the task of church preaching to say: here is the church, where Jew and German stand together under the word of God; here is the proof whether the church is still the church or not...'

The dimensions of the first part of this article have dawned only slowly upon German Protestantism – in part only after 1945. On the other hand, as Künneth's paper also shows, there was a decisive group in the Protestant church which from the beginning held fast to the second point without being aware of the consequences which this simple truth actually required of the church.

For the time being, however, at the end of April politics and church politics triumphed over all Christian objections and hesitations over the whole issue.

On 25 and 26 April Kapler had called the Kirchenausschuss to Berlin for an extraordinary meeting. The church-political situation and the Jewish question were on the agenda. The group was completely dominated by the storm which the Reich Conference of German Christians had unleashed at the beginning of April. An additional shock was the surprising attack by the government on the Landeskirche of Mecklenburg which had taken place shortly beforehand and which had caused many people to fear an imminent political co-ordination of the whole Protestant church. The interest of members was thus, understandably enough, focussed primarily on the church-political problems of the moment and of the immediate future. These circumstances made a church statement on the Jewish issue, which for many people was in any case controversial and problematical, seem even more open to question.

Nevertheless, the following day Wilhelm von Pechmann tried to change the minds of the Kirchenausschuss with a moving statement. By way of introduction he described 'how appeals for help from men of Jewish extraction who had come to believe as Christians had been brought to him, and what spiritual agony he had encountered as a result. He was seized with the thought that we owe protection to these members of our communities and our churches. We should not abandon them to the feeling that at a time of most terrible distress they were being forsaken, silently and without a word, by the church to which they had long belonged.'[101] However, the discussion which then followed demonstrated all the confusion, the blindness, the faint-heartedness and the weakness of the Protestant church. Time and again talk turned to the difficulties, the possible misunderstandings, the danger that a declaration could be 'misused against Germany by foreign powers', the right of the state to settle the Jewish problem, and the necessity to stand behind the state. In view of these doubts, the great majority manifestly followed the judgment of the President who, the day before, in a conversation with Hitler, had expressed the church's hope for peace and reconciliation only in general terms. Kapler had 'not specifically mentioned' the Jewish question, as he explained: 'I considered it imprudent to say more at this first meeting.'

On the Catholic side, at crucial points the picture was very similar. Here, the representatives of the church provinces met – by chance, also on 25 and 26 April in Berlin – in order to discuss further steps by the bishops. And here too church politics was in the foreground. The five points on the agenda all centred on the protection of the freedom and the independence of the church. Specific issues were the question of the Catholic organizations, the development of Catholic Action, the establishment of a liason body between church and state, schools and educational questions, and the problem of the co-ordination of the church.[102] All these points were dealt with in detail and with obvious care. There was general agreement to do all that might be necessary for the defence of the church and to avoid anything that might be a burden on relations with the new régime. In these circumstances, here too, the Jewish issue shifted to the periphery. A single suggestion that there should be 'an intervention on behalf of the clergy designated by the new government law as non-Aryan and Jews converted by pedagogy' seems to have received no response.[103] Among the numerous resolutions there was only one that took up the problem, namely the suggestion that the racial question should be examined carefully 'by Catholic theologians in conjunction with racial theorists'.[104]

After Hitler had received the first representatives of German Protestantism on 25 April and been given by Kapler the impression that while the Protestant church would defend its independence it would not protest against Jewish policy, on 26 April he had his first interview with a representative of the German bishops. Notes made by Bishop Berning of Osnabrück make it clear that in this conversation, too, the decisive emphasis was on the protection of church rights. The bishop submitted four points to the Chancellor as being the special concern of the church, namely: the freedom of the church, the freedom of the Catholic schools, the freedom and independence of the Catholic associations, and the dismissal of Catholic civil servants.[105] And so there was no challenge to what in other circumstances the bishop would certainly have repudiated emphatically, namely Hitler's appeal to the Catholic church for it, too, 'to regard the Jews as anti-social' and therefore banish them to the ghetto.[106]

The two conferences at the end of April determined the courses both churches would take for the time being. They resembled each other in the fact that, for all the dissimilarity in the specific problems they faced, basically they were agreed that the defence of the freedom and independence of the church *vis à vis* the state was now the first and most important task, in the face of which all other undertakings had to take second place.

If the church decisions of those weeks are critically examined in retrospect, a surprising fact emerges. The minority in both churches which did not keep silent, but rather spoke up, had no common criterion other than uneasy consciences. Having an uneasy conscience was obviously independent of age, confession, estate or political alignment. It bound together the old Bavarian nobleman with the young socialist pastor in the Rhineland, the liberal professor of theology in Hessen with the Berlin Dominican father, the Protestant German Nationalist with the Catholic Centre Party member. These uneasy consciences remained, and remain, underivable, personally as well as socially.

We can well understand why in an extremely difficult situation the church administrations yielded to the quite rational and convincing arguments which at this moment made silence on the part of the church seem advisable. However, what Wilhelm von Pechmann wrote to Martin Rade on 8 September 1934 about the disturbed minority is true: 'I know that I am free from any trace of arrogance when I say how happy a later church historian will be about each one of those who have not bent the knee before the Baal of this era.'[107]

4

Protestant Church Reform
(April)

Whereas in retrospect the Jewish question takes on crucial significance for the conduct of the churches during these weeks, contemporaries almost without exception thought another problem of disproportionately greater importance. That was the new pattern of the relationship between church and state and, on the Protestant side, the problem of church reform associated with it. The aim of this reform had a name as promising as it was vague: the Evangelical Reich Church.

The idea of an Evangelical Reich Church as an amalgamation of the Protestant confessions and the Landeskirchen was not new. Like so much that was revived during this era, it originated early in the nineteenth century, and since then had come up at every nationalist turning point in German history.[1] The realization of it had, however, always been frustrated on two fronts. First, the interests of the church governments, controlled as they were by local rulers, and later the growing self-awareness of the Landeskirchen, had resisted any closer alliance. Secondly, neo-Lutheranism had brought the question of the *status confessionis* so strongly into the foreground that the Lutheran churches objected to a Reich church for that reason also and preferred to contemplate a general Lutheran merger. The 1922 Kirchenbund, with its extremely federalistic constitution, provided a very visible symbol of these tendencies.

At the beginning of the 1930s, however, the subject suddenly reappeared in public discussion. The unsatisfactory state of the ponderous and rarely-effective Kirchenbund, combined with the powerful upsurge of the völkisch-nationalist movement, had the effect in broad circles of German Protestantism of making common church representation seem once again a worthwhile goal. Typically, it was above all the Evangelischer Bund, at whose conference in Magdeburg in June 1931 'the divisions of the Protestant church in Germany' were vigorously deplored amid calls for the mobilization of the Bund 'for a more effective concentration of the forces of the church' which voiced these desires and hopes. As the President of the Bund suggested, 'a vast number of Protestant Christians in all the German Landeskirchen' cherished this, 'as a passionate yearning in their hearts'.[2] In the following year the German Christians took up this idea in a much more radical way, putting the 'amalgamation of the twenty-nine churches combined in the German Evangelischer Kirchenbund' into an Evangelical Reich church at the head of their 1932 'guidelines' as a winning slogan.[3]

But even the Kirchenbund was obliged to concern itself with the problem. The discussion of the reform of the Reich constitution provided the opportunity. In view of the growing weakness of the Reich, this discussion had entered a new stage after 1930, and at the end of 1931 suggested the possibility of an early demolition of federalism and a strengthening of centralism.[4] The Lutherans from Lower Germany first brought this up. In particular August Marahrens, Land Bishop of Hanover, urged a clarification of the problem. While he would welcome a merger of the Lutheran churches of Lower Germany, at all events he wanted to avoid a union with Reformed or United areas.[5] For a reform of the Reich that redrew the borders of the Länder in Lower Germany could easily create a highly undesirable situation for Lutherans. Hence in February 1932 the Federation of the Lower German Lutheran churches resolved to press the Kirchenausschuss for a thorough consideration of the question of Reich reform.[6]

The first comment made by the Kirchenausschuss coincided with the tenth anniversary of the Kirchenbund, which was solemnly celebrated in Wittenberg in May 1932. Precisely because of the lively public discussion over the future of the church prompted by this anniversary,[7] the Kirchenausschuss thought it necessary, contrary to all the Reich church ideas of unity – to refer to the federative and confessional foundations of the Kirchenbund. In a resolution it therefore declared itself to be against 'earth-shaking innovations' in the relationship between Reich and Länder, in any case asked that the church's point of view be heard at the appropriate time, and emphasized the basic autonomy of the church in all matters relating to the organization of the Landeskirchen.[8] A further statement in 1932 confirmed this line. After public discussion during the course of the year had again moved more strongly towards the federalist solution, the Kirchenausschuss expressly welcomed the fact 'that the plans recently published by the Reich government for Reich reform are aimed at preserving the independence of the Länder, including the Land of Prussia, within the framework of the Reich constitution...' At the same time there was a further recommendation to the President 'also to continue... to protect the interests of the church energetically in the face of the effort to reform the Reich....'[9]

These resolutions were remarkable in several respects. Not only did they emphasize the undiminished aversion of the Landeskirchen to any plans for a Reich church but they also demonstrated how closely the Kirchenbund felt its own constitution to be tied to the Reich constitution. Moreover, the November resolution contained a mandate for President Kapler in all situations to protect the interests of the Evangelical Church in the face of the Reich.

This was the state of affairs when Hitler took power on 30 January.

It explains why the step into the Third Reich inevitably had far-reaching consequences not only for church consciousness but – in contrast to Catholicism – also for the ecclesiastical organization of German Protestantism.

For it soon became evident that the new government was dominated by a concern to centralize the Reich which far exceeded all centralist plans in the past. Hence the longer the Kirchenbund clung to a strictly federalist approach over the Landeskirchen, the less possible and advisable it appeared. It did not take the German Christians to make this clear, however much they later took credit for having first launched the whole development. In the Protestant consciousness of the time there was such a close connection between Reich and church that a reconstruction of the Reich could not be imagined without a simultaneous reconstruction of the church. This was the decisive motivation behind the reform of the church in spring and summer 1933.[10]

It seems as though Kapler understood these implications quite early. However, the actual impetus for him to take immediate action in this direction did not first arise out of the matter itself but rather out of Catholic church policy.

The news of 23 March that Hitler had offered the Catholic side the possibility of concluding a Reich concordat put the chief authorities in the Protestant church in a state of the utmost concern. They feared that Hitler's manifest efforts towards Rome might represent a basic Catholic orientation in his policy and that by comparison German Protestantism would lose in influence and importance. Danger seemed to be looming for the Protestant side, and prompt action seemed to be called for.

Kapler's first reaction matched the level of his anxiety. He gave the news to the Reich President the same day in a personal letter,[11] and added that he thought himself 'officially authorized and obliged at this very moment to request the immediate, special and thoughtful vigilance of the Reich President – as chief guardian of the law and confessional peace – to ask for a proportionate safeguarding of Protestant church interests'. He went on: 'Especially in respect of the possibility of a Reich concordat with the Catholic church, may I mention that on the Protestant side. According to the constitution of the German Evangelischer Kirchenbund, which embraces all the German Protestant Landes-kirchen, there would be in the German Evangelischer Kirchenausschuss a legitimate organ for the conclusion of a corresponding treaty between the Reich and the German Evangelischer Kirchenbund.'[12] The supreme authority in the Reich was thus directly drawn into the concerns of the Protestant church. And in this respect Kapler had undoubtedly come to the right man. For not only did the confidence of the Reich President play an important role in Hitler's politics at the beginning, but he was, and remained until his death, responsive and sensitive in matters affecting his ancestral church. So his Secretary of State, Otto Meissner, immediately reported that the Reich President had taken an interest in the letter and had referred it to the Reich Minister of the Interior for his in-formation.[13] In this way Frick, too, was already involved in the whole proceedings.

The important confidential circular letter of 1 April in which Kapler informed the chief agencies of the German Landeskirchen of the situation revealed how deeply the President was impressed by the plans for a concordat and how vigorously the Kirchenbundesamt had taken the initiative in connection with it. Kapler let the Landeskirchen know that among other things he had 'devoted increasing attention to the action of the Catholic church. The declaration of the Fulda Bishops' Conference,' he went on to state, 'along with various signs of increased activity for the preservation of – or rather the increase in – the number of personnel at Reich and Land level, and for strengthening Catholic influence, put the development of relations with the Papal see mentioned in the program-matic statement of the Reich government in a special light'. However, Kapler's important conclusion from these observations ran: 'On the Protestant side, the Kirchenbund will necessarily have to be set up as an equally strong counter-balance to the obvious efforts to establish the Catholic Church in the Reich as a self-contained, united power factor.'[14] Kapler did not say as much openly, but every well-informed person knew what this 'equally strong counter-balance' meant, namely a step in the direction of an Evangelical Reich Church.

That the President had already had these thoughts in mind for a long time was evident from the fact that as early as autumn 1932 he had asked the Marburg constitutional lawyer Gustav Adolf Walz for an opinion on the constitutional problems of an Evangelical Reich church. Walz came to the conclusion that 'an inter-territorial church with a federative or centralist structure, recognized as a corporation with a special legal status answerable to the Reich alone', should be designated as 'a Reich Church'. The Reich alone would be responsible for its 'legal control and supervision', in accordance with Article 132 II of the Reich constitution.[15] The most important step for Kapler was now therefore to obtain direct information as to how the relevant Reich authorities, the Reich Minister of the Interior and the Reich Chancellor, might react to these plans. In these circumstances it was especially significant that on 1 April the President could inform the Landeskirchen that he now thought that the time had come for 'personal contact with the leading figures in the Reich government', and that 'a visit by me to the Reich Minister of the Interior and the Chancellor is being planned and prepared for as soon as possible'.[16]

While Kapler was considering all this, a direct stimulus now also came from the Protestant side. Again it was the Federation of Lower German Churches which first made a move. Their fears, however, were focussed less on Catholicism than on a threat to the purity of the Lutheran confession. On the initiative of Paul Fleisch, the Hanover Vice-President, a man who more than anyone had fought all his life for an exclusively Lutheran church policy, on 29 March the federation condemned all plans so far made for a Reich church with the argument that 'the confessional factor... fundamentally and decisively' stood in their way. 'For Lutheranism is not only quite sharply distinct from Christianity... but also above all lays crucial emphasis on *pura doctrina* and on a church government that watches over the purity of the *publica doctrina*, whereas an Evangelical Reich church has to acknowledge several *doctrinae*'.[17] Instead, a confessional alliance would bring German Protestantism close to the unity it also desired here. At the same time Marahrens and Traugott von Heintze, the President of Schleswig-Holstein, were authorized to go to Berlin the next day and report to President Kapler 'that 1. in north-west Germany there was a desire to form a closer alliance and 2. there was a feeling that the Kirchenbund needed a more forceful and more active head than the present German Evangelischer Kirchenausschuss, perhaps a directorate of between three and five men'.[18] The visit of the two Lutherans took place on 30 March and would presumably have made the difficulties of his own plan even clearer to Kapler.

However, his visit could not dissuade the President from his conviction that German Protestantism had to form as close an alliance as possible as quickly as possible, not least because on 31 March 1933 the 'Provisional Law for the Co-ordination of the Länder with the Reich' was published.[19] Its centralism naturally impinged directly upon the interests of the Protestant church.

On 1 April it emerged how far the plans of the President along these lines had progressed. The conversation with the Reich Minister of the Interior which had been announced in the circular letter of 1 April took place that very day.[20] In the report on this conversation which Kapler gave on 11 April he informed the general superintendents that he had 'conveyed the readiness of the church for co-operation, but only with its freedom safeguarded. Furthermore he had discussed the problem of the Reich Church with reference to the proposals put forward in the Kirchenbund. He had talked over the question of a Reich concordat, and in this connection had pointed out that the Kirchenbund was an instrument which could serve in connection with the possible conclusion of an Evangelical Reich Church treaty.'[21] This amounted to a declaration that the Protestant church not only urged the conclusion of a church treaty comparable to the concordat but that under the impact of the nationalist revolution and its results it was also ready to alter its traditional Landeskirche-federalist structure.

A discussion in Berlin on 7 April to which Kapler had invited the representatives of the major Landeskirchen – Prussia, Saxony, Hanover, Württemberg, Bavaria, Thuringia and Schleswig-Holstein – also served this end. Kapler opened the discussion by asking 'whether or not it could in fact be certified that the constitution still meets present requirements and whether or not practical changes might be necessary'. Bishop Marahrens of Hanover thereupon presented the plans of the Lower German Church Federation to the meeting. The collaboration that was so necessary, he said, could only take place on a confessional basis. According to Marahrens, this amounted to 'a threefold organization of German Protestantism into a United, a Lutheran and a Reformed type'. 'The independence of the Landeskirchen would then be destroyed, but the question arises whether the present moment does not call for special sacrifices from the Landeskirchen.' For the moment, above all an action committee had to be formed which was capable of acting quickly and resolutely. The general agreement to the plan for such a committee also led to the model of the three-man committee which not long afterwards was for some time in fact to determine the fortunes of German Protestantism.[22]

In view of the tremendous confusion which very quickly began to spread throughout the Protestant camp, this must be taken as being initially the real church line. German Protestantism, in the form of its most important elected and legitimate authorities, was ready and determined to reform the Evangelical Church, legally and practically, following the model of the new Reich and on the basis of the Kirchenbund – with the aim of arriving at an independent Reich Church by means of close collaboration between the Landeskirchen. The plans for achieving this purpose seemed quite dissimilar in detail, but the willingness was there even before the German Christians arrived on the scene. It did not take their appearance to provoke their willingness, which was merely strengthened and accelerated by it. On 14 April Marahrens, quite correctly, expressly rejected the charge that the churches had left the initiative to the German Christians. 'On 29 March of this year,' he wrote to a concerned critic, 'the Lutheran churches of Lower Saxony spoke about the Reich Church. On 30 March I negotiated with President Kapler on their behalf. On 7 April, in a small group under the chairmanship of Dr Kapler in Berlin, I made a report on a Reich Church and a reorganization of the German Evangelischer Kirchenbund. You will agree with me that the Lutheran churches at any rate have not let their own behaviour be dictated by the German Christians.'[23]

However, this development was now interrupted by an event which, contrary to Kapler's cautious procedure, proclaimed the legitimacy of a church revolution.

284

This event quite quickly upset all plans, tangled all the various threads, provoked numerous actions and reactions, and in a matter of a few months finally plunged German Protestantism into almost total chaos. It was the first Reich Conference of the Faith Movement of German Christians which took place in Berlin between 3 and 5 April 1933.

After 30 January the German Christians, whose development we must now consider, found themselves in a remarkable position. In spite of the relatively high number of votes they had gained in the November 1932 church elections,[24] there could be no question of their having gained a foothold in the Prussian church, far less of the existence of a functioning national organization. At this time, if their national leader, Joachim Hossenfelder, and his deputy, Fritz Lörzer, mustered all their forces, they could count on a fairly reliable band of followers only in Berlin and Brandenburg. East Prussia, as shown by the considerably milder guidelines which had been introduced there, was already going its own way, while after the elections the daily routine had once again largely taken over in the other Prussian church provinces. Furthermore the German-Christian groups in Baden, Hessen-Nassau and Thuringia, all of which had developed independently of the activities in Berlin, in part remained independent into May and saw no reason why they should put themselves under a Reich administration. How difficult the construction of an organization in other Landeskirchen was, and how modest the successes initially remained, emerges from the records in the Faith Movement in North Germany, the only complete collection of German Christian files to have survived from this early period.[25]

The organization of the entire North German area only began, after some hesitations, on 24 November 1932 with a letter from Hossenfelder's adjutant, Gotthard Rachner, to the forty-five-year old Hamburg businessman Hans Aselmann. As chairman of the Northern Federation of Protestant Men's and Young Men's Associations, Aselmann seemed to the Berlin group obviously qualified for this task, though he was completely unknown to them personally. In the pompous style characteristic of the time, it said: 'Please organize the Faith Movement of "German Christians" in Schleswig-Holstein. I am sending you under separate cover at printed rate a copy of "The Guidelines of the German Christians" and a copy of our Sunday newspaper, *Evangelium im Dritten Reich*. You will also receive by parcel post 1000 order forms for this Sunday paper...' The letter gave two names as Party spokesmen and technical consultants on church questions in Schleswig-Holstein: Pastors Ernst Szymanowski from Kaltenkirchen near Neumünster and Johann Peperkorn from Viöl near Husum. The end of the letter stated quite casually: 'Immediately take the Hanseatic cities of Hamburg, Bremen and Lübeck under your wing and appoint campaign managers there'.[26] Impressed not least by the splendid official Party letterhead, on 28 November Aselmann promised Hossenfelder that he would undertake the task. However, by way of a precaution he let him know that because he held office in a church association he thought it 'inopportune for the time being to make too prominent a public appearance' as part of his efforts for the German Christians.[27]

Aselmann noted quite early that there was no question of any enthusiasm for the German Christians in the north; Szymanowski's address proved unproductive; Peperkorn had only a few addresses of possible subscribers to *Evangelium im Dritten Reich* and in any case did not feel that there was any hurry about organizing the German Christians in Schleswig-Holstein.[28] Instead, an additional collaborator, Gustav Rössing, the pastor of the Kiel City Mission, came forward in December.[29] At the beginning of January Aselmann succeeded in winning over the hesitant Hamburg Gauleitung and commending to it the self-important and ambitious pastor Franz Tügel, Gau spokesman for the Party from 1932 and later Land Bishop of Hamburg.[30] In spite of this, on 30 January Aselmann was virtually the only member of the German Christian movement in North Germany. This did not prevent Hossenfelder that same day, in Circular Letter no.15, from calling for the organization of fourteen specialist departments for every Landeskirche and for all the provinces of the Prussian church, and at the same time announcing the new official organization of the Faith Movement. In future it was to be divided into Reich leadership, Land inspectorates, provincial leadership, Gau leadership, Kreis leadership and community groups.[31]

Even after 30 January the organization of the German Christians in the north made only very slow progress, despite Hossenfelder's grandiose plans. At the end of March the nucleus of the movement in Schleswig-Holstein consisted at the most of between thirty and forty people; however, they already included two members of the church administration, consistory councillors Nikolaus Christiansen and Dr Christian Kinder. Both were chosen as speakers for the first meeting of the German Christians, which took place on 31 March at Neumünster.[32] At the same time – the end of March – Tügel, as 'Gau supervisor of the preparation for church elections' appointed 'by the Reich leadership of the NSDAP' began his attacks in Hamburg on the national unreliability of the church administration.[33] In Bremen, a pastor Paul Thyssen was said to have been active on behalf of the Faith Movement since December.[34] But there was no news from there. From Lübeck, the Bundeswart of the YMCA, Albert Meyer, reported on 25 March in a typical letter that only one pastor was a member of the NSDAP, and he 'unfortunately disapproved' of the YMCA. How unknown the Faith Movement still was at this time was shown by Meyer's report that unfortunately he had 'not yet come into contact' with it, although – he added – 'I would very much like to.'[35] So just before the opening of their first Reich conference, the situation was that either there was no serious organization of German Christians outside Berlin and Brandenburg whatsoever, or it consisted of individuals or small groups which still played virtually no role in the Landeskirchen. A few exceptions made no fundamental difference to this picture.

This observation coincides with the results of an inquiry which the Kirchenbundesamt sent to the the Landeskirchen on 20 March. It was trying to establish a body of general election statistics for the church elections, which was also supposed to provide specific information about the political groupings. Most Landeskirchen announced that they were willing to supply information. However, more detailed statistics could be established at this time only in Baden, Thuringia and Prussia. The rest of the Landeskirchen – including Bavaria, Württemberg and Hanover – answered in very much the same way as the office of the Schaumburg-Lippe Landeskirche. On 22 March, in the most exquisite official style, it told Berlin that in response 'to your kind letter of the 20th inst… concerning the formation of groups of deputies, we respectfullly reply that we have not yet observed anything of the kind here. In future we shall take this into account and will supply the Church Statistics Office with information'.[36]

However, not only had the Faith Movement still made hardly any progress in the building up of an organization by the end of March; its public activity, too, was largely taken up with being busy for the sake of being busy, as a reflection of the Party. It seemed that without a specific political goal such as that provided by the church elections, the German Christian mobilization of the communities largely took place at the level of petty-bourgeois evening meetings. Here the Reich cultural director of the movement, a certain Alfred Bierschwale, played an important role. As a zealous organizer and orator, this shady figure knew how to make himself indispensable until in October he dropped out of sight, evidently because of criminal offences.[37] The cultural evenings which Bierschwale organized in Berlin were typical of the spirit of the Berlin group as a whole; unlike that in Thuringia, for instance, it did not have even a trace of a distinctive religious consciousness. Thus along with one or two speeches about the struggle of the German Christians, the heroic Luther, and Hitler's mission, the standard repertoire of those evenings consisted of the chorale 'Ein feste Burg...', marches, opera tunes and songs from operettas.[38] In addition to this there was 'training', which took place in barely twenty of the more than four hundred Berlin communities – to take the second week of February as an example.[39] The welcome to all the opportunities which the nationalist revolution offered for public appearances at services and celebrations after 30 January was therefore all the more joyful. The packed thanksgiving service on 3 February at the Marienkirche, the service of mourning on 5 February in Berlin Cathedral,[40] and the festal service for the opening session of the Prussian Landtag on 22 March all had Hossenfelder as preacher. Goebbels' party organ, *Der Angriff*, gave a vivid description of the festal service. After the National Socialist Landtag group had gathered in the Landtag, the report went on: 'The march started... with the leader of the Group, Party Member Kube, at its head. In a long brown line the procession marched... to Christus-Kirche.' On Hossenfelder's sermon with the Good Shepherd (John 10.12) as its text, the paper reported: 'Christianity is a matter of struggle... Leaders of the church who negotiate with Marxism or who cower before it surrender the soul of the German Volk to godlessness. Such leaders are no shepherds, but rather hirelings... Jesus... is the one who leads redeemed human beings to God... After times of bondage, after times in which hirelings ruled, he has now sent us men whom he has called to be leaders... We thank God that he has sent us a leader again.' After the service, *Der Angriff* subsequently reported, Kube led off 'the parade of the parliamentary group'.[41]

Managing the organization, festal services, cultural evenings and educational lectures, and – not least – recruitment for the Party – these were the things that kept the Reich administration busy in February and March. In addition, there were those who busied themselves as informers, like Pastor Karl Eckert, a parliamentary deputy and Kube's consultant for church affairs, who wrote to the Prussian Ministry of the Interior on 16 March that the Bürgomeisters of Arnswalde and Neuwedell were very unreliable politically, and also that the Landrat should 'not be forgotten when it comes to demolition'.[42]

In view of this weakness, which was hardly concealed by the general activity, it was quite understandable that when the national leadership of the Faith

Movement gathered on 6 February for its first meeting after the seizure of power, it perceived its future above all in a closer dependence on the Party. It was decided to approach Dr Robert Ley, Strasser's successor as Reich Organization Leader, that very day and to ask him to create a Reichstag mandate for Hossenfelder. At the same time the following points were mentioned as the next task for Hossenfelder and the German Christians: '1. Expansion of the movement, above all in Bavaria and over all southern Germany, by means of personal lectures, meetings of officials, contact with the NSDAP and its Gauleiters... 2. Removal of the obstructions which exist as a result of people acting independently... particularly in Protestant circles, which are in fact already divided into twenty-seven churches. 3. Strengthening the position of the Faith Movement of German Christians in the face of the church authorities... by means of his [Hossenfelder's] legitimation from outside, from the NSDAP side.' The letter identified the goal as being the conquest of 'the Protestant church by the Faith Movement, lock, stock and barrel for National Socialism'. Dr Krummacher, Landrat in Gummersbach, Land leader of the Faith Movement in the Rhineland and a close friend of Ley, who wrote this letter, added as a personal note that the matter was really urgent: Hossenfelder had 'the right Lutheran fighting spirit'; and Kube had a high opinion of him, 'whereas Goebbels apparently could not understand him at all'.[43]

After that a conversation took place as early as 10 February between Hossenfelder and Dr Ley, at which the latter promised to support the plan of the German Christians.[44] But by now the whole cause was not important enough to the Party actually to go ahead with a Reichstag mandate for Hossenfelder. So the campaign evidently petered out very quickly. The disappointment among the German Christians over this slight on their Reich leader was doubtless considerable. That made the preparations for the first major public activity of the Faith Movement all the more energetic. It was an event which was finally to bring the attention and recognition that was so longed for from the Party as well as from the church.

The First Reich conference had originally been planned for 19-22 February and was supposed above all to deal with questions of organization and propaganda.[45] However, on 8 February Hossenfelder announced that the conference was to be postponed to the first week in April because of the impending Reichstag election campaign, which would totally pre-empt all the energies of the Faith Movement. The order closed with a statement which was and remained typical of Hossenfelder's military conception of the mission of the German Christians: 'So go with God in the political election campaign that lies before us, in which the watchword is "German Christians to the front!".'[46]

The new and final programme for 3 and 4 April appeared on 26 March in *Evangelium in Dritten Reich*. It clearly showed the effort that had been taken to impress the Party with a demonstration of broad support from the Faith Movement and at the same time by the inclusion of topics related to the church and theology to show the church that there was a serious movement here. So an 'honorary committee' was created for the conference, which among others included the Reich Ministers Frick and Göring; Count Helldorff, the leader of the Berlin SA; Hans Hinkel, the leader of the Fighting League for German Culture; Hanns Kerrl, the President of the Prussian Landtag; and also, of course,

Wilhelm Kube, Gauleiter and Chairman of the National Socialist party in the Landtag. As quite soon became apparent, Kube was the only one who had an interest in the event and made a personal appearance. In spite of this array, the response in the church remained exceedingly modest. The *Tägliche Rundschau* counted only seventeen pastors from Berlin and eighteen from the rest of the Reich among the participants. 'From a total of 16,000 pastors,' the paper noted quite correctly, 'that is not many'.[47] So in fact it was thanks almost exclusively to Kube's preparation and public appearance that the first Reich Conference became that lightning-stroke which abruptly changed the whole church scene.

After his vigorous efforts in the winter of 1931/32 which had finally led to the founding of the Faith Movement in the summer of 1932, the Gauleiter of Brandenburg had for the time being devoted himself to other issues and left the further development of the movement to Hossenfelder.[48] Only in January 1933, in an article in *Evangelium im Dritten Reich*, did he again seize the chance to speak out. He maintained that since he, Kube, no longer led the movement, 'a quite disgraceful witch hunt was being staged' against Pastor Hossenfelder. The unmistakable threats which he attached to this statement were of course again directed above all against the reactionary general superintendents, and against some 'Berlin gentlemen' in particular.[49] Whereas in January there was no more behind this article than the well-known hatred of a Party functionary, eight weeks later the situation had changed fundamentally. In the interim Kube had become Senior President and thus the highest-ranking official in the province of Berlin-Brandenburg. When he spoke now, his word had also to be regarded as the voice of the Prussian government. This lent quite different weight to his representation of the church. Whether at this point Kube had heard of Kapler's plans and feared that the Faith Movement might lose the initiative, or whether he simply considered the time and opportunity ripe for finally getting even with the Prussian church authorities, at all events he decided to give the Reich conference a political impact that the German Christians would never have achieved under their own steam. The occasion he needed for a fight was offered him by the confidential circular letter which Dibelius had sent to all the Brandenburg pastors on 8 March.[50] Under the headline 'The True Face of General Superintendent Dr Dibelius', on 2 April Kube's party newspaper the *Märkischer Adler* described this circular letter as a 'disgraceful libellous tract against the National Socialists', and printed the complete text with the appropriate emphases. 'The open-hearted clerical custodian of Protestant Prussia.' the newspaper commmented, 'writes on it "Confidential! No.1, 1933"'. This loyal guardian of souls probably has still further stylistic exercises of the same type in mind.'[51]

In spite of this preparation, Kube's short speech of welcome at the large public rally on the afternoon of 3 April was a sensation. A crucial contribution to this effect was the fact that the whole event was broadcast on the radio and thus made public. According to the report of the Telegraphic Union, the only source of information about it that we have, Kube first of all declared that here he was speaking not so much in his capacity as Senior President as in his function as the leader of the strongest parliamentary group in the Prussian Landrat. And then came the crucial sentences: 'In the sphere of church politics,' he assured the assembled German Christians, 'you may be certain that no matter what, the

National Socialist group in the Prussian Landtag, with all state means at its disposal and the personal politics available to us through the church treaty, will take account of the revolution among our people.' This, of course, was the emphasis that the German Christians wanted to hear, so the report recorded 'tumultuous applause' at this point. 'So,' continued Kube, 'here and now I reject the unprecedented attack of the General Superintendent of Brandenburg, Dr Dibelius, upon our movement (loud applause). You, my friends, will find the 211 men of the Prussian group to be your protection and your protagonists in the effort to carry forward the German revolution in the spirit of Martin Luther in the twentieth century (tumultuous applause).'[52]

If these statements were taken seriously – and there was no reason whatsoever not to do so – then they could only meant that the Party in Prussia had now made the cause of the German Christians its own and at the same time had declared the goals of the German Christians to be a task of state policy. And this was precisely the way in which Kube was understood, not only in the numerous press reports but above all in the church administration. But this meant that the intention of the Oberkirchenrat to make as little fuss about the Reich Conference as possible was frustrated. There was no future for the kind of friendly, well-meaning neutrality represented by Kapler's letter declining the official invitation.[53]

Kube's speech now also gave extraordinary significance to the church-political reports published in the next few days, which otherwise would have created hardly any stir in the Prussian church. Indeed the fact had to be faced that these were now more than just the well-known utterances of an extreme right-wing minority: such views might be forced on the church in the imminent future by the use of state power.

The most important of the twelve working parties (others dealt with theology, culture, women's questions, religious education, social questions, liturgy and the hymn book, missions, personnel matters and national issues) proved to be the one dealing with church law. Here the young Berlin lawyer Dr Friedrich Werner gave a report on 'The Legal Basis of the Coming Reichskirche'. Werner, one of the few from these first tumultuous days who managed to keep himself at the top until the 1945 collapse, outlined the picture of a coming Reich Church which 'will stop only at the border of the Reich and will embrace all Protestant Christians in a Reich whose borders will one day reach from Riga to Strassburg and from the North Sea to the eastern borders of our Austrian brothers'. The National Socialist state, Werner asserted, could not and did not want to dispense with the church. It called for the co-ordination of state and church because that alone could 'bring forth the unprecedented increase in power which the nation requires to achieve its goals'.[54]

The specific political ideas for achieving these goals which Werner's report lacked were added in the discussion that followed. Since the existing church was not of itself capable of such a reform, it had to be assisted by the appointment of state commissioners. A new constitutional assembly was necessary which could either be called after repeal of the basic Prussian state law of 1924 or could even be formed simply by means of a co-ordination with the Prussian Landtag. Until the new order, all state subsidies to the church were to be suspended.[55] Misgivings that in all of this there was too little mention of theology and dogmatics were brushed aside with a reference to the requirements of a 'revolutionary period'. 'We stand,' it was claimed, 'before a great new formation of the church. Revolution is life, not theorizing about life.'[56]

It was clear that the Berlin group, which was behind this first Reich conference, was meanwhile receiving its impulses and ideas almost exclusively from the nationalist revolution. Drunk with the enthusiasm of these weeks and fascinated by Hitler's successes, each of the individuals involved here felt himself to be a little Führer attempting to emulate the great Führer in audacity, swiftness and unscrupulousness. Also characteristic of this tendency was the group working on 'personnel questions' in which the Berlin pastor Siegfried Nobiling read a paper on 'Leadership in the Church'. Nobiling was convinced that the 'appropriate incorporation of the empirical church into the Volksstaat of the nationalist revolution' which he demanded also meant the introduction of the so-called Führer principle. However, only 'someone who feels within himself the call of the Lord of the church out of his Volk into leadership' could be a church leader. The völkisch implications of this observation were obvious, and Nobiling went on to draw them: 'A dignity in the church can be held only by someone who has no alien blood in him... Only a person of purely German blood can be admitted to the office of pastor.'[57] This was a call for an Aryan paragraph in the church, too – only a few days after the great boycott and before the Civil Service law had yet appeared. In the thinking of this Berlin group the völkisch idea, Aryan blood, leadership and the Reich idea formed a unity. Their great aim was now to convert it into power in church politics.

At the closing session on the Tuesday evening this goal was formulated by Hossenfelder in a resolution as follows: 'In the face of a state that promotes the powers of darkness, the true believer has the right of revolution. He also has this right over against a church administration that does not acknowledge the nationalist uprising without reservations. For a German Christian, the church is the community of the faithful which is obligated to fight for a Christian Germany. 'The goal of the Faith Movement of "German Christians" is an Evangelical German Reich church. The state of Adolf Hitler calls upon the church; the church must hear the call.'[58]

These statements were quite simply the consequences of a radicalized political theology. According to the basic confession of the Lutheran churches, the Augsburg Confession of 1530, the church is 'the assembly of all believers among whom the gospel is preached in its purity and the holy sacraments are administered according to the gospel'.[59] The basic principle of political theology was immediately evident in the understanding of the church as 'a community of the faithful which is obligated to fight for a Christian Germany'. Word and sacrament were superseded by the political mission which, according to the German Christians, was not to displace word and sacrament but rather to represent a modern, up-to-date understanding of them.

The reaction of the Prussian church administration to this unmistakable challenge followed quickly and resolutely. However, it did not begin at the point where the real damage lay, namely in theology. The Protestant church took more than a year to notice and articulate this damage. Only at the Barmen Synod of May 1934 did it achieve clarification on this point. In April 1933 the entire attention of the church administrations was concentrated, rather, quite simply on the preservation of their legal independence.

The official protest of the Prussian Oberkirchenrat on 5 April therefore limited itself strictly to Kube's speech. The Senior President of Berlin and Brandenburg had 'emphatically announced the intention of the NSDAP group in the Prussian Landtag to influence church politics', and had given the 'impression of a deliberate state intervention in the church sphere'. However, this intention (the nub of the protest) was 'incompatible with the declaration of the Reich government, delivered before the assembled Reichstag in a fateful hour by the Reich Chancellor' on the inviolability of church rights. Only a church free and independent of the authority of the state could render the Volk the service for which the church was 'joyfully ready'. Therefore the Oberkirchenrat made the 'strongest protest' against Kube's statement. At the same time the letter called Kube's attacks on Dibelius 'a most extraordinary public attack by a senior Prussian state official on a high dignitary of our church', which the contents of the circular letter of 8 March 'could in no way justify'.[60] This letter went to the Prussian Kultusminister, to Papen as Reich Commissioner for Prussia, to the Reich government in the person of the Reich Chancellor and to all the supreme church authorities in Prussia.

If we recall Kapler's church-political plans, then the theses of the Reich Conference and this protest from the church clearly mark out the basic positions of the coming confrontations. The issue on both sides, for the church authorities as well as among the German Christians, was church reform and the Reich Church in the Third Reich. Here was a common basis on which there could be meetings and negotiations for a long time to come. However, the issue of autonomy and independence was controversial. In the mind of the church administrations the future Reich Church was to enjoy political and legal independence. The German Christians, on the other hand, called for a close legal and practical integration of state and church. This was the core of the conflict which, with shifting fronts, dragged on into the summer.

The first immediate effect of the Reich Conference became apparent on 8 April. The first meeting between Hitler and Kapler was planned for this day, and in the circumstances the church administration attached the utmost importance to it. However, as the President entered the Reich Chancellery on this 8 April an unexpected disappointment awaited him. Hitler declined to appear at the reception and had the Secretary of State in the Reich Chancellery, Hans Heinrich Lammers, take his place. The reason for this snub to Kapler can be reconstructed from Lammers' notes. In the meantime Kapler's protest letter of 5 April about Kube had been received in the Reich Chancellery. Under the date 7 April Lammers wrote about this letter: '1. The Chancellor has been alerted. 2. To be brought up again at tomorrow's reception of Dr Kapler.' But on 8 April there were new instructions to the official responsible. '1. The reception of President Dr Kapler by the Chancellor had to be cancelled. Herr Kapler was received by me. 2. Note an interview for President Dr Kapler with the Chancellor on 25 April, noon. Inform the office of Herr Kapler, but only at the end of the week after Easter.'[61] It is not difficult to conclude from this note that Hitler, put off his stride by the German Christian attack and the church's protest, was seeking time to prepare his own decision in the matter. The man whom he summoned for consultation on this, and with whom he then met on Easter Monday for a detailed discussion, was the army chaplain from Königsberg, Ludwig Müller.

With Hitler's provisional refusal, for the time being the urgency seemed to have gone out of the situation for Kapler. At all events, soon afterwards he suggested to those involved in the 7 April discussion that they should propose the immediate formation of an action committee on which they had already agreed. Since in the meantime an extraordinary session of the Kirchenausschuss had been called for 25 April, he believed that he 'should keep the final selection of an action committee for this gathering'.[62]

However, the expectation of calmer developments on which Kapler was obviously counting at this point proved deceptive as early as the next day. Surprisingly, on this day – Maundy Thursday, 13 April – an appeal was published which gave the question a further and completely new dimension.

The problem which Kapler saw and upon which he concentrated all his attention was the relationship between Reich Church and state. In his belief, the future of the Protestant church in the Third Reich depended on the church's solution to this problem. However, the problem that this appeal put at the centre had a very different aspect, namely that of the relationship between a Reich Church and the confession. And – in the view of those responsible for this appeal – the future of the church depended upon how this problem was clarified.[63]

The proclamation of the question of the confession at this point was a direct and forced reaction to the German Christian plans for a Reich Church. For as had already been demonstrated in the case of the Lower German Federation, the formation of a Reich Church in fact not only raised the question of the relationship of such a church to the state but inevitably revived the old problem of the confession within the church. The first Reich Conference had indicated that the question whether one was Lutheran, Reformed or United was virtually irrelevant to German Christians. Rather, in their opinion – at least as far as the Kube-Hossenfelder tendency was concerned – all confessions were to be merged in the Evangelical Reich Church. The reaction of the Lutherans, for whose understanding the only conceivable Evangelical church was a Lutheran church with a Lutheran confession, thus inevitably seemed that much more vigorous. This, in turn, could not but arouse the Reformed and the United Christians, who defended their own traditions and convictions against the Lutheran claims. This led to a new front, which cut straight across the camps of the German Christians and the church administrations and considerably increased a confusion that was already great. Later on, this thrust was to have quite different and unusually far-reaching consequences. On the one hand, in connection with activities in Lower Germany, it led to the formation of a Lutheran block which helped Hitler's Reich Bishop to victory; on the other side, however, it also brought the whole confessional issue into play, thus leading via a series of intermediate stages directly to the Synod of Barmen and thence to the Confessing Church.

The author of the 'Appeal to All Lutherans' was Wilhelm Zoellner, a former Westphalian general superintendent, at that time seventy-three and highly respected in church circles. He was one of those Prussian Lutherans who saw the Old Prussian Union more as a political and administrative creation of the nineteenth century than as a church. According to his Lutheran understanding a church could be founded only on a confession. For the Union, this meant that the three denominations represented in it – Lutheran, Reformed and United – ought in each case to unite around its own confession. The United Church still had to develop a confession of its own.[64]

However, only traces of this fundamental idea could be recognized in the Appeal itself. Frightened by the first Reich conference, the political danger of which had become clear to him only during a visit to Berlin early in Holy Week, Zoellner had believed that he ought not to delay another moment in confronting the German Christian claims.[65] Hence the Appeal bore all the signs of being a hasty draft. In essence, it contained two demands. The first was over the new form of church organization, which needed 'bishops at the top… and no church parliaments'. Zoellner was certainly not urging the introduction of the leadership principle along German Christian lines. His concern was, rather, the implementation of the Lutheran concept of ministry, which could understand church government only in terms of the responsible ministry of the individual and not in the majority decisions of synods. As Zoellner had declared as early as 1931, 'I support a concentration of the ministry in individual leaders. I would like to see this concentration carried out beyond the diocese… to a single leader for this ministry of the word in the church as a whole.' Only in this way, Zoellner was convinced, was not only administration but also effective spiritual leadership of the church possible.[66] The second demand related to the foundations of the new church. In contrast to the concept of the Reich Church, in which Zoellner quite correctly saw an indifference to the confessional issue, he called for 'the formation of an Evangelical Church of the German nation upon a clear confessional foundation'. This meant quite simply that the new church should abolish the old borders between the Landeskirchen and in their place should re-establish the confessional organization of German Protestantism.

The appeal did not stop at mere proclamation. Rather, Zoellner asked the church public for their collaboration and announced that 'by calling on a series of leading men' he would shortly create a group which would 'start the practical work'.[67]

The response to this appeal was quite extraordinary. 'With it I have now thrown a stone in the water which is making a remarkable number of waves,' wrote Zoellner to his friend Wilhelm Laible, editor of the *Allgemeine Evangelisch-Lutherische Kirchenzeitung*, as early as 15 April.[68] But the diversity of this response also showed how complicated the whole church question was. As Zoellner's comments as well as his later conduct proved, the appeal was undoubtedly meant as support for the Prussian church administrations – and especially Kapler – against the assertions of the German Christians.[69] At the same time it put the Prussian church in immediate danger. For if Lutheranism across Germany in fact consolidated itself into one confessional church, that would mark the end of the Church of the Prussian Union. Certainly Zoellner always denied that he intended a break-up of the Union. But he could not prevent many younger pastors, precisely those who had long been tired of Prussian church bureaucracy, from seeing this as a desirable goal. For example Günther Koch, a young pastor from Dortmund, doubtless spoke for many when at the end of April he recorded categorically in a memorandum: '1. Because of the confusion in its confession… the Union is in an internal crisis which for decades has been driving it towards disintegration. 2. Almost all the younger theologians, therefore, have little idea of what to make of the Union. 3. The Union is the stronghold of reaction simply because of its inner apathy... So those in favour of the Union are above all the reactionary element in the church bureaucracy and the old church-political parties.' Koch therefore called for the dissolution of the Union and the formation of a Lutheran Reich Church. 'Under the joint attack of the German Christians, more recent theology and older spiritual leaders... the new church organization would certainly prove victorious.'[70]

In a period of unusual oppression, then, the Prussian church administration could not but feel its existence directly attacked by the appeal and its results. This basically amounted to a strengthening of the German Christian position, which was seen to be aligned with Lutheran attacks on the Union, though that was certainly not Zoellner's intention.

On the other hand, Zoellner's appeal undoubtedly had an element of truth, indeed a decisive point, to it, and the great response to it proved that this was also understood in the church. For the old General Superintendent was the first publicly to make church reform a question of the confession. In contrast to the policy of Kapler and the Landeskirchen, which until the summer remained to a certain extent the policy of the church cabinet, for the first time Zoellner offered the beginnings of a theological solution to the problem. The most remarkable thing here was that Zoellner's concept of a confession already came surprisingly close to the later understanding in the Confessing Church. This applied both to the function of the confession and its contemporary form. As to the function, Zoellner stated in a memorandum dated 23 April that particularly at that time the confession was 'indispensable for preaching and instruction, and for public witness in the response of the church to the most urgent questions of the day. In the face of the rise of a new syncretism of revelation and völkisch myth, the confession cannot be dispensed with.'[71] However, Zoellner felt that a repetition of the confessional formulae of the sixteenth century would not be enough to cope with the crucial task of distinguishing between the true teaching of the church and the political heresy of the time. In contrast to a Lutheran theology which proceeded on the basis that the formulation of its confession had basically been concluded at the Reformation, Zoellner was convinced that the time had come for a reformulation of the confession. 'For this reason,' he wrote, 'those who love the confession of their church have with increasing energy been making the demand that the confession should give an answer to the present distress on the basis of the gospel and in the language of the present.' 'To preserve the substance of our old confessions and apply it as a confession in the midst of today's distress' was the difficult task with which the author of the appeal saw himself confronted.[72]

Now all this was in no way abstract theorizing. Rather, Zoellner had in mind a specific incident in which pastors and community had actually made a new confession of their faith: the Altona Confession of January.[73] Zoellner had evidently been in touch with the Altona group as far back as the beginning of April. For on 15 April Pastors Hasselmann and Asmussen, who had played a decisive part in shaping that confession, published an article which pointed precisely in the direction of Zoellner's ideas. Under the title 'The Reich Church' the two pastors approved 'without reservation' the efforts for a concentration of the Protestant churches into a Reich Church and did not hesitate to suggest a process for the church similar to the co-ordination of the Länder with the Reich. At the same time, however, they emphasized 'that living churches live only from the confession', and that the Reich Church, too, could become what it was supposed to be 'only on the basis of the confession of faith'. This was 'the most urgent question even for the Reich Church', namely, whether it found its way to a new and vigorous confession of faith, 'and that the Reich Church, too, could become what it was supposed to be only on the basis of the confession'. This was 'the most urgent question even for the Reich Church', namely whether it had found its way to a new and vigorous confession. 'Therefore,' the two pastors declared, 'this collective answer of the Evangelical Church must first of all be sought. This answer must be an answer to the question: how does the church judge the revolution in the state that has now taken place? How does the church understand its relationship to state and Volk? This answer' – and here the Altona pastors hit on the crucial point – 'can be given only in the light of the word of God. It must agree with the earlier confessions of the church. It must not emerge from political perceptions and convictions.' This was in the first place true of the proclamation of the church. It was also true, however, of its constitution, 'for the organization of the Reich Church which has yet to be created can only be set up on the basis of a confession which has already been formulated'.[74]

These few sentences in fact embodied the theological programme which from the late summer of 1933 on was then translated into reality step by step, and led to the Barmen Confession and the Confessing Church.

That Zoellner already had something similar in view – although he certainly never had the remotest idea of the conflicts which this course of action was to bring – was shown by his formation of several working parties in connection with this appeal. These included one which was to devote itself primarily to a new confession for the church. The leadership of this working party was entrusted to Hans Asmussen. The Altona pastor soon succeeded in gaining further collaborators, among them such diverse people as his colleague Karl Hasselmann; Karl Barth's young friend and collaborator Georg Merz; the Frankfurt pastor Robert Frick – at that time still close to the German Christians – and Paul Althaus, Professor of Theology in Erlangen.[75] Zoellner's idea was that working parties should immediately be formed in all the Landeskirchen to take up the suggestions of the Asmussen group, work through them, and return the results for re-examination. As Zoellner said, summarizing the goal of his campaign: 'This should help the blood to circulate. A new "we" should emerge in the confession on the basis of the old data... Times of change like the present are God-given necessities in which the church must again confess her faith.'[76] Hence it was no accident that the crucial slogan of the church struggle was formulated for the first time in Zoellner's theses of June 1933: 'The church must become a confessing church.'[77] The personal link to these beginnings was, however, Hans Asmussen. He was the one who, a year later, in May 1934, presented the binding interpretation of the Barmen Confession to the Synod of Barmen.

A further direct reaction to Zoellner's appeal understandably came from the Reformed side. Two representatives of the Reformed Alliance, Professor Wilhelm Goeters of Bonn and the young Elberfeld licentiate Wilhelm Niesel, had made contact with Zoellner on the very day of the appeal and in a lengthy conversation had indicated 'full understanding and completely unqualified endorsement' of his plans.[78] At the same time the Reformed Alliance invited the Reformed communities to a meeting in Rheydt on Easter Monday. It was an indication of the effect of Zoellner's Appeal, as well as of the church situation generally, that in spite of the short notice not just a 'few hundred' from the city and surrounding area came but that more than 1,200 filled 'the spacious rooms of the main church ... to the last seat', rather than the community house.[79] The resolution which was issued in the evening in fact followed Zoellner's line completely. The first thesis ran: 'We joyfully dedicate ourselves to the building up of the "one Evangelical Church of the German nation" and trust in the solemn promise of the Reich Chancellor to grant the church full freedom for its work and its service to our people.' The second thesis then took up Zoellner's approach directly. 'The building up and service of the church,' it said, 'can happen only on the basis of its confession...' The fourth thesis, however, repeated something that was self-evident – at least to the Reformed. 'The organization of the church is built up from its confession.'[80]

However, the approval in principle of Zoellner's ideas expressed here by the Reformed concealed the difficulties which inevitably followed from this approval. For the Lutherans, to build up the church on the basis of the confession meant the unconditional introduction of a bishop at the head of the church; for the Reformed, on the other hand, it meant the strengthening and renewal of the synodical organization of their communities as required by their confession. This was the point at which the differences between the two confessions became most conspicuous. Behind this, however, were fundamental theological differences in understanding the faith generally, differences which made themselves felt in a great variety of ways. To be sure, the extreme Lutheran and Reformed positions had been toned down over centuries of mutual Protestant co-existence. But if, as happened here, one fell back so resolutely upon the confessions of the sixteenth century, it was inevitable that the awareness of these differences should also be revived. So the Reich Church was not only burdened with the political question of independence or co-ordination; it also had to deal with the centuries-old question of confessional differences.

As early as 30 April an article in the *Reformierte Kirchenzeitung* indicated that the German Reformed would defend their rights quite emphatically. Its author, Pastor Wilhelm Kolfhaus of Vlotho, as editor of the paper, could also be seen as a kind of spokesman for the Reformed Alliance. As Kolfhaus wrote: 'The Lutherans will no doubt already know how to bring the influence of their confession to bear. We demand for ourselves no more than a recognition of our duty and our right to make possible for our congregations a life in accordance with Reformed convictions'. That it was hoped that such a statement would win back communities from the Prussian Union for the Reformed Confession was demonstrated by Kolfhaus's remark that not only those 'who have retained their confessional designation' belonged to the Reformed congregations, 'but also the numerous others who, while having lost the old and honourable name, have preserved the Reformed catechism.' The rejection of the utterly intolerable demand to live 'under a crozier' was unequivocal; so, too, was the rejection of new church elections 'based on the political right to vote'. 'Moreover,' the article ended – and here Kolfhaus knew that he was again at one with the Lutherans, 'not the slightest impression should be given that the church, whether Lutheran or Reformed, might receive its mandate from anywhere other than its head, Christ.'[81]

For Kapler, a convinced advocate of the Union, the confessional issue had so far had no basic significance. He had obviously not even thought of inviting a Reformed representative to Berlin on 7 April to discuss the necessary first steps. Only the reactions to Zoellner's appeal showed him the forces he had to reckon with here. Hence from now on he made every effort to maintain a balance in this respect also.

The development of the discussion of church reform during these weeks was marked by a constant series of divisions and new, surprising turns of events. This was also true of the Zoellner action. Exactly ten days after the appearance of the appeal it had already come to an end. That its impetus nevertheless had further and enduring effects along several different lines will emerge from the course of events.

For the time being, however, new and frightening news moved into the foreground for those in the churches.

A large, self-aware and well-administered church like the Old Prussian Union could not be upset all that quickly. Neither Kapler's negotiations nor the thunderbolt of the first Reich Conference nor Zoellner's appeal had proved powerful enough to shake the supreme church authorities in Prussia. This was shown at the session of the Prussian Church Senate which took place in Berlin on 21 April. According to the Prussian church constitution of 1922 the church senate – a body, incidentally, the total age of whose members, as the German Christian Pastor Georg Probst of Frankfurt remarked not without humour, was 15,000,[82] was the most important church body in the Union. Kapler, who made a detailed report to the meeting on 'the general situation in church politics', hoped for the consent of this body to a proposal on which the general superintendents had agreed on 21 April. The issue was a kind of enabling law which was to transfer the powers of the church senate, 'in important cases which brook no delay', to three plenipotentiaries: the President himself, a member of the church senate and a general superintendent. The aim of the proposal was obvious. It was to give Kapler, as president, legal room to manoeuvre over decisions which, in view of the situation over the negotiations with the state that were anticipated, might perhaps have to be made very quickly. The political model, of course, played an essential role in this authorization. Surprisingly, however, the majority of the church senate flatly rejected the proposal. Although Kapler argued vigorously for this solution, the church senate decided to adhere in principle to a synodical constitution. Where rapid decisions were necessary, a five-member commission of the church senate under its president was to have the powers of the senate.[83] A further proposal to co-opt a representative of the German Christians on to the commission was also rejected.

However, the prepared statement that was issued in the afternoon gave no indication of these discussions. It was completely in tune with the lofty nationalist tone of those days; it welcomed 'with deep joy and thankfulness to God' the 'mighty movement... which has seized the soul of our people', emphasized the urgency of the merger of all Protestant churches and also expressed the

298

willingness of the church senate to take 'the needs of the moment in the Old Prussian Church' into account. The delicate question of the participation of the German Christians in the work of the committee was taken up with the non-committal formula that it was the will of the church senate 'that in the leadership of the church and its administration the energy and forward thrust of the younger members should be combined with the experience of the older ones'.[84].

When the members of the church senate left the session in the evening they could do so with the feeling that essentially they still had basic control of church affairs. By the very next morning, however, the situation looked completely different. That day – it was the Saturday after Easter, 22 April – Protestant Germany was startled by the news that a state commissioner had taken over the church government of the Lutheran Landeskirche of Mecklenburg-Schwerin. As matters stood, in Berlin this could only be construed as the beginning of the long-feared direct intervention of the state in the Protestant church. In truth, however, it was a small, local action, behind which stood the muddled völkisch ideas of Richard Walther Darré, the agricultural expert in the Munich-based Reich administration of the Party, who later became leader of the farmers in the Reich and Minister of Food. Neither he nor his helpers had any idea of the extreme political complications they were causing with their action.

The prehistory of the Mecklenburg incident extends back to the beginning of the 1930s. In the course of his efforts on behalf of North Germany,[85] Darré, the most important representative of the Nordic 'blood and soil' ideology in the Party, had become aware of a certain Walter Bohm. Bohm was a former Baltic landowner who, after many years as a soldier, was now studying law in Hamburg. He had followed Darré's line completely in a book about farmers and the relationship between state and church.[86] In various conversations between Darré and Bohm, the question of the government of the Landeskirche, its dissolution and possible renewal was also discussed. Presumably all of this belonged in the context of Darré's ideas about 'a new nobility based on blood and soil', on rule and religion.[87] After the seizure of power, rural Mecklenburg seemed to Darré to be an ideal experimental field for these ideas, the more so since he had a follower in the National Socialist Minister President Walter Granzow, who was a Mecklenburg farmer, and since the latter had complained to Darré about difficulties with the Protestant church. To what degree plans for a restoration of the monarchy were also involved at this juncture can no longer be clarified conclusively.

At all events, Darré and Granzow visited Bohm in Hamburg before Easter 1933 in order to ask whether he would like to take over control of the church of Mecklenburg as state commissioner. The fact that early on the 22nd everything had been carefully prepared gives us every reason to believe that the plan of action, to the day and hour, was already fixed during this Hamburg discussion.[88] In order to prepare for the event and to give at least the impression of a revolutionary movement, on Easter Tuesday Bohm had published an article in the Nationalist Socialist *Niederdeutscher Beobachter* under the splendid pseudonym of Walter zur Ungnad, which summoned the farmers to the conquest of the church. There was a danger that 'reaction' might become established in the church government. Besides this, there was the threat of priestly domination. According to Bohm, with an obvious reference to Zoellner's appeal, the free

Protestant Christian was 'to be humbled under the domination of bishops... of bishops who want to arrogate to themselves the power of the crozier over against the parishes and the Landeskirchen'. 'Farmers,' the article concluded, 'take over the government of the church for yourselves along with all functions of church government down to community level.'[89]

Now the potential of the Mecklenburg farmers to revolutionize the church was doubtless not so great that the church administration had cause to fear a sudden storm. The members of the Oberkirchenrat of Mecklenburg were therefore all the more surprised when, four days later, they were informed at eight o'clock in the morning by a letter from the Minister President 'that for the purpose of the co-ordination of the church government with the government in the state and the Reich, Herr Walter Bohm has been appointed by him State Commissar for the Lutheran Church of Mecklenburg-Schwerin, and took over his duties at eight o'clock this morning in the offices of the Oberkirchenrat'.[90] At the same time Bohm made use of the 'legislative, judicial and executive power in the Landeskirche' thus conferred on him by issuing a decree disbanding all synodical bodies. In their place he appointed a three-man regional synodical committee. This decree was dated '22 Easter Moon 1933', in a fashion typical of the Nordic-völkisch groups. When the perplexed Church President, who meanwhile had arrived in the office building, together with members of the Oberkirchenrat, asked whether Article 137 of the Reich Constitution with its guarantee of independence for the church had been revoked, Bohm replied that he could not 'engage in legal discussions' and would act in accordance with his assignment. Thereupon the Church President and Land Bishop went to the Minister President, who also received them readily, and told them that the pastors had failed and that the people wanted a co-ordination of the church 'with the national awakening'; he was acting on his own responsibility on the basis 'of the nature of the national revolution'. The Oberkirchenrat then decided to send an immediate telegram of protest to the Reich President, the Reich Chancellor and the Reich Minister of the Interior, and in addition to alert the Kirchenausschuss. At the same time Rendtorff telephoned Secretaries of State Meissner and Lammers about the whole development. It is an indication of the innocence of those involved that Granzow, for his part, obtained the approval of the Reich Interior Minister in Berlin within whose competence the matter lay, by telephone, only as a result of the complaints from the Land Bishop.

Meanwhile, however, the matter had already become an affair of state. For Lammers, terrified by Rendtorff's call, had immediately called the matter to Hitler's attention. 'The Reich Chancellor,' Lammers afterwards noted tersely, 'has declared that he does not approve of the action of the Minister President of Mecklenburg-Schwerin and has charged me with conveying this view to Minister President Granzow. I have done this at once.'[91] Thus by the afternoon of 22 April the position of Granzow and his state commissioner had already become untenable. In fact the whole affair in Mecklenburg ended five days later with the resignation of Bohm, who had thus been left in the lurch. Granzow did not survive the defeat either, and in November was replaced by the Reich governor.[92]

Meanwhile, however, the action in Mecklenburg had triggered off in Berlin decisions of far-reaching consequences at the highest levels in the Reich as well as among the supreme church authorities.

The starting point for these developments on the political side was Hitler's unequivocal rejection of the Schwerin church revolution. The reasons for this attitude are not hard to guess. First of all there was a risk that the affair might offend the Reich President, something which Hitler doubtless feared.[93] But second and more important was that in conversation with the Königsberg chaplain Ludwig Müller on Easter Monday Hitler had just become clear about what were to be the main outlines of his policy towards the Protestant church and accordingly had invited Kapler to a reception, already once postponed, which was now planned for 25 April – only three days later. In these circumstances it must have mattered a good deal to Hitler to leave scope for his plans. But this required a rapid settlement of the Mecklenburg incident. And since Hitler still wanted to keep in the background as much as possible over the whole church question, Frick was entrusted with this task.

Everything went according to plan. In the telephone call from the Reich Chancellery on the Saturday, Granzow had asked permission to explain the reasons for his action to Hitler the next Monday. Granzow, Bohm, Darré and Frick therefore met in Wilhelmstrasse about noon on 24 April. After a short conversation with Granzow, Hitler invited everyone to lunch. However, to the great disappointment of the still unsuspecting Bohm, Hitler did not say a word about the church conflict during the meal. Instead, the people from Mecklenburg learned that they would have to meet Rendtorff at the Ministry of the Interior immediately afterwards. According to Rendtorff's report Frick, acting as chairman, opened with the forthright statement 'that the measures of the Mecklenburg-Schwerin government were illegal; though it had to be remembered that these were revolutionary times. As for settling the matter, he felt that an arrangement had to be made which avoided any loss of face for either side.'[94] And that is how things worked out. Agreement was reached on a statement which to some extent concealed the state's defeat in a general and cheerful assent to reforms.[95] What at first looked like the hastily-improvised resolution of an unwanted conflict proved the next day to reflect a basic decision on Hitler's part. That was the day on which the reception for Kapler was scheduled, and on this occasion Hitler also had to make some statement about his intentions in church politics.

In the meantime, on the church side the situation had developed as follows. Of course there had been no lack of activity in the Kirchenbundesamt over the previous fourteen days. The plan for the action committee, upon which the major Landeskirchen had agreed on 7 April, had been quite quickly rejected as inappropriate and impractical in the form in which it had been presented. For this era committees no longer seemed appropriate: the only possibility was the individual, responsible leader. So Hosemann, the Director of the Kirchenbundesamt, had worked out a kind of enabling act for Kapler. The Zoellner action, however, made it clear that this authorization would not find any endorsement in the church unless consideration were given to the confessional problem. Hosemann had therefore planned that Kapler, as representative of the Union, should summon prominent representatives of the Lutheran and Reformed confessions 'to his side'. The Kirchenausschuss was supposed to decide on this plan and its implementation in terms of personnel at a special meeting on 25 April. But consent to this plan was still by no means certain, for as late as 21 April the same plan for Prussia had been rejected by the church senate.

Deliberations had got this far when on the Saturday news of the state intervention in Mecklenburg arrived in the Kirchenbundesamt. In the first shock it was believed that the forcible co-ordination of the church by the state had now begun. Kapler had not forgotten Kube's threats any more than he had forgotten the German Christian statements at the first Reich Conference, in which, in fact, the talk had been unmistakably about state commissioners and co-ordination. In fact, since the end of March Kapler's main concern, along with keeping an eye on Catholicism, had been to ward off any government intervention in the church. On 11 April he had reported to the Prussian general superintendents on tendencies in the Party 'arising out of efforts towards a totalitarian state... to take over the church as well, so as to integrate it as a department of state into the totalitarian state, that is, the National Socialist state'. He added that attempts of this kind would also be made within the church camp, as the resolutions of the Reich conference showed.[96] Since then the activity of the German Christians had hardly been such as to dispel these fears. And the news from Mecklenburg fitted in so precisely with this picture that no one could believe it to be a mere coincidence. Only on the Tuesday, when it became evident that the German Christians in Berlin were just as perplexed about events as the church administrations, because there was as yet no Faith Movement in Mecklenburg,[97] and Rendtorff declared to the Kirchenausschuss that he was convinced that the Reich was 'in no way behind the measures',[98] was it understood in Berlin that the affair was in fact only a local and isolated action.

On the Saturday, however, that was not yet clear at all. On the contrary, Berlin was rife with rumours that something similar to what had happened in Mecklenburg was imminent for the Prussian Landeskirche and the Kirchenbund. Thereupon Kapler and Hosemann resolved on attack as the best form of defence. In the afternoon they asked the former spokesman for national reform, the Lutheran bishop August Marahrens, and Dr Hermann Albert Hesse, a Reformed pastor in Elberfeld, whether they were ready to assume responsibility with Kapler to reform the church. Both agreed.[99] So on the Sunday Kapler issued the following appeal: 'The hour calls without delay for the introduction of a reform of the constitution of German Protestantism. The goal of the reform is the Federal German Evangelical Church, built on the foundation of and under the full protection of the confession. Having grown up out of vigorous Landeskirchen, it should retain all the powers it requires for the nurture of all-German Protestant church life and its relationship to Volk and state at home and abroad.' At the same time, the appointment of Marahrens and Hesse was announced.[100]

This was quite simply an attempt to forestall suspected political action from the German Christians by means of an emphatically ecclesiastical plan of the future Reich Church. However, the formula also already revealed the difficulties facing this concept. For endorsement of the full protection of the confession of faith and emphasis on vigorous Landeskirchen were the two factors which had hitherto prevented any closer merger of the churches, and in the future, too, they would hardly give up their rights voluntarily.

Nevertheless, to a considerable extent Kapler's appeal acted as a deliverance in the church. As early as Sunday, and increasingly during the days which followed, a profusion of endorsements from the whole of Protestant Germany arrived at the Kirchenbund in Berlin.

This was the situation when, on the afternoon of 25 April, the first official meeting finally took place between the supreme representative of the new state and the representative of the Protestant church. For Kapler the timing, after the quasi-revolutionary move and before the meeting of the Kirchenausschuss, was beyond doubt highly unfavourable. Nevertheless, he did not give a bad account of himself. Kapler's detailed report of the afternoon of 25 April tells us about the content of the conversation, which lasted almost an hour and a half. Granted, the official protocol is silent about this confidential point; instead we have the handwritten notes of two people involved in the meeting: Kirchenrat Johannes Kübel from Frankfurt and Wilhelm von Pechmann, the former President of the Kirchentag. These notes agree in all important points and make quite an accurate reconstruction of the conversation possible.[101]

According to them Kapler first of all expressed the thanks of the church and its readiness to co-operate, though this co-operation could come about only in complete freedom. The state, Kapler went on to declare, had indeed to be hard, but the church must and might ask for clemency and reconciliation. Then he went into his chief concerns, the protection of parity and the safeguarding of the promises in the government policy statement of 23 March, which had been broken time and again by subordinate officials in the Party – here the name of Kube was mentioned – by the press and by the German Christians. In this connection Kapler brought up the Mecklenburg incident, which in a few hours had triggered off the greatest indignation on all sides. No one would dare to show the brutality shown to the Bishop of Mecklenburg to even the most humble Catholic chaplain. According to Kapler, such state interventions prevented the church from being the church. Adolf Hoffmann apart, nothing like this had happened even in 1918.

At this point, both reports agreed that Hitler interrupted the church president. Who wanted state intervention? 'He had known nothing of the goings on of the Mecklenburg government; and in any case the matter was now settled. Besides, quite different things had been expected of the Catholic church: it had been told that he would not touch the church, and had adapted itself accordingly.' This remark sheds significant light on Hitler's view of the bishops' 28 March declaration, which he obviously considerd a capitulation that he had forced on them.[102] 'In matters affecting the Protestant church,' Hitler then continued, 'he was in a difficult situation since he himself was a member of the Catholic church. Whatever position he took, it was always held against him.' Pechmann here supplements Kube's report with the interesting remark that he – Hitler – had first heard that there were twenty-eight Landeskirchen from Pastor Müller. Following this, Hitler vigorously criticized both churches. 'Both churches, the Protestant and the Catholic, were in danger of losing contact with the Volk and spoke a language that the Volk did not understand. The German Christians wanted to re-establish contact with the Volk.' Moreover the churches had themselves to blame for their situation. 'Had the churches taken their place earlier at the side of National Socialism, the relationship would be much better.'

After these general statements Hitler came to the political heart of the matter. 'He did not have the slightest thought of a state commissioner for the churches,' he declared, 'but the time could come when the churches would turn to him and ask for his assistance.' This cloaking of massive interests in the form of an offer of help was a very characteristic approach on Hitler's part. In fact what followed could be understood as a direct political decision: 'His official liaison in Protestant church affairs was Frick. Today he had appointed Pastor Müller as his personal adviser in these matters. As a statesman he had the utmost interest in a unified Protestant block, indeed as a counter-balance to Catholicism.'[103] Kapler replied that 'if this was what he wanted, then the first precondition was for the state not to intervene in church affairs. Otherwise there would be an exodus from the church towards the free church, and Protestantism would only be weakened.' Moreover, the Landeskirchen were already on the point of a closed and more solid union, to be brought about as quickly as possible.

With this the conversation ended. It contained no less than the basic principles of Hitler's policy for the Protestant church, to which he held firm until the end of 1934.[104]

Immediately after this interview, at three o'clock on the Tuesday afternoon, the Kirchenausschuss convened. In these circumstances there could no longer be any doubt about its decision. After a detailed report by Rendtorff about the Mecklenburg incident and a subsequent report by Kapler about the developments to date, by far the majority of the participants enthusiastically endorsed the President's action. When questions were asked, Hosemann expressly declared that 'in respect of the limits on the enabling action, all that was laid down was that the confessions might not be attacked; but on the other hand it should not be said that the constitution and administration were untouchable'.[105] Apart from a few expressions of suspicion, the only one to speak out seriously against this far-reaching enabling action was Wilhelm von Pechmann. Once again the clarity of the old Bavarian nobleman's vision was manifest. It was the task of the Kirchenausschuss, he declared, to prevent 'the churches, too, from being forced under the domination of political movements. With due deference to the wish of the Reich Chancellor, who would guarantee the freedom of the church if the thousand-year-old rights of the Länder could be swept away with the stroke of a pen?' He could not, he concluded, disregard the danger 'that the impression might be given that the Kirchenbund was reacting to outside pressure'.[106] However, Pechmann did not succeed in finding supporters for his critical approach, especially since Kapler fought with great determination for unlimited authorization, and even declared that restricted authority would be no use at all.[107] In fact the need to act felt by all sides – whether out of enthusiasm, worry, or just the general agitation – proved to be so overpowering that Pechmann's was the only voice against the prepared resolution. With it the Kirchenausschuss gave its President authority 'to take all measures necessitated by the reorganization of civil life and required for the welfare of the whole of German Protestantism, as well as for the requisite declarations to the authorities of the Reich and the Land and to other authorities in public life.' The appointment of Marahrens and Hesse was also approved. Finally, the Landeskirchen were requested to enact similar authorizations.[108] The next week, almost all the Landeskirchen followed this recommendation.

The day after these turbulent events, the treatment of the Jewish question was on the agenda of the Kirchenausschuss.[109] Only when all the circumstances of this meeting are kept in view does it become quite clear why the Protestant church kept silent on this issue. In the conflict between church politics and conscience, church politics carried the day.

The conclusion of these decisive days of meetings and decisions consisted of the negotiations in the Kirchenbundesamt in which the representatives of the Landeskirchen met on the Thursday. These discussions were completely overshadowed by the preceding developments. Hosemann repeated to the representatives of the Landeskirchen, too, that nothing was further from Berlin's intentions than 'to have a revolution in the Kirchenbund'. But it was also necessary to be clear that if offence was now taken at legal technicalities, then 'events would probably pass over our heads. So it was our belief that we could regain the initiative from our opponents only through prompt action.'[110] At the end of the long discussion, as expected, the Kirchenbundesrat unanimously approved Kapler's action and authorization.

The result of these decisions as seen by the Protestant church was reflected in an announcement published under the signatures of Kapler, Marahrens and Hesse and dated 25 April. In its combination of political faith and church confession it was typical of the attitude of those men who now bore responsibility for the Protestant church – and to a large extent it was typical of the church, too.

A powerful nationalist movement has seized and uplifted our German people. A comprehensive reformation of the Reich is going forward in the awakened German nation. To this turning point in history we say a grateful Yes. God has given us this. To him be the glory!

Bound by God's Word, we recognize in the great events of our day a new commission given by our Lord to his church. It has to do with the proclamation of the living God, who has created us, who governs and still preserves us; of the Lord and Saviour Jesus Christ, who died and rose again for us; and of the Holy Spirit, who alone gives true faith and real renewal. It has to do with a living, contemporary testimony to the Reformation confessions. It has to do with the reorganization of the church on the basis of the imperishable powers of these confessions founded on the word of God.[111]

For all its doubtful politics, this was undoubtedly a word from the church. And in this way the church might hope to remain the church.

At this point hardly anyone had a thought for Ludwig Müller, Hitler's newly-appointed and authorized representative. Nevertheless, only a short time later it became apparent that the Königsberg chaplain was to become the key figure in the church question.

5

The Protestant Church Asserts Itself
(May)

During April 1933 Hitler developed his church policy into a unified concept. His special attention here was at first directed solely towards Catholicism. Only when matters were decided here, when the agreement with Kaas was certain and Papen was already on his way to Rome with precise instructions, did Hitler turn his attention to the Protestant church. The policy which he pursued here and which he finally clarified on Easter Monday in a conversation with Ludwig Müller was completely shaped by his Catholic concerns and understandings. For his major interest in supporting the plans for a Reich church lay in the creation of a counter-balance to the Catholic church, which he hoped would result from a close consolidation of Protestantism.

In this connection during the last week of April, in personal meetings with key representatives of both churches, Hitler for the first time formulated certain basic principles to which he continued to hold even later. They consisted of three main points: 1. to prevent the church from having any influence in politics; 2. to avoid a Kulturkampf, i.e. an open confrontation between church and state: 3. to treat the two confessions in strict parity. These three points were the logical extension of the basic decision on church politics which Hitler had made as party leader during the 1920s and which had led to the split with Ludendorff and Dinter. At that time Hitler had understood that power could not be gained through a völkisch religion, but only through a political organization. He had gradually transformed the Party into such an organization.[1] If he transferred those experiences to his present situation, then what was true at that time for the Party had to be true now for the leadership of the state: namely, the elimination of religious influences in politics and the avoidance of any kind of religious confrontation with the churches and among them. Hitler reconsidered these basic principles time and again in the course of his régime: at the end of 1934, when his policy towards the Protestant church had failed; in summer 1937 when, in connection with the encyclical 'Mit Brennender Sorge' he considered a termination of the Reich concordat; and in January 1939, when in the Reichstag he threatened a fundamental change in his church policy. But each time he resolved to give these basic principles one more try. In fact they survived in the Third Reich until the end of the Second World War. In the hotch-potch of different opinions, intentions and interests, they formed a kind of basic model which prevailed again and again in the critical moments of the government's church policy.

The chance to express these things for the first time was provided by the coincidence that not only the Evangelischer Kirchenausschuss but also an extraordinary conference of representatives of the Catholic dioceses were meeting in Berlin at the same time: on 25 and 26 April. Oppressed by the same worries about the freedom of the church as the German Protestants, this conference requested its chairman, Bishop Berning of Osnabrück, to make immediate personal contact with the Reich government. The importance which Hitler attached to church politics in those days is indicated by the fact that a telephone call was enough to obtain appointments that very day and the next day with Papen, Rust, Hitler and Goering.[2] Thus it came about that Hitler received the Protestant President Kapler on Tuesday afternoon and then the Catholic Bishop Berning at the same time on the Wednesday. The two conversations, which also took about the same length of time, ran along surprisingly similar lines. Both gentlemen assured Hitler first of all of their gratitude and enthusiastic readiness to co-operate in the new state. They then emphatically expressed their fears for the freedom and independence of the church;[3] here Berning evidently also referred to the Mecklenburg incident.[4] Hitler then replied to both conversation partners that this incident was an exception and at the same time stated as a fundamental point that he had no plans to intervene in the church through state commissioners. He further declared that he felt obligated to maintain parity in respect of both confessions; because of this, however, as a Catholic he was in a difficult position over against the Protestant church. As he asserted to Berning, he could 'not get used to the Protestant church and its structure'. 'No matter what position he took,' he said to Kapler, it would 'be held against' him as a member of the Catholic church.[5]

In fact alongside the agreements in principle on the fundamentals of church policy the difference in Hitler's relationships to the two confessions was now unmistakable.

Towards the Catholic church Hitler the Catholic clearly seemed far more secure and independent. This security was not feigned. For he knew Catholicism, and he also thought that he knew how it had to be dealt with. Moreover he had already set his course in church politics and knew from Papen that his concordat plans had found the favourable reception in Rome that he had hoped for.[6] So in conversation with the unsuspecting Bishop of Osnabrück he found himself in a superior position: he was already treating the Catholic church as a firm ideological ally in the struggle against godless Bolshevism and pernicious Jewry. 'He spoke cordially and calmly,' the report said, 'and here and there with passion. Not a word was said against the church – only appreciation of the bishops.'[7] With the same apparent agreement he gave far-reaching though indefinite guarantees for the freedom of the church, the schools and the Catholic associations, and assurances that he would tolerate no irregularities in any reduction in the number of Catholic civil servants.

In contrast to this conversation, which revealed Hitler as a skilled and superior politician who had everything under control, the interview with Kapler betrayed a certain reserve. What Pechmann noted from Kapler's report is true; Hitler had first heard of the complicated Landeskirche structure of German Protestantism through Ludwig Müller,[8] and it is likely that he did not have the slightest feeling for the special Lutheran mentality in the Protestant church. So it was obvious that after a statement of the basic principles, he should give direct responsibility for Protestant affairs to men better versed than he in this tricky subject. Moreover this was the crucial content of the conversation with Kapler. So Lammers quite correctly noted as the 'result of the discussion: (*a*) Dr Kapler should refer to the Reich Minister of the Interior in all matters concerning the Protestant church, and in addition to Pastor Müller as the adviser of the Reich Chancellor.'[9]

This double authorization, deliberately left unclear, was typical of Hitler's style of rule, as Ernst Fraenkel has analysed it in his 'Double State' with reference to legal policy.[10]

The Reich Minister of the Interior, a Protestant who in fact looked after the affairs of the Protestant church benevolently within the limits of his capacity until the end of 1934, came from the competent department and was suited to the post by virtue of his own church membership.[11] As was to be demonstrated, within the limits of his portfolio, Frick's authorization guaranteed the church that at least some attention would be paid to existing laws during the vigorous struggle of the subsequent period.

By contrast, Müller's mandate was of a purely political kind. Through him Hitler created the possibility of influencing the development of Protestant church affairs without himself having to enter the field. The goal he was pursuing here was evident from the wording of the authorization, which was published on 25 April. 'Since it has become necessary because of recent events,' ran the decree, 'to decide on a series of questions connected with the relationship between the state and the Protestant church, I appoint Army Chaplain Müller of Königsberg as my authorized representative for Protestant church affairs. Moreover he has the special assignment of promoting all efforts towards the creation of a German Evangelical Reich Church.'[12] This authorization and the plan for a Reich concordat must be seen as parallel steps by Hitler towards the solution of the church question on the basis of his three principles. The Evangelical Reich Church was important above all for reasons of parity. Hitler was doubtless sincere in assuring Kapler that as a statesman he had 'the greatest interest in a unified Protestant bloc... merely as a couter-balance to Catholicism.'[13] Moreover, when on 4 May Müller explained Hitler's attitude towards the Reichskirche to the Committee of Three, he once again confirmed these connections explicitly. Müller said that Hitler did not want to conclude a Reich concordat without a Protestant Reichskirche. Moreover, he would sign a concordat only if in exchange he could eliminate the Centre Party.[14]

Hitler's desire to deal symmetrically with the two confessions in the church question and to resolve it as concurrently as possible proved so powerful that in fact the law dealing with the new constitution of the German Evangelical Church and the Reich concordat were settled at the same cabinet meeting on 14 July. However, the way to 14 July took the two churches along very different routes. On the Catholic side, developments were systematic and followed a plan; on the Protestant side there were spectacular interventions and stormy incidents. Hitler's desire to bring church problems to an end without delay and in his own way remained crucial for both developments. Only this desire can explain why in spite of all the difficulties Hitler stood by his man until the end of 1934 and, despite everything, ventured upon or permitted constantly new attempts to save the Evangelical Reichskirche.

Ludwig Müller, who suddenly emerged from anonymity as a result of Hitler's 25 April decree, and who in the autumn was for a time to become the first and only Reich Bishop of the German Evangelical Church, was a weak character. Fifty years old at the time, he came from Westphalia, had become a naval chaplain during the War and had continued his career in the services, becoming chaplain at Königsberg in 1926. As a chaplain, he was the sort of pious old hand who knew how to adapt himself to all situations and was as much a master of the language of the pietistic circles in Westphalia as he was of the brash tone of the Reichswehr casinos.

Since he began with some signs of good will and evidently knew how to radiate a degree of trustworthiness, at first he was largely successful in giving a misleading impression to the church. But the further course of events very quickly and almost cruelly demonstrated his inner emptiness and instability. Under the influence of questionable advisers, from summer 1933 on he became increasingly entangled in a web of lies and intrigues until he finally proved intolerable to church and state alike and not even Hitler was willing or able to keep him any longer. After being quietly deprived of power in spring 1935, almost forgotten, he then led a curious marginal existence which ended in Berlin in 1945, possibly in suicide.[15]

There was a simple reason for Hitler's choice of this particular man. He knew only a few Protestant pastors, and no others who would have been suitable for this task. However, he had known for quite some time that Müller had certain ideas about church politics and that he – Hitler – could depend on him. The details of the prehistory of Muller's call can no longer be established. His first encounter with Hitler probably took place in Königsberg in 1926 or 1927. If Müller's reports about it are correct, even at this meeting he gave Hitler some ideas about the future of the Protestant church.[16] Just as important for Hitler may have been the fact that Müller – who meanwhile had become his devoted follower – had propagandized for the Party, not without success, among the officers of the Königsberg command. And in 1932, in a difficult situation, he had established contact between Colonel von Reichenau, the Chief of Staff in Königsberg, and Hitler.[17] As for his church activities, in the same year Müller had joined the German Christians in East Prussia and, probably with Erich Vogelsang and Horst Schirmacher, had drawn up their distinctive guidelines, which differed from those of Berlin in placing greater emphasis on the church.[18] We do not know when Müller and Hitler met after the seizure of power and on whose initiative. Presumably it was in connection with the first Reich Conference of German Christians at the beginning of April. At all events, by 6 April Müller was already known as 'the Reich Chancellor's adviser on Protestant church affairs', and it was in this capacity that he explained Hitler's wishes and intentions to Kapler and Zoellner, who happened to be there. Müller told both men that Hitler was 'urgently concerned to consolidate Protestantism... The existing situation of fragmentation into twenty-eight Landeskirchen is incomprehensible to the Chancellor. He wants a block that will serve as a counter-balance against the uniform organization of Catholicism.' Müller further declared that Hitler found 'far-reaching agreement with this view among the ranks of the "German

Christians". How the future Reich Church was to be shaped was, however, still uncertain: 'there was a desire for an organic union of the church with the state', if possible through appointing church leaders to a primary chamber, to be newly created.[19] At the same time a first mention was made in this conversation of considerable tension between Müller and Hossenfelder, which may have given Zoellner the crucial impetus towards his action on 13 April. In fact – as will soon emerge – Müller's special relationship to Hitler necessarily posed considerable problems to Hossenfelder from the beginning. A circular letter from Hossenfelder dated 15 April already contained a reference to rumours to that effect and an indignant rejection of them.[20]

On Easter Monday an evidently more extended conversation between Hitler and Müller took place at Berchtesgaden, at which all the problems were discussed and the plan for an official authorization of Müller was made.[21]

The events in Mecklenburg which then took place could only strengthen Hitler in his desire to settle Protestant affairs as quickly as possible. So even if Müller's name was still largely unknown, the Königsberg chaplain was by no means without information or connections when he emerged into the public eye on 25 April with Hitler's commission and soon afterwards moved into an office in the Ministry of the Interior.[22]

Innocent as to what this commission meant, but convinced that a great period was now dawning for the Reich, for the church and above all for himself, in a declaration on 26 April Ludwig Müller affirmed: 'The confidence of the Reich Chancellor has called me to a great and difficult task. I am going to work with trust in God and in consciousness of my responsibility before God. My goal is the fulfilment of the longings of Protestant Germany since the Reformation.' This is how he saw the situation: 'The "German Christians" want an Evangelical German Reich Church. They have considerably shaken the people of the church. The church governments also want a great "Evangelical Church of the German nation". This church must now be built.' The declaration left no doubt that from now on its architect was to bear the name of Ludwig Müller. 'It is the wish and the desire of the Reich Chancellor that Protestant Christianity should begin the great work with cheerful trust in God and complete it in trustful co-operation with the Reich.' Then came the pious encouragement, 'May the Lord of the church give us all the spirit of unanimity', accompanied by the pious threat that the same Lord might also give the power 'inexorably to suppress all attempts at interference'. But Müller asked 'the Evangelical communities throughout the German fatherland... to carry forward our work with a compassionate heart'.[23] This declaration was typical of the language which Müller loved, and which – as he used it – revealed an embarrassing degree of stereotyped vacuity.

With the events and decisions of 23, 24 and 25 April the affairs of the Protestant church, which had developed so perplexingly during the course of April, finally appeared to be on a clear course again. The danger of state intervention had been averted. Through the appointment of an official and personal representative the Reich Chancellor had apparently respected the freedom of the church and at the same time clearly indicated his interest in church reform. With the appointment of Müller, the *Niederdeutsche Kirchenzeitung* exulted, Hitler had 'now intervened personally in the destiny of the Protestant church and in a way that assures the freedom of the church. We Protestants should not forget that about him, the Catholic. His greatness is beyond all praise.'[24] With this was bound up at the same time the hope that the revolutionary political forces of the German Christians might be directed towards the course of co-operation with the church administrations. With the virtually unanimous endorsement of the Committee of Three, responsibilities in the church also appeared to be clarified. Zoellner, whose arbitrary action had caused so much unrest, gave assurances that from now on everything would be exclusively the concern of the new officials; the plenipotentiaries of the Prussian church senate which had denied power to Kapler as late as 21 April accepted the situation and on 26 April transferred their authority to him.[25] Moreover, as Müller had rightly perceived, there was at least basic unity over the goal. All those involved wanted a major church reform which would turn the Evangelischer Kirchenbund, divided into Landeskirchen and with a synodical constitution, into a unified and powerful Reich Church. In these conditions people went energetically to work at the end of April. And initially the Committee of Three in fact kept things largely under control.

The first observations on the new constitution were made by the legal adviser to the Kirchenbund, the Bonn church lawyer Johannes Heckel, in a discussion with Kapler and Hosemann on 2 May. The very next day Marahrens and Hesse, the representatives called in by Kapler, appeared, and on 4 May there was the first official conversation between the Committee of Three, Heckel and Hosemann on the one hand and Müller and the East Prussian pastor Horst Schirmacher, whom Müller had meanwhile named his adjutant, on the other.[26]

At this first official meeting, Heckel presented the gathering with the results of previous reflections and discussions. It became clear that the crucial problem over the new church did not lie in its institutional organization. On the contrary, the Reformed churches apart, there was agreement on all sides as to the need for a strong spiritual leader at the head, the concentration of executive power, and the dismantling of church parliamentarianism at all levels. The difficulties emerged, rather, in the problematical area of the confession. It was this that turned the drafting of a Reich Church constitution into an attempt to square a circle. For by Lutheran conviction it was a mark of every church that was a church in the full sense of the word that it should have the same confession in common. In Protestant Germany, however, there were three forms of confession: the Lutheran, the Reformed and the variety found in the Union churches. Thus either a truly unified Protestant Reich Church could be created, in which case the confessional question had to be relativized, and for the Lutherans that meant that such a church ceased to be the church (this was the course that the German Christians would gladly have taken, but it soon proved impossible), or one could start from the inviolability of the forms of confession, in which case it was impossible to arrive at a unified Reich Church: the result could only be another federation, which would not be a church federation but a confessional federation. This second course was advocated almost unanimously by all the church administrations and in the end it prevailed.[27]

Interestingly enough, Ludwig Müller at first attempted a third course. Its direction became clear in the joint press release which Hosemann issued on the evening of 4 May. This stated that 'a most gratifying agreement as to the means and end of this extraordinarily significant task' had emerged among those taking part in the discussion. The concern was to create something 'fundamentally new', so that the message of the gospel could again reach all circles of the German Volk. However, complete reconstruction of the church – and here Ludwig Müller's ideas emerged – would prove lasting only 'if what the various historical confessions have in common is brought to the fore and made central. The Reformation message must be proclaimed to the Protestant people at this new turning point of history as this basis of what is held in common. To find and secure this common ground must be the object of prayer by all German Evangelical Christians.'[28]

Müller indicated what he understood by this search for common ground the next week. After a conversation between the Committee of Three and the Berlin German Christians on 5 May, which I shall be describing shortly, the Committee of Three again met with Müller on 10 May. In the communiqué there was again talk of 'full agreement', and again the issue of the confession was highlighted. This time there was an explicit statement: 'Before the details of the new constitutional work reach the stage of final discussion, an attempt must be made to demonstrate to our generation what it means to be Protestant. The Reformation confessions, which four hundred years ago gave classic and inviolable expression to this on the basis of the Word of God, summon us today to an act of confession which uses the language of our time and deals with the questions confronting us today.'[29]

It was quite obviously Ludwig Müller's plan to overcome the dilemma of the confessional issue with a modern confession, intended to be added to the historical confessions and to make the Reich Church a theological possibility. He already envisaged the content of such a confession. In two different interviews in this connection, on 11 and 12 May, he referred emphatically to the East Prussian guidelines of the German Christians, in the formation of which he had been involved. In fact there was already a suitable statement in these guidelines which Müller now only needed to quote: the demand for an elaboration of the German Protestant confession, accompanied by full safeguarding of the confessional standard of the Reformation. For Müller, there was no question but that this confession had to be shaped as the German Christians understood it and the East Prussian guidelines expressed it: 'The eternal truth of God, as Christ taught it, should be proclaimed in a language and a manner understandable to the German soul.' In the same interview he emphasized that a unanimous confession was 'the most important and decisive element in the form of the German Evangelical Church', and that when this foundation had been laid, 'a unified external edifice' could also be 'built...such as the present age demands'.[30]

Without doubt Müller, with this surprising emphasis on the confession, found himself in agreement with the great confessional movement which had gripped the Protestant church for some time and which had found its first clearly visible expression in the Altona confession. How much all this was in the air had been shown by Zoellner's ideas and also, early in May, by approximately two hundred East Prussian pastors who, following the model of the Altona confession and incorporating ideas from the East Prussian guidelines, had unanimously issued a 'Word for the Hour'.[31]

Hans Asmussen also welcomed this tendency. In contrast to the others, however, the young Altona pastor understood the direction in which the confessional question was moving the church. In May he formulated sharply and clearly the consequences which he saw emerging for the church in this respect. 'Are the Protestant churches of Germany ready to issue a binding statement that Christian salvation needs even more passionate dedication than political salvation? Are they prepared to testify that anyone who has staked his entire life on political salvation cannot possibly have found the pearl of great price and the treasure in the field? Are they prepared to issue a binding statement that political salvation, if it is attained, is nevertheless still damnation when measured against the salvation which is in Christ? Are they then prepared to testify that in this sense all earthly powers are within the realm of disaster? Are those in positions of responsibility prepared to defend any pastor who preaches in this manner against the charge that such preaching does not match up with the national interests?'[32]

This, however, could not be Müller's own conviction. So he soon let the confessional question drop, especially as it became increasingly apparent that his real problem was not so much Kapler as Hossenfelder. As Müller emphasized, collaboration with the Committee of Three 'was far more cordial than could ever have been expected and extraordinarily good'.[33] That could not be said, however, of the Berlin German Christians.

Since its spectacular Reich Conference at the beginning of April, Hossenfelder's Faith Movement had undergone a series of astounding changes. First of all, immediately after the conference Kapler had summoned four of the pastors responsible (Hossenfelder, Lörzer, Kessel and Freitag) to the Oberkirchenrat and made clear to them the displeasure of the church authorities. On this occasion Hossenfelder had defended himself with the comment that the ideas about government intervention had not come from the German Christians but from the National Socialists.[34] Because of the great response to the Reich conference, the self-confidence of the Berlin group had increased in the following days, especially since membership of the Faith Movement had also increased considerably outside Berlin. On the other hand Hossenfelder, caught between the unfriendly attitude of the church authorities and Hitler's plans for Ludwig Müller, saw little chance of any promising ventures of his own. On 15 April, he therefore wrote a letter to Kapler attempting to persuade him immediately to involve representatives of the Faith Movement in meetings of the church authorities, since the other church-political groups were also represented there. But neither Kapler nor the Old Prussian Church Senate was prepared to make such concessions.[35]

At the same time a circular letter from Hossenfelder indicated that soundings were being taken in Berlin about the immediate nomination of Müller. The churches, wrote Hossenfelder, were unfortunately rejecting the Faith Movement even more vehemently after the Reich Conference than before. 'Just as before Hitler's seizure of power Papen attempted to "go it alone", so the churches are now attempting to do everything as quickly as possible, indeed over-hastily, to force us, the Faith Movement of German Christians, to the wall. Above all, an attempt is being made to sow distrust between the Führer, Adolf Hitler, and me. Rumours spread by the church that Adolf Hitler has disbanded the Reich leadership of the Faith Movement of German Christians and has entrusted further work to the Königsberg chaplain Ludwig Müller are filthy lies.' Hossenfelder reassured the German Christian leaders that precisely the opposite was the case. 'I have entered into a closer connection with the Party in order to heighten our impact.'[36] The indication that 'a few changes' would follow from this, namely that the leader of the Faith Movement would no longer be allowed to use the title Gauleiter, also showed the direction in which these connections pointed: to the Staff Director of Political Organization, Robert Ley.[37] In fact, on 24 April Robert Ley expressly pointed out to the Gauleiter of the Saarland, Josef Bürckel, 'that the German Christians are carrying out their work within the framework of the Party organization and that the Reich Leader of the German Christians, Pastor Hossenfelder, is subordinate to the senior leadership of the Political Organization of the Party.'[38] Now the support of Ley and the Political Organization was undoubtedly important, especially for publicity and propaganda. But it did not bring the German Christians one step closer to what they longed for: power in the church.

On the other hand the situation was different in respect of a decision which was at first noted only in passing, although it set the scene for the first great clash between church and state in the Third Reich. On 20 April Hossenfelder – whether at the request of Kube, Göring or Rust is unknown – was appointed a consultant to the Prussian Kultusministerium. Here, of course, his influence was initially quite small, because the head of the Church Department, Ministerial Director Dr Friedrich Trendelenburg, was an impeccable civil servant of the old school who would tolerate no high-handed abuses of any kind. But the fact that the ambitious and power-hungry Reichsleiter of the German Christians, with his considerable knowledge of church personnel, now had a place in the largest and most important governmental church department in Germany, was indeed an alarm signal. Under the headline 'Commissioner of Churches for Prussia?' the *Tägliche Rundschau* not incorrectly remarked that Hossenfelder's appointment had to be viewed as 'belated approval of the proceedings at the Reich conference'.[39]

Finally it was also evident that membership of the German Christian movement increased during the first half of April. Appeals to the Berlin church administration to work with the German Christians mounted. 'The two largest Reformed communities in Germany, Elberfeld and Barmen,' sent a telegram at the end of April with the postscript 'at night' to the Kirchenbund in Berlin that they attached 'utmost importance to calling on German Christians for collaboration...' The Superintendent of Flöha in Saxony, Dr Krönert, for example, wrote on 22 April in similar terms that in his church district opinion was unanimous that the German Christians 'ought to be received into our church with joy and trust'.[40]

Typical of the mood of awakening that now seized above all the younger generation in the church was a letter written by the young pastor of Rüstring, Heinz Kloppenburg, to the Party Kreisleiter of his area on 28 April. Kloppenburg, like the signatories of the telegram from Elberfeld and Barmen, was later to become a leading figure in the Confessing Church, but in those April days things still looked quite different: 'What you said in yesterday's meeting with Pastor Meyer in your capacity as Kreisleiter moved me very much. What struck me more than ever before was the utter earnestness and profound responsibility with which National Socialism is fighting for the soul of the German people as a Christian people. To this I would add that the attitude of the Reich Chancellor and Führer towards the Protestant church, as indicated in the nomination of Pastor Müller, seems to be truly pioneering, so I really see no further possibility of avoiding the logic of joining the NSDAP.' Kloppenburg went on to say that he wanted to take part 'with all my energy in the controversies, or rather in the reordering of the relationships between state and church; and if he might already be appointed representative for Rüstring by Pastor Hollje, the leader of the German Christians in Oldenburg, he believed that he could serve the cause still better by joining in the party. The letter ended by expressing his hope that his admission could be arranged 'before the 1 May ban on membership',[41] In fact from the beginning of May Kloppenburg went on to engage in a vigorous propaganda and lecture campaign for the German Christians in the villages along the Jade Canal.

With the support of the Office of Political Organization, the appointment of Hossenfelder to the Kultusministerium and their increasing membership across the country, the German Christians had come a long way – but evidently not far enough to be able really to influence the course of events. For the clarification of the church question brought about by the events of 24-26 April took place completely without the involvement of the Berlin group. So it looked as though the Committee of Three, together with Müller, would produce a *fait accompli* before the German Christians really had a chance. In this situation Hossenfelder saw only one way left of putting himself at the head of the church reform, namely through primary elections. With the polling of the entire membership of the Protestant church he could bring his strength, the propaganda backing of the Party, fully to bear, and given the general political mood, could hope to win a clear majority for his radical course. Thus on 30 April the Berlin-based national leadership made an announcement which simply ignored the decisions taken in the meantime: 'Now drive the movement towards its final goal. God is with us. Our Reich Conference was the mobilization. It has swept like a storm throughout the country and far beyond the borders of Germany.' For the first time the political denunciation which was henceforth to play a major role also made an appearance here: 'The enemies of the Third Reich are hiding themselves behind the church. To them, in faith, we retort, "Nevertheless..." The hour has come to give the church of the gospel which has loved the German Volk and is loved by the German Volk to the glorious Reich of Adolf Hitler. May God bless our struggle!' At the same time the national leadership made its most important demand: 'No renewal of the outward form is any use to us unless the inward part is filled with real life. However, the church can receive true life only through the mass of Protestant church people who are still strangers to the official church. This mass, however, already stands behind our Faith Movement and demands more and more vigorously the co-ordination of state and church... We therefore call for immediate new elections on the basis of an equal, secret and direct vote.'[42]

The Committee of Three, of course, had no inclination to agree with these demands. However, it was thought right to invite the German Christians to present their ideas for the reconstruction of the church to them. So on 4 March Hossenfelder, who saw this as an opportunity for direct intervention, in the absence of Müller, called some members of the national leadership, including the still unsuspecting Friedrich Wieneke, to a meeting at the Kultusministerium, at which a programme 'The Evangelical Reich Church according to the principles of the German Christians' was worked out. It consisted of ten points, and for the first time presented the ideas of the Berlin group fairly precisely. The most important slogans ran: 'A Protestant Reich Church of a Lutheran kind, incorporating the Reformed communities'; no state church but rather a church 'which by faith acknowledges the sovereignty of the National Socialist state'; 'a church of German Christians, i.e. of Christians of Aryan race'; leadership by a – Lutheran – Reich Bishop; organization 'into no more than ten church Länder, at the head of each of which there is a Land bishop'; seat of the Reich Bishop to be in Wittenberg; decision about the Reich Church and the identity of the Reich Bishop – 'this in accordance with a proposal from the ranks of the German Christians' – by means of a primary election on 31 October, with only Christians of Aryan race entitled to vote; preparation for the election by a sixteen-member committee under Müller's leadership, composed half of German Christians and half of representatives of the Landeskirchen.[43]

The very next day, a delegation of German Christians presented this programme to the Committee of Three, where it was noted, evidently without further comment – 'matter-of-factly and coolly', as Wieneke observed. Wieneke also thought, even after the war, that these ten points 'bore witness to a healthy, stimulating venture of faith and – over and above all the politicizing – strove for a course of action that really was the church's'. However, that was now out of the question. Still, the principles possessed at least the virtue of clarity: more than almost any other document from this period they made clear what co-ordination of church and state in fact meant to the German Christians. What was at stake was no less than the complete organizational and ideological adaptation of the church to the National Socialist state, which would have meant that the church in fact ceased to be the church in any conceivable Christian theological sense.

The first person to fly into a rage over these principles was Ludwig Müller. That very evening he had a vigorous argument with Hossenfelder in his hotel. What disturbed him was certainly not just the 'invasion of his territory',[44] however unpleasant this self-confident man might have found it that Hossenfelder had simply taken advantage of him. Obviously he still had sufficient awareness of tradition to be well aware of the effect of these statements upon his partners in church dialogue. Müller saw clearly that an agreement between the church authorities and the German Christians on the basis of these statements was unthinkable.

That explains Müller's next steps. First of all, it was now of the utmost importance to him to gain control of the German Christians in order to prevent any further radical escapades. And at the same time he had to find a programme of his own upon which the representatives of the Kirchenbund and the German Christians could agree. By the middle of May he had achieved both these goals.

First of all Müller planned to make short shrift of the German Christians. He sent his adjutant, Horst Schirmacher, to Hossenfelder with the message that 'the Chancellor personally wishes the church to be led by Müller, and therefore Müller proposes to take over leadership of the Faith Movement'.[45] But although Ludwig Müller apparently held all the trump cards, the Reichsleiter of the German Christians had no desire to throw in his hand completely. So he gave in for the moment, nominated Ludwig Weichert, an Inspector of Missions, highly respected in church circles, as his liaison officer in the work of church reform, and then declared that the Reich leadership had 'the utmost confidence in the Committee of Three'.[46] He did not, however, relinquish the leadership of the Faith Movement. Instead he suggested that Müller should take over supervision of the German Christians as 'patron'.

During this development and parallel to it Müller had been pushing ahead vigorously in search of a programme of his own, which in his view was to be a kind of new confession, forming a common basis for all those involved in church reform. In this he had found an important helper: German university theology in the person of the Tübingen theologian Karl Fezer.

Fezer, a Swabian, and forty-two at the time, was one of the most respected of the younger generation of theologians. In 1925, in a work entitled *The Word of God and the Sermon*, he had developed Karl Barth's proposals for the theory of preaching; he was then called as Professor for Practical Theology to the Land university in Württemberg and soon afterwards was made head of the theological Stift. To Fezer's personal reputation was added the importance of his department; with almost 900 theological students it was the largest in the Reich – even larger than Berlin.[47] Fezer's move into church politics, in which until late autumn he was to play a role as significant as it was problematical, began with an extraordinary meeting in Berlin, to which Hans Schmidt, the Halle Old Testament scholar, impressed by the first Reich Conference of the German Christians, had invited the deans of all the Protestant theological faculties as their President.[48] Given the point in time – it was 27 April and both Hitler and the church had just made important decisions – a heated debate on the tasks of theology and the theological faculties in this era developed among an almost full complement of deans and assistant deans. This showed that there was also a deep rift in university theology. 'A great many people are waiting for a word from the church against the injustice which is now taking place,' asserted Friedrich Mahling, the sixty-eight-year old Berlin Professor of Social Ethics. 'The church ought to renounce state support in order to save the freedom of the spirit, of culture and of proclamation.' Hermann Mulert, the Kiel systematic theologian, and Hans von Soden, the Marburg New Testament scholar, expressed themselves in similar vein.

By contrast, many from a much larger group of younger professors passionately demanded unconditional solidarity of the church with the new state. Among their spokesmen were Emanuel Hirsch, who announced that he was joining the Faith Movement; the church historians Hermann Wolfgang Beyer of Greifswald and Heinrich Bornkamm of Giessen; the Old Testament scholars Anton Jirku of Breslau, Johannes Hempel of Göttingen and Artur Weiser of Tübingen; and not least Karl Fezer. Many of these names were very soon also to be found on the list of German Christians. In the end the faculty conference agreed on a solution which was natural at that time, of authoritarian commissioners and church plenipotentiaries. At the suggestion of Beyer and Hirsch, Karl Fezer was unanimously elected 'liaison officer of the Theological Faculty Conference in respect of the questions to be resolved'. Fezer had already indicated in the meeting that he was sympathetic to the German Christian cause. 'Our authorized representative,' he had declared, 'must be a theologian who 1. has reverence for the blood which has flowed all around Germany; 2. has reverence for the blood that has flowed in the service of the National Socialist cause; 3. of course has reverence above all for the cause which he represents as a theologian'.[49] In keeping with this approach he first sought co-operation with Ludwig Müller and only later visited Kapler.[50] In the circumstances it could not have been hard for Ludwig Müller, who moreover shared a common Pietist background with Fezer, to win over the Tübingen theologian as a defender and collaborator. This was a decisive step, for very soon other theologians appeared on the scene and formed a kind of personal working party to support Müller's mandate and approach. Along with Fezer, this working party included first and foremost Emanuel Hirsch, who from the middle of May fought for Ludwig Müller's cause with his typical blind determination; Friedrich Karl Schumann, the Lutheran systematic theologian from Halle; and the Bonn theologian Wilhelm Goeters from the Reformed side.

The benefit that this working party brought to Ludwig Müller can hardly be exaggerated. The extraordinary reputation which German university theology enjoyed at home and abroad was transferred to the hitherto unknown military chaplain, concealing his theological and moral weaknesses. And it was felt beyond Württemberg that a man in whom Karl Fezer had confidence could and should be followed blindly.

It is certainly doubtful whether Fezer's affiliation with Müller exactly reflected the intention of the faculty conference. But at that time the position of critical adviser on the great questions relating to the future of Germany was thought so improper, and partisanship and partiality were so bluntly demanded, that Fezer could imagine that he could fulfil the terms of his assignment precisely in approaching Müller.

Müller's theological working party, which originated in a kind of rivalry with the Reich leadership of the German Christians, did not limit itself to providing him with personal support. Rather, Fezer set to work immediately to co-operate with Müller in formulating that new confession of faith to which Müller hoped to commit both church administrations and the German Christians. In fact it proved possible within a short time to produce a text that appeared to satisfy all requirements.

The new 'Guidelines of the Faith Movement of "German Christians"' – now called the Fezer or Müller guidelines, to distinguish them from those of Hossenfelder – fell into two parts. The first part, entitled 'Goal of the Movement', contained the formulation of the theological starting-point; the second section represented an enlarged and revised version of the East Prussian guidelines. All in all, this new programme represented a theological and church line the substance of which could be subscribed to by all those who were more or less directly influenced by the political theology of the 1920s. And as the 1927 Königsberg Kirchentag had demonstrated, that comprised the majority in the Protestant church.[51]

The crucial sentences in the first part, sentences that clearly revealed the theology of Emanuel Hirsch, ran: 'A German church alongside the German Volk is nothing but an empty institution. It is the Christian church in the German Volk only when it is a church for the German Volk; when, in selfless service, it helps the German Volk to be able to recognize and fulfil the calling laid upon it by God.'[52] That expressed the fundamental thesis of political theology: solidarity

318

with the Volk as the prerequisite of all true Christian proclamation. Only a theology which understood the Volk as a direct creation of God and therefore also saw God himself at work in the destiny of the Volk could thus interpret the gospel as a Christian theology for this era. So the conclusion ran: 'To give the Christian churches a form which makes them capable of performing the service to the German Volk laid upon them through the gospel of Jesus Christ precisely for the sake of their Volk is the goal of the Faith Movement of "German Christians".' There followed the new version of the East Prussian guidelines. Particularly in view of the ten principles of the Berlin German Christians which had been published not long before, they seemed theologically moderate and responsible. The most important aims of church organization were said to be the demolition of the democratic electoral system, the establishment of a personally responsible spiritual leadership, and the uniting of the Landeskirchen in a German Evangelical Church – 'with reverent preservation of historically based special rights'. The concept of a Reich Church had been dropped, to be replaced by the concept of a German Evangelical Church, because Reich Church suggested a legal and territorial identity of Reich and church, and this appeared to jeopardize the connection with the German communities abroad.[53] This decision also held in the days to come.

The seven demands contained here sounded far more Christian-nationalist than German-völkisch. At their head stood the demand for a further development of the confession, while 'fully preserving the Reformation confessions'; a second, new point was an article which, in forthright contradiction to the Hossenfelder guidelines, defended 'the work of the German Protestant missions' as ' "a lapidary statement in stone of the church's act of confessing" (Martin Kähler)', though this was to be done 'with recognition of the diversity of peoples and races as an order intended by God for this world'. It was also difficult to raise any objection to another demand which had just been incorporated, namely that as soon as possible hard-working fellow-countrymen should be allowed to establish a 'German-Christian household... in which joy at the progress of a cheerful host of children' would bring 'happiness and blessing'.

Nevertheless, these theses were also a sign of the corruption of political theology. For here the proclamation of the church was completely at the service of the people and thus had lost its freedom – the freedom of Christian discernment as well as the freedom of Christian action. The Jewish question was only one example of this, albeit the most important.

By Monday 15 May the new theses had been formulated and the agreements with the Berlin German Christians had been reached. On the morning of 16 May Müller reported to Hitler on general progress and as a precaution had his plans approved explicitly.[54]

The report on these events which Fezer gave in a meeting in Stuttgart early in June demonstrated how far and how readily Protestant theology and piety had already let themselves be deceived by this time. Fezer reported that Müller had wanted to know what the Führer himself would say to the new guidelines. He then continued: 'It was enthralling for us when Pastor Müller made inquiries at the Reich Chancellery on Monday evening. This very busy man immediately agreed to a reception, talked over the guidelines with Pastor Müller and gave his consent to them. Let me stress this: the Chancellor has read these statements, has approved them, and in order to achieve a clear line of march has transferred the supervision of the Faith Movement of "German Christians" to Pastor Müller. That took place on Tuesday between 11 a.m. and noon.'[55]

So Hossenfelder was beaten. That very day he fell in completely with Müller's line. He announced that to secure united action 'the Chancellor's authorized representative, Pastor Müller', had taken over the supervision of the Faith Movement and that the Chancellor and Führer had 'approved the arrangement'. At the same time he added his name to those of Wiechert, Fezer and Müller under the new guidelines which the movement was to observe in the future. In its next number *Evangelium im Dritten Reich* printed both the agreement and the guidelines, though bad make-up and placement revealed the displeasure of the Berlin group clearly enough.[56]

Ludwig Müller, on the other hand, seemed to be almost home. Charged with the 'supervision' of the German Christians, and with the signed guidelines in his pocket, that very day he travelled to Hanover in high spirits, in order first to confer with his theological working party and then to go on to the monastery of Loccum nearby. Here, from 18-20 May, the concluding negotiations with the Committee of Three were to take place.

By the end of the next week, however, the Reich Chancellor's representative already faced the ruins of all his compromises.

The main responsibility for the ruin was borne by a group which at first seemed to have been organized in his support, but then quite soon embarked on embittered opposition to him. If Hitler and those whom he sponsored in the church were successful neither in 1933 nor later in co-ordinating the Protestant church, a major part of the credit is due to the group which now began to fight – in May 1933, when the struggle seemed almost decided.

The foundation of the Young Reformers Movement was a direct reaction to the 4 May theses of the German Christians and their claim to leadership. It was a concentration of a generation of forty-year-olds who had in some way or another been deeply affected by the church movement of the 1920s. Hitherto the whole burden of church reform had lain upon the old church government. The young and dynamic element had been represented only by the German Christians. But this scenario in no sense represented the real situation in German Protestantism. The picture of church development up to 1933 had indeed been stamped more by a growing desire for church renewal, like the desire which became visible in the dispute over the church in 1930-31.[57] The German Christians had come into the fight only late, in 1932, and only the auspiciousness of the hour had put them in a position from which they could lay claim to leadership. The younger generation, in so far as they had not gone over to the German Christians, had kept silent for three months – confused, vacillating and spellbound by the dynamic force of events into which state and church had been drawn so abruptly. Now, early in May, because of the German-Christian claim to leadership, it began to speak for the first time. A small group of Berlin pastors became its mouthpiece, just as by and large all essential decisions during these months up to the approval of the constitution on 14 July were almost without exception made in Berlin.

Three representatives of this generation had also already taken part in the 5 May meeting at which the German Christians had presented their church theses to the Committee of Three: they were Otto Riethmüller from the Burckhardthaus in Dahlem, Walter Künneth from the Central Office for Apologetics in Spandau, and Hanns Lilje – since 1927 General Secretary of the German Student Christian Movement.[58] Shocked by the open claim to leadership made by the German Christians, to which the Kapler Committee seemed to have made little response, these three began to organize a group to oppose the German Christians and at the same time to support Kapler. Five days later, on 9 May, Künneth and Lilje presented the 'Appeal of the Young Reformers Movement for the Reconstruction of the Church' at a press conference in the Hotel Adlon.

This appeal, like the Young Reformers generally, was later often categorized as the expression of a problematical church-political group, hardly different from the German Christians.[59] This was above all a consequence of the harsh criticism which Karl Barth made of the group soon afterwards. But this judgment is not correct. Of course the church wing of the German Christians and the Young Reformers had features in common. Both started from the idea that a nationalist revolution was God's gift; both shared almost unlimited enthusiasm for the Third Reich and its Führer; both felt united in a youth front against the old church (to Dibelius's anger, the appeal spoke of 'senile decay in ministries and corporate bodies'); both wanted a speedy and comprehensive reform of the church. Moreover an article like Article 11 of the Young Reformers' Appeal could also have been subscribed to by German Christians: 'We demand that in joyful affirmation of the new German state the Protestant church should fulfil, in full freedom from all political influence, the mission given it by God and at the same time bind itself in inalienable service to the German people.' Moreover the demand of Article 8 for a new confession which 'on the basis of the existing individual confessions' must 'afford to today's men and women the answer of the gospel to the question of race, Volk and state', largely coincided at least with the East Prussian guidelines.[60]

But none of this was decisive. What was decisive was the fact that none of these common interests was sufficient to eliminate the one difference between the German Christians and the Young Reformers. This difference was formulated in Article 1 and made specific in Articles 3 and 7. The basis of Article 1 ran: 'We demand that the coming decisions are made solely in accordance with the nature of the church.' This led to a decisive confrontation with the German Christian programme at two points. The Young Reformers rejected primary elections (Article 2) and demanded the immediate appointment by the Committee of Three of a Reich Bishop (Article 3). Only in this way, it was asserted – correctly, as was to be demonstrated in July – could the influence of National Socialist agitation be headed off. However, it was the second point that was decisive for the present and the immediate future. With it the Protestant church remained at this moment a Christian church, whatever it might otherwise advocate by way of political and church-political ideas, plans, right ways and wrong ways. The point was made in Article 7 and ran as follows: 'We profess faith in the Holy Spirit and therefore fundamentally reject the exclusion of non-Aryans from the church; for that rejection rests upon a confusion of church and state. The task of the state is to judge; the task of the church is to save.'[61]

Many of the political and church-political decisions which required so much effort and argument in German Protestantism in spring and summer 1933 were –

from a theological point of view – matters of judgment, which a Protestant Christian could make either way without separating from the church of the third article, the one holy Christian church of the apostolic confession. The Aryan Paragraph in the church was not of this kind. At this moment – even if neither Lutheran nor Reformed theology understood the point – it was the true *articulus stantis et cadentis ecclesiae*, the truth by which the church stood or fell. And with this truth, with its confession or with its denial, the Jewish issue became the hidden theme of the church struggle.[62] Elly Heuss-Knapp, the wise and resolute wife of the Liberal deputy who later became Federal President, had understood this point perfectly when on 18 May she wrote in a letter: 'All our friends belong to the Young Reformers group and have at least proclaimed loud and clear that the Aryan paragraph is impossible in the church. I go even further and tell everyone that on the day on which it is implemented I shall leave the church. That I will then join the Catholic church is something that I don't say to everyone so plainly, but I'm thinking of it.'[63]

The 9 May Appeal of the Young Reformers Movement bore a whole series of signatures in addition to those of Künneth, Lilje and Riethmüller.[64] They included well-known systematic theologians like Karl Heim of Tübingen, Friedrich Gogarten of Breslau and Wilhelm Lütgert of Berlin; and practical theologians like Wilhelm Stählin of Münster and Helmut Schreiner of Rostock. Other names stood for complete groups or schools: like Gerhard Jacobi the 'Diary Pastor', now at the Kaiser Wilhelm Memorial Church in Berlin; for a circle of young Berlin pastors who sympathized with Karl Barth; Georg Schulz of Wuppertal, for the pastors of Sydow; and Karl Bernhard Ritter of Marburg for the Brotherhood of St Michael. This indicated the great breadth of the movement. It was far more united over what it did not want, namely the hegemony of the NSDAP in the church, than over what it did want. And many a signature that was given in the haste of those days soon lost all value.

When Künneth and Lilje gave their press conference on 9 May the movement consisted of little more than the small Berlin group, the appeal, and perhaps a dozen signatures. But how long Protestant Germany had waited for a programme of this kind was shown by a real flood of declarations of assent. Only a week later, Marahrens learned from Berlin that 3,000 signatures had already arrived, representing even more actual supporters.[65]

In the meantime another man had joined the Young Reformers, who quickly became the real head of the whole movement: the forty-one-year-old Dahlem pastor Martin Niemöller.[66] The former navy captain had been a successful U-boat commander on UC 67 during the War; already the father of a family, he had then literally starved himself during his theological studies and through the good offices of Zoellner had become chaplain to the Westphalian Inner Mission in Münster. In 1931 he was chosen for a pastorate in the community of Berlin-Dahlem, which at the time was one of the best and wealthiest parishes of the Old Prussian Union. Decidedly a German nationalist, Niemöller combined an unusual determination, courage and stability with a certain theological flair, based less on reflection than on a very direct understanding and grasp of Christian truth. With these qualities he was the born leader for the struggle which now began to take shape. Exactly a week after Niemöller had made contact with the Young Reformers he had already joined Künneth and Lilje in the leadership of the new movement.

In the meantime, the focal point of events had shifted for a few days to Hanover. Here, on the 16th, Müller met with his advisers Fezer, Hirsch and Goeters to discuss the guidelines once again and to set the line of approach for the concluding negotiations. As a result the text was revised, and corrected at one point, a point to which the Lutherans above all took exception. There was no more talk of a 'further development of the confession of faith', which according to Lutheran understanding must inevitably lead to the dreaded Union, but only of a 'confession-like message from the church on the burning issues of the present'.[67] Again it was Fezer who, in his report of this discussion, introduced that tone of false piety which was soon to be strained to such an intolerable degree, especially by Müller. 'On the Wednesday morning, Pastor Müller said – I am telling you this so that you get a picture of this man – "Each of us will now go to his room in silence, and there he should listen for what will be given to him." Less than an hour can have passed when Pastor Müller asked me to come to him. He put something before me and said, "Can you sign this?", and I answered: "From the first word to the last."'[68]

At the same time as Müller and his advisers, the Kapler Committee was also meeting in Hanover to arrive at clarity on the most important questions.

The first joint session of that closed meeting – at which the final decisions about church reform were to be made – took place on the afternoon of 17 May at Loccum. It revolved above all round the new guidelines. Müller, who in the meantime had grasped how complicated the confessional question was, vigorously denied that a confession of faith was involved here. At the same time he revealed the tactical purposes of the new programme when he declared that this agreement meant a great deal to him: it was a way of arriving at 'a clear line over the attitude of the German Christians, who so far had viewed the church governments as their opponents, and in whose ranks the hybris after the Reich Conference had destroyed any sense of reality'. The church plenipotentiaries were of course delighted to hear this, and moreover Marahrens assured Müller that the new guidelines represented 'a relief and an easing of the situation'. 'However,' Marahrens continued, and in so doing touched on the decisive problem which had now emerged, 'in his opinion, a difficulty had arisen in that the Reich Chancellor's authorized representative was at the same time the leader of a church party; and so the demand of other church-political groups (the Young Reformers) for involvement in the negotiations was justified'.[69]

The pressure to which all those involved were already subjected at this time is indicated in an extraordinarily significant way by the fact that the Committee of Three did not even consider the obvious question whether, in these circumstances, the concluding negotiations should not be conducted without Müller. Of course the exclusion of the 'Führer's spokesman' from the negotiations would have met with the misunderstanding, indeed the indignation, of broad circles of the public, and it would have triggered off reactions, above all among the German Christians, for which the Kapler Committee believed itself to be no match. On the other hand the Committee of Three now ran into the difficulty of having to negotiate in the presence of precisely those forces for whose elimination it was striving. The unsatisfactory result of the Loccum negotiations, to which such expectations had been attached, can largely be explained by this situation.

These negotiations – in which Heckel and Hosemann now also participated again – were about two particular problems, namely the basic outlines of the new organization and how it was to be implemented.

There was rapid agreement over the outlines, especially since all concrete statements were avoided. The so-called Loccum Manifesto which was issued at the end of the negotiations and published on 27 May listed the following points: legal continuity between the Kirchenbund and the German Evangelical Church; a federation composed of confessional groups of equal status; the confession of faith as an inviolable foundation; removal of the geographical fragmentation, but preservation of the vigorous Landeskirchen; a Lutheran Reich Bishop and ministry for the clergy, a National Synod and advisory offices. These key words already to a large extent anticipated the 11 July constitution. At the same time the Manifesto also contained a short, joint confession which surprisingly formulated Christian faith and Christian hope in trinitarian language in a way almost totally free of political theology. 'Amidst the cares and distresses of earthly life,' the Manifesto concluded, in an attitude of openness to the future which was remarkable at a time when everything was so completely motivated by present fulfilment, 'we wait in responsibility and with confidence. Christ is coming again and is bringing a final consummation in the kingdom of his glory'.[70]

Agreement over the second problem, how the programme was to be implemented, proved much more difficult to achieve. For here were the real political problems in the whole affair. The main question was the nomination of the Reich Bishop. Ought the state to have any right of participation or co-determination in these negotiations? Müller repeatedly attempted to build such a right into the method of nomination, but on this point the church representatives stood firm. The lesson which the Landeskirchen had learned after the termination of government by local rulers had had its effect. The church alone could and might nominate its first Reich Bishop – otherwise it would lapse back into the dependency and constraints of a state church. Thus the Committee of Three decided on a *modus procedendi* which Müller also finally acknowledged and signed. By this decision the personal wishes of the various church groups were first to be heard; then a confidential agreement about the constitution and about the person of the Reich Bishop was to be produced by authorized representatives of the Landeskirchen; only after this was the result to be communicated to Hitler – by the Committee of Three. Following that, everything was to be confirmed in religious celebrations throughout the Reich on one and the same day, and the constitution was to be ratified in agreement with the Ministry of the Interior.[71] This arrangement explicitly rejected the primary elections that the German Christians wanted, as well as Ludwig Müller's desire for state partici-pation. Thus the church side had prevailed at the crucial point, even if the whole reform programme and its implementation was problematical in more than one respect. What this meant in specific terms was very soon to emerge.

In describing the turbulent events that followed, we must proceed on the assumption that ever since the time of his appointment Müller had envisaged that he himself would become the first Reich Bishop. The singleness of purpose with which he engaged in the negotiations, and the matter-of-fact way in which he appeared everywhere suggest that he knew what he wanted from the beginning. And until Loccum, everything had apparently run so smoothly that when Ludwig Müller put his name to the *modus procedendi*, he presumably did not have the remotest idea that the church might make someone else Reich Bishop. However, to his surprise and annoyance this was precisely what now happened.

The Young Reformers Movement provided the impetus. If this movement had any goal from the beginning, it was to bring to the head of the Reich Church a man with experience in the church – and to impede Ludwig Müller's candidacy at all costs. This had less to do with the person of Müller than with the perception generally shared in the church that the nomination of Hitler's plenipotentiary and spokesman as Reich Bishop would prejudice the state church to a considerable degree. The Young Reformers therefore quickly started searching for a candidate of their own. Their first choice at this point fell upon August Marahrens, Land Bishop of Hanover. He was experienced, had good support ecumenically, and was above all unquestionably a Lutheran. Therefore Walter Jeep, the executive director of the Central Board of the Inner Mission, in a letter dated 16 May in the name of the Young Reformers, asked Marahrens if he would allow himself to be considered for this office. In view of the fact that the Bishop of Hanover immediately and decisively rejected this offer, special significance came to be attached to the alternative formulated in the letter. 'Should insurmountable difficulties stand in the way of the personal solution requested here, in spite of this wish which we express clearly and once again which is also the conviction of many,' Jeep wrote, 'then we may perhaps refer to the possibility of a solution which, with the mention of the name of Pastor Friedrich von Bodelschwingh, has been suggested here and there in the last few days...'[72]

On 16 May – the very day on which Müller had come to an arrangement with the German Christians and on which he seemed to be only a short distance from his goal – the *Tägliche Rundschau* published an article under the title 'Peter or Stephen?' which made the alternative a demand. 'In the foreground, therefore,' it stated, 'today we do not need a Peter but a Stephen. The first deacon of the church now belongs at the head... We do not mention his name, but the poor know him and the workers know him. He comes from the place where this promise is still customary: "The blind see and the lame walk, the lepers are cleansed and the deaf hear, the dead are raised and the gospel is preached to the poor."'

The man who was referred to in this solemn way was Friedrich von Bodelschwingh, aged fifty-six, and Director of the famous Bodelschwingh Institutes in Bethel near Bielefeld. He had taken them over from his father in 1910 and in the meantime had developed them into a widely-diversified and model centre of Christian aid to the poorest of the poor. Almost all of that which was false in Ludwig Müller was genuine in Bodelschwingh. His piety was genuine, like his modesty and his love. By nature rather shy, and certainly not born to be a church leader, he nevertheless possessed undaunted courage, as was very soon to be demonstrated, especially in critical situations. He was thus undoubtedly a good choice.[73]

At first, however, Bodelschwingh reacted to the article with unmistakable alarm. That very day he wrote an agitated letter to his colleague Pastor Gerhard

Stratenwerth, who happened to be in Berlin at the time, saying that he wanted, please, utterly to blot out 'every trace of this idea' from the mind of the writer of the article 'so that he never comes back to it. I hope that no one pays any attention to this suggestion.'[74]

This remark, however, betrayed a total innocence about conditions in Berlin. For here, while the Kapler committee and Müller were meeting in Loccum, news and rumours had followed head over heels. They all amounted to the idea that the German Christians were determined at all costs to make Ludwig Müller Reich Bishop and had been for a long time. In fact to judge from the article in the *Tägliche Rundschau* now the other side was no longer willing to keep silent either. On 17 May the young Königsberg university junior lecturer Erich Vogelsang, spokesman for the German Christians in East Prussia, persuaded an assembly of East Prussian pastors to send a telegram to Berlin with the demand that since Müller possessed the Führer's confidence, he should become Reich Bishop.[75] Discussions between the Young Reformers and Fezer and Vogelsang on 18 May confirmed 'that among the new national leadership of the German Christians, too, no other person than Ludwig Müller was being contemplated as Reich Bishop'.[76] For the Young Reformers, all this was an alarm signal. So that very same day, Künneth and Niemöller sat down together and drew up sixteen theses which were presented the next day at a press conference. In content these theses largely agreed not only with the Loccum decisions but also explicitly with the new Fezer guidelines. At three points, however, there was an obvious difference. Along with the Fezer guidelines, the Young Reformers demanded 'a rejection of all modern heresies'; they also wanted to see this rejection expanded to 'resolute defence against völkisch heresies'. This was the beginning of the confrontation with the völkisch foundations of the Party. The second point concerned the church's attitude to the victims of political persecution. In the conflict between nationalist conviction and Christian commandment, the theses affirmed that general declarations by the church for the poor and needy were no longer enough. Rather, it was necessary 'to help to bear the bitter distress of those human beings who are deeply affected in their spiritual and social existence by the unavoidable impact of political struggle'. This was a clear affirmation of government measures, but it was just as clearly a rejection of the underlying ideology which was so destructive of humanity. Most conspicuous, however, was the third point, upon which all attention began increasingly to concentrate: the repetition of the demand for the immediate appointment of the Reich Bishop. He was to be a clergyman 'who has the confidence of the praying and working communities', a man 'like Friedrich von Bodelschwingh'.[77] Thus the ball was set rolling and the *modus procedendi*, signed on the same day in Loccum, was no longer sufficient to stop it.

Bodelschwingh, however, still hoped to be able to head off the mandate. In a moving letter to Marahrens on 23 May he reiterated his reasons. 'No one who truly knows me and my work will believe that I could be considered for such a task. Here I am a pastor of the epileptics and of the brethren of the road, and I have attempted to carry on quietly the work of our Father.... I do not understand church politics. Apart from a short time as a curate I have never been in a pastorate. My theological notions are inadequate for an office in the church.' And then followed a sentence which makes clear what the nomination of this man really meant for the church in the summer of 1933. 'I belong neither to the German Christians nor to the National Socialist Party, nor would I see any possibility of taking on any external or internal activity for this approach.' He concluded with the declaration: 'I am capable of any personal sacrifice which may serve our church at this solemn moment. But for the sake of conscience, I could not undertake a step by which I might damage the church.'[78] However, before this letter could reach the person to whom it was addressed, events took place in Berlin which once again dramatically changed the whole scene.

Since 16 May Ludwig Müller had evidently deluded himself into believing that with Hossenfelder's signature under the new guidelines and the formal assumption of 'supervision' he had the German Christians in hand. A meeting of the German Christian leaders which had been called for Tuesday 23 May in Berlin was supposed to confirm the agreements made on 16 May and thus finally to secure Müller's position. But the victory for which Müller had hoped proved to be his first striking defeat. There were several different reasons for this defeat. The discrepancy between the German-Christian demands as they had been voiced at the Reich Conference and the church line which Müller represented was so great that the radical wing of the German Christians could only regard Müller's activity as a betrayal of the revolutionary goal of the Faith Movement. The fear that Müller would make common cause with the old church (which in fact he did) and that the German Christians would once again be betrayed was a contributory factor. Finally, the beginning of discussions over the Reich Bishop had weakened Müller's position considerably, because everyone now knew that in these circumstances he could gain the office he coveted only with the aid of the Faith Movement. So at the meeting of the German Christian leaders there were heated arguments which were resolved in favour of the radical representatives – in the end, apparently, almost by brute force. At all events the Frankfurt pastor Georg Probst plausibly reported that when he contradicted Hossenfelder, Hossenfelder had thrown a beer glass at him. Other moderate representatives remained terrified over the next few days.[79]

The consequence of the meeting was an almost complete surrender by Müller to the German Christians. The gathering did designate him its candidate for the office of Reich Bishop and also accepted the new guidelines. However, there was no longer any talk of his 'supervision' of the Faith Movement. The organization remained firmly in the hand of Hossenfelder and his people. Müller was merely made 'patron', and was not even successful in keeping a promise given at Loccum to expel the two worst Berlin demagogues, Grevemeyer and Bierschwale.

The triumph of the radical national leadership seemed complete. In a letter dated the following day, Pastor Karl Jakubski, Hossenfelder's liaison to the Fellowship Movement, left no doubt as to this basic decision. Unfortunately, as he wrote to a friend, on that day he had not been able to speak personally with Müller and Hossenfelder. 'Here they are going from meeting to meeting. This morning they have been with Adolf Hitler and I can tell you the latest news – that Müller will become Reich Bishop. No other person is under consideration at all. It is also completely out of the question that the new church will be any other than National Socialist and following the German Christian line. That was confirmed to me again today by Hossenfelder's adjutant, who is in fact very well informed about everything.' How sure people felt of their ground and how little thought was given to bothering about any kind of agreement was demonstrated by the rest of the letter. 'All other attempts to intervene and to give the church a new face are to be seen as nothing but childish efforts from some other quarter to tackle the big questions of the new church – whether that happens in Loccum or in the Committee of Three, by Kapler, etc., or by the Young Reformers Movement...'[80]

The tragedy of Ludwig Müller and his collaborators and followers in the church and theology began with the 23 May meeting. For since the truth would have meant the immediate end of all their ambitious plans, they now had to lie. As early as the following day Müller lied to Meiser when he said that he was the only leader of the German Christians and would definitely bring his influence to bear in the movement.[81] Fezer lied two weeks later in Stuttgart when he said that there was no doubt that the new guidelines were the 'marching orders' by which the German Christians would proceed. Whereas immediately after that meeting the Tübingen professor had even told Kapler that he was considering leaving the German Christians, he now emphasized that he should be judged by his statement and 'not by any sort of individual press notices'.[82] Wurm in turn built his confidence in Müller upon Fezer's lie.[83] So soon the whole Müller group was caught in a net of lies which no one could now break. For the irresponsible Müller himself this apparently presented no serious problem; at any rate he never showed any kind of scruples or inhibitions. Serious men like Fezer, however, to the very end of their lives were unable to come to terms with their own conduct in this period.

The German Christian nomination of Müller was brought to Kapler the morning after that stormy meeting by a small delegation led by Hossenfelder. Kapler, who had evidently understood that it was meant to be a *fait accompli*, replied that he would note the information; he added that the churches 'were already agreed on the matter of the individual'. In fact, however, so far there had been no official decision at all in the Committee of Three about particular individuals. But now there was no longer any choice. In view of the reports coming in from all sides that Müller had already been nominated Reich Bishop, the plenipotentiaries agreed on the name of Bodelschwingh. Marahrens was commissioned to telephone Bethel immediately. Bodelschwingh, completely surprised by the call, finally gave in to the increasingly urgent pleas of the Bishop of Hanover and consented to be nominated provisionally, but on two conditions: that he continued to have 'full freedom of decision and that there were discussions with Ludwig Müller beforehand'.[84] The first condition quickly proved to be an illusion. The other was met, but in such a vague manner that Ludwig Müller and his advisers, Fezer and Hirsch, apparently felt themselves deceived.

The result of a short press release in the evening by the Committee of Three to the effect that Bodelschwingh had been selected as a 'future Reich Bishop' and of long, unpleasant negotiations during the night made large headlines in the press on the morning of Ascension Day: 'Bodelschwingh Nominated Reich Bishop'. The result was rage and indignation among Müller's following, and uncertainty and fear among the church delegates. Hirsch in particular had behaved so scandalously during the night and had so ruthlessly threatened to fight against Bodelschwingh that Marahrens and Hesse were already of the opinion that Bodelschwingh's candidacy could not be upheld. Bodelschwingh himself, informed of this new turn of events by telephone, was relieved; in the train to Berlin he drew up a declaration which was supposed to contain his final refusal of the nomination. On arrival in the capital, however, he found yet another mood. Both Hosemann and above all the representatives of the Young Reformers now entreated the Bethel pastor to hold fast to his candidacy at all costs. To back down would mean the end of the Kapler committee, lead to a capitulation of the church to the state and give the politically fettered Ludwig Müller the leadership. By contrast, Bodelschwingh would assure a broad base in favour of the new church. Detailed discussions with Müller convinced Bodelschwingh that the man would really be intolerable as Reich Bishop. So he decided to let things take their course, though with a heavy heart.[85]

The provisional decision in this question, which anyone could see was just as much a matter for the church as a political decision, now lay with the representatives of the Landeskirchen who had been called together for that day – 26 May – in Berlin. Originally – in line with the Loccum agreements – only the outlines of the new constitution were supposed to be issued at this meeting, and a confidential agreement was to be reached on the person of the Reich Bishop. Now the situation had turned into an open declaration of war. Whereas the church question had largely been debated over past weeks by a mere handful of people, and behind closed doors, the horizon had once again expanded: the Protestant church had to demonstrate where it really stood.

This day in fact once again brought out the old rift that separated South German and North German Lutherans from the Prussian Union Church. Many factors had contributed to this rift and its recent deepening: the great mistrust on the part of the Lutherans of all unionism; their traditionally greater friendliness towards the state; their openness to a right-wing political theology; and also quite simply the provincialism of the Landeskirchen and old anti-Prussian resentments. Most of the Lutheran Landeskirchen had meanwhile determined to collaborate with the German Christians, though these were more moderate than in Prussia. In Bavaria and Württemberg, Hamburg and Schleswig-Holstein, Thuringia and Mecklenburg, it was thought that simply for reasons of state a struggle with the Faith Movement at this time would be disastrous; moreover it was asserted that only through close co-operation with them could the best for state and church be achieved. It thus became apparent when the Lutheran representatives met in the morning for preliminary discussions that there was strong support for Ludwig Müller, who appeared to guarantee just such co-operation.[86] However, this group was very much in the minority in numerical terms, and all the more so in votes, especially since Lutheran Hanover stood firm with Marahrens on the side of Bodelschwingh. For this reason alone there was no clear vote for Müller's candidacy in the Lutheran group. Rather, it was agreed first of all to insist upon the completion of the constitution and to reserve any decision about the person of the Reich Bishop until afterwards.[87]

The session itself began late in the afternoon with a surprise. Kapler asked the assembly first of all to allow Ludwig Müller, the Chancellor's representative, to make a speech. At his request Marahrens and Hesse had agreed to this the evening before. So Müller – who up to this point had been unknown to most of the gathering – was given the opportunity to present himself and his cause to the

Landeskirchen, which he did in his typical way, with a mixture of false piety and actual threat. He began by saying that he stood before the gathering as 'a poor sinner', and that for him 'just as much as for Brother von Bodelschwingh' the office did not mean a 'shining crown' but rather 'a heavy cross'. In contrast to this feigned humility, however, in the next sentences he made it unmistakably clear to the church's representatives that all roads led to him. As National Socialism had conquered the Reich, so the Faith Movement would conquer the church. He had taken over supervision of it and with the 'best and leading heads of theological faculties' had compiled new guidelines. His goal was 'to interest the masses in the innermost matters'. For him and his people there now could be no turning back. 'See things the way they are,' he concluded. 'Do not be deceived by the talk that is popular today. But if the fight is avoided, then we will fight with them as true warriors.' Bad as this speech was, the threats did not fail to have their effect.

The beginning of the discussion showed that the assembly found itself in the most difficult situation imaginable. Since it was not an official body of the Kirchenbund, it had neither procedural rules nor authority, and there was a dispute, which continued to the very end, as to whether it could pass binding resolutions at all. On the other hand, a decision could hardly be avoided on the question of the Reich Bishop if things were not to get completely out of control. The attempt of the Lutheran representatives in accordance with their morning agreement to escape the dilemma by asking first for the Kirchenausschuss to vote on the new constitution and then to adopt a position on the question of the person of the bishop was therefore thwarted by the general conviction that only an immediate decision by the church could keep the initiative in its hands.

However, the very first round of negotiations, which lasted until midnight, clearly demonstrated that the assembly was hardly in a position to accomplish this. To the extreme disappointment of Kapler, who had counted on a unanimous vote by the churches for Bodelschwingh, a series of Lutheran Landeskirchen asserted that the moment called for an unconditional Yes to the National Socialist movement, to the new Reich and therefore to Ludwig Müller. In addition to Simon Schöffel, chief pastor of Hamburg, Bishop Mordhorst of Kiel who had already toed the Party line along with his whole staff in the Landeskirche and the Württemberg Church President Theophil Wurm, who was influenced by Fezer, the Bishop of Mecklenburg made himself the main spokesman for this group. 'At the moment,' Rendtorff declared with enthusiasm, 'Bodelschwingh is the symbol of the church's boundaries and limitations. Müller is the symbol of a step towards a movement filled with a longing to be allowed to believe. Müller has the Chancellor's confidence. Spiritually, the fresh forces of youth are with him. He is the daring Yes of the church to this hour.' Against him, Dibelius spoke for the Prussian Church and demanded an immediate decision: 'I am for Bodelschwingh. His name does not represent a retreat but rather a Yes to spirituality and service. We shall take up the fight. Political force will do no violence to the name of von Bodelschwingh.' A first straw vote moved by Rendtorff ended with a narrow defeat for Müller. Thirteen churches with fifty-five votes had declared against him; eleven churches with thirty-one votes were for him. A second vote did not produce essentially different figures.[88]

Bodelschwingh, to whom this result was communicated during the night, knew that some of the Lutheran representatives were now awaiting his withdrawal, so that the way would be free for an easy solution. However, it was precisely this that now moved the Bethel pastor to abandon his hesitations and to show courage. 'During the night,' he wrote in retrospect, 'I arrived at the conviction that at this moment I could not forsake the coming young church. Though the undertaking appeared hopeless, in this hour it was not a matter of success or failure but rather of raising a flag for the future to which a new troop could rally.' Whatever might happen, above all he had 'the certainty of an inner compulsion that sets the nevertheless of faith and obedience over against an anxious consideration of human factors, and which confidently entrusts whatever happens to God'.[89]

At noon the following day the assembly convened once more. And again all the legal, technical, political and personal difficulties of the situation were thrashed out in a long discussion. Heckel, himself the legal adviser of the Kirchenbund, also urged an immediate decision and advised against dwelling on hesitations about legality: 'The constitutional limits of the office are nothing. The new man makes the office... If everyone stands behind the bishop, then he is it.' Again it was Dibelius especially who urged the gathering not to capitulate 'at the point of a revolver': 'If they open the floodgates, then we in Old Prussia are lost. The appointment of the Reich Bishop is only the first act. After that comes the appointment of Hossenfelder as Land Bishop for Prussia.' Again Rendtorff, in his utterly innocent enthusiasm, declared that it was not a revolver that the churches faced 'but rather an extended hand'. Finally, towards five o'clock a new vote brought a decision in an already agonizingly confused situation. In Kapler's motion, a surprising majority now approved the nomination of Bodelschwingh and at the same time entrusted him with continuation of the work on the constitution. Only three churches voted against him: Württemberg, Mecklenburg-Schwerin and Hamburg. The voting was ninety-one to eight.

Clear though this decision turned out to be in the end, from the beginning its binding force was problematical. For a motion in the afternoon by Schöffel had demonstrated the limits of Lutheran loyalty. If the Committee of Three, the motion ran, decided to nominate Bodelschwingh as Reich Bishop, then the signatories would 'stand by this choice loyally, but with the explicit reservation that it does not involve us in a struggle, or a decision, against the German Christians'. The motion bore the signatures of Schöffel, Rendtorff, Reichart, Tilemann, Mordhorst, Wurm and Bernewitz.[90] Further developments showed clearly and very quickly that the Lutheran group in fact insisted upon their reservation. But this meant that for all practical purposes Bodelschwingh was lost even before he took office.

At first, however, joy and relief predominated among the gathering. Marährens was the one who communicated the decision to Bodelschwingh. Both then drove immediately to the Kirchenbundesamt, where Kapler ceremonially greeted the Reich Bishop designate among a group of church representatives.

Thus the Protestant church had once again prevailed against the state. It had called to be its bishop a man who was determined to make no concessions to the new era. This became impressively clear in a greeting which Bodelschwingh published on the very evening of 27 May. Where everything was attuned to power and grandeur, violence and dominion, triumph and victory, this message

331

began with a call for repentance and a confession of guilt. It was a starting point similar to that which the Stuttgart Confession of Guilt would repeat twelve years later.

> The German church confesses that it has been guilty of much and has neglected much. We Christians have not taken seriously enough the responsibility that God has given us in the gospel. We should have been more truthful, more humble, more active. We should have resisted more bravely the powers that make the human being the slave of money, and put selfishness in the place of service.
>
> With its distress and guilt, the church comes into the light of the One who alone can cleanse us and make us alive. We place our trust completely in the God who has redeemed us from death through the dying and rising of our Lord Jesus Christ, so that we may be obedient to him from the bottom of our hearts.

If the church, in this attitude, understood itself as 'the free helper of the state'; if it thanked God for the government and made itself available for service to the Volk, it still remained the church. For it was clear that when Bodelschwingh said 'service' he really meant service – and not the secret or open political collaboration of the church with an ideology.

Just how seriously Bodelschwingh meant this was shown by the conclusion of his word of greeting, which mentioned his own personal position:

> I have not coveted this episcopal office for myself: I am following the path of obedience. If those in authority in the church have entrusted me with a task, coming as I do from work among the poor and the sick, then that shows the way on which I have to continue. It is the way of the diaconate. If it were up to me, I would be rather called Reich Deacon than Reich Bishop. But the name does not matter. The ministry should receive its content from a will not to rule but rather to serve, in humble imitation of the one who 'came not to be served but to serve and give his life a ransom for many'.[91]

Bodelschwingh's work began with this greeting. The very next day, a Sunday, the new Reich Bishop embarked on his first negotiations.

6

The Fall of Bodelschwingh
(June)

The election of Bodelschwingh as Reich Bishop was an event of extraordinary significance. In retrospect it even appears as a crucial turning point in the development of the relations between church and state in the Third Reich.

Until this moment everything had apparently yielded to Hitler's will. The unification of the nation, his declared political goal in early 1933, had gone forward vigorously, just as he wanted. The reconciliation with tradition on 'Potsdam Day' had been a success. The 'Festival of National Labour' on 1 May had to all appearances brought the endorsement of German labour. And on 17 May in the Reichstag all parties had backed the government foreign policy statement by the National Socialist Chancellor.[1] A unanimous declaration for Ludwig Müller by German Protestantism would without doubt have been an effective continuation of the series of declarations of unity. Instead, with the selection of Bodelschwingh, the Protestant church had demonstrated that it would not give up freedom of decision, at least in its own sphere. And this had created a new situation for the state as well as for the church.

While hitherto Hitler could assume a stance of benevolent neutrality, now he saw himself compelled to act. For if he did not want to let the church's decision for independence rest – and merely as a precedent this caused problems – he had no alternative but to impose Ludwig Müller upon the church by force, since it had not chosen him of its own free will. To be sure, this went against his basic church-political decision to avoid direct intervention in church questions, but the internal logic of the political process in the spring and summer of 1933 allowed of no other solution. Hitler – albeit hesitantly and reluctantly – decided on this action, and in the following weeks he openly lent his power and that of the Party to Ludwig Müller in the pastor's struggle for the office of Reich Bishop.

This put the church in precisely the situation which hitherto it had carefully tried to avoid. It had to decide whether it should capitulate to this pressure or go on insisting upon its independence. The Church Struggle began with the struggle over this decision. In its first stage it split German Protestantism into several different camps, led to the first serious crisis in the relationship between church and state and ended in a compromise, the tolerances of which were already almost exhausted by autumn 1933.

From the beginning the church struggle was a struggle for the church, and it largely remained so even into the Second World War. But from the beginning this struggle was also a political issue of the first importance. This was shown pointedly in the dramatic confrontations which followed the election of Bodelschwingh.

Ludwig Müller himself gave the signal on the very evening of the election day. In a statement on the election, which was broadcast on Berlin radio, the Führer's spokesman blamed the Protestant church administrations for not having heard 'the call of the hour'. 'You have not heard the voice of God which, through the movement in our Volk, calls us to daring action... The Reich Bishop ought to be a man whose name arouses a response in our fighting groups, a man whom the whole awakening Volk looks on with trust with all its heart. He ought to be the church's leader for a new birth and a new energy.' There was no doubt that Ludwig Müller was describing himself at this point. And so it was quite consistent that now, contrary to the Loccum agreements, he should suddenly change his mind about Hossenfelder's demands for primary elections. It was an 'abnormality', he thought, that the Reich Bishop had been elected by men 'the majority of whom are advocates of the *status quo*'. Therefore 'we say No to this solution and an even stronger No to the way in which it has been arranged. Only through the confidence of the church people, acknowledging him by its own decision, can the Evangelical Reich Bishop be elevated to his position... Forward with God for a new Evangelical Church...'[2]

And so the battle began. And at the same time the German Christian organizations got their first instructions. In them Müller, supported by his theological advisers, attempted first of all to persuade the German Christians to fall in with a moderate church line. 'Important, strictly confidential guidelines,' dated 26 May and evidently directly from Müller's theological circles, clearly suggested this goal. In a section dealing with basic principles they stated that the struggle over the coming weeks was 'to be directed exclusively towards the goal of making Pastor Müller the Evangelical Reich Bishop'. In this connection Müller's personality was to be described in the following way: 'He is a German who has stood faithfully by the Führer in the most difficult years of the struggle... He is by God's grace a pastor with great kindness of heart... His power lies in the unshakable trust in God which God gives to this believer... He is obedient to the gospel... Those of us who know Pastor Müller stand in prayer to God for him and seek to support him through this difficult period of struggle.' The individual points which followed made even clearer the effort to take a church line. Thus there were instructions, among other things, to make contact with professors of theology and to seek their advice; to put special emphasis on the validity of the confessions; 'to overwhelm' the church authorities 'with telegrams and letters'; to avoid attacks on individuals; 'at all events to respect... the person of Pastor B'; and in no way to damage 'the Christian dignity of our struggle'.[3] A leading article written for the *Völkischer Beobachter*, in which Emanuel Hirsch justified the German-Christian support for Ludwig Müller, followed exactly these lines. There was no talk of political co-ordination in it but rather of a give and take between church and state. 'Not one people in the world,' wrote the Göttingen theologian on the front page of the main newspaper of the National Socialist Party, 'has a statesman who takes Christianity so seriously. When Adolf Hitler ended his great speech on 1 May with a prayer, the whole world felt the wonderful sincerity in it.'

The political movement, said Hirsch, could offer the church 'an inner, positive relationship to the basic ethical and religious presuppositions of the Christian faith'. But precisely for this reason it also had a demand to make of the church. 'Minds cannot be so educated that the state pulls one way and the church another. That would tear Germans to pieces.' But for this reason the church should never be subjected to co-ordination. 'We do not want any church in which the National Socialist state is in command. Only an independent church has worth in our eyes. But,' and here Hirsch drew the crucial conclusion, 'this independent church should be bound spiritually to the German Volk, with the very new, impetuous concern of the hour for constructive work...'[4]

The summons to battle was accepted enthusiastically by the German Christians. In the provinces where the Party took charge of things from the beginning scarcely anything of the church line could be detected. The Kirchentag which the German Christians staged on 28 May in Bad Freienwald, a small country town north of Berlin on the Oderbruch, was typical of the numerous similar events which took place in this period.

The day began with a sermon in the town church, packed to the doors, by Pastor Freitag from Berlin, on St Paul's words, 'By the grace of God I am what I am' (I Cor.15.10), which the preacher interpreted entirely in terms of Hitler and his government policy statement ('May God incorporate our work into his grace'). In the solemn hour which followed, a speech by the Kreisleiter of the Faith Movement, Pastor Gustav Nahrgang of Neulewin, was followed by one from the Ortsgruppenleiter of the NSDAP. According to the detailed report he spoke 'of the special satisfaction for the National Socialists that today for the first time, from this very pulpit, an open confession of faith has been made in our Führer Adolf Hitler.' The Kreisleiter was undoubtedly expressing the general views of the German Christians among the Party officials when he continued: 'Without a cultural revolution, our church would not be able to exist... The idea of struggle must once again become the life-meaning of the church; only through the annihilation of the enemy can we build anew. All must fight alongside us so that Luther's chorale may again take on its old meaning.' Following this, Pastor Freitag, in an 'excellent speech, stirring to the last detail and received with much applause', explained to the assembly the church-political proceedings of recent days. The issue today, he said, was the 'spiritual co-ordination of the church with the state', which only Ludwig Müller could achieve. Nationalism and socialism were the pillars which supported the nation. Therefore, he said, we want a 'German Christian who is inwardly committed to Nationalist Socialism'. In a resolution which was passed unanimously the gathering endorsed this view. In a closing speech, another German Christian pastor, Eberhard Wagner of Wriezen, introduced with the title Assistant Gau Propaganda Leader of the Faith Movement, connected the election of Bodelschwingh with the 'process of senile decay in the nation' which Hitler had terminated so inexorably. We want a Reich Bishop, Wagner exclaimed, 'who is elected by the Volk, not by a clique which is seeking to save what it can'. 'With the community singing of the first verse of "Ein feste Burg ist unser Gott"', the report in the local newspaper concluded, 'the Freienwald Kirchentag came to an end, certainly not without having made an indelible impression upon all the faithful'.[5]

Similar reports from this period can be compiled from many parts of Germany.

They all demonstrate how successful the German Christians had been meanwhile in mobilizing the Protestant population. But they also demonstrate that the motive power of the movement was provided almost exclusively by the NSDAP. Even in those places where the gatherings were not directly influenced by the radical wing of the Reich leadership, the interest, fascination and personal magnetism came almost solely from the Party. This was true in respect of personnel as well as subject matter. In terms of personnel, numerous participants were regularly provided from the ranks of the Party; as to the subject matter, Hitler, the new Reich and the new community of the Volk almost monopolized the field. In view of this concentrated desire for action, for youth, for change, for the nation and for socialism, there was just no room left for theological reflection. Hossenfelder's radical rejection of all theology was not just his personal opinion. It matched the essential nature of the German Christian movement.

The German Christians still, however, lacked the crucial political legitimation, namely the support of Hitler himself. So far Hitler had, for well-considered reasons, avoided directly taking sides in the church question, and had limited himself to general statements and indirect influence through his spokesman. Now, however, the way in which the situation had developed required his intervention, especially since no very great effort seemed to be required finally to subject German Protestantism to his will. So in a lengthy conversation with Ludwig Müller on 30 May Hitler made the unusual decision to employ the political organization of the Party in support of the German Christians. The press reported this conversation as merely the usual 'basic agreement on all pending questions',[6] but that very day a member of the Berlin Reich leadership, Pastor (later Bishop) Friedrich Peter, boasted at a meeting of having information that the Führer had 'placed the entire Party apparatus at the disposal' of Ludwig Müller for four weeks, 'for his fight',[7] and on 2 June the order already existed in black and white. Its wording showed that Hitler still wanted to avoid committing the Party openly to the German Christians, and that he had limited its involvement to four weeks. Within this period, however, he had obviously decided to help his man to victory.

'Pastor Müller, the Führer's authorized representative for the Protestant Church,' so the senior officials and Gauleiter learned from the Staff Director of the Political Organization, 'informs me that the Führer wishes the German Christians to drive reaction from its last bastion. The German Christians will embark on a four-week campaign. The NSDAP must support this campaign with all means, but without itself becoming actively involved in it. The Gauleiters will take the necessary steps on their own initiative.'[8] This order marked the beginning of the direct commitment of the Party to the German Christians. It lasted barely eight weeks, up to the church elections on 23 July, and came to a climax with Hitler's election speech on the eve of election day. Immediately afterwards he returned to his old line: the neutrality of the Party in all matters relating to church politics. For these eight weeks, however, we may proceed on the assumption that the Party and its Führer were actually behind the German Christians.

Even before the Party's order had been issued in Munich, Hitler's promise had already been converted into new campaign instructions for the German

Christians. This was the second set of guidelines for the conduct of the campaign to go out into German Christian territory within a few days. Their style and content revealed that now, finally, the radical wing around Hossenfelder had prevailed. They were concerned only with preparation for a change of power, systematically staged in the well-tried forms of propagandistic mass agitation. 'All the departments of the Political Movement,' ran the first point of the new instructions, 'are as soon as possible to come to an agreement over *the organizational apparatus of the political movement to further and support our struggle*. 2. It is to be arranged that the Protestant members of all SA, SS, NSBO and other formations of the National Socialist Movement *send off protest telegrams immediately*. The sooner they are sent, the better will be their effect. The opposing side must have no time at all to turn the popular vote to its advantage. 3. A wave of meetings of the most intensive kind is to be organized everywhere, even in the smallest community...' All this, the addressees were told, had to be done as quickly as possible because, 'for reasons which cannot be discussed here in greater detail', only three weeks were available for the entire campaign. Berlin, therefore, expected reports of success 'without fail within fourteen days, that is, by the middle of June'.[9]

From now on the Berlin Reich administration pursued the struggle against Bodelschwingh with the utmost determination. Wherever local conditions allowed, mass demonstrations were organized in association with the Party and according to instructions telegram and letter campaigns were staged and petitions presented to the public. A report of success from Lübeck, for example, listed no fewer than twelve campaigns for the small Hanseatic Landeskirche between 30 May and 27 June, among them a public appeal to the Protestant population on 2 June; a rally on the same day at an open-air theatre with approximately 2,000 participants; a protest rally in co-operation with the local group Holstentor in the Concert Hall on 15 June; protest rallies in the Flora Concert Hall and in the Matthäi community house on 21 June and so on.[10] The German Christians were not, however, as active everywhere as they were in Lübeck. There were other Landeskirchen – as for example in Bavaria – in which there was hardly any trace of direct activity.[11] Nevertheless by the end of June in Protestant Germany there could have been no pastor, no church-minded Christian who had been left untouched by the question 'Müller or Bodelschwingh?'

Evangelium im Dritten Reich regularly expressed the general tenor of the German Christian attack. The 12 June edition began with Ludwig Müller's Whitsun sermon, which spoke of the boisterousness of the spirit of Pentecost. Müller himself was sure that the Spirit of that time 'was the very spirit which passes through our age as a gift of God – again runs through the songs of the young, awakened German fighters. That is what makes men of us, to pledge ourselves utterly... To be triumphant bridges to the new era, ready to make the final sacrifice in victorious anticipation!' After this, Emanuel Hirsch outlined the church basis for the fight against Bodelschwingh and for Müller, and a lawyer the legal basis. A contribution on 'The Co-ordination of the Church' maintained that Hitler was building the new state 'with the deepest sense of responsibility to God' and that therefore 'the leadership of the state and the church' had to 'be in the most vital positive contact with each other'. Under the title 'The Era of Intrigues in the Church', a Pastor Knolle from Nowawes described the nomination of Bodelschwingh as 'the last attempt of a greatness in collapse'. Finally, the national press officer of the Faith Movement, Pastor Albert Freitag, also attacked Bodelschwingh personally in the central political article of the paper. Freitag cited as 'facts from Bethel' that the sentiment there was 'anti-nationalist, opposed to the government, anti-National Socialist. 'It stands to reason,' the article asserted, 'that it is quite impossible for the Evangelical Church to be filled with such a sentiment in the new Germany, or indeed that it can even remotely have anything to do with it. But since Dr von Bodelschwingh has tolerated it in his very own domain, he certainly cannot be considered to be the bishop of this church.'[12]

A last decisive fact for the significance and expansion of the campaign was that the daily press, which to a large extent had already been taken over – also adopted the German Christian views. Under the direction of the central press office of the German Christians which supplied the entire German press with information and articles produced by leading German Christians,[13] the impression was thus given to the public mind that the great majority of Protestant Germany in fact backed the Faith Movement and its behaviour. In terms of propaganda, the German Christians had achieved an essential aim among both friend and foe: they were now generally known; every attention had been paid to them; and both within the church and outside it the name of Ludwig Müller was at least as familiar as that of Bodelschwingh.[14]

The time limit on the campaign, the tone of the speeches and the self-assured bearing of the German Christian leaders made it clear that the national administration counted on a quick conquest of the church. This, however, proved to be a mistake. Rather, the German Christians met with unexpected resistance, especially among the pastors, which intensified even more during the month of June.

The Faith Movement already had considerable difficulties within its own hastily constructed organization. Thus great attention was paid to the resignation of Inspector of Missions Ludwig Weichert from the Faith Movement on 31 May. Only in May, Weichert had been entrusted by Hossenfelder with the task of liaison with the Kapler Committee; he had been a signatory to the Fezer Guidelines, and was widely regarded as the spokesman for the new course of the Faith Movement within the church. In a statement, Weichert now clearly backed Bodelschwingh and his legitimation. He said that it was a mystery to him why the German Christians protested against this. So he had to resign from the Faith Movement, 'the more so since, to say the least, the contest which has been declared, in its forms and implications, puts in question the achievement of the great goal of reform within the church'.[15] On the same day Hossenfelder received a telegram from Oldenburg: 'All seven pastors Ruestringen members of Faith Movement expect from national administration acknowledgment of Bodelsch-wingh and energetically protest against unleashing a church struggle over person of Reich Bishop.' The instigator of this telegram was Pastor Heinz Kloppenburg, who as late as May had made propaganda so zealously and successfully for the German Christians in the towns of the Jade valley. Hossenfelder, however, in his sharp manner made short work of the matter. 'The pastors,' he informed his north-west regional leader, Hans Aselmann, 'are to be expelled immediately and the public is to be informed of this.'[16] On 12 June, at the district synod in

Sillenstede, Kloppenburg in fact combined an ardent confession of faith in the new state and its Führer with vigorous criticism of the Faith Movement. Under the headings 'authentic state' and 'authentic church' he declared: 'I say as a National Socialist and I say quite openly that they are bad friends of the state who today, in opposition to the clear line of Hitler, seek to force through certain concerns in the church with the aid of the SA and NSBO, with instruments of political power... They are also bad friends of the church,' Kloppenburg continued, thus showing how difficult it was to get one's bearings in this question, 'who think that the church today must wrest something from the state, who attach no value to the fact that... Adolf Hitler can say "Yes" with joy to what has been reconstructed in the church.'[17]

Doubts began to arise elsewhere, too. From Lübeck on 6 June Canon Schaade, one of the leading German Christians of the Hanseatic city, informed Aselmann of certain misgivings, 'personally and in the strictest confidence.' Hitherto, he said, an effort had been made to conduct the struggle in an orderly manner. This had been successful until the beginning of the dispute over the Reich Bishop. 'From this moment on,' Schade wrote, shedding significant light on the situation, 'the leading politicians locally have jumped up as though stung by a tarantula.' Because of this the Faith Movement in Lübeck had been 'misled and compelled to use means which, though they may be usual in the political struggle, are hardly likely to be considered the correct thing in the church.' In his answer of 9 June Aselmann, after a few words of reassurance, expressed the hope that the opposite side would capitulate 'in advance because of the force of the campaign now being mounted.' There was no question of a retreat, but only of 'unwavering adherence to the course already adopted'.[18] The question whether in these circumstances to continue or resign was a personal decision for every German Christian pastor. Two other pastors, Schulz from St Gertrud and Jensen from Travemunde, resigned. It is no coincidence that in the autumn these two names then appeared as signatories to the endorsement by the Lübeck pastors of the Pastors Emergency League. For almost all the decisions of this kind which were made in June in connection with the struggle over the Reich Bishop were of a fundamental character and determined the attitude those who made them would have to the church right down to the end of the Third Reich.

The greatest difficulties for the German Christians arose in Bodelschwingh's home church of Westphalia. Here the national administration failed to impose its radical course. Rather, there was an agreement on 1 June with the Gauleiter of the Party, Dr Alfred Meyer, on the vague formula: 'The German Christians in Bodelschwingh's homeland are marking time. The national administration is asked to be understanding about this.'[19] Westphalia, however, remained an exception. Everywhere else the struggle was conducted with increasing political ferocity.

This ultimately made Ludwig Müller's circle of theological advisers also ask whether they could, and should, continue to back this course. The Greifswald church historian Hermann Wolfgang Beyer raised this question on 22 June in a long letter to his colleagues Fezer, Hirsch and Schumann. Beyer rightly thought that broad sections for the Faith Movement were kept in it 'only through the confidence which they have in Pastor Müller and us professors'. This, he said, gave rise to a special responsibility. 'It is an intolerable situation that quite specific methods of struggle are commended to the public, and then authoritative statements are constantly heard from the national administration which directly contradict these methods and frankly give the lie to one's words.' Beyer therefore called on his colleagues, along with Ludwig Müller, to commit the national administration – if need by threatening to resign – to a course which clearly bore witness to the fact 'that we do not want to do violence to the masses by the use of organizational power, but rather to win hearts for the church which is in the process of formation and for the victorious power of our cause.'[20] The letter was a sign of the remarkable mixture of doubt and enthusiasm which was and remained so characteristic of the church wing of the Faith Movement. But it did not lead anywhere. As matters, stood, it too had arrived too late.

More important than these difficulties in problems in the Faith Movement itself, however, was the major process of influencing church opinion and decision-making as a whole which was going on during these weeks among Protestant pastors and in many communities in Germany. The significance of this process for the further development of church affairs can hardly be underestimated. Until the election of Bodelschwingh, the overwhelming majority of pastors had not yet become committed in the church-political discussions. They restrained themselves and left the action and decisions to the church administrations, the more so as the major lines of action had in any case been laid down in Berlin. This now changed abruptly. During June there were pastors' and community meetings in many Landeskirchen in which there were heated arguments over the question 'Müller or Bodelschwingh?' The aggressive behaviour of the German Christians ensured that the traditional church apathy vanished and the seriousness of the situation became clear to everyone down to the last country pastor.

One of the first gatherings of this kind took place in Mecklenburg. The situation here was especially confused because of the attitude of the Land Bishop. After the successful repulse of state intervention at the end of April, on 4 May Rendtorff, overwhelmed by the unification of the Reich, became the first Protestant Land Bishop to announce that he had joined the Party. Consistently right to the end he had also shown his support for the election of Ludwig Müller.[21] In a meeting on 29 May to which almost all the pastors of Mecklenburg had come, he justified himself in a long speech and at the same time attempted to commit the approximately 350 assembled pastors to a moderate German Christian declaration. Opposition from the assembly to the formulations, which went too far, led to a counter-draft by the small group of radical German Christians who, after vehement arguments, finally left to cries of 'Heil Hitler'![22] Soon afterwards, some pastors from Rostock began to collect votes for Bodelschwingh among the pastors of the Land and almost immediately obtained 1500 signatures. Since Rendtorff continued to support the German Christians, the next step was also consistent. On 7 June twenty-one pastors and three church elders in Schwerin founded a 'League of German Lutherans' which, like the Young Reformers movement, understood itself to be a gathering of all those forces faithful to the confession. On 20 June the League presented itself to the public for the first time, with a declaration and ten principles.[23] On the same day Ludwig Müller spoke at a major rally of the German Christians in the town hall in Schwerin, attended by between two and three thousand people. There could

340

1. For a short time after the November revolution Adolf Hoffmann (USPD), one of the best-known agitators for the Kirchenaustritt movement, was responsible for Prussian church policy.

2. Until 1923 Ludendorff was the undisputed leader of the Völkisch. The 'civilian' Hitler and Frick are still standing clearly beside him.

RNET   Dr. WEBER   FRICK   KRIEBEL   LUDENDORFF   HITLER BRÜCKNER   RÖHM   WAGN

3–5. German-völkisch antisemitism also had a decisive effect on Hitler. Its most influential representatives in Germany included (from left to right) the writer Dietrich Eckart, the former mill engineer Theodo Fritsch and the writer Dr Art Dinter.

6. Ludendorff and Mathilde von Kemnitz were among the champions of a new völkisch religion. This led to the final break with Hitler, who was intent on keeping the NSDAP out of confessional disputes.

7. An antisemitic pamphlet issued by the Deutsch-Völkischer Schutz- and Trutzbund.

haltet den Dieb!!

ruft die Menge, die den Verbrecher verfolgt, um ihn zu fangen, ihm seine Beute abzujagen. Der Dieb schreit mit „haltet den Dieb", um seine Verfolger irrezuführen, um sie von seiner Person abzulenken, und oft gelingt es ihm durch diesen Trick zu entwischen.

Genau so machen es die Juden!

Die Juden mischen sich unter das Volk und stellen sich, als seien sie Sozialdemokraten. Sie schreien, schimpfen und hetzen am lautesten gegen den Kapitalismus und täuschen dadurch das Volk.
Die Juden haben ungeheure Reichtümer an sich gerafft.
Aus Geschäften, die sie unter sich, unter ihren Stammesgenossen gemacht haben, konnten sie diese Reichtümer nicht erwerben, dazu ist ihr Volkskreis zu klein.

Der ungeheure Reichtum der Juden ist erworben durch die Arbeit, den Fleiß und den Schweiß des arbeitsamen deutschen Volkes!

Arbeiter, Soldaten, Bürger, passet auf!

vergesset das nicht, laßt Euch durch das Geschrei, Geschimpfe und Gehetze der Juden nicht von der richtigen Fährte ablenken.
Laßt Euch nicht irreführen! Die Juden sind die Großkapitalisten, durch Eure Arbeit, Euren Fleiß!

Haltet Euch die Juden vom Leibe!
Wählet deutsche Männer zu Euren Führern, keine Juden!

| Um Nachdruck wird gebeten! | Reicht schnell dies Blatt von Hand zu Hand, von Brief zu Brief. Schlagt's an die Wand, und was es sagt, beherzigt tief. | Um Nachdruck wird gebeten! |

The first NSDAP Party
Conference after its
rehabilitation took place in
Weimar in 1926. Artur Dinter,
the Gauleiter of Thuringia (on
the left beside Hitler) still
played an important role in it.
Alongside Dinter in the first
row (from right to left) are
Feder, Rosenberg, Strasser and
the treasurer of the Black
Party.

After 1925 Hitler firmly
insisted that his party should
be neutral in church politics.

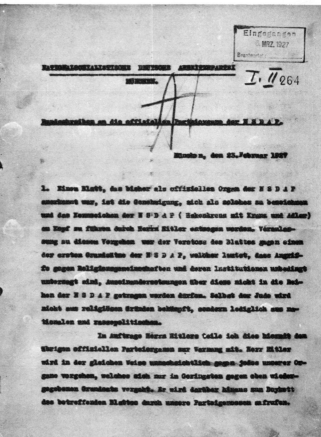

45. Ausgabe · 42. Jahrg. Einzel-Nummer 20 Pf. Österreich 30 Groschen **Bayernausgabe** „Freiheit und Brot!" **Bayernausgabe** München, Freitag, 22. Februar 1929

VÖLKISCHER BEOBACHTER

Herausgeber Adolf Hitler

Kampfblatt der national-sozialistischen Bewegung Großdeutschlands

Eine Rede Hitlers über die Lösung der Römischen Frage

Der Römische Friede und der Nationalsozialismus

Adolf Hitler
über den Friedensschluß zwischen dem Faschismus und dem Vatikan

Die Anerkennung des faschistischen Staatsgedankens durch den Papst — Liberalismus und Nationalismus — Die Rechtfertigung der nationalsozialistischen Außenpolitik

Damit maßen sich diese Organe an, aus ihren parteipolitischen Gründen heraus die weltanschauliche Auffassung des heiligen Vaters einer Korrektur zu unterziehen.

Denn wenn die Kirche heute mit dem faschistischen Italien zu einer Verständigung kommt, die mit dem liberaldemokratischen undenkbar gewesen wäre, dann ist damit unzweifelhaft bewiesen, daß die faschistische Gedankenwelt mit dem Christentum näher verwandt ist, als die jüdisch-liberale, oder gar atheistisch-marxistische, mit der sich die sog. katholische Partei des Zentrums heute zum Schaden jeglichen Christentums und unseres deutschen Volkes so sehr verbunden fühlt. Wenn der Papst heute mit dem Faschismus zu einer solchen Verständigung kommt, dann ist zumindest er der Ansicht, daß der Faschismus und damit der Nationalismus für die Gläubigen vertretbar und mit dem katholischen Glauben vereinbar ist. Wie kann dann aber z. B. der Münchener „Bayerische Kurier" als sog. „katholisches Organ" die Gläubigen der Politik des Papstes gegenüber mit Zweifel über ihre eigene Einstellung erfüllen? Ich sehe die Zeit noch kommen, da der Papst es begrüßen wird, wenn die Kirche vor den Parteien des Zentrums durch den Nationalsozialismus dereinst in Schutz genommen werden wird.

Eines steht fest, und darin sehe ich die große Bedeutung des zwischen dem Papst und Mussolini abgeschlossenen Vertrages: es ist nunmehr durch ein historisches Ereignis nachgewiesen, daß der Nationalismus nicht, wie das deutsche Zentrum und seine Organe lügenhafterweise behaupten, an sich antichristlich und antikirchlich ist. Die nationalistische Weltanschauung — gleichgültig, ob in Italien faschistisch oder in Deutschland nationalsozialistisch — ist eine positiv christliche, und jeder gute Katholik kann ebenso wie jeder überzeugte Protestant ein Gegner des Parlaments und ein Anhänger der Diktatur der nationalen Idee sein.

10. The 1929 Lateran Treaties were evidence for Hitler that the Curia would also negotiate with a National Socialist government in Germany.

11. After the conclusion of the Lateran Treaties Mussolini gave the Pope a motor car; here Pius XI is looking at the new vehicle.

12. The General Superintendent of Brandenburg, Otto Dibelius – here in the year 1930 – was already one of the leading figures of the Prussian Church in the Weimar period.

13. Dibelius speaking at a rally of the Evangelical Reich Alliance of Parents in Potsdam.

14. As President of the Prussian Oberkirchenrat and the German Evangelischer Kirchenausschuss Hermann Kapler (right) occupied a central position within German Protestantism. Next to him is the Bavarian Church President Friedrich Veit, who resigned in 1933.

15. The members of the Kirchenbundesamt, the central authority of the Deutscher Evangelischer Kirchenausschuss, in 1932.

Those depicted are Heckel, Troschke, Schreiber, Hosemann (the Director of the Kirchenbundesamt) with his famous Tirpitz beard, President Kapler, Scholz, Gisevius and Besig.

16. Matthias Erzberger, who was murdered in 1921 by right wing extremists, played an important role as intermediary between German politics and the Curia.

17. The Centre Party Deputy, Prelate Ludwig Kaas, also represented Germany at international negotiations. Here he is in Geneva in 1926 with Rheinbaben and Breitscheid on the occasion of the acceptance of Germany into the League of Nations.

18 and 19. At the brilliant Magdeburg Katholikentag in 1928 the papal Nuncio Pacelli (above with the monstrance) announced the beginning of Catholic Action in Germany.

20. The conclusion of the concordat between the Vatican and Prussia, 1929. Pacelli is leaving the Prussian Ministry of State with the treaty in his hand.

21. After his nomination as Cardinal Secretary of State at

the end of 1929 Pacelli returned to Rome. The picture shows him leaving the palace of the Reich President after handing over his letter of recall.

22. Farewell from the Foreign Minister Dr Curtius (far left), Bishop Schreiber of Berlin and the Prussian Kultusminister Carl Heinrich Becker (left behind the Nuncio).

23 and 24. The Swiss pastor Karl Barth, above left in 1920 with his friend Eduard Thurneysen; on the right a picture from the 1930s. After the War he became the founder of a revival of Protestant theology. From

Professor Pfarrer Dehn

Deutscher Volksgenosse,

dieser Mann will ein christlicher Geistlicher sein und verkündete vom Katheder einer deutschen Hochschule, daß die Verweigerung des Kriegsdienstes sittliche Pflicht ist.

Und er wurde nicht entlassen!

1921 to 1935 he taught at the universities of Göttingen, Münster and Bonn.

25 and 26. Günther Dehn, a representative of Barthian theology, was called as professor to Halle in 1931. Thereupon the National Socialist students launched a witch-hunt against him – a prelude to coming events. On a postcard (left) the National Socialist Students' Association called for his dismissal.

Wir halten fest am Wort Gottes!

Wählt deutschnational

KPD
LISTE
3

Schluss mit diesem System

Wir
schaffen das neue Deutschland!
Wählt Nationalsozialisten Liste 1

27–30. Election posters at the
end of the Weimar republic.
Communists and National
Socialists mobilized the voters
against the system with heroic
figures. The DNVP appealed
to National Protestantism while
the Centre Party bridged the
abyss of 'Terror' and 'Chaos'
with the banner of the cross.

31. Reich Chancellor Heinrich
Brüning and his Secretary of
State Pünder at a polling booth,
April 1932.

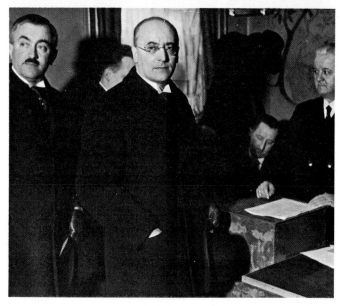

Left poster

Die Kirchen geschlossen!
Tausende Priester ermordet!
Die Religion verlästert und verspottet!

So melden täglich die Zeitungen aus Sowjetrußland. Das ist das Land, in dem der Marxismus offen und brutal das betreibt, was der Kern seines Wesens ist. Und ein Sturm der Entrüstung geht durch die ganze übrige Welt!

Die christlichen Kirchen rufen zum öffentlichen Protest auf!

Während sich so eine Abwehrfront gegen den in Rußland herrschenden religionsfeindlichen Bolschewismus bildet, nimmt die bolschewistische Unterwühlung der Religion und Kultur

in Deutschland selbst

erschreckende Formen an.

Magnus Hirschfeld, Lilienstein, Grünow sind mehr als bloße Namen. Die Jugend wird systematisch verdorben, die Erwachsenen durch Film, Theater, Literatur und Presse immer mehr entwurzelt.

Schleichend geht die Bolschewisierung durch unser Land, bereits soweit vorgeschritten, daß es Millionen schon nicht mehr merken.

Hier Aufklärung zu schaffen und die Front der Charaktere zu erweitern,

ist es der Zweck der großen

Protestkundgebung

die am Freitag, den 14. März, abends 8 Uhr, im

Gürzenich

Abgeordneter Schemm - Bayreuth

Kulturbolschewismus in Deutschland

Nationalsozialistische Deutsche Arbeiterpartei

Right poster

Papst Leo XIII.

nannte das Zentrum die Gefahr für Deutschland.

In seiner Rede in Köln am 27. Juli erklärte der bayerische Ministerpräsident Dr. Held die Solidarität der bayerischen Volkspartei mit dem Zentrum. Also gilt das Wort des Papstes Leo XIII. auch für die **Bayerische Volkspartei.**

In seiner Rede in München am 20. Juli 1932 nannte Dr. Brüning **die Sozialdemokratie seine treueste Helferin.** Also stehen Sozialdemokratie, Bayerische Volkspartei und Zentrum **in einer Linie.**

Die Sozialdemokratie aber ist die Schrittmacherin des Bolschewismus. So mußte die Politik der drei Parteien, Zentrum, Bayerische Volkspartei und Sozialdemokratie zur Bolschewisierung Deutschlands und damit zur Zerstörung Deutschlands führen. Papst Leo XIII. hat also schon zukunftsschauend die Entwicklung der Dinge richtig gesehen. Bayern und das Reich stehen vor dem Abgrund.

Auch die deutsche Kultur lag nie so darnieder wie jetzt. Alle Zweige der Kunst sind verjudet und bolschewisiert. **Die Gottlosenbewegung** ist unter der Herrschaft des Systems, das von **Zentrum, Bayerischer Volkspartei und Sozialdemokratie** getragen ist und erhalten wird,

zu einer Millionenbewegung geworden.

Darum: Bayer, erhalte Dein Bayern!
Deutscher, erhalte das Reich!
Katholik, rette Deine Kirche!
Christ, rette den christlichen Gottesgedanken!

Zerbrich das System! Zerschlage Zentrum, Bayerische Volkspartei und Sozialdemokratie und damit den Bolschewismus!

Adolf Hitler an die Macht!
Wählt Liste 2 Nationalsozialisten!

---

32. The annihilation of the Christian church in Soviet Russia was an important theme for the National Socialists in winning over Christian voters. This is an advertisement for a rally in Cologne with the Gauleiter of Franconia, Hans Schemm, in 1929.

33. The NSDAP also exploited the traditionally tense relationship between the Curia and the Catholic parties in its election propaganda. In Bavaria it laid claim to Pope Leo XIII in its fight against the Centre Party.

34. The rise of the NSDAP: Hitler giving a speech in 1929. The typical gesture makes clear his will to win.

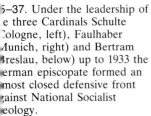
5–37. Under the leadership of the three Cardinals Schulte (Cologne, left), Faulhaber (Munich, right) and Bertram (Breslau, below) up to 1933 the German episcopate formed an almost closed defensive front against National Socialist ideology.

Evangelium im Dritten Reich
für Groß-Berlin

Jahrgang 2, Nr. 6   Sonntag, 5. Februar 1933

Mit uns der Sieg, mit uns das Feldgeschrei: Deutschland erwache! Deutschland du bist frei!

Diese Worte aus dem Sturmlied unseres Wilhelm Kube haben wir in den Jahren der Schmach und Schande so oft als heiligen Schwur gen Himmel schallen lassen. Jawohl, wir glaubten an den Sieg, wir kämpften um den Sieg, und unser Herrgott gab uns den Sieg. Heute steht unser Führer

Adolf Hitler

als Reichskanzler an der Spitze des Deutschen Reiches.

Nach all dem Kampf, nach all den blutigen Opfern der hinter uns liegenden 14 Jahre, falten sich für einen Augenblick nun unsere Hände und stille zieht durch unsere dankerfüllten Herzen des alten Martin Rinckart's schlichtes Dankgebet:

„Nun danket alle Gott mit Herzen, Mund und Händen, Der große Dinge tut an uns und allen Enden."

Wer so denkt und mit uns Gott danken will, der komme zu unserem nachstehend angezeigten Dankgottesdienst in St. Marien.   Karl Fahrenhorst.

Die Glaubensbewegung „Deutsche Christen" veranstaltet am Freitag, dem 3. Februar 1933, in der St. Marienkirche, abends 8 Uhr

einen

Dankgottesdienst

Die Predigt hält der Reichsleiter, Pfarrer Hossenfelder.

Alle Nationalsozialisten und Deutsche Christen, die mit uns Gott danken wollen für den Sieg des 30. Januar 1933, nehmen an diesem Gottesdienst teil.

Telegramm unseres Reichsleiters an den Führer des neuen Deutschlands Adolf Hitler.

Sie und das Deutsche Volk beglückwünsche ich zu dem durch Gottes Fügung gestalteten Ergebnis des 30. Januar. Als Reichsleiter der Glaubensbewegung „Deutsche Christen" versichere ich Sie, mit unserem Gebet hinter Ihnen zu stehen.

Hossenfelder.

Aufruf!

Evangelische Volks- und Glaubensgenossen!

Der evangelische Christ, der sein Volk und seine Kirche lieb hat, wählt am 6. November die Hitler-Bewegung.

Die Hitler-Bewegung ist das gewaltige Sammelbecken nationaler und christlicher Kraft; sie bürgt allein für einen Wiederaufstieg des deutschen Volkes und der evangelischen Kirche.

In Hitler sehen wir den von Gott gerufenen und begnadeten Menschen, durch den der lebendige Gott unserem armen deutschen Volke helfen will. Darum wird jeder, dem es um die Güter des Volkstums und des Evangeliums geht, nationalsozialistisch wählen!

Hossenfelder.

38. Volkstum and Christianity were the key words with which the newly founded 'Faith Movement of German Christians' called for votes for the NSDAP in November 1932 in their journal *Evangelium im Dritten Reich*.

39. The Gauleiter of Brandenburg, Wilhelm Kube (left), political initiator and most important supporter of the German Christians.

40. The Reichsleiter of the German Christians, the young Berlin pastor Joachim Hossenfelder, here at the climax of his career in Autumn 1933 as Vice President of the Prussian Oberkirchenrat and Bishop of Berlin-Brandenburg.

41. While the Protestant church governments were still restrained, the German Christians celebrated the seizure of power with a service of thanksgiving.

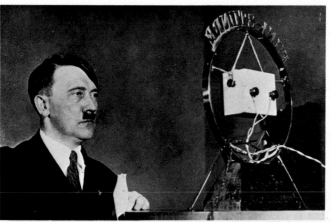

42. Hitler deliberately adopted an air of gravity and trustworthiness when on the evening of 1 February 1933 he read out the appeal of the new government over the radio: 'May the Almighty God take our work into his grace'.

43. One of the last rallies of the Centre Party, on the occasion of the Reichstag elections of March 1933, with Brüning (right) and Prelate Kaas (far left).

44. The 'Potsdam Day', 21 March 1933. Reich President von Hindenburg going to the festal service in the Nicolaikirche.

45. State opening of the new Reichstag, Hindenburg and Hitler in the Garrison Church. Hitler stood in front of the altar and gave his short address from the desk which usually served for the biblical readings.

46. The famous handshake
between the field marshal and
the corporal is a vivid
illustration of the illusion many
Germans had: the Reich
President, whom one could
trust, and the respectful Reich
Chancellor, who served the old
field marshal.

47. The practising Catholics in
Hitler's cabinet included Vice
Chancellor Franz von Papen
(left) and Eltz von Rübenach,
the Minister of Transport; here
at the head of the Berlin
Corpus Christi procession, 15
June 1933.

8. Hitler began his rule with a comprehensive campaign for the confidence of Christians which was not without effect: church communities asked for and received altar Bibles with a dedication by the Reich Chancellor in his own hand.

9. The terrorism of the authorities which was now beginning was often justified by reference to Bolshevik threats to the Reich. The first concentration camps (this picture is of Oranienburg) initially posed above all a pastoral problem to the church. 'This work will usually be done by the community clergy in whose parish such a camp is situated' (Degree of the Prussian Evangelischer Oberkirchenrat, 21 July 1933).

50. First Reich Conference of the German Christians in the former Prussian Herrenhaus in Berlin, April 1933. The storm over the Protestant church begins. Pastor Peter is giving his lecture on 'Church and Volk'. Hossenfelder is in the chair.

51. The two largest Reformed communities in Germany, Elberfeld and Barmen, already centres of church resistance in the west of the Reich in Autumn 1933, speak out for the 'enlisting' of the German Christians.

52. On the morning of 23 March, the day of the Enabling Act, President Kapler learned of an agreement over a Reich concordat and thereupon wrote to the Reich President.

Telegramm **Deutsche Reichspost**

wuppertalbarmen f 53/52 23 2300 =

Deutsches Evangelisches
Kirchenbundesamt
Eing. 24. APR 1933
KA L 1069 Anl.

Aufgenommen
Jahr   Zeit

4.4 0005

Berlin-Charlottenburg

nachts = kirchenbund
praesident kapler
jebenstr 3 berlincharlottenburg =

n groessten wert auf heranziehung der deutschen christen
zur mitarbeit bitten dringend bei herausstellung des
kirchendirektorius wehrkreis pfarrer mueller koenigsberg
einzuschalten leitung fest in kirchlicher hand behalten =
die beiden groessten reformierten gemeinden deutschlands
elberfeld und barmen p windfuhr d humburg kirchenmeister
dr mensing kirchenmeister frohwein +++

Raum für dienstliche Rückfragen

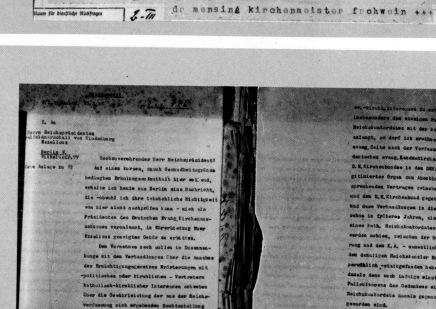

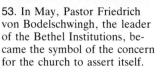

53. In May, Pastor Friedrich von Bodelschwingh, the leader of the Bethel Institutions, became the symbol of the concern for the church to assert itself.

54. Bodelschwingh's opponent was 'the Reich Chancellor's authorized representative', Ludwig Müller, military chaplain in Königsberg. The picture shows him at the Luther celebrations in Eisleben in August 1933.

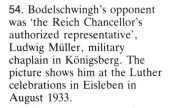

55. Bodelschwingh, accompanied by General

perintendents Vits (left) and
row (right), on the way to a
ntecost service. Behind
delschwingh is his colleague
artin Niemöller.

. (left, bottom) Pentecost
mon by Bodelschwingh in
Zionskirche, Berlin.
delschwingh's choice of a
rking-class community with a
h proportion of Communist
ers was exploited by the
rman Christians as a sign of
political unreliability.

. The National Socialist state
ervenes in the church. On 24
ne, August Jäger was
pointed State Commissioner
all the Protestant churches
Prussia by Kultusminister
st. Jäger (centre) with, from
t to right, Hossenfelder the
ichsleiter of the German
ristians, Assessor Kettner,
stors Dietrich and Lörzer.

. The Prussian
ltusminister Bernhard Rust
eaking at a mass meeting of
rman Christians on 'God
d Volk, Church and State',
rlin, 29 June 1933.

59. As a result of massive intervention by the NSDAP the church elections of 23 July 1933 were a great success for the German Christians. Election propaganda at the church door. On the right the opposition list Evangelium und Kirche, supported by the Young Reformers Movement.

60. The leaders of the German Christians. Sitting, from the left: Kessel, Freitag, Peter, Hossenfelder, Kettner, Nobiling. Standing, from the left, Kersten, Jacubski, Rachner, Propp, Thom, Pichottka, Wieneke-Soldin, Koch, Krüger, Lörzer, de la Croix. Hossenfelder.

ationalsozialistische Deutsche Arbeiterpartei

Reichsleitung

Reichsgeschäftsstelle: München, Briennerstraße 45 ...
Reichs-Nummer: 14901, 15346 u. 16081
Postscheckkonto München 23319

58

Reichspropagandaleitung
Sekretariat.

E i l t !
Streng vertraulich !

An alle Gauleiter.

München, den 14. Juli

Eingeg.
17. JULI 1933
Beantwortet

Sehr geehrter Herr Gauleiter !

Zu den in Kürze stattfindenden Evangelischen Kirchenwahlen ersuchen wir Sie, den "Deutschen
Christen" jede Unterstützung angedeihen zu lassen.

Wir bitten Sie, die Gaupropagandaleitungen
anzuweisen, sofort mit dem zuständigen Vertreter der
"Deutschen Christen in Ihrem Gau Fühlung zu nehmen und
dieser Organisation im Wahlkampf mit Rat und Tat zur Seite
zu stehen.

Aus Prestigegründen muss der Wahlkampf von
den "Deutschen Christen" siegreich durchgeführt werden.
Wir müssen ihnen daher alle Unterstützung geben. Wie Organisation von Massenversammlungen, Plakatierung, Flugzettel-
und Presewerbung zuteil werden lassen. Presse und Rund-
funk werden auch vom Ministerium für Volksaufklärung und
Propaganda eingesetzt.

Die "Deutschen Christen" führen den Wahlkampf, jedoch wird derselbe von der Bewegung gestützt
und organisiert.

Diese Anordnung verbinden wir mit dem Wunsch
des Führers, den "Deutschen Christen" einen vollen Erfolg
zu verschaffen.

Für die Richtigkeit:

Heil Hitler!
gez. Fischer
Reichspropaganda-
Leiter.

Walter Schulze

Zur Kirchenwahl
ein Wort an alle Gemeindeglieder!

Die kirchliche Lage bringt uns plötzlich

Wahlen am 23. Juli.

Wir rufen alle Freunde einer staatsfreien, allein auf Gottes Wort gegründeten Kirche zur Beteiligung an der Wahl auf. Die Not der Stunde zwingt alle, die ihre Kirche lieb haben, zum Zusammenschluß. Es gilt jetzt nicht Partei noch Gruppe, sondern gemeinsame Arbeit am Aufbau unserer Kirche aus dem Glauben allein.

Wir stehen dankbar und entschlossen hinter Hindenburg und Hitler als den Führern unseres Staates, die jetzt durch ihr Eingreifen auch der Kirche den Weg in die Freiheit gebahnt haben. In Treue zu diesem Staate wollen wir für Volk und Vaterland in unserer Kirche arbeiten.

Wir wollen eine deutsche evangelische Kirche, die von volksverbundenen und gegenwartsnahen Männern geleitet wird, eine Volkskirche, deren Pfarrer — wie es auch Hitler fordert — nicht Vertreter einer politischen Weltanschauung sind, sondern wahre Seelsorger und Helfer in den Nöten unserer Tage.

Wir wollen eine Kirche, die im Glauben unserer Väter wurzelt und eine Stätte des Friedens und der Wahrhaftigkeit ist, in der Luthers Wort von der Freiheit eines Christenmenschen sich im Dienst an den Brüdern bewährt.

Wir haben mit schmerzlichem Bedauern erlebt, wie man in den letzten Monaten mit politischen Methoden rücksichtslos die Macht in der Kirche erobern wollte. Um des Gewissens, um der Ehre unserer Kirche und um des Evangeliums willen lehnen wir uns gegen diese Kampfesart auf.

Wer eine Kirche will, die ohne Menschenfurcht Gottes Wort verkündigt und in hingebender Treue unserem Volke dient, der wähle unsere

Liste: „Evangelische Kirche!"

Kirche muß Kirche bleiben!

Wählen kann nur, wer in die kirchliche Wählerliste eingetragen ist. Darum laßt Euch noch heute von Eurem Pfarrer in die Wählerliste eintragen. Wer sich früher schon gemeldet hat, vergewissere sich, daß sein Name in der Wählerliste steht.

---

1. The Reich leadership of the
SDAP instructs the
auleiters to support the
erman Christian church
ection campaign.

62. 'The church must remain
the church'. The church
opposition entered the election
campaign with this slogan
against state intervention.

63. In Bonn Karl Barth had his
own election campaign 'For
the Freedom of the Gospel',
against both German Christians
and Young Reformers.

64. Hitler entrusted his Vice Chancellor Franz von Papen with the negotiations over the concordat in Rome; here he is at an audience with the Pope. Frau von Papen is on the left.

65. Pope Pius XI.

66. The signing of the concordat between the German Reich and the Holy See on 20 July 1933 in the Vatican. From the left, Kaas, von Papen, Mgr Pizzardo, Pacelli, Mgr Ottaviani, Ministerial Director Buttmann, Mgr Montini, Counsellor Klee.

67. Abbot Alban Schachleiter, a Hitler enthusiast, was a constant scandal to the Bavarian episcopate. On this picture which shows him under a portrait of Hitler he wrote: 'Faithful to the Führer but also faithful to Christ and his Church!' 'Heil Hitler!'

68 and 69. The papal Nuncio in Berlin, Cesare Orsenigo, leaving St Hedwig's Cathedral, 7 September 1933, after a solemn service of thanksgiving to mark the ratification of the concordat.

70 and 71. Mass wedding in SA
uniform in the Lazaruskirche in
Berlin, 2 July 1933. 'Won back
to the church by the Faith
Movement of German
Christians', commented
Goebbels.

72. Karl Barth's battle-cry
Theological Existence Today
became a signal which was
widely listened to. The original
title of the manuscript, which
can still be seen clearly, betrays
its theological thrust: 'From
Church Politics to the Church!'

73–76. The community of
Dahlem in Berlin became a
focal point for opposition in the
Prussian church. The
preaching of Pastors (from the
top) Röhricht, Niemöller and

Müller in the Jesus-Christus-
Kirche drew large
congregations.

77 and 78. The Prussian
General Synod of 5 September
1933 – the 'Brown Synod' –
marked a turning point. With
the passing of the 'Aryan
Paragraph' and the withdrawal
of the opposition the split in the
Prussian Church began.
Above, the President of the
Synod, at the same time
President of the
Oberkirchenrat, Dr Werner,
giving the Hitler salute. Below,
a view of the chamber. To the
right at the front are Werner's
representatives Hossenfelder
and Jäger.

79. The 450th anniversary of the birth of Luther was celebrated all over the Reich in countless rallies. This is a Luther festival at Eisleben on 20 August 1933.

80. The National Synod in
Wittenberg on 27th September
1933 was to mark the end of the
church revolution. The
participants are welcomed by
the Oberbürgermeister of
Wittenberg. In the front row on
the far left is Professor Fezer;
second from left the Land
Bishop of Prussia, Ludwig
Müller; next to him the Land
Bishop of Hamburg, Simon
Schöffel.

81. Land Bishop Theophil Wurm of Württemberg gave the festal sermon in the Schlosskirche.

82. Professor Fezer of Tübingen (at the microphone) proposes Ludwig Müller as Reich Bishop.

83. The new Reich Bishop giving his first declaration of principles. Alongside him are the members of the first 'Clergy Ministry', from the left Hossenfelder, Schöffel, Weber and Dr Werner.

84. After the election. The new
Reich Bishop, surrounded by
SA men, raises his arm in the
Hitler salute.

85. The National Synod closes
in the evening with a great
torchlight procession in front of
the Luther monument.

86. The heroic picture of Luther characteristic of the German Christians: the fruit of a centuries-old nationalist misunderstanding of the Reformer.

87. Christian cross and Swastika. The symbol of the co-ordination of the Evangelical Church with the Third Reich.

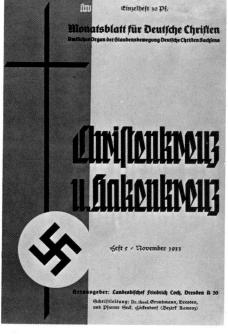

88. Barely twenty-five, Baldur von Schirach became Reich youth leader. At the end of 1933 Ludwig Müller negotiated an agreement with him which handed over Protestant youth to the Hitler Youth.

89. Ludwig Müller loved wearing medals and showing off in the company of the military and the nobility (here he is with Prince August Wilhelm of Prussia, on the right). His Turkish Order of the Crescent (on the right side of his chest), from the Dardanelles front, was much mocked.

Warum muß der Katholik die Reichstagsliste Adolf Hitlers wählen?

Weil im nationalsozialistischen Staat an sich und durch das

Reichskonkordat

1. die Religion geschützt ist,
2. der kirchliche Frieden gesichert ist,
3. die öffentliche Sittlichkeit gewahrt bleibt,
4. der Sonntag geheiligt wird,
5. die Bekenntnisschule erhalten ist,
6. das katholische Gewissen nicht mehr belastet ist,
7. der Katholik vor dem Gesetz und im Staatsleben gleichberechtigt ist,
8. die katholischen Vereine u. Verbände, soweit sie ausschließlich religiösen, charitativen und kulturellen Zwecken dienen, frei arbeiten können.

Deshalb muß der Katholik am 12. Nov. so wählen:

Volksabstimmung ➡ Ja ⊗

⊕ ⬅ Reichstagswahl Adolf Hitler

Ein feierlicher Augenblick von der Grundsteinlegung zum Haus der deutschen Kunst.

Der päpstliche Nuntius Vasallo di Torregrossa spricht eben zum Führer:

„Ich habe Sie lange nicht verstanden. Ich habe mich aber lange darum bemüht. Heute versteh' ich Sie."

Auch jeder deutsche Katholik versteht heute Adolf Hitler und stimmt am 12. November mit:

„Ja"!

90 and 91. At the election and plebiscite of 12 November Hitler reaped the fruits of the Reich concordat by surprisingly high 'yes' votes, above all in predominantly Catholic circles of the electorate.

92. Papen, too, involved himself in the election campaign with a major speech to the 'Arbeitsgemeinschaft Katholischer Deutscher'. Here he is at the vote on 12 November.

93 and 94. The beginning of the end of the German Christians; the meeting of German Christians from the Gau of Greater Berlin in the Sports Palace, 13 November 1933. At the presidential table, from the left Gauobmann Krause, Gau Executive Director Thieder, an unknown figure, Pastors Tausch and Jacubski, President Werner, Provost Lörzer, Bishop Peter, and consistory councillors Freitag and Nobiling.

no longer be any doubt; the Protestant church had been caught up in quite unusual turmoil.

Events took a similar course in Ludwig Müller's homeland of East Prussia. On 8 June the East Prussian Pastors' Association convened in Königsberg. A motion by the German Christians calling for a legal investigation of Bodelsch-wingh's election was rejected, after vigorous discussion, by 105 votes to 51. Here, too, about 30 German Christians then left the assembly, which thereupon almost unanimously passed a declaration in support of Bodelschwingh. On June 11 the core of the group that championed Bodelschwingh published another appeal calling for the mobilization 'of all the constructive forces of the church' for the 'lawfully elected Reich Bishop'. Here, too, the names were those which later appeared in support of the Pastors' Emergency League and the Confessing Church in East Prussia.[24]

In Hanover it was the Pentecost Conference that gave the impulse to organizing a 'Landeskirche Assembly'. Its first leaflet, dated 17 June, contained the slogan of the fight for Bodelschwingh up and down the country: 'The church must remain the church; the church must become the church.' The signatories – who again became the nucleus of the later Confessing community in Hanover – declared: 'We are confident that our Land Bishop Pastor Dr Friedrich von Bodelschwingh, chosen to be Reich Bishop, will carry through the work of reconstructing the church upon a Reformation foundation.'[25]

While in Hanover it was a matter of strengthening the position of the Land Bishop, in Württemberg – as in Mecklenburg – the gathering of the Confessing group began against the will of the church administration. The report on a meeting of the theological study groups in the church in Stuttgart early in June demonstrated how carefully the pastors of Württemberg were moving in view of the vote of the Württemberg Church President Theophil Wurm for Müller and his moderate German Christian approach. In order to avoid a schism in the church, the group refused to acknowledge two camps 'into which the pastors of Württemberg might divide. Rather,' the report continued, 'we remind each of our colleagues of the charge laid upon him at ordination, which clearly obliges him to proclaim the biblical gospel.' Otherwise the working groups did not dispute the fact that in many respects they simply felt 'united in solidarity with the Young Reformers'.[26] This approach, which sought – even at the cost of some lack of clarity – at all events to avoid, or at least to mitigate, the polarization of the church, still remained typical of the pastors of Württemberg even later, and very soon made them incur vigorous criticism, even in their own church.

But the question 'Müller or Bodelschwingh?' was not only being discussed by pastors and parishes, church associations and groups up and down the country; the universities, too, were increasingly being drawn into the controversy. Surprisingly – when one thinks of the radical nationalism that expressed itself so readily in the Dehn case – here, too, the German Christians did not find everywhere the support that they expected. To be sure, in Tübingen the thoroughly German Christian faculty succeeded in persuading the student body to make a declaration of support for Müller,[27] but the 'Young Church' reported a devastating failure from Breslau.[28] There was also a defeat in Berlin. The German Christians here had called for a student rally on 19 June, but the majority of those present left the hall – not without powerful prompting from Bonhoeffer –

before there could be a vote for a resolution supporting Müller.[29] Three days later, Bonhoeffer and the Berlin student pastor Ernst Bronisch-Holtze organized a discussion between Young Reformers and German Christians. The strong response to it – two thousand students came – was an impressive demonstration of the interest in the church question. In contrast to the propaganda meetings of the German Christians, which in the end were simply concerned to mobilize the masses, the entire emphasis of this meeting lay upon the theological arguments from both sides. In it Bonhoeffer repeated some thoughts from his paper 'The Church and the Jewish Question'. He argued that the weak, as understood in Romans 14, were precisely those who now seemed so strong, since they were setting up a racial law. The others had to bear this in faith as brothers. Should, however, the law of the weak actually be made the law of the church, an Evangelical Council would have to make a decision. 'The last possibility that Protestantism recognizes is then separation.'[30]

Decisions and divisions took place over these weeks throughout the Protestant church. The innumerable discussions and declarations, meetings and confessions of faith, the whole feverish activity which, in retrospect, characterizes the picture of this period, should not, however, conceal the essential point. Every individual pastor who decided in public against the German Christians in June 1933 was making a personal decision which – as things stood – had incalculable consequences. 'The Bodelschwingh Front against Hitler'[31] ran the newspaper headlines. Anyone who joined this front in future risked being counted an enemy of state.

Pastor Hugo Hahn of Dresden, a brother of the Pastor Traugott Hahn who was shot dead by the Red Army in Dorpat in 1919, who later was to become an important figure in the Confessing Church, recorded this move towards a decision in his memoirs. Originally a naive Lutheran nationalist, open to the Faith Movement, Hahn understood the necessity of taking a public step in view of the dispute over Bodelschwingh. 'I felt,' he reported, 'that for conscience' sake I could no longer remain silent. The struggle in the church was repugnant to my nature. At the same time I was conscious of the fact that a public stand against the German Christians would put me in personal danger.' After encouragement from his wife and an unhelpful last exchange of views with the leading figure of the Faith Movement in Dresden, Pastor Friedrich Coch, on the second day of Pentecost Hahn went into the pulpit in the Frauenkirche with the resolve to lay matters openly before the congregation. As he later described this moment: 'In the course of the sermon I read a statement, written down word for word, that as the pastor of the congregation entrusted to me I could no longer remain silent about what was going on in the church. The ungodly struggle of the German Christians against Reich Bishop von Bodelschwingh was an offence against the church... I based my declaration on the passage Matthew 18.1ff., where our Lord speaks sharply about giving offence. The impression on the congregation was strong. It was the first time in Dresden – and moreover in such a prominent place as the pulpit of the Frauenkirche – that such an open and sharp attack on German Christians had been made.'[32]

The picture of these June weeks differs from Landeskirche to Landeskirche, from town to town, indeed from community to community. Much still held together; there were surprising common factors but also shifting boundaries which again and again obscured the dividing lines between the Party, the German Christians, the church administrations and the Young Reformers. Yet it is possible to note as a result of these turbulent weeks for the Protestant church as a whole some facts which decisively determined the further development of the church question in Germany. First of all these confrontations led to an alertness in the church of a kind that had not existed for centuries. This alertness was a precondition for the formation in all the Landeskirchen of groups which understood the decisive character of the situation. At this time no one yet knew exactly what the decision was all about – whether it was about Bodelschwingh or Müller, about Landeskirche or Reichskirche, about confessionalism or unionism, or simply about the confession of faith in a broad sense. Nevertheless, in these groups the Confessing Church was already in the making. The groups were just waiting, as it were, for the cue to band together and together establish the substance of the decision on the basis of which their separation from the church would come about. The continuity in both personnel and concerns between these groups and the later Councils of Brethren is so great that there can be no doubt about this.

At first the outcome of the struggle, which from early June on had gradually come to grip the whole church, still appeared open. On the Sunday after his election Bodelschwingh had asked Pastors Martin Niemöller and Gerhard Stratenwerth 'to stand by his side as personal adjutants' for a few weeks, and as early as Monday, 29 May, he and a few colleagues had started work in two rooms of the Kirchenbundesamt. He still had no intimation of the resolve of the Faith Movement. Rather, he thought that he could establish a reasonable, fraternal relationship with Ludwig Müller by means of a frank conversation.[33] He was strengthened in his conviction by a flood of declarations of approval – on a completely unexpected scale, from both inside and outside Germany – which arrived in Berlin and Bethel over the next few days. 'From all over the Reich,' reported the *Vossische Zeitung* as early as 29 May, 'and from German Protestants abroad, telegrams keep arriving which indicate delighted approval of this choice. Youth and study associations, theology students and professors, pastors' organizations and charitable organizations – all place themselves behind the man called to be leader of the Protestant church.' The paper surely reflected a widespread hope when in a reference to the continuing opposition of the German Christians it pointed out 'that the cohesive force that radiates from Bodelschwingh's personality will yet be successful in resolving this conflict'.[34]

There can be no doubt that Bodelschwingh could in fact count on an extraordinarily broad base of support within the Protestant church. But Pentecost already demonstrated that this base was not as unified as it appeared.

On the Wednesday before Pentecost, still in the first week of his office, Bodelschwingh had sent a greeting to the church administrations, asking that it should be read at the services on the first day of Pentecost. It was formulated in a biblical style and on behalf of the whole church prayed 'that it should build its new house upon the solid ground which alone endures in the storms of time'.[35] It was hardly surprising that Hossenfelder should have immediately protested to Kapler, and even announced 'spontaneous protest demonstrations during worship'.[36] In fact there were incidents in only a few places, as in Berlin-Friedenau. There, while the greeting was being read to a packed church, a small group stood up and interrupted with cries of 'In the name of the National Socialist Party, we object!' Nothing could be heard in the confusion which followed; but after that the greeting was read without disturbance.[37]

Much more disquieting than such incidents was the fact that a series of Lutheran church administrations refused to forward the greeting to the community pastors. These were the churches that had already voted against Bodelschwingh and for Müller on 26 and 27 May: Bavaria, Württemberg, Brunswick, Hamburg, Mecklenburg and Schleswig-Holstein. The reason given was always the same. As Hans Meiser, Land Bishop designate of Bavaria, put it to his Hamburg colleague Schöffel: 'We in Bavaria are taking no orders of any kind from the Reich Bishop designate as long as his legal position is not clarified beyond dispute. So we have not even had the Pentecost declaration read here, and we have decided to follow a very clear line in order to force the gentlemen in Berlin, too, to make things completely clear.'[38] The Württemberg Church President noted laconically von Bodelschwingh's appeal: 'In view of the legal situation and the attitude of the Bavarian Landeskirche, the Pentecost message has not been sent on to the pastors.'[39]

The fact that no fewer than six Landeskirchen refused to pass on the Pentecost greeting demonstrated just how insecure Bodelschwingh's position really was. Certainly the legal status of the 27 May election was doubtful. But it was equally certain that in the circumstances the demand for a legal review of the elections in fact amounted to a revision of the decision for Bodelschwingh. The increasingly urgent inquiries about the legal situation which arrived in Berlin from the same Landeskirchen during June also leave no doubt that the legal problems were merely being used as a pretext. Bodelschwingh was not wanted and there was a wish to get rid of him, as he was increasingly regarded as the crucial obstacle to the desired collaboration of state and church. Although the Lutheran Marahrens fought for Bodelschwingh to the end, alone and uncompromisingly, it was certainly no accident that these six churches were without exception Lutheran. For them, the idea of having to build the church outside, or even against, the new state was even harder to bear than it was for the Protestant church as a whole.

Württemberg started things off on 30 May with a telegram conveying the urgent request 'that the final selection of the Reich Bishop be carried out only after acceptance of the constitution'.[40] Quite obviously Wurm was so much under Fezer's influence that he accepted the German Christian version of Bodelschwingh's election completely. Already on 2 June an additional inquiry arrived from Schwerin by telegram, signed by Rendtorff: 'Request urgently immediate public clarification of legal basis of Reich Bishop. Confusion intolerable, grows daily.'[41] But in Mecklenburg the confusion did not result from the legal questions about the election, but solely from Rendtorff's action in joining the Party, his support of Müller, and his attempt to commit the Mecklenburg pastors to a German Christian line. No less transparent was the letter from the Schleswig-Holstein church government dated 9 June.[42] For the unanimous resolution of this church administration to convene a meeting of the leading organs of the Kirchenbund to review the 27 May election originated in a body which in the meantime had firmly endorsed the new direction in state and church. At this time Bavaria was operating in an especially unfortunate way. A declaration inspired by the church administration which was passed on 12 June at a meeting of the Bavarian pastors' association contained the remarkable sentence: 'It is imperative that the authorities responsible immediately settle the dispute, if need be at the cost of the personal sacrifice of individuals.' And something of the motive behind the declaration was revealed when it continued: 'The course originally taken must be resumed. First of all the office and constitution must be created. As representatives of a Lutheran Landeskirche we expect the Lutheranism intimately bound up with German Volkstum to retain its full force here.' So that Bodelschwingh could not possibly overlook this declaration, it was sent to him by the Bavarian Dean Friedrich Langenfass with the open comment that the 'personal sacrifice' referred to him, Bodelschwingh.[43]

On 13 June Schwerin followed again with a formal petition to the Kirchenausschuss for a resolution that the steps so far taken were to represent 'no obligation of any kind for the final decision as to the person of the future Reich Bishop'. The reason given made it clear that the legal question was only a pretext: 'If the nomination of the first Reich Bishop takes place without the co-operation of the representatives of national renewal, then the work of reform is endangered and perhaps even shown from the beginning to be under an illusion as to its external objective.'[44] On 14 June the Council of the Thuringian Landeskirche let it be known that 'a hallmark of the nationalist revolution' was 'that the reform had always been accomplished lawfully... We are of the opinion that in the reconstruction of the church... the procedure must accord with this principle all the more.'[45] Finally, on 17 June, in accordance with the regulations, six members proposed by telegram the convening of the Kirchenausschuss 'for the purpose of reviewing the questions connected with the procedures in the appointment of Pastor Dr von Bodelschwingh as Reich Bishop'. The signatories once again brought together the whole group of those Landeskirchen which were the less willing, the longer the situation continued, to engage in confrontation with the state over Bodelschwingh: Meiser of Munich, Mordhorst of Kiel, Reichardt of Eisenach, Rendtorff of Schwerin, Schöffel of Hamburg and Wurm of Stuttgart.[46]

Given this situation, the outcome of the decisive last session of the Kirchenausschuss, which was called on 19 June for 23 and 24 June at Eisenach, became increasingly doubtful.

This was all the more the case because even in Berlin – where innumerable conversations, negotiations, meetings and telephone calls took place during those weeks – Bodelschwingh's position began to be increasingly difficult, in spite of continuing approval from the church and powerful efforts on the part of the Young Reformers. This was connected above all with political developments. In the week after Pentecost the Reich Minister of the Interior became the first official government authority to intervene in the dispute. In a lengthy conversation with Bodelschwingh on 10 June he expressed his unease about the difficulties which had arisen and at the same time suggested a compromise. Bodelschwingh 'should certainly remain in and carry on the office, but declare that the final decision on the question of the bishop should be made by the Reich Synod'. This could happen either through an election or through a vote of confidence.[47] This compromise suggestion was presumably meant quite honourably. At this time Frick was certainly more on Bodelschwingh's side, even if as matters stood he could make his influence felt in this direction only to a limited extent.[48] Bodelschwingh nevertheless saw matters correctly when he rejected the Reich Minister of the Interior's suggestion. By leaving open the question as to who should occupy the office, he asserted, it would remain an object of German Christian agitation right up to the time the Reich Synod met. The victory of the Faith Movement would become all the more probable, 'the more the government bodies take a one-sided position, as they have already begun to do'.[49] One result of this rejection, however, was that the Reich Minister of the Interior was out of the game for the time being. And that gave Ludwig Müller a free hand.

On 12 June Müller had again met with Hitler. The very next day he explained to the Director of the Kirchenbundesamt, Johannes Hosemann, in a long and confidential conversation that the Chancellor could 'only give his approval to the Reich Bishop... if in some way the people had been consulted and had given its approval'. Until that time the Chancellor did not wish to receive either the Reich Bishop or the Committee of Three. The Chancellor had also agreed with the Reich President 'for the time being to discontinue receptions until the situation was clarified'.[50] Soon afterwards, Ludwig Müller also officially informed the Committee of Three of these facts. A letter dated 15 June – which Müller simultaneously released to the press – stated: 'The Chancellor has expressed to me his extraordinary regret that the labours for the reconstruction of the German Evangelical Church have taken a difficult and thoroughly disagreeable turn. He has rejected my request to receive its authorized representatives. He also refuses to receive Pastor Dr von Bodelschwingh. Similarly, any reception by the Reich President is at present impossible.' For the Kapler Committee, as well as for Bodelschwingh himself, all political paths were thus blocked. More than that, the letter was understood by the public to be a clear rejection on the part of the Reich government of the church's action. That made the opinion expressed by Ludwig Müller in the same letter, that a recognized office of Reich Bishop did not yet exist as long as the new constitution was not in force, all the more telling. The new constitution required 'the assent of the people of the church as well as of the Reich'. In conclusion Müller therefore suggested to the Kapler Committee that new negotiations should be undertaken with the aim 'of preparing new elections in all the Landeskirchen, or of finding another way out of the existing difficulties'.[51] The inconspicuous last clause was, of course, a suggestion that the German Christian assault on the Landeskirchen could be avoided by dropping Bodelschwingh and nominating him, Müller, as Reich Bishop.

In spite of the rapidly deteriorating situation, Bodelschwingh and his friends did not give up. After long joint discussions, Marahrens, Bishop of Hanover, who continued to be the only Lutheran to give Bodelschwingh unconditional support, made a last attempt to get to Hitler. As he declared on 17 June in a long letter to the Chancellor, he was well aware that Hitler believed he 'should refuse to receive the churches at this time'. However, Marahrens would be neglecting 'the conscientious duty weighing on him' if he did not attempt 'to express with all candour, in the presence of the Chancellor, what no other person in our people has such a clear right to hear...'

Marahrens ended by saying that his house had been 'devoted to the movement for years' and was 'open, as the house of a Protestant pastor, to the onrushing life of the awakened German nation'.[52] The letter went unanswered.

Bodelschwingh put the same request to the Reich President the same day. 'I see,' he wrote to him, 'that final decisions are at stake, including decisions about the future of our Volk and Fatherland.' But Ludwig Müller had evidently done his homework quite well. For Hindenburg wrote back on 21 June that although he shared Bodelschwingh's concerns, he would ask him to refrain from pressing his request. A reception at the present moment would be interpreted 'as taking a one-sided position' and would draw him – Hindenburg – 'into the dispute between the two trends'. 'I consider it advisable,' continued the Reich President, thus taking the line that Hitler wanted him to, 'that first you and perhaps a representative of the other trend should meet for a personal discussion – perhaps under the chairmanship of the Minister of the Interior, whose responsibility it is, and make an effort to build a bridge between the opposing positions.' He would be very glad to convey a request to this effect to the Minister of the Interior.[53]

On 19 June Bodelschwingh finally sent an urgent letter to Rudolf Hess, who since the end of April had been Hitler's official deputy 'in all questions of Party leadership'.[54] In it, he asked for a reply to three questions: '1. Are the Protestant National Socialists obliged by an order of the Reich leadership of the NSDAP to support the German Christians or take a position along their lines? 2. Would non-affiliation to the German Christians in terms of the first question result in expulsion from the Party? 3. If not, would it lead to an official Party investigation?'[55] These were in fact the crucial points. They showed how clearly Bodelschwingh saw things. However, they also showed how little he was able to change the situation. This letter, too, went unanswered. And public opinion which could have compelled such an answer no longer existed.

Within the church, too, the last attempts were made from Berlin and Hanover to shore up the crumbling front. Here the most important figure was without question the Bavarian Land Bishop Hans Meiser. Meiser was the leader of the Lutheran group, and if he stood by Bodelschwingh, then Württemberg would follow. A divergent vote from other, smaller Landeskirchen would then have been tolerable. Marahrens therefore asked Paul Althaus, the Erlangen theologian, to bring his influence to bear on Meiser. Surprisingly, Althaus had meanwhile split from his friend Hirsch and informed Marahrens of the fact. On 19 July the Bishop of Hanover wrote back and urgently requested the hesitant Althaus for an opinion. 'In my view,' ran the most important sentence, 'the question is the decisive one as to whether the course is to be set in the direction of the state or in the direction of the church. For me, the answer is quite clear. Everything, but absolutely everything, shows that the groups rallied around Müller are heading in the wrong direction.'[56] Althaus had in fact already decided that very day to write a letter to Meiser. Although the theology about which he wrote was the very theology which he himself had founded and advocated along with Hirsch, he now proved to be frightened of the consequences. 'As I see it,' he now entreated Meiser, 'I can only ask: please take care that the German Christians do not win: I see no alternative than to stand by Bodelschwingh. I will publicly declare my position in the next few days. I hope my Erlangen colleagues will follow me... If we must suffer defeat by the German Christians and others – why does Bavaria abandon Hanover in advance and not stand by the first nomination to the very end?'[57]

It was easy for Bavaria to answer this question. Meiser himself gave his reasons to the Kirchenausschuss a few days later. To the Bavarian Land Bishop, who had been installed in his position not long beforehand with the ceremonial assent of the state and the Party,[58] peace in his Landeskirche was more important than the struggle for a remote Reich Bishop who was suspected of being a supporter of union and who in addition could provoke incalculable political problems. It is hard to avoid the conclusion that the provincialism of the Landeskirchen was an essential reason for the fall of Bodelschwingh.

In other respects even the innermost circle of leading figures was seized with helplessness during these days. On 21 June Niemöller asked the Reich Bishop to release him 'from his more intimate staff group', at the same time indicating that in his own opinion, in the impending decision at Eisenach the only question was 'whether it will be those who want to preach an alien gospel who are forced into schism or those who stand upon the ground of the reformed confessions'.[59] Hermann Hesse, the Reformed representative in the Kapler Committee, reacted in a different way. He told the Reich Bishop designate to his face that his position was 'impossible'. 'We have to reckon with the opposition of at least six Lutheran churches. Moreover, there are the German Christians with their claim to total power. Finally, according to the statements of last week the Reich Chancellor and the Reich President regard us with considerable reserve.' Hesse's advice was as ill-fated as his role in the Committee of Three. He advised Bodelschwingh to stand down voluntarily along the lines of the proposal made by the Reich Minister of the Interior.[60]

In spite fo all this resistance, doubt and suspicion, Bodelschwingh held firm. While on all sides general accommodation was winning the day, he continued to stand by his task unperturbed. He was strengthened in this by the undiminished approval which was coming to him from church people. Just as important, however, was the certainty that outside Hanover he could go on depending on what was still by far the largest and most important German Landeskirche: the Old Prussian Union. On 8 June its supreme body, the Old Prussian Church Senate, had welcomed Bodelschwingh's election with only two votes in opposition, and that very day, 21 June, only two days before the crucial session in Eisenach, had welcomed him to give a personal greeting.[61] But despite the Lutheran resistance it was still an open question how a decision in the Kirchenbund might turn out if Prussia and Hanover backed Bodelschwingh with equal determination.

In the meantime, however, a development was under way in Prussia which was finally to lead to a dramatic heightening of the conflict and after that to a complete change in the situation.

On 6 June the sixty-six year old Hermann Kapler, the man who had nominated Bodelschwingh and on 27 May had finally got him accepted, and who at the same time in his office held all the reins of the Prussian Church along with the Kirchenbund, had asked the Prussian Church Senate to release him at the end of the month. The ailing President had been thinking of resigning for a long time. That he now so quickly turned his thoughts into reality was connected not least with his disappointment over the lack of unity in the Landeskirchen, revealed in the negotations on 26 and 27 May.[62] Kapler no longer felt up to the struggle that now loomed.

348

Few resignations can have been more untimely than this one. For with Kapler's departure Bodelschwingh lost his most important supporter, whom no one even began to match in reputation and influence. At the same time the Prussian Church found itself in an extraordinarily difficult situation. And the Kirchenbund, which was difficult to hold together anyway, literally became leaderless at the most dangerous moment of its history.

As early as 8 June the Church Senate accepted Kapler's resignation. Even before the conclusion of the meeting Kapler left Berlin to begin a vacation from which he returned only once – on 23 June – to take leave of the Kirchenausschuss as well.

The negotiations over a replacement began immediately after Kapler's departure. In this connection one point was especially delicate. The so-called 'political clause' of the Prussian church treaty of 1931 provided for the possibility of questioning the civil government in advance of a nomination for such an office. And Kube had already declared early in April, at the first Reich conference, that the NSDAP would 'ruthlessly' exploit the personal political potential of this treaty. Hence the concern that the state would use the opening to appoint a man of its choice to the top post was justified. In addition, there was the general insecurity over the future of the church, which could cause problems over an appointment at this moment. All of this resulted in the position for the moment being administered only provisionally, by Ernst Stoltenhoff, General Superintendent of the Rhineland. The decisive element in the selection of this emphatically nationalistic man was the expectation – as the Oberkirchenrat itself put it soon afterwards – 'that by the evidence of his whole personality and the conduct of his office, he gave the best guarantee that he would work on the best terms with the state, the National Socialist Party and finally the Faith Movement of German Christians.'[63] After the relevant official in the Oberkirchenrat had established in a meeting with Ministerial Director Trendelenburg, head of the Church Department in the Kultusministerium, that the state 'had no interest, according to the terms of the church treaty',[64] in a merely provisional appointment, on 21 June the Church Senate unanimously passed the relevant resolution. This seemed to settle this difficult question for the time being.

All of these developments, intentions and plans – and in addition all the hopes, anxieties, desires and fears that had built up in the meantime – now concentrated on 23 and 24 June, when the Kirchenausschuss and Kirchenbundesrat gathered in Eisenach for the crucial meeting. All down the history of German Protestantism since the time of the Reformation, hardly any church assembly had faced more difficult decisions than this one. And that was also clear to all the participants.[65]

The long series of meetings began on 22 June with a conference of Lutheran bishops to which Meiser had invited his colleagues. It showed – even more plainly and openly than the discussion in the Kirchenausschuss on the following day – how resolutely the majority of these bishops opposed Bodelschwingh. Even Marahrens' detailed report on the situation and his plea that the important thing now was for the churches to remain 'undivided and united' did not change anything. Rather, Schöffel, who was the first to reply, demonstrated the basic political and theological considerations governing the Lutheran support for Müller. Müller, he asserted, was indeed a 'political candidate'. But the same was true of Bodelschwingh. Was the latter not, Schöffel argued, 'the candidate of politically reactionary forces? ...the symbol of the wish at all events to be free from this state? Should the church offer the state a battle on the Marne?' Bishops Mordhorst of Kiel and Rendtorff of Schwerin agreed emphatically with Schöffel, Rendtorff all the more emphatically, with the remark that he would rather leave the assembly than say '*pater peccavi*'. Wurm, who found no theological difficulties in siding with the Young Reformers, saw things more in terms of church politics. The influence of Fezer was unmistakable when Wurm argued in favour of strengthening the church line of the German Christians against the radical line of Hossenfelder. Schöffel, on the other hand, once again justified his vote in a specifically theological way. The old liberal interpretation of the relationship between church and state had finally to disappear. The ideal he had in mind was 'how the old bishops used to stand by a Kaiser or a king. A Reich Bishop is not the same as a President elected by a Synod.' However, he had not noticed any leadership qualities of this kind in the pastor from Bethel. 'If Bodelschwingh gets to the top, that means the death of our church.' Without any formal resolution, the discussion, despite Marahrens' persistent objections, finally ended in a decision to compel Bodelschwingh in one way or another to declare that he considered himself merely a candidate for the office of Reich Bishop, and that he was proceeding on the assumption that a final election had still to take place.[66] The aim of the bishops was obvious. They were interested above all in avoiding a confrontation with the state and in uniting the church on a moderate German Christian line – on what, for example, they thought to be the Müller-Fezer line.

While the Lutheran bishops were discussing, and the committee members of the Kirchenbund were on their way to Eisenach from all over Germany, a completely different decision had been taken in Berlin. Its consequences increasingly began to overshadow the Eisenach negotiations. The morning papers of 23 June published the following letter from the Prussian Kultusminister, Bernhard Rust, to the Director of his Church Department, Dr Trendelenburg: 'Dear Dr Trendelenburg, The appointment of a Provisional President of the Evangelischer Oberkirchenrat without instruction and consultation with the Prussian Minister for Science, Art and National Education represented a step by the Old Prussian Landeskirche which cannot fail to have serious consequences for the relationship of the state to the church. To resolve the questions to which this gives rise, an official is needed to protect me from surprises of that kind and whose conception of the nationalist state completely coincides with the one I represent. I am therefore suspending you from your office with immediate effect.' 'Kultusminister Rust,' the papers went on to report, 'has at the same time entrusted Landesgerichtsrat Jäger with the leadership of the Church Department in the Kultusministerium.'[67]

Not one of those who read this news in the hotels of Eisenach that morning with a greater or lesser sense of disquiet could have had even the remotest idea of what it really meant. For it introduced for the first time the name of a man who, as a key figure of National Socialist church policy from this point until its temporary defeat at the end of 1934, was to contribute more to the suppression and destruction of the Protestant church than any other individual.

August Jäger,[68] at that time forty-six years old, was the son of a Nassau pastor and consistory councillor who at one time had sought in vain the position of

Land Bishop of Nassau. Jaǧer himself, as a member of the conservative Nassau Alliance for Bible and Christianity, had belonged to the church council of the Marktkirche in Wiesbaden. But in 1931 he had had to resign his office because of a divorce. It is therefore possible that, being as ambitious as he was ruthless, Jäger had personal reasons for seeking prominence above all in the church-political field after joining the Party on 1 March 1933.[69] Be this as it may, as early as April he appeared as a speaker at the first conference of the German Christians in Wiesbaden, and at the beginning of May he functioned as leader of the Faith Movement church district of Greater Wiesbaden. In this capacity, on 8 April he wrote a letter to August Kortheuer, Land Bishop of Nassau, which already contained his complete view of church politics and is the key to all that followed: 'The particular reason why I am writing today is that it is certainly high time now to settle certain main issues. In order for the way to be made clear for the pending reorganization of church affairs, it appears necessary to dissolve all church bodies, from community councils to the Landeskirchentag.' Jäger went on to make it crystal clear that he did not feel himself restricted by legal scruples, but rather represented a new and revolutionary legal interpretation. 'In this respect,' he continued, 'as indeed in general I might point out that in all the questions to be discussed a legalistic standpoint is far less important than the determination to create something new. So if purely legal scruples, based merely upon the current formal legal position of the church, should in any way prevail, then in the final analysis crucial and decisive significance cannot be attached to such considerations. In transitional periods like this it is often asked what in fact is now lawful; and this question can be resolved satisfactorily only if there is a will really to use the established law, or the spirit of the existing law, as a tool for the purpose of opening the way to the development of law in the future.' And Jäger already had even the Aryan Paragraph in view when he added that in addition 'the question of the extension of the Civil Service Law to the church, or at least its application in conditions which call for co-ordination, have to come up for discussion'.[70]

In fact, even later Jäger never left any doubt that the only goal of his activities in church politics was the radical, political co-ordination of the church, and that he would make use of every means to this end.

However, this concept, like its implementation, proved to be impractical in the long run, even for the Third Reich. Thus at the end of 1934 Jäger was thwarted by his own narrow-mindedness. After a year of forced retirement in 1936 he was nominated President of the Senate in the Berlin Kammergericht. In September 1939 the ambitious careerist was remembered in the Reich Ministry of the Interior and made District President and civil deputy to the Gauleiter of the new Reich district of Wartheland. Here, in Posen, Jäger – who meanwhile had left the church – could finally implement his political and church-political views, which had meanwhile become even more radical, without paying any heed to legal considerations. After the collapse Jäger was brought before a Polish court in Posen on 13 December 1948 on charges of aiding and abetting the 'organization and execution of war crimes and crimes against humanity', and was executed on 17 June 1949. A petition for mercy from Dibelius was of no avail.

As long as Jäger was still Landgerichtsrat in Wiesbaden, his church-political views could at most cause unrest in the small church of Nassau. However, that changed in May 1933. Presumably through Dr Wilhelm Stuckart, Rust's young Secretary of State, who had known him from his days as a junior lawyer in Wiesbaden, Jäger was called at this time to be assistant chief of the department for church constitutional questions in the Prussian Kultusministerium. Here he met a fellow spirit in Hossenfelder, and these three – Stuckart, Jäger and Hossenfelder – sketched out a plan to conquer the refractory Prussian church as it were by stealth. Perhaps surprised by the provisional filling of the position of President, which avoided state involvement, they induced the Kultusminister, Bernhard Rust, who himself had virtually no interest in church affairs, to dismiss Trendelenburg and put Jäger in charge. This created the conditions for a radical change in Prussian church policy.[71]

Of course the delegates of the Kirchenausschuss were still unaware of all this when they convened on the morning of 2 June in order, first of all, to bid farewell to their President. It was the last moment when the Kirchenbund remained intact. Kapler knew that a turning point was imminent when he assured the Kirchenausschuss that he saw 'a higher force' in his resignation. 'The environment in which we work has become completely different. We have a new Volk, a new state, a new theological conception of the relationship between state and church.' The outgoing President indicated clearly that he, at any rate, was no longer willing to adapt himself to these new conditions, and that he was therefore making way for other and younger forces.[72] His deputy, the Consistory President of Saxony, Friedrich Seetzen, who chaired the meeting from this point, lauded Kapler's long years of work for the church. The President then took his leave of each individual and left the meeting.

The major debate on the Reich Bishop began at about eleven o'clock. As the result of a resolution by the Lutheran bishops, the legal question was to be taken first.[73] After a lengthy discussion, however, the vote revealed that the Lutheran bishops were clearly in the minority in this body. A referral to the legal comittee was rejected by a vote of twenty-five to eight. Support for Bodelschwingh also emerged in the further course of the meeting. Among the numerous contributions during the morning, that by the Frankfurt Kirchenrat Johannes Kübel was especially impressive. If the election of Bodelschwingh were reversed, he declared, then the Landeskirchen which had voted for him were finished. The German Christians were 'not a movement of faith but rather of unbelief'. Therefore, Kübel declared, it was better to accept subjugation than 'to raise a hand to give the leadership of the church to this movement'.[74] At this point Niemöller, who had accompanied Bodelschwingh to Eisenach, noted in his official diary, 'Situation good'.[75] In the afternoon, the main representatives of the standpoint of the Lutheran bishops were Meiser and Schöffel, an unscrupulous politician. The aims of the Lutheran opposition were seldom expressed more plainly than at this point. 'The question is,' the Bavarian Land Bishop asserted, 'whether we are serving the National Socialist movement as we should. Let us not be deceived about the power of this movement. Something has to be done to bring about calm in our communities. We are facing the issue of state and church. If we do not prevent the outbreak of a conflict, then there is only one course: that of becoming a free church. I deny that my church is obliged to do this.'[76] This was nothing short of a declaration of surrender even before the

352

struggle had really begun. How different, by contrast, was the position of Bodelschwingh, who once again explained his standpoint to the Kirchenausschuss. Involuntarily the peaceful Bethel pastor now used warlike imagery. He had assumed this office and would remain in it: 'I feel responsible for the banner that I have taken over. I must stand by it. This thought has sustained me through all four weeks of difficult struggle. Now I hear the call that I should resign. But I keep thinking of the banner. If I retreat even one step during the attack, the battle is lost. I cannot accept such a responsibility.' Bodelschwingh also asked for 'the barrier to be torn down' that isolated 'the leaders of our church from the Chancellor'. But he put this forward as a demand to the new state by the United Protestant Church, and not as a condition for its life and survival in this state – and this was the crucial difference between him and the Lutherans.[77]

Even before a vote in the evening finally clarified matters, however, the delegates were surprised by two pieces of news which caused grave confusion and unrest. First of all, Land Bishop Wurm of Württemberg announced that Professors Fezer and Schumann had come to Eisenach on behalf of Ludwig Müller and were available for negotiations. A motion to give them a hearing before the Kirchenausschuss was rejected. In lieu of this, the official representatives – Marahrens, Hesse and Seetzen, who had now taken Kapler's place – declared themselves ready to meet the professors that same evening. At the same time public mention was made of a telegram which the Prussian Kultusministerium had sent to the Prussian representatives. It ran: 'Now that the Evangelical Landeskirche of the Old Prussian Union has left solid legal ground, I point out emphatically to its representatives that their actions have no legal validity.'[78] While Fezer's mission permitted various interpretations, the intention of the telegram was unequivocal. Both actions, however, were ultimately aimed at preventing a decision in favour of Bodelschwingh in any circumstances.

It cannot be completely ruled out that both of these actions were ploys worked out beforehand by Müller and Jäger. However, it is more probable, as Müller always asserted, that Jäger and Hossenfelder were attempting with a revolutionary determination to outflank the desperate manoeuvres of Müller and all his theological advisers. Be this as it may, the effect of the two actions was decisive. The Kirchenausschuss adjourned its meeting. No more resolutions were passed.

In the evening and into the night the Committee of Three negotiated with the two professors. The discussion began with a partial capitulation. It was suggested that Bodelschwingh could be persuaded to state that his designation was only temporary and that he would submit to the provisions of the future constitution. The opposition was asked what price it would pay for this. Fezer had the audacity to reply that 'it would immediately be announced that in future any intervention by force and any constraint on conscience through the use of power structures would be eliminated. Doubtless the Party's political apparatus would be withdrawn.'[79] About three o' clock in the morning the meeting broke up, with those involved thinking that they had found a compromise.

However, the decision that the Lutheran bishops made that same night was more important. Meiser had spoken on the telephone at about ten o'clock to the Bavarian pastor Friedrich Klein, through whom he maintained contact with the

Berlin German Christians. What he learned there seemed to him to be alarming to the highest degree. Müller, Klein told his Land Bishop, had been enjoined not to agree to any more compromises in dealing with the Kirchenbundesamt. 'It was the last chance for the leading men of the church in Prussia (Kirchenbundesamt and Oberkirchenrat) to resign of their own accord.' The election of Bodelschwingh was construed as a 'deliberate snub' to the state; for the sake of its 'self-respect and dignity', the latter now had 'to resort to the most stringent measures. The church itself must act (by withdrawing Bodelschwingh's candidacy) before it gives the state the chance to intervene. Situation enormously aggravated,' Meiser was further told. 'Guilt lies not with the state but rather with the leading figures in the church.'[80] This report undoubtedly reflected the mood, opinion and purposes of Jäger and Hossenfelder exactly.

These threats were the last straw for the Lutheran bishops. The resolutions which they went on to pass immediately amounted to no less than the irrevocable abandonment of Bodelschwingh, the termination of church fellowship in the Kirchenbund, and thus also the end of this federation itself. At the same time they provide the most important key to understanding further developments on the church side. The unanimous election of Ludwig Müller as the first Reich Bishop of the German Evangelical Church in triumph three months later was not least a direct result of the decisions taken on this night.

For instead of informing the Prussian church administration of the ominous situation and considering joint steps that might be taken, the Lutherans resolved from now on to go their own way. First of all, as Meiser noted, it was 'now absolutely necessary... to induce Bodelschwingh to make a suitable statement. Should the Lutheran bishops be outnumbered, they would refuse allegiance.' This in fact put an end to the church fellowship. However, the effect of the final decision was still worse. Though nothing was said, there was obviously deep satisfaction in the Lutheran group that the Prussian group had now finally been eliminated, both politically and ecclesiastically. At all events, the Lutheran bishops resolved not to intercede for the Prussian church but to take its place as the leaders of German Protestantism. As the minutes put it: 'Should the Prussian churches be considered incapacitated for negotiations, for the sake of the whole of Protestantism the Lutheran churches are willing to resume relations with the state and to press forward with the church question. Meiser, Schöffel and Reichardt should be considered the leaders of the negotiations.'[81] At about 3.30 that night and again at 4.48 telephone calls were made to Fezer to ensure that these decisions were made known immediately in Berlin.

But in Berlin Meiser's attitude was already known. At about two o'clock in the morning Emanuel Hirsch was still sitting at his desk writing a long letter to Althaus. In it he informed his friend that he knew quite a lot about Eisenach. 'Presumably one of two things will happen: either the actions of Ascension Week will be withdrawn without reservation or Meiser and some others will break with the Kirchenbund and become something like allies.'[82] And now indeed the Lutherans became 'something like allies' with Müller, Hirsch and Fezer.

At first the assembly which reconvened the following morning, 24 June, at 8.30, still had no inkling of these developments. At the request of Marahrens it was decided to continue the negotiations over a compromise in a larger body, and the meeting was adjourned until 11 a.m. While the Prussian representatives met and entered a 'solemn protest' against the accusation of the Prussian Kultusminister,[83] the enlarged committee was agreeing to pursue the path of compromise over the question of the Reich Bishop.

At 11 a.m. the meeting was resumed. The Kirchenausschuss and the Kirchenbundesrat had a joint briefing on the position over the church constitutional question. Until lunchtime Heckel, Hosemann and Karnatz gave reports on the main features of the planned reform of the church.[84] But the assembly with its almost one hundred members was hardly able to concentrate on these matters. Unrest, nervousness and worry spread. Nevertheless, the news which circulated in Eisenach around two o'clock in the afternoon came as a shock. It was a decree from the Prussian Kultusminister to the following effect: 'The situation of Volk, state and church calls for elimination of the present confusion. I am therefore nominating Jäger as Director of the Church Department in the Prussian Kultusministerium, to be Commissioner for the area of all Protestant Landeskirchen in Prussia, with authority to take any necessary steps.'[85] Thus the long-feared event had taken place. The state had intervened directly in the church.

The first devastating consequences of the Lutherans' nocturnal decisions immediately became evident. Instead of forming a united front against the obviously unlawful state intervention, they were all the more concerned finally to get rid of Bodelschwingh. Marahrens, who with the plenipotentiaries had once again negotiatied with Fezer in the afternoon, reported to the Kirchenausschuss when it reconvened at about five o'clock that the other side would no longer accept any compromise and demanded Bodelschwingh's complete withdrawal. Thereupon Seetzen declared that further developments depended entirely on the decision of the Reich Bishop. 'The tone and import of the statement,' Kubel recalled, 'all too plainly added up to the question: Will he now at last resign?'[86] Bodelschwingh now went to discuss the matter one last time with the Committee of Three. Towards seven o'clock things were finally settled. When discussions resumed, the pastor from Bethel, who for four controversial weeks had been a true bishop, read the following statement: 'The appointment of a State Commissioner for the sphere of all Evangelical Landeskirchen in Prussia has deprived me of the possibility of carrying out the task entrusted to me. This compels me to hand back the charge laid upon me by the German Evangelischer Kirchenbund.'[87] He then left the Kirchenausschuss.

Immediately afterwards the long pent-up emotion poured out. The spokesman for the Prussian church, Präses Winckler, deplored with passionate words the inglorious end of the Kirchenausschuss. He had no doubt as to where the guilt lay: a lack of unity and the existence of special interest groups were the factors which had led to this disgraceful end. The Lutherans reacted promptly. As if he were not the very one who had been aiming at exactly this result, Schöffel protested against this assertion 'with the utmost indignation'. Meiser was even clearer: 'After this bitter declaration which has been a great blow to a large number of Lutheran leaders, it is my duty as chairman of the Lutheran group and in the name of all the Lutheran leaders to reject most emphatically the accusations raised here.' Anyone who knew about the noctural decisions made by the bishops could, however, hardly believe his ears when Meiser continued: 'Believe us, certainly no one has gone through more difficult weeks than we have. Day and night we have struggled for a decision, and innumerable times we have beseeched God to show us the right way. But these accusations are the bitterest experience of all.'[88]

The breach could no longer be healed. Only with great difficulty could the mandate for Seetzen, Marahrens and Hesse be renewed. Then the Kirchenausschuss broke up. Winckler, the Prussian President, was to be proved right. It was the last meeting of this body.

From now on all substantial church decisions in Protestant Germany were confronted with the question: 'Do we resist the State Commissioner or collaborate with him?' The Old Prussian Union, which was the hardest hit, always opted for resistance; the majority of the other churches, however – and above all the Lutherans – pursued a policy of compromise with the authorities.

This was demonstrated that very evening in Eisenach. The Kirchenbundesrat had convened for the settlement of a few formalities and had by rotation elected the secular Vice-President of the Protestant Oberkirchenrat in Berlin, Ernst Hundt, to be its Acting President. In the meantime, however, the news had arrived that Hundt had that afternoon been suspended by Jäger. Thereupon Tilemann, Seetzen and Meiser attempted to reverse the election. And again it was above all Meiser who expressed his 'serious misgivings' about 'electing a man who has been suspended by the State Commissioner, at a time when it is most important to restore a tolerable relationship with the state'.[89] Another momentous decision was made later in the evening by a few representatives of the Prussian Landeskirche. Only gradually had it become clear that the state intervention not only affected the Old Prussian Church but also applied to all the Landeskirchen situated in Prussia. So the decision was made to send a joint telegram to Hindenburg and a joint protest to Rust. Schleswig-Holstein, however, did not dare even to do this, and withheld its signature.[90] After that, the question of collaboration with the State Commissioner was the key issue. Against the opposition of Kübel, who demanded that all of the church administrations affected should tender their resignations,[91] representatives of Hanover above all decided to collaborate 'as far as was consistent with conscience and the church's vow, and as long as unworthy actions were not demanded'.[92] In fact, Kübel was the only one who resigned his office, a few days later.[93] Thus for the time being Jäger had no opposition in Kiel and Hanover, in Kassel, Nassau and finally in Frankfurt. In contrast to this, developments in the Old Prussian Church were to prove all the more awkward for the State Commissioner.

The Struggle over the Prussian Church and the Completion of the Reich Church Constitution (July)

Jäger's rule over the Prussian churches, which lasted just three weeks, was one of the most turbulent periods ever of German church history. Never before nor after were there so many appointments and dismissals, so many competing measures, decrees and actions in so short a time. Three groups with completely different aims, instruments of power and supporters now struggled to exercise decisive influence on the further development of the Protestant church – each along its own lines.

Jäger headed one group. Together with Hossenfelder, the Berlin Reich leadership and the radical wing of the Faith Movement, he attempted to create *faits accomplis* as quickly as possible in a ruthless co-ordination of the church. This group had the political support of the Prussian Kultusminister Bernhard Rust, of the Prussian Minister President Hermann Göring and also of the Party. The front that offered resistance to this group was made up of the Prussian Oberkirchenrat, the General Superintendents and the Young Reformers. This opposition had wide church support among the pastors and some political support from the Reich President. A third group, under the leadership of Ludwig Müller, very quickly inserted itself between the other two. It included Müller himself, his theological advisers the Lutheran bishops, and all those who were in search of compromise. Crucial for this group was the fact that it received the support of the Reich Ministry of the Interior and of Hitler. So in the end it proved victorious.

When August Jäger took up his post as Commissioner of Churches at noon on 24 June, he at first planned to have the affairs of the Prussian Oberkirchenrat carried on by its former lay Vice-President Ernst Hundt.

This would have maintained the appearance of legal continuity, at least externally. But Hundt – although a member of the Party and close to the German Christians – refused to co-operate. Even an urgent plea by Jäger and Stuckart could not make him change his mind.[1] Most of the departmental officials in the Oberkirchenrat joined in this refusal. Because of this surprising resistance, which for all concerned meant at least a risk to profession and career, Jäger was forced to put his cards on the table. He did this in his own drastic way. That very evening he suspended Hundt and Martin Schian (the General Superintendent in Silesia, who was especially hated by the German Christians) 'with immediate effect'. At the same time – in accordance with the ideas that he had outlined early in May in his letter to Kortheuer – he dismissed 'all the elected church bodies in the Protestant Landeskirchen of Prussia',[2] also with immediate effect. That made these churches legally incapable of conducting negotiations. The very next day, a Sunday, the change of power was completed by means of a further decree. 'For the free development of the Evangelical Church according to its fundamental nature,' Jäger informed all consistories and church administrations in Prussia by telegram, 'a reconstruction is necessary.' The Old Prussian Church was given a completely new provisional leadership: its President was the young Berlin lawyer Dr Friedrich Werner, well-known from the first Reich Conference; its lay Vice President a German Christian consistory councillor from Silesia, Dr Fürle; and its clergy Vice-President none other than the pastor and national leader Joachim Hossenfelder. Soon afterwards half the Reich leadership of the German Christians entered the Oberkirchenrat in triumph.[3] In the same decree authorized representatives were nominated for the eight Old Prussian church provinces and the seven Prussian Landeskirchen. Most of these representatives were well-known German Christians, like pastors Thom of Pomerania; Eckert of Brandenburg; Adler of Westphalia; and Landrat Krummacher for the Rhine province. For Nassau and Frankfurt Jäger appointed his brother-in-law, Pastor Walther of Wiesbaden-Bierstadt; and for Schleswig-Holstein, the church government of which was already Socialist anyhow, Consistory Councillor Dr Kinder. For Reformed Hanover, evidently the only name to occur to Berlin was that of the Bonn professor Wilhelm Goeters, but that soon proved to be a misunderstanding.[4] No less important than the elimination of the church administrations was the take-over of the two largest Protestant associations: the Press Association and the Inner Mission. Here, the legal situation was more difficult, because these were not public authorities but private companies. But Jäger took no notice of such difficulties. 'The State Commissioner,' he emphasized in the first official discussion with his authorized representatives, 'has all the rights of the Ministry of State; it therefore makes no difference whether one is dealing with a "Ltd" or not'.[5] Nevertheless, since these associations embraced not only Prussia but the whole territory of the Reich, as a precaution Jäger had also got Müller's signature for this intervention, as the authorized representative of the Reich Chancellor. Accordingly, on Saturday at 6 p.m., Dr Michael Müller, university instructor at Jena, and Max Grevemeyer, publications expert in the Reich administration, appeared at the office of the Press Association and declared that they were 'authorized to take over the direction of the Protestant Press Association for Germany'. Legal objections from the Director, Profesor Hinderer, 'were disposed of with the declaration that this was a revolutionary act'. Later, SA teams occupied the office building and official residence.[6] Thus access to publicity, so crucial at precisely this moment, was blocked to the legal church government. From now on the Press Association, along with the Evangelische Pressedienst and *Evangelisches Deutschland*, the most influential instruments of the church's public relations work, reported exclusively for the German Christians.

The entire state intervention which Jäger made this weekend was simply a copy of the political co-ordinations taking place everywhere at this time. This was the only reason for it and its only justification. A semi-official commentary dated 24 June expressed this openly. The National Socialist revolution, it said, was 'even now far from reaching its goal,' but would prefer to 'fight to the end for its claim to exclusive leadership and sole rule'. 'The struggle over the Reich Bishop,' the commentator went on, 'and the achievement of parity with the Catholic Church, the struggle for the church's youth associations which is still to come and proceedings against the leaders of the German trade unions which have now been eliminated completely, are further phases along the course indicated'.[7]

While Jäger pursued the political conquest of the Prussian church in this way, the dissenting members of the Oberkirchenrat and the general superintendents met as early as the Saturday for a first discussion. As a result Dibelius asked Niemöller to sketch out a statement expressing protest and opposition. After long discussion this statement was published on the Monday afternoon in the name of all the Prussian general superintendents. It contained an unequivocal challenge to the Prussian state government and to the church administration imposed by it. The leading clergymen of Prussia protested against the employment of instruments of political power in the church and against the political falsification of the gospel. They declared Hossenfelder to be intolerable and called upon communities and pastors to join with them. 'Next Sunday we want to bring this whole distressing matter before the face of the living God in our worship. This should be a service of repentance and prayer.' The proclamation closed with words from Romans 8 which had a special significance in this context, because they had so often marked the climaxes of the nation's history: 'If God be for us, who can be against us?'[8]

What could not be overlooked was the fact that these remarks were no mere paper protests, but directly summoned pastors and communities to resistance against the new church government. Granted no German newpaper dared to print this statement, but church papers and mimeographed copies ensured that it reached pastors and communities in a short time.[9] Jäger and the new church administration reacted promptly. That same day the State Commissioner suspended Dibelius, whom he rightly considered to be the spokesman of this resistance. Vice President Hossenfelder responded with his own 'Message to the Communities', which called upon them 'to place yourselves, enthusiastically and ready for action, at the disposal of the great work of church reorganization which has now begun – in praise, prayer, thanksgiving and action'. Moreover his colleague Friedrich Werner, the new President, ordered that this message should be read in Sunday services. At the same time he pointed out to all pastors that any type of church-political activity carried with it 'the danger of prosecution because of the criticism of government measures which might be connected with it'. 'Therefore we recommend all clergy,' those concerned could read in the official gazette, 'to refrain from such church-political activity. Any attack on the state or on the authorities appointed by the state, any attack on measures undertaken or contemplated by such authorities will result in disciplinary punishment and if necessary removal from office.'[10]

On this Monday afternoon – it was 26 June – two remarkable meetings took place. Jäger had summoned his authorized representatives to Berlin for preliminary talks and instructions on that day. He made it clear to them that their primary task was the reorganization of the church bodies dissolved by his first decree. Thereafter, he thought, everything would 'develop naturally'.[11] At this time Jäger was still thinking of implementing this reorganization by means of a proportional allocation of votes. But quite possibly the reports of his commissioners from the various areas dissuaded him from this idea. At all events, two days later he decided in favour of the safer course of having the members of the new church bodies nominated on the spot by his representatives.[12] The different reports in fact revealed that in a whole series of church provinces no majority for the Faith Movement could be expected. This was especially true of Brandenburg, Saxony, Westphalia, the Rhine province and Frankfurt. From Westphalia Pastor Adler reported that all the pastors stood united against the Faith Movement, and in the Rhine province Krummacher guessed that seventy-five per cent were still opposed. To all the anxious objections of his officials, however, Jäger always gave the same answer: 'Don't get involved in discussions. Act. You are accountable to no one but me; I am accountable to no one but Rust; and Rust is accountable to no one but Göring.' He spoke even more bluntly to Adler: a war was going on, and if necessary, 'Let them have it.' 'If one cannot rely on numbers, then revolutionary rights must take centre stage.' Accordingly, the question of finances presented no difficulties. 'Every commissioner has the right,' affirmed the new Vice-President Günther Fürle, 'to strip the till and use it.'[13] The second point under discussion, the co-ordination of the press, was dealt with similarly. The press official in the Reich government, Kurt Freitag, told the commissioners that the church press had 'as a rule taken such a terribly hostile attitude towards us that the result must be a take-over by us.' To this Jäger could only agree. At the same time Müller's special role in the affair also became clear. He declared that he would negotiate with the board of the Protestant Press Association 'and really try to persuade it to put itself at our disposal. If it refuses, the other course will be adopted.' After a concluding word from Hossenfelder, Jäger ended the meeting with a triple 'Sieg Heil': 'Our Führer, our Volk and our true church: Heil!'[14]

At the same time the national assembly of representatives of the Young Reformers Movement was meeting in Niemöller's apartment in Dahlem. Here the situation was far less clear. But in spite of a series of voices advising church-political restraint in the tense situation, the meeting ultimately decided – at the urging of the Berlin representatives – to stand solidly behind the general superintendents. 'The struggle for the inner freedom of the church of the gospel continues', was the heading to their statement. It carried a call to disseminate the proclamation of the general superintendents in as many different ways as possible, and to organize the coming Sunday service everywhere as a service of repentance and prayer. What was expected now was, as it said, 'courage to confess and if necessary also to suffer'.[15]

The next day brought further heightening of the situation.

First Dibelius declared in a letter to Jäger – tens of thousands of copies of which were immediately circulated – that while the state might discharge him from his administrative functions, it could not do so from the spiritual leadership of his community. 'At this point it is a matter of episcopal and priestly functions. However, episcopal and priestly functions can be conferred only by the church, and can be revoked only by the church; not arbitrarily by it... That is the basis of the independence and the authority of the office of the clergy. On account of these solemn duties of our office, I cannot therefore allow myself to be suspended by any state commissioner.' 'Nothing is more essential to our people,' the letter closed, 'than to have men who know how to live according to the word of Holy Scripture: one must obey God more than men.'[16]

No less remarkable was a step decided upon by the suspended council of the Prussian Oberkirchenrat that same morning: to file a suit against the Land of Prussia with the civil court of justice in Leipzig. The short but impressive complaint had been discussed in the morning and had been delivered to the chancellery of the civic court about noon. In it the Oberkirchenrat demanded the annulment of Jäger's orders and, until the final decision, a temporary injunction to prohibit any activity by the Land of Prussia, its commissioners and authorized representatives.[17] This step by the Oberkirchenrat caused an extraordinary stir. It was not only courageous, but also clever, because no one could actually foresee the outcome of such a dispute.

Jäger reacted vigorously. Sending telegrams to all administrative presidents, district presidents and chiefs of police in Prussia, he now mobilized the state machinery. With reference to the proclamation by the general superintendents, he reported: 'Since the state, in its own interest, that of the Volk and that of the church, cannot tolerate any kind of resistance, but must rather consider attempts at such resistance to be treason against the Volk and the state, I request that you give your keenest attention to seeing that my orders and those of my publicly authorized representatives are not sabotaged. Such an attempt would be revolt and rebellion against the authority of the state... As a precaution I recommend giving a word of warning to the pastors.'[18] In the afternoon Göring strengthened the position of his Kultusminister with a letter in which he explicitly confirmed the latter's authority to end the church dispute and transferred to him all his powers as Minister President and deputy to the Reichsstatthalter.[19] In the evening Jäger spoke on German radio and explained the purposes behind his action. In his speech he did not stint threats against 'resistance of such a base kind' as that represented by the Oberkirchenrat's filing of a suit in imitation of Severing's example, and he announced that Rust would give an important speech on the Thursday.[20]

Under cover of this complete mobilization of the government, the new masters in the Oberkirchenrat decided to risk an ecclesiastical test of strength. In contrast to the general superintendents, who had called for a service of repentance, an official decree dated the same day ordered all pastors in the Old Prussian Church 'to decorate all the churches, manses, community houses and church administrative buildings... not only with the church flag but also with the black-white-red and the swastika flag', and to organize services on Sunday 2 July 1933 'as a celebration in thanksgiving and intercession'.[21] This action carried the conflict into every manse and every community. No one could evade making a decision.

Among the bitter facts of this history is that on the very day on which matters in Prussia came to such a head the Lutheran bishops handed over the Kirchenbund to Hitler's official representative. On the Monday Ludwig Müller, who had been precisely informed about the proceedings in Eisenach, had invited Meiser, Wurm, Schöffel, Rendtorff, Reichardt and Kühlewein, the new Land Bishop of Baden (but significantly not Marahrens) by telegram to a conference in Berlin on the following day.[22] In accordance with their decision in Eisenach 'to resume relations with the state and to press forward with the church question',[23] if the Prussian church proved incapable of carrying on negotiations, the bishops in fact accepted this invitation. The meeting, in which Müller's team of theologians (Professors Fezer, Schumann and Hirsch) also took part, made it clear that the Lutherans were really perplexed over the intervention of the state. At the same time, however, they were obviously of the opinion that because of its refractoriness the Prussian church essentially had only itself to blame for this situation. Müller exploited this situation quite skilfully when he expressed his wish 'that this affair should remain limited to Prussia, and that we should protect our freedom for the German church as a whole'. Immediately afterwards he came out with his own plan. 'Would not the correct thing,' he asked, 'be for me to act with the Chancellor's authority?' On the basis of this authority, for example, he wanted to make the following statement: 'The German Protestant churches are now in a state of emergency... The state of emergency calls for extraordinary measures. Therefore I am taking over the leadership of the Evangelischer Kirchenbund.' Thereupon he would immediately convene a committee which would prepare the church constitution, and this would be 'followed by a thorough missionizing of the whole Volk'. This was the way he saw things; but he had not wanted the decree to be issued before 'I had discussed the whole situation with you'. None of the bishops raised any objection. In the evening they did complain about individual points: above all the appointment of Hossenfelder and the State Commissioner for the Inner Mission. But no one took fundamental exception to Müller's suggestion. Not even the comment by Jäger, who arrived during the course of the meeting and declared that the state intervention in Prussia had taken place because the church had 'not done its duty', could make the bishops prick up their ears.[24]

How much all this was political blindness, and how much Landeskirche provincialism and Lutheran self-righteousness, was demonstrated by Wurm when, a few days later, he reported about this meeting to his Oberkirchenrat. 'The present desire to lay the blame for the muddled situation at the door of the Landeskirchen,' he asserted, looked to him 'like someone blaming those who warned against setting the points wrongly because they didn't get on board the train which had the accident.'[25] He could hardly have said more plainly that the Prussians had to fight their Kirchenkampf alone, whereas he himself was determined to lead his own church in a much more intelligent manner.

The consequences of this attitude were revealed the very next day.

In the Prussian conflict, on that day Jäger had summoned the general superintendents to Berlin to take them sharply to task for their proclamation. Very much in line with his radical approach, he declared that this proclamation was a subversive act and that in this context the conclusion 'If God be for us, who can be against us!' was sheer blasphemy. In spite of these threats the general superintendents stood firm. They would not engage in any discussion with Jäger. Instead, they simply presented him through their spokesman, General Superintendent Karow of Berlin, with the declaration that they rejected the charge of blasphemy and continued unanimously to stand by their proclamation.[26] That very same evening Karow paid the price: a decree by Jäger ordered his suspension 'with immediate effect'.

362

The same decree contained an additional surprising message. Müller had promised the bishops to ensure that Hossenfelder was withdrawn. Evidently he had been successful in actually convincing Jäger that this was now tactically wise. At all events, Hossenfelder was given leave of absence until further notice, with orders 'to place himself at the disposal of the Chancellor's authorized representative for the purpose of carrying out work in mission to the Volk'.[27] The whole affair was purely a diversion, but it did not fail to have its effect. The Prussian opposition took hope from it, and the Lutheran bishops saw it as emphatic confirmation of their course.

After these preparations and assurances, late in the evening Ludwig Müller made a grab for the Evangelischer Kirchenbund. In an undercover operation by night, he had the building of the Kirchenbundesamt occupied by the SS. Seetzen, the Acting President, and Hosemann, the Director of the Kirchenbundesamt, who had been informed by a third party and had hurried to Marchstrasse, learned from the men in uniform only that they were acting for Müller. Müller himself, as a precaution, remained unavailable that evening.[28] Instead, on the following day he issued a 'Decree towards Removing the State of Emergency in Church and Volk'. It was worded entirely in the style of the new era and corresponded almost literally to the procedure for which he had secured the backing of the Lutheran bishops the day before. The church, the decree stated, was in a state of emergency; the unity of Volk and church was in danger; this called for extraordinary measures. Therefore he, Müller, was taking over 'the leadership of the Evangelischer Kirchenbund, as the official representative of the Chancellor' for the time being. In particular he was taking over 'the Presidency of the Kirchenbundesamt, the powers of the Kirchentag, the Kirchenausschuss and its subsidiary committees'. In contrast to Jäger, Müller concluded with pious declarations: 'With trust in God and consciousness of my responsibility before God and our Volk, I go to work, obedient to the truth of the pure and untainted gospel of Jesus Christ.' It obviously did not disturb him that his first official action was another suspension. Hosemann, who had supported Bodelschwingh so long and so effectively, had to go. His place was taken by an old acquaintance of Müller's, the retired Admiral Ernst Meusel.[29]

That very same day Müller also withdrew the authorization from the Kirchenbund of the Committee of Three, Seetzen, Marahrens and Hesse, and announced the appointment of a new constitutional committee. The composition of this committee clearly reflected Müller's views. Besides Jäger, four Lutheran bishops, four German Christians and one representative each from the Young Reformers and the Old Prussian Church were to make it up.[30] However, before this commission could begin serious work it was once again overtaken by events.

In the tense and complicated situation of those days, Müller's action seemed 'a surprise of the highest degree'.[31] Not only was the Committee of Three, which legally represented the Kirchenbund, in the dark about the background to this action: in Prussia too, everyone was completely baffled. The true circumstances, the arrangement between Müller and the Lutheran bishops, were unknown at the time and strangely enough have remained so to this day. But at this juncture those two courses of action which were to become so extraordinarily typical of the development of events in subsequent years already began to emerge: the resolute attitude of the Prussian group and the readiness of the Lutheran Landeskirche for compromise.

On 29 June the situation in Prussia became even more tense for both sides. On this day Bodelschwingh, in a letter to the new President of the Oberkirchenrat, urgently asked for the decrees ordering the flying of flags and services of thanksgiving to be withdrawn, since it represented 'a heavy burden upon the conscience of many pastors'.[32] At the same time an anonymous 'group of determined pastors' called on all colleagues to offer open resistance. In this connection, the group referred to a written pledge demanded of all pastors to conduct all church affairs according to the orders of the State Commissioner.[33] 'What is most important now is that the clergy of our Evangelical Church should summon up the courage to resist an unlawful intrusion of force into the church. The general superintendents and the members of the Oberkirchenrat have set the example. A significant number of superintendents and pastors have already decided, in part through a joint declaration, in part by individual decisions, not to sign without reservations the form laid before them. They have declared that the demand to call the communities on the coming Sunday to praise and thanksgiving, and to fly flags on manses and churches, goes against their conscience and that therefore they will not comply with the summons. *Only by strengthening this front can we keep our church!*... Unless resistance is offered from the beginning, in a short time we will have a church whose preaching is no longer believed, because it is no longer permitted to preach what its conscience tells it that it must preach!'[34]

As a matter of fact many Prussian pastors found themselves plunged into deep inner conflict by Jäger's decrees and by the new church government. This conflict was made especially acute by the fact that to oppose these decrees it was necessary to resist a state which they would have obeyed and served happily and with all their hearts. In spring 1933 the hopes of a large part of German Protestantism were set on the fulfilment of the Königsberg message of 1927, which had proclaimed an indissoluble bond between Deutschtum and Christianity, between God and Volk.[35] And now in the Prussian church there was a growing suspicion that the Third Reich might mean not the fulfilment but rather the end of this bond. The passion with which the young nationalist pastors in particular resisted this suspicion demonstrated that this conflict struck at the very roots of their being as Germans and as Christians. In the middle of June a 'Working Group of National Socialists in the Young Reformers Movement' was founded, which called upon all Party members to stand up for a proper relationship between state and church. 'We do not permit our National Socialism to be challenged,' their declaration, which was widely distributed, stated, 'just because for reasons of conscience we cannot stand on the German Christian front. We have given to the state and to the Führer Adolf Hitler what belongs to the state, and we are ready day by day to support this state and its Führer with our blood and our lives. But we also want to be permitted to give to God what belongs to God. In matters of faith we want to have freedom granted to us in exactly the same way that it has been granted to the "German Christians".'[36] Another indication of the rift which was beginning to open up here was a letter which Wilhelm Niemöller, a younger brother of the Dahlem pastor, at that time thirty-five, sent to Ludwig Müller from Bielefeld on 30 June. In this letter Niemöller held the Reich leadership of the German Christians responsible for the fact that he, along with many other pastors in Westphalia, found himself in a situation in which his ordination vow – 'I have learnt it by heart in order to be able to help confused consciences' – compelled him to resist authority. The degree to which this conflict came as a surprise became clear when Niemöller continued, 'That I personally am among those who have been manoeuvred into a situation in which they must confess their faith, must even confess it in opposition to the state, is a strange and unexpected thing for a man who has belonged to Adolf Hitler's movement for ten years.' However, his personal confidence in Hitler was still unbroken. 'I request one thing of you,' the letter ended. 'If you understand the nature and distress of an *evangelical* conscience... then give this letter to my Führer Adolf Hitler. He should know, and he must know, the situation we are in – we who are, and wish to remain, his most loyal followers.'[37]

Certainly the path to opposition to the state was not everywhere as long as it was for this group. But in those days no one in Prussia was likely to have walked it easily, naturally and freely.

On the evening of 29 June the outbreak of open struggle appeared almost unavoidable. At a mass meeting of the German Christians in the Berlin Tennis Halls, the Prussian Kultusminister Bernhard Rust delivered his programmatic speech on 'God and Volk – Church and State' which had already been announced by Jäger. It turned out to be an unprecedented indictment of Prussian church officialdom, which it alleged to be incompetent and obstructive, and simultaneously for the first time disclosed the political motives behind the state intervention. The Kultusminister declared that he could no longer stand by and watch the public dispute over the Reich Bishop. 'Nor was there any justification for the church dispute to turn into the first centre of resistance to the progress of the German Volk towards unity.' The state had therefore wanted to put in Kapler's place a man who 'at the same time is in the deepest personal solidarity with the new völkisch movement of Adolf Hitler, so that he can reconcile the two parties in the dispute from within without the state having to lift a finger'. This necessity had been frustrated by the church through a breach of the church treaty, 'with a petty trick'. Thereupon he, Rust, had done 'what I had to do as a representative of the state. I appointed a commissioner.' The commissioner had the task of making up for what the old church officialdom had neglected, namely the creation of 'a bond between church and Volk'. Along with this, said Rust, Ludwig Müller – together with 'all serious movements within the Evangelical Church' – was to complete the constitutional work of the Reich Church. After that no one would say a word about church affairs: 'So there is no need to worry about the church.' 'I want to be proved right by history,' declared the Minister, very much in the style of Hitler's speeches of this time, 'and not by a so-called Civil Court of Justice to which these gentlemen have appealed.'[38]

The tone and content of this speech, which was broadcast by all German stations and was published by all the leading newspapers, did not indicate the slightest readiness for compromise. On the contrary, everything seemed to indicate that the state was determined to bring the Prussian and the German Evangelical Church to heel in the shortest possible time and with all possible means. But before it came to a decisive test of strength, things again took a new and surprising turn.

Hitler had undoubtedly observed the church dispute with growing displeasure. Early in June Müller had promised that he would conquer the church – with the Party's help – in four weeks. Rust might well also have assured Hitler that the old and decayed Prussian church would put up no resistance to the energetic grasp of his state commissioner. Instead of this the confrontations here were beginning to develop into an open scandal – mainly through Bodelschwingh's steadfastness and the resistance of the Oberkirchenrat and the general superintendents. In spite of rigorous control of the press, unrest and concern were growing both at home and abroad. The major Swiss newspapers, for example, saw the proceedings in the Prussian church as a 'climax to the crises of the year 1933'.[39] The Anglo-Saxon and Scandinavian public were also following matters with great interest.

This was a development which could only be very inconvenient for Hitler, precisely at a time when he was insisting upon a rapid conclusion to the revolution. On 26 June he had finally secured the co-ordination of the nationalist organizations. The German National Party and the State Party had disbanded on 27 and 28 June. His major political and church-political goals – the end of the Centre Party and his signature to the Reich Concordat, and with that the conclusive stamp of approval upon his power – seemed about to be realized. An open struggle with the Protestant church, with its unavoidable effects upon the general political climate, might well have disturbed this development at the last moment. This alone must have made the utmost restraint seem advisable to Hitler in this matter.

This was the situation when the Chancellor, in a conversation on 28 June, surprisingly found himself personally confronted with the church dispute. He had delivered a speech in the administration building of the Association of German Newspaper Publishers and was in the foyer with his entourage. At this moment Erich Backhaus, a Berlin pastor, who happened to have just visited the superintendent of the building, went up to him and called out, 'Mr Chancellor, protect the Evangelical Church from schism and violence!' In his answer Hitler, who according to the report replied 'seriously, but in a friendly way', first of all maintained and then emphatically repeated that he had no knowledge of what was going on and was not responsible for it. Only on the insistence of Backhaus, who openly and persistently advocated the position of the church opposition, did Hitler admit that the church had antagonized him with the election of Bodelschwingh and that he had been receiving completely different information about the church situation from Rust and the German Christians. His undoubtedly genuine annoyance became obvious when he declared in so many words that the whole church affair had become more and more a millstone round his neck and that he wanted nothing more to do with it. He had even stopped receiving Müller, his right-hand man. He had only wanted the unity of the church. Now it should see how it coped by itself.[40]

This conversation is likely to have reflected fairly exactly Hitler's approach to the church question at that time. It looked very different from Rust's resonant, inflated style. But of course in the circumstances there was no question of Hitler withdrawing in disgust. Rather, the following day made it clear to him that he could no longer avoid taking an initiative of his own in the church question. That

366

this initiative could only end up in a compromise in line with his plans followed logically from the situation and the circumstances.

The occasion of this initiative was, once again, the Reich President. Hitler met him on 29 June in Neudeck, where he gained the President's approval for the resignation of Hugenberg and for the appointment of a new Reich Minister of Economics, Kurt Schmitt. But while Hindenburg no longer had any scruples about endorsing this decisive step towards the co-ordination of the Reich Cabinet,[41] he requested the Chancellor, evidently quite emphatically, immediately to restore law and order in the Protestant church. Here Hindenburg was reacting to a volume of complaints and protests about the state intervention which had reached him since the first telegrams from Eisenach. This intervention by Hindenburg became extraordinarily significant by virtue of the fact that in this situation – for the first and only time during Hitler's Chancellorship – he resorted to the media. On 1 July all the German morning papers, typically with the exception of the *Völkischer Beobachter*, printed a letter from the Reich President to the Chancellor – in some cases under a banner headline. In it the President, 'as a Protestant Christian as well as the supreme head of the nation', expressed his deep concern over the dispute in the church. Hindenburg's critical view of the action of the Prussian government was evident when he wrote that numerous telegrams and letters had confirmed to him 'that German Evangelical Christians are deeply disturbed by these confrontations and by concern for the internal freedom of the church. A continuation or intensification of this situation can only bring the most grievous harm to Volk and fatherland...' At the same time the President publicly held the Chancellor to the specific promises he had made the day before. 'From my discussions of these problems with you yesterday,' said his letter, 'I know that you, Mr Chancellor, have the fullest understanding of these concerns and are ready for your part also to help in bridging the differences.' He was therefore confident that Hitler's statesmanlike vision would be successful in restoring peace through negotiations with both trends in the Protestant church, and with the Prussian government, 'and upon this foundation bring about the union of the various Landeskirchen that we so hope for.'[42]

Understandably enough, this clear letter was initially welcomed with rejoicing and relief in the camp of the church opposition. However, its effect very soon proved to be divisive. To be sure, it in fact put an end to Jäger's radical plans; at the same time, however, it also tied up the church opposition, which now had to defend itself against the charge that only its obstinacy prevented an amicable agreement. For the church this letter represented pressure to compromise which no one was able to escape. For who would have ventured to call in question the honesty of the efforts of the Reich President and the Reich Chancellor to achieve a united and strong German Evangelical Church? And who would have wanted to refuse to co-operate in this? Thus it was now possible to get all parties round a table and to complete the new Reich Church constitution within twelve days. As the compromise candidate, however, there was naturally only one possible name, Ludwig Müller. So now there began a period of hollow peace, about which virtually the whole church allowed itself to be deceived – by no means reluctantly!

Hindenburg's intervention now finally compelled Hitler to take the solution of the church question into his own hands. His quick and skilful reaction was again a typical example of his ability to turn muddled situations into successes. On 30 June, immediately after his return from Neudeck and even before the Reich President's letter had been published, he summoned Frick, as his government representative for the Evangelical Church, along with Rust and Ludwig Müller. At first a vigorous confrontation evidently developed at this juncture between Frick, who from the beginning had considered the state intervention wrong, and Rust, who had justified and defended it in his sensational speech only the evening before. In the end there was agreement on the following procedure: Frick was given the task of taking in hand the negotiations for the Reich. With his help Müller was to secure the agreement of all groups to a new Reich Church constitution as quickly as possible. The commissioners in Prussia were to remain in office until then – not least as a means of exerting pressure; after the agreement on the constitution they were to be withdrawn immediately. The political point of the whole procedure, however, lay in the decision to hold church elections immediately afterwards with the full support of the Party, in order in this way to set the church apparently unassailably on the desired course.[43]

This plan undoubtedly offered Hitler a whole series of advantages. It would satisfy the President, and at the same time provide the Reich church constitution that he urgently needed because of the imminent conclusion of the concordat. In addition he could keep Müller and did not have to disown Rust. And finally, there was the hope of a highly desirable general stabilization of the church problem. Further developments up to the middle of July actually worked out exactly according to the plan made in the Reich Chancellery on 30 June.

Not least with a view to foreign opinion, at the beginning of the very next week Hitler received the Dean of Chichester, A.S. Duncan-Jones, and let him know that he hoped for a swift conclusion to the crisis. 'He had been compelled to intervene,' Duncan-Jones reported in *The Times* about Hitler's statements, 'because there was a "Notstand", conflicts and controversies. He hoped those would now be overcome and that the new constitution which Church leaders were making would really unify the Church.' Hitler had also spoken candidly about his motives. 'He pointed out that when he dealt with the Roman Catholic Church he could deal with one united thing. He wanted to be in the same position in regard to the Protestant Church.' Finally, Hitler's concluding remark was no less candid. 'If the churches would abstain from politics they would have complete freedom in religious matters.'[44]

The German public also learned very quickly that something was up. At the same time as the publication of Hindenburg's letter, Frick's commission 'to begin negotiations along the lines of the Reich President's letter'[45] was announced officially. Frick himself wrote to Müller and wished him 'total success and God's blessing for the work under your leadership and for the first session of the committee for the creation of a new constitution for the German Evangelical Church'.[46]

Müller thereupon once again issued a statement to the church public: 'The constitution of the German Evangelical Church should be and must be set up in the shortest possible time. The people of the church must then say their Yes, so that I can go to the Führer and tell him that the German Evangelical Church is ready to serve the Volk and fatherland in obedience to the gospel... May God help us all!'[47]

368

The impression that Frick totally agreed with Müller's views was, however, deceptive. At the same time it was announced by his ministry that the Minister had ordered the investigation of all questions to do with 'the incorporation into the public law of the Reich of the Protestant church which was to be reconstructed', and that for this purpose he had directed the official in charge of church affairs, Oberregierungsrat Dr Conrad, to make contact 'with the German Evangelischer Kirchenbund and the Chancellor's official representative, Pastor Müller'.[48] This announcement was the reaction of the Ministry of the Interior to a communication from the Committee of Three that work on the constitution had progressed so far that discussions with the state could now be undertaken.[49] Evidently Müller's 'seizure of power' in the Kirchenbund was being ignored here; instead the basic presupposition was that he continued to be legally independent. The Committee of Three also understood things in these terms when immediately after the public announcement they sent a protest to Frick in which they denied that there was a state of emergency throughout the territory of the Kirchenbund and protested emphatically against Müller's action.[50]

While things gradually got going in the Kirchenbund in this way, in Prussia everything stayed as it was for the time being. In keeping with the results of 30 June, Frick showed little haste to enter into negotiations on the Prussian question. In the meantime Jäger and his officials could continue unchecked their goal of creating *faits accomplis* in the Prussian church. A circular letter dated 30 June showed that the State Commissioner had already been informed of the discussion that same day and now insisted on the greatest possible speed. He suggested that his task could be finished off in two to three weeks if the officials worked 'reliably, quickly and correctly'. The principal perspective in the formation of the new bodies was 'the absolute certainty that the constitution produced under the leadership of Pastor Müller would later be accepted by the provincial synods and Landeskirchentage concerned without a struggle'.[51]

At the same time the State Commissioner made a new effort to persuade the general superintendents to toe the line. During the discussion as to whether his invitation ought to be accepted, the first problematical consequences of the Hindenburg letter became evident. For whereas some of the general superintendents flatly rejected it, others were of the opinion that it was necessary to support the work of reconciliation initiated by the Reich President. After vigorous discussions they eventually agreed on a negative answer. A short letter dated 1 July informed the State Commissioner that the general superintendents did not at present consider themselves 'competent... to conduct fundamental discussions' and that the accusations made by Jäger and Rust must first be withdrawn.[52]

At the same time this meant that the conflict over Sunday 2 July remained unresolved. Every pastor now had to decide for himself whether he should comply with the call of the general superintendents for a service of repentance or obey the order of the new church administration for a service of thanksgiving and the flying of flags on churches.

Instructions from both sides, the German Christians and the church opposition, sought to influence matters in one way or the other, albeit with the difference that one side had the power of the state and all the media at its disposal, while the other could only use its own devices – and moreover found itself in an unclarified situation of semi-legality.

The German Christian Gauleiter of the Ostmark, Pastor Karl Eckert, while being unusually radical, issued a decree that left no doubt as to the political significance of the day. Among other things it stated that: 'Both church groups and the local political groups of the NSDAP must see that their members come to church in large numbers next Sunday, 2 July 1933, in as much solidarity as possible, to take part in services of thanksgiving arranged on the occasion of the reorganization of our church. In church, too, all National Socialists must turn this Sunday into a powerful confession of the new church and state of Adolf Hitler. Pastors who have preached in a cowardly or spiteful manner are to be reported... to me.'[53]

On the other side, a circular letter from the church opposition, with a mention that this was 'by order of the State Commissioner', asked for Hossenfelder's decree first to be read out. After that the call of the general superintendents and Bodelschwingh's letter were to be read. How serious the situation was thought to be was revealed by the conclusion to the circular letter. 'Now, if ever, is the *status confessionis*... If there is suffering, then we are not the first, nor are we the last. At all times the blood of the martyrs has been the seed of the church.'[54]

Anyone who had been to services held by each side this Sunday, say in Berlin, would hardly have thought that this was still one church. In the Kaiser Wilhelm Memorial Church, for example, Hossenfelder preached in the morning on Romans 13: 'Let every one be obedient to those in authority.' The church was packed to the doors; SA banners had been put on both sides of the altar. The large congregation was all in brown uniform. In the evening service in the same church, but to a completely different congregation, the local pastor, Gerhard Jacobi, preached on Matthew 21.12-16, the passage dealing with the cleansing of the temple. Given the state of affairs, v.13 required no special exegesis: 'My house shall be called a house of prayer; but you have made it a den of thieves.' At the end of this service Jacobi announced that a meeting of Berlin pastors had decided to make known the names of those involved in any arrest. Accordingly, he had to inform the congregation of the arrest of the sixty-six year old Pastor Otto Grossmann on Sunday morning after the service in Steglitz.[55]

In the Lazarus-Kirche in east Berlin on this Sunday the German Christians staged the first of their mass weddings, which soon became so popular. More than forty couples, the men all in brown shirts, were married in a retrospective church wedding in the presence of the entire Horst Wessel Sturm – won back to the church, Goebbels declared that afternoon, by the Faith Movement of German Christians.[56]

At the same time, three pastors, Fritz Müller, Martin Niemöller and Eberhard Röhricht, held a service of repentance and prayer in Jesus-Christus-Kirche in Dahlem. It was particularly significant in that here, for the first time, an attempt was made which was then to become a characteristic of the whole Confessing Church: to express resistance through the liturgy. That service in Dahlem on 2 July began with the reading of the various declarations and proclamations, in accordance with the circular letter from the church opposition. Then followed texts from Luther on authority, the church and the gospel; a congregational hymn; scriptural lessons on the lordship of Christ; the confession of faith, for the first time spoken in unison; another congregational hymn, and only then three short addresses by the pastors. The service ended with the prayer for the church, congregational recitation of the Lord's Prayer, the blessing and – after the blessing – Bodelschwingh's comments on his resignation.

We can see in retrospect the significance of this discovery of the possibilities in the liturgy. For while the affirmations of fatherland, Volkstum and the authority in the three sermons raise problems today, the liturgical parts of the service seem as powerful and as fresh as ever. Here the church had found its own form of resistance – more impressive than proclamations, declarations and speeches could ever be.[57]

It is hardly possible to sum up the overall attitude of the Old Prussian Church on this Third Sunday after Trinity 1933. The situation in the individual church provinces was too varied and the possibilities of reaction were too manifold. From the Grenzmark, from Pomerania, Silesia, Brandenburg and the Rhine province the general superintendents gave contradictory reports. On the whole the majority of pastors here would have complied with the decree to fly flags and would have read out Hossenfelder's proclamation; only a small minority would have held real services of thanksgiving. The assertion in the press that in Berlin only three violations of the orders of the church authorities had occurred was certainly incorrect; only a few days later 106 pastors signed a public protest.[58] The situation in Westphalia left no doubt. Here the almost unanimous resistance of the pastors had already led to surrender on the part of Jäger's official representative, Bruno Adler. Instead, Hindenburg's letter was now read on this occasion in most Westphalian churches along with the declaration that they were unanimously 'behind the desire of the two leaders of our people for peace'.[59]

Thus if this was not a victory for the church opposition, it was even less a breakthrough for the German Christians. There could be no question of a 'powerful confession of the new church and state of Adolf Hitler', as the Reich leadership and church officials had hoped. Rather, it became clear how far confusion, unrest and concern had spread in the meantime, and how necessary they had made a solution to the church problem – even for the state.

A further extraordinarily significant event this weekend stressed the seriousness of the situation for the Protestant church. Until then only the Prussian churches, among them above all the Old Prussian Union, had suffered the direct assault of the state. But the action by Rust and Jäger inevitably had an irresistible attraction for the new administrations wherever the situation was similar to that in Prussia. This was true of the second-largest of the German Landeskirchen, that of Saxony. Here, on 7 June, Land Bishop Ihmels had died. The new election, in accordance with the constitution, lay with the Saxon Land synod. Its composition, however, gave the German Christians no chance whatever of electing their man. After a dispute had broken out over the question of new elections, on 30 June the Ministry of the Interior for Saxony intervened, following the Prussian example. Without hesitation it declared a state of emergency in the church and, on the basis of the Decree for the Protection of Volk and State dated 28 February, transferred the rights and powers of all leading church bodies to the German Christian pastor Friedrich Coch. Coch appeared in the consistory of the Landeskirche on the morning of 1 July with his German Christian collaborators, dismissed the old officials and began work. One of his first decrees consisted in the compulsory suspension of seven superintendents and fourteen pastors.[60] There was also unrest in the North German city-states. In Bremen SS

Oberführer and Senator Otto Heider was appointed at the end of June to be state commissioner for the church in Bremen.[61] In Lübeck the church administration fell into National Socialist hands through a special law dated 4 July.[62]

All of this, Hindenburg's initiative, growing oppression in Prussia, and the danger that additional Landeskirchen would be co-ordinated by state commissioners, had the result that now practically everyone in the church hoped for a rapid conclusion to the negotiations over the constitution, on the assumption that with it a new, secure legal status could finally be achieved. At this point the situation was now very similar to that on the Catholic side: in both instances the traps had been so skilfully set that the churches as it were pushed themselves into them.

At the beginning of the new week the question of who was now responsible for the conclusion of work on the constitution – Ludwig Müller or the Committee of Three – was still not settled. At first Müller attempted to settle this issue in his own favour. On Monday 3 July he therefore invited his newly-formed committee to Berlin for a first meeting. However, it became apparent that neither the representative of the Old Prussian Church nor the Lutheran bishops were willing to co-operate with him. As the representative of Old Prussia, the Westphalian General Superintendent Wilhelm Weirich told the committee that he had come only to demonstrate his basic willingness to co-operate. However, he would take no further part in the morning session but return to Westphalia, where 'hundreds of pastors and communities' were 'in the deepest confusion and moral perplexity'. As long as Westphalian pastors were given orders by the police in the name of the Prussian state government, he said, he had to make sure that he stood beside his pastors, who would not understand if he 'were to collaborate with this committee now, given the conditions existing in Old Prussia'.[63] The Lutheran bishops now spoke. In a long and convoluted declaration they emphatically defended their former conduct, confirmed that the church had to make allowances for 'the necessities of state', but nevertheless requested the Reich government 'respectfully and urgently' as soon as possible 'to put an end to the state of emergency in state and church by restoring the church's freedom of action and resposibility for itself.'[64] Under the impact of these proceedings and under powerful pressure from the Ministry of the Interior Müller finally brought himself to work with the Committee of Three. In a statement on 4 July to this effect at the same time he expressed the expectation 'that these three gentlemen would co-operate in the restoration of legal continuity between the Kirchenbund and the German Evangelical Church'. The Committee of Three for their part agreed to this offer on condition that their legal custodianship was reinstated. Frick confirmed the agreement and recommended that they get together 'for positive work', leaving aside the legal questions.[65]

With this practical compromise Frick had taken the crucial step. Clarification of the legal situation would have been almost hopeless and would have taken months. Talk about getting together 'for positive work' met with the sense of impatience among all those involved; it left all possibilities open and it allowed everyone to hope. Only three days later, on 7 July, the reconstituted, last and definitive constitutional committee convened. It now consisted of Ludwig Müller; Admiral Meusel, the new Director in the Kirchenbundesamt; the

Committee of Three, Marahrens, Hesse and Seetzen; the Bavarian Land Bishop Hans Meiser; the Bavarian Oberkirchenrat Hans Meinzoldt; the Reformed pastor Otto Weber, and Professors Fezer and Heckel.[66]

While these events were taking place the confrontations in Prussia continued for the time being with undiminished sharpness. On 3 July they reached a new climax with Jäger's decree that 'all church bodies' were to be reorganized 'by nominations so that at least eighty per cent of the members were drawn from the ranks of the German Christians'. At the same time a series of superintendents were suspended and replaced by commissioners. That same evening, the church opposition emphatically protested to Frick against this attempt 'to create permanent conditions before the conclusion of work on the constitution'.[67] An action originating at that time from Gerhard Jacobi's group was also quite remarkable. This was a public statement by pastors from Greater Berlin who, 'not to achieve parity with the Roman Catholic Church but in principle...' demanded 'freedom for the Evangelical Church because only that church is the Evangelical Church which derives its doctrine and its ethics exclusively from Holy Scripture'. The statement went on to list all the violations of this freedom: the restrictions on press and radio, the appointment of state commissioners, the appeal of the new church government, the disciplining of the general superintendents and the arbitrary reorganization of church bodies. Within a week no fewer than 106 pastors from Greater Berlin – about a quarter of all the clergy in this area – had signed the statement. On 12 July it went with all the signatures to the Reich President, the Reich Chancellor, the Reich Minister of the Interior and the Prussian Kultusminister.[68] In view of the threats by the state and the propaganda by the Faith Movement, in the midst of the general enthusiasm and the confusion and uncertainty in the church this was a remarkable sign of courage and determination.

In Prussia at this time the first consequences of the political statement of principle which Hitler had made to a gathering of Reich governors also emerged: the revolution was 'no permanent condition'; nor ought it to 'develop into a permanent condition'. It was necessary 'to direct the flowing stream of revolution into the secure bed of evolution'.[69] Frick took up this slogan a few days later in an uncommonly sharp and clear letter to the chief authorities in the Reich and the Länder, the Party and the SA. As Frick saw it, in his last few addresses the Chancellor had 'clearly established that the German revolution is concluded. In so far as political parties still existed alongside the National Socialist German Workers Party, they have disbanded themselves. There is no question of their ever returning. The National Socialist German Workers Party has thus become the sole vehicle of the state. All the power of this state lies in the hands of the Reich government, led by the Reich Chancellor alone, in which all decisive offices are occupied by reliable National Socialists.' Any kind of disturbance – especially economic – had to be avoided completely in the new phase of 'normal legal work of reconstruction'. In no case in the future could any other organizations or Party authorities 'assume the powers of government'. In this connection Frick instructed the chief authorities of the Reich and Länder 'to ensure that for these reasons they dispense with the previous practice of the appointment of commissioners and official representatives and enter into an accelerated investigation of 'how those commissariats, etc., which now exist can be dismantled in the fastest possible way or, in so far as they are indispensable, how they can be incorporated into the regular apparatus of state...'[70]

Hence even Jäger's days were numbered. In fact the State Commissioner now found himself compelled to withdraw his decree of 3 July,[71] and on 6 July to transfer 'the authority of the chief church administration' of the Old Prussian Church to Ludwig Müller, so as to mitigate the offence caused by a church governed only by the state. Müller immediately let it be known that at this point he too wanted to help 'to complete as quickly as possible the work of unifying the German Evangelical Church which has already begun, by means of church self-help'.[72]

Still more important was the fact that on 7 July Frick received representatives of the suspended Prussian Oberkirchenrat and Emil Karow, the spokesman of the general superintendents who had also been suspended, and asked them to indicate their understanding of 'the actual and legal situation' of the Old Prussian Church.[73] This was an unmistakable indication that the Reich Minister was dissociating himself from the measures of the Prussian government. The restoration of law appeared closer at hand.

It is almost impossible to overestimate the compulsion of those days, what was felt to be the overpowering pressure to come to an agreement without delay. All participants felt it. Before the imminent publication of the concordat settlement Hitler's absolute will bound the government to reach a comparable result on the Protestant side. Moreover the revolutionary phase, the time of disturbance, was now supposed to be over. The church side was no less committed. It saw itself confronted with the wishes of the Reich President; with the necessity of returning to clear legal relationships; but above all with a development which made a schismatic church seem an impossibility in a nation which seemed rapidly to be becoming a unity. This alone is the explanation of the surprising fact that on 7 July Jäger, Müller, Meiser and Marahrens found themselves round a table in the Reich Ministry of the Interior, and that the new constitutional committee concluded its discussions after only three sessions. On the evening of the last day of the meetings – it was 10 July – Frick personally took the chair. He stressed that the speedy passage of the draft was essential because of the concordat. At the same time he agreed to all the conditions made on the church side for a constitutional settlement: the inclusion of the legitimate church administrations – Kirchenführer had now become the general term – in the concluding discussions, an the abolition of the coercive measures in Prussia and the other churches. Finally, he held out the prospect of a state treaty comparable to the concordat. After this, the final protocol was signed. Its wording demonstrated how much the semblance of legal and technical continuity mattered to Frick. 'The work begun by the committee constituted by the German Evangelischer Kirchenbund to create a constitution for the German Evangelical Church, in joint consultation with' – here followed, with full titles, the names of Müller, Fezer, Heckel and Jäger – 'has today been concluded. Tomorrow work on the constitution will be completed with its submission to the representatives of the German Evangelical Landeskirchen.' Then followed the signatures in this order: Frick; Marahrens, Hesse and Seetzen; Meiser; Müller; Fezel; Heckel and Jäger.[74]

The text of the constitution which was completed on the evening of 10 July had a turbulent history behind it. It began early in May with the negotiations of the Kapler Committee, in the course of which the basic principles of the new constitution were worked out. These basic principles, which were set down in the 'Loccum Manifesto' at the end of May, already revealed all the problems of rewriting the constitution. The difficulty was that while all those involved wanted a unified and strong Reichskirche, the large Landeskirchen did not want to give up their fundamental independence, and the confessions did not want to give up their exclusiveness.[75] These two reservations, the significance of which increased during the course of the negotiations, ensured that even the new Reich Church would not be a universally recognized church, but still only a federalistic church alliance. Since in the circumstances there was no way of changing this situation, all attention was concentrated upon the office of the Reich Bishop. The creation of this office was the really new element. However, from the beginning its significance was controversial and unclear. For the Lutheran episcopalians, this office was a further stage in completing the Reformation; a broad middle group saw it more as a political and a church-political necessity, i.e. a way of representing the unity of the church in a unified state and thus also of standing one's ground in the face of Catholicism; for the German Christians, finally, the Reich Bishop was above all the Führer, and the creation of this office was the first step towards the leadership principle in the church.[76] The struggle over Bodelschwingh was not least also a struggle over the understanding of the new office: the Lutherans denied him support because they did not consider him a true Lutheran; and the German Christians knew that the pastor from Bethel could not be expected to develop along the lines of the leadership principle.

Since the significance of the new office was unclear, the organization of the leading bodies generally also remained unclear. The guidelines had stated that a 'clergy ministry' was to stand alongside the Reich Bishop and direct the church in co-operation with him; a German Reich Synod was to assist in legislation and in the appointment of the church administration. However, what 'stand beside' and 'assist' were supposed to mean in legal terms was left open. And further negotiations brought no clarity on this point.

After Bodelschwingh's election at the end of May, Heckel worked out the first specific text of the constitution. It already contained all the important elements of the final version. These included the confession as 'the inviolable foundation' of the German Evangelical Church (Article 2); the division 'into vigorous Landeskirchen' and their independence 'in confession and worship, as well as in the ordering of the constitutional foundation of church life' (Article 3). They also included a strong legal position for the Reich Bishop, which was among other ways expressed in his right to appoint the members of the Clergy Ministry (Article 7) and a weak Reich synod which, according to this draft, needed to meet only once every two years (Article 8). The right of legislation lay with the Clergy Ministry or with the Reich synod in co-operation with it (Article 10). Financial resources were to be procured through contributions from church members, or through a sharing of costs by the Landeskirchen.[77]

The negotiations of the second constitutional committee under the chairmanship of Bodelschwingh led via various intermediary stages to a further draft which was presented on 24 June to the Eisenach assembly. It had now been enlarged with a preamble which went back to a draft by Martin Niemöller and which revealed the degree to which the church opposition was also dominated by a sense of the magnitude of the times. 'In the hour when God allows our German Volk to witness a great historical turning-point,' ran the preamble, some of which was to be included in the final version word for word, 'the German Protestant churches bind themselves, in continuation and completion of the agreement introduced by the German Evangelischer Kirchenbund, to a united German Evangelical Church. It combines the confessions emerging from the Reformation, setting them side by side with equal rights, and in so doing bears witness to that which they have in common, that which binds the churches united in it on the basis of Holy Scripture and the Reformation confessions.' Here followed a freely formulated, trinitarian confession, but this soon fell victim to Lutheran second thoughts and was replaced with the passage about the unity and unanimity of the community from Ephesians 4.4-6.[78] Moreover, the 17 June draft posited more of a unity: for example, preliminary talks with the Reich Church were to proceed the appointment of the senior officials in the Landeskirchen (Article 2.6); the Reich Church was to strive 'for a uniform attitude in the church' and to give a 'goal and direction' to the work of the church (Article 4). In addition, the Reich Bishop acquired the right 'to take necessary steps for the protection of the constitution' (Article 6) – in the circumstances this was an extraordinarily problematical provision which virtually invited abuse. On the other hand, the right of legislation was now tied to an agreement between clergy synod and Reich synod (Article 10).

In spite of the obvious weaknesses of this draft and the problems it presented in terms of church law and church politics, there were no serious objections to it at Eisenach. On the contrary, the protocol explicitly remarked that the discussion had resulted in 'agreement over essentials'.[79] Up to this moment, then, the constitutional work was still in church hands, and the fact that the Kirchenbundesrat and the Kirchenausschuss approved its main features showed that this constitution in fact corresponded to the wishes of a large majority in the church.

After the collapse of the Kirchenbund, Heckel, who in the meantime had fallen into line with Müller,[80] applied himself anew to a revision. The text was tightened up and above all Article 6, on the Reich Bishop, was shaped even more strongly by the leadership principle. This was the draft which was to be the basis of the concluding discussions of the new constitutional committee in July. Only now did the official representatives have misgivings. These were over the relationship of the Reich Church to the Landeskirchen and the position of the Reich Bishop. While the existence of the Landeskirchen and their independence in confession and worship was guaranteed by Article 2, Article 3 stated: 'The German Evangelical Church regulates the entire legal system of the German churches.' When asked by Meiser and Marahrens how this provision was to be understood, Jäger declared clearly and concisely: 'The provision means: Reich law prevails over Land law. Where Reich law does not exist, Land law is valid. That makes it clear.'[81]

Efforts to bind the Reich Bishop more tightly to the Clergy Ministry also failed, the more so since Heckel now joined Jäger and Müller in emphatically advocating the leadership principle. When Jäger declared that the basic ideas behind the constitution were 'the confession of faith and the leadership idea',

Meiser rightly expressed doubt as to whether the church recognized a ' "Führer" at all, rather than simply a chief minister'. However, Jäger and Müller, supported by Heckel, successfully resisted all attempts to reshape the constitution at the last moment in a collegial and synodical direction. 'The incorporation of security factors,' Jäger remarked, 'is not in keeping with the significance and nature of the work.'[82] The text of the constitution thus remained unchanged in its essential provisions. All that Marahrens, Meiser and Fezer achieved was to record certain misgivings in the protocol.

That was the state of affairs when on the morning of 11 July the official delegates of all the German Landeskirchen gathered in Berlin for the ratification of the constitution. It was a remarkable gathering. Frick, who wanted above all to rule out later objections, had ordained that to be safe, both sides – the old church administrations and the new commissioners – were to vote and sign the document. Thus Prussia was represented not only by Müller and Jäger but also by the suspended members of the Oberkirchenrat, Hundt and Karnatz, and the commissary president Ernst Stoltenhoff (appointed by the church and removed by the government). The church of Saxony was represented by its old President, Friedrich Seetzen, and its new provisional bishop, Friedrich Coch. The Bremen delegation was likewise mixed.

Müller opened the meeting. Not unskilfully he anticipated possible objections to the draft of the constitution, which had been distributed simultaneously, by reading the minutes of the previous day's proceedings. In fact they appeared to remove many of the misgivings: the Reich Church was not able to enact any laws against the opposition of the Landeskirchen; the provision of regular discussions between Reich Bishop and leaders of the Landeskirchen was to be legally binding; the removal of the Reich Bishop was to be regulated by law; and above all, where there was opposition between the Clergy Ministry and the Reich Bishop, no law could be enacted. Then Müller pointed out the state's concern to create 'full freedom of action' for the church as quickly as possible; he requested that no further exception be taken 'to the church renewal movement by way of pettiness and exaggeration' and he concluded with a remark that once again suddenly illuminated Hitler's skill in playing off one confession against another. 'I ask you to bear in mind something that I am telling you in confidence. The concordat with Rome will be brought to a rapid conclusion. Obedience is also part of the leadership idea. The concordat does not represent a final end to the struggle against the Catholic Church. If Catholic infringements against us should occur, then we shall have no better and tougher protector of our interests than the Führer. So the Führer also attaches importance to a church treaty with the Evangelical Church. In addition, it is essential that we do not come to a conclusion here which enables us to reach our goal only with the greatest difficulty. Show the Catholic Church that you can achieve a work which, seen from the outside, is joyful and united, and which puts back the labours of Catholic Action for fifty or a hundred years!'[83]

After discussions in smaller working groups, the whole constitution was worked through in a few hours during the afternoon. Heckel silenced a critical inquiry from the Reformed side with the observation that there should be confidence that the Reich Bishop would apply the constitution loyally. When Schöffel, of all people, having made a considerable contribution to this result by means of his audacious theology and his ruthless intriguing, raised 'theological doubts' about the presentation, Jäger retorted in the same tone as Heckel's that 'every residue of mistrust towards the future leadership of the... church' might really be abandoned.[84] Finally the draft, with a few corrections, was passed unanimously. This decision was confirmed in a session of the Kirchenbundesrat which followed immediately. Thereupon all those involved went to the Minstry of the Interior, where, at about 8 p.m., Marahrens reported the acceptance of the constitution to the Minister with grandiose, dignified words. Frick expressed his thanks and at the same time gave his assurance that the measures in Prussia would be rescinded in the shortest possible time, 'during the course of this week'.[85]

Then late in the evening the final act of signing the constitution took place in the Kirchenbundesamt. The longest-serving person present, Senior Pastor Möller of Kassel, made the last speech. He recalled the 1906 Eisenach Conference at which the Reich Church had already been mentioned. At that time, Möller said, no one had believed in a church alliance. That made him all the more delighted that this work was a success. 'Thus we experience this day,' he concluded with some emotion, 'as a bright day in this life of ours which is drawing to a close. The church is alive.'[86]

The constitution of the German Evangelical Church dated 11 July 1933 was in many respects a highly problematical compromise. That is, in its inclination towards the leadership principle, it only too clearly bore the characteristics of its times and of the history of its origin. Nevertheless, it was a church constitution and not merely an instrument of German Christian domination. This was above all expressed in its first article, which ran: 'The inviolable foundation of the German Evangelical Church is the gospel of Jesus Christ, as it is testified to us in the Holy Scriptures and has come to light again in the confessions of the Reformation. By this means the powers which the church requires for its mission are determined and limited.' It was significant that neither Jäger nor Müller paid the slightest attention to this article in the concluding negotiations. Quite obviously they considered it to be an empty formula without real significance. However, the article in fact soon proved the most important provision of the whole constitution. For it became the critical criterion for the implementation of the office of Reich Bishop and later became the legal foundation of the whole Confessing Church. Whether, as a noted church lawyer asserted after the war, in other circumstances, the 11 July constitution really would have been suited to 'a further development, in a favourable sense, of the office of Evangelical Bishop' may remain open.[87] However, its character as church, in terms of canonical legitimacy, is demonstrated beyond question by the explicit reference of the Confessing Church to the ecclesiastical intent of this constitution.

With the passing of the new church constitution Hitler had achieved his main goal. Satisfied, on 12 July he sent a telegram to the Reich President: 'The constitutional work of the German Evangelical Church having been concluded yesterday, the negotiations on the settlement of the Prussian church conflict have today been brought to an end in a manner equally satisfying to state and church. The inner freedom of the church, to which I also attach especially great importance, has been placed beyond doubt by the withdrawal of the commissioners and sub-commissioners of the state. The internal reconstruction of the Landeskirchen will be brought to an immediate conclusion, in accordance with church law, through a free election by members of the Evangelical Church.' A brief telegram also went off to Ludwig Müller, expressing Hitler's satisfaction.[88]

In the meantime the Reich Minister of the Interior worked with the utmost speed on a law which was to ratify the constitution according to Reich law. On 13 July the draft went to the Secretary of State in the Reich Chancellery with the request that it be placed 'on the agenda of the cabinet meeting on 14 July'.[89] A final version of the law, as well as the justification for it, followed on the very day of the meeting.[90]

In its abundance of new legislation the cabinet meeting on 14 July, not incorrectly characterized as an 'epoch-making date', betrayed Hitler's determination to complete the co-ordination and to conclude the revolutionary phase of the seizure of power.[91] The joint treatment of Protestant and Catholic churches at the same meeting once again made clear the internal connections of his church policy. Item 17 on the agenda was the Reich concordat, which was passed after a short but remarkable discussion.[92] The draft of the law on the constitution of the German Evangelical Church was the next and last point. In this context the protocol noted only that, 'The Reich Minister of the Interior presented the content of the bill, which the cabinet approved'.[93]

Hitler was convinced that the essential church-political decisions had now been made. He felt what happened next to be no more than routine: the use of the instruments he had created for a church policy along National Socialist lines.

That same day Rust, as arranged, announced the end of Jäger's state commissariat. Jäger withdrew the commissioners for the Prussian church provinces.[94] To be sure, it was still some time before the old authorities could work again everywhere, and in particular there were considerable difficulties over the return of the Prussian Oberkirchenrat. But in principle the Reich Minister of the Interior appeared to be keeping all his promises.[95]

So on this 14 July peace appeared to be restored. Widespread hope filled the church that the terrible period of legal uncertainty, of confusion, of dispute and of confrontation had finally been overcome by the decisions of this day. A new and great future seemed to be opening up. The leaders of the Landeskirchen everywhere expressed their joy and gratitude. Thus for example Wurm organized an announcement to be read from the pulpit the following Sunday in which he spoke of the 'merciful hand of the Lord of the church', who in this week had prospered a work of unification about which there had been doubts even a short time before. 'In total unanimity, the official representatives of all the German Evangelical Landeskirchen have concluded the foundation of a united German Evangelical Church which stands upon the ground of the old inviolable gospel and the faith of the Reformation, and which desires to commit itself with complete dedication to the tasks which God himself has set before it through the course of the history of our people...'[96]

More vigorous still was the tone of *Junge Kirche*, which on 17 July wrote: 'We bear before God in deep joy the awareness that now, through the events of recent days in the Third Reich, the way has become free for the Volkskirche under the gospel. Talk of schism, all the distress and despair which the Young Reformers Movement in spite of everything has always rejected as irresponsible, are now at an end among the people of the Evangelical Church. *All energies must now go to the building up of the church!* The way to a new Reformation is open.'[97]

8

The Conclusion of the Reich Concordat
(April-September)

Hitler's major political goal in the spring and summer of 1933 was the unification of the nation. His church policy was also directed towards this aim. But while he expected from Protestantism nothing other than a nationalist attitude,[1] which it was only necessary to exploit and steer in the right way, things on the Catholic side were obviously more difficult. Here – as had already been demonstrated - he faced two apparently contradictory tasks. He had to destroy political Catholicism. At the same time he needed Rome's recognition of himself and the new state. The destruction of political Catholicism was the precondition for completion of the one-party state, and hence for the safeguarding of political power. Without the recognition of Rome, however, the internal incorporation into the Third Reich of that part of the people faithful to Catholicism, which was no less important, remained uncertain and problematical. He had attained both goals in July 1933, by means of the Reich concordat.

The planning, execution and conclusion of the concordat negotiations with Rome were unquestionably a political masterpiece. Hitler's passing remark about himself that 'Bismarck was Protestant and therefore unable to conduct his Kulturkampf with the necessary expertise; but he himself, as a Catholic, understood the matter better',[2] hit the nail on the head. It was typical of his approach that, in the cleaning up of his relationship with the Catholic Church which was needed, he did not spend a moment on those diplomatic proposals which as late as March had still recommended to him discussions 'between leading representatives of the Party and the German bishops'.[3] Endless difficulties would in fact have been to be expected from such an approach. Instead, from the beginning he had been convinced that the key to this relationship lay in Rome, and that only a major solution would bring him the rapid and permanent success that he desired. Hence he pursued this major solution energetically and brilliantly, free of those anti-Catholic feelings which had always made negotiations with Germany difficult for the Curia and with a nose for the weakness of his opponents which hardly gave them a chance.

To his good fortune, at this juncture Rome came a long way towards meeting him. For Hitler's behaviour appeared to the Curia to match exactly the description of the behaviour of Italy by Ludwig Kaas, in his study of the Lateran Treaties. Kaas had said: 'The aggressive instinct which is characteristic of Fascism in the purely political sense and is to a large extent the key to its success also revealed itself after initial waiting and hesitation in the difficult area of the further development of church policy and state-church law, which in Italy was especially difficult. With a frontal initiative at a favourable moment, it seized what six decades had sought in vain and abandoned as hopeless in a relatively short period, considering the practical and psychological barriers in the way. The Lateran Treaties are a "Battaglia della Pace", the bringing about of a consolidation and a concentration for the new Italy which only a later era will be able to appreciate.'[4] This could be transferred almost word for word to German conditions. How in these circumstances could Rome have hesitated?

Contrary to the view of almost all more recent literature on the concordat – according to which such plans were spoken of for the first time only at the beginning of April[5] – essential preliminary decisions had probably already been made by then. Kapler's 23 March letter to the Reich President in which a connection was made between the acceptance of the Enabling Act by the Centre Party and the conclusion of a Reich concordat[6] presumably marked not the beginning but already the end of the development which had begun immediately after the March elections. In the course of this development a basic agreement on the Reich's intentions on the concordat had been reached between Hitler, Papen and Kaas. In view of the difficulties and resistance which such notions had encountered in both camps – the Party and the church – it is improbable that anything about this had already been put down in writing. But in this context Hitler's government declaration of 23 March, with the pledge to 'nurture and further develop friendly relations with the Holy See', and the subsequent unanimous Centre Party approval of the Enabling Act, were political declarations of intent which were now unmistakable to those involved.

Among the fatal errors which the ambitious prelate made during these weeks was to set out for Rome, the very next day and obviously in great haste, in order – as he wrote later – to explain there 'the situation created by the Reich Chancellor's statements' and to investigate 'the chances of a comprehensive understanding between church and state'[7]. A direct result of the new information was Pacelli's instruction of 29 March to the Nuncios in Berlin and Munich to inform the German episcopate 'confidenzialmente e oralmente' that a revision of the church's attitude towards National Socialism was required.[8] However, the instruction came too late: manifestly upon Papen's urging, Cardinal Bertram had already decided this himself and published the 28 March declaration.[9]

Kaas's haste was more questionable for another reason. Although the prelate had presumably prepared for a lengthy stay and thorough discussion in Rome, Hitler compelled him to return quicky to Berlin by suddenly summoning the Working Committee for 31 March.[10] As matters stood, the Chancellor could thus expect that at this time Kaas would bring back a first answer from the Holy See. Immediately after his return Kaas is in fact likely to have assured Hitler at least of Rome's basic agreement to enter into negotiations over a Reich concordat.[11] This gave Hitler the initiative. Now Berlin could determine when, where and how negotiations were conducted. And from that moment on Hitler in fact kept the reins firmly in his hands. Even in retrospect no situation can be seen – comparable, say, to the election of Bodelschwingh – between the formal beginning of the negotiations in April and their conclusion in July in which there was even a possibility for the Catholic Church to decide other than as Hitler wanted it to.

As so frequently happened, Hitler surprised his negotiating partners by his unusual speed. As early as 2 April – Kaas had only just returned from Rome – the Papal Nuncio in Berlin, Cesare Orsenigo, informed the Cardinal Secretary of State that Vice-Chancellor von Papen would travel to Rome even before Easter and wished to be received by him there.[12] Five days later Papen was already sitting in the train. The day he left he explained the purpose of his journey to the Chief of Vatican Affairs in the Foreign Office, Legationsrat Fritz Menshausen. As he confirmed to the diplomat, he in fact wanted to encourage 'the conclusion of a Reich concordat in the Vatican'. To Menshausen's question 'whether he had in hand a definite draft of a new Reich concordat', the Vice-Chancellor replied in the negative. But he added in strict confidence – and this was, and from the beginning remained, the crucial point for the Reich – that he 'intended to demand as one of the chief concessions the acceptance of a provision which was also contained in the Italian concordat, according to which the clergy were forbidden to be active for, or to join, any political party'.[13]

The speculation that Papen himself set this concordat plan in motion is improbable.[14] For in his own thoughts on a concordat a few months earlier the former Chancellor had not even hinted that he had any information about the Lateran Treaties and their possibilities. Rather, all this clearly bore Hitler's signature. The lightning-quick reaction, the exclusion of the diplomats and the concentration on the one essential point – namely the withdrawal of the Catholic Church from politics and with it the destruction of political Catholicism: all this was typical of Hitler's policies. Welcome though Papen was to the Chancellor as a negotiatior, the concordat issue was thought out, planned and decided by Hitler alone.

In the meantime the press had got hold of the topic and among all sorts of speculations there appeared in the Paris *Journal* of 6 April a news item that reflected the state of affairs fairly accurately. The Berlin correspondent for the paper believed he could report 'that Chancellor Hitler has ordered... representations to be made to the Vatican over the conclusion of a concordat. One of the main points would be to forbid German Catholic clergy being elected as representatives to parliament.'[15]

At the same time the intrinsic connection between the concordat and developments in German Protestantism also became visible. The *Tägliche Rundschau* of 7 April discussed the merits of the Reich concordat as seen by the German Christians. That is, it forced the Landeskirchen 'finally to shape the German Evangelischer Kirchenbund as quickly as possible into an organ capable of negotiations, so that a partner might emerge on this front capable of concluding an analogous treaty between the Protestant churches and the Reich'.[16] The fact that Ludwig Müller first told Kapler and Zoellner on 7 April that this very idea was Hitler's opinion,[17] like further developments leading up to the joint conclusion on 14 July, showed that Hitler was in fact translating a great church-political concept for both confessions into reality.

However, he would not have been so successful so quickly and easily all along the line had he not found willing collaborators in both camps. On the Protestant side they were the German Christians, Ludwig Müller and the Lutheran bishops;

on the Catholic side Papen, Kaas, and later a part of the episcopate, above all the Archbishop of Freiburg, Conrad Gröber.

Whether and how far Papen and Kaas collaborated in this matter as early as March has not been clarified. However, the story which is supposed to explain their joint appearance and their close co-operation in Rome after 9 April is so improbable that it is difficult to accept that Kaas is honest on this point. According to it, without knowing much about each other's plans, both Papen and Kaas had departed on the evening of 7 April in different trains from Berlin via Munich to Rome. In the express train from Munich to Rome on the morning of 8 April Kaas had then 'unexpectedly' met Papen in the dining car and in the course of a discussion prompted by Papen established 'that the plans for the conclusion of a concordat, which had been repeatedly discussed, even in public, were a real possibility'.[18] This version of his intervention in the concordat negotiations which Kaas himself gave later has been largely taken over in more recent literature.[19] We are expected to imagine that the Chairman of the Centre Party, who shortly beforehand had celebrated the historic significance of the Lateran treaties, disregarded and left uninvestigated the rumours buzzing around since 23 March about Hitler's plans for a concordat; that on 24 March he travelled hastily to Rome in order there to negotiate with Pacelli about an already archaic political dispute over nationalities in the Eupen and Malmedy area;[20] that after his return the preparations in the Foreign Office – with which he personally had excellent connections – remained just as hidden from him as Papen's intentions and the latter's travel dates and finally that in a private interview with Hitler on 7 April he spoke only about the protection of Catholic schools and Catholic societies. Only if we consider all this plausible could Papen's presence in the train to Rome and his concordat plans have been a genuine surprise to the prelate.

It is much more probable to suppose that the chief German concordat specialist and also Pacelli's confidant not only wanted to have established the historic contact between Berlin and Rome but was also keenly interested in the further negotiations. There was hardly any official status for him in this; because of his position between the two sides, neither one nor the other could officially entrust him with the negotiations. Even later, in spite of his efforts, significantly Kaas never received any official authorization.[21] So the only possibility for him was to insert himself, so to speak, into the negotiations (though in the course of them both sides – Hitler and Papen a well as Pius XI and Pacelli – knew his great value as a go-between). This is the only explanation for the position which Kaas occupied in the following weeks, as the confidant of all those involved.

If participation in the substantive negotiations over a concordat was Kaas's goal, then sharing the journey to Rome with Papen completely served his purpose. For in a series of conversations the Vice-Chancellor explained to him the basic principles of the planned treaty – that is, negotiating the security of the church's rights in exchange for depoliticizing the clergy and abandoning the Centre Party. However, this was not new to Kaas. From his notes it emerges that at this time the Centre Party chairman did consider his party to be no more than a bargaining chip. 'Basically I did not contradict this line of thought,' he noted on Papen's statements, 'but rather above all pointed out that first of all some evidence had to be given of the creation of adequate cultural-political guarantees. If the latter were the case, then I certainly would not be petty.'

Crucial for Kaas personally was the end of the conversation, during which he declared to Papen his willingness 'if necessary, to be available to him, say, for working out any statements'. The latter accepted the offer 'with thanks'.[22] Kaas had thus obtained the mediator's position that he had hoped for and aspired to, and he then remained active in it until autumn 1933.

Thus the team of persons crucial to the Reich concordat was already in place when Papen and Kaas arrived in Rome on the morning of 9 April. And anyone in Germany who read the newspapers attentively could suspect the direction in which things were supposed to move. On 11 April even the official Party newspaper *Völkischer Beobachter* reported on Papen's mission. It could be assumed, wrote the paper, 'that in the visit to the Holy See the question of *the future attitude of the government towards the Centre Party* will play a decisive role, and it is already believed that *the Pope will raise no objections to Hitler's government, since the government view that first of all order must prevail in a state is thoroughly in keeping with that of Christianity. As long as the Reich Cabinet fights against Communism, the Vatican will not cause the slightest difficulty for it.*' The article then went into Papen's intention to found a new, nationalist Catholic party in Germany and continued: 'Von Papen is also thought to want a *concordat* between Germany and the Holy See, the basic features of which would correspond exactly to the concordat that exists at present between Italy and the Vatican.'[23]

The official negotiations began on the Monday of Holy Week, 10 April, with a conversation between Papen and Pacelli. It presumably confirmed the basic agreement on the treaty project and resolved to carry through negotiations quickly. At all events the next discussion was scheduled for as early as Holy Saturday, and it was agreed that Papen was to prepare it with Kaas. The two Germans met on the evening of Good Friday. The Vice-Chancellor had brought with him the old 1924 concordat draft,[24] which Kaas revised overnight and supplemented with Hitler's most important demand, the depoliticizing article. On the afternoon of Holy Saturday, Pacelli, Papen and Kaas then met in the study of the Cardinal Secretary of State. On this occasion, according to Kaas's notes, the 'oath of allegiance, prayers for the state, depoliticizing article, marriage in cases of moral emergency, article on the protection of minorities, military chaplaincies, articles on the embassy and nunciature' were discussed as parts of a new concordat. In the afternoon Kaas then dictated a first complete draft which he discussed with Pacelli on Easter Day and Easter Monday. The revised version was presented to the Pope on the evening of Easter Monday and he discussed it the next morning with Pacelli and indicated a series of changes that were wanted.[25] The haste was obviously because Papen intended to take back a finished draft with him when he left on the Tuesday evening. That did not quite work, because the Pope's wishes still had to be taken into consideration. But the delay was only brief. Only two days later, on 20 April, the draft of the treaty left by courier for Berlin.[26] This ended the first round of negotiations.

Even in retrospect the whole proceedings have lost nothing of their strangeness. If it was already surprising that the German Vice-Chancellor should abruptly leave for Rome without any kind of diplomatic preparation in order to offer the Curia a concordat with the German Reich, it was almost incomprehensible that the heads of the Roman world church – Pope and Cardinal Secretary of State – should produce within a few days, in the midst of the celebration of Holy Week and Easter, the text of a treaty over which the Vatican would normally have negotiated for years. With the Prussian concordat, for example, it took two years – from 1926 to 1928 – to get even to the first complete draft. In spite of long preliminary discussions the negotiations over the Austrian concordat also still took two full years – from 1931 to 1933.[27] The Reich concordat is certainly the only treaty of the Roman Church the draft of which was conceived, so to speak, to the tones of the Good Friday liturgy and worked through and concluded amidst the bells of the Easter celebrations.

The question of what moved Rome to this haste can be answered on the basis of previous history. The safeguarding of canon law by treaty, which determined the policy of the Curia from 1917; Pacelli's decades-long futile efforts for a Reich concordat; the model of the Lateran Treaties; and not least the belief of the Cardinal Secretary of State and his closest German adviser that the historical situation was unique: all this combined to make this unusual procedure possible.

At this time neither Kaas nor Pacelli believed in the survival of the Centre Party. Therefore there had to be prompt action while the purchase price – i.e. the depoliticizing article – still had some value. However, because of their fixation on safeguards guaranteed by a concordat, and under the impact of a rapidly changing situation, the church partners in the negotiations overlooked the fact that the direct elimination of political Catholicism was only a small part of the advantage which Hitler gained from the treaty. He had formulated this advantage as early as 1929 in connection with the Italian concordat, and there is certainly no reason to assume that in 1933 he did not still look at things in the same way in respect of his own situation. As he declared at the time, 'the fact that the church can come to an understanding with Fascist Italy which would have been unthinkable with liberal-democratic Italy establishes beyond doubt that the Fascist world of ideas is more closely related to Christianity than is the Jewish-liberal or atheistic-Marxist world to which the so-called Catholic Party of the Centre now feels itself to be so closely bound, to the detriment of Christianity and our German Volk. If the Pope today comes to such an understanding with Fascism, then he is at least of the opinion that Fascism – and therefore nationalism – is justifiable for the faithful and compatible with the Catholic faith.'[28]

The haste with which the Catholic side engaged in negotiations demonstrated its burning interest in the treaty. But this gave Hitler a decisive trump card. In the certainty that Rome neither could nor would turn back, he was now able to steer the negotiations almost as he wanted. The records prove that he exploited this situation to the full.

On 20 April Kaas, 'in view of the urgency of the matter', had forwarded the draft to Papen and asked for him to give his opinion on it 'speedily... after confidential consultation with the Chancellor'.[29]

On the same day Kaas sent Hitler a birthday telegram, the most notable indication of the understanding between the Chancellor and the Chairman of the Centre Party, which in the circumstances amounted to an explicit endorsement of the concordat plans. The telegram read: 'Sincere good wishes for today and assurances of unswerving collaboration in the great work of the creation of a Germany united within, socially at peace, and outwardly free.'[30]

386

Papen's answer went off to Rome a week later, on 27 April. Following immediately on a 'general' discussion of the draft with Hitler, in this answer he markedly drew attention to the crucial points. Hitler was willing 'to grant far-reaching guarantees in the matter of the schools'; however, the wording of the depoliticizing article appeared to him 'quite inadequate'.[31]

In fact, apart from the actual concordat principle these were the two real issues in the whole concordat question between Berlin and Rome. For the Catholic side, the school provision (i.e. above all the safeguarding of confessional schools) had from the beginning of the 1920s been the 'heart of the concordat', 'a *conditio sine qua non*', 'the salient point'. If it was eliminated, Pacelli declared as early as 1921, 'the church would have no interest at all in the conclusion of a concordat'.[32] Exactly the same phrases, '*conditio sine qua non*', 'the salient point', were employed by the German side in connection with the demands for depoliticizing.[33] This and nothing else was the core of the treaty negotiations: the granting in full of the Catholic demands over schools in exchange for compliance in full with depoliticizing. As a negotiating tactic, Hitler guaranteed concessions to the demands over schools from the beginning and thus forced the Curia to adapt the depoliticizing article step by step to his views.

Here for reasons of canon law Kaas had at first tried to fall back on a provision of canon law which made the acceptance by clergy of a seat in Parliament dependent on episcopal authorization. At first, the article shown to Hitler at the end of April promised no more than to expand this requirement of authorization for holding office in political organizations and at most gave the impression that in the future this authorization would be construed more restrictively.[34] Whether this was a 'showpiece of Kaas's skill in drafting'[35] can remain open. However, Kaas certainly considerably underestimated Hitler if he acted on the assumption that he could get all he wanted on the school issue out of the Chancellor and then avoid complying in full with the demand for depoliticizing by a canon law ploy. Moreover Hitler had in fact never shown any kind of readiness to fall in with the negotiating ploys of the prelate. Rather, he insisted on a hard and clear formulation of this point - successfully, as was ultimately demonstrated.

Another point in Papen's letter of 27 April also called for Catholic attention. Discreetly but clearly, the Vice-Chancellor pointed out 'the efforts being made on the Protestant side towards the foundation of a Reich Church', efforts which seemed to him to make the current arrangements 'seem quite especially valuable' to the Holy See. In fact only two days before, Hitler had appointed Ludwig Müller as his official representative for Protestant church affairs and had given him the task of promoting a German Evangelical Reich Church. And as Hitler obviously had drawn the attention of the Catholic negotiators to the significance of this event for the Catholic side, he also informed the Protestant representatives similarly. For when on 4 May Ludwig Müller for the first time confidentially informed the Kirchenbund Committee of Three of Hitler's intentions, Marahrens made a note: 'Müller; no Reich concordat *without* Evangelical Reich Church. Hitler; a Catholic concordat only when *I* can ban the Centre Party.'[36]

Exactly fourteen days after Papen's letter Rome had made up its mind on the changes called for by the Germans. On 11 May a new version of the text of the preliminary draft of the concordat, which in many points already agreed with the final treaty, went to Berlin. In the most important article, however, the depoliticizing issue, the Curia was still far from a statement clear enough to satisfy Hitler. In comparison with the first draft Kaas had merely added an additional paragraph to this article stating that authorization for the involvement of the clergy in political activity would be granted by diocesan superiors 'only in exceptional instances and other cases especially justified by church interests'.[37] With this the treaty had evidently reached its optimal form for the Vatican, for soon afterwards Kaas informed the Vice Chancellor that he thought he could assume 'that an agreement can be reached upon the basis now established'.[38] Only a few days later, however, Papen had to inform the go-between in Rome that the Chancellor wanted 'a clear decision' on the depoliticizing question. At the same time he suggested a textual change that stood Kaas's regulation on its head: all official political activity by clergy was to be categorically forbidden, and an exception was to be possible only on the basis of a special agreement.[39]

The peculiarity of the negotiations which took place between Berlin and Rome during these weeks becomes really evident only when we visualize the situation in which German Catholicism found itself at this time. As early as Holy Week Professor Eggersdorfer of Munich had spoken in a letter to Vicar-General Riemer of Passau about the willingness on the part of both the Pope and Pacelli for a concordat and summarized his impression of the development in the prophetic sentences: 'Future of German Catholicism appears to be decided entirely in Rome. A result of the progressive centralism.'[40] In fact, up to the middle of May, when the essentials of the text of the concordat were already established, neither the Centre Party nor the German bishops had even been informed officially in any way, not to mention having been asked for their advice or in any way involved.

To be sure, strictly speaking there was no need for this participation since, according to Catholic canon law, as a so-called *causa major* the conclusion of a concordat is reserved to the Pope alone. In the conclusion of the previous concordats, however, both the political and the church Catholics of the countries concerned had always been involved as a matter of course. Thus during the 1920s the Centre Party had generally – through outstanding individual representatives such as Prelates Kaas and Föhr – contributed decisively to the form of the concordats with the German Länder. And the Austrian concordat of 1933 had even been prepared and essentially co-determined by an initiative on the part of the bishops.[41] The complete exclusion of the Catholic bishops and the Catholic parties from results obtained from negotiations up to the middle of May had been quite unusual. This also betrayed the unfortunate willingness of the Curia to go along all too quickly with the style of the new Reich.

In the light of this development, the Centre Party above all found itself in an almost hopeless situation. Since its Chairman had again left Germany for Rome on 7 April, it remained without any leadership or instruction from this side. Not even the top men of the Centre Party knew whether or when Kaas would return. Thus on 17 April the chairman of the parliamentary group thought that the party leader would be back in Berlin the next day. On 28 April, however, he wrote that 'contrary to expectations' he had not seen Kaas, though it seemed that the return of 'the chief' from his 'journey abroad' would not be for some time.[42] Even a statement entitled 'Centre Party People in City and Country' which the party vice-chairman, Joseph Joos, issued 'by instruction' on 14 April was ultimately no more than an expression of general helplessness. For lack of clear direction, which the Centre Party did not give because the Chairman was away and no one could act or decide in his place, its voters could only guess what might be meant by the following sentences: 'We are working together, with broad minds and open hearts, along with all the forces concerned to conserve the state and build up the nation, on the renewal and strengthening of our fatherland. In the spirit of a great tradition, we wish to use the forces we have gathered so that they become more fruitful for the whole enterprise.'[43]

For four full weeks, throughout April, Centre Party supporters saw themselves confronted with silence on the part of their leader. The consequences of this must have been all the more severe since at the same time the opposing side were increasingly loudly and emphatically asserting their claim to be the one party which united all good Germans, regardless of confession and in the best interests of the fatherland. During these weeks confusion spread through the already bewildered and perplexed party and among its followers which was irremediable. This confusion led to the final disintegration of the Centre Party, which had hitherto held up relatively well, so that it finally collapsed almost silently, without requiring any further push from the authorities.

Kaas doubtless bore the chief responsibility for this silence. That during these weeks he so manifestly failed in his duties as a leader was less a matter of 'negligence'[44] than of the desire, or at least the accepted consequence, of the policy he pursued. For he could hardly lead the party on a course of self-definition and renewal at a time when he was involved in crucial negotiations over its demise. On the other hand he could not easily give up control of it, because he still needed it as a bargaining chip for the 'adequate cultural-political guarantees' which he had mentioned to Papen on 8 April as the price.[45] This explains why Kaas neither took his party chairmanship seriously in April nor gave it up – in spite of urgent requests from his friends in the party.

In these circumstances the attempt by the Centre Party in early May at a new start was hardly more than an act of desperation. The party executive committee, the party group in the Reichstag and the Prussian parliamentary group had been summoned to Berlin for 5 and 6 May in order, finally, to make 'crucial decisions in matters of personnel and policy' relating to the reorganization of the party.[46] Kaas, who at first had evidently still warned against electing a new chairman because 'it would upset things in Rome',[47] had shortly beforehand finally been persuaded by telephone to resign the chairmanship. Heinrich Brüning was elected his successor on 6 May; he was the only person whose experience, courage and integrity were trusted to hold the party together in this situation. But in spite of the enthusiastic approval for the new chairman from all over the country, and in spite of the almost dictatorial powers which that the party delegated to him, there was really no hope. For not even Brüning could alter the fact that not only did Hitler find himself in possession of actual power but the process of the conquest of the minds of the German people had already advanced so far that it was no longer within the realm of the possible to pursue a policy against Hitler. Thus Brüning had no alternative than to attempt once more to lead the party along a path of national co-operation with Hitler while strictly protecting its independence and autonomy – an attempt which in the circumstances was doomed to failure.

It is perhaps no accident that Brüning is the only one of the prominent Catholics of this period who mentioned and understood the role of Bodelschwingh in his memoirs. Only he assessed the election of the first Reich Bishop as a 'Protestant success' which should have taught Rome and the bishop 'that their hour of resistance had also come, on a common front with the Protestants'.[48] In fact there are remote parallels between the fates of Brüning and Bodelschwingh during these weeks. Both made an attempt, in limited co-operation with the new Reich, to preserve autonomy and independence; both experienced the increasing undertow from the Nazi movement's resistance; and both were ultimately thwarted by church politics – Bodelschwingh by the whole-hearted willingness of the Lutheran bishops to compromise; Brüning by the no less whole-hearted willingness on the part of the Vatican to compromise. For in spite of all objections,[49] it is indisputable that Rome's lack of interest in the continued existence of the Centre Party, which was obvious to every member from the way in which its chairman abandoned it, was a crucial factor in its collapse.

During these weeks the German episcopate stood between the determination of Rome and the lack of leadership in the Centre Party. Like the Centre Party, but with rather more reason for confidence, since their 28 March declaration the German bishops had found themselves compelled for the time being to sit things out.

Evidently as early as the beginning of April, at least in Munich, there was fairly reliable information about Hitler's demand for the depoliticizing of the clergy and about Rome's readiness in principle to conclude a concordat. Thus on 10 April the Munich canon lawyer and Landtag deputy Anton Scharnagl reported to the Cardinal Secretary of State a relevant decision by Cardinal Faulhaber, who after discussion with the cathedral chapter rejected any exclusion of the clergy from the parliaments because this would 'be interpreted as a submission to National Socialist demands' and would, moreover, bring confusion into their own ranks.[50] And on 12 April his university colleague, Franz Eggersdorfer, noted laconically to the Vicar-General of Passau: 'Concordat; both Pope and Pacelli for a Reich concordat.'[51] Given the extreme importance of this information for the whole church, the knowledge of it was certainly not restricted to Munich. The intention to conclude a concordat was also known at the beginning of April through personal contacts. This was especially true in the case of the Archbishop of Freiburg, Conrad Gröber, known to be well disposed to a concordat, who was a friend of Kaas as well as of Pacelli's closest confidant, Father Leiber. Quite early on he showed himself to be well informed. At all events a phrase in a letter of 15 April – 'If only the Reich concordat does not again rob us of our chances for a Baden concordat'[52] – indicated that a decision had been made to conclude a treaty.

Beyond this, however, the bishops had no official information of any kind. So all that their official spokesman, Cardinal Bertram of Breslau, could do was to convey in general terms to the Cardinal Secretary of State the manifest unease felt about the negotiations in Rome. He did this on 18 April by communicating a series of petitions which concerned the protection of the Catholic associations and especially of the Catholic youth organizations, and with a reference to the limited influence of Papen. At the end he referred to the concordat negotiations with the significant phrase, 'In the endeavours of the Reich government for an understanding with the Holy See, I ask Your Eminence kindly to note these written statements which express the joint concerns of all the German bishops.'[53] However, Pacelli stood firm on his policy. In his answer of 1 May, the imperious and didactic tone of which was not very appropriate to the situation, there were only allusions to 'discussions initiated and possible negotiations between the Holy See and the Reich';[54] and as late as 22 May – long after the Vatican had given its consent to Kaas's draft – he maintained to Cardinal Faulhaber of Munich that there had indeed been talk with Papen and Göring about a Reich concordat, but so far there was 'nothing concrete'.[55]

The disparate state of information when the representatives of the church provinces met in Berlin on 25-26 April 1933 seems especially striking.[56] Whereas at this time Papen already had the first draft from Kaas in his hands and discussed it with Hitler on 26 April, the representatives of the German church were still completely dependent on news at second or third hand. The best-informed man proved to be the chairman of the Baden Centre Party, Prelate Föhr. On the basis of the connection between Archbishop Gröber and Father Leiber he could report that a Reich concordat had in fact been discussed in Rome. It was said to contain the essential provisions of the previous concordats with the Länder. However, a depoliticizing article on the Italian model was 'out of the question'. He reported that in general Rome was watching things carefully and wanted to avoid anything that could 'complicate the situation between state and church'.[57] In the middle of the discussions the chairwoman of the Catholic Women's Association, Maria Hessberger, made a surprise appearance. She had come directly from Rome and was supposed to convey to the chairman of the meeting, Bishop Schreiber, Kaas's anxiety that all the Catholic organizations would be smashed to pieces; his feeling that Papen was unreliable but that negotiations with Hitler were promising.[58] The purpose of these statements remained Frau Hessberger's secret. This interlude was also important simply as an indication of the chance sources of information upon which Rome still made the German church depend.

There were good reasons for the strict secrecy with which the plans for the concordat were surrounded until the middle of May. Evidently feelings about Hitler and the new situation in the Vatican and in the German episcopate at first differed completely. This was also one of the decisive impressions of Cardinal Faulhaber of Munich, who had stayed in Rome for ten days in mid-March. As he noted on 20 April for a report to the Bavarian bishops, his journey had confirmed to him that in Rome 'National Socialism, like Fascism, was thought to be the only salvation from Communism and Bolshevism'. Everything in Rome was seen reflected through the Italian newspapers, which naturally reported 'in Fascist colours'. So Faulhaber cited as a typically Roman opinion that it was time 'for the German Catholics to make another policy (that is, one no longer against Hitler)'.[59] Other visitors to the Vatican during these weeks had similar impressions. Thus on 25 April Bishop Schreiber of Berlin also knew 'from circles around the Cardinal Secretary of State... that not all the measures of the German bishops are approved. People are now very hopeful in Rome.'[60]

While this certainly reflected the basic mood in the Vatican, Pacelli was well aware that the German episcopate as a whole did not share this optimism. In April the two conference chairmen, Bertram and Faulhaber, were undecided but rather sceptical. The third German cardinal, Schulte, was considered a resolute opponent of National Socialism. What individual bishops thought was not always clear. But without question it had to be assumed that at least a minority were unreconciled opponents of Hitler. In addition, while there was hope of the rescue of the Centre Party, the bishops would hardly have given up their close connection with it. This differing assessment of the situation, which in turn inevitably had a crucial effect upon the basic willingness for a concordat, could not be balanced out. Thus Pacelli obviously saw – probably quite correctly – that his plans would be endangered, if not doomed to failure, by a premature inclusion of the German bishops in the concordat negotiations. Hence in this first phase he kept everything to do with the concordat secret – evidently without considering what a triumph it must be for Hitler when the Curia had more confidence in him than in its own bishops.

But the significance of this policy of secrecy may extend still further. That is, it prevented a discussion in the Catholic Church like that which a little later almost tore the Protestant church apart. This was undoubtedly an advantage in the eyes of the Curia. But perhaps in an open discussion in the struggle against the Reich concordat, as well as against the Reich Church, the obstinate minority of both churches would have been able to find themselves. As it was, on the Catholic side things happened in such a matter-of-fact and silent way that the Protestant opposition did not have the slightest point of contact. On the contrary, here too a hasty pact with Hitler must have seemed the necessity of the moment.

On 13 May Kaas assured the Vice Chancellor, after renewed consideration of the draft by the Vatican, that he believed an agreement to be possible on this basis.[61] Two weeks later, the German ambassador to the Holy See, in a letter to the Reich Foreign Minster, also confirmed the wide-ranging agreement of the two partners. With a bad grace, because to that point he had been almost totally excluded, the diplomat declared that there was no question of his having any 'influence over the shape of the planned concordat'. 'The discussions with Pacelli have moved on so far, and the commitments entered into are already so strong (it looks as if the draft has also been submitted to the Pope for unofficial approval in principle), that no more suggestions for major change can be made without seriously endangering the hoped-for treaty.' He could therefore take no credit for work on concluding the treaty nor responsibility for any concessions.[62]

Only at this stage of the negotiations was the German episcopate officially informed. For this purpose the Curia used the *visitatio liminum* in the Holy City of two German bishops, Bishop Berning of Osnabrück and Archbishop Gröber of Freiburg.[63] Both were particularly well suited to be go-betweens in the concordat plans in a manner to Rome's liking: Berning because since his conversation with Hitler on 26 April he was convinced of the Chancellor's good will;[64] Gröber because, as the friend of Pacelli, Leiber and Kaas, from the begining he had sympathized with the Vatican. Pacelli received Berning on 18 May. The most important topic of discussion was the concordat. The Cardinal Secretary of State now told the Bishop of Osnabrück that it was 'not to be done without the bishops'. They were to consolidate their wishes for the conference scheduled for 30 May at Fulda and send them to him. In addition they were to nominate a bishop who would then take part in further negotiations. On 20 May these instructions were explicitly confirmed at a reception of Berning by the Pope.[65]

However, even the Bishop of Osnabrück did not yet see the text of the concordat draft. For its communication Pacelli made use of the Archbishop of Freiburg, who thus clearly gained a key position in the further course of the negotiations.[66] That in using Gröber Rome had trusted an explicit friend of the concordat to be go-between emerged from a letter which the Archbishop of Freiburg sent to Kaas immediately on his return. In it he repeated that the draft of the concordat was 'very good in both content and wording'. In view of the growing radicalism everywhere, he increasingly realized that the Reich concordat had to be completed 'as soon as practicably possible'. And he added: 'That would finally bring about clarity, and guarantee co-operation towards holding everything together.'[67] In fact Gröber was one of those in the Catholic Church who had an unshakeable trust in the possibility of an understanding with the Third Reich and who thought that it was to their own side that they had to appeal again and again for loyalty and co-operation.[68]

How successful Pacelli's concordat policy had been so far was demonstrated at the great plenary conference at the end of May, which for the first time since 1905 again brought together all the German bishops in Fulda. With the assignments to Gröber and Berning, this conference had surprisingly been given a new, definitive theme. Having originally planned the meeting in order to come to an understanding of the standpoint of the episcopate in the new Reich, to discuss necessary measures and to issue a joint pastoral message, the bishops now saw themselves confronted with an initiative from Rome which had already to a certain degree pre-empted their basic decisions. That there was still some room for manoeuvre for the church in Germany at the end of May was shown by the Protestant church's decision for Bodelschwingh, which was made at almost the same time. However, in this situation a critical dissociation on the Catholic side like that suggested by Bishop Preysing would have amounted to a disavowal of Rome. Even in other circumstances it would have been difficult to find a majority for this position among the bishops.

Obliged to strict secrecy by the chairman, Cardinal Bertram, the comprehensive official record revealed almost nothing of the dominant theme during these days.[69] Only the notes – albeit quite fragmentary – of the Bishop of Speyer, Ludwig Sebastian, show that the question of the Reich concordat governed the discussion from the beginning.[70] Thus on the very first day in the 'debate on the present situation', Gröber and Berning put forward the desires and ideas of the Vatican, while the Bishop of Berlin, Christian Schreiber, presented the government view on behalf of Papen. Here the bishops learned that Hitler considered the total depoliticizing of the clergy to be the *conditio sine qua non* for the concordat, while the Vice-Chancellor was arguing for a more moderate solution. Since Gröber reported truthfully that the concordat had already made a good deal of 'progress' and Berning added that 'haste is called for', it seemed rather pointless to discuss the fundamental problem any further.

All the more remarkable, then, was the objection of Cardinal Schulte of Cologne, who declared that 'the government is a revolutionary government; law and right do not at present exist. No concordat could be concluded with such a government'.[71] The Bishop of Eichstätt, Konrad von Preysing, attempted to influence things in another way. In a short memorandum to the conference on 31 May he expressed his views on the content of the planned pastoral letter. As clear-sighted as he was determined, he asked for no acknowledgment 'of the "new order" or the "new state" to be included' in it, arguing that 'the new state is identified by its creators with the National Socialist Party. Consequently it has basic principles, like those of the Party, which are incompatible with our view of the world.' In addition, he asked for an explicit repetition of the dogmatic and ethical rejection of National Socialist errors. The bishops, he said, 'owe it to the Catholic people to open its eyes to the dangers to faith and ethics which emerge from National Socialist ideology'. That Preysing did not share the Roman optimism, but considered a struggle to be almost inevitable, was shown by his remark, 'We must be able to refer to this pastoral letter in a conflict which is probably coming.' Finally, he pointed out – in a way similar to critical voices on the Protestant side – that the apparently pious language of the Third Reich was false and corrupt. 'Today,' his memorandum concluded, 'all meaning is taken out of the words God, Christ, morality, law and they are given an empty, or rather a depraved, sense.'[72] This memorandum not only contained a devastating criticism of National Socialism but also represented an unspoken condemnation of the Roman plans for a concordat. For if Preysing was right, then the church could not conclude a treaty with this state which certainly also amounted to a recognition of the civil partner in the treaty.

It is not known whether Preysing's memorandum was discussed at the conference at all, and whether there were confrontations among the bishops similar to those taking place at the same time on the Evangelischer Kirchenaus- schuss. The only certain thing is that in the end the majority took Gröber's position. And the concordat, in its turn, contributed decisively to this. For the Archbishop of Freiburg was the only one who was really familiar with the text of the draft – which on the Wednesday morning was merely read, but not distributed. And he was also the only one in a position 'to report in detail about the state of affairs'.[73] At the same time he was evidently successful in really convincing the majority of the bishops of the quality as well as of the necessity of the concordat. For when soon afterwards, in a conversation with Papen, Cardinal Faulhaber of Munich affirmed that 'the draft is good, so good that I can hardly believe that it will be passed', his enthusiasm was undoubtedly caught from Gröber.[74] In a choice between unforeseeable difficulties on the one hand and the apparently hopeful way towards a better future on the other, the bishops decided for the latter, all the more happily because the responsibility for it lay not with them but with Rome.

The fundamental decisions of these days made themselves felt in two respects. On 3 June a joint pastoral message appeared, the wording of which was entrusted by the conference to the Archbishop of Freiburg – another sign of his dominant position.[75] Already drafted before the conference began and in accord with its conviction, the message was completely attuned to the idea of hopeful co- operation. Catholic Germany could now see that the opinion of its bishops was that if only the state would respect certain rights and demands of the church, the church would thankfully and joyfully support the newly-created state. In particular the pastoral message welcomed the 'national awakening'; the 'strong emphasis on authority' for which the church had always had a special appreciation; 'the goals to which the new state authority' aspired 'on behalf of the freedom of our people'; and the solemn professions of Christianity by leading figures. Critical misgivings like references to the injustice to which 'exclusive emphasis on race and blood' led were formulated so carefully that they hardly disturbed its basically affirmative tenor. This was also true of the paragraphs on the rights and demands of the church, the necessity of its freedom and independence, its right to confessional schools and protection for its societies and associations. All this was included in the acknowledgment of the new state and co-operation in it. 'We German bishops do not make the demands listed here on the basis of some concealed reserve towards the new state. We do not want at any price to withhold the forces of the church from the state nor may we, for only the power of the people and the power of God which flow inexhaustibly out of church life can save us and raise us up. Standing aside to see what happens, or even hostility on the part of the church towards the state, could fatally affect church and state.'[76]

If we connect this pastoral letter with the concordat plans, the context in which it obviously belongs, then it simply represented the bishops' consent to the policy of the Curia and, at the same time, the preparation of German Catholicism for the impending treaty. Moreover, it was no coincidence that Gröber enclosed a copy of this message in his first report to Kaas on the course of the conference, along with the comment: 'Praise God I succeeded in getting approval for the accompanying pastoral letter, which I had drafted last Sunday.'[77]

The details of the result of the discussions on the concordat were no less gratifying to Rome than this pastoral letter. In any case they would have been a 'high point of the conference', as Gröber told his friend Kaas. And with some relief he noted that the bishops 'do not just agree with most of the paragraphs, but they welcome them gratefully'. The extent of his own share in this result emerged from the remark that 'a series of wishes' had been 'expressed but I could easily reject them because they demand the impossible'.[78] Some individual results, which Gröber passed on to his friend in Rome, were more concerned with incidental matters. By contrast, he kept remarkably quiet about the main point, namely the depoliticizing question. Here the conference had made emphatic objections to the draft, and in a formulation of its own had suggested a version which was to leave to the bishops far-reaching rights in this question. The arguments used showed that the German bishops saw the purpose and danger of this provision far more clearly than did the Curia. That is, the state demand was in line with 'the effort of the National Socialists to drive the clergy from each and every activity in public life. This is very disadvantageous for Germany, where the church is a Volkskirche to a quite exceptional degree. In other words, it is not confined to the sacristy. It will deprive the clergy of a very great many spheres of activity which belong within the social context of the influence of Catholic Action.'[79] However, in spite of these misgivings the bishops did not make the depoliticizing article in its church version the *conditio sine qua non*, a move which would certainly have led to a breakdown of negotiations. Rather, Faulhaber now indicated, to Papen of all people, that he personally was willing to yield on this point. 'The concordat as a whole is so important,' he noted on the question of Article 31, 'for instance confessional schools, that I feel that it ought not to fail on this point.'[80] With this comment, the significance of which Papen of course grasped immediately, the church's room for manoeuvre had shrunk to almost nothing.[81]

Nevertheless, the result of the Fulda Conference appeared to be a brilliant success for the Curia. Publicly as well as internally, the German bishops had now committed themselves to the Vatican's concordat policy. Now all that was necessary was to bring matters to a conclusion as quickly and as advantageously as possible.

However, before this conclusion could be achieved, the church's negotiating position deteriorated rapidly. This was a direct result of the progress made at this time in the National Socialist seizure of power. From the beginning of March the Chancellor had succeeded almost week by week not only in improving his internal political position but also in gaining the support of more and more groups in the population. Anyone who was not completely firm in his conviction now moved more and more towards Hitler. This affected the Catholic population in two respects. For the first time the Party now dared to let the church feel its power directly. And at the same time the Centre Party fell apart with a speed which surprised even the National Socialist camp.

The first, major and widely noticed clash took place in Munich early in June. The second German Apprentices Rally, the Kolping Rally, had been called for 8-11 June in the Bavarian capital. With 20-25,000 non-resident participants, this great meeting was to give evidence of the commitment of the Catholic apprentices to both church and fatherland. In a city like Munich, of course, this meeting also amounted to a demonstration of Catholic self-confidence and Catholic independence. This was probably the real reason why the Bavarian political police suddenly banned the event on 2 June.[82]

Since the beginning of April this authority had been in the hands of two men whose names were later to become the epitome of the National Socialist reign of terror: Heinrich Himmler and Reinhard Heydrich. Himmler, a thirty-three year old graduate agriculturalist from Munich, Reichsführer of the SS, which was still small, and also since 2 June the newly appointed Reichsleiter, had begun his police career at the beginning of April as Commandant of the political police in Bavaria, a position which was to take him on to head the whole German police. His deputy Heydrich, only twenty-nine, a former Navy officer, became chief of the Security Police only three years later and was thus among the most powerful men in the Reich. Now, at the Munich Kolping Rally in June 1933, both were evidently rehearsing their steps on the way to power through terror. The third member of this alliance was the Gauleiter of Munich and Bavarian Minister of the Interior, Adolf Wagner; it was he who, as the most powerful political figure in the Bavarian cabinet, furthered and covered Himmler's activity.[83]

This unusual Bavarian team gave a special importance to the 2 June ban. Nevertheless, in a conversation with Adolf Wagner, the two leading figures in the Apprentices Association – General President Theodor Hürth and General Secretary Johannes Nattermann, supported by protests from Papen and Faul-haber,[84] succeeded in obtaining a reversal of the ban on condition that 'any public demonstration, marching in closed groups would be avoided, and banners would only be carried furled'. The intention here soon emerged in a further conversation between Wagner and Cardinal Faulhaber. In it the Minister of the

Interior declared that Hitler had authorized him to give the assurance that in no circumstances was anything to be done against the church or the clergy. At the same time, however, he uttered vigorous threats against the Bavarian People's Party and demanded the withdrawal of the associations from the streets 'for at least a few months'.[85] The course of the Apprentices Rally showed impressively just how these threats were meant. After numerous attacks on individuals during the first two days, on the Saturday evening the acts of violence increased to the point of systematic terror. An order from the political police which with immediate effect prohibited the wearing of the orange-coloured Kolping shirts reached the Rally towards the end of a major celebration, at which Papen had just given a patriotic speech. The prohibition left the apprentices, as planned, to the whim of the waiting SA, who pursued them, beat them up, and tore the shirts from their backs. Since the leaders of the Rally did not manage to get a guarantee of the life and safety of the participants from the police, the meeting broke up even before the festal mass on the Sunday. Beatings and insults followed the departing apprentices as far as the station platforms.[86]

The target of this violent action was political Catholicism in the broadest sense; the whole affair was a kind of commentary on the depoliticizing article. And Catholic reactions showed that the blow struck home. Karl Scharnagl, a prominent member of the Bavarian People's Party, and former Chief Bürgomeister of Munich, advised the Cardinal the very next day to pursue Catholic interests 'through complete dissociation from all political groups and the expulsion of all politically-suspect persons'. 'Only the church authorities, our bishops, are called to act in these matters.'[87] Although the clarity of Faulhaber's protests to Hitler, Wagner, Siebert Röhm and Himmler left nothing to be desired,[88] in a letter to the Bavarian bishops the Cardinal showed at the same time that the proceedings had produced the effects for which those who instigated them had hoped. In this letter Faulhaber quoted the declaration of the Minister of the Interior 'that given the current fury of the SA troops against the Catholic associations, all demonstrations of the Catholic associations in closed columns and uniforms' had to 'be discontinued "for at least two or three months"' and added: 'After what we have experienced at the Apprentices Rally we have no alternative, if we do not want to risk the lives of our young men and a government ban on the youth organizations.'

At the same time the letter contained a remark which was very typical of the church's situation between the National Socialist revolution and the Reich concordat. 'Stern action will be taken against clergy who speak imprudently. Such people do not realize that we are living in the middle of a revolution, indeed that this revolution is only beginning.'[89] This meant quite simply that any kind of public criticism of and resistance against the new régime by the clergy would not only be prosecuted by the state but would also be reprimanded and punished by the church authorities. Where this course led was shown by the fact that at the end of June this already could become the subject of official agreements between church and Party. Thus after violent clashes on 26 June the Gauleitung in the Palatinate promised the Bishop of Speyer to release all arrested clergymen in exchange for the bishop's promise to instruct the clergy to abstain in the exercise of their office 'from all political activity and improper criticism of the measures of the national government'.[90] And even after the conclusion of the Reich concordat this forced self-limitation of the church also remained the general line of the episcopate. At the end of 1933, for example, Gröber complained to Pacelli that unfortunately it had not always been possible 'to obtain among the clergy that prudent discretion and expedient reflection which, while fully safeguarding principles, protects the individual priest from inappropriate words and actions'.[91]

In view of this open dissociation of the church from political Catholicism, it was not surprising that the Catholic parties, the Centre Party and the Bavarian People's Party, fell apart with increasing rapidity. By the middle of the month the Centre Party was in effect finished. The complete hopelessness of the situation, the end of all leadership and all solidarity, was reflected in the image of the lonely Reichstag deputy Eugen Bolz, until not long before State President of Württemberg. On 16 June he wrote to his wife from Berlin, 'Nor is there anyone with whom I can talk... At present I'm in the Reichstag, but couldn't converse with any one.'[92] Nor did anyone help him when he was arrested three days later in Stuttgart, dragged through the city in triumph, and then taken into 'protective custody'. Not long afterwards Karl Bachem noted from the former stronghold of Cologne, 'The Centre Party is quite incapable of action; today all activity is quite impossible for it.'[93]

Hitler, however, still distrusted his hated and feared opponent. Therefore a new wave of house searches and arrests, of threats and humiliations, was launched to contribute towards hastening and completing the disintegration of the Catholic parties. In Bavaria in particular, the government of the Land exploited its new power to the full. At the climax of the campaigns against the Bavarian People's Party, almost 2,000 supporters and officials were in prison – including even the chairman, Fritz Schäffer.[94] Under the headline 'The Black Saboteurs in Protective Custody', on 27 June the press reported that 'the actions against political Catholicism' had clearly revealed that 'these circles' were not at all serious in their affirmation of the new Reich. 'Rather, the investigations have shown that Catholicism aims in every way to sabotage the orders of the government and to work against it.'[95]

The organizations and members of both parties were far from being able to stand up to these stresses any more. The resignations now piled up everywhere; whole parliamentary groups went over *en bloc* to the NSDAP.[96] The official self-dissolution of the party was only a question of time.

The pressure which resulted from the whole situation at the end of June can hardly be overestimated. The Evangelical Church in Prussia was under a state commissioner, and between rebellion and co-ordination was on the way to being a Reich Church. Political Catholicism was at an end; however, the Catholic Church, wavering between fear and hope, kept a spellbound eye directed on Rome and waited for the result of the Roman negotiations.

For it was precisely in this period that the concordat discussions now entered their last, decisive phase. On 22 June Papen had given Hitler a 'detailed report on the state of the negotiations' and had been authorized to return immediately to Rome to conclude them. The announcement of his journey to the German ambassador to the Vatican contained two important pieces of information. One was about the depoliticizing article and indicated that Hitler would insist upon a clear formulation on this point. The other revealed knowledge of the special role of Gröber, whose involvement Bergen was to suggest to the Curia.[97] The

Archbishop of Freiburg was in fact summoned to Rome by telephone on 28 June as the representative of the German episcopate and took part in the negotiations from 1 July.[98]

The very day Papen arrived in Rome, 28 June, as a basis for negotiation he sent Pacelli a draft concordat 'as discussed by us in the preliminary negotiations and as proposed by the German government'. For the first time the Curia could read the depoliticizing article Hitler had in mind: 'In consideration of the guarantees created by the provisions of the aforesaid treaty, and of legislation preserving the rights and freedoms of the Catholic Church in the Reich and its Länder, the Holy See establishes provisions which exclude the participation of all clergy and members of orders in party political activity.'[99]

Here the most important demand of the Reich, the *conditio sine qua non*, 'the salient point', lay upon the negotiating table. The crucial question was whether the Vatican would accept this formulation.

Of course the rapid deterioration of its negotiating position in June had not escaped the Curia. Whereas in April and May, with Hitler's apparent need for support and lack of stability it was certainly still possible to hope to obtain a kind of concordat of the century, the scene was now known to have changed fundamentally as a result of the rapid increase in the power and security of National Socialist rule. In the course of this change, however, Pacelli's attitude to the treaty also changed. If early in the year it still seemed to the Cardinal Secretary of State that a uniquely favourable combination of political circumstances might put into his hands the fulfilment of all his efforts over long years for a German concordat, he now began to understand that the treaty could be justified only as a line of defence. The most important evidence for this altered assessment lies in the comments of his closest confidant, Father Robert Leiber, on the draft presented by Papen. These comments explain why the Curia finally signed in spite of everything. The depoliticizing article was again crucial in this context. Leiber saw that the suggestion made by the German government was even more restrictive than the wording of the Italian concordat. But he also saw how far the Curia had already been pushed into a defensive position. So he suggested a new compromise version to be used if the Holy See, *ad maiora mala vitanda* (i.e. in order to prevent something worse), had 'to look for a way out'. 'After the dissolution of the German National Party,' he added, 'we must expect similar consequences for the Centre Party very soon. If that happens, then Article 31, the only one for which the government is making the concordat, would no longer be a concession by the church. I would not like to bear this responsibility. Any delay carries within it a great *periculum in mora*.' But there is a concluding sentence in Leiber's version which makes the humiliating assent to the depoliticizing of the church ordered by the government even appear to be an advantage: 'After the dissolution of the Centre Party, the formula proposed is a safeguard for the church against a National Socialist invasion of the clergy.'[100] There had been no talk of this before, nor did this factor play any role later; but for the moment it might in fact have helped Pacelli to overcome his last objections to agreeing to this article.[101]

The concluding negotiations began on Friday 30 June. Only two days later, on the Sunday afternoon, the text was finalized. Gröber had a considerable share in making it possible to arrive at an agreement so quickly, even though the news reports about the persecution and suppression of the church in Germany were coming in one on top of another. In a letter to Pacelli on 1 July the Archbishop of Freiburg, since the middle of May unswervingly on a concordat course, himself raised the obvious question whether now was really the time for a concordat. But in Germany, Gröber affirmed, there was agreement 'among the bishops, the clergy and leading lay people that the concordat had to be concluded, and the sooner the better'. The treaty was a good one and would 'put things in order, at least temporarily'. Misgivings about the Centre Party were 'inappropriate in the present situation'. As he explained the opinion of the German church, in contradiction to the decision at Fulda: 'I believe that even a harsh prohibition of the political activity of the clergy will be readily tolerated if it succeeds in saving our organizations, and if the Protestant clergy are affected as well as the Catholic. Hundreds of people who are facing protective custody, and are now in great distress along with their families because of it, would be exceedingly grateful to the Holy See if they could be spared this fate.' Of course the German government would have to agree 'that now, at last, the German Kulturkampf has been called off'.[102]

This now became a condition for the approval of Pius XI, who discussed the text of the treaty with Pacelli on the Sunday. 'Guarantees,' as Pacelli noted to himself at the end of the morning audience with reference to the Pope's position, 'that the acts of violence will be made good. Here the Holy Father is unyielding. Here negotiated with; there abused. Hitler to make a declaration. I will initial only if there is compensation.'[103] With this reservation the Pope, too, finally gave his consent to the agreed text on the afternoon of 2 July.

For Papen, this declaration by Hitler was no problem since the latter had authorized him by telephone the day before to give the Cardinal Secretary of State all the assurances he wanted 'for a comprehensive and full settlement between the Catholic part of the Volk and the Reich government'.[104] Thus the Vice-Chancellor could send on to Hitler that very Sunday the text of the concordat together with a covering letter which all too clearly indicated his pride at the scope of what had been achieved. In the short explanation of the individual articles, expressions like 'in accordance with your wishes' (Article 14); 'the formula... which corresponds... to your wish' (Article 27) recurred repeatedly. On Article 29 the Vice-Chancellor remarked that here he had 'obtained a concession for the rights of minorities which is of quite extraordinary importance for German policy'. Finally, he explained the transposition of the concluding article 'so that what was Article 31 concludes the concordat as its most important article'. This new article, now no.32, produced the solution 'which you, Mr Chancellor, have wished, in that the Holy See is enacting regulations which exclude all members of the clergy and all members of orders from membership of and activity in political parties'.[105] Hitler received this letter in Munich on the afternoon of 3 July. However, Papen's hope that he would now be authorized to initial the treaty that very evening was not fulfilled. Rather, a delay suddenly occurred which surprised all those involved.[106]

These days also saw the formal end of the Centre Party in Germany. The most important man in this connection was the Baden Deputy Albert Hackelsberger, a friend of Gröber and Kaas and like them determined on a policy of accommodation. On 28 June, the day that Papen arrived in Rome, the busy Hackelsberger entered into negotiations with the Reich Interior Minister over how the 'process of adjustment which can no longer be avoided' could take place in 'as smooth a way as possible', since a 'schematic co-ordination' might gain nominal members but certainly not 'happy colleagues'.[107] This was a periphrasis for Hackelsberger's attempt to obtain, if possible, an associate status in the NSDAP for all parliamentary members of the Centre Party. Negotiations on this question dragged on and on, especially since the Bavarian People's Party still sought an arrangement with the Centre Party. On 5 July everything was finally ready. 'The political revolution,' the national leadership of the party announced, 'has placed German civil life upon a completely new foundation which no longer leaves any room for a party-political activity which was possible only a short time ago. Therefore the German Centre Party is disbanding with immediate effect, in agreement with Reich Chancellor Hitler.' Hackelsberger's hand was unmistakable in the next passage: 'This disbanding gives its supporters the chance to make their energies and experiences wholly available for the national front under the leadership of the Chancellor, for positive co-operation towards the stabilization of our national, social economic and cultural conditions, and collaboration in the restoration of law and order.'[108]

Here Hitler had achieved one of his oldest and most important domestic political aims. For it was not just any political party that had disappeared; the bastion of dreaded political Catholicism had now finally fallen. Possibly Hitler had overestimated the political and ideological power of this opponent from the beginning. However, that did not diminish his triumph and the impression made by his victory. The totalitarian state was now within reach.

Whereas the German press celebrated this victory at length, Rome proved remarkably taciturn. According to a report from Robert Leiber, on hearing the news of the disbanding Pacelli remarked, 'A pity that it had to come now.'[109] But this regret could in all honesty be only over the time of the end. For from the beginning – presumably from as early as 23 March – the negotiations over the Reich concordat were conducted at the expense of political Catholicism, and the Curia should have been the last to show itself surprised at the dissolution of the Centre Party. In fact, in Rome, too, the party had been finally written off for a long time. This was shown by Leiber's remarks of 29 June about the expected end of the party[110] and by Kaas's flippant comment in a telephone conversation with Joos early in July: 'You still haven't disbanded?'[111] Although the surrender of the party had thus been agreed upon for a long time, Papen once more brought up the question officially in a discussion with Pacelli, Gröber and Kaas on the evening of 3 July, and that same evening reported to Berlin that 'disbanding of the Centre Party is approved here and considered to be settled with the conclusion of the concordat'.[112] In these circumstances Pacelli's official denial of April 1934, understandable though it is – seems somewhat questionable. 'The disbanding of the Centre Party,' maintained the *Osservatore Romano* at that time, 'which occurred even before the signing of the concordat, was never an object of negotiations between the Holy See and the Reich government. The Holy See did not have the least thing to do with it.'[113] Given all that we know, this is untrue.

On 2 July all the parties in Rome believed that the initialling of the concordat by the Cardinal Secretary of State and the Vice-Chancellor was only hours away.

Hitler, however, had a new surprise. Instead of approving on the spot a text which in essentials accorded with his wishes, he now decided, to Papen's dismay and Pacelli's annoyance, that the Reich Minister of the Interior should also deal with the treaty. On 4 July he summoned the head of the division responsible, Ministerial Director Dr Rudolf Buttmann, and gave him the text of the concordat with instructions to work out an opinion on it immediately from the Ministry of the Interior.[114] Thereupon Buttmann and his associate Walter Conrad sat up deep into the night looking at the detailed provisions. On 5 July Buttmann presented the results of this work to Hitler, who in addition had invited the Minister of the Interior, the Foreign Minister and the Finance Minister.[115] The very day the Reich Chancellor had approved the suggestions for changes, Buttmann flew to Munich in Hitler's special plane, and next day on to Rome to present and explain the Reich's new demands.

While Hitler's step was surprising, it was not at all incomprehensible. Once the basic decision had been made, it seemed advisable to have the particulars of the treaty, which hitherto had been negotiated completely in a Catholic environment, reviewed independently by a third party. Frick and Buttmann, whom Hitler could trust absolutely, were especially qualified for this. Besides, there were in fact still two technical questions to clarify, the so-called protection of associations and the declaration from Hitler which the Curia categorically demanded. Finally, a delay was highly desirable in view of the Protestant situation. For it was only on 4 July that the declarations by Müller and Frick had shown a way of resolving the church conflict which would also leave Hitler's way free on the Catholic side. All this together explained Buttmann's mission. Despite the delay, neither Hitler nor Pacelli contemplated that the negotiations would fail at the last moment. Thus Buttmann did not arrive as a National Socialist agitator, as was feared, but quite quickly proved to be a serious and co-operative negotiating partner with whom it was possible to have 'a frank and open discussion' – as Gröber reported to Faulhaber and Bertram soon afterwards. In fact in a first preliminary discussion Buttmann let himself be convinced by the German negotiators 'that some of the changes which he was demanding on behalf of the Ministry could not be accepted by the Holy See'.[116]

Nevertheless, on 7 July the climate was obviously worse at the beginning of the negotiations with Pacelli. The Cardinal Secretary of State spoke of a 'spirit of distrust' behind the suggestions for changes, and he let it be understood that in these circumstances it was virtually out of the question for the concordat to be concluded. Buttmann skilfully retorted that it was better to review everything thoroughly now than to get into difficulties in implementing the concordat later. At the same time, to Pacelli's displeasure, he also demonstrated that he regarded himself as a representative of Protestant interests. He declared that the Italian concordat was not applicable to Germany in all respects, 'because in Italy there is only one confession, whereas the Reich government always has to discover what the overwhelming Protestant majority of the German people has to say to individual provisions'.[117]

Immediately afterwards, and at Buttmann's suggestion, the two parties entered into substantive negotiations. It then became evident that after the decision over the depoliticizing question it was Article 31 – supposed to control the protection of the Catholic associations – which had now moved into the centre of interest for both sides. This was not at all surprising. For after the end of political Catholicism the associations provided crucial public support for the Catholic church; whereas conversely the Party's radical co-ordination policy fundamentally ruled out the existence of independent confessional associations and had already affected some of them. So in the draft of 2 July a compromise had been arrived at which divided the associations into those with 'purely religious, cultural and charitable purposes' and others which 'for example, also serve social or professional purposes'. The former group was to be fully protected; the latter to enjoy this protection on certain conditions, 'without prejudice to their possible integration into civil associations'.[118] Buttmann, for whom this went too far, had brought from Berlin the suggestion that the article should be retricted to the purely religious associations and that references to the other associations should be deleted. However, he could not get approval for this suggestion from Pacelli, who was unyielding here. This left the complicated and impractical provision, supplemented by an additional paragraph, which reserved 'the definition of the organizations and associations which fall under the provisions of this article' to a 'settlement to be agreed on' between the Reich government and the bishops. The fact that the Curia did not insist on unequivocal arrangements here but relied on future agreements would soon prove to be a serious mistake.[119]

No less controversial than Article 31 was the question of Hitler's political declaration, which Pius XI personally had made the condition for his assent. Presumably Buttmann had not left Berlin without instructions on this point, too. At all events, on the Friday, even before the beginning of the negotiations, he drew up 'at Kaas's request' a text which was then refined during the course of the day and was finally settled personally by Hitler in a long evening telephone conversation.[120]

That solved the essential problems. Nothing more stood in the way of initialling the treaty.

Even in retrospect, Buttmann's account of the solemn act of the signing on the afternoon of 8 July 1933 reveals something of the unusualness of the situation. Pacelli evidently also felt it strongly. 'The bell rings at 6 p.m. precisely. First of all, after a few ceremonial greetings during which I speak Italian with Pizzardo, Pacelli and Papen take their seats and sign with initials. Pacelli by mistake signs one copy of the final protocol with his full name; Kaas notices this and induces him to keep the copy for himself. Then Pacelli discusses some recent rumours, one from the Palatinate (Königsbach!), where a pastor had been hauled out of his manse at night, "barefoot and without stockings", brought to a car a quarter of an hour's walk away and beaten until he collapsed, etc. I take the opportunity to speak: this would probably be a pastor with a high political profile; the people of the Palatinate are very temperamental; besides, the Gauleiter was a Catholic.'[121]

On the Monday morning the whole German press reported the conclusion of the treaty in large headlines. At the same time it published the 'Decree of the Reich Chancellor on the Conclusion of the Concordat', agreed upon in Rome on the Friday. In its way, this decree was a masterpiece. It certainly contained the concessions demanded by the Vatican, at any rate the two most important ones, without deletions and qualifications. But an introductory sentence put

403

these concessions in a context which made them seem a success for the politics of national renewal.[122] The decree ran:

> The conclusion of the concordat seems to me to give sufficient guarantee that the Reich members of the Roman Catholic confession will from now on put themselves without reservation at the service of the new National Socialist state.
>
> Therefore I am ordering as follows: 1. The disbanding of such organizations as are recognized by the present treaty, and whose disbanding occurred without the order of the Reich government, is to be rescinded immediately. 2. All coercive measures against the clergy and other leaders of these Catholic organizations are to be revoked. Repetition of such measures in the future is not allowed and will be punished on the basis of existing laws.[123]

Seldom did it become as clear as in this decree to what extent Hitler's church policy was also part of his general policy. The disbanding of the parties, the collapse of political Catholicism, the conclusion of the concordat and the end of the revolution: during these days all this merged into a unity which provided a victorious conclusion to the seizure of power. These connections became evident once again in the closing sentence of the decree, which directed attention to the Protestant side. 'The treaty concluded between the Reich and the Catholic Church will also serve to restore the peace for which all are calling in this area' – namely, in the controversies between state and church. 'I have high hopes that the settlement of the issues of present concern to the Protestant confession will soon happily complete this act of settlement.' Three days later, on 11 July the new constitution of the German Evangelical Church was signed.

All of this, but especially the concordat, was Hitler's personal achievement. In the history of the Third Reich there is hardly a treaty to which he devoted such intensive attention as this one. When Buttmann made a detailed report to him on the Obersalzberg on 10 July, he again went into 'all the details with the greatest interest and spoke,' as Buttmann wrote to his wife, 'a few very confident words which were of psychological interest to me'.[124]

Also on 14 July, when the treaty came to the great cabinet meeting which put a political end to all these developments, he could not conceal his triumph, nor did he want to. 'The Reich Chancellor,' the protocol recorded, 'rejected a debate on the details of the Reich concordat. He was of the opinion that here only the great success should be noted. An opportunity had been given to Germany in the Reich concordat, and a sphere of confidence had been created which would be especially significant in the urgent struggle against international Jewry. Possible defects in the concordat could be remedied later, when foreign relations had improved.' Hitler then put special emphasis on three advantages: 1. 'that the Vatican had negotiated at all'; 2. that it 'could be persuaded to create a good relationship with this one nationalist German state'; this represented 'without doubt an open recognition of the present government'; 3. 'that with the concordat the church had withdrawn from organizations and party life'. Moreover, now for the first time the disbanding of the Centre Party could be 'regarded as final'. At the end of his statement Hitler once again made clear how much this treaty had in fact been his personal goal from the first day of his chancellorship. 'That the goal of an agreement with the Curia, to which as Reich Chancellor he had always aspired, was reached so much more quickly than he would have thought possible, even on 30 January, was such an indescribable success that all critical objections were unimportant compared to it.'[125]

Only a few days later, on 20 July, the concordat was signed formally in Rome.[126]

Immediately after the signing of the treaty the tension of the past relaxed in a flood of votes of thanks, articles, declarations and statements. They demonstrated how difficult and controversial the appraisal of this extraordinary event was from the beginning. Certainly in the perspective of the major goals of his policy Hitler had every reason to celebrate the conclusion of the concordat as an 'indescribable success' for his government. But anyone who saw things from the Roman perspective could come to the conclusion that at the least the treaty was just as much an indescribable success for Catholicism. Even a year before, the Holy See had only been able to dream of the concessions which the concordat contained. And the fact that on the Catholic side the concordat was accordingly described as 'something very great', indeed as nothing short of a 'masterpiece',[127] must have aroused a very deep suspicion in many National Socialist circles.

The treaty with Rome in fact came up against vigorous criticism in the radical wing of the Party. As matters stood, of course, this was hardly heard in public. Nevertheless the Prussian Kultusministerium, with Stuckart and Jäger, had made a last-minute attempt to prevent its being passed in the cabinet by pointing to the 'most far-reaching special position' which was granted to the Catholic church by the treaty. Very much in keeping with the Prussian tradition, the Prussian Kultusminister wrote that he believed that 'in comparison with the Prussian concordat, the Reich concordat' was 'discrimination against the state' and that 'the rights of the Curia' would be considerably expanded.[128] The proceedings at the general meeting of the Bavarian Teachers' Association in Nuremberg were undoubtedly also typical of the mood among a section of the German teachers. 'We ought not to conceal the fact,' the chairman declared, 'that the conclusion of the concordat has been particularly disappointing to us teachers and educators (tumultuous applause). Our demand was for the state to be the only patron of the schools. We have not come any closer to this goal... We have sworn not to find fault with the action of the Führer, Hitler. And even today I am not unhappy, because I am absolutely convinced that Hitler knows why he has done this.'[129] The treaty also caused considerable disquiet in sections of German Protestantism, as for example Ludwig Müller indicated when he pointed out at the conclusion of the constitutional negotiations that 'the struggle against the Catholic church' was by no means 'completely over' as a result of the concordat, and that the Führer would definitely safeguard Protestant interests against all 'Catholic encroachments'.[130]

This hostile mood in the radically anti-Catholic circles of the state, the Party and German Protestantism could undoubtedly only confirm the view of Rome and the German episcopate that the conclusion of this treaty was a quite extraordinary windfall. Guardedly but clearly, Pacelli expressed this conviction when he wrote on 22 July to Bishop Bornewasser of Trier 'that in the most difficult circumstances and at a time of widespread helplessness and serious discouragement, something has been created by a determined use of the general situation under God's benevolent and gracious help. If it is implemented in an equally loyal way it will prove to be a blessing to the church as well as the state, and can protect immortal souls from the infinitely many dangers which we have all faced, even yesterday, with trembling hearts.'[131] Cardinal Bertram's letter of thanks to Hitler also showed satisfaction over the fact 'that the harmonious co-operation of church and state' had 'found a solemn expression and firm, clear outlines in the Reich concordat'. At the same time, however, Bertram expressed 'the urgent desire' of the episcopate 'that heartfelt and sincere co-operation might prevail in the execution and effect' of the agreement.[132] Cardinal Faulhaber expressed open enthusiasm. As he wrote to Hitler: 'What the old parliaments and parties could not accomplish in sixty years, your statesmanlike vision has translated into a real piece of world history in six months. For Germany's reputation in the West and in the East, and before the whole world, this handshake with the papacy – the greatest moral power of world history – is a feat of immeasurable blessing.' Nor did Faulhaber forget to express the hope 'that the articles of the concordat do not remain written on paper', and that the subordinate authorities might not lag too far 'behind the statesmanlike greatness of the Führer'. Besides this, he asked that 'the great hour' be crowned 'with a magnanimous amnesty'.[133] Very much in line with these expressions of felicitation was a suggestion from Bishop Berning that a solemn service of thanksgiving should be held in all Catholic churches in Germany to mark the conclusion of the concordat, a service 'in which Christ the King is publicly thanked for this demonstration of grace'.[134] Bertram, however, would have none of this. The situation remained serious and it was not yet the right time 'to chime in with the general kling-klang Gloria', as he told Faulhaber.[135]

The almost unanimous enthusiasm of official German Catholicism over the concordat, albeit tempered by worries about how it would be implemented, was so striking that Hitler now thought it advisable to inform the Party of the significance of the treaty as he saw it. An article meant to achieve this appeared on 22 July in the National Socialist Party Letter. In contrast to Buttmann's official commentary, which emphasized above all 'the restoration of confessional peace',[136] the Party Letter totally represented Hitler's viewpoint. Down to the very wording, the article corresponded to Hitler's remarks to the cabinet in perceiving the significance of the Reich concordat above all in the following points: 'The fact that the Vatican is concluding a treaty with the new Germany means the acknowledgment of the National Socialist state by the Catholic Church. This treaty shows the whole world clearly and unequivocally that the assertion that National Socialism is hostile to religion is a lie invented for the purpose of political agitation... Through the concordat the church is forbidding priests to engage in any party-political activity. Beyond this the Catholic Church is instructing its priests to support the new state, the current German Reich... The church is abandoning existing Catholic-political associations. This takes the ground from under the Centre Party and once and for all puts an end to its disastrous effect.' And like Hitler on 14 July in the cabinet, the article also rejected all petty misgivings. 'An aim has been achieved which even a few months ago many people thought impossible. Any kind of misgivings over non-essential details of the treaty which could be brought forward by over-anxious minds are of no consequence and disappear in the face of the tremendous improvement on previous circumstances which has been achieved through the concordat.'[137]

406

This, however, was an interpretation of the treaty which Pacelli could in no circumstances accept. So the Cardinal Secretary of State answered personally with two articles which appeared on 26 and 27 July in *Osservatore Romano*, though without bearing his name. At root it was a dispute as to which side might now justify and celebrate the concordat as a success. So Pacelli emphatically disputed the assertion that the conclusion of the concordat signified an acknowledgment of National Socialism. The Holy See negotiated 'with states as such' and in the process refrained 'from any other consideration or value judgment'. Moreover, the prohibition of party-political activity on the part of the clergy in no sense meant 'keeping aloof from involvement in the true and universal welfare of the state and the prosperity of the fatherland'. Therefore the Catholic organizations ought 'even to enjoy state protection in the development of their activity'. But above all – and here the genuine Roman understanding of the treaty emerged – it was to be emphasized 'that the *Codex juris canonici* is the foundation and the essential legal presupposition of the concordat'. This meant 'not only official recognition of the legislation of the church, but also the adoption of many provisions of this legislation and the protection of all church legislation'.[138] Thus the concordat was incorporated into Roman church policy, and the success of the treaty was claimed almost solely for the church. It did not in any way represent the recognition by the church of the state, but on the contrary complete recognition by the state of the new church law.[139]

These theses in their turn posed a critical challenge to the state side. So it was now Buttmann – though again without his name being mentioned – who drew up an answer to *Osservatore Romano*. In it he rejected Pacelli's ideas point by point and with unusual sharpness. There could be no question of a general recognition of church legislation by the state; 'precisely the opposite' was the case. 'The removal of the clergy and members of orders from political parties, and the elimination of their activity in such parties' ought 'not to be construed too narrowly'. The purpose of this provision was 'to restore the clergy to their pastoral task'. Finally, the author of the article said that he was especially disconcerted by the protest against seeing the conclusion of the concordat as an acknowledgment of National Socialism. Of course the treaty had been concluded 'with the German Reich as such'. But this Reich was totally controlled by National Socialism, 'a fact which is not likely to be unknown even to private authors of articles in Rome'. Thus the conclusion of the treaty signified 'the actual and legal recognition of the National Socialist Government'.[140]

With this tough reply Buttmann – without knowing it – was getting at Pacelli personally. Several days later Counsellor Klee, who represented the ambassador during these weeks, felt the consequences emphatically. Klee reported to Berlin on 31 July that the Cardinal Secretary of State had declared to him 'in an agitated tone' that the reply contained interpretations 'which the Vatican could not leave uncontradicted'.[141] Thus a serious conflict over basic problems in understanding and interpreting the treaty seemed imminent – with the ink on the treaty barely dry. And this was all the more serious because while the treaty had been signed, it had not yet been ratified. And only with the exchange of documents would it have legal force. Thus the possibility had to be considered that a further intensification of the rhetoric might delay the ratification of the treaty, if not prevent it altogether. However, now it emerged just how much both treaty partners were interested in finally concluding the treaty.

In the conversation with Klee, Pacelli had already given the counsellor to understand that he might possibly dispense with a reply if no further statement were made on the concordat in Germany. This suggestion was taken up in Berlin immediately. Both the Foreign Office and the Ministry of the Interior tried to the best of their abilities to dampen down the conflict. As early as 3 August, Secretary of State Bülow stressed, via Klee in the Vatican, that 'no other significance could be attached' to the German reply than to 'the articles in the *Osservatore Romano* which have already been mentioned'. Although both statements in fact portrayed an authentic understanding of the treaty for the respective sides, this question could not in fact be clarified further. Instead, Pacelli learned that 'on condition that the Holy See' gave the appropriate instructions to the media associated with it, 'all further discussion of the concordat might now be forbidden to the entire Reich press'.[142]

An additional concession by the Reich government also contributed towards soothing the Vatican. Since the concordat had been signed in Rome, according to diplomatic custom the exchange of documents should take place in Berlin. For Pacelli it was obviously a recognition of the special position of Rome in international relations for both the signing and the ratification to take place in Vatican City, 'within the jurisdiction of the sovereign Pope'.[143] So he declared to the German Embassy counsellor that 'a concession by the Reich government on this matter would help to disperse the clouds that might have gathered'.[144] In Berlin not much time was spent on such subtle considerations. The very next day the Foreign Office informed the Vatican Embassy that the Reich government was ready and happy for the ratification to take place in Rome.[145] Soon afterwards Klee could report that in these circumstances the episode was 'finally settled'. At the request of the Cardinal Secretary of State, the exchange of documents was to take place if possible before he went on holiday on 8 September.[146] Thus for the first time a definite date was set.

While the basic interpretation of the treaty was in dispute at the highest level, in Germany, too, the situation remained unclear. The arguments between Party and church continued almost undiminished after 20 July and above all affected with full severity those who could least defend themselves: the Catholic associations and youth groups in the south and the west of the Reich.

It had been easy for both sides to predict that there would be difficulties in the interpretation of Article 31, with its poorly-defined formulations on the protection of Catholic associations and groups. Therefore even before the signing of the concordat in Berlin on 17 July, Buttmann and Bishops Gröber and Berning had come to agree on 'principles of interpretation' which seemed to guarantee the church a reasonably acceptable application of Article 31. According to these principles the purely religious associations in paragraph 1 were to 'be able to lead a complete life of their own', while the mixed organizations in paragraph 2 were at least guaranteed 'their Catholic character and independence in fulfilling their tasks' in a possible integration. It was further established that the members of the Catholic organizations were 'not to experience any legal disadvantage in school and state because of their membership'.[147] In view of the hard-pressed situation of many loyal Catholics in Germany, this was undoubtedly an agreement of great significance. That made the way in which it was handled in Rome all the more incomprehensible. Among the many mistakes that the Curia made during the concordat negotiations, negligence in dealing with the principles of interpretation was without doubt one of the most reprehensible. For in the haste to conclude the negotiations, not only was there a failure to establish that the agreement was binding, but the point was evidently completely lost sight of after the signing. No one in Rome insisted that the agreement, the final wording of which, moreover, was known only there, should be published at the same time as the text of the concordat. So everything lay in the hands of Buttmann, who finally released the principles of interpretation to the press on 29 July.

Once again the German bishops learned only through the daily newspapers of the content of an agreement between Rome and Berlin which ultimately concerned them more than anyone else. How difficult the situation had become in the meantime for the associations, under constantly increasing pressure from the Party, was demonstrated by a letter from Bertram to the members of the Fulda Bishops' Conference. It entreated them to point out 'repeatedly and promptly', because of the numerous disbandings and co-ordinations, that according to Article 31 and the principles of interpretation 'the existing Catholic organizations are to be kept in being, and that the pastors and presidents require specific permission if they want to disband an association or agree to co-ordination'.[148]

Furthermore, completion of the list of associations, which was to establish specifically which groups fell under paragraph 1 and which under paragraph 2, was delayed. This was due not so much to the Reich Ministry of the Interior, to which a rapid conclusion meant a great deal, as above all to the bishops' ponderous and complicated information-gathering apparatus, which had come to a standstill simply because Buttmann had sent only three copies of the list to Breslau for examination.[149]

An impressive picture of the real situation of German Catholicism during these weeks between the signing and the ratification of the concordat was outlined by the General President of the Catholic Young Men's Association, Ludwig Wolker, in a detailed report which he presented to the German bishops on 20 August. This report was in fact only concerned with youth organizations, but in principle the same experiences were true of all other branches of activity in Catholic associations, and numerous individual Catholics in Germany who displayed their links with the church all too openly. One report out of many made it clear that economic pressure had a crucial role at this juncture. 'Report from Köttingen, 11 August: in spite of the concordat which sounds so splendid, the Catholic Young Men's Movement in our brown coal district has been greatly harmed, since the unemployed are hired at the works only if they are in the SA or the NSDAP. So the first question put to my unemployed prefect when he looked for work at a pit was: Are you in the SA or the NSDAP? As the son of a family with many children he had no alternative but to enrol in the SA. Other people who have work are induced in a great variety of ways, almost forced, to join the Hitler movement or to enrol their children in the Hitler Youth. Many leaders, especially leaders at a lower level, look on us as enemies...'[150]

Wolker himself summarized the situation as follows: 'Over recent months all the presidents have been faced with a most difficult task. The majority have worked with great devotion, patience and wisdom. Some, however, have failed, partly worn down by endless and trying difficulties in the community, partly as a result of a "change of mind"... By and large the young people themselves have been extraordinarily good and brave, especially those in the community organizations. However, in the long run there is one thing that the youth cannot cope with: the economic boycott which is already directed on a large scale against all those who are not in NS organizations and often especially against those who bear the sign of Christ.'[151]

It was in this situation that the German bishops met in Fulda on 29 August for their second plenary conference of the year. Bertram had originally suggested, immediately after the signing of the concordat, that an opportunity should be provided to discuss the 'general questions arising out of this settlement, and details of its implementation'.[152] However, developments since then had called for a far more fundamental decision. It was Pacelli himself, for the first time evidently uncertain, who through Kaas and Gröber had put to the bishops the question 'whether it might be advisable to work for an acceleration of the ratification of the concordat or to insist on the removal... of the abuses before the ratification'.[153] This was now in fact the crucial point both for Rome and for the German episcopate.

The comprehensive report of the three-day conference contained the mass of worries which beset the bishops. The first issue was that of the school articles in the concordat, which were discussed and explained in detail. At this point, on the whole, the positive elements seemed to prevail. On the other hand, the outlook was grim for the associations, which were rightly seen to be in great danger, and it was also particularly grim for the Catholic press; indeed it was said that 'if the persecution and suppression... continues unhindered as it has done over recent weeks', there would soon 'be no Catholic German press at all'. The discharged Catholic civil servants and employees were a source of worry. As the protocol reported: 'The number of those who have been slandered as politically unreliable because they professed "political Catholicism" and who have lost their positions and every possibility of making a new life, is very large.' Finally, serious misgivings were caused by the 'Law for the Prevention of Offspring with Hereditary Diseases', the so-called Sterilization Law, which had already been passed at the 14 July cabinet meeting but typically was published only after the signing of the concordat on 25 July. This law, undoubtedly an important step in National Socialist racial legislation,[154] with its provisions for the forced sterilization of those with 'hereditary diseases', directly conflicted with the Catholic doctrine of the sanctity of marriage and the inviolability in principle of the human body, which Pius XI had expressly repeated, first in December 1930 in the encyclical *Casti connubii*.[155]

In the light of all these difficulties, the question whether the ratification ought to be pressed and thus the legal force and protection of the treaty should be finally established, or whether the whole situation called, rather, for delay, was in fact difficult to answer. In spite of this there was evidently a clear majority among the bishops for immediate ratification. The reasons for this decision, which Bertram disclosed to Pacelli immediately after the close of the conference, were typical of the general appraisal of the situation. The fear of losing the treaty altogether was obviously greater than the hope of obtaining further guarantees by negotiating over ratification. Bertram spoke of a feeling against the concordat and of rumours that 'the Reich Chancellor was only aiming at… gaining prestige in foreign affairs without fully and completely wanting its domestic political effect'. Bertram also seemed disturbed over large groups which felt that 'the government had gone too far in making concessions; a reversal of direction was called for. All this spoke urgently for an immediate exchange of documents.' The argument which the Interior Ministry was happiest to use, namely that only through ratification was there a chance really to enforce the rights in the concordat, appeared only in third place. At the same time, however, Bertram suggested asking along with the ratification for the 'end to the gravamina' which 'had to be demanded… for an honest implementation' of the treaty, Bertram appended a highly impressive list of these gravamina.[156]

Thus the die had been cast. At the same time it meant that because of the planned start of Pacelli's holiday on 8 September only a few days were left for the preparation and conclusion of the ratification. But the brevity of this period virtually ruled out obtaining even modest guarantees from the German side.

Even if all the difficulties of the situation are taken into consideration, and in addition it is remembered that the Cardinal Secretary of State was utterly exhausted, in restrospect we have to see the way this question was treated as a manifest failure of the much-vaunted Vatican diplomacy. For Pacelli could and indeed did know that the Reich government was just as interested in a rapid ratification as was the church, because decisions of considerable importance for Germany would be made that September at the League of Nations in Geneva, for which the moral backing of a ratified concordat seemed eminently desirable. Pacelli ought therefore at least to have insisted on the unequivocal establishment of the points already negotiated, i.e. on the completion and publication of the list of associations and the legal clarification of the principles of interpretation. Failure on these two points meant losing the last chance still to persuade the Reich to give certain guarantees – at least on Article 31. The very next weeks were to demonstrate the fatal effects of this failure.

Instead of this, in connection with the ratification Pacelli only demanded a declaration which stated the most important points of contention along with the Reich government's willingness 'to negotiate as soon as possible on the specific points in order to come to a mutual agreement corresponding to the wording and to the spirit of the concordat'.[157] With this declaration, which was intended for publication, came a secretly-prepared Promemoria from Pacelli that – as a supplement to a 'short note' which he had already submitted – once again expressly made the suppression of the Catholic associations and the Catholic press the object of future negotiations.[158]

After this had been arranged, the ceremonial exchange of documents signed by the Pope and by the German Reich President took place on Sunday 10 September at 5.30 p.m. in the Apostolic Palace of the Vatican. This gave the concordat legal force.

At the same time the president of the Deutscher Caritas Verband, Prelate Benedikt Kreutz, wrote an imploring memorandum on the situation of the associations as a last attempt to warn Rome against an over-hasty settlement. But Kreutz learned of the ratification of the treaty even before the memorandum left Freiburg. The concluding sentence, which he thereupon added to the finished letter in his own hand, may have reflected the feeling of other leading Catholics at this moment. 'I have just seen in the newspaper,' he wrote, 'that the ratification has taken place. A shame, it was... too early!!?'[159]

After the ratification the question of the thanksgiving service was raised again. On 13 September Bishop Buchberger of Regensburg sent a letter to Faulhaber in the hope that this was 'perhaps also a favourable opportunity to pave the way for peace between the organizations'.[160] Faulhaber passed this suggestion on to the Bavarian bishops the next day, but not without adding emphatically his own critical misgivings.[161] The answers of the Bavarian bishops which he received on this question were – with the exception of Bamberg – amazingly unanimous. For example the Bishop of Passau wrote in reply: 'The idea of holding a service of thanksgiving for the Reich concordat is so very repugnant to all my feelings and sensibilities that I would prefer to respond to the suggestion with a strong protest rather than with a simple *Non placet*.'[162]

However, the situation was not as tense everywhere as in Bavaria, so in other places there may have been more of an inclination to sing a Te Deum.[163] But the decision whether to have a great festive service of thanksgiving for the entire church was left to the Papal Nuncio Cesare Orsenigo, who thus once again gave a tangible demonstration at the conclusion of the ratification of the way in which the whole set of agreements was Rome's affair.

The suggestion for this thanksgiving service had been conveyed to the Nuncio by the Gauleitung of Berlin as early as the beginning of August, and in an obviously well-meaning way Orsenigo had promised to consider it.[164] A note from the Gau propaganda director dated 23 August left no doubt as to the purpose of this event. The majority of the erstwhile Centre Party Catholics, it said, formed a solid block which still disapproved of the movement. And their leaders, the clergy, were 'also still hostile'. But since the majority of Catholics were nationalist by conviction, 'a redeeming act on the part of the church will dispel all personal inhibitions among these Catholics and make them convinced supporters of our movement'. Since this act was not to be expected from senior clergy, contact had been made with the Nuncio. A declaration 'made with great force' which indicated 'the solemn recognition of the National Socialist movement by the representative of the Holy Father' would 'suddenly show the German Catholics that all the earlier accusations made but the Centre Party clergy... were unjust. Millions of compatriots freed from personal inhibitions will become supporters of our movement on this day.'[165]

These were certainly exaggerations which hardly indicated an informed knowledge of Catholic circumstances. Nevertheless the celebration of the Reich concordat at a service of thanksgiving on 17 September in a packed St Hedwig's Cathedral and on the broad square in front of the church was an unmistakable sign. 'On the Bishop's throne,' reported the *Katholisches Kirchenblatt* in Berlin, 'sits the representative of the Holy Father, the Apostolic Nuncio Cesare Orsenigo, and through his pontifical presence gives the service a deeply significant character. Around the altar stand the flags of the Reich, the Catholic student fraternities, the banners of the Catholic youth associations, of the Associations of St Hedwig... In front of the cathedral the standards are marshalled on the steps of St Hedwig and thus give the altar before the portal a broad, dignified setting. Very near to it stand the delegations of the National Socialists with the

412

NS flags. The loudspeakers make the "Kyrie" and the "Gloria" of the cathedral mass ring out loud and clear to the thousands outside the house of God. After the gospel the cathedral preacher, Fr Marianus Vetter, ascends the pulpit to explain the meaning and the great significance of the hour: the spirit of the concordat.'[166]

There has been much argument since then about this spirit. The treaty between the Curia and the German Reich was the only one among Hitler's major foreign policy treaties to survive the collapse, and it is still valid law in the Federal Republic, though no longer enforceable at crucial points. In the church-political sense this treaty could hardly have been avoided by a church which was determined to have the legal security of a concordat. Morally, however, the treaty will certainly remain controversial.

In summer 1933 the Bavarian nobleman Erwin von Aretin, who had been in protective custody since March, had a conversation in the notorious Stadelheim prison in Munich with a young Nuremberg Communist which suddenly illuminated this moral problem. 'So where are your bishops?', the young Communist asked Aretin, the convinced Catholic. 'In the old days, if a stage play was given that didn't suit them, they were always there. But now, when thousands of people are being murdered, no one gets up in the pulpit and breathes even a word... You'll see that the bishops want to make a concordat so that they are protected and we can all go to hell together.' 'It wasn't a very kind thing to say,' Aretin commented on these remarks, and continued, 'but on the day after the concordat I really felt rather foolish when my Nuremberg friend grinned at me from a distance.'[167]

This was certainly only one aspect of this complex treaty. But it was significant enough for the concordat not to be seen as a 'work of resistance against National Socialism', which should have been resisted by means of this treaty.[168]

The verdict on the concordat given by the Jesuit Friedrich Muckermann in his memoirs, written during the war and as a refugee, is clearer: 'The Catholics of Germany and of the whole world were so to speak morally compelled to believe in a compromise with National Socialism, at least for the future. In their view there had to be a feeling that in the end the young movement, wild as it was, would despite everything take the path of purification... Anyone who still fought against National Socialism as the arch-enemy of the church now came under the suspicion of being a pessimist, of opposing the supreme authority in the church; he was decried as a fanatic; and above all, he had great difficulty in protecting himself against this suspicion. That is, he was always being told that there was peace, indeed there were friendly relations, between the church and National Socialism. These men were even blamed for sabotaging the concordat, for contributing to the intensification of the differences. And so the real champions of the church were put in a situation in which they were exposed to attacks from within as well as from outside.'[169]

9

Theology in the Summer of 1933

For both churches the spring and summer of 1933 were totally dominated by church politics. The speed, depth and violence of the upheavals which had gripped Germany seemed to leave neither room nor time for fundamental theological reflection. The only thing that seemed to matter was to stand one's ground to some extent in the midst of this torrential flood, and to secure positions that might guarantee the survival of the churches even in the Third Reich. To make a theological examination and to take into account what had to be held on to and what could be given up for this cause, what finally would be won or lost, obviously had to be left to a later time.

In the Catholic church this attitude did not come up against any substantial difficulties. For the hierarchical organization of this church, which also produces a close connection between the theological teaching office and the church leadership, excluded in principle any conflict between church-political and theological decisions. To be sure, Catholic university theology was by no means silent in 1933, but – like Protestant university theology – developed its own theological interpretation of events. However, the Holy See's concordat policy was not an object of theological inquiry either in 1933 or later. And of course there was no question of developing an opposing theological position in the church. Only long after the war – at the beginning of the 1960s – did German Catholicism, too, begin to engage in theological discussion over the significance of the church-political decisions of 1933.

The situation in German Protestantism looked utterly different. Here was a traditionally independent university theology, well aware of itself, whose considerable church-political potential had been shown once again precisely in the 'struggle for the church'.[1] The significance of this university theology for the church was undoubtedly considerable, even if its influence in particular instances was frequently difficult to gauge. This different status of theology alone inevitably made theological discussion in German Protestantism much more significant than that in Catholicism.

However, at first even here developments appeared to leave less and less room for theological argument. The German Christians, who had staked everything on church political action, appeared to have taken the right course: the basic decisions had obviously already been made, even before the theological discussion about them had got underway. Surprisingly, however, this supposition proved to be false. The German Christians were compelled to note with growing perplexity how – contrary to their specific expectations – the course of events since the summer of 1933 was being increasingly determined by the discussion of theological positions. In the end of the day it was not politics and church politics but theology and faith which decided the future of the Protestant church in the Third Reich. This was the really surprising, astonishing and moving result of developments in the Protestant church during 1933.

The most intense theological confrontation which the twentieth century had yet seen in Germany began with the renunciation of all theology. That from the beginning the Faith Movement deliberately dispensed with any theological foundation for its programme and its aims was already demonstrated in the Hossenfelder Guidelines of 6 June 1932. By professing to desire 'neither to be nor to replace a confession of faith, nor to undermine the confessional foundations of the Evangelical Church', but rather to be 'a confession of a way of life', these guidelines clearly betrayed an effort to avoid engaging in theological discussions in any circumstances.[2] Moreover for Hossenfelder this was not just a question of policy: it was also a matter of conviction. He was sure that the triumph of the National Socialist movement over political argumentation would repeat itself in the church with a triumph of the Faith Movement over theology. Thus at the end of April he explained to two Lübeck pastors who were seeking to gather information in Berlin about the aims of the German Christians that the Faith Movement had 'no special theology and dogmatics', and he continued: 'Theology is nonsense; it stands between Volk and church.' His instructions about how to organize Lübeck were in keeping with this point of view, as was his confidence in the power of mere action. 'Get an SA man who doesn't yet have a post, if possible one with a clean slate, and put him in the communities; he doesn't need to have a clue about theology; and let him get on with the job.' Somewhat surprised, the Lübeck pastors noted that Hossenfelder vigorously emphasized the value of this 'church mercenary' type.[3]

In these circumstances it was only logical that the Reich leadership should in fact devote all its power and attention almost exclusively to questions of organization and propaganda. And the greater the successes it scored with this approach to begin with, the more of course it found the approach confirmed. Friedrich Wieneke, the 'Reich Expert on Theology and University', a pastor on the staff of Soldin Cathedral, who in any case was a weak figure and at first had merely been pushed into the foreground, notably lost influence.[4]

A 'German Christian series' of publications started by Hossenfelder ended as early as July 1933 with Volume 6, not least because no one was bothered about theological contributions. And the Sunday paper *Evangelium im Dritten Reich*, the only medium of communication of any significance beyond regional borders for the Faith Movement, eventually proved so inadequate at the theological level that in the long run it could not meet even modest demands. The shallow addresses, sentimental meditations and primitive political and church-political agitation it contained clearly showed how little regard the editor had for any kind of theological reflection.

Basically, Hossenfelder advocated action, pure and simple. For him the guarantee for the community lay quite definitely in the fact that all were fighting under the same symbol: the swastika. 'Struggle,' began the only programmatic

415

text that he ever wrote, 'struggle is the father of life. This is the law of God which is inscribed on the face of our time.'[5] However, in Hossenfelder's view differences within the church and theology from a past age had become completely unimportant in this struggle. They no longer had a role to play and belonged to that old, bourgeois academic world which those fighting for the Third Reich had left behind them long ago. A direct result of this attitude was that by the end of April the 'German Christians' had still received hardly any theological support worth mentioning. And presumably the crucial link between the Faith Movement and German theology would still have taken a long time to forge had not Ludwig Müller now appeared on the scene.

In contrast to Hossenfelder, Müller obviously felt from the beginning that the German Christians could not achieve a breakthrough in the church without support from theology. Here Müller's experiences are likely to have played a larger role than his convictions. In the end of the day, the formulation of theological questions was probably as alien to his pious routine as it was to Hossenfelder's preoccupations with action. But Müller knew German Protestantism better, and was aware of the important status that university theology enjoyed in it. So the visit which the recently appointed 'Spokesman for the Theological Faculty Conference', the Tübingen professor Karl Fezer, paid at the end of April to Ludwig Müller, also recently appointed as Hitler's spokesman on church affairs, to offer Müller his help in the name of the theological faculties, had a significance for the course of events that can hardly be overestimated.[6]

For this visit led to the collaboration of the two men, which very rapidly led to the 'theological working party' that gave theological support to Müller's task and policy.[7] Over and above this direct support, however, the significance of the working party lay above all in the fact that Müller used it to demonstrate his basic readiness to listen to theology and to call on it to justify and direct the Faith Movement. It was this readiness which created the conditions for German university theology now to devote itself to the Faith Movement along a broad front. Here people were to some extent looking past Hossenfelder and the Reich leadership; the preoccupation of the latter with action, and the persistent rejection of all theology associated with it, left a bad taste for which apologies had to be made.

The stormy encounter between the Faith Movement and university theology in the summer of 1933 is one of the most important events in the history of recent German theology. However, details of the course and the circumstances of the encounter are still obscure. The fact that the complete collapse of the German Christians by the end of 1933 proved this encounter to be a terrible mistake caused many of those involved to forget their mistakes as quickly as possible. One significant feature is that books and articles from summer 1933 are absent from the biographies and bibliographies of many scholars. At the time only Emanuel Hirsch had correctly perceived the risk in this decision, when he wrote 'on the present spiritual situation': 'By venturing to behave with daring at a given moment, having the courage to state the substance and meaning of this moment, an individual becomes exposed to the most effective and striking of all refutations, that made by future events. This refutation does not catch him out in some random error, but rather affects his very will to decide, that is, the heart of his historical humanity.'[8] In fact, summer 1933 remained an implicit and unfinished topic for a whole generation that was cut to the quick; it was difficult, sensitive and bitter, but nevertheless it had a deep and enduring after-effect.

The critical precondition for the rise of German-Christian theology in summer 1933 lay in the increasing persuasiveness of Hitler and the National Socialist revolution, which at this time could be felt all over Germany. Obviously, during the first months of the Third Reich, particularly in the universities, there was an increasing feeling that what was happening was not just a change in government but also a turning point in human destiny; that this was a time of revolution which in one way or another would decide the future of Germany – and not of Germany only. The spiritual dissociation from the Weimar Republic, which was considered a non-state, had triggered off a tremendous and highly-charged expectation, an expectation which Hitler had met most closely with the religious tone of his speeches; with the Potsdam Day and the 1 May celebrations; with his claim to be master of German destiny; and with the determination of all his actions. Hence to a large extent, also in theology and the church, it quickly became an indubitable certainty that what mattered most was the whole of the future; that in this period of time everything was to be won or lost; that now, no matter how questionable, difficult or even offensive particular aspects might be, it was important to stand up for the new era with all one's strength. Not everyone was seized with this conviction, but many people were. It was the common factor behind the general revival of German theology in summer 1933.

Hanns Rückert, a young Tübingen church historian from the school of Karl Holl, gave particularly clear and impressive expression to this presupposition in a lecture to Tübingen students on 17 May 1933. His subject, 'The Revival of Reformation Piety in the Present', had been announced as early as the previous semester and undoubtedly had had the so-called 'Luther Renaissance' in mind. Now events had removed this theme 'from the sphere of academic discussions, of tranquil theological reflection and faithful pastoral routine' and made it a 'vital question of the first order for church and nation', as Rückert's definition of the great new task for theology now ran: 'The church is asked, not by a party outside or within itself, but rather by history, whether it has the inner strength to interpret a great turning point in German destiny as coming from the hand of God, and to take a creative part in it. If the church ignores this question, or if it does not summon up this power, then despite its best intentions it will *ipso facto* have become a sect and be condemned to historical impotence. For anyone who does not hear the command to mobilize or who has to stay at home as being unfit for active duty has certainly forfeited the intrinsic right to play a role in German history for the foreseeable future.'[9]

'To interpret a great turning-point in German destiny as coming from the hand of God and to take a creative part in it' – that was a precise description of the problem with which German theology saw itself confronted in summer 1933. Certainly there were very different theological ways and means of solving this problem. But the very existence of the task, the characterization of the time as a call which simply could not be refused, had at first largely gone unchallenged. The young pupils of Karl Holl, Emanuel Hirsch and (along with Hanns Rückert) the church historians Heinrich Bornkamm, Hermann Wolfgang Beyer and Erich Vogelsang, took up this call with special passion. But even theologians from the circle of Young Reformers like Walter Künneth and Helmuth Schreiner had no doubt about this way of posing the problem. When at Pentecost 1933 they wrote the foreword to their major theological symposium *The Nation before God*, they started from 'the basic conviction that the great work of national renewal can be carried out beneficially only if it is in touch with the eternal forces which Volk and state do not control in their own right. So the German nation stands before God at the turning point of its destiny.' So here too the task could be put in one sentence: 'The issue is the theological word of the church on the inward questions of national rebirth.'[10] The urgency attached to this task up and down the country was shown by the titles of the flood of publications which now appeared: Paul Althaus, *The German Hour of the Church*; Friedrich Gogarten, *The Unity of the Gospel and the People*; Adolf Schlatter, *The New German Nature in the Church*; Ethelbert Stauffer, *Our Faith and Our History*; Karl Heim, *German State Religion or Protestant Volkskirche*. All felt the political upheaval as a challenge which theology should in no circumstances avoid. 'At the times in which something great occurs,' wrote Karl Heim, 'in which storms churn up the depths of the sea, out of their inner emptiness and insecurity human beings always ask after God again. This happened in the wars of independence; it happened in August 1914; and so it is happening anew today. There is an open door into which we must enter... We have opportunities present which were not previously there, and which perhaps will never return.'[11]

The task of 'interpreting a great turning-point in German destiny as coming from the hand of God and taking a creative part in it' was acknowledged almost throughout German theology in summer 1933. However, this way of putting it already amounted to a far-reaching theological decision. That is, the very fact that the task was posed and acknowleged in this way at the same time presented and acknowledged certain theological themes which in this form had hitherto been a serious preoccupation only for political theology: 'God and Volk, history and salvation history, the historical experience of God and biblical revelation'.[12] For the 'greatest turning-point in German destiny', the interpretation and creation of which were at issue, was not just any turning point, but rather a quite specific one; the reconstruction of the nation and the Reich out of the forces of völkisch ideology. And if theology wanted to interpret and help to create in a responsible way at this juncture, the only way in which it could do this meaningfully was by turning towards this völkisch ideology. Even where theological judgment finally had critical reservations, the völkisch movement had first to be accepted, examined and taken seriously before its problems and limitations could be pointed out. However, the new themes almost automatically assigned a leading role to political theology. In fact Hirsch and Stapel now became the most important representatives of that approach which undertook to provide a theological interpretation of the National Socialist revolution.[13]

That as early as the Faculty Conference at the end of April Emanuel Hirsch became one of the first German university theologians to announce his imminent entry into the Faith Movement[14] was hardly surprising for a man who since 1920 had made 'Germany's Destiny' the crucial theme of his theological ethics.[15] Indeed, this book had arisen out of the conviction that it was the task of the theologian to interpret to the Volk its spiritual and political mission in the name of God. So he had called on this Volk to recognize a strong state, and to convey through this state its moral responsibility in the world. Hirsch was convinced that

418

this was no optional, no arbitrarily chosen path; rather, it was the historical will of God as recognized by conscience. Given these presuppositions, the year 1933 had to be seen as a year of divine fulfilment. 'In September 1920, when *Germany's Destiny* was published,' Hirsch now wrote, 'I would not have dared to dream of experiencing so turbulently a German awakening for which I had wanted to create the foundations...'[16] What this year meant for Hirsch the theologian, he described at its end in a publication which without doubt contained the most concise and impressive presentation of German Christian theology: 'The Present Spiritual Situation as mirrored in Philosophical and Theological Reflection. Academic Lectures towards Understanding the German Year 1933'.[17] The heart of this work was the chapter, 'The German Turning Point'.[18] 'All spiritual Germans,' this chapter began, 'to whom the events of the German year 1933 are disclosed by their own living roots in the destiny of their Volk, agree involuntarily and surprisingly on one point: that at this very moment we are passing over the crest between two ages.' Hirsch saw the rise of nothing less than 'a new, great possibility of historically significant life in Germany', shining out from Germany 'over the peoples and cultures which still stand at the threshold between eras'.[19] Hirsch tried to describe this new 'possibility of historically significant life' with two concepts: *horos* and *nomos*. *Horos* denoted the divine-natural limit which the new era had perceived and to which it held fast; blood and race. Hirsch was convinced that only the unconditional observance of this limit secured the future for a Volk; for this limit was 'the original, of which reason and freedom are only servants'.[20] The *nomos* meant the Volk's 'order, mode of life and thinking' as defined by this limit,[21] the 'appropriateness of all orders and forms' which at the same time was in tune with the divine and for which, therefore, German theology and the German church bore a unique responsibility. This whole design, remote from reality though it was, nevertheless had a peculiar coherence and force. That derived from the consistency with which a position opposite to the foundations of the modern world was developed: the German revolution appeared to have transcended both the French and the Russian revolutions.

Of course the crucial theological question in this connection lay in the theological foundation of this outline, which Hirsch himself called 'Christian philosophy of history'. Hirsch's answer to this was clear. In his view there was not only a recognition of the will of God in his Word Jesus Christ; there was also a recognition of the will of God in history. This was the insight which young Lutheranism, with which Hirsch identified himself, had regained during and after the War: 'that the right decision in the questions of life generally could always ultimately be found only in the risk of faith, looking back on the steps of the Lord of history. From listening amidst historical human life and its commitments he thus developed a concept of the orders of creation; this became a listening to the moment now given to him, the hour of Volk and state... the central goal of a life-sustaining historical development of German Volklichkeit and statehood.' In this 'faith looking back', this 'listening', upon which all the significance of Volkstum dawned, the concept of revelation and grace was 'liberated from mere christological narrowness: God's history knows prevenient revelation and prevenient grace'.[22] Hirsch, however, saw such prevenient revelation and prevenient grace at work in the events of the year 1933: prevenient revelation of *horos* and *nomos* in Volkstum; prevenient grace in the new beginning. This established the locus of theology and the church. It was their mission, entrusted to them by God, to interpret to the German Volk that prevenient action of God and at the same time to help to shape it in unconditional solidarity with the Volk.

So the text ended logically with the sentence 'Recent German Protestant theology and the present moment of Volk and state belong together.' It was the unshakable conviction of the Göttingen theologian that 'If we in theology and the church do not measure up to this moment, if we are unable to risk giving up all the prejudices stemming from the past and all the need for security and certainty in the boisterous new age, in the vigorous movement of our own Volk, then we are lost. There is no middle way; there is only the either/or.'[23]

This theological outline established Hirsch's position in church politics. Inevitably it was completely and unreservedly within the Faith Movement. This radical either/or itself demonstrated that for this theology mere approval of political change of the kind expressed even by the church administrators, indeed even by Bodelschwingh, was not enough. Here, in fact, was radical political theology for sure, which no longer wanted to keep anything for the church, because only unreserved commitment, only complete risk, matched the magnitude of the task.

From the beginning of May until the end of the year, after Fezer, Hirsch was the most important theological adviser to Ludwig Müller. With him and for him he fought for a Reich Church which, in its order and proclamation, would accord with the National Socialist revolution. For Hirsch this accord was not a coordination in the sense that the church was simply to be brought into political conformity with Volk and state; rather, it was the precondition for the intelligibility and credibility of its proclamation in the Third Reich. 'If we build up our Evangelical Church in inner homogeneity with the National Socialist state, i.e. if we above all stress the leadership idea in it and correctly select and train the people who are to give leadership in it, then our Protestant church can become a truly German Volkskirche, i.e. a church which is loved by the Volk as its own church and which for its part can move the Volk with its Word.'[24]

Political theology, as was also demonstrated by Hirsch and his friends, necessarily led to a political hermeneutic for the proclamation of the gospel. So Hirsch repeated again and again: 'If the Protestant church in genuine inner solidarity with the German Volk, as that Volk is now emerging, wishes really to proclaim the gospel, then it has to take as its natural standpoint the circle of destiny of the National Socialist movement. If it does not do this, then it becomes alien and different, and loses the natural precondition for speaking and hearing the gospel in proclamation.'[25]

Next to Hirsch, in the 1920s Wilhelm Stapel had been paramount in shaping the modern political theology of his age. Though not himself a university theologian, beyond question he nevertheless had a marked effect on university theology. Initially Stapel entertained the conviction that the German Volk – as he put it in 1922 – was 'not an idea of human beings but rather an idea from God'.[26] Since this time he had attempted, in a series of new approaches, to develop the significance of this insight for a modern Lutheran theology. The result finally emerged in 1932 in *The Christian Statesman. A Theology of Nationalism*, which sparked off a long and lively theological discussion.[27]

420

In fact Stapel's crucial thesis had been thought out with considerable spirit and consistency, and where the argument grew weaker a glib solemnity readily came to its aid. If the Volk was an idea of God, this thesis ran, then it must also have had its own order implanted in it by God: 'a law of life that determines its internal and external form, its cultus, its ethics, its constitution and its law in accordance with its nature': the *nomos*.[28] So there was no universal ethic applying to humanity, as maintained by the Enlightenment which Stapel so hated. Rather, there was only völkisch law, the Volksnomos. The theological focus of this thesis, however, lay in its apparently bold exaltation of the German Volksnomos to an autonomous status, which Stapel achieved by drawing a parallel with the Jewish Volksnomos. Just as Israel had its Volksnomos in the Ten Commandments, which were therefore a law valid only for Israel, so too the German Volk ought to have its *nomos* – the *Nomos Germanikos* – in the articulation of what it felt to be morally good, a *nomos* which would find its fulfilment in the concept of the Reich.[29] Stapel did not hesitate to describe this parallelism in quite specific terms: 'When Israel apostatized from Yahweh, God punished Israel – as we can read in the Old Testament. When we apostatized from the Reich, God punished us, as German history demonstrates. That is the German Testament, And the question of this book is: How can we be Christians without apostatizing from the Reich? Has Christ come to fulfil our law too? (Matt.5.17).'[30] So any leadership which really brought the German Volk to the Reich could consider itself to be a direct instrument of the divine will. Any leadership which acted in this way – the truly nationalist state – thus also had full and unlimited power over morality; the nationalist state was its master, not its servant. The Christian church had to acknowledge unreservedly this state control of morality. Any interference was strictly forbidden. For the preaching of cross and resurrection, which in the final analysis Stapel wanted to be able to maintain absolutely and genuinely, applied only to the kingdom of heaven: the forgiveness of sins, grace, the future life.

The attempt to give autonomy to the Volksnomos made by Stapel necessarily led to the radicalization of the doctrine of two kingdoms, to the point at which state and church simply had nothing more to say to each other: whatever the state had to do for the sake of God's will it knew better than the church on the basis of the Volksnomos; the church could only confirm this. And what the church had to proclaim was something that the state could not know.

Stapel's approach was doubtless directly connected with Emanuel Hirsch. Both saw in the Volk and Volkstum something of the reality of God's creation which revealed itself in the change of destiny which took place in 1933. Nevertheless, it was clear that in this definition of the relationship between state and church in the Third Reich Stapel had inevitably come to conclusions which differed from those of Hirsch. In fact the notion that state and church, theology and revolution, were urgently directed to each other was almost completely lacking in Stapel's work. Stapel felt that proper demarcation was the issue of the moment, even more than the subordination for which he so passionately fought. Moreover, when in summer 1933 he presented his ideas about 'The Church of Christ and the Hitler State' to packed audiences in Tübingen, Bonn and Königsberg, each time at the invitation of the theological faculties, he was above all concerned with this problem. In accordance with his doctrine of the Volksnomos, he resolved the issue rigorously in favour of the totalitarian state:

'The totalitarian state controls all law, all morality. The church has all that concerns the kingdom of heaven.'[31] Specifically, this meant: 1. 'Law and order in the church are subordinate to the state. What must be conceded to the church is that its members should be able to gather undisturbed in the name of Jesus Christ, that the gospel should be properly preached to them and the sacraments correctly administered. Even how that happens, and under what order and law is a secular matter'; 2. 'The morality which the church teaches must be that which grows in the hearts of the Volk to which the church brings the gospel, for morality belongs to the "nomos" of the Volk.' Stapel answered the question of what in these circumstances the church still had left by referring to the third article of the confession: it still had the Holy Spirit, the holy catholic church and the communion of saints.[32] In the end all this amounted to a monstrous state church, and later Stapel in fact confirmed this explicitly in the dispute with the Confessing Church. 'Does that mean that the state not only can but "may" do with the church what it wishes, and the church may not say a word to rebel? Certainly the state can do that. It can appoint bishops when it likes, and as many as it likes. It can establish community boundaries as it likes. It can transcend the Landeskirchen and organize a Reich Church to suit itself... in short, it can exercise the most rabid control over the Landeskirchen.' According to Lutheran understanding, Stapel continued, the church was subject to the law and power of the state. The only thing which was inviolate was 'the source of faith: the gospel and the sacraments'.[33]

This approach could hardly be a basis for the Faith Movement, to the degree that it really sought to be a religious renewal movement, and in fact Stapel does not seem to have joined it. That made it all the more important for the Führer's agent, Ludwig Müller, to have Stapel on his side in his attempts at reorganization. The editor of *Deutsches Volkstum* in fact saw the dispute over the independence of the church as nothing but a 'purple passage in the confusion in the church'[34] which the state had to end quickly. He found the 'anxious Melanchthonisms' of church diplomacy; the circumstances surrounding Bodelschwingh's nomination; the 'Reich Bishop's worshipping in the working-class area of Berlin', which made the church the 'franchised assembly point for enemies of the state' all highly suspicious.[35] Would 'a united front between Judaism, Catholicism and Protestantism really be allowed to form and express 'mistrust of the new state'?[36] So for the sake of the church 'the angry thunderbolt from the Prussian Kultusministerium which put an end to the confusion and the wrangling...' was 'the most genuine act of Christian love in the whole church dispute'.[37]

Stapel's doctrine of the Volksnomos was one of the most discussed theological models of 1933. Almost all the theologians who joined the Faith Movement were indebted to him in one way or another. And this doctrine had, in fact, been thought out so consistently, and appeared so convincing in the context of events, that it was by no means easy to show where its crucial error actually lay. In retrospect it is obvious that this error also consisted in a grandiose misapprehension of the Third Reich. But in 1933 this was no argument at all. Anyone who wanted to challenge Stapel's approach at this time had to do so theologically.[38] And it was around this point that the discussions began quite quickly.

In taking such a position, Hirsch and Stapel were keeping to the line that they had already developed and advocated in the 1920s. In it the connection between

422

theological and church-political decisions was clearly evident. But summer 1933 also demonstrated that this connection was evidently less inevitable than it appeared. To everyone's surprise, two of the most respected German systematic theologians changed places in this period. Paul Althaus, who was quite certainly expected to be among the German Christians, did not appear among them, and Friedrich Gogarten, whom with equal certainty no one expected to find there, took his place among them in the summer.

Gogarten's step caused an extraordinary stir in the theological world. Heinrich Vogel, who like many others had followed Gogarten's theological work 'for a long time with passionate interest', spoke of 'puzzled astonishment, indeed... shock'.[39] In fact no line whatsoever seemed to lead from that critical approach which since 1920 had united the young pastor of Stelzendorf with Karl Barth in a belligerent partnership to the position that he now held. But in truth for a long time Gogarten had been going his own way, which had brought him close to political theology. Much more interested in the problem of faith and history than Barth, he had looked for the roots of the German distress in terms of the radical criticism of culture that they both shared, and thought that he had found it in the total lack of order and commitment which marked the age of individualism. So in 1930 he opened his polemical treatise 'Against Contempt for Authority' with the statement: 'Until we succeed in overcoming the moral contempt for authority and the power related to it, there can be no healing for all our spiritual and political life.'[40] Two years later, having become Ordinarius professor in Breslau, in his *Political Ethics* he called for the authoritarian state, since only under the pressure of the demands of the state could human beings find their way back to those orders in which the truth of law and gospel are revealed. It was therefore only consistent that Gogarten should give the new state a warm welcome in summer 1933. 'The German of the present,' he declared at the end of May, 'whose deepest distress has been that, as I have put it in my *Political Ethics*, he no longer belonged to anyone, God or individual, again knows that he belongs to his Volk and through and in his Volk to the state in which the will of the Volk has become sovereign.'[41] What he had suggested previously only as a vague assertion, the central significance of political ethics for the preaching of law and gospel, he now transferred to the new state with the help of Stapel's categories. As he formulated this crucial point in the summer: 'The Lordship of Jesus Christ affects human beings in their earthly reality. For it affects them at the point where they stand under the law and at the point where by nature – or as I should prefer to say – in their earthly history – they stand under the law. Being under the law means governing one's existence from one's history. And that is the law, the Nomos of the Volk, indeed, as one must say with emphasis, the law of one's Volk.'[42]

This standpoint, however, was only one step short of justifying the German Christian election slogan, 'Unity of Gospel and Volkstum', which to the dismay of many of his friends Gogarten took at the end of July in a widely-distributed polemical tract. In it Gogarten also committed himself to the task to which almost all German theology committed itself that summer: contemplating 'with all seriousness how through political events God's leadership gives us reason to listen anew to his Word'.[43] This task led Gogarten first of all to affirm the new state in the most comprehensive way imaginable. Because the Volk was corrupt, its law had to be 'very harsh, very uniform'. For if a Volk, his bold thesis continued, having 'lost its form to the degree that ours has, is to be put into shape, then it must first be put in uniform. Those who complain about the impoverishment of life do not understand that at present the most important thing is to save our very existence.'[44] However, this struggle could not leave the church's proclamation untouched either. For the church was involved in this struggle at that point where it understood that the German Christian election slogan 'is about nothing other than the unity of law and gospel. For the law is given us in our Volkstum. Here I cannot but agree with Stapel.'[45] This law and the assertion of its claim to dominion belonged completely within the sphere of the state. However, it was the task and mission of the church – and here Gogarten was evidently more sceptical than Hirsch and Stapel – to preserve the purity of 'Volkstum in its character of moral law'. 'Race and blood, too, which are certainly not inseparable from Volkstum, are not be understood on this basis. The preservation of their purity cannot occur in a naturalistic way... It must be moral, in terms of morality...' At precisely this point, however, 'the task of the church begins'.[46]

In the summer of 1933 the consistency of this position could only lead straight to the German Christians. Though it had only been May when Gogarten had signed the proclamation of the Young Reformers, along with a group of younger Silesian pastors, on 4 August he made it known that he no longer wanted to go on fighting 'on false fronts'. 'A group of theologians and church lawyers, which has worked seriously for weeks under the leadership of Professor Gogarten of Breslau on contemporary theological questions, has therefore decided as a group, in making the enclosed declaration, to join the Faith Movement of German Christians.' This declaration was worded entirely along the lines of Gogarten's theology and justified the application for admission with the observation that the National Socialist state, with its new order, had created 'a necessary precondition' for 'the unhindered proclamation of the risen Lord, crucified for our sins, to fall upon productive soil.'[47] In the autumn, when Gogarten explained this step once again, to Georg Merz, the tone was already considerably more cautious. One had to take 'state and Volk – which, and here I want to express myself carefully, are concerned with law, and apply and represent law in some way – seriously if we are to be allowed to turn against them in the name of the gospel when they overstep their bounds'.[48] Gogarten certainly never did this. But the year was not yet over before he announced his resignation from the Faith Movement – not without having the German Christians of Silesia say of him that he could not resign because he had never been a proper member.[49] This was an ironical point in that mistaken encounter between German theology and a movement which considered theology as a whole to be utter nonsense.

The caution of Gogarten's contemporary Althaus remained as surprising as Gogarten's membership of the Faith Movement. In the 1920s the systematic theologian from Erlangen had been one of the most important advocates of political theology in Germany. He had made basic theological contributions to it with his doctrine of the 'primal revelation', the self-witness of God, even in the historical orders of Volk and state.[50] More cautious than that of his friend Hirsch, Althaus's political theology always remained a 'yes-but' theology: the self-witness of God in the order of creation of the Volk stood under the 'but' of his full revelation in Jesus Christ. And Althaus now held fast to this, even in the 'German hour of the church'. He could certainly go a long way with those who directly perceived the voice of God in the upheavals of the time. 'If the historical order of Volkstum or of the state,' he wrote under the impact of events, 'gains authority over our hearts... then we experience in earnest, and directly, what a volunteer soldier of 1914 said for the multitude: "God calls us." And if the determination of our Volk for true and worthy life in times of delusion and forgetfulness again becomes law for the multitude, through the demands of a Führer, then indeed they have heard more than the voice of a human being.'[51] But at the same time he also thought that 'the substance of historical experience must be brought back into the light of the biblical witness to God. Otherwise it becomes a victim of pagan interpretation. Volkstum, state and Führertum become absolutized and thus demonized. To guard against this is the first great task of proclamation.'[52]

In church politics, this attitude led straight to the middle course which the Bavarian Landeskirche adopted – certainly not uninfluenced by the arguments from Erlangen. In fact Althaus's position at this time may largely have corresponded to the standard theology of the Landeskirche, which opened itself wide to the Faith Movement without completely abandoning the final 'but' in church politics: the demand for church autonomy.

Political theology is tied to no confession. Where political ethics becomes the key question for theological understanding and church action, the political theme determines theology and not theology the political theme. The summer of 1933 provides a surprisingly impressive proof of this state of affairs, to which too little attention has so far been paid. For this summer there was also an encounter between Catholic university theology and the National Socialist revolution which developed hardly less violently than on the Protestant side. In many respects this was surprising. Catholicism had previously developed no comparable political theology.[53] Rather, up to March 1933 the völkisch ideology of Nationalist Socialism had been explicitly banned by the church, and university theology had observed this ban. Nor was there any pressure for a decision from the church point of view. The Curia's concordat policy was theologically unassailed; there was no dispute like that in the Protestant church. So it was the spiritual force and conviction of the German hour of destiny which now also gripped Catholic theology. This theology became increasingly open to the conviction that – as the young Münster systematic theologian Michael Schmaus put it – there is not just 'a self-evident demand of the time', namely 'to take one's place unreservedly in the new state, but also' – and here the move towards political theology began – 'to consider the intellectual foundations of the National Socialist view of the world'.[54]

The Braunsberg theologian Karl Eschweiler was one of the first to take a stand. Of the same generation as Hirsch, Gogarten and Althaus, Eschweiler had held the chair of systematic theology at the highly respected Ermsland Academy since 1928, and was without doubt regarded as one of the most profound representatives of his discipline. His 1926 book *The Two Ways of Recent Theology*, a brilliant defence of Neo-Scholasticism – which he distinguished, as the 'way of dogmatic reflection', from a rationalist theology of 'apologetic controversy' – was justifiably one of the most discussed theological works of the era.[55] However, it was the Neo-Scholastic Thomism, which advocated a contemporary reinterpretation of the doctrine of the great Aquinas, that in its German form now proved to be surprisingly open to the political theology of this age. In addition to Gogarten's sensational article on 'The Independence of the Church', the first June issue of *Deutsches Volkstum* contained an article by Karl Eschweiler, 'The Church in the New Reich', which for the first time clearly developed this Neo-Thomist approach to National Socialism. The article began with an analysis of the church-political situation, which Eschweiler thought had been eased on the one side by the guarantees in the government policy statement of 23 March and on the other by the bishops' answer of 28 March. In Eschweiler's view an essential contribution towards this easing had been made by the bishops' dissociation from the Centre Party, which he believed he could note since early April. Only after this clarification did Eschweiler come to the crucial point: völkisch ideology. 'Is the völkisch idea which dominates National Socialist ideology,' he asked, 'in fact in irresolvable contradiction to Catholic truth? Or is not the difference, intensified politically to the point of episcopal condemnation, a misunderstanding which, while having a very real basis in the intellectual constitution of German Catholicism and the literary expression of the völkisch struggle for freedom, nevertheless a misunderstanding that can be removed?' Eschweiler's contribution to the resolution of this misunderstanding was no less than a demonstration that Article 24 of the Party programme – 'We demand the freedom of all religious confessions in the state, so long as they do not... offend against the moral and ethical feeling of the German race' – in fact repeated one of Thomas Aquinas's basic philosophical doctrines. Aquinas had taught that the soul which perceives God, the *anima intellectiva*, was alive in the *una et unica forma corporis*, the 'unity and uniqueness of the essential form': 'Not although, but precisely because the intellectual soul as the substantial basis of the person has its source directly in the will of the Creator, with its *anima* which is determined by heredity, it forms a unity that is more intimate than that between blood and bones in this living being.' According to Eschweiler this was more than a mere scholastic opinion. 'Where the view prevails that the so-called biological factor is incidental and unimportant to human thought, desire and action, any genuine philosophy, true morality and good law has at the same time become impossible.'[56] But Eschweiler found a justification for the völkisch approach not only in Aquinas' philosophical anthropology; the great scheme of nature and supernature also proved to be capable of absorbing it. Eschweiler defined the concept of the 'moral and ethical feeling of the Germanic race' theologically as '*natus primus vel naturalis, in quo Creator nos conservat et parentes nostros*'. He could then continue: 'It is a Catholic truism that the grace of divine faith in those born German does not destroy their peculiar, God-given natural dispositions; rather, it presupposes, indeed implies as the most holy duty, that they assert and develop them against evil inclinations – there are also similar products of original sin.' Eschweiler was simply coming to the same conclusion as Hirsch, Stapel and Althaus and many, many others on the Protestant side when he declared: 'Anyone who disregards the creative will of God, in so doing shuts himself off from God's gracious will; and the gracious mystery of being a child of God does not presuppose that the natural Volksgemeinschaft is a chance prelude of no importance: rather, it is its elevation and fulfilment.' But precisely for this

426

reason – and here too the Protestant and Catholic patterns of thought were similar – National Socialism and the church needed each other. No one, Eschweiler thought, would guard National Socialism against the danger of falling victim to the heroic unbelief of a Friedrich Nietzsche if he did not find 'his discipline and order in the church of Christ'.[57]

Eschweiler's approach contained a pattern of interpretation that was now frequently accepted and repeated by Catholic university theology – almost totally orientated as it was on Neo-Thomism. At the end of July one of the best known of all German theologians, Karl Adam, systematic theologian at Tübingen, went even further in this direction. Now fifty-seven, Adam had become famous in the middle of the 1920s with his book *The Spirit of Catholicism*. Immediately translated into all the major world languages, this book stood for that German reform Catholicism which spoke with new passion and warmth of the Catholic Church as the body of Christ. It was a self-confident Catholicism that spoke here, a Catholicism which – in comparison with Protestantism – felt completely up to date 'as the full and strong affirmation of the whole man, in the complete sum of all his life relations'.[58] This determination to make the church modern, combined with the traditional rejection of 'Western' ideas, now led Adam to interpret Catholicism in 1933, too, in terms of the nationalist revolution. His article 'German Volkstum and Catholic Christianity' which appeared in late summer in the oldest academic journal of German Catholicism, the *Theologische Quartalschrift*, displayed not only general enthusiasm over the change in German affairs but also a concern to shift Catholic thought, over against that of Protestantism, into an even closer proximity to Volk and Volkstum.

How strongly the Tübingen theologian felt the historical power of the nationalist revolution was shown in his interpretation of Hitler, with its messianic overtones, as the man who had come, at first unknown, 'from the south, the Catholic south'. 'But the hour came when we beheld and recognized him,' wrote Adam. 'And now he stands before us as the one for whom the voices of our poets and sages called, as the liberator of the German genius, who took the blindfold from our eyes and – through all the political, economic, social and confessional veils – let us again see and love the one essential: our unity of blood, our German self, the *homo Germanus*.'[59]

The question and the task which Adam saw raised by this historical moment were: 'What real, fruitful connections exist between Christianity and Volkstum? And what demands emerge from this for us Catholics..?'[60] The answer followed two lines; what German Volkstum had to contribute to Catholic Christianity and, conversely, what Catholic Christianity had to contribute to German Volkstum.

The first sentence in the exposition of the first part already pointed to the Thomistic scheme. 'The dependence of Catholic Christianity upon living national Volkstum is a direct consequence of that principle with which the Catholic church and its theology describes the relationship of supernature to nature: "Grace presupposes nature (*gratia supponit naturam*)."' Because this was the foundation of Catholic Christianity, it was already clear at this point 'how Catholic Christianity understands and perceives its relationship to Volkstum much more comprehensively and intimately than does Protestant Christianity'. According to the Protestant understanding, there was absolutely no point of contact for

427

grace in fallen nature; the new righteousness was and remained an alien righteousness (*justitia Christi extra nos*). Between nature and the unfolding of grace in Volkstum there therefore yawned 'a deep, unbridgeable gulf'. Thus for the Protestant approach, 'an air of weary resignation lay over the powers of Volkstum, over its "blood"'. The light of the gospel may shine over it, but not in it.' By contrast, the Catholic Christian saw matters quite differently. According to the second major principle of Catholic theology, 'Grace does not destroy nature, but rather completes and perfects it (*gratia non destruit, sed complet et perficit naturam*)', 'nature and supernature, blood and spirit' presupposed each other. The basis and the vehicle of the new synthesis, however, was 'not the new spirit but rather the old blood, the *natura humana*'. The spirit becomes effective 'on the blood, in the blood, through the blood'.[61]

Continuing to think consistently here, Adam finally arrived at a resolute endorsement of the National Socialist racial policy. To protect and to secure through laws the 'purity and freshness' of German blood was 'a requirement of German self-expression' which originated in that ordered self-love 'which, in Christian morality, is the natural presupposition of the love of our neighbour.' Since the Jewish legislation to secure the purity of the race was legitimated by God's revelation in the Old Testament, it could be maintained that 'the German demand for the purity of the blood is in line with God's revelation in the Old Testament'. However, the Christian conscience would insist upon 'justice and love in the implementation of government decrees' and would reject 'combining a moral defamation of the Jewish character with the national-political defence against Jewry'.[62]

Typical though this contribution was of the political fashion of the year 1933, it was also typical that the sequel announced at the end never appeared. In both churches, the illusions which had led to such bold theological designs also came to an end with the year's end. As early as January 1934 Karl Adam came under intense fire from the Party because of public criticism of Hauer's German Faith Movement, and only Papen's intervention prevented something worse.[63]

Whereas Eschweiler and Adam laid the foundation for an encounter between Catholicism and National Socialism, above all in systematic terms, Michael Schmaus proceeded more along practical lines. At that time thirty-six, having made a name through works on Augustine and Thomas, in spring 1933 he had been called to the chair of systematic theology at Münster and, at the request of the Catholic theological faculty, had given a lecture in July, much noted, on 'Encounters between Catholic Christianity and National Socialist Ideology'. This lecture appeared in August as the first number of a newly-founded series *Reich und Kirche*, which – 'sustained by the conviction that there is no basic contradiction between the natural völkisch rebirth of our days and the supernatural life of the church' – was 'to serve the building up of the Third Reich by the united forces of the National Socialist state and Catholic Christianity'.[64]

Schmaus first of all described the nature of the National Socialist movement, which he understood to be 'the sharpest and most important protest against the spirituality of the nineteenth and twentieth centuries'. It replaced 'the mechanistic image of the world, the organic view of the world, the liberal and individualistic attitude towards life, with commitment to the given, to the earth, to the community.' Its dominant ideas were 'community, Volk, commitment,

428

authority'.[65] On this basis, it was now a simple matter to find the points of contact for encounters between National Socialism and Catholicism: anti-liberalism; affirmation of the naturally-developed community, of the Volk, and of Volkstum; strong emphasis on authority; finally, the shared experiential nature of the political movement and of faith. All of this, in Schmaus's conviction, bound the church closely to the new state. As on the Protestant side, with explicit reference to Stapel, so with Schmaus there was something of the völkisch nationalist philosophy of history. 'Since the Divine Will stands in the background of all history,' he declared, 'we can read from history, without self-deception, that God intended one of the greatest responsibilities for the German Volk.'[66] For Schmaus as for all Catholic theology the theological scheme for perceiving and interpreting these 'encounters' was the scheme of nature and supernature. The 'common interest' of National Socialist ideology and Catholic Christianity which Schmaus saw was ultimately simply evidence 'that supernature acknowledges and presupposes nature; that supernature perfects nature; that the God of creation and the God of redemption is one God'.[67]

The Braunsberg church historian Joseph Lortz was also ultimately concerned with 'the recognition of fundamental affinities between National Socialism and Catholicism'. The work which made Lortz famous, *The History of the Church seen from the Standpoint of the History of Ideas*, had just been published in 1932 (in 1965 it achieved its twenty-third edition).[68] Now, in the summer of 1933, Lortz expressly referred to this work as the 'vindication and support' and 'further interpretation' of his position.[69] In origin, character and theology there were hardly two more different men than the Braunsberg Reformation historian Joseph Lortz and the Tübingen Reformation historian Hanns Rückert. The latter was a Prussian, stern to the point of gruffness, and to the end of his life convinced of the unchanged, lasting truth of Luther's case against Catholicism. The former was from Luxembourg, vigorous and active by nature, and one of the first to attempt to secure some modest recognition for Luther's cause in the Catholic Church, too. It was therefore all the more remarkable that in the summer of 1933 Lortz described the great problem of the age to the students of Königsberg in the same way as Hanns Rückert did to the students of Tübingen. For Hanns Rückert, in the nationalist revolution the church was confronted with the question 'whether it possesses the inner power to interpret a great turning point in German destiny as coming from the hand of God, and to take a part in shaping it'.[70]

And for Lortz, too, the most important thing was to find 'an assent that arises from within'. 'National Socialism today,' ran his crucial argument, 'is not just the legitimate holder of state power in Germany; barely a few short months after the take-over of power, it is the German state itself. This state is involved in a truly decisive struggle for the deliverance of the whole Volk in every respect; through the declarations already mentioned and the concordat with the Curia it has made its peace with the church: with a power hitherto unknown in Germany it is striving to realize the inner unity of all our fellow members of the Volk. German Catholicism is thus confronted in the most urgent way possible, and in a great variety of areas, with the task of giving to National Socialism an assent arising from within. This task will be decisive for the church in Germany, and not less so for National Socialism.'[71]

The sentences with which Lortz concluded his work contained the common conviction of political theology, a conviction that was prior to all confessional differentiations. Rückert and Hirsch, Stapel and Gogarten, Eschweiler, Adam and Schmaus, and many, many others would have been able to formulate it in the same, or a similar way: 'Either this movement fights its way through to a deliverance or we end up in chaos. No one denies this inexorable logic any longer. But chaos would mean the destruction of the nation and the ruin of the German church. That closes the discussion.'[72]

Political theology was undoubtedly one of the most astonishing developments of the year 1933. For, in contrast to the German Christians, power was obviously not the issue here, but rather perception. It was not church-political domination that was at issue but theological truth. In fact the distinctive feature of political theology was not just assent to National Socialism, even if that was specially emphasized. The number of those in both churches who endorsed National Socialism extended far beyond the circle of political theology. The distinctive feature lay, rather, in the fact that at this juncture the political revolution became a principle of theological epistemology – the starting point for a way of theological thinking which felt that it had to understand itself anew from this point. Only in this way can the surprising parallelism of the developments in both churches be explained. For while the nationalist revolution as a principle of theological epistemology was put before a theological system and thus the need was recognized to see here an event to be understood and interpreted in purely theological terms by theology, the systematical interpretation as it were came to take second place. No matter whether the nationalist revolution was interpreted within the framework of a Christian philosophy of history as by Emanuel Hirsch or whether it was rediscovered in the relationship of law and gospel by Friedrich Gogarten, or whether the Thomistic scheme of nature and grace was called in as by Eschweiler and Adam, the result was the same: National Socialism and Christianity, Third Reich and church mutually conditioned and explained one another, disclosed themselves and were responsible to one another. Solidarity with the National Socialist movement not for political but for theological reasons was the demand of political theology in summer 1933. And this was clearly only superficially a political problem: basically it was a theological problem.

In this question, however, the arguments now proved extraordinarily difficult. For political theology could not simply be opposed by another political theology – in which the place of National Socialism was taken, for example, by Western democracy or Marxism. An argumentation on this level, of the kind the Religious Socialists had attempted in the 1920s, would not have affected political theology one way or the other. Here one ideology would merely have stood over against another, perhaps a theologically interpreted National Socialism over against a theologically interpreted Marxism. There was little to be gained from this, the more so since in summer 1933 this ideological confrontation seemed to have been settled for the time being. The possibility of arguing against political theology by setting another political theology over against it made no sense either in principle or in practice. But the other possibility, that of countering political theology by denying the church *qua* church any right to political judgment, was hardly convincing. Rather, political theology was undoubtedly right in maintaining that theology and the church were always political, regardless of whether they were making political judgments or not, and that a proclamation that did not affect political reality in principle was certainly not a proclamation of the word of God.

So if one could not argue against political theology in principle or non-politically, all that was left was theological argumentation, namely the question whether the political judgment of political theology withstood the test of theology as having an essentially theological basis. So it was not a question whether the political decision of German theology for National Socialism was correct, nor even whether theology might make political judgments at all. The key question was simply whether this political judgment had been arrived at in a theologically correct manner. The man who made this question the key to all church controversies was Karl Barth.

After his split with the Religious Socialists Karl Barth's total passion was devoted to the battle for the freedom of theology from all alien bonds, including those of alien politics. How little he was willing in this connection to concede the arguments of political theology, even in extreme situations, had been demonstrated in 1931 by his position in the Dehn case. When after long hesitation he finally intervened in this dispute, he did not make a real statement of political solidarity with Dehn, but demanded that the whole issue finally be discussed at the level at which it belonged, namely that of theology. And when once again he explained his position to Hirsch, he did so with a series of extremely typical expressions which demonstrated the reason for this demand. 'How could I want to remind you,' he replied at the time to Hirsch, 'of what is Above and Beyond the political excitement?... perhaps a "God", perhaps a "gospel", perhaps a "church" to which a really independent and dominant passion could lay claim?... Perhaps a theology which, in respect to politics as well, did not become politics but instead remained theology?'[73]

When Barth the next year wrote the Foreword to the new first volume of his *Dogmatics*, he again expressly took up the theme of the primacy of theology. Among the reasons which justified 'undertaking a dogmatics of the Evangelical Church today' he emphatically also mentioned his belief 'that we cannot reach the clarifications, especially in the broad field of politics, which are necessary today and to which theology today might have a word to say (as indeed it ought to have a word to say to them!), without having previously reached those comprehensive clarifications, in theology and about theology itself, with which we should be concerned here.' So the important thing here was neither a political theology nor a non-political theology, but rather a theology which 'first of all' – that is, before it made political judgments – had become clear about itself. In contrast to political theology, which in his conviction let its position arise from political events, Barth was determined to give political events their place within theology. Hence his declaration, 'Ethics so-called I regard as the doctrine of God's command and do not consider it right to treat it otherwise than as an integral part of dogmatics, or to produce a dogmatics which does not include it.' In this way, any attempt to make political ethics independent of dogmatics, so typical of all models of political theology, was ruled out. He also went on to indicate where ethical concepts were to be given detailed treatment. 'The concept of the command of God in general' was not to be discussed within the framework of the doctrine of creation – i.e., God's command in history or in nature – but

431

rather at the end of the section on the doctrine of God. 'The commandment of God from the viewpoint of Order will be dealt with at the close of the doctrine of Creation, from the viewpoint of Law at the close of the doctrine of Reconciliation, from the viewpoint of Promise at the close to the doctrine of Redemption.'[74]

Karl Barth himself felt the point which he had reached with this new first volume of his *Dogmatics* to be both a conclusion and a starting point. He felt it to be the conclusion of a development in which step by step he had eliminated from theology all philosophical, political and social conditioning as the conditioning of theological knowledge. In his conviction, this development went back a long way. For more than two hundred years it had controlled Protestant theology. This explains the radical way in which Barth now argued. He mentioned the line from Schleiermacher through Ritschl to Herrmann and declared: 'in any thinkable continuation of this line I can only see the plain destruction of Protestant theology and the Protestant church.' Either theology should base itself solely upon the word of God or it had to follow the Catholic path. In Barth's conviction there was now 'no third possibility between play with the *analogia entis*, legitimate only on Roman Catholic ground, between the greatness and the misery of a so-called natural knowledge of God in the sense of the Vaticanum, and a Protestant theology self-nourished at its own source, standing upon its own feet, and finally liberated from such secular misery'. Because this was now clear, however, the point arrived at was at the same time also a starting point. For upon this basis a theology which set out to be and remain nothing other than theology could be established and developed anew.[75]

Barth's first lecture to be written in the Third Reich, which he delivered on 10 and 12 March 1933 in Copenhagen and Aarhus, repeated and confirmed the position he had reached here. It was entitled 'The First Commandment as a Theological Axiom'. Among the abundance of much more famous articles by Barth, there is not one that explains his later theological and political decisions more concisely, clearly and impressively than this one.

His starting point was the simple First Commandment which everyone knew: 'I am the Lord your God. You shall have no other gods but me!' Referring to Luther's Lesser Catechism, Barth explained the other gods as that 'upon which man places his trust, in which he believes, for which he expects it to give him that which he loves, and to protect him from that which he fears'. The commandment explicitly concedes that there really are such gods, as it also presupposes 'that there are Völker which have them as gods, which give their heart to these gods'.[76]

The question which Barth attached to this was the significance of the first commandment for theology. This commandment, he thought, involved a three-fold responsibility. If theology considered it necessary to form pairs of concepts, such as 'revelation and creation, revelation and primal revelation, New Testament and human existence, the commandment and the ordinances', then it would demonstrate its responsibility first of all in the fact 'that it will speak about revelation with notably increased seriousness and interest – and of that other authority only incidentally and for the sake of revelation'. And if theology could not in fact refrain further 'from also speaking about human beings, about reason and experience, history and creaturely existence, and then certainly also about

432

Volkstum, morality and state when it speaks of revelation, then' – and this is where the whole weight of the argument now lay – 'this responsibility will be demonstrated in the fact that it will interpret those other authorities by the criterion of revelation and not interpret revelation by the criterion of those other authorities. It will not seek to investigate heaven with a searchlight set up on earth, but rather will attempt to see and to understand the earth in the light of heaven.' Finally, in all these relationships theology would demonstrate its responsibility in the fact that 'in any case, there will be no possibility whatsoever of the mixing or exchange, no possibility of an identification of the two concepts'.[77]

If, however, in Protestant theology the question thus raised about the 'other gods' could not definitely be answered in the negative, if something else determined it, then in truth it was Catholic. For this was the nature of the Catholic church, the *analogia entis*: 'It also knows about Christ, also about grace, also about faith. But it is a master in the art of dividing its heart between God and the gods. It knows, alongside Christ, a second authority essential to salvation; it knows as something "below", analogous to that "above" in its existence and being as it is and, in its immanent structure, is ordered by it; it knows about the human being, with his capacity to collaborate on the basis of grace with grace for the honour of God and his own salvation.' If so many paths led back to Rome, that was all the more reason to insist that in the present Protestant theology 'should dismiss all and every natural theology, and should venture in that question, in that isolation, to cling solely to the God who has revealed himself in Jesus Christ'.[78]

So the unconditional primacy of theology over politics which Barth demanded – a theology which, 'even in respect of politics, would not become politics but remain theology' – was not only a formal decision but corresponded to the content of theology, to the first commandment as a theological axiom, which absolutely forbade other gods alongside God.

In specific terms, this meant that where fundamental decisions were at issue theology and church could not espouse Fascism, but could not espouse anti-Fascism either; they could not espouse either Communism or anti-Communism.

Karl Barth remained faithful to this line all his life. When after 1945 he confused and angered many people by not wanting to toe the anti-Communist line of Western politics, this was after all the same decision which in 1933 kept him from constructing a church anti-Fascism.

Barth's position over politics and the church in the Third Reich was thus marked out by his theological position. It was a position which allowed, indeed required, one's own political judgment, but which was absolutely opposed to making the future of theology and church dependent upon this political judgment.

As to political judgment, even in the Third Reich Karl Barth was and remained a member of the SPD until it was banned. Early in April he made clear to Paul Tillich how he understood this membership. 'For me, membership of the SPD does not mean a profession of the idea and ideology of socialism. Given my interpretation of the exclusive nature of the Christian confession, I cannot "confess" an idea or ideology in a serious way.' Thus Marxism, too, was as close and as distant for him as, for example, the nationalism then dominant. That nevertheless he wanted to be and remain a member of the SPD was an utterly practical political decision.

'Confronted with the various possibilities which the human being has in this respect, I consider it important *rebus hic et nunc sic stantibus* to adopt the party 1. of the working class, 2. of democracy, 3. of non-militarism and 4. of a conscious but sensible affirmation of the German people and state.' He would adhere to this political decision as long as that was possible.[79] In fact he informed the Prussian Kultusminister, Bernhard Rust, of this in exactly the same way, and at the same time asked whether in the circumstances he was permitted to continue to teach during the summer semester. To everyone's surprise, Rust raised no objections.[80]

Thus the practical political decision was clear, and remained so. The state had no power over one's convictions, nor might anything be conceded to it. But, given Karl Barth's theological starting point, it was and remained just as clear that this practical political decision could not readily have the last word on either the office or the task of the theologian. The Word of God alone decided on this office and this task. And as long as the state permitted the office, i.e. free theological teaching and free church proclamation – there was no reason to put it at risk for the sake of a practical decision.

So during April Barth defended himself against both left and right in the face of an attempt to require certain political decisions of him. On the left, he declared to his faculty colleague and friend Karl Ludwig Schmidt – who, as a Social Democrat member of the City Council, was threatened with dismissal and expected a declaration of solidarity – that 'on purely political grounds' this was conceivable and could well happen. 'Neither of us, however, thinks in purely political terms. We have also, indeed above all, a church office to discharge and to hold.' Barth explained the specific conclusion that he drew from this once again in the following statement: 'If the Reformed Alliance and the Elberfeld community send a special courier to me in Switzerland in order to tell me that I am requested to do everything possible to support church efforts to keep me, then I can truly tell them that this could in no way include the surrender of my party card. However, I cannot possibly say (and the incident took place here just fourteen days ago) that your mandate will be more important to me than the continuation of my own work, for which I was again asked just as urgently.'[81]

On the right, that same day he assured his young friend and fellow pilgrim of many years, Georg Merz, who stated as a condition for further collaboration in the Christian church in Germany that Barth must declare himself 'for the destiny of Germany' and was not to offer opposition, that in no circumstances would this happen. For by this token the new church order would be a failure from the very start. 'Dear Georg,' wrote Barth, 'I have not resisted Religious Socialism (already at a time when you thought that you could detect "religious approaches" in socialism) in order now to find myself ready to affirm that it is German destiny to combine Christ and Caesar with the other side because the sacred stream of history is for the moment running in this direction, and for the sake of the church I may not stand "against" (e.g. what is now happening to the German Jews).' Rather, he stood, quite strongly, 'against' most of what was happening in Germany, 'and if it is still not my task to apply this view politically, I still emphatically refuse for the sake of the "Christian Church in Germany" to show any kind of solidarity with these "things".' There then followed in one sentence the precise formulation of the standpoint which Karl Barth held from then until his dismissal in the summer of 1935: I will certainly oppose, 'directly and indirectly, not the new political system, but certainly the system of any special substantive connection between the church and this system'.[82]

This position was certainly not without problems. Barth's report in the same letter that he had dispatched to Bonn proof of his Aryan extraction revealed where the problems lay. They did not in any way lie where they are frequently located today, namely in a refusal to offer 'political resistance'. Rather, Barth's objections to any political theology remain theologically valid, as does his assertion of the theological clarifications needed 'first of all' before the church expressed itself on political questions. But for the church there is certainly not only the preaching of reconciliation but also the act of reconciliation, which expresses itself in a helping and compassionate solidarity with the victims of this and every age. Perhaps the fact that Barth did not perceive and did not ponder this possibility was the only real weakness in his position.

On the other hand, the way things stood it was undoubtedly true that in the summer of 1933, in the face of a political theology which was expressing itself increasingly loudly and becoming increasingly self-confident, only one approach in fact had a chance: that which reminded the Church Struggle exclusively of the theological problems. The extraordinary response to Barth's first contribution to the Church Struggle demonstrates that he had found here how the Protestant church even now, and indeed in the Third Reich for the future, could remain a church and could preach and teach as a church.

The publication which fundamentally changed the church situation bore the title *Theological Existence Today*. It was published early in July. Since then something of a legend has grown up around its origin. As Helmut Gollwitzer tells it on the authority of Hellmut Traub, Barth's fellow-lodger at that time, Barth had first written 'a quite political, unprecedentedly sharp manifesto'. Advised by Traub and Charlotte von Kirschbaum, a close friend, that this could not possibly be published, Barth had 'crossly' laid the manuscript aside and immediately started writing again. The result was *Theological Existence Today*. Both his audience had been enthusiastic about it and moreover had been satisfied with it 'because this could now be published'. Barth, however, so ran the nice ending, 'threw the pages in a blazing rage at their feet and rushed out of the room with the words, "There's your co-ordinated theological existence!"'[83]

The attempt to explain and excuse the political composure of the theologian Karl Barth, which seems so hard to bear, is understandable. But it fails to understand the reason for this composure, namely his theological approach. According to Barth's development and everything he said before and after 1933 on the relationship between theology and politics, it would be not only surprising but quite inexplicable had he decided in June on a 'quite political, unprecedentedly sharp manifesto'.

In fact the real prehistory was far less dramatic. Charlotte von Kirschbaum reported it on 15 June in a letter to Karl Barth's mother in Switzerland. According to this account, on 13 June a few of Barth's friends – his colleagues Wilhelm Vischer, Fritz Lieb and a young pastor from Bochum – had attempted to persuade the famous Bonn theologian finally to make a statement in favour of Bodelschwingh. It was the time when the struggle over Bodelschwingh was reaching a climax, and the visitors were of the opinion 'that every church-minded man now had to stand behind this name'. In a long conversation, however, Barth told them 'what frightened him about this position and how completely the church turned into church politics in this way of thinking'. The three visitors impressed on him 'that precisely this had to be said now, for once loudly and openly', so Barth decided to write this message. It was obvious that the message could not be just a political, or even a church-political message. In fact the letter also said that 'essentially it will consist of an appeal to the theologians among our contemporaries not to give up their theological existence now'. And Charlotte von Kirschbaum continued, 'Of course it is inevitable that this appeal must at the same time mean drawing a sharp line over against those who have been "co-ordinated", so perhaps he will start up a very agitated debate, or perhaps not.' In spite of that, she thought that he had finally taken a position, albeit a position – as she once more assured Barth's concerned mother – 'only as a theologian. He will abstain from all political statements.'[84]

This was now confirmed in the famous first sentences of *Theological Existence Today*. The crucial thing, Barth declared, was that 'the essence of what I attempt to contribute today bearing upon these anxieties and problems cannot be made the theme of a particular manifesto, for the simple reason that at Bonn here, with my students in lectures and courses, I endeavour to carry on theology, and only theology, now as previously, and as if nothing had happened. Perhaps there is a slightly increased tone, but without direct allusions: something like the chanting of the hours by the Benedictines near by in the Maria Laach, which goes on undoubtedly without break or interruption, pursuing the even tenor of its way even in the Third Reich. I regard the pursuit of theology as the proper attitude to adopt: at any rate it is one befitting church politics, and indirectly, even politics.'

What he now proclaimed to theologians in Germany was simply what he had been saying all through the years: 'The one thing that must not happen to us who are theological professors, is our abandoning our job through becoming zealous for some cause we think to be good. Our existence as theologians is our life within the church and, of course, as appointed preachers and teachers within the church.' The other gods which threatened theological existence in the present bore the names 'politics and church politics'. In the light of this threat the most important thing was 'that now, one and all, within the church as she has borne us by means of the Word, and within the incomparable sphere of our vocation we must *abide*, or (if we have left it) *turn back* into the church and into the sphere of our vocation, at all costs, by putting all regards and concerns behind'.[85]

This passionate appeal was given concrete form in three examples which Barth used to explain the situation. Thus he criticized all the church reform of the summer for not having arisen out of obedience to God's word but rather out of a human, purely political decision. He thus asserted that the introduction of an office of Reich Bishop was 'clearly the imitation of a certain "governmental model"'. This was nothing less than a new dogma, but a dogma 'not only without authority but even without a shade of a theological argument'. So he ended by declaring 'emphatically and distinctively, yet only in passing' because basically it went without saying – in respect of the doctrine of the German Christians: 'I say, absolutely and without reserve, No! to both the spirit and the letter of this doctrine.' 'Their growth and increase is a reason for anxiety', but not for theological reasons – their teaching was really only a 'small collection of odds and ends from the great theological dustbins of the despised eighteenth and nineteenth centuries' – but rather because they had demonstrated 'that there can be a "Faith-Movement" which even possesses form and force by using violence after the manner of political mass demonstrations and forced recruiting campaigns'.[86]

Though this was already clear enough, it was only now that the work achieved the last sharpness which gave it its decisive effect.

Barth said that much worse than the German Christians was the 'point-blank amazing lack of resistance' with which 'pastors and church members, professors and students of theology, educated and illiterate, old and young, Liberal, Fundamentalists and Pietists, Lutherans and Calvinists, have surrendered in droves at the noise of this movement which bears so distinctly on its brow the brand of topsy-turvydom. That already a candidate for confirmation has had to take note, that in a healthy church he cannot remain alone for a single hour, with either the Lutheran or the Heidelberg Catechism in his hand, and get on with it, under any pretext. Where in all this was the plain but critical question as to Christian truth? When could all this be possible? Or is it that this question dare not be put at all in the present Evangelical Church? Has the quest for truth been totally suppressed in one jubilation or groaning by the shouts of Revolution, Reality, Life, Mastery or Destiny...?'

The question about Christian truth, however, not only affected the church in general; to a special degree it applied to those offering resistance to the German Christians: the Young Reformers Movement. Karl Barth saw these on the same course as their opponents, distinguished from them not by theology but only by 'the idea of the formal independence of the Church as regards the state and political influences'. 'Anyhow, both these opponents of yesterday come alike from the calamitous theology of the nineteenth century.' And 'as architects of a serious reconstruction of the church neither of them should have been called in.' If one keeps in mind what happened in Prussia, such sweeping criticism of the Young Reformers was doubtless unjustified. And yet it was precisely this uncompromising one-sidedness which made a decisive contribution to the clarification of the church situation. For only through this criticism was the Young Reformers Movement brought face to face, in connection with church-political events, with the significance of the confession, which was then to become the key concept of the Confessing Church.

Barth consistently went on to say that what was needed was not church political 'movements' but rather trust in God's help and commitment to the confession. The important thing was to form not a centre of church-political resistance but rather a spiritual one, 'one that would, for the first time, give a meaning and a content to church politics'.[87]

Was this insistence too self-centred? Did 'theological existence' here become an end in itself? At the very end of the work, in a few almost prophetic sentences, Karl Barth suggested what all this meant politically: 'All that was called Liberty, Justice, Spirit only a year ago and for a hundred years farther back, where has it all gone? Now, these are all temporal, material, earthly goods! "All flesh is as grass..." No doubt. There is no doubt that many people in olden times, and later, have had to do without these proffered goods, and have been able to if the bold enterprise of the "Totalitarian State" demanded it. "But the Word of our God abideth for ever", and consequently, it is true and indispensable every day; for every day hastens into Eternity. Because of this, theology and the church cannot enter upon a winter sleep within the "Total State"; no moratorium and no "assimilation" can befall them. They are the natural frontiers of everything, even of the "Totalitarian State". For even in this "Total State" the nation always lives by the Word of God, the content of which is "forgiveness of sins, resurrection of the body and life everlasting". To this Word the church and theology have to render service for the people. Because of this, church and theology are the frontier, the bounds, of the state.'

Therefore, vigilance was necessary: 'In the particular concern entrusted to us, we theologians must be awake, "as a sparrow on the house-tops"; on the earth also, but under the open, wide, but infinite open heavens. If it so be that the German Evangelical theologian should still remain awake, on the watch, or if he have gone to sleep, today, today once more, Oh! that once more he were awake!'[88]

Barth completed the manuscript of *Theological Existence Today* on 25 June 1933, one day after the appointment of the State Commissioner in the Prussian Church. The document was available from 1 July; fourteen days later four impressions totalling 12,000 copies had already been printed. The eighth impression in October appeared at the same time as the first issue of a new series, founded by Barth and Thurneysen together, which as a whole now bore the title which meanwhile had become famous: Theologische Existenz heute. Altogether, the publication achieved a circulation of 37,000 copies before it was confiscated in July 1934.[89] But these statistics say little about the actual effect which *Theological Existence Today* had in summer 1933 and for a long time afterwards.

'When we read this,' wrote Hans Asmussen on the occasion of Karl Barth's fiftieth birthday in 1936, 'a great sobering came over us, and with the sobering came the confidence that our cause would also carry us through.'[90] And many other reports say much the same thing. In a country manse, a young pastor read what the teacher of the *Church Dogmatics* was saying. He read it aloud 'and under its liveliness and clarity, the oppressive cloud began to break up'.[91] At the same time in Tübingen it was for a young student as though scales fell from his eyes: 'Here was a clear understanding in things eternal and temporal. Here a theological teacher finally showed us a way forward that was in accordance with the gospel!'[92] Nor was this true only for assenting young pastors and students. From Dresden, for example, the Saxon Lutheran Hugo Hahn remembered the enthusiasm with which *Theological Existence* was welcomed. To be sure, he probably would not have 'been led in any really different direction', even without Karl Barth. Yet the whole Dresden group was much indebted to the Bonn theologian 'for clarification and strengthening'.[93] And from Marburg Barth's famous colleague Rudolf Bultmann wrote as early as 13 July that he stood by the work with all its consequences, 'even if I regret your verdict on the Young Reformers'.[94]

The strong impact of the document was also demonstrated among its opponents. Hirsch, deeply affected, published a criticism as early as the middle of July, *The Purpose of the German Christians for the Church. On Assessing the Attack by Karl Barth*, in which he accused Barth, with his lack of a sense of

438

history, of making a new law out of the gospel. Hirsch could not think, he said, using an expression of which he was fond at that time, that Barth would be so blind about church and Volk 'if he were German from top to toe, like us; if he had experienced as his own the fate of our Volk in war and defeat and self-alienation, and the National Socialist revolution in the way we did, with trembling and joy.'[95] Friedrich Gogarten replied in agitation, 'For my part, however, I am convinced that we lose our "theological existence"... unless we reflect in all seriousness on the way in which God's guidance through political events gives us occasion to listen anew to his Word.'[96] And even years later he charged his one-time comrade-in-arms with having 'hopelessly confused the church at a crucial moment'.[97] On 19 and 20 August the leading German Christian theologian in Hamburg, Franz Tügel, wrote *Impossible Existence! A Word against Karl Barth*. Not entirely without justification, in it he stated that 'thinking out to the end' Barth's position would 'mean a direct path into the concentration camp'. 'No thread of understanding, however delicate, binds us to the neutrality of one who can do theology today in this German land "as if nothing had happened"... Not theology but politics separates us.'[98] And even Catholic theology now began to draw a line. Joseph Lortz, for example, pointed out in the third edition of his book that the history of the church proved 'that nature does not represent just an eternal point of contact for grace, above which the latter hovers as "the wholly Other"; rather, it confirms the fact that in the kingdom of the God of order, an inner relationship between nature and grace is of the essence of reality.'[99] But Barth had expected nothing else from this quarter.

With the publication of *Theological Existence Today*, Barth's approach began to make itself felt in the Protestant church in a church-political way as well. Within about a year – at the Confessing Synod of Barmen in May 1934 – it had prevailed. And the 1945 collapse brought completely to light the truth and falsehood in the theological decisions of the summer of 1933. The result of this development was that Barth's approach appeared for a long time far less problematical than it was.

Its crucial weakness lay in the fact that the church's concentration on theological existence blocked direct insight into the significance of the Jewish question. This was no accidental omission, but rather a deliberate result. When Barth discussed the Jewish question in a sermon in December 1933 he explicitly stated that he was doing so only as a result of the text for the day. 'As a theme, neither the Jewish question nor any other of the questions concerning us today belongs in the pulpit.'[100] And he said exactly the same thing in answer to a letter that reached him early in January 1934, which spoke of the misery of the Jews and the misery of a church that remained silent on this question. 'I agree with anyone who says to me today that he would like the Protestant church to be *different* – but only on condition that he realizes that it must become *different* in an exceedingly fundamental way.'[101] Only later did Barth see that this was a crucial weakness in his position.[102]

Moreover, the concentration of the content of all discussions on the question of natural theology was not without problems. It obscured any view of the fact that the theological landscape, even in summer 1933, was after all considerably more complex than the formula 'Scripture or 1933' suggested.[103] The way from natural theology to the 'German Christians' was by no means as straight and as clear as Barth maintained. This was true of Protestantism, where resistance was also offered on the basis of quite different theological arguments, and all the more so – despite all the amazing agreement over political theology – of the Catholic Church. So it was also no accident, but rather a consequence of the radical one-sidedness of Barth's approach, that during the war even the Confessing Church became involved in a severe theological crisis from which two of its most important theologians, Dietrich Bonhoeffer and Rudolf Bultmann, attempted to free themselves, each in his own way, with new approaches.

An additional problem lay in the difficulty of conveying Barth's approach in any form of church organization. Barth himself at first transferred his deep distrust of the Young Reformers, as of all church movements in general, to the Pastors Emergency League as well; only after a long time and considerable effort did it prove possible to establish a close connection here.[104]

And finally, all this also had its human side. The impatience with which Barth presented his position and the forthrightness with which he dissociated himself from all those who did not want to share that position created deep divisions which in many cases – as for example in the case of Gogarten – could never be bridged again.[105] Even more problematical in this respect were some of his disciples who disseminated a degree of self-righteousness in the Confessing Church which many people found almost intolerable.

In spite of all these objections and weaknesses, however, Barth's theological approach, particularly in the critical situation of 1933, proved to be one of the truly great theological models of Christian theology. Here again something of Christian truth, something of Christian faith, Christian consolation and Christian confidence emerged which many people had for a long time believed to be lost. For this reason, this one voice was heard amid the tremendous din of the church-political turmoil. For this reason, the longer it was heard the more it determined the theme of the discussions. And for this reason it finally prevailed in the church. And even if this theology certainly was, and remained, partial (I Cor.13.9), it nevertheless was, and remained, great and special in its partial way.

10

The Establishment of the Reich Church
(July-September)

On the Catholic side, the major decisions had been made with the passing of the Reich concordat in the cabinet on 14 July and its signing in Rome on 20 July. Even the eventful history up to its ratification on 10 September brought no further change.

On the Protestant side, however, the cabinet decision of 14 July on the new Evangelical Church constitution meant the reorganization of the whole church. First of all the church elections which Hitler had arranged on 30 June[1] were now to be held; after that, on the basis of the election returns, the church bodies – community representatives and synods – were to be reconstituted; and finally the National Synod had to convene in order to complete and conclude the reconstruction of the church with the election of the first Reich Bishop. The eight weeks up to this election on 27 September demonstrated how strong the political influences on the Protestant church now were. They also showed, however, the fragile nature of the foundation upon which the Reich Church was erected.

Like so many important decisions during this year, the Protestant church elections were also marked by tremendous haste, which simply swept away objections, misgivings and reservations. Probably one of Hitler's most outstanding political qualities was his general feeling for the importance of timing. Here, too, this played its part.

Over 12 July most of the representatives of the Landeskirchen returned home from the strenuous negotiations in Berlin on the church constitution, undoubtedly feeling that they had now earned a lengthy rest for the moment. But the very next morning they again received a telegram from the Reich Ministry of the Interior summoning them back to Berlin for a meeting on 14 July at 10 a.m.[2] To the utter surprise of the assembly, the Secretary of State in charge of affairs, Hans Pfundtner, now laid before it the draft of a Reich law which was to be passed that very day by the Reich cabinet. It contained not only the expected legal recognition of the church constitution of 11 July but also a provision that the new elections for all church bodies, which were also expected, were to be held as early as 23 July. This date was a bold risk. The original draft from the Ministry of the Interior had provided for an interval of at least four weeks – until 20 August. On the personal orders of Hitler, however, this period had now been shortened to nine days. Since this timing naturally violated all the election rules

441

of the Landeskirchen, at the same time the law included an authorization that if necessary the Landeskirchen might deviate 'from the provisions of the church laws and church constitutions governing the external course of election procedure'.[3]

An orderly completion of the election at such short notice was impossible. For example, all regulations for church elections made it a condition that voters should be personally entered on the voting lists of their communities – a procedure that normally took weeks in large city communities in which 15-20,000 votes were eligible. A representative of the ministry therefore recommended using the old lists, simply appending additions and otherwise proceeding 'not too formally'. All protests against this drastic intervention in the church's freedom of decision, like those made above all by Bavaria, Württemberg and Baden, were ineffectual. However, they were not very persuasive. For in Prussia the situation was still difficult. And since the Landeskirchen had already accepted state involvement to such an extent, there was no reason why they should not also accept this latest step towards the state pacification of the church. Moreover, Pfundtner emphatically referred to the imminent signing of the Reich concordat which, to give the Protestant church full equality, called for an immediate agreement on the Protestant side, too. Finally, the church delegates were again assured that the Reich would guarantee the smooth and impartial completion of the election.[4]

The unusual circumstance that Hitler had this law presented to the official delegates of the Landeskirchen before it was given cabinet approval raises the question whether an extension of the period might have been achieved had some individual Landeskirchen refused to accept it. Of course this can no longer be ascertained, but we may surely suppose that Hitler would hardly have let his plans be thwarted on this point. And even fourteen days more for the election preparations might have been enough to change the picture fundamentally. But after all that the previous weeks had brought, no one seemed willing to run the risk of refusing the state.

That same 14 July two central directives were issued which laid down the terms of the church elections for state and party. The Reich Minister of the Interior wrote from Berlin requesting all governments of the Länder 'respectfully to instruct all appropriate authorities... to facilitate the completion of the elections for the church agencies through the distribution of information, etc.' And the next day he made it known that he had appointed Secretary of State Pfundtner to be the 'official representative for the supervision of the impartial implementation' of the church elections.[5]

Also on 14 July the Reich propaganda leadership in the Party likewise wrote in the strictest confidence from Munich to all Gauleiters requesting them 'to give the German Christians full support'. At all costs the election had to be won by the German Christians 'for reasons of prestige'. All methods of propaganda were to be mobilized. Press and radio were also brought into action by the Ministry of Propaganda. The letter ended with the 'desire of the Führer to secure a complete victory for the German Christians'.[6] If hitherto the relationship between the Faith Movement and the Party had remained somewhat ambiguous, clarity now obviously prevailed. The performance of the Party in the individual areas had become a matter of honour for each Gauleiter.

442

There is hardly any example which gives a better indication of Hitler's double strategy than these two directives. The apparent conflict between state and Party which emerged here was as typical as it was confusing. For it kept the notion of the rule of law and to some degree put it to the test. However, it did not in any way prevent the illegitimate realization of political goals.

In these circumstances, then, feverish preparations for the church elections began throughout Protestant Germany on the very evening of 14 July. While the church administrations everywhere were revising and adapting the electoral rules, the church groups were attempting to mobilize their followers throughout the country. In this connection it was certain from the beginning that by and large there were only two electoral choices: either the Faith Movement of German Christians or the church opposition.

The initiative for the concentration of the church opposition came from Berlin. Here, immediately after the announcement of the date of the election, the leadership of the Young Reformers Movement had agreed upon a common list of candidates and had given it the name Evangelische Kirche. At the same time a national executive was formed for this list, which basically lay in the hands of Dietrich Bonhoeffer, Eitel-Friedrich von Rabenau and Gerhard Jacobi. An office was set up in a church hostel for the unemployed in Mirbachstrasse. During the night of 14-15 July Niemöller, Künneth and Lilje immediately drew up an appeal to all the communities along with guidelines for the election, while Bonhoeffer and Jacobi composed a circular letter to the pastors. All the appeals made at this time kept to the line of the Young Reformers, which combined the demand for an independent church with unconditional loyalty to the state. For example, the message of the church members ran: 'We call on all friends of a church free from the state and founded solely on the Word of God to participate in the election. The present emergency compels all who love their church to form an alliance.' The appeal then continued: 'We stand thankfully and resolutely behind Hindenburg and Hitler as the leaders of our state, who now, too, have paved the way to freedom for the church by their intervention.' The church's independence and loyalty to the state were again combined in the concluding sentence: 'Anyone who wants a church which proclaims God's Word without fear of persons and which serves our Volk in devout loyalty should vote for our list: Evangelische Kirche. Let the church be the church.'[7] Without doubt the church opposition differed widely in its appraisal of the situation and what it called for. Thus, for example, Bonhoeffer was far more sceptical about Hitler than were Niemöller, Künneth and Lilje; and this was also expressed in many announcements.[8] But generally speaking, the whole group still backed the united Young Reformers' programme.

How quickly the church opposition had worked emerged from the fact that the group's election materials were on the way to all Prussian clergy and non-Prussian church administrations as early as the evening of 15 July.[9]

The German Christian counter-stroke followed promptly. Since they had certainly not acted as quickly, and still did not have real support among the pastors, on 17 July Hossenfelder obtained an injunction against the name 'Evangelische Kirche' – probably on the suggestion of August Jäger, on the grounds that this name defamed the German Christians.[10] At the same time Jäger, through an official in his ministry, mobilized the Gestapo. That evening they confiscated the entire supply of election material – in all about 320,000 copies of a wide variety of pamphlets and leaflets – from the office of the opposition's national headquarters in Mirbachstrasse. The next day Jacobi and Bonhoeffer personally visited the Gestapo chief, Rudolf Diels. On the basis of their complaints that this was a serious infringement of the promised electoral freedom, they obtained a partial release of the material on condition that the name of their election list, 'Evangelische Kirche', be changed to 'Evangelium und Kirche'. Bonhoeffer and Jacobi announced this the same evening in a circular letter. Obviously encouraged by their success with Diels, at the same time they requested that all infringements of free elections or of preparations for the election should be reported to them immediately.[11] In spite of this partial victory, the opposition had lost precious time.

Despite everything, however, the German Christians would still not have become masters of the situation had not the impact of the 14 July letter to the Gauleiters now taken effect throughout the Reich. This letter had arrived in the district offices on Monday 17 July. Until this moment the leadership of the Faith Movement itself had not managed very much more than an injunction and an appeal that contained little that was new, even when it demanded: 'Build Christ's new church in Adolf Hitler's new state. Build it in the new spirit, on the ground of the old gospel. Close ranks!'[12] However, from 18 July on the whole Party apparatus threw itself with full force into the election campaign. The day before, Goebbels had already given the press to understand in a directive that the government's verdict on individual newspapers would be dependent upon their 'participation in the publicity campaign for the German Christians'.[13] Thus from that day the propaganda wave was also rolling. More important than this public support, however, was the intervention of the Party organization. On this day, up and down the country, district leaders and local group leaders were given strict orders to arrange for the immediate 'registration of all Protestant Volk members on the voting lists'.[14] Ambition to fulfil the Führer's wishes gave the individual Gaue the most surprising ideas. In Lübeck, for example, the Party organization itself distributed the electoral roll cards to its members, gathered them in again, and warned that there would be 'strict supervision of the registration as well as of the use of the vote'. Moreover, candidacy on any list other than that of the German Christians was forbidden with threats of expulsion from the Party. Chief Pastor Jannasch, who was campaigning in the church magazine for the 'Evangelische Kirche', was at once prohibited from doing any 'official work' by the – German Christian – church council.[15] In Hamburg, in place of individual registrations on the voting lists, it proved possible on the responsibility of a representative to hand in closed lists which were provided for the purpose by the Gauleitung.[16] In Franconia, too, the lists of candidates for the election were to be worked out 'by the local Party leaders'.[17] Where all this was still not yet enough, there was open coercion, confiscations, prohibitions of assemblies – in short, all the tried means available to the Party for controlling public opinion. And the zeal of the minor and intermediate-level Party function-aries was not at all restrained in the choice of such means. Wherever there was active resistance to the German Christians the Party spread a climate of fear and terror.[18]

In these circumstances there could be no talk of the 'impartial completion' of the election which had been solemnly promised. So the complaints and protests immediately began to pile up in the Reich Ministry of the Interior. A telegram from the Prussian church administration on 19 July to Secretary of State Pfundtner suddenly made the situation clear. 'Nomination of lists other than those of German Christians designated a subversive act by official authorities in the Rhine province. In many places expulsion from the NSDAP threatened for candidates on list Evangelium und Kirche. Numerous acts of violence. Free choice thus endangered... Request appropriate notification to authorities responsible for enforcing Reich law of 14 July.'[19] Pfundtner took the protests quite seriously. On 27 July he had already made the 'sharpest protest' to the Prussian Kultusministerium because of Jäger's high-handed confiscation operation.[20] On 20 July he publicly repeated the Reich government's guarantee of 'the free and impartial completion of the election'. As he declared explicitly, 'Attempts to influence a free election by coercive means are not in accord with the will of the Reich government.'[21] At the same time he requested the Secretary of State in the Reich Chancellery 'to leave to the consideration of the Chancellor' whether he might not want to make a similar statement. However, Hitler did not now have the remotest intention of doing this. Rather, he immediately informed Pfundtner that the assurance of free elections meant 'that the authorities in Reich and Länder must be concerned to prevent any violent disruption of preparations for the election and of the electoral act'. However, this was in no sense a promise 'that the NSDAP and its organization would be required to refrain from all kinds of electoral agitation'. The Chancellor was not, Pfundtner learned, 'in a position to issue a directive to that effect to Party officials of the NSDAP'.[22] It was hard to argue against this, so Pfundtner kept quiet then and also on subsequent days.

On 21 July, however, Hitler went to Bayreuth, where the 1933 season was opened in the afternoon with *Meistersinger*. And from the festival he now also intervened personally in the church election campaign.

This unusual step originated in an agreement with Ludwig Müller of which Müller again reminded the Chancellor just before the elections. Müller's letter in this connection was a sign of the complete dependence of the German Christians on Hitler, and at the same time was an indication of the significance of the confessional problem in German politics. 'It is good,' wrote Müller to his Führer at this time, 'that you have set the date for the church elections so soon; otherwise the campaign would take on the ugliest forms. The reactionaries in their final fury are using all – and I mean all – means, including the most vile slander, to deprive us of control of the new Reich Church. I urgently need your help, because otherwise the instrument of power we have forged will fall into the hands of the enemy. And it is essential to be clear that in the final analysis this so-called "church struggle" is none other than a struggle against you and against National Socialism. We need help in two ways: 1. You had promised to speak on the radio on the Saturday, i.e. the last day before the election. I must earnestly ask you to keep this promise, for the Volk must know that you stand by us as we stand by you. 2. I need renewed confirmation of your trust to put before the "princes of the church", because the reactionaries are spreading the news that you have disowned us and me personally and have withdrawn your authorization from me.'

Ludwig Müller had crossed out the next sentences from his rough draft, probably because they seemed to him to be a criticism of Hitler: 'There is much more at stake in these weeks than there might seem. For with my name and the whole Faith Movement of German Christians, I argued that the lie that you want to make Germany Catholic is nothing but a lie. Now after this concordat, in which the Catholic church has obtained what it has sought for seven hundred years, namely complete freedom from the state and full independence in the church, it is doubly necessary that you recognize the National Socialism in our Faith Movement. Therefore,' the unaltered text continued, 'I once again ask you: Do not leave us alone now, at the last moment, but put the whole weight of your person and the movement which you lead behind us.'[23]

The morning papers on 22 July published a notice that the Führer would speak about the church election on all German stations from 11.30 to 11.45 p.m. In fact, after the end of *Parsifal* which, conducted by Richard Strauss, was a highpoint of the 1933 season, Hitler began a speech in which he once again explained his whole approach to church politics. It is the most important and at the same time the most conclusive proof of the basic outline and uniformity of this approach.

State and church, Hitler declared in this speech, are dependent on each other. The churches required 'government protection'; on the other hand, however, in exchange the state also had to demand from the churches that support which it required 'for its existence'. Therefore there could be no indifference, either of the state towards the churches or of the churches 'towards the völkisch political events and changes'. This was especially true of the struggle against Bolshevism. In the Lateran treaties the Roman church had for the first time adopted a position on Fascism: 'the German concordat which has now been signed' was 'the second, equally clear, step in this area'. As a National Socialist, Hitler continued, he had 'the most ardent desire to be able to make an equally clear arrangement with the Protestant church'. However, this presupposed that 'one united Reich Church' would take the place of the multitude of Protestant churches. To have seen and understood this great goal would also go down in history as the merit of the German Christians. Hitler's final declaration was very much in his solemn, convoluted style of speaking: 'In the interest of the renaissance of the German nation, which I regard as being inseparably bound up with the National Socialist movement, I therefore understandably want the new church elections to result in support for our new national and state policy. For by being thus willing to guarantee the inner freedom of religious life, the state has the right to hope that those forces in the confessions will be welcomed which are resolute and determined to play their part in standing up for the freedom of the nation... I see these forces above all assembled in that sector of the people of the Protestant church who as "German Christians" have deliberately trodden the ground of the National Socialist state.'[24]

The impact of this speech was tremendous. Church opposition, which in any case was small, and had worked in good faith with the argument that Hitler himself was in no way committed to the German Christians,[25] found itself forced literally overnight into the camp of its opponents. One clear indication of a widespread mood was the action in Brunswick early one Sunday morning by which the Evangelium und Kirche list was officially withdrawn 'under the impact of the Chancellor's speech and out of loyalty to Adolf Hitler'.[26]

With the Party's massive involvement and Hitler's public support for the German Christians, the elections had been settled. What the propaganda of the Faith Movement had previously not been able to do was now achieved by the confusion, fear, illusions and opportunism which took control of the Protestant church at this time. Thousands of Protestant pastors – not a few of them with bad consciences – went over to the German Christians, or at least no longer dared to take a public stand against them. Thus the election became a triumph for the Faith Movement.

Just how limited was the readiness for resistance during these July days emerged from the mere fact that in most communities no genuine election took place at all. Rather, up and down the country use was made of the possibility for an agreement that was provided for in the election rules of all the Landeskirchen. An election could be dispensed with if there was only one list of candidates in a community. So the German Christians, with powerful assistance from the Party, demanded and received a two-thirds or even three-quarters majority with innumerable so-called agreed lists. In this way whole Landeskirchen spared themselves a public election campaign, and formed their synods by agreement. This was the case, for example, for Baden, Württemberg and the Palatinate; for Frankfurt and Hamburg; and largely also for Hanover and Saxony, and particularly for Schleswig-Holstein, where in the end no fewer than seventy-five of the seventy-nine seats in the Landessynode fell to the German Christians.[27]

Even at points where the Evangelium und Kirche group had nominated its own list of candidates, things hardly looked any better. In these communities, too, the German Christians achieved considerable majorities almost everywhere – not least through the mobilization of former non-voters.

The election took on decisive significance in the largest Protestant Landeskirche, the Old Prussian Union. Here, according to the election rules, only the representative bodies in the communities were to be elected. These then settled the composition of the higher bodies, the provincial synods and the General Synod. The opposition was strongest in the Prussian Church; there were also vigorous confrontations here. But here too agreed lists were frequently drawn up even in large church-conscious communities. Nevertheless, in Berlin there was an election in approximately 80 out of about 130 communities. As the *Kreuzzeitung* reported the next day, 'the rush of voters' started 'immediately after the close of the services; the election organizers could often hardly manage their work. Even the mostly very small communities in the city, where normally the elections could be expected to go off very quietly, were at times heavily overrun by voters.'[28] The result was an overwhelming victory for the German Christians. On this day they gained a majority in all the Berlin communities, with a single exception, which subsequently very soon became a centre of church resistance: in Dahlem the Evangelium und Kirche list won a narrow victory with pastors Martin Niemöller, Fritz Müller and Eberhard Röhricht.[29]

Another community which was later to play an outstanding role in the Church Struggle also stood its ground on this day: the Reformed community of Barmen Gemarke. Whereas in most of the Rhineland communities – as, for example, also in neighbouring Elberfeld – agreed lists with large German Christian majorities were also nominated, the six pastors of Barmen-Germarke together represented the Evangelium und Kirche list. The result was that the German Christians took only five of the twenty-one seats in the presbytery. Above all it was pastors Karl Immer and Paul Humburg who later made the Gemarke church a centre of the Confessing Church far beyond Barmen and the home of its First National Confessing Synod.[30]

During these days Karl Barth conducted his own election campaign in Bonn. What he had so resolutely argued for in *Theological Existence Today* he now represented in the church elections. At a rally on the eve of the election he attacked both the German Christians and the Young Reformers. For the sake of the freedom of the gospel, he said, neither of these two lists could be voted for. For 'the Protestant church people say secretly, in a hushed and restrained tone, what the German Christians say loudly and continuously. That is all. Here, too, the gospel is not free – and at the same point, by virtue of the fatal "and" with which one God is put next to the other.' Both presented a message in which the freedom of the gospel and thus the gospel itself was done away with.[31] For this reason, too, the list which Barth himself led was called 'For the Freedom of the Gospel', and on it he was elected to the presbytery with ten per cent of the vote.[32]

However, given the overall result of the election such things appeared trifling incidentals. For the reports which arrived in the following days confirmed that in Prussia the overwhelming majority of representative bodies in all the Prussian church provinces, from the Rhineland to East Prussia, and from Silesia to Pomerania, were solidly in the hands of the German Christians. Accordingly, the provincial synods and the General Synod would also be controlled by the Faith Movement. That the Westphalian provincial synod was the one exception was a surprise with which no one had reckoned.[33]

Thus all over the Reich the Protestant church elections ended with a complete triumph for the German Christians. In jubilant telegrams, the next day Hossen-felder reported 'the decisive electoral victory' of the Faith Movement to Hindenburg, Hitler, Müller and Jäger.[34] At the same time Dibelius and eight members of the opposition in the Prussian Oberkirchenrat, 'in loyal recognition of the altered situation', asked to resign.[35] Nothing more seemed to stand in the way of a final co-ordination of the church with the Third Reich.

Even if we take into account all the circumstances of this election, 23 July remains a dismal date for the Protestant church. It demonstrated how easily the church could be led astray by a political theology if such a theology tied itself to political power and political fashion. For despite all the vagueness as to specific details, the failure of the church at this moment to resist was an acknowledgment of the course which the German Christians had previously taken.

On the other hand, however, we should not overlook the fact that this politically secure victory was far less clear cut than the election results suggested. It was still impossible to assess what the Faith Movement had achieved during these weeks. At all events, its scope ranged from the moderate churchman and theologian to the radical German-völkisch sectarian. How the German Christians would cope with this tension was a completely open question. And the degree of scepticism and perplexity remaining in the manses was revealed, for example, by the letter of a Hamburg pastor who wrote on 27 July to a young German

448

Christian friend: 'The success of this conquest, which is a worthy successor to the brilliant victory over the defenceless Jews and freemasons, will consist in the fact that many of our most spiritual church people will stay away and the victors will not attend.'[36]

The conviction that the electoral victory of the German Christians marked a great decision governed not only the Faith Movement itself but all of German Protestantism after 23 July. It also shaped those developments in church politics which were visible to the public during the following weeks. The developments seemed to lead directly and immediately to the German Christian Reich Church and the election of Ludwig Müller as the first Reich Bishop. But while the German Christians were still unsuspectingly enjoying their victory and at the same time systematically going about consolidating their power, changes were taking place in the background which after only a few months effectively put in question the victory and power of the Faith Movement. The most important of these changes had to do with the attitude of Hitler and the Party.

The astonishing election speech of 22 July had proved that a German Christian victory in fact mattered a great deal to Hitler. Understandable though the massive commitment by the Party to the Faith Movement was, Hitler could hardly want a permanent arrangement to come out of this connection. On the contrary: with this involvement he had taken himself so far from his own basic decision over church politics, namely at all events to keep the movement out of all church controversies, that a correction now appeared urgently necessary. In the long run the Gauleiters were hardly credible as electoral officers in church elections. An additional reason also prompted such a correction. In the concluding protocol to the Reich concordat, Article 32 had expressly recorded the agreement 'that the Reich will order similar arrangements over party-political activity in respect of the non-Catholic confessions as well'.[37] This, however, could only mean that in the foreseeable future the Party also had to dissociate itself from its Protestant clergy – who now held more or less official Party posts, up to and including Hossenfelder. The decision to make this correction was undoubtedly easier for Hitler as a result of the victory of the German Christians. In the future, he probably thought, it would be sufficient to give the Reich Bishop the appropriate instructions from time to time so that the church was steered in the direction he wanted. Nothing else interested him any longer.

So it was not at all surprising when on 5 August, barely fourteen days after the church elections, Hitler already issued new guidelines for the Party. On this day he had assembled the Reichsleiters and the Gauleiters on the Obersalzberg in order to instruct them, in a major speech, about the domestic political situation and his next aims. The official report of this 'guideline speech' may not contain any indications that during his three-hour-long remarks Hitler had also dealt with the church question. But there is hardly any doubt that on this day he declared to the Gauleiters that the church-political goal had been achieved and that from now on the Party would return to its old path of neutrality in church politics.[38]

Hitler was not thinking at this point of a radical change. And indeed it would have been foolish to give up again a position which he had just secured with considerable effort. The process of detachment could only be gradual, restoring freedom of movement to the Party without upsetting the German Christian position. In fact this process extended over a period of many months, during the course of which quite diverse layers of interest became visible.

It was no coincidence that the first official signal for an alteration in the Party's course in church politics, and one that was widely noted, came from Alfred Rosenberg. The author of the *Myth*, who saw himself playing the role of völkisch religious thinker, must have observed with deep unease the movement's involvement on behalf of a German Christian Evangelical Church. Now, however, he saw his time approaching. In a leading article in the *Völkischer Beobachter* of 16 August entitled 'Politics and Church', he announced the imminent changes. He could have been quoting Hitler's own remarks of 5 August when he said, '...just as, by means of the concordat, the encroachment of church interests into the political sphere has been stopped, so too the political movement will withdraw from the strife over confessional questions. Though it is understandable that those groups whose leaders in the past openly and honestly declared themselves for the fight for a new Germany generally appear welcome to the National Socialist movement, we have nevertheless entered a stage in which National Socialism cannot turn itself into the political support of one or another church group. This position corresponds exactly to our paragraph 24, according to which the NSDAP cannot bind itself confessionally in any way.' That Rosenberg also had great personal hopes of the declaration of neutrality was shown by his remark that now the confessions had to struggle 'for the soul of the Germans... from their innermost and primal power', and that the 'life feeling of the future' could produce further innovations in this sector, too.[39] Anyone who had read the *Myth* knew what 'new forms' Rosenberg had in mind here.

Hitler's declaration of neutrality was supposed to restore the independence of the Party, but it was not to mean an abandonment of the German Christians. This was demonstrated by the fact that Hitler continued his unconditional support for Ludwig Müller. And it was also demonstrated by the fact that the relevant directives from the Party were slow in coming and were formulated very cautiously. Thus only on 6 October did Martin Bormann, since early July the Stabsleiter for the Führer's representative, declare in a letter to the Gauleiters that Party members who, against the Party's recommendation, had not voted for the German Christians in the church elections were not to be discriminated against. 'The intended aim of the church elections,' wrote Bormann, 'has been achieved. The Führer does not want to have further action over the issues of the election.'[40]

Hess, too, publicly affirmed the neutrality of the Party in church questions in a statement a few days later, on 13 October.[41] And in early 1934 he confidentially reminded the Gauleiters once again that the support of the German Christians by the Party had come to an end. Political leaders who still held the 'office and title of "Consultant for Protestant Church Questions", etc.', had to discontinue their work immediately. In this connection Hess referred expressly to the remarks which the Führer had made 'on the subject of the Party and the church on 5 August 1933 at the Gauleiters meeting on the Obersalzberg'. Accordingly the Führer had also 'forbidden any influence upon the development of affairs in the Protestant Church'.[42]

Even if the Party moved away from the German Christians only very hesitantly and carefully, the consequences were immense. While as early as the middle of

450

September Martin Niemöller considered the church-political possibilities to be exhausted, on the other hand he thought the situation as a whole to be 'considerably more favourable since the official Party press has moved away from the GC and instead makes propaganda for Hauer and company'.[43]

The reference to 'Hauer and company' indicated an additional problem which emerged from the declaration of neutrality and which to an increasing extent disturbed both churches during the coming year. This problem was connected with the ideological roots of the movement. From the beginning Hitler's party had in fact by no means been ecclesiastically neutral: rather, it had arisen upon the soil of völkisch ideology, with all its special religious notions and claims. To be sure, it became crucial for its victory that Hitler had succeeded in separating himself from Ludendorff and Dinter, repressing these völkisch religious claims and concentrating the Party organization entirely on the political acquisition of power.[44] But this had in no way settled the problem. As before, part of the old core of the movement stood far closer to a German-völkisch faith than to a völkisch Catholicism or to a 'German Christian' Reich Church. The official church policy, with its emphatic focus on the two major Christian confessions, had for a long time caused considerable annoyance in these circles.

The most important mouthpiece of this movement was Count Ernst zu Reventlow's journal *Reichswart*. Reventlow was a typical representative of the völkisch religious tendency within the Party and had some prominence there in that since 1927 he had belonged to the NSDAP group in the Reichstag. The *Reichswart*, which in view of Hitler's efforts towards the churches had since March constantly pointed to the 'divisive effect of political propaganda for religion and indeed politics conducted by the government',[45] now in June published a startling article with the title 'Equal rights for German Non-Christians'. It described the millions of Germans who had long since turned away from the Christian churches and from Christianity in general but who nevertheless had the desire to form a religious community. All of these various associations were agreed 'in rejecting the churches and wishing to conduct, to promote further and to develop their religious life in a free community. There is just as much religion in them as in the Christian churches of Germany. The time seems to us to have come,' Reventlow therefore demanded, 'indeed it is more than high time for these associations to be granted equal rights in the state with the Christian churches.' There had to be, he concluded, 'a community of faith with full rights, however broadly conceived... parallel to the Christian churches, alongside Christianity. This is a demand of German life and of the German people which is really urgent today.'[46]

So long as Hitler pursued his active church policy, however, the realization of this demand was virtually unthinkable. But as soon as it became clear, through Rosenberg's article, that the Party had begun to distance itself from the German Christians, the supporters of a German faith in the Party found themselves greatly encouraged. At the centre of all the efforts to found a 'German Faith Movement' stood the Tübingen professor Jakob Wilhelm Hauer.[47]

Hauer, at that time fifty-two, came from Württemberg. After a Protestant theological education he was sent to India by the Basel Mission in 1906 and returned from there with deep impressions of the Indian religion. Since that time he had devoted himself – alongside his pastorate – to studies in comparative

451

religion; he had qualified as a university teacher at Tübingen in 1921 and had become Professor for Indian Studies and Comparative Religion there in 1927. At home in a great variety of völkisch religious notions, in the summer of 1933, like so many others Hauer also thought that his time had come. His house in Tübingen – named 'Breidablick' after the mystical residence of the god Baldr – became the centre for vigorous activity throughout the Reich. A first success from this activity came on 29-30 July 1933, only one week after the church elections, when a serious of German Faith leagues and associations which had previously been hopelessly split merged in the 'Working Group of the German Faith Movement'. To this belonged such distinctively völkisch groups as the Germanische Glaubensgemeinschaft, Volkschaft der Nordungen, Nordische Glaubensgemeinschaft, the Rig-Kreis and others – including, surprisingly, the large League of Free-religious Communities, which came from the free-thinking Marxist tradition. Appointed chairman of this Working Group, which he then led in partnership with Reventlow, at the end of August Hauer presented his request for public, legal recognition of the German Faith Movement in a memorandum to Hitler, Frick and Jäger. It was 'no coincidence, but intrinsically necessary, that many of the most significant spiritual leaders in the Third Reich either explicitly or at least in their basic attitude' belonged to it. Above all, the National Socialist youth were waiting in their thousands only 'for the liberating word of the Führer 'in order finally to be able to join the Faith Movement without reservation'. The German workers, too, so Hauer claimed, wanted 'in the main not Christianity but rather a German faith'. The memorandum clearly indicated that Hauer's intentions were aimed at the formation of a new, third confession. For in his conviction the German people would then organize itself 'into the three great religious domains: ...Catholic Church... Protestant Church.. and German Faith Community'. All three, however, were to work together in a 'Religious Working Group of the German Nation'.[48]

One year later, in autumn 1934, the tightly organized German Faith Movement had meanwhile emerged from the loose Working Group – Hauer himself drew up the 'Fundamentals for a German Faith' which was published under the title *The German Vision of God*. The basic idea was that of the entire völkisch movement: the world-historical 'struggle between the Near Eastern-Semitic and the Indo-Germanic world of faith'. This struggle was supposed to take place in a threefold form: 'biological-racial, political-economic and ideological-religious'.[49] The chapter titles alone made Hauer's programme clear: 'Race and Volk as Fundamental Values of German Faith', 'Teutonic-German View of the World', 'The Teutonic-German Faith in Life', 'The Teutonic-German View of God'. The relationship to Christianity was to be that of superiority and tolerance. To be sure, there would certainly 'always be a community of Jesus in the German Volk', but 'the normative, i.e. the authoritative religious power' in the future could only be the 'German Faith', since the 'epoch of Christianity' was 'at an end'.[50]

In his own words, Hauer's *German Vision of God* was intended 'for the Volk', not 'for theologians and philosophers of religion'.[51] But the way in which a 'faith from primal Germany' was constructed here indiscriminately out of the Edda, Bhagavadgita and Upanishads; Neoplatonism and mysticism; Goethe, Schiller, Hölderlin, Hegel, Kant, Wagner, Nietzsche, Kolbenheyer, Rosenberg and many

452

others, betrayed the fact that here was no more than a new and Nordic-völkisch articulation of nineteenth-century German academic religion. Moreover, it was above all political fashion which led so many followers to the pseudo-profundity of the *German Vision of God* in the first years of the Third Reich that the churches actually thought that the German Faith Movement was one of their most dangerous opponents. Hauer's enterprise, however, was real competition only for the German Christians. The blanket term 'Faith Movement' alone showed that they found it difficult to defend themselves against this opponent.

Hitler's declaration of neutrality on 5 August and as a result the tangible growth of the German Faith tendencies made themselves felt only gradually in church politics. But they played a crucial role in the major change of climate in the relationships between Party and church and in the church itself, a development which took place in the late summer and which made a considerable contribution to the fact that the great project of the founding of a Evangelical Reich Church came to such a rapid and deplorable end.

On the evening of 23 July and in the days that followed, however, there was no hint of this. Instead, the period following the triumphant electoral victory of the German Christians was completely dominated by the conviction that the decision had been made. For the church opposition in particular, this raised the difficult question of how it ought to adjust to the new situation.

Here again the developments in Prussia became crucial. As early as the election day itself the leadership of the church opposition had come together to discuss further action by the Young Reformers Movement. The decision which was already made in this first discussion[52] became extraordinarily important for the future of the whole church. As formulated in a declaration dated the end of July, it was 'that with the church elections held on 23 July 1933 the Young Reformers Movement considers its church-political activity to be at an end, and henceforth seeks to turn its energies to the work of theology and community within the church'. As justification, the leadership of the Young Reformers referred to the events of recent weeks which had forced the movement to form a front in national politics which it could not possibly maintain. As a result individuals had been exposed to the suspicion 'of being unreliable in state politics'. The leadership could not assume responsibility for this. Therefore there was no other way left than 'to withdraw from this misguided frontal position in order to make possible once again the development of an authentic and substantial line within the church'.[53]

This decision did not go undisputed. On 27 July, when the members of the national leadership of the 'Evangelium und Kirche' electoral list met, Gerhard Jacobi in particular vigorously criticized the announced withdrawal from church politics. 'This is like Pilate washing his hands in innocence,' he asserted. 'Politics arises out of politics, and we cannot give up the work of shaping the church...' Others supported these statements and objected emphatically to 'defeatism when the wood is green'; in view of Hitler's 22 July speech this might be understandable but, given the impending synods, would be fatal.[54]

The retreat from church politics could in fact be understood as a capitulation. But that was not what it was meant to be. So under the impact of the criticism, Martin Niemöller elucidated the aim of the new direction and summarized it in sixteen theses.

After an analysis of the situation, the eleventh thesis contained the nucleus of the new approach. 'The main concern must now be to create new, clear fronts and to see that a community of Jesus Christ develops in the church, which is now decisively shaped by the German Christians, fronts which are also ready to confess when a confession is really demanded of them.' This, however, was not a 'church-political' but rather a 'practical-community' and a 'church-theological' task. The 'practical-community' task consisted in 'gathering the faithful members of the community and in bringing the proclamation to them in all seriousness'. The church-theological task, however, was as it were directed outwards: it was important to confront the German Christians 'with the question of the confession'. So Niemöller now asked quite sharply: 'Is there theologically a basic difference between Reformation doctrine and what the German Christians proclaim? We fear: Yes! They say: No! This lack of clarity must be removed by a modern confession.'[55]

Here was the crucial slogan: 'a modern confession'. This slogan was not new. It had accompanied developments in the church from the time of the Altona Confession, through the attempts of Zoellner and Müller to find a common confessional statement for the new Reich Church, up to the many confession-like declarations which had been produced up and down the country during the dispute over Bodelschwingh. But now the slogan had again taken on a new dimension. At a time when power and violence were so obviously triumphing in the church; when theological confusion had simultaneously reached an almost inconceivable level; when opportunism and illusion ruled and hardly anyone could say where the church of Jesus Christ was now and where it was not – at this moment the demand for a modern confession became a last opportunity, an extreme attempt to rediscover truth, certainty and reassurance in the gospel.

What Niemöller called for here was in essence parallel to Karl Barth's appeal in no circumstances to lose 'theological existence', but rather first to build up a spiritual centre of resistance' which was needed 'to give meaning and a content to church politics'.[56] This was now the issue; but in Berlin in a way that was more resolute, prompt and pragmatic than Barth had imagined. Niemöller's hasty imperious style long remained alien to Barth. So although in Bonn the efforts in Berlin were at first viewed with deep distrust, it was nevertheless foreordained that the two approaches, and indeed the two men, must ultimately meet and join forces. Karl Barth, too, had not in any way concluded from his text that he must refrain from all church politics. On the contrary, he had entered vigorously into the election campaign with an election rally of his own, and his own list of candidates. Similarly, Niemöller now explained the misleading 'retreat from church politics' by saying that this did not mean the voluntary surrender of church-political positions, but rather that the Young Reformers Movement would 'join the various synods on the basis of free association' in order to hold the group which now held power in the church to its responsibility for the church. 'In this sense,' the theses concluded, in a sentence which four weeks later was to acquire an unsuspected significance, 'we think it important also to raise our voice where that is possible and necessary.'[57]

The same issue of *Junge Kirche* in which these theses were published also carried a reprint of the article by Rosenberg in the *Völkischer Beobachter*, with the comment that these remarks 'presaged significant proceedings within the

454

NSDAP'.[58] And in the very next issue the problem of the German Faith Movement was raised as the question of the pagan, Germanic forces on the heels of the German Christians, forces which could 'be overcome only on the basis of pure doctrine and a clear confession'.[59] From now on the church opposition did not lose sight of either the incipient retreat of the Party or the advance of Hauer and Reventlow: the one viewed as a hope and the other as a motivation for the 'modern confession'.

In subsequent weeks, however many individual questions continued to remain disputed within the church opposition, there was agreement that the two tasks formulated by Niemöller – the church-theological and the practical-community work – were now in fact the demand of the moment. Both were begun as early as August.

The practical-community work began with the coming together of pastors and church members who continued to maintain opposition in spite of the new circumstances. It was a modest beginning which at first depended entirely upon the initiative of individual pastors. Since an organization was to be avoided, Bodelschwingh assumed the role of a personal and spiritual focus; in his modest and restrained manner he maintained it until the autumn made harder decisions necessary. In Greater Berlin it was the pastors Gerhard Jacobi and Eitel-Friedrich von Rabenau who had gathered about a hundred colleagues around themselves and invited them to weekly meetings.[60] In the Niederlausitz three pastors – including Eugen Weschke and Günter Jacobi – began to organize a brotherhood of pastors.[61] In the Rhineland Joachim Beckmann and others had led the way with a similar idea as early as 19 July.[62] They were followed on 4 August in Westphalia by Karl Lücking, who suggested that pastors and community members true to the confession should join together 'in services, community evenings and conferences'.[63] In Brandenburg the young Sachsen-hausen pastor Kurt Scharf – later Bishop and Council Chairman of the Evangelical Church in Germany – wrote on 4 August to the colleagues who until then had stood by Dibelius: 'We know... that many Protestant Christians in pulpit and community look with concern upon recent developments in our church and feel that they are responsible for keeping alive the Christian way of life and the proclamation of the Word in it. The important thing for us now is to reach these Christians who are aware of their responsibility, both pastors and laity.' And he continued very much along the lines of the principles decided by the Young Reformers Movement: 'I would be grateful if you would let me know personally whether we can also continue to count on your co-operation; whether, for instance, you and the members of the community who remain true to the church and to the gospel can start small working groups for fundamental discussions of the chief questions of Reformation Christianity – above all questions relating to the confession.'[64] Of roughly 650 pastors in Brandenburg about 50 participated. That was not many. And at first it was impossible to see immediately where all this was to lead. People were just clinging on to one another so as not to be swept away by the overwhelming current of the new era. Only four weeks later, after the Prussian General Synod, did it become clear what in fact was at stake.

Not only the practical-community work but also the church-theological work began in August. Since the church opposition had intensified all the confrontations over the confession, it could not just leave this issue aside. So

Bodelschwingh, at the suggestion of Berlin, invited 'a small group of younger theologians' to Bethel early in August in order to work out together in the seclusion of the Bodelschwingh Institutes a 'modern confession of faith'.[65] The most important participants in this work, which lasted from the middle to the end of August, were Dietrich Bonhoeffer and Hermann Sasse, the former editor of the *Kirchliches Jahrbuch*, who meanwhile had become Professor of Church History in Erlangen. In addition Georg Merz and Wilhelm Vischer, of the Bethel teachers, were close collaborators. Pastor Stratenwerth, who with Niemöller had been among Bodelschwingh's closest advisers in June, functioned as a kind of editor. The result of this work was the so-called 'Bethel Confession'.[66]

The Bethel Confession had a remarkable history. The original version which was written during those August days in a 'happy collaboration' of all the participants[67] was never published. This version became known only in 1959 when Eberhard Bethge – quite correctly – included it in the *Collected Works* of Dietrich Bonhoeffer. What appeared at the beginning of 1934 under the title 'The Confession of the Fathers and the Confessing Community', on the responsibility of Martin Niemöller, was a revised version, toned down and adapted at crucial points. For that reason this version, too, had no recognizable effect, because circumstances in the Protestant church had meanwhile changed completely. Whereas in August the authors still proceeded on the basis that it would be necessary 'to challenge the German Christians over their intentions',[68] and that therefore it was necessary to enter into theological dialogue with them – though people differed over the prospects of such a dialogue – by the beginning of January 1934 the time for such a plan was long since past.[69]

Nevertheless the original version of the Bethel confession remains a brilliant, sharp and impressive witness to what theological work was still capable of achieving in summer 1933 – indeed specifically because of the great German Christian upsurge in German theology at this time. Ponderous though it was and loaded with numerous passages from the Bible, from Luther, and above all from confessional texts, this confession was nevertheless theologically and politically clearer and more exact in some passages than the famous Barmen declaration of May 1934.

The Confession developed the doctrine of the Lutheran church in six classical, dogmatic chapters.[70] The first chapter bore the title 'On Holy Scripture' and began: 'The Holy Scripture of the Old and New Testaments is alone the source and criterion of the church. Valid in its unity, it testifies that Jesus of Nazareth, who was crucified under Pontius Pilate, is the Christ, that is, the promised Messiah of Israel, the King of the church, the Son of the living God.' Anyone who thought that this sentence sounded merely traditional learned from its exposition what it meant. For what was at issue was in fact the difference between sound doctrine and heresy. And the heresies to which the authors believed this statement to refer were, in their opinion, not at all traditional but rather very modern and highly virulent. The confession rejected in principle the heresy, 'in whatever form it might appear, that Christ also bears witness to himself without the scriptures and outside them, and that the Holy Spirit is also given without the "external Word" of preaching founded upon scripture, and without the sacrament'. The 'uniqueness and historicity of God's revelation' which was thus expressed was aimed at both völkisch historical theology, with its idea of the

456

election of the German people, and Stapel's Volksnomos. And it was aimed at all those who in one way or another attempted to relativize, reinterpret or eliminate the Old Testament. Chapter 2 attacked the völkisch-nationalist misuse of Luther and the Reformation; chapter 3, with the doctrine of the Trinity, contained the theological basis for a defence against any kind of independent doctrine of creation. This was then specified in chapter 4, 'On Creation and Sin'. This expressed Barth's theological approach and at the same time made one of the central statements which distinguished doctrine and heresy at this time: 'We recognize the Creator only through obedience to the Word of God from scripture, not through any interpretation of events in the world.' Therefore, it went on to say, 'We reject the heresy that God speaks directly to us from a particular "historical hour"... the heresy that the voice of the people is the voice of God... The voice of the people cries "Hosanna" and "Crucify him".'

The authors used especially impressive formulations, finally, in chapter 6, 'On the Holy Spirit and the Church'. If everything up to this point had been discussed as a theme within the church and within theology, although the ideology of the Third Reich was always kept in view, in the three sections 'Church and Volk', 'Church and State', and 'The Church and the Jews', there were now statements the political relevance of which was immediately clear. And it was here that the most considerable alterations and changes were made in the course of the revision. The crucial features of the relationship between church and Volk had already been expressed in the first chapters. Thus this section could limit itself to a sober portrayal of the church's accord with the Volk and the limits to it 'in the content of the proclamation'. But an unmistakably distinctive tone crept in when this section spoke of the indissoluble solidarity which bound Christians to both Volk and church. 'They share in the guilt of their people. They are at the same time members of the people of God, whose citizenship is in heaven.' Today the message of these sentences would probably be overlooked had not the revised version considered a clear correction necessary: 'They have a share in the fame and guilt of their people and in the promise and guilt of their church.'[71] The sentence was still correct but – and this was typical of the revision – it had lost its salt. The published text simply took over all the essential distinctions and definitions in the relationship between church and state which the first version had developed. What was sketched out here was an extraordinarily tense relationship in which the church was given the task of showing the secular authorities 'the limits of their own order... by means of the appropriate proclamation', so that they did not become 'a tool of the devil... who in the end seeks only disorder, that he may thus destroy all life'. In summer 1933 it was impossible to ignore the special overtones of the statement: 'With this service, the church preserves those under authority from the deceit of the devil, who wants an unlimited authority to have him worshipped as lifegiver and saviour.' Here too the corrected version robbed the statement of its crucial sharpness when it spoke of 'an authority fused with the church' which the devil wanted to have worshipped as 'lifegiver and saviour'.[72] Finally, the language of the Bethel authors was also resolute in the section on 'The Church and the Jews'. This section followed Bonhoeffer's line of argument completely in seeing the attempt to transform the German Evangelical Church 'into a Reich Church of Aryan race' as an enterprise which robbed the church of its promise. 'For this would establish a racial law before the entrance to the church, and such a church would itself have become the community under the law.' In the many contributions to this question in 1933, nowhere else was the demand for the irrevocable communion of all Christians so clearly expressed as here. 'Christians descended from the Gentile world must expose themselves to persecution rather than give up, voluntarily or by force, even in one respect, their brotherhood with the Jewish Christians in the church which has been established through Word and sacrament'.[73] In the final version the whole argument was compressed into one sentence. 'Gentile Christians can no more – i.e. than the church from its responsibility for mission to the Jews – separate themselves from Christians than from the people of Israel.'[74]

The text ended with a chapter 'On the End of All Things'. and this chapter also made clear once again how relevant the doctrine of the church could be when it was taken seriously.

From the beginning the Bethel Confession was not intended as a private theological work, but as a draft for a modern confession by the church. However, there was not yet a synod which could have accepted and endorsed it. At that very time the very first steps were being taken on the way from church opposition to Confessing Church, and no one yet had any inkling of where they would lead. So at the end of August Bodelschwingh, in order to broaden the base of support, sent the draft 'to an expanded circle of perhaps twenty brethren... with a heartfelt request for examination and collaboration'.[75] The date by which answers had to be returned – 15 September – indicated an intention to produce it as a 'real confessing front' at the first National Synod, planned for the end of September.[76] Among those to whom the confession was sent, along with the theologians of the Young Reformers Movement, were a series of theology professors whom Bodelschwingh trusted, including Karl Barth, Karl Heim and Adolf Schlatter. However, the response was evidently hesitant and on the whole disappointing. Schlatter, for example, flatly rejected the draft and declared that if there were to be a repudiation it should be of the 'Bonn heresy' – i.e. Karl Barth.[77] Barth answered only on 11 October, with the legitimate question as to whether a Lutheran confession was enough for the present, or whether it was not rather necessary 'to work through the draft together so that it... could appear before the public as an Evangelical confession of faith?'[78] In fact the decisive point in which the Barmen Declaration was to be superior to the Bethel Confession was that it was a common confession of faith by Lutheran, Reformed and United Christians. The delay in receiving answers also delayed the concluding work. When the new draft was finally available, this was so altered that Bonhoeffer – who meanwhile had become pastor to the German community in London – spoke out bluntly against its publication.[79] Other co-authors had also expressed misgivings in the meantime. But since Niemöller insisted, because in November he was concerned 'daily and hourly' about the text, which had been announced long beforehand, Bodelschwingh finally consented to the last version being published under the name of Martin Niemöller.[80] But by then the course was already set in another direction.

While all this was going on in the background, in the foreground the German Christians loudly and conspicuously took over control of the German Evangelical Church. Their election victory throughout the Reich was so complete, and the

458

impression of their power was so universal, that as a result they did not encounter serious resistance from a single Landeskirche. With a few exceptions – for example in the Prussian Oberkirchenrat – no one in the church administrations resigned and no one refused to co-operate. Instead, everywhere – in Munich and Stuttgart, in Hanover and Hamburg, Brunswick and Dresden – there was willingness and eagerness to come to terms with the new masters in the church. Even in Berlin, where people knew best of all whom they were dealing with, there were discussions and agreements between the German Christians and the Evangelium und Kirche group.[81] Nothing further appeared to stand in the way of the final subjugation of the Evangelical Church to the will of the German Christians and its co-ordination with the Third Reich. Consequently the Faith Movement now set about its work quickly and systematically.

The crucial man in this process was the former Prussian State Commissioner August Jäger. Far more than was suspected at the time, it has subsequently become known that he was the driving force behind the whole development. His plans were as comprehensive as they were clear: he wanted all the power throughout the new Reichskirche.

That from the beginning things did not run quite as Jäger intended was the result of a decision that was made even before the elections – a decision that very quickly exposed all the tensions within the Faith Movement.

Mindful of the confusion which Bodelschwingh's undefined authority had produced, the fathers of the new church constitution had given it an introductory decree which was also to regulate the administrative authorities clearly during the transitional period. Article 5 of this transitional decree provided that 'until the election of the Reich Bishop the latter's authority shall be exercised by a person chosen by the official delegates of the German Protestant churches'. The four representatives for the Clergy Ministry were also to be determined in the same way.[82] Thus the body of official delegates of the Landeskirchen – as the legal organ of a church which did not even exist – was summoned to a last action, finally to direct the rather muddled legal relationships in the German Evangelical church back into clear paths.

However, it very soon emerged that this regulation was extraordinarily difficult to implement. Simply to appoint Ludwig Müller, as the German Christians no doubt expected, would have looked like an anticipation of the decision of the National Synod – an action that the advocates of an independent course for the church did not want to take in any circumstances. On the other hand, to pass over Müller appeared to be an affront to the Chancellor and the German Christians which was equally unacceptable to the majority. So the thirty-six delegates of the Landeskirchen were deeply perplexed when they reconvened in Berlin on 20 July – three days before the election.[83] After the numerous encroachments on the freedom of the election had been excitedly discussed, and a stiff complaint had been lodged with Pfundtner, in long and difficult negotiations a compromise on the question of the leadership finally emerged. It consisted in the formation of a five-member committee, to which the German Christians nominated three members and the church delegates two. The German Christians suggested Ludwig Müller and his two theological advisers, Fezer and the Halle professor Friedrich Karl Schumann, who incidentally had conducted the negotiations from the German Christian side together with the church law

459

specialist Johannes Heckel (who meanwhile had gone over to Ludwig Müller). The church representatives agreed on Bishop Schöffel of Hamburg and Otto Koopmann, the Reformed Church President. In order to avoid any reference to the future Reich Bishop, a chairman was deliberately not named: the chairmanship of the committee was 'to change in alphabetical order' among the members from meeting to meeting. Since this procedure undoubtedly did not conform legally to Article 5 of the introductory decree, that article was suspended forthwith 'until the assembling of the German Evangelical National Synod'.[84]

Finally, the church representatives decided almost unanimously to send a delegation to Munich to the Führer, which was at last to present to him personally the concerns and difficulties of the Protestant church.

Thus even before the elections the church again had a provisional church administration, one which again caused legal problems – the fifth one within three months after the Kapler Committee of Three, Bodelschwingh's term as Reich Bishop, the committee which succeeded the Committee of Three and the commissariat led by Ludwig Müller. When the committee was welcomed that evening in the meeting of official delegates, once again it was Ludwig Müller who could find a pious word to crown one of the many great hours of this year: 'When I opened the Bible just now,' he affirmed, 'the first thing which I read was the passage, "I command you to love one another." If in such a difficult time we are confronted with such a difficult task, then let us accept it with a confident gaze towards the Lord of the church and with a vow to exert all our strength in selfless devotion, so that the church of our Lord may be built up...'[85]

The new committee, which officially called itself the 'Provisional Administration of the German Evangelical Church',[86] played an important role in the church politics of the following period – until the meeting of the National Synod on 27 September. However, to a large extent this role was concealed from the public. The committee was of a predominantly moderate German Christian character in its composition and thus appeared to offer a certain guarantee that the radical tendency would be checked. Fezer and Schumann had already indicated that there was a problem here, when they pointed out to the church delegates that their proposal 'had at least as much symbolic importance for the radical wing of the German Christians' and in this regard was 'no small matter'.[87]

However, this hardly gave any idea of what was really going on in the camp of the radical German Christians at this time. August Jäger, who held the reins here, was almost beside himself with rage. In a confidential memorandum on the proceedings, almost certainly intended for the Reich leadership, he gave free rein to this rage. Of the five members of the Provisional Administration, he declared, only Ludwig Müller could be considered a German Christian; in the cases of Schöffel, Fezer and Schumann 'their German Christian quality... and above all whether if necessary they will submit to the discipline of the Movement' was uncertain; Koopmann was even a 'declared opponent'. This arrangement was 'unlawful', 'a reactionary act' and offended against the spirit of the constitution which was built 'upon the leadership principle'. He derided 'that conception which, three days before the election, had given power to the opposition'. All of this called for 'the fiercest struggle'. What had 'to be achieved at all costs' was 'immediately after the elections to implement the rules laid down in the introductory decree'. The following telegram was to be sent immediately to

460

Müller, Hitler and Frick: 'Reactionary church officials, not supported but rather opposed by churchpeople, sabotaging church constitution by recreating an illegal instrument to keep themselves personally in power. The whole churchpeople in outright revolt. We request immediate measures.'[88]

However, the time for direct interventions in the church dispute by the Party or the state, of which Jäger was obviously still thinking, was now long past. Hitler's 5 August speech and Rosenberg's article of 16 August heralded a completely new situation. This situation did not, of course, exclude local acts of violence and individual abuses. But a general mobilization of the party apparatus or of the Political Police on behalf of the aims of the German Christians after the church elections did not happen. So to a large extent Jäger remained dependent in the coming confrontations on the means of power at his own disposal. And these were not slight. As Ministerial Director and leader of the Church Department of the Prussian Kultusministerium, he was the highest-ranking civil servant in charge of church affairs in Prussia; he had the full support of his Minister, Bernhard Rust; and he totally controlled the Reich leadership of the German Christians, which was completely dependent on him – not least financially.[89]

The electoral victory of 23 July could only increase Jäger's malicious and reckless resolve, but it was nevertheless significant at this point that he could no longer dismiss the hated Provisional Administration out of hand. Rather, he had to seek, via the Reich leadership, an agreement with Ludwig Müller 'to have the authority of the provisional bishops' committee' – this meant the Provisional Administration – 'transferred and dissolved' immediately after the election. That, at any rate, was what had been said in a telegram by Hossenfelder which was published in the *Völkischer Beobachter* on 18 July.[90]

This, however, put Ludwig Müller in an extraordinarily painful situation. For at the first meeting of the Provisional Administration on 1 August his colleagues naturally wanted to discover from him whether there was any substance to the rumour that their committee was to be dissolved. Müller evidently succeeded in talking himself out of the situation. After he had given assurances that he had not agreed to anything of the kind, he added significantly that the Führer had, however, told him in Bayreuth that the leadership of the committee had to pass to the German Christians. The Provisional Administration did not want to refuse this wish, so as its first act it passed the resolution that 'in order to take into account the results of the church elections of 23 July, the permanent chairmanship of the Committee of Five is transferred to the patron of the Faith Movement of German Christians, Pastor Müller.'[91]

The first task with which the new body had to deal was the reorganization of the Prussian Church administration, which had fallen into total confusion because of the state commissariat.[92] But Prussia was the place where August Jäger was in a position to bring his entire influence to bear. The only person still left from the old leadership, the President of the Prussian General Synod and Chairman of the Church Senate, Dr Friedrich Winckler, a well-known former delegate of the German National People's Party in Prussia and long associated with the Prussian Church, was the representative of the Prussian Church on the Provisional Administration.[93] Little resistance was to be expected from this man, who had been stripped of his political power. Jäger arranged for the Prussian

461

Kultusminister Bernhard Rust to receive Winckler and instruct him on the intentions of the Prussian government.[94] As early as 3 August Winckler passed on these intentions to the Provisional Administration. Whether the committee considered the suggestions unavoidable in view of the election results, whether it had no idea of their implications, or whether it simply baulked at a confrontation, must remain an open question. At all events it consented, and so at the suggestion of the Provisional Administration of the German Evangelical Church the cold-blooded seizure of power by the German Christians in the Prussian Church officially took place on 4 August. The proposal of the Provisional Administration ran: 'The Church Senate may want to elect Pastor Müller as President of the Evangelical Oberkirchenrat; it further may wish, by means of an emergency decree with a two-thirds majority, to abolish the collegial character of the Oberkirchenrat and thus give the new President special authority so that he is not bound to majority decisions of its council; further, to bestow on this President the official designation of Land Bishop; finally, in order to make rapid action possible, the church senate may wish to transfer its powers to its present chairman, President Dr Winckler.'[95]

At its fifty-third session on 4 August the Church Senate accordingly decided on exactly this. Even the old chairmen of the provincial consistories and the general superintendents voted for this suggestion. Anyone who did not want to consent, like Dibelius and the venerable Vits, did not appear.[96] The power of resistance in the Old Prussian Church was finally extinguished.

So three weeks after the withdrawal of the state commissioners for the second time, but now in an apparently legal manner, the Prussian Church had a German Christian church government. Ludwig Müller, with the office and title of Prussian Land Bishop, had finally left his title of 'Military chaplain' behind him and achieved a key official church post. And August Jäger must have been satisfied too, since the whole affair was the first successful step in a long-range plan for the ambitious Ministerial Director. According to this plan Ludwig Müller was soon to get his own Prussian episcopal office, but Jäger had marked out for himself the post of President – Kapler's old office, which had thus become vacant.[97] And this would at the same time give him the power in the Reich Church, since according to Article 4.7 of the new Reich Church constitution the offices of the first jurist of the Prussian Church and the first jurist of the Reich Church were associated in a personal union. With the weak and spineless Müller at his side, and a Reich Church cabinet which according to the constitution could be manipulated almost at will, Jäger would thus in fact have become master of the German Evangelical Church.

This plan was thwarted by resistance which no one – least of all Jäger himself – still expected after 23 July from the Protestant church. For quickly though the Provisional Administration had yielded in the Prussian question, it now showed itself surprisingly resolute in defence of the authority given it by the Reich Church constitution.

The question which the conflict was about was the territorial reorganization of German Protestantism. The merger of many smaller Landeskirchen into a few large churches had indeed been a chief motive for church reform from the beginning.[98] Without doubt this question now fell under the authority of the new Reich Church. Hence the Provisional Administration had also dealt with this matter from the beginning. In its third session Koopmann had already given a report on the state of the mergers and, a short time later, had already made the first specific recommendations.[99]

The committee was therefore all the more surprised when on 22 August Professor Fezer read it a report which spoke of a meeting 'which has taken place under the chairmanship of Ministerial Director Jäger in the Prussian Kultusministerium under the chairmanship of Herr Jäger as "the authorized representative of the German Evangelical Church", for the purpose of discussing the constitution of the future Church of Greater Hessen, a meeting in which' – and this was the particular point of the report – 'Land Bishop Müller had also participated'.[100] For at this very moment Ludwig Müller was sitting at the table with the Provisional Administration, and had taken part in all its discussions about church mergers without having said a word about his co-operation with Jäger's rival project. But if the future Reich Bishop deserved admiration for anything, it was for the way in which he could talk himself out of situations like this. Of course he had not authorized Herr Jäger, he loyally assured the committee, and in all innocence continued: 'He had received news that he should come to the Kultusministerium since there were representatives there from Hessen who wanted a merger. So he had gone to the Kultusministerium and expressed his delight that the churches wanted to merge.' And although in fact he had been informed about all the proceedings and had all the documents in his hands, he hastily declared himself willing to establish who might have issued the invitation to this meeting, 'on whose inititiative' and 'with what justification'.[101]

Almost a year later, in September 1934, Müller's disappointed former friends from the theology faculty in Tübingen – headed by Karl Fezer – were to put together a comprehensive memorandum about Ludwig Müller's untrustworthiness, mendacity and treachery. And at the top of this devastating list of examples stood the incidents in the Provisional Administration.[102]

In fact at this time Ludwig Müller was already well aware of Jäger's intentions. Since the beginning of August, Jäger had felt himself to be complete master of the church – in anticipation of the future. So he had now decided to create conditions in his home church in Hessen which were to be an example to the entire future Reich Church. He therefore not only pursued the merger of Hessen-Darmstadt, Hessen-Nassau, Frankfurt and Hessen-Kassel into one Church of Greater Hessen – this was an old and hardly revolutionary plan – [103] but also immediately drew up a constitution for the new Landeskirche that he considered a model for all Landeskirchen.[104] All Jäger's notions about church constitutions were limited to the two concepts of united leadership. He had already viewed the Reich Church constitution in this way,[105] and he now fashioned the new model constitution in this way too. It dispensed with any kind of confessional formulation; instead, the leadership principle was implemented strictly: the Reich Bishop nominated the Land Bishop; he in turn appointed the three-man Kirchenrat in the Land, along with the provosts, deans and pastors. The deans, on the suggestion of the pastors, nominated the members of the community councils, each of which consisted of the pastor, the so-called 'duty leaders' and two additional advisers. The Land Synod and the projected Advisory Chambers had no exclusive and clearly-defined responsibilities, and therefore merely served the function of acclamation. Jäger's mistrust of the theologians was typical and expressed itself in a somewhat vague separation of the spiritual and legal leadership of the church: the chairman of the church council was not as a rule to be the pastor, but rather one of the duty leaders; also, a degree of independence was granted to the administrative officials.[106] This was a constitution precisely as Jäger understood it: certainly suitable for his purposes, but without the least sign of any understanding of the complicated and tense relationship between order and confession, community pastor and church administration, which is so typical of most Protestant churches in the European tradition.

On 16 August, Jäger had invited a small group of acquaintances to the Prussian Kultusministerium for the purpose of discussing this constitution. Two regular official delegates, Prelate Diehl of Darmstadt and Kirchenrat Trommershausen of Frankfurt, had appeared on behalf of the four churches. The Land Bishop of Nassau, August Kortheuer, and the President of the Kassel Landeskirchenamt, Dr Bahr, were absent, and for good reason: Jäger knew that neither would comply with his demands. Instead, Jäger had himself appointed by Hossenfelder as the 'Leader of the Parliamentary Group of the German Christians in the Nassau Landeskirchentag' in his old home territory of Wiesbaden.[107] Now in this capacity he personally took over the representation of Nassau. For Kassel, he had won over the seventy-year-old chairman of the previous Landeskirchentag, Metropolitan Dr Dithmar. No less revealing was the composition of the rest of the group. This included, alongside Hossenfelder and Dr Werner, the two Schleswig-Holstein Consistory Councillors Drs Kinder and Christiansen, both absolutely devoted to Jäger, and the Dresden Consistory Councillor Dr Klemich.[108] This indicated that Jäger had not only intended his constitution for Greater Hessen but was also pressing for its introduction in Saxony and northwest Germany too.

After the negotiations had ended on 16 August, the very same day Jäger sent the draft of the constitution to Ludwig Müller, at the same time asking him to take part in the concluding discussion the next day.[109] This was the meeting about which Fezer informed the Provisional Administration. Müller in fact appeared there too and expressed his delight that here was to be concluded a merger of churches 'which truly, without doubt, belong together internally'. It was imperative to gather the twenty-eight Landeskirchen together 'into a very small group. I thank you especially, Ministerial Director, for beginning on this,' he concluded, 'because you have again placed yourself in the service of the cause. And so I wish God's blessing on your work.'[110] After this word of greeting Müller left in a hurry, as so often when serious or unpleasant things were being discussed. For the participants, however, after these words there could not be the slightest doubt that Jäger was in fact acting on behalf of Müller.

In the meeting itself Jäger brusquely rejected all objections and misgivings. 'The ideas of leadership and unity' were 'developed consistently' in the new constitution. He had no intention whatsoever 'of organizing major discussion in the Land synods'. 'The law will just be presented and accepted... Every Landeskirchentag is made up of two-thirds German Christians. And these will be informed beforehand.' The fears of individual participants that the Party members would not fall in unanimously with this were swept aside by Jäger. 'That would be indiscipline. Anyone who does not obey will be thrown out.' He himself would inform the Reich leadership and it would then take the necessary steps.[111] Moreover, he said, the plan was to be treated in strict confidence so that the church administrations would have no opportunity for counter-actions. Jäger named 12 September as the date for the simultaneous meeting of all Hessen synods[112] – a date which was in fact kept.

In spite of the confidentiality which Jäger asked to be kept, these plans did not of course remain concealed from the church administrations in Wiesbaden and Darmstadt. Land Bishop Kortheuer and President Bahr filed a complaint with Jäger on 22 August, and at the same time expressly asked the Provisional Administration for assistance and protection.[113] The committee (but without Müller, who was once again on his way to the Führer at Berchtesgaden) responded two days later with the resolution 'that discussions and negotiations over a merger of churches may in future be conducted only in agreement with the administration of the German Evangelical Church'.[114] Jäger, however, acted as though there were no Provisional Administration at all. Instead, he immediately wrote officially to the government of the Landeskirche in Wiesbaden and requested it 'to convene the Landeskirchentage for Tuesday, 12 September 1933'. This convening served the purpose, he maintained, of 'implementing the plans of the German Evangelical Church for the formation and standardization of the Reich Church'. As his authority he referred explicitly to a mandate from Ludwig Müller, 'a leader of the Reich Church' (by this he probably meant Müller's permanent chairmanship of the Provisional Administration), to his own capacity as a member of the national leadership of the German Christians and his status as a delegate of the Nassau Landeskirchentag. Should the church administration, contrary to expectations, not comply with his request, then 'regrettably an atmosphere of strife would be created from the beginning'. At the same time Jäger pointed out that on the same day the 'smaller Landeskirchen of the Nordmark' would convene their Landeskirchentage.[115]

In fact Jäger had also almost simultaneously set in motion an action in northwest Germany, which aimed at the merger of the Landeskirchen of Hanover, Oldenburg, Bremen, Hamburg, Schleswig-Holstein, Lübeck, Eutin, Brunswick and the two Mecklenburgs into one large Church of Lower Saxony. A resolution to this effect had been passed in Hamburg on 24 August at a discussion among the leaders of Organization Group I of the German Christians.[116]

Thus the situation seemed somewhat difficult for Ludwig Müller when the full Provisional Administration met again on 30 August. But Müller was able in his usual way to impress the committee for the time being, with a report on his visit to Hitler. In this connection, among other things he confirmed the party's change of course, though the importance of this news had not become clear to him or to any of the other members. Müller reported that a Party order would be issued for the purpose of 'stabilizing and strengthening the general church situation' which would prohibit 'any intervention by Party officials in church affairs'. He was able to report further that the visit by Marahrens, Meiser and Tilemann on 24 July to Bayreuth had had 'a most undesirable effect'. Terrified, his colleagues therefore requested him at the coming Reich Party conference 'to rectify the objectively false impression of the situation in the church which the Führer had received from those three men', and if possible to see to it that in his cultural-political speech Hitler said 'something positive and encouraging' about the Protestant church.

After Ludwig Müller had once again demonstrated his importance and indispensability in this way, it was not difficult for him, in answer to pressing questions about Jäger's plans in Hessen and Lower Saxony, to assure his questioners that these plans were of a 'purely private nature' and did not come from the Reich leadership of the German Christians. On further urging he even promised pompously 'to turn off these private efforts'.[117] Only two days later, however – with Müller again absent – it became clear to the group that there could be no talk of 'turning off'. 'The juxtaposition,' the protocol noted with remarkable frankness, 'of the work of Ministerial Director Jäger on the one side and the "Provisional Administration" on the other becomes embarrassingly clear.' So it was then decided for the third time 'to have the question of Dr Jäger's authorization clarified' conclusively by Ludwig Müller.[118] However, before this clarification could be given, an event of unexpectedly far-reaching significance had once again considerably sharpened the general situation.

August Jäger had not only pushed ahead in Hessen and Lower Saxony, but he had also continued to influence decisively the development in the Prussian Church. Here, after the conquest of the key Berlin positions on 4 August, the issue was first of all the reorganization of the principal synods in the eight provinces of the giant church, and then the final German Christian transformation through the highest body, the General Synod. In this context Jäger also pursued his personal goal of becoming President of the Oberkirchenrat in September and thus Kapler's successor.

All the newly elected Prussian provincial synods met between 22 and 24 August. On the basis of the election result of 23 July, the German Christians controlled two-thirds majorities everywhere; in some places their majority was even higher. Only in the Westphalian Synod, because of the special electoral law, did the German Christians remain in the minority over against the parliamentary group Evangelium und Kirche, with sixty seats to eighty. So here the synodical conference took a completely different direction from that in the other provinces. Here the previous President, Karl Koch, was re-elected unanimously. Almost nine months later to the day, as President he was to open the first National Confessing Synod of the German Evangelical Church at Barmen. The representatives on the provincial Kirchenrat and the General Synod were also elected unanimously. Finally, a German Christian motion which spoke out for the continued independence of the Westphalian Provincial Synod and for the preservation of its presbyteral-synodical organization was accepted unanimously.[119]

Whereas the Westphalian Synod took three days for its detailed business, and thus kept outwardly, too, within the usual framework, the other German-Christian dominated provincial synods completed their tasks in a few hours. Here, on orders from Berlin, substantive negotiations were completely dispensed with. The German Christian majorities merely elected new German Christian chairmen, appointed the representatives for the provincial Kirchenräte and the General Synods and finally transferred all the powers of the synods to the provincial Kirchenräte, which thus took over the leadership in the provincial churches. After a hymn and a blessing, these synods closed with a'Sieg Heil' to the Führer, the German national anthem and the Horst Wessel Song.

Although taken together the course and the results of these so-called 'brown synods' seemed uniform, the picture they presented was nevertheless different in each particular case. Whereas in Saxony there were riotous scenes which even led to a complaint to the Provisional Administration,[120] in the Rhineland moderation and traditional churchmanship obtained – even if here too the German Christians made ruthless use of their majority.[121] In East Prussia, on the other hand, the course of the synodical conference proved decisive for the particular approach taken by the church of this province, an approach which made it very difficult for the province to find its way to the Confessing Church. Here, in Ludwig Müller's home territory, was the only case of the Gauleiter of the Party and the First President of the province, Erich Koch, himself being elected President of the Provincial Synod. The speech which he delivered after his election was indicative of the complexity of the church events in this period. For Koch, a former YMCA man, was undoubtedly expressing his own views when he said: 'Outwardly, much has changed. But in our church the Word of Christ according to the doctrine of Luther remains... We East Prussians want to do pioneering work for the blessing of our church, work that can and must be done. Righteousness, truth and love should guide us here, not merely at the level of charity but also in the joyful and active struggles for our Evangelical confession of faith.'[122] In fact Koch remained the only senior National Socialist official to hold on to his church posts after the collapse of the German Christians at the end of 1933. Even such a critical, markedly Reformation-minded theologian as the Königsberg systematic theologian Hans Joachim Iwand – two years later to become director of the Confessing Church's preachers' seminary in East Prussia, wrote at that time to his teacher Rudolf Hermann of Greifswald that the Gauleiter spoke 'with the deepest understanding of our church'; he consistently dealt with 'the central themes of Christianity' and in so doing was 'so directly sensitive that we still find this a miracle'.[123]

However, it was another of the provincial synods that was to set the tone: Brandenburg. It had been formed after 23 July through an agreement between Hossenfelder and Jacobi with a proportion of seventy-five per cent to twenty-five per cent in favour of the German Christians.[124] The special significance of this synod derived from the simple fact that the leading men from both sides were represented in it. Almost all the prominent members of the Reich leadership belonged to the German Christian group. Next to Jäger himself, who took part as a co-opted member, sat Hossenfelder, Peter, Kessel, Freitag, Nobiling, Tausch, Eckert, Wieneke, Grell, Werner, Bierschwale and many others. The leader of the group was a forty-year-old secondary-school teacher, still largely unknown at that time, Dr Reinhold Krause, Gauobmann of the Faith Movement in Greater Berlin. Three months later this same Krause was to achieve questionable fame overnight through a single speech at the Berlin Sports Palace, and at the same time to seal the fate of the German Christians in Prussia and in the Reich. The spokesman for Evangelium und Kirche was Gerhard Jacobi. To this small group belonged, among others, Niemöller, von Rabenau, Görnandt, Diestel, Harder and the church historian Hans Lietzmann – sent by the Berlin faculty.

How the majority intended to deal with the minority was already demonstrated by the speech of the newly-elected President, Superintendent Johannes Grell. 'Our wonderful National Socialist revolution,' he declared (and it could be seen here why the East Prussians treasured their Gauleiter), 'created through the dedication of a hundred thousand Brown Shirts ready to sacrifice their blood, and above all by the heaven-sent Führer and saviour of our Volk and fatherland, for whose sending our Protestant church cannot thank God enough, and must always thank him again and again – our wonderful National Socialist revolution needs must also set the church in motion, the Volkskirche.' The important thing now, at this great turning point in time, was to rebuild the church totally. 'Revolutionary times,' continued Grell, 'are hard times, brutal times. They are seen through by hard fists; hands in kid gloves are no good. Anyone who cannot free himself from the past... is not fit to join in the reconstruction of the Evangelical Church in our beloved people.' 'All hail to my land of Brandenburg!' Grell ended his speech, 'All hail, you Brandenburg Provincial Church!' The minutes went on to note: 'Tumultuous shouts of "Heil" "Bravo" and applause. Call from the German Christian group: "A threefold 'Sieg Heil' for our new President, Superintendent Grell!" The Synod joins vigorously in the shouts.'[125]

The very first elections in the synod made it clear that the majority was determined to follow this tone. More important, however, was the passing of a series of substantive motions. The fact that all these motions were aimed at the General Synod revealed that the future course of the whole Prussian church was to be determined here. Thus one motion called for a church law which would fix the retirement age for senior clergy – 'should this appear appropriate for reasons of service' – at sixty. According to another motion, 'all church agencies, administrative organs and associations and institutes supported by the church' were to be 'co-ordinated in line with the recent church election', also by a church law.[126] While these demands remained within the parameters of what had been expected, another motion became a signal the effect of which neither its author and his frantically applauding supporters nor the church opposition expected at this time.

The author of the motion was the leader of the German Christian group, Dr Krause himself. Krause, who came from the German Church, was fanatically antisemitic. So the motion he introduced was 'that the General Synod should decree through a church law that the same principles should apply to the further employment and reappointment of pastors, church officials, community officials and church employees as applied to Reich, state and municipal officials in accordance with the Law for the Protection of the Civil Service'. This amounted to the introduction of the government's Aryan Paragraphs as a precondition for employment in a church post. Theology and church which, for so long and with such apparently good and understandable reasons, had evaded the Jewish question, were now inescapably challenged to make a decision. Neither the question of the Reich Bishop nor the church elections nor the outrages of the German Christians even began to acquire the significance for the conscience of the church opposition that this Aryan Paragraph had. It became the point which showed most clearly what separated the spirits in the church.

Immediately after Reinhold Krause had introduced his motion, Gerhard Jacobi made the following statement in the name of the Evangelium und Kirche group: 'A transfer of the principles of state laws relating to the Civil Service to those holding church offices goes against the nature of the church. Therefore we reject the motion.' The protocol noted here: 'Vigorous shouts: Hear, Hear! and laughing on the right.' In a roll-call vote demanded by the German Christians the motion was then passed by 133 to 48.[127]

Weeks later, the University of Berlin, among other bodies, received a letter from the Gau leadership of the NSDAP with the information that Professor Dr Lietzmann, who was 'employed there', had voted against Krause's motion at the Brandenburg Provincial Synod. 'It follows that either the person concerned does not recognize what this actually means or that he is deliberately working against the government's measures. If the former, he is incapable of holding a post of this kind; if the latter he will always be against the government. In either case he is intolerable... I request you to take the necessary action.'[128]

However, what was typical of the spirit of the Brandenburg Synod was not only its results but also the way in which they were achieved. In the report of a Swedish journalist for the *Svenska Morgenbladet*, the methods by which the revolutionary or pseudo-revolutionary majorities were accustomed to reducing the opposition to silence became oppressively clear. 'In Swedish conditions it would certainly be inconceivable that up to two hundred Swedish clergy in brown uniforms, riding boots, waist and shoulder straps, with swastikas, badges of rank, and medals of all sorts, should assemble in the First Chamber of the country. Among them, however, there were still perhaps one hundred men in the auditorium, in correct middle-class suits, with peaceful faces, some of them going grey. From these a middle-aged man comes forward and timidly requests consideration for the minority wearing civilian clothes. The majority thereupon begin to protest, some with derisive laughter. When he appeals to the Christian brotherly love of those present, he is told that no one wants a dispute about matters of taste, whereupon he goes silently back to his seat.' After the reporter had described the conditions and the purposes of the synod further, he went into Krause's motion and Jacobi's statement and continued: 'The statement was met with gales of laughter, whereupon the vote was taken. From the ranks of the Brown Shirts the motion for a roll-call vote was heard, and now every negative vote was greeted with shouts of "Aha!", ironic cheers and laughter. One could only sincerely admire the men who risked their entire reputation, and perhaps their existence, in order to follow their honest convictions. The whole affair could only be characterized as religious barbarism.'[129]

The course of the Brandenburg Provincial Synod raised storm signals for the impending General Synod.

The supreme church body in the Old Prussian Union had been summoned for 5 September, immediately after the conclusion of the first Reich Party conference in the Third Reich which, held on Albert Speer's gigantic stage, without doubt represented a new propaganda high point of the year.[130] Although a rapidly distributed photograph showed Hitler with Ludwig Müller and the Catholic abbot Alban Schachleiter in the market place of Nuremberg, the Party conference was undoubtedly a disappointment for the German Christians. For despite the hope of the Provisional Administration that the Führer would say 'something positive and encouraging' about the Evangelical Church in his culture-political speech, Hitler was totally silent on the church issue. This was all the more striking since he used the Nuremberg meetings specially to clarify the spiritual and ideological principles of his politics. The fact that there was no longer any talk in this context about Christianity and the church indicated that he actually considered the church question settled. Instead, for the first time since the seizure of power Hitler publicly and again with great emphasis stressed the importance of the racial question. As he assured the tens of thousands, 'Ideologies... see in the attainment of political power only the precondition for the beginning of the fulfilment of their true mission.' This 'true mission' consisted in the implementation of the racial principle. 'National Socialism declares itself for a heroic doctrine of the value of blood, race and personality, as well as of the eternal law of natural selection. It thus deliberately enters into an unbridgeable opposition to the ideology of pacifist-international democracy and its consequences.'[131]

For the German Christians this could only mean redoubling their effort for the complete co-ordination of the church – also specifically through the introduction of the Aryan paragraph. And the proper platform for this was the meeting of the Prussian General Synod, an event which was likely to attract extraordinary attention both at home and abroad – simply because it took place in Berlin and involved by far the largest German church.

In preparation for the Synod the Prussian Church Senate, which meanwhile had also become a German Christian body through the new chairmen of the provincial synods, met once again at the end of August. How far the hopes and ideas of the German Christians extended was shown by the co-options to the General Synod which the Church senate undertook in accordance with the constitution. Presumably only Hitler's Catholic affiliation kept this body from nominating him personally as a member of the Prussian General Synod. Instead, Reich Interior Minister Wilhelm Frick, the Prussian Minister Hermann Göring and Prussian Kultusminister Bernhard Rust were elected to the highest body of the Prussian Church, and the respective Secretaries of State were designated deputies. Whether there was ever any response to these co-options is not known. Be that as it may, they made clear the grotesquely false estimate of the significance and possibilities of the situation which prevailed among the German Christians.[132]

Within the church, however, they were in fact the undisputed masters of the situation, and let there be no doubt about this.

When the Evangelium und Kirche group met on the morning of 4 September for a first preliminary discussion the basic expectation was still that given their one-third share of the vote the church opposition would be taken into account and that where motions were contested, compromise would indeed be sought, in committee discussions.[133] In the Council of Elders, which met at the same time, however, Jäger put forward the view that the elections to the various committees had to follow the majority rule. The Evangelium und Kirche group were allowed only three representatives in the National Synod and three in the Church Senate. The German Christians claimed the chairmanship of the Synod, the Legal Committee, the Court of Arbitration for Educational Affairs, and the Committee for Clergy Placement exclusively for themselves. Only vague information was given about the motions to be expected.

On the basis of this information from the Council of Elders, in the evening the church opposition was confronted with the question whether it should take

470

part in the synod at all. The Westphalian President Karl Koch having first been elected spokesman for the group, Martin Niemöller moved to boycott the Synod – so as not to give even the appearance of sharing in the responsibility for the resolutions that were anticipated. But the roughly seventy-man group was so divided, and the actual intentions of the German Christians appeared to many to be so inconceivable, that Niemöller's proposal did not gain a majority. In the end there was an agreement to prepare a statement which the spokesman was to present at the synod if the situation made it necessary.

The meeting itself began on the Tuesday morning with a service. Here, too, the majority and the minority were already different, even in dress. While the general superintendents and the pastors in the Evangelium und Kirche group appeared in gowns, the German Christians all wore uniforms – a brown block of SA and officials which almost completely filled the nave.[134] 'The picture of the Synod,' so *Evangelium in Dritten Reich* rejoiced, 'is clearly defined spiritually by the Faith Movement and outwardly by the brown uniform of the Hitler movement.'[135] Indeed, the synod ran in the afternoon in a way which the little Hitlers seemed to have learned from their great model. To be sure, the dissolution of the old Presidium still took place in the traditional forms, with almost a plea from Winckler that the independence of the local communities should be respected and the pastors spared.[136] But as soon as the new President, Dr Werner – the man who had acted as commissioner for the Prussian Oberkirchenrat from the end of June – had taken over the chairmanship along with his two deputies Hossenfelder and Jäger, things went 'blow by blow and in rapid succession'.[137] More than twenty motions were literally whipped through in two hours. Objections and replies from the opposition, which in any case operated irregularly and unhappily, were either disallowed or interrupted by noise and shouts. Among these motions were two which changed the mandate and organization of the Prussian church from the very foundations. These were the 'Church Law concerning the Legal Status of the Clergy and Church Officials' and the 'Church Law for the etablishment of the office of Land Bishop and of Bishoprics'.[138] The first of these two laws contained the so-called Aryan Paragraph, which was thus formulated for the first time in a church context: 'Anyone who is of non-Aryan extraction, or is married to a person of non-Aryan extraction, may not be called as a minister or official in the general church administration. Clergy and officials of Aryan extraction who marry persons of non-Aryan extraction are to be dismissed. Who is to be considered a person of non-Aryan extraction is determined by the prescriptions of the Reich law...' And, like the corresponding state law, the new church law also stipulated that all clergy and officials affected were to be retired retroactively. Moreover, the law contained a blanket clause which in principle associated the pastorate with complete support of the nationalist state.

The second of these two laws reorganized the Prussian Church. It completely reflected the spirit of the new era in its laconic brevity: '1. The Land Bishop represents the Evangelical Church of the Old Prussian Union without prejudice to the powers of the Church. 2. Land Bishop Müller is called to the office of Land Bishop. With 3., Jäger fulfilled his personal wish: 'The position of President of the Evangelical Oberkirchenrat is occupied by a person who has the qualifications for holding judicial office or performing higher administrative service.' Paragraphs 4 and 5 finally contained Jäger's reward for the radical Reich leadership and especially for Hossenfelder: 'The office of general superintendent is abolished. The following bishoprics will be established: Brandenburg, Cammin, Berlin, Danzig, Königsberg, Breslau, Cologne-Aachen, Münster, Magdeburg-Halberstadt, Merseburg-Naumburg. The bishop is the head of the bishopric. The Bishop of Brandenburg is the permanent representative of the Land Bishop. At the same time he is the clergy vice-president of the Oberkirchenrat.' In the justification for this law Pastor Peter gave the assurance 'in all modesty but with joyful emphasis' that the real creator of the idea of the bishoprics had been the Reichsleiter, Pastor Hossenfelder himself.[139] In fact, however, here too Jäger is likely to have dictated the crucial points.[140]

The most important motions having been introduced, after a short pause the voting was to take place. This was the moment at which the opposition spokesman, Karl Koch, called for a point of order and read out the text prepared that morning. At first in silence, then to increasing unrest among the German Christians, he declared that in spite of everything his group had still hoped for brotherly collaboration. However, this hope had been disappointed by the manipulation of the elections and by the treatment of the draft laws for the reorganization of the Prussian Church and the introduction of the state civil service law. For all of this was taking place, he said, 'without the church making the theological reflection that was so desperately needed and without preliminary clarification and discussion'. In the growing tumult Koch's next sentences were barely comprehensible. 'We are deeply shaken to see how, in an hour of the most serious decision for the highest synod of our Landeskirche, the form and nature of the church is to be decided on not by the co-operation which we confidently expected and solely in accordance with the spirit of the church, but rather by the ruthless use of power. This procedure,' Koch continued, addressing the German Christians, 'for which you have the opportunity and the power on the basis of your majority, carries the methods of the world into the sphere of the church and is incompatible with the Christian obligation to brotherly co-operation.'[141] Here the spokesman for the opposition finally had to break off. In wild tumult, amidst incessant shouts of 'Shame! Insolence! Stop it! You're through! Shut your mouth! Get out!', the whole group left the synod together. It was, as one of the participants noted, 'a primitive proceeding' which ruled out any arrangement.[142]

The forced departure of the church opposition from the General Synod was an event of extraordinary importance. It meant nothing less than the division of the Prussian Church, and was the immediate point of departure for the development leading to the Confessing Church in Prussia.

For the time being, however, the majority which remained considered this departure a famous victory. How many of the German Christians may have felt unease at the scene is unknown. There will have been quite a few of them. But in a situation like this, where group processes of sudden, intoxicated awareness of power take over, the individual conscience fights a losing battle. At all events no recognizable objection was raised when the spokesmen for the majority now finished their work. Thus, after the Law for the Reorganization of the Prussian Church had been accepted unanimously, Pastor Eckert called on the Synod to appoint the creator of the Bishops' law, Pastor Hossenfelder, the first Bishop of

Brandenburg (and thus at the same time the clergy vice president of the Oberkirchenrat). In addition he declared that the German Christians would now claim all the seats in the National Synod because, as the cynical justification ran, 'the Evangelium und Kirche group has left the field without any excuse, and thus has shown that it does not wish to have any part in the building up of the church by the National Synod'.[143]

Ludwig Müller, the Prussian Land Bishop, closed the Synod. His address once again demonstrated where he now stood. He wanted to use this opportunity, he declared, 'once more to say to all those beyond the borders of our land who may and must hear it that we – with our church here in Germany – are free'. Anyone who spread untruths about this abroad would be shown 'where he belongs'. 'I have just come from Nuremberg,' Müller continued, 'Anyone who has experienced the Nuremberg rallies cannot escape the powerful impression made upon those who were at all of them. I can well understand that when the word "race" is uttered among us in church life there are many who do not see and do not understand this great, tremendous issue. But I must say that I myself now feel and understand with redoubled intensity what has moved the Führer to deal with this problem so firmly.' The church was summoned to give the Volk, thus stirred, 'at this moment of time the strong spiritual support which can come only from Eternity and which no one can bring so inwardly near to the Volk as this very church.' Finally he also spoke of the need for a reconciliation with those who stood apart, and asked the synod – this synod! – 'In all your labours and all your desires, always look beyond what is past to the Everlasting and the Eternal. All of us must draw optimum strength from the stillness before our God and Father, and anyone who derives... new power and new joy from this stillness will stand his ground in order with clear eyes, a joyful heart, hard hands and a final iron will – to bring the truth of God, as the Saviour has brought it, to this our dear German fatherland... May God grant us this!'[144]

An interview which took place this same evening between delegates of the opposition and Ludwig Müller remained as empty, hollow and rhetorical as these words. 'Clearly offended' by the course of the Synod, Ludwig Müller spoke 'of an excited atmosphere and of the necessity of coming together and working with each other'. 'The same desire,' noted a participant, 'was emphasized by our side, but along with the conviction that collaboration was impossible given the methods applied hitherto, and that in this way our church would not be built up but destroyed.'[145] And this was exactly the way things turned out.

The following evening the Church Senate, under its new Praesidium, which consisted of Dr Werner, Hossenfelder and Jäger, completed the pseudo-legal side of the reorganization. In this small group it also became clear who in fact was holding the reins. Without exception, on a motion by Jäger, and carried throughout with a vote of all against four, in precisely one hour the body decided to approve all the motions of the General Synod: to appoint Hossenfelder Bishop of Brandenburg; on the basis of the new Civil Service Law to retire nine Oberkirchenrat members or transfer them to pastorates, and to bring in eight German Christians; similarly to retire six general superintendents and at the next session to appoint nine bishops and seven deans; to plan for Dr Werner as secular vice-president and – on the motion of Pastor Lörzer – Jäger as President of the Oberkirchenrat. Furthermore, the co-ordination of the Inner Mission was decided upon, and finally Jäger had the powers of the church senate transferred to a small committee to which he himself belonged.[146] The goal of this ambitious and unscrupulous man – the domination of the Prussian and the German church – seemed virtually in his grasp.

As early as 9 September Ludwig Müller officially informed the Prussian Kultusminister that Jäger was to become the new President, and formally asked for confirmation 'that there were no objections of a political nature against the nominee'. However, scarcely fourteen days after this letter another one followed with the surprising sentence: 'Circumstances arising in the meantime lead me to request you for the time being not to implement my letter of the 9th inst.'[147] Meanwhile August Jäger's first major defeat had taken place. It was due to a few courageous men in the Nassau church, led by Land Bishop August Kortheuer.

When on 2 September, immediately after the conclusion of the reorganization in Prussia, Jäger reported in writing to his Minister, he saw only the Provisional Administration as an obstacle 'to development along our lines'. However, the majority for Ludwig Müller in the National Synod was secure. As for the rest, everything was as good as could be: 'the principle of unity and leadership' had not only prevailed in Prussia, but was also valid for the constitutional work in Greater Hessen-Nassau, in Lower Saxony and in the Saxon Landeskirche, which likewise was willing to 'take over word for word' the planned constitution.[148] Here, however, Jäger had obviously underestimated the resistance inside and outside the church. For at this point the Reich Church again put in an appearance.

The far-reaching decisions of the Prussia General Synod for the reconstruction of the Prussian Church naturally violated the order issued by the Provisional Administration of the Reich Church and also supported by Ludwig Müller, according to which the Landeskirchen were temporarily to refrain from changing their constitutions, or at least were to submit them beforehand. The Prussian Church, however, had done nothing of the sort. Therefore Ludwig Müller chose, for safety's sake, to stay away from the meeting of the Provisional Administration on 6 September. But its furious members, who after the goings on in Hessen and Nassau now felt themselves duped in Prussia, too, summoned their chairman to the meeting by telegram.[149] When Ludwig Müller actually appeared in the afternoon, a statement was presented to him which culminated in the question whether, given the Prussian development, the Provisional Administration of the church could continue at all in the circumstances. Embarrassed, Müller thereupon conceded that 'formally, a constitutional change' had taken place, and that 'formally, too', there had been actions 'against that order'. 'But the thought had not occurred to him that the spirit of that order had been violated here.' Moreover, he had heard of the Bishops' law 'only shortly before the session'.[150] This time, however, the committee was no longer satisfied. Rather, it was stated officially that the situation could be cleared up only by a frank explanation from Müller and that this explanation was expected on the following day.[151]

This situation, however, at last put too many demands on Ludwig Müller. And so the drama now temporarily became grotesque. Since the Prussian Land Bishop neither dared to oppose August Jäger's policy nor wanted to forfeit the support of the Provisional Administration, his expectant colleagues were told the next morning that their chairman was sick, and when the next day the committee insisted on establishing at least telephone contact with Müller, his confidant, Admiral Meusel, declared that the Land Bishop was 'out of town in a sanatorium... he didn't know the address'. This, however, in no way hindered Müller, only twenty-four hours later, from ceremonially receiving the Swedish Archbishop Erling Eidem with members of the Provisional Administration.[152]

Other people now also withdrew from the firing line. Johannes Heckel, for example, who as creator of the Reich Church constitution was almost beseeched for help by the Provisional Administration, said that he did not want 'to be the corn which was ground between two millstones', and would not change his mind even at the urgent remonstrations of Schöffel and Fezer.[153] Thus the four remaining members of the Provisional Administration stood alone when they once again instructed all the Landeskirchen to make no changes to the constitution at their impending synods and at the same time entered a protest against Hossenfelder's appointment by the Prussian Church Senate.[154]

However, such protests could not impress August Jäger. He was determined to push through his plans now by hook or by crook. His schedule was so tightly calculated in this respect that there was no longer time for negotiations, even if he had wanted them. The Prussian General Synod had met on Tuesday, 5 September, and the Church Senate on the 6th. On the 7th Jäger had ordered the German Christian representatives of the future Church of Greater Lower Saxony to Berlin and secured their commitment to the new draft constitution in writing.[155] This gave him just four more days to arrange everything as he wanted it before the assembly of the four Hessen synods on 12 September. On the 8th, Jäger and Hossenfelder were therefore already on their way to Kassel, where they expected the chief resistance to the merger. And it was here that Jäger suffered his first defeat. He was in fact thwarted not by the church but rather by the local state and Party authorities, which suspected that the planned Church of Greater Hessen was a first step towards the abolition of the independence of the Gau and Land of Hessen-Kassel, and therefore resolutely opposed Jäger's plans.[156] Accordingly, only three churches remained for the merger: Darmstadt, Frankfurt and Nassau.

Back in Berlin on 9 September, Jäger prepared to travel again on the 10th in order personally to take things in hand in his home territory of Wiesbaden. But Nassau was not Berlin. Whereas there was no support for the resistance in Berlin because no recognized church administration existed any longer, in its Land Bishop August Kortheuer the Nassau church had a man whose reputation was unshaken and in whom, at a pastors' meeting as late as the end of August, almost two-thirds of all Nassau pastors had expressed their confidence.[157] It thus became apparent at a meeting of the German Christian group in Wiesbaden on the morning of 11 September, to Jäger's surprise, that the synod was in no way prepared to bow meekly to his commands. A German Christian Gauleiter, of all people, the young pastor Georg Gründler, not only criticized the draft constitution but also protested emphatically against Jäger's methods. Gründler was not only responsible to the Faith Movement, he declared, but had also been elected to the Landeskirchentag 'as a representative of the community'. He certainly set great store on unanimity, but he was also concerned 'that the conscience of the individual should not be infringed by any orders'. He believed that here he spoke not only for himself; nor could he guarantee that at the Synod next day no one else would take the floor. This could only be a warning signal for Jäger, all the more so as Gründler remained firm in spite of threats and insults. The church environment, the young pastor repeated, was 'a different one from the political arena. The leadership issue in the church is that of the Lord Jesus Christ. Therefore I cannot say that the matter is clear.' The lack of sensitivity here on the part of Jäger was demonstrated by his concluding comment, in which he declared that he would 'regard it personally as a shame if, in the homeland of the Church Commissioner, the Synod presented a less than united picture. What you see here is the spirit of Dr Kortheuer, which must disappear as fast as possible.'[158]

The whole course of the morning showed Jäger clearly that he could not be at all certain of the German Christian majority in the Landeskirchenrat – at any rate, not as long as Kortheuer was in office. Thereupon he decided to rid himself of the hated man that very day. On the afternoon of 11 September there was an unprecedented scene in the office of the unsuspecting Land Bishop. Jäger and Dr Fink, a senior Party leader, appeared there at about four o'clock, both in brown uniforms. Jäger claimed first of all that Kortheuer had spread lies about church plans for Greater Hessen. When Kortheuer denied this, Jäger asked whether Kortheuer had examined his – Jäger's – divorce files. When Kortheuer admitted this and declared that he had done so because of an official enquiry from Dibelius,[159] Jäger lost his temper. 'What!', he cried, 'Dibelius, that swine, that swine, that swine! I'll get him yet. And you, Herr Land Bishop, get down on your knees and thank God tonight that I don't have you put immediately into a concentration camp, as you deserve. I have the power to do this. If I show mercy,I do so only in memory of my father, who worked with you. But I require you, in the name of fifty-six delegates to the Land synod, to tender your resignation tomorrow morning at nine o'clock.' When Kortheuer asked whether Jäger wanted to do all this for personal reasons, Jäger answered that Kortheuer was against the Church of Greater Hessen, had lowered his standing in Berlin, and was therefore intolerable.[160]

Kortheuer, who at first had determined not to yield, wrote out his resignation that very evening in order to avoid an explosion.

The next day, Landeskirchentage took place in Wiesbaden, Frankfurt and Darmstadt. The intimidation had had its effect. Under Jäger's chairmanship in Wiesbaden, Kortheuer's immediate dismissal was decided on with only three votes against, and the new Civil Service Law of the Prussian Church, with the Aryan Paragraph, was now accepted for the Nassau Church also, with eight votes against. All other motions, above all the merger and the new model constitution, were passed unanimously; also unanimously, the powers of all church bodies were transferred to the young pastor Dr Ernst-Ludwig Dietrich, who thus became the dominant figure in the church of Hessen. The entire agenda was finished in barely two hours, on the already-proven Prussian pattern.[161] Jäger thus had time to take part personally in the Frankfurt Synod too. This meeting began in the late afternoon and its course ran completely parallel to that of the Wiesbaden synod. Here too a small group of only nine representatives still raised opposition. Pastor Georg Probst, who had started the Faith Movement in Frankfurt,[162] took over the powers of the church bodies. In Darmstadt, however, where Jäger could not be present at the same time, difficulties quickly arose. Here Prelate Diehl, the leading member of the clergy, followed the instructions of the Provisional Administration and withdrew the motion for the foundation of the Church of Greater Hessen, even though he too had signed the draft in Berlin on 16 August. Instead, a constitutional committee was formed and empowered to work out a new constitution according to the Reich Church guidelines. An appendix expressed the expectation that the Church of Hessen, 'as the largest', would 'participate in the leadership of the new church in line with its importance' – an arrangement which was quite quickly to lead to vigorous confrontations between the three churches. However, the delay in Darmstadt lasted only two days. Presumably under massive pressure from Jäger, as early as 15 April Diehl succeeded in persuading the constitutional committee and church administration to accept the original draft. Thus here too Jäger seemed to have prevailed.[163]

The founding of the Church of Hessen on 12 September 1933 was undoubtedly illegal and invalid in almost every conceivable aspect of church law. Yet the normative force of historical facts now went on to apply to its founding. After a period of transition, the three churches which had been merged by force remained together, even after 1945, and today form the Evangelical Church in Hessen and Nassau.[164] Kassel, however, continued to retain its independence, and after Waldeck joined it in July 1934 it became the present-day Evangelical Landeskirche of Kurhessen-Waldeck.

The destruction of the German Landeskirchen had begun in Prussia; in Hessen it continued without a pause. And now the great clearing-up began in the other Landeskirchen too. In these first weeks of September 1933 Protestant Germany experienced that rigorous reorganization which was to become decisive for the Church Struggle in the years to come.

The second largest Landeskirche, Lutheran Saxony, had already made progress on 11 August with the election of Friedrich Coch as Land Bishop. Here the Brown Synod had had only to confirm what had already in fact occurred through the provisional appointment of Coch after the death of Ludwig Ihmels. Jäger did not miss this synod on 11 August either. Now, on 16 September, the new church administration adopted the Prussian Civil Service Law with the Aryan Paragraph, in a 'Decree for the Introduction of a Church and National Socialist Civil Service'.[165] But Coch, hurt because he had not been sufficiently heeded, refused the consent of Saxony to Jäger's model constitution for which Jäger had hoped.[166] In Brunswick, the old Land Bishop, Alexander Bernewitz, had to go on 12 September, although for a long time he had joined in echoing the slogans of the German Christians. Typical of the trend of the times was the fact that a thirty-year-old pastor, Wilhelm Beye, was elected his successor and was welcomed with a threefold 'Sieg Heil' by the Synod, which soon afterwards passed the new Civil Service Law in similar fashion. The joy over the 'youngest bishop in the world' was, however, only short-lived; by February 1934 he had resigned all his offices after a mysterious legal process for embezzlement and fraud.[167] In Schleswig-Holstein, too, it was no help to Bishops Nordhorst and Völkel that they had welcomed the German Christians into their churches with open arms. On 12 September the Brown Synod in Rendsburg under the chairmanship of its new President, Hans Aselmann, abolished their offices and sent them into retirement. The Civil Service Law and Enabling Act also followed here. Satisfied, the next day Aselmann sent telegrams in all directions: 'On basis of preparatory constitutional draft Land Synod Schleswig-Holstein decided unanimously to approve formation of Church of Lower Saxony.'[168] In Mecklenburg, immediately after the church elections Land Bishop Rendtorff tasted the bitter fruits of his muddled course and his political gullibility. Despite his public support of the Party and his emphatic endorsement of the German Christian orientation of Ludwig Müller, in August he became involved in a vigorous dispute – in which the Provincial Administration also intervened intensively – with the Mecklenburg government and the Gauleiter and governor Fritz Hildebrand. Suspended from office and after much argument restored to it, he was finally deprived of power by the Landessynode on 13 September. To be sure, formally he still remained in office, but the Synod transferred his responsibilities to the young pastor Walter Schultz, not yet thirty-three, who henceforth led the Mecklenburg church as 'Führer of the Landeskirche'. Until the end of the year Rendtorff, still hopeful that all this was just a mistake, attempted to clear up the alleged misunderstanding, and as late as November declared himself still to be 'a champion of co-operation between the church and National Socialism'. Only in January 1934 did he resign, give up his office as bishop and in the course of the year join the church opposition as a pastor in Stettin. Nationalist credulity, political blindness and above all that devastating enthusiasm for missionizing the Volk which caused so much mischief during these years were combined in an almost exemplary way in the figure of the Land Bishop of Mecklenburg until his change of mind.[169]

When one looks towards the future, in the brown flood which overwhelmed the Protestant church in those September days and swept away the old church administrations there were only three notable exceptions. In Hanover, Land Bishop Marahrens was successful at the Synod on 28 August in preventing the loss of his power and in maintaining himself in office – though only just, and with some difficulty. The church administrative bodies, however, the Landeskirchenamt and the Church Senate, were shaped in accordance with German Christian wishes. Marahrens attempted to get this situation under control through extensive compromises, which contributed much to the problematical course of the Hanover Church in subsequent years.[170] In Württemberg, Land Bishop Wurm surprisingly held out unchallenged. Supported by a stable group of moderate German Christians orientated on Fezer, with whom he largely concurred, on 12 September Wurm even succeeded in persuading the Landeskirche to confirm the Enabling Act for the Land Bishop dated May 1933. Thus it was clear that Wurm's position in his Landeskirche was unshaken, a fact which no one in Württemberg could get round even in subsequent years. The Civil Service Act with the Aryan Paragraph, proposed by the radical group in the Synod, was referred to committee and not discussed again.[171] And finally, in Bavaria, too, Land Bishop Meiser remained at the head of the Landeskirche, likewise legally secure as a result of an unlimited extension of his authority passed by the Synod at its meeting of 12-14 September.[172] The special development in Hanover, Württemberg and Bavaria which was to acquire crucial significance for future events, had essentially the same basis. All three churches had an outstanding personality at their head and possessed a group of pastors of a rather conservative kind which was not at all inclined to make too radical decisions. In their rural

478

church areas, which were relatively united in confessional terms, the organization of the Berlin Reich leadership could gain only a small footing. Instead, in Württemberg and Bavaria (Hanover followed here only in September) the bishops themselves resolutely pleaded for the goals of the moderate German Christian movement, and thus for the time being created a common basis upon which the different trends could meet. In this way, while they in fact avoided schism and the destruction of their Landeskirchen, they were constantly compelled to support Ludwig Müller's candidacy and later his conduct in office – even against the church opposition in Prussia which had nothing more to lose and had moved towards increasingly resolute resistance.

In these weeks, while the concepts were still foreign and the consequences known to none, in fact after the synods of 12 September, destroyed Landeskirchen and intact Landeskirchen continued in German Protestantism side by side. Those Landeskirchen which were later considered to have been destroyed were all the ones which had a German Christian church administration, such as Prussia, Hessen, Brunswick, Schleswig-Holstein and Mecklenburg. Only three remained essentially intact: Hanover, Württemberg and Bavaria. The different points of departure which were thus created for future controversies could never be completely balanced in the Confessing Church. In spite of many difficulties over individual issues, on the whole developments up to the middle of September seemed to favour the German Christians. Only one more step had to be taken towards the crowning achievement: the assembly of the National Synod and the election of the first Reich Bishop. At the same time, however, during this period resistance was making itself felt which went far deeper and had a far more lasting effect than might appear on the surface.

First of all, it became apparent immediately after 12 September that August Jäger had gone much too far in Hessen. Only the day after the scene in the Landeskirchenamt in Wiesbaden, Kortheuer had been requested by the Provisional Administration to come to Berlin immediately and to give a personal report. And in contrast to many people who during this period had learned the advantages of silence, the indignant Land Bishop complied with the request and on the following day presented to the committee a detailed and unvarnished account of events in Hessen. In this situation, however, neither Ludwig Müller nor Hossenfelder, who was immediately informed, could continue to keep the Ministerial Director, nor did they want to. Possibly even relieved to escape their inexorable slave-driver in this way, both agreed with the view of the Provisional Administration 'that it is impossible to consider Jäger the legal minister for the German Evangelical Church, and that Jäger must withdraw from the Reich leadership of the German Christians'. On the same day Ludwig Müller declared once again: 'Jäger is through, because of the episode with Kortheuer', and also that Jäger's church constitution would be suspended.[173]

Kortheuer was assured by the relieved members that the whole church would thank him once again for having been the sacrificial offering which had made it possible 'to keep the evil spirit' – i.e. Jäger – 'away from the church'.[174] And Müller, for a change, actually kept his word. On 21 September he wrote to the Prussian Kultusminister that the planned appointment of Jäger as President of the Prussian Oberkirchenrat was no longer feasible. 'Circumstances arising in the meantime lead me to request you for the time being not to implement my letter of the 9th inst.'[175] Thus Jäger's church career seemed at an end. The following months demonstrated, however, that in the realization of their goal the German Christians could not do without either Jäger's position of power or his brutality. Thus April 1934 still found him next to Ludwig Müller, in the highest legal office of the Reich Church, until his church politics were finally wrecked in the autumn of that year. In September 1933, however, Jäger's forced withdrawal represented a decisive weakening of the German Christian front which undoubtedly facilitated the resistance of the church opposition, especially in Prussia.

The merger and the reorganization of this opposition was the most important event of these dramatic weeks in September. It was, however, ultimately to change the German Protestant understanding of the state more deeply than any other event since the Reformation.

After its withdrawal from church politics, the church opposition in Prussia had occupied itself throughout August with its two new tasks: church theological clarification and practical-community consolidation. In Bethel the first draft of the confession was produced which, to Bonhoeffer's disappointment, no one was then prepared to support. And at different places, in Berlin, in the Kurmark and the Neumark, in the Rhineland and Westphalia, the concentration of pastors willing to stand up for scripture and the confession in the church had begun. All these activities were planned with a lengthy period of time in view. Long and laborious work was foreseen before the fronts were really clarified. The earliest date for a public stand was thought to be the first assembly of the National Synod at the end of September, though it was not known whether anything ought to be said there, and if so what. But this situation was changed by the Prussian General Synod. The brutal scenes, the walk-out, and the laws which were ultimately passed acted on the church opposition like a shock. If they had previously proceeded on the assumption that the German Christians had to be challenged by means of a confession, they now saw themselves challenged. At the centre of all the concerns stood the Aryan Paragraph. It, above all, led to the rise in less than a week of the first major opposition organization: the Pastors Emergency League.

When the church opposition gathered in Berlin on 6 September, the day after the General Synod, in the St Michael Hospice, to discuss the situation, there was deep despondency and perplexity. Here Dietrich Bonhoeffer and his friend Franz Hildebrand were the most resolute, attempting to gain the support of the assembly for a radical decision. With the incomparable clarity which had characterized him – and almost only him – in this whole question from the beginning of April, in August Bonhoeffer already drafted a memorandum on the Aryan Paragraph in the church, before or alongside the Bethel Confession. Still uncertain as to what was to be expected in this respect, the memorandum distinguished between a radical form of the Aryan Paragraph – the exclusion of all non-Aryans from the German Reich Church – and a more moderate procedure, which to begin with would affect only church officials and pastors. In connection with the radical form, Bonhoeffer took up his most important April theological theses, according to which a church that excluded the Jewish Christians today had 'itself become the Jewish-Christian church and thus fallen away from the gospel to the law'. In developing this thesis, the brief work seized

480

upon the German Christian arguments of the time and rejected them in an uncompromising way. 'The GC say that the church may not dissolve nor despise divine ordinances. Race is one of these ordinances; therefore the church must be racially determined. We reply that the given ordinance of race is no more misunderstood than that of the sexes, estates, etc... In the church the Jew remains a Jew, the Gentile a Gentile, the male a male, the capitalist a capitalist, etc... But the call of God summons and gathers all into one Volk, God's Volk, to which all belong in the same way and to one another...' 'The GC say: We do not have in mind the thousand Jewish Christians, but rather the millions of our fellow countrymen who are alienated from God. For their sake the others must be sacrificed, if need be. We answer: We too have them in mind, but in the church no individual is sacrificed, and it may be that the church does not gain the millions for the sake of the thousand faithful Jewish Christians who may not be sacrificed. But what would be even a gain of millions if it were bought at the cost of the truth and the love of even one individual?' The consequences were formulated clearly and distinctly; the Aryan Paragraph is 'a false doctrine of the church and destroys its basic nature. Therefore only one service to the truth can be performed in respect of a church which implements the Aryan Paragraph in the radical form: withdrawal.' As to the second possibility, which now in fact came about, the memorandum stated that the German Christian demand for the dismissal from office of Jewish Christian pastors destroyed the nature of this office in that it turned 'members of the community into brothers with inferior rights, second-class citizens'. 'The others who remain unaffected by this demand, the privileged, will themselves prefer to stand by the side of the brothers with inferior rights rather than to make use of their privileges in the church. They will therefore have to see that the service which they can yet render to their church in truth is to resign the pastorate that has become a privilege.'[176]

In the discussion within the church opposition group Bonhoeffer and Hildebrandt now advocated precisely these consequences: resignation from one's office and possibly withdrawal from the church.[177] The majority, however, did not endorse this radical demand. As its spokesman, the Berlin Director of Missions, Siegfried Knak, argued that the foundation in Germany of a distinctively Jewish Christian church could not be excluded, at least for the future, and that the resistance of the opposition had to direct itself above all against the retroactive force of the new church law. In view of these extreme contrasts, an agreement was unthinkable. It was decided, therefore, to wait for the time being and with an eye to the National Synod, to plan on a 'message from opposition pastors'. Bonhoeffer and Niemöller were to work out a draft.[178]

In the course of the session a decision was taken the significance of which for the future development of the church question no one could yet see – as so often happened in this period. For on this day it was decided that the church opposition would not withdraw from the church and found a free church, as Bonhoeffer demanded, but rather assert and hold fast in the church to the claim to be the true Evangelical Church in Germany. And so far as this can be said historically, this was the correct decision, even if its theological justification was questionable. For there can hardly be any doubt that following Bonhoeffer's advice at this moment would have meant the end of the church resistance. It would have been all too easy to isolate and to silence the small group of those who withdrew. The opportunity for resistance lay in the church, and it became that much greater the more people could be won over to this resistance in the church.

Bonhoeffer and Niemöller already went to work on the evening of 6 September. In the laconic language of his official diary, Niemöller recorded: '8 p.m., Bonhoeffer and many students, Röhricht, Hildebrandt... 2.15 a.m. to bed.'[179] The result was a short statement which, in three paragraphs, described the Aryan Paragraph as a violation of the confession, declared the undiminished and continuing validity of the ordination of all clergy affected, and demanded the repeal of the law 'which separates the Evangelical Church of the Old Prussian Union from the Christian church'.[180]

The personal and spiritual centre of church opposition in these days was still Friedrich von Bodelschwingh. So the declaration went off immediately to Bethel with the request that it should be signed by as many pastors as possible and then be used against the Prussian church administration. Bodelschwingh, however, delayed. The consequences of the declaration evidently seemed to him to be too radical. So immediately afterwards he wrote a letter to Ludwig Müller, explicitly endorsing only the second point, which was directed against the removal of clergy who were already in office. Otherwise he urged the Prussian Land Bishop to dissuade the German Christians from their violent methods, which could produce 'nothing but untruth and a curse'.[181] Now this was certainly not the reaction which the resolute group of opponents had expected. So it was already a preliminary decision of considerable significance.

In Berlin, initially nothing of Bodelschwingh's hesitation was known. Here all attention was concentrated on 11 September when – as on every Monday – the opposition pastors met at Jacobi's manse. At noon on this day two young colleagues from the Lausitz, Eugen Weschke and Günther Jakob, appeared at Niemöller's manse. They brought from home, where as country pastors they were far more exposed to political pressure than in the city, a plan to bring into being a merger of all pastors in the German Evangelical Church who were loyal to the confession, under the leadership of Bodelschwingh, a development which would go beyond the fraternal groups which already existed. It was an idea which was so to speak in the air as a result of all that had happened in the meantime. Niemöller agreed. That very afternoon Eugen Weschke explained the plan to the pastors at Jacobi's manse, while Günter Jacob presented a similar declaration of commitment which he had composed in the meantime. After a short discussion the plan and the declaration were approved. This was the moment of the foundation of the famous Pastors Emergency League.

The declaration of commitment, which was signed that day by the first sixty pastors, consisted of five sentences. They ran: '1. I commit myself to use my office as a servant of the word solely in commitment to Holy Scripture, and to the Reformation confessions as the correct interpretation of Holy Scripture. 2. I commit myself to protest with uncompromising dedication against any violation of such a state of confession. 3. I trust the fraternal leadership and the representative service of Dr von Bodelschwingh in exercising vigilance over such a state of confession. 4. I consider that to the best of my ability I share the responsibility for those who are persecuted for the sake of such a state of confession. 5. In such commitment I bear witness to the fact that the application of the Aryan Paragraph in the domain of the church of Christ brings about a violation of the state of confession.'[182]

If the whole action was still to have any effect on the national synod and possibly prevent a decision on the Aryan paragraph there, then literally no more time was to be lost. For the meeting of this supreme synod was scheduled for 19 September, leaving precisely one week for the preparation. So the dispatch of the declaration of commitment to the supporters of the Young Reformers Movement began the same night. 'Moved by the distress of so many isolated colleagues,' wrote Martin Niemöller in reference to this, 'we have committed ourselves in a wider circle of friends to the attached declaration and now wish to seek throughout the German fatherland first of all pastors who will likewise join this league. We need this solid alliance for the sake of the many lonely people, for the sake of our church, and for the sake of all those who are threatened by the passage of resolutions in the Prussian General Synod which violate the confession. After our experiences we hope that a quite considerable portion of the body of Protestant pastors will join this emergency league.' If in the course of the week over a thousand signatures were collected, Niemöller wrote, the wording of the commitment and the number of signatures could perhaps be used at the National Synod. '*Speed is of the essence.*'[183]

The short time at the disposal of the new League before the National Synod meant that even Bodelschwingh could only now be informed of the role conceived for him in Berlin. 'Please forgive us,' Weschke asked on 12 September, 'for having committed your name on our own initiative. There was no time to inform you. Point 3 is supposed to enable you to take action outside, so that you can act and speak independently in the name of all the pastors who have signed without first having to ask any individual. Please do not deny the cause and us in this hour of decision, which for many people is a last rally to defend themselves.'[184] Bodelschwingh, however, hesitated. The speed of the Berlin people surprised him; moreover, he doubted whether the radical formulation of the commitment was in fact the right way, however firmly he too rejected the Aryan paragraph. So he invited Weschke and Niemöller to Bethel to discuss the whole matter on 15 September. After a long discussion Bodelschwingh finally let himself be convinced, but on condition that Marahrens also joined in the leadership of the new League. However, Marahrens, who at this particular time could remain at the head of his Landeskirche only by making far-reaching concessions to the German Christians, did not feel able to participate. After these discouraging experiences it might have seemed advisable to give up the whole plan. But this was most decidedly against Niemöller's nature. So during his journey home from Hanover to Berlin, he decided to take over the leadership of the League himself.[185] After Bodelschwingh once again had asked particularly not to be committed to the specific leadership 'of even one group',[186] the third point in the Emergency League declaration was eliminated. On 21 September, then, in its final form it was sent to all the available addresses of the Young Reformers Movement along with a detailed letter from Niemöller. 'At the present time,' he reported, 'about 1300 have signed this, not including Westphalia, which already has its own brotherhood... In addition we must see to it that there is one such league in every Landeskirche and in every province; that these leagues support one another (otherwise one district after another will be "purged"); and that the members of this league actively commit themselves to the building up of the Christian community in their province (lay assembly).' At the end of this letter Niemöller then found the tone that was to become characteristic of the resistance in Germany, arising out of Christian responsibility. At its innermost core this resistance was no longer based on a hope for a turning point in things, or even for the victory of the opposition, but rather on the need to do what conscience demanded. 'I am aware,' Niemöller concluded, 'that this League cannot save the church and move the world; but I am equally aware that we owe it to the Lord of the church and to the brethren to do today what lies within our power, and that caution and restraint today already signify failure, because those in great distress lack proof of our fraternal solidarity. So let us act.'[187]

With the leadership of the Pastors Emergency League Martin Niemöller had found his mission, and the German Christian church government its most determined opponent. The system of mutual solidarity which was immediately developed proved to be extraordinarily stable; and the strict limitation to church and confession and along with it the deliberate openness of its approach also made the League politically almost impregnable.[188] Thus the organization of the Pastors' Emergency League became the heart of the Confessing Church and remained so until the collapse of the Third Reich.

The Aryan paragraph, which the Prussian General Synod had passed, did not only affect the Berlin-Brandenburg church. Parallel to the founding of the Pastors' Emergency League in Essen, the Rhineland Brotherhood also decided, that very day, for a close alliance under the leadership of a religious community. On the application and implementation of the new law, 'spiritual resistance (non-violent resistance in the Word and in love)' was to be offered 'through a joint protest by a public confession of faith (pulpit)', 'through public support for those affected', and finally – as in Berlin – 'through fraternal aid in emergencies involving those affected.' The basic principles of the Rhineland Brotherhood were, in sum: 'suffering violence and outrage, but making a protest against a church government which is incompatible with the gospel and unspiritual on the basis of the confession.'[189]

Another sign of the deep unrest that had seized the church was that on this same 11 September, even the Synod of Kurhessen, that fourth church in Hessen which had just escaped Jäger's grasp, though with a German Christian majority, resolved to request the theological faculties of Marburg and Erlangen for 'a solemn and responsible instruction to German Evangelical Christianity' on 'whether the law on the conditions of employment for clergy passed recently by the General Synod of the Church of the Old Prussian Union and planned for the whole German Evangelical Church – containing the Aryan Paragraph – is in conformity with or contradicts the teaching of Holy Scripture, the gospel of Jesus Christ and the teaching of the apostles... the ecumenical confessions and the doctrine of the Reformation... as well as the preamble of the constitution of the German Evangelical Church'. The answer from Marburg, signed by the Dean, the church historian Hans Freiherr von Soden, was clear and unequivocal. 'The Faculty considers the two basic principles of Sections 1 and 3 (or 11) respectively to be incompatible with the nature of the Christian church as it is defined by the authority of Holy Scripture and the gospel of Jesus Christ, which alone is binding, and attested by the Reformation confessions.' The detailed substantiation contained the German Christian theses point by point along with a refutation of them from the Bible and theology. The answer from Erlangen which the two systematic theologians Paul Althaus and Werner Elert had drawn up for the faculty was far less unequivocal. It declared that the 'völkisch diversity of external church organization' expressed 'a necessary consequence of the divisions of the peoples which are to be affirmed in terms of destiny as well as ethics', and that account was therefore also to be taken of this 'in admission to the ministry of the church'. 'In present circumstances, the occupation of its ministry by persons of Jewish origin generally would be a severe burden and a hindrance to the church's new task of being a Volkskirche of the Germans.' The church had therefore 'to require the withholding of its Jewish Christians from office'. In finally stating the possibility of exceptions, and seeking to have these exceptions applied especially to clergy already in office, the two Erlangen theologians carefully made their own position that of that middle group which thought the Aryan Paragraph acceptable in principle but rejected its retroactive application.[190]

In contrast to this opinion, twenty-one New Testament specialists at the same time declared 'that according to the New Testament, the Christian Church is a church of "Jews and Gentiles"... who come together visibly in a community', that 'faith and baptism alone' are decisive for membership of this community; and also that 'Jews and Gentiles are qualified to hold office in the church in fundamentally the same way'.[191] Thus began a theological controversy which extended far into 1934.

Now the unrest spread beyond the German church. The fact that Protestants abroad now also began to be intensively concerned with the question of the Aryan Paragraph became even more significant for the impending decisions. Alongside individual initiatives from Scandinavia, two ecumenical bodies above all discussed the problem in detail. First, the Executive Committee of the Ecumenical Council for Practical Christianity – the so-called Stockholm Movement ('Life and Work') – had its annual meeting in Novi Sad, Yugoslavia, from 9-12 September. This was of special importance for the German situation in two respects. First, from the beginning this movement was especially interested in political and social issues, so that the problem of antisemitism had a high priority for it. Secondly, the German church was officially represented as such in this ecumenical body. Just how serious was the situation was shown by a letter from the French representative Wilfred Monod, who spoke for the Reformed Churches of France. As he wrote to the leading members of the council: 'Unless we resist today, unyieldingly and compassionately, the pressure of Hitlerite racism which seeks to penetrate the Ecumenical Council, our movement will have lost its *raison d'être*...'[192] For this very reason, however, the Provisional Administration had decided to have the German church represented as strongly as possible in Novi Sad – by Ludwig Müller, Fezer and Schöffel. The increasing strain to which the committee saw itself exposed after the end of August shattered this plan. Because of August Jäger's attitude it did not seem wise for them to leave Germany at this moment. So Heckel and Schreiber were sent as delegates to Novi Sad. In addition Hans Wahl, who had been involved with the Jewish question in the Kirchenbundesamt, went along as an escort. The leader of the delegation was Theodor Heckel, thirty-nine years old, brother of the Bonn church lawyer, who had at first belonged to the Young Reformers Movement and then, like his brother, had quickly fallen in with Ludwig Müller's German Christian line.[193]

In Novi Sad Heckel appeared for the first time in the role which which he was subsequently to play from 1934 until well into the Second World War, as Bishop and Director of the Church Foreign Office. He had to convey the German position to Protestantism abroad so decisively that even under the far more severe circumstances of the later period he still appeared useful to Reich and Party authorities; abroad, however, he had to appear critical enough still to retain a degree of credibility.[194] Heckel's appearance in Novi Sad was a first proof of his skill as a harmonizer. For his position was certainly not easy. The mandate given him by Fezer ran 'on the one hand to avoid breaking off relations; on the other hand to prevent a resolution which made substantial comments on the problems raised'. However, this was made more difficult by information given to various members of the committee by the church opposition in Germany. It was more or less summarized by a telegram in English from Bonhoeffer on the evening of the General Assembly: 'General Synod finished, all General Superintendents dismissed, only teutonic Christians admitted to National Synod, Aryan Paragraph now in action, please work out memorandum against this and inform press at once, separation at hand, further information in Sofia.'[195] Heckel thus found himself exposed to numerous unpleasant questions from the English bishop George Bell, the Frenchman Monod, the Norwegian bishop Valdemar Ammundsen, and others. He answered at length, and ended by saying, in irritation, that one could not 'gain from specific details today a final picture as to what might be a permanent feature and what a passing incident'; moreover, the Executive Committee had no right at all 'to pass judgment on developments in Germany'. When the committee nevertheless insisted on a plain letter to the German church, Heckel threatened to break off relations and as a compromise finally suggested an instruction from the committee to its chairman to write to the Provisional Administration on its own responsibility; there should be no decision about its content. In spite of Heckel's protests, however, a statement on 'the results of the discussion' expressing the concerns of the European and American churches about the persecution of the Jews and the suppression of freedom of opinion in Germany could not be prevented.[196] In any case it was clear by the end of the meeting that the ecumenical movement would not tacitly accept the introduction of the Aryan Paragraph throughout the German church, and that pressing the matter could have highly undesirable repercussions for Germany's foreign affairs.

By contrast, the state of affairs in the Executive Committee of the World Alliance for Promoting International Friendship through the Churches, to the Sofia meeting of which, in the middle of September, Bonhoeffer had referred in his telegram, was rather different. Here there were no member churches sending official delegates but only representatives from the individual national groups. A co-ordination of the German branch had not yet occurred, so only the old missionary scholar Julius Richter and Dietrich Bonhoeffer, who as Youth Secretary was on the Executive Committee of the World Alliance and was scheduled to speak at the planned 1934 Youth Conference, went to the Bulgarian capital. The resolution which the committee passed under the heading 'Racial Minorities' also clearly revealed Bonhoeffer's hand: 'We protest against the decision of the Prussian General Synod and of other synods which transfer the state Aryan Paragraph into the church...' We consider this 'to be a denial of the clear teaching and spirit of the gospel of Jesus Christ'.[197] From a report which Bonhoeffer and Richter made to the German mission in Sofia while the discussions were going on, the legation gained the impression that while the two German delegates had made an effort 'to adopt a position which took German interests into account' in the matter under dispute, they considered it out of the question 'to establish at the conference the lie that the application of the Aryan Paragraph to the church is not to be condemned from the Christian standpoint'.[198]

Far more lasting in its effect than the congresses and resolutions, though, was a personal visit to Berlin by the Swedish archbishop Erling Eidem. Eidem's great reputation, his undisputed love for Germany and the special connection that existed between Scandinavian and German Lutheranism gave extraordinary significance to this visit. Having been kept well informed about developments in the church by the pastor of the Swedish community in Berlin, Birger Forell, on 9 September Eidem met the Provisional Administration and implored it to do whatever it could to prevent the National Synod passing the Aryan Paragraph. Pressed by the representatives of the church opposition, with whom he spoke soon afterwards at Forell's home, he repeated this request once more after his return, in a letter to Ludwig Müller. The 'final acceptance of the Aryan Paragraph and of the exclusively nationalistic civil service laws', wrote the Swedish archbishop, would 'pose the utmost threat to fellowship with the rest of the Protestant churches or even make it impossible and mean an isolation of the German church.'[199] Müller and the Provisional Administration were apparently unimpressed. When on 20 September Professor Lietzmann gave the committee the opinion of the twenty-one New Testament specialists on the racial question, he also learned from it of the letter from Uppsala. But now the Cultural Department of the Foreign Office, alarmed by Lietzmann, intervened. In a conversation with Fezer, Envoy Friedrich Stieve learned that if the Aryan Paragraph were accepted 'the break of the Swedish Evangelical Church' from the German church was to be expected, that the Provisional Administration was 'under pressure from a radical group', and that therefore an appropriate letter from the Foreign Office would be gratefully received. That Fezer was not concerned with theological questions here, but that he was thinking merely in terms of a political ploy was shown by his assertion – made with no basis whatsoever – that Eidem had indicated in his letter 'that the removal of the Jewish clergy from the German Evangelical Church through administrative processes would not result in such a step'. In fact, that same day Secretary of State von Bülow decided on a letter in strict confidence to the Provisional Administration in which he expressed his concern that with the passage of a resolution on the Aryan Paragraph at the National Synod 'the witch-hunt against Germany because of the Jewish question' would increase still further, which was all the more problematical since 'in any case Germany will probably be exposed to malicious attacks over the Jewish question at the autumn assembly of the League of Nations, which is just beginning'. 'I therefore consider it my duty,' wrote the Secretary of State, '...to point out the above-mentioned danger and respectfully submit for your consideration whether implementing the Aryan Paragraph through administrative channels rather than through an official adoption of the law might not be possible.'[200] The topic was thus settled for the National Synod.

For the Foreign Office, however, from now on the church question stayed on the agenda. Shortly afterwards, on 30 September, the German delegation to the League of Nations in Geneva reported by telegram a visit by representatives of world Protestant organizations, and requested 'detailed instructions immediately whether the Aryan Paragraph, the greatest stumbling block, is to become a resolution at the National Synod'. And two days later another report, from the German embassy in London, about the effects of Novi Sad, went off to Berlin. According to this, 'considerable practical significance' was to be attached to the resolution, at all events in connection with England, 'since it must certainly be understood as the deliberate enlistment of English Protestant church circles among the groups of those organizations which are actively concerned with the German Jewish problem and the organized welfare work for Jewish emigrants.'[201] From this time on the Foreign Office followed church developments in Germany with increasing concern until, in October 1934 – essentially under pressure from the London Embassy and the Reich Foreign Minister – Ludwig Müller was finally toppled.[202]

And so the day of the National Synod, 27 September, arrived. Just eight weeks had passed since the triumphant election victory of the Faith Movement. And although during this period the German Christians had succeeded in occupying the most important posts in German Protestantism and in giving themselves the semblance of an impregnable position, developments as a whole were posing problems for them. With the withdrawal of the Party their political base was beginning to crumble, and at the same time a serious rival had arisen in Hauer's German Faith Movement. The Prussian General Synod had ended with an explosion and the Aryan Paragraph had provoked resistance which gradually became increasingly tangible: in the formation of the Pastors Emergency League, the protests from abroad, and now even the objection from the Foreign Office. Furthermore, Jäger's ruthless church policy had brought not only successes but also a scandal that had ruled out his nomination for the leadership of the Reich Church; and this also severely burdened the radical Reich leadership of the German Christians.

If the National Synod presented a picture of unity despite an almost unbroken series of difficulties and scandals, the responsibility for this lay above all with the Lutheran bishops. Since Meiser, Wurm, Schöffel and the other Lutherans had decided in that remarkable night session of 23-24 July in Eisenach to drop Bodelschwingh, the Church of the Prussian Union and the old Kirchenbund, and instead to attempt to secure the nationalist and Lutheran leadership of the new Reich Church through Ludwig Müller, in principle they had held to that line.[203] It had preserved Meiser and Wurm as leaders of their Landeskirchen and had at least protected Marahrens, who had come along only after the church elections, from a vote of no confidence by his synod. Pressed by the difficult situation in their Landeskirchen and at the same time still convinced of the national mission of the Lutheran Church in the Third Reich, the Lutherans remained prisoners of this church-political line even at the National Synod.

The Lutheran church leaders came together in Halle on 22 September to prepare for the Synod. Here Schöffel, who as a member of the Provisional

Administration had the best information, gave a detailed report on the events of recent weeks. He described the misgivings abroad over the Aryan Paragraph; he went into the Jäger case in detail, describing Jäger as the 'evil spirit'; in addition to other co-ordinations of Landeskirchen singled out specifically the procedure of the German Christians in Schleswig-Holstein, which bordered 'on knavery'; and repeated without comment Müller's assertion that everything had been done by Jäger and that he, Müller, was completely innocent.

Although this report put a good deal of truth on the table, none of the bishops was capable of seeing it. The talk was not about the church opposition and its theological arguments. For this company everything was a matter of church politics. The Aryan paragraph was only a problem abroad; Jäger's actions were questionable only because they endangered the 'status of the Lutheran confession'. It was not the imminent removal of Jewish clergy nor the ruthless suppression of the church opposition in Prussia and in the other Landeskirchen ruled by the German Christians that troubled the Lutherans, but solely the idea that Jäger's policy could ultimately end up in Union churches in which the purity of the Lutheran confession might perish. For the sake of the Bremen church, which notoriously had no confession, Johannes Heckel reported, the word 'Lutheran' was to be deleted from the constitution of the 'Evangelical Lutheran' Church of Lower Saxony; and the Reformed President Otto Koopman, who was participating as a guest, reported amidst general consternation that even the Reformed church in Aurich had been invited to join the Church of Lower Saxony![204] The most dangerous sign of this development, however, appeared to the Lutheran bishops to be the intention of Ludwig Müller, which had meanwhile been announced, to retain his office as Land Bishop of the (United) Prussian Church even after his election as (Lutheran) Reich Bishop. Meiser was therefore commissioned to express to Ludwig Müller personally the conference's urgent wish that he resign this combination of offices.

However, the Prussian Land Bishop and future Reich Bishop had no thought of giving up his position of power in Prussia. So in his usual way he asked for time to think and promised to send a message next day. It never arrived. When the Lutheran bishops met again for discussion – in Wittenberg on 26 September, the day before the Synod – they found the situation in no way improved. On the contrary, they found that Ludwig Müller had also included Hossenfelder in the Clergy Ministry and that Hossenfelder also wanted to keep his office as Clergy Vice President of the Prussian Oberkirchenrat, which would in fact produce a triple connection between the Reich Church and the United Prussian Church. Ten church leaders, the most prominent of whom were Meiser, Marahrens, Wurm and Schöffel, thereupon entered a protest in the minutes against this 'endangering of the status of the confession which is guaranteed by the constitution of the German Evangelical Church'.[205] Since Ludwig Müller was once again unavailable to receive the protest and a public confrontation at the National Synod was to be avoided, on the morning of 27 September Meiser sent this declaration to Müller's permanent quarters in Wittenberg, the 'Golden Eagle', along with a detailed letter in which he once again made the 'most resolute protest possible' against the fact that the 'confessional-political situation within the new church was shifted to such a degree to the detriment of Lutheranism', and also registered certain misgivings about the person of Hossenfelder.[206]

Müller's colleagues from the Provisional Administration also endorsed these misgivings in a joint letter and declared themselves 'in no way' able to share 'in the responsibility for them'[207] – which did not prevent Schöffel entering the new Reich Church administration as a Lutheran the very same day.

Ludwig Müller, however, supported by the new German Christian bishops and with the goal tangibly before his eyes, now made very short work of the Lutheran church leaders. It appeared to him to be incompatible with the constitution, he wrote back immediately, 'to buy the election of the Reich Bishop through arrangements with church leaders who were appointed to make suggestions. It would go against the leadership principle expressed clearly in the constitution and would give rise to the dangers of electoral capitulation which are well known from church history.' He was not pressing for such a double office, he hypocritically maintained, and looked forward to the moment when he could devote himself 'exclusively to the whole church'; the choice of this moment should, however, be left to his 'responsible decision'. At the end of the letter he then added in his own hand one of those pious remarks with which he so readily and successfully deceived himself and others: 'The whole affair is ultimately a matter of trust. I ask you and the other Lutheran brother bishops to trust that I will conduct my office in deep awareness of my responsibility before God. – After all, we pray together to the same Father in Heaven – He will reveal the future ways – and we must walk them together full of trust and in brotherly love. John 13.34-35.'[208] Anyone who looked up the passage would find there Jesus' commandment to his disciples to love one another.

On the other side, too, among the German Christians the preparations for the National Synod were obviously just as difficult as for the Lutheran bishops. Here the Reich leadership and the 'Grand Council of Leaders' also met on the day before the Synod in order finally to sort out the composition of the government of the Reich Church.[209] Ludwig Müller's nomination as Reich Bishop was of course taken for granted, and as early as 26 September he held in his hand a telegram from the Reich Chancellery with the assurance that 'no objections would be raised' to his elections 'on the part of the Chancellor'.[210] However, the composition of the so-called Clergy Ministry, i.e. the Reich Church leadership, which according to Article 7.2 was to consist of three theologians and a trained lawyer, caused problems. For the three theological posts the Lutherans had suggested Schöffel, the United (i.e. Ludwig Müller himself) Hossenfelder and the Reformed Otto Weber, thirty-one and a secondary school teacher from Elberfeld. Apparently the controversial figure here was Schöffel, to whom a young radical German Christian Lutheran would certainly have been preferred. However, the struggle over the legal post, which in fact Jäger had originally earmarked for himself, was still more difficult. Evidently the Ministerial Director had made further attempts in Berlin to put pressure on Hossenfelder to nominate him for the highest legal office in the Reich Church in spite of the scandal in Hessen. But Hossenfelder stood fast and in so doing earned Jäger's implacable hatred. Instead of Jäger the young lawyer Dr Werner was nominated. Werner had kept himself inconspicuously and skilfully at the head of the Faith Movement and then also of the Prussian Church after the first Reich Conference, and thanks to these qualities he was also the only one to survive all the church upheavals down to the end of the war.[211] On the morning of 27 September Ludwig Müller

490

sent the final list of his first Clergy Ministry to the Reich Chancellery with the comment that Hossenfelder, Weber and Werner were Party colleagues and Schöffel was 'spiritually a National Socialist'; he vouched for those nominated. The Reich Chancellery thereupon immediately indicated Hitler's agreement by telegram.[212]

Thus nothing further stood in the way of the demonstration of unity.

'And then dawns the day, 27 September 1933! A splendid sun again smiles from the cloudless sky, and the bells ring festively and ceremonially. All of Wittenberg is on its feet. Shortly after eleven o'clock the huge procession starts to move to the Stadtkirche: the flags of the SA storm groups from Wittenberg, the flags of the Protestant youth organizations, of the craft guilds, of the associations; the theological faculties in festive robes, the clergy of Luther's city in gowns, the members of the Synod, the Lutherans in brown shirts, the bishops of the German Landeskirchen with the golden pectoral crosses of their office, and – the man whom all eyes seek in awe, inquiringly and full of hope: the future Reich Bishop Ludwig Müller.'[213]

To anyone who kept to the outward picture the whole affair could indeed have seemed to be a festive high point. But the Potemkinesque character of this event could not remain hidden from anyone who did not allow himself to be blinded. Although only the evening before in a 'weighty report of activities' Hossenfelder had set the National Socialist Party and the Faith Movement of German Christians side by side, the struggle for one Volk and the struggle for one church,[214] Party and state showed virtually no interest in the Reich Church. That Hitler had declined his invitation was understandable.[215] But it was a critical sign that none of the invited Ministers appeared – no Secretary of State, no official representative of the Party; only one ministerial councillor as a representative of Papen and the appropriate civil servants of the Ministry of the Interior, among them Dr Buttmann and Dr Conrad, had been entered in the lists of the guests of honour.[216] Moreover, the festive procession of flags, uniforms and gowns which moved to the Schlosskirche did not remain undisturbed. On the edge of the street, among the spectators, stood Niemöller, Jacobi, Bonhoeffer, Hildebrandt and others who had driven over early that morning from Berlin, and they pressed into the hands of the surprised participants a petition to the National Synod from two thousand pastors. Later the members of the Synod also found this petition on their desks, and soon it hung throughout the city on trees, telegraph poles and the walls of buildings. It represented the first public protest of the Pastors Emergency League and expressed what no one wanted to say in Wittenberg itself: 'The National Synod should not give the impression of a united church through its festal character so long as its communities are torn apart by the deepest divisions.' There followed a list of the most important points to which there were objections: the pressure of violence on church life; the Aryan Paragraph's contradiction of scripture and confession; the endangering of the church's ministry. The petition then appropriately repeated the commitment of the Pastors Emergency League and concluded: 'So we will not cease to fight against everything that destroys the very nature of the church. We will not cease to raise objections loudly and clearly to every violation of the confession. We will not cease to work unswervingly, in true obedience to our ordination vows, for the building up of the German Evangelical Church.'[217] This petition could not change the external course of the National Synod in any way. But it became significant because it showed those at home and abroad that the picture of unity was deceptive, that there could be no talk of an uncontested victory of the German Christians, and that there was an opposition which knew what it wanted and was willing to stand up for it.[218]

Land Bishop Wurm preached at the festal service. The remark of a female observer was precisely to the point: 'He had the beautiful text about the marriage garment, but he made no further use of it at all.' So the attention of the congregation apparently turned more to the 'theological storm troops' which Land Bishop Coch of Saxony had organized from theology students. In field grey uniform, with a purple cross and the SS runes on their arms and heavy field packs on their backs, these theological storm troops stood in the choir throughout the service and in their own way demonstrated the new era in the church.[219]

After a short meeting in the morning for the Provisional Administration's report of activities, the synod adjourned until the actual voting in the afternoon. 'At 5.55,' so the official report described the proceedings, 'the guests, the press and the sixty members of the National Synod are assembled in their places in the Stadtkirche. The lights of the great chandeliers flare out; the sound of the organ floods through the church. Professor Fezer, on behalf of the Provisional Administration of the German Evangelical Church, steps to the lectern and announces that Land Bishop Ludwig Müller has been nominated unanimously as Reich Bishop by all the leaders of the Landeskirchen. At this moment the whole assembly rises silently in their places. "I ask the Synod for a declaration of its will," rings out the voice of Professor Fezer round the church. A unanimous "Yes" is the answer. Then objections are asked for. Anyone against should raise his hand. Not a movement. *Ludwig Müller has been elected Reich Bishop unanimously by the First German Evangelical Reich Synod. Protestant Germany has its Führer.*'[220]

Ludwig Müller had achieved his goal.

Immediately afterwards the new Reich Bishop summonded the members of the Clergy Ministry and delivered his first, tensely-awaited declaration of principles.

Its tone was courteous. Yet it contained, unchanged, a confession of the mission of the church in the Third Reich, a cautious but clear affirmation of the Aryan Paragraph, and an unqualified declaration of confidence in the new state. The declaration concluded with three evocative sentences which were often quoted later, and with which Ludwig Müller might certainly have hoped to silence all resistance: 'The Old is ending,' he exclaimed; 'the New is dawning. The church-political struggle is over. The struggle for the soul of the Volk is beginning.'[221]

At the sentence 'the church-political struggle is over,' Jacobi later reported, 'Bonhoeffer in the gallery gave a short sharp laugh...'[222]

In fact it soon proved that the struggle was not over at all.

11

Catholicism after the Concordat
(September 1933-January 1934)

In autumn 1933 the church question in the Third Reich appeared to be settled politically. On 10 September the Reich concordat had been ratified in Rome and had thus taken on legal status. Scarcely three weeks later the Evangelical National Synod had met in Wittenberg and, with the election of the first Reich Bishop, had completed the reconstruction of the Protestant church. Hitler's will had evidently triumphed. For it had unquestionably been his will that Catholicism had to thank for the concordat and Protestantism for the Reich Church. And his will alone had made it possible for this to be implemented in just a few months, between March and September, contrary to all experience.

However, the political parallel disguised the fact that the Reich concordat and the Reich Church formed two completely different starting points.

In the hierarchical episcopal church of German Catholicism, the concordat was never in doubt for a single moment. Although previously there might have been voices among the bishops which were thoroughly critical of the timing and circumstances of this treaty, once it was concluded every critic fell silent. Instead, confidence in the decision of the Holy See increased, the more it became clear how great the threat to the existence of believing Catholicism in the Third Reich remained. Of course the German bishops were not unanimous about everything. On the contrary, complaints of disunity were the order of the day in autumn and winter 1933. But this disunity was always confined to assessments of the situation and the tactics to be adopted. The leadership of the Vatican was never in question even to the slightest degree, nor were the basic points of the treaty. Archbishop Gröber of Freiburg was quite correct in this respect when at the end of the year in a long personal letter among other things he assured the papal Secretary of State that in his opinion 'the disunity among the German bishops, already complained about from several directions', was 'not inward but purely outward and accidental', conditioned by the different situations in the dioceses and the different levels of information.[1] In fact, if there was one comfort for German Catholicism at this time it was that the church stood united, unassailed and secure in its basic principles.

The situation on the Protestant side was quite different. The new Reich Church constitution, passed precipitately under political pressure, had solved none of the problems which had impeded the unity of German Protestantism for generations. Neither the relationship of the Landeskirchen to the Reich Church nor the relationship of the confessions to one another had been settled. The legal relationship of the church to the state had also been left open, and was still to be defined in a church treaty. In all of these questions, concerned with the basic understanding of the church, there were far-reaching differences of opinion within German Protestantism, which were by no means removed during the negotiations on the constitution, but only postponed. The office of Reich Bishop, the only really new institution which the church constitution had produced and on which many hopes were thus pinned, had neither a tradition nor a serious theological foundation in the pastors' and theologians' church of German Protestantism. So despite the strong legal position which he had been given in the new church constitution, the Reich Bishop remained dependent upon the consent and agreement of the church public. The sort of obedience which could be taken for granted, as was accorded the Catholic hierarchy in decisive matters, was unthinkable in the Protestant church. In contrast to the conclusive character of the Reich concordat, the founding of the Reich Church was not so much a conclusion as a beginning. For its foundation set in motion a development that was to lead to an entirely new understanding of the church in German Protestantism, and also in due course to a new understanding of the state. While on the Catholic side a rumbling skirmish began over the principles for interpreting the concordat, on the Protestant side there was a theological and church-political battle over the basic understanding of the church itself, which seized and changed the Protestant church at its deepest level. And enviable though the closed ranks and firmness of the Catholic church seemed to many Protestants, at the end of the year the Swiss Church President Alphons Koechlin could nevertheless report about 'prominent Roman Catholics who expressed the opinion that with voices like those of Karl Barth and others, and with their fight for the independence of church life, the Protestant churches were standing up much better than the Roman Catholic Church, which in spite of the concordat had lost the chance openly and freely to utter its convictions about the life of the nation'.[2]

The conclusion of legal and political developments with the ratification of the Reich concordat did not, of course, mean that all questions between the National Socialist state and the Catholic Church were instantly resolved. On the contrary, from the very first day it became evident that a whole series of party and government officials scarcely felt themselves bound by the concordat and went on unhindered with their old battle against the hated Catholic church. What made the situation so difficult for the church in all this was the fact that this evidently happened without any unified plan. This created such varied conditions in different parts of Germany that it made a united programme extraordinarily difficult.

From the start the most important point of dispute was Article 31, which was meant to secure state protection for Catholic organizations and associations.[3] Here the interests of the state and those of the church overlapped to the greatest extent. While the church was of course interested in achieving the co-ordination of all organizations and associations, for the church it seemed almost a matter of life and death to retain at least this support in the public sphere after the demise of the Centre Party. Article 31 had created two categories of association: in the first paragraph purely religious associations, which were to have total protection; and in the second paragraph those with a social or professional focus, for which relative protection had been provided 'without prejudice to possible

494

inclusion in state associations'. The business of these categories appeared difficult enough, given the different kinds of interest. But it now proved fatal that Rome had relied on a future agreement between the Reich government and the German bishops on this question and had not even insisted on basic lists before ratification of the concordat. For as long as this agreement did not exist, it could be argued from the state side that the associations were unprotected; so nothing was more natural than that the negotiations over the agreement should be delayed until the most important associations had dissolved themselves automatically under the massive pressure and been co-ordinated and Article 31 had thus lost its significance.

While the Reich Ministry of the Interior was concerned to fulfil the concordat provisions as quickly and as loyally as it could, and on 18 September Buttmann had already inquired in Rome whether the papal Secretary of State was ready for negotiations to complete the Reich concordat, a series of Land governments created thoroughly anti-Catholic conditions.[4] Bavaria proved to be the most radical of them.[5] Thus a good deal of the concern of state and church was initially devoted to the Bavarian situation.

The Council of Ministers and the Reich governor in Munich were under the influence of the Gauleiter and Minister of the Interior, Adolf Wagner, and of the Political Police, which under the leadership of Himmler and Heydrich began to develop into a tool for the suppression of Catholicism. While immediately after the ratification of the concordat some relaxation of tension had made itself felt even in Bavaria, the Political Police struck a heavy blow on 19 September. Referring to the continuing lack of agreement over Article 31, a circular not only explicitly confirmed the 13 and 20 June bans on meetings but made them even stricter. The only permissible activities were 'choir practices which are absolutely necessary and to a limited degree meetings of the leaders of the St Vincent Associations to deal with requests for help'.[6]

This was such an obvious and blatant assault on the spirit of the concordat as soon as the circular became known that there were vigorous reactions on every side. On 25 September Vicar General Riemer of Passau informed the Berlin Nuncio Cesare Orsenigo, the Vice-Chancellor, and the two episcopal representatives for negotiations with the government, Bishops Gröber and Berning, about the Bavarian situation and asked for appropriate steps to be taken 'so that through the Reich government just treatment – i.e. in accordance with the concordat – may be secured for the Catholic associations in Bavaria as well'.[7] Soon afterwards Berning, who was specifically responsible for compiling the lists of associations, was personally put in the picture over the situation in Bavaria by a leading member of the Bavarian committee of associations. This made it clear how varied the situation in Germany actually was. Berning was apparently flabbergasted and declared that the circular was 'incomprehensible' to him; there were 'no complaints' anywhere in Prussia in this respect. Moreover he astonished the Bavarian delegate by saying that if he had known all this he would naturally have speeded up the negotiations; the list of associations had been completed three weeks before and was circulating among the several Land governments.[8] Nevertheless Berning now wrote to Buttmann immediately, and received from him by return the confirmation he sought, namely that Buttmann had already made contact with the Reich government representative in Munich 'in order to point out that such decrees went against the Reich concordat'. The Reich Ministry of the Interior would see to it that once the protected societies had finally been listed, 'the provisions of the concordat' would 'be stringently observed towards them'.[9]

But this by no means ended the course of protests. Faulhaber, who had been deeply affected by the whole situation, now requested and received the support of the Munich Nuncio Vasallo di Torregrossa, who on 4 October personally delivered a protest note to the Bavarian chancellery. It was stated that the 19 September decree was 'synonymous with the destruction of the entire life of the Catholic societies' and was thus 'in absolute contradiction to the Reich concordat'. Unless the Bavarian government repealed the decree completely and officially, the Holy See would make an 'energetic protest' to the Reich government. Attached to it was a memorandum by the Munich Vicar General Ferdinand Buchwieser, which went in detail into the ban on assemblies, the discrimination against members of Catholic organizations, the prohibition of uniform, the confiscation of the property of Catholic associations, and other complaints, and in general gave a depressing picture of the situation of the Catholic associations.[10]

While the situation in Bavaria involved direct violation of rights under the concordat, the list of the serious issues that Bertram gave the Pope during his *ad limina* visit of 4 October dealt more with the general difficulties which the Catholic Church faced in the Third Reich even after the conclusion of the Reich concordat. Among the twelve points, Bertram started with 'basic errors in the broadest circles of National Socialism', and mentioned first the 'totalitarian claims of the state, characterized by nationalist and völkisch tendencies', with all the consequences that this had for state, family and public life. The problem of church associations followed as Point 2, and Point 3 was about the restrictions on the Catholic press, which Bertram adjudged 'worse than the pressure on the press during the Prussian Kulturkampf'. The cardinal also complained about the dismissal of Catholic civil servants, the violation of the sanctity of Sunday, and the difficulties of Catholic theology students. He rejected the application of the Aryan paragraph to Catholic teachers and resisted the complete take-over of charitable work by the state. A kind of concluding statement argued that 'this would complete the confinement of the church to the sacristy'. Finally, he perceived the first serious conflict as arising in the 'Law for the Prevention of Offspring with Hereditary Diseases', the so-called sterilization law, which conflicted directly with the encyclical *Casti Connubii*.[11]

On the whole, Bertram's memorandum presented a remarkably realistic picture of the situation. And it was known in Rome that a majority of the German bishops agreed with this view of things. Nevertheless, it was found very difficult to come to an unequivocal decision. For a minority, whose spokesman was Archbishop Gröber of Freiburg, vigorously contradicted Bertram, who was always apprehensive, and his followers. Gröber had outstanding contacts with the Curia. Personal friendships bound him to Kaas, who was still functioning as a versatile negotiator, and to Robert Leiber, Pacelli's closest colleague. Nor was his opinion without influence upon the Cardinal Secretary of State himself.[12] Where Bertram saw only difficulties, expressed misgivings and counselled restraint, Gröber represented the opposite opinion: that openness and a dependable co-operation within the Third Reich was equally decisive for state and church. And in public, too, he left no doubt about this conviction. Thus on 10 October, i.e. about the same time as Bertram was presenting his memorandum in Rome, at a Catholic mass meeting in Karlsruhe Gröber was thanking 'the government men' for their attendance. 'I am betraying no secret,' he then went on, 'in declaring that in the course of recent months dealings between the church administration in Freiburg and the government in Karlsruhe have been most friendly. Nor do I think that I am betraying any secrets to them and to the German people if I say that I unreservedly support the new government and the new Reich.'[13]

These utterances not only represented Gröber's convictions; with them he associated the hope that this openness would lead to a good relationship with the state and an improvement in the general church situation. Nor did this appear to be mere fantasy. For instance, that same 9 October the Baden Minister of the Interior informed his colleagues in the Kultusministerium that he intended to instruct the Land police no longer to permit any more illegal acts against Catholic priests. It was 'in the interest of making peace between the nationalist movement and the Catholic priesthood... to draw a line under the past and to give an opportunity to priests who had been hostile to the national movement before the conclusion of the concordat to conduct themselves loyally now the concordat is in force'. In his response the Kultusminister held this to be 'not only desirable but urgently necessary'. In the future care must quite emphatically be taken that 'the use of force against the clergy which is often so popular' should be refrained from because this 'stands in the crudest contrast to the provisions of the concordat' and could give rise to 'foreign policy difficulties'.[14] Thereupon, in fact, a broader, tangible peace began in Baden. What made the picture so confusing for the Curia was that Gröber, with his view of things, could point to tangible successes, and this did not help to decide whether developments in Germany might not be more easily improved by openness than by mistrustful resistance.

This openness was also to be helped by another process, which took place at the same time and was hardly calculated to clarify the confusing picture. For not only did Gröber see things this way but Papen, the Vice-Chancellor, also watched the heightening of tensions with concern. In the spring, at the beginning of April, he had already attempted to gain support for his politics by means of his own organization, the League of Catholic Germans, under the resounding title 'Cross and Eagle'.[15] Now, in the changed circumstances, there was reason to found a new organization which could relate more readily to the Party and stand more openly for the aims of the new state. Evidently under the impact of the growing difficulties, most untimely at this particular point, Hitler approved the plan. Thus 3 October saw the founding of the Arbeitsgemeinschaft katholischer Deutschen, AKD for short. The Arbeitsgemeinschaft seemed in many ways to be a kind of counterpart to the German Christian Faith Movement. At least the German Christian model was betrayed by the fact that the call for its founding came from the Party chancellery and was signed by the deputy Führer, Rudolf Hess. Its aims, too, were like those of the Protestant movement, carried over into a Catholic setting. As was said in the call for its founding, the association was: 1. 'To strengthen national consciousness among the Catholic part of the

Volk, to deepen and augment honourable and unqualified collaboration with National Socialism, to enlarge the ranks of active Party supporters' and 2. 'In particular to provide for a clear relationship between church, state and NSDAP to the last detail, to do away with misunderstandings from the start, and to nip in the bud all attempts to bring about discord.' Taught by the difficulties which had arisen from the agitation of the German Christians, the Brown House, however, had made it clear that the Party would tolerate no competition. As it stated, the Arbeitsgemeinschaft was 'no mass organization'; it refrained 'from mass recruitment' and did not accept 'corporate membership'. The leadership consisted entirely of 'tried warriors'. Those named were Hans Dauser, the Bavarian Secretary of State; the former Major Hermann von Detten, who was later also to play a role in the church politics of the Third Reich; and Rudolf zur Bonsen, President of the Cologne administration. In these circumstances the Party leadership was able to instruct its membership 'to support the Arbeits-gemeinschaft in its activity at every opportunity'.[16] This created the same vague relationship to the Party as that of the German Christians. And like that movement, the Arbeitsgemeinschaft also sought to build up an organization like that of the Party, in that Papen as a kind of 'Reich supremo' nominated 'Gau deputies' for NSDAP Gaue.[17] That, however, exhausted the similarities. Papen's leadership, the restrictions on a basis for agitation, and not least the situation of the Catholic Church, from the start ruled out the possibility of the Arbeitsgemein-schaft taking over on the Catholic side the kind of revolutionary role played by the German Christians on the Protestant side during the summer.

Naturally the response in German Catholicism to the founding of the Arbeits-gemeinschaft was divided. Whether in fact, as the *Germania* of 28 October claimed, a flood of applications was sent in in the very first days cannot be checked.[18] Precisely because of the stance of many university theologians, the possibility cannot be excluded. Certainly it was no accident that Papen's programmatic speech to the Arbeitsgemeinschaft in Cologne appeared in the same series, Reich und Kirche, as that in which the contributions of Michael Schmaus and Josef Lortz had been published,[19] and that the Catholic Vice-Chancellor expressly referred to the 'list of well-known theologians' who had recently devoted their efforts to deepening 'the encounter between Catholic Christianity and the National Socialist world-view'.[20]

The reactions among the bishops clearly differed. Cardinal Bertram, whom Papen had told about the new association on 3 October, at the same time pleading 'for the full and unreserved support and co-operation of the episcopate and clergy', responded with marked reserve. His letter consisted merely of reser-vations and scruples and indicated clearly that he considered the new venture to be totally superfluous.[21] Gröber reacted quite differently. When the Reich Executive Director of the Arbeitsgemeinschaft, Roderick Graf Thun, asked the Archbishop of Freiburg for 'some encouraging and challenging words' for the first number of the newsletter, the Archbishop responded immediately. He assured the AKD that he 'honestly' welcomed its founding and wished it the 'widest spread'.[22] This in turn irritated Archbishop Klein of Paderborn so much that he complained bitterly to Bertram about Gröber's new commendation, 'which was disapproved of in many Catholic circles'.[23]

In spite of all the efforts of Gröber and Papen, by the middle of October things were heading for an explosion – in view of the increasingly unpleasant reports from Germany. On 11 October Leiber hastily told the Archbishop of Freiburg that the Prussian bishops, who had been in Rome that week, almost all took a 'very pessimistic' view of the situation, and the Pope would probably, not least because of Bertram's memorandum, 'bring up for discussion in the next consistory the relationship of the Catholic church to National Socialism as a world-view'.[24] The German Embassy at the Holy See also showed alarm. On 12 October a detailed report from the ambassador on 'the attitude of the episcopate to the general church situation in Germany since the conclusion of the concordat' was sent on to the Foreign Office. This report, which Bergen had again taken over virtually word for word from Kaas, whether through haste or complacency, noted an unmistakable 'setback in feelings' among the bishops during the previous months and contained a full collection of complaints which obviously stemmed directly from Bertram's memorandum. The Ambassador did not yet seem to take really seriously a hint by Kaas that if something did not happen soon the Vatican, 'under pressure from the official reports of the Nuncio and the bishops arriving here from Germany, as well as other news', would come out with 'undesirable declarations', as these were abruptly deleted.[25] Shortly afterwards, however, he was told personally by the Cardinal Secretary of State that the Pope had indicated his intention to make a sharp protest 'against the steadily increasing infringements of the concordat and pressures against Catholics, in spite of all the official German promises', and that he planned 'to make a public stand in an address... against the things that had happened in Germany'.[26]

Even in normal circumstances this report would no doubt have caused real concern in Berlin. But on the afternoon of 14 October when the telegram from the German embassy at the Vatican reached the Foreign Office, it acted as an alarm signal. For that same afternoon a foreign policy decision had been announced, the effect of which was still quite unpredictable: the German resignation from the League of Nations. With this decision Hitler had taken a risk that made it seem urgently advisable to eliminate where possible all causes of conflict, both internal and external. It had also created a new situation for all participants in the concordat: the Curia, the bishops, the Reich government and the governments of the Länder. It demonstrated almost paradigmatically both the possibilities and the limitations of the concordat church.

Hitler's decision had a long prehistory. In the first seven months of his rule the Chancellor had stayed out of foreign affairs completely. With the exception of the Reich concordat, which, however, seemed conceived above all in the light of internal political considerations, he had undertaken no substantive initiatives. Even the famous peace speech to the Reichstag on 17 May, which brought him the assent of all groups, seemed to contain no new ideas. Yet in this speech he had already set in place the lever which he would use in the autumn to take European security politics off its hinges, to broaden the scope of Germany's foreign policy at a stroke and at the same time to make his domestic political position virtually unassailable: the question of equal international rights for Germany.

The strength of this position for domestic and foreign policy lay in the fact that at this point Germany without doubt had moral justification on its side. The

499

heart of the problem was the arms limitation which had been imposed on the German Reich by the Treaty of Versailles, and which in fact left the country virtually defenceless. This arms limitation inevitably seemed even more of a discrimination against Germany, the less the other powers showed themselves ready and able to reach agreements on disarmament themselves. So it was the truth when in this convention on 17 May Hitler called the demand 'for a tangible expression of equal rights in concrete form a moral, legitimate and rational demand', and he was right when he went on to say that 'the disqualification of a great nation' could not be maintained 'historically, for all eternity'.[27] And this remained true and right even if Hitler misused the arguments for purposes which no longer had anything to do with truth and justice. In May Hitler already indicated his point of view when he declared that the German government and the German Volk would 'in no circumstances let themselves be coerced to some signing or other that would mean a permanent disqualification of Germany'. If this were nevertheless attempted, say by means of a majority ruling in the disarmament conference, then Germany would abandon its co-operation and leave the League of Nations.[28]

The fact that Hitler had evidently already fastened on this point during the summer explains why the Reich government pressed so hard for ratification of the concordat. For in the autumn it had to put to the test for the first time the larger, much more important question of the future role of Germany. On 12 September, two days after the exchange of documents in Rome, the Minister of Foreign Affairs gave the Reich cabinet a first report on the new session of the League of Nations in Geneva to open on the 22nd. The situation was grim. The atmosphere in Geneva was bad, the Minister reported, with attacks on Germany to be expected because of the Jewish issue. At the present time the League of Nations was achieving virtually nothing. Nevertheless Neurath advised against leaving the field without a battle. Only with a 'total collapse of the disarmament conference' would the time be ripe to leave the League of Nations.[29]

Although in Geneva it was clear very early on that on the disarmament question a hard line would again be taken against Germany, and that a further extension of the discrimination against the Germans must be expected,[30] towards the end of the month Hitler was still weighing all his options carefully. On the 30th the Foreign Minister noted as the Chancellor's opinion 'that in any case it would be desirable to hold a disarmament conference, even if not all of our wishes were fulfilled at it'.[31] This radical shift may have been caused by a report from London, which brought about precisely the situation which Hitler had foreseen in May and from which he had urged drawing the appropriate conclusions. Specifically, the German embassy reported that the British government believed that it could 'force through' a new draft convention against Germany at the negotiating table, because 'Germany today is weaker in foreign affairs than ever before, being not only disarmed but isolated'.[32]

Now Hitler threw the helm right over. And as always, everything moved very fast. On the evening of 11 October the German delegation in Geneva discovered that a German withdrawal from the disarmament conference was possible.[33] Two days later Hitler informed the cabinet. Following his unmistakable political style with its unique mixture of delay and decision, he stated: 'In such a situation, driven by the course of events, one must resolve to act. The path of negotiation is now terminated.'[34] This statement had the same finality about it as the one that was uttered almost exactly six years later, 'Since 5.45 a.m. we have been returning fire', also in substance as a result of the decision of 11 October 1933.[35]

Soon afterwards, Hitler made clear to the President of the Danzig Senate, Hermann Rauschning, that he did not just intend this decision as a political manoeuvre but also meant it to change the whole political situation. What he said there no doubt went to the heart of the whole action. 'I had to do it... A grand, universally intelligible liberating action was necessary. I had to tear the German Volk out of this whole clinging net of dependencies, slogans and false ideas, and regain the capacity for us to act. I am not concerned here with everyday politics. For the time being the difficulties may become greater. That must be balanced out against the trust which I am gaining among the German Volk as a result.'[36]

In order to make this trust visible externally as well as internally, Hitler seized upon a surprising method. He submitted his decision to leave the League of Nations to a plebiscite and combined the issue with new elections to the Reichstag. The German public discovered all this on 14 October, and from this moment until 12 November, the day of the elections, the entire public life of Germany was dominated by the plebiscite. Although there could be no doubt as to the outcome of the plebiscite, and for the election there was only the united list of the Party, a propaganda campaign began which the British ambassador in Berlin in a report dated 15 November quite rightly regarded as being 'without parallel'.[37] Hitler himself opened it with a speech over all German radio stations on the evening of 14 October. In it he affirmed peace, honour and equal rights as being the foundations of any continuing international order. And he concluded, 'may this mighty proclamation of peace and honour by our people succeed in giving to the internal relationship between the European states that foundation which is necessary not only to end centuries of discord and strife but also in rebuilding a better community: the recognition of a higher common duty arising out of common equal rights'.[38] After 22 October he appeared nearly every day at mass meetings throughout the country. He spoke in Berlin, Hanover, Cologne and Stuttgart; in Weimar, Breslau, Kiel and Munich. He ended with an election speech to the workers of the Siemens factory in Berlin. The British ambassador called Hitler's appearance in the giant dynamo hall of the factory, where he campaigned from a platform for the votes of workers throughout Germany, a moment 'which was unforgettable'.[39] Along with Hitler, the entire Party threw itself into the election campaign and until 12 November turned Germany into a sea of flags, slogans, meetings and proclamations.

Without question, the resignation from the League of Nations was extraordinarily popular in Germany. For far too long people had felt Germany to be the whipping boy of the world. Now a kind of sigh of relief in fact passed through the German people. How completely this was the case for both churches as well is shown by two telegrams sent to Hitler on 15 October: the agreement in their content betrays the unity of convictions among Catholic and Protestant Christians on this point. For Catholic Action in the Berlin diocese, Capitular Vicar Paul Steinmann and Chairman Erich Klausner sent a telegram: 'In the hours of our nation's destiny the Catholics of the Berlin diocese, in unshakable love for Volk and fatherland, stand solidly behind the Führer and Chancellor in his fight for the equal rights and the honour of the nation, and the restoration of a just peace between the nations.'[40] And five Berlin pastors, among them Martin Niemöller, Fritz Müller and Eberhard Röhricht from Dahlem, sent a similar telegram the same day for the Pastors Emergency League which was in process of being set up: 'At this decisive hour for Volk and fatherland we greet our Führer. We give thanks for the manly action and the clear word which safeguard Germany's honour. In the name of more than 2500 Protestant pastors who do not belong to the Faith Movement of German Christians we pledge loyal obedience and remembrance in prayers.'[41] Of course the two telegrams did not represent all Christians in Germany, but they did represent a large majority, Catholic as well as Protestant.

The decision of 14 October in fact influenced the church situation too, deeply and permanently. While – as we shall see – on the Protestant side the Reich Bishop attempted to shore up the already shaky structure of the Reich Church with the slogan of national unity, Hitler's decision seemed at first to open up new and favourable prospects for Catholic church politics. For apparently the need to get the support of the whole people at this moment would inevitably make Hitler and the Party more responsive to the remonstrations and protests of the bishops. At least that is evidently how it seemed to the Archbishop of Freiburg when on the evening of 14 October he replied to Robert Leiber's warning of the 11th from Rome: 'I meant to reply this morning, but it was a good thing that I didn't... an entirely new situation, which will also substantially influence what you have written to me about. Perhaps now is the time to gain what could not be achieved before the ratification...'[42]

In Rome, Pacelli was clearly now at the helm. The Cardinal Secretary of State would only give up the threatened public declaration by the Pope and the protest note that was also threatened in exchange for a promise that the representative of the Reich government, Ministerial Director Rudolf Buttmann, would come to Rome without delay and deal with the whole range of complaints. After a fruitless discussion on the 16th, on the 17th the German ambassador yielded to Pacelli's conditions and asked Berlin to send the German negotiatiors 'as fast as possible'.[43] The next day Hitler instructed Buttmann to travel to Rome 'in the course of this week' – which meant the next day or the day after.[44] Buttmann in fact set out on 20 October and reached Rome on the 22nd, after a short stop in Munich.[45]

Pacelli had meanwhile prepared a clear memorandum. It was the first official complaint that the Reich government received from the Vatican, and in style as well as in its manner of arguing it was typical of a long series of similar messages which from now on would be exchanged between the Holy See and the Reich government with almost monotonous regularity. In the first place the Holy See warned the German government against continuing the 'often clearly planned reduction of the assets of the Catholic part of the German people, publicly defined and protected according to treaty by the signing of the concordat', and then enumerated the acknowledged complaints in nine points: 'the suppression and repression of Catholic societies and organizations by all possible means', 'the deliberate paralysis, economic destruction and indeed fettering of the views of the Catholic press', 'the dismissal without compensation of countless Catholic civil servants, administrators and trade union secretaries', the failure to observe the sanctity of Sunday, the demands made on Catholic students of theology, the confiscation of church assets, the 'attempted application of the so-called Aryan Paragraph to members of the priesthood', the endangering of Catholic confessional schools, the compulsory course in ideological training and finally the sterilization law. The document ended in typical curial style: 'Unless the convincing language of facts soon makes sufficiently clear to the Catholic world that the justified claims of the Catholic Church have been met, the Holy See will not be able to avoid making known, in whatever way seems appropriate to it, what it has done in the interest of peace, justice and freedom, and to indicate that a silence on the part of the supreme office of the church which glosses over offences against justice and against the freedom of the church and its members in Germany which have not been done away with cannot prevent their well-deserved condemnation.'[46]

Buttmann, to whom the document was given immediately on his arrival, thus knew what awaited him when on 23 October he met the Papal Secretary of State for the first round of negotiations. The situation of the German negotiator was tricky. Personally loyal throughout, and concerned to safeguard the rights of the church within the terms of the concordat, he was just as critical of many things as the Catholic side but had no chance of making his view felt. So one of Pacelli's first questions was directed at the contradiction between Hitler's purported good will and the deeds of his subordinate leaders. Buttmann answered, not unskilfully, that two-thirds of the Germans were Protestant and did not want to know about the concordat, and that by no means all Catholics were in agreement with it either, so that the Chancellor was having to deal with 'tremendous resistance' in implementing the concordat.[47] Considering the many currents in the Party, this was no doubt the truth, although it omitted the fact that Hitler, too, had only a political interest in the concordat. Then Kaas, whom Pacelli had brought in in the meantime, spoke on the point which was now most important to negotiating tactics: the plebiscite of 12 November. This must, Kaas felt, call for 'a moderate attitude towards the Catholic section of the people'. But here, as in all other matters, Buttmann kept things so general that in the end the consultation ended without concrete results.

This day also saw the end of the remarkable role played by Prelate Kaas. Buttmann categorically rejected his offer to work out a position statement. At the same time the German negotiator requested that the former Chairman of the Centre Party be no longer involved in the official negotiations. And in fact his name disappeared from the protocol after the end of the year.[48] Obviously Kaas still had many contacts, but the very speed with which things changed in Germany meant that he gradually disappeared from view. Later, at the request of Pacelli, who also remained loyal to him as Pope, he undertook the excavations in St Peter's, Rome, and in so doing discovered the disputed grave of Peter. He died in Rome in 1952.

At the second discussion, on 25 October, in which the Archbishop of Freiburg took part as a representative of the German episcopate, there were vigorous arguments about how Article 31 was to be implemented. When Buttmann indicated that the Catholic youth organizations, like all other youth organizations, could be incorporated by law into the Hitler Youth, the Cardinal Secretary of State declared this to be 'an open breach of the concordat by the Reich government, which would be intolerable for the Curia'.[49]

Only the third round of negotiations, on 27 October, showed definite progress. Buttmann confirmed the validity of the principles of interpretation on 20 July and also promised before 12 November to examine any specific infringements, which were to be pointed out to the Ministry of the Interior as soon as possible.[50] In return, Gröber promised to stir the German bishops to make a statement on the plebiscite. Whereas the Papal Secretary of State summed up the results of the discussion on the principles of interpretation in writing on 28 October, on the evening of the 27th Gröber had already reported the agreements arrived at to the chairmen of the two German bishops' conferences, Bertram and Faulhaber, by express letter. The submission of complaints, he wrote, should follow 'in the next few days', because what position the German bishops took in reference to 12 November would depend upon that. The government would welcome a proclamation from the bishops 'as a national act at the highest level'. Of course the concerns and misgivings here could not be hidden; but in his opinion a proclamation 'could not be avoided'. The difficulty in which the German bishops found themselves here became evident in the remark that it would be a matter of 'reconciling episcopal dignity with love of fatherland, and combining the pain over things that have taken place in recent times with trust in a speedy end to them'.[51]

In view of the overall situation it would perhaps in fact have been possible to extract specific promises along these lines from the Reich government. But that would have required united negotiation by the German bishops, and such unity was out of the question. Gröber himself had contributed to the confusion because in his haste he had forgotten to advise the recipients of his letter that he was communicating with both simultaneously. So Bertram sent the news from Rome to the German bishops on 30 October, and a couple of days later Faulhaber did exactly the same thing.

The old tensions between the two German bishops' conferences, the shortness of time, the vastly different situations in the different dioceses, and not least the pressure on everyone concerned – all this combined from the very beginning to negate a common approach. Thus, instead of the action planned step by step, there were a series of very different episcopal declarations which certainly did not contribute to a strengthening of the church front. Kaas was right when he reported from Rome four weeks later that 'the misused approach by the bishops over the elections' have 'made a sorry impression here, and not just here. The Vatican, the government or NSDAP, and the Catholic people are all more or less dissatisfied with it – albeit for different reasons.'[52]

In fact, the different opinions of their bishops could not but confuse the German Catholics. The Archbishop of Freiburg went furthest. Although he and Berning had achieved nothing, or virtually nothing, in Berlin at the beginning of November – a small concession from the Reich government over the regulations governing the implementation of the sterilization law was hardly worth mentioning[53] – on 8 November he issued an appeal calling on Catholics for unqualified support of the government. 'Equal rights, peace and work' were 'three goals' congruent with 'both national honour and the Christian law of morality and the law of nations'. 'Therefore it seems to us a patriotic duty to

504

accord the German fatherland and Volk loyalty and love in the present hour of destiny, as in the past, and on 1 November to give evidence of that united feeling with the rest of our fellow countrymen.' Gröber's conviction that trust and openness had to be displayed was shown clearly at the end of the appeal: 'Here we trust the Chancellor's statement that now at last a line has been drawn under the past, which is so painful to many true citizens, and that for us Catholics the peaceful work of the concordat has been guaranteed, to the exclusion of deletions, reinterpretations and infringements.'[54] Rottenburg, Berlin, Paderborn and Osnabrück joined in this appeal.[55]

Bertram's proposal was more restrained. Somewhat morosely he had informed the bishops that he would prefer 'not to take part in such a declaration as that on 12 November which dealt with purely political matters, in order to avoid creating a precedent for any other situations which might occur in the new Reich and could be even more difficult.' But he would submit to the will of the majority. His draft declaration distinguished between the Reichstag election and the plebiscite. As the final text put it, the former was left to the conscience and discernment of the voters as 'the purely political aspect of this vote...'; in connection with the latter, on the other hand, the Cardinal drew attention to the duty 'of protecting the authority of the government according to one's best knowledge and conscience, and of supporting those efforts – which were also encouraged by the bishops at all times – to restore Germany's equal rights in the family of nations, furthering work in the fatherland and preserving peace'. Compared with the memorandum which Bertram had delivered only four weeks earlier in Rome, however, the Cardinal sounded astonishingly mild when with just a single phrase he referred 'to that basis of inner peace... which consists of protection of religion, freedom for a full development of all branches of church life, the education of all in Christian morality, and equally favourable treatment of all subjects who are loyal to the fatherland.'[56] Only someone who knew exactly what was going on could discern the Cardinal's accusations behind these general remarks.

Worst of all, however, was the situation in Bavaria. To be sure, the combined efforts of Buttmann and Papen, who in mid-October had been fully informed of the Bavarian situation by the active head of the Munich chapter, Johannes Neuhausler, achieved an initial success to the extent that on 25 October the Bavarian cabinet declared that the Bavarian state government was 'ready for its part to do everything to implement the concordat meaningfully in Bavaria as well'. The church discovered what 'meaningful implementation of the concordat' meant in Bavarian during the next few days when again the Catholic Apprentices Association was forbidden to hold a meeting in its own premises and the Association of Catholic Shopgirls was forbidden its Annual General Meeting which was due.[57] Vicar General Franz Riemer of Passau was quite right when he told Papen's secretary in early November that the concordat was indeed 'implemented meaningfully', according to a cabinet decision, i.e. disregarded whenever convenient'.[58] It was in fact possible to get the ban on meetings of 19 September lifted, by Heydrich, on 2 November, only through further pressure from Berlin. But even this ruling, which significantly was not to be made public, and the text of which was made known to the Munich ordinariate only some days later, was formulated in such a way that it was clear that it had been forced on the authorities and led to fears for the worst in the future.[59]

In these circumstances it was sheer impertinence nevertheless to require a unanimous appeal for 12 November from the Bavarian bishops. But evidently precisely that was expected, above all by the Bavarian Kultusminister, Hans Schemm. On 28 October two Kreisleiters appeared at the Passau ordinariate with this request. On 2 November the Bishop of Speyer was visited by representatives of the Gau leadership who insisted on a service and the ringing of the church bells; and on the same day Archbishop Hauck of Bamberg was faced with the same question. Here, however, the representatives of the state had a surprise. For when soon afterwards the two ministers of state, Hermann Esser and Hans Schemm, made a personal approach to the archbishop, there was a 'dramatic and passionate' discussion, of which Hauck reported to Munich that at least the ministers could not say 'That I did not speak the full truth to them, or handled things too delicately, or without clarity.' The electioneering of the two men, Hauck noted, not without satisfaction, had then become 'rather mute and tame'.[60]

When Faulhaber weighed all this up – the general conviction of the bishops that a declaration was unavoidable; the mood among the populace, who were without doubt in favour of Hitler's decision; the attitude of the Party and the state; and the actual conditions in Bavaria, which seemed to rule out the Breslau proposal and even more that of Freiburg – everything indicated the path which he in fact took, after sounding out the other Bavarian bishops. He issued a declaration of his own, making the Catholic affirmation of the plebiscite as clear as its rejection of the continued oppression of the church. The third episcopal proclamation about 12 November from Bavaria was accordingly divided into three clearly distinct sections. The first section contained the unqualified support of Catholics 'for peace among the nations, for the honour and equal rights of the German Volk'. The second section explained sharply and clearly what was not contained in this statement of support, namely the state actions against the associations and the desecration of Sundays. On the other hand the Reichstag election, which was mentioned in the third section, was 'left to the conscience and discernment of the voters' as in the Breslau text, 'according to Article 22 of the Reich concordat'.[61]

In contrast to Bertram's colourless text, despite the affirmations of loyalty to the Führer, the criticism here just could not be missed. The Bavarian government obviously felt that way, so on 9 November, one day after the text was published, there was a general ban on publications. After turbulent scenes in Munich, it was explicitly repeated the day before election Sunday. According to the 11 November instruction of the Bavarian Minister President to the police authorities, 'Because of its illegitimate criticism of government actions, with the permission of the Reich Chancellor and the Reich Minister of Propaganda there is a ban on the publication of the declaration. I am trying to reach an immediate agreement with the Ordinariate that readings from pulpits which may have been planned shall not in any circumstances take place...'[62]

Perhaps such a ban might have been accepted by the bishops had their silence at least sharpened the issues. Instead, however, something quite different happened. When the Cardinal turned on his radio on the evening of 11 November,

506

what he heard in the new report as 'A statement by the Bavarian bishops' was only the first section of the appeal. No listener discovered that this was by no means everything that the Bavarian episcopate had to say about the vote.

This possibility had in fact been discussed during the afternoon in Munich, but there could be no question of Faulhaber having agreed to this procedure,[63] as was claimed later. The whole episode displayed a degree of deception and a contempt for the bishops that was unusual even by Bavarian standards. The lively controversies over these events were in any case dominated by the fact that on 12 November Hitler had scored a triumphant victory at the polls.

Without doubt, 12 November marked a wide, conclusive break in the internal and external development of the Third Reich. According to the official final count, in the plebiscite 95.1% of all voters supported the Reich government policy and only 4.9% opposed it. The results of the parliamentary election were somewhat less favourable to the Party. Here 92.2% had voted for the union list of the NSDAP and 7.8% against.[64] Now of course this election could hardly be called 'free'. This was not so much due to a breach of electoral secrecy or direct falsification, although both also occurred.[65] Much more decisive was the storm of propaganda which had swept over Germany since 14 October, and which had created a climate of coercion which only a few were able to escape. The fear that a 'No' vote could perhaps be identified and have unforeseeable consequences certainly also played a major role in the voting. In addition to this, withholding one's vote by staying away from the election was made virtually impossible, for a perfect electoral organization reached even the last voter and compelled a trip to the ballot box.[66] But even if all this is taken into account, Hitler doubtless still had a giant majority of votes which went to him voluntarily and out of conviction, and supported his politics. The landslide which had occurred in Germany since 5 March had now become visible in the statistical tables too.

The election results also demonstrated how far Hitler had succeeded in achieving one of his most important domestic political goals, namely the defeat of political Catholicism. That block of nearly five and a half million committed Catholic votes, which in the March elections had shown itself so astonishingly capable of resistance, had largely been won over – and only eight months had passed![67] The election positions in Catholic and Protestant areas had virtually balanced out and in part had even been reversed. Among the four Gaue with the lowest share of the votes for the Union list – Hamburg 78.1%, Berlin 78.6%, Schleswig-Holstein 84.1%, and Cologne-Aachen 84.4% – only one had a definitely Catholic population, and traditional Catholic areas like Koblenz-Trier (90.2%), Munich-Upper Bavaria (90.9%) and Silesia (89.9%) even surpassed traditionally Protestant areas like Hessen-Nassau (88.7%), Thuringia (88.8%) and South Hanover-Brunswick (89.7%). Certainly, in view of the conditions of this election it is hardly possible to draw detailed conclusions. But on the whole the tendency towards an equalization of the confessionally influenced differences in voting was unmistakable.[68]

The consequences of 12 November were profound and varied. This day further increased the Germans' trust in Hitler. His domestic political position was almost unassailable. He knew that himself, and anyone who had to deal with him after 12 November knew it too. Naturally that changed things – in Rome, too, where people became more cautious; and also in the German episcopate, which knew that it could count on only slight support for opposition among the Catholic church people.

When Buttmann resumed his negotiations in Rome in the middle of December he did not hide the changed situation. He declared to Pacelli right at the beginning of the first discussion that the 12 November election result 'had certainly not strengthened the authority of the bishops, for the election result – even in the overwhelmingly Catholic areas – exceeded our keenest expectations. Germany today,' continued Buttmann, 'is completely National Socialist... I do not need to assure your eminence that with their reservations, Archbishop Bertram and the Bavarian bishops have not played an especially happy role in this.'[69]

So it was no accident but a direct consequence of the overall situation that on election day itself Papen wrote Gröber a long letter bringing up the problem which – along with the Bavarian situation – most disturbed relations between state and church: the future of the Catholic youth organizations. Papen's solution was simple. The Catholic youth organizations should be dissolved and incorporated into the appropriate Party organizations. In return the Party should give guarantees for the fulfilment of the church obligations of the Catholic members. Only through such a 'voluntary act of trust' in the Führer could the 'necessary and desirable measures for protecting and furthering the religious interests of the Catholic youth be taken'.[70]

This letter was to have extraordinary importance for the future of Catholicism in the Third Reich. For because of an inquiry by Gröber, it prompted in Rome the fundamental decision 'that no negotiations were to be conducted on the whole business of the episcopate, since this came under the concordat and exclusively concerned the Holy See and the German government'.[71] This saved the unity of the episcopate, which seemed seriously endangered on this question.[72] The price, however, was an ever closer bond between the German bishops and the political line of the Curia. In material terms, this decision meant that in spite of the changed situation in Germany Rome did not approve the Gröber-Papen line at this juncture, but undertook to defend the concordat positions. This had to do above all with Article 31 and in that context especially with the independence of the Catholic youth organizations.

The quite different paths taken by the Protestant and Catholic youth at the end of the year followed from this decision.

The question of the future of organized church youth in the Third Reich had become increasingly urgent from the spring of 1933 on. At the end of the Weimar Republic, both churches had flourishing youth activity. At this time the Catholic youth associations numbered around 1.5 million members; the Protestants had about 700,000, but with the free community groups, there too the total came to about 1.5 million.[73] However, the degree of organization was definitely higher on the Catholic side: about one third of all Catholic youth between fourteen and twenty-one belonged to a Catholic youth organization, while on the Protestant side the figure was only around 10%.[74] Still, within the 'Reich Committee of German Youth Associations' the two churches provided almost half of all youth organized into associations and groups.

Among the many different youth organizations of the two churches, the erstwhile young men's associations provided a focal point on which, in the nature of things, the battle chiefly concentrated. The Catholic Young Men's Association,

508

comparatively tightly organized and uniformly led, was the largest male youth association in Germany with 365,000 members.[75] In 1933 it was headed by General President Monsignor Ludwig Wolker, aged 46, a born youth leader with considerable verve. With about 265,000 members, the Protestant counterpart, the 'Reich Alliance of German Protestant Young Men's Associations', was smaller and had only a loose organization. The Reichswart was Pastor Erich Stange, almost the same age as Wolker, an enthusiast with a somewhat aimless faith, which in autumn 1933 he unfortunately placed in Ludwig Müller.

At the beginning of 1933, over against these large and well-led church youth organizations, stood a Hitler Youth which with little more than 100,000 members seemed hardly able to compete in numbers.[76] But as in all other sectors, in the course of the year a powerful geological shift occurred which involved not only an outward and violent co-ordination but also – as 12 November indicated – an inner change and new direction. At the end of the year this left only one independent youth organization: Catholic Youth. All the others had been shattered, dissolved or voluntarily assimilated into Hitler Youth.

Baldur von Schirach, National Youth Leader of the NSDAP, played a decisive role in this development. Schirach was twenty-four years old when in 1931 Hitler named him Führer of the Hitler Youth. In contrast to the cramped mentality of many Party leaders, he came from a home with artistic inclinations which was open to the world. He had no trace of the rowdyism that opened the taverns for Hitler in the years of struggle. Travel and camping, fighting and play, adventure and fellowship – everything which he was later to organize for Hitler Youth with such enormous success – lay far outside his personal interests. Much more characteristic was the mixture of sentimentality and enthusiasm expressed in his numerous poems. One of the first of these poems, written in 1925 under the impact of a personal meeting with Hitler when he was seventeen, later became one of his most famous. Millions of young Germans read it and memorized it:

> You are many thousands behind me,
> and you are me and I am you,
> I have had no thoughts
> which do not vibrate in your heart.
>
> And if I speak, I know no word
> which is not one with your will.
> For I am you and you are me
> and we all believe, Germany, in you.[77]

Belief in Germany, personalized in belief in Hitler, was and remained Schirach's confession of faith. He sought to lead the Hitler Youth along the lines of this confession, and probably a considerable measure of his success lay precisely in the youthful sentimentality with which he communicated the experience of the Führer to the generation of Rilke's 'Cornet'.

However, in 1933 the issue was not just poetry, but also decisive action. Here the twenty-six-year-old Reich Leader and his twenty-five-year-old deputy, Carl Nabersberg, lost no time. Without preliminaries, on 3 April Schirach had Nabersberg take over the office of the 'Reich Committee of German Youth Associations', thus acquiring a splendid organizational base for operations.[78] No

509

less important was the powerful movement which set in after the March elections, especially among the youth leagues, leading numerous individual groups and leagues to join the Hitler Youth directly. By the middle of June, with the exception of the church youth organizations, large areas of the youth leagues, professional youth associations and sports clubs were already either incorporated or so weakened that serious resistance was no longer to be expected of them. On 17 June Hitler rewarded Schirach's efforts by naming him 'Youth Führer of the German Reich'. According to the citation he headed 'all associations of male and female youth'. From now on 'the founding of youth organizations' could occur only with his permission.[79]

Schirach had hardly been nominated when by a decree of 23 June he dissolved the All German League, which combined the association youth and the Hitler Youth, and at the same time announced the dissolution of the Reich Committee, its tasks now to be taken over by the Youth Leader.[80] Although this seemed to indicate a clear change of direction, it did not necessarily mean the compulsory co-ordination of all the youth associations. For as Youth Leader Schirach was under the National Ministry of the Interior, and at this point the Minister of the Interior stuck stubbornly to his prerogatives. Accordingly, in a decree of 8 July, Hitler's proclamation of 17 June was officially confirmed and at the same time the Youth Leader was bound by precise guidelines. While these guidelines among other things confirmed the dissolution of the Reich Committee, at the same time they announced the creation of a Leader's Council in which all the important branches of the youth organizations were to be represented. Moreover the decree expressly stated that while the Youth Leader could call on the help of government bodies, he was 'not authorized' to 'intervene forcibly in any way'.[81] This meant that the Hitler Youth could only take over those youth organizations which more or less willingly fell in with the general development. For all other associations, and very soon that meant only the churches, the Hitler Youth had to seek another course. That was the nature of the situation in summer and autumn 1933.

Especially on the Catholic side, from the very beginning the whole development was watched with great attention and understandable concern. While the Protestant youth associations could still not arrive at any united position, because under the impact of the national enthusiasm there was general uncertainty over the way forward, the General Praesidium and National Executive of the Association of Catholic Young Men decided at the beginning of May to tighten up the organization and to give the Reich Leadership a kind of general authorization 'to make the necessary decisions, at the appropriate time and independently, on its own, in agreement with the church authorities'.[82] At the end of May Wolker, who had been negotiating tirelessly during these weeks, gave a comprehensive report on the situation of the church youth associations to the German hierarchy at its plenary conference in Fulda. This situation was characterized on the one hand by solemn assurances that the independence of the church youth associations would not be attacked, and on the other by constant encroachments which laid heavy burdens on the boys and girls associated with the church. In fact, since March small-scale open warfare had broken out in many places between the church youth and the Hitler Youth, in which political-ideological conflicts, local rivalries and youthful delight in brawling were often

510

inextricably combined. The skirmishes focussed on youth hostels and tents, banners and badges, neckties and shoulder insignia. In good Catholic territories, Hitler Youth was by no means always victorious. The situation was made more difficult when the Party began to exert ever-increasing pressure on schools, places of work and teaching posts, which in turn produced counter-pressure on the church side, so that later here and there resolute leaders could form cells of resistance which held together all the more strongly the more the outside pressure increased.

Wolker's May memorandum described the whole extent of the difficulties realistically, and ended by asking whether in these circumstances the associations should not be dissolved in their present form and a new form of youth fellowship be created. The General President himself decisively rejected this solution. 'A violent solution' was impossible, both 'spiritually and economically'. So only the second solution remained: 'To maintain the associations recognized by the church even in the changed circumstances and to secure a basis which would allow them to fulfil their roles.' To achieve this goal, Wolker requested the help and support of the hierarchy.[83]

The episcopate responded whole-heartedly to this request. The resolutions of the plenary conference on 'The Requests of the Youth Associations' show the bishops' resolve to defend the independence of the church youth. With the concordat, of which they had just been informed, in view, the bishops called, in the name of the church, for 'full community rights for the church youth organization and educational rights, in terms of the physical, spiritual and professional training of their members'. 'A state of legal uncertainty and discrimination... in school and at work' would be intolerable for Catholic youth. It would also be intolerable for them 'to be looked on and treated as second-class German youth with inferior rights...' 'But because the church youth organization is of vital importance to the church, the church unyieldingly maintains the rights of Catholic youth in the community and in education, and considers the church youth organization a treasured part of its fellowship.'[84]

This was a clear statement. And the signing of the concordat on 29 July also seemed to guarantee this position by treaty. That put Schirach in a difficult position. The Catholic youth associations had now been protected from direct attack by the Hitler Youth, and it was by no means clear whether, with their solid anchorage in the church, the tactic of wearing them down would be successful in the long run. So the National Youth Führer chose another course. On 29 July, the very day on which the principles for interpreting Article 31 were published, he announced that dual membership of the Hitler Youth and the church youth associations was prohibited, on the grounds that 'the confessional organizations' were not restricting themselves 'to their specific responsibilities in the church'.[85] The purpose of this prohibition was clear. The church organizations were to be driven back into church territory, while Hitler Youth alone spoke for the whole community of the German Volk. Taken along with the many material advantages which membership of the Hitler Youth now offered, and which especially affected schooling and employment, the prohibition in fact proved to be a very effective weapon. Wolker, who on 20 August gave the bishops a further report on the situation, now had to report a substantial loss of membership. He wrote that on the whole the youth had 'shown themselves extraordinarily good and brave... However, there is one thing with which the youth cannot cope in the long run: the economic boycott which is now directed across the board against all who are not in Nazi organizations – and especially against those who bear the sign of Christ.' An appendix illustrated how the Schirach decree worked: 'On one hand, many members are compelled to join the Nazi organizations at work... On the other, members of the Nazi youth organizations and the SA are now forbidden at the same time to be members of the confessional associations. Thus they are driven out of our ranks.'[86]

In the nature of things, this report, which with its twenty-one supplementary documents was for all practical purposes a cry for help from the tottering and collapsing associations, could achieve nothing more in the second plenary session of the bishops at the end of August than a further reference to the importance and necessity of the concordat. In connection with the beleaguered state of the Catholic associations the protocol maintained that there was 'an agreement that the Reich concordat had to be fully maintained in respect of Article 31, so a dissolution of the organizations by the bishops is utterly out of the question.'[87]

But it was precisely here, in the storm of these first months, that the problematical aspect of the concordat first emerged. For while it was meant to restrict the state, and indeed did limit it to a certain extent, it limited the church far more. As long as the concordat was there, and as long as the church appealed to it – indeed had to appeal to it, just because it was there – the church was incapable of resistance. For Hitler that was probably more the significance of the concordat the longer it lasted. Wolker himself, who as General President knew the reality of the Third Reich better than many others, demonstrated this two-edged aspect of the concordat clearly. In a message to Catholic young men which appeared in September in *Wacht*, he described how the concordat not only gave Catholic youth equal rights but also placed it 'with equal obligations alongside the other associations of German youth in the German state'. 'Yes, equal obligations,' he continued. 'Yes, indeed, dear friends, we must be clear that the conclusion of the concordat also involves duties. By recognizing the church and by a solemn treaty binding itself to a joint activity among the German people, the new state has also put obligations on the youth of the church over against the new state. And not only in the sense that as Catholics we of course for conscience' sake give the state what belongs to the state, but in the further sense' – and in *Wacht* this was printed in bold type – '*that we recognize the German state with its National Socialist stamp, its concept, its leadership, its forms, and put ourselves at its disposal in utter readiness and loyalty.*'[88] Of course the reciprocal relationship between the conclusion of the concordat and loyalty to the state was not formulated so enthusiastically in all sectors of the Catholic church. But even where thinking was much more critical in this respect, the concordat called for loyalty – though sometimes with gnashing of teeth.

In autumn 1933, like innumerable others, Wolker was undoubtedly one of Hitler's admirers. And even if the suppression of Catholic youth hit him hard, the scene that autumn seemed politically so diverse and rich that he would not let his judgment be determined by this one issue. So in his September statement he had declared that the Reich government had succeeded 'in approaching quickly, and with an incredible show of strength, a solution to the basic problems of the new state', which could mean nothing less than 'the fulfilment of a divine

512

will'. Thus 'the injustice and contempt' which still burdened the Catholic youth could not and must not prevent them from 'seeing the total picture and serving it all'.[89] It was also in line with this picture that Wolker, regardless of all continuing difficulties, declared on 17 October in connection with the Germany's resignation from the League of Nations: 'On 12 November German Catholic young men who are entitled to vote will without exception do their duty.'[90] Thus all the preconditions had been fulfilled for making the General President feel the political change represented by 12 November very strongly. For a moment he too was no longer certain whether it was right and possible to maintain and fight for the independence of the Catholic youth organizations against the will of the state leadership. The consequent isolation of Catholic Youth seemed almost irresponsible, especially in view of Hitler's convincing victory.

This was precisely the moment at which the Archbishop of Freiburg received Papen's letter with its proposal – contrary to the guarantee of church influence – that the Catholic youth organizations should be dissolved and transferred to the appropriate Party sections. This certainly put the organizations in extreme danger. For Papen and Gröber were not alone in thinking this the right way, or at least a possible course. In the meantime, many association leaders had also become uncertain. This was shown at a meeting which the Archbishop of Freiburg quickly called to discuss the whole matter with the most important association leaders. At the beginning of the session Gröber first presented the arguments for and against dissolution. In essentials, the argument *for* dissolution amounted to saying that the associations were lost in any case and that a voluntary dissolution might at least achieve 'pastoral care over the Hitler Youth' which would be 'a tremendous gain in terms of pastoral care'. His pastoral clergy also agreed. Finally, dissolution would 'remove a dangerous source of conflict'. The factors *against* dissolution, in Gröber's view, were the 'enormous vitality of these organizations which still exists' and the suspicion that Berlin's intentions could not be honourable. 'Our suicide,' Gröber commented vivvidly, 'relieves our opponents of the unwelcome task of killing us.' And if Berlin wanted a Kulturkampf, it would not be 'prevented by concessions at this point'.[91] The discussion which followed constantly focussed on the same problems. It was clear to all those involved that the whole matter was a question of power. But it remained open what Hitler really wanted; whether the unity of the bishops could be depended upon; whether the Catholic people still stood behind the associations; and whether – as Wolker put it – there was a possibility of an overall influence on the National Socialist organizations in place of the Catholic associations, in other words the whole in place of the part.' In the general perplexity there was finally assent to Gröber's proposal that to begin with above all there should be clarity as to Hitler's intentions. If Hitler wanted the dissolution of the associations, then guarantees for Catholic work among the Hitler Youth had to be negotiated; if Hitler did not want dissolution, everything should stay as it was. Moreover, Rome should be informed without delay and asked 'whether negotiations with Berlin were permissible or not'.[92]

For all practical purposes the result of this meeting was capitulation. For to make the future of the associations entirely dependent on Hitler's intentions amounted in essence to their betrayal. Everything now depended on Rome's decision. And that followed immediately and unequivocally.

On the same day as the meeting Gröber had sent a copy of Papen's letter and a report of the course of the discussion by courier to Kaas.[93] Pacelli, informed without delay, did not hesitate for a moment. He had Kaas telephone Freiburg to say that this was 'a *causa major* which could only be negotiated between Rome and Berlin'.[94] And soon afterwards – on November 24 – Gröber wrote a letter to Bertram in which he informed the Chairman of the Fulda Bishops Conference of this decision and at the same time assured him that the entire problem was resolved as far as he was concerned. 'Now that Rome has spoken, the matter is no longer in our hands.' 'I personally am glad,' he added, 'that I am thus relieved of all responsibility'.[95]

It was high time for this clarification. For the German bishops had come close to splitting on this issue. On 22 November Bertram – with every sign of disgust – had informed the German bishops that he had heard that four bishops had decided to abandon the Catholic youth associations. Was this not a betrayal of the youth, a surrender of the concordat, 'and a rejection of the Holy Father'?[96] From the answer he requested it emerged that under the pressure of the Bavarian situation Faulhaber had already worked out a plan for incorporation.[97] The Archbishop of Bamberg proposed that the youth associations should be withdrawn to purely religious territory,[98] while his colleague from Paderborn, referring to the Reich concordat, declared in unusually sharp language that he felt obliged 'to argue forcefully for the continuation of the Catholic youth associations without exception'.[99] But all the replies had in common a deep concern for the unity of the German bishops.

Rome's decision had terminated this discussion for the time being. And the whole responsibility again rested with the Curia.

In fact Pacelli had meanwhile had a wealth of reasons for urging a resumption of the negotiations with Buttmann which had been interrupted in October. But in Berlin after 12 November no one any longer showed signs of being in a hurry. After an enquiry to the German ambassador on 23 November had gone unanswered, on 3 December Pacelli indicated plainly that the patience of the Curia was being exhausted. Now things speeded up. Only three days later the Foreign Office informed the ambassador that Buttmann would arrive in Rome the following week.[100] However, Pacelli's desire for Buttmann to be authorized to conclude a definitive agreement was not fulfilled. Rather, the German ambassador was confidentially informed in advance that final agreements were out of the question. For the moment, what was needed was 'a clarificatory discussion of some important points in the context of the overall situation'. At the same time, Neurath intimated that Buttmann would bring a surprise with him: namely, the news that in view of the impending reform of the constitution the Reich government intended 'to enter into negotiations in the near future over a new Reich concordat, eliminating Land concordats'.[101]

Thus the negotiations which had longingly been awaited by the German church were turned into a 'clarificatory discussion' without binding character – and at the same time expanded to include a topic which on the side of the Curia could only cause surprise and confusion. The whole development proved to be an unusually skilful diplomatic ploy. For in this way Buttmann was able to avert for the time being the dreaded public statement by the Pope against the Third Reich, without having to make a single concession worth mentioning.

514

On 18 December the German representative began negotiations with a declaration of the friendly nature of his visit. The Reich government wanted to allay the anxieties of the Curia. In the opinion of the Führer specific questions of interpretation and implementation could best be answered 'in connection with the negotiations on a new Reich concordat, which in any case would come up soon'. Pacelli responded, as expected, that the Holy Father was 'very disturbed by the situation in Germany'. He had told Pacelli that very morning that in his Christmas allocution 'he must unquestionably speak about Germany'. If only he – Pacelli – 'could produce some good news,' he believed 'that the Pope's mood would be much improved'. In this way the negotiating positions were marked out. Pacelli went on to introduce a series of complaints, beginning with conditions in Bavaria and the difficulties over Article 31. Buttmann answered, not unskilfully, that these difficulties lay partly with the leaders of the Catholic associations, who were still those who had long opposed the movement. This occasioned unrest and mistrust. It would certainly be in the interest of the church if there could be a 'renewal of leadership' and a 'unification of the Catholic associations'. While the Cardinal Secretary of State evidently expected no specific concessions on these points, he made it clear that the Pope expected a decision in other matters. The issues were above all the election of a Bishop of Berlin, the application of the Aryan paragraph to Catholic teachers, the exemption of Catholic theology students from SA service, and the continuation of certain obligations under the state concordats. Buttmann promised to make inquiries in Berlin by telephone and give the Cardinal Secretary of State an answer the next morning. In fact Hitler made the relevant decisions the very same day. Thus on the 19th Buttmann was able, as promised, to tender a short memorandum in which all the immediate wishes of the Curia were met – with the exception of the Aryan paragraph, on which the document was silent.[102] Given the situation of the church in Germany, this was not a substantial achievement. But again it must have seemed that it was possible to negotiate with the Reich government and that much could be achieved through skill and stubbornness.

At the same time Pacelli was peristently strengthened in this conviction by all those who had pursued the conclusion of the concordat during the spring and summer, headed by Kaas. Shortly before Christmas, a long letter from the Prelate to his friend Gröber provided a good view of this aspect of the Roman scene. And even if this letter was perhaps intended more for the eyes of the state censor than for those of his friend, it still revealed the situation quite clearly. Even Robert Leiber, Kaas reported to Freiburg 'in strict confidence', now urged 'firm action by the Vatican'.

His own situation could hardly be worse. Referring to the concordat negotiations, he wrote that 'it was then stated on all sides that the Holy See should not make the effort to conclude a treaty, because it was dealing with professional treaty-breakers. Today the people who then argued in that way – thank God without success – seem to be having a good time and are maliciously pointing to the difficulties and delays, past and present, over the concordat. You do not need telling that I am suffering terribly in this situation.'[103] That made the visit of their mutual friend, Albert Hackelsberger, who had 'managed his affairs splendidly', all the more important.

In fact Pacelli clearly thought the former Centre Party deputy – not least on the basis of commendations from Gröber and Kaas – an especially trustworthy political informant on the political situation. But what Hackelsberger had noted about 'the balance of power in Germany' only showed how rapidly the developments had moved beyond the old politicians, and how little Hackelsberger had in fact understood the new political reality in Germany. The central government, he assured the Cardinal Secretary of State, could not yet penetrate everywhere and steer a middle course to achieve reform of the Reich, which could then afford it the populist power that it needed. Hackelsberger concluded: 'If before the end of this process a statement is issued from Rome, above all now, which is irritating to the Chancellor, the Protestants and the circles hostile to the church, the result will be that the resistance of the central government to these negative forces will be dangerously weakened. The enemies of the church will rejoice and devote all their efforts to winning over the Chancellor, who in spite of many regrettable weaknesses is not ill disposed and is reluctant to have a Kulturkampf. As a culmination to his explanations he compared Hitler with Kerensky, and said that 'more than a Lenin' lurked behind the scenes. The situation in Germany could scarcely have been more deeply misunderstood and with more disastrous consequences. And no less devastating was the misunderstanding of the development in German Protestantism, from the controversies in which Hackelsberger expected 'future possibilities of a positive nature for German Catholicism, given certain conditions'. A hard word from Rome 'would most probably unite the spirits that now find themselves in a healthy struggle, and battle against the "old Roman enemy..."'.[104]

Here the decision by Rome in principle to retain all negotiations over the concordat showed its other side. For as a consequence Pacelli was dependent on informants selected more by subjective factors and accident than for their knowledge and responsibility. Even more important to the creator of the concordat, as was only human, was to pay more attention to those voices that pressed for accommodation and further negotiations than to those that called for a clear word from the Pope.

So the various diplomatic efforts from this side were not without their effect. In his Christmas address to the cardinals, which was eagerly awaited, Pius XI said nothing about the German situation. Only a reference to the law on sterilization revealed the dissatisfaction of the Holy See.

The fact that at the end of the year the Pope let the German ambassador know plainly that the reports from Germany filled him with pain and concern was no substitute for a public statement.[105] And even an unusually frank pastoral letter from the Austrian bishops, dated 21 December, could not compensate for the silence. On the contrary. For the statement that while any judgment on the observation and implementation of the Reich concordat was the concern of the Holy See, 'the whole world' knew 'the tense relations between state and church in the German Reich' and the 'deep concern' that they justified,[106] inevitably raised even more questions about the Pope's silence. Moreover, such remarks gave the German side the possibility of complaining about 'an unprecedented interference by the Austrian bishops in internal German affairs and in German or German-Vatican concerns'.[107]

One can only guess what a sharp and clear word from the Pope about the

National Socialist ideology and infringements of the law by Hitler's government might have meant to the German Catholics at the end of 1933. Certainly it would hardly have changed the real situation. But equally certainly it would have strengthened many loyal Catholics among the clergy and the laity, and given a stimulus to them at least to continue to resist the undertow of co-ordination.

It is clear that the Pope's silence was celebrated as a victory by the German embassy. And even if Bergen claimed too much for his efforts, it was evident that he was very satisfied by the prevention of 'the Vatican offensive (a sharp note of protest from the Cardinal Secretary of State followed by an official proclamation by the Pope)'. From now on, he reported to the Foreign Minister in a personal letter, one could 'count on some weeks of comparative calm' and he recommended 'coming off the defensive and sending a lengthy protest note to the Cardinal Secretary of State'.[108] On 12 January the ambassador already had in hand the text of a memorandum which to a considerable degree corresponded to his proposal. In it the Reich government rejected all the Vatican's complaints in well-chosen phrases. The concluding section was without question a masterpiece of political-diplomatic drafting, and at the same time an illustration of how it was hoped to influence the Vatican from the German side. 'The disciplined course of the national revolution in Germany, which is unique in history,' the conclusion read, 'allows its great depth and breadth to be missed all too easily. The goals of National Socialism are clearly marked out. Its great tasks of secular significance for Germany and peace generally can only be accomplished by a hard struggle over a lengthy period of time. It was inevitable that in this tremendous new construction, especially in the first stage, stones would fall from the scaffolding and injure passers-by. The injuries are to be regretted; an attempt will be made to heal the wounds. But attention must be directed beyond these unfortunate isolated incidents towards the future. The same thing must be said, in the view of the Reich government, about the concordat and its implementation, to which the fullest attention and care will be given.'[109]

Pacelli certainly did not let his view of what was really going on in Germany be clouded by this. But his inclination to see this real situation as part of a larger picture, and to deal with it diplomatically – a tendency which must inevitably be close to the central authority of a world church – was undoubtedly strengthened by such needs.[110]

A correspondence at the end of the year between Gröber and Pacelli again clarified some of the essential elements in German-Roman relations. At the end of a long report on the situation Gröber put 'the crucial question', namely as to which was the right method, 'that of detached and careful waiting or that of approach and positive co-operation to the degree that Catholic principles allow it'. Gröber left no doubt that he stood for the latter course and at the same time expressed the hope 'that we are over the hump of our difficulties, and that the mountain shaking from the earthquake will slowly settle again'.[111] In his answer Pacelli revealed that he shared Gröber's optimism on the 'basic issue'. The Cardinal Secretary of State wrote that the Nuncio in Berlin had been given the task 'of preparing a final solution for guiding the associations protected by the concordat, and finding a form in connection with the re-organization of the so-called list to meet the desires of the government without damaging the material interests of the church'. Given the disputes among the German bishops, the master of Vatican policy declared that in times like these there was always the possibility 'of occasionally different shades of opinion over the methods to be used from time to time, among such personalities about whose loyalty to the church and submission to the highest authority of the Holy See there could not be the slightest doubt'. But precisely for that reason the Holy See must now 'most emphatically protect the uniformity of that action'.[112] This once again emphasized something about which there could be no doubt during 1933: Pacelli considered the German question as a whole a *causa major*, on which decisions were to be made only in Rome.

With so much optimism, diplomacy and lofty viewpoints, it was a good thing that there was nevertheless one place in Catholic Germany where attention was publicly drawn to the conflict between Christian belief and the National Socialist world-view. In the largest church in Munich, St Michael's, from the First Sunday in Advent to New Year's Eve, Cardinal Faulhaber preached five sermons on the relationship between Judaism, Christianity and Germanhood. Faulhaber was doubtless better equipped for this task than others. He had been able to observe the beginning and rise of the movement on the spot, and was quite clear about its völkisch-religious nucleus. Despite Hitler's basic decision on church politics, which increasingly concealed this nucleus from many people, at the end of 1930 Faulhaber had plainly called National Socialism a 'heresy' which 'could not be reconciled with the Christian world-view'.[113] Now, three years later and in a totally changed situation, the Cardinal repeated this judgment in the form of a defence of the Old Testament. Specifically in view of what had happened in the Berlin Sports Palace, which at that time had shocked German Protestantism,[114] he was aware that what was at stake was not just a Christian-Catholic position but a Christian position generally. Given the tense confessional situation in Germany, it was quite unusual for a German cardinal to look over the confessional fence and declare: '*We extend our hands to our separated brethren*, to defend together with them the sacred books of the Old Testament...' Though, as Faulhaber said in the fourth sermon, a storm was raging through Germany which sought to 'sweep away the Holy Scriptures from German soil, because they are Jewish books', he was convinced that this storm would 'spark, rather, the holy fire of a new enthusiasm for the holy books in all confessional communities'. 'Our separated brethren,' he went on, 'do not kneel with us at the communion rail. *But believing trust in the holy gospel* is *spiritual communion with our Lord and Saviour*.'[115]

Of course not all the arguments which Faulhaber produced for the religious, moral and social value of the Old Testament were of equal weight. But in the matter of central importance, condemning the basic teaching of National Socialism by defending the Old Testament, the line was clear enough, despite Faulhaber's distinction between Judaism before Christ and Judaism after Christ. Thus the cardinal already made it clear in the first sermon that the Old Testament was to be interpreted from the standpoint of the New. This meant that blood and race were no longer decisive for Christians. For it was obvious that Christ rejected the 'ties of blood' and stood for 'the ties of faith'. So the question was not 'Was Christ born a Jew or an Aryan?' Rather, it was: 'Are we incorporated into Christ by baptism and faith? "In Christ whether or not one is a Jew is not important, but only the new creation" (Gen.6.15). The Old Testament was erected on blood ties, the New Testament is established on ties of faith. More serious' – and here the Cardinal took up Artur Dinter's well-known antisemitic title – 'than the "sin against the blood" is the "sin against faith"'.[116]

In the final sermon, on New Year's Eve, which specifically took up the issue of 'Christianity and Germanhood', the Cardinal repeated this thought once again and developed it into a memorable formulation. 'In the fullness of time... the dogma of race – i.e. the racial dogma of the Old Testament – is dissolved by the dogma of faith. Jews and Gentiles, shepherds from the land of the Jews and wise men from the East, found their way to the crib at Bethlehem. In the kingdom of this child, according to the word of the one who announced him, there is "no distinction between Jews and Greeks; there is one and the same Lord of all" (Rom.10.12).' And no one among the thousands who crowded in to follow the sermons could be in doubt as to what the Cardinal meant when he finally said in this connection: 'We may never forget: We are not saved by German blood. We are saved by the precious blood of our crucified Lord (I Peter 1.19).'[117]

The response to these sermons was quite extraordinary. In addition to St Michael's, Sunday by Sunday the two nearest churches, the Studienkirche and the Bürgersaal, connected by loudspeakers, were also full. The sermons, printed individually, sold like hot cakes. By the beginning of February 150,000 copies had been distributed, along with a pamphlet which had been necessitated by 'innumerable requests from near and far'.[118] A secret situation report by the Chief of the Security Office of the SS Reich Leader (May/June 1934) also gave a vivid impression of the effect of Faulhaber's Advent sermons, deriving a considerable number of his accusations against the Catholic church from them. The report even stated that the Cardinal was 'generally considered the spiritual leader of the Catholic resistance to the National Socialist state, especially the foreign press... His occasional admonitions to the clergy "to co-operate with the state" did not outweigh the disruptive effect of his Advent sermons about Judaism and especially his New Year's Eve sermon on Germanhood'.[119]

However, Himmler's security officer was mistaken here. The Cardinal did not wish 'in any way to set out on a course of fundamental opposition'. Rather, he felt he had made a gesture of conciliation when he turned over the royalties from the printed sermons, RM 700, to winter aid.[120]

Thus in spite of all the differences among the bishops, at the end of the year German Catholicism presented a picture of solidarity. It was a solidarity that was essentially dependent on the politics of the Holy See, aimed at still achieving a balance of interests through negotiations with Hitler.

This policy was a mistake.

But it was not just the mistake of the Holy See.

It was the mistake of Europe.

The Reich Church between Illusion and Reality
(October-November)

The offices of Prussian Land Bishop and German Reich Bishop made Ludwig Müller the most important church-political figure in German Protestantism. However, his astonishing career said more about Hitler's authority than about his own. For Ludwig Müller owed everything that he had become simply to his personal connection with Hitler. And the fact that in Wittenberg, for all their experiences with this weak and undependable man, no one dared any longer to oppose his candidacy, also demonstrated the extent to which between April and September 1933 internally, too, Germany had become a Führer state.

But at the same time Ludwig Müller's election expressed a conviction that was held in those days by large areas of German Protestantism – reaching right into the circles of the Young Reformers. That was the belief that Hitler himself, and with him the state and the Party of the Third Reich, really desired and wanted the work of a German Christian Evangelical Church. Hossenfelder had expressed this conviction in a succinct remark at the first Reich conference in April: 'Adolf Hitler's state calls to the church. The church must heed that call.'[1] All through the summer this conviction had fed on Hitler's affirmation of Christianity, his efforts towards a union of the Protestant church, the intervention of the Party on behalf of the German Christians, their organized church-going, the battle against pornography and filth, and much more besides. And all that seemed only the start of a powerful new beginning for Germany and Christianity.

However, the few months up to the end of 1933 would show that this belief was nothing more than a grandiose illusion. As it fell apart piece by piece in late autumn, the Faith Movement also collapsed, and along with it the dream of the new German Church. The Reich Church did not come to grief on the resistance of the Confessing Church. It came to grief on the illusory character of its basic conception.[2]

However, at the end of September all this was still to come. On the contrary, many signs seemed to point to a great future for the church in the Third Reich. In this connection the greatest impression was made by the growth in church admissions. In the second half of the year, the turn of the Party towards the church also began to make itself felt visibly, in numbers. The movement to leave the church, a nightmare of the church leadership since 1919, swung sharply round to become a movement to join the church. In Thuringia, for example, the number of admissions grew from about 6,300 in the first half of the year to 11,700 in the second half. That totalled 18,000 people who turned to the Protestant church – almost nine times as many as in the year before. Correspondingly, the numbers leaving the church, which in 1932 were still 5,300, fell to 1,800. In Saxony, in just this one year almost 10,000 returned to the church; the figures for those leaving fell from 28,000 to 8,000. And even in churchgoing Bavaria, which had had no comparable movement to leave the church, the number of admissions doubled.[3]

The amazing reports of mass baptisms and mass weddings coming particularly from the large Berlin city communities were also much cited, and indeed much advertised. For instance, on 26 August Pankow reported the marriage of 147 couples in the Alte Kirche and the Hoffnungskirche. On 10 September Wittenau had 32, on 17 September Johannisthal had 34 couples who jointly celebrated a church wedding. On 23 September, in the Passionskirche in Neu-Kölln, not exactly famous for its churchgoing, 117 children of the Eighty-Third Volksschule were baptized together. Here something happened that could in fact have scarcely been conceivable during the Republic: at the great baptismal celebration, college heads and school teachers took part alongside parents and godparents. And it kept being said, as in a report on the Harvest Festival at Friedenau, that there had not been so many people at a service for fifteen years: the church 'was so packed before the start that more than 400 visitors could not be admitted'.[4]

It is hard to say what was really going on among the people and in the churches. From his experience of the work of the Volksmission, Walter Birnbaum thought that: 'The reports of my colleagues from all over Germany indicated beyond any doubt that a strong and genuine trend towards the church has set in among the people; and these Volksmission veterans were critical men and very well capable of distinguishing wheat from chaff, authentic life from a superficial appearance.'[5] But there were also other quite different experiences. Thus at the same time, on 1 September, the Hamburg pastor Walter Windfuhr wrote to his young German Christian friend Ernst-Ludwig Dietrich that he could imagine how things were in Hamburg. 'Of course, we are a long way from having a "Faith Movement of German Christians" here. My young colleague Fischer gets very worked up maintaining even a semblance of such a thing: half a dozen men brought together laboriously for this purpose.' In deep resignation, Windfuhr added: 'The Protestant church is on the rocks as a result of National Socialism. The various shots of morphine in the form of Luther festivals, etc., to give the picture of new life don't help in the least. The moment the SA came through the front door to "conquer" the church, God fled out through the back. And now he has retreated into the synagogue, as the only place for divine worship which is not ruled by the swastika.'[6]

In September hope and scepticism, enthusiasm and resignation, illusion and reality, could still be found side by side in the Protestant church. But the majority no doubt clung to the illusion: to the colourful life, to the torches, banners, festivals and marches, and not least to the church statistics.

As he returned to Berlin from Wittenberg on 28 September, the Reich Bishop, too, trusting in his political support and surrounded by the jubilation of the masses, might have felt that he was in his prime. The Secretary of State in the Reich Chancellery personally handed him a telegram with Hitler's warmest congratulations. And the Prussian Kultusminister assured him 'with loyal

521

support': 'You know that I understand the difficulty of your task. From my position I will help you as much as I can.'[7]

On the evening of this day, the Protestant Youth of Berlin, together with the German Christians, the Free Churches and the Salvation Army, staged a huge rally for the new Reich Bishop. It was a kind of counterpart to the Catholic celebration of the concordat in St Hedwig's church, with which the week had begun. 22,000 people, among them about 16,000 young men and women, marched past Ludwig Müller 'with resounding music and waving banners and pennants'. And it was a precise expression of the illusory hopes of those days when the Reich leader of the Protestant Youth, Erich Stange, thanked the Reich Bishop in his address 'for pointing us to the almost unimaginable task of winning back Germany's younger generation for the gospel of the Reformation. Be sure, Reich Bishop,' Stange declared, 'that Protestant Youth is ready for the offensive. We are already working in preparation for a great youth mission in November... And we support you, our Reich Bishop, who have received this responsibility from the faithful hands of our God, with the prayers of the young hearts of our church, putting them deep, deep into our greeting, Sieg Heil!' There then followed, the report has it, the address by the Reich Bishop, listened to in breathless stillness by the great crowd.[8] Here, too, the end of the illusions was not far off. Three months later Stange had been dismissed and Ludwig Müller had handed over Protestant Youth to the Hitler Youth.

Immediately afterwards, the Clergy Ministry of the German Evangelical Church began its work. The very first decision of this body was very typical of the understanding that the church leadership of the Reich Church had of itself and its role. In response to the question what name the main authority in the church should bear in the future, it was decided to call the Clergy Ministry the Reich Church Cabinet and to give the authorities as a whole the title Reich Church Government. Accordingly the members were called Church Minister, a title for which Ludwig Müller later personally solicited the approval of the Reich Minister of the Interior.[9] The choice of these titles could not have been more appealing. The parallels between Reich Cabinet and Reich Church Cabinet, Reich Government and Reich Church Government, Reich Minister and Church Minister, was obviously intended to express the fact that Reich and Reich Church had entered into a new, equal, reciprocal, mutually acknowledged relationship, and that the representatives of the Reich Church leadership also regarded themselves as senior officials in the Reich.

The four tasks which the Reich Church had to tackle urgently were also sorted out very quickly. The most important was without doubt the ending of controversies within the church. Then the reform of the constitutions of the Landeskirchen was essential for unifying the church. Next, the matter of financing the Reich Church had to be resolved, and finally, the great, centrally directed Volksmission was to begin, the 'missionary penetration' of the Germans, which was the main goal for the German Christian upsurge, for Ludwig Müller and for the whole Faith Movement. There were good reasons why Ludwig Müller attempted first of all to settle the controversies within the church. For in Hitler's eyes the whole significance of previous developments had lain in the aim of a united, pacified Protestant church loyal to the state, which would stabilize its authority and at the same time create a counterbalance to Catholicism, which was politically uncertain. Disturbance, conflict and controversies in the church were certainly the last thing the Reich Chancellor wanted and could use, and Ludwig Müller was well aware of that.

Thus an appropriate suggestion made at the beginning of October by the Reich Ministry of the Interior fell on fertile ground. In late July, the Secretary of State of this ministry, Hans Pfundter, had received a letter from the head of the United Patriotic Societies of Germany, General Graf Rüdiger von der Goltz, who was well known at the time, vigorously complaining about the church conflict because it had 'brought bitter division and animosity to our people, who at this moment should stand together against the outside world... For the sake of peace in our Evangelical Church, I urgently request that the pastors who have hitherto been unable to join the German Christian Faith Movement out of inner conviction – essentially, in fact, because of its misuse by non-Christian elements – should not suffer any disadvantage in their official duty.' These very clergy who out of conviction had not become opportunists, were among the most valuable pastors and were thoroughly 'friendly and co-operative' to the new state. Pfundtner now delivered this letter to the Reich Bishop as he entered office and added that 'a word from this source was certainly worthy of serious attention'.[10] Ludwig Müller reacted promptly. On the following day – it was 11 October – he issued a 'Proclamation for the Whole Pastorate' which included word for word the admonition from the Ministry of the Interior. This proclamation, which quickly became public knowledge, declared that 'there are senseless rumours that a wave of dismissals and displacements is soon to break over the German clergy. In particular it is said that all those pastors are in danger who do not belong to the Faith Movement of German Christians. Let me state that these rumours represent an especially malicious misleading of public opinion... I will never allow anyone to suffer a disadvantage simply because he is not a German Christian. I repeat what I said at Wittenberg: "The church-political battle is over. The battle for the soul of the Volk is beginning." Let me appeal to all pastors: Take your place confidently in this battle!'[11] When this proclamation did not have the hoped-for effect, two weeks later Pfundtner wrote to the Reich Bishop over a similar appeal. On this occasion the Secretary of State was even plainer. Referring to the increasing polarization in the church he spoke of the grave dangers that could arise for the whole renewal work of the government. The Reich Bishop was therefore to use all his influence to bring about peaceful co-operation of all groups in the church. In his reply the Reich Bishop again referred to his Wittenberg speech and to the proclamation of 11 October. Moreover he had 'commissioned Church Minister Weber by means of negotiations with the leaders of all the groups hitherto in conflict as far as possible to take the existing conflicts out of the area of power politics into that of theological struggle'. Within a foreseeable time he would strengthen the measures taken so far by a newsletter to all pastors. After their previous experiences, on the whole the church people had begun to quieten down nicely.' He was 'further concerned to advance this trend as vigorously as possible.'[12] But on 6 November, as this letter went off, a development emerged which suggested anything but a quieter time.

Ludwig Müller's peace announcement had provoked a response in a place where the Reich Bishop had doubtless least expected it: in the Reich leadership of the NSDAP.

Since Hitler had returned to his basic church-political decision on 5 August on the Obersalzberg, in the presence of the Reich leaders and the Gau leaders, and had ordered the withdrawal of the movement 'from the fight over confessional questions', very little had appeared in public about this decision. Only Alfred Rosenberg's leading article of 16 August had attracted attention here and there. Otherwise the state and the Party still seemed to stand right behind the German Christians. Apparently in Germany the view was increasingly making itself felt that a good National Socialist must of necessity also be a good Christian. In any case, the Reich Minister of the Interior felt compelled at the end of September 'at the special request of the Reich Chancellor' to make the request 'for restraint from any measures by subordinate civil servants that could be perceived and interpreted as official influence towards a return to the church'.[13]

Of course this apparent move towards the church inevitably caused even more displeasure in the Party than in the state. Its völkisch centre had in any case fallen into line with Hitler's church politics only hesitantly, and was just waiting for the moment when the movement could again draw a demarcation line from the churches. This moment seemed to have arrived with the end of the Reich church development. From local units of the Party – for example particularly Schleswig-Holstein, which was almost 100% German Christian, the idea was criticized with marked irritation 'as if now for all eternity the Faith Movement of German Christians is to be supported by the NSDAP with all possible means'. Rather, the Party had supported the Faith Movement only 'to defeat the most *reactionary* circles in the church, which did not have the slightest sympathy for our movement.' But that certainly did not mean 'that we, as National Socialists, approve of everything that happens in the churches or in the church organization.'[14]

There was also a similar reserve in a letter from the Reich leadership of the NSDAP, which introduced the dissociation of the Party from the German Christians throughout Germany. 'A constant stream of complaints,' wrote Stabsleiter Bormann in it to the Reich leaders and the Gau leaders, 'is going to the Führer's representative through the Reich Ministry of the Interior that the National Socialists who did not vote for the German Christian list commended by the Führer's representative have been excluded from the Party and the Women's Auxiliary, or have suffered other disadvantages because of their position. The aim of the church elections has been achieved. It is not the Führer's intention to take further action over matters to do with the election. Expulsions and the like will therefore not take place.'[15]

At first these were only internal instructions, which need not necessarily have troubled the German Christians. The misfortune came only when Ludwig Müller, pressed by the Reich Ministry of the Interior, evidently went very directly counter to the further wishes of the grass-roots and leadership of the Party with his Peace Declaration. For the Reich Bishop's announcement of the church-political neutrality of the Reich Church suggested that the Reich leadership of the NSDAP was affirming the church-political neutrality of the Party. Thus, to the dismay of the German Christians and the delighted satisfaction of the German Faith Movement, on 17 October a regulation appeared from the

Führer's Deputy which took precisely this position. 'In connection with the declaration by Reich Bishop Müller,' it read, briefly and tersely, 'according to which no pastor shall suffer because he does not belong to the Faith Movement of German Christians, I ordain that no National Socialist may suffer any detriment because he does not belong to a particular line of belief or confessional community, or because he does not belong to any confession at all. Faith is a deeply personal matter, for which the individual is answerable only to his own conscience. Coercion of consciences may not be practised.'[16]

The German Christians immediately perceived that in this regulation nothing less than their existence was at stake. For this existence was grounded in the conviction that the German Christian movement fulfilled Article 24 of the Party programme – the Party's confession of positive Christianity – as understood by Hitler and the Party. But this very conviction was done away with by the new announcement. As Friedrich Wieneke later noted quite rightly in his memoirs, it detached 'as it were the whole world-view of the Party from the church and Christianity', and in fact amounted to something like a 'change in fortunes' for the German Christians.[17] The German Christian hope for the positive Christianity of the Third Reich proved to be what it had always been: an illusion.

If the German Christians wanted to know what the regulation meant for them, they had only to read the triumphant commentary of their German faith opponents in the *Reichswart*. 'Freedom of conscience is here!', Reventlow wrote as the headline to his first comment on Hess's regulations, and declared: 'Now we have an end to the pestering of those who are not Christian. There will be an end to compulsory church-going with threats of fines and other punishments... The high and mighty pastors may no longer command prayers aloud. They and their fellow workers must now also deny themselves the special pleasure of forcing the gospel down the throats of non-Christians and attempting to compel them to be saved with the fists of the SA... It will soon be evident how much missionary attraction is left.'[18] From now on the *Reichswart* reprinted the new regulation incessantly, and urged readers to do everything possible to secure its dissemination. 'To make a clear distinction and separation between politics and religion, and everything that goes with them', had been Hitler's point of view from the beginning up to the present, and anyone who supported this also supported Hitler and the Party.[19]

In a desperate leading article in *Evangelium im Dritten Reich* Provost Fritz Lörzer, Hossenfelder's deputy, attempted to avert these consequences. The title was 'German Freedom of Conscience!' and the emphasis was evidently on the word 'German'. The Hess regulation, the article said, openly expressed 'what was self-evident to every Evangelical Christian, every Protestant'. 'We must come to God not as bondsmen but as free. Compulsory "faith" is a contradiction in terms.' The German Christians also affirmed, of course, 'with full hearts that the promotion of freedom of conscience is to be taken for granted'. But – and here Lörzer repeated the fundamental belief of the whole Faith Movement – this freedom of conscience did not alter the fact that Christianity was 'the norm... for Adolf Hitler's Third Reich'. 'For us it is something to be taken for granted, something about which we have never wondered,' he affirmed, 'that National Socialism and Christianity belong together'. The Party was tied to Christianity 'with a thousand unbreakable threads – spiritually, at the roots'. 'In this movement of Adolf Hitler there is no place for the thoroughly Marxist, basically liberal phrase "Religion is a private matter". Without doubt' – and here Lorenz was of course referring to the representatives of German Faith – 'the many little groups and circles of mystical enthusiasts or free thinkers disguised as nationalists will attempt to twist the self-evident, clear decree of Rudolf Hess in this liberal direction... Woe to us if we do not perceive the danger in time.' There followed once again in one sentence the creed of the German Christians: 'Adolf Hitler did not put Christianity alongside a thousand other world-views, all of equal worth or equal lack of worth; rather, he founded the Party on the basis of a positive Christianity, just as he himself, as all who know him are aware, is a believing and praying Christian.'[20]

These evocative phrases could not, of course, do away with the impression that the Party was in the process of dissociating itself from the German Christians and at the same time opening itself up to the new völkisch religion.

The German Christians had been troubled by fears of this kind since at the end of July Hauer and Reventlow had united the German Faith leagues and associations with the German Faith Movement, and in the meantime much had happened that could only justify those anxieties. That the völkisch ideas fell on fertile soil in the Party and especially in the Hitler Youth is evident, for example, from reports in the youth press agency *Wille und Werk*, which under the heading 'The young generation in the German Faith Movement' wrote that the German Faith ideas were working powerfully and that the 'forces of the young generation, ready for sacrifice' were now being concentrated in working groups in order to assist the deepest religious longing of the German Volk to find fulfilment.[21] In this connection Baldur von Schirach, the young Reich Youth Leader, aroused extraordinary attention at a regional leaders conference in Frankfurt an der Oder on 5 October when he spoke of a Reich Church and to tumultuous applause declared: 'I belong to no confession. I am neither Protestant nor Catholic. I believe only in Germany.'[22] Among students, too, völkisch ideas were having an increasingly favourable reception. The training leader of the National Socialist German Student Union, Dr von Lees, was a member of the Führerrat of the German Faith Movement along with the Leipzig philosopher Ernst Bergmann, who, in a much-noted lecture in Berlin University on 12 October sharply contrasted Christianity with Nordic-Germanic faith and virtually declared that National Socialism and Christianity were incompatible.[23]

In view of all this, the 1 October Hess's announcement inevitably had the effect of being a first step towards official Party endorsement of the German Faith Movement, which finally gave völkisch forces a free hand in the Party. And that is the way in which Hauer himself understood it. In his memorandum to Hitler, Frick and Jäger dated 24 August in the name of the German Faith Movement he had already called for 'the official recognition of the validity of our German Faith – that is, the free exercise of this German Faith and independent instruction in the faith and the education of our children in Germanic models'.[24] And now he declared in Stuttgart that the first goal of the German Faith Movement, the establishment of freedom of faith and conscience in the religious sector, would be quickly achieved through Hess's published decree. The second goal was the struggle for recognition and the right to organize parallel to the church. The third goal was to win for the movement its share in the religious training and leadership of German youth.[25]

In this development the German Christians suddenly saw themselves faced with the danger that the Party might decide as it were to pass them over in favour of the völkisch religion of the German Faith movement. And this now inevitably led to vigorous criticism within the Faith Movement too. The Wittenberg compromise began to break up. It was especially the radical völkisch group of the former German Church supporters which raised the question who was to blame for the apparently startling turn round of the Party. This group, which with the Gauobmann Dr Krause and Johannes Schmiedchen, the vigorous church Kreisleiter of Berlin Land II, firmly controlled the Berlin Gau of the German Christians, was in any case dissatisfied with the compromises of Ludwig Müller. Thus the answer to the question of the Party's attitude was not difficult. The Peace Declaration of the Reich Bishop, to which Hess had in fact explicitly referred, bore the blame for the whole mistaken development. For with this Peace Declaration the Reich Bishop had given a hand to the church opposition, and thus made clear to the Party that he, too, merely intended to restore the old church, instead of building the new German Volkskirche by means of a radical völkisch revolution. As early as 15 October the newly founded Sunday paper of this group, *Unsere Volkskirche*, had warned of the danger that a 'prelates' church' might replace the previous 'pastors' church', 'ruled over high-handedly by the princes of the church, on the basis of an authority which comes to them automatically in the age of the Führer principle'. The connection was obvious when the statement went on to say: 'We must be clear that to disappoint the church Volk again will prepare the ground for a new "cult of the Germanen" which certain circles are propagating.'

That the criticism of the group was in addition aimed at the whole ceremonial officialdom of the Reich Church was shown by the next issue of the paper, which carried a massive attack on the church leadership. In the author's opinion, 'church people will fail to understand how the millions which, for example, the Prussian state pays the church go entirely in church administration...Church people will have little understanding of how in the consistories and so on an administrative apparatus has been constructed which has little to do with Christianity but a great deal to do with bureaucracy... Nor do church people understand why, for example, certain senior clergy are paid RM 40,000 annually (and more). RM 500 a month for rent seems sheer hypocrisy at a time when the unemployed receive scarcely that much in support for an entire year.'[26] The unrest and dissatisfaction of the Berlin group were, finally, expressed in two official resolutions, in which Ludwig Müller was accused of demanding too much of the Party with his Peace Declaration and of having given an advantage to the opponents of the German Christians.

On 28 October Ludwig Müller struck back. He could only warn, he wrote to the Greater Berlin Gau of the Faith Movement, against 'interpreting decrees from the highest post in the Party in unauthorized ways. Rudolf Hess most gladly authorized my Declaration and also took the opportunity to make it clear that as far as the Party was concerned no one church position was to be regarded as the only one possible. Here, a breach of Point 24 of the Party Programme was as far from his mind as any thought of advancing our religious opponents.' His

527

declaration, continued the Reich Bishop, was in no sense meant to leave everything in the church the way it used to be, and for example to fail to dismiss preachers unfit for their task. Rather, it is the intention to prevent illegitimate violent measures against our church opponents... the coming missionary campaign among the Volk will show our opponents how we work.' At the end of the letter Ludwig Müller attempted to make a decisive impact on everyone. 'I resolutely reject the idea that our opponents have been given the advantage by my Declaration. No compromises will be made. I insist on my purpose to see an end to the church-political struggle, and I declare that this is also the will of the Führer.'[27]

But this half step towards the radical side, to which the revolutionary criticism compelled the Reich Bishop, could only increase the difficulties which had arisen long before on the other side – the moderates. This was clear especially in Württemberg. Here the small radical leadership group of the German Christians, with the young pastor Wilhelm Rehm at its head, had not succeeded in standing up to the Bishop. The substantial tensions within the Württemberg Faith Movement had led in September to a split which ended on 14 October in the official resignation of more than 200 pastors.[28] Those who still remained loyal to the Land leadership of the German Christians after that rapidly lost all status and influence. Wurm had told the Reich Bishop at the beginning of October what was at stake: 'Is the church parallel government which was being advocated by certain advocates of the Faith Movement now being brought to an end? Or is it to go on, in such a way that no work can be done, because constant attacks have to be fought off from this quarter?' Wurm had justifiably been able to point out how much he had endeavoured to have every assistance given to the Faith Movement in Württemberg 'and to overcome the misgivings of the best of the clergy, with such success that 300 pastors have joined it. But now a split has come about, which has to do with the carrying over of methods of political struggle into the life of the church against the wishes of the majority... If you, Reich Bishop, could speak a word of clarification in this matter, many servants of the church would be eternally grateful to you.' At the same time Wurm urgently requested a confidential personal discussion with the Reich Bishop.[29] On 13 October the Bishop of Württemberg wrote another letter to Berlin on the same subject, which he also disclosed to Land Bishop Meiser of Bavaria six days later, with the observation that he – Wurm – had reasons for assuming 'that the leadership of the German Evangelical Church' was considering 'an action against the Bavarian and Württemberg Landeskirchen'.[30] Obviously the south was beginning to mobilize against the radical demands of the Berlin leadership. A letter which was kept very confidential, from Wurm to Professor Fezer of Tübingen, who in October was still standing by Ludwig Müller, makes this especially clear. 'Everybody in Württemberg knows,' wrote the Land Bishop, 'that it is a question of Rehm or Wurm, the triumph of brutal political methods or the establishment of a genuine ecclesiastical and nationalist line. Neutrality is no longer possible.' At the same time the letter showed the willingness and ability of Fezer, who had previously been one of the strongest supporters of Ludwig Müller, openly to admit his mistakes. With the intention of encouraging Fezer to emerge from the shadows of corrupting compromises, he stated frankly: 'I do not hesitate to admit that in the agreements which led to the production of the Unity list and voluntarily opened the way to a German Christian majority in the Landeskirchentag I presupposed a totally different attitude to the group from the one that emerged later. I do not find that this has damaged my authority in any way. No one is obliged to be infallible, but everyone is obliged to deal honestly according to the circumstances...'[31] Not least because of this rare readiness and ability to take note of past mistakes and openly acknowledge them the Land Bishop of Württemberg was later to become the undisputed leading authority in the Protestant church in Germany.

By contrast, Fezer could not find a way to admit his mistakes. Nevertheless he showed himself so impressed by Wurm's arguments and also by his experiences in Berlin that at the beginning of November he began carefully to dissociate himself from Ludwig Müller and the German Christians. After long hesitation, on 6 November he informed the Reich Bishop that he had decided not to accept a call to Berlin (which he had already received during the summer) and so at the same time he would also take leave 'of the circle of your Berlin colleagues'.[32]

Fourteen days later the whole group of Tübingen professors had already been expelled from the Faith Movement.

As early as October, then, the beginnings of a 'southern line' emerged which was soon to play a substantial role in the Reich Church. When at the beginning of November Pastor Heidenreich, Hossenfelder's colleague, negotiated with the leaders of the secession, the first announcement that he made was: 'The behaviour of the Württemberg group (and moreover the use of the word "north wind" and the conspiracy with Bavaria) was anti-Hossenfelder, anti-Prussian and an attempt to form a new main line! But it was worth noting – and from the perspective of Berlin very suspicious (not least from a political perspective) that Bavaria, Württemberg and recently also Baden were demanding that the Land leadership be put under the Land Bishop. That could not be permitted by the Reich Church. For the revolutionary struggle against outdated church institutions that was needed could not be led by the authorities themselves.'[33]

But it was not only in the south that difficulties arose. A church territory which the German Christians firmly controlled, namely the new church of Greater Hessen, proved to be an almost insoluble problem. Although in early October, as Church Minister and Reich Leader, Hossenfelder had personally attempted to reach an agreement on future developments between the German Christian representatives from Darmstadt, Wiesbaden and Frankfurt, he was unable to resolve the rivalry between the three former Landeskirchen.[34] This was all the more painful for the Reich Bishop in that August Jäger took this manifest failure as an excuse to make very vigorous accusations against the Reich Church government. With reference to the scandalous events in Hessen which Jäger attributed especially to the boundless ambition of the Frankfurt pastor Georg Probst, he declared that it was incomprehensible 'how the trust which should exist between state and church should be trifled with in this way'.[35] And soon afterwards, in an official express letter from the Prussian Kultusministerium, he urged the Reich Bishop at last to give some attention 'to the elimination of all ambiguities' and by virtue of his position as Führer to clarify the situation by an authoritative pronouncement.[36] The letter contained an undisguised threat that he might take things in Hessen back into his own hands – a step which, after all that had happened, could only plunge the Reich Bishop and the Reich Church government into incalculable difficulties.

Thus already by the end of October it was plain that the Reich Church was on shaky ground. And this was true regardless of the church opposition, which at this time began to marshal its forces further – organizationally, and above all theologically.

In these circumstances Müller and Hossenfelder decided to retreat by advancing. For neither the one nor the other, the Reich Church Cabinet nor the Reich leadership of the German Christians, was willing and able to work on the difficulties in detail. So at a session of the Reich leadership which Hossenfelder had called in Berlin for the evening of 17 October, he passed on the new slogan. 'The movement's drive,' he told the gathering, 'must not slacken. It must go on growing. It must be therefore the first call of the Reich Bishop to accomplish the most difficult tasks. And these tasks may be briefly summed up in one word: Volksmission. Mission to the Volk was the new magic notion to which Müller and the whole movement began increasingly to cling. Then the Reich Bishop, who took part in the session as patron of the Movement, also took up the slogan. After again explaining the 13 October decree to the meeting, he stressed (as the minutes put it) 'most urgently the need for a great offensive directed at the whole clergy, to win them for more vigorous, more direct work in the reconstruction of the church'.[37]

The whole session was visibly aimed at winning back for the German Christians the initiative which everywhere was slipping out of their hands. And in this connection the Reich Bishop evidently felt it necessary again to be more open on a matter which in the past for many reasons he had kept in the background: the Jewish question.

Without doubt Ludwig Müller had been a convinced adherent of the National Socialist racist ideology – at the latest from the time of the Nuremberg Reich Party Conference.[38] Only concern for foreign opinion had restrained him from calling in his Wittemberg programmatic address for the Aryan paragraph also to be introduced into the Reich Church. To reassure the Anglo-Saxon churches in particular the Reich Bishop had sent Fezer and Hossenfelder to England with direct instructions to explain 'to all official posts' with which they came into contact, 'especially the English bishops, but also the German Embassy and perhaps in church assemblies, that the official position of the Reich Church government was that there was no thought of implementing the Aryan Paragraphs in the German Evangelical Church'.[39] The journey, which took the two prominent leaders of the Reichskirche to London, Oxford and Cambridge, was a great success, above all because of this declaration and also because of the vigorous support from Frank Buchman and the Oxford Group.[40]

By contrast, the wretched reality of the situation in the church of the Prussian Land Bishop Ludwig Müller is revealed in a petition which arrived on his desk the very day his representatives were giving their soothing reassurances in England. The writer was a puzzled father who had to explain to his son, a third, semester theology student, that on his mother's side he was not of pure Aryan descent and therefore had to give up his studies. 'And now I take the liberty,' the letter said, 'of addressing this petition, on the advice of the Dean of the Theological Faculty of the University of Halle, Dr Schomerus, to Your

530

Excellency, with the urgent plea to let my son continue his studies and not to deny him the calling of a minister. I plead sincerely that he be restored to the German community; that he be regarded as an Aryan and may serve his fatherland in the study of which he has become so fond and in subsequent posts. Because I have faith in the goodness of Your Excellency, I place the fate of my son in your hands in confident trust.' Ludwig Müller had the letter answered by one of his theological advisers, the Jena Professor Hans-Michael Müller. 'The Reich Bishop,' the answer went, 'cannot disregard the regulation just introduced by the state, even in your case. The issue is not essentially a matter of church law, on which the Reich Bishop is free to rule. Rather, the church must recognize the principles and ordinances of the völkisch state. In cases involving new training and new appointments it is impossible to deviate from this rule.'[41]

The Reich Bishop now thought it necessary to repeat this openly to the Reich leadership. According to *Evangelium im Dritten Reich* he stressed urgently 'how important it is to be unyielding in *implementing the Aryan principle*. Here no attention is to be paid to misunderstandings which might arise as a result. The person who does not know the full German distress of the last fifteen years does not have the right to judge our present measures. We must take harshness over individual cases on our consciences, where necessary, so that the future may be built.'[42]

The hope that this declaration would again bring the Party, even far into völkisch circles, behind the German Christians, was, however, disappointed. But the Reich Bishop's phrases triggered off a reaction in the church opposition which directly endangered the existence of the Reich Church, which was fragile enough anyhow. For however disunited the church opposition still was in October, in the matter of the Aryan Paragraph clarity obtained.

A short time beforehand, *Evangelischer Ruf*, a weekly appearing in Breslau, had made the whole question clear in an unforgettable image.

'A Vision'

Church service. The opening hymn has ended. The pastor stands at the altar and begins:
'Non-Aryans are requested to leave the church.'
No one moves.
'Non-Aryans are requested to leave the church immediately.'
Again all remain quiet.
'Non-Aryans are requested to leave the church immediately.'
Thereupon Christ comes down from the altar cross and leaves the church.

When the editor of this paper was sent to a concentration camp for this contribution, Martin Niemöller protested to the Reich Minister of the Interior in the name of the whole Pastors Emergency League. The letter was sent at the very time when Ludwig Müller was again calling for the ruthless implementation of the Aryan Paragraph. It was therefore only consistent that the Council of Brethren of the Pastors Emergency League should decide on 9 November to break off all discussions with the Reich Church government and the German Christians until the Reich Bishop's statements had been clarified.[43]

During these October days of 1933, the church opposition had two clearly different focuses. One was in the Rhineland, the other in Berlin.

It was no accident that the church opposition was concentrated in the Rhineland in particular. There the church, like all the other Prussian provincial churches, had been reorganized into a diocese by the bishops' law of the Prussian General Synod. While this law was vigorously disputed everywhere, in the Rhineland it touched the nerve of the church. For here were large Reformed communities aware of their character, which would rather bring persecution upon themselves than make the slightest compromise over their presbyteral-synodical order and obey a bishop. And on 10 October the thirty-eight-year-old pastor Dr Heinrich Oberheid took up his post in Koblenz as the first Rhineland bishop.

Oberheid, who was soon also to play an important role in Berlin, was beyond doubt a special figure among the leaders of the German Christians. At first successful as an economist in a Rhineland industrial concern, he had started the study of theology late and had been called to his first pastorate in early 1933. The Landrat of Gummersbach, Dr Krummacher, German Christian Gau Führer in the west, had noticed the gifted and lively young preacher, and so it happened that in a certain sense Oberheid's church career led directly from his second examination to one of the largest and most difficult episcopal sees in the Prussian church.

The new bishop knew very well what difficulties awaited him. Thus the word of greeting with which he entered office was more balanced than many that appeared at this time. It began with a thanksgiving for the new order that God had allowed Germany, and defined the task of the church within the new political reality as a task which was 'at all times... one and the same...', namely to proclaim the gospel of Jesus Christ, crucified and risen, who came into the world to save sinners. 'The church must carry out this task. With this message it may not allow itself to be limited by any power.' On the other hand, the structures within which the church carries out this task changes, depending on the times. In the past that was disputed; but now the battle was at an end. 'In fellowship with all of you,' Oberheid proclaimed to the Rhineland communities, 'the task appointed to me as the first Rhineland bishop is to urge and to maintain that the newly created office of bishop shall have the spirit, content and form of a truly evangelical episcopal ministry'.[44]

At the same time Oberheid attempted to start a theological discussion of the principles of the German Christians. At a small conference of ten clergy and laity whom he invited to Rengsdorf, seven theses were worked out which, as 'Rengsdorf Theses', were sent to all Protestant manses in the Rhineland. Once again they presented that political-theological approach which negated a 'universal Christianity', 'Christianity as such', and took as its point of departure, rather, the roots of Christianity in German Volkstum. The Theses accordingly claimed that there could be no conflict in 'an unlimited commitment to the gospel on the one hand and likewise an unlimited commitment to German Volkstum on the other'.

These theses provoked the expected lively opposition. In addition to Karl Barth, it was above all the young Düsseldorf pastor Joachim Beckmann who disputed the German Christian understanding of the gospel and Volkstum. 'The gospel is the word of God; state and Volkstum are not. Therefore the Christian gives only the Word of God the honour of an unlimited commitment.'

Joachim Beckmann's work *Generic Christianity or Scriptural Faith in Christ?* rightly regarded the political theology of the German Christians as enthusiasm, and thus clearly added a new critical note to that of Karl Barth. Beckmann caught the spirit and the sensibility of the time precisely when he concluded that in all controversies with the Faith movement one kept coming up against the same thing: 'Being seized by the national revolution, the experience of National Socialism, being caught up in the dynamic of this rhythm – that is the source of the theological teachings, the church-political demands and the unrestrained fighting methods of the German Christians. And it is *precisely the incursion of the national experience into the domain of the Lordship of Christ which makes the German Christian movement enthusiasm*. Where that occurs, the possessed, enthusiastic human being, fanatically convinced of the truth of his experience, becomes the one who shapes, and thus the lord of the faith and the church who goes at will beyond the Ten Commandments: John 10.1ff. Since the Reformation we have called this enthusiasm, and we must continue to do so today.'[45]

However, the church opposition in the Rhineland received its real direction less from this discussion than from a group which made a first public appearance at this time: the Coetus of Reformed Preachers in Germany. It was above all the idea of the Barmen pastor Karl Immer, in connection with the rise of the Rhineland Pastors Brotherhood, to found an alliance of Reformed pastors who were loyal to the confession. The first communication (dated 21 September) mentioned as a starting point 'the church's need, especially the condition of the clergy, whose theological innocence and brittle character shame us deeply.' Completely under the influence of earnest and strict Reformed Pietism, of the kind typical of Wuppertal, this circular letter declared as its aims 'to gather around word and sacrament for mutual upbuilding those servants of the word who have not succumbed to the spirit of the times (*censura morum, consolatio fratrum mutua*) and for encouragement in ministry through prayer, daily deepening in the Word of God, serious theological work and a monthly meeting of the brethren (compulsory)'. The old Reformed self-awareness still rang out in the statement: 'We mean to arm ourselves to fulfil the task which the Reformed church has had of old, to be a bulwark against Rome.'[46] In contrast to the more open Pastors Emergency League, in which liberal theologians could also find a home, the Reformed Coetus was from the beginning committed to a strongly biblical stance and remained so. But the Reformed basis of this circle worked in a direction which was decisive for the rise of the Confessing Church. According to the Reformed Confession, the Coetus could only recognize church decisions reached in the communities and in synods formed from communities. The Rhineland Coetus had a decisive part in the success at the end of 1933, in taking the church question out of the hands of church-political groups and making it the concern of the communities. The September circular letter already stated: 'We are convinced that church-political negotiation is possible only for living communities – not through individuals or through groups. We therefore demand of those who unite in a covenant: "Get out of all church-political fronts, groups and movements... Our struggle is over the community, so that as the body of Christ it may be brought into obedience to its exalted head. Our struggle is over the position of the servants of the word to whom we know that we are responsible for loyal intercession, admonition and comfort, for every service of brotherly love".[47]

The first instructions, which were sent out a week later, consisted of the biblically based opposition to the two most important laws of the General Synod – the Bishops' Law and the Aryan Paragraph. Because these laws, it was finally stated, 'conflict with the clear wording of Holy Scripture, they may not be recognized by any community bound by the Word of God.' At the same time the instructions contained the duty of all preachers to teach their communities and call on them to take the appropriate measures.[48]

One of the first communities to accept this invitation was the great Reformed Church of Barmen-Gemarke. Immediately after Oberheid took office, the presbytery passed a resolution which left no doubt as to where this church stood. 'In the light of Holy Scripture,' it stated, 'such a so-called bishop's office, superior to other church offices, is neither enjoined nor blessed, and it cannot be imposed in any legal manner upon a community of the church which is reformed according to the Word of God, because it conflicts with its confession. In particular, we make the sharpest protest against the establishment of the bishopric of Cologne-Aachen... We emphasize in all seriousness that any infringements of the presbyteral-synodical rights and ordinances of our community, especially of the right of the free election of elders and preachers, must be excluded.'[49]

Soon afterwards, on 13 October, the first assembly of Reformed preachers took place in Elberfeld. About forty pastors had attended. The new fellowship now for the first time called itself a Coetus – after the Coetus which John à Lasco had founded 400 years earlier in Emden, in order to exercise church discipline in the circle of preachers of the young Reformed Church of East Friesia. Karl Barth, too, took part in this first assembly. And from then on the Coetus provided the Bonn theologian with his closest fellowship within the church opposition – the group within which he felt that he was best understood. Karl Barth's mistrust of the Berlin business and its speedy success had been unmistakable when the Coetus refused to join the Pastors Emergency League. 'We find it suspicious,' their report stated, 'when 2000-3000 pastors immediately combine in a league. "The crowd is too big."'[50] Barth's resolution was equally unmistakable when the Coetus decided not to have the bishop's greeting read in the communities and requested all brethren to respond in the same way. In conclusion Barth admonished the gathering: 'The Word of God makes its own way. The Word takes care of us. We do not have to take care of the Word. When we know that, we can stand in this hope by our Leader in all decisions, firm and unmoved. Our church does not need heroes now but just plain ordinary *men*, who hear God's word and act accordingly; who do not just repeat the words of the fathers but like them also make them a reality: "Here I stand. I can do no other."'[51]

Furthermore, only a few weeks later, the Coetus also had its own organ – a biblical weekly with the programmatic title *Unter dem Wort*. The introduction stated that the editors were committed 'to provide for the community in which we are called as elders and servants of the Word and seek to be obedient to the gospel by means of a free weekly newspaper drawing on the divine text of the Old and New Testaments. In this way we seek to provide help towards standing firm in time of temptation. As far as we can, we mean to prevent any clouding of the issues. We seek to call to repentance under the judgment of God. And we seek to be ambassadors of free grace: Be reconciled with God!'[52] *Unter dem Wort* soon became the watchword of the church opposition in the Rhineland. It had its own special biblical style, though later it was not free from a tendency towards narrowness and legalism. But at this time, under the leadership of Karl Barth, it led to a clarity and decisiveness which was scarcely reached anywhere else in German Protestantism.

In Berlin developments differed, and were in open tension with the Rhineland. Here Ludwig Müller had commissioned Church Minister Otto Weber to enter into theological discussions with the church opposition over a possible way forward together. The group which Otto Weber invited for this was colourful enough. For the church opposition he invited Jacobi, Künneth, Lilje, Merz and Niemöller; the German Christians involved, apart from himself, were Leffler, Hans-Michael Müller, Schirmacher and Wieneke.[53] Remarkable as this conversation appears in retrospect, at the time it did not seem to be totally hopeless. For the clearest and most decisive theologian of the Berlin circle, Dietrich Bonhoeffer, had already resigned in September and decided to leave his position in Berlin to take over a German pastorate in London. Unlike Barth, who was not only older and professionally more independent, but had also begun to find support for his activity in Berlin in the Coetus, the twenty-seven-year-old Bonhoeffer was almost alone in his convictions. It was understandable that he did not feel prepared for this situation in the long run. He justified his decision to Barth at the end of October: 'I felt that I was incomprehensibly in radical opposition to all my friends, that my views of matters were taking me more and more into isolation, although I was and remained in the closest personal relationship with these men – and all that made me anxious, made me uncertain. I was afraid I would go wrong out of obstinacy – and I saw no reason why I should see these things more correctly, better than so many able and good pastors to whom I looked up, so I thought that it was probably time to go into the wilderness for a while and simply do pastoral work...'[54] Karl Barth knew what he was doing when he passionately criticized this decision four weeks later. 'What is all this about "going away", "the quietness of pastoral work", etc., at a moment when you are just wanted in Germany. You, who know as well as I do that the opposition in Berlin and the opposition of the church in Germany as a whole stand on such weak feet! That every honest man must have his hands full making it sharp and clear and firm! That now perhaps everything is going down the drain not because of the great power and deceit of the German Christians, but because of the pig-headedness and stupidity, of the desperate shallowness of, of, of all people, the anti-German Christians... No, to all the reasons and excuses that you might perhaps still be able to put in front of me, I will only give one answer: "And the German church? And the German churches?" – until you are back again in Berlin to attend faithfully and truly to the machine-gun which you have left behind there...'[55]

In fact, with Bonhoeffer's departure, in principle the way to a theological compromise no longer seemed blocked in Berlin. This was demonstrated by an article which Künneth published on 19 October in *Junge Kirche*, in which under the headline 'Authentic Fronts' he declared that the demand of the hour was 'readiness for legal co-operation specifically in this Reich church, specifically in this Volk and their national revival, specifically in Hitler's state'. This co-operation was necessary both for the sake of maintaining the Volkskirche and because of the need of the Volk, which politically was like 'a besieged fortress'. Künneth saw the coming 'authentic front' in the awakening of 'völkisch-German religious feeling', on which the spirits would very soon part company.[56] This article clearly took Ludwig Müller's line completely, and so long as the issue was not the Aryan Paragraph – and throughout October this was not a public issue – a compromise between the Reichskirche and the church opposition in Berlin seemed by no means completely out of the question.

During these occurrences and reflections, the construction of the organization of the Pastors Emergency League was completed. The first joint meeting of delegates from throughout the German Evangelical Church which in practice represented the constituency of the League took place in Niemöller's Dahlem manse on 20 October. The thirty-seven participants in this session came from eighteen different Landeskirchen and Prussian provincial churches.

Their reports demonstrated how varied the situation was in the individual church territories. Above all relations with the already existing church opposition groups like the Silesian working group Evangelium und Kirche, the Westphalian Brotherhood, the Landeskirche groups in Hanover and Württemberg was unclear and remained so. Accordingly the number of those who were counted members or potential members fluctuated betwen 700 and 3000. By contrast, the proportion of German Christian pastors in the separate areas was estimated at about a quarter, though with great disparities. From Schleswig-Holstein, for example, Pastor Johannsen reported that of the 450 pastors in the Landeskirchen 300 were German Christians. In Hessen-Kassel, by contrast, Karl Bernhard Ritter claimed 60-70% of the clergy for the Pastors Emergency League, including the whole Marburg faculty.[57]

The most important decision that the gathering reached in the course of its consultations was the formation of its own pattern of leadership, the so-called Council of Brethren, to which eight pastors were elected. Almost all of those who belonged to the first Council of Brethren were later leading figures in the Confessing Church. This was true of Martin Niemöller, himself the unchallenged leader; likewise Hugo Hahn of Dresden, Gerhard Jacobi of Berlin, Eberhard Klügel of Hanover, Karl Lücking of Dortmund and Ludolf Müller of Heiligenstadt im Eichsfeld.[58] There were difficulties in the discussion of the nature of this new League. While some wanted to see the League as a brotherhood of pastors, others opposed that with the argument that there was no basis for this and the Emergency League could really be a League only for those pastors who found themselves in an emergency over the confession. In fact this issue was never totally clarified, even later. The Pastors Emergency League was never a clergy brotherhood like the Sydow Brotherhood or the Michael's Brotherhood. However, it was still much more than a mere emergency fund for pastors. The decisions of 20 October already showed that the common theological orientation was considered essential. Thus beginning with the First Sunday in Advent a common set of Bible readings was provided for all members. And in the first circular letter attention was emphatically drawn to the principles of the Rhineland Pastors Brotherhood, which were to serve as a point of reference for the creation of individual groups. However, the emphasis in the discussions, as in the circular letters, was on a series of specific communications. Thus questionnaires from

536

the church authorities aimed at establishing Aryan descent were not to be answered; the question of co-operation with the church leadership was left open, but was first to be discussed with the Council of Brethren. The theological discussions with the Reich church leadership – that is, the round of discussions begun by Otto Weber – were to be continued; but there was no reason, Niemöller added, to look on their further continuation 'with special optimism'.[59]

This first session also demonstrated how much the understanding of the tasks and significance of the Pastors' Emergency League depended upon the situation in a particular Landeskirche. Whereas for example the report of Hugo Hahn, who in Saxony was under the church government of Friedrich Coch, clearly expressed delight at joining a larger group, the representative of the church-theological working group in Württemberg, the young pastor Karl Vöhringer, was comparatively cool and detached. A Bavarian representative had not appeared at all. Moreover Vöhringer reported on his return that there was certainly no question that Württemberg should join the Pastors Emergency League, though they were in solidarity with it in its struggle and also wanted to demonstrate this with a financial contribution.[60]

Thus the picture which the church opposition presented in late autumn 1933 was anything but uniform. Meanwhile there were larger or smaller groups in all the Landeskirchen which had joined forces to resist. Courage, decisiveness and loyal conviction were on the increase. But this resistance was not an organized unity, nor was there agreement as to what it should be directed against. It was all the more important that in Berlin, too, a process of theological clarification now began which brought closer together the various approaches – such as were to be found, for example, in the Reformed Coetus and in the formation of the Emergency League. The occasion was the Reformation Festival, for which the church opposition had invited Karl Barth to Berlin. In thirty-six hours, from the afternoon of 30 October to the evening of 31 October, the Bonn theologian managed to persuade the Berlin circle even more of the need for theological decisions and demarcations.

The theme of the address which Karl Barth gave on the evening of 30 October in the Berlin Singakademie was 'The Reformation as Decision'. Although for fear of a ban the event was not publicized much, the Great Hall was filled to overflowing. Barth described the essence of the Reformation as the decision for the rule of God, a decision in which man has irrevocably bound and binds himself 'without any prospect of a future alternative, without leaving open any possibility of a future reversal of this decision'.[61] Then as now, the only authentic Reformation teaching was that which derived from this unconditional decision and repeated it, as for example it was expressed in the Reformation doctrines of Holy Scripture, original sin, justification and predestination. However, Barth continued, often enough this Reformation decision and the teaching derived from it had been strange and unbelievable even in the Protestant church itself: 'People choose faith with good reasons, out of earnestness and conviction; but they choose it as one of their own possibilities. They confess it, but they do not wish to ignore the many other possibilities besides faith, which they could indeed also choose in this freedom.'[62] The possibilities which were there for the choosing varied: at one time it was morality, then reason, humanity, culture, and now Volkstum and the state. But in all these expressions, Barth reiterated, there was one and the same disloyalty to the Reformation decision, and in the movement which was now dominant in the Protestant church, this disloyalty had reached its 'last, most vital, most consummate form'. And in this connection it now seemed quite clear what those who had not succumbed to this movement had to do. 'What do they have to do? Strengthened by what the Reformation has to say to us today, they have to offer *resistance*. In the name of the true evangelical church, against the dominant false church which is embodied in this movement. And this resistance will consist in the fact that in contrast to the dominant movement it will again heedlessly and joyfully stand behind the decision that has been made, as was done 400 years ago.'[63] This one word 'resistance' spontaneously seized the listeners and was given a tremendous response. Barth had to interrupt his address for several minutes.[64] And when he went on, he described the whole situation in a memorable picture which soon took on symbolic power throughout the church opposition. 'When of old the Swiss went into battle near Sempach against the armed phalanx of Leopold of Austria, one of them is said to have cried out, "Strike their spears, for they are hollow!" They *are* hollow!'[65]

Almost more important than the lecture were the three major discussions which Karl Barth had during these days with the 150 pastors who comprised the Emergency League in and around Berlin. In these discussions he attempted to make clear to those present the specific significance of the Reformation decision for their action in the present. At stake were the four questions which Barth understood as 'controlling questions': whether resistance was to be offered only in individual instances, and hence whether it would be a chance and uncertain resistance, or whether there would be a resistance which came out of a 'centre of spiritual resistance'.[66] The first question, put by Jacobi, concerned the Aryan Paragraph. Here there was widespread agreement that uncompromising resistance was called for against its implementation. The second question, which Barth associated with it, was that of the limits of loyalty to the state. Barth thought that on the basis of the same law governing church civil servants a signature might be required which committed the pastor to affirm the National Socialist state without reservation and unconditionally. 'In my opinion,' Barth continued, 'in principle this would raise the same questions as the Aryan Paragraph. And I would like... to know whether we are agreed on that. Do we have the same view here, namely the independence of the church and the freedom of the gospel?' Barth made clear at a later stage in the discussion that the issue involved specific political consequences. The only decisive issue was and remained that the church 'sought to be free in its words towards the whole event'. Specifically, this freedom meant 'certainly sometimes also saying what Goebbels says, but perhaps at others saying something quite different. In that case the specific message could be very dangerous. The specific question might, for example, be asked: What happened this summer in Germany? Did it happen justly or unjustly? This kind of seizure of power? This elimination of other parties? This confiscation of property? What has happened in the concentration camps? Can Germany, can the German church, explain this volume of suicides? Does not the church share the guilt in this because it was silent? I am only asking questions,' Barth declared. But it was obvious that these were anything but mere questions. In the late autumn of 1933 there was probably no other meeting in

Germany of similar size and openness in which speech was still so free. But this freedom was to be none other than the freedom of the gospel. 'Anyone who is to proclaim the Word of God must say to such occurrences what the Word of God says.' Once again Barth repeated emphatically: 'Truly I am not concerned about political resistance. I am concerned with the freedom of the gospel.'

Beside these specific dangers, the two other 'controlling questions' seemed to be of somewhat subordinate significance. Both of them had to do with attitudes to the church government of Ludwig Müller. But Barth was convinced that the decisive point lay here, because it was here that the decision would be made on that common understanding of gospel and church which made the political questions possible at all. So the third question was as follows: should decrees and proclamations by the Reich Church government or the Prussian Church leadership be read out in the community or not? And the decisive fourth question was: should one co-operate in any way at all with the new church government? This question had already been decided in the negative by the Reformed Coetus, and Barth now emphatically repeated this decision. And in fact on this issue depended no more and no less than the whole future course of the Protestant church in Germany. In this group of 150 pastors, Barth now developed those ideas which to a certain extent had already been worked out in the Rhineland, and which were in fact to shape the future. 'If our attitude to the present church government,' he said as the basis for a radical rejection of any co-operation, 'is such that we have to perceive it as a heretical and illegimate church government, then our attitude to it must be that of Paul to Nero. (It is well known that he did not become a Roman senator.) For anyone who sees things in this way I see no other possibility than that those who take their stand on the basis of the confession will confront heresy by coming together in a free synod. There will be no more talk of "brotherhood" and "circle", but you will know that you are there as the legitimate representatives of the true German church. And if you ask: where is the church government? the answer must be: Here in our midst.'

This was the decisive theological step which in the New Year in fact totally altered the church situation in Germany. Wherever this was understood, there were suddenly no longer church parties facing one another which could negotiate compromises. Rather, the true church stood over against the false church. This, however, opened up a perspective which was so new, so surprising, indeed almost dizzying in its effect that even more powerful impetus was needed before it began to establish itself.

At the end of October the time for so fundamental a choice was far from ripe. When the young Heinrich Vogel in his enthusiasm wanted to see an immediate decision, and called upon the assembly to assent to a confession he had drawn up,[67] Barth, shocked, pulled back. 'That won't work,' he declared. 'Up to now I have not asked for a vote. Nor should you. The issue is spiritual. You press the brethren too far when you ask them to say Yes or No to it. However important and correct your confession was – and I could vote for it myself – at this stage do we not want to avoid anything that is a mere gesture? Perhaps things may one day necessarily come to that. But out of reverence for God I do not want any mere gesture.' Heinrich Vogel understood, and withdrew his resolution. Günther Dehn, who perhaps understood Barth best at this time, later confirmed the need for a confession and the need to wait for the right moment. 'I have the feeling,' he said, looking back on the discussion, 'that we keep trying to run away from the existing situation. It is understandable that people keep trying to avoid being obedient to God. Only when we understand "Speak, Lord: thy servant heareth," have we reached the moment for a confession.'

But even if this was not yet the time for a confession, the way leading in that direction had now been indicated. It was the way that led the church opposition in Prussia to the Confessing Synod of the Evangelical Church of the Old Prussian Union, which became one of the most moving signs of spiritual resistance in the Third Reich.[68] Jacobi, who brought the meeting to a close, was right when he commented: 'Yesterday one of us said: These two days could be a turning point in church history. That is going too far, but we do sense that things have come to a turning point...'

Yet this way had hardly been begun. And a piece of news which burst upon the meeting of the 150 showed how hard it was to find, amidst the confusing mass of political and church-political slogans of the time. Once again the news was about Hitler. Charles Macfarland, a well-known American church representative who had long had contacts with Germany, had been travelling around since the beginning of October on his own initiative in order to gain his own impressions of the situation, especially of developments in the church, which were so vigorously argued over abroad. To conclude his trip, he had succeeded in arranging an interview with Hitler for mid-day on this 31 October, in order to present his findings and offer his services as a mediator. Early in the morning of this same day Macfarland met first with Barth, who sought to make three points clear: 1. The German church opposition should not be compromised abroad by being interpreted and presented as 'political opposition'; 2. Stabbing the opposition in the back by recognizing Ludwig Müller should be avoided; 3. It should be indicated that, in contrast to the Reich Church government, the German opposition represented 'the cause of the Christian church as a whole'.[69] What Barth suppressed in this later report of his discussion, he had revealed that afternoon to the 150 pastors, to their very great amusement. Barth said that in addition he had told Macfarland that he might let Hitler know 'that his having entrusted the German church to Ludwig Müller was like entrusting the army to the Captain of Köpenick'.[70] For understandable reasons Macfarland did not pass this on. But in addition Barth rightly had the feeling that the American had not understood him at all, and had gone to Hitler with the idea that there were two church groups of more or less equal size in Germany, both of which had a case, and between which mediation must therefore be undertaken.[71] Macfarland indeed described things like this during his interview with Hitler. This suggestion raised the obvious question whether Hitler himself, 'as someone who was trusted by both sides, might not receive representatives as a way of bringing about a union through his authority'. The sensation seemed perfect when Hitler declared that he was ready to do so if he was asked 'by one of the interested parties'.[72]

Soon afterwards Jacobi was called to the telephone from the gathering of the 150 and returned with the news that 'Hitler had let him know through Macfarland that he was ready to receive him, Jacobi'. It was characteristic of the pressure on all those involved that there was immediately a great spontaneous outburst of joy. Here at last a way out seemed to be emerging. And there was further great jubilation when Jacobi went on to declare: 'I will take Barth with me.' 'For a moment,' the minutes stated in showing the change of mood, 'all the comments focussed on this forthcoming event, proposals were made as to what was to be said to Hitler and the mood became more optimistic as a result of this interlude.'[73] However, it very soon proved that there was little cause for optimism. The way in which Macfarland had handed on the news was presumably a misunderstanding. In fact this great summit conversation with Hitler only took place at the end of January 1934, with quite other personnel, and ended in a complete fiasco for the church opposition.

Reactions within Berlin circles were more important for the moment. They demonstrated how little there could be any question of a real decision having been made and how difficult Karl Barth's position was even among his friends. The Council of Brethren of the Emergency League in particular found it intolerable that Barth should be the one to represent the church opposition to Hitler. The brief report which Jacobi sent to Bonn on 11 November left no doubt on the matter. 'On Thursday the Council of Brethren of the Pastors Emergency League met... Here Niemöller raised the question who should take part in the audience as a representative of the church opposition. Except for me, all took the following position: You are Swiss, and in addition a former member of the Social Democrats. If Hitler subsequently discovered this, he would feel we had gone behind his back. The whole church opposition would appear to be political opposition... I spoke against this as best I could, consistently stressed the church point of view, and repeatedly declared: That is not the issue. The issue is exclusively this, that Hitler should understand the nature of the Evangelical Church. Finally they hit on the idea that an outspoken supporter of Hitler had to be present, and the choice fell on Wilhelm Niemöller of Westphalia. A desolate situation.'[74]

Thus the two days in Berlin, with their intensive discussions, had only made a beginning. The Barth line, pressing for a resolute theological confession, and the line of Niemöller and the Council of Brethren, aiming at a church-political exclusion of the German Christians and a nationalist compromise, ran side by side largely unreconciled. Karl Barth left Jacobi in no doubt as to his opinion of this course of action. He called it 'desperately opportunistic church politics which this Council of Brethren evidently feels that it can pursue again and again', and included the whole situation in the 'chapter of examination which the whole opposition still has to go through before it can consider taking itself seriously as a church in the face of apostasy. I would not object,' he added, 'if you took the appropriate opportunity to let the Council of Brethren know my opinion of it.' Nevertheless Barth was also not without confidence in referring to the Berlin session. He concluded his letter: 'The nervousness of the German Christians is unmistakable all along the line. We can all smoke our pipes with considerably greater calm than Ludwig the Child and his people.'[75]

In fact, after all these happenings at the beginning of November Ludwig Müller could only look upon the state of the Reich Church with great uneasiness. But at least at this time the plans were complete by which the Reich Church government hoped to resolve the great tasks before the German Evangelical Church: the guidelines for achieving uniformity in the constitution of the Landeskirchen, the budget, and an emergency plan for Volksmission. These plans, taken together, indicate as nothing else the sweeping ideas with which the

Reich Church began. However, in their rapid demise they also indicate the illusory character which marked them from the beginning.

One of the major aims of the Reich Church was to be accomplished legally with the unification of the constitutions of the Landeskirchen, namely the unitary consolidation and direction of church work throughout the Reich. Hence the constitution of the Reich Church had emphatically maintained in Article 2.4 that the German Evangelical Church could provide 'uniform guidelines for the Landeskirchen in their constitution, to the extent that these are not confessionally bound'. For only in this way could the problem of the relationship of the Reich Church to the Landeskirchen – still one of the chief difficulties of the new church – be resolved. For this reason the Provisional Leadership had devoted itself intensively to this issue in August and September, and at its last Wittenberg meeting – immediately before the National Synod met – had even fixed appropriate guidelines which on 26 September were sent out to the supreme authorities in the Landeskirchen. The reason for this haste was no doubt the anxiety felt by the former leadership over the adoption of the constitutional guidelines which Jäger had laid down for the churches of Greater Hessen and Lower Saxony.[76] In fact the guidelines of the Provisional Leadership, unlike those of Jäger, strikingly stressed the independence of the Landeskirchen. This was expressed above all in certain collegial and synodical provisions. Thus the Land Bishop was not chosen – as in Jäger's proposals – by the Reich Bishop, but rather was to be selected in accordance with the proposal of a smaller body from the Land synod. Moreover the Land synod was at least to retain the right of veto in the promulgation of decrees governing the Landeskirche. In conclusion, the method of decision clearly displayed the method of German Christian rule. 'In a Christian synod,' it read, 'the conscience of its members may not be bound by parliamentary party discipline.'[77] At its second session on 6 October the Cabinet of the Reich Church had already decided to state this preparatory work and produce 'now with the utmost speed a constitutional framework for the Landeskirchen'. Otto Weber, the Minister for Church Affairs, and Professor Heckel were assigned this task. But apparently it was Heckel alone who submitted a new proposal on 19 October and then revoked it on the basis of consultations in the Reich Church Cabinet. At the request of this body, special guidelines were to be issued for the Reformed churches which would make possible an almost total elimination of the synodical element. The Reich Bishop's right to nominate the Land Bishops was similarly formulated, and thus a decisive characteristic of the Führer principle was adopted. After further consultations, on 24 October the Cabinet decided to present the guidelines to the representatives of the Landeskirchen before they were finally adopted. Surprisingly, the church leaders who met in Berlin on 3 November raised no basic objections,[78] for on 7 November the guidelines were unanimously adopted by the Reich Church Cabinet,[79] along with a law governing their introduction.

If they had ever taken effect, the 'Constitutional Guidelines for the German Evangelical Landeskirchen with the exception of the Reformed Churches'[80] would have meant a far-reaching assimilation of the Reich Church to the structural principles of the Third Reich. The same structure was uniformly provided for all the Landeskirchen, namely: Landeskirche, episcopate, deanery, district, community. The old controversy in church law between 'church principle' and 'community principle' was rigorously settled along the lines of superiority and subordination.[81] This was shown by the recommendation that the new structural principle should be clarified 'by a statement on the relationship between the highest and the lowest organizations (Landeskirche and community). The traditional formulation of the so-called community principle, "The church is based on the community", is to be avoided.' In view of these statements, which were unmistakably connected with the general tendencies of the period, a further statement was added that the community principle should be replaced with 'a new declaration on the vocation of the community itself' meant little, especially because the communities were mentioned only at the end of the guidelines and then essentially only in terms of their leadership. Superiority and subordination also defined the relationship of the church offices to one another. 'At the head of the Landeskirche,' it was clearly stated, 'stands the Land Bishop. The Land Bishop heads the Landeskirche.' His powers in this respect were practically unlimited. Just as he himself could be called and discharged only by the Reich Bishop, so in turn he nominated the members of the church government and the bishops and provosts. He was at the head of the administration, summoned the members of the synod, a third of them at his own nomination, and determined the time and place of its meetings. The bishops had the same powers for their sphere of authority, without prejudice to their 'subordination to the Land Bishop', and this also applied to the other offices. All synodical bodies from the Land synod to the council of elders in the individual communities had only advisory functions: in cases of doubt, those in office could always win. At first glance the whole thing looked like a return to Catholic constitutional principles. But since there was no basis for this understanding in Protestantism, whether in theology or in church law, it was clear that here in fact was a leadership principle which was meant to structure Reich and church according to the same basic principles. However, even before these guidelines could be sent out the Reich Church was already in process of dissolution.

No less indicative of the great hopes with which the Reich Church began was the draft of a budget for its first financial year 1934 – and its short and inglorious history. The church government had already been asked to produce this draft budget at its first meeting. At the beginning of November the budget had been sent to the Ministry of the Interior and the Reich Chancellery. Attached to it was a memorandum which explained the new budgetary approach. The tasks of the Reich Church, it pointed out, were 'far more comprehensive, independent and responsible' than those of the Kirchenbund. The new church should seize the leadership 'in all areas of church work, and by clearly stating goals and indicating directions should control the work of the Landeskirche to the last bodies and staff members. To this end,' and here the memorandum quickly got to the heart of the matter, 'it is essential that the bodies envisaged for the central government of the Reich Church provided for in the church constitution of 11 July 1933 *be fully set up and manned by the necessary complement of able, competent staff*. In addition, it is essential that bodies should be financially in a position *to guide all measures in such a way as to fulfil completely the task laid upon the new church* of an enlivening and spiritualizing united German Evangelical Christianity'.[82] Expressed in sober figures, this meant raising the budget of the Kirchenbund by about 700%. For the central church administration, which had previously required about RM 300,000, the draft budget provided about RM 1,700,000 for 1934. By the decision of the Reich Church government only the Reich Bishop was moved up into income category B-2, comparable to a Reich Minister, and was to receive a discretionary fund of RM 100,000 for his personal staff in addition to substantial expenses. In addition there was the increase in the offical staff, which with forty-five new posts was to be more than tripled. The draft budget also revealed where the Reich Church perceived the focus of its work to be, namely in a 'large-scale Volksmission', above all also in the 'SA, SS, Stahlhelm, Hitler Youth, "League of German Maidens"; the creation of Volk High Schools and other institutions for the ideological training of the broadest range of the Protestant sector of the people, especially the SA, and also among men and women, particularly the young'.[83] So the draft budget earmarked the largest new item, over RM 1,000,000 for these tasks which Hossenfelder had taken over.[84] At a time when the average weekly wage of a labourer barely amounted to RM 320, this was an almost monstrous amount. All in all, it emerged from the draft that the new Reich Church would have a financial requirement of RM 5,800,000 – as opposed to the previous RM 730,000.

Naturally, the decisive question was where this money was to come from. The Kirchenbund had previously been financed by quotas from the Landeskirchen and in an off-hand way the budget outline therefore saw extra money coming from increased Landeskirche assessments. But at the same time the memorandum left no doubt that given the extremely tight financial situation of the Landeskirchen there could in fact be no question of increased contributions. The Reich Church government therefore saw only one way out, namely 'that the Reich helps the new German Evangelical Church, formed under its protection, to carry on towards the goal also aimed at by the Reich for Volk and fatherland... *by itself covering the financial increase (RM 4,750,000 per year) at the expense of the Reich*. Without the provision of such a contribution from the Reich... fruitful Reich Church work, the speed and effectiveness of which may also prove to be the requirement of the hour from the Reich point of view, is impossible.'[85]

But the Reich evidently had a decisively different opinion as to the 'requirement of the hour'. The relevant official in the Reich Ministry of the Interior, Ministerialrat Conrad, stated at the very first consultations that the draft presented could 'certainly not be considered as the basis for a discussion'.[86] And in the Reich Chancellery at the beginning of December 1933 it was noted on the draft as the personal view of the Minister of the Interior that the Reich 'would in no way contribute more in the year 1934 than in the year 1933, but if anything rather less. According to the view of the Reich Minister, Dr Frick, the consolidation of church administration should produce savings rather than costs.'[87] After that the outline disappeared into the files without further comment.

Thus nothing had remained of the high flying financial expectations when the Reich Church Cabinet – with its second set of members, the legal standing of whom was already disputed – settled on an emergency budget for the first quarter of 1934.[88] In place of the hoped-for RM 5,800,000 only RM 1,500,000 were provided for the whole year, and even this beginning was to prove far too high. For one year later, in the emergency budget of 1936, the income assigned contributed only RM 728,000 – over RM100,000 less than the old Kirchenbund

544

had at its disposal in 1932![89] The whole increase in personnel had already been eliminated in the December 1933 budget. So too had all the plans for Volksmission and work within the church. What remained – carefully hidden under various headings – were above all the high expenses for the Reich Bishop. Thus the Reich Church which the German Christians had hoped for came to an end in financial terms, too, before it had even begun its work.

However, at the beginning of 1933, when the great plans for the Reich Church were presented one after the other in rapid succession, there was still no hint of the impending disaster. On the contrary, now at last Hossenfelder, too, finally presented his grand programme which had been conjured up time and again since the Reich Bishop's Wittenberg speech: the programme for the Volksmission to all Protestant Germans. No doubt this was close to the heart of the German Christians. Here it was that they saw their task, their hope, and their future. They had in view a comprehensive role for the church in educating the Reich, as Ludwig Müller had described it in Wittenberg: 'A new Reich is on the way. There will also be new men in the new Reich. The church must not wait until people come to her, but the church must seek the people, the people as they are now to be found: the SA and SS man, the man from the Arbeitsdienst, the man at the plough, at the lathe, in the study, the growing youth and most particularly the German wife and mother – to plant in the soul of the rising generation a living faith, a reverent trust in God, and a joyful and strong awareness of responsibility.'[90]

In view of the approach of 10 November, the 450th anniversary of Luther's birth, during these weeks plans for the great Volksmission were connected increasingly closely with the figure of Luther. The Reformer was to become as it were the spiritual patron of the new Reich Church. Since early summer 1933 a Reich working party specially set up by the German Christians had been at work for a 'German Luther Day 1933', in order to make 10 November a triumph of the völkisch Luther.[91]

The Luther text most frequently quoted at this time came from a 1521 letter, originally about the translation of Bible texts into German: '*Germanis meis natus sum, quibus et serviam*'.[92] Now this remark appeared in the form: 'I was born for my beloved Germans; it is them I want to serve,' repeated *ad nauseam* as evidence of Luther's völkisch mission to the German nation. And from one end of the country to the other it was proclaimed, as at the Jubilee celebrations in Göttingen: 'Let us be instructed by the prophet of the Germans to hear the call given to us and respond in the decisive hour. For both belong inseparably together: Luther and Germany.'[93]

The Erlangen church historian intensified this further by demonstrating 'basic parallels' and 'remarkable agreements' between Luther and Hitler. As Preuss pointed out, both had emerged 'from the cry for a great man to bring salvation'; both cames from 'peasant stock' and 'were despised as "Czechs" because of their origin'; they had experienced 'the whole misery of their age' and only in their thinking emerged 'as quite unknown and powerless people'. Finally, after many further examples, the whole portrayal issued in an 'illuminating concluding parallel': 'Before their people, Luther and Hitler felt themselves *deeply bound to God*'.[94]

In view of such bold interpretations it was natural to associate the summons to the great Volksmission with the Luther Jubilee, and thus to make it clear that the German Christians intended no more and no less than the completion of the Reformation in the German Third Reich. Indeed, at one of the first innumerable Luther celebrations that year, at the end of August in Eisleben, Luther's birthplace, Ludwig Müller stated that the Reich Church was the fulfilment of a dream 'which had inspired the pious German heart since the days of the great Reformer'. For Luther had 'always hoped and laboured to build a great German church, free of Rome'. And Alfred Bierschwale, at that time still in the Reich leadership of the Faith Movement, gave specific form to this declaration with the promise that the Reich Working Party for the German Luther Day would take pains to see to it that 'from the year 1934 on, 31 October was declared a public holiday in Germany and celebrated as a Protestants' day'.[95]

These reports disturbed the Nuncio in Berlin so much that on 7 September he personally expressed his deep concern about the plans to the Reich Minister of the Interior. Ultimately, he told Neurath, what was involved was 'the celebration of an action (the nailing of the theses on the church door in Wittenberg) which had had a plainly hostile tendency towards the Catholic Church. He, the Nuncio,' the notes on the conversation went on, 'indeed feared for the ratification of the concordat were this celebration to take place on a large scale and with government involvement'. Neurath – at this point very much the convinced Protestant – retorted 'that on the Catholic side, too, celebrations were held in Germany which were in no sense always filled with a friendly spirit towards the Protestant church', and let the whole matter rest.[96]

Characteristic as this episode was of the deep mutual distrust between the confessions in Germany, it apparently remained without influence on the attitude of the state. The Luther celebrations continued to enjoy the benevolent attention and involvement of the state, and it was entirely in keeping with the high expectations of the Reich Church when on 3 October the Reich Minister of the Interior informed the supreme Reich authorities that he intended to propose that the German Luther Day, 10 November, should be an official holiday.[97]

However, before this intention could be realized, on 14 October came word of Germany's withdrawal from the League of Nations and the announcement that on 12 November a plebiscite and new elections would be held. From then on the entire apparatus of state and Party were directed towards just one goal: propaganda for 12 November. The Friday before the day of voting, the 'German Luther Day', for which preparations had so long been made, was marked out for a climax to this propaganda campaign. It was on that day that Hitler was to make his speech in the Siemens factory, which was to become so famous.[98]

Even the Reich Church leadership was clear that the Luther celebration had no chance against this rivalry. And its decision 'to ask the Reich Chancellor to work towards keeping 10 November clear of political rallies' was just one further indication of its complete failure to understand the situation.[99] In fact the Reich Bishop sent a telegram to Hitler on 20 October: 'German Evangelical Church with forty million Protestants urgently requests Friday 10 November be kept free of political rallies if possible because already... extensive preparations have been made for celebration 450th anniversary of German Reformer Martin Luther...'[100] However, there could be no question of such a compromise, so there was no alternative for Ludwig Müller but to transfer the Luther Day to 19

546

November. It was in fact celebrated then, but without the great public attention that was hoped for.

Thus the plan to make 10 November into a grandiose Protestant national festival and at the same time to begin on the mobilization of Protestant church people had failed. Instead, this day saw the appearance of the long-heralded programme of the German Christian church administration: an appeal, guidelines and an immediate programme for Volksmission, which was to indicate the direction for the future. It was the first and last programmatic statement by the Reich Church, and once against it betrayed how far even in church affairs those with responsibility in it were living in a world of illusion. 'For the first time,' declared the appeal of the Reich Church leadership, 'one German church is celebrating one great Luther festival. The anniversary, which only looks backwards, will become the dedication festival for a new house of the German church of Martin Luther. This day should at the same time be the beginning of a joint work. The task which the present hour of German destiny presents to our church is a great one. This is the decisive battle for the soul of the German people. The hour of Volksmission is at hand.' The declared aim was: 'The face of the new Germany is to be that of a Christian Volk!'[101]

The guidelines were apparently meant to indicate how that was to be accomplished. They were put emphatically in church language and defined the task as that of Volksmission, 'proclaiming the strong and joyful message of Jesus Christ to all classes and ages of the Volk'. Beginning 'from the centre of the gospel', the group of tasks was to expand 'into three concentric circles: 1. To call people to Christ and involve them in the community. 2. To build up living communities and prepare them for service. 3. To strive with all means for the growth of evangelical piety among the people.' Here, the Volksmission was to seek 'especially a way to reach the fighters for the Third Reich, the military groups and the National Socialist youth'. There followed eight points of instruction as to substance and organization, which combined traditional experiences in popular evangelism with new demands. But the general principle behind the whole enterprise was this: 'All those working in the Volksmission must be as clearly grounded in the gospel as they are convinced members of the Third Reich.' Finally, the immediate programme, which was probably above all Hossenfelder's idea,[102] laid down uniform worship for the entire Reich Church in each month with a uniform service intended especially for Christian fathers of households, and went on to remind them of 'the priestly office of the father of the house and his responsibility for wife and child, Volk and church'. But Hossenfelder had no luck with his immediate programme either. The Württemberg Landeskirche took official exception to this 'invasion of the worship of the Landeskirche'.[103] And very soon the new programme began to be mocked and, with reference to the recent economy programme in which the state had commended dishes like stew, was called 'Stew for the Soul'.[104]

In spite of these great plans, and in spite of the apparent self confidence of the Reich Church leadership, at the beginning of November there was no mistaking the fact that barely six weeks after its foundation the Reich Church had already been seriously shaken. The Party leadership had publicly dissociated itself from the German Christians and in so doing had deprived them of their credentials for continuing to present themselves as those who were carrying out the Christian will of the Party. At the same time, this endorsed the claim of the third confession – the German Faith Movement of Hauer and Reventlow – to have equal rights as a religion in the Third Reich. The advance of this movement, specifically within the Party, was unmistakable. And this in turn had the effect of bringing out growing interest on the radical wing of the German Christians, especially in Greater Berlin and Thuringia. The Berlin Gau was poised to make revolutionary changes in the Reich Church with a new offensive. On the other side, bringing up the Aryan Paragraph had severed connections with the church opposition and it was only a matter of time until there were clashes here. A foretaste of this was given by an action of Hossenfelder: on the basis of a circular letter from the Pastors Emergency League and an 11 November article in *Junge Kirche*, he secured the dismissal from office of Pastors Martin Niemöller, Kurt Scharf and Eitel-Friedrich von Rabenau. The immediate occasion was the protest against the Aryan Paragraph, but the goal was the elimination of the opposition expected in the church to the programme of the Volksmission. On the evening of the 11th the Reich Chancellery withdrew the regulation, but after the election day it was reimposed by the President of the Oberkirchenrat, Dr Werner.[105] Finally, the South German Landeskirchen of Württemberg and Bavaria, previously Ludwig Müller's most dependable church support, decided to oppose a Reich Church which seemed largely controlled by Hossenfelder.

That the Reich Church nevertheless still largely held together during the first weeks was more for national than for church reasons. For in the Protestant church, too, Hitler's decision to leave the League of Nations and the 12 November elections resulted in all groups of the church coming together to proclaim the honour and freedom of the nation. And at those points where the German Christians had meanwhile taken control in connection with this day it again became more and more clear how far German Protestantism had in the meantime laid itself open to unbounded theological enthusiasm. For what was now expressed in many church declarations was not just enthusiasm for Hitler and his decision. Rather – and here there was no doubt an essential difference from the Catholic declaration – this was a direct interpretation of events, a piece of political theology.

'On this 12 November,' wrote *Evangelium im Dritten Reich*, 'God has put the German Volk and its destiny in the balance. Every German knows his responsibility. This is the hour of a new birth, which the Christ spirit creates in the individual as well as the whole Volk, as the new purifying will of God. Whether we realize it or not, it is God who wills our "Yes", who calls us out of doubt and anxiety to new faith, out of decline into a new future.'[106] From this it was only a step to the pulpit declaration for the Twenty-First and Twenty-Second Sundays after Trinity (5 and 12 November) signed by Land Bishop Reichardt, who had been in office since 1921, which stated: 'If the world is not to go under in deceit and betrayal, a Volk must arise as standard-bearers of the gospel of Christ, in belief in God and his realm of light. Faith in the victorious power of the saviour of the nations should be shown triumphantly in the political testimony of the German Volk to the Führer sent to it by God.'[107] In Mecklenburg, where in the meantime the young Land Bishop Walter Schulz had supplanted Land Bishop Rendtorff, the decision for Hitler was even transformed into a formal act of confession. There, after an appropriate sermon, the congregation was to stand and be asked: 'Members of the church, if this is your resolute purpose, then reply with a loud "Yes"!' 'After the congregation has said "Yes",' the rubric went on, 'without announcement or interlude the organ introduces the singing of the first verse of Ein Feste Burg.'[108]

12 November once again marked a climax in Protestant illusions. And Hitler's triumphant election victory seemed once again emphatically to justify them.

But in fact the end had long since begun.

The Collapse of the German Christians and the Beginnings of the Confessing Church (November 1933-January 1934)

The problem of every successful revolution is the transition from the revolutionary phase to the continuity of the new régime. Between April and September 1933 the German Christians doubtless brought about a real revolution in the Protestant church. Their man was at the head of the Reich Church; they had firm control of the largest Landeskirche, that of Prussia. In the meantime Saxony, Thuringia, Schleswig-Holstein, Mecklenburg, Brunswick, Hessen and a series of smaller churches had come under the domination of the German Christians. Everywhere the church leadership had been taken over by young men, totally unknown a year before. Everywhere revolutionary orders were being put into effect. Only the Landeskirchen of Bavaria, Württemberg and Hanover stood like rocks under their former church leadership. In view of this almost total victory of the revolution in the churches, everything depended upon whether the German Christians would be able to consolidate their rule. All their actions and programmes proposed in October pointed to this end. It was an illusory goal, but perhaps this goal – like so many other illusions in the Third Reich – could have been maintained longer had the German Christians in fact accomplished the transition to continuity. But it was this transition which now failed. The transition did not fail because of the resistance of the church opposition, which in October did little more than rally its forces and wait for developments. Rather, the transition failed because of the conflict typical of revolutions, that is, because of a contradiction between the desire on the part of those in power to end the revolutionary phase and the dissatisfaction with what had been achieved which continued to spur on the radical wing. In principle it was the same conflict that Hitler resolved six months later in his favour with the liquidation of the SA leadership. But the German Christians shattered on this polarization. And their collapse mercilessly revealed the illusory character of their whole endeavour.

The radical wing of the Faith Movement, which wanted to push things further in the church, had its most important stronghold in the Gau of Greater Berlin. Here, from the beginning of October, preparations were being made for a great rally of the general membership in the Sports Palace, at which the Gau leadership, above all the Gauobmann Dr Krause himself, were to proclaim the new revolutionary aims. At first planned for 21 October, then for 26 October, this rally, too, had finally to give way to the propaganda for 12 November. The Gau leadership of the German Christians thereupon selected 13 November as the final date.[1] And in fact this day proved tailor-made for the planned occasion. For here the Berlin German Christians could celebrate their völkisch Luther just before the official Luther celebration on 19 November. And Hitler's election victory, which was welcomed in these circles as a triumph for their own cause, could not but intensify greatly the radical enthusiasm of the gathering.

Unsere Volkskirche, the newspaper of the Berlin group, again made clear in its issue of 12 November what was involved. Under the headline 'Is That the Meaning of the Luther Year?' it reported deep unrest among Protestant church people. The new church constitution (this was a reference to the constitutional guidelines which the Reich Church Cabinet had recently issued on 9 November) would exclude the lay component and permit only the leadership principle to remain. But this would preserve only the old and reactionary system in the church. 'We were promised,' wrote the anonymous 'Nicodemus', probably a pen name for the Kreisleiter, Johannes Schmiedchen, 'the true German Volkskirche. But so far we have only been given bishops, provosts and deans, while church people have already been excluded and (if things go on in this way) will be even more excluded in the future.' The Gau leadership in Berlin was obviously determined not to let things go on in this way. 'We had hoped that the clergy from our ranks would know what avails us, as the Augustinian friar once comforted a hungry and cold people. But if those who were called do not want to proceed, then some non-theologians will have to. Indeed our Lord and Saviour took fishermen when the theologians refused to follow him...'[2] In the storm of protest which soon swept away this whole group there was a complete failure to note that here they in fact had a point. With the new constitutional guidelines the Reich Church was coming close to exceeding even the old official and authoritarian church controlled by the local rulers – at least in the way in which it tied the church people and communities to its apron strings.

So, after the failure of the theologians to act, the non-theologians were to set to work. This was the particular solemnity of the rally at the Sports Palace on 13 November. The community groups of the German Christians, who came in closed ranks with their banners from all over Berlin, filled all of the 20,000 seats in the giant hall. Among others, those on the dais beside the Gauführer Dr Krause were Bishops Hossenfelder and Peter, Provost Lörzer, and practically the whole Prussian Oberkirchenrat led by its President, Dr Werner. After the opening by Kreisleiter Schmiedchen, Hossenfelder spoke first. The Reichsleiter of the Faith Movement, who meanwhile as bishop, church minister and vice-president had himself become a typical representative of the new church leadership which was under attack from the radicals, was well aware of the sentiment in Berlin. So he not only appealed for the Volksmission but at the same time tried to be convincing about the unchanged fighting spirit of the Reich leadership. The most important matter was the Aryan paragraph. Although in England just four weeks earlier Hossenfelder had solemnly declared that the Reich Church had no thought of introducing the controversial paragraph, he now asserted that he had personally objected to the proposal by the Swedish Archbishop Erling Eidem that the Aryan paragraph should be dropped in the interest of inter-church co-operation. Rather, only three days beforehand he had instructed the Prussian Oberkirchenrat to carry out the resolution of the

General Synod regardless.[3] This was an open declaration of war on his opponents in the church. And so disaster for the German Christians had begun to run its course.

While after this address the assembly was singing the inevitable 'Ein feste Burg', accompanied by SA bands, Hossenfelder left the Sports Palace in order to appear the next day in Nuremberg in the assembly of the representatives of the German pastors' associations. Now the Berlin Gauobmann, Dr Krause, gave the main speech. Interrupted by growing and ultimately repeated and almost frenetic applause, he laid out the programme for the second revolution in the Protestant church.

Krause began with the overwhelming experience of 12 November. 'One Volk, one Führer,' he said, had now become the truth. 'One God and one church' was yet to be achieved by the Germans. The issue now was the most precious legacy that Luther had left behind: 'the fulfilment of the German Reformation in the Third Reich'. 'The Volk, awakening,' Krause declared, wanted to build a new church, 'so in these days we call upon the fiery spirit of Dr Martin that he may help us to complete, to give form to, his work; not a Lutheran, not a Reformed, not a United nor a synodical or consistorial church; not a church of the bishop or the general superintendents – but this one, powerful, new, all-inclusive church, the German Volkskirche.' This church could never grow up alongside the state, but only within it, and to it 'the same laws of life without exception' applied, namely 'heroic piety' and 'generic Christianity'.

After that, the Berlin Gauobmann turned to sharp criticism of the Reich Church. The new constitutional guidelines were not yet made public, but he wanted to say quite clearly in the name of the Berlin movement: 'We cannot use a church of pastors (very loud applause). We can only have a church in which it is still the case, as of old, that the church is built up on the community' (very loud applause). That Krause here was not concerned about the right of the community but putting forward the claims of the revolutionary position emerged from his comment that in no circumstances would people be allowed 'to impose themselves as leaders' about whom there were reservations because 'it was impossible properly to trust either their National Socialism or their German faith'. In this connection Krause also attacked the peace message from the Reich Bishop. It had unleashed 'boundless uncertainty' among the German Christians and evoked 'a triumph' among their opponents – 'a triumph that is expressed in the fact that these people are now again at their peak' (Hear, hear!) and think that when they are offered peace they can respond with a fight. The 'leaders of the German Christians in high office' had to decide to which side they belonged: the side of the old authoritarian pastors' church with its confessional ties or the side of the new German Volkskirche.

And then Krause went on to give a description of the substance of this new Volkskirche, which was to become the real scandal of the assembly. For it emerged that Reinhold Krause, leader of the German Christians in Berlin, member of the provincial synod of Brandenburg, the Prussian General Synod and the Prussian Church Senate, and deputy member of the National Synod,[4] was putting forward nothing short of Alfred Rosenberg's völkisch religion. 'A new feeling for the homeland,' he proclaimed to the assembly, must arise in the church, and the first step towards it was 'liberation from everything un-German in worship and the confession; liberation from the Old Testament with its Jewish morality of rewards, these tales of cattle-traders and pimps.' 'If we National Socialists are ashamed to buy a necktie from a Jew,' he continued with constant applause from the audience of 20,000, 'then we should even more be ashamed to accept from Jews something of central religious importance, that speaks to our souls.' And, once having got going, Krause urged the Prussian Landeskirche also to purge the New Testament of all 'clearly distorted and superstitious stories' and totally to abandon 'the whole scapegoat- and inferiority-complex of the Rabbi Paul'. The 'whole line of development in dialectical theology from Paul to Barth' had 'made an intellectual mockery of our Father God'. It had attempted to separate God and men. But the pure teaching of Jesus knew no such separation. This pure teaching of Jesus had again to become the foundation of the church. 'When we draw from the gospel,' Krause summarized in conclusion, 'that which speaks to our German hearts, then the essentials of the teaching of Jesus clearly and revealingly emerge, coinciding completely with the demands of National Socialism – and of that we may be proud'. Therefore an 'exaggerated presentation of the crucified Jesus' was also to be avoided, for the Third Reich needed proud men, and not slaves. The Reich Church would have to decide where it stood. For the völkisch church was the church of the future. 'And we will experience,' Krause ended emphatically, 'how close is the relationship of the Nordic spirit to the heroic spirit of Jesus. Then it will be clear that the fulfilment of Martin Luther's Reformation means the final victory of the Nordic spirit over eastern materialism. Heil! (long sustained applause).'[5]

None of this was new nor surprising in principle. It belonged in the broad stream of völkisch religious feeling which had begun in the nineteenth century with Fichte, Richard Wagner and Paul de Lagarde, was carried on in the 1920s by the German Church, and from which Alfred Rosenberg had also fashioned his *Myth*.[6] But what was new and startling was that in spite of all the experiences with the German Christians, this völkisch religion now appeared right in the middle of the Protestant church with the claim to be no less than the future of this church and the fulfilment of the Reformation. In order to lend strength to this claim, a resolution was adopted in connection with Krause's speech which repeated his central demands in six points.[7] It was later reported that only one hand among the 20,000 had been raised in opposition when the vote was taken. The first reports of this meeting appeared on 14 November in the Berlin morning papers. The same morning the leadership of the Pastors' Emergency League sounded the alarm. Barth and Bodelschwingh were summoned by telephone to Berlin for a discussion. And the same afternoon Jacobi and the Niemöller brothers, Martin and Wilhelm, visited the Reich Bishop to make clear to him the seriousness of the situation. Ludwig Müller, who until that moment had obviously hardly been aware of what had happened, sought desperately to gain time. But the three pastors left him no choice. Their ultimatum, with an 8.00 p.m. deadline, contained three demands: '1. The Reich Bishop must give up his patronage of the German Christian Faith Movement. 2. Bishop Hossenfelder and the church leaders who were present at the Sports Palace on Monday are immediately to be suspended from their posts in the church government. 3. The pastors, church elders, community officials and church administrators are again to be committed to their ordination vows.' Unless the Reich Bishop fulfilled these demands, there would be a split in the church the next day.[8]

Thus driven into a corner, Ludwig Müller partly gave in. Manoeuvring as always, he decided to sacrifice Krause to save Hossenfelder. Perhaps he even wanted this separation, as he had already indicated that afternoon, because it would free the Reich Church of an extremely unpleasant critic, and because people like Krause were certainly a burden to the Faith Movement. So by an order of the Prussian Oberkirchenrat dated 14 November, Krause and the church leader Fritz Arendsee, who had introduced the resolution, were provisionally dismissed from all the offices they held in church bodies.[9] At the same time the Reich Bishop published a statement in which he emphatically dissociated himself from Krause. He was speaking 'as the leader of the church, answerable before God for the protection of the confession' (the original draft had had 'spiritual leader', but Ludwig Müller had deleted the word 'spiritual' with his own hand), and therefore was combatting 'the attacks on the substance of our Evangelical Church'. Krause's views and demands were nothing short of 'an intolerable attack on the church's confession'. 'The direction and leadership of the German Evangelical Church sharply' rejected such a spirit. And in order to meet the demands of the Pastors' Emergency League on at least one point – one which did not cost anything – he requested the Landeskirchen, their clergy and community officials 'sharply and clearly to remember their vows of ordination and office'.[10]

The evening that Ludwig Müller dismissed Krause and dissociated himself from the Sports Palace demonstration, there was a vigorous argument at the Jacobi manse between Barth and Niemöller as to what the church opposition was to do next. Niemöller was resolved to use the demonstration to split the German Christians and finally to keep the Reich Bishop and the Reich Church to a church line. So he insisted on negotiations with Ludwig Müller, who along the lines of the three demands was to separate himself from the German Christians and draw the consequences for those persons responsible for the Sports Palace demonstration. Here Hossenfelder above all was the issue. He was regarded as the most important representative of the German Christians in the church leadership and his resignation was therefore regarded as a prerequisite for a new direction in the Reich Church. And in fact until the end of the year the battle over the church was largely one as to whether Hossenfelder's head should roll.

For Barth, on the other hand, all this was merely a continuation of the tactical course that he had already criticized in the Young Reformers during the summer. Here he saw once again only the same church-political compromise, and not the basic renaissance in faith which he was convinced could alone help the church. Therefore he called for the negotiations with Ludwig Müller to be broken off and an appeal to be made directly to Hitler, with the request to give the church back its freedom and allow it to make a new decision without pressure from the Party. Behind this was Barth's unshakable confidence that the power of the Word of God could show its might even against Hitler, a confidence shown not least in the fact that Barth had personally sent Hitler *Theological Existence Today*, and also had the later issues sent to the Reich Chancellor.[11]

Because everything was now at stake, as Barth explained that evening to the church opposition, it could not be just a matter of calling for 'Hossenfelder's head'. 'But the question must be asked: Can or cannot things go on like this in the Evangelical Church? We are of the opinion that they cannot. And if that is where we are, then we have to communicate this conviction to those responsible for this development who have helped the German Christians into control of the administration: the state... We demand that the church be once more given the freedom which it enjoyed before 24 June. The church elections must be rescinded. Must not the state be required to restore to the church enough of its freedom so that it can overcome by its own powers the sickness with which it is now infected?'[12]

Although a majority of those present, including Jacobi, Dehn and Schultz-Sydow, inclined more to Barth's view, in the end Niemöller had his way. The minutes which, however, were not unbiassed, ended by noting that 'Niemöller continued to insist on going to Müller and only Müller. He clearly does not want Barth to go to Hindenburg and Hitler. Finally it is decided that Barth undertakes his approach as an individual action (Bodelschwingh is considered unsuitable for the approach to Hitler, but suitable for Hindenburg), and the initiative of the Council of Brethren is unaffected by it.'[13]

In all probability, in the circumstances Niemöller's decision to join battle with the German Christians was right. Whether Barth made any attempt to contact Hitler is unknown. But Bodelschwingh's visit to Hindenburg, which took place the next day, demonstrated the fruitlessness of trying to achieve anything in this way. In almost a caricature of a Prussian casino conversation, more was said about the 1907 battle of Friedland in which a Hindenburg and a Bodelschwingh had both fought than about any serious intention or possibility of the President's helping the Protestant church in its acute emergency.[14]

As for Barth, the result of that evening's argument was a deep, long-lasting ill humour. A few days later he candidly told the Osnabrück pastor Richard Karwehl of the 'whole anthill of agitated pastors' that he had found in Berlin 'ready for action' – as he sarcastically noted – 'under the dictatorship of the U-boat commander Niemöller, who was all set to turn the Sports Palace scandal into a "Tannenberg" for the German Christians and in the name of "fellowship"' forbade any theological misgivings.' 'If sooner or later there is a catastrophe for the German Christians,' Barth went on – and this comment shows how totally alienated he felt from the Berlin group – '...and if then the so-called Council of Brethren of the Pastors Emergency League should become our future conference of bishops, my dear pastor, we shall then be in no better shape than at present under the rule of the German Christians or earlier under that of the Dibeliuses.'[15] And at the end of that dramatic week the Bonn theologian repeated his criticism publicly in the Foreword to the fourth volume of Theologische Existenz. To a terrifying degree 'during those days in Berlin' he had found confirmation of 'everything, but everything' which had troubled him about the 'Young Reformers' during the summer. Once again the church opposition was thinking only along church-political lines, and not basically theologically, so precisely because of events at the Sports Palace incident there was the disastrous danger 'that those who are supposed to be better among the German Christians and all those opposition groups who have so far fought well but not correctly, i.e. not for principles, will unite in some kind of bad middle ground under the leadership of the church governments'. No church politics would help further, nor would any compromise. The opposition would in no sense be equal to the German Christians with 'a Saul's armour consisting in a kind of thought which was continually all too historical, political and tactical and supposedly (only supposedly!) practical'.

'What shall we do?' Barth asked at the end, and concluded in his typical manner:

> One thing and only one thing:
> Let each one set his face
> and turn his whole body
> straight towards Jerusalem.
>
> In all the weakness and foolishness and perversity, in which none of us will be lacking, let us be 'straight' and turn our 'whole body'. Where that happens, everything has happened. Where that does not happen, nothing has happened.[16]

All this did not arise out of sudden offence, even if personal feelings may have been involved. Rather, it was precisely the line that Barth had taken since the summer and to which he held quite firm under the impact of the Sports Palace demonstration. So in December he still assured a troubled pastor who had attacked him for his public criticism of the Pastors Emergency League: 'All the trouble and anxiety that this year has cost will have been in vain if the only difference is that the future Reich Bishop is – for example – called Niemöller... My great concern, which I cannot suppress, is that while there is now a fight, it is not the right one.'[17]

Meanwhile the Emergency League was implementing Niemöller's line in Berlin. On the morning of 15 November the leaders agreed on a statement to the Reich Bishop and a pulpit declaration which was to be read by all the pastors of the Emergency League on the next Sunday or on the following Day of Repentance. This statement, which was handed over to Church Minister Weber in the afternoon, contained the conditions which had been indicated – separation from the Faith Movement and suspension of all the leading church officials and clergy who had taken part in the Sports Palace Rally, supplemented by demands for complete freedom of preaching and 'also freedom for us to make full and effective use of the radio and press in the struggle within the church' and 'guarantees of the safety of the Emergency League, standing by the Bible and the confession'.[18]

Even more important was the pulpit proclamation which was read on 19 and 22 November in thousands of communities. For the first time since the summer it involved the pastors and communities directly in the church controversies. 'We preachers of the gospel do not wish to incur the reproach of the prophets that we were dumb dogs. Rather, we owe it to our communities and our people to oppose this adulteration of the truth. We therefore emphatically confess the Holy Scriptures of the Old and New Testaments to be the only rule and criterion of our faith and life, and the confessions of the fathers to be their true interpretation in the Reformation. Only the community that bases itself on them has the promise of its Lord that the gates of hell shall not prevail against it, even if in the eyes of the world it remains a little flock.' The proclamation closed with the words of Jesus in Matthew 10.32f.: 'Every one therefore who shall confess me before men, him will I also confess before my Father which is in heaven. But whosoever shall deny me before men, him will I also deny before my Father which is in heaven.'[19]

The solemnity of this proclamation did not fail to find an echo in the communities. Unlike the usual declarations which were read on many occasions during divine services, it was clear that this had been read because of a personal decision by the pastor, and that therefore the community, too, had been called upon for a decision. As Hugo Hahn reported from the Frauenkirche in Dresden, the impact of this proclamation 'was tremendous. A profound stir was caused in the community, but the German Christians present... were of course dismayed by my attack. A few days later I was summoned to a meeting of the church council because of my Repentance Day sermon. There was a sharp clash...'[20] In fact there were not only sharp clashes but also the first mass measures. On 23 November in a circular letter Martin Niemöller reported the first suspensions in Pomerania, Berlin and Mecklenburg and asked for public intercessions in services for those involved.[21] But the unrest in the Protestant church could no longer be pacified. Accurately informed by surprisingly thorough reporting in the daily press, in a few days the protest movement began to spread from Berlin throughout the Reich.

Against this movement Krause was a lost cause. Even the fact that the *Völkischer Beobachter* of 15 November came to his assistance and published the full text of the resolution adopted in the Sports Palace could not alter the situation. The day after the Prussian Oberkirchenrat had suspended the Berlin Gauobmann from all church offices, 14 November, Hossenfelder dismissed him from all functions in the Faith Movement. An indication of the way in which the Reich leader of the German Christians had no inkling of the situation was the fact that he nominated as Krause's successor none other than the Pastor Rausch who had dedicated the banners after Krause's speech.[22] The others who had taken part in the Sports Palace demonstration also hastened to dissociate themselves from their former Berlin leader. In a statement the 'German Christian' bishops and members of the Oberkirchenrat asserted that on the evening immediately following Krause's speech 'they had made the sharpest protests... on the spot'. The argument over the truth of this claim, which was vigorously disputed by Krause and his friends, continued for a long time. But the visible evidence of the assembly, during which many of those present had evidently seen the platform party enthusiastically applauding, told so plainly against any protest that virtually no one gave any credence to the solemn assurance of Peter, Lörzer, Werner and the other participants.[23]

Without doubt the person most astonished by this sudden reaction from his friends was Krause himself. He sounded completely plausible when, immediately after his suspension, he assured the Reich Bishop that 'from the very beginning' he had worked in the Faith Movement along the lines of what he had said, and that in his view he was 'fully in agreement with Bishop Hossenfelder here'. He wrote that he had 'argued not for an abolition of the confession but for broadening it, so that all the members of the Volk could be united in one Volkskirche'. 'I am and remain a Christian,' concluded Krause, 'and stand by my Saviour and his uncorrupted joyful tidings. If nevertheless the church finds me unacceptable, if I must leave this church, then for the sake of my fellow members of the Volk who have trusted me I will go on fighting for a church that has room for all German God-seekers.'[24] In fact, only a few days later Krause informed the German Christian leadership in a circular letter of his resignation from the Faith Movement of 'German Christians',[25] and soon afterwards, together with Johannes Schmiedchen, he founded the German Volkskirche Faith Movement. The enterprise had little success, so in 1935 Krause finally joined the 'German Faith Movement' which at this time was increasingly developing into a radical, anti-religious fighting movement.[26] Krause had no further significance for the church.

On 15 November yet another prominent member of the Protestant church already drew the consequences of Ludwig Müller's dissociation of himself from Krause. Alfred Rosenberg declared that he was leaving the church. He told the 'Chancellery of the Reich Episcopate' that since the Reich Bishop had considered it correct to use the expression 'false doctrine' of views which were 'already for the most part being advocated today among the Volk' with the feeling that they 'represent a further development of the German Reformation', there was no longer any hope for a progressive change in the church. Whether Rosenberg was right in suggesting that his resignation was 'very welcome'[27] to the Reich Bishop may, however, be doubted, given Ludwig Müller's dependence on the Party. But now there was obviously nothing more to be salvaged from the situation.

Meanwhile the Reich Church Government desperately tried to control the growing unrest in the country. On the morning of 16 November the Reich Church Cabinet met and unanimously voted to drop the disputed Aryan Paragraph and at the same time to stress in a decree from the Reich Bishop the church's commitment to Bible and confession. Whereas in the previous weeks up to the Sports Palace rally Ludwig Müller and the German Christians had repeatedly called for a ruthless application of the Aryan Paragraph, now a Reich Church law abruptly terminated 'the implementation of laws issued in the German Evangelical Landeskirchen'.[28] The sudden decisiveness over Bible and confession expressed in the decree of the Reich Bishop dated 16 November sounded no less surprising. Soon mockingly called the 'morphia decree',[29] it at least communicated Ludwig Müller's tactical plan in one sentence. All unions and associations, it stated, were in future to devote themselves solely to service to the community and the church. 'No association may take upon itself the powers of church government.'[30] What Müller meant by this he communicated at midday to the leaders of the Pastors Emergency League through the Lutheran Church Minister Simon Schöffel. The Reich Bishop would immediately disband the German Christian Faith Movement if the Pastors Emergency League was also prepared to disband. However, this plan, with which the Reich Bishop evidently would be rid of all his problems at a stroke, came to grief on the refusal of the Emergency League to acknowledge that both groups had equal rights in the church.[31] When in the evening Niemöller insisted on the demands he had put forward, the Reich Bishop broke off the negotiations with the remark. 'You will have to bear your responsibilities, as I bear mine.'[32]

It is hard to say whether this plan was meant seriously, and above all whether it could have been carried out. But the mere fact that Ludwig Müller declared his readiness under certain conditions to drop even the German Christians must have shown Hossenfelder that now his head was at risk. Hence he again staged, for the last time, a grand propaganda campaign on his own behalf. On 16 November instructions went out from Berlin to all senior Gau officials of the Faith Movement to send a telegram to Berlin 'in the following terms': 'Loyally behind Hossenfelder and the Reich Church Government. Confession may not be attacked. Repudiate Berlin Sports Palace Rally.'[33]

Evangelium im Dritten Reich thereupon reported triumphantly under the headline 'United Front for Hossenfelder' 'the hundreds of declarations of support... from all over the Reich' which had 'expressed the unshakable trust and loyal following of the vast majority of the church people represented by the movement'.[34] Hossenfelder himself spoke of 'reactionaries and apostles of disintegration' – by which he probably meant the Emergency League and the 'Krause group', which 'in this most glorious period of German church history' were attempting to tear apart 'the marching front of the Faith Movement'.[35] For Hossenfelder, in fact, everything now depended on whether he would succeed in holding the Faith Movement together in spite of the Sports Palace débacle, and in again committing the vacillating Ludwig Müller to the German Christian line. The most important thing here was to save the Berlin district. On the evening of 17 November about 1200 community officials from Greater Berlin attended a dramatic debate between Wieneke and Peter on one side and Krause on the other, which ended in victory for the representatives of the Reich administration. The great majority of those present evidently backed the Reich administration. Only a minority finally left the hall with Krause in order to resolve on a continuation of the fight along Krause's lines.[36]

However, this victory in Berlin did not yet amount to a final decision. That had to take place at the great leadership conference which Hossenfelder had called for 23 and 24 November in Weimar. The aim of this leadership conference was obvious. Hossenfelder and the Reich leadership needed as solid a declaration as possible in support of its previous line and for Hossenfelder personally. And in fact in the closing session of the Reich leadership council the Reich leader succeeded in pushing through two resolutions which fully achieved this goal. 'The Faith Movement of German Christians,' the first resolution stated, 'stands on the foundation of the Party programme as a movement founded by old warriors of the NSDAP. It 'exists as a movement founded by Christians on the basis of the pure gospel'. It 'is built up on the leadership principle and stands solidly behind Bishop Hossenfelder'. The second resolution emphatically attacked the reactionaries within the church and pledged unshakable loyalty to Hossenfelder 'and our patron, Reich Bishop Müller'.[37]

If people were ready to believe the enthusiastic reports in *Evangelium im Dritten Reich*, no less than a new Pentecost miracle had taken place at that time in Weimar. 'In all truth mention must and may be made of the living faith, of the painful, heroic wrestling,' stated the report, ' "Lord, I will not let thee go until thou bless me" is found amidst the Faith Movement of German Christians.' And the reporter felt able boldly to report 'in all earnestness... that even elderly clergy who took part in the consultations, drawing on their spiritual resources, spontaneously exclaimed, "We can feel the rushing wind of Pentecost."'[38] In fact, however, 'the plain truth' was quite different. The resolutions which were to put an end to 'rumours of disintegration' were passed only by a centre group whose church politics were orientated on Berlin. The two wings – the moderate, church-orientated and the radical völkisch, orientated on a National Church – had split off during the Weimar days.

Representing the moderate wing in Weimar was the tripartite Bavarian delegation, under the leadership of the Nuremberg pastor Hans Greifenstein. During the summer the German Christians in Bavaria, like the great majority of the Faith Movement in Württemberg, had placed themselves under the leadership of their Land Bishop, clearly dissociating themselves from the Berlin Reich leadership.[39] In accord with this decision, the Bavarian representatives arrived in Weimar with a clear programme. This programme included a resolute condemnation of the events at the Sports Palace and otherwise largely kept to Ludwig Müller's statements of 15 and 16 November. In addition, the Bavarians called for the reconstruction of the Reich leadership and Reich leadership council of the Faith Movement. To their consternation, however, the South Germans had to face the fact that a decisive number of representatives of the Faith Movement in North Germany firmly rejected the Reich Bishop's 'morphia decree'. Rather, this group was attempting to force the resignation of the Lutheran Church Minister Simon Schöffel in order to take complete control of the Reich Bishop and the Reich Church leadership. In these circumstances the unconditional subordination of the Bavarian Land leadership to the Reich leadership which Hossenfelder demanded was out of the question. In spite of persistent political pressure, on the morning of 25 November the Bavarian group therefore announced its withdrawal from the Faith Movement and left Weimar.[40]

The break with the völkisch-national church wing was also to be no less successful. It had already been a blunder on Hossenfelder's part to hold the leadership conference in Weimar, of all places, since the Thuringian German Christians, under the leadership of Pastors Leffler and Leutheuser, had from the start pursued their own völkisch line,[41] which they maintained even after their formal incorporation into the Reich movement. Hossenfelder knew that very well, since only at the beginning of November Leutheuser had presented the Thuringian view of the content of the Volksmission in Berlin, declaring that Adolf Hitler was 'the spokesman for a saviour who wills to be, and indeed has become, flesh and blood in the German Volk'. For the Thuringians, basically even more radical than Krause, 'the formation of a new church' was being accomplished in the Party itself. According to Leutheuser, in National Socialism 'there is already the new body of Christ'. To go back to the old Protestant church was out of the question, for 'Hitler has brought Christ to us. We do not bring Christ to Hitler.'[42]

With this radical religious enthusiasm, the Thuringians felt far superior to the church politics of the Berlin Reich leadership. A great evening celebration in the Weimar hall on 23 November, for which the Thuringian group had issued invitations, clearly expressed this position. This evening was marked by readings, new songs by the Wieratal SA and speeches by Leffler and Leutheuser. Hossenfelder, the final speaker, evidently attempted to keep a careful distance, but then in conclusion assured Leffler: 'That was splendid. The Führer must know about it and experience it.'[43] So the two Thuringians were all the more surprised when at the leadership council the next morning Hossenfelder clearly dissociated himself from their position. The open letter which Leffler thereupon addressed to Hossenfelder developed into a devastating criticism of the whole Faith Movement. 'We have deceived ourselves,' it said, 'and are deeply shaken by the ecclesiastical, spiritual level which emerged at the various meetings during the conference... But, most respected bishop, our sorriest discovery was that your German Christian Faith Movement had no faith at all in which one could find life, strength, love... The world is today asking: What is Christ to us? And in response so far you have had only one answer: a purely church-political one! You have thrown out the former church rulers! Certainly that was necessary! And you and your Berlin friends have occupied dioceses and bishops' thrones instead. But truly you have not achieved more than that. You have turned the good idea of German Christianity into a matter of church politics, and in so doing have finished all faith down to the last tiny spark. For that you even called your movement a "faith movement". It is impossible for anyone like you, Lord Bishop, who applies criteria of political power in the church sphere, to build up the church in the spirit of Christ. Such a person cannot bring people together; at best he furthers the ruin of the church.'[44] Soon after this the 'Thuringian Land Community' left the Faith Movement and established itself independently as 'The German Christian Church Movement (Movement for a National Church)'. It soon began also to recruit outside Thuringia and later became the only German Christian group to grow steadily in significance up to the war.[45]

However, at the close of the Weimar conference this development was still in the future. Instead, Hossenfelder believed that with the adoption of the two resolutions after the departure of the Bavarians he had won a complete victory. In order to exploit the victory it was decided to travel in a special coach with a delegation of fifty to Berlin and persuade the Reich Bishop to return to Hossenfelder and the Reich leadership.[46] When the group entered the Oberkirchenrat late in the evening, things there were on a knife-edge.

In the meantime, because of the events at the Sports Palace a new front had formed in the Protestant church which from then on would be decisive for the future: the alliance between the Pastors Emergency League and the South German Landeskirchen. On 14 November Martin Niemöller had not only mobilized the church opposition in Prussia but also informed Bishops Meiser and Wurm by telephone as to what had happened.[47] Plainly his concern was to enlist the two bishops as allies in the Emergency League's fight to get Hossenfelder removed. That was the very tactic that Barth had rejected at all costs. And in fact it would soon prove that the alliance with the South German churches was in no sense without problems. On the other hand, a realistic assessment of the church situation – and on this point Niemöller was a realist – almost inevitably led to the conviction that the elimination of Hossenfelder and the saving of the church were possible only by a concentration of all non-German Christian forces. These two positions, one theologically radical and uncompromising and the other mediating, extending far into the centre of the church, remained typical of the Confessing Church throughout the changing conditions of the coming years. A real solution to this problem was never found.

At first, however, during those November days Niemöller's strategy seemed entirely justified. Under the impact of the Sports Palace demonstration, even the Bavarian Lutherans forgot their mistrust of the rebels in the Prussian Union Church. It fortunately came about that the Lutheran Church Minister Simon

Schöffel happened to be in Munich on 14 November to speak at a big Luther celebration. Thus that very evening at the end of this address Meiser was able to call publicly upon 'all true Lutheran spirits in our Reich Church to make a blazing protest'. 'And may I also express the expectation,' he continued, looking at Schöffel, 'that our Reich Church leadership, beginning with our Lutheran Church Minister, will resist these attacks in a clear statement, all the more so because the Reich Church leadership is the chosen defender of the church constitution, and this church constitution declares the Reformation confessions to be the inviolable basis of the German Evangelical Church.'[48] Meiser took things so seriously that on 16 November he paid a personal visit to Berlin to have a private conversation with the Reich Bishop. Having been thoroughly informed by the Niemöller brothers about the negotiations with Ludwig Müller, he reached an agreement with Land Bishops Wurm in Stuttgart and Marahrens in Hanover and at the same time took over in their names the most important demands of the Emergency League.

'We declare once again,' Meiser then wrote to the Reich Bishop on the 17th, 'that to us as Evangelical-Lutheran Land Bishops any person in the Reich Church leadership who has permitted damage to the confessional status of the church in a public assembly without immediately protesting is unacceptable to us... We... are compelled to demand most urgently that any such persons in the church government be made to refrain immediately from all official activity.'[49] No names were mentioned in this letter, but of course everyone was clear that it referred above all to Hossenfelder.

This letter received powerful support from a whole series of protest meetings that took place at this time – especially in south and west Germany. For example on 22 November there was a packed rally in Augsburg, as also in Pforzheim, Dortmund and elsewhere. These rallies consistently concluded with resolutions calling for the resignation of the church leaders who took part in the Sports Palace demonstration.[50] Numerous protests also came from specifically German Christian circles which had joined the movement in good faith in the summer and now found themselves in company utterly remote from what they had in mind. For example the Untergau of Wuppertal bluntly required the Reich Bishop to secure the resignation of all those who 'had failed by their persistent silence' and in addition expected 'that all the members of the Reich leadership of the Faith Movement of German Christians should be pledged to the Bible and the confession'.[51]

In Württemberg, too, Hossenfelder was increasingly felt to be an intolerable burden. This was especially true of the Tübingen theological faculty, which under Fezer's influence had joined the Faith Movement almost *en bloc* and had thus contributed substantially to its credibility in the church. So Professors Fezer and Weiser decided to travel to Berlin for a personal discussion in which they hoped to persuade Hossenfelder – with whom Fezer had appeared in England only in October – to resign. Hossenfelder, however, had no thought of acceding to this request. Instead, after the inconclusive discussion he picked up the telephone and informed the Land leader of the German Christians in Württemberg, the young pastor Wilhelm Rehm, that the professors were expelled from the Faith Movement. Since Fezer had until then been the most prominent representative of the German Christians in Württemberg, this news came as a

562

bombshell to the Land. The uproar was intensified by an obscure toing and froing which compelled the professors, almost immediately after they had got back, to return to Berlin, on the evening of 23 November – this time as a threesome. In spite of all their experiences with the Reich Bishop and the Reich leadership, the Tübingen professors still had not realized, and even later did not want to realize, that by joining the Faith Movement they had committed themselves to a venture which was full of illusions politically, questionable theologically and – at least as far as Müller and Hossenfelder were concerned – mendacious personally. So when after further vain conversations in Berlin on 25 November the three professors in turn solemnly announced their departure from the Faith Movement, this was more as a result of a feeling of hurt and disappointment than as a change in conviction. At any rate Fezer apparently did not feel the least guilt when in December he publicly affirmed: 'But we,' i.e. the Tübingen people, 'have followed a clear course. We are still loyal to the cause of a genuine Evangelical Faith Movement of German Christians.'[52]

On the same 24 November on which Hossenfelder celebrated his victory in Weimar and the three Tübingen professors were negotiating in Berlin, there was a first meeting in Stuttgart of those men who from now on would form the so-called Confessional Front in Germany. In contrast to the Confessing Church, which understood itself to be a church, this term then and for the future denoted the joint church-political front of all those church leaders, Landeskirchen and communities which did not belong to the German Christians. On this day the gathering consisted of Martin Niemöller and Gerhard Stratenwerth for the Pastors Emergency League, Land Bishops Meiser, Wurm and Marahrens, and Präses Karl Koch of Westphalia, representing the only Prussian provincial church that had not been captured by the German Christians. The gathering came to the unanimous decision to ask Müller to dismiss Hossenfelder and to stay away from Müller's solemn installation as Reich Bishop, scheduled for 3 December. Both points were communicated without delay to the Lutheran Church Minister Simon Schöffel, who was to pass this decision on to the Reich Bishop.[53]

In view of this ultimatum, on the evening of 24 November in the Church Cabinet Müller had to decide between Hossenfelder and Schöffel – and at the same time decide on the future direction of the Reich Church. But even before the cabinet session began, the fifty men who had left Weimar at midday after the close of the leadership conference appeared in the Oberkirchenrat building. Conscious of their supposed victory, they pressed the Reich Bishop again to take the line of the Reich leadership, to dismiss Schöffel and Weber from the leadership of the Reich Church, and ruthlessly to impose the Aryan Paragraph on the Reich Church. After vigorous debate, Ludwig Müller finally gave in. And soon afterwards a saying of his went the rounds: 'Hossenfelder and I are inseparable.'[54]

True, Ludwig Müller avoided dismissing Schöffel directly. But when the late night cabinet meeting at last ended, the German Christians clearly felt that victory was theirs. According to the report in *Evangelium im Dritten Reich*, the Horst Wessel Song rang powerfully out through the quiet building, 'followed by the old battle song of the Protestants: "Ein feste Burg ist unser Gott"'.[55] Soon afterwards a solitary pastor, still waiting for Schöffel, told his Württemberg friends about this moment. 'The line "with force of arms we nothing can" never sounded so frivolous as on that evening.'[56]

The next morning the Hamburg representative of the German Christians sent a triumphant telegram home about the result: 'After stormy night session sale of Santa Clauses assured. Conference resonance means great turning point...'[57]

The Reich Bishop now disclosed to Schöffel that he could not dismiss Hossenfelder and intended to add another Lutheran General Church Minister, namely Land Bishop Coch of Saxony. This was the signal for Schöffel to ask the Reich Bishop to accept his resignation. The Bishop of Hamburg had certainly not realized what was going on any better than the Tübingen professors,[58] but it had become clear to him that he had to go. The morning papers of 26 November reported Schöffel's resignation and the crisis in the Reich Church government.[59]

Ludwig Müller's retention of Hossenfelder soon proved to be a serious mistake. The outcome of the controversies was indeed a 'great turning point', but not as the German Christians had imagined. For on 26 November – it was the Sunday before Advent, on which the dead were commemorated – and during the following days an avalanche of declarations came in from all over Germany, in which prominent individual members, communities and whole districts dissociated themselves from the Berlin leadership. Bavaria had already done so. The Thuringians – albeit for opposite reasons – followed. A flood of protests came from the Rhineland and Westphalia, among them a letter from Dr Gustav W.Heinemann, legal advisor to the Rhineland Steel Works of Essen and presbyter of the Protestant community of Essen-Altstadt. On 29 November he wrote that seventeen pastors of the church district of Essen had announced their resignation from the Faith Movement that day. 'Of perhaps fifty-four pastors in this church district only five or so remain with the German Christians.'[60] In Württemberg about 800 pastors in two different groups joined the Emergency League. The Gau of Pomerania opposed Hossenfelder. The same was true of Greater Hessen, whose German Christian leadership sent a telegram on the 27th: the Faith Movement of German Christians in Greater Hessen 'detaches itself from the Reich leadership and demands the immediate resignation of the Reich leader'.[61] Gogarten and his circle, who had aroused so much attention in the summer by joining the Faith Movement, dissociated themselves from the Berlin heresies in a remarkably clear theological declaration. In Halle, Professors Friedrich Karl Schumann and Ernst Kohlmeyer protested; in Giessen their colleagues Bornkamm and Haenchen.[62]

With all the fickle resignations, only Emanuel Hirsch stood by the decision he had made. 'I believe,' he wrote to the Reich Bishop on 27 November, 'that what I perceive your path and intention to be are definitive for me, so I am staying with the German Christians and not taking the course of Fezer and Schumann. I am glad to run the risk of being called a heretic. My feeling is simple; *I do not abandon a standard when the bombardment becomes heavy*.'[63]

The protest movement reached a climax with a new ultimatum from the Confessing Front, which was handed to the Reich Bishop by Meiser on midday of 29 November. It now called not only for the resignation of Hossenfelder but for the restoration of orderly church relationships in the Landeskirchen, and the total abolition of the 'Parallel Church Government' hitherto exercised by the Faith Movement. The declaration was worked out by the Lutheran Land Bishops who were not, or were no longer, to be counted among the German Christians, and subscribed to by Martin Niemöller for the Emergency League and Karl Koch for the church province of Westphalia.[64]

However, the list of signatures indicates that Barth was not completely wrong when he expressed the opinion that the church could hardly stand fast behind this front. For along with Meiser, Wurm and Marahrens were people like the Thuringian Land Bishop Wilhelm Reichardt, whose Landeskirche was in part way beyond Krause; the Baden Land Bishop Julius Kühlewein who co-operated happily with the German Christians in Karlsruhe, and Bishop Schöffel of Hamburg, who remained unchanged in his belief in the mission of the German Christians in the Third Reich. Still, through this joint action it had become clear that something had at last to happen.

But what was to happen now once again depended utterly upon the behaviour of the state.

While the crisis over the Reich Church was coming to a head, both sides – the Berlin church leadership and the church opposition – had attempted to sway government offices in their direction. Ludwig Müller had already justified his retention of Hossenfelder by saying that he was protected by 'the highest Party authorities' and regarded his dismissal as 'a source of conflict'.[65] And now the Reich leadership was apparently testing whether a new state commissioner and the intervention of the Gestapo might not restore calm in the church by force, as it had during the summer. Provost Lörzer in Prussia introduced the appropriate measures, and at the same time in a circular letter advised all Gau officials 'to approach the Gestapo with the request' to dissolve the Pastors Emergency League.[66] But the circular letter received no response in the movement, which was now disintegrating.

Much more influential, by contrast, was the position which Meiser and Wurm had meanwhile established in the Reich Ministry of the Interior. Here, in Ministerial Director Buttmann and Ministerialrat Conrad, the Confessional Front had two friends whose help was now increasingly called upon by the South German bishops. In fact, immediately after the Sports Palace demonstration Meiser – probably through the mediation of Pastor Klein – had discussed the church-political situation with Conrad and Buttmann.[67] On 25 November Wurm then described the situation in a lengthy letter to the Reich Minister of the Interior and while emphatically stressing his unconditional political loyalty warned against any government suppression of the church opposition, which could only have 'direct consequences' for internal peace as well as foreign relations.[68] This letter, too, would not have lacked influence in the Ministry.

In the meantime the Ministry of Propaganda had also gone into action. The reporting of the controversies had caused lively unrest far beyond the circle of immediate participants, and this had been picked up especially by the foreign press. The public rejection of the Faith Movement, personally supported by Hitler, seemed to indicate a weakness in the National Socialist united front of 12 November. So on 27 November the Ministry of Propaganda ordered a substantial reduction in the reporting 'of the pastors' conflict inside and outside the German Christian movement'. There was no point 'in giving the foreign press the impression that the German people is totally embroiled in religious conflicts...' The next day this admonition was heightened by an official ban on publishing 'any more lines about the conflict within the German Christian movement'. 'Any infringement of these guidelines will result in an immediate ban on the newspaper concerned.' It is worth noting the emphatic statement that this prohibition also applied to official statements by the church administration and the Reich Bishop, which indeed was already a hint of the impending downfall of the German Christians.[69]

From this direction, too, everything was forcing a decision which in the nature of things only Hitler personally could make. Now, however, it proved that in contrast to the summer, this time the Confessional Front had the better position. Ludwig Müller's plans were aimed at dissolving the Faith Movement and the Pastors Emergency League with Hitler's approval. But in the Reich Ministry of the Interior it was realized that in the circumstances this would inevitably result in a one-sided ban on the church opposition. And in fact the Reich Minister of the Interior succeeded in convincing Hitler, even before the decisive discussion with the Reich Bishop, that the government must maintain 'strict neutrality' *vis à vis* the church controversies.

So when the Reich Bishop met with Hitler on the afternooon of 29 November, the ultimatum from the Confessional Front in his pocket, he evidently discovered only that the government would in no way intervene in church affairs, and that he would have to cope with the difficulties himself.[70] On the following day an express letter from the Reich Ministry of the Interior to the Land governments endorsed this decision. 'Within the German Evangelical Church,' ran the decisive first section, 'there are currently discussions aimed at clarifying the entire church situation. The Reich Chancellor has made the unequivocal decision that since this is purely a church matter, there will be no outside interference in the conflict of opinion. In particular, all police intervention – protective custody, confiscation of mail, etc. – is to be avoided. For the reason given,' the letter ended, evidently having plans by the German Christians in view, 'I am giving instructions that church offices are also not entitled to enlist the intervention of state agencies in the church's battle over opinions.'[71]

In view of developments since early 1933, this was a decision of inestimable importance. Following the Party, the state too clearly backed away from a policy which had been thought capable – by means of direct or indirect intervention – of steering the Protestant church in a specific direction. And even if Hitler could scarcely have been aware of it at this moment, here lay the admission of a political weakness. The Protestant church proved to be too complicated, too full of contradictions, or – as Hitler saw it – simply too chaotic to be comprehended and integrated from the centre like other major organizations, for instance the trade unions or the army. It was typical of the whole situation that at the beginning of December the chief of the Prussian Gestapo telephoned the Reich Ministry of the Interior and declared: 'I can no longer keep track of the situation.'[72] And it was no less typical that at the same time Hitler should spontaneously tell Buttmann that he despised 'the "squabbles of the theologians"'. If the Protestant church should blow into pieces, that would be a disgrace on Christianity'.[73] However, at the same time this indicates that Hitler here preferred to refrain from radical solutions because he scarcely expected any serious resistance. Nevertheless, this decision brought into being – amidst the ideological totalitarianism of the Third Reich – a kind of free space, a place where things could be said that could be uttered publicly nowhere else in the Third Reich.

And this decision was no less consequential for the Protestant church also. It meant nothing less than the failure of the basic idea of the German Christians. Their claim to be the genuine representatives of a new church, co-ordinated with the state – a claim that Hitler had emphatically endorsed in his speech the evening before the church elections – had been rejected by that very state. That meant that the stigma of illegality was lifted from the church opposition. That in the coming months a Confessing Church was able to emerge from the Confessional Front, and could present itself, despite all the tricks and impediments, as the true Evangelical Church – something without a parallel in the history of the Third Reich – was also a result of this basic change of course.

Thus the decision of 29 November, however little those involved may have had a detailed awareness of the fact, was a turning point. And even if in retrospect this turning point can be clearly demonstrated in historical and political terms, it was also a lesson for the leadership of the church: *confusione hominum, Dei providentia.*

The results of Hitler's refusal to provide government support for the Reich Bishop's plans were already evident on the evening of this eventful day. For without this support Ludwig Müller had nothing more to set against the demands of the Confessional Front. Therefore that night he had to call on the remaining members of the Clergy Ministry – Hossenfelder, Weber and Werner – to offer their joint resignation.[74] The first Reich Church Cabinet had come to an end after scarcely eight weeks of activity. And – as would subsequently emerge – this also marked the end of the idea of a Reich Church, at least one with any constitutional status. For in spite of all the efforts made, it was no longer possible to set up a second Clergy Ministry capable of functioning fully. From now on the guidelines for the Reich Church consisted only of makeshift expedients and emergency rulings of doubtful standing, which legally, too, plunged the Protestant church into almost incalculable difficulties.

For the moment, however, all the representatives of the Confessional Front who had remained in Berlin welcomed the news of the resignation of the Clergy Ministry with undisguised relief. The way towards a basic restructuring of church conditions now seemed open. But they had once more deceived themselves over Ludwig Müller. The Reich Bishop had sought new friends in this difficult situation, and this introduced a new stage in the developments. During the crisis, the young Bishop Oberheid of the Rhineland had surprisingly become Ludwig Müller's closest adviser. And behind Oberheid was the man who during the summer had been the driving force of co-ordination: August Jäger. After his defeat at the Reich Synod, the Prussian Ministerial Director now apparently perceived a new chance of coming closer to the goal he so passionately sought, taking over the leadership of the Protestant church. Thus it was probably Jäger's plan, if the Reich Bishop now showed himself to be resolute, to push through his own candidates for the Clergy Ministry against the wishes of the Confessional Front, even without the support of the state. In Jäger's view, all this made sense. For if the theological positions were occupied by insignificant figures, and Werner retained his position as the only commissioner, as a so-called legal member, then it was only necessary to overthrow him at a given moment for Jäger to reach his desired goal.[75] This was the plan that he actually set in motion in the spring of 1934, in other circumstances. But for the time being Jäger had overestimated his chances, and in the coming weeks this was to cause Ludwig Müller further difficulty.

On 30 November the Confessional Front had proposed – as an ultimatum – three names of members for the new Clergy Ministry: Oberkirchenrat Schaal of Stuttgart for the Lutheran post, and at the same time to be the official representative of the South German churches; Präses Koch for the United churches, and at the same time as representative of the Pastors Emergency League; and finally the Reformed Pastor Udo Smidt, who was at the same time to stand for the church associations.[76] However, discussions on the next day, 1 December, in which according to the constitution everyone now participated, including the new German Christian church leaders, did not produce a united opinion on this proposal. Ludwig Müller exploited this disunity. After considerable toing and froing he called in all the church leaders on the afternoon of 2 December and told them – probably on the advice of Oberheid and Johannes Heckel, both of whom were present – 'that a Reich Bishop cannot and may not accept non-negotiable demands from any group'. 'I feel conscience-bound,' he asserted in his old tone of voice, 'in commitment to scripture, to make a decision achieved through careful counsel and reflection, and fought for in prayer. Here I have kept strictly to the constitution, as in Wittenberg I pledged that I would.'[77] Then he called on those present to make their suggestions for the positions in the Clergy Ministry. After a series of names had been mentioned, and the requirements of the Reich Church constitution had thus formally been fulfilled, Ludwig Müller informed the astonished gathering that he was 'appointing to the Clergy Ministry Rector D.Lauerer of Neuendettelsau as representative of the Lutherans, Professor Dr Beyer as representative of the United Churches, and Church Minister Weber as representative of the Reformed. The post of Church Chancellor remains open for the time being.'[78]

At this point Ludwig Müller was not as strong as he seemed. For it very soon emerged that the Neuendettelsau Rector Hans Lauerer was by no means prepared to take the post offered him. In his place, over Meiser's objections, the Reich Bishop appointed the Bavarian Pastor Friedrich Klein as Lutheran delegate.[79] Moreover, the appointment of Otto Weber as Reformed Church Minister was legally problematical, to say the least. So Wurm was no doubt correct when he remarked on 9 December that such a cabinet could 'not rely on a firm foundation of trust from the church as a whole'. The 'rump cabinet' that there was called to mind 'in a fatal way the coalition cabinets of such unhappy memory'.[80]

Nevertheless, the new Reich Church Cabinet immediately went ahead with its task. And the first and most important consequence of the new direction soon made itself evident. The dominant position of the German Christians in the Reich Church rapidly came to an end. Ludwig Müller had only one aim: to secure his own position. But he saw this security as lying only in maintaining or restoring the close connections with the Party and the state. So as soon as he perceived that Hossenfelder and the Faith Movement were no longer any use to him, all pledges of loyalty were forgotten. He now turned to Jäger and Oberheid, from whom he anticipated the political influence which the Faith Movement had evidently forfeited. At the same time it was necessary to calm the Confessional Front, at least sufficiently for them to desist from major public protests. These were the two goals which Ludwig Müller pursued during December.

At the first meeting of the new Church Cabinet on 4 December, an important decision was already made in this direction. The 'Church Decree concerning the Church-Political Independence of the Reich Church Government' forbade the members of the Clergy Ministry and the officials of the church government to be 'members of church-political parties, groups and movements'.[81] The only point of this law was to make it possible for the Reich Bishop and the Reich Church Government to distance themselves from the Faith Movement, which had become so inconvenient. Accordingly, two days later Ludwig Müller issued a statement to the German Christians in which he announced that he was giving up his role as sponsor. The great aim, he wrote, 'that this church should not be a state within a state, but that it should find a vital position in the Third Reich', could only be achieved 'by a clear and unified leadership. Therefore I had to release the church leadership from ties to all of the conflicting groups. In obedience to the law which had to be passed on this... I must be the first to obey this law and give up the role of sponsor. This decision has been a hard one for me. It has pained me. I struggled over it for a long time. But I am sure that you, as National Socialists, will also follow the leadership where obedience commands!'[82]

Hossenfelder still sought to parry this stroke with a statement in which he declared that the German Christians were 'a Faith Movement and not a political party'. He was withdrawing the movement 'from the church-political struggle as of today'; but the existing groups of the German Christians should be maintained within the church bodies. In a personal letter at the same time he asked Ludwig Müller to recognize that the Faith Movement now no longer fell 'under the church decree of 4 December 1933'.[83] But no one in the Reich Church leadership took any notice of the letter.[84] Instead, during those days Ludwig Müller was negotiating, unknown to his old ally, on the latter's place as Clergy Vice President of the Prussian Oberkirchenrat. The proposal of someone for this post who was also highly regarded in the Pastors Emergency League, the Westphalian President Karl Koch, was evidently thought to be a clever ploy against the church opposition in Prussia. Koch wrote back on 7 December that he was ready to accept the post provided that the Clergy Ministry were set up in accordance with the wishes of the Confessional Front and that he himself was provided with the plenary powers needed 'in order to overcome the present internal difficulties in the Old Prussian Church'.[85] This was naturally unacceptable to Ludwig Müller. But the discussions dragged on until the end of the year, thus hindering immediate action by the Emergency League. For as long as there was still hope of an agreement, they did not want in any circumstances to disturb these approaches.

Meanwhile, even Gaue which until recently had been loyal to Hossenfelder began to abandon him. At a combined meeting on 11 December the whole north and west of the Reich – Hamburg, Schleswig-Holstein, Mecklenburg, Lübeck, Brunswick and the Rhineland – broke off from the Berlin leadership. The explanation given showed that only one thing was held against the national head of the movement: political failure. 'The Reich leadership in Berlin,' the report of the meeting stated, 'ultimately no longer had any contact with the political leadership, which is intolerable to us National Socialists.' At the same time the discussion also already revealed Ludwig Müller's new line. The theological interests of the Reich Church would be represented in the future by three 'Confessional Ministers' but the administration was 'to correspond to the structure of the Third Reich'. To this end a Chancellor was to be installed, a proven National Socialist who would be 'the guarantor of the unconditional implementation' of German Christian principles.[86] This meant August Jäger.

In these circumstances it was little more than a sign of helplessness when on 17 December *Evangelium im Dritten Reich* published a statement by Hossenfelder in which he indicated 'that the movement is led solely by me, and anyone acting against the Reich leadership automatically excludes himself from the Faith Movement'.[87] For Ludwig Müller was now insisting at least on getting rid of his fellow fighter, who was finished as far as politics and the church were concerned, in order to have a free hand for his new plans. In a long conversation on 20 December he compelled Hossenfelder to give up all his church posts – Bishop of Brandenburg, deputy Land Bishop and Clergy Vice President of the Oberkirchenrat, and in addition simultaneously to surrender the Reich leadership of the German Christians.[88] After Hossenfelder's agreement, Müller asked him straight away – for simplicity's sake – personally to draft a letter of resignation of the kind he would expect from him, Müller. In doing this, Hossenfelder returned once more to his old German Christian pathos. 'Dear Brother Hossenfelder,' he made the Reich Bishop write to him in his draft, 'you (and here he used the familiar Du) have put your offices in the Evangelical Church at my disposal because of the church-political situation. In so doing you have made a sacrifice for the church which as Reich Bishop and National Socialist I cannot praise too highly. You have thus set yourself above the petty charges laid against you, and demonstrated that as a National Socialist and a German Christian you are not concerned for your person or your positions, but only for the cause... If you now go into the wilderness at your own request, as you are longing to do, and place the burden of your task on other shoulders, be certain that the hour will strike when you will be needed again. Be assured that we two, who have become comrades in the struggle, still stand together in true comradeship.'[89] However, Hossenfelder's hope that the Reich Bishop would adopt this draft was not realized. On 21 December he announced his resignation from all offices. Ludwig Müller no longer felt it necessary even to acknowledge the fact.

Thus at the end of the year one of the most controversial personalities of the German Protestant church disappeared astonishingly quickly and finally from the church-political stage. And the departure of its first natural leader brought the great era of the Faith Movement of German Christians to an end. The beginning of the year 1934 marked a new period in the history of the 'German Christians', a period that no longer had anything in common with the upsurge, the force, the passion and the successes of the first year.

Nothing made the depth of this change clearer than the fact that Hossenfelder's successor had altered everything even before the end of 1933: the organization, the guidelines and even the name. The man to whom Hossenfelder in his last official letter transferred the office of Reich leader[90] was the Vice President of the Schleswig-Holstein Landeskirche, Dr Christian Kinder, a thirty-seven-year-old lawyer. He had belonged to the German Christians in Schleswig-Holstein from the very beginning,[91] and had played a substantial part in the rapid and total victory of the Faith Movement between the Elbe and the Southern Au. This, plus the impression that Kinder represented an indeterminate German Christian middle ground, and that as a non-theologian he might possibly be less vulnerable to the attacks of the church opposition, may above all have governed Hossenfelder's selection of him. But the weak and superficial man never had the slightest chance of bringing the German Christian movement back into the great church-political game. When he produced his memoirs in 1965 he mentioned a surprise that probably also never left him as Reichsleiter. 'I could never understand that then as even today the erroneous assertion is made that the German Christians wanted to combine National Socialism and Christianity. Perhaps this slogan was used by my predecessors, but after I took over the leadership no one can justifiably attribute such a concern to the German Christians.'[92]

On 21 December 1933 the new Reichsleiter, in a statement 'To the Evangelical Members of the Volk', announced the basic changes. In the changed task of building a Reich Church 'the pattern of mere struggle is no longer useful, especially in a church in which the areas of outward form and faith are so clearly distinct'. So the Faith Movement now had to 'return to its original starting point, and be definitively involved in the building up of the German Volk. Though for a time it seemed,' Kinder continued somewhat enigmatically, 'that within the church there was a movement parallel to National Socialism within the state, this was dictated by the development of National Socialism itself, which had to struggle very hard and could only conquer the ground step by step. But now the triumph of National Socialism makes it necessary to abandon the appearance of parallelism and direct the development of the German Christian Movement more widely and more generally.'[93]

Kinder decided that in order to achieve this aim new guidelines for the future were necessary. These were the so-called 'Twenty-eight Theses of the Saxon Volkskirche for the Internal Development of the German Evangelical Church' which the German Christian theologians of the Saxon Landeskirchenamt – especially Oberkirchenrat Walter Grundmann – had drafted after the Sports Palace demonstration and had had passed by the Saxon Land synod on 10 December. These twenty-eight theses were an attempt to endorse and establish the decisive points of a German Christian church – recognition of the total claims of the National Socialist state and commitment to blood and race – with the use of confessional formulae. They were equally opposed to the 'rigid dogmatism' of the church position and a religion of 'racial experience' and in this way demonstrated where the German Christians now had to seek their new position.[94] As these guidelines required 'a new name', at the end of his statement Kinder ruled: 'As National Socialists of the Evangelical Church we bear the name German Christians'.

So here was a new man; a development towards 'more widely and more generally'; and new hybrid guidelines, dropping the term 'faith movement'. At the end of the 1933 that was the new programme of the German Christians. 'In your person, most esteemed Lord Bishop,' Kinder told Ludwig Müller on 29 December, 'is embodied the confidence of the Führer in our efforts and the unity of the German Evangelical Church. So the broad front of our compatriots in Volk and faith who as National Socialists will call themselves German Christians, will stand behind you. As Reichsleiter I ask for your endorsement of this.'[95] But the church-political collapse of the splintered and defeated party was so great that Ludwig Müller let almost three weeks elapse before on 16 January he expressed to the new Reichsleiter his 'warmest good wishes for the development begun here'.[96]

While the Faith Movement was thus disintegrating and Hossenfelder had fallen, the Reich Bishop tried to get things under control through his new Reich Church Cabinet. Unconcerned at the ultimatum from the Confessional Front; unconcerned, too, at the legal objections to its composition, at the beginning of December the new church government decided on three major church laws with far-reaching effect. These included a 'Church Law for Resolving Church-political Disputes' which – on the Party model – provided for special 'Arbitration Committees' and a 'Church Law for the Uniting of Smaller Landeskirchen' which was intended to give the Reich Church sweeping authority for the reorganization of the church in Germany. But the most controversial was the 'Provisional Church Law concerning the Legal Position of Clergy and Officials of the Landeskirchen', which reached deep into the rights of the Landeskirchen. It was to provide uniform control over the removal of clergymen 'in the interests of service', if 'positive effectiveness' in the community seemed impossible.

Even if the decisions involved were to be entrusted to a regular church court, it was still clear that this was primarily a means of political discipline. The first dispute in the Clergy Ministry was over whether the Aryan paragraph was again to be incorporated into the law, in that clergy were to be dismissed 'who enter into marriage with a person of non-Aryan descent'. Given the tense situation on precisely this point, it was decided instead to adopt a contingency formula which concealed the same intention behind general terminology: 'The clergy must receive permission to enter into marriage'.[97]

In the face of this obvious contempt for the Confessional Front, Meiser decided again to invite the opposition church leaders to Berlin for a discussion on 18 December.[98] At the evening session, in which the representatives of the Pastors Emergency League also took part, after a draft proposal by Wurm an endorsement of the ultimatum of 29 November was decided upon and personally delivered to the Reich Bishop by Wurm and Meiser at noon on the 19th. At the heart of this declaration was a demand for the reconstruction of the Clergy Ministry that week according to the concerns of the Confessional Front, along with the threat that in the case of a refusal the Reich Church government would no longer be in accord with the 'authority of the Landeskirchen'.[99]

While this petition did not as yet directly question the office and person of the Reich Bishop, in its own statement the next day the Pastors Emergency League went a step further. 'The trust of pastors and communities in the Reich Bishop,' ran the statement decided on by the Council of Brethren, 'has been turned into mistrust, against which we are neither ready nor able to act unless a resolution of the cabinet crisis, which must be achieved by Sunday 23 December 1933, finally opens the way to truly church action within the church.'[100]

The attempt in this way to compel Ludwig Müller to surrender failed all along the line. But the second Clergy Ministry now collapsed under the growing

572

pressure. On 22 December the Reformed Church Minister Otto Weber announced his resignation, while the lawyer Dr Werner, in any case functioning only provisionally, was dismissed by Ludwig Müller before Christmas, in order to make way for August Jäger. Pastor Klein, who held the Lutheran post, continued to lack recognition by the Landeskirchen and ended his activities on 31 December. So at the beginning of the year the entire Reich Church government consisted only of the Reich Bishop and the United Church Minister, Professor Hermann Wolfgang Beyer, until he too resigned at the beginning of January.[101]

However, the Reich Bishop was apparently unaffected by all this. For on the same 19 December, the day on which the bishops issued their statement, Ludwig Müller believed that he had again secured the full support of Hitler. This was a step which in his memoirs Wurm called 'a real dirty trick':[102] the delivery of the Evangelisches Jugendwerk into the hands of the Hitler Youth.

From the spring of 1933 on, the future of church youth work in the Third Reich had also been the topic of a vigorous dispute on the Protestant side. The 700,000 members were for the most part covered in three large associations, substantially independent: the National Federation of Associations of Protestant Young Men, the National Federation of Protestant Young Women and the League of German Bible Circles, which was especially active in the upper schools. And, as on the Catholic side,[103] here too the growing claims of Hitler Youth to power were watched with a concern which was also expressed openly when Schirach was nominated Youth Leader of the German Reich on 17 June 1933. After the end of June nearly all the non-Christian youth organizations – the federated, the professional and the sports associations – were incorporated into Hitler Youth; only the two church youth groups were left as large independent groups. So the efforts of the Reich youth leadership were aimed especially at their conquest and incorporation. The reaction to this development on the Protestant side was the same as that on the Catholic side. Although the Protestant youth generally welcomed the new Reich and its Führer with almost unqualified enthusiasm, there was nevertheless widespread agreement that the special contribution of church youth work unquestionably made it necessary to maintain its organizational independence.[104] This conviction was reinforced by the surprising fact that in the spring and summer of 1933 the number of members of Protestant Youth grew from month to month – probably an extension of the Christian German enthusiasm of the hour, as well as of the search for its own style of common life, not provided by the state.[105] Regardless of all the difficulties and in spite of the prohibition of uniforms, the tricks and manifold interferences,[106] during the summer Protestant youth still stood substantially unshaken: full of hope for a great task of Volksmission in the Third Reich and ready for broad co-operation with Hitler Youth, even to the point of corporate membership of it; but not ready for self-surrender and co-ordination which would mean the end of church youth work.

Similar organizational conclusions were drawn from this development to those of the Catholic youth associations. Just as already at the beginning of May the Catholic young men's associations decided to tighten up their organization and give the national leadership plenary powers, so too a shift towards unified leadership was achieved in the Protestant youth organizations. Here the organizational model of the leadership principle, now generally recognized, played as great a role as the wish and hope, by the consolidation of all forces, to maintain and secure the independence of the youth associations. After a series of unions of the smaller associations, almost all Protestant youth associations were combined at the end of July in the Evangelisches Jugendwerk Deutschlands.[107] Dr Erich Stange, previously Reichswart of the young men's associations, was appointed Reichsleiter with almost unlimited plenary powers. Although this solemn enthusiasm was regarded by the sceptics – like Udo Schmidt, who led the Bible Circles, or Leopold Cordier, who headed the Christian German Youth – as being all too ready to make concessions,[108] this action, like the corresponding nomination of General President Wolker on the Catholic side, clearly indicated the central importance of the young men's associations.

The great majority of the associations and their leaders thought that they had created a guarantee of the preservation of their independent church youth work by founding the Evangelisches Jugendwerk and by introducing the leadership principle. But what was conceived as salvation led to disaster. For the leadership principle called for the transfer of final responsibility and power of command to the supreme leader. And this supreme leader was Ludwig Müller.

Even at the foundation of the Jugendwerk, according to the leadership principle the patronage of the Protestant youth was transferred to Hitler's representative and future Reich Bishop.[109] And Ludwig Müller did not hesitate to strengthen his new authority by an appeal of his own. 'I expect,' he told the Protestant youth, 'that the Jugendwerk, with its more than 700,000 members, will be prepared together to dedicate itself to the tasks of Volksmission, now that it has honoured me with its leadership. Anyone who breaks ranks here or goes his own selfish way will make it more difficult to accomplish the tremendous task whch the proclamation of the gospel in the Third Reich presents to us.'[110] A response to this appeal was expressed by the great rally with which on 29 September the Protestant youth of Berlin greeted the newly elected Reich Bishop, and at which Reichsleiter Stange assured the Reich Bishop that the young men of the Reich were ready for sacrifice, 'as we have promised you'.[111]

At the same time the new Reich Church government set to work to provide a basic solution to the difficult problem of the relationship of the Hitler Youth to Evangelisches Jugendwerk. At a meeting of the most important youth leaders and Land youth pastors, invited to Berlin on 13 October by Hossenfelder, all sides virtually unanimously stated that while Protestant youth unconditionally supported National Socialism, there was no question of a dissolution and a take-over by Hitler Youth. The predominant view of most of the participants was that Evangelisches Jugendwerk should rather enter into a close co-operation with Hitler Youth. The training of the church youth in politics and military sports was to be left to Hitler Youth, while in return church youth were to be accorded broad opportunities for mission among Hitler Youth. 'Our task in the Hitler Youth,' declared Stange in this meeting, 'cannot be fulfilled by dissolution of the youth associations. This idea is not without appeal. It is as if one were to throw salt out among all the youth; but where does the next handful of salt come from? What then? We are the shock troops in the church's Volksmission, the troops with fighting spirit. So we need the youth associations, again growing within their ranks, shaping themselves.'[112]

The decisive question, of course, was how the government youth leadership would respond to this proposal. On this, Stange reported at the next meeting that he had 'made a far-reaching proposal for the affiliation or federation of the church youth' to Schirach, 'but this was turned down on the grounds that the Hitler Youth demanded total incorporation: for "we are getting you anyway"'. In time the Catholic Church would also give way 'under pressure'.[113] In this difficult situation, which was heightened by the fact that the members of the German Christian leadership were now increasingly clearly slipping towards capitulation, the hopes of the youth leaders turned more than ever to the Reich Bishop. Only direct negotiations between Ludwig Müller and Hitler, so the argument ran, could now clarify the situation. So Ludwig Müller, evidently seeing a chance to extend his influence, thereupon asked the youth leaders for a statement that the church youth put themselves under the Reich Bishop 'without reservations'.[114]

Meanwhile the situation of the church youth had markedly worsened. Reports of conflicts, attacks and interference came from all parts of the country. Worst of all, as also for Catholic youth, was the requirement of Hitler Youth membership for getting teaching posts and jobs. A decree along these lines was issued at the beginning of November in Baden: 'Members of Hitler Youth are to be given preference in every respect in filling teaching posts and other jobs.' In future, Hitler Youth would take on 'all appointments to teaching posts and jobs by our youth'. The Land Bishop of Baden, who reported this to Berlin on 8 November, expressed the opinion that along with 'political discrimination against non-National Socialist youth' this economic measure was 'the severest test for the youth of the church'.[115]

Influenced by the rising pressure on the one hand, and by the tremendous undertow of the 12 November plebiscite on the other, things came to a crisis at almost the same time in both Catholic and Protestant youth organizations. On 12 November Papen wrote a letter to Gröber which led to a consultation of the Catholic youth leaders in Freiburg on 15 November, and soon afterwards to a direct intervention by the Holy See.[116] Only two days later, on 17 November, the Protestant Youth met in Berlin. The confusion and uncertainty which characterized the Freiburg meeting was, if anything, surpassed here. In retrospect, the decisions which the youth leaders reached that day seem crassly contradictory. But for the participants they were evidently meant to be a saving solution – and this demonstrated once again the almost unintelligible situation for the future. That 17 November the Sports Palace scandal was only four days past, and the agitation in the church was still growing from day to day. Nevertheless, the Reich Bishop put before the youth leaders the draft of an agreement which in essence provided for the full and unconditional compulsory incorporation of Protestant youth into Hitler youth. Although Ludwig Müller obscured the situation in his usual way and claimed that the only issue was 'that we carry the Saviour to the Volk', the majority of the youth leaders expressed their lasting reservations about this agreement and declared that 'compulsory incorporation' was intolerable. But rather than drawing conclusions from this contradiction and pulling back from Ludwig Müller, the exact opposite was done: the Reich Bishop was solemnly given 'the power of command over the church youth' – evidently on the assumption that only under Ludwig Müller's leadership could the independence of Protestant youth be saved.[117]

On 4 December the Protestant youth leaders again met in Berlin, to respond to Ludwig Müller's draft agreement. The conclusion of the group was as clear as could be. 'We have... come to the definitive conclusion,' the youth leaders wrote to the Reich Bishop that same day, 'that the agreement is intolerable to us and would make the task of Evangelisches Jugendwerk in the church practically impossible.' At the same time Arnold Dannenmann, Reichswart of the Jungvolk, was authorized to put his personal standpoint to the Reich Bishop, 'to the effect that all further negotiations were to be rejected'.[118]

So the Reich Bishop could have had no doubts about the clear rejection of the agreement by the Jugendwerk. But the weaker his church-political position became, the less prepared he was to take it into account. The possibility of demonstrating his unconditional submission to the Party, and the hope that this would again strengthen his relationship to Hitler far outweighed all criticism in the church. So now there was a dramatic final act.

On 9 December the Reich Bishop and the Reich youth leader announced that negotiations over the incorporation were almost complete.[119] When countless protests followed this announcement, three days later Ludwig Müller abruptly dismissed Reichsleiter Stange and dissolved the Council of Leaders.[120] At the same time, however, Church Minister Beyer gave the assurance in the name of the Reich Church Government that before any final decision, the Council of Leaders 'would in all circumstances be given due hearing'.[121] Nevertheless, the Protestant youth leaders who relied on this promise were again disappointed. To be sure the Council of Leaders were again summoned to Berlin, on Saturday 16 December, where there was long and fruitless discussions with Oberheid. Thereupon on the Sunday Stange composed a statement which once again gave detailed reasons for the rejection of the agreement and at the same time contained the counter-proposal of the Jugendwerk.[122] On the Monday there was a direct discussion with the Reich Bishop who, while thinking that he would sign the agreement, at the same time promised that he would do nothing 'before listening again to the leadership of the Jugendwerk'.[123]

On this day – it was 18 November – the whole question was finally also discussed in the circles of the non-German Christian church leaders, gathered in Berlin. Now both problems – the reconstruction of the Clergy Ministry and the preservation of the Evangelisches Jugendwerk – appeared to be the decisive demands which Meiser and Wurm were to present to the Reich Bishop the next day as an ultimatum. In fact, on 19 December, in handing over this ultimatum, the two bishops told Ludwig Müller 'not to conclude the youth agreement without once again giving the youth leaders an opportunity to express themselves'. The Reich Bishop promised this 'quite definitely', as both Meiser and Wurm later explained.[124] In this state of affairs a surprise conclusion of the agreement by Ludwig Müller seemed totally ruled out. Yet this is precisely what happened.

If Schirach's recollections are accurate, the capitulation of Protestant youth to the Hitler Youth took place on the very evening of this day, during a meal at the Hotel Esplanade – to the accompaniment of music by Barnabas von Géczy, a well-known violinist of whom the Reich Bishop was 'especially fond'. 'Reich Bishop Müller told me,' Schirach recalled, 'that Protestant youth had given him total control, and that he now wanted to transfer all Protestant boys and girls under the age of eighteen to the Hitler Youth. We would soon reach agreement on the details. He responded immediately to my proposal that the agreement should be announced to the *Wochenschau* in my office in the Reich youth headquarters. That took place on 19 December 1933.'[125] The signing of the agreement the next day was therefore only a formality.

If this were not revolting and scandalous enough, the Reich Bishop brought things to a final head only in the late evening. At the same time, the youth leaders had been talking things over and were agreed at the meeting which they expected to 'withdraw the power of command given directly and personally, on specific conditions, to the Reich Bishop on 17 November of this year'.[126] Ludwig Müller in fact received the representatives of the Council of Leaders once again, around 9.00 p.m., apparently to keep his promise. The Reich Bishop and the youth leaders negotiated for nearly two hours over the terms of the agreement without Ludwig Müller ever revealing by so much as a word that the outcome had long since been decided. Finally, the youth leaders gave the Reich Bishop their prepared statement on the withdrawal of the power of command and that same night composed a letter to the entire Jugendwerk, which called for resistance 'to the infringement of this constitution and the destruction of its status'.[127] However, on 21 December they read the report about the signing of the agreement – in the morning newspapers.

The agreement to incorporate the Protestant youth into Hitler Youth in fact meant the unqualified and compulsory surrender of the church youth to Hitler Youth. The first sentence left no doubt that this was precisely the intention. 'Evangelisches Jugendwerk,' it stated, 'recognizes the uniform political education of German youth by the National Socialist state and Hitler Youth as the bearers of the vision of the state. The young people of Evangelisches Jugendwerk under the age of eighteen will be incorporated into Hitler Youth and its subsidiary units. From now on, anyone in these age groups who is not a member of Hitler Youth cannot be a member of Evangelisches Jugendwerk.' All further regulations,[128] according to which e.g. two afternoons a week and two Sundays a month were to be kept free for Evangelisches Jugendwerk were hardly of comparable importance. The agreement meant the end of the flourishing church youth associations. What came next was a laborious search for new ways for Protestant youth work.[129]

The action of the Reich Bishop almost immediately let loose a flood of protests. Quite rightly they were directed not against the régime and the Party but against the Reich Bishop and the church government. It was not hard to see that, quite unnecessarily, a purely political decision had been made. Typical of this awareness was a protest telegram from Hagen, which arrived in Berlin on 21 December. 'Westrundfunk announces betrayal of Evangelisches Jugendwerk by Reich Bishop. Apart from lack of representative authority, stab in back from that direction was unexpected. Church dies at hand of bishop. Ashamed and sad for such a church. Gerstein, Licensed Engineer, Hagen Community Councillor.'[130] This was the Kurt Gerstein who later made a career in the SS in order to sabotage the crimes of the régime – or at least to be able to give eye-witness testimony. One of the few direct reports of the proceedings in the killing of Jews in Belzec and Treblinka in 1942 comes from him.[131]

However, Ludwig Müller was not very bothered by these protests. For him, the only important telegram was the one sent to Hitler on 20 December. 'I have just completed,' the Reich Bishop reported, 'the incorporation of the Evangelisches Jugendwerk into Hitler Youth, in agreement with the Youth Leader authorized by you. May God bless this hour for our Volk and our church...'[132]

And now everything depended on whether Hitler would send the Reich Bishop the official confirmation he expected, from which he promised himself that his position would be decisively strengthened. How completely Ludwig Müller depended upon Hitler was shown by the discussion he had with Bodelschwingh the next day, 21 December. Müller assured him that no other solution to the question of the Jugendwerk was possible, because Hitler wanted it that way. Hitler had declared to him only the day before that 'the conclusion of the agreement was his best Christmas present'. This saying quickly went the rounds. Otherwise, Müller went on, he felt quite isolated. Only the trust of the Führer sustained him. 'If the Führer ever lost confidence in him,' Bodelschwingh recorded Müller as saying, 'he would be out any day. Otherwise he has to stay.'[133]

All of this, however – Hitler's supposed wish, the matter of the Christmas present and the assurance of trust – was a sheer lie. In reality, at the end of the year Hitler was extremely angry at the situation in the Protestant church and refused even to have any contact with any representatives of this church.[134]

The handwritten draft of a letter from Ludwig Müller to Hitler at the end of the year exposes the totally illusionary duplicity of the Reich Bishop during these days. In it Müller reported a heightening of the situation and 'new ultimatums' from 'bishops opposed to me' which compelled him 'now to take quite drastic measures. The occasion of this heightened opposition,' Ludwig Müller wrote, 'was my agreement with the Reich Youth Leader. Baldur von Schirach told me that you were very pleased with this agreement. I had asked him to ask you to express in a short telegram your agreement and your pleasure at my telegram about the conclusion of this agreement. Unfortunately this has not happened, and my opponents have concluded that you are not at all in agreement... with this great and important work. Therefore for your sake and mine I must urgently request you to be so kind as to send me such a telegram as soon as possible.'[135] But although Hitler on his own initiative liberally sent letters of appreciation at the end of the year to his trusted associates, no recognition of Ludwig Müller was forthcoming. He had every reason to fear for his position.

With the surrender of the Jugendwerk the church opposition had had enough of Ludwig Müller. Now the opinion gained ground that a change in the cabinet was not enough; the Reich Bishop himself had to go. The only question was how to secure a tolerably honourable departure for him. On 22 December Meiser, Wurm and Bodelschwingh visited him to advise him to create a new cabinet with Dr Lauerer, the Neuendettelsau Rector, to fill his deputy post, and to go on indefinite leave. But Ludwig Müller refused.[136]

Thereupon the Confessional Front met on 30 December in Würzburg, now strengthened considerably by the Protestant youth leaders, and agreed on a joint letter containing a new ultimatum. By 2 January 1934 a new Church Ministry was to be set up consisting of Dr Lauerer, Oberkirchenrat Zentgraf of Mainz, Pastor Udo Schmidt of Barmen and Reichsgerichtsrat Flor; the Reich Bishop was to be represented by a deputy, and Praeses Koch was to be called as Clergy Vice-President in Prussia.[137]

Again Ludwig Müller refused. In a letter to Meiser on 2 January he declared that for the sake of the respect and authority of his office a 'group ultimatum' could not be accepted, and that in addition he was 'also legally quite unable to fulfil the demands'.[138] Thereupon the Confessional Front met again – on 4 January, this time in Halle/Saar. And here it became perfectly clear that all the toings and froings of the Reich Bishop, all the ultimatums, rejoinders, rumours and intrigues had reduced church politics to the level of a farce.

Even in retrospect, the grotesque situation can be seen in the laconic minutes of the meeting:

10 a.m.: Meiser reports on Ludwig Müller's letter of 2 January.

11 a.m.: Pastor Klein telephones from Berlin. The Reich Bishop wants 'to investigate Zentgraf and Flor'. He will decide by 8 January. The meeting decides to accept no compromises and stick to the ultimatum. Ludwig Müller refuses. Reliable reports arrive from Berlin that the Reich Bishop plans a 'dictatorship' under Article 6.1 of the Reich Church constitution. The meeting does not know what to do.

4.30 p.m.: New telephone call from Berlin. Church Cabinet supposed to be planned: Beyer, Klein, Oberheid, Jäger. Extraordinary measures against the Emergency League.

7.00 p.m.: Further reports from Berlin. The Reich Bishop taken to a clinic. The meeting asks: 'Can we let ourselves be put off once again?'

9.00 p.m.: Reich Bishop has offered resignation on 1 February. Coch to become commissioner. 'Message from Munich. Discussion with the Führer. Over one hour. Total impression crushing. Church: Führer extremely angry, neither Bishop nor Reich Bishop granted audience. We are to do what we want! – But the Protestant church is even worse than the Catholic... Said *loudly!*'

So the reports and rumours went on, until shortly before midnight Ludwig Müller warned the meeting by telegram against 'illegal and unconstitutional' decisions. Only then was there agreement on a letter that repeated the demands of 30 December and rejected participation in further negotiations.[139]

The same day the Reich Bishop responded to the obvious inconclusiveness and indecision of this meeting with a 'Decree concerning the Restitution of Orderly Conditions in the German Evangelical Church'. In 'responsible exercise of the office of leadership constitutionally granted me, on the basis of Article 6 paragraph 1 of the constitution', with this decree the Reich Bishop forbade all church-political controversies and rallies, and threatened all church officials with 'immediate provisional suspension from office' and the prompt initiation of disciplinary proceedings on those 'who attack the church government or its measures publicly or by the dissemination of writings – especially by flysheets or circular letters'.[140] This decree was intended finally to bring the Reich Bishop the peace and quiet he longed for.

On this date, 4 January 1934, the church-political situation looked almost equally hopeless from all sides. The Reich Bishop could only keep his position by means of a 'muzzling order', and had almost entirely forfeited support and respect in the church. But the church opposition, too, did not appear in a very good light. For obviously there was no possibility of changing things. It was trapped within the provisions of a constitution to which it had itself largely assented; in a leadership principle which made the Reich Bishop legally unassailable; and in its own convictions, according to which nation and church, national revolution and church renewal could still not be separated. Thus on 4 January this was not the path that pointed to the future. That distinction belonged to an event that from the centre of church politics seemed quite peripheral: the first 'Free Synod' of the Reformed communities which met that day in Barmen.

The calling of a free synod was wholly in keeping with the strict line which had become established in the west of Germany in autumn 1933, not least under the influence of Karl Barth. The decision was taken in a wider circle of Reformed preachers and elders which had met in Barmen on 22 December. The letter of invitation was addressed to 'Reformed preachers and elders from all the Reformed and United communities of Germany' and at the same time indicated the conditions for admission, which wholly reflected the Reformed tradition: 'Only those will be admitted to the synod who can show that they are preachers or elders... of their community and on solemn oath to the synod affirm that free of any control from outside the community in matters of faith without reservations they hold completely to the Word of God in the Old and New Testaments as the only source of revelation for our faith.' At the same time the agenda indicated that more was at stake than merely seeking advice and discussing the situation. For a lecture by Karl Barth was scheduled for 10 a.m. on 4 January which directed the synod to the basic theological question: 'The Confession of a Free Church Synod'.[141]

320 pastors and elders from 167 communities gathered in Barmen on the evening of 3 January for the first lecture, on 'The Reformed Churches and Communities in the Storm of the Year 1933'. They heard a critical and self-critical account of developments which ended in the question how there could be such a powerful incursion of heresy into the communities.

The next morning Karl Barth then presented the 'Confession of a Free Church Synod'. He called it a 'Declaration on the Correct Understanding of the Reformation Confessions Today' because, as he said, the confession was 'only an action of the church and not of an individual professor', and because his declaration could therefore only be a question to the Synod, 'which as representatives of the communities they must take up and answer in the name of the church'.[142]

This first Barmen Confession was the direct forerunner of the famous Barmen Declaration, which united the whole Confessing Church in May 1934. It was more detailed, more comprehensive and therefore less influential, but it already contained, sometimes down to the exact wording, all the decisive theological statements of its great successor. This started with the form. For the first time since the Reformation a confession was not content with a positive statement but declared clearly and emphatically what false teachings were at the same time rejected and repudiated. 'In view of the church events of the year 1933,' ran the first article, 'the Word of God calls on us to repent and be converted. For in these events a heresy which has devastated the Protestant church for centuries has become ripe and visible. It consists of the view that alongside God's revelation, God's grace and God's majesty a legitimate human independence has to determine the gospel and the form of the church – i.e., the temporal path to eternal salvation. This rejects the view that the church development since the Reformation has been a normal one, and that the present emergency in our church is only a passing disruption, after dealing with which we proceed along the same line of development.'[143]

Occasionally interrupted by short explanations and discussion, Karl Barth then put before the Synod a total of seventeen theses which dealt with five sets of topics: 'The Church Today', 'The Church under Holy Scripture', 'The Church in the World', 'The Message of the Church' and 'The Form of the Church'. The decisive statement which then came to a focus in the Barmen Declaration was found here in Paragraph II.1: 'The church has its origin and its existence solely from revelation, from the authority, the consolation and the guidance of the Word of God, which the Eternal Father has uttered once for all in Jesus Christ, his Eternal Son, in the power of the eternal Spirit, when the time was fulfilled. This is a rejection of the view that apart from the revelation of the triune God the church may and must base itself upon and find recourse to divine revelation in nature and history.'

In two respects the development of this central statement pointed in a special way towards the future. First, it affected the relationship of the Reformation confessions one to another. 'Who is meant,' Barth asked, 'when we speak of the church which must repent and be converted?' and he answered: ' "We" are addressed. That cannot just mean we Reformed, or in the east we Lutherans, or in the Rhineland, we United... When we do not have this responsibility in a vacuum but in the context of the year 1933/34, we are inevitably reminded of the Evangelical Church, and when we say that, we are at all events saying more than just Reformed Church; we are saying, "The church of Jesus Christ!"' And that meant clearly and unambiguously: 'We have experienced that there are all kinds of Reformed and all kinds of Lutherans; the real division cuts right through both. Our much-vaunted Reformed concerns are to be placed under, and not over, the claims of the common evangelical confessions of faith.'[144] This statement did not remain unchallenged, especially among the Reformed, but it did become a decisive presupposition for the Confessing Church.

Finally, the last two theses pointed in a special way towards the future – though towards a future which was as yet scarcely imagined. The penultimate one affirmed the unity of the church of Jesus Christ 'in the various times, races, peoples, states and cultures' and explicitly rejected the Aryan Paragraph. And the last attempted to define the authority and limits of the state, in so doing taking up a theme which was increasingly to become the decisive theme of the years to come. For the assertion of the 'fundamentally free church in a state which is fundamentally just as free in connection with its task' meant the emphatic rejection of totalitarianism, i.e. the view that 'the state is the supreme or even the only (total) form of historical reality with a visible, temporal form, to which therefore the church with its message and form has to be co-ordinated, subjected or even incorporated'.

The synod ended with a solemn resolution: 'The 320 Reformed elders and preachers from 167 Evangelical communities of Germany, assembled in a free Reformed synod, make it known that the "Declaration concerning the Right Understanding of the Reformation Confessions in the German Evangelical

Church Today", written by Professor Dr Barth, which they have heard, bears witness to the truth of Holy Scripture, and take responsibility for it in gratitude.'

The decision to pass this resolution succeeded where the Bethel Confession had not, namely in the acceptance of responsibility by the church. It was only a start, but it was a start along a course on which the church could proceed further. So when Barth published the theses in *Theologische Existenz* at the end of January, despite the desolate condition of church politics, for the first time there was confidence. And the statements which he formulated in this context in fact became marks of the church, far beyond their time and occasion.

'Now especially,' he wrote, 'it is impossible to deny that however things may go for the confessor, the confession was and is the issue. And although people may go round with grim faces in the much-vaunted "sphere of the church", in no circumstances may they go around with anxious, sour faces. Wherever it is believed – *credo unam sanctam catholicam et apostolicam ecclesiam* – the church is there, and one has reason to be joyful.'[145]

Notes

Part One

1. Between Yesterday and Tomorrow (1918-1919)

1. *Kirchenbuch für evangelisch-protestantische Gemeinden*, produced by the Evangelische Konferenz in Baden, Leipzig 1915, 50.

2. *Kirchenbuch für die Evangelische Kirche des Grossherzogtums Hessen*, 1, Darmstadt 1904, 51. These prayers were part of the general intercessions after the sermon. As the prayer books show, it was also possible to choose prayers without special intercessions for the local rulers, but these may have been the exception.

3. G.Mehnert, *Evangelische Kirche und Politik 1917-1919. Die politischen Strömungen im deutschen Protestantismus von der Julikrise 1917 bis zum Herbst 1919*, Düsseldorf 1959, 114f.; *Kirchliches Jahrbuch für die evangelischen Landeskirchen Deutschlands*, 1919, 351.

4. C.Cordes, 'Hannoversche Pfarrer und Politik 1918-1929', *Hannoversche Pfarrerblatt* 74, 1967, 80f.

5. Faulhaber to the Bavarian episcopate, 15 November 1918; Henle to Faulhaber, 17 November 1918; L.Volk (ed.), *Akten Kardinal Michael von Faulhabers 1917-1945*, I, Mainz 1975,40-4.

6. Examples for the Catholic side can be found in e.g. H.Müller, 'Der deutsche Katholizismus 1918-19', *Geschichte in Wissenschaft und Unterricht* 17, 1966, 532f.

7. *Verhandlungen des Deutschen Evangelischen Kirchentags 1919*, published by the Deutscher Evangelischer Kirchenausschuss, Berlin nd [1920], 57f., address of welcome by President D.Moeller, Berlin.

8. G.Mehnert, *Evangelische Kirche und Politik*, 99f. We must agree with Mehnert in his view that 'the thanksgiving addresses given to local rulers and the Kaiser during the first weeks' cannot be regarded as 'explicitly political statements'. However, this changed with the formation of political fronts against the Republic (cf.ibid., 113 n.69). K.W.Dahm, *Pfarrer und Politik, Soziale Position und politische Mentalität des deutschen evangelischen Pfarrerstandes zwischen 1918 und 1933*, Cologne and Opladen 1965, 168f., gives a somewhat one-sided account of these connections. C.Motschmann, *Evangelische Kirche und Preussicher Staat in den Anfängen der Weimarer Republik*, Lübeck and Hamburg 1969, 18ff., tends to be more balanced.

9. G.Mehnert, *Evangelische Kirche und Politik*, 129-39; R.Morsey, *Die deutsche Zentrumspartei, 1917-1923*, Düsseldorf 1966, 94-109, 290f.

583

10. W.Göbell (ed.), *Kirche, Recht und Theologie in vier Jahrzehnten. Der Briefwechsel der Brüder Theodor und Julius Kaftan*, 2, Munich 1967, 674, letter of 17 November 1918.

11. *Kirchliches Jahrbuch für die evangelische Landeskirchen Deutschlands* 46, 1919, 137-41; P.Troschke, *Evangelische Kirchenstatistik Deutschlands*, Kirchliche Statistik I, Berlin 1930, 94f.; J.Jacke, *Kirche zwischen Monarchie und Republik. Der preussische Protestantismus nach dem Zusammenbruch von 1918*, Hamburg 1976, 25-8, 88-94, puts special stress on the financial dependence of the Prussian church.

12. K.-W.Dahm, *Pfarrer und Politik*, 140. For the situation of the individual Landeskirchen cf. *Kirchliches Jahrbuch* 48, 1921, 334-8.

13. B.Doehring (ed.), *Ein feste Burg – Predigten und Reden aus eherner Zeit*, I, Berlin nd [1914], 14f. (emphasis in the original). After the Second World War a whole series of works on German war theology and war preaching during the First World War appeared. They have been covered in a recent account which makes the welcome attempt to arrive at a balanced judgment which goes beyond the obvious criticism that can be made of this position: W.Huber, *Kirche und Öffentlichkeit*, Stuttgart 1973, 135-219.

14. Cf. p.11 below and S.Miller, *Burgfrieden und Klassenkampf. Die deutsche Sozialdemokratie im ersten Weltkrieg*, Düsseldorf 1974, 68-74.

15. Thomas Mann, *Betrachtungen eines Unpolitischen*, Stockholmer Gesamtausgabe, Frankfurt 1956, 39f.

16. *Jahrbuch des Evangelischen Bundes für 1918 – Vertraulich – Nur für unsere Mitglieder*, Berlin 1919, 3.

17. *Kirchliches Jahrbuch* 46, 1919, 312.

18. Ibid., 313f. The text of the announcement also appears in the very instructive collection of sources edited by M.Greschat, *Der deutsche Protestantismus im Revolutionsjahr 1918-19*, Witten 1974, 26f.

19. Quoted from G.Mehnert, *Evangelische Kirche und Politik*, 97 n.13. There are similar statements in ibid., 103ff., and in C.Motschmann, *Evangelische Kirche und preussische Staat*, 19ff.

20. A significant light is shed on the general uncertainty, for example, by the fact that when the delegates discussed the location for the National Assembly, the problem of security was the decisive factor in the choice of Weimar, *Quellen zur Geschichte des Parlamentarismus und der politische Parteien*, 1.R., 7.II, *Die Regierung der Volksbeauftragten*, 2, Düsseldorf 1969, 223-33.

21. G.Köhler, *Die Auswirkungen der November Revolution von 1918 auf die altpreussische Evangelische Landeskirche*, Diss.theol. Kirchliche Hochschule Berlin 1967, 43. J.Jacke, *Kirche zwischen Monarchie und Republik*, 60-2, is critical of the proceedings. The full text of the statement is quoted by A.Hoffmann, *Sitzungsberichte der verfassungsgebenden Preussischen Landesversammlung* 1919/21, 6, 719f. Hoffmann links the quotation with the scornful comment that 'with such a majority the gentlemen' should have been 'delighted with the separation of state and church...' Cf. also the statement by the Protestant pastors of Frankfurt am Main, *Christliche Welt* 50/51, 12 December 1918, 485.

22. C.Motschmann, *Evangelische Kirche und preussische Staat*, 24ff.

23. Wilhelm Philipp in *Die Reformation. Deutsche Evangelische Kirchenzeitung für die Gemeinde*, 17, 1918, 24 November 1918. The text also appears in M.Greschat, *Deutscher Protestantismus*, 37. The 'Positive Union' was the dominant Prussian church party which was closely connected with the conservative forces in church and state. For the function of Rom.13 in this connection cf. also G.Mehnert, *Evangelische Kirche und Politik*, 97ff.

24. F.Thimme and E.Rolffs, *Revolution und Kirche*, Berlin 1919, 372. The quotation from Karl Muth, editor of the journal *Hochland*, occurs in an article 'Die neuen "Barbaren" und das Christentum', *Hochland*, March 1919, 588. Cf. 13 below.

25. For the attempts at reform cf. the texts in M.Greschat, *Der deutsche Protestantismus*, ch.IV, 'Kirchliche Erneuerungsbestrebungen', 143-84.

26. For details see J.Jacke, *Kirche zwischen Monarchie und Republik*, 158-70.

27. C.Motschmann, *Evangelische Kirche und preussische Staat*, 94.

28. *Christliche Welt*, no.52 of 26 December 1919, col. 499.

29. *Christliche Welt*, nos.48/49 of 28 November 1918, 466. For Martin Rade and the *Christliche Welt* cf. also F.W.Kantzenbach, 'Kirchlich-theologischer Liberalismus und Kirchenkampf. Erwägungen zu einer Forschungsaufgabe', *Zeitschrift für Kirchengeschichte* 87, 1976, 302ff.

30. *Christliche Welt* 52, 1919, 499.

31. G.Köhler, *Auswirkungen der November Revolution*, 70ff.

32. 'Volkskirchenräte, Volkskirchenbund, Volkskirchendienst', in Thimme und Rolffs, *Revolution und Kirche*, 208.

33. C.Bauer, 'Carl Muths und des Hochland Weg aus dem Kaiserreich in die Weimarer Republik', *Hochland* 59, 1966, 234f.

34. R.Morsey, 'Die deutschen Katholiken und der Nationalstaat zwischen Kulturkampf und Erstem Weltkrieg', *Historisches Jahrbuch der Görresgesellschaft* 90, 1970, 62.

35. Ibid., 60f.

36. H.Lutz, *Demokratie im Zwielicht. Der Weg der deutschen Katholiken aus dem Kaiserreich in die Republik*, Munich 1963, 46.

37. Cf. on this e.g. S.Merkle, 'Konfessionelle Vorurteile im alten Deutschland', in *Süddeutsche Monatshefte*, December 1914, 390-406.

38. The phrase appeared first in the speech given by Wilhelm II on the evening of 31 July from the balcony of the Berlin Schloss. It was repeated in the address from the throne on the opening of the Reichstag on 4 August. Cf. also R.Morsey, *Deutsche Zentrumspartei*, 53f.

39. Quoted from L.Hüttl, 'Die Stellungnahme der katholischen Kirche und Publizistik zur Revolution in Bayern 1918/19', *Zeitschrift für bayerische Landesgeschichte* 34, 1971, 653f. For Faulhaber's biography see the excellent 'Lebensbild' by L.Volk, in id., *Faulhaber-Akten* I, XXV-LXXXI.

40. K.Hammer, *Deutsche Kriegstheologie 1870-1918*, Munich 1971, 79. The author sees the assimilation of the substance of Catholic faith to nationalist faith as being the reason 'why we dare at all to combine Protestant and Catholic war theology in the same book', ibid.

41. H.Lutz, *Demokratie im Zwielicht*, 44f.; R.Morsey, *Deutsche Zentrumspartei*, 55f.

42. H.Lutz, *Demokratie im Zwielicht*, 43f.; C.Bauer, *Carl Muths Weg*, 237.

43. Text of Pastoral Letter of 1 November 1917, etc., in M.Meinertz and H.Sacher, *Deutschland und der Katholizismus. Gedanken zur Neugestaltung des deutschen Geistes- und Gesellschaftslebens* I, Freiburg 1918, 429-46. This extremely instructive two-volume collection produced under the auspices of the 'Arbeitsausschusses zur Verteidigung deutscher und katholischer Interessen im Weltkrieg' is one of the extensive pieces of Catholic war propaganda largely directed by Matthias Erzberger. Cf. K.Epstein, *Matthias Erzberger und the Dilemma of German Democracy*, Princeton 1959, 102. For the conservative attitude of the episcopate over the question of the suffrage cf. also R.Patemann, 'Der deutsche Episkopat und das preussische Wahlrechtsproblem 1917/1918', *Vierteljahrsheft für Zeitgeschichte* 13, 1965, 345-71.

44. Quoted in R.Morsey, *Die deutschen Katholiken*, 63.

45. J.Schmidlin, *Papstgeschichte der neuesten Zeit* 3, Munich 1936, 278. However, the political background to this collection was more questionable. It amounted to nothing less than an attempt by the German war propaganda directed by Erzberger to exercise massive influence on the attitude of the Holy See. That Benedict XV was not unreceptive

to this is evident from the fact that he gave Erzberger his own cardinal's hat, a ring, and other valuable presents. For the whole matter see K.Epstein, *Matthias Erzberger*, 102ff. and above all Karl Bachem's memorandum on Erzberger's relations with the Vatican 1914-1915, ibid., 460f.

46. For the pontificate of Benedict XV cf. G.Schwaiger, *Geschichte der Päpste im 20. Jahrhundert*, Munich 1968, 77-95. According to K.O.von Aretin, *The Papacy and the Modern World*, New York 1970, 173, Benedict XV brought the papacy 'new heights of world prestige'.

47. J.Schmidlin, *Papstgeschichte* 3, 281f. The Centre Party deputy Peter Spahn had given similar reasons why the Reich needed to be represented at the Vatican in the Reichstag session of 28 February 1919. F.von Lama, *Papst und Kurie in ihrer Politik nach dem Weltkrieg. Dargestellt unter besonderer Berücksichtigung des Verhältnisses zwischen dem Vatikan und Deutschland*, Illertissen 1925, 83.

48. An impressive piece of evidence for Pacelli's standing in German Catholicism is the *Laudatio* by his colleague Ludwig Kaas from the year 1929, in L.Kaas (ed.), *Eugenio Pacelli. Erster Apostolischer Nuntius beim Deutschen Reich. Gesammelte Reden*, Berlin 1930, 7-24.

49. O.Köhler, in *The Church in the Industrial Age*, History of the Church, ed.H.Jedin and J.Dolan, London and New York 1981, IX, 235.

50. Denzinger-Schönmetzer, *Enchiridion Symbolorum Definitionum et Declarationum de rebus fidei et morum*, [32]1963, no.3165.

51. These circumstances are stressed above all by K.O.von Aretin, *Papacy*, 161, 167, etc.

52. *Wiederbegegnung von Kultur und Kirche in Deutschland* was the title for the Festschrift which friends and colleagues gave Karl Muth on his sixtieth birthday: R.van Dülmen, 'Katholischer Konservatismus oder die "soziologische" Neuorientierung. Das Hochland in der Weimarer Zeit', *Zeitschrift für bayerische Landesgeschichte* 36, 1973, 256.

53. R.van Dülmen, op.cit., 265.

54. Quoted from van Dülmen, op,cit., 267. For Scheler's significance in this period cf. also H.Lutz, *Demokratie im Zwielicht*, 22-42, and – for its effect – W.Spael, *Das katholische Deutschland im 20.Jahrhundert*, Würzburg 1964, 260ff.

55. Erzberger to Faulhaber, 27 December 1917: L.Volk, *Faulhaber-Akten*, 24-26.

56. For details see R.Morsey, *Deutsche Zentrumspartei*, 83ff.

57. Ibid., 85f.

58. Ibid., 91ff.

59. Ibid., 94-109.

60. For political developments in this period cf. G.Schulz, *Zwischen Demokratie und Diktatur*, Berlin 1963; E.Kolb, *Die Arbeiterräte in der deutschen Innenpolitik 1918-1919*, Düsseldorf 1962. There is a bibliography of this period arranged by subject matter in E.Kolb (ed.), *Vom Kaiserreich zur Republik*, Gütersloh 1972, 405-25.

61. G.Köhler, *Auswirkungen der Novemberrevolution*, 34.

62. F.Thimme, 'Das Verhältnis der revolutionären Gewalten zur Religion und den Kirchen', in Thimme und Rolffs, *Revolution und Kirche*. 24.

63. For A. Hoffmann cf. e.g. Thimme, op.cit., 25-35, 38-43; R.Morsey, *Deutsche Zentrumspartei*, 111-17; Jacke, *Kirche zwischen Monarchie und Republik*, 44-7; M.Greschat, *Der deutsche Protestantismus*, 88f.

64. Haenisch later expressly established that only the threat of workers' and soldiers' councils forced him to give in over important points in order to avoid worse, *Sitzungsberichte der verfassunggebenden Preussischen Landesversammlung* (cf. n.21), 7251, and 7259 for Hoffmann's reply. Hoffmann, however, criticized Haenisch: 'Herr Haenisch has

wanted to destroy the revolution from the beginning', ibid., 7186. For the course of events cf. the account by J.R.C.Wright, *'Above Parties'. The Political Attitude of the German Protestant Church Leadership 1918-1933*, Oxford 1974, 1ff.

65. Quoted from C.Motschmann, *Evangelische Kirche und preussische Staat*, 28f.

66. *Christliche Welt* 48/49 of 28 November 1918, 466. For the effect of this news on the Catholic side cf. R Morsey, *Zentrumspartei*, 111f.

67. For the history of this law up to its revision on 30 November 1920 cf. G.Köhler, *Auswirkungen der Novemberrevolution*, 172-81: for the Kirchenaustritt movement after the War, ibid., 181-97.

68. Thus in the introduction to the decree. The text of the extensive document is contained in *Preussisches Pfarrarchiv. Zeitschrift für die Rechtsprechung und Verwaltung auf dem Gebiet der Landeskirche*, 1918, 290ff. Cf. G.Köhler, *Auswirkungen der November-revolution*, 126ff.

69. F.Thimme, in Thimme and Rolffs, *Revolution und Kirche*, 29. O.Zimmermann SJ, 'Revolutionäre Trennung von Kirche und Staat', *Stimmen der Zeit* 96, 1919, 345-59, gives a good survey of the various measures and an impression of the dismay in the church.

70. 'A Kulturkampf attack on the violent treatment of the church' was the way in which the *Allgemeine Evangelisch-Lutherische Kirchenzeitung* described an account of the wave of protest (52, 1919 of 10 January 1919, 36f.). Text in M.Greschat, *Der deutsche Protestantismus*, 101-3. Cf. also the reports, ibid., 128ff.

71. Quoted from Mehnert, *Evangelische Kirche und Politik*, 108.

72. Text in *Archiv für katholisches Kirchenrecht* 79, 1919, 124-8.

73. G.Mehnert, *Evangelische Kirche und Politik*, 165.

74. Ibid.

75. Morsey, *Deutsche Zentrumspartei*, 135f.

76. There is a detailed account in Mehnert, *Evangelische Kirche und Politik*, 173-9.

77. H.Müller, *Der deutsche Katholizismus*, 528-31.

78. For this see below 000ff.

79. See e.g. the article by F.Thimme, 'Das Verhältnis der revolutionären Gewalten zur Religion und den Kirchen', in Thimme und Rolffs, *Revolution und Kirche*, esp. 44-50.

80. G.Mehnert, *Evangelische Kirche und Politik*, 179.

81. Quoted from G.Köhler, *Auswirkungen der Novemberrevolution*, 137.

82. Ibid., 138. The figures were examined by H.Dymke in the Archive of the Evangelischer Oberkirchenrat. H.D.Dymke, *Die Auseinandersetzungen um Schule und Religionsunterricht in den ersten Monaten nach der Novemberrevolution 1918*, Wissenschaftliche Zulassungsarbeit, Tübingen 1970 (unpublished).

83. A.Milatz, *Wähler und Wahlen in der Weimarer Republik*, Bonn ²1968. The total number of votes cast was around 30.4 million (34): the ratio between Protestant and Catholic was about two-thirds: one-third.

84. K-.W.Dahm, *Pfarrer und Politik*, 134-7.

85. Karl Rieker, *Zur Neugestaltung der protestantischen Kirchenverfassung in Deutschland*, Leipzig and Erlangen 1919, 5.

86. For W.von Pechmann see below, 229f., 266f., 304.

87. 'Zur neuen Kirchenverfassung', in *Neue Kirchliche Zeitschrift* 31, 1920, 19.

88. A.Krose, SJ (ed.), *Kirchliches Handbuch für das katholische Deutschland* 9, 1919-20, Freiburg 1920, 109. For the so-called 'constitutional dispute' in German Catholicism and its consequences see the details in R.Morsey, *Deutsche Zentrumspartei*, 236-42.

89. *Kirchliches Handbuch* 9, 110.

2. The New Orientation of the Protestant Landeskirchen (1919-1930)

1. There is a clear account of this development, full of detail despite its brevity, in G.J.Ebers, *Staat und Kirche im neuen Deutschland*, Munich 1930, esp. 26ff., 108ff.

2. Ibid., 29 n.1, 46.

3. Ibid., 44ff.

4. K.Scholder, '100 Jahre Württembergische Landessynode', in *Verhandlungen der 7. Württemburgischen Landessynode*, Stuttgart 1969, 849-56.

5. For details of the constitutional law of the German Landeskirchen as this applied up to 1918 see E.Friedberg, *Lehrbuch des katholischen und evangelischen Kirchenrechts*, Leipzig ⁶1909, 248ff. The last General Synod order in the larger Länder was given to the eastern provinces of Prussia in 1876. For this see J.Heintze, *Die Grundlagen der heutigen preussischen Kirchenverfassung in ihren Vorstadien seit der Generalsynode von 1846*, Greifswald 1931, 55f.

6. 'Synode', *Realenzyklopädie für protestantische Theologie und Kirche*, third edition, vol.19, 1907, 277.

7. Cf. the comprehensive account of these events in G.Besier, *Die preussische Kirchenpolitik 1866-1872*, Tübingen Protestant Faculty dissertation 1976, 317-98.

8. Cf. R.Smend, 'Zur neueren Bedeutungsgeschichte der evangelischen Synode', *Zeitschrift für evangelischen Kirchenrecht* 10, 1963/64, 248-64, esp. 252ff.

9. *Kirchliches Jahrbuch* 1920, 313.

10. *Verhandlungen der verfassungsgebenden Deutschen Nationalversammlung*, Vol.336 (report of the constitutional committee), 188.

11. For the course of the negotiations cf. the account by C.Israel, *Geschichte des Reichskirchenrechts*, Berlin 1922, esp. 20ff. (the making of the compromise) and 52ff. (second and third reading in the plenary session).

12. For what follows cf.also G.Anschütz, *Die Verfassung des Deutschen Reiches. Ein Kommentar für Wissenschaft und Praxis*, Berlin ¹⁴1933, 629ff.

13. R.Morsey, *Deutsche Zentrumspartei*, 217f.

14. For the basis of the necessity for a national legal regulation relating to the intervention of the Länder in church law cf. the remarks by Düringer and Delbrück of the DNVP and Heinze of the DVP at the first reading in the constitutional committee, *Verhandlungen*, Vol.326, pp.474, 388, 398, etc.

15. However, for the problems of this definition for the Weimar period cf. G.Anschütz, *Reichsverfassung*, 629ff., esp. 636ff.

16. For the legal problems of the concept of the corporation cf. now A.von Campenhausen, *Staatskirchenrecht. Ein Leitfaden durch die Rechtsbeziehungen zwischen Staat und den Religionsgemeinschaften*, Munich 1973, 93-9.

17. Ibid., 95.

18. G.S.Ebers, *Staat und Kirche*, 132.

19. The quite negative assessment of the Weimar regulation in J.Jacke, *Kirche zwischen Monarchie und Republik*, 119-49, measures the result by an ideology of separation which does not do justice to the conditions of the time.

20. Morsey, *Deutsche Zentrumspartei*, 220 n.13.

21. *Kirchliches Jahrbuch* 1920, 340f.

22. Thimme and Rolffs, *Revolution und Kirche*, 208: see also above, 10.

23. W.Beyschlag, in *Realencyklopädie für protestantische Theologie und Kirche*, Vol.3, 1897, 549.

24. E.Schubert, *Die deutsch-evangelischen Einheitsbestrebungen vom Beginn des 19. Jahrhunderts bis zum Gegenwart*, Volksschriften zum Aufbau, Vol.6, Verlag des Evangelischen Bundes, Berlin 1919, 33.

25. See 9 above.

26. Cf. G.Mehnert, *Evangelische Kirche und Politik*, 214-18.

27. *Niederschrift der Verhandlungen der Vorkonferenz zur Vorbereitung eines allgemeinen deutschen evangelischen Kirchentages. Cassel-Wilhelmshöhe, den 27. und 28. Februar 1919*, Berlin 1919, 53.

28. *Verhandlungen des 1.Deutschen Evangelischen Kirchentages 1919*, published by the Deutscher Evangelischer Kirchenausschuss, Berlin nd [1920], 26ff. The counting of the Kirchentage is confusing because after the official foundation of the Kirchenbund it began again, so that the Bethel Kirchentag of 1924 is also cited as the 'First German Evangelical Kirchentag'.

29. Ibid., 293ff.

30. Ibid., 215.

31. Ibid., 223,237.

32. *Verhandlungen des 2.Deutschen Evangelischen Kirchentages 1921, Stuttgart 11-15 September 1921*, Berlin nd [1922], 30ff.

33. Ibid., 202 (emphasis in the original).

34. This regulation was explicitly based 'on the independence of the individual churches' with the aim of avoiding any undesirable pressure, ibid., 40. For more details on the legal structure of the Kirchenbund cf. M.Berner, *Die rechtliche Natur des Deutschen Evangelischen Kirchenbundes*, Berlin 1930.

35. For details of the work of the DEKB see the two reports *Der Deutsche Evangelische Kirchenbund in den Jahren 1924-27* and ibid., *1927-30*, published by the Kirchenbundesamt, Berlin 1927, 1930.

36. The most important instance was Prussia, where in March 1919 the assembly of the Land which produced the constitution transferred the rights of the king to three Protestant ministers of state – called *Minister in evangelicis* or even 'The three wise men'. The initiative for this came from the Protestant theologians in the DDP group in the Prussian Land assembly (R.Otto, M.Rade and E.Troeltsch), who in this way sought above all to establish a system of primary elections. (For this see Martin Rade, 'Demokratisierung der Kirche', *Christliche Welt*, 14 August 1919, 522-6.) This unwise step did a good deal of damage to the democratic cause inside and outside the church and also contributed to the DDP losing ground so quickly in the Weimar republic. For the whole process cf. C.Motschmann, *Evangelische Kirche und preussische Staat*, 55ff., and above all Jacke, *Kirche zwischen Monarchie und Republik*, 171ff.

37. *Kirchliches Jahrbuch*, 1925, 17. The constitutions were collected in F.Giese and J.Hosemann, *Die Verfassungen der Deutschen Evangelischen Landeskirchen*, Vols 1 and 2, Berlin 1927, and *Das Wahlrecht der Deutschen Evangelischen Landeskirchen*, Vols 1 and 2, Berlin 1929. There is a good survey in P.Schoen, *Das neue Verfassungsrecht der evangelischen Landeskirchen in Preussen*, Berlin 1929.

38. Thus also J.Jacke, *Kirche zwischen Monarchie und Republik*, 298-303, though with much more critical final conclusions.

39. In addition to the ongoing information in the *Kirchliches Jahrbuch* there is a summary of statistics on the Protestant churches in the Weimar period in P.Troschke, *Evangelische Kirchenstatistik Deutschlands*, Kirchliche Statistik I, Berlin 1930. There is a survey of the Landeskirchen on 9ff.

40. *Kirchliches Jahrbuch* 1920, 43.

41. Cf. Hesse's twelve theses 'Warum sind wir gegen den Bischofstitel?', in *Reformierte Kirchenzeitung*, 1926, 3ff.

42. For details of the controversy over the title 'bishop' in Prussia cf. H.Vorländer, *Aufbruch und Krise. Ein Beitrag zur Geschichte der deutschen Reformierten vor dem Kirchenkampf*, Neukirchen 1974, 51ff.

43. *Das Jahrhundert der Kirche*, Berlin ⁵1928, 76f. Also *Nachspiel. Eine Aussprache mit Freunden und Kritikern des 'Jahrhunderts der Kirche'*, Berlin 1928. Hesse reviewed the book in a very polemical way ('Jahrhundert des Bischofs'); cf. his contributions in the *Reformierte Kirchenzeitung*, 1927, 62ff., 122ff.

44. *Nachspiel*, 33.

45. Ibid., 29.

46. *Das Jahrhundert der Kirche*, 277; cf. also *Nachspiel*, 15-26.

47. *Das Jahrhundert der Kirche*, 228f.

48. *Kirchliches Jahrbuch*, 1929, 380f.

49. *Handbuch der Evangelischen Presse*, ed. A. Hinderer, Leipzig ³1929, XIX, XXIV.

50. P.Troschke, *Evangelische Kirchenstatistik Deutschlands*, Kirchliche Statistik II, Berlin 1931, 56.

51. Walther Wolff, *Zehn Jahre Deutsche Geschichte 1919-1928*, Berlin 1928, 423.

52. *Kirchliches Jahrbuch*, 1929, 315f.

53. H.Priebe, *Kirchliches Handbuch unter besonderer Berücksichtigung der Evangelischen Kirche der altpreussischen Union*, Berlin ³1928, 35, 36 (with an almost literal echo of Dibelius).

54. H.G.Haack, *Die evangelische Kirche Deutschlands in der Gegenwart*, Berlin 1929, 14f., 34, 35f., etc.

55. *Die evangelische Kirche der Neuzeit in Deutschland und in den benachbarten Gebieten deutscher Sprache*, ed. M.Schian, Schuber, Schoell, Buntzel, Matthes, etc.

56. W.Wolff, in *Zehn Jahre Deutsche Geschichte*, 423f.

3. The Revival of Protestant Theology (1919-1930)

1. See above, 29f.

2. W.Herrmann, *Ethik*, Tübingen ⁵1913, 12.

3. Ibid,. 59.

4.Ibid., 139f.

5.Ibid., 180ff.

6. Ibid., 177.

7. So the criminal statistics for the year 1911 listed only a total of 667,541 indicted crimes and offences. If one compares the number of convictions with the size of the population subject to criminal law, it follows that for 1911 1,182 out of every 100,000 people were sentenced. Between 1890 and 1914 this ratio remained almost constant. In the 1920s the criminal element then clearly increased. Thus the statistics for 1924 show a total of 917,960 crimes and offences. That means that of every 100,000 people 1,494 were convicted (*Statistik des Deutschen Reichs*, NF, Vols. 257, 335, Berlin 1913/1925).

8. Cf. K.Hammer, *Deutsche Kriegstheologie*, 136ff.

9. *Kirchliches Jahrbuch*, 1919, 308.

10. H.von Schubert, *Unsere religiös-kirchliche Lage in ihrem geschichtlichen Zusammenhange. Eine Vorlesung während Weltkrieg und Revolution*, Tübingen 1920, 14.

11. Thus the greeting from Gottfried Traub to the Dresden Kirchentag, *Verhandlungen des Deutschen Evangelischen Kirchentages 1919*, 63. Traub was politically on the extreme right wing. His phraseology is typical of the nationalist Protestant trend within the Evangelical Church.

12. Ibid., 148f.

13. Ibid., 152.

14. G.Merz, 'Die Begegnung Karl Barths mit der deutschen Theologie', *Kerygma und Dogma* 2, 1956, 157.

15. According to the report by G.Dehn, who also took part in Tambach, *Die alte Zeit, die vorigen Jahre. Lebenserinnerungen*, Munich 1962, 217.

16. Karl Barth – Eduard Thurneysen, *Briefwechsel*, 1, 1913-1921, Zurich 1973, 334 n.1.

17. Karl Barth, *Revolutionary Theology in the Making*, ed. J.D.Smart, London and Richmond, Va. 1964, 47.

18. G.Dehn, *Die alte Zeit*, 219.

19. *Briefwechsel Barth-Thurneysen* 1, 336f.

20. It was first published by Patmos Verlag, Würzburg 1920, and then included in Karl Barth, *The Word of God and the Word of Man* (1924), ET New York 1957, 272-327, from which quotations are taken. For the 'Tambach Lecture and its consequences' see now also the detailed biography by E.Busch, *Karl Barth. His life from letters and autobiographical texts*, London and Philadelphia 1976, 109-16.

21. *The Word of God and the Word of Man*, 273 (emphasis in original).

22. Ibid., 277.

23. Ibid., 283.

24. Ibid., 292f.

25. Ibid., 294f.

26. Ibid., 319f.

27. Ibid., 311f.

28. First published Munich 1920. Reprinted in *The Word of God and the Word of Man*, 51-96, from which the quotations are taken.

29. *The Word of God and the Word of Man*, 61.

30. Ibid., 62.

31. K.Barth, *Epistle to the Romans*, ET Oxford 1933, 1.

32. *The Word of God and the Word of Man*, 68.

33. Ibid., 70f.

34. Karl Barth, *Letzte Zeugnisse*, Zurich 1969, 21.

35. *Karl Barth – Rudolf Bultmann Letters 1922-1966*, ed. Berndt Jaspert, Grand Rapids and Edinburgh 1982, 153; cf. E.Busch, *Karl Barth*, 46ff.

36. Ibid., 154. For criticism of political socialism cf. also Karl Barth, *Church Dogmatics*, II.1, Edinburgh 1957, 634f.. W.Härle, 'Der Aufruf der 93 Intellektuellen und Karl Barths Bruch mit der liberalen Theologie', *Zeitschrift für Theologie und Kirche* 72, 1975, 206-24, is critical of Barth's account of himself.

37. *Barth-Bultmann Letters*, 158f.

38. For the biographical and bibliographical details of the 1927 autobiographical sketch which has already been mentioned, see the correspondence between Barth and Thurneysen, 1913-1921, which has also been mentioned often; also Karl Barth's Preface to the emended reprint of the first edition of *Romans* (1919), Zurich 1963, and the Prefaces to the second to fifth editions; also E.Busch, *Karl Barth*.

39. An extreme product of this misunderstanding is the confused book by F.W.Marquardt, *Theologie und Sozialismus. Das Beispiel Karl Barths*, Munich and Mainz 1972. After reading it one will find the 'all powerful impact of the social and political' less 'in Barth's thought' (313) than in the author's convictions.

40. Cf. the account of the two stages of development in W.Kopp, *Die gegenwärtige Geisteslage und die dialektische Theologie*, Tübingen 1930, 34ff.

41. *Christliche Welt*, 1920, 374-8. Reprinted in *The Beginnings of Dialectical Theology*, ed. James M.Robinson, Richmond, Va. 1968, 277-82.

42. Ibid., 277.

43. Thus Jürgen Moltmann in the German edition, *Anfänge der dialektischen Theologie*, 2, Munich 1963, 278f.

44. *Anfänge der dialektischen Theologie* 2, 96f.

45. *Beginnings of Dialectical Theology*, 279.

46. Ibid., 282.

47. Thus according to Gogarten's own account in P.Lange, *Konkrete Theologie? Karl Barth und Friedrich Gogarten 'Zwischen den Zeiten' 1922-1933*, Zurich 1972, 387 n.5.

48. *Briefwechsel Barth-Thurneysen* 1, 399.

49. However, far-reaching differences of opinion between the two men had already emerged before 1933 and often put further collaboration in question. In a letter to Ihlenfeld dated 4 June 1955, Barth writes in retrospect that 'already at that time I regarded Gogarten as one of those responsible for the ideology of National Socialism because of utterances like the speech on authority that he made during the 1920s' (quoted from E.Busch, *Karl Barth*, 223; cf. ibid., 196ff., 229ff.).

50. *Beginnings of Dialectical Theology*, 292f.

51. Ibid., 294.

52. Ibid., 298.

53. Ibid., 295.

54. Ibid., 300.

55. *Briefwechsel Barth-Thurneysen* 1, 432.

56. Ibid., 435.

57. E.Brunner, *Die Mystik und das Wort. Der Gegensatz zwischen moderner Religionsauffassung und christlichem Glauben, dargestellt an der Theologie Schleiermachers*, Munich 1924 (²1928).

58. *Briefwechsel Barth-Thurneysen* 2, 100. Cf. also the 'report from the front', 16; 'scene of considerable battles' (the year 1922), 32; 'pause between two fights', 102; 'General chief of staff in Munich' (Georg Merz), 112; 'break-through battle' (Emden), 114; 'the capture of Dordeney', 187; 'real cross-fire' (Leipzig), etc., etc.

59. Ibid., 111, 114.

60. Ibid., 285.

61. Ibid., 341.

62. Ibid., 479.

63. P.Schempp, 'Randglossen zum Barthianismus', *Zwischen den Zeiten* 6, 1928, 529-39. Quoted from *Die Anfänge der dialektischen Theologie*, 305f.

64. Ibid., 305.

65. Cf. P.Lange, *Konkrete Theologie?*, 158-65 and n.57 above.

66. Despite many objections made in the meanwhile, I stick to the thesis of the political problems of dialectical theology in the Weimar period which I developed at length for the first time in my article 'Neuere deutsche Geschichte und protestantische Theologie', 510ff.

67. A.von Zahn-Harnack, *Adolf von Harnack*, Berlin ²1951, 414f.

68. J.Rathje, *Die Welt des freien Protestantismus*, Stuttgart 1952, 377.

69. Ibid., 363.

70. T.Heuss, *Erinnerungen 1905-1933*, Tübingen ⁵1964, 177.

71. *Briefwechsel Barth-Thurneysen* 1, 362. Letter from Thurneysen dated 23 December 1919.

72. Ibid., 2, 68. Letter from Thurneysen dated 24 April 1922.

73. *Die Anfänge der dialektischen Theologie* 1, 197. For the contributions of Tillich and Barth to this controversy cf. ibid., 165ff. For the question cf. also P.Lange, *Konkrete Theologie?*, 161, and the account of Barth's theological criticism of religious Socialism in R.Breipohl, *Religiöser Sozialismus und bürgerliches Geschichtsbewusstsein zur Zeit der Weimarer Republik*, Zurich 1971, 237-57.

74. *The Word of God and the Word of Man*, 276.

4. Church, Curia and Concordats (1919-1929)

1. U.Stutz, *Der Geist des Codex iuris canonici*, Stuttgart 1918, is still a good introduction.

2. So too Stutz with a much-quoted phrase: 'Basically the codex does not introduce much that is new', ibid., 57.

3. Ibid., 50f.

4. The Pope has 'the supreme and most complete jurisdiction throughout the church both in matters of faith and morals and in those which affect discipline and church government throughout the world'.

5. Nomination of bishops, canon 329 § 2; clergy houses, canon § 465.1; sacrifice of the Mass, canon 802; banning of books, canon 1395 § 1; jurisdiction, penal law, Books IV, V.

6. For more recent Catholic criticism of CJC cf. e.g. the new approach by J.Neumann, *Das Kirchenrecht – Chance und Versuchung*, Graz, Vienna and Cologne 1972, with further bibliography; P.Shannon, 'The Code of Canon Law. 1918-1967', *Concilium*, Vol.8.3, 1967, 26-30. The discussion over the possibility of a *lex fundamentalis ecclesiae* also belongs in this context, cf. J.Neumann, 'Zum Entwurf einer *Lex fundamentalis ecclesiae*', in M.Seckler, Otto H.Pesch, Johannes Brosseder and Wolfhart Pannenberg (eds), *Begegnung. Beiträge zu einer Hermeneutik des theologischen Gespräches*, Graz, Vienna and Cologne 1971.

7. Cf. e.g. CJC, canon 1063 § 3. Marriage law as a whole (CJC Book III, VII, canons 1012ff.) is for the first time no longer discussed as independent law but in the framework of the sacraments as 'sacramental law' (U.Schutz, *Geist des CJC*, 38, 89).

8. Cf. e.g. the brief biographical introduction by Ludwig Kaas in *Eugenio Pacelli, Erster Apostolischer Nuntius beim Deutschen Reich, Gesammelte Reden*, Berlin 1930, 7-24, which comes to a climax in the comment of a converted Protestant theologian about Pacelli: '*Angelus non Nuntius…*' (ibid., 24).

9. Ritter to Herting, 8 February 1914, quoted from G.Franz-Willing, *Die Bayerische Vatikangesandtschaft 1803-1934*, Munich 1965, 135.

10. Letter from Ritter of 7 February 1914, ibid., 146 n.7.

11. K.Epstein, *Matthias Erzberger*, 149f., 188, 216, etc.

12. Thus the British Ambassador Lord D'Abernon: L.Volk, *Das Reichskonkordat vom 20.Juli 1933. Von den Ansätzen in der Weimarer Republik bis zur Ratifizierung am 10 September 1933*, Mainz 1972, 252.

13. Epstein, *Matthias Erzberger*, 188.

14. Gaspari to Pacelli, 24 August 1917; Pacelli to Michaelis, 30 August 1917, in F.von Lama, *Papst und Kurie in ihrer Politik nach dem Weltkrieg. Dargestellt unter besonder Berücksichtigung des Verhältnisses zwischen dem Vatikan und Deutschland*, Illertissen 1925, 35f.

15. There is still vigorous dispute over the question of guilt for the failure of the papal peace action. Cf. K.Epstein, *Matthias Erzberger*, 219 n.12.

16. The text of the 1817 Bavarian concordat is now in the excellent collection of sources edited by E.R. and W.Huber, *Staat und Kirche im 19.Jahrhundert. Dokumente zur Geschichte des deutschen Staatskirchenrechts* I, Berlin 1973, 170-7.

17. Instruction for the Prussian chargé d'affaires in Rome, 22 August 1802, ibid., 48, 46.

18. Ibid., 169.

19. Thus also A.Hollerbach, *Verträge zwischen Staat und Kirche in der Bundesrepublik Deutschland*, Frankfurt 1965, 9.

20. Text of *De salute animarum* and *Quod de fidelium* in E.R. and W.Huber, *Staat und Kirche*, I, 204-23.

21. Ibid., 22-6.

22. E.R. and W.Huber, *Staat und Kirche* II, Berlin 1976, 536-43, 823-7.

23. Ibid., 540.

24. Ritter to the Bavarian Minister President Georg von Hertling on 24 May 1917 and 22 February 1918, G.Franz-Willing, *Bayerische Vatikangesandtschaft*, 146 n.12, 148 n.28.

25. E.Deuerlein, *Das Reichskonkordat, Beiträge zu Vorgeschichte, Anschluss und Vollzug des Konkordates zwischen dem Heiligen Stuhl und dem Deutschen Reich vom 20.Juli 1933*, Düsseldorf 1956, 4f.

26. For the whole proceedings cf. also G.Franz-Willing, *Bayerische Vatikangesandtschaft*, 138ff.

27. F von Lama, *Papst und Kurie*, 78.

28. Ibid., 84f.

29. Quoted from H.Trippen, *Das Domkapitel und die Erzbischofswahlen in Köln 1821-1929*, Cologne and Vienna 1972, 490.

30. Text: *Archiv für katholische Kirchenrecht* 99, 1919, 141f. For the controversy over the interpretation of the school article cf. G.Grünthal, *Reichsschulgesetz und Zentrumspartei in der Weimarer Republik*, Düsseldorf 1968, esp. 80ff.

31. G.Franz-Willing, *Bayerische Vatikangesandtschaft*, 165f.; G.Anschutz, *Reichsverfassung*, 419-21.

32. Graf Hertling to Frühwirth, 12 March 1917; ibid., 139.

33. Report by Ritter, 22 July 1921, ibid., 185.

34. Protocol of the Conference of the Bavarian Episcopate, 3-4 September 1919; L.Volk, *Faulhaber-Akten* I, 90.

35. E.Deuerlein, *Reichskonkordat*, 42.

36. N.Trippen, *Domkapitel*, 484f.

37. Ibid., 500.

38. L.Volk, *Reichskonkordat*, 6 n.23.

39. N.Trippen, *Domkapitel*, 504.

40. Ibid., 506f., 516f.

41. F. von Lama, *Papst und Kurie*, 83.

42. *Akten der Reichskanzlei. Weimarer Republik. Das Kabinett Scheidemann, 13. Februar bis 20.Juni 1919*, Boppard 1971, 127, 128 n.10.

43. K.Epstein, *Matthias Erzberger*, 216 n.6, etc. Pacelli's assent is in R.Morsey, 'Zur Vorgeschichte des Reichskonkordats aus den Jahren 1920 und 1921', *Zeitschrift der Savigny-Stiftung für Rechtsgeschichte* 75, Kanonistiche Abteilung 54, 1958, 240 n.14a. For Erzberger and Bergen cf.also G.Schreiber, *Zwischen Demokratie und Diktatur. Persönliche Erinnerungen an die Politik und Kultur des Reiches (1919-1944)*, Münster 1949, 89f. Ibid., n.6, also quotes the extremely critical remarks by Bülow to Erzberger and Bergen.

44. E.Deuerlein, *Reichskonkordat*, 8f.

45. Report by Preger, 31 December 1919, in G.Franz-Willing, *Bayerische Vatikangesandtschaft*, 164.

46. Ibid., 167.

47. Ibid. Franz-Willing quotes this declaration only from the perspective of keeping the Munich Nunciature. How important this matter was for the Curia is also evident from the comments by Benedict XV and Gasparri to the Bavarian and Prussian envoys at the beginning of 1920, ibid., 168.

48. Ibid.

49. K.Epstein, *Matthias Erzberger*, 386f.

50. E.Deuerlein, *Reichskonkordat*, 12.

51. For these connections see 249 below.

52. Texts: E.Deuerlein, *Reichskonkordat*, 12f.

53. It is put like this by Bergen, 18 January 1922, in L.Volk, *Reichskonkordat*, 20.

54. Text: G.Franz-Willing, *Bayerische Vatikangesandtschaft*, 215-17.

55. R.Morsey, *Vorgeschichte des Reichskonkordats*, 248.

56. Report of 20 October 1922 in G.Franz-Willing, *Bayerische Vatikangesandtschaft*, 193.

57. R.Morsey, *Vorgeschichte des Reichskonkordats*, 249.

58. L.Volk, *Reichskonkordat*, 17-19.

59. Pacelli to Bertram, 30 August 1920, in L.Volk, *Reichskonkordat*, 7.

60. Report of 6 November 1921, in G.Franz-Willing, *Bayerische Vatikangesandtschaft*, 186.

61. R.Morsey, *Vorgeschichte des Reichskonkordats*, 248.

62. Text: G.Franz-Willing, *Bayerische Vatikangesandtschaft*, 184. The Reich Foreign Minister was the Independent Walter Simons, a lawyer, who at the same time played a leading role in the Evangelical Social Congress.

63. For the attempts of the Reich government to dissociate themselves from Simon's assurance cf. for 1921 E.Deuerlein, *Reichskonkordat*, 27f.; for 1928 in the context of the discussions over the Reich school law G.Franz-Willing, *Bayerische Vatikangesandtschaft*, 213f.

64. F. von Lama, *Papst und Kurie*, 199f.

65. D.Golombek, *Die politische Vorgeschichte des Preussenkonkordats* (1929), Mainz 1970, 13f. The Prussian suspicions are given in detail in G.Schreiber, *Persönliche Erinnerungen*, 77-83.

66. E.Deuerlein, *Reichskonkordat*, 18. The text of the Koch-Weser guidelines, which goes back to Delbrück, and Delbrück's preliminary work can be found in A.Kupper, *Staatliche Akten über die Reichskonkordatsverhandlungen 1933*, Mainz 1969, 435-41. The so-called Pacelli understanding I of 1 May 1920, which is similar in tendency to the proposals for the Bavarian concordat, is in L.Volk, *Kirchliche Akten über die Reichskonkordatsverhandlungen 1933*, Mainz 1969, 277-81.

67. L.Volk, *Reichskonkordat*, 8.

68. Letter from the Prussian Kultusministerium of 16 and 20 June 1921 in D.Golombek, *Preussenkonkordat*, 17.

69. Ibid.

70. L.Volk, *Reichskonkordat*, 38.

71. D.Golombek, *Preussenkonkordat*, 7.

72. The protocol of the negotiations in Berlin on 11 November 1921 relating to a Reich and Land concordat are in E.Deuerlein, *Reichskonkordat*, 24.

73. For Joseph Wirth cf. R.Morsey, *Zentrumspartei*, 386f.; 433ff. etc.

74. E.Deuerlein, *Reichskonkordat*, 26f.

75. L.Volk, *Reichskonkordat*, 11 n.64.

76. The text of the so-called Pacelli understanding II of 15 November 1921 is in A.Kupper, *Akten*, 441-7. For an assessment cf. Bergen's letter of 18 January 1922, ibid., 448 n.1, where it is said that Pacelli's proposals went 'much too far', assigning 'the rights to the Holy See and the duties to the state.'

77. L.Volk, *Reichskonkordat*, 13.

78. Note by Secretary of State Becker. Text: R.Morsey, *Vorgeschichte des Reichskonkordats*, 262-6.

79. Letter of the Prussian Kultusminister of 6 January 1922, in L.Volk, *Reichskonkordat*, 18f.

80. Pacelli to Bertram, 9 January 1922, ibid., 19.

81. Letter of Bertram of 5 January 1922 and Schulte of 9 January 1922, ibid., 19f.

82. Text of the so-called Delbrück outline I in A.Kupper, *Staatliche Akten*, 458-64. Delbrück's list, ibid., 458f. n.1. On 22 June 1922 Ritter reported to Munich that the outline gave the church 'virtually all' that it wanted, G.Franz-Willing, *Bayerische Vatikangesandtschaft*, 191.

83. Delbrück's notes are in A.Kupper, *Staatliche Akten*, 458.

84. L.Volk, *Reichskonkordat*, 22f. As things are it is not completely comprehensible that Volk, who otherwise made such balanced judgments in this connection, speaks of a 'simplification of the situation' and of 'a criticism excessive in extent and sharpness' from Bergen and accuses the ambassador of 'being off the point, one-sided and prejudiced'. For according to Delbrück's notes this visit to Rome was specifically to overcome the resistance of Prussia by a 'theoretical agreement with the Curia'. And so as the Nuncio had dealt with Prussia, it was natural to suspect collusion with the Reich.

85. L.Volk, *Reichskonkordat*, 24.

86. Against Volk, ibid., 30f.

87. Report by Ritter, 8 September 1922, in G.Franz-Willling, *Bayerische Vatikangesandtschaft*, 192.

88. Report by Ritter, 9 January 1925, ibid., 202.

89. E.Deuerlein, *Reichskonkordat*, 50f.

90. Report by Ritter, 16 January 1925, in G.Franz-Willing, *Bayerische Vatikangesandtschaft*, 203.

91. Text of the Bavarian concordat of 29 March 1924 with skeleton law and declaration by the government in W.Weber, *Die deutschen Konkordate und Kirchenverträge der Gegenwart*, Göttingen 1962, 38-66.

92. G.Franz-Willing, *Bayerische Vatikangesandtschaft*, 207.

93. Text of the outline dated 24 November 1924 in A.Kupper, *Staatliche Akten*, 473-8.

94. D.Golombek, *Preussenkonkordat*, 48.

95. For the Prussian fears cf. ibid., 51 n.8.

96. Ibid., 49-56.

97. Ibid., 92.

98. O.Braun, *Von Weimar zu Hitler*, Hamburg [3]1949, 278.

99. Text of the Prussian concordat of 14 June 1929 with government justification in W.Weber, *Die deutschen Konkordate*, 86-8.

100. So also D.Golombek, *Preussenkonkordat*, 113ff.

101. Note from Pacelli, 5 August 1929. Braun's answer 6 August 1929. Text in W.Weber, *Die deutsche Konkordate*, 86-8.

102. Text: E.R.and W.Huber, *Staat und Kirche* I, 246-57, 268-79.

103. E.Föhr, *Geschichte des badischen Konkordats*, Freiburg 1958, 14; A.Hollerbach, 'Streiflichter zur Entstehungsgeschichte der Badischen Staatskirchenverträge von 1932', in *Zeitschrift der Savigny-Stiftung für Rechtsgeschichte* 92, Kanonistische Abteilung 61, 1975, 342ff.

104. Föhr, *Geschichte des badischen Konkordats*, 14f.

105. E.Deuerlein, *Reichskonkordat*, 85.

106. Farewell speech and a farewell article from *Germania* of 18 December 1929 in L.Kaas, *Pacelli*, 187ff., 191ff.

107. U.Stutz, *Konkordat und Codex*, Sitzungsberichte der preussischen Akademie der Wissenschaften, Philosophisch-Historische Klasse XXXII, 1930, 694, 707.

5. The Völkisch Movement, Hitler, and the Beginnings of the NSDAP (1919-1923)

1. Cf. e.g. *Brockhaus Enzyklopädie* 19, Wiesbaden 1974, 690, in which the term völkisch has only seven lines.

2. C.C.Bry, *Verkappte Religionen*, Gotha and Stuttgart 1924, 15. This work, which

unfortunately has remained virtually unknown, is one of the wisest analyses of the growth of ideologies in the 1920s, in essay form. Bry's critique of antisemitism is particularly good.

3. A.Mohler, *Die konservative Revolution in Deutschland 1918-1932. Ein Handbuch*, Darmstadt ²1972, is an indispensable basis for any future account. It contains all the important names of the völkisch movement, with biographies and bibliographies. For the lack of an overall account see ibid., 213. E.Nolte, *Der Faschismus in seiner Epoche*, Munich 1963, 345-55, gives a short survey of its origins in the nineteenth century. The best current account of the connections is in E.Goldhagen, 'Weltanschauung und Endlösung. Zum Antisemitismus der nationalsozialistischen Führungsschicht', *Vierteljahrshefte für Zeitgeschichte* 24, 1976, 379-405.

4. Cf. M.Broszat, 'Die völkische Ideologie und der Nationalsozialismus', *Deutsche Rundschau* 84, 1958, 65.

5. Ibid., 79f. For Gerstenhauer cf. also A.Mohler, *Konservative Revolution*, 344f.

6. Cf. G.Altner, *Weltanschauliche Hintergründe der Rassenlehre des Dritten Reiches*, Theologische Studien 92, Zurich 1968; G.Zmarzlik, 'Der Sozialdarwinismus in Deutschland als geschichtliches Problem' (1962), in id., *Wieviel Zukunft hat unsere Vergangenheit?*, Munich 1970, 65-85.

7. E.Reichmann, *Flucht in den Hass. Die Ursachen der deutschen Judenkatastrophe*, Frankfurt nd [1956], 205-11. gives an impressive account of the total destruction.

8. P.W.Massing, *Vorgeschichte des politischen Antisemitismus*, Frankfurt 1959, 222f. Similarly H.G.Zmarzlik, 'Der Antisemitismus im Kaiserreich von 1871' (1962), in id., *Wieviel Zukunft hat unser Vergangenheit?*, 32-50, esp. 41. A recent work which is in basic agreement despite its socio-historical assessment of the Jewish question is R.Rürup, *Emanzipation und Antisemitismus*, Göttingen 1975, 109: 'The antisemitic groups became sect-like structures.' For the significance of the World War for the development of völkisch antisemitism cf. U.Lohalm, *Völkischer Radikalismus. Die Geschichte des Deutschvölkischen Schutz- und Trutz-Bundes 1919-1923*, Hamburg 1970, 46ff. and 71-6. Similarly A.Kruck, *Geschichte des Alldeutschen Verbandes*, Wiesbaden 1954, 130ff.

9. *Eine Zusammenstellung des wichtigsten Materials zur Verurteilung des jüdischen Volkes*, Hamburg ²⁸1919. T.Fritsch, born in 1852, was by profession a mill engineer and had already for decades been an unshakable völkisch-antisemitic propagandist. For Fritsch and the Reichshammerbund cf. U.Lohalm, *Völkischer Radikalismus*, 58-66, and A.Mohler, *Konservative Revolution*, 356.

10. Dinter, who will be mentioned quite often in due course, was originally a natural scientist. His novel was the völkisch best seller. A first edition appeared from Verlag Matthis and Thost, Leipzig and Hartenstein im Saareland 1918; the sixteenth edition (bringing the total circulation to 200,000) appeared from the same firm in 1921. In 1921 there followed 'The Sin against the Spirit' and in 1922 'The Sin against Love', again with large editions (cf. U.Lohalm, *Völkische Radikalismus*, 126: A.Mohler, *Konservative Revolution*, 378f.). 'The sin against blood and race' appears as a formula in Hitler's *Mein Kampf*, 226. This trilogy, with the overall title 'The Sins of the Time', was prefaced by John 13.17, 'You know these things, blessed are you if you do them', as a motto. Dinter's books were among the most objectionable to appear on this theme. See 94ff. below.

11. Dietrich Eckart, born 1868, a Munich journalist and playwright, was Hitler's most important spiritual mentor. For Eckart and his role cf. G.Franz-Willing, *Die Hitlerbewegung, 1. Der Ursprung 1919-1922*, Hamburg 1962, 127; Ernst Nolte, *Der Faschismus in seiner Epoche*, 398, 401-9; and above all M.Plewnia, *Auf dem Weg zu Hitler. Der völkische Publizist Dietrich Eckart*, Bremen 1970.

12. T.Fritsch, *Handbuch zur Judenfrage*, 641; similarly, ibid., 16.

13. *Die Sünde wider das Blut*, ⁶1919,243, 245.

14. *Auf gut Deutsch. Wochenschrift für Ordnung und Recht*, ed. Dietrich Eckart, ²1920, Vol.30/34, 350, quoted from M.Plewnia, 47.

15. Cf. the summary of Eckart's thought in M.Plewnia, 56f.

16. Ibid., 55f.

17. The main source for this conspiracy theory was the so-called 'Protocol of the Wise Men of Zion', an antisemitic forgery from the late nineteenth century. Cf. the edition by U.Fleischhauer – dedicated to Theodor Fritsch and Dietrich Eckart - *Die echte Protokolle des Richteramtes V in Bern*, Erfurt 1935. For the conspiracy theory cf. also E.Goldhagen, *Weltanschauung*, 381ff.

18. Fritsch, *Handbuch*, 547. Fritsch here takes up the so-called Lehnin Prophecy, a forgery from the eighteenth century. Cf. *RGG*³, 4, 266f.

19. For Judah's way to world rule cf. M.Plewnia, 48f.; Fritsch, *Handbuch*, 497ff., 516, 544ff. etc.; Dinter, *Die Sünde wider das Blut*, 295ff., etc.

20. *Auf gut Deutsch*, 1, 1919, 44/45, 521. Quoted from M.Plewnia, *Auf dem Weg zu Hitler*, 86.

21. Ibid., 88.

22. A.Dinter, *Die Sünde wider das Blut*, 297.

23. T.Fritsch, *Handbuch zur Judenfrage*, 641.

24. Ibid., 29. Similarly, 646.

25. *Die Sünde wider die Liebe*, 1922, 79. Dinter doubtless comes closest to the later National Socialist legislation. His five demands ran: 1. Abolition of equal rights for the Jewish religion. 2. 'No Jew may be a teacher, official and jduge in Germany.' 3. 'German blood must be protected against Jewish shaming and bastardizing. Marriages between Germans and Jews are to be forbidden by law.' 4. No Jew may inherit land in Germany. 5. Jewish immigration is forbidden, ibid., 81-4. Eckart, too, is against a solution of the Jewish question 'with the sword'. Cf. M.Plewnia, 56.

26. Dietrich Eckart, *Auf gut Deutsch*, 19/20, 1919, 297; M.Plewnia, 53.

27. It is also possible to explain this situation as an 'expression of a failure of theorizing in a bourgeois society in a state of crisis', R.Rürup, *Emanzipation und Antisemitismus*, 91.

28. From the unpublished notes of Class quoted in A.Kruck, *Geschichte des Alldeutschen Verbandes*, 135. For Class cf. also U.Lohalm, *Völkischer Radikalismus*, 32-40.

29. E.Ludendorff, *Vom Feldherrn zum Weltrevolutionär und Wegbereiter Deutscher Volksschöpfung. Meine Lebenserinnerungen 1919-1925*, Ludendorff-Verlag, Munich 1940, 12f. Cf. also W.Brecker, *Die Tragik Ludendorffs*, Stollhamm, Oldenburg 1953, 567f.

30. *Mein Kampf*, 187.

31. Cf. the flysheet of the Deutschvölkischer Bund reprinted in W.Jochmann, *National-sozialismus und Revolution. Ursprung und Geschichte der NSDAP in Hamburg*, Frankfurt 1922, 5-9.

32. For the problem of the relationship between ideology and reality which is touched on here see K.Scholder, 'Ideologie und Politik', in *Aus Politik und Zeitgeschichte*, supplement to the weekly *Das Parlament*, 1962, 377-82.

33. R.H.Phelps, 'Before Hitler Came: Thule Society and Germanen Order', in *The Journal of Modern History* 53, 1963, 249.

34. U.Lohalm, *Völkischer Radikalismus*, 38.

35. A.Kruck, *Geschichte des Alldeutschen Verbandes*, 131; U.Lohalm, *Völkischer Radikalismus*, 53f.

36. The Bamberg declaration is reprinted in W.Jochmann, *Nationalsozialismus und Revolution*, 10-24. Cf. esp. 17,21.

37. All the figures come from U.Lohalm, *Völkischer Radikalismus*, 88-90.

38. Ibid., 90f.
39. These are the so-called 'Jewish memorandum' of 16 September 1919 (first published in E.Deuerlein, 'Hitlers Eintritt in die Politik und die Reichswehr', in *Vierteljahrshefte für Zeitgeschichte* 7, 1959, 203-5; now also in W.Maser, *Hitlers Briefe und Notizen. Sein Weltbild in handschriftliche Dokumenten*, Düsseldorf and Vienna 1973, 223-6), and the speech of 13 August, the first speech of which we have the complete wording (reprinted in R.H.Phelps, 'Hitlers grundlegende Rede über den Antisemitismus', *Vierteljahrshefte für Zeitgeschichte* 16, 1968, 390-420); also the collected reports of the Reichswehr and police from the years 1919 and 1920. (The Reichswehr reports are in Deuerlein, 'Hitlers Eintritt in die Politik', 177-227; the police reports are in R.H.Phelps, 'Hitler als Parteiredner im Jahre 1920', *Vierteljahrshefte für Zeitgeschichte* 11, 1963, 274-330.
40. Joachim C.Fest in particular has convincingly brought out the special link between Richard Wagner and Hitler in his Hitler biography: *Hitler. Eine Biographie*, Frankfurt, Berlin and Vienna ²1973, 522ff., etc.
41. Thus e.g. W.Daim, *Der Mann, der Hitler die Ideen gab*, Munich 1958, in his otherwise interesting and important work has surely overestimated the influence of the völkisch sectarian Lanz v.Liebenfels on Hitler. Phelps aptly remarks: 'In most cases it is, rather, parallels which prove to be the sure sources for Hitler's arguments', *Vierteljahrshefte für Zeitgeschichte* 16, 1968, 396.
42. E.Deuerlein, *Hitlers Eintritt in die Politik*, 203-5 (see n.39 above).
43. R.H.Phelps, 'Hitlers "grundlegende" Rede' (n.39), 406.
44. Ibid., 415.
45. Ibid., 417.
46. Final sentence of Hitler's political testament of 29 April 1945, W.Maser, *Hitlers Briefe und Notizen*, 375.
47. This is the final conclusion of H.J.Gordon Jr, *Hitlerputsch 1923. Machtkampf in Bayern 1923-1924*, Frankfurt 1971, 522f.
48. E.Jäckel, *Hitlers Weltanschauung. Entwurf einer Herrschaft*, Tübingen 1969, 141.
49. Ibid., 157 and passim.
50. 'Über das Verhältnis des deutschen Staates zu Theologie, Kirche und Religion. Ein Versuch Nicht-Theologen zu orientieren', in *Deutsche Schriften*, Göttingen ⁵1920, 67. For the whole question see also K.Scholder, 'Paulus und die Aufklärung', in G.C.Berkouwer and H.A.Oberman, *De dertiende apostel en het elfde gebod. Paulus in de loop der eeuwen*, Kampen 1971, 124-34; and now above all F.Regner, *Paulus und Jesus im 19. Jahrhundert. Beiträge zur Geschichte des Themas Paulus und Jesus in der neutestamentlichen Theologie von der Aufklärung bis zur Religionsgeschichtlichen Schule*, Protestant Faculty dissertation, Tübingen 1975, esp. 154-84.
51. P.de Lagarde, *Deutsche Schriften*, 62.
52. H.G.Reimarus, *Apologie oder Schutzschrift für die vernünftigen Verehrer Gottes*, ed. G.Alexander, no place or date (Insel Verlag 1972), 332.
53. *Die Grundzüge des gegenwärtigen Zeitalters*, Sämtliche Werke, ed. J.H.Fichte, Vol.VII, Leipzig nd., 190.
54. F.Regner, *Paulus und Jesus*, 163.
55. Cf. H.W.Schütte, *Lagarde und Fichte. Die verborgenen spekulativen Voraussetzungen des Christentumsverständnisses Paul de Lagarde*, Gütersloh 1965.
56. P.de Lagarde, 73. For the understanding of Lagarde as a forerunner of the völkisch movement cf. e.g. F.Krog, *Lagarde und der deutsche Staat*, Munich 1930, especially on Lagarde's antisemitism, 78-90.
57. Quoted from the third edition, Berlin 1906, 189.
58. Ibid., 296.
59. W.Daim, 55 (n.41). Daim describes Lanz's religion in analogy with trashy novels

as 'trashy religion', ibid., 239. For Lanz cf. the extensive bibliography in A.Mohler, *Konservative Revolution*, 350-4.

60. T.Fritsch, *Der falsche Gott. Beweismaterial gegen Jahwe*, Leipzig ⁴1916, 227f.

61. *Grundlagen des neunzehnten Jahrhunderts*, first edition 1899, tenth edition (popular ed.) Munich 1912. All editions have the page numbers of the first edition. The remarks on Jesus' racial affinity are on 210-20. Chamberlain, however, limits himself to the negative judgment 'that Christ was not a Jew' (219). He leaves open what race Christ belonged to.

62. Fritsch, *Der falsche Gott*, 228-31. An extensive account of the renewal of Christianity as Fritsch imagined it appeared from Hammer Verlag (T.Fritsch), Leipzig, under the title: *Vom neuen Glauben. Bekenntnis der Deutschen Erneuerungs-Gemeinde* (nd).

63. Quoted from M.Plewnia, *Auf dem Weg zu Hitler*, 45.

64. Ibid., 46, 53, etc.

65. *Die Sünde wider die Liebe*, 1922, Epilogue, 328.

66. Ibid., 330 (emphasis in the original).

67. A.Steiger, *Der neudeutsche Heide im Kampf gegen Christen und Juden*. Verlag der Germania, Berlin 1924, gives an account of these groups and their aims. For the Alliance for a German Church see below, 117.

68. G.Franz-Willing, *Die Hitlerbewegung*, 62-75, and W.Maser, *Die Frühgeschichte der NSDAP. Hitlers Weg bis 1924*, Frankfurt and Bonn 1965, 141ff.

69. *Mein Kampf*, 331-6.

70. Ibid., 336f.

71. G.Franz-Willing, *Die Hitlerbewegung*, 71f.

72. R.H.Phelps, 'Hitler als Parteiredner' (n.39), 292, 294.

73. W.Maser, *Frühgeschichte*, 211.

74. G.Franz-Willing, *Die Hitlerbewegung*, 78f.; W.Maser, *Frühgeschichte*, 206f.

75. A.Rosenberg, *Das Parteiprogramm. Wesen, Grundsätze und Ziele der NSDAP*, Munich (1922) ²⁷1943, 15ff., 57f. The formula 'public advantage comes before individual advantage' goes back to the programme of the 'German Socialist party' as presented in an appeal of the 'Germanen order' in the winter of 1918/1919. Cf., R.von Sebottendorff, *Bevor Hitler kam*, Munich 1933, 175.

76. A.Rosenberg, *Das Parteiprogramm*, 14.

77. Ibid., 58.

78. W.Maser, *Hitlers Briefe und Notizen*, 292-7 (facsimile and transcription). Maser dates the sketch 'shortly after the "opinion" on the Jews', ibid., 386 n.146. Moreover this is not a matter, as Maser assumes, of the outline for a 'Monumental History of Mankind'. Rather, this key word clearly belongs with the term 'Bible'. The whole thing is in fact the systematic outline of a völkisch world-view.

79. T.Fritsch, *Handbuch zur Judenfrage*, 333f.

80. R.von Sebottendorff, *Bevor Hitler kam*, 44f.

81. *Mein Kampf*, 372.

82. *Rede des Pg.Adolf Hitler in der Versammlung vom 12.April 1922 im Bürgerbräukeller in Munich*, offprint from no.32, 1922 of the *Völkischer Beobachter*, BA Koblenz NZ 26/59 (emphasis in the original). Also in E.Klöss, *Reden des Führers*, Munich 1967, 42f.

83. Niederschrift über ein Führer-Gespräch, Führerhauptquartier, 30 November 1944, BA Koblenz NS 6/133.

84. *Mein Kampf*, 60. Emphasis in the original.

6. Hitler's Basic Decision on Church Policy (1924-1928)

1. E.Jäckel, *Hitlers Weltanschauung*, 42f.

2. *Mein Kampf*, 263f.

3. Ibid., 326f.

4. Ibid., 329.

5. U.Lohalm, *Völkischer Radikalismus*, 255-72.

6. Cf. the embarrassed account in Sebottendorff, *Bevor Hitler kam*, 167. On this R.H.Phelps, 'Before Hitler came', 259.

7. *Mein Kampf*, 327-30. Cf. also the comment on 'völkisch splintering', ibid., 467.

8. Ibid., 107.

9. Ibid., 313f. That Hitler rightly estimated the different starting points of Catholicism and Protestantism over this question is clear from his comments on the possibilities and limitations of collaboration with Protestantism, ibid., 101ff.

10. Ibid., 513.

11. Ibid., 346. The parallels with Marxist theory are not fortuitous. Hitler himself drew them, 347f.

12. Ibid., 329.

13. W.Nolte, 'Eine frühe Quelle zu Hitlers Antisemitismus', *Historische Zeitschrift* 192, 1961, 584-606. The quotation is from 606. See, similarly, id., *Der Faschismus in seiner Epoche*, 404.

14. Saul Esh, 'Eine neue literarische Quelle Hitlers', *Geschichte in Wissenschaft und Untrerricht* 15, 1963, 487-93, and above all M.Plewnia, *Auf dem Weg zu Hitler*, 94-112.

15. D.Eckart, *Der Bolschewismus von Moses bis Lenin*, 50.

16. *Das Geistchristentum. Monatsschrift zur Vollendung der Reformation durch Wiederherstellung der reinen Heilandslehre*, ed. A.Dinter 1, 1928, 71-3. Moreover Dinter claims that Eckart had essentially copied the example from him.

17. D.Eckart, *Der Bolschewismus von Moses bis Lenin*, 18.

18. Ibid., 29.

19. Ibid., 33; cf. also 35.

20. Ibid., 31.

21. Ibid., 36.

22. Ibid., 30, 32.

23. M.Plewnia, *Auf dem Weg zu Hitler*, 9. There is further evidence there of Hitler's close relationship to Eckart.

24. There are no fairly recent works on Ludendorff. The dissertation by G.Borst, *Die Ludendorff-Bewegung 1919-1961. Eine Analyse monologer Kommunikationsformen in der sozialen Zeitkommunikation*, Munich 1969, is important only as a collection of material. For Ludendorff's significance alongside Hitler cf. the quotations in ibid., 113-23. There is a comprehensive bibliography on the Ludendorff movement in A.Mohler, *Konservative Revolution*, 388-96.

25. W.Breucker, *Die Tragik Ludendorffs*, 97.

26. Thus W.Breucker, ibid., 108. A different view is taken by H.Buchheim, 'Die organisatorische Entwicklung der Ludendorff-Bewegung und ihr Verhältnis zum Nationalsozialismus', in *Gutachten des Instituts für Zeitgeschichte (1)*, Munich 1958, 363, where Hitler's acquaintance with M.von Kemnitz is dated to the year 1922.

27. The speech appears in E. Ludendorff, *Vom Feldherrn zum Weltrevolutionär*, 269-314. For Ultramontanism cf. above all 270-87.

28. F.von Lama, *Papst und Kuria*, 626f.

29. W.Breucker, *Die Tragik Ludendorffs*, 107.

30. F. von Lama, *Papst und Kurie*, 624-9.

31. E.Ludendorff, *Vom Feldherrn zum Weltrevolutionär*, 350f.

32. Ibid., 352.

33. Ibid., 376.

34. Alan Bullock, *Hitler. A Study in Tyranny*, Harmondsworth 1969, 123-6; also J.C.Fest, *Hitler*, 316.

35. Quoted from the documentation 'Aus dem Kampf der Bewegung', in *Nationalsozialistische Monatshefte* 9, 1938, 647-9. Cf. also the ban on religious disputes in the 'Basic Guidelines for the Refounding of the NSDAP' in the same number of the *Völkische Beobachter*, in A.Tyrell, *Führer befiehl... Selbstzeugnisse aus der 'Kampfzeit' der NSDAP*, Düsseldorf 1969, 107.

36. Ludendorff stood on 20 March 1925 as a candidate for the NSDAP and got only 1.6% of the votes, H.Buchheim, *Ludendorff-Bewegung*, 366.

37. Of the numerous contemporary accounts of this development I would mention K.Witte, 'Der Tannenbergbund', in W.Künneth and H.Schreine, *Die Nation vor Gott*, Berlin ²1934, 416-63.

38. A.Tyrell, *Führer befiehl*, 165f.

39. H.Buchheim, *Ludendorff-Bewegung*, 359-60.

40. Quoted from E.Kloss (ed.), *Reden des Führers. Politik und Propaganda Adolf Hitlers 1922-1945*, Munich 1967, 26.

41. There is a 'biographical description' by one of his followers in *Das Geistchristentum* 1, 1928, 238-42.

42. For the Grossdeutsche Volksgemeinschaft cf. A.Tyrell, *Führer befiehl*, 81-3.

43. Thus in Dinter's communication of 20 January 1925 to Esser and Streicher, DC Berlin, OPG-Akte Dinter.

44. Report in the *Völkischer Beobachter*, 26 May 1926. Quoted from Tyrell, *Führer befiehl*, 134. Cf. also ibid., 180; report of the Reichsparteitag 1927.

45. The letter is reprinted in *Das Geisteschristentum* 1, 1928, 353-6.

46. Cf. A.Dinter, *197 Thesen zur Vollendung der Reformation. Die Wiederherstellung des reinen Heilandslehre*, Leipzig 1928.

47. A.Dinter, 'Politik, Religion und Rasse', in *Das Geisteschristentum* 1, 1929, 4.

48. Ibid., 9.

49. Letter of 28 June 1928, DC Berlin, OPG Akte-Dinter.

50. Original with signatures of the Reichsleitung, BA Koblenz, Sammlung Schumacher, 260 (reproduced in R.Kühnl, *Die nationalsozialistischen Linke 1925-1930*, Meisenheim 1966, 340f.).

51. According to the OPG-Akte quoted in A.Tyrell, *Führer befiehl*, 202, Sauckel was organization leader from 1 February 1927, ibid. 164.

52. Ibid., 202f. The account of events in P.Hittenberger, *Die Gauleiter, Studien zum Wandel des Machtgefüges in der NSDAP*, Stuttgart 1969, 44-6, sees things above all in terms of the history of the organization and therefore does not focus on the decisive themes and their significance.

53. *Das Geistchristentum* 1, 1928, 11-35: constitution and assembly.

54. The letter has evidently been lost. However, it is in the catalogue of OPG-Akte Dr Dinter under no.21. The catalogue has 145 numbers, beginning with 8 December 1927 and ending with 27 November 1937. It was evidently finished in July 1939 and shows that in 1927/28 almost all the prominent people in the Party were concerned with the Dinter case.

55. A.Tyrell, *Führer befiehl*, 196f.

56. Ibid., 197.

57. Ibid., 203.

58. *Das Geistchristentum* 1, 1928, 357.

59. Letter of 12 June 1928, DC Berlin, OPG-Akte Dinter, copy without heading or signature. The sender is given in the catalogue.

60. DC Berlin, OPG Akte-Dinter.

61. See n.58.
62. *Das Geistchristentum* 1, 1928, 354, 356. Abbreviated quotation in A.Tyrell, *Führer befiehl*, 203.
63. A.Tyrell, *Führer befiehl*, 208ff. Cf. also 206f. The wording of the order is in *Das Geistchristentum* 1, 1928, 283f.
64. *Das Geistchristentum* 1, 1928, 274.
65. Strasser's letter is in A.Tyrell, *Führer befiehl*, 210f.; the statement is in DC Berlin, OPG-Akte Dinter, and in *Das Geistchristentum* 1, 1928. 377f.
66. The catalogue (n.54 above) indicates at least eighteen returns including the names of Kube, Goebbels, Buttmann, Kerll and Göring.
67. The text of the order for expulsion is in *Das Geistchristentum* 1, 1928, 379f. A discussion between Hitler and Dinter which surprisingly took place in Coburg after the expulsion on 30 October 1928 got nowhere. Cf.ibid., 386, and for the content of the conversation, ibid. 2, 1929, 183, 275.
68. DC Berlin OPG-Akte Dinter. Personnel card from the Reichsleitung to the official Party scrutinizing committee for the protection of National Socialist writing, 27 July 1937. Dinter died in Offenburg, Baden on 21 May 1948 (A.Mohler, *Konservative Revolution*, 378).
69. *Das Geistchristentum* 2, 1929, 414. This charge is regularly repeated in seven further issues.
70. According to the word-for-word record by a supporter, BA Koblenz, NS 26/55, 17f.

7. The Origin of Political Theology and the Jewish Question in German Protestantism (1917-1930)

1. See above, 37f.
2. For this prehistory cf. K.Scholder, *Neuere deutsche Geschichte*, 525-30, and above all W.Tilgner, *Volksnomostheologie und Schöpfungsglaube. Ein Beitrag zur Geschichte des Kirchenkampfes*, Göttingen 1966, esp. 36-87.
3. Works which are important for the political theology of figures mentioned are detailed in A.Mohler, *Die konservative Revolution*, 424-7. For Stapel see ibid., 410f.
4. In P.Althaus, *Die deutsche Stunde der Kirche*, Göttingen (1933), ²1934, 56.
5. Ibid., 55, 57.
6. Ibid., 58, 60.
7. P.Althaus, *Das Erlebnis der Kirche*, Leipzig (1919) ²1924, 7.
8. Ibid., 14.
9. Ibid., 21.
10. Quotations are taken from the third edition of 1925. Cf. also the analysis of this work in G.Schneider-Flume, *Die politische Theologie Emanuel Hirschs 1918-1933*, Europäische Hochschulschriften, Reihe XIII.5, Berne and Frankfurt 1971.
11. Cf. above, 6f., 77ff.
12. E.Hirsch, *Deutschlands Schicksal*, 143.
13. Ibid.
14. Ibid., 152.
15. Ibid., 153.
16. E.Hirsch to E.Geismar, 31 December 1922, Geismar archive, Copenhagen. I am grateful to J.H.Schørring for this information.
17. P.Althaus, *Die deutsche Stunde der Kirche*, 26f.
18. K.Sontheimer, *Antidemokratisches Denken in der Weimarer Republik*, Munich 1962, 308.
19. Ibid. 34f. and n.6; 310ff.

20. H.Kessler, *Wilhelm Stapel als politischer Publizist. Ein Beitrag zur Geschichte des konservativen Nationalismus zwischen den beiden Weltkriegen*, Nuremberg 1967,23f.

21. W.Stapel, 'Volk und Volkstum', in *Die neue Front*, ed. Moeller van den Bruck, H. von Gleichen and M.H.Boehm, Berlin 1922, 81f.

22. Ibid., 89.

23. H.Keller, *W.Stapel*, 51-3.

24. Ibid., 81f.

25. Ibid., 92.

26. Ibid.,101f.

27. *Deutschlands Schicksal*, 159.

28. K.Holl, 'Was verstand Luther unter Religion?' (speech given at the Reformation Celebrations of the University of Berlin on 31 October 1917), in *Gesammelte Aufsätze zur Kirchengeschichte* I, *Luther*, Tübingen [7]1948, 35. One of the best contributions on the problem is E.Wolf's article 'Vom Problem des Gewissens in reformatorischer Sicht' (1942), in id., *Peregrinatio. Studien zur reformatorischen Theologie und zum Kirchenproblem*, Munich [2]1962, 81-112.

29. E.Hirsch, *Deutschlands Schicksal*, 157.

30. Ibid., 161f.

31. Ibid., 165.

32. K.W.Dahm, *Pfarrer und Politik*, 185.

33. See below, 111f.

34. 'The Hitler trial has stirred people up a great deal', wrote W.Stählin in the April issue of the magazine *Christentum und Wirklichkeit*. The article is one of the earliest remarks about Hitler in a church context, *Christentum und Wirklichkeit* 2, 1924, 88f.

35. *Kirchliches Jahrbuch* 1925, 373-6. For the Evangelischer Bund see also 6, 140, 230f.

36. *Reden und Vorträge, gehalten bei der 28.Generalversammlung des Evangelischen Bundes in München*, Verlag des Evangelischen Bundes, Berlin 1924. The lecture which is discussed in the next paragraphs is not contained in it.

37. Hoefler, born in 1878 the son of a teacher, was a chaplain to the Fifth Bavarian Reserve Division in the War and after 1920 a teacher at the Girls' Gymnasium in Nuremberg, LKA Nürnberg, Personalakte Hoefler.

38. Verlag der Buchhandlung des Vereins fur Innere Mission, Nuremberg nd [1924], 5, LKA Nürnberg.

39. Ibid., 9.

40. *Mein Kampf*, 326f., 329 and above, 108.

41. *Kirchliches Jahrbuch* 1925, 375.

42. No. 244 of 4 September 1924. See also F. von Lama, *Papst und Kirche*, 628f.

43. *Vorstandsblatt des Evangelischen Bundes*, published by the Praesidium (printed as a confidential manuscript for the leaders of the associations), No.4, October 1924, 22f.

44. E.Moering, 'Selbstbesinnung des Protestantismus', *Vossische Zeitung*, 2 December 1931. Fahrenhorst's answer with a commentary in the (Catholic) *Märkische Volkszeitung*, 6 February 1932.

45. Cf. W.Stählin, *Via Vitae. Lebenserinnerungen*, Kassel 1968, here esp. 176-91.

46. Buchverlag des Bundes Deutscher Jugendvereine, Sollstedt nd [1924].

47. Ibid., 29.

48. Ibid., 22.

49. Ibid., 34.

50. Ibid., 47.

51. Ibid., 55.

52. Cf. his article 'Der Hitler-Prozess', in *Christentum und Wirklichkeit* 2, 1924, 88f.

53. *Kirchliches Jahrbuch* 1925, 557.

54. *Kirchliches Jahrbuch* 1926, 588. Cf. also J.Rathge, *Die Welt des freien Protestantismus*, 351.

55. K.Themel, 'Der religiöse Gehalt der völkischen Bewegung und ihre Stellung zur Kirche', Lecture given on Reformation Day 1925 at the Church Week of Free Protestantism in Hamburg, *Protestantische Studien* 3, Berlin 1926, 80. On pp.6f. there is a bibliography which shows how modest was the interest of the church in this question at the time.

56. Letter of 19 September 1927. Althaus archive, Barth fascicle.

57. See above, 100ff.

58. *Verhandlungen des zweiten Deutschen Evangelischen Kirchentages 1927, Königsberg 17-21 June 1927*, Berlin-Steglitz nd [1928], 205. The lecture is also reprinted in P.Althaus, *Evangelium und Leben, Gesammelte Vorträge*, Gütersloh 1927, 113-43.

59. Verhandlungen des zweiten Deutschen Evangelischen Kirchentages 1927, 208.

60. Ibid., 207ff., 213ff.

61. Ibid., 209.

62. Ibid., 215.

63. Ibid.

64. Ibid., 224.

65. Ibid., 216.

66. Ibid., 216, 220.

67. Text, ibid., 338-40.

68. Protocol and statement in AEKD Berlin A2/489.

69. For Pechmann's attitude see above 19 and below 266f.

70. *Deutsches Pfarrerblatt* no.29 of 22 July 1930. Quoted from I.Arndt, *Die Judenfrage im Licht der evangelischen Sonntagsblätter von 1918 bis 1933*, Tübingen philosophical dissertation 1960 (ms), 62-66.

71. *Kreuz und Hakenkreuz*, Leopold Klotz Verlag, Gotha 1926, 19-20.

72. Ibid., 20.

73. Ibid., 31-6.

74. Ibid., 31, 36.

75. *Evangelische Kirche und Judentum*, no place or date [privately published Stuttgart 1928], reprinted in R.R.Geis and H.J.Kraus (eds.), *Versuche des Verstehens. Dokumente jüdisch-christliche Begegnung aus den Jahren 1918-1933*, Munich 1966, 256-302. Cf. also E.Lamparter, *Das Judentum in seiner kultur- und religionsgeschihtlicher Erscheinung*, Leopold Klotz Verlag, Gotha 1928.

76. E.Lamparter, *Evangelische Kirche und Judentum*, 55f.

77. Cf. on this P.E.Lapide, *The Last Three Popes and the Jews*, London 1967, 86-116.

78. E.Lamparter, *Evangelische Kirche und Judentum*, 60.

79. Ibid., 1.

80. There is a biography of the 'German Church' and its most important representatives (Andersen, Niedlich, E. and P.von Wolzogen, etc.) in A.Mohler, *Konservative Revolution*, 222-4, 371-5.

81. For Andersen cf. H.Buchheim, *Glaubenskrise im Dritten Reich*, Stuttgart 1953, 45f.

82. *Eine Laientheologie auf geschichtlicher Grundlage*, Schleswig 1907. For what follows cf. C. Nicolaisen, *Die Auseinandersetzung um das Alte Testament im Kirchenkampf 1933-1945*, Protestant theological faculty dissertation, Hamburg 1967, 92f.

83. The whole episode is covered in *Kirchliches Gesetz- und Verordnungsblatt für den Amtsbezirk des Königlichen evangelisch-lutherischen Konsistoriums in Kiel*, no.13 of 8 August 1913, 127-34.

84. *Deutschchristentum auf rein-evangelischer Grundlage*, Leipzig 1917. The individual

series of theses are each marked with the name of the author; there is a bibliography of the four authors at the end of the work.

85. From H.Buchheim, *Glaubenskrise im Dritten Reich*, 46.

86. K.Hutten, *Christus oder Deutschglaube?*, Stuttgart 1935, 11. There is also a detailed account of German Church teaching in G.Gloege, 'Die Deutschkirche', in W.Künneth and H.Schreiner, *Die Nation vor Gott*, Berlin 1934, 393-415.

87. *Kirchliches Jahrbuch* 1924, 467.

88. *Niederschrift über die Sitzung des Deutschen Evangelischen Kirchenbundesrates, 8-9.6. 1931 in Eisenach*, Berlin 1931, 32, 42.

89. Ibid., 22ff.

90. K.Witte, 'Deutschtum und Christentum', in *Das religiöse Deutschland der Gegenwart*, 1, Berlin 1928, 133.

91. Ibid., 133f.

92. As emerges from a letter to Paul Althaus of 25 April 1932, Hirsch had voted for Hitler in the Reich Presidential elections in spring 1932 and, as he writes, 'also stated this publicly in the newspaper'. At the same time, however, his view of Hugenberg's anti-Brüning policy was: 'We who have remained with Hugenberg would have all run away from him without thinking and would today all be Nazis had he had another policy,' Althaus bequest, Hirsch fascicle.

93. H.Kesler, *Wilhelm Stapel*, 201f., 266ff. (Stapel's own account).

94. At a lecture to Erlangen students in July 1933 on 'Worthless Life in the Light of Christian Faith' he was given a sharp warning by the Bavarian Ministry of the Interior on 4 August 1933. Althaus bequest, Kirchenkampf fascicle.

8. The Struggle for the Church (1929-1931)

1. The whole episode – letter from the President of 14 February 1928 and replies from the Landeskirchen – is documented in AEKD Berlin, A2/493.

2. *Tagebuch eines Grossstadtpfarrers*, Berlin (Furche Verlag), [2]1929, [17]1931 (!), numerous translations. Quoted here from the eighth edition, nd [1930].

3. Ibid., 135; cf. also 111f., 125, etc.

4. Ibid., 138, 154 etc.

5. Ibid., 150.

6. Ibid., 147.

7. Cf. *Das Tagebuch im Spiegel der Presse. Pressestimmen zum 'Tagebuch eines Grossstadtpfarrers'*, gesammelt und herausgegeben vom Furche Verlag, Berlin 1930. Motions critical of the church were also passed at the 'Young Evangelicals Conference' in Marburg in 1929, *Kirchliches Jahrbuch* 1930, 442ff.

8. H.Ehrenberg (ed.), *Credo Ecclesiam, Festgabe W.Zoellner zum 70 Geburtstag*, Gütersloh 1930.

9. L.Thimme, *Im Kampf um die Kirche. Versuch einer Lösung der Spannungen zwischen Kirche, Theologie und Gemeinschaft*, Gotha 1930.

10. See 44f. above.

11. K.Barth and E.Thurneysen, *Briefwechsel* 2, 1921-1930, Zurich 1974, 293.

12. Ibid., 252, circular letter of 18 May 1924.

13. Ibid., 696, letter of 12 January 1930.

14. K.Barth, '*Quousque tandem...?*', in *Zwischen den Zeiten* 8, 1-6; reprinted in K.Kupisch, *Der Götze wackelt*, Berlin [2]1964, 27-32.

15. See above, 35f.

16. Kupisch, *Der Götze wackelt*, 30f.

17. Ibid., 31. Barth had already told Thurneysen in December 1928 that the work was 'a worthless book', *Briefwechsel Barth-Thurneysen*, 2, 639.

18. *Verhandlungen der 9. Generalsynode der Evangelischen Kirche der altpreussischen Union*, 1, Berlin 1930, 34f. Other speakers in the debate also evidently found Barth's criticism ludicrous, cf. 36, 48, etc.; there is another view in 58f.

19. K.Barth, *Die Christliche Dogmatik im Entwurf*, 1, *Die Lehre vom Worte Gottes*, Munich 1927, 25. Barth did not continue the *Christliche Dogmatik*, but began all over again in 1932 with I.1 of the *Church Dogmatics*.

20. K.Barth, *Christliche Dogmatik*, 66.

21. K.Barth, 'Die Not der evangelischen Kirche', *Zwischen den Zeiten* 9, 1931, 89-122. Also in K.Kupisch, *Der Götze wackelt*, 33-42.

22. K.Kupisch, *Der Götze wackelt*, 53-5.

23. Circular letter of 22 January 1931, Karl Barth Archive, Basle.

24. O. Dibelius, *Die Verantwortung der Kirche*, Berlin nd [1931], 33.

25. Postscript to 'Die Not der evangelischen Kirche', in K.Kupisch, *Der Götze wackelt*, 62. (emphasis in the original).

26. The German pastors' associations which had been founded in various Landeskirchen in the 1890s and soon were also combined in a Reich organization were the basic organizations of the German Protestant pastors. The *Deutsches Pfarrerblatt* was compulsory reading for all members of the pastorate; in 1929 it had the significant circulation of 18,500 copies and was regarded as the 'only organ which reaches the whole of the pastorate' (A.Hinderer, *Handbuch der Evangelischen Presse*, Leipzig 1929, 127). However, it seems to have been little read in southern Germany. Despite the wide circulation, library copies are quite rare.

27. *Deutsches Pfarrerblatt* 1930, 113, 180, 257, 278, 291, 323, 369ff., 407, 469, 771 etc. Cf. K.W.Dahm, *Pfarrer und Politik*, Cologne and Opladen 1965, 74f.

28. *Kirchliches Jahrbuch* 1930, IXf., 444ff.

29. M.Schian, *Ecclesiam habemus. Ein Beitrag zur Auseinandersetzung zwischen Karl Barth und Otto Dibelius*, Berlin 1931.

30. *Kirchliches Jahrbuch* 1930, 445f.

31. *Kirchliches Jahrbuch* 1931, 24ff.

32. *Church Dogmatics* I.1 (1932), ET Edinburgh 1936, IX.

9. Catholicism, Protestantism and National Socialism after the Elections of September 1930

1. For the Young referendum cf. H.Heiber, *Die Republik von Weimar*, Munich [5]1971, and G.Schulz, *Aufstieg des Nationalsozialismus, Krise und Revolution in Deutschland*, Frankfurt am Main, Berlin and Vienna 1975, 462-5.

2. Letter of 25 April 1932. Althaus bequest, Hirsch fascicle.

3. Cf. A.Milatz, *Wähler und Wahlen*, 124f.

4. For the political side of the formation of the formation of the Thuringian government cf. F.Dickmann, 'Die Reigierungsbildung in Thüringen als Modell der Machtergreifung. Ein Brief Hitlers aus dem Jahre 1930', in *Vierteljahrshefte für Zeitgeschichte* 14, 1966, 45-64. For Frick's religious policy see below, 189.

5. There are details of the results of the Landtag elections in A.Tyrell, *Führer befiehl*, 383f. For the whole question see G.Schulz, *Aufstieg des Nationalsozialismus*, 479-83.

6. There is a table of election results in G.Schulz, *Aufstieg des Nationalsozialismus*, 845f. For the conquest of the universities by the National Socialist students see the instructive study by A.Faust, *Der nationalsozialistische Studentenbund*, two vols, Düsseldorf 1973, esp. 1, 88-105; 2, 7-42.

7. A.Milatz, *Wähler und Wahlen*, 133.

8. For the development in the vote between 1924 and 1933 see table 8 in the study by A.Milatz, *Wähler und Wahlen*, 134.

9. H.Christ, *Der politische Protestantismus in der Weimarer Republik, Eine Studie über die politische Meinungsbildung durch die evangelische Kirchen im Spiegel der Literatur und der Presse*, Bonn philosophical dissertation 1967, investigates the vote (3-52) but merely explains Protestant voting in terms of 'anti-republicanism' (ibid., 51, 53, 170, etc.).

10. H.Mulert, 'Konfession und politische Parteistellung in Deutschland', in *Zeitschrift für Politik* 21, 1932, 339.

11. Details of the election results in A.Milatz, *Wähler und Wahlen*, 70ff.

12. H.Mulert, *Konfession und politische Parteistellung*, 338ff. J.Schauff, *Das Wahlverhalten der deutschen Katholiken im Kaiserreich und in der Weimarer Republik. Untersuchungen aus dem Jahre 1928*, ed. with an introduction by R.Morsey, Mainz 1975, 132, comes to the same result for the first years of the Republic: 'The Social Democrats had the largest share of the Protestant vote (in 1924) with 31.5%.'

13. A.Grabowsky, 'Nach den Wahlen. Betrachtungen aus Amerika', *Zeitschrift für Politik* 20, 1931, 441-3.

14. T.Geiger, 'Die Mittelschichten und die Sozialdemokratie', in *Die Arbeit. Zeitschrift für Gewerkschaftspolitik und Wissenschaftskunde* 8, 1931, 620ff. Against the thesis of F.Tönnies 'neo-proletariat', ibid., 782f.

15. Ibid., 626.

16. G.Schmidtchen, *Protestanten und Katholiken. Soziologische Analyse konfessioneller Kultur*, Berne and Munich 1973, 225.

17. *Christliche Welt* 44, no. 23 of 1 December 1930, 1162. However, for W.Laible, the editor of the *Allgemeine Evangelisch-Lutherische Kirchenzeitung*, Rade's reaction was only an 'aesthetic shudder of horror'. Laible himself saw the influx of youth as 'a basically delightful phenomenon', ibid. 64, 1931, 160f.

18. *Die Furche* 17, 1931, 226. The Catholic Church also observed the same thing among its own young people. Cf. E.Matthias and R.Morsey (ed.), *Das Ende der Parteien 1933*, Düsseldorf 1960, 297 n.40, where there is a quotation from the October number of *Junges Zentrum*: 'The young voters went over to the National Socialists and Communists in large groups.'

19. LKA Berlin-Brandenburg, G III 94 a I. There is a series of similar reports there.

20. M.H.Kater, 'Zur Soziographie der frühen NSDAP', *Vierteljahrshefte für Zeitgeschichte* 19, 1971, 157.

21. G.Schulz, *Aufstieg des Nationalsozialismus*, 556. Cf. also the statistics for the Berlin SA in A.Tyrell, *Führer befiehl…*, 274. This shows that of 1800 Berlin SA men in 1931, only 10% were over thirty.

22. W.Dirks, 'Katholizismus und Nationalsozialismus', *Die Arbeit* 8, 1931, 201f.

23. E.Deuerlein, *Der deutsche Katholizismus 1933* (1961), Osnabrück 1963, 51.

24. The correspondence, which was much quoted and commented on at the time, is now in H.Müller, *Katholische Kirche und Nationalsozialismus, Dokumente 1930-1935*, Munich 1963, 13-15, and in B.Stasiewski, *Akten deutscher Bischöfe über die Lage der Kirche 1933-1945*, I, *1933-1934*, Mainz 1968, 787ff.

25. H.Müller, *Katholische Kirche und Nationalsozialismus*, 15.

26. L.Volk, *Der bayerische Episkopat unter Nationalsozialismus 1930-1934*, Mainz ²1966, 31.

27. This problem was spelt out in the letter of a Berlin doctor to the Bishop of Berlin which the *Völkischer Beobachter* published in autumn 1931, H.Müller, *Katholische Kirche und Nationalsozialismus*, 37f.

28. L.Volk, *Der bayerische Episkopat*, 24.

29. Ibid., 26.

30. H.Müller, *Katholische Kirche und Nationalsozialismus*, 15-19.

31. Ibid., 21-23.

32. In fact 'throughout Bavaria not a single person who died was refused a funeral train because of being a member of the NSDAP', L.Volk, *Der bayerische Episkopat*, 35.
33. It appears in the reprint of the declarations in H.Müller, *Katholische Kirche und Nationalsozialismus*, on pp. 25 (Cologne), 33 (Paderborn) and 36 (Freiburg).
34. L.Volk, *Der Bayerische Episkopat*, 29.
35. H.Müller, *Katholische Kirche und Nationalsozialismus*, 6.
36. K.Trossmann, *Hitler und Rom*, Nuremberg 1931, 196.
37. A.Wild, *Hitler und das Christentum*, Augsburg 1931, 54, 46.
38. J.Nötges SJ, *Nationalsozialismus und Katholizismus*, Cologne 1931; *Der National- sozialismus und die deutschen Katholiken*, published by the Zentralstelle des Volksvereins für das katholische Deutschland, München-Gladbach 1931. There are further titles, though the list is not complete, in H.Müller, *Katholische Kirche und Nationalsozialismus*, 413.
39. *Prophetien wider das Dritte Reich. Aus den Schriften des Dr Fritz Gerlich und des Pater Ingbert Naab*, ed.J.Steiner, Munich 1946, 202.
40. Cf. above 158f.
41. For Schachleiter cf. L.Volk, *Der bayerische Episkopat*, 53-5. The confessional reason for his activity is interesting, namely 'to keep open access to National Socialism for Catholics, so that the German freedom movement does not become exclusively Protestant', ibid., 54. Cf. also L.Volk, *Kirchliche Akten über die Reichskonkordatsver- handlungen* 1933, Mainz 1969, 36 n.2.
42. For Haeuser cf L.Volk, Der *Bayerische Episkopat*, 27f. The quotation comes from an article by Haeuser, 'An meine Kritiker', *Völkische Beobachter*, 20 January 1931.
43. W.M.Senn, *Halt! Katholizismus und Nationalsozialismus. Meine zweite Rede an den deutschen Katholizismus und – nach Rom*, (Franz Eher Verlag), Munich nd (1932), 93. Cf. also *Katholizismus und Nationalsozialismus. Eine Rede an den deutschen Katholi- zismus*, Karlsruhe ²1931. Both booklets were directed above all against the Centre Party and put forward a radical völkisch Catholic National Socialist line.
44. H.E.Friedrich, 'Nationalsozialismus', in *Christliche Welt* 45, 1931, 406-10, 471-4, 553-9, 617-20; the quotation is from 619. There is a characteristic underestimation of Hitler on 407, 554. According to this, while Hitler has 'many characteristics of a Führer, he does not have the one that could make him the real Führer: the power of decision born out of ultimate solitude'.
45. See above, Ch.8, n.26.
46. *Deutsches Pfarrerblatt* 34, 1930, 709-11. In 1933 Wieneke became theological consultant in the Reich leadership of the German Christians, see below 199f., 204f., 212f.
47. *Deutsches Pfarrerblatt* 34, 1930, 788-9.
48. Ibid., 789.
49. *Deutsches Pfarrerblatt* 35, 1931, no.2 of 13 January 1931.
50. *Deutsches Pfarrerblatt* 34, 1930, 710.
51. Report of the *Allgemeine Evangelisch-Lutherische Kirchenzeitung* 64, 1931, 118f. Putz's theme was: 'The development of National Socialism – a question to theology and church people'.
52. W.Stapel, *Sechs Kapitel über Christentum und Nationalsozialismus*, Hamburg ⁵1931, 26.
53. Ibid., 29.
54. Ibid., 13.
55. A.Hinderer, *Handbuch der evangelischer Presse*, 95.
56. *Allgemeine Evangelisch-Lutherische Kirchenzeitung* 64, 1931, 253-7. Cf. also Laible's first opinion, ibid., 160f.
57. *Verhandlungen des Bayerischen Landtags, IV. Tagung 1930/1931*, Vol.5, 15th

session of 29 April 1931, 690-2. Buttmann's statement of principles was printed in the *Völkische Beobachter* of 1 May 1931 under the heading, 'The "Positive Christianity" of the NSDAP'. Cf. W.Laible in *Allgemeine Evangelisch-Lutherische Kirchenzeitung* 64, 1931, 474. For Buttmann see also below, 191ff.

58. Ibid., 403.

59. Aurel von Jüchen, 'Der Faschismus, eine Gefahr für das Christentum', in *Zeitschrift für Religion und Sozialismus*, 1930, 299-311. The statement, ibid., 311. See R.Breipohl, *Religiöser Sozialismus und bürgerliches Geschichtsbewusstsein zur Zeit der Weimarer Republik*, Zurich 1971, 24 n.47.

60. *Reich Gottes, Marxismus, Nationalsozialismus*, ed. Georg Wünsch, Tübingen 1931. Cf. the detailed critical review by E.Bizer in *Die christliche Welt* 46, 1932, 420-6. A 'Report on the Religious Socialists' theological course from 7-10 April at Caub am Rhein' appeared in the *Zeitschrift für Religion und Sozialismus*, 1930, 251f.

61. For the Eckert case, which in its time caused a considerable stir and was a major burden on the Religious Socialists, see below, 170f.

62. G.Wünsch, *Evangelische Ethik des Politischen*, Tübingen 1936, 652ff.

63. *Neue Blätter für den Sozialismus*, ed. E.Heimann, F.Klatt, A.Rauthmann and P.Tillich, 2, 1931, 176f.

64. G.Opitz, *Der Christlich-soziale Volksdienst. Versuch einer protestantischen Partei in der Weimarer Republik*, Düsseldorf 1969, 181f. Opitz's sweeping statement about the Christian-Socialist service to the Volk in the community movement needs to be corrected. Cf. H.Lehmann, *Pietismus und weltliche Ordnung in Württemberg*, Stuttgart-Berlin-Cologne-Mainz 1969, 312-18. For the differences between them and the NSDAP see ibid., 256f.

65. Strathmann was only pushed by the German Nationalists into the Volksdienst in 1930 and from January 1931 was Reichstag deputy for this party. Cf. G.Opitz, *Der Christlich-soziale Volksdienst*, 178 n.67 and 215. For the political position of the Christian-Socialist Volksdienst, cf.ibid., 256f.

66. *Christentum und Volkstum. Schriften in zwangloser Folge im Auftrag des Christlichen Volksdienstes*, ed. Prof. D.Strathmann, Erlangen, Volksdienst Verlag, Nuremberg nd [1931], second enlarged ed. 1932.

67. Ibid., 10ff.

68. Ibid., 18ff.

69. Ibid., 35.

70. G.Opitz, *Der Christlich-soziale Volksdienst*, 292-4. For the capitulation of the Christlich-soziale Volksdienst, ibid., 298ff.

71. Thus the account in the *Allgemeine Evangelisch-Lutherische Kirchenzeitung* 64, 1951, 441-3, though it is partisan.

72. The lectures by Künneth, Wilm and Schemm were published by the Verlag des Landesvereins für Innere Mission des evangelisch-lutherische Kirche in Sachsen, Dresden 1931. Martin Rade discussed them in a remarkably critical review in *Christliche Welt* 45, 1931, 620.

73. *Allgemeine Evangelisch-Lutherische Kirchenzeitung* 64, 1931, col.443.

74. The statement of 23 April 1931 appeared in all the Mecklenburg daily papers, in the *Niederdeutsche Kirchenzeitung* 1, 1931, 176ff., in the *Allgemeine Evangelisch-Lutherische Kirchenzeitung* 64, 1931, cols. 424-6, etc.

75. Vol.35 of the *Volkschriften des Evangelischen Bundes*, Berlin 1931. It is quoted here from the fourth enlarged edition (12th to 25th thousand!), Berlin 1932, 68. For the attitude of the Bund in this period see also F.v.d.Heydt, *Gute Wehr. Werden, Wirken und Wollen des Evangelischen Bundes*, Berlin 1936, 152f.

76. 'Die Grundlagen des Nationalsozialismus und ihr Verhältnis zum Evangelium.

Gutachten, erstattet an den Evangelischen Oberkirchenrat in Berlin von Lic.Dr Helmuth Schreiner, Berlin-Spandau, Johannesstift.' Cf. on this F.W.Kantzenbach, ' "Zeitenwende". Zum Weg einer Kulturschrift und ihrer Münchner Redaktion im Dritten Reich', *Zeitschrift für bayerische Landesgeschichte* 37, 1974, 577f.

77. Memorandum of 18 June 1931, AEKU Berlin, EO Gen. VI. 27f. I (I am grateful to R.Bunz for this information). The lecture was also sent out by the Kirchenausschuss; thus for example at the request of the German Provost of Porto Alegro in Brazil for 'a statement at the highest level from the Evangelical Church in Germany' on National Socialism. The answer from Berlin was that there was no such statement but that the Provost would certainly find the enclosed document – Schreiner's lecture – interesting. Letters of 11 April and 16 October 1931, AEKD Berlin A2/491.

78. H.Schreiner, *Der Nationalsozialismus vor der Gottesfrage* (1-10 thousand), Berlin-Spandau 1931, 43.

79. Ibid., 51.

80. Ibid., 30f.

81. Ibid., 51.

82. E.Klügel, *Die lutherische Landeskirche Hannovers und ihr Bischof 1933-1945*, Berlin and Hamburg 1965, 12f.

83. R.Karwehl, 'Was ich als lutherischer Prediger von Karl Barth gelernt habe', in *Antwort. Karl Barth zum 70. Geburtstag*, Zurich 1956, 897-905.

84. 'Politisches Messiastum', *Zwischen den Zeiten* 9, 1931, 519-43. Here quoted from W.Fürst (ed.), *Dialektische Theologie in Scheidung und Bewährung 1933-1936*, Munich 1966, 26-8. Cf. also 32f.

85. Ibid., 28.

86. Ibid., 40f.

87. *Kirchliches Jahrbuch* 1931, 65.

88. *Kirchliches Jahrbuch* 1932, 65-7.

89. Vols I,II, Leopold Klotz Verlag, Gotha (March and August 1932). For this see L.Siegele-Wenschkewitz, *Nationalsozialismus und Kirchen*, 27-35.

90. The difference between National Socialism and patriotism was already argued at that time among the younger generation. Cf. e.g. H.-D.Wendland, 'Sozialismus und Nationalismus. Fragen zur politischen Ethik der Gegenwart',in *Neue kirchliche Zeitschrift* 42, 1931, 425f.

91. *Preussische Zeitung* no. 155 of 4/5 July 1931. Quoted from *Zeitschrift für Religion und Sozialismus* 1931, 381f.

92. See above, 132f.

93. G.Schäfer, *Die evangelische Landeskirche in Württemberg und der Nationalsozialismus*, I. *Um das politischen Engagement der Kirche 1932-1933*, Stuttgart 1971, 34f.

94. Individual texts in *Kirchliches Jahrbuch* 1932, 126-68.

10. Concordat Policy and the Lateran Treaties (1930-1933)

1. R.Morsey, 'Die deutsche Zentrumspartei', in E.Matthias and R.Morsey (eds.), *Das Ende der Parteien 1933*, Düsseldorf 1960, 285-9. The problems of this decision were already noted at the time, cf. ibid., 287 n.31, and H.Brüning, *Memoiren 1918-1934*, 135. Also now the critical evaluation in L.Volk, *Reichskonkordat*, 41.

2. Cited from L.Volk, *Reichskonkordat*, 41.

3. J.Schmidlin, *Papstgeschichte der neuesten Zeit*, 4, *Pius XI (1922-1939)*, Munich 1939, 175-9.

4. Ritter's report of 2 June 1928; G.Franz-Willing, *Bayerische Vatikangesandtschaft*, 229.

5. See below, 151ff.

6. Klein to Pacelli, 1 October 1928. Quoted from L.Volk, *Reichskonkordat*, 45.

7. Ibid.

8. Telegram from Bergen of 31 December 1929, Archive AA Bonn, *Botschaft Rom-Vatican*, Vol.193. Cf. also L.Volk, *Reichskonkordat*, 45f. The Foreign Office also paid the expenses of this stay.

9. Ritter to Held, 9 March 1930. Text: A.Kupper, 'Zur Geschichte des Reichskonkordats', *Stimmen der Zeit* 171, 1962/63, 31f.

10. Ibid., 27.

11. Bergen to Foreign Offfice, 2 June 1930. Archive AA Bonn, *Botschaft Rom-Vatikan*, Vol.193.

12. E.Föhr, *Badisches Konkordat*, 16f.

13. Ibid., 17f., 21f., etc.

14. For Brüning's government cf. now G.Schulz, *Aufstieg des Nationalsozialismus*, 539-47, 599-604.

15. The term comes from the Catholic *Allgemeine Rundschau*, L.Volk, *Der bayerische Episkopat und der Nationalsozialismus 1930-1934*, Mainz ²1966, 41.

16. Report by Ritter of 8 November 1930; G.Franz-Willing, *Bayerische Vatikangesandschaft*, 230f.

17. *Osservatore Romano* no.238 of 11 October 1930. Quoted from F.Sandmann, *Die Haltung des Vatikans zum Nationalsozialismus im Spiegel des Osservatore Romano von 1929 bis zum Kriegsausbruch*, philosophical dissertation Mainz 1965, 99.

18. J.Nötges, *Nationalsozialismus und Katholizismus*, 27. Against E.Deuerlein, *Der deutsche Katholizismus*, 51, who sees this declaration as an endorsement of the first.

19. Report from Ritter, 11 May 1931, G.Franz-Willing, *Bayerische Vatikangesandschaft*, 231 and 250 n.17.

20. Report from Ritter of 11 May 1931, E. Deuerlein, *Katholizismus*, 53f.

21. Report from Bergen, 20 March 1931. Wording in Pacelli's Promemoria of 23 April 1931, A.Kupper, *Geschichte des Reichskonkordats*, 33.

22. Ibid., 27.

23. R.Morsey, 'Zentrumspartei', 301.

24. Cf. H.Irmler, 'Bankenkrise und Vollbeschäftigungspolitik (1931-1936)', in *Währung und Wirtschaft in Deutschland*, published by Deutsches Bundesbank, Frankfurt 1976, 283-308, esp. 291f.

25. The authenticity of Brüning's reminiscences on this point has, however, been disputed. Given other unreliable points and weaknesses in the *Memoiren* and on the basis of demonstrable mistakes over detail, R.Morsey in particular regards the political nucleus of the conversation as 'improbable (though not completely to be ruled out)' (*Zur Entstehung, Authentizität und Kritik von Brünings Memoiren 1918-1934*, Rheinland-Westfälische Akademie der Wissenschaften, Vorträge G 202, Opladen 1975, 45-9). In fact, however, the conversation fits well into Pacelli's thoughts and aims of this time as they are known to us. Brüning, overburdened and on edge, may have delineated some things excessively sharply, but in my view there can hardly be any doubt that he indicates Pacelli's intentions correctly. So too – though with some qualifications – L.Volk, *Reichskonkordat*, 48f.

26. Brüning to Bertram, 22 July 1930. Quoted in a letter from Reichswehrminister Schleicher to Klein, 13 July 1932, A.Kupper, *Geschichte des Reichskonkordats*, 34.

27. The Vatican was already offended over the identification of concordat and church treaty on the occasion of the Bavarian concordat, report from Ritter of 10 November 1924, G.Franz-Willing, *Bayerische Vatikangesandtschaft*, 202.

28. H.Brüning, *Memoiren 1918-1934*, Stuttgart 1970, 358-60.

29. For Pacelli's determination see L.Volk, *Reichskonkordat*, 49.

30. Quoted from R.Morse, 'Zentrumspartei', 302.

31. Report from Ritter, 20 December 1931, ibid., 310 n.23.

32. G.Franz-Willing, *Bayerische Vatikangesandtschaft*, 231.

33. R.Morsey (ed.), *Die Protokolle der Reichtagsfraktion und des Fraktionsvorstandes der deutschen Zentrumspartei 1926-1933*, Mainz 1969, 553.

34. Cf. above, 72, 149f., and A.Hollerbach, *Streiflichter*, 333.

35. E.Föhr, *Badisches Konkordat*, 24-6.

36. For Eugen Baumgartner, the only Kultusminister in the Weimar period to come from the ranks of the Centre Party, cf. now A.Hollerbach, *Streiflichter*, 328ff.

37. Pacelli to Baumgartner, 8 January 1932; E.Föhr, *Badisches Konkordat*, 25f.

38. E.Föhr, ibid., 26f.

39. Ibid., 39f.

40. Ibid., 50f.

41. Text with basis in W.Weber, *Konkordate und Kirchenverträge*, 100-28.

42. A.Hollerbach, *Streiflichter*, 324f.

43. G.Schulz, *Aufstieg des Nationalsozialismus*, 688.

44. R.Morsey, *Protokolle*, 572.

45. L.Kaas, 'Der Konkordatstyp des faschistischen Italien', in *Zeitschrift für ausländisches öffentliches Recht und Völkerrecht* III.1, 1933, 488-522. For this article see the comments on 165f. below.

46. B.Stasiewski, *Akten deutscher Bischöfe über die Lage der Kirche 1933-1945*, I, *1933-1934*, Mainz 1968, 843f.

47. L.Volk, *Der bayerische Episkopat und der Nationalsozialismus 1930-1934*, Mainz ²1966, 46.

48. Freising, 7 September 1932, L.Volk, *Faulhaber-Akten* I, 632.

49. Report from Ritter of 2 August 1932; G.Franz-Willing, *Bayerische Vatikansgesandtschaft*, 231f.

50. Meissner's notes of 13 August 1932. Quoted from T.Vogelsang, *Reichswehr, Staat und NDSAP*, Stuttgart 1962, 479f.

51. D.Junker, *Die Deutsche Zentrumspartei und Hitler 1932/33*, Stuttgart 1969, above all 86ff., in particular has brought out this dilemma for the Catholic party – with a reference to the Catholic doctrine of the state.

52. R.Morsey, *Protokolle*, 583f. Emphasis in the original.

53. Gerlich-Naab, *Prophetien wider das Dritte Reich*, 517. As a motto also in D.Junker, *Zentrumspartei*, 8. For the seriousness of the efforts by the Centre Party see ibid., 100-5.

54. Ibid., 109.

55. Papen to Bergen, 6 June 1932, Archive AA Bonn, *Botschaft Rom-Vatikan*, Vol.1042.

56. Schleicher to Klein, 13 August 1932, A.Kupper, *Geschichte des Reichskonkordats*, 35-37.

57. Decision of the Fulda Bishops' conference, 17-19 August 1932, ibid., 28.

58. Promemoria of 25 October 1932, ibid., 37f. For the statement mentioned cf. above 64.

59. Pacelli to Papen, 29 October 1932, ibid., 39f.

60. Papen to Pacelli, 17 November 1932, quoted from L.Volk, *Reichskonkordat*, 54.

61. A.Kupper, *Geschichte des Reichskonkordats*, 42-4, cf. also L.Volk, *Reichskonkordat*, 55f.

62. A.Kupper, *Geschichte des Reichskonkordats*, 30f. II Vat. 129 (secret) was the reference of Menshausen's first document of 5 April 1933 on the new possibilities for a Reich concordat. Text in A. Kupper, *Staatliche Akten über die Reichskonkordatsverhandlungen 1933*, Mainz 1969, 3-5.

63. For Mussolini as a Marxist cf. E.Nolte, *Faschismus*, 200-19.
64. For the development of Fascism see ibid., 261-87.
65. J.Schmidlin, *Papstgeschichte* 4, 104f., and above all on the political context, K.Neundorfer, 'Die Kirchenpolitik des italienischen Faschismus', *Hochland* 23 II, 1926, 36-71.
66. J.Schmidlin, *Papstgeschichte* 4, 67-79, gives an account of Catholic Action and its world-wide propagation which is full of information.
67. K.Neundörfer, *Kirchenpolitik* (n.65).
68. E.Pacelli, *Gesammelte Reden*, 137-40. According to E.Schmidlin, *Papstgeschichte* 4, 73, 'From the start Catholic Action was a dead letter on German soil.'
69. *Die Lateran-Verträge zwischen dem Heiligen Stuhl und Italien vom 11 Februar 1929. Autorisierte Ausgabe mit einer Einleitung des Päpstlichen Nuntius Eugenio Pacelli in Berlin*, Freiburg 1929, 9. Cf. also Art.26., ibid., 31. This edition will be cited below.
70. The significance of this clause is underlined by the fact that in the 1930s outside Italy only Bolivia, Colombia, S.Salvador and Nicaragua had similar ones L.Kaas, *Konkordatstype*, 501 n.13.
71. Ibid., 516.
72. Ibid., 507.
73. Ibid., 517.
74. *Die Lateran-Verträge*, 5f.
75. R.Leiber, 'Die Lösung der römischen Frage durch die Lateranverträge', *Stimmen der Zeit* 59, 1929, 161-81, above all 173f., 179. Similarly also J.Lulvès, 'Der Lateran-Vertrag zwischen dem Heiligen Stuhl und Italien', *Preussische Jahrbücher* 216, 1929, 61-76.
76. H.Liermann, 'Staat und Kirche in den Lateranverträgen', *Archiv des öffentlichen Rechts* 57 (NF 18), 1930, 399, 410.
77. Thus, as a representative of many, e.g. John S.Conway, *The Nazi Persecution of the Churches*, London 1968, 1.
78. For the role of Italy in Hitler's policy of alliances cf. E.Jäckel, *Hitlers Weltanschauung. Entwurf einer Herrschaft*, Tübingen 1969, 33ff.
79. *Völkischer Beobachter* no.45, 22 February 1929, Bavarian edition. The sub-headings of the article on p.1 run: 'Roman Peace and National Socialism – Adolf Hitler on the Peace Treaty between Fascism and the Vatican – The Recognition of the Fascist Idea of the State by the Pope – Liberalism and Nationalism – The Justification of National Socialist Foreign Politics'. Remarkably, the article has hitherto remained unknown in the concordat literature as a whole. My colleague L.Siegele-Wenschkewitz, *Nationalsozialismus und Kirchen. Religionspolitik von Partei und Staat bis 1935*, Düsseldorf 1974, 90-108, drew my attention to it for the first time.
80. J.Stark, *Nationalsozialismus und katholische Kirche*, Munich [2]1931, 31, 20. This section is also quoted in L.Volk, *Reichskonkordat*, 60 n.4.
81. W.Köhler, 'Konkordatswehen in Baden', *Völkischer Beobachter*, Munich edition, no. 327 of 22 November 1932 (emphasis in the original).
82. L.Kaas, *Der Konkordatstyp der faschistischen Italien*. 494, 497f. As far as I can see, this 1933 article by Kaas, which is of decisive importance for politics and church politics, has not yet been mentioned in any of the concordat literature. There is no reference to it in Deuerlein or in Morsey, Kupper, Volk or Repgen. The explanation may possibly be that the concern to demonstrate the continuity between the concordat negotiations in the Weimar period and the Reichskonkordat of 20 July 1933, which governed above all Ernst Deuerlein's first great monograph (1956), has shifted attention from the direct political significance of the Lateran treaties. But cf. L.Stegele-Wenschkewitz, *Nationalsozialismus und Kirchen*, 105f.

83. L.Kaas, *Konkordatstyp*, 510f.
84. Ibid., 517.

11. The Formation of Fronts in Protestant Theology and the Protestant Church (1931-1933)

1. Cf. A.Boyens, *Kirchenkampf und Okumene, 1933-39. Darstellung und Dokument-ation*, Munich 1969, 17f.
2. *Kirchliches Jahrbuch*, 1931, 478.
3. Special documentation appeared on this in 1931: W.Zoellner, *Die Ökumenische Arbeit des Deutschen Evangelischen Kirchenausschusses und die Kriegschuldfrage*, Berlin 1931. It also went in detail into the Stuttgart Declaration on the question of war guilt by the German Association of the World Alliance for Promoting Friendship of 24 September 1924, which argued for an international investigation of this question and against a dictatorial solution of it, ibid., 20-22. Cf. also the clear speech by F.Siegmund-Schultze at the seventh anniversary conference in Kassel in August 1929, ibid., 45f.
4. Quoted from *Theologische Blätter* 10, 1931, cols.177f.
5. On 4 June 1931 Karl Barth wrote to Georg Merz: 'Have you also already seen the Hirsch-Althaus declaration? Isn't Althaus a thoughtless sheep (Prov.1.10)! Hirsch paid him a visit at Pentecost and evidently dictated... this nonsense to him then' (Karl Barth archive, Basle). There is a critical comment and a short survey of reactions to the joint statement by Hirsch and Althaus in *Theologische Blätter* 10, 1931, 230-4.
6. *Allgemeine Evangelisch-Lutherische Kirchenzeitung* 64, 1931, col. 709.
7. Ibid., 65, 1932, 62-5.
8. *Christliche Welt* 45, 1931,606f.
9. *Allgemeine Evangelisch-Lutherische Kirchenzeitung* 64, 1931, 709.
10. F.-M.Balzer, *Klassengegensätze in der Kirche. Erwin Eckert und der Bund der Religiösen Sozialisten*, Cologne 1973, 93f. This interesting work, which is essentially written from Eckert's perspective, otherwise involuntarily confirms that the Baden church government was right in instituting proceedings against Eckert. The Mannheim pastor held forty-one political meetings in autumn 1930 and about 100 in the first half of 1931 (ibid., 90). In fact for a long time he had been far more a political agitator than a pastor and theologian.
11. H.Schafft, 'Der Fall Eckert', in *Neuwerk* 12, 1930/31, 356-8.
12. For Schafft see the impressive composite volume *Hermann Schafft. Ein Lebenswerk*, ed. W.Kindt, Kassel 1960, which makes Schafft's significance clear. For his relations with religious socialism and especially Paul Tillich cf. ibid., 90-6. For the Neuwerk circle see also G.Dehn, *Die alte Zeit, die vorigen Jahre*, 230-46.
13. G.Wünsch, 'Zum Fall Eckert', in *Zeitschrift für Religion und Sozialismus*, 1931, 249-31.
14. G.Dehn, 'Kirche und Politik. Bemerkungen zu den Angriffen auf Hermann Schafft', *Neuwerk* 13, 1931/2, 117-20. Cf. also Barth's similar comments in *Christliche Dogmatik*, above 124.
15. There is an extensive literature on the Dehn case. In addition to Dehn's own documentation I would mention: *Kirche und Völkerversöhnung. Dokumente zum Halle-schen Universitätskonflikt*, Berlin nd [1931], and his reminiscences, *Die alte Zeit, die vorigen Jahre*, Munich 1962, esp. 247-85; the contribution by E.Bizer, 'Der Fall Dehn' in *Festschrift fur Günther Dehn*, ed. W.Schneemelcher, Neukirchen 1957, 239-61; W.Prokoph, 'Die politische Seite des Falles Dehn', in *Wissenschaftliche Zeitschrift der Universitäts Halle* XVI, 1967, 2/3, 249-71; A.Faust, *Der nationalsozialistische Studenten-bund*, Düsseldorf 1973, Vol.2, 62-73.
16. G.Dehn, *Kirche und Völkerversöhnung*, 15-21f.

17. Ibid., 27-34.

18. Cf. A.Faust, *Der nationalsozialistische Studentenbund*, 2, 9ff.

19. H.Mulert, *Baumgarten und die Nationalsozialisten*, Neumünster 1930, 4-15 (reprint of the justification for the verdict).

20. G.Dehn, *Die alte Zeit, die vorigen Jahre*, 260.

21. Traub, who had himself become well known before the First World War through a 'case' of his own and was dismissed from his pastorate in 1911 in the so-called Apostolicum dispute, was rehabilitated during the War for service to the nation; in *Eiserne Blätter* he advocated a radically nationalist course. Towards the end of the Second World War, in a letter to Dehn he asked forgiveness for his conduct at the time, which Dehn gave, G.Dehn, *Die alte Zeit, die vorige Jahre*, 260.

22. For the 'Gumbel case' cf. A.Faust, *Der nationalsozialistische Studentenbund* 2, 57-62.

23. Both opinions are contained in *Kirche und Völkerversöhnung*, 40-3.

24. Ibid.,46.

25. G.Dehn, *Die alte Zeit, die vorigen Jahre*, 272. Cf. also the eye-witness account in *Kirche und Völkerversöhnung*, 68f.

26. There are numerous similar instances in A.Faust, *Der nationalsozialistische Studentenbund* 2, 51-81.

27. *Kirche und Völkerversöhnung*, 81.

28. Ibid., 89f.

29. Cf. esp. E.Bizer, 'Der Fall Dehn', 256-9.

30. DAZ 71, 1932, 31 January 1932.

31. Barth to Knak, 13 March 1931, Karl Barth archive, Basel.

32. Barth to Dehn, 20 October 1931, ibid.

33. Barth to Dehn, 9 February, ibid.

34. 'Warum führt man den Kampf nicht auf der ganzen Linie? Der Fall Dehn und die dialektische Theologie', *Frankfurter Zeitung* 122 of 15 February 1932; also in *Neuwerk* 13, 1931/32. 366-72.

35. *Deutsches Volkstum* 14, 1932, 266f.

36. Reply to Emanuel Hirsch of 17 April 1932, ibid., 390-4.

37. W.Prokoph, 'Die politische Seite des "Falles Dehn"', 271 n.128.

38. G.Schulz, *Aufstieg des Nationalsozialismus*, 472ff., 672ff., 723.

39. Resolution of the Landessynode of Hessen-Kassel of 15 April 1931, *Kirchliches Jahrbuch* 1931, 145. Cf. also Wright, *'Above Parties'*, 102-4.

40. AEKD Berlin, A2/478. Cf. also K.Scholder, 'Die Kapitulation der evangelischen Kirche vor dem nationalsozialistischen Staat', *Zeitschrift für Kirchengeschichte* 81, 1970, 183ff.

41. AEKD Berlin, A2/479.

42. The sermon at this service was given by Pastor Hans Asmussen, who later became one of the crucial figures in the composition of the Altona confession (see 184ff. below). The text for the sermon was the fifth commandment, 'Thou shalt not kill!', H.Asmussen, 'Erinnerung an das Altonaer Bekenntnis', *Evangelisch-Lutherische Kirchenzeitung* 12. 1958, 54.

43. According to the report in the *Deutsche Allgemeine Zeitung* 71, 1932, 331-2, of 19 July 1932. Cf. also J.C.Fest, *Hitler*, 471.

44. The printed liturgy, 'Notgottesdienst der Propstei Altona am 21 Juli 1932', and the message are in AEKD Berin A2/479.

45. Cf. H.Asmussen, 'Zur jüngsten Kirchengeschichte. Anmerkungen und Folgerungen, Stuttgart 1961, 30; 'In my view a confession had to be made. It was

immaterial in what part of Germany that insight dawned. But I believe that we in Altona were the ones who had it.'

46. P.Kluke, 'Der Fall Potempa', *Vierteljahrshefte für Zeitgeschichte* 5, 1957, 279-97.

47. M.Domarus, *Hitler. Reden und Proklamationen 1932-1945. Kommentiert von einem deutschen Zeitgenossen*, Vol. I.1, Munich 1965, 130. For the political motives behind the telegram cf. J.C.Fest, *Hitler*, 475f.

48. *Völkischer Beobachter* no.239, 26 August 1932.

49. G.Schäfer, *Die Evangelische Landeskirche in Württemberg und der Nationalsozializmus. Eine Documentation zum Kirchenkampf, 1. Um das politische Engagement der Kirche 1932-33*, Stuttgart 1971, 155f.

50. Ibid., 157f., cf. also 168.

51. Ibid., 171f.

52. Ibid., 156f.

53. Ibid., 161-3.

54. *Allgemeine Evangelisch-Lutherische Kirchenzeitung* 65, 1932, 832-4.

55. *Christliche Welt* 46, 1932, col.816 (H.Mulert).

56. A.Tyrell, *Führer befiehl*, 383.

57. *Nachrichten für Stadt und Land*, no. 251 of 14 September 1932. Press cuttings and all following sources in StA Oldenburg AII – 24 no.24.

58. Memorandum signed Ahlhorn, 14 September 1932.

59. *Nachrichten für Stadt und Land*, 15 September 1932.

60. *Oldenburger Nachrichten*, 21 September 1932.

61. *Nachrichten für Stadt und Land*, 15 September 1932.

62. *Bremer Nachrichten* no.263 of 21 September 1932.

63. According to the account in the *Delmenhorster Kreisblatt* no.219 of 17 September 1932. Similarly the account in the National Socialist *Freiheitskämpfer* of 20 September 1932.

64. *Bremer Nachrichten* no. 263 of 21 September 1932.

65. Wording of the complaint in StA Oldenburg A II Varia.

66. There was a report of this on the front page of the *Frankfurter Zeitung* on 26 September 1932.

67. *Das Evangelische Deutschland* 9. 1932, 408. Text also in K.D.Schmidt (ed.), *Die Bekenntnisse und grundsätzlichen Äusserungen zur Kirchenfrage des Jahres 1933*, Göttingen 1934, 18f.

68. *Das Evangelische Deutschland* 10, 1933, 10-12.

69. *Oldenburgische Volkszeitung*, 19 September 1932.

70. H.Beyer, 'Das Altonaer Bekenntnis vom 11 Januar 1933', *Ostdeutsche Wissenschaft* V, 1958, Munich 1959, 530.

71. J.Bielfeldt, *Der Kirchenkampf in Schleswig-Holstein*, Göttingen 1964, 22 n.6, and H.Beyer, 'Das Altonaer Bekenntnis', 524. For Steltzer cf. Ger van Roon, *Neuordnung im Widerstand*, Munich 1967, 132-40.

72. H.Asmussen, 'Erinnerung an das Altonaer Bekenntnis', *Evangelisch-Lutherische Zeitung* 12, 1958, 54.

73. The Altona Confession has often been reprinted. It is here quoted from K.D. Schmidt, *Die Bekenntnisse und grundsätzlichen Äusserungen*, 18-25. It is now also readily accessible in J.Beckmann, *Kirchliches Jahrbuch 1933-1945*, Gütersloh ²1976, 17-22. For its interpretation cf. M.Pertiet, *Das Ringen um Auftrag und Wesen der Kirche in der nationalsozialistische Zeit*, Göttingen 1968, 63, 66, and H.-J.Reese, *Bekenntnis und Bekennen*, Göttingen 1974, 141-8.

74. H.Asmussen, *Politik und Christentum*, Hamburg 1933, 118.

75. Ibid., 163.

76. Ibid., 170.
77. Ibid., 172f.
78. H.Asmussen, *Erinnerungen*, 55.
79. There is a short summary account of the most important voices in G.Christiansen, 'Der Ruf und sein Echo', *Niederdeutsche Kirchenzeitung* 3, 1933, 523-4. Further details in H.Beyer, *Das Altonaer Bekenntnis*, 528 n.28.
80. All quotations from G.Christiansen, *Der Ruf und sein Echo*.
81. For the reaction of the church press cf. H.Beyer, 'Das Altonaer Bekenntnis', 528 n.28.
82. Supplement to no.3 of *Niederdeutsche Kirchenzeitung* 3, 1933.
83. *Niederdeutsche Kirchenzeitung* 3, 1933, 91.
84. Ibid., 105f.
85. Cf. H.J.Reese, *Bekenntnis und Bekennen*, 147.
86. Thus E.Wolf, *Barmen. Kirche zwischen Versuchung und Gnade*, Munich 1957, 65.
87. E.Bethge, *Dietrich Bonhoeffer* (1967, ET 1970), paperback ed. London 1977, 167.

12. The German Christians (1931-1933)

1. See above, Chapter 10, 163ff.
2. See above, Chapter 9, 127f.
3. See above, Chapter 5, 75.
4. See above, Chapter 7, 117f.
5. *Christliche Welt* 44, 1930, 350f.
6. The wording of the five prayers is in *Christliche Welt* 44, 1930, 500f. Cf. also the report, ibid., 403, 550f., 609, 709, 758, 851.
7. Quoted here from *Der Mythus des 20.Jahrhunderts*, Munich [23,24]1934. By 1944 the book had attained a circulation of 1.1 million. For Rosenberg cf. the admirable study by J.C.Fest, *Das Gesicht des Dritten Reiches*, Munich 1963, 225-40. For *The Myth* cf. ibid., 230ff.
8. A.Rosenberg, *Der Mythus des 20.Jahrhunderts*, 8, 114. For mysticism cf. ibid., 221-59.
9. Ibid., 2f.
10. Quoted from K.Meier, 'Die Religionspolitik der NSDAP in der Zeit der Weimarer Republik', in *Zur Geschichte des Kirchenkampfes, Gesammelte Aufsätze* II, Göttingen 1971, 21, and G.Feder, *Das Programm der NSDAP und seine weltanschaulichen Grundlagen*, Munich, [41-50]1931 (201-250,000), 2.
11. G.Feder, *Das Programm der NSDAP*, 17.
12. Confidential minutes of the conversation, 7 March 1931 (five pages), AEKD Berlin A 2/490. See also J.R.C.Wright, *'Above Parties'*, 81f.
13. See above, Chapter 6, 94.
14. The speech, covering six pages in the Landtag protocol, was somewhat abbreviated in the *Völkischer Beobachter*, but all its essential statements remained unchanged. Here I have quoted from the *Verhandlungen des Bayrischen Landtags IV.Tagung 1930/1931*, V, 115th session of 29 April 1931, 690-6.
15. See above, Chapter 9, 133f.
16. *Hans Schemm spricht. Seine Reden und sein Werk*, ed. G.Kahl-Furtmann, Bayreuth 1936, 124.
17. On 22 December 1932, for example, the *Völkischer Beobachter* reported on an 'elevating Christmas celebration by the Breslau National Socialists': 'Deeply rapt, the thousands listened to what he (Schemm) said, which was a confession of faith in German and Christian Christmas thoughts.' For the church response cf. above, Chapter 9, 140.
18. Memorandum: *Der nationalsozialistische Lehrerbund, seine Gründung, sein Wirken*

und Wachsen, seine Bedeutung und die ersten schulpolitischen Massnahmen nach der Machtergreifung (printed, 28 pp nd, presumably May 1933), DC Berlin.

19. Exact numbers are not known. However, on the basis of the various estimates at the time it is hardly possible to be wrong about the degree of magnitude, cf. J.R.C.Wright, *'Above Parties'*, 87 n.61.

20. According to a letter from the leader of the Race and Culture Division in the Reichsleitung, H.Konopath, to the Reich Executive Director of the NS Alliance of Teachers, Max Kolb, 10 March 1932, DS Berlin, OPG Akte Konopath. There is a similar letter dated 7 June 1932 in J.R.C.Wright, *'Über den Parteien'* , 147 n.88a (only in the expanded German edition, see bibliography; this is also true of other references, see below).

21. *Christliche Welt* 45, 1931, 522.

22. AEKD Berlin, A2/491.

23. According to information in the memorandum (p.8, see n.18), Schemm spoke from 1930 on at church meetings in Dresden, Leipzig, Bremen, Hamburg, Berlin and Sttutgart. Topics mentioned are: Christianity and National Socialism, Race and religion, Confessional or community school, Racial materialism, *The Myth of the Twentieth Century*, the Germanic world-view, Christianity, Protestantism, Catholicism and the Centre Party.

24. For this and the following pages cf. the account by K.Meier, *Die Deutschen Christen. Das Bild einer Bewegung im Kirchenkampf des dritten Reiches*, Halle 1964, 4ff. (edition licensed for the Bundesrepublik, Göttingen 1964).

25. Ibid., 6.

26. S.Leffler, *Christus im Dritten Reich der Deutschen. Wesen, Weg und Ziel der Kirchenbewegung 'Deutsche Christen'*, Weimar nd [1935], 29.

27. Ibid., 27.

28. Ibid., 59.

29, Ibid., 33.

30. *Christliche Welt* 45, 1931, 238, and *Das Evangelische Deutschland* 8, 1931, 133. There are precise statistics for this election in P.Troschke, *Evangelische Kirchenstatistik Deutschlands*, Kirchliche Statistik III, Berlin 1932, 14f. According to this the church unity list had 76.5% and the Christian nationalist Confessors' League 23.4%. In his own church district Lehr achieved 32%, whereas in Wiesbaden city and Land he had less than 14%.

31. E.Eckert, *Was wollen die religiösen Sozialisten?*, Schriften der religiösen Sozialisten 1, Mannheim 1927, 12, etc. Elsewhere, too , the work reads like a model for the German Christians. It is governed by the same contempt for 'dogmatics' in favour of life, which is so characteristic of the German-Christian enthusiasm. 'Dead forms and formulas of past piety are more important to the existing churches than the revelations and testimonies of the living piety of the present, more important than the desire of the proletariat for the fulfilment of life and the content of life,' ibid., 3.

32. K.Dürr, *Notizen über die kirchlichen Verhältnisse Badens in den Jahren 1933 bis 1937* (ms 1969), LKA Karlsruhe.

33. *Allgemeine Evangelisch-Lutherische Kirchenzeitung* 65, 1932, 1051.

34. Cf. H.Heiber, 'Aus den Akten des Gauleiters Kube', *Vierteljahrshefte der Zeitgeschichte* 4, 1956, 67f.

35. Letter from W.Kube to the *Evangelische Pressedienst*, 16 January 1932, BA Koblenz NS 226/1240.

36. *Sitzungsberichte des preussichen Landtages, 3.Wahlperiode, 92 Sitzung*, six vols, Berlin 1929, 7610, 7614, 7616.

37. Ibid., *244. Sitzung*, 151 vols, Berlin 1931, 21393f.

38. Letter from the President of the Evangelischer Oberkirchenrat, Kapler, to the

Prussian Kultusminister Carl Heinrich Becker, 31 March 1936. Quoted from E.von Rittberg, *Der preussische Kirchenvertrag von 1931. Seine Entstehung und seine Bedeutung für das Verhältnis von Staat und Kirche in der Weimarer Republik*, philosophical dissertation Bonn 1959, Bonn 1960, 95.

39. At this period, with about 300,000 members, the Evangelischer Bund collected three million signatures against a concordat, D.Golombek, *Preussenkonkordat*, 39 n.1.

40. Cf. E.von Rittberg, *Der preussische Kirchenvertrag von 1931*, 95f.

41. Ibid., 206.

42. See above, Chapter 2, and J.R.C.Wright, *'Above Parties'*, 35-38.

43. *Sitzungsberichte des preussischen Landtags* (cf.n.36), 21393.

44. Kube to Strasser, 7 January 1931. Also quoted in J.R.C.Wright, *'Über den Parteien'*, 148.

45. Thus F.Wieneke, *Die Glaubensbewegung Deutsche Christen*, Schriftenreihe der Deutschen Christen 2, Soldin ⁵1933, 9f. Wieneke, who is one of the most important sources of information for the history of the German Christian movement, includes it in his accounts of the prehistory of the German Christians. He is followed by K.Buchheim, *Glaubenskrise im Dritten Reich*, 60f.; H.Baier, *Die Christen Bayerns in Rahmen des bayerischen Kirchenkampfes*, Nuremberg 1968, 8f. I shall go on to demonstrate that this is right only with major qualifications.

46. Kleist-Schmenzin was executed on 9 April 1945 as having been involved in the 20 July plot. Cf. A.Leber (ed.), *Das Gewissen steht auf. 54 Lebensbilder aus dem deutschen Widerstand 1933-1945*, Berlin and Frankfurt 1954, 149f. This also contains excerpts from Kleist's 1932 flysheet.

47. See above, 135f.

48. F.Wieneke, *Kirche und Partei. Erlebte Kirchengeschichte 1920-1945* (ms), Institut für Zeitgeschichte München, MA/15, 22f.

49. *Deutsches Pfarrerblatt* 34, 1930, 790, of 16 December 1930.

50. G.Schulz, *Aufstieg des Nationalsozialismus*, 662f.

51. Letter from the Bund für Deutsche Kirche to the Reich leadership of the NSDAP, 23 October 1931, H.Baier, *Die Deutschen Christen*, 355.

52. Kube to Strasser, 14 October 1931, J.R.C.Wright, *'Über den Parteien'*, 149.

53. Letter of 23 October 1931, see n.51 above.

54. F.Wieneke, *Kirche und Partei*, 25f. For a description of the 'Harzburg front on church ground', cf. H.Mulert, 'Volkskirche und Parteipolitik (April 1932)', in *Christliche Welt* 46, 1932, 374.

55. Reprinted in *Kirchliches Jahrbuch* 1932, 74f. Sasse wrongly dates the guidelines to summer 1932. However, they had already been given to Theophil Wurm, the Württemberg church president, on 10 December 1931, cf. G.Schäfer, *Dokumentation* 1, 80-3.

56. *Kirchliches Jahrbuch*, 1932, 75. Cf. also H.Rendtorff, *Das Wort Gottes über das Volk*, Schriftenreihe der Christlich-deutschen Bewegung 1, Verlag Deutscher Osten, Küstrin 1931.

57. G.Schäfer, *Dokumentation* 1, 78. Cf. also 84. For the dissociation from the NSDAP in the north, ibid., 88f.

58. Letter from Lohss to Wurm, 8 November 1932, G.Schäfer, *Dokumentation* 1, 99-102.

59. Letter from Kube to Strasser, 27 October 1931, quoted from J.R.C.Wright, *'Über den Parteien'*, 149.

60. The announcement by the Evangelischer Oberkirchenrat is in *Das Evangelische Deutschland* 8, 1931, 408.

61. Letter from the Evangelische Pressedienst to Kube, 14 January 1932. Kube's answer is dated 16 January 1932, BA Koblenz NS 26/1240.

62. Quoted from J.R.C.Wright, *'Über den Parteien'* , 150.

63. Letter from Strasser to Kube, 17 December 1931, BA Koblenz, NS 26/1240,

64. *Völkischer Beobachter* of 10/11 January 1932. Second supplement, extract also in Buchheim, *Glaubenskrise*, 73f.

65. F.Wieneke reports this function in a memorandum of June 1942, 'Zehn Jahre Deutsche Christen' (ms), BA Koblenz R 43II/165a. Cf. also J.R.C.Wright, *'Über den Parteien'* , 148.

66. The circular letter was then 'disseminated by a large part of the German daily press' (*Materialdienst*, produced by the Landesgeschäftsstelle des Evangelischen Volksbundes für Württemberg 4, 1932, no.6 of 29 March 1932, col.44) and has now been reprinted in H.Baier, *Die Deutschen Christen*, 357-9.

67. LKA Berlin-Brandenburg, Ho 107, Vol.1, Personalakte Hossenfelder.

68. W.Ulmenried, *Hossenfelder*, Die Reihe der Deutschen Führer 6, Berlin 1933, 6.

69. F.Wieneke, *Kirche und Partei*, 34.

70. F.Wieneke, *Denkschrift* (n.65). Those Wieneke mentions as belonging to the first advance include: Nobiling, Dr Thom, D.Freitag, Kessel, Peter (Berlin), Karl Eckert, Ludwig Sylvester, Weitz (Mark Brandenburg), Zarnikow, Jenetzky (Silesia), Kirste (Sydow in Pomerania), Adler (Westphalia), Meyer (Aurich), Wagner (Homberg am Niederrhein).

71. F.Wieneke, ibid. In his notes on 'Church and Party', Wieneke wrongly dates this meeting to 6 June. K.Meier, *Die deutschen Christen*, 12, and H.Baier, *Die Deutschen Christen*, 12f., make the same mistake.

72. This division did not come under Strasser's command, but was subordinate to the Reich Organization Leader II, Konstantin Hierl, cf. A.Tyrell, *Führer befiehl*, 362, 363 (no.14e).

73. DC Berlin, OPG Akte-Konopath, Beschluss USCHLA Reich leadership of 30 June 1932.

74. F.Wieneke, *Kirche und Partei*, 35f.

75. It is uncertain whether the suggestion came from Hitler. Perhaps it was also taken over from the Thuringians. Incidentally, the final naming, which took place only on 11 February, is an indication that the Silesian special circular letter was in fact composed *before* this meeting, although it was only circulated later.

76. Appendix to the consistory letter to the Evangelischer Oberkirchenrat of 7 March 1932, AEKU Berlin, EO Gen III 15.1, supplement. The Thursday was 11 February 1932.

77. F.Wieneke, *Kirche und Partei*, 35f.

78. Kube to Konopath, BA Koblenz, NS 26.1240.

79. LKA Hamburg, Bestand Deutsche Christen no.204/1.

80. Orders from the Reichsleitung, Series 24 of 31 May 1932, HStA Wiesbaden 483/1650.

81. USCHLA Reich leadership decision of 30 June 1932, DC Berlin, OPG-Akte Konopath.

82. Written communication from Hossenfelder to the author, July 1970. F.Wieneke, *Kirche und Partei*, 36, reports vigorous arguments over the 'Guidelines' between him and Hossenfelder on the one side and Konopath on the other. The establishment of the 'Guidelines' by Hossenfelder on 27 May is in Ulmenried, *Hossenfelder*, 8.

83. For the connections with the Berlin Missiongesellschaft cf. H.Beyer, 'Volk, Staat und Kirche in der Übergangs- und Krisenzeit 1932-1934', in *Ecclesia und Res Publica, K.D.Schmidt zum 65. Geburtstag*, Göttingen 1961, 149.

84. The 'Guidelines', reprinted countless times and distributed by the hundred thousand, are here quoted from the version in *Evangelium in Dritten Reich* 1, 1932, Vol.2.

Some later versions differ slightly. There is an English translation in J.S.Conway, *The Nazi Persecution of the Churches*, 339-41.

85. E.Bunke, 'Die Kirche und das Dritte Reich', in *Die Reformation*, 4 September 1932.

86. This is F.Wieneke, *Die Glaubensbewegung 'Deutsche Christen'*, Schriftenreihe der DC no.2, Soldin ⁵1933, 16-31, and the running commentary on the individual points by various authors in the first issues of *Evangelium in Dritten Reich*, October-December 1932.

87. F.Wieneke, op.cit., 16.

88. Point 4, which stated, 'Our church must not stand aside from the struggle for the physical and spiritual rebirth of the nation. Your place is in this battle, at the front...', was evidently inspired by the programme of the Baden National Socialists, letter of the German Evangelischer Kirchenausschuss to the Evangelischer Oberkirchenrat, 30 August 1932, AEKU Berlin EO Gen.,III, 51.1, supplement.

89. *Verhandlungen des Zweiten Deutschen Kirchentags*, 215. See also above, 000f.

90. J.Hossenfelder, *Eine Stellungnahme, Potsdam, den 7 August 1945*, LKA Berlin-Brandenburg.

91. The whole proceedings are in AEKU Berlin, EO Gen.III, 51 1, Beiheft. Sammlung zur Verfügung von 2 März 1935 betr. Richtlinien d.NSDAP Gau Schlesien zu Kirchenfragen.

92. Ibid., appendix on the confidential letter of the Evangelischer Oberkirchenrat to the general superintendents of 25 May 1932, 9. Cf. also J.R.C.Wright, *'Über den Parteien'*, 157ff.

93. There is a copy in LKA Berlin-Brandenburg J IX 66. There is also a copy in AEKU Berlin (n.91).

94. AEKU Berlin (n.91).

95. Ibid., memorandum of 9 September 1932.

96. LKA Hamburg, *Bestand Deutsche Christen*, no.204/1, no date. This archive contains the only known complete collection of circular letters from the beginnings of the German Christians. Article 19 § 2 of the Prussian Church Constitution contained the oath of office for elders and community officials. It consisted in assent to the following question: 'Do you swear before God and this community to perform the office laid upon you carefully and faithfully, in accordance with the Word of God, the ordinances of the church and the community, and conscientiously to see that all is done in the community in order and honourably?', F.Giese and J.Hosemann, *Die Verfassungen der Deutschen Evangelischen Landeskirchen* 2, Berlin 1927, 7f.

97. LKA Hamburg, circular letter 7 of 21 June 1932.

98. Ibid., circular letter 8 of 31 July 1932.

99. This was RM 1 per candidate. Of this. 50 pfennigs were to go to Berlin, circular letters 8 and 9, ibid.

100. For the independence of Koch and the special role of East Prussia cf. P.Hüttenberger, *Die Gauleiter*, 52f., 72f. and J.R.C.Wright, *'Über den Parteien'*, 149, 153.

101. AEKU Berlin, EO Gen III, 51,1.

102. Cf. J.R.C.Wright, *'Über den Parteien'*, 152f. and below 309.

103. See above, 210.

104. Circular letter 11, LKA Hamburg (n.96).

105. Circular letter 8, ibid.

106. *Der Reichsbote*, no.173 of 2 August 1933, supplement 'Die Führer der Deutschen Christen'.

107. J.Hossenfelder, *Unser Kampf*, Schriftenreihe der Deutschen Christen 5, Berlin 1933, 25.

108. For Themel see above, 111.

109, For Peter cf. A.Dannenmann, *Die Geschichte der Glaubensbewegung Deutsche Christen*, Dresden 1933, 25-33.

110. Ibid., 26f.

111. Letter from Hossenfelder to the author, July 1970.

112. J.Hossenfelder, *Unser Kampf*, 8.

113. *Kirchliches Jahrbuch*, 1932, 71f.

114. 'Hakenkreuz über dem Kreuz!?', *Vorwärts* no.421, 7 September 1932. Cf. also E.von Harnack, 'Kreuz und Hakenkreuz', ibid., 482 of 16 September 1932, and 'Nazi-Rummel in der Kirche', ibid., 435 of 15 September 1932.

115. Copy in AEKU Berlin, EO Gen III 51.1.

116. 'Von den Deutschen Christen', *Vossische Zeitung* 511 of 30 October 1932.

117. General church voting statistics for the Kirchenbund were prompted by the Kirchenausschuss only in their letter of 20 March 1933. AEKU Berlin EO Gen. III, 51,II. For the difficulty in assessing the outcome of the vote cf. also J.R.C.Wright, *'Über den Parteien'*, 161f.

118. Report in *Reichsboten*, 16 October 1932: letter of the Evangelischer Presseverband für Deutschland to Geheimrat Oberkonsistorialrat Karnatz of 1 November 1932: report on the German Christian assembly in Wilmersdorf of 19 September 1932, etc., AEKU Berlin, EO Gen.III, 51 II.

119. O.Dibelius in *Der Tag* of 10 November 1932. The results from all the Berlin communities are in *Evangelium im Dritten Reich* 1, no.7, of 27 November 1932. Supplement for Greater Berlin.

120. J.R.C.Wright, *'Über den Parteien'* ,161.

121. *Evangelium im Dritten Reich* 1, no.7, of 27 November 1932.

122. No. 447 of 20 November 1932.

123. Letter from the Kirchenstatistisches Amt to Oberkonsistorialrat Fischer of 23 February 1933, AEKU Berlin, EO Gen.III, 51 II.

Part Two

1. The Seizure of Power and Protestantism (February-March)

1. G.Rühle, *Das Dritte Reich. Dokumentarische Darstellung des Aufbaus der Nation. Das erste Jahr 1933*, Berlin ²1934, 26.

2. B.Stasiewski (ed.), *Akten Deutscher Bischöfe über die Lage der Kirche, 1933-1945* I, Mainz 1968, 31.

3. W.Niemöller, *Die Evangelische Kirche im Dritten Reich. Handbuch des Kirchenkampfes*, Bielefeld 1956, 76.

4. The author of the diary was Luise Solnitz. Text in W.Jochmann (ed.), *Nationalsozialismus und Revolution. Ursprung und Geschichte des NSDAP 1922-1933*, Frankfurt 1963, 422f.

5. F.Tügel, *Mein Weg 1888-1946. Erinnerungen eines Hamburger Bischofs*, Hamburg 1972, 229.

6. L.Solnitz on 30 January, in W.Jochmann, *Nationalsozialismus und Revolution*, 421.

7. G.Schäfer, *Dokumentation* 1, 234. The commentary in the *Allgemeine Evangelisch-Lutherische Kirchenzeitung* 66, 1933, 114, of 3 February 1933 takes exactly the same line.

8. R.Morsey, 'Die Zentrumspartei', in E.Matthias and R.Morsey, *Das Ende der Parteien 1933*, Düsseldorf 1960, 346. Similarly F.Maassen in the Catholic journal *Junge Front* of 5 February 1933: 'For in fact Hitler today is the prisoner of Hugenberg, who is directing this new cabinet...', K.Gotto, *Die Wochenzeitung* Junge Front/Michael, Mainz 1970, 26. Further examples in K.Repgen, 'Hitlers Machtergreifung und der deutsche

Katholizismus. Versuch einer Bilanz' (1967), in D.Albrecht (ed.), *Katholische Kirche im Dritten Reich. Eine Aufsatzsammlung zum Verhältnis von Papsttum, Episkopat und deutschen Katholiken zum Nationalsozialismus 1933-1945*, Mainz 1976, 4f.; also in D.Junker, *Zentrumspartei*, 163f.

9. E.Matthias, 'Die Sozialdemokratische Partei Deutschlands', in E.Matthias and R.Morsey, *Ende der Parteien*, 163f.

10. O.K.Flechtheim, *Die KPD in der Weimarer Republik* (1948), Frankfurt 1969, 269ff.; S.Bahne, 'Die Kommunistische Partei Deutschlands', in E.Matthias and R.Morsey, *Ende der Parteien*, 637ff.

11. S.Bahne, op.cit., 696f.

12. Ibid., 658.

13. Karl Barth to Anna-Katharina Barth, 1 February 1933, Karl Barth Archive, Basel.

14. Letter of 17 March 1933 to the Revd John McConnachie, ibid.

15. The significance of 'illusionism and opportunism' on the right wing and 'deception and self-deception' on the left wing is also stressed by K.D.Bracher, *Die deutsche Diktatur. Enstehung, Struktur, Folgen des Nationalsozialismus*, Cologne ⁴1972, 214ff., 217f.

16. M.Domarus, *Hitler. Reden und Proklamationen 1932-1945*, I, Munich 1965, 191-4.

17. G.Kretschmar (ed.), *Dokumente zur Kirchenpolitik des Dritten Reiches, I, Das Jahr 1933*, ed. C.Nicolaisen, Munich 1971, 4-6.

18. *Das Evangelische Deutschland* 10, 1933, 54; letters to eastern Germany, No.53 of 15 March 1933, 6; protocol of the forty-ninth session of the Church Senate of 23/24 February 1933, 3f. (AEKU Berlin).

19. Kretschmar and Nicolaisen, *Dokumente* I, 2-4.

20. Cf. ibid., 6-8.

21. M.Domarus, *Hitler* I, 208.

22. Ibid., 211. Cf. also Kretschmar and Nicolaisen, *Dokumente* I, 8-10.

23. G.Schäfer, *Dokumentation* I, 263, n.6.

24. *Völkischer Beobachter*, Berlin edition, 16 March 1933.

25. *Christliche Welt* 47, 1933, 239. The assembly of Kassel pastors made a remarkably detached declaration on this, ibid.

26. BA Koblenz, R 43 II/150. The proceedings, with a wrong reference and not reproduced wholly correctly, are also in Kretschmar and Nicolaisen, *Dokumente* I, 11-13.

27. In a conversation with Cardinal Faulhaber on 1 March 1933 Vice-Chancellor Papen repeated the description of the Communist plans for revolution which Göring had presented in the cabinet meeting on the previous day: L.Volk, *Faulhaber-Akten* I, 652.

28. K.D.Bracher, W.Sauer and G.Schulz, *Die nationalsozialistische Machtergreifung. Studien zur Errichtung des totalitären Herrschaftssystems in Deutschland 1933/34*, Cologne and Opladen ²1962, 87.

29. There is ongoing information about conditions in Russia and the anti-Christian propaganda in Germany in e.g. the *Materialdienst* published by the Evangelischer Volksbund for Württemberg, for which this was one of the most important themes after its foundation in 1929. The *Materialdienst* also reported in detail on the Communist plans for unrest and revolution in 1933 (ibid., 5, 1933, no.6 of 5 April 1933, 42-6). The closing comment, which is typical, runs, 'It has become clear to everyone as a result of developments during the last month that we face an unexpected abyss to which no one is willingly ready to close his eyes.'

30. Bracher, Sauer and Schulz, *Machtergreifung*, 91.

31. The 'Netherlands Thanksgiving' was the favourite chorale of Wilhelm II and was played at countless solemn occasions above all during the War.

32. W.Laible in *Allgemeine Evangelisch-Lutherische Kirchenzeitung* 66, 1933, 260.

33. M.Koschorke (ed.), *Geschichte der Bekennenden Kirche in Ostpreussen 1933-1945*, 1976, 36f. Lenkitsch's report is not completely correct about the outcome of the declaration. But cf. H.Linck, *Der Kirchenkampf in Ostpreussen 1933-1945*, Munich 1968, 27f.

34. Bracher, Sauer and Schulz, *Machtergreifung*, 147.

35. According to Kretschmar and Nicolaisen, *Dokumente* I, 21 n.2, the Reich President will also have played a role in this.

36. Memorandum of 3 March 1933 in AEKU Berlin, Gen.I, 63, vol.1.

37. Thus on the afternoon of 7 March Hitler reported the course of events to the Reich cabinet (cf. the record of the ministerial discussion, BA Koblenz R 43 I/1460). The official report followed with the letter of Reich Minister of the Interior Frick to the President of the Evangelischer Oberkirchenrat on 8 March 1933: Kretschmar and Nicolaisen, *Dokumente* I, 21f.

38. Memorandum of the Kirchenbundesamt, 16 March 1933, AEKD Berlin C 3/207.

39. *Der Tag von Potsdam*, souvenir edition of *Die Woche*, nd [6 April 1933]. For the course of the day and its impact cf also Bracher, Sauer and Schulz, *Machtergreifung*, 149-52. Celebratory services also took place in other cities on this day. Cf. e.g. the report on the packed service of thanksgiving in the Stiftskirche in Stuttgart in G.Schäfer, *Dokumentation* 1, 276f.

40. *Verhandlungen des Reichstags, VIII.Wahlperiode 1933*, Vol.457, Berlin 1934, 28f., 31f. The version which was published in the *Völkischer Beobachter* on 24 March 1933, which does not differ substantially, is in M.Domarus, *Hitler* I, 229-237. The main omission is the statement about schools and education.

41. From this perspective it is very improbable that the excessive statements of Hitler that he would not pause until he had 'exterminated Christianity in Germany root and branch, with every sinew and fibre', which Hermann Rauschning records as dating from early 1933, were in fact stated like that at the time (H.Rauschning, *Gespräche mit Hitler* [Zurich 1940], Vienna 1973, 50). In fact, clear as Rauschning's conversations are in many points, they are not an authentic source for the historian who is working chronologically. By his own acknowledgment the former President of the Senate – and also a member of the Prussian General Synod – had 'woven together an overall picture of Hitler from notes, from memory and even from reports about Hitler from others' (cf. T.Schieder, *H.Rauschnings Gespräche mit Hitler als Geschichtsquelle*, Rheinland-Westfälische Akademie der Wissenschaften, Vorträge G 178, Opladen 1972, 25). The description also, of course, incorporates events and experiences up to the time the conversations were written down at the end of 1939, and it is now impossible to distinguish details. Parts of Hitler's comments from the section 'The Antichrist', which according to Rauschning's account were made in a conversation on the evening of 6 April 1933 (Rauschning, 49; Schieder, 63), only fit into the time after 1937, when the failure of Hitler's church politics and its defeat had become evident. This is also supported by the fact that Rauschning stands completely alone in handing down sayings of such a kind from this period, and they can hardly be brought into line with Hitler's actual church-political activities at this time. Cf. also K.Scholder, 'Die evangelische Kirche in der Sicht der nationalsozialistischen Führung bis zum Kriegsausbruch', *Vierteljahrshefte für Zeitgeschichte* 16, 1968, 16f. J.R.C.Wright, *'Über den Parteien'*, 183f., is judicious.

42. See Part One, Ch.11, 184ff. above.

43. *Christliche Welt* 47, 1933, 239.

44. K.Dienst (ed.), *Dokumentation zum Kirchenkampf in Hessen und Nassau, I*, Jahrbuch der Hessische Kirchengeschichtliche Vereinigung 25, Darmstadt 1974, 370.

45. Cf. Part One, Ch.2.

46. Protokol of the session of the Kirchenausschuss of 2/3 March 1933 in Berlin, AEKD

Berlin, A2/28, 22f. Text also in G.Schäfer, *Dokumentation* 1, 248-50. The preliminary history and the various outlines can be found in ibid., 233ff.

47. G.Schäfer, op.cit., 250.

48. Protocol of the session (n.6), 25-9.

49. Text of the resolution with the alterations in G.Schäfer, *Dokumentation* I, 251f.

50. Ibid. For the discussion in the committee see Pechmann's letter to the former Stuttgart Consistory President Zeller of 12 April 1933, F.W.Kantzenbach (ed.), *Widerstand und Solidarität der Christen in Deutschland 1933-1945. Eine Dokumentation zum Kirchenkampf aus den Papieren des D.Wilhelm Freiherrn von Pechmann*, Nuremberg 1971, 38.

51. *Das Evangelische Deutschland* 10, 1933, 83.

52. W.Niemöller, *Die Evangelische Kirche*, 70.

53. F.W.Kantzenbach, *Widerstand und Solidarität*, 72.

54. *Christliche Welt* 47, 1933, 322. There are further names there.

55. Instructions from the Election Propaganda Directorate for the Reich and the Land of Prussia to all Gau propaganda leaders, 25 February 1933, NStA Hannover Des.310 I B no.3. For the lamentable role of the 'Catholic Association for National Politics' cf. B.Stasiewski, *Akten* I, 403 n.1, and A.Kupper, *Staatliche Akten über die Reichskonkordatsverhandlungen 1933*, Mainz 1969, 73 nn.4,5.

56. G.Schäfer, *Dokumentation* I, 261f.

57. Ibid., 263f. For the March elections cf. also K.H.Götte, *Die Propaganda des Glaubensbewegung 'Deutsche Christen' und ihre Beurteilung in der deutschen Tagespresse. Ein Beitrag zur Publizistik im Dritten Reich*, Münster philosophical dissertation 1957, 230-3.

58. Pastor W.Rehm in the *NS-Kurier* of 11 March 1933, G.Schäfer, *Dokumentation* 1, 359.

59. As far as I know the letter has so far remained unknown with the exception of the short quotations in J.Gauger, *Chronik der Kirchenwirren (Gotthard-Briefe 138-145), 1.Teil 1932-1934*, Elberfeld 1934, 68. There is an original in the Karl Barth archive, Basel.

60. Reply by Barth of 17 March 1933, Karl Barth archive, Basel.

61. Ibid.

62. For Dryander's sermon see 6 above. The complete text of Dibelius's sermon can be found in *Das Evangelische Deutschland* 1, 1933, 101f. Dibelius's own recollection of this day, with a reference to the generally hostile criticism from the National Socialists and praise for the sermon from Göring, is contained in O.Dibelius, *In the Service of the Lord*, London and New York 1964, 140f.

63. J.Gauger, *Chronik* 1, 68.

64. Ibid. The full text is in AEKU Berlin, Gen.II, 42, Vol.1, 186f.

65. AEKU, ibid., 60f. For the whole event see Ch.4 below, 289f.

66. K. Dienst, *Dokumentation* 1, 203.

67. H.Baier, *Die Deutschen Christen Bayerns*, 42.

68. Both appeals are printed in *Das Evangelische Deutschland* 10, 1933, 105.

69. Ibid., 117.

70. Ibid., 127.

71. Protocol of the session in AEKU Berlin, Gen.III, 17, Vol.III, 225-36.

72. The whole proceedings are in ibid., Gen.II, 42, Vol.I, 47-53.

73. Ibid., 140. Text also in W.Niemöller (above n.3).

2. The Capitulation of Catholicism (February-March)

1. R.Morsey, 'Hitlers Verhandlungen mit der Zentrumsführung am 30.Januar 1933', *Vierteljahrshefte für Zeitgeschichte* 9, 1961, 186f. Cf. also R.Morsey, *Protokolle*, 612ff., and D.Junker, *Zentrumspartei*, 156ff.

2. D.Junker, op.cit., 165-70.

3. R.Morsey, 'Ende der Zentrumspartei', 348.

4. B.Stasiewski, *Akten* I, 3-6.

5. J.Maassen, 'Schreie, Wahrheit!', K.Gotto, *Die Wochenzeitung Junge Front/Michael*, Mainz 1970, 32. Because of this article the newspaper was banned by the senior president of the Rhine province between 24 February and 17 March, ibid., 32f. Cf. also the articles in H.Müller, *Katholische Kirche*, 62f. (*Westdeutsche Arbeiterzeitung*) and 66ff. (Youth Praeses).

6. H.Brüning, *Memoiren*, 65f.

7. L.Volk, *Bayerischer Episkopat*, 51.

8. Text in J.Neuhäusler, *Kreuz und Hakenkreuz* II, Munich 1946, 120-2.

9. B.Stasiewski, *Akten* I, 1f. The possibility indicated in ibid., 1 n.1, that the pastoral letter could also have been written on 30 January, has much to be said for it.

10. Text of the pastoral letter of 12 July 1932 in H.Müller, *Katholische Kirche*, 41. Text of 20 February 1933 in Stasiewski, *Akten* I, 6f., against Morsey, who regards the declaration as an 'important moral support for the Centre Party' ('Ende der Zentrumspartei', 350).

11. J.Pieper, *Noch wusste es niemand. Autobiographische Aufzeichnungen 1904-1945*, Munich 1976, 105.

12. R.Morsey, 'Ende der Zentrumspartei', 354.

13. Account of the ministerial discussion on 7 March 1933, BA Koblenz R 43 I/1460.

14. Thus e.g. J.Becker in his unfortunate polemic against K.O.von Aretin ('Das Ende der Zentrumspartei und die Problematik des politischen Katholizismus in Deutschland', *Welt als Geschichte* 23, 1963, 149-72, also expanded in G.Jasper (ed.), *Von Weimar zu Hitler*, Cologne and Berlin 1968, 344-76. But cf. also K.O.von Aretin, 'Prälat Kaas, Franz von Papen und das Reichskonkordat von 1933', *Vierteljahrshefte für Zeitgeschichte* 14, 1966, 252-79). Then with firm emphasis by K.Repgen ('Das Ende der Zentrumspartei und die Enstehung des Reichskonkordats', in *Militärseelsorge* 11, 1969, 83-122, now also in K.Repgen, *Historische Klopfsignale für die Gegenwart*, Münster 1974, 97-127), who is certain that the history of the origin of the Reich concordat does not begin before 2 April (*Militärseelsorge*, 89). W.Mussmann, 'Der Deutsche Katholizismus im Jahre 1933', in *Festschrift für Hermann Heimpel*, I, Göttingen 1971, 180-204, esp. 186-8, and now above all L.Volk, *Das Reichskonkordat*, 60f., 77, and passim also think that the question of the concordat was not yet a live issue in March.

15. K.Repgen, 90f., draws attention to this. But the argument loses weight because of decisive gaps in the sources. Thus rightly L.Siegele-Wenschkewitz, *Nationalsozialismus und Kirchen*, 118f.

16. J.Lulvès, *Der Lateran-Vertrag*, 76.

17. Arch.AA Bonn, Ref.D.Pol.7, Deutschland, Vol.5, s.v. Ministerien.

18. L.Volk, *Reichskonkordat*, 64 n.24.

19. Faulhaber's notes of 10 March 1933, L.Volk, *Faulhaber Akten* I, 660.

20. L.Volk, *Reichskonkordat*, 65 n.25.

21. L.Volz, *Faulhaber-Akten* I, 715. Also in the protocol of the conference of 20 April in B.Stasiewski, *Akten* I, 58. The attempts by Volk to attribute the pronounced description by Faulhaber to his search for a 'help in orientation' and to describe the reference itself as an inconsequential matter is only tenable to any degree if one leaves Hitler's interest in the whole question completely out of account, as Volk does. Cf. L.Volk, 'Päpstliche

Laudatio auf Hitler?', in *Stimmen der Zeit* 173, 1963/64, 221-9, and again in *Reichskonkordat*, 65.

22. Text in L.Volk, 'Zur Kundgebung des deutschen Episkopats vom 28. März 1933', *Stimmen der Zeit* 173, 1963/64, 431-56, here 433 n.7.

23. Text in L.Volk, *Reichskonkordat*, 221-3.

24. Thus according to Gröber's letter to Pacelli, 18 March 1933, B.Stasiewski, *Akten* I, 10.

25. L.Volk, *Reichskonkordat*, 71.

26. W.Dirks, *Katholizismus und Nationalsozialismus*, 206f.

27. Letter of 19 March 1933, B.Stasiewski, *Akten* I, 11f.

28. H.Brüning, *Memoiren*, 652-5.

29. R.Morsey, 'Ende der Zentrumspartei', 382.

30. L.Volk, *Reichskonkordat*, 67.

31. J.Becker, 'Ende der Zentrumspartei', in G.Jasper (ed.), *Von Weimar zu Hitler*, 348.

32. K.D.Bracher, 'Nationalsozialistische Machtergreifung und Reichskonkordat. Ein Gutachten zur Frage des geschichtlichen Zusammenhangs und der politischen Verknüpfung von Reichskonkordat und nationalsozialistischer Revolution', in F.Gese and F.A.von de Heydte (eds.), *Der Konkordatsprozess*, Munich nd [1957-1959], 947-1021, esp. 976-90.

33. H.Brüning, *Memoiren*, 656.

34. A.Kupper, *Staatliche Akten*, 237.

35. Papen to Bergen, 7 April 1934, quoted in G.Lewy, *Die katholische Kirche und das Dritte Reich*, Berlin 1965, 79. Similarly also in his address to Catholic academics in Maria Laach on 22 August 1933 (*Die katholische Gedanke* 6, 1933, 331-6). Because they are so close in time these accounts are to be preferred to those of Papen to the Spruchkammer in 1946, where he gave the date as April 1933. Quoted in E.Deuerlein, *Reichskonkordat*, 110.

36. Praschma to Papen, Schloss Repten, Post Tarnowitz (Polish Upper Silesia), 25 March 1933. It emerges from the letter that Praschma had been dealing with the Mixed Commission in Poland for two days and therefore had 'no direct news of the most recent events'. His information must therefore have been older, BA Koblenz R 53/76. This rules out Volk's assumption that Papen could have planned his journey to Rome after the bishops' declaration of 18 March (*Reichskonkordat*, 93).

37. L.Volk, *Reichskonkordat*, 60f., esp. n.5.

38. Official copy of 18 March 1933. Text in *Der Prozess gegen die Hauptkriegsverbrecher vor dem Internationalen Militärgerichtshof Nürnberg (IMT)*, Vol.31, Nuremberg 1948, 402-9, here 404.

39. Ibid., 406.

40. *Vom Kaiserhof zum Reichskanzlei*, Berlin 1934, 284.

41. Quoted from L.Volk, *Reichskonkordat*, 80f. n.114. There is a similar comment from April 1933 in this passage.

42. F.G.von Tschirschky, *Erinnerungen eines Hochverräters*, Stuttgart 1972, 99f.

43. The author of this account of 22 April 1933 was Karl Bachem. Text in R.Morsey, *Ende der Zentrumspartei*, 434f. For the authenticity of the scene see ibid., 357 n.32. Given the time of the conversation the negotiations mentioned cannot have been the official conversations of Hitler with the Centre Party, which only began on 2 March.

44. Kapler to Hindenburg, who was at Eisenach at the time, 23 March 1933, AEKD Berlin B 3/240.

45. See below 281f.

46. Meissner to Kapler, 25 March 1933. Date of receipt at the Kirchenbundesamt stamped as 27 March 1933. For the record of 5 July 1933 cf. AEKD Berlin B 3/240.

47. AEKD Berlin C 3/207. Text also in G.Schäfer, *Dokumentation* 2, 32-37, here 34.

48. Protocol of the session of 11 April 1933, AEKU Berlin Gen.III 17, Vol.II, 226. For the date of the discussion see below, 283f.

49. Manuscript notes on the session of 25 April 1933 by W.von Pechmann, LKA Nürnberg 101/XXIII, no.34. Pechmann's notes on Kapler's report on this point run: 'I. IV Frick... for Frick fin[ally] parity of the R[eich] c[on]cordat dis[cussion] be[tween] the R[eich] g[overnment] a[nd] the Cath[olic] rep[resentatives] ov[er] the [Reichsc]oncordat situation of Cath[olic] ch[urch] sup[ports] enabl[ing act]. Kap[ler] inf[orms] by tele-phone... K[apler] m[anu]s[cript] to R[eich] P[resident] K[irchenbund] a[nd] R[eich] Concordat]? Letter s[ent on] to Frick. Dis[cussions] ab[out] R[eich] concordat held[...] von Papen (Reich concordat) seems to have ret[reated], can very soon reappear.'

50. A.Kupper, *Staatliche Akten*, 496.

51. Thus L.Volk, *Reichskonkordat*, 87. The assertion by J.Becker, that Kaas's journey related to the clarification of a German-Belgian dispute and had already been planned by the Foreign Office in January 1933 is refuted by the wording of the letter and also shows little awareness of the situation. J.Becker, *Ende der Zentrumspartei*, 346. By contrast see L.Volk, 86f.

52. K.Repgen, 'Ende der Zentrumspartei', 92f., differs.

53. Letter of 11 November 1958 to R.Morsey, L.Volk, *Reichskonkordat*, 84 n.132.

54. R.Leiber, 'Pius XII', *Stimmen der Zeit* 16, 1958/59, 95. Now also in D.Albrecht, *Katholische Kirche*, 103-27.

55. Thus according to the report of a former deputy in R.Morsey, 'Ende des Zentrums-partei', 364.

56. The ongoing significance of the Kulturkampf for the attitude of Catholicism in this period has rightly been stressed by W.Bussmann, *Der Deutsche Katholizismus*, 181ff.

57. The prototol of the session of 29 March is in R.Morsey, *Protokolle*, 630-2. The morning session of the group began at 11.15 and was postponed until after the government statement had been made without a decision being taken. The plenary session in the Kroll Opera opened at 14.05. The afternoon session with the decisive vote lasted from 15.12 to 16.00. For the details see R.Morsey, 'Ende der Zentrumspartei', 361-6. For the attitude of the Bavarian People's Party, which steered a resolute course towards assimilation, see now K.Schönhoven, 'Zwischen Anpassung und Ausschaltung. Die Bayerische Volks-partei in der Endphase der Weimarer Republik 1932/33', *Historische Zeitschrift* 225, 1977, 372f.

58. R.Morsey, 'Ende der Zentrumspartei', 364.

59. Text, ibid., 429-31.

60. L.Volk, *Reichskonkordat*, 84.

61. Text, *Archiv für katholisches Kirchenrecht* 100, 1920, 128. Cf also G.Schreiber, 'Deutsche Kirchenpolitik nach dem ersten Weltkrieg', *Historisches Jahrbuch der Görres-gesellschaft* 70, 1951, 309f., and L.Siegele Wenschkewitz, *Nationalsozialismus und Kirche*, 10f. Morsey's conjecture ('Zentrumspartei', 363 n.59) that the passage came into the government declaration from a memorandum of Bergen's is refuted by the fact that this memorandum spoke only of a 'maintaining' and not of the decisive 'cultivating'.

62. B.Schneider (ed.), *Die Briefe Pius' XII an die deutschen Bischöfe 1939-1944*, Mainz 1966, 308.

63. A.Kupper, *Staatliche Akten*, 496.

64. On 2 April Orsenigo announced to Pacelli that Papen would be coming in Holy Week, L.Volk, *Kirchliche Akten*, 79. But even earlier, on 30 March, the *Tägliche*

Rundschau, which was admirably informed on church affairs, had already said that 'the way was already being taken' towards a concordat, L.Volk, *Reichskonkordat*, 80 n.113.

65. Cf. L.Volk, *Der bayerische Episkopat*, 53-5.

66. Text, Kreschmar and Nicolaisen, *Dokumente* I, 22f.

67. Letter of 24 March 1933, L.Volk, *Reichskonkordat*, 72.

68. Gröber to Cardinal Bertram, 22 March 1933, B.Stasiewski, *Akten* I, 14.

69. Faulhaber to the Bavarian episcopate, 24 March 1933, ibid, 17.

70. L.Volk, *Reichskonkordat*, 73.

71. *Germania* of 24 March and *Kölnische Volkszeitung* of 29 March, R. Morsey, 'Ende der Zentrumspartei', 362 n.60.

72. No. 36, 1933. Quoted from *Das Evangelische Deutschland* 10, 1933, 110f. (no.14 of 32 April 1933).

73. B.Stasiewski, *Akten* I, 125f.

74. Ibid., 29,

75. L.Volk, *Reichskonkordat*, 76f.

76. L.Volk, 'Zur Kundgebung des deutschen Episkopats vom 28 März 1933', *Stimmen der Zeit* 173, 1963/64, 431-56, here 441. Against L.Volk, *Reichskonkordat*, 77.

77. L.Volk, 'Kundgebung', 443.

78. Text in B.Stasiewski, *Akten* I, 3-32.

79. Ibid., 31 n.1.

80. Ibid., 44.

81. L.Volk, *Faulhaber-Akten* I, 710.

82. Ibid., 714f.

83. L.Volk, 'Kundgebung', 454. Text of the pastoral instruction 'On Criticism of the Attitude of the Episcopate', of 30 May 1933 in B.Stasiewski, *Akten* I, 214.

84. L.Volk, *Faulhaber-Akten*, 714. similarly to Bishop Gföllner on 3 April 1933. Stasiewski, *Akten* I, 48f. L.Volk, *Der bayerische Episkopat*, 73, differs.

85. Thus R.Leiber SJ, 'Reichskonkordat und Ende der Zentrumspartei', *Stimmen der Zeit* 167, 1970-71, 217.

86. *Allgemeine Evangelisch-Lutherische Kirchenzeitung* 66, 1933, 325f.

3. The Jewish Question (March-April)

1. W.Sauer (in Bracher, Sauer and Schulz, *Die nationalistisch-sozialistische Machtergreifung*, 871), reckons that up to autumn 1933 there were about 500-600 dead and about 100,000 imprisoned for a shorter or longer time. In Prussia alone the number of those taken into custody by the police in the months of March and April was 'at least 25,000' without the 'wild' arrests of the SA, M.Broszat, 'Nationalsozialistische Konzentrationslager 1933-1945', in *Anatomie des SS-Staates* II, Olten and Freiburg 1965, 20.

2. T.Vogelgesang, 'Zu den Anfängen der Verfolgung im Dritten Reich (Februar-April 1933)', in *Gutachten des Instituts für Zeitgeschichte* II, Stuttgart 1966, 1f.

3. T.Vogelgesang, ibid, 12.

4. R.Diels, *Lucifer ante portas... es spricht der erste Chef der Gestapo...*, Stuttgart 1950, 217ff. This book is still the only detailed account of internal happenings at this time. Despite its clearly recognizable apologetic tendency, in essentials seems to give the broad outlines accurately. New studies of this theme are, however, urgently needed.

5. An impression of this gruesome scene is given in: the account by Diels, ibid., 251-67, etc.; the 'Brown book on the Reichstag Burning and the Hitler Terror (July 1933)', which was compiled abroad, facsimile reprint, *Das Braunbuch über Reichstagbrand und Hitler Terror*, Frankfurt 1973; the statements by the former American Consul in Berlin, Raymond H.Geist, for the Nuremberg Trial (IMT, Vol.XXVII, esp.241-7) and above all the description by F.Boll, 'Eine Nacht im Gestapokeller (30. März 1933)', in

G.Schoenberner (ed.), *Wir haben es gesehen, Augenzeugenberichte über Terror und Judenverfolgung im Dritten Reich*, Hamburg 1962, 23-34.

6. W.Sauer, 873. Frick, Himmler etc. publicly announced the setting up of such camps in March (W.Sauer, ibid.). Newspapers and even illustrated magazines reported on them.

7. W.Maser, *Hitlers Briefe und Notizen*, Düsseldorf and Vienna 1973, 225. Cf also above, 80.

8. The action took place on 11 March. Quoted from *Das Schwarzbuch. Tatsachen und Dokumente. Die Lage der Juden in Deutschland 1933*, published by the Comité des Délégations Juives, Paris 1934, 94. Precisely because of its restrained account, this Black Book is especially impressive. There is an eye-witness report, which describes the terrors of this day from the perspective of one of those involved, in L.Foerder, 'SA-Terror in Breslau', in G.Schoenberner, *Wir haben es gesehen*, 18-22.

9. See L.Foerder, 21: 'Had this procedure been followed in all the many courts in which equally unworthy scenes had taken place, who knows what course the "national uprising" would then have taken...'

10. Quoted from the *Schwarzbuch*, 96.

11. Ibid. 101.

12. Ibid., 105.

13. Ibid., 140ff.

14. J.Klepper, *Unter dem Schatten Deiner Flügel. Aus den Tagebüchern der Jahre 1932-1942*, Stuttgart 1956, 41-6.

15. See above, 40, 50.

16. *Neue Wege, Blätter für religiöse Arbeit*, 1933, 174f. Quoted from M.U.Kaiser, *Deutscher Kirchenkampf und Schweizer Öffentlichkeit in den Jahren 1933 und 1934*, Zurich 1972, 210f.

17. See above, n.6.

18. At the beginning of January 1934 Diels presented to Hitler a memorandum on the atrocities of the SA, R.Diels, *Lucifer ante portas*, 384.

19. For H. von Dohnanyi cf. E.Bethge, *Dietrich Bonhoeffer*, London 1977, 318, 358, 368, etc.

20. F.G.von Tschirschky, *Erinnerungen*, 103.

21. Letter from E.Rotten to F.Siegmund-Schulze, 13 March 1933, ÖA Soest, H.II 1,1. On F.Siegmund-Schulze cf. H.Maas in *Ökumenische Profile*, I, 1961, 253-62.

22. A. Boyens, *Kirchenkampf und Ökumene*, 1, 45.

23. The Thomas theory runs: 'If people define situations as real, then their consequences are real', R.K.Merton, 'Die Eigendynamik gesellschaftlicher Voraussagen', in E.Topitsch (ed.), *Logik der Sozialwissenschaften*, Cologne and Berlin [7]1971, 144f.

24. See above, 75ff.

25. *Das Schwarzbuch*, 22.

26. For this cf. for the Protestant church the detailed account above, Part 1, ch.7. For the Catholic Church see R.Lill, 'Die deutschen Katholiken und die Juden in der Zeit von 1850 bis zur Machtübernahme Hitlers', in K.H.Rengstorf and S. von Kortzfleisch, *Kirche und Synagoge. Handbuch zur Geschichte von Christen und Juden* II, Stuttgart 1970, 394-412.

27. Cf. e.g. A.Hitler, *Mein Kampf*, 529, 536-51, 567, etc.

28. 'Staatsgewalt und Glaubensfreiheit', *Tägliches Rundschau* no.62, 14 March 1933.

29. L.Colk, *Faulhaber-Akten* I, 714.

30. For this ecumenical organization cf. above 169.

31. The French text is in A.Boyens, *Kirchenkampf und Ökumene*, 1, 291-5.

32. Cf. H.A.Jacobsen, *Nationalsozialistische Aussenpolitik 1933-1937*, Frankfurt and Berlin 1968, 392f.

33. *Vossische Zeitung* 147, 28 March 1933.
34. A.Boyens, *Kirchenkampf und Ökumene*, 1, 38.
35. *Frankfurter Zeitung*, 23 March 1933. 'The Jewish Question – America's Interest'.
36. A.Boyens, *Kirchenkampf und Ökumene*, 1, 290 and 440.
37. Ibid., 41.
38. AEKD Berlin, C I 22, Vol.1 = D 1/29.
39. Telegram of 24 March 1933, ibid.
40. Manuscript draft by Richter of 25 March; Schreiber's memorandum of 17 March, ibid.
41. 'Sonntagsspiegel', in *Der Tag*, no.73 of 26 March 1933.
42. Manuscript draft by Kapler with date stamp of 27 March, AEKD Berlin, C I 22 Vol.I = D 1/29. Text also in A.Boyens, *Kirchenkampf und Ökumene*, 1, 39.
43. A.Boyens, ibid.
44. Text, *Das Evangelische Deutschland* 10, 1933, 126.
45. Notes of 28 March, date stamp 29 March, AEKD Berlin, C I 22l, Vol.I = D1/29.
46. *Das Evangelische Deutschland* 10, 1933, 126.
47. Thus e.g. through John Mott, the President of the Council of World Mission, ibid.
48. 'Reassurance in New York', *Vossische Zeitung* 148, of 28 March 1933.
49. BA Koblenz R 43 II/472.
50. J.Goebbels, *Vom Kaiserhof zur Reichskanzlei. Eine historische Darstellung in Tagebuchblättern (Vom 1 Januar 1932 bis zum 1.Mai 1933)* [1934], Munich 1943, 288. According to this the boycott was clearly on Hitler's orders. There is no evidence for H.A.Jacobsen's view (*Nationalistisch-sozialistische Aussenpolitik*, 393) that the initiative came from Goebbels.
51. According to Goebbels' account, ibid., 288, he himself will have composed the appeal. But the style and layout of the whole clearly point to Hitler, even if he did not sign it himself, but only the 'Party leadership' signed. Text in M.Domarus, *Hitler*, I, 248-51.
52. See above, 95. For the further composition of this central committee cf. K.D.Bracher in Bracher, Sauer and Schultz, 278 n.86.
53. E.g. in the Stuttgart *NS Kurier* of 1 April 1933. Text in P.Sauer, *Dokumente über die Verfolgung der jüdischen Bürger in Baden-Württemberg durch das nationalistisch-sozialistische Regime 1933-1945* I, Stuttgart 1966, 5f.
54. Ibid., 8. Facsimile of the title page of the *Führer* of 1 April with the headline 'All-Judah wants the Fight' and the text of the appeal, ibid., II. The slogans for the most part derive from instructions by the central committee, cf. *Schwarzbuch*, 30.
55. J.Goebbels, *Revolution der Deutschen. 14 Jahre Nationalsozialismus. Goebbels-reden mit einleitenden Zeitbilder*, ed. H.Schlecht, Oldenburg 1933, 155-61. The speech was given before officials in the evening of 31 March in the Berlin Tennis Halls and broadcast over all German radio stations, J.Goebbels, *Vom Kaiserhof zur Reichskanzlei*, 290.
56. There is a good survey of the course of the boycott and its consequences, on the basis of press cuttings from all over Germany, in the *Schwarzbuch*, 292-314. There are press reports from Stuttgart and other cities of Württemberg in P.Sauer, *Dokumente* I, 9-13. Examples from Cologne in *Widerstand und Verfolgung in Köln 1933-1945*, published by the Historischer Archiv der Stadt Köln, Cologne 1974, 150-2. There is an account for the Rhineland in *Monumenta Judaica. 2,000 Jahre Geschichte und Kultlur der Juden am Rhein*, ed. K.Schilling, Cologne ²1964, 609-12.
57. *Schwarzbuch*, 312f.
58. Thus the report of the British ambassador in Berlin, in K.D.Bracher, Bracher, Sauer and Schulz, 279 n.92.

59. *Schwarzbuch*, 313.

60. E. Bethge, *Bonhoeffer*, 201.

61. *Schwarzbuch*, 303.

62. Cf. Pechmann's short 'theological-political creed' in F.Kanzenbach, *Widerstand und Solidarität der Christen in Deutschland 1931-1945. Eine Dokumentation zum Kirchenkampf aus den Papieren des D.W.Freiherrn von Pechmann*, 108f.

63. Note by H[osemann], 30 March 1933 and copy of the telegram in AEKD Berlin C3/207. Hosemann's comment on the attitude of the Reich Chancellor related to the press statement about the cabinet meeting of 29 March, M.Domarus, *Hitler* I, 251. It was impossible to establish which 'normative side' in Berlin sought to influence the churches.

64. F.W.Kantzenbach, *Widerstand und Solidarität*, VII.

65. Ibid., 37. Cf. also 39 (letter to Dr Pehrsson of 15 April); 42 (letter to Dr Pehrsson of 10 May); 47 (letter to Oberkonsistorialrat Hosemann of 7 June, etc.).

66. Note by H[osemann], 31 March 1933, AEKD Berlin C3/207.

67. Letter of 4 April 1933, ibid.

68. Letter of 18 April 1933 (copy), ibid.

69. Menn to Stoltenhoff, 1 April 1933, G.von Norden, *Kirche in der Krise*, 59f. Cf. also Stoltenhoff's answer, ibid., 60, Menn's retort of 8 April, ibid., 177 n.89. and Menn's letter to Dibelius of 18 April, ibid., 61f.

70. Letter to Dibelius of 18 April, ibid., 61. Cf. also Menn's letter to Pastor Harney of 11 April, ibid., 179.

71. Circular letter from the Cologne superintendent Georg Klingenburg to the Cologne pastors, 5 April 1933, *Widerstand und Verfolgung in Köln*, 152 no.151. A monograph on this question which collected and evaluated all the available material is urgently needed.

72. R.Diels, *Lucifer ante portas*, 251.

73. A detailed account of the messages from Nuelsen and Dibelius appeared in the *Reichsanzeiger* no. 8 of 6 September 1933, English text in J.S.Conway, *The Nazi Persecution of the Churches 1933-1945*, London 1968, 342-4.

74. AEKD Berlin, C3/207.

75. Protocol of the negotiations in AEKU Berlin, Gen.III 17, Vol.3.

76. B.Stasiewski, *Akten* I, 42f. n.3.

77. Ibid., and L.Volk, *Der bayerische Episkopat*, 77.

78. L.Volk, *Faulhaber-Akten* I, 701. Individual Catholic papers do, however, seem to have printed similar articles; e.g. the *Rhein-Mainische Volkszeitung* no.80 of 4 April 1933 printed an article by Pastor Eckert. Text in H.Müller, *Katholische Kirche und Nationalsozialismus*, 87-89.

79. Ibid., letter of 8 April 1933, 705. Cf. also the answer from Wurm of 8 April, as open as it is decisive, according to which he is ready to risk even 'protective custody' for the confession 'of so fundamental a Catholic truth', ibid., 706f.

80. Thus in a letter to Pacelli of 10 April 1944, L.Volk, *Der bayerische Episkopat*, 78. Similarly in the letter to the Bavarian episcopate of 31 March 1933, L.Volk, *Faulhaber-Akten* I, 684.

81. P.Franziskus Stratmann OP to Faulhaber on 10 April 1933, L.Volk, *Faulhaber-Akten* I, 711.

82. Ibid.

83. *RGBl* I, 1933, 175. The full text is also in B.Blau, *Das Ausnahmerecht für die Juden in Deutschland 1933-1945*, Düsseldorf ³1965, 13-18. The regulations for exceptions for those who fought at the front went back to a desire of Hindenburg's, U.D.Adam, *Judenpolitik im Dritten Reich*, Düsseldorf 1972, 62f.

84. H.Seel, 'Die Erneuerung des Berufsbeamtentums', in *Das Recht der nationalen Revolution*, Vol.4, Berlin 1933, 4. For Seel's role cf. U.D.Adam, *Judenpolitik*, 62 n.191.

85. W.Niemöller (ed.), *Texte zur Geschichte des Pfarrernotbundes*, Berlin 1958, 26.
86. R.Morsey, 'Ende der Zentrumspartei', 372-7.
87. B.Stasiewski, *Akten* I, 49f.
88. Ibid., 51.
89. Ibid., 59f.
90. Buchberger's draft of 11 April 1933, ibid., 54-8; advice of 20 April, ibid., 68f.; the final version of 5 May, ibid., 126-32. For ths see also L.Volk, *Der bayerische Episkopat*, 82-4.
91. R.Morsey, 'Ende der Zentrumspartei', 376 n.50.
92. Pechmann to Kapler, 12 April 1933, F.W.Kantzenbach, *Widerstand und Solidarität*, 37.
93. Letter to Kapler, 18 March 1933, AEKD Berlin C3/207.
94. Letter from Bishop Kumpfmüller to Cardinal Faulhaber of 24 April and Faulhaber's answer of 26 April, L.Volk, *Faulhaber-Akten* I, 716f.
95. For the foreign enquiries in April see A.Boyens, *Kirchenkampf und Ökumene*, Vol.I, 43f.
96. Protocol of the session of 11 April 1933 in AEKU Berlin, Gen III 17, Vol.3, 8.
97. The German Evangelischer Kirchenausschuss had the same paper at its session of 25/26 April in Berlin. It is quoted here (AEKD Berlin A 2.28). Künneth published the paper in an extended version under the title 'The Jewish Problem and the Churches' in summer 1933 in the collected volume, W.Künneth and H.Schreiner, *Die Nation vor Gott*, Berlin (1933) [3]1934, 115-37.
98. In *Der Tag*, no.73 of 26 March 1933.
99. The English text is available in Dietrich Bonhoeffer, *No Rusty Swords*, London and New York [2]1970, 217-25. For the preliminary history cf. E.Bethge, *Bonhoeffer*, 206ff. However, Bethge's criticism of 'some very conservative emphases' in the article (ibid., 208) overlooks the tension which makes it so topical today.
100. This is the reading of the original manuscript, according to Eberhard Bethge, as opposed to that in the printed text.
101. According to the protocol of the session in AEKD Berlin, A 2/28. A basis was provided both by Künneth's list and by a Baden outline, which contained far more about the injustice done to the Germans than about church fellowship with persecuted Christians of Jewish descent. Cf. also J.R.C.Wright, *'Über den Parteien'*, 193f.
102. B.Stasiewski, *Akten* I, 87 (Rottenburg protocol); 104 (Freiburg protocol); 117ff. (Passau protocol).
103. Ibid., 91.
104. Ibid., 122.
105. Text of the list in H.Müller, *Katholische Kirche*, 102-2. Cf. also B.Stasiewski, *Akten* I, 100-3.
106. H.Müller, *Katholische Kirche*, 121.
107. F.W.Katzenbach, *Widerstand und Solidarität*, 90.

4. Protestant Church Reform (April)

1. For the efforts towards a Reich church in 1866 and 1870/71 cf. G.Besier, *Die preussische Kirchenpolitik 1866-72*, Protestant faculty dissertation, Tübingen 1976, 219, etc.
2. *Kirchliches Jahrbuch* 1932, 171.
3. Cf. above Part I, ch.12, 208.
4. There is a thorough treatment of this up to 1930 in G.Schulz, *Zwischen Demokratie und Diktatur. Verfassungspolitik und Reichsreform in der Weimarer Republik*, I, *Die Periode der Konsolidierung und der Revision des Bismarckschen Reichaufbaus 1919-1930*,

Berlin 1963. Volume 2 is still to come. For the particular problem of the north-west German area in this connection, cf. W.Kothe, 'Die Gedanken zur Neugliederung des Reiches 1918-1945 in ihrer Bedeutung zur Nordwestdeutschland', *Westfälische Forschungen* VI, Münster and Cologne 1953.

5. E.Klügel, *Hannoversche Landeskirche*, 20f.

6. P.Fleisch, 'Das Werden der Vereinigten Evangelisch-Lutherischen Kirche Deutschlands und ihrer Verfassung', *Zeitschrift für evangelischen Kirchenrecht* 1, 1951, 22f.

7. *Kirchliches Jahrbuch* 1932, 127.

8. Ibid., 132.

9. Proceedings of the German Evangelischer Kirchenausschuss on 24/25 November 1932 in Berlin, appendix 2: report of the legal committee, 9, AEKD Berlin 12/28. Cf.also J.R.C.Wright, *'Über den Parteien'*, 178.

10. This connection is also emphatically stressed by Kapler's representative, Friedrich Seetzen, the president of the Saxon church authorities, *Lebenserinnerungen*, 1939. 16. (Unpublished manuscript, EAKiZ Munich).

11. See above, Chapter 2, 246f.

12. Kapler to Hindenburg, who was at Eisenach, 23 March 1933, AEKD Berlin B3/240. Kapler occasionally went to the Reich President over questions of particular Protestant interest; thus also in November 1932, where he intervened for the nomination of a Protestant Minister of the Interior, cf. Wright, *'Über den Parteien'*, 180.

13. Meissner to Kapler, 25 March 1933, stamped as received 27 March 1933, ibid.

14. Confidential circular letter from Kapler to the supreme church authorities, dated 1 April 1933, AEKD Berlin C3/207. Text also in G.Schäfer, *Dokumentation* 2, 32-7.

15. Opinion by G.A.Walz. Received 10 February 1933, AEKD Berlin A 2/484. Quoted from H.Baier, *Um Reichsbischof und Verfassung der Deutschen Evangelischen Kirche 1933*, 71f. (unpublished MS, LKA Nürnberg).

16. See n.14.

17. Text of the theses of 29 March 1933 in *Zeitschrift für evangelische Kirchenrecht* I, 1951, 404f.

18. P.Fleisch, *Erlebte Kirchengeschichte. Erfahrungen in und mit der Hannoverschen Landeskirche*, Hanover 1952, 155.

19. Bracher, Sauer and Schulz, *Machtergreifung*, 464f.

20. The date of this conversation is confirmed by Kapler's own statement to the Kirchenausschuss on 26 April 1933, protocol of the German Evangelischer Kirchenausschuss on 25/26 April in Berlin, AEKD Berlin A2/28, 14: 'Thus in my conversation with Reich Minister Frick, which took place on 1 April, the day of the boycott on the Jews.' This refutes the view of almost all previous research that the plans for a Reich Church were first set in motion by the German Christians.

21. AEKU Berlin, Gen.III 17, Vol.3, 225.

22. Confidential report on a conversation with representatives of the supreme church authorities on the revolution which the Kirchenbund faced as a result of the political situation; the conversation took place on Friday, 7 April 1933 at 10 a.m. in the Kirchenbundesamt, Berlin, AEKD Berlin A2/48. Cf. also the letter from the Kirchenbundesamt relating to this and addressed to those who were involved, dated 12 April 1933, in G.Schäfer, *Dokumentation* 2, 38.

23. Marahrens to Professor Johannes Meyer, 14 April 1933, LKA Hannover, Akte Reichskirche 1933.

24. For the origin and development of the German Christians up to the church elections in November 1932, cf. Part I, Chapter 12, 189ff.

25. LKA Hamburg, re German Christians. From what follows see also H.Wilhelmi,

Die Hamburger Kirche in der nationalsozialistichen Zeit 1933-1945, Göttingen 1968, 23f., 63-6.

26. LKA Hamburg, ibid., no.206.

27. Ibid. It was a typical and deliberate misunderstanding of Hossenfelder's position that Aselmann addressed this letter to 'Reich organization leader Pastor Hossenfelder' which indicated that he assumed that Hossenfelder was at the head of the Party hierarchy. Tügel (see below n.30) also took his commissioning to be a 'Party order', H.Wilhelmi, *Hamburger Kirche*, 66.

28. Aselmann to Hossenfelder, 8 December 1932, ibid.

29. Rössing to Aselmann, 16 Deceber 1932, ibid., Akte no.51.

30. Gauleitung Hamburg to Aselmann, 6 January 1933, ibid., Akte, no.212; Aselmann to Hossenfelder, 13 January 1933, ibid., Akte no.206. For Tügel, cf.F.Tügel, *Mein Weg 1888-1946. Erinnerungen eines Hamburger Bischofs*, Hamburg 1972.

31. Circular letter no. 15, 30 January 1933, ibid., Akte no.204/1.

32. Ibid., Akte No.51. C.Kinder, *Neue Beiträge zur Geschichte der evangelischen Kirche in Schleswig-Holstein und im Reich 1924-1945*, Flensburg 1966, 38, 40f., asserts that he and Christiansen only became members of the German Christians after the church elections in July. According to the Hamburg Akte this is just not true.

33. Tügel to the Hamburg Kirchenrat, 22 March 1933, F.Tügel, *Mein Weg*, 424f.

34. Rachner to Aselmann, 19 December, LKA Hamburg, Akte, no.206.

35. Meyer to Aselmann, 25 March 1933, ibid., Akte no.2.

36. AEKD Berlin C2/1.

37. *Junge Kirche* I, 1933, 288, and AEKD Berlin A 4/248.

38. There is a typical programme for June in J.Gauger, *Chronik* I, 85.

39. *Evangelium im Dritten Reich* 2, no.6, of 5 February 1933, announcements of meetings for Greater Berlin.

40. *Evangelium im Dritten Reich* 2, 1944, 54. See also above, 222f.

41. *Der Angriff*, No.69 of 22 March 1933.

42. Eckert MdL to Commissioner z.b.V. Daluege, BA Koblenz, Schumacher collection.

43. Dr.Krummacher to Dr Ley, 6 February 1933, DC Berlin OPG Akte Hossenfelder.

44. Hossenfelder to Dr Ley, 10 February 1933, ibid.

45. Circular letter no.14, 30 January 1933, LKA Hamburg, re German Christians, Akte, No. 240/1. The planned programme is in *Evangelium im Dritten Reich* 2, 1933, 6, of 5 February 1933, 48.

46. Order of 8 February 1933, ibid., no.7 of 12 February 1933, 56.

47. J.Gauger, *Chronik* I, 69. This figure also appears in the important memoirs of the then Land Bishop of Nassau, August Kortheuer, *Das Ende der Evangelischen Landeskirche in Nassau*, Wiesbaden 1943. Manuscript in AEKHN Darmstadt 0201, 76.

48. See above, Part I, Ch.12, 207ff.

49. *Evangelium im Dritten Reich* 2, 1933, no.5, of 29 January 1933.

50. See above Part 2, Ch.1, 231ff.

51. *Märkischer Adler* no.1, of 2 April 1933. Cutting in AEKU Berlin, Gen.II, 42, Vol.1, pp.60f.

52. Copy in AEKU Berlin, ibid., p.16. Text also in Kretschmar and Nicolaisen, *Dokumente* I, 29f.

53. Letter of Kapler as President of the Oberkirchenrat, 31 March, AEHN Darmstadt 1/92. Letter of Kapler as President of the Kirchenausschuss, 3 April 1933, AEKD Berlin C2/1.

54. Report of the Telegraphic Union, AEKU Berlin (n.51), 19f.

55. Report from the *Tägliche Rundschau*, 5 April 1933. Partial extract also in J.Gauger, *Chronik* I, 71.

56. Report of the Telegraphic Union, AEKU Berlin (n.51), 120.

57. Ibid., 123.

58. J.Gauger, *Chronik* I, 73.

59. Article VII of the Augsburg Confession, quoted from J.H.Leith, *Creeds of the Churches*, Atlanta ³1982, 70.

60. Outline and text in AEKU Berlin (n.51), 3-35.

61. BA Koblenz, R 43 II/161. Cf. also Kretschmar and Nicolaisen, *Dokumente* I, 39 n.9.

62. Letter from Kapler to Veit, Seetzen, Burghart, Marahrens and Wurm, 12 April 1933, AEKD Berlin C3/207.

63. For the development and significance of the question of the confession in German Protestantism, see above Part I, Ch.2.

64. Zoellner presented this in a memorandum of 23 April 1933 to the Prussian Oberkirchenrat, in which he gave detailed reasons for, and a defence of, his appeal, AEKU Berlin, Gen.II, 42, Vol.1, 207ff. This is contained in a more developed form as structural principles for the Reich Church in Zoellner's 'Requirements for Today' of June 1933, in W.Zoellner, *Die Kirche der Geschichte und die Kirche des Glaubens. Beiträge zum Neubau der Kirche*, Berlin 1933, 191, theses 8-10.

65. Zoellner to Kapler, 15 April 1933, AEKD Berlin 1933, 140f.

66. W.Zoellner, *Kirche der Geschichte*, 43.

67. Text of the appeal in K.D.Schmidt, *Bekenntnisse* 1933, 140f.

68. F.W.Kantzenbach, 'Generalsuperintendent D.Zoellner und der Herausgeber der *Allgemeinen Evangelisch-lutherischen Kirchenzeitung*', in *Jahrbuch des Vereins für Westfälische Kirchengeschichte* 64, 1971, 143.

69. 'I resolved not to make any kind of difficulties for the church government, but to put the church government in a position to disown me if the whole matter turned out differently from what I hoped; but if not to take whatever success ensued from it', Zoellner to Kapler on 15 April 1933, AEKD Berlin, C2/1.

70. G.Koch, *Erwägungen zum Bau des Reichskirche*, manuscript annotation 'written April 1933'. Paul Althaus bequest, fascicule 'Kirchenkampf'. Cf. also H.-J.Reese, *Bekenntnis und Bekennen. Vom 19.Jahrhundert zum Kirchenkampf der nationalsozialistischen Zeit*, Göttingen 1974, 164ff., but he does not want to 'overestimate' the significance of these radical voices.

71. W.Zoellner, *Denkschrift* (n.64), 209.

72. Ibid., 211.

73. For the origin and significance of the Altona confession, cf. Part 1, Ch.9, 184ff.

74. 'Die Reichskirche', *Niederdeutsche Kirchenzeitung* 3, 1933, of 15 April 1933, 139-42. Similarly also in the independent work by H.Asmussen, *Reichskirche*, Hamburg 1933, 13ff.

75. Asmussen to Kapler, 23 April 1933, AEKD Berlin C2/1.

76. W.Zoellner, *Denkschrift* (n.64), 212.

77. W.Zoellner, *Die Kirche der Geschichte*, 191, thesis 11.

78. Zoellner to Kapler, 15 April 1933, AEKD Berlin C2/1.

79. *Reformierte Kirchenzeitung* 83, 1933, No.17 of 23 April 1933, 125.

80. Ibid.

81. *Reformierte Kirchenzeitung* 83, 1933, No.18 of 30 April 1933, 132f.

82. K. Dienst, *Dokumentation*, Vol.1, 37.

83. Protocol of the transactions of the fiftieth session of the Church Senate on 21 April 1933, AEKU Berlin.

84. Special edition of the *Kirchliche Amtsblatt* of the church province of Brandenburg, 25 April 1933. Text also in W.Niemöller, *Die Evangelische Kirche*, 78f.

85. Cf. Strasser's letter to the Hamburg Gauleiter Hinrich Lohse of 24 December 1931 in A.Tyrell, *Führer befiehl...*, 340. For Darré's ideas see especially R.Walther Darré, *Das Bauerntum als Lebensquell der Nordischen Rasse*, Munich 1929 (⁴1934).

86.For the preliminary history, cf. Bohm's own account from the year 1956 in K.D.Schmidt, 'Eine folgenreich Episode. Der Staatskommissar für die Kirche in Mecklenburg', *Evangelische Theologie* 22, 1962, 379-92.

87. Cf. R.Walther Darré, *Neuadel aus Blut und Boden*, Munich 1930, 27ff.

88.So W.Bohm in K.D.Schmidt, 'Episode', 387.

89. J.Gauger, *Chronik* I, 70.

90. Promemoria of the President of the Mecklenburg Oberkirchenrat, Dr Lemcke, of 22 April, with manuscript annotation by Land Bishop Rendtorff to Kapler, 24 April, 'as material for the discussion with the Reich Chancellor', AEKD Berlin A 4/1. Rendtorff's report to the Kirchenausschuss of 25 April follows this note from the President word for word, but supplements it with the events of 24 April. Protocol of the session, ibid., A2/28. The account essentially follows these sources.

91. BA Koblenz R 43 II/161, Kretschmar and Nicolaisen, *Dokumente* I, 37f.

92. Ibid., 41 (Bohm's announcement of his resignation, 27 April 1933), and 38 n.5 (Granzow).

93. K.D.Schmidt, 'Episode', 388f.

94. Thus Rendtorff's report to the Kirchenausschuss, cf. n.90.

95. Text in Kretschmar and Nicolaisen, *Dokumente* I, 40.

96. AEKU Berlin, Gen. III 17, Vol.3, 226.

97. J.Gauger, *Chronik* I, 70.

98. See n.90.

99. Cf.E.Klügel, *Hannoversche Landeskirche*, 30f.; H.A.Hesse, 'Elberfeld', in G.Harder and W.Niemöller, *Die Stunde der Versuchung, Gemeinden im Kirchenkampf 1933-1945*, Munich 1963, 203.

100. J.Gauger, *Chronik* I, 74.

101. J.Kübel, *Erinnerungen. Mensch und Christ, Theologe, Pfarrer und Kirchenmann. Zum 100. Todestag*, privately published by his daughter, Dr Martha Frommer, Villingen-Schwenningen, 1973, 89f. The editor has kindly confirmed that the basis of the account which was already finished by 1947 was written notes which Kübel used to make during the sessions and usually worked over on his journey home. That is the only explanation of the sometimes word-for-word agreement with Pechmann's handwritten notes on the sessions (LKA Nürnberg 101/XXIII no.34). Research has so far taken no account of the content of this important conversation and has in some respects arrived at quite major errors of judgment on the basis of other reports. Thus e.g. H.Buchheim, *Glaubenskrise*, 94f.; Kretschmar and Nicolaisen, *Dokumente*, 39 n.9; and even J.R.C.Wright, *'Above Parties'*, 122f. Only in the revised German version of Wright's book, *'Über die Parteien'*, 203ff. are the sources evaluated.

102. For this cf. above, Ch.2, 250ff.

103. There is clear evidence for this decisive declaration by Hitler in both sources. It also corresponds with the notes made by Lammer, who was also present at the conversation, BA Koblenz R43/II 161. Text also in Kretschmar and Nikolaisen, *Dokumente* I, 39. Speculations based on the observations of Senior Pastor Reichardt of Thuringia are thus untenable. (ibid., n.9).

104. For the significance of this conversation see below, Ch.5, 306ff.

105. Protocol of the session of 25 April (see n.90), 8.

106. Ibid., 9.

107. Ibid., 10.

108. Ibid., appendix 1; the text of the resolution is also in G.Schäfer, *Dokumentation* 2, 40f.

109. Cf. above 277f.

110. Protocol of the extraordinary session of the German Evangelischer Kirchenbundesrat on 27 April 1933 in Berlin, A3/92.

111. Complete text in G.Schäfer, *Dokumentation*, 42.

5. The Protestant Church Asserts Itself (May)

1. Cf. above, Part 1, Ch.6.

2. B.Stasiewski, *Akten* I, 118.

3. For the content of the conversation with Kapler, cf. Kübel and Pechmann (above Ch.4 n.101). The most extensive report on the conversation with Berning is in the conference minutes by the Rottenburg representative in B.Stasiewski, *Akten*, 100-3. Another essentially similar note in the archive of the Foreign Office is reproduced in A.Kupper, *Staatliche Akten*, 28-30. The text of this note is also in Kretschmar and Nicolaisen, *Dokumente* I, 45-7.

4. B.Stasiewski, *Akten* I, 100.

5. J.Kübel, *Erinnerungen*, 90; Stasiewski, *Akten*, 102.

6. Kaas had sent the outline from Rome on 20 April. A.Kupper, *Staatliche Akten*, 18f. and 30ff. However, already on the evening of 19 April Papen could personally inform the Reich Chancellor in Munich 'at least summarily on the result of his journey to Rome', L.Volk, *Reichskonkordat*, 105.

7. B.Stasiewski, *Akten* I, 101.

8. Thus according to Pechmann's notes of 25 April 1933, LKA Nürnberg 101/XXIII no.34.

9. BA Koblenz, R 43 II/161. Text also in Kretschmar and Nicolaisen, *Dokumente* I, 39.

10. E.Fraenkel. *The Dual State*, New York 1941.

11. For the situation in the Reich Ministry of the Interior cf. the reminiscences of the former Oberregierungsrat in the Reich Ministry of the Interior, W.Conrad, *Der Kampf um die Kanzeln*, Berlin 1957, 13f. etc.; further L.Siegele-Wenschkewitz, *Nationalsozialismus und Kirchen*, 171ff.

12. J.Gauger, *Chronik* I, 74; the text in Kretschmar and Nicolaisen, *Dokumente* I, 43, is to be corrected to 'churches'.

13. J.Kübel, *Erinnerungen*, 90.

14. LKA Hannover, Marahrens bequest 4/II, manuscript notes by Marahrens on the negotiations of 4 May 1933, 11 a.m.

15. In spring and summer 1933 Müller was celebrated above all as the faithful and loyal fighter for Hitler's idea. Cf. e.g. W.Ulmenried, *Ludwig Müller, Die Reihe der Deutschen Führer*, Vol.7, Berlin 1933, and the typical commemorative article for his fiftieth birthday in *Evangelium im Dritten Reich* 2, 1933, no.26 of 25 June 1933, 236-8. In retrospect almost all his contemporaries come to a more or less devastating verdict on Ludwig Müller. Cf. e.g. W.Conrad, *Kampf um die Kanzel*, 23f.; O.Dibelius, *In the Service of the Lord*, 140f.; T.Wurm (who joined in electing him Reich Bishop), *Erinnerungen*, 90f.; also F.Tügel (who for a long time stuck up for him as a German Christian), *Mein Weg*, 249f. Bodelschwingh's verdict in W.Brandt, *Bodelschwingh*, 116, is rather more favourable; a former colleague, W.Birnbaum, was still almost enthusiastic about him in *Zeuge meiner Zeit*, 196ff. There is some dispute over the cause of Müller's death in Berlin in July 1945. Whereas according to the documents in the church chancellery he is said to have committed suicide, this was disputed by his family. Moreover Pastor Emeritus Dr G.Luntowski, who was still meeting Müller regularly in the summer of 1945, regarded suicide as quite out of

the question, as it would not have fitted in with Müller's 'childlike belief and unconditional trust in God' (letter from Luntowski to K.Themel of 22 March 1971, AKZG Tübingen).

16. This first conversation is regularly mentioned, e.g. in an interview between Müller and the Reich ambassador of 12 May 1933; in an account in the same newspaper dated 5 August 1933 ('The Leader of the German Christians'); in F.Wieneke's reminiscences, *Kirche und Partei*, 13, and in numerous speeches by Müller, thus e.g. on 28 February 1934 in the Sports Palace. Cf. *Der Reichsbischof. Die Deutschen Christen. Die Reden des Reichsbischofs und des Reichsleiters der Deutschen Christen, Dr Kinder am... 28.2.1934*, Berlin 1934, 7. For the date of the first meeting cf., also J.R.C.Wright, *'Above Parties'*, 123.

17. Müller's advocacy of the Party and his mediation are reliably attested by the statements of two staff officers of that time, Oberleutnant von Mellenthin and Major von Salmuth (IfZG München, ZS 105 and ZS133). Müller's mediation is mentioned in a letter from Hitler to Reichenau dated 4 December 1932. T.Vogelsang, 'Hitlers Briefe an Reichenau von 4.Dezember 1932', in *Vierteljahrshefte für Zeitgeschichte* 7, 1959, 429-37. Cf. also T.Vogelsang, *Reichswehr, Staat und NSDAP*, Munich 1962, 310, 375.

18. Cf. above, Part 1, 212.

19. Thus Kapler's account to the general superintendents on 11 April, AEKU Berlin, Gen III 17, Vol.3, 227. The date in Pechmann's notes is 25 April, LKA Nürnberg, 101/XXIII, no.34. Zoellner's presence is similarly noted by Pechmann.

20. See below, 313f. and n.36.

21. The fact and date of the conversation emerge from an interview with Müller published in the *Reichsbote* on 12 May 1933. The *Tägliche Rundschau* was already speaking of a call to Müller on 21 April, Kretschmar and Nicolaisen, *Dokumente* I, 42f. n.1.

22. Cf. W.Conrad, *Kampf um die Kanzeln*, 24.

23. J.Gauger, *Chronik*, 75f.

24. *Niederdeutsche Kirchenzeitung* 3, 1933, 162.

25. *Das Evangelische Deutschland* 10, 1933, of 30 April 1933, 157.

26. The dates and participants in the negotiations between 24 April and 28 June, the day on which the Kirchenbundesamt was occupied, are listed complete in a diary kept by Hosemann. There were all in all fifty-one sessions and discussions, AEKD Berlin, A 4/2.

27. LKA Hannover, Marahrens bequest Vol.4/II, notes on the negotiations of 4 May 1933, 11 a.m. and 4.30 p.m.

28. Text, G.Schäfer, *Dokumentation* 2, 44f.

29. This paragraph is in *Das Evangelische Deutschland* 10, 1933, of 14 May 1933, 177.

30. 'Wehrkreispfarrer Müller über Reichskirche und Deutsche Christen', *Der Reichsbote* of 12 May 1933. Cf. also 'Adolf Hitler und die evangelische Kirche. Eine Unterredung mit Wehrkreispfarrer Müller', *Kreuzzeitung* no.128 of 11 May 1933. Text also in *Niederdeutsche Kirchenzeitung* 3, 1933, 183f.

31. Text in *Niederdeutsche Kirchenzeitung* 3, 1933, 178f. and H.Linck, *Kirchenkampf in Ostpreussen*, 37.

32. H.Asmussen, *Neues Bekenntnis? ein Beitrag zum Neubau der Kirche*, Berlin 1933, 21.

33. *Der Reichsbote*, 12 May 1933 (n.30).

34. LKA Berlin-Brandenburg J IX 66 and Kapler's report of 25 April 1933, Pechmann notes, LKA Nürnberg 101/XXIII, no.34.

35. AEKU, Gen.II, 42. Vol.I, 175-81; J.Gauger, *Chronik* I, 75.

36. Circular letter No.16 of 15 April 1933, LKA Hamburg, Deutsche Christen, no.204.1.

37. Cf. also Hossenfelder's letter to the senior leadership of the Political Organization

on the same matter, dated 14 August [should be September] 1933, H.Baier, *Die Deutschen Christen*, 370f.

38. Kretschmar and Nicolaisen, *Dokumente*, I, 41f.

39. Ibid., 42 n.1.

40. Telegram of 19 April and letter along with other similar statements in AEKD Berlin, A 4/2.

41. Copy of the letter and press reports in LKA Oldenburg, Präsident der Bekennender Synode, Presse-Ausschnitte DC.

42. J.Gauger, *Chronik* I, 75.

43. *Evangelium im Dritten Reich* 2, 1933, of 14 May 1933, 175. For the origin and evaluation and the ensuing controversies, cf. F.Wieneke, *Kirche und Partei*, 46f.

44. Thus F.Wieneke, ibid.

45. J.Hossenfelder, *Eine Stellungnahme*, Potsdam 7 July 1945, LKA Berlin-Brandenburg.

46. J.Gauger, *Chronik* I, 77. Text of the report of the Reich leadership also in LKA Darmstadt, I/92.

47. *Kirchliches Jahrbuch* 1933 (only Part I, the church statistics, appeared), 88. According to this there were 893 Protestant theologians studying in Tübingen in the Summer semester of 1932, 840 in Berlin. The next largest faculties were Breslau with 595, Marburg and Leipzig with around 380. The smallest faculty was Kiel with 138 students.

48. The invitation also appears as a manuscript addition by the President of 10 April on a circular letter of 5 April which was originally meant to be an invitation to the Faculty Day in Erlangen in October, UA Tübingen 12/XIIIa.

49. Copy of the negotiations, ibid.

50. This emerges from a manuscript note by Kapler on Fezer's visit on 28 April 1933, AEKD Berlin A4/2.

51. For political theology and the Königsberg Kirchentag cf. above Part One, Chapter 7.

52. J.Gauger, *Chronik* I, 79.

53. Thus L.Müller as early as 11 May in his interview with the *Kreuzzeitung*, above n.30.

54. *Tägliche Rundschau*, no.11, dated 16 May 1933.

55. Fezer's report of 7 June 1933 in a gathering in Stuttgart organized by the Evangelischer Volksbund, text in G.Schäfer, *Dokumentation* 2, 118f.

56. *Evangelium in Dritten Reich* 2, 1933, no. 21 of 21 May 1933, 187f.

57. See above Part I, Ch.8.

58. For Künneth see above 139f. For Lilje see K.Kupisch, *Studenten entdecken die Bibel. Die Geschichte der Deutschen christlichen Studenten-Vereinigung*, Hamburg 1964, 136ff.

59. Thus e.g. E.Wolf, *Barmen*, 44. M.Pertiet, *Das Ringen um Wesen und Auftrag*, 81ff., differs.

60. One of the co-signatories to the appeal has emphatically pointed out these common features and has described the assertion 'that the Young Reformers Movement was from the beginning opposed to the German Christians' as 'a part of that lamentable formation of legends', W.Stählin, *Via Vitae*, 274.

61. Text in J.Gauger, *Chronik* I, 77f.; W.Niemöller, *Die Evangelische Kirche*, 82f.; K.D.Schmidt, *Bekenntnisse* 1933, 145f.

62. In view of the annihilation of Jews, the 'holocaust', this is also the conviction of a group of American theologians who are concerned with the 'Final Solution' and its significance for Christian theology and the church and Judaism. There is now a survey

in A. and R.Eckart, 'Christentum und Judentum: Die theologische und moralische Problematik der Vernichtung des europäischen Judentums', *Evangelische Theologie* 36, 1976, 402-26.

63. E.Heuss-Knapp, *Bürgerin zweier Welten. Ein Leben in Briefen und Aufzeichnungen*, Tübingen 1961, 228.

64. The details in *Allgemeine Evangelisch-Lutherische Kirchenzeitung* 60, 1933, 476, quoted in W.Niemöller, *Die evangelische Kirche*, 82, and P.Neumann, *Die Jungreformatorische Bewegung*, Göttingen 1971, 22 n.1, differ. The most extensive – and possibly later – list with 26 names is in P.Neumann.

65. W.Jeep to Marahrens, 16 May, LKA Hannover, Marahrens bequest, Vol.4/1.

66. For M.Niemöller see his autobiography, *Vom U-Boot zur Kanzel*, 1934 (85-87th thousand 1940!), and now the careful account by Jürgen Schmidt, *Martin Niemöller im Kirchenkampf*, Hamburg 1971.

67. This final version of the guidelines is in K.D.Schmidt, *Bekenntnisse 1933*, 143f.

68. G.Schäfer, *Dokumentation* 2, 120.

69. LKA Hannover, Marahrens bequest, Vol. 4/II, Protocol of 17 May 1933, 5 p.m.

70. Text in K.D.Schmidt, *Bekenntnisse 1933*, 153f.

71. Wording LKA Hannover, Marahrens bequest Vol.4/II, *modus procedendi* of 19 May 1933. Cf. also J.Gauger, *Chronik* I, 78.

72. E.Klügel, *Lutherische Landeskirche Hannovers*, 40 n.59.

73. For F.von Bodelschwingh, cf.W.Brandt, *Friedrich von Bodelschwingh, 1877-1946. Nachfolger und Gestalter*, Bethel 1967. For 1933 esp. 113ff.

74. HA Bethel, Akte Reichsbischof, letter of 16 May 1933, quoted from H.Baier, *Um Reichsbischof und Verfassung*, 213f.

75. H.Linck, *Kirchenkampf in Ostpreussen*, 38, thinks that the text of the telegram was manipulated by Vogelsang.

76. W.Künneth, "Denkschrift der Jungreformatorischen Bewegung über Reichsbischofsfrage' (published end of May 1933), *Junge Kirche* I, 1933, 3.

77. The text of the theses is in K.D.Schmidt, *Bekenntnisse 1933*, 146-8. For their origin cf. Schmidt, *Niemöller*, 58-60.

78. Bodelschwingh to Marahrens, 23 May 1933. LKA Hannover Marahrens bequest, Vol.4/1. Quoted from H.Baier, *Um Reichsbischof und Verfassung*, 215f.

79. The scene with the beer glass is described in J.Kübel, *Erinnerungen*, 101f. There is a wealth of accounts of the turbulent events of these days, e.g. Kapler's extended confidential memorandum of 25 May 1933 in AEKD Berlin, A4/24; an account by Oberkirchenrat Meinzolt of the discussions in the period between 2 and 25 May 1933 in LKA Nürnberg, Meiser 96; Pastor Hesse's reminiscences of the decisive events which led to the nomination of Bodelschwingh as Reich Bishop, end of May 1933, in LKA Hannover, Marahrens bequest, Vol. 4/II; report of the Kirchenbundesamt of 2 June 1933, reprinted in G.Schäfer, *Dokumentation* 1, 94-98; account by Professor Dr Emanuel Hirsch, Göttingen, in *Allgemeine Evangelisch-Lutherische Kirchenzeitung* 66, 1933, cols 511f.; F. von Bodelschwingh, *Dreissig Tage an einer Wegwende deutscher Kirchengeschichte*, manuscript taken down from recording on 29 October 1935, in HQ Bethel E 17 (partly reproduced in W.Brandt, *Bodelschwingh*, 119ff.). Meinzolt and Hesse are here quoted from H.Baier, *Um Reichsbischof und Verfassung*, 217f.

80. Jakubski to Krawielitzki, 24 May 1933, quoted from E.G.Rüppel, *Die Gemeinschaftsbewegung im Dritten Reich. Ein Beitrag zur Geschichte des Kirchenkampfes*, Göttingen 1969, 75 n.39. For Jakubski's doubtful role and the collapse of the community movement, cf. ibid, 64ff. and esp. 101ff.

81 Copy by Meinzolt, see n.79.

82. Memorandum by Kapler, see n.79, and G.Schäfer, *Dokumentation* 2, 121f.

Notes to pages 328–337

83. T.Wurm, *Erinnerungen*, 86.

84. F.von Bodelschwingh, *Dreissig Tage*, see n.79.

85. F.von Bodelschwingh, *Dreissig Tage*, see n.79. Cf. also J.Schmidt, *Niemôller*, 63f.

86. According to the report by Schöffel in H.Wilhelmi, *Die Hamburger Kirche*, 70f.

87. Notes on the meeting of the representatives of the Landeskirchen on 26 and 27 May 1933 in the Kirchenbundesamt (27 ms folios), AEKD Berlin A 4/24. Copy of the details of the negotiations AEKD Berlin A 13/93. The following pages quote from the more detailed 'Notes'. Cf. also J.Kübel, *Erinnerungen*, 92f. The outcome of the Lutheran preliminary discussion is based on the remarks of Meiser in the notes, 10.

88. Ibid. The results of the vote are recorded in a letter from the Kirchenbundesamt to the supreme church authorities dated 6 June 1933, Arch AA Bonn Kult A 1/2.

89. F.von Bodelschwingh, *Dreissig Tage*, see n.79.

90. Accredited copy of the motion and the relevant letter from Schöffel to the Kirchenbundesamt of 14 June 1933 in AEKD Berlin A 4/24. In his own account of February 1946 Schöffel kept quiet about the all important proviso of the motion and claimed that he was the one who had shown the way to the 'unanimous choice of Bodelschwingh'. This does not accord with the truth. H.Wilhelmi, *Die Hamburger Kirche*, 69 and 72.

91. Quoted from F.von Bodelschwingh, *Dreissig Tage*. There is a rather different text in *Das Evangelische Deutschland* 10, 1933, 203; *Allgemeine Evangelisch-Lutherische Kirchenzeitung* 66, 1933, 520, etc.

6. The Fall of Bodelschwingh (June)

1. For the significance of 1 May and 17 May, cf. Bracher, Sauer and Schulz, *Machtergreifung*, 181ff., 197f. J.C.Fest, *Hitler*, 577ff., makes an apt comment on the vote on 1 May.

2. Text of the declaration in *Evangelium im Dritten Reich* 2, 1933, 206.

3. Circular letter no. 17 of 26 May 1933, signed Pastor Lörzer as representative of the Reichsleiter, LKA Hamburg, Deutsche Christen 204/1.

4. *Völkischer Beobachter* of 28/29 May 1933, also in E.Hirsch, *Das kirchliche Wollen der Deutschen Christen*, Berlin 1933, 23-5.

5. *Oberbarnimer Kreisblatt und Freienwalder Zeitung* No. 123 of 29 May 1933, supplement, 'New Revival of German Church Life' (LKA Berlin-Brandenburg J IX, 66).

6. Thus e.g. *Die Christliche Welt* 47, 1933, col.570.

7. F.von Bodelschwingh, *Dreissig Tage*, 20. Bodelschwingh gives 30 May or 1 June as the date for this meeting. Similarly P.Fleisch, *Erlebte Kirchengeschichte*, 165.

8. Order no.28/33. Signature: Stabsleiter of the Political Organization, Dr R.Ley, circulation to Amtsleiters, *Gauleiters*, Pastor Hossenfelder, Pastor Müller. Emphasis in the original, NStA Hannover Des. 310 I B No.3; HStA Munich, Division II, Secret State Archive, Reichsstatthalter 632/5, Evangelische Kirche. There is also the content of a later copy in Kretschmar/Nicolaisen, *Dokumente*, I, 56.

9. Although it was confidential, this circular letter no.4 of 1 June 1933 was already generally known at that time. It was released on 9 June by the Evangelischer Presseverband of East Prussia (LKA Berlin-Brandenburg J II 81), and appeared in the *Tägliche Rundschau*, no.137 of 15 June 1933; in the *Junge Kirche* 1, 1933, no.1 of 21 June 1933, 7ff., in J.Gauger, *Chronik* I, 83-85: text also in H.Buchheim, *Glaubenskrise*, 103f., etc. Emphasis in original.

10. R.Schwebcke to Aselmann, 27 May (must be June) 34, LKA Hamburg, Deutsche Christen no.52. Text of the appeal with the signatures of senators, Party members, pastors and numerous teachers, K.F.Reiners, *Lübeck im Kirchenkampf*, 40-2.

11. H.Baier, *Die Deutschen Christen Bayerns*, 48.

643

12. *Evangelium im Dritten Reich* 2, 1933, 24 of 11 June 1933, 214-19.

13. K.H.Götte, *Die Propaganda der Glaubensbewegung*, 19f.

14. Ibid., 62.

15. J.Gauger, *Chronik* I, 83. For Weichert's decision, cf. also P.Fleisch, *Erlebte Kirchengeschichte*, 167f.

16. Rachner to Aselmann, 31 May 1933. LKA Hamburg, Deutsche Christen no.206. For Kloppenburg see above, 314.

17.'Volk, Staat und Kirche im neuen Reich', lecture by Pastor Kloppenburg, Rüstringen, to the Kreis synod in Sillenstede, LKA Oldenburg, Präsident der Bekennender Synode Presseausschnitte DC.

18. Schaade to Aselmann, 6 June 1933; Aselmann's reply to Schaade of 9 June; Schwebcke to Aselmann, 14 June, LKA Hamburg, no.52.

19. Pastor Niemann to Gauleiter Meyer, 2 June, quoted from Bernd Hey, *Die Kirchenprovinz Westfalen 1933-1945*, Bielefeld 1974, 37, and W.Niemöller, *Bekennende Kirche im Westfalen*, Bielefeld 1952, 44.

20. Beyer to Fezer, Hirsch and Schumann, 22 June 1933, AEKD Berlin A 4/245.

21. J.Gauger, *Chronik* I, 72 and above, 330f.

22. N.Beste, *Der Kirchenkampf in Mecklenburg 1913-1945. Geschichte, Dokumente, Erinnerungen*, Göttingen 1975, 35ff. Texts of the two declarations in K.D.Schmidt, *Bekenntnisse 1933*, 157f.

23. Text in N.Beste, *Kirchenkampf in Mecklenburg*, 40f.

24. H.Linck, *Kirchenkampf in Ostpreussen*, 40-2.

25. E.Klügel, *Die Lutherische Landeskirche Hannovers*, 49f. Text of the leaflet, ibid, Vol.2, *Dokumente*, 20f.

26. G.Schäfer, *Dokumentation* 2, 109.

27. Ibid., 170ff.

28. *Junge Kirche* 1, 1933, no.2 of 30 June, 24.

29. J.Glenthøj (ed.), *Dokumente zur Bonhoeffer-Forschung 1928-1945*, Munich 1969, 82, 93f.

30. Discussion report, ibid., 95f. There is also a report in *Junge Kirche* 1, 1933, 22. Cf. also E.Bethge, *Bonhoeffer*, 218f.

31. Headline in *NS Kurier*, Stuttgart, 21 June 1933, G. Schäfer, *Dokumentation* 2, 173.

32. G.Prater (ed.), *Kämpfer wider Willen. Erinnerungen des Landesbischof von Sachsen D.Hugo Hahn aus dem Kirchenkampf 1933-1945*, Metzingen 1969, 19f.

33. F.von Bodelschwingh, *Dreissig Tage*, 17ff.

34. 'After the accession of the Reich Bishop. The "German Christians" again in Opposition', *Vossische Zeitung*, 29 May 1933. Wright reports about 600 greetings, *'Über den Parteien'*, 222 n.153.

35. Text in K. Dienst, *Dokumentation* 1, 45.

36. J.Gauger, *Chronik* I, 85.

37. *Germania* no. 154 of 7 June 1933.

38. Meiser to Schöffel, 6 June 1933, LKA Nürnberg, Meiser 77, quoted from H.Baier, *Um Reichsbischof*, 266.

39. Note of 29 June, G.Schäfer, *Dokumentation* 2, 144.

40. Ibid., 138.

41. Text: Appendix 3 to the account of the transactions of the German Evangelischer Kirchenausschuss on 23/24 June 1933 in Eisenach, AEKD Berlin A 2/28.

42. Appendix 4, ibid.

43. The whole proceedings are in W.Brandt, *Bodelschwingh*, 131f.

44. Account of 23/24 June, appendix 5.

45. Appendix 6, ibid.

46. Appendix 7, ibid.
47. W.Brandt, *Bodelschwingh*, 134.
48. For the situation in the Reich Ministry of the Inerior cf. above Ch.5, n.11 and J.R.C.Wright, *'Über den Parteien'*, 225f.
49. W.Brandt, *Bodelschwingh*, 134.
50. Confidential note by Hosemann of 13 June 1933, AEKD Berlin, A4/24.
51. J.Gauger, *Chronik* I, 82.
52. Marahrens to Hitler, 17 June 1933. Copy for Ludwig Müller, AEKD Berlin A4/525.
53. Bodelschwingh to Hindenburg, 17 June 1933. Hindenburg's reply of 21 June 1933, HA Bethel. Quoted fom H.Baier, *Um Reichsbischof und Verfassung*, 287ff. Hindenburg's answer is also in Kretschmar and Nicolaisen, *Dokumente* I, 59f.
54. Decree of 27 April 1933, M.Domarus, *Hitler* I, 257.
55. Bodelschwingh to Hess, 19 June 1933, HA Bethel, quoted from H.Baier, *Um Reichsbischof und Verfassung*, 290.
56. Marahrens to Althaus, 19 June 1933, Althaus bequest, fascicule Reich Bishop elections.
57. Althaus to Meiser, 19 June 1933, LKA Nürnberg, Meiser 114, quoted from H.Baier, *Um Reichsbischof und Verfassung*, 281; see also H.Baier, *Die Deutschen Christen Bayerns*, 48.
58. H.Baier, *Die Deutschen Christen*, 49.
59. J.Schmidt, *Niemöller*, 83f.
60. Hesse to Bodelschwingh, 21 June 1933; W.Brandt, *Bodelschwingh*, 133.
61. AEKU Berlin, Protocol of the fifty-first and fifty-second sessions of the Church Senate on 8/9 June and 21 June 1933.
62. For the detailed motives of the President, cf. the account by the the Geheimrat and Oberkonsistorialrat B.Kanatz, 'Der Rucktritt von D.Dr Hermann Kapler von seinem Amt als Präsident des Evangelischen Oberkirchenrats in Berlin', in O.Söhngen, *Die erste Phase des Kirchenkampfes (24 Juni bis einschliesslich 2 Juli 1933)*, privately printed 1972, 125-32. [The work is in university libraries]. The contribution by Karnatz is a retort to my article 'Die Kapitulation der evangelische Kirche vor dem nationalsozialistischen Staat', *Zeitschrift für Kirchengeschichte* 81, 1970, 182-206. I have gratefully adopted many corrections relating to details, but generally speaking I do not want to change my view. There is a balanced view in J.R.C.Wright, *'Über den Parteien'*, 219f.
63. Letter of the Evangelischer Oberkirchenrat to the Reich Chancellor, 24 June 1933, BA Koblenz R 43 II/161. For the collaboration of Niemöller and Bodelschwingh in this decision, cf. J.Schmidt, *Niemöller*, 81f.
64. Letter of the Oberkirchenrat, see n.63.
65. The course of this decisive session has not so far been described in detail. It is not even mentioned in G. van Norden, *Kirche in der Krise*, and even J.R.C.Wright, *'Über den Parteien'*, 226f., gives only a short survey. The following account is based – where there is no indication to the contrary – on the following sources: account of the transactions of the German Evangelischer Kirchenausschuss on 23/24 June 1933 in Eisenach (44 folios), AEKD Berlin A 2/28 (copy I); copy of the negotiations over the combined session of the German Evangelischer Kirchenbundesrat and the German Evangelischer Kirchenausschuss on 24 June 1933 at 11 a.m. in Eisenach (3 folios), ibid., A 3/93 (copy II); copy of the transactions of the session of the Deutscher Evangelischer Kirchenbundesrat on 24 June 1933 in Eisenach (12 folios), ibid. (copy III); also manuscript notes of Land Bishop Dr Hans Meiser from the time of the Church Struggle, typescript transcription of recording, LKA Nürnberg (Notes by Meiser). There are individual extracts fom this in H.Baier, 'Das Verhalten der lutherischen Bischöfe gegenüber dem

nationalsozialistischen Staat 1933/45', in *Tutzinger Texte, Sonderband I, Kirche und Nationalsozialismus*, ed. P.Rieger and J.Strauss, Munich 1969, 94-8. There is a short and, as ever, reliable account of events in J.Kübel, *Erinnerungen*, 95-8.

66. Notes by Meiser, 1-12.

67. Kretschmar and Nicolaisen, *Dokumente*, I, 68.

68. For the political and private biography of Jäger see J.Gauger, *Chronik* I, 85, 170. There is a detailed personal file in DC Berlin; a small archive with a variety of memoranda, opinions and personal letters in the Archivum Panstwowe Poznan under 'August Jäger'. The information about Jäger's end is in AEKU Berlin, Gen I, 66 I. Jäger's activity in church politics in the Warthegau (cf. P.Gürtler, *Nationalsozialismus und evangelische Kirchen im Warthegau*, Göttingen 1958) will be reported on later on the basis of extensive archive material in Posen and Warsaw.

69. This is conjectured e.g. also by Jäger's protégé, Ernst Ludwig Dietrich, who later became German Christian Land Bishop of Hessen, in a letter to the author of 29 December 1971. The divorce was later to have unsuspected consequences for the Nassau church, see below, 476.

70. Jäger to Kortheuer, 8 May 1933, AEKHN 1/92. Extracts also in K. Dienst, *Dokumente* 1, 211f.

71. We have no information about the events in detail. Even the acts of the Prussian Kultusministerium in the Central State Archive in Merseburg, to which Wright had access, do not seem to contain any further information.

72. Copy I, 5.

73. Notes by Meiser, 13.

74. Copy I, 20; Notes by Meiser, 17. Cf. also J.Kübel, *Erinnerungen*, 98.

75. J.Schmidt, *Niemöller*, 86.

76. Copy I, 27.

77. Ibid., 28-30.

78. Kretschmar and Nicolaisen, *Dokumente*, I, 69.

79. According to the account by Marahrens, Copy I, 333f., notes by Meiser, 30f. The recollections of Seetzen differ (EVAKiZ München 20f.).

80. Notes by Meiser, 24.

81. Ibid., the decisive note is also in H.Baier, *Lutherische Bischöfe*, 98.

82. Hirsch to Althaus, 23 June 1933, 'after 2.am', Althaus bequest, Hirsch fascicule.

83. O.Söhngen, *Die erste Phase*, 5.

84. Notes by Meiser, 25-30. There is also a more detailed, very accurate account on the state of affairs in G.Schäfer, *Dokumentation* 2, 100-6. The dates of 24, 27 May should be corrected to 24, 27 June.

85. Kretschmar and Nicolaisen, *Dokumente* I, 69.

86. J.Kübel, *Erinnerungen*, 97.

87. J.Gauger, *Chronik* I, 84.

88. Copy I, 39-42.

89. Copy III, 11.

90. Texts in O.Söhngen, *Die erste Phase*, 19f.

91. J.Kübel, *Erinnerungen*, 91f.

92. E.Klügel, *Die lutherische Landeskirche Hannovers*, 54.

93. J.Kübel, *Erinnerungen*, 103.

7. The Struggle over the Prussian Church and the Completion of the Reich Church Constitution (July)

1. For this and what follows cf. O.Söhngen, *Die Erste Phase* (here 9,14, etc.); the documentation in J.Gauger, *Chronik* I, 85-92, and the documentation in Kretschmar and Nicolaisen, *Dokumente* I, 67-99, which is unfortunately incomplete.

2. Text, Kretschmar and Nicolaisen, op.cit., 70. For Schian, cf. G.Ehrenfort, *Die schlesische Kirche im Kirchenkampf 1932-1945*, Göttingen 1968, 34f.

3. J.Gauger, *Chronik* I, 87.

4. Letter from Jäger to the Landeskirche of Nassau, 26 June 1933, written confirmation of a telegram of 25 June, AEKHN Darmstadt 1/93. Text without date also in O.Söhngen, *Die erste Phase*, 29f.

5. H.Baier and J.R.C.Wright, 'Ein neues Dokument zum Staatseingriff in Preussen (1933)', *Zeitschrift für Kirchengeschichte* 86, 1975, 220-41, here 240.

6. Report of the leadership of the Evangelischer Presseverband to the Reich Minister of the Interior, 25 June 1933, Buttmann archive. See O.Söhngen, *Die erste Phase*, 22f.

7. *Kölnische Volkszeitung*, no.124 of 24 June 1933.

8. O.Söhngen, *Die erste Phase*, 23ff., and J.Schmidt, *Niemöller*, 89f. Text also in *Junge Kirche* 1, 1933, 16f.

9. Cf. K.H.Götte, *Propaganda der Glaubensbewegung*, 81-91.

10. Decree of 26 June 1933, *Kirchliche Gesetz- und Verordnungsblatt* no. 9 of 27 June 1933, quoted from O.Söhngen, *Die erste Phase*, 27f.

11. Baier and Wright, 'Ein neues Dokument', 225.

12. J.Gauger, *Chronik* I, 87.

13. Baier and Wright, 'Ein neues Dokument', 225-38.

14. Ibid., 238-41.

15. P.Neumann, *Jungreformatorische Bewegung*, 98; J.Schmidt, *Niemöller*, 91; also id., 'Studien zur Vorgeschichte des Pfarrernotbundes', *Zeitschrift für Kirchengeschichte* 79, 1968, 47f.

16. Text: *Junge Kirche* 1, 1933, 17.

17. Text: O.Söhngen, *Die erste Phase*, 38-42.

18. Text: Kretschmar and Nikolaisen, *Dokumente* I, 74.

19. Text of letter of 27 June 1933, ibid.,75.

20. Text: ibid., 71-4.

21. *Kirchliches Gesetz-und Verordnungsblatt* 10, 28 June 1933, quoted from O.Söhngen, *Die erste Phase*, 44f.

22. Notes by Meiser, 34.

23. See above, Ch.6, 354.

24. Notes by Meiser, 36-40.

25. Report by Wurm, 30 June 1933, G.Schäfer, *Dokumentation* 2, 260. The report was communicated on 10 July to the Württemberg deans' office 'for the attention and confidential information of the pastors', ibid., 256 n.1. See also T.Wurm, *Erinnerungen*, 87.

26. O.Söhngen, *Die erste Phase*, 51f.; *Junge Kirche* 1, 1933, 48.

27. Text: Kretschmar and Nicolaisen, *Dokumente* I, 76.

28. F.Seetzen, *Lebenserinnerungen*, EAKiZ München, 22f.; O.Söhngen, *Die erste Phase*, 80ff.

29. Kretschmar and Nicolaisen, *Dokumente* I, 76. Meusel died as early as November 1933.

30. J.Gauger, *Chronik*, I, 90.

31. O.Söhngen, *Die erste Phase*, 80f.

32. Bodelschwingh to Werner, 29 June 1933, AEKD Berlin A 4/245.

33. According to a leaflet from the church resistance front in AEKU Berlin, Gen.II 42, I, 296.

34. Copies of the appeal of 29 June 1933 are in AEKD Berlin, A 4/245 and AEKU Berlin, Gen.I, 66, Vol.1. Address 'Dear Brother in Office', no signature.

35. See above, 111ff.

36. Invitation to join in *Junge Kirche* 1, 1933, no. 2 of 30 June 1933, 21. Text of the appeal in AEKD Berlin A4/103.

37. AEKD Berlin, A4/245. For Wilhelm Niemöller's commitment to the movement in early 1933 cf. in detail F.Baumgärtel, *Wider die Kirchenkampflegenden*, 24-30. Baumgärtel's polemic in this connection against a simplistic picture of the Confessing Church is justified if it helps to see things as being as complex as they really were.

38. Text from the report by the *Reichsbote* of 1 July 1933 in Kretschmar and Nicolaisen, *Dokumente*, I, 77-82. Cf. also K.H.Götte, *Propaganda der Glaubensbewegung*, 82-4.

39. M.U.Kaiser, *Deutscher Kirchenkampf und Schweizer Öffentlichkeit*, 40ff.

40. There are a shorter and a longer tradition of the conversation in J.Glenthøj, 'Unterredung im Vestibul. Das Gespräch zwischen Pfarrer Backhaus und Hitler am 28 Juni 1933', *Kirche in der Zeit*, 1962, 389-94. The longer version is also in Kretschmar and Nicolaisen, *Dokumente* I, 94-98.

41. Bracher, Sauer and Schulz, *Machtergreifung*, 212f.

42. Letter of 30 June 1933, text e.g. in Kretschmar and Nicolaisen, *Dokumente* I, 83; *Junge Kirche* 1, 1933, 68f.

43. There is a report of this discussion in W.Conrad, *Der Kampf um die Kanzeln*, 16f., and a short reference also in O.Söhngen, *Die erste Phase*, 87. The date follows from Frick's official statements of the same day. Fezer's account in G.Schäfer, *Dokumentation* 2, 1937, is to be corrected accordingly.

44. 'The Church in Germany, Herr Hitler's aims', *The Times*, Friday, 7 July 1933, 15.

45. O.Söhngen, *Die erste Phase*, 93. Cf. also the memoranda of the Reich chancellery of 30 June in Kretschmar and Nicolaisen, *Dokumente* I, 83 n.38.

46. Kretschmar and Nicolaisen, 83f.

47. O.Söhngen, *Die erste Phase*, 81.

48. Report of 30 June, ibid.,87.

49. F.Seetzen, *Lebenserinnerungen*, EAKiZ München, 21.

50. Text of the letter of the authorized representatives of the German Evangelischer Kirchenbund to the Reich Minister of the Interior of 30 June 1933, O.Söhngen, *Die erste Phase*, 84f.

51. Text in Kretschmar and Nicolaisen, *Dokumente* I, 84f. The rendering does not show that the important reference to 'between two and three weeks' is underlined in the original regulation (AEKU Berlin Gen.I, 66, Vol.1, 127f.).

52. O.Söhngen, *Die erste Phase*, 103f., text also in *Junge Kirche*, 1933, 70f.

53. Text of the Gau order of 30 June 1933 in O.Söhngen, *Die erste Phase*, 88f., and extracts in *Junge Kirche* 1, 1933, 71f.

54. LKA Nürnberg, Meinzolt 2. Quoted from H.Baier, *Um Reichsbischof und Verfassung*, 365.

55. According to the account from the *Tägliche Rundschau* of 4 July in O.Söhngen, *Die erste Phase*, 111f., and J.Gauger, *Chronik* I, 91.

56. O.Söhngen, *Die erste Phase*, 109, and *Evangelium im Dritten Reich* 2, 1933, 262. See also below Ch.12.

57. Text of the liturgy and the addresses in K.Kampffmeyer (ed.), *Dein Wort ist Deiner Kirche Schutz. Predigten von der Kirche*, Göttingen 1934, 159-74.

58. J.Glenthøj, *Dokumente*, 99ff.

59. The impressions of the general superintendents are given in O.Söhngen, *Die erste Phase*, 114-23; for Westphalia, ibid., 108 and 119f.; also J.Gauger, *Chronik* I, 91f., and *Junge Kirche* 1, 1933, 3f., etc.

60. Text of the regulation by the Minister of the Interior for Saxony of 30 June 1933 in Kretschmar and Nicolaisen, *Dokumente* 1, 98f. For the events cf. Hahn, *Kämpfer wider Willen*, 22ff., and a detailed memorandum on the church situation in Saxony which Hugo Hahn sent on 13 July 1933 to a 'senior German Reich government', BA Koblenz R 53/203.

61. J.Gauger, *Chronik*, I, 90.

62. F.K.Reimers, *Lübeck im Kirchenkampf*, 46-52.

63. Text of the statement of 3 July in *Junge Kirche* 1, 1933, 70.

64. Text of the statement of 4 July in G.Schäfer, *Dokumentation* 2, 270. Signatures Wurm, Meiser, Reichardt, Schöffel, Rendtorff.

65. O.Söhngen, *Die erste Phase*, 85f.; F.Seetzen, *Erinnerungen*, 34f.; H.Kater, *Die Deutsche evangelische Kirche in den Jahren 1933 und 1934. Eine rechts- und verfassungsgeschichtiche Untersuchung zu Gründung und Zerfall einer Kirche im nationalsozialistischen Staat*, Göttingen 1970, 87.

66. E.Klügel, *Die Lutherische Landeskirche Hannovers*, 61. Apparently Seetzen and Hesse only took part in the closing session: H.Kater, *Die Deutsche evangelische Kirche*, 88.

67. J.Schmidt, *Niemöller*, 101.

68. Text of the statement of 6 July and signatures, D.Bonhoeffer, *Gesammelte Schriften* 6, Munich 1974, 269-72.

69. M.Domarus, *Hitler*, I, 286f.; Bracher, Sauer and Schulz, *Machtergreifung*, 216.

70. Circular letter of 10 July 1933, BA Koblenz R 43 II/1263, but the text is also in the *Völkischer Beobachter* of 12 July.

71. *Junge Kirche* 1, 1933, 49.

72. *Das Evangelische Deutschland* 10, 1933, 259.

73. J.Gauger, *Chronik* I, 90.

74. Copy as appendix to the record of the negotiations of 11 July 1933, in AEKD Berlin, A 3/93.

75. Text of the Loccum manifesto in K.D.Schmidt, *Bekenntnisse 1933*, 153f. For the whole development cf. also above chs.4 and 5.

76. Cf. H.Kater, *Die Deutsche Evangelische Kirche*, 104-7.

77. Text of the draft constitution of 1 June, ibid., 195-8. The protocols of the constitutional committee – which are not evaluated here – are in BA Koblenz R 79/27.

78. J.Schmidt, *Niemöller*, 78f. Text in H.Kater, 201 (incomplete) and 105; Meiser's objections, ibid., 94.

79. Record of negotiations of 24 June 1933, morning 11 a.m., AEKD Berlin A 3/93 (cf. above Ch. 6, n.65); Notes by Meiser, 25-30, LKA Nürnberg. Detailed account of the session and its consequences for the Württemberg Oberkirchenrat in G.Schäfer, *Dokumentation* 2, 100-6 (the date is to be corrected to 24 June).

80. H.Kater, *Die Deutsche Evangelische Kirche*, 87.

81. Ibid., 101.

82. Ibid., 104-10.

83. Record of the session of the representatives of the Landeskirchen on 11 July 1933, 10 a.m., in the Kirchenbundesamt, AEKD Berlin A 3/93, 2-4.

84. Ibid., 7, 9, 11.

85. E.Klügel, *Die Lutherische Landeskirche Hannovers*, 61; Notes by Meiser, 43; W.Conrad, *Der Kampf um die Kanzeln*, 20f.

86. Record (n.83), 18.

87. H.Liermann, 'Das evangelische Bischofsamt in Deutschland seit 1933', *Zeitschrift für evangelische Kirchenrecht* 3, 1953/54, 4.
88. Text: Kretschmar and Nicolaisen, *Dokumente* I, 87f.
89. BA Koblenz R 43 I/1464.
90. Pfundtner to Lammers, 14 July 1933, copy in Arch AA Bonn, Kult A1, 2. See below, 441f.
91. Bracher, Sauer and Schulz, *Machtergreifung*, VII, 214ff.
92. Text in A.Kupper, *Statliche Akten*, 234-8. For the Reich concordat see below, 404.
93. BA Koblenz, R 43 I/1464.
94. Kretschmar and Nicolaisen, *Dokumente* I, 89.
95. See the report on a discussion with the Prussian Minister President Hermann Göring on 15 July, which is unfortunately not printed in full, ibid., 89f., and Frick's letter to Rust of the same day, ibid., 93. Also J.Gauger, *Chronik* I, 91.
96. G.Schäfer, *Dokumentation* 2, 274f.
97. *Junge Kirche* 1, 1933, 50f. The contribution comes from the editor, F.Söhlmann, emphasis in original.

8. The Conclusion of the Reich Concordat (April-September)

1. Cf. e.g. *Mein Kampf*, 103: 'Protestantism as such is a better defender of the interests of Germanism, in so far as this is grounded in its genesis.'
2. F.Muckermann, *Im Kampf zwischen zwei Epoche, Lebenserinnerungen*, Mainz 1973, 583.
3. Memorandum by Bergen, 16 March 1933, Kretschmar and Nicolaisen, *Dokumente* I, 20.
4. L.Kaas, *Konkordatstyp*, 492.
5. E.Deuerlein, *Reichskonkordat*, 110; K.Repgen, 'Zentrumspartei', *Militärseelsorge* 19, 1970, 89f. (*Klopfsignale*, 102f.); L.Volk, *Reichskonkordat*, 84-89, 93 etc.; R.Morsey, *Protokolle*, XVII n.1.
6. See above, 246f.
7. See above, 249f.
8. This assumption is more probable than Volk's reference to Pacelli's conversation with the Bavarian Prince Albrecht on 28 March, which unfortunately did not contain any really new political information, L.Volk, *Reichskonkordat*, 87f.
9. See above, 251f.
10. A.Kupper, *Staatliche Akten*, 12; L.Volk, *Reichskonkordat*, 87.
11. In connection with this date it should be recalled that on 1 April Kapler raised the question of the concordat with the Reich Minister of the Interior on 1 April without being contradicted and referred to the consequences for the Protestant side. See above, 247f. and 283f. For the problems of the whole matter see A.Kupper, *Staatliche Akten*, 12 n.2.
12. L.Volk, *Kirchliche Akten*, 7ff.
13. A.Kupper, *Staatliche Akten*, 9-11.
14. Thus e.g. K.Repgen, 'Zentrumspartei', in *Klopfsignale*, 103f., 107.
15. A.Kupper, *Staatliche Akten*, 11 n.10.
16. Ibid., 9 n.9.
17. See above, 309.
18. Thus the account by Kaas to Bergen on 19 November 1935, A.Kupper, *Staatliche Akten*, 496.
19. K.Repgen, 'Zentrumspartei' (*Klopfsignale*, 110); W.Bussmann, *Der deutsche Katholizismus*, 197; L.Volk, *Reichskonkordat*, 97ff.
20. Thus L.Volk, *Reichskonkordat*, 86.

21. See e.g. the letter from Kaas to Papen of 23 May 1933, A.Kupper, *Staatliche Akten*, 663; L.Volk, *Kirchliche Akten*, XXIIf.

22. Diary-like notes by Kaas for the period from 7 to 18 April 1933, A.Kupper, *Staatliche Akten*, here 12-14. It is interesting that Kaas's attempt once again to offer his services as a mediator came to grief with Buttmann in October 1933, L.Volk, *Reichskonkordat*, 204f.

23. *Völkischer Beobachter* (north German edition), no.101 of 11 April 1933 (emphasis in the original).

24. A.Kupper, *Staatliche Akten*, 15. For this draft of the concordat see above 69f.

25. Text of Pacelli's manuscript notes in L.Volk, *Reichskonkordat*, 224-6.

26. The account of the course of the negotiations follows the notes by Kaas in A.Kupper, *Staatliche Akten*, 14-16. Kaas's letter to Papen of 20 April, ibid., 18f. The text of the draft sent on 20 April (the so-called Kaas Draft I) is unknown; there is a reconstruction in L.Volk, *Kirchliche Akten*, 20-2.

27. D.Golombek, *Preussenkonkordat*, 52, 90; Erika Weinzierl-Fischer, *Die österreisch-ischen Konkordate von 1855 and 1933*, Munich 1960, 160, 201, 221.

28. *Völkischer Beobachter* no. 45 of 22 February 1929, see above, 164f.

29. A.Kupper, *Staatliche Akten*, 67f.

30. R.Morsey, 'Zentrumspartei', 379. Kapler's birthday letter was much more markedly official by contrast, to the degree that the Protestant President also stressed the collaboration of the church. J.R.C.Wright, *'Über den Parteien'*, 190f.

31. A.Kupper, *Staatliche Akten*, 30-2.

32. D.Golombek. *Preussenkonkordat*, 12f.,22f.; L.Volk, *Reichskonkordat*, 13.

33. A.Kupper, *Staatliche Akten*, 59, 72f., etc.

34. Text of the article in a first draft in L.Volk, *Reichskonkordat*, 127 n.14.

35. Ibid., 127.

36. LKA Hannover, Marahrens bequest Vol.4/II, manuscript record of 4 May, emphasis in the original, cf. also above, 308f.

37. Kaas to Papen, 11 May 1933, A.Kupper, *Staatliche Akten*, 40f., the so-called Kaas II draft, ibid., 41-5. The new article 31, ibid., 54.

38. Kaas to Papen, 13 May 1933, ibid., 56.

39. Papen to Kaas, 17 May 1933, ibid., 58f.

40. Eggersdorfer to Riemer, 12 April 1933; L.Volk, *Kirchliche Akten*, 12ff.

41. E.Weinzierl-Fischer, *Die österreichischen Konkordate*, 375 n.48.

42. Quoted from R.Morsey, 'Zentrumspartei', 375 n.48.

43. Text ibid., 433f.

44. Thus L.Volk, *Reichskonkordat*, 209.

45. See above, n.22. What role was played in the prelate's decision not to return to Germany by a possible concern not to get involved in the bankruptcy proceedings over Görreshaus-AG in Cologne must remain an open question. In L.Volk, *Reichskonkordat*, 202f., some influence is claimed; in A.Kupper, 'Reichskonkordat', *Stimmen der Zeit*, 163, 1958/9, 288 n.37, this is answered in the negative.

46. R.Morsey, 'Zentrumspartei', 82f.

47. H.Brüning, *Memoiren*, 666.

48. Ibid.

49. Thus characteristically e.g. L.Volk, *Reichskonkordat*, 209: 'None of those who accused him of treachery saw how in these very weeks Ludwig Kaas, flexible in form and uncompromising in substance, fought in his own way with no less dedication for the continued existence of the Centre Party. He himself could not make speeches or give answers, and where the depoliticizing article, toned down by Kaas, could have borne witness for the author, Heinrich Brüning, blind to the difficult rescuing tactics of his predecessor, abruptly repudiated the standpoint.' Cf. also 181ff., etc. In fact Kaas was

fighting here less for the 'continued existence of the Centre Party' than for a canonistically correct formulation of his prohibition. According to canon law it was to be a church ban and not a state ban.

50. L.Volk, *Kirchliche Akten*, 12f.

51. Ibid., 14.

52. Ibid., 16. There is indirect information from Faulhaber from 1 May in ibid., 282f.

53. Ibid., 19.

54. Ibid., 25f.

55. Ibid., 50.

56. See also above, 278, 307f.

57. B.Stasiewski, *Akten* I, 88ff. Cf. also the accounts, 106f., 116.

58. Ibid., 89, 107, 117.

59. L.Volk, *Faulhaber-Akten* I, 715.

60. B.Stasiewski, *Akten* I, 106.

61. A.Kupper, *Staatliche Akten*, 56f.

62. Bergen to Neurath, 26 May 1933, ibid., 70f.

63. Berning stayed in Rome from 17 to 25 May, Gröber from 11-23 May, L.Volk, *Kirchliche Akten*, 28ff., 31 n.4. For Gröber see also his 1946 report, ibid., 316f.

64. B.Stasiewski, *Akten* I, 100-3.

65. L.Volk, *Kirchliche Akten*, 29, 33.

66. L.Volk, *Bayerischer Episkopat*, 112.

67. L.Volk, *Kirchliche Akten*, 51-3.

68. For the particular role of Gröber and his experiences in Baden, cf. K.Scholder, 'Baden im Kirchenkampf des Dritten Reiches. Aspekte und Fragen', in *Oberrheinische Studien* II, ed. A.Schäfer, Karlsruhe 1973, 225-30.

69. Protocol of the first plenary conference of the German episcopate, Fulda, 30 May to 1 June 1933, B.Stasiewski, *Akten*, 196-210, appendices 1-7, ibid., 210-28.

70. Notes by Sebastian, ibid., 230-7.

71. Ibid., 232.

72. Preysing to the Fulda Bishops' Conference, ibid., 238.

73. For the reading, B.Stasiewski, *Akten* I, 235, and L.Volk, *Kirchliche Akten*, 62; for the draft, Gröber's account, ibid., 316.

74. Faulhaber on 10 June 1933 to Papen, L.Volk, *Kirchliche Akten*, 62.

75. Gröber's account, ibid.,317.

76. Pastoral letter of the German episcopate, B.Stasiewski, *Akten* I, 239-48, for the models see ibid., 239 n.1.

77. L.Volk, *Kirchliche Akten*, 59.

78. Ibid.

79. Comments on the outline in 'Sachen Reichskonkordat, Breslau, 22 Juni 1933', 62.

80. Faulhaber's notes on a conversation with Papen, 10 June 1933, ibid., 62.

81. For the consequences of this observation cf. ibid., 78, 86, and A.Kupper, *Staatliche Akten*, 90.

82. L.Volk, *Bayerischer Episkopat*, 92-101.

83. For the particular political constellation in Bavaria cf. e.g. P.Diehl-Thiele, *Partei und Staat im Dritten Reich, Untersuchungen zum Verhältnis von NSDAP und innerer Staatsverwaltung 1933-1945*, Munich 1969, 75-91.

84. Faulhaber's letter of 5 June 1933 to Wagner and Himmler in L.Volk, *Faulhaber-Akten*, 732f.

85. L.Volk, *Bayerischer Episkopat*, 94.

86. Faulhaber's account is in a letter to the Bavarian episcopate of 13 June 1933, L.Volk. *Faulhaber-Akten* I, 737f.

87. K.Scharnagl to Faulhaber, 12 June 1933, ibid., 735.

88. Cf. Faulhaber's two letters of 12 June 1933 in B.Stasiewski, *Akten* I, 249f., and 250ff.

89. See above, n.86.

90. L.Volk, *Faulhaber-Akten*, I, 743f. n.3, cf. also L.Volk, *Bayerischer Episkopat*, 106.

91. Gröber to Pacelli, 28 December 1933, B.Stasiewski, *Akten* I, 493.

92. R.Morsey, 'Zentrumspartei', 395 n.69; Max Miller, *Eugen Bolz*, Stuttgart 1951, 458f.

93. R.Morsey, 'Zentrumspartei', 395f.

94. K.Schwend, 'Die Bayerische Volkspartei', in E.Mathias and R.Morsey, *Das Ende der Parteien*, 504ff.

95. *Bayerischer Kurier*, 27 June 1933, text, ibid., 514f.

96. R.Morsey, 'Zentrumspartei', 399; K.Schwend, *Bayerische Volkspartei*, 507; H.Brüning, *Memoiren*, 673.

97. A.Kupper, *Staatliche Akten*, 118f.

98. L.Volk, *Reichskonkordat*, 138f.

99. L.Volk, *Kirchliche Akten*, 82-5.

100. Ibid., 86-9.

101. K.Repgen, 'Zentrumspartei', differs.

102. L.Volk, *Kirchliche Akten*, 92f., cf. also Gröber's letter to Pacelli of 3 July, ibid., 107.

103. L.Volk, *Reichskonkordat*, 231.

104. A.Kupper, *Staatliche Akten*, 131.

105. Ibid., 128-31.

106. Ibid., 133 and n.1.

107. According to the *Kölnische Volkszeitung* of 30 June 1933, quoted in R.Morsey, 'Zentrumspartei', 396.

108. Text ibid., 439f.

109. R.Leiber, 'Reichskonkordat und Ende der Zentrumspartei', in *Stimmen der Zeit*, 167, 1960/61. 220.

110. See above n.100.

111. For the dispute over this remark cf. R.Morsey, 'Zentrumspartei', 398, and Volk's attempts at a psychological explanation, *Reichskonkordat*, 209f.

112. A.Kupper, *Staatliche Akten*, 134.

113. R.Leiber, *Reichskonkordat*, 200.

114. Notes by Buttmann, A.Kupper, *Staatliche Akten*, 139.

115. Diary entries by Buttmann, ibid., 139 n.1 and 149 n.1, cf. also Buttmann's memorandum, ibid., 176.

116. Letter from Gröber of 11 July 1933, L.Volk, *Kirchliche Akten*, 140. For this see also Buttmann's notes of 6 July, A.Kupper, *Staatliche Akten*, 164.

117. Buttmann's notes, 8-9 July 1933, A.Kupper, *Staatliche Akten*, 166f.

118. Ibid., 159f.

119. For the development and significnace of Article 31 cf. especially L.Volk, *Reichskonkordat*, 151-68, and Ch.11 below.

120. A.Kupper, *Staatliche Akten*, 166; for the sequence of events, cf. ibid., 257 n.1.

121. Ibid., 175.

122. Thus rightly K.D.Bracher, 'Nationalsozialistische Machtergreifung und Reichskonkordat. Ein Gutachten zur Frage des geschichtlichen Zusammenhangs und der politischen Verknüpfung von Reichskonkordat und nationalsozialisticher Revolution', in *Der Konkordatsprozess*, Munich 1958, 1006.

123. A.Kupper, *Staatliche Akten*, 219f.

124. Ibid., 223.

125. Ibid., 235-7.

126. For the negotiations between 8 and 20 July see L.Volk, *Reichskonkordat*, 151-68.

127. Ivo Zeiger SJ, 'Das Reichskonkordat', *Stimmen der Zeit* 126, 1933.34, 1, 7.

128. The Prussian Kultusminister only received a copy of the text of the treaty on the afternoon of 13 July (!), Rust to Hitler, 14 July 1933, A.Kupper, *Staatliche Akten*, 238f. Letter and opinion by Stuckart of the same day, ibid., 239-43.

129. B.Stasiewski, *Akten* I, 347f.

130. Cf. above, 377f.

131. Pacelli to Bornewasser, 2 July 1933, L.Volk, *Kirchliche Akten*, 180f.

132. Bertram to Hitler, 22 July 1933, A.Kupper, *Staatliche Akten*, 290f.

133. Faulhaber to Hitler, 24 July 1933, ibid., 293f.

134. Berning to Bertram, 24 July 1933, L.Volk, *Kirchliche Akten*, 187f.

135. Bertram to Faulhaber, 10 August 1933, ibid., 219f.

136. Official commentary on the Reich concordat of 11 August 1933, A.Kupper, *Staatliche Akten*, 283-6.

137. 'Die Bedeutung des Konkordats', article in the *Nationalsozialisticher Parteikorrespondenz*, 22 July 1933, 287-90.

138. 'Randbemerkungen zum Konkordat zwischen dem Heiligen Stuhl und dem Deutschen Reich', 26 July 1933; 'Nochmals zum Konkordat zwischen dem Heiligen Stuhl und Deutschland', 27 July 1933, ibid., 298-303. For Pacelli as author cf. ibid., 297 n.3.

139. For the central significance of canon law in this connection cf. e.g. also R.Jestaedt, 'Das Reichskonkordat vom 20.Juli 1933 in der nationalsozialistischen Staats- und Verwaltungspraxis unter besonderer Berücksichtigung des Artikels 1', *Archiv für katholisches Kirchenrecht* 124, 149/50, 343f.

140. Buttmann's reply of 28 July 1933, A.Kupper, *Staatliche Akten*, 304-7.

141. Klee to the Foreign Office, 31 July 1933, ibid., 314f.

142. Bülow to the Vatican Embassy, 3 August 1933, ibid., 319.

143. This was stressed by Ivo Zeiger SJ in *Stimmen der Zeit* 126, 1933/34, 1.

144. Klee to the Foreign office, 7 August 1933, A.Kupper, *Staatliche Akten*, 327-9.

145. Bülow to the Vatican Embassy, 8 August 1933, ibid., 330f.

146. Klee to the Foreign Office, 11 August 1933, ibid., 335f.

147. Text; A.Kupper, *Staatliche Akten*, 280f.: L.Volk, *Kirchliche Akten*, 294f.; D.Albrecht, *Notenwechsel* I, 174. For the negotiations over the principles of interpretation cf. in detail L.Volk, *Reichskonkordat*, 158-62, 166f., 187-92.

148. Bertram's circular letter of 1 August, L.Volk, *Kirchliche Akten*, 207f., text also in B.Stasiewski, *Akten* I, 273f.

149. Bertram to Buttmann, 15 August 1933, L.Volk, *Kirchliche Akten*, 209f.

150. From the appendices to Wolker's report in B.Stasiewski, *Akten* I, 301.

151. Wolker's report of 20 August 1933, ibid., 283. For the whole development in the question of the youth movements see Chapter 11 below.

152. Bertram to the episcopate, 23 July 1933, L.Volk, *Kirchliche Akten*, 185.

153. Bertram to Pacelli, 2 September 1933, ibid., 237f.

154. For the significance of the 'Law for the Prevention of Offspring with Hereditary Diseases' cf. e.g. G.Rühle, *Das Dritte Reich*, I, 268f.

155. Protocol of the second plenary conference in B.Stasiewski, *Akten* I, 319-65. The school questions, ibid., 322f.; associations, 328; press, 332f.; officials, 331; sterilization law, 336.

156. Bertram to Pacelli, 2 September 1933, L.Volk, *Kirchliche Akten*, 237-42, *Staatliche Akten*, 410.

157. Press release from the Foreign Office, 11 October 1933, A.Kupper, *Staatliche Akten*, 410.

158. For the 'short notice' of 5 September 1933, cf. ibid., 357-60; the Promemoria of 9 September, ibid., 378-80.

159. Kreuz to Noppel, 12 September 1933, L.Volk, *Kirchliche Akten*, 252.

160. Buchberger to Faulhaber, 13 September 1933, L.Volk, *Faulhaber Akten*, 746.

161. Faulhaber to the Bavarian Episcopate, 14 September 1933, B.Stasieweski, *Akten* I, 394-6.

162. Ow-Felldorf to Faulhaber, 18 September 1933, L.Volk, *Faulhaber-Akten* I, 769f. Cf. also the other letters, ibid., 766-8.

163. Thus evidently in the Archdiocese of Cologne, cf. A.Kupper, *Staatliche Akten*, 347 n.1.

164. According to a note by Menshausen on a conversation with Orsenigo of 4 August, ibid., 321.

165. Note of 23 August 1933, ibid., 346.

166. The account is in H.Müller, *Katholische Kirche*, 202-6.

167. E.von Aretin, *Krone und Ketten. Erinnerungen eines bayerischen Edelmannes*, Munich 1955, 23.

168. Thus E.Iserloh, 'Vom Abschluss des Reichskonkordats bis zur Ratifikation', *Trierer Theologische Zeitschrift* 72, 1963, 42f.

169. F.Muckermann, *Lebenserinnerungen*, 584.

9. Theology in the Summer of 1933

1. See above, Part One, ch.8.

2. See above, 207f.

3. K.F.Reimers, *Lübeck im Kirchenkampf*, 33ff.

4. For Wieneke see above, 199, 210 etc.

5. J.Hossenfelder, *Unser Kampf*, Schriftenreihe der Deutschen Christen 5, Berlin 1933, 8.

6. For Fezer see above, 317.

7. See above, 318ff.

8. E.Hirsch, *Die gegenwärtige geistige Lage im Spiegel philosophischer und theologischer Besinnung. Akademische Vorlesungen zum Verständis des deutschen Jahres 1933*, Göttingen [30 January] 1934, 3.

9. H.Rückert, *Das Wiedererwachen reformatorischer Frömmigkeit in der Gegenwart*, *Öffentliche Vorträge der Universität Tübingen, Sommersemester 1933. Deutsche Gegenwart und ihre geschichtliche Wurzeln*, Stuttgart 1933, 1.

10. W.Künneth and H.Schreiner, *Die Nation vor Gott. Zu Botschaft der Kirche im Dritten Reich*, Berlin [1]1933, [3]1934, 5f.

11. K.Heim, *Deutsche Staatsreligion oder Evangelische Volkskirche*, Stimmen aus der deutschen christlichen Studentenbewegung 85, Berlin 1933, 3.

12. P.Althaus, *Die deutsche Stunde der Kirche*, Göttingen (1 October 1933) [3]1934, 3.

13. The most important comprehensive account of German Christian theology is W.Tilgner, *Volksnomostheologie und Schöpfungsglaube. Ein Beitrag zur Geschichte des Kirchenkampfes*, Göttingen 1933.

14. Account of the transactions of the Faculty Day in Berlin on 27 April 1933, US Tübingen, 162/XIII 3 a.

15. See above, 102ff.

16. E.Hirsch, *Die gegenwärtige geistige Lage*, 4.

17. On this see Karl Barth's verdict: '...a book well thought out in every respect and ultimately also a readable book which is written in an interesting way, in which certainly

for the moment the very best is said about the German Christian cause that can be said', *Offenbarung, Kirche, Theologie*, Theologische Existenz heute 9, 1934, 4f.

18. Cf. G.Schneider-Flume, *Die politische Theologie Emanuel Hirschs 1918-1933*, 135ff.

19. *Die gegenwärtige geistige Lage*, 26.

20. Ibid., 33.

21. Ibid., 5.

22. Ibid., 116f.

23. Ibid., 132f.

24. 'Die wirkliche Lage unserer Kirche', *Monatsschrift für Pastoraltheologie Mai/Juni 1933*, 182-5, in *Das kirchliche Wollen der Deutschen Christen*, Berlin 1933, 22.

25. 'Freiheit der Kirche, Reinheit des Evangeliums (30.Juni 1933)', in *Das kirchliche Wollen*, 28.

26. See above, 104.

27. Cf. H.Kessler, *Wilhelm Stapel*, 168 n.3.

28. *Der christliche Staatsmann. Eine Theologie des Nationalismus*, Hamburg 1932, 174.

29. Ibid., 174-85.

30. Ibid.

31. *Die Kirche Christi und der Staat Hitlers*, Hamburg 1933, 65. The work went through four impressions with a total print number of 12,000 copies, H.Kessler, *Wilhelm Stapel*, 306.

32. *Die Kirche Christi*, 65-70.

33. W.Stapel, *Volkskirche oder Sekte?*, Hamburg 1934, 57.

34. W.Stapel, 'Die violette Kirchenverwirrung und ihre Lösung', *Deutsches Volkstum* (second July volume) 1933, 610ff.

35. *Die Kirche Christi*, 77f.

36. *Deutsches Volkstum*, 1933, 612.

37. *Die Kirche Christi*, 79.

38. One of the earliest and best critical analyses can already be found in Bonhoeffer's lectures from the winter semester 1932/1933, *Gesammelte Schriften* 5, 1972, 331-4.

39. H.Vögel, 'Wider die Gleichschaltung von Gottesgesetz und Staatsgesetz', *Junge Kirche* 1, 1933, 333.

40. F.Gogarten, *Wider die Ächtung der Autorität*, Jena 1930, 5.

41. F.Gogarten, 'Die Selbständigkeit der Kirche', *Deutsches Volkstum* (first June volume), 1933, 445.

42. Ibid., 448.

43. F.Gogarten, *Einheit von Evangelium und Volkstum?*, Hamburg 1933, 7.

44. Ibid., 17.

45. Ibid., 17f.

46. Ibid., 22.

47. E.Hornig, *Der Kirchenkampf in Schlesien*, Göttingen 1976, 79f.

48. Reported by G.Merz in *Zwischen den Zeiten* 11, 1933, 552.

49. The details of Gogarten's entry and departure have not been completely clarified. It is certain that Gogarten regarded himself as a member of the Faith Movement (*Zwischen den Zeiten* 11, 1933, 552) even if it is possible that he never had a membership card. Cf. E.Hornig, *Kirchenkampf in Schlesien*, 79 n.2, and 85f.; *Junge Kirche* 1, 1933, 357f.; K.-W.Thyssen, *Begegnung und Verantwortung, Der Weg der Theologie Friedrich Gogartens von den Anfängen bis zum Zweiten Weltkrieg*, Tübingen 1970, 220-6.

50. P.Althaus, *Grundriss der Dogmatik* I, Erlangen 1929, 10-14.

51. P.Althaus, *Die deutsche Stunde*, 12.

52. Ibid., 13.

53. But the Catholic Reich ideology rightly stressed by Klaus Breuning, *Die Vision des*

Reiches, was only in isolated instances understood as a theologumenon and did not have a völkisch orientation.

54. M.Schmaus, *Begegnungen zwischen katholischem Christentum und nationalsozialistischer Weltanschauung*, Reich und Kirche 1, Münster 1933, 3.

55. K.Eschweiler, *Die zwei Wege der neueren Theologie, Georg Hermes – Matthias Joseph Scheeben. Eine kritische Untersuchung des Problems der theologischen Erkenntnis*, Augsburg 1926, 2.

56. K.Eschweiler, 'Die Kirche im neuen Reich', *Deutsche Volkstum* 1933, 454-6. For the theological prehistory of this article cf. K.Eschweiler, 'Politische Theologie', in *Religiöse Besinnung. Vierteljahrschrift im Dienste christlicher Vertiefung und ökumenischer Verständigung* 4, 1931/32, 72-88.

57. *Die Kirche im neuen Reich*, 456f.

58. K.Adam, *The Spirit of Catholicism*, London and New York 1930, 12. The twelfth German edition of the book appeared in 1949. Cf. R.Aubert, 'Karl Adam', in *Tendenzen der Theologie*, 156-62.

59. K.Adam, 'Deutsches Volkstum und katholisches Christentum', *Theologische Quartalschrift* 114, 1933, 41f.

60. Ibid., 44.

61. Ibid., 48-53.

62. Ibid., 60-3.

63. The whole extensive proceedings which dragged on until June 1934 can be found in Papen's file in BA Koblenz R 53.

64. Thus the publisher's text on the backs of Volumes 1 and 2.

65. M.Schmaus, *Begegnungen zwischen katholischem Christentum und nationalsozialistischer Weltanschauung*, Reich und Kirche 1, Münster 1933, 12f., 22.

66. Ibid., 30.

67. Ibid., 45f.

68. J.Lortz, *Geschichte der Kirche in ideengeschichtlicher Betrachtung. Eine Sinndeutung der christlichen Vergangenheit in Grundzügen*, Münster [1]1932, [3]1933, [22/23]1965!

69. J.Lortz, *Katholischer Zugang zum Nationalsozialismus*, Reich und Kirche 2, Münster [2]1934, 9, 2.

70. See above, 417.

71. J.Lortz, *Katholischer Zugang*, 7.

72. Ibid., 26.

73. See above, 176f.

74. Karl Barth, *Church Dogmatics* I/1, XIIIf.

75. Ibid., X.

76. K.Barth, 'Das erste Gebot als theologisches Axiom', *Zwischen den Zeiten* 11, 1933, 297-314, here 304-6; also in Karl Barth, *Theologische Fragen und Antworten, Gesammelte Vorträge*, Zurich 1957, here 134f.

77. *Zwischen den Zeiten*, 308-12; *Theologische Fragen und Antworten*, 138-41.

78. *Zwischen den Zeiten*, 312-14; *Theologische Fragen und Antworten*, 141-3.

79. Letter to Paul Tillich, 2 April 1933, text *Evangelische Kommentare* 10, 1977, 111f.

80. E.Busch, *Karl Barth*, 225. Although in this connection Barth clearly and unambiguously rejects any 'confession of the idea and world-view of Socialism', this seems hardly comprehensible. For F.W.Marquardt, for example, the decisive sentence in the letter to Rust is 'Socialist praxis in the form of a confession' (*Theologie und Sozialismus*, 49). The literature which wants to make Barth the key-witness of a left-wing theology is full of remarkable assertions and misunderstandings. Thus U.Dannemann (*Der Zusammenhang von Theologie und Politik im Denken Karl Barths*, Bochum Protestant Theological Dissertaion 1975, 197f.) emphatically stated: 'It is not a matter of indifference to the

theologian Karl Barth whether the Socialism of the SPD or the Fascism of the NSDAP gets the upper hand in state and society.' As if anyone had ever claimed that Barth was indifferent in this way! What is more important is the absolutely fundamental distinction between Fascism and Communism as new 'religions' and the 'generally modest affair that we knew and still know as Social Democracy...' ('Fragen an das Christentum' [1931], in *Theologische Fragen und Antworten*, 94. When a woman student asked Barth in summer 1933 whether one could be a Christian and a theologian and a National Socialist all at the same time, Barth gave as the reason for his doubts in this respect the 'religious' character of National Socialism. He went on: 'I have always felt that in this respect it had a feature in common with Communism which for the same reason I have never been able to accept. The density of the world-view-religious, which is doubtless also haunting the SPD, cannot remotely be concerned with the density of the parallel feature among the National Socialists and the Communists. I would not conclude from this that it is impossible to reconcile National Socialism and Communism. But I must concede that I personally would find this impossible: because I would not know how at the same time I could take the National Socialist ideology honestly and fundamentally seriously and then accept my responsibility to the first commandment' (Letter to Fräulein Dallmann, 1 September 1933. Copy in the Karl Barth Archive, Basel).

81. Letter to Karl Ludwig Schmidt, Berlin-Oberrieden (Canton Zurich), 21 April 1933, Karl Barth Archive, Basel.

82. Letter to Georg Merz, 21 April 1933, ibid.

83. H.Gollwitzer, *Reich Gottes und Sozialismus bei Karl Barth*, Theologische Existenz heute, NF 169, Munich 1972, 58. Werner Koch has taken over the popular legend with further reminiscences (W.Koch, 'Wechselwirkungen zwischen Kirchenkampf und Theologie beobachtet an Karl Barth', in *Freispruch und Freiheit, Theologische Aufsatz für W.Kreck zum 65 Geburtstag*, ed. H.-G.Geyer, Munich 1973, 276f.). E.Busch also thinks that there was a 'first draft, in a sharp tone and couched in political terms', although the letter to Thurneysen of 27 June 1933 cited as evidence does not support this conclusion (E.Busch, *Karl Barth*, 226). In fact in the first draft Barth seems only to have had a sharper theological criticism of the Young Reformers Movement than in the final version. The title which he originally intended, still clearly recognizable on the manuscript, 'From Church Politics to the Church!' also indicates that the work cannot have been political.

84. C. von Kirchbaum to Frau Anna Katharina Barth, 15 June 1933, copy in the Karl Barth Archive, Basel.

85. Karl Barth, *Theological Existence Today*, Hodder and Stoughton 1933, 9f.

86. Ibid., 47-54.

87. Ibid., 55-76.

88. Ibid., 84f.

89. Karl Barth to Pastor Steinbach, 17 July 1933, copy in the Karl Barth Archive, Basel; W.Niemöller, 'Karl Barth's Mitwirkung im deutschen Kirchenkampf' (1954) in id., *Wort und Tat im Kirchenkampf, Beiträge zur neuesten Kirchengeschichte*, Munich 1969, 297 n.14.

90. H.Asmussen, *Begegnungen*, Wuppertal-Barmen nd [1936], 7. The work was intended as a contribution to the Festschrift for Karl Barth's fiftieth birthday, but was excluded for political reasons and published separately.

91. G.Schwenzel, 'Wirkung der *Theologische Existenz heute* in einem Pfarrhaus auf dem Lande', in *Antwort. Karl Barth zum 70. Geburtstag*, Zurich 1956, 909.

92. J.Hamel, 'Begegnungen mit Karl Barth', *Stimme der Gemeinde* 18, 1966, col.290.

93. G.Prater, *Kämpfer wider Willen*, 32f.

94. *Briefwechsel Barth-Bultmann*, 137 (only a précis of this letter is contained in the

English translation, Karl-Barth-Rudolf Bultmann, *Letters 1922-1966*, Grand Rapids and Edinburgh 1982, 69).

95. E.Hirsch, *Das kirchliche Wollen der Deutschen Christen*, 7 (15-16 July 1933).

96. F.Gogarten, *Einheit von Evangelium und Volkstum*, 7.

97. F.Gogarten, *Gericht oder Skepsis. Eine Streitschrift gegen Karl Barth*, Jena ²1937, 151.

98. F.Tügel, *Unmögliche Existenz!*, Hamburg 1933, 17 (emphasis in the original).

99. J.Lortz, *Katholischer Zugang zum Nationalsozialismus*, Münster ²1934, 24f.

100. Karl Barth, *Die Kirche Jesu Christi*, Theologische Existenz heute 5, Munich 1933, 3.

101. Dr Elisabeth Schmitz to Karl Barth, 1 January 1934, copy in the Karl Barth archive, Basel. Barth's answer of 18 January 1934, copy, ibid. (emphasis in the original).

102. See the letter to Bethge of 22 May 1967, in K.Barth, *Letters, 1961-1968*, Grand Rapids and Edinburgh 1981, 250.

103. Thus rightly P.Lange, *Konkrete Theologie*, 266f.

104. J.Schmidt, *Martin Niemöller*, 96, etc. and below Ch.13.

105. Cf. the accounts in P.Lange, *Konkrete Theologie*, 274-6.

10. The Establishment of the Reich Church (July-September)

1. For Hitler's decision on this point see 367f. above.

2. Telegram from Frick to Meiser, 13 July 1933, LKA Nürnberg, Meiser 114. Quoted from Baier, *Um Reichsbischof und Kirchenverfassung*, 417.

3. Undated (1.) draft of the Law on the Constitution of the German Evangelical Church, Buttmann, papers, Hitler's order in Conrad, *Der Kampf um die Kanzeln*, 22. (2.) Draft of the Reich Ministry of the Interior of 13 July 1933 in BA Koblenz, R 43 I/1464. This second draft was presented to the gathering on the morning of 14 July. A series of minor emendations suggested by this group was accepted and by afternoon was incorporated into a new (3.) draft. This third draft was then passed by the Reich Cabinet in the late evening. Cf. the letter from Pfundtner to the Secretary of State in the Reich Chancellery of 14 July 1933. Copy in Arch AA Bonn, Kult A 1,2. Text of the law in *Gesetzblatt der Deutschen Evangelischen Kirche*, 1933, 9; also – but with mistakes, in Kretschmar and Nicolaisen, *Dokumente* I, 107-9.

4. Protocol of the session in BA Koblenz, R 79/28, and in the notes by Meiser, LKA Nürnberg, 43-7. Cf. also the account by Wurm of 24 July in G.Schäfer, *Dokumentation* 2, 280f.

5. The Reich Minister of the Interior to all Land governments, 14 and 15 July 1933, Bad Gen. Karlsruhe, 223/27784.

6. 'Express! Strictly Confidential', Munich, 14 July 1933, signed Fischer pp. Reich Propaganda Leader, NStA Hannover Des I B No.3. This central piece of evidence is lacking from Kretschmar and Nicolaisen. The letter from the Gauleiters was in part handed on to the Kreisleiters almost word for word, as in Westphalia (B.Hey, *Die Kirchenprovinz Westfalen*, 231). Significantly Hossenfelder knew nothing of this order, as is betrayed by his own letter to the Gauleiters of 17 July (F.Zipfel, *Kirchenkampf*, 267).

7. Appeal and guidelines in *Junge Kirche* 1, 1933, 43f. The statement in ibid., printed with the date 14 July, was evidently written before the date of the elections was known. In general the detailed sequence of these events, in both chronology and substance, coming one on top of another as they do, needs a very much more accurate examination than we have in any of the accounts so far. Neither E.Bethge, *Bonhoeffer*, 224-9, nor P.Neumann, *Die Jungreformatorische Bewegung*, 120-9, nor J.Schmidt, *Niemöller*, 102-6, makes things clear.

8. Cf. P.Neumann, *Die Jungreformatorische Bewegung*, 126f.

9. Letter from the Reich leadership of the Evangelische Kirche list to the Oberkirchenrat in Oldenburg, 15 July, with material enclosed, LKA Oldenburg, OKR A I – 24 I. In Munich both the letter and the material were put on record with the note 'not relevant in Bavaria', H.Baier, *Die Deutschen Christen*, 56.

10. Copy of the Provisional Decree in the *Völkischer Beobachter* no.203 of 22 August: 'List name "Evangelische Kirche" not allowed'.

11. For these events see E.Bethge, *Bonhoeffer*, 226-8; Bonhoeffer, *Gesammelte Schriften* 2, 58f., partial English translation in D.Bonhoeffer (ed .E.H.Robertson), *No Rusty Swords*, 204f.; J..Glenthøj, *Dokumente*, 102f.; *Junge Kirche*, 1933, 60.

12. *Evangelium im Dritten Reich* 2, 1933, 276.

13. Kretschmar and Nicolaisen, *Dokumente* I, 113.

14. 'The Kreisleiters', one of these typical orders ran, 'are responsible for seeing that this order is made known as quickly as possible to all OG and support leaders. The Gauleiter makes the Kreisleiters personally responsible for handing on the report.' 'Gau Hessen-Nassau, urgent, strictly confidential', written confirmation of a telephone conversation of 18 July 1933, HStA, Wiesbaden, 483/2718.

15. F.Reiners, *Lübeck im Kirchenkampf*, 58-62, text also in Kretschmar and Nicolaisen, *Dokumente*, 115.

16. P. Langmann to the representatives of the Faith Movement, 17 August 1933, LKA Hamburg Deutsche Christen 2.

17. Kretschmar and Nikolaisen, *Dokumente*, 115.

18. Among the numerous examples, W.Harnisch's report on the Berlin Samaritan community is particularly vivid and typical; G.Harder and W.Niemöller (eds.), *Die Stunde der Versuchung*, 97ff. There is a wealth of instances in AEKU Berlin, Gen.III 51, vol.3.

19. E.V.Benn, 'Die Einstweilige Leitung der Deutschen Evangelischen Kirche (July-September 1933)', *Zeitschrift für evangelische Kirchenrecht* I, 1951, 368 n.13.

20. Letter from Pfundtner of 17 July 19e3 in J.Glenthøj, *Dokumente*, 102f. Also in Kretschmar and Nikolaisen, *Dokumente* I, 114f.

21. Kretschmar and Nikolaisen, *Dokumente* I, 118.

22. Ibid., 116, 119.

23. Manuscript note by Ludwig Müller, no date. It cannot be established whether the letter was actually sent, AEKD Berlin 14/246.

24. Text: Kretschmar and Nikolaisen, *Dokumente* I, 119-21.

25. Cf. e.g. *Junge Kirche* 1, 1933, 61f.

26. O.Palmer, *Material zur Geschichte des Kirchenkampfes in der Braunschweigischen Landeskirche*. Unpublished manuscript LKA Braunschweig, 15.

27. There are typical examples of such agreements e.g. in Württemberg in G.Schäfer, *Dokumentation* 2, 210ff.; in Hanover in E.Klügel, 65f.; in Schleswig-Holstein in J.Bielfeldt, 38f.

28. *Kreuzzeitung* no.189 of 24 April 1933.

29. J.Schmidt, *Niemöller*, 107.

30. For Elberfeld see H.Vorländer, *Kirchenkampf in Elberfeld*, 58-63; for Barmen-Gemarke, R.Steiner in Harder and Niemöller, *Stunde der Versuchung*, 286-302.

31. *Für die Freiheit des Evangeliums*, Theologische Existenz heute 3, 13. Cf. also the flysheet on the elections in W.Fürst (ed.), *Dialektische Theologie*, 5.

32. E.Busch, *Karl Barth*, 228.

33. For the German Christian victory in Westphalia and the reasons which led to a shift of the balance of power in the provincial synod, cf. now the careful investigation by B.Hey, *Kirchenprovinz Westfalen*, 41-9.

34. *Evangelium im Dritten Reich* 2, 1933, 286.

35. J.Gauger, *Chronik* I, 95.

36. P.D.Walter Windfuhr to Dr Ernst Dietrich, 27 July 1933, AEKHN Darmstadt, 44/126.

37. L.Volk, *Reichskonkordat*, 244.

38. For the basic significance of this speech for church politics see L.Siegele Wenschkewitz, *Nationalsozialismus und Kirchen*, 127-31.

39. *Völkischer Beobachter* No.218, 16 August 1933, Kretschmar and Nikolaisen, *Dokumente* I, 124.

40. Ibid., 143.

41. Ibid., 145. See in detail below, Ch.12.

42. Circular letter to all Reichsleiters and Gauleiters of 12 January 1934, ibid., 371f.

43. M.Niemöller to Chief Pastor Jannasch, Lübeck, 13 September 1933, W.Niemöller, *Der Pfarrernotbund. Geschichte einer kämpfenden Bruderschaft*, Hamburg 1973, 16.

44. Cf. above, Part One, Chs.5, 6.

45. 'Staat und Religion', *Reichswart* 14, 1933, of 19 March.

46. 'Gleichberechtigung für deutsche Nichtchristen!', *Reichswart* 14, 1933, of 11 June.

47. For Hauer and the German Faith Movement cf. K.Hutten, 'Die Deutsche Glaubensbewegung', in Künneth and Schreiner, *Die Nation vor Gott*, 1934, 506-33, and above all the account and evaluation in H.Buchheim, *Glaubenskrise*, 157-204, which is probably too positive.

48. Memorandum of 24 August 1933, BadGenA Karlsruhe, 235/12851.

49. W.Hauer, *Deutsche Gottschau. Grundzüge eines Deutschen Glaubens*, Stuttgart 1934, 4.

50. Ibid., 246.

51. Ibid., Foreword.

52. J.Schmidt, 'Studien zur Vorgeschichte des Pfarrernotbundes', *Zeitschrift für Kirchengeschichte* 79, 1968, 54.

53. *Junge Kirche* I, 1933, 80f.

54. P.Neumann, *Jungreformatorische Bewegung*, 136f.; J.Schmidt, *Niemöller*, 110.

55. M.Niemöller, 'Die Jungreformatorische Bewegung und die Kirchenpolitik, 16 Thesen', in *Junge Kirche* 1, 1933, 99-101.

56. K.Barth, *Theological Existence Today*, 76.

57. *Junge Kirche*, 1933, 101.

58. Ibid., 106.

59. Willy Praetorius, 'Kampf um Wahrheit und Glauben, Sollen wir Deutsche Christen werden?', ibid., 107-9. Cf. also the article 'Deutsche Glaubensgemeinschaft', with a detailed account of the Eisenach agreement and Hauer's intentions, ibid., 113-17.

60. Jacobi to H.Ehrenberg, 12 August 1933, J.Glenthøj, *Dokumente*, 105. K.Scharf to about fifty Brandenburg pastors, 11 August 1933, in K.Scharf, *Für ein politisches Gewissen der Kirche. Aus Reden und Schriften 1932-1972*, Stuttgart 1972, 29f.

61. K.Kupisch, 'Zur Genesis des Pfarrernotbundes', *Theologische Literaturzeitung* 91, 1966, 725f.

62. J.Schmidt, *Studien*, 60.

63. J.Schmidt, *Niemöller*, 114.

64. K.Scharf, *Politisches Gewissen*, 28.

65. Circular letter from Bodelschwingh, 11 August 1933, Glenthøj, *Dokumente*, 105.

66. The work began on 15 August, and on 26 August the redaction of th first form was completed, J.Glenthøj, *Dokumente*, 105. For the origin and history of the Bethel Confession see the preliminary comments by E.Bethge in D.Bonhoeffer, *Gesammelte Schriften* 2, 80-9 and id, *Bonhoeffer*, 231-4. For the interpretation cf. M.Pertiet, *Das Ringen um Wesen und Auftrag*, 97-102, and H.J.Reese, *Bekenntnis und Bekennen*, 200-6.

Also Dorothea Friedrich, *Das Betheler Bekenntnis*, Wissenschaftliche Zulassungsarbeit, Tübingen 1973 (unpublished).

67. On this cf. D.Bonhoeffer, *Gesammelte Schriften* 2, 82.

68. Thus Bonhoeffer to his grandmother on 20 August, ibid., 78f.

69. M.Niemöller, *Das Bekenntnis der Väter und die bekennende Gemeinde. Zu Besinnung dargeboten von einem Kreise vom evangelischen Theologen und in ihrem Namen*, ed M.Niemöller, Munich 1934. Here quoted from the reprint in K.D.Schmidt, *Bekenntnisse 1933*, 105-31.

70. D.Bonhoeffer, *Gesammelte Schriften* 2, 91-119.

71. Ibid., 112f.; K.D.Schmidt, *Bekenntnisse*, 125.

72. D.Bonhoeffer, ibid., 114; K.D.Schmidt, ibid., 127.

73. D.Bonhoeffer, ibid., 117; K.D.Schmidt, ibid., 127.

74. K.D.Schmidt, *Bekenntnisse 1933*, 128.

75. Letter from Bodelschwingh of 26 August 1933, D.Bonhoeffer, *Gesammelte Schriften* 2, 90f.

76. Stratenwerth to M.Niemöller, 30 August 1933, ibid., 84.

77. The documents seem to be lost so that the events so far can only be reconstructed from the recollections of those who took part. Cf. ibid., 87, 85.

78. K.Barth, *Grundsätzliche Vorbemerkung zum Betheler Bekenntnis*, 11 October 1933, in J.Glenthøj, *Dokumente*, 106f.

79. Merz to Niemöller, 5 December 1933, D.Bonhoeffer, *Gesammelte Schriften* 2, 86.

80. Ibid., 85f., and J.Schmidt, *Niemöller*, 87.

81. For the agreement between Jacobi and Pastor Heidenreich as Hossenfelder's representative cf. J.Schmidt, *Niemöller*, 116; P.Neumann, *Jungreformatorische Bewegung*, 143f., and the corresponding report in the *Völkischer Beobachter* no.216 of 4 August: 'United list for the provincial synod elections', with the signatures of Hossenfelder, Eckert, Schulz and Jacobi.

82. *Gesetzblatt der DEK*, 1933, 7.

83. There are two detailed records of this meeting: 1. Account of the transactions of the session of the authorized representatives of the German Evangelical Churches on 20 July 1933, at 10.30 a.m. in the offices of the German Evangelical Church Chancellery (29pp.), AEKD Berlin, A 3/93; 2. notes by Meiser, LKA Nürnberg, 48-56.

84. The resolution is in E.-V.Benn, 'Die Einstweilige Leitung', *Zeitschrift für evangelische Kirche* 1, 1951, 364.

85. Transactions (n.83), 28f.

86. Records of the transactions of the sessions of the Provisional Leadership of the German Evangelical Church, AEKD Berlin, s.v Handakten Benn, first session of 1 August 1933, 2, point 3.

87. Record of transactions (n.83), 22f.; notes by Meiser, 55f.

88. E.V.Benn, 'Die Einstweilige Leitung', 376f. Both content and expression certainly indicate that the unsigned note of 20 July 1933 from Müller's Handakten (ibid., 366 n.6) comes from Jäger. However, telegrams with a similar content will hardly have been sent.

89. On 25 July Jäger was also called officially to the Reich leadership of the German Christians with the task of taking over the report on 'State and Church', J.Gauger, *Chronik* I, 96.

90. No. 209. Also in J.Gauger, *Chronik* I, 96.

91. Records of transactions (n.86), first session of 1 August, 1 point 1. Müller's visit to Hitler took place on 28 July. For Hitler's alleged wish cf. Schöffel's comment at the fourth session on 8 August, ibid., 7, point 1; E.V.Benn, 'Die Einstweilige Leitung', 366 n.9 (statement by Koopman).

92. Because of state pressure (discussion with the Prussian Minister President Hermann

Göring on 15 July 1933, Kretschmar and Nicolaisen, *Dokumente* I, 89f.) some 'commissioners' – above all Hossenfelder and Dr Werner – remained in office in the Prussian Oberkirchenrat alongside the members of the Evangelischer Oberkirchenrat who had returned. After the church elections a series of members had asked for leave. This left the church authorities almost incapable of functioning.

93. G.Mehnert, *Evangelische Kirche*, 145.

94. Record of transactions (n.86), second session of 2 August, 2, point 1.

95. Ibid., third session of 3 August 1933, 6, point 8.

96. Protocol of the 53rd conference of the Church Senate on 4 August 1933, AEKU Berlin.

97. On 16 August Dibelius wrote on behalf of the Prussian general superintendents to August Kortheuer, Land Bishop of Hessen, and asked him for personal information about Jäger because he had been 'selected' as President of the Evangelischer Oberkirchenrat, K. Dienst, *Dokumentation* 1, 239.

98. See ch.4 above.

99. Record of transactions (n.86), third session of 3 August 1933, 5f., point 7, and fifth session of 9 August 1933, 9f., point 5.

100. Report of the Telegraph Union, 18 August 1933. Read out in the thirteenth session of 22 August 1933, 22f. point 3.

101. Ibid., 23.

102. 'Concerning Reich Bishop Ludwig Müller, compiled by members of the Protestant Faculty', Tübingen 1934 (29pp.), US Tübingen from 162/XIV, 6.

103. Negotiations over this alliance had already been in process since 1926, W.Lueken, *Kampf, Behauptung und Gestalt der Evangelischen Landeskirche Nassau-Hessen*, Göttingen 1963.

104. Records of negotiations (n.86), 42.

105. In an opinion of Jäger's dated 19 July on the Reich Church constitution we find: '1. It is unitary...'; 'The second main concept is that of leadership', Arch. Panstw.Poznan, s.v. August Jäger, 6.

106. The original draft of the constitution for Greater Hessen dated 17 August 1933 is in AEKHN Darmstadt, 44/125. There is a draft with similar wording for Lower Saxony in Kretschmar and Nicolaisen, *Dokumente* 1, 201.

107. K. Dienst, *Dokumentation* 1, 239.

108. The participants are in the appendix of the protocol to the original draft (n.106), folios 10f.

109. W.-V.Benn, 'Einstweilige Leitung', 370 n.20.

110. Protocol of the session in the Prussian Kultusministerium on 17 August 1933, 1-3, AEKHN Darmstadt, 44/125.

111. Ibid., 3, 16-18.

112. Ibid., 30.

113. K. Dienst, *Dokumentation* 1, 242f.

114. Records of transactions (n.86), fifteenth session of 15 August 1933, 32f. point 7.

115. Jäger to the Landeskirche government in Wiesbaden, 25 August 1933, Kretschmar and Nicolaisen, *Dokumente* 1, 126f.

116. 'Report on the discussion with the Führer... on 24 August 1933', LKA Hamburg, s.v.Deutsche Christen, no.1216.

117. Records of transactions (n.86), sixteenth session on 30 August 1933, 34ff., point 2, and 36f., point 3.

118. Ibid., eighteenth session of 1 September 1933, 42.

119. B.Hey, *Kirchenprovinz Westfalen*, 50f.; W.Niemöller, *Bekennende Kirche im Westfalen*, 64-6.

120. Records of transactions (n.86), eighteenth session on 1 August 1933, 47, point 10.

121. Transactions of the regular twenty-third Rhenish Provincial Synod in its conference on 23 and 24 August at Koblenz, J. Beckman, *Rheinische Synoden im Kirchenkampf*, Neukirchen 1975, 11-33.

122. Transactions of the conference of the provincial synod of East Prussia on 23 August 1933, Kònigsberg 1933, 2.

123. H.J.Iwand, *Briefe an Rudolf Hermann*, Nachgelassene Werke 6, Munich 1964, 251f. (letter of 9 September 1933). See also the letter of 21 December 1933, ibid., 258f. The special course taken by East Prussia already began with the development of distinctive German Christian guidelines in summer 1933 (see above, 211f.). For Erich Koch's double role cf. M.Koschorke (ed.), *Geschichte der Bekennenden Kirche in Ostpreussen 1933-1945*, Göttingen 1976, 33-5, 43, 122-9, 410, 510-13. Similarly also H.Linck, *Der Kirchenkampf in Ostpreussen*, 32, 42-44, 49, etc. For Iwand's activity in East Prussia cf. M.Koschorke, *Geschichte der Bekennenden Kirche im Ostpreussen*, 65-75.

124. See above n.81.

125. *Verhandlungen der 21. ordentlichen Brandenburgischen Provincialsynode im Jahre 1933*, [Berlin] 1933, 22-5. There is an account of the course of the synod e.g. also in the *Allgemeine Evangelisch-Lutherische Kirchenzeitung* 66, 1933, 845.

126. *Verhandlungen*, 41ff., 47ff.

127. Ibid., 4-6.

128. Hans Lietzmann was one of the best known church historians of his time. There is a copy of a similar letter to the Administrative Court of Charlottenburg for Oberverwaltungsgerichtsrat von Dryander, AEKD Berlin C 4/17. There is also a reproduction of an undated copy in *Junge Kirche* 1, 1933, 251f. The signature was that of the adjutant representing the Gauleiter, attorney Wilhelm Woy, who was a member of the synod. The whole proceeding was written on the record on 29 May 1934 by the secretariat of the Reich Bishop as 'superseded'.

129. Quoted from H.Schmid, *Apokalyptisches Wetterleuchten. Ein Beitrag der Evangelische Kirche zu Kampf im 'Dritten Reich'*, Munich 1947, 39-41. For Jacobi's verbal communication see the transactions (n.125), 32f.

130. A.Speer, *Inside the Third Reich*, 41f., also 67f., 71-5.

131. Hitler's three main speeches are printed in *Nürnberg 1933. Eine Sammlung der wichtigsten Reden auf dem Parteitag der NSDAP von 30 August – 3 September 1933*, Berlin 1933, 11-41; the quotations come from ibid., 19f. Otherwise the whole Party conference was unmistakably dominated by the race question.

132. 54th meeting of the Church Senate on 28 August 1933 in Berlin, AEKU Berlin.

133. Evidently because the constant pressure of events, the transactions were no longer printed. There is a manuscript ready for press, 'Transactions of the Tenth General Synod of the Evangelical Church of the Old Prussian Union in its regular meeting on 5 and 6 September 1933', in AEKU Berlin (which on the whole is quoted in what follows) in AEKU Berlin; there is a further – incomplete – copy in the possession of the EvAGKiZ Munich. From the side of the Young Reformers (Evangelium und Kirche) there are three reports from the Westphalian church on the preliminary history and course of events. They come from: Dr Georg Müller, director of studies, 'Events taking place in connection with the last General Synod of the Old Prussian Union of 8 September 1933'; from the Dortmund Pastor Karl Lücking, who was at the same time a member of the synod's Council of Elders, 'Report on the Course of the Tenth General Synod on 5 September in Berlin' (both reports in AEKHN Darmstadt, no.62.1040); also the account by the representative of the theological faculty of the University of Münster, W.Stählin, in *Via Vitae*, 276-9. There is a brief German Christian account in *Evangelium im Dritten Reich*

2, 1933, 364; a comprehensive account in *Evangelisch-Lutherische Kirchenzeitung* 66, 1933, 859-62; cf. also *Junge Kirche* 1, 1933, 192ff.

134. W.Stâhlin, op.cit.

135. *Evangelium im Dritten Reich*, ibid.

136. Transactions, 1-11.

137. *Allgemeine Evangelisch-Lutherische Kirchenzeitung*, ibid.

138. Texts: J.Beckmann, *Kirchliches Jahrbuch 1933-1944*, Gütersloh ²1976, 3f.

139. Transactions, 52.

140. Thus also Hossenfelder in his 'Opinion' of 7 July 1945, though in it he says explicitly that Jäger was author only of the Law for Civil Servants and the Enabling Act, LKA Berlin-Brandenburg, Akte Hossenfelder.

141. Quoted from the original draft of the statement, AEKHN Darmstadt, no. 62/1040.

142. Thus G.Müller, op.cit.

143. Transactions, 77, 85f.

144. Transactions (Munich MS), 39-41.

145. Thus the account by Karl Lücking (n.133). Cf. also the accounts by G.Müller and W.Stählin, ibid.

146. 55th session of the Church Senate on 6 September 1933, AEKU Berlin.

147. Drafts of the letter of 9 and 21 September with memoranda in AEKU Berlin, Präs.I, 2 IX.

148. Memorandum of 7 September 1933, Archive Panst.Poznan, s.v August Jäger, no.6.

149. Record of transactions (n.86), nineteenth session on 6 September 1933, 48.

150. Ibid., 51f.

151. Ibid., 53.

152. Ibid., 20th session on 7 September 1933, 55; twenty-first session on 8 September, 66f., and 74f. For the reception of Eidem on 9 September cf. E.Murtorinnen, *Erzbischof Eidem zum Deutschen Kirchenkampf 1933-1934*, Helsinki 1968, 26ff.

153. Record of transactions, twentieth session on 7 September 1933, point 5, 63, and 21st session on 8 September, 65, point 1.

154. Ibid., twentieth session on 7 September 1933, 55ff., point 2, and 57ff., point 3.

155. There is a brief protocol of this session in Kretschmar and Nicolaisen, *Dokumente* I, 128.

156. Record of transactions (n.86), 21st session on 8 September 1933, 72-4, point 8. The Provisional Administration received information about the proceedings on the same day from a lengthy telephone conversation with Kassel. Cf. also K. Dienst, *Dokumentation* I, 108, 241, 250 and above all 254. There is also an account of the resistance of the Gauleiter of Kurhessen to Jäger's plans in Kortheuer, *Das Ende der Evangelischen Landeskirche im Nassau*, AEKHN 0201, 89.

157. The Landeskirche of Nassau had 293 pastorates in 1928 (Troschke, *Evangelische Kirchenstatistik*, 6/7, 1931, 429). 177 pastors took part in the gatherings of pastors in Limburg on 23 August, K. Dienst, *Dokumentation* 1, 243.

158. Protocol of the session of 11 September by an unkonwn participant, Kirchliche Dienst, *Dokumentation* 1, 249-53.

159. For this enquiry see n.97 above.

160. Thus the wording according to Kortheuer's report to the Provisional Leadership on 13 September, Transactions (n.86), 23, twenty-third session, point 4, 84-7. The account in K. Dienst, *Dokumentation* 1, 255f. is essentially similar.

161. K. Dienst, *Dokumentation* 1, 257-69.

162. Ibid., 392-8.

163. Ibid., 84-110.

164. For the legal problems of these events see W.Lueken, *Nassau-Hessen*, esp. 118-84.

165. For developments in Saxony cf. J.Fischer, *Sächsiche Landeskirche*, 19-22. For the Brown Synod of 11 August, *Junge Kirche* 1, 1933, 189f.; also 'Christenkreuz und Hakenkreuz', *Monatsblatt für deutsche Christen* 1, 1933, Vol.3, September 1933, 1f.

166. Coch to the Provisonal Leadership, 14 September 1933.

167. While Beye was acquitted, he had obviously become impossible, J.Gauger, *Chronik* I, 134, 154, and in more detail O.Palmer, *Braunschweigische Landeskirche*, unpublished MS, LKA Braunschweig, 18-23 and 50-4.

168. For the course of the synod, J.Bielfeldt, *Schleswig-Holstein*, 40-6. The telegram is in LKA Oldenburg OKR A I – 24 I and Transactions (n.86), 92. For the Greater Church of Lower Saxony see also K.F.Reimers, *Lübeck*, 72-5.

169. For Rendtorff cf. N.Beste, *Mecklenburg*, 50-6; documents, ibid., 263-81; also records of transactions (n.86), passim.

170. E.Klügel, *Hannover*, 67-78. Marahrens went so far as to declare that 'on the basis of the last guidelines the concern of the German Christians, in full personal affirmation of the National Socialists, is largely my own', letter of 26 August 1933, E.Klügel, *Dokumente*, 26f.

171. For the enabling of the Land Bishop in May 1933 see G.Schäfer, *Dokumentation* 1, 285-98; for the course of the synod, G.Schäfer, *Dokumentation* 2, 346-81.

172. H.Baier, *Die Deutschen Christen Bayerns*, 62-6.

173. Records of transactions (n.86), twenty-second session on 12 September 1933, 78 point 2 (invitation to Berlin); twenty-third session of 13 September 133, 84-7, point 4 (report) and 88f. point 9 (discussion); twenty-fourth session of 14 September 1933, 91-3, consequences, and 97f., point 7 (Müller's confirmation).

174. K. Dienst, *Dokumentation* 1, 256.

175. Memorandum with annotation 'Today!' of 21 September 1933, in AEKU Berlin, Präs. I, 2 IX.

176. D.Bonhoeffer, 'Der Arierparagraph in der Kirche', *Gesammelte Schriften* 2, 62-9. Cf. E.Bethge, *Bonhoeffer*, 235ff., and J.Glenthøj, *Dokumente*, 86.

177. Gerhard Jacobi also attests Bonhoeffer's initial resolution to leave the church on the evening of the General Synod, in W.D.Zimmermann (ed.), *I Knew Dietrich Bonhoeffer*, London and New York 1966, 71. Cf. also Bonhoeffer's letters to Sasse and Karl Barth of 9 September 1933, *Gesammelte Schriften* 2, 71 and 126f.

178. For the course of this session cf. the account by Georg Müller of 8 September 1933 (n.133); the statements by Knak on 13 September in J.Glenthøj, *Dokumente*, 86f., and W.Stählin, *Via Vitae*, 279. The accounts in E.Bethge, *Bonhoeffer*, 248f., and J.Schmidt, *Niemöller*, 119f., are to be corrected accordingly.

179. J.Glenthøj, *Dokumente*, 87.

180. Text in D.Bonhoeffer, *Gesammelte Schriften* 2, 70f.

181. Bodelschwingh to Ludwig Müller, 11 September 1933, AEKD 1933 Berlin A 4/328.

182. W.Niemöller, *Texte zur Geschichte des Pfarrernotbundes*, Berlin 1958, 26f. There is a later version without point 3 in K.D.Schmidt, *Bekenntnisse 1933*, 77f.; *Kirchliches Jahrbuch 1933-1944*, ²1976, 35 and many other passages. The role of Weschke and Jacob was indicated for the first time by K.Kupisch, 'Zur Genesis des Pfarrernotbundes', *Theologische Literaturzeitung* 91, 1966, 722-30. Otherwise cf. W.Niemöller, *Pfarrernotbund*, 15-18; J.Schmidt, *Niemöller*, 121-4 and above all id., 'Studien zur Geschichte des Pfarrernotbundes', *Zeitschrift für Kirchengeschichte* 79, 1968, 64-7.

183. Quoted from W.Niemöller, op.cit., 16. Cf. also the circular letter from Kurt Scharf of 14 September, in K.Scharf, *Politisches Gewissen*, 30f.

184. W. Niemöller, op.cit., 18.

185. J.Schmidt, *Niemöller*, 125f.

186. W.Niemöller, *Pfarrernotbund*, 17.

187. W.Niemöller, *Texte*, 22f.

188. Cf. Kurt Scharf, 'Der Pfarrernotbund', in *Bekennende Kirche, Martin Niemöller zum 60. Geburtstage*, Munich 1952, 136-41.

189. Results of the consultations in Essen, 11 September 1933, W.Niemöller, *Texte*, 20-2.

190. Texts of the enquiry and both opinions e.g. in K.D.Schmidt, *Bekenntnisse 1933*, 178-86.

191. 'Neues Testament und Rassenfrage', opinion of 23 September 1933, ibid., 189-91.

192. Monod's letter of 13 August 1933, quoted from A.Boyens, *Kirchenkampf und Ökumene 1933-1939*, 60.

193. Records of transactions (n.86), resolutions of the Provisional Leadership of 17 August (17) and 30 August (37).

194. For Heckel's role cf. now E.Gerstenmaier, 'Das Kirchliche Aussenamt im Reiche Hitlers', in *Kirche im Spannungsfeld der Politik, Festschrift D.Hermann Kunst am 70. Geburtstag*, Göttingen 1977, 307-18.

195. A.Boyens, *Kirchenkampf und Ökumene 1933-1939*, 62-4. Cf. also Bonhoeffer, *Gesammelte Schriften* 2, 70. The telegram arrived in Geneva at 5 p.m. (Boyens, op.cit., n.163). For the whole matter cf. also E.Bethge, *Bonhoeffer*, 242, 246; above all Heckel's letter of 6 November 1933, ibid., 371f.

196. English text in A.Boyens, op.cit., 311f.

197. Text in ibid., 312.

198. Complete text of the letter from the German Embassy in Sofia to the Foreign Office in Berlin dated 26 September 1933 in J.Glenthøj, *Dokumente*, 341. For the conference in Sofia cf. E.Bethge, *Bonhoeffer*, 241-6; A.Boyens, *Kirchenkampf und Ökumene*, 66-9; there is a more subtle account in J.Glenthøj, *Dokumente*, 47-52.

199. Archbishop Eidem to the Provisional Administration and Land Bishop Müller, Uppsala, 15 September 1933, text in E.Murtorinne, *Erzbischof Eidem zum deutschen Kirchenkampf, 1933-1934*, Helsinki 1968, 88f.; A.Boyens, op.cit., 312f.

200. Stieve's notes of 22 September and letter from the Foreign Office of the same date in Kretschmar and Nicolaisen, *Dokumente* I, 130-2. For the course of Eidem's visit see E.Murtorinne, *Eidem*, 26-32.

201. Geneva, German delegation telegram of 30 September 1933, signed Roediger; letter of the German embassy in London of 2 October 1933, signed Bismarck, Arch AA Bonn, Kult A 2,2.

202. K.Scholder, 'Die evangelische Kirche in der Sicht der nationalsozialistischen Führung bis zum Kriegsausbruch', *Vierteljahrshefte für Zeitgeschichte* 16, 1968, 23-5.

203. For this session see above 353f.

204. Notes by Meiser, LKA Nürnberg, 57-62; Baier and Henn, *Chronologie*, 38.

205. LKA Nürnberg, Meiser 115, memorandum, 'Was haben wir Lutheraner jetzt zu tun?'. Quoted from H.Baier, *Reichsbischof*, 229. Text also in J.Gauger, *Chronik* 1, 104.

206. Meiser to Müller, 27 September 1933, in H.Baier, *Reichsbischof*, 453.

207. Letter of 27 September 1933, AEKD Berlin A 4/18.

208. H.Baier, *Reichsbischof*, 444f.

209. So far no consecutive accounts or minutes of these sessions have appeared. The following account is based on individual documents and references. For the 'Grand

Council of Leaders' cf. J.Gauger, *Chronik* I, 99; also *Evangelium im Dritten Reich* 2, 1933, 468.

210. BA Koblenz, R 43 II/161:; Kretschmar and Nicolaisen, *Dokumente* I, 135.

211. For the discussions between Hossenfelder and Jäger cf. F.Weineke, *Kirche und Partei*, 20f.; J.Hossenfelder, 'Eine Stellungnahme' (1945), LKA Berlin-Brandenburg; F.Tügel, *Erinnerungen*, 248.

212. BA Koblenz, R 43 II/161; telegram of 27 September 1933.

213. *Evangelium im Dritten Reich* 2, 1933, 409. There is a similar account from a German Christian writer (Pastor Schairer, a synod member from Württemberg) in G.Schäfer, *Dokumentation* 2, 393-7; also F.Tügel, *Erinnerungen*, 246-9. W. Conrad, *Kampf um die Kanzeln*, 29-31, is critical; cf. above all a detailed account from Gertrud Staewen to Karl Barth of 27 September in the Karl Barth Archive, Basel. Members, participants and negotiations are listed in the official printed volume, *Verhandlungen der Ersten Deutschen Evangelischen Nationalsynode am 27. September 1933 in der Lutherstadt Wittenberg*, published by the Deutscher Evangelischer Kirchenkanzlei, Berlin 1934.

214. *Evangelium im Dritten Reich*, ibid., 409.

215. Hitler's refusal of 23 September is in Glenthøj, *Dokumente*, 90.

216. List of guests, *Verhandlungen*, 19.

217. Text e.g. in J.Beckmann, *Kirchliches Jahrbuch*, 35f. and 495. For its composition see J.Schmidt, *Niemöller*, 127ff.

218. Cf. the reports from Wittenberg to Eidem and Berggrav, J.Glenthøj, *Dokumente*, 110f.

219. Thus the account by Gertrud Staewen. The theological storm troops from Saxony made such an impression that they were also explicitly mentioned in most of the other accounts. The most detailed report was in *Christenkreuz und Hakenkreuz* (Saxony), 4, October 1933, 18f.: There – on the Elbbrücke in Wittenberg – 'stand with the banners of the Third Reich our theological storm troops, who came overnight from Augustusburg. The young men look sturdy and fresh in their grey uniforms and jackboots, with their knapsacks packed for a route march, bread bags and water flasks. Some sharp commands resound from the splendid leader of our theological storm troops, and to the sound of music the future pastors of the Third Reich enter Wittenberg. Our Land Bishop stands before the Court of Wittenberg, and the theological storm troops pass in front of him in an impeccable march past...'

220. *Evangelium im Dritten Reich* 2, 1933, 410 (emphasis in the original).

221. Complete text in *Verhandlungen*, 39-45; *Gesetzblatt der Deutschen Evangelischen Kirche*, 1933, 11f.

222. J.Glenthøj, *Dokumente*, 50.

11. Catholicism after the Concordat (September 1933-January 1934)

1. Gröber to Pacelli, 28 December 1933; B. Stasiewski, *Akten* I, 494.

2. Alphons Koechlin to George Bell, 11 December 1933, *George Bell – Alphons Koechlin. Briefwechsel 1933-1954*, Zurich 1969, 83.

3. For this see above, 402f.

4. E.Deuerlein, *Reichskonkordat*, 135, and W.Conrad, *Kampf um die Kanzeln*, 72ff. The negotiations did not take place at first because Pacelli was having a long holiday. Telegram from the German embassy at the Holy See to the Foreign Office, 20 September 1933, *Akten zur deutschen auswärtigen Politik*, Serie C, Vols. 1, 2, Göttingen 1971, 911 n.3.

5. For the particular situation in Bavaria cf. above all L.Volk, *Der Bayerische Episkopat*, 123-30, 137ff., and above 395f.

6. Text, Kretschmar and Nicolaisen, *Dokumente* I, 129f.

7. Letter of 25 September 1933, B.Stasiewki, *Akten* I, 400f.

8. Neuhäusler to Faulhaber, 28 September 1933, L.Volk, *Faulhaber-Akten* I, 770ff.

9. From a letter from Buttmann to Berning of 28 September , ibid., 773 n.3.

10. D.Albrecht, *Notenwechsel* I, 1-8.

11. Text in L.Volk, *Kirchliche Akten*, 263-9. Cf. on this also Bertram's circular to the German episcopate of 23 October 1933, B.Stasiewski, *Akten* I, 416.

12. On this cf. e.g. the letter from Kaas to Gröber of 12 December 1933, B.Stasiewski, *Akten* I, 482-4.

13. Quoted from *Germania*, 11 October 1933, in H.Müller, *Katholische Kirche*, 207.

14. Letter from the Minister of the Interior, 9 October 1933; answer from the Kultusministerium, 24 October 1933. BadGenA Karlsruhe 235/12754. For these whole proceedings cf. also K.Scholder, 'Baden im Kirchenkampf des Dritten Reiches', esp. 225-30.

15. For *Kreuz und Adler* ('Cross and Eagle') cf. K.Breuning, *Vision des Reiches*, 225-35.

16. Text, Kretschmar and Nicolaisen, *Dokumente* I, 137f.

17. Newsletter of the Arbeitsgemeinschaft of 15 December 1933, text: K.Breuning, *Vision des Reiches*, 342.

18. Quoted from K.Breuning, op.cit., 237.

19. See above, 428.

20. F. von Papen, *Der 12. November 1933 und die deutschen Katholiken, Rede gehalten vor der Arbeitsgemeinschaft katholischer Deutscher in der Messehalle zu Köln am 9. November 1933*, Reich und Kirche 3, Münster 1934, 6.

21. Papen to Bertram, 3 October 1933, Bertram's answer from Rome, 7 October 1933, B.Stasiewski, *Akten* I, 430 n.1, and 403-5. Cf. also the comments by Leiber to Gröber about this letter, 11 October 1933, L.Volk, *Kirchliche Akten*, 272.

22. Thun to Gröber, 17 November 1933. Gröber's answer of 19 November 1933, B.Stasiewski, *Akten* I, 461 n.1 and 363f.

23. Klein to Bertram, ibid., 869-71.

24. Leiber to Gröber, 11 October 1933, L.Volk, *Kirchliche Akten*, 270-2.

25. Bergen's original account is in A.Kupper, *Staatliche Akten*, 426-9; Kaas's draft is in L.Volk, *Kirchliche Akten*, 300-4.

26. Telegram from Bergen to the Foreign Office, 14 October 1933. Note in the margin: 'Presented to the Herr Reich Minister', *Akten zur deutschen auswärtigen Politik*, Serie C, Vol.1, 2, 910f.

27. M.Domarus, *Hitler* I, 274. For Hitler's decision cf. also above all J.C.Fest, *Hitler*, 600-5.

28. M.Domarus, op.cit., 277f.

29. Ministerial discussion on 12 September 1933, *Akten zur deutschen auswärtigen Politik*, Serie C, Vol.1, 2, 785f.

30. Cf. on this e.g. the notes by Neurath on a conversation with the British Foreign Minister, Sir John Simon, of 24 September 1933, ibid., 824-6; also H.A.Jacobsen, *Nationalsozialistische Aussenpolitik*, 397f.

31. *Akten zur deutschen auswärtigen Politik*, Serie C, Vol.1, 2, 868.

32. Telegram from the Embassy in London, 4 October 1933, ibid., 870f.

33. Telegram from Neurath, 11 October 1933, ibid., 890f.

34. Ministerial discussion of 11 October 1933, ibid., 907.

35. Hitler's Reichstag speech of 1 September 1939, M.Domarus, *Hitler* II, 1315.

36. H.Rauschning, *Gespräche*, 102f.

37. Report by the British ambassador in Berlin, Sir Eric Phipps, to the Foreign Minister,

Sir John Simon, 15 November 1933, on the 12 November elections, *Ursachen und Folgen*, X, 57.

38. M.Domarus, *Hitler* I, 314.

39. M.Domarus, op.cit., 330, extracts from the speech in *Ursache und Folgen* X, 53-6. The report by the British ambassador, ibid., 59.

40. H.Müller, *Katholische Kirche*, 212. There are other appeals from the Catholic side in E.-W.Böckenförde, 'Der deutsche Katholizismus im Jahre 1933. Eine kritische Betrachtung' (1961), in id., *Kirchlicher Auftrag und politische Entscheidung*, Freiburg 1973, 72.

41. *Junge Kirche* 1, 1933, 252. After the Second World War F.Baumgärtel was the first to refer emphatically to this telegram. He combined with it criticism of an over-simplistic account of the beginnings of the Church Struggle (*Wider die Kirchenkampflegenden*, Neuendettelsau ²1959, 4-13. There is a retort by W.Niemöller, ibid., 17-21). Both Martin Niemöller and Wilhelm Harnisch, the author of the telegram, described the situation quite accurately in retrospect, when they spoke – as did Niemöller - of a 'spontaneous expression', 'participation in the general shouting' (J.Schmidt, *Niemöller*, 472 n.269) or – like Harnisch, declared: 'At that time my position, which I still hold today, was that the League of Nations was then no more than an organization with the aim of keeping down Germany' (*Junge Kirche* 18, 1975, 222).

42. Gröber to Leiber, 14 October 1933, L.Volk, *Kirchliche Akten*, 273.

43. Cf. the telegrams from Bergen to the Foreign Office of 16 and 17 October, *Akten zur deutschen auswärtigen Politik*, Serie C, Vol.1, 3f., 8f.

44. Telegram from Neurath to Bergen, 18 October 1933, ibid., 9 n.6.

45. E.Deuerlein, *Reichskonkordat*, 137.

46. D.Albrecht, *Notenwechsel* I, 10-14, *Akten zur deutschen auswärtigen Politik*, Serie C, Vol.1, 24-28.

47. W.Conrad, *Kampf um die Kanzeln*, 76.

48. Ibid., 78. Cf. also the reminiscences by Gröber in L.Volk, *Kirchliche Akten*, 326, and *Reichskonkordat*, 204f., above all nn. 18,19.

49. W.Konrad, *Kampf um die Kanzeln*, 81.

50. D.Albrecht, *Notenwechsel* I, 14-17.

51. Gröber to Bertram and Faulhaber, 27 October 1933, B.Stasiewski, *Akten* I, 420-2.

52. Kaas to Gröber, 12 December 1933, B.Stasiewski, *Akten* I, 482-4.

53. Gröber and Berning to Bertram, 3 November 1933, ibid., 433-6.

54. Draft of 3 November 1933, ibid., 436. Final version as distributed at Osnabrück in H.Müller, *Katholische Kirche*, 220.

55. G.Lewy, *Katholische Kirche*, 200; W.J.Doetsch, *Württembergs Katholiken*, 147.

56. First draft in Bertram's letter to the episcopate of 30 October 1933, B.Stasiewski, *Akten* I, 427. Final version ibid., 437 n.3; also L.Müller, *Katholische Kirche*, 216-18. A chapter title in L.Volk, *Bayerischer Episkopat*, 121, runs ' "Meaningful Implementation" of the Concordat'.

57. Thus Faulhaber in the letter to the episcopate of 30 October 1933, B.Stasiewski, *Akten* I, 427.

58. L.Volk, *Bayerischer Episkopat*, 147.

59. Text, Kretschmar and Nicolaisen, *Dokumente* I, 169f. For the delaying tactics by Heydrich cf. B.Stasiewski, *Akten* I, 438, and above all L.Volk, *Faulhaber-Akten* I, 795-8.

60. Riemer to Faulhaber, 8 October 1933; L.Volk, *Faulhaber-Akten* 1, 776; Sebastian to Faulhaber, 2 November 1933, ibid., 787; Hauck to Faulhaber, 2 and 4 November 1933, ibid., 783, 791.

61. Text e.g. in B.Stasiewski, *Akten* 1, 440f., and L.Volk, *Faulhaber-Akten* I, 806f. The

preliminary drafts are also included in these volumes. First draft in Stasiewski, *Akten* I, 426f.; the second, beyond doubt the clearest, draft is in L.Volk, *Faulhaber-Akten* I, 789; third draft, ibid., 800.

62. Decree of the Bavarian Minister President, 9 October, B.Stasiewski, *Akten* 1, 441 n.4; and of 11 November 1933, L.Volk, *Faulhaber-Akten* I, 809 n.3.

63. On this see L.Volk, *Episkopat*, 57f., and above all the notes by Faulhaber on his conversations with Vassalo on 11 November 1933 in L.Volk, *Faulhaber-Akten* I, 807-9.

64. *Ursachen und Folgen* X, 56.

65. On this cf. Bracher, Sauer and Schulz, *Machtergreifung*, 355-8.

66. On this see the very vivid account by the British ambassador in Berlin, 16 November 1933, *Ursache und Folgen* X, 56-60.

67. See above, 239f.

68. For details of the election results cf. Bracher, Sauer and Schulz, *Machtergreifung*, 358-68.

69. Notes by Buttmann, *Akten zur deutschen auswärtigen Politik*, Serie C, Vol.2.1, 234f.

70. Papen to Gröber, 12 November 1933, B.Stasiewski, *Akten* I, 422-46.

71. Gröber to Bertram, ibid., 865.

72. L.Volk, 'Die Fuldaer Bischofskonferenz von Hitlers Machtergreifung bis zur Enzyklika "Mit brennender Sorge"' (1969), in D.Albrecht, *Katholische Kirche*, 44f.

73. Numbers of members of Catholic youth in a letter from the Bavarian episcopate to Hitler and Schemm, 24 April 1933, B.Stasiewski, *Akten* I, 81ff. Cf. also B.Schellenberger, *Katholische Jugend und Drittes Reich. Eine Geschichte des Katholischen Jungmännerverbandes 1933-1939 unter besonderer Berücksichtigung des Rheinlandes*, Mainz 1975, 191f. For Protestant youth see H.Riedel, *Kampf um die Jugend. Evangelische Jugendarbeit 1933-1945*, Munich 1976, 13f. The statistical information can only be estimates which clarify the proportions, given the rapidly changing circumstances in the youth associations.

74. B.Schellenberger, *Katholische Jugend*, 6.

75. Ibid., 15.

76. H.W..Koch, *Geschichte der Hitlerjugend. Ihre Ursprünge und ihre Entwicklung 1922-1945*, Percha 1975, 154.

77. B. von Schirach, *Ich glaubte an Hitler*, Hamburg 1967, 22f.

78. Ibid., 177f.

79. Text: *Ursache und Folgen* IX, 517f.

80. Text: ibid., 518.

81. Text: ibid., 518f.

82. B.Schellenberger, *Katholische Jugend*, 95; text, B.Stasiewski, *Akten* I, 193f.

83. Text of Wolker's memorandum, ibid., 180-92, quotation on 186.

84. Protocol of the plenary conference, ibid., 296f.

85. Text, etc. in Kretschmar and Nicolaisen, *Dokumente* I, 122f.

86. Wolker's report of 20 August 1933, B.Stasiewski, *Akten* I, 282f., 287.

87. Protocol of the plenary conference, ibid., 206f.

88. H.Müller, *Katholische Kirche*, 191f. Cf. the qualifications in B.Schellenberger, *Katholische Jugend*, 107.

89. H.Müller, op.cit., 192f.

90. Circular letter to the Presidents and Prefects, 17 October 1933, B.Stasiewski, *Akten* I, 419 n.1.

91. Gröber to Kaas, 15 November 1933, ibid., 452-5.

92. Protocol of the session of 15 November 1933, ibid., 467-73.

93. See n.91 above.

94. Report by Bornewasser to Bertram of 24 November 1933, ibid., 463f. According

to Canon 220 of the *Codex Juris Canonici* so-called *causae majores* fall solely within the competence of the Holy See.

95. Gröber to Bertram, 24 November 1933, ibid., 865. See also above, 507f.

96. Bertram to the German episcopate, 22 November 1933, ibid., 462f.

97. Faulhaber to Bertram and Berning, 25 November 1933, and appendix, ibid., 866-8.

98. Hauck to Bertram, 27 November 1933, ibid., 476-8.

99. Klein to Bertram, 28 November 1933, ibid., 869-71.

100. *Akten zur deutschen auswärtigen Politik*, Serie C, Vol.2.1, 99.

101. Ibid., 205f.

102. Notes by Buttmann, 18 December 1933, ibid., 233-88; Hitler's reply to Buttmann 18 December, ibid., 239; Buttmann's note of 19 December, ibid., 240; Buttmann's notes of 19 December, ibid., 241-3.

103. Kaas to Gröber, 21 December 1933; B.Stasiewski, *Akten* I, 484-8.

104. Hackelsberger's memorandum, ibid., 489f.

105. Bergen's report of 27 December 1933, *Akten der deutschen auswärtigen Politik*, Serie C, Vol.2.1, 270.

106. Text of the Austrian Pastoral Letter in *Archiv für katholisches Kirchenrecht* 114, 1934, 247-56.

107. Notes by Bergen on a conversation with Pacelli of 27 December 1933, *Akten zur deutschen auswärtigen Politik*, Serie C, 2.1, 270f.

108. Bergen to Neurath, 28 December 1933, ibid., 277.

109. Memorandum of the Reich government; transmitted to Pacelli on 15 January 1934. All the source material is also in D.Albrecht, *Notenwechsel* I, 37-44.

110. For Pacelli's critical reaction cf. the report by Bergen of 20 January 1934 in D.Albrecht, op.cit., 44f. n.6.

111. Gröber to Pacelli, 28 December 1933, B.Stasiewski, *Akten* 1, 491-5.

112. Pacelli to Gröber, 4 January 1934, ibid., 507f.

113. Report on the diocesan synod of the archdiocese of Munich and Freising, 19 November 1930, L.Volk, *Faulhaber-Akten* I, 513.

114. See below, 550ff.

115. Kardinal Faulhaber, *Judentum, Christentum, Germanentum. Adventspredigten, gehalten in St Michael zu München 1933*, Munich nd [1934], 20, 97 (emphases in the original).

116. Ibid., 23f. For Artur Dinter's title see above 76ff.

117. Ibid., 118. Volk's judgment that 'the Cardinal did not dare to touch the hot potato of antisemitism' (*Bayerische Episkopat*, 172) overlooks the allusions to Dinter which were topical at the time.

118. Faulhaber, *Judentum*, 3f.; L.Volk, *Bayerischer Episkopat*, 171 n.46.

119. H.Boberach, *Berichte des SD und der Gestapo über Kirchen und Kirchenvolk in Deutschland 1934-1944*, Mainz 1971, 21. Cf. also ibid., 6, 7,41, 45. The Security Office under Heydrich was at that time still in Munich, ibid., XXXIV.

120. Volk, *Bayerischer Episkopat*, 172.

12. The Reich Church between Illusion and Reality (October-November)

1. See above, 291.

2. G.Kretschmar, 'Die Auseinandersetzung der Bekennenden Kirche mit den Deutschen Christen', in *Tutzinger Texte*, ed. P.Rieger and J.Strauss, *Sonderband I, Kirche und Nationalsozialismus*, Munich 1969, 131f.

3. W.Birnbaum, *Zeuge meiner Zeit*, 132f. Birnbaum, himself a committed German

Christian, still sees these numbers as an indication of the great possibility for the church in Volksmission at this time.

4. All the accounts are in *Unsere Volkskirche. Sonntägliches Nachrichtenblatt aus den Berliner Kirchengemeinden*, 1933, no. 1 of 8 October 1933. There is a similar account of the collective baptism of 140 children in the Osterkirche in Wedding, Berlin, in *Das Evangelische Deutschland* 19, 1933, 487f.

5. W.Birnbaum, *Zeuge meiner Zeit*, 131.

6. Windfuhr to Dietrich, 1 September 1933, AEKHN Darmstadt, 44/126.

7. Kretschmar and Nicolaisen, *Dokumente* I, 136.

8. J.Gauger, *Chronik* I, 124.

9. Protocol of the first session of the Reich Church Cabinet on 3 October 1933, AEKD Berlin A4/37. Müller to the Church Minister, 20 October 1933, ibid.

10. Von der Goltz to Pfundtner, 27 July 1933 (copy). Pfundtner to Ludwig Müller, 10 October 1933, AEKD Berlin A4/103.

11. Declaration from the Reich Bishop to all the pastorate, 11 October 1933, *Gesetzblatt der Deutschen Evangelischen Kirche* 1933, 16.

12. Pfundtner to Ludwig Müller, 22 October 1933. Müller's answer (fair copy), 6 November 1933, AEKD Berlin, A4/238.

13. Confidential circular from the Reich Minister of the Interior, 26 September 1933, Kretschmar and Nicolaisen, *Dokumente* I, 134f.

14. Circular letter from the Gau Propaganda Leader of the Gauleitung of Schleswig-Holstein, 6 October 1933, ibid., 143.

15. Circular letter from the Reich Leadership to all Reichleiters and Gauleiters, 6 October 1933, ibid., 144f.

16. Regulation of the Reich Leadership of the NSDAP of 13 October 1933, ibid., 145.

17. F.Weineke, *Kirche und Partei*, 87f.

18. *Reichswart* 14, 1933, no.42 of 22 October 1933.

19. Ibid., no. 44 of 5 November; no.47 of 26 November, etc.

20. *Evangelium im Dritten Reich* 2, 1933, 442f.

21. Quoted from *Junge Kirche* 1, 1933, 282.

22. Ibid., 248.

23. According to the account in *Christliche Welt* 47, 1933, 1008. Cf. also *Das Evangelische Deutschland* 10, 1933, 379.

24. Memorandum of 24 August 1933, Bad Gen A Karlsruhe 235/12851. Cf. also above, 452.

25. *Das Evangelische Deutschland* 10, 1933, 449f.

26. Quoted from *Junge Kirche* 1, 1933, 305f.

27. The Reich Bishop to the Faith Movement of German Christians, Gau of Greater Berlin, 28 October 1933, copy to the Supreme Church Authorities of 3 November 1933, LKA Oldenburg OKR A1-24 II. Cf. also *Junge Kirche* 1, 1933, 308.

28. The whole proceedings are documented at length in G.Schäfer, *Dokumentation* 2, 479-709. The statement about Germany's withdrawal of 14 October 1933 is quoted there on 589f.

29. Draft of 2 October 1933, G.Schäfer, *Dokumentation* 2, 636-8. The draft very probably went off, as is indicated by the reference to the vigorous conversation of 20 October, ibid., 642.

30. Wurm to Ludwig Müller, 13 October 1933, ibid., 638-41; Wurm to Meiser, 19 October 1933, ibid., 655f.

31. Wurm to Fezer, 20 October 1933, ibid., 641-3.

32. Fezer to Müller, 6 October 1933, AEKD Berlin A4/38.

33. Pressel to Wurm, 2 November 1933, G.Schäfer, *Dokumentation* 2, 672.

34. Hossenfelder's report at the second session of the Reich Church Cabinet of 6 October 1933, protocol of the session, AEKD Berlin A 4/37.

35. Jäger to Müller, 28 October 1933, AEKD A 4/179.

36. Express letter from Jäger to Reich Bishop Müller, 10 November 1933, AEKD A 4/179.

37. *Evangelium im Dritten Reich* 2, 1933, 467f.

38. See above, 469f., 473.

39. Memorandum of the Protestant Theological Faculty of Tübingen, UA Tübingen, from 162/XIV,6.

40. Cf. on this the references in J.H.Schjørring, 'Moralische Aufrüstung und westeuropäische Politik bis 1954', in *Zeitschrift für Kirchengeschichte* 87, 1976, 71 n.12, and above all also Hossenfelder's own report in *Eine Stellungnahme* of 7 July 1945, LKA Berlin-Brandenburg.

41. Retired Corvette Captain D.W.Schmidt-Henrici to the Reich Bishop, 15 October 1933. Answer from Hans-Michael Müller, Jena, 3 November 1933, AEKD Berlin C4/17.

42. *Evangelium im Dritten Reich* 2, 1933, 468. The declaration did not prevent Ludwig Müller from assuring the Foreign Office two weeks later that there was no intention of introducing the Aryan Paragraph into the German Evangelical Church. Letter to the Foreign Office of 9 November 1933, *Akten zur deutschen auswärtigen Politik*, Serie C, Vol.2.1, 96-8.

43. The article from *Evangelischer Ruf* is in Niemöller's protest letter to the Reich Minister of the Interior, 25 October 1933, LKA Berlin-Brandenburg J II 67 I (copy); the resolution of 9 November 1933 in the Lücking protocol, Notbund, Bruderrat, 9 November 1933, Berlin, LKA Bielefeld, Best.5.1, No.837 fasc.1.

44. The Bishop of the Evangelical Bishopric of Cologne-Aachen, at that time Koblenz, 10 October 1933, printed leaflet, 'Greetings to the Rhineland Communities', AEKD A4/179.

45. J.Beckmann, *Artgemässes Christentum oder schriftgemässer Christusglaube? Eine Auseinandersetzung mit der Lehre der Glaubensbewegung Deutsche Christen*, Essen 1933, 5 and 20 (emphases in the original). The Rengsdorf theses and the counter theses of Karl Barth, Walter Bach and Joachim Beckmann are in K.D.Schmidt, *Bekenntnisse 1933*, 91-6. There is an account of the discussion with especial reference to Beckmann in G.van Norden, *Kirche in der Krise*, 102-8.

46. K.Immer, *Die Briefe des Coetus reformierte Prediger 1933-1937*, ed. J.Beckmann, Neukirchen 1976, 3. For the beginnings of the Reformed Coetus cf. also W.Niesel, 'Kirche unter dem Wort. Die Entstehung und Entwicklung der Bekennenden Kirche der altpreussischen Union', in *Freispruch und Freiheit, Theologische Aufsätze für Walter Kreck*, Munich 1973, esp. 357-62.

47. K.Immer, *Coetus*, 3.

48. First recommendation of 28 September 1933, ibid., 5-9.

49. *Reformierte Kirchenzeitung* 83, 1933, 322.

50. K.Immer, *Coetus*, 10f. The quotation is an allusion to Judges 7.2.

51. Ibid., 13.

52. *Unter dem Wort* 1, 1933, 1. Quoted from H.Vorländer, *Kirchenkampf in Elberfeld*, 85.

53. Invitation from Weber, 10 October 1933, AEKD Berlin C2/2. Cf. also J.Schmidt, *Niemöller*, 139.

54. Bonhoeffer to Barth, London, 24 October 1933, *Gesammelte Schriften* 2, 130-4; *No Rusty Swords*, 231.

55. Barth to Bonhoeffer, 20 November 1933, ibid., 134-7; 233f.

56. W.Künneth, 'Echte Fronten', *Junge Kirche* 1, 1933, 239-42. Niemöller's request to

Franz Hildebrandt, Bonhoeffer's friend to reply to the article was refused by the latter 'for reasons of principle' ('I cannot say with the whole *Junge Kirche* and the whole Pastors League anything like or even approaching what Barth says by himself'). Hildebrandt to Niemöller, 24 October 1933, Bonhoeffer, *Gesammelte Schriften* 6, 277f.

57. Record of the discussion of representatives of the Pastors Emergency League in Berlin-Dahlem at the home of Pastor Niemöller on 20 January 1933, AEKD Berlin, KKA 698, 106ff.

58. Circular letter no.1 of 2 November 1933, text in W.Niemöller, *Pfarrernotbund*, 166-9.

59. Ibid.

60. G.Prater, *Hugo Hahn*, 35f.; G.Schäfer, *Dokumentation* 2, 725-7.

61. K.Barth, *Reformation als Entscheidung*, Theologische Existenz heute 3, 1933, 12.

62. Ibid., 19.

63. Ibid., 23.

64. Thus according to Barth's own recollection, quoted in M.U.Kaiser, *Kirchenkampf und Schweizer Öffentlichkeit*, 77.

65. *Reformation als Entscheidung*, 24.

66. What followed is based above all on the 'Protocol of the meeting in the House of Pastor Jacobi (about 150 pastors), Tuesday 31 October 1933, p.m.' prepared by Barth's colleague Charlotte von Kirschbaum (11 pp.), LKA Bielefeld 5,1, no.312, fasc.2. According to a letter from Erika Küppers dated 11 November 1933 (Karl Barth archive, Basel), a first conversation with about 150 pastors took place immediately after Barth's arrival on the afternoon of the 30th. A second conversation followed on the morning of the 31st in a smaller group (about twenty; this included Dehn, Künneth, Knak, Niemöller and Hildebrandt). There are fragmentary minutes of this conversation in LKA Bielefeld 5,1, no.312 fasc.c (2 pp.). The third conversation, on which there are detailed minutes, on the afternoon of 31 October, began about 2 p.m. and lasted until 8 p.m. In the evening there was an 'Open Evening' with members of Berlin churches (Küppers' letter). For the whole event cf. also the account by W.Niemöller, 'Vor fünfundzwanzig Jahren (1933)' (1958), in W.Niemöller, *Wort und Tat im Kirchenkampf*, Munich 1969, 69-74.

67. These are the 'Acht Artikel evangelischer Lehre', printed in K.D.Schmidt, *Bekenntnisse 1933*, 80-9.

68. Texts; W.Niesel (ed.), *Um Verkündigung und Ordnung der Kirche, Die Bekenntnissynoden der Evangelische Kirche der altpreussischen Union 1934-1943*, Bielefeld 1949.

69. Barth to the Foreign Office, 13 March 1934; A.Boyens, *Kirchenkampf und Ökumene*, 1, 322f.

70. Notes of 31 October (n.66), 6.

71. Barth's letter (n.69).

72. Notes by Oberregierungsrat Thomsen (Reich Chancellery), 31 October 1933. Text: *Akten zur deutschen auswärtigen Politik*, Serie C, Vol.2.1, 57-9, and Kretschmar and Nicolaisen, *Dokumente* 1, 166-9.

73. Protocol of 31 October (n.66), 6.

74. Jacobi to Barth, 11 November 1933. The original is in the Karl Barth archive, Basel. Wilhelm Niemöller, who was involved here, does not seem to have known anything of the events. Cf. his article 'Vor fünfundzwanzig Jahren (1933)' (n.66), 74. Lücking's notes on the session of the Council of Brethren of 9 November 1933 (LKA Bielefeld 5, 1, no. 837 fasc.1) remarkably do not have anything to say about the decision.

75. Barth to Jacobi, 13 November 1933. Copy in the Karl Barth Archive, Basel. The term 'examination', 'Sichtung', comes from the vocabulary of the Herrnhutter Community of Brethren.

76. See above, 463ff.

77. Constitutional guidelines of the Provisional Leadership of the German Evangelical Church, 26 September 1933, LKA Oldenburg OKR A I-24 II.

78. No minutes of this meeting have yet been found. *Evangelische Deutschland* (10, 1933, 413) reports on 'the discussions of the leaders of the German Landeskirchen', that the draft of the guidelines worked out by Professor Heckel 'on the whole met with the approval of the church leaders'.

79. Protocol of the sessions of the Reich Church Cabinet of 6 October, 19 October, 24 October and 9 November, AEKD Berlin A4/37.

80. The text of the constitutional guidelines, so far unpublished, are in ibid., Appendices to the Eighth Session of the Reich Church Cabinet on 9 November 1933.

81. For this dispute cf. e.g. H.Frost, *Strukturprobleme evangelischer Kirchenverfassung. Rechtsvergleichende Untersuchungen zum Verfassungsrecht der deutschen evangelischen Landeskirchen*, Göttingen 1972, 33f.

82. Memorandum of the Reich Church Government on the financial situation of the German Evangelical Church, 11 November 1933, BA Koblenz, R 3 II/161, emphases in the original.

83. Ibid.

84. Reference draft of a budget plan for the German Evangelical Church for 1934, ibid.

85. Memorandum (n.82).

86. W.Konrad, *Kampf um die Kanzeln*, 57f.

87. Initialled W(ienstein), 6 December 1933 (see n.82).

88. 'Kirchengesetz über die vorläufige Sicherung des Haushalts der Deutschen Evangelischen Kirche', 12 December 1933. Emergency budget for the period from 1 January to 31 March 1934, *Gesetzblatt der Deutschen Evangelischen Kirche*, 1933, 39-41.

89. Emergency budget for the first quarter of 1935, dated 1 January 1935, circular letter from Dr Werner, 'Haushaltsführung der Deutschen Evangelischen Kirche ab 1 Januar 1935', AEKD Berlin C1/177.

90. *Gesetzblatt der Deutschen Evangelischen Kirche*, 1933, 21.

91. Reichsgeschäftsstelle Deutscher Luthertag 1933 to Hitler, 15 August 1933, BA Koblenz 43 II/168.

92. Luther to Nikolaus Gerbel, 1 November 1521, Weimarer Ausgabe, *Briefe* 2, no.435, 397.

93. H.Dörries, *Luther und Deutschland. Sammlung gemeinverständlicher Vorträge* 169, Tübingen 1934, 19.

94. H.Preuss, 'Luther und Hitler', *Allgemeine Evangelisch-Lutherische Kirchenzeitung* 66, 1933, 970-3, 994-9. Also printed as a pamphlet by Freimund Verlag, Neuendettelsau 1933. Emphasis in the original.

95. Eisleben, 20 August. Newspaper report of unknown origin in BA Koblenz R 43 II/168.

96. Noted by Neurath of 7 September 1933, stamped 'The Reich Chancellor knows' and initialled L(ammers), 12 September, BA Kobelnz R 43 II/168.

97. The Reich Minister of the Interior to the Supreme Reich Authorities, 3 October 1933, Kretschmar and Nicolaisen, *Dokumente* I, 140f.

98. For this speech see above, 501.

99. Protocol of the fifth session of the Reich Church Cabinet on 19 October 1933, AEKD Berlin A4/37.

100. Telegram from the Reich Bishop, 20 October 1933, Kretschmar and Nicolaisen, *Dokumente* I, 142. The official statement by the Reich Bishop on the transfer to 19 November, etc., is in *Das Evangelische Deutschland* 10, 1933, 394.

101. Text in *Gesetzblatt der Deutschen Evangelische Kirche*, 1933. The authorship is not clear. In his memoirs W.Birnbaum claims that he worked out the guidelines and draft

and that Hossenfelder took both over 'almost unaltered' (*Zeuge meiner Zeit*, 151). On the other hand Wieneke also states that he played a 'normative' part in working out the guidelines (*Kirche und Partei*, 94). And finally it emerges from a protocol of a session on the formation of a chamber for Volksmission on 3 November 1933 that a commission was entrusted with the composition of the programme (AEKD Berlin A/41).

102. Thus W.Birnbaum, *Zeuge meiner Zeit*, 153.

103. Letter from the Württemberg Evangelischer Oberkirchenrat to the Reich Bishop, 24 November 1933, G.Schäfer, *Dokumentation* 2, 790 n.92a.

104. W.Conrad, *Kampf um die Kanzel*, 61.

105. A note by Vice-President Fürle of 11 November 1933 in KLA Berlin-Brandenburg J III 67 I gives information about the internal proceedings. The issue was a circular letter from Kurt Scharf dated 1 November 1933 in which Scharf stated that questionnaires on Aryan descent would not be filled in (AEKD Berlin A 4/107) and an article by Rabenau against Künneth, 'Unsere Verantwortung', in *Junge Kirche* I, 1933, 267f. Cf. also J.Gauger, *Chronik* I, 109, and J.Schmidt, *Niemöller*, 145f.

106. *Evangelium im Dritten Reich* 2, 1933, 474 (no. 46 of 12 November 1933). Cf. in ibid. also the article by Hossenfelder 'Der 12. November' and the position of the German Christian bishops.

107. Quoted from *Junge Kirche* I, 1933, 323f. But cf. the protest of Protestant church members from Jena, ibid., 326-7.

108. Ibid., 324f.

13. The Collapse of the German Christians and the Beginnings of the Confessing Church (November 1933-January 1934)

1. The original date is in *Unsere Volkskirche* 1933, no.1, 10. The postponement to 26 October was decided upon on 13 November, Krause to the Consistory of the Mark of Brandenburg, 30 October 1933, LKA Berlin-Brandenburg J IX 66.

2. 'Ist das der Sinn des Lutherjahres?', *Unsere Volkskirche* 1, 1933, no.6 of 12 November 1933, 81f.

3. According to the reports in *Deutsche Allgemeine Zeitung* and the *Vossische Zeitung* of 14 November 1933, reprinted in *Junge Kirche* 1, 1933, 309-11. Cf. also *Christliche Welt* 47, 1933, 1086, and K.Meier, *Kirchenkampf* I, 132f. The wording of Hossenfelder's speech does not seem to have been recorded.

4. J.Gauger, *Chronik* I, 109.

5. *Rede des Gauobmannes der Glaubensbewegung 'Deutsche Christen' in Gross-Berlin Dr Krause gehalten im Sportpalast am 13. November 1933* (based on two stenographic reports), ed. Dr Reinhold Krause, pamphlet without place or date [Verlag Unsere Volkskirche 1933].

6. For the history of völkisch religion see 81ff. above. For the parallels between Krause and Rosenberg cf. *Der Mythus des 20.Jahrhunderts*, e.g. 74f. (Paul against Jesus); 129 (Judification through the Old Testament); 603 (abolition of the Old Testament); 606 (inferiority of Paul); 607 (simple good news of the kingdom of heaven); 604 (heroic Jesus), etc.

7. The text of the resolution appeared in the *Völkischer Beobachter* on 15 November. It is printed e.g. in J.Gauger, *Chronik* I, 11, and *Junge Kirche* 1, 1933, 312.

8. Protocol of the conversation between Ludwig Müller, Otto Weber, Martin Niemöller, Wilhelm Niemöller and Gerhard Jacobi on 14 November 1933, 16.00-17.15, in W.Niemöller, *Pfarrernotbund*, 162-6. The summary of the three demands follows the circular letter of the Pastors Emergency League of 16 November 1933, ibid., 174.

9 Decree of the Evangelischer Oberkirchenrat, 14 November 1933, LKA Berlin-Brandenburg J IX 66.

10. Berlin-Charlottenburg, 14 November 1933. Draft corrected in Ludwig Müller's own hand, AEKD Berlin A4/245. Text etc. also in J.Gauger, *Chronik* I, 110.

11. Barth to Hitler, 1 July 1933 (Vol.1), 28 November 1933 (Vols 2 and 3), Karl Barth Archive, Basel.

12. Protocol of the conversation on Tuesday, 15 [should be 14] November 1933 in the evening in the house of Pastor Jacobi, Berlin (produced by Charlotte von Kirschbaum), LKS Bielefeld 5, 1, no.343.

13. Ibid.

14. Notes by Bodelschwingh on his reception with the Reich President on 16 November 1933, Kretschmar and Nicolaisen, *Dokumente* I, 172-5.

15. Barth to Karwehl, 17 November 1933, Karl Barth Archive, Basel.

16. Karl Barth, Theologische Existenz heute 4, Munich 1933. Preface of 19 November 1933, 3-7. The verses come from the hymn 'Come, children, let us go', written by the Rhineland Reformed mystic Gerhard Tersteegen (*Evangelisches Kirchengesangbuch* 22).

17. Barth to Licenciate Leonhard Jacob, 15 December 1933, Karl Barth Archive, Basel.

18. Text of the declaration of 15 November, W.Niemöller, *Pfarrernotbund*, 40f. For the course of events cf. M.Niemöller's lengthy circular letter of 16 November 1933, ibid., 72-7. The later version of the leaflet is in *Junge Kirche* 1, 1933, 353.

19. Text of the proclamation in J.Gauger, *Chronik* I, 111-13, and W.Niemöller, *Pfarrernotbund*, 176f. For the 'dumb dogs' cf. Isa. 56.10.

20. G.Prater, *Kämpfer wider Willen*, 38f.

21. Circular letter no. 3 of 23 November 1933, W.Niemöller, *Pfarrernotbund*, 177-9.

22. J.Gauger, *Chronik* I, 111.

23. For this whole dispute cf. e.g. J.Gauger, ibid., 111-3; *Junge Kirche* 1, 1933, 354, 361f.; *Evangelium im Dritten Reich* 2, 1933, 512f.; W.Niemöller, *Pfarrernotbund*, 178f.

24. Krause to the Reich Bishop, 15 November 1933, AEKD Berlin, A 4/249.

25. Circular letter of 18 November 1933, *Junge Kirche* 1, 1933, 362f.

26. Guidelines of the Faith Movement 'Deutsche Volkskirche', LKA Hamburg, Deutsche Christen, no.1. Cf. also J.Gauger, *Chronik* I, 115, and H.Buchheim, *Glaubenskrise*, 132f.

27. Rosenberg's declaration that he was leaving the church, 15 November 1933, is in Kretschmar and Nicolaisen, *Dokumente*, 171f.

28. 'Gesetz betreffend die Rechtsverhältnisse der Geistlichen und Beamten der Landeskirchen, 16 November 1933', *Gesetzblatt der Deutschen Evangelischen Kirche*, 1933, 33.

29. H.Wilhelmi, *Hamburger Kirche*, 104,

30. Text etc. in *Gesetzblatt der Deutschen Evangelischen Kirche*, 1933, 34.

31. Circular letter of 23 November 1933, W.Niemöller, *Pfarrernotbund*, 178.

32. J.Schmidt, *Niemöller*, 151.

33. Rachner to all senior Gau officials, 15 November 1933, LKA Hamburg, Deutsche Christen, no.206.

34. *Evangelium im Dritten Reich* 2, 1933, 504.

35. J.Hossenfelder, 'Deutsche Christen', ibid., 499f.

36. F.Wieneke, *Partei und Kirche*, 82, speaks of a 'small pile'; Krause of 'hundreds' (*Junge Kirche* 1, 1933, 352f.). However, further developments show that the movement had in fact stabilized in Greater Berlin (K.Meier, *Die Deutschen Christen*, 81f.).

37. *Evangelium im Dritten Reich* 2, 1933, 511.

38. 'The Fire is Burning! The Conference of the German Christian Faith Movement in Weimar', ibid., 511f.

39. Cf. H.Baier, *Die Deutschen Christen*, 62-4.

40. There is a vivid account of events from a Bavarian perspective, presumably written by Greifenstein, in ibid., 75-77.

41. For the development of the Thuringian German Christians see above, 194ff.

42. Record of the preparatory session for the formation of a chamber of Volksmission on 3 November 1933, AEKD Berlin A4/41. Leutheuser's contribution is also in E.G.Rüppel, *Die Gemeinschaftsbewegung im Dritten Reich. Ein Beitrag zur Geschichte des Kirchenkampfes*, Göttingen 1962, 246.

43. K.Meier, *Die Deutschen Christen*, 45f.; J.Gauger, *Chronik* I, 117.

44. Text in *Junge Kirche* I, 1933, 369f.; H.Buchheim, *Glaubenskrise*, 140-2.

45. For the foundation and expansion of the German Christian church movement cf. K.Meier, *Die Deutschen Christen*, 75ff.

46. *Evangelium im Dritten Reich* 2, 1933, 515.

47. J.Schmidt, *Niemöller*, 15.

48. H.Baier, *Die Deutschen Christen*, 73f.

49. Meiser, at the same time in the name of Marahrens and Wurm, to Ludwig Müller, 17 November 1933, AEKD Berlin A 4/38.

50. There is an account of the Augsburg declaration with a literal transcription of the speeches in *Allgemeine Evangelisch-Lutherische Kirchenzeitung* 66, 1933, 1121-26. Further reports ibid., 1132ff.; J.Gauger, *Chronik* I, 113f.

51. Untergau Wuppertal to Ludwig Müller, 23 November 1033; H.Vorländer, *Kirchenkampf in Elberfeld*, 93.

52. All the events are documented in detail in G.Schäfer, *Dokumentation* 2, 850-60. Professor Kittel followed the step taken by his three colleagues on the same day (Kittel to Hossenfelder and Müller, 25 November 1933, AEKD Berlin A 4/249). For the vacillating attitude of Fezer cf. the critical account by Pastor Schuler in G.Schäfer, op.cit., 882. But cf. the report by Wurm, ibid., 929f.; and Fezer's own account, ibid., 936-41. Fezer's quotation, ibid., 940f.

53. J.Schmidt, *Niemöller*, 55; G.Schäfer, *Dokumentation* 2, 900 and 930.

54. J.Gauger, *Chronik* I, 116; F.Wieneke, *Kirche und Partei*, 93.

55. *Evangelium im Dritten Reich* 2, 1933, 515f.

56. Schuler to Dipper, 8 December 1933, G.Schäfer, *Dokumentation* 2, 883. There is also further detailed information about the events there.

57. Holt to Aselmann, 25 November 1933, LKA Hamburg, Deutsche Christen 206. On this see H.Wilhelmi, *Hamburger Kirche*, 108.

58. In a letter of 28 November he complained to the Reich Bishop about the suspicion that he had supported 'agents of reaction' and urgently asked him to protect his 'honour and existence'. 'They know,' the letter literally said, 'that I supported you from the first moment on and have been loyal to you, precisely because you have been the authorized representative of Adolf Hitler' (AEKD Berlin A, 4/245). In a memorandum the same day Schöffel put forward the aims of the German Christians unaltered (H.Wilhelmi, *Hamburger Kirche*, 105ff.). He also continued to play an obscure role until in March 1934 he was overthrown by the radical political wing of the Hamburg German Christians.

59. Thus e.g. *Deutsche Allgemeine Zeitung* 72, 1933, no.524, of 26 November 1933. Cf. also *Junge Kirche* 1, 1933, 360.

60. Heinemann to Hitler, 29 November 1933, copy to the Reich Bishop, AEKD Berlin A 4/249.

61. G.Schäfer, *Dokumentation* 2, 860-7; K. Dienst, *Dokumentation*, 137; J.Gauger, *Chronik* I, 113; *Junge Kirche* 1, 1933, 358-60.

62. *Junge Kirche* 1, 1933, 357f.; Bornkamm and Haenchen to Müller, 26 November 1933, AEKD Berlin A4/249.

63. Hirsch to Ludwig Müller, 27 November 1933, AEKD Berlin A 4/249.

64. Text: J.Gauger, *Chronik*, 116. Original with copies AEKD Berlin A4/245. For the course of events cf. Wurm's report in G.Schäfer, *Dokumentation* 2, 941f.

65. Thus Wurm to Frick, 25 November 1933, ibid., 900.

66. Circular letter no.39 of 27 November 1933, LKA Hamburg, Deutsche Christen 204/1. Cf. also J.Schmidt, *Niemöller*, 474 n.342, and G.Schäfer, *Dokumentation* 2, 884.

67. H.Baier, *Chronologie*, 45.

68. Wurm to Frick (n.65), 901.

69. Instructions no.79 of 27 November and no.81 of 28 November 1933, Kretschmar and Nicolaisen, *Dokumente* I, 177f. Cf. also W.Conrad, *Kampf um die Kanzeln*, 59: 'Call by the Propaganda Ministry that abroad the dissolution is already being regarded as a symptom of the inner collapse of the NSDAP'. There are similar Swiss voices in M.U.Kaiser, *Deutscher Kirchenkampf und Schweizer Öffentlichkeit*, 79-83.

70. Thus the course of events in W.Conrad, *Kampf um die Kanzeln*, 58-60.

71. Express letter from the Reich Minister of the Interior to the Land governments, copy to the Reich Governor, 30 November 1933, Bad Gen. A Karlsruhe 233/27784. The text appeared on 2 December 1933 in the *Völkischer Beobachter* and was often reprinted in the church press. There is also a reprint, rather full of mistakes, in Kretschmar and Nicolaisen, *Dokumente* I, 181.

72. W.Conrad, *Kampf um die Kanzeln*, 61.

73. Ibid.

74. J.Gauger, *Chronik* I, 116; G.Schäfer, *Dokumentation* 2, 943; 'Official Declaration' of the Reich Bishop. Undated and unsigned draft, AEKD Berlin A 4/245.

75. For Jäger and Oberheid see F.Wieneke, *Kirche und Partei*, 97ff. Altnough there is no direct evidence for Jäger's plans during these days, there is much to indicate that he in fact was the decisive man in the background. Cf. e.g. W.Conrad, *Kampf um die Kanzeln*, 61f.; the declaration of the leaders of the Landeskirchen of 30 November (G.Schäfer, *Dokumentation* 2, 942) and Wurm's comment of 9 December (ibid., 944). Also Hossenfelder's statement of 7 July 1945 (LKA Berlin-Brandenburg).

76. Cf. the statement of the leaders of the Landeskirchen in Wurm's report of 9 December 1933, G.Schäfer, *Dokumentation* 2, 942ff.

77. Ibid., 943. J.Gauger, *Chronik*, 118.

78. Report by Wurm of 9 December, G.Schäfer, *Dokumentation* 2, 944.

79. H.Baier, *Die Deutschen Christen*, 80. Lauerer's refusal may not have been published; press release of 5 December 1933, Kretschmar and Nicolaisen, *Dokumente* I, 178.

80. G.Schäfer, *Dokumentation* 2, 945.

81. Session of the Reich Church Cabinet on 4 December 1933, AEKD Berlin, A 4/37, *Gesetzblatt der Deutschen Evangelischen Kirche 1933*, 35.

82. Text: *Junge Kirche* 1, 1933, 399f.

83. The 'new line' was established on 6 December at a session of the Berlin group, *Evangelium im Dritten Reich* 2, 1933, 541. Text of the decree as an appendix in no.50, ibid., and – an extract only – in J.Gauger, *Chronik* I, 119.

84. Hossenfelder to Ludwig Müller, 11 December 1933. The letter is stamped as having been received on 9 January 1934 (!) and is marked 'Found on 8 January 1934 at the place of Pastor Hoff', AEKD Berlin A 4/219.

85. Koch to Ludwig Müller, 7 and 11 December 1933, AEKD Berlin A4/245.

86. Confidential account of the discussion on 11 December 1933 in Hamburg, LKA Hamburg, Deutsche Christen 216, 205.

87. *Evangelium im Dritten Reich* 2, 1933, 541. J.Gauger, *Chronik* I, 119.

88. According to the report from Müller to Bodelschwingh on 21 December there had been a 'hard fight'. 'Until the last special resistance from his wife', notes by Bodelschwingh, 27 December 1933, Archiv Bethel from Akte 2/39-5.

89. Hossenfelder to Müller, 21 December 1933, AEKD Berlin, A4/245.

90. Hossenfelder to the Faith Movement of German Christians, 21 December 1933. Text J.Gauger, *Chronik* I, 119-21.

91. See above 286.

92. C.Kinder, *Neue Beiträge*, 53.

93. Text: *Evangelium im Dritten Reich* 2, 1933, 561-3.

94. Text of the twenty-eight theses, etc., in J.Gauger, *Chronik* I, 121-3; K.D.Schmidt, *Bekenntnisse 1933*, 98-102. For the origin and history of the theses and the controversies over them see J.Fischer, *Sächsiche Landeskirche*, 24-26 and 109, esp. n.92.

95. Kinder to Müller, 29 December 1933, AEKD Berlin 4/ 249.

96. G.Gauger, *Chronik I, 121.*

97. Sessions of the Reich Church Cabinet of 5, 7 and 8 December, AEKD Berlin A 4/ 37. Texts: *Gesetzblatt der Deutschen Evangelischen Kirche 1933*, 35-7.

98. Text and invitation list in G.Schäfer, *Dokumente* 2, 954.

99. Draft and final version of the petition of 19 December 1933, ibid., 954-7.

100. Ibid., 957f. and W.Niemöller, *Pfarrernotbund*, 46.

101. J.Gauger, *Chronik* I, 118; H.Baier, *Die Deutschen Christen*, 80.

102. T.Wurm, *Erinnerungen*, 91. Cf. also W.Conrad, *Kampf um die Kanzeln*, 62 (on 22 December).

103. For the development of this question on the Catholic side cf. above, 508ff.

104. M.Priepke, *Die evangelische Jugend im Dritten Reich 1933-1936*, Hanover and Frankfurt 1960, 44-53.

105. Ibid., 52. The increasing membership is probably to be seen in connection with the growing number of those returning to the church.

106. On this see D.von Lersner, *Die evangelischen Jugendverbände Württembergs und die Hitler-Jugend 1933/1934*, Göttingen 1958, 22-31.

107. H.Riedel, *Kampf um die Jugend*, 50-6.

108. M.Priepke, *Evangelische Jugend*, 52, 55, 59f.

109. *Allgemeine Evangelisch-Lutherische Kirchenzeitung* 66, 1933, 666.

110. *Junge Kirche* 1, 1933, 133.

111. See above, 521f.

112. Record of the preliminary discussion at the Clergy Ministry with Bishop Hossenfelder over the formation of a Youth Chamber of the Evangelische Reichskirche, 13 October 1933, AEKD Berlin A4/42.

113. Record of the second preparatory session for the establishment of a Reich Youth Chamber on 23 and 24 October 1933, ibid.

114. Record of the third preparatory session... on 27 October 1933, ibid.

115. The Land Bishop of Baden (Bender) to the Reich Church government, 8 November 1933. Attached, copy of a decree on the institution of a social office of Hitler Youth', from *Die Volksjugend*, November 1933, AEKD Berlin, A 4/56.

116. See above, 507f., 513.

117. Protocol of the session of the Leader of Evangelisches Jugendwerk in the presence of the Reich Bishop on 17 November 1933, AEKD Berlin A4/42. For an assessment of the events cf. especially the circular letter of the spokesman of the opposition to the treaty, Udo Smidt, of 1 December. According to this the negotiations of the last weeks had shown 'how decisive powerful intervention from the most senior church leadership was for our Evangelical youth work' and that people were confident that the church government would 'resolutely take up ourcase', M.Priepke, *Evangelische Jugend*, 182.

118. Account of the session in the Leadership Council and group of officials of the Evangelisches Jugendwerk Deutschlands, 4 December 1933, text in M.Priepke, *Evangelische Jugend*, 182f.

119. M.Priepke, *Evangelische Jugend*, 183.

120. Ibid., 196.

121. Ibid., 71.

122. Extracts from the text in ibid., 184-6.

123. Re Reich Bishop Müller, US Tübingen from 162/ XIV, 6, p.10.

124. Ibid.

125. B.von Schirach, *Ich glaubte an Hitler*, 193.

126. Stange to the Reich Bishop, 19 December 1933, M.Priepke, *Evangelische Jugend*, 189f.; J.Gauger, *Chronik* I, 125.

127. Re Reich Bishop Müller (n.123) and letter from the leaders of 19 December 1933 in M.Priepke, *Evangelische Jugend*, 205-7.

128. Text, etc., in Kretschmar and Nicolaisen, *Dokumente* I, 183f. A facsimile of the original agreement dated 20 December can be found in H.Riedel., *Kampf um die Jugend*, 315.

129. Cf. the letter from the Council of Leaders, 3 February 1934, in M.Priepke, *Evangelische Jugend, 205-7.*

130. Ibid., 194. There are further protests in ibid., 193f.; H.Riedel, *Kampf um die Jugend*, 315.

131. S.Friedländer, *Kurt Gerstein oder die Zweispältigkeit des Guten*, Gütersloh 1968. Cf. also Gerstein's speech on the dissolution of the Bible Circle on 8 February 1934.

132. Text, H.Riedel, *Kampf um die Jugend*, 66f.

133. Notes by Bodelschwingh, 27 December 1933, Archive Bethel 2/39-51. Similarly also in W.Conrad, *Kampf um die Kanzeln*, 62.

134. Thus the reports on a conversation with Hitler at the Church Leaders' Conference on 4 January in Halle/Saar, AEKHN Darmstadt Best.6/1023, H AI/II Pfarrernotbund 1933/34.

135. Manuscript draft by Ludwig Müller, no date, AEKD Berlin A 4/246.

136. Thus according to Niemöller's report to the Council of Brethren of the Emergency League on 3 January, AEKHN Darmstadt, Best. 6/1023 HA I/II Pfarrernotbund 1933/34.

137. Text, ibid.

138. Draft in AEKD Berlin A 4/38.

139. Manuscript minutes, 4 January,Halle a./S., 10 a.m., AEKHN Darmstadt (n.134), J.Schmidt, *Niemöller*, 162f. No note is made of Hitler's conversation partners.

140. *Gesetzblatt der Deutschen Evangelischen Kirche* 1934, 1.

141. K.Immer, *Briefe des Coetus*, 20-2. For the course of the synod cf. also the account by Heinrich Graffmann in *Reformierte Kirchenzeitung* 84, 1934, 13f.

142. J.Beckmann, *Rheinische Bekenntnissynoden*, 36f.

143. Text of the declaration, etc., also in *Junge Kirche* 2, 1934, 118-22; K.D.Schmidt, *Bekenntnisse 1934*, 22-5; *Kirchliches Jahrbuch 1933-1944*[2], 48-51.

144. J.Beckmann, *Rheinische Bekenntnissynoden*, 36f. Cf. also H.-J.Reese, *Bekenntnis und Bekennen*, 246-9.

145. Karl Barth, *Gottes Wille und unsere Wünsche*, Theologische Existenz heute 7, Munich 1934, 5.

Sources and Bibliography

A. Unpublished sources

1. Documents from state archives in the Federal Republic of Germany

Bundesarchiv, Koblenz (BA Koblenz)
Document Center, Berlin (DC Berlin)
Politisches Archiv des Auswärtigen Amtes, Bonn (Arch AA Bonn)
Generallandesarchiv Karlsruhe (BadGen A Karlsruhe)
Bayerisches Hauptstaatsarchiv Abt II, Geheimes Staatsarchiv, Munich (GStA München)
Geheimes Staatsarchiv Preussischer Kulturbesitz, Berlin (GStA Berlin)
Hessisches Hauptstaatsarchiv Wiesbaden (HStA Wiesbaden)
Niedersächsisches Hauptstaatsarchiv, Hanover (HStA Hannover)
Niedersächsisches Staatsarchiv in Oldenburg (StA Oldenburg)
Staatliches Archivlager in Göttingen

2. Documents from state archives abroad

Archivum Glownej Komisji Badania Zbrodni Hitlerowskich w Polsce, Warsaw (Arch.Glow.Kom.Warschau)
Archivum Panstwowe Miasta Poznania Wojewodztwa Poznanskiego, Posen (Arch.Panst.Poznan Posen)

3. Documents from church archives

Archiv der Evangelischen Kirche in Deutschland, Berlin (AEKD Berlin)
Archiv der Evangelische Kirche der Union, Berlin (AEKU Berlin)
Landeskirchliches Archiv der Evangelisch-Lutherischen Kirche in Bayern, Nuremberg (LKA Nürnberg)
Archiv des Evangelischen Konsistoriums Berlin-Brandenburg, Berlin (LKA Berlin-Brandenburg)
Landeskirchliches Archiv der Braunschweigischen Evangelisch-lutherischen Landeskirche, Brunswick (LKA Braunschweig)
Archiv der Evangelisch-lutherisch Kirche im Hamburgischen Staate, Hamburg (LKA Hamburg)
Landeskirchliches Archiv der Evangelisch-lutherischen Landeskirche Hannovers, Hanover (LKA Hannover)
Archiv der Evangelischen Kirche in Hessen und Nassau, Darmstadt (AEKHN Darmstadt)

Landeskirchenarchiv der Evangelisch-Lutherischen Kirche in Oldenburg, Oldenburg
(LKA Oldenburg)
Landeskirchenarchiv der Evangelischen Kirche von Westfalen, Bielefeld (LKA Bielefeld)

4. Documents from other archives, collections and bequests

Universitätsarchiv Tübingen (UA Tübingen)
Hauptarchiv der von Bodelschwinghschen Anstalten, Bethel (HA Bethel)
Institut für Zeitgeschichte Munich (IfZ München)
Archiv der Evangelischen Arbeitsgemeinschaft für kirchliche Zeitgeschichte, Munich
(EvAKiZ München)
Arbeitsstelle für die Geschichte des Kirchenkampfes, Tübingen
Karl Barth Archive, Basel
Rudolf Buttmann bequest, Stockdorf
Paul Althaus bequest, Traunstein

5. Major unpublished manuscripts

Baier, Helmut, *Um Reichsbischof und Verfassung der Deutschen Evangelischen Kirche
1933* (LKA Nürnberg)
Bodelschwingh, Friedrich von, *Dreissig Tage an einer Wegwende deutscher Kirchenge-
schichte* (Hauptarchiv Bethel)
Kortheuer, August, *Das Ende der Evangelischen Landeskirche in Nassau* (LKA
Darmstadt)
Palmer, Otto, *Material zur Geschichte des Kirchenkampfes in der Braunschweigischen
Landeskirche* (LKA Braunschweig)
Wieneke, Friedrich, *Kirche und Partei. Erlebte Kirchengeschichte 1929 bis 1945* (Institut
für Zeitgeschichte, Munich)

B. Printed Sources and Bibliography

Adam, K., *The Spirit of Catholicism*, London and New York 1930
—, 'Deutsches Volkstum und katholisches Christentum', *Theologische Quartalschrift*
114, 1933, 40-63
Adam, U.D., *Judenpolik im Dritten Reich*, Düsseldorf 1972
*Akten der Reichskanzlei. Weimarer Republik. Das Kabinett Scheidemann, 13. Februar bis
20.Juni 1919*, Boppard 1971
Akten zur deutschen auswärtigen Politik 1918-1945, Serie C: 1933-1936, Göttingen 1971ff.
Albrecht, D., *Der Notenwechsel zwischen dem Heiligen Stuhl und der deutschen Reichsregi-
erung*, 1. *Von der Ratifizierung des Reichskonkordats bis zur Enzyklika 'Mit brennender
Sorge'*; 2. *1937-1945*, Mainz 1965-9
— (ed.), *Katholische Kirche im Dritten Reich. Eine Aufsatzsammlung*, Mainz 1976
Althaus, P., *Das Erlebnis der Kirche*, Leipzig (1919) [2]1924
—, *Evangelium und Leben. Gesammelte Vorträge*, Gütersloh 1927
—, *Grundriss der Dogmatik* I, Erlangen 1929
—, *Die deutsche Stunde der Kirche*, Göttingen (1933) [3]1934
Altner, G., *Weltanschauliche Hintergründe der Rassenlehre des Dritten Reiches. Zum
Problem einer umfassenden Anthropologie*, Zurich 1968
—Andersen, F., *Anticlericus. Eine Laientheologie auf geschichtliche Grundlage*, Schleswig
1907
—, Bartels, A., E.Katzer and H.von Wolzogen, *Deutschchristentum auf rein-evangelischer
Grundlage. 95 Leitsätze zum Reformationsfest 1917*, Leipzig 1917

684

Anschütz, G., *Die Verfassung des Deutschen Reiches vom 11. August 1919. Ein Kommentar für Wissenschaft und Praxis*, Berlin ¹⁴1933

Aretin, E.von, *Krone und Ketten. Erinnerungen eines bayerischen Edelmannes*, ed. K.Buchheim and K.O.von Aretin, Munich 1955

Aretin, K.O.von, *Das Ende der Zentrumspartei und der Abschluss des Reichskonkordats am 20 Juli 1933*, Frankfurter Hefte 17, 1962, 237-43

—, 'Prälat Kaas, Franz von Papen und das Reichskonkordat von 1933', *Vierteljahrshefte für Zeitgeschichte* 14, 1966, 252-79

—, *The Papacy and the Modern World*, New York 1970

Arndt, I., *Die Judenfrage im Licht der evangelischen Sonntagsblätter von 1918-1933*, Tübingen philosophical dissertation 1960 (ms.)

Asmussen, H., *Politik und Christentum*, Hamburg 1933

—, *Neues Bekenntnis? Ein Beitrag zum Neubau der Kirche*, Berlin 1933

—, *Reichskirche?*, Hamburg 1933

—, *Begegnungen*, Wuppertal-Barmen nd [1936]

—, *Zur jüngsten Kirchengeschichte. Anmerkungen und Folgerungen*, Stuttgart 1961

Aubert, R., 'Karl Adam', in *Tendenzen der Theologie im 20. Jahrhundert*, Stuttgart and Berlin 1966, 156-62

Bahne, S., 'Die Kommunistische Partei Deutschlands', in E.Matthias and R.Morsey (ed.), *Das Ende der Parteien*, Düsseldorf 1960, 655-739

Baier, H., *Die Deutschen Christen Bayerns im Rahmen des bayerischen Kirchenkampfes*, Nuremberg 1968

—, 'Das Verhalten der lutherischen Bischöfe gegenüber dem national-sozialistischen Staat 1933/34', Tutzinger Texte, Sonderband 1, *Kirche und Nationalsozialismus*, ed. P.Rieger and J.Strauss, Munich 1969, 87-116

— and E.Henn, *Chronologie des bayerischen Kirchenkampfes 1933-1945*, Nuremberg 1969

— and J.R.C.Wright, 'Ein neues Dokument zum Staatseingriff in Preussen (1933)', *Zeitschrift für Kirchengeschichte* 86, 1975, 220-41

Balzer, F.-M., *Klassengegensätze in der Kirche. Erwin Eckert und der Bund der Religiösen sozialisten Deutschlands*, Cologne 1973

Barth, K., 'The Christian's Place in Society' (1919) in id., *The Word of God and the Word of Man*, New York 1928, 272-327

—, 'Biblical Questions, Insights, and Vistas' (1920), in ibid., 51-96

—, *Der Römerbrief*, Bern 1919

—, *The Epistle to the Romans* (ET of second edition of *Der Römerbrief*), Oxford 1933

—, 'The Word of God and the Task of Ministry' (1922), in *The Word of God*, 183-217

—, *Die christliche Dogmatik im Entwurf, 1. Die Lehre vom Worte Gottes*, Munich 1927

—, '*Quousque tandem...?*', in *Zwischen den Zeiten* 8, 1930, 1-7. Reprinted in K.Kupisch (ed.), *Die Götze wackelt*, Berlin ²1964, 27-32

—, 'Die Not der evangelischen Kirche', *Zwischen den Zeiten* 99, 1931, 89-122. Reprinted in K.Kupisch (ed.), *Die Götze wackelt*, Berlin ²1964, 33-62

—, *Church Dogmatics* I.1 (1932), ET Edinburgh 1936

—, 'Das erste Gebot als theologisches Axiom', *Zwischen den Zeiten* 11, 1933, 297-314. Reprinted in id., *Theologische Fragen und Antworten*, Gesammelte Vorträge 3, Zurich 1957, 127-43

—, *Theological Existence Today*, London 1933

—, *Reformation als Entscheidung*, Theologische Existenz heute 3, Munich 1933

—, *Lutherfeier 1933*, Theologische Existenz heute 4, Munich 1933

—, *Die Kirche Jesu Christi*, Theologische Existenz heute 5, Munich 1933

—, *Offenbarung, Kirche, Theologie*, Theologische Existenz heute 9, Munich 1934.

Reprinted in id., *Theologische Fragen und Antworten*. Gesammelte Vorträge 3, 158-84

—, *Letzte Zeugnisse*, Zurich 1969

— and E.Thurneysen, *Suchet Gott, so werdet ihr leben!*, Munich 1928

— and Eduard Thurneysen, *Briefwechsel, 1, 1913-1921*, Zurich 1973; *2, 1921-1930*, Zurich 1974. Partial ET of 1 in James D.Smart (ed.), *Revolutionary Theology in the Making*, Richmond, Va. and London 1964

—, *Rudolf Bultmann, Briefwechsel 1922-1966*, Zurich 1971. Partial ET in *Karl Barth-Rudolf Bultmann. Letters 1922-1966*, Grand Rapids and Edinburgh 1982

Bauer, C., 'Carl Muths und des Hochland Weg aus dem Kaiserreich in die Weimarer Republik', *Hochland* 59, 1966/67, 234-47

—, 'Das Reichskonkordat', *Hochland* 49, 1956/57, 169-76

Baumgärtel, F., *Wider die Kirchenkampf-Legenden*, Neuendettelsau [2]1959

Baumgarten, O., *Kreuz und Hakenkreuz*, Gotha 1926

— et al., *Geistige und sittliche Wirkungen des Krieges in Deutschland*, 1927

—, *Meine Lebengeschichte*, Tübingen 1929

Becker, J., 'Prälat Kaas und das Problem einer Regierungsbeteiligung der NSDAP 1930-1932', *Historische Zeitschrift* 196, 1963, 74-111

—, 'Das Ende der Zentrumspartei und die Problematik des politischen Katholizismus in Deutschland', *Die Welt als Geschichte* 23, 1963, 149-72

Beckmann, J., *Artgemässes Christentum oder schriftgemässer Christusglaube? Eine Auseinandersetzung mit der Lehre der Glaubensbewegung Deutsche Christen*, Essen 1933

— (ed.), *Kirchliches Jahrbuch 1933-1945* (1928), Gütersloh [2]1976

— (ed.), *Rheinische Bekenntnissynoden im Kirchenkampf*, Neukirchen 1975

Benn, E.-V., 'Die Einstweilige Leitung der Deutschen Evangelischen Kirche (Juli-September 1933)', *Zeitschrift für evangeliches Kirchenrecht* 1, 1951, 365-81

Berner, M., *Die rechtliche Natur des Deutschen Evangelischen Kirchenbundes*, Berlin 1930

Beste, N., *Der Kirchenkampf in Mecklenburg 1933, Geschichte, Dokumente, Erinnerungen*, Göttingen 1975

Besier, G., *Preussische Kirchenpolitik 1866-1872*, Protestant theological dissertation Tübingen 1976 (ms)

Bethge, E., *Dietrich Bonhoeffer*, London and New York (1970) [2]1977

Beyer, H., *Das Altonaer Bekenntnis vom 11.Januar 1933*, Ostdeutsche Wissenschaft, V, 1958, Munich 1959

—, 'Volk, Staat und Kirche in der Übergangs- und Krisenzeit 1932-1934', in *Ecclesia und Res Publica. K.D.Schmidt zum 65. Geburtstag*, Göttingen 1962, 142-61

Bielfeldt, J., *Der Kirchenkampf in Schleswig-Holstein*, Göttingen 1964

Bierbaum, M., *Nicht Lob, Nicht Furcht. Das Leben des Kardinals von Galen nach unveröffentlichten Briefen und Dokumenten*, Regensburg [7]1974

Birnbaum, N., *Zeuge meiner Zeit. Aussagen zu 1912-1972*, Göttingen, Frankfurt and Zurich 1973

Bizer, E., 'Der "Fall Dehn"', in *Festschrift für Günter Dehn*, ed. W.Schneemelcher, Neukirchen 1957, 239-61

Boberach, H. (ed.), *Berichte des SD und der Gestapo über Kirchen und Kirchenvolk in Deutschland 1934-44*, Mainz 1971

Böckenförde, E.W., 'Das Ethos der modernen Demokratie und die Kirche', *Hochland* 50, 1957/58, 4-19

—, 'Der deutsche Katholizismus im Jahre 1933. Eine kritische Betrachtung' (1961), in id., *Kirchlicher Auftrag und politische Entscheidung*, Freiburg 1973, 30-65

—, 'Der deutsche Katholizismus im Jahre 1933. Stellungnahme zu einer Diskussion' (1962), in id, *Kirchlicher Auftrag und politische Entscheidung*, Freiburg 1973, 66-104

Bollmus, R., *Das Amt Rosenberg und seine Gegner*, Stuttgart 1970

Bonhoeffer, D., *Gesammelte Schriften 2: Kirchenkampf und Finkenwalde: Resolutionen, Aufsätze, Rundbriefe 1933-1945*, Munich 1959; 6. *Tagebücher, Briefe, Dokumente 1923-1945*, Munich 1974. Partial ET of 2 in E.H.Robertson (ed.), *No Rusty Swords*, London and New York (1965) [2]1970

Borst, G., *Die Ludendorff-Bewegung 1919-1961. Eine Analyse monologer kommunikationsformen in der sozialen Zeitkommunikation*, Munich philosophical dissertation 1969

Bracher, K.D., 'Nationalsozialistische Machtergreifung und Reichskonkordat. Ein Gutachten zur Frage des geschichtlichen Zusammenhangs und der politischen Verknüpfung von Reichskonkordat und nationalsozialistische Revolution', in *Der Konkordatsprozess. In Zusammenarbeit mit H.Müller*, ed. F.Giese and F.von der Heydte, Munich 1957-59, 947-1021

Bracher, K.D., W.Sauer and G.Schulz, *Die nationalsozialistische Machtergreifung. Studien zur Errichtung des totalitären Herrschaftssystems in Deutschland 1933/34*, Cologne and Opladen [2]1962

Bracher, K.D., *The German Dictatorship*, London 1971

Brandt, W., *Friedrich von Bodelschwingh 1877-1946. Nachfolger und Gestalter*, Bethel 1967

Braun, O., *Von Weimar zu Hitler*, Hamburg [3]1949

Breipohl, R., *Religiöser Sozialismus und bürgerliches Geschichtsbewusstsein zur Zeit der Weimarer Republik*, Zurich 1971

Breucker, W., *Die Tragik Ludendorffs. Eine kritische Studie auf Grund persönlicher Erinnerungen an der General und seine Zeit*, Stollhamm (Oldenburg) 1953

Breuning, K., *Die Vision des Reiches. Deutscher Katholizismus zwischen Demokratie und Diktatur (1929-1934)*, Munich 1969

Broszat, M., 'Die völkische Ideologie und der Nationalsozialismus', *Deutsche Rundschau* 84, 1958, 53-68

Broszat, M., H.A Jacobsen and H.Krausnick, *Anatomie des SS-Staates II*, Olten and Freiburg 1965

Brüning, H., *Memoiren 1918-1934*, Stuttgart 1970

Brunner, E., *Die Mystik und das Wort. Der Gegensatz zwischen moderner Religionsauffassung und christlichen Glauben dargestellt an der Theologie Schleiermachers*, Munich 1924

Bry, C.C., *Verkappte Religionen*, Gotha and Stuttgart 1924

Buchheim, H., *Glaubenskrise im Dritten Reich. Drei Kapitel nationalsozialistischer Religionspolitik*, Stuttgart 1953

—, 'Die organisatorische Entwicklung der Ludendorff-Bewegung und ihr Verhältnis zum Nationalsozialismus', in *Gutachten des Instituts für Zeitgeschichte* (1), Munich 1958, 356-9

Bullock, A., *Hitler. A Study in Tyranny*, Harmondsworth [2]1962

Bultmann, R., 'Liberal Theology and the Latest Theological Movement', in *Faith and Understanding*, London and New York 1969, 28-52

Busch, E., *Karl Barth. His life from letters and autobiographical texts*, London and Philadelphia 1976

Bussmann, W., 'Politische Ideologien zwischen Monarchie und Weimarer Republik. Ein Beitrag zur Ideengeschichte der Weimarer Republik', *Historische Zeitschrift* 190, 1960, 55-66

—, 'Der deutsche Katholizismus im Jahre 1933', *Festschrift für Hermann Heimpel* 1, Göttingen 1971, 180-204

Campenhausen, A.von, *Staatskirchenrecht. Ein Leitfaden durch die Rechtsbeziehungen zwischen Staat und den Religionsgemeinschaften*, Munich 1973

Chamberlain, H.S., *Die Grundlagen der neunzehnten Jahrhunderts* ([1]1899), Munich [10]1912

Christ, H., *Der politische Protestantismus in der Weimarer Republik. Eine Studie über die politische Meinungsbildung durch die evangelischen Kirchen im Spiegel der Literatur und der Presse*, Bonn philosophical dissertation 1967

Codex Juris Canonici, (1917) 1965

Conrad, W., *Der Kampf um die Kanzeln. Erinnerungen und Dokumente aus der Hitlerzeit*, Berlin 1957

Conway, J.S.. *The Nazi Persecution of the Churches*, London 1968

Cordes, C., 'Hannoversche Pfarrer und Politik 1918-1929', *Hannoversches Pfarrerblatt* 74, 1967, 78-99

Cordier, L., *Das eigentliche Anliegen in der Kirchenfrage. Volkskirche als christliche Volksreligion oder als Kirche Jesu Christi*, Schwerin 1934

Dahm, K.-W., *Pfarrer und Politik. Soziale Position und politische Mentalität des deutschen evangelischen Pfarrerstands zwischen 1918 und 1933*, Cologne and Opladen 1965

Daim, W., *Der Mann, der Hitler die Ideen gab. Von der religiösen Verirrungen eines Sektierers zum Rassenwahn des Diktators*, Munich 1958

Dannemann, U., *Der Zusammenhang von Theologie und Politik im Denken Karl Barths*, Protestant theological dissertation Bochum 1975

Dannenmann, A., *Die Geschichte der Glaubensbewegung 'Deutsche Christen'*, Dresden 1933

Darré, W., *Neuadel aus Blut und Boden*, Munich 1935

Dehn, G., *Proletarische Jugend. Lebensgestaltung und Gedankenwelt der grossstädtischen Proletarierjugend*, Berlin 1930

—, *Kirche und Völkerversohnung. Dokumente zum Halleschen Universitätskonflikt*, Berlin nd [1931]

—, *Die alte Zeit, die vorigen Jahre. Lebenserinnerungen*, Munich 1962

Denzinger, H. and A.Schönmetzer, *Enchiridion symbolorum definitionum et declarationum de rebus fidei et morum*, Freiburg [32]1963

Deuerlein, E., *Das Reichskonkordat. Beiträge zu Vorgeschichte, Abschluss und Vollzug des Konkordates zwischen dem Heiligen Stuhl und dem Deutschen Reich vom 20.Juli 1933*, Düsseldorf 1956

—, 'Hitlers Eintritt in die NSDAP und die Reichswehr', *Vierteljahrshefte für Zeitgeschichte* 7, 1959, 177-227

—, *Der Deutsche Katholizismus 1933*, Osnabrück 1963

Der Deutsche Evangelische Kirchenbund in den Jahren 1924-27, Geschäftsbericht des Deutschen Evangelischen Kirchenausschusses zum Kirchentag 1927, nebst einleitendem Vorwort und den einschlägigen Beschlüssen des Kirchentags, published by the Kirchenbundesamt, Berlin-Charlottenburg 1927

Dibelius, O., *Das Jahrhundert der Kirche. Geschichte, Betrachtung, Umschau und Ziel* (1927), Berlin [5]1928

—, *Die Verantwortung der Kirche. Eine Antwort an Karl Barth*, Berlin nd [1931]

—, *In the Service of the Lord*, London and New York 1964

Diehl-Thiele, P., *Partei und Staat im Dritten Reich. Untersuchungen zum Verhältnis von NSDAP und innerer Staatsverwaltung 1933-1945*, Munich 1969

Diels, R., *Lucifer ante portas. Es spricht der erste Chef der Gestapo*, Stuttgart 1950

Dienst, K. (ed.), *Dokumentation zum Kirchenkampf in Hessen und Nassau 1*, Jahrbuch der Hessische Kirchengeschichtliche Vereinigung 25, Darmstadt 1974

Diem, H., *Ja oder nein. 50 Jahre Theologie in Kirche und Staat*, Stuttgart and Berlin 1974

Dinter, A., *Die Sünde wider das Blut. Ein Zeitroman*, Leipzig und Hartenstein im Saar ([1]1918) [16]1921

—, *Die Sünde wider den Geist*, Leipzig und Hartenstein im Saar 1921

688

—, *Die Sünde wider die Liebe*, Leipzig and Hartenstein im Saar 1922

—, *197 Thesen zur Vollendung der Reformation. Die Wiederherstellung der reinen Heilandslehre*, Leipzig 1926

Dirks, W., 'Katholizismus und Nationalsozialismus', *Die Arbeit* 8, 1931, 201-9

Doehring, B. (ed.), *Eine feste Burg – Predigten und Reden aus eherner Zeit. Zum Besten der Nationalstiftung für die Hinterbliebenen der im Kriege Gefallenen* 1, Berlin nd [1914]

Dörries, H., *Luther und Deutschland*. Sammlung gemeinverständlicher Vorträge 169, 1934

Doetsch, W.J., *Württembergs Katholiken unterm Hakenkreuz 1930-1935*, Stuttgart 1969

Domarus, M., *Hitler. Reden und Proklamationen 1932-1945. Kommentiert von einem deutschen Zeitgenossen*, 1. *Triumph 1932-1938*; 2. *Untergang 1939-1945*, Munich 1965

Dülmen, R.van, 'Katholischer Konservatismus oder die "soziologische" Neuorientierung. Das *Hochland* in der Weimarer Zeit', *Zeitschrift für bayerische Landesgeschichte* 36, 1973, 254-301

Ebers, G.J., *Staat und Kirche im neuen Deutschland*, Munich 1930

—, *Reichs- und preussiches Staatskirchenrecht. Sammlung der religions- und kirchenpolitischen Gesetze und Verordnungen des Deutschen Reiches und Preussens nebst den einschlägigen kirchlichen Vorschriften*, Munich 1932

Eckard, A. and R., 'Christentum und Judentum: Die theologische und moralische Problematik der Vernichtung des europäischen Judentums', *Evangelische Theologie* 36, 1965, 402-26

Eckart, D., *Der Bolschewismus von Moses bis Lenin. Zwiegespräch zwischen Adolf Hitler und mir*, Munich 1924

Eckert, E., *Was wollen die religiösen Sozialisten?*, Schriften der religiösen Sozialisten 1, Mannheim 1927

Ehrenberg, H. (ed.), *Credo Ecclesiam. Festgabe für Wilhelm Zoellner zum siebzigsten Geburtstage*, Gütersloh 1930

Ehrenforth, G., *Die schlesische Kirche im Kirchenkampf 1932-1945*, Göttingen 1968

Epstein, K., *Matthias Erzberger and the Dilemma of German Democracy*, Princeton 1959

Eschweiler, K., *Die zwei Wege der neueren Theologie, Georg Hermes – Matthias Joseph Scheeben. Eine kritische Untersuchung des Problems der theologischen Erkenntnis*, Augsburg 1926

—, 'Politische Theologie', *Religiöse Besinnung. Vierteljahresschrift im Dienste christlicher Vertiefung und ökumenischer Verständigung* 4, 1931/32, 72-88

—, 'Die Kirche im neuen Reich', *Deutsches Volkstum* 1933, 454-6

Faulhaber, M. von, *Judaism, Christianity and Germany*, New York 1934

Faust, A., *Der Nationalsozialistische Deutsche Studentenbund. Studenten und Nationalsozialismus in der Weimarer Republik*, two vols, Düsseldorf 1973

Feder, G., *Das Programm der NSDAP und seine weltanschaulichen Grundlagen*, 41st-60th editions, 201-250,000, Munich 1931

Fest, J.C., *Das Gesicht des Dritten Reiches. Profile einer totalitären Herrschaft*, Munich 1963

—, *Hitler. Eine Biographie*, Frankfurt, Berlin and Vienna [2]1973

Fichte, J.G., *Die Grundzüge des gegenwärtigen Zeitalters*, Sämtliche Werke 7, ed. J.H.Fichte, Leipzig nd

Fischer, J., *Die sächsische Landeskirche im Kirchenkampf 1933-1937*, Göttingen 1972

Fischer, O., *Der Parlamentarismus in den evangelischen Landeskirchen Deutschlands*, Erlangen law dissertation 1931

Flechtheim, O.K., *Die KPD in der Weimarer Republik* (1948), Frankfurt 1969

Fleisch, P., 'Das Werden der vereinigten Evangelisch-Lutherische Kirche Deutschlands und ihrer Verfassung', *Zeitschrift für evangelische Kirchenrecht* 1, 1951, 15-55

689

Fleisch, P., *Erlebte Kirchengeschichte. Erfahrungen in und mit der hannoverschen Landeskirche*, Hanover 1952

Fleischhauer, U. (ed.), *Die echten Protokolle der Weisen von Zion. Sachverständigengutachten, erstattet im Aufträge des Richteramtes V in Bern*, Erfurt 1935

Föhr, E., *Geschichte des Badischen Konkordates*, Freiburg 1958

Foerster, F.W., *Erlebte Weltgeschichte 1869-1953. Memoiren*, Nuremberg 1953

Fraenkel, E., *The Dual State*, New York 1941

Franz-Willing, G., *Die Hitlerbewegung*, 1. *Der Ursprung 1919-1922*; 2. *Krisenjahr der Hitlerbewegung 1923*, Hamburg 1962/75

—, *Die Bayerische Vatikangesandtschaft 1803-1934*, Munich 1965

Freyter, H., *Revolution von rechts*, Jena 1931

Friedberg, E., *Lehrbuch des katholischen und evangelischen Kirchenrechts*, Leipzig [6]1909

Fritsch, T., *Der falsche Gott*, Leipzig [4]1916

— (ed.), *Handbuch der Judenfrage. Eine Zusammenfassung des wichtigsten Materials zur Beurteilen des jüdischen Volkes*, Hamburg [28]1919

—, *Vom neuen Glauben, Bekenntnis der Deutschen Erneuerungsgemeinde*, Leipzig (nd)

Fromm, E., *Anatomy of Human Destructiveness*, New York 1975

Frost, H., *Strukturprobleme evangelischer Kirchenverfassung. Rechtsvergleichende Untersuchungen zum Verfassungsrecht der deutschen evangelischen Landeskirchen*, Göttingen 1972

Fürst, W. (ed.), *Dialektische Theologie in Scheidung und Bewährung 1933-1936. Aufsätze, Gutachten und Erklärungen*, Munich 1966

Gaede, R., *Kirche – Christen – Krieg und Frieden. Die Diskussion im deutschen Protestantismus während der Weimarer Zeit*, Hamburg 1975

Gauger, J., *Chronik der Kirchenwirren (Gotthard-Briefe 138-145)*, 1. *1932-1934*, Elberfeld 1934

Geiger, T., 'Die Mittelschichten und die Sozialdemokratie', *Die Arbeit* 8, 1931, 620ff.

Das Geistchristentum. Monatsschrift zur Vollendung der Reformation durch Wiederherstellung der reinen Heilandslehre, ed. A.Dinter, 1, 1927; 2, 1929

Gerstenmaier, E., 'Das Kirchliche Aussenamt im Reiche Hitlers', in *Kirche im Spannungsfeld der Politik, Festschrift D.Hermann Kunst zum 70.Geburtstag*, Göttingen 1977, 307-18

Gesetzblatt der Deutschen Evangelischen Kirche, published by the Deutsches Evangelische Kirchenkanzlei, 1933 and 1934

Giese, F., and J. Hosemann (eds), *Die Verfassungen der Deutschen Evangelischen Landeskirchen. Unter Berücksichtigung der kirchlichen und staatlichen Ein- und Ausführungsgesetze*, 2 vols, Berlin 1927

Giese, F., and F.A.von der Heydte (eds.), *Der Konkordatsprozess*, Munich nd [1957-1959]

Glenthøj, J., 'Unterredung im Vestibul. Das Gespräch zwischen Pfarrer Backhaus und Hitler am 28 Juni 1933', *Kirche in der Zeit* 17, 1962, 388-94

—, 'Dokumente zur Bonhoeffer-Forschung 1928-1945', Munich 1969

Gloege, G., 'Die Deutschkirche', in W.Künneth and H.Schreiner, *Die Nation vor Gott*, Berlin 1934, 393-415

Goebbels, J., *Revolution der Deutschen. 14 Jahre Nationalsozialismus. Goebbelsreden mit einleitenden Zeitbildern*, ed. H.Schlecht, Oldenburg 1933

—, *Vom Kaiserhof zur Reichskanzlei. Eine historische Darstellung in Tagebuchblättern (Vom 1.Januar 1932 bis zum 1.Mai 1933)* (1934), Munich 1943

Göbell, W. (ed.), *Kirche, Recht und Theologie in vier Jahrzehnten. Der Briefwechsel der Brüder Theodor und Julius Kaftan* 2, Munich 1967

Götte, K.-H., *Die Propaganda der Glaubensbewegung Deutsche Christen und ihre*

Beurteilung in der deutschen Tagespresse. Ein Beitrag zur Publizistik im Dritten Reich, Münster philosophical dissertation 1957

Gogarten, F., 'Between the Times' (*Christliche Welt* 1920, 374-8), reprinted in James M.Robinson (ed.), *The Beginnnings of Dialectical Theology*, Richmond, Va 1968, 277-82

—, 'The Crisis of our Culture' (*Christliche Welt* 1920, 770-7), reprinted in ibid., 283-300

—, *Wider die Ächtung der Autorität*, Jena 1930

—, *Politische Ethik*, Jena 1932

—, 'Die Selbständigkeit der Kirche', in *Deutsches Volkstum*. 1933

—, *Einheit von Evangelium und Volkstum?*, Hamburg 1933

—, *Gericht oder Skepsis. Eine Streitschrift gegen Karl Barth*, Jena ²1937

Goldhagen, E., 'Weltanschauung und Endlösung. Zum Antisemitismus der nationalsozialistischen Führungsschicht', *Vierteljahrshefte für Zeitgeschichte* 24, 1976, 379-405

Gollwitzer, H., *Reich Gottes und Sozialismus bei Karl Barth*, Theologisches Existenz heute NF 169, Munich 1972

Golombek, D., *Die politische Vorgeschichte des Preussenkonkordats* (1929), Mainz 1970

Gordon, H.J., Jr, *Hitlerputsch 1923. Machtkampf in Bayern 1923-24*, Frankfurt 1971

Gotto, K., *Die Wochenzeitung* Junge Front/Michael. *Eine Studie zum katholischen Selbstverständnis und zum Verhalten der jungen Kirche gegenüber dem Nationalsozialismus*, Mainz 1970

Grabowski, A. 'Nach den Wahlen. Betrachtungen aus Amerika', *Zeitschrift für Politik* 20, 1931, 435-45

Greschat, M. (ed.), *Der deutsche Protestantismus im Revolutionsjahr 1918-19*, Witten 1974

Grünthal, G., *Reichsschulgesetz und Zentrumspartei in der Weimarer Republik*, Düsseldorf 1968

Gürtler, P., *Nationalsozialismus und evangelische Kirche im Warthegau. Trennung von Staat und Kirche im nationalsozialistischen Weltanschauungsstaat*, Göttingen 1958

Haack, H.G., *Die evangelische Kirche Deutschlands in der Gegenwart*, Berlin 1929

Härle, W. 'Der Anruf der 93 Intellektuellen und Karl Barths Bruch mit der liberalen Theologie', *Zeitschrift für Theologie und Kirche* 72, 1975, 206-24

Hahn, H., *Kämpfer wider Willen. Erinnerungen des Landesbischofs von Sachsen D.Hugo Hahn aus dem Kirchenkampf 1935-45*, revised and edited G.Prater, Metzingen 1969

Hamel, J., 'Begegnungen mit Karl Barth', *Stimme der Gemeinde* 18, 1966, 289-92

Hammer, K., *Deutsche Kriegstheologie 1870-1918*, Munich 1971

Handbuch der Evangelischen Presse, ed.A.Hinderer, Leipzig ²1929

Harder, G., and W.Niemöller (eds.), *Die Stunde der Versuchung. Gemeinden im Kirchenkampf 1933-1945. Selbstzeugnisse*, Munich 1963

Hauer, W., *Deutsche Gottschau. Grundzüge eines Deutschen Glaubens*, Stuttgart 1934

Heer, G., *Der Glaube des Adolf Hitler. Anatomie einer politischen Religiosität*, Munich and Esslingen 1969

Heiber, H., 'Aus den Akten des Gauleiters Kube', *Vierteljahrshefte für Zeitgeschichte* 2, 1956, 657-92

—, *Die Republik von Weimar*, Munich ⁵1971

Heim, K., *Deutsche Staatsreligion oder Evangelische Volkskirche*, Stimmen aus der deutschen christlichen Studentenbewegung 85, Berlin 1933

Heinonen, R.E., *Die Bremer Deutschen Christen. Ein Beitrag zu Theologie und Kirchenpolitik der Deutschen Christen im Dritten Reich*, Tübingen Protestant theological dissertation 1972 (ms)

Hermelink, H., *Kirche im Kampf. Dokumente des Widerstandes und des Aufbaus der Evangelischen Kirche in Deutschland von 1933-1945*, Tübingen 1950

Herrmann, W., *Ethik*, Tübingen (1901) ⁵1913

Hesse, H.A., 'Elberfeld', in G.Harder and W.Niemöller, *Die Stunde der Versuchung. Gemeinden im Kirchenkampf 1933-1945. Selbstzeugnisse*, Münster 1963, 302-18

Heuss, T., *Erinnerungen 1905-1933*, Tübingen [5]1964

Heuss-Knapp, E., *Bürgerin zweier Welten. Ein Leben in Briefen und Aufzeichnungen*, Tübingen 1961

Hey, B., *Die Kirchenprovinz Westfalen 1933-1945*, Bielefeld 1974

Heydt, F. von der, *Gute Wehr. Werden, Wirken und Wollen des evangelischen Bundes. Zu seine 50jährigen Jubiläum*, Berlin 1936

Hirsch, E., *Deutschlands Schicksal. Staat, Volk und Menschheit im Lichte einer ethischen Geschichtsansicht* (1921), Göttingen [3]1925

—, *Staat und Kirche im 19. und 20. Jahrhundert*, Göttingen 1929

—, *Das kirchliche Wollen der Deutschen Christen*, Berlin 1933

—, *Die gegenwärtige geistige Lage im Spiegel philosophischer und theologischer Besinnung. Akademische Vorlesungen zum Verständnis des deutschen Jahres 1933*, Göttingen 1934

—, *Geschichte der neuern evangelischen Theologie im Zusammenhang mit den allgemeinen Bewegungen des europäischen Denkens*, Gütersloh 1949-54

History of the Church, ed. Hubert Jedin and John Dolan, Vol.IX, London and New York 1981

Hitler, A., *Mein Kampf* (1925/27), ET London 1972

—, 'Zum Wiedererstehen unserer Bewegung' (1925), reprinted in the documentation 'Aus dem Kampf der Bewegung', *Nationalsozialistische Monatshefte* 9, 1938, 647-9

Hoefler, K., *Protestantismus und Völkische Bewegung*, Nuremberg nd [1924]

Holl, K., 'Was Verstand Luther unter Religion?' (speech given at the Reformation Festival of the University of Berlin, 31 October 1917), in *Gesammelte Aufsätze zur Kirchengeschichte, 1, Luther*, Tübingen (1923) [7]1948, 1-110

Hollerbach, A., *Verträge zwischen Staat und Kirche in der Bundesrepublik Deutschland*, Frankfurt 1965

—, 'Streiflichter zur Entstehungsgeschichte der Badischen Staatskirchenverträge von 1932', *Zeitschrift der Savigny-Stiftung für Rechtsgeschichte* 92, Kanonistische Abteilung 61, 1975, 324-47

Horn, W., *Führerideologie und Parteiorganisation in der NSDAP (1919-1933)*, Düsseldorf 1972

Hornig, E., *Die Bekennende Kirche in Schlesien 1933-1945, Geschichte und Dokumente*, Göttingen 1977

Hornung, K., *Der Jungdeutsche Orden*, Düsseldorf 1958

Hossenfelder, J., *Unser Kampf*, Schriftenreihe der Glaubensbewegung Deutsche Christen no.5, Berlin 1933

Huber, E.R. and W., *Staat und Kirche im 19. Jahrhundert und 20. Jahrhundert. Dokumente zur Geschichte des deutschen Staatskirchenrechts*, 2 vols., Berlin 1973-76

Huber, W., *Kirche und Öffentlichkeit*, Stuttgart 1973

Hüttenberger, P., Die Gauleiter. Studie zum Wandel des Machtgefüges in der NSDAP, Stuttgart 1969

Hüttl, L., 'Die Stellungnahme der katholischen Kirche und Publizistik zur Revolution in Bayern 1918-19', *Zeitschrift für bayerische Landesgeschichte* 324, 1971, 652-95

Hutten, K., *Christus oder Deutschglaube? Ein Kampf um die deutsche Seele*, Stuttgart 1935

—, 'Die Deutsche Glaubensbewegung', in W.Künneth and H.Schreiner, *Die Nation vor Gott*, Berlin [3]1934, 157-204

Immer, K. (ed.), *Die Lebensordnungen einer nach Gottes Wort erneuerten Kirche. Vorträge auf einer Rüstzeit von Pastoren und Ältesten*, Barmen 1935

—, *Die Briefe des Coetus reformierter Prediger 1933-1937*, ed. J.Beckmann, Neukirchen 1976

692

Irmler, H., 'Bankenkrise und Vollbeschäftigungspolitik (1931-1936)', in *Währung und Wirtschaft in Deutschland*, published by Deutsche Bundesbank, Frankfurt 1976, 283-308

Iserloh, E., 'Vom Abschluss des Reichskonkordats bis zur Ratifikation', *Trierer Theologische Zeitschrift* 72, 1963, 39-52

Israel, C., *Geschichte des Reichskirchenrechts*, Berlin 1922

Iwand, H.J., *Briefe an Rudolf Hermann*, Nachgelassene Werke 6, ed. H.Gollwitzer et al., Munich 1964

Jacke, J., *Kirche zwischen Monarchie und Republik. Der preussische Protestantismus nach dem Zusammenbruch von 1918*, Hamburg 1976

Jacobi, G., *Tagebuch eines Grossstadtpfarrers. Briefe an einen Freund*, Berlin (1929) [8]1930

Jacobsen, H.-A., *Nationalsozialistische Aussenpolitik 1933-1938*, Frankfurt am Main and Berlin 1968

Jäckel, E., *Hitlers Weltanschauung. Entwurf einer Herrschaft*, Tübingen 1969

Jasper, G. (ed.), *Von Weimar zu Hitler 1930-1933*, Cologne and Berlin 1968

Jestaedt, R., 'Das Reichskonkordat vom 20.Juli 1933 in der nationalsozialistische Staats- und Verwaltungspraxis unter besonderer Berücksichtigung des Artikels 1', *Archiv für katholisches Kirchenrecht* 124, 1949/50, 335-430

Jochmann, W., *Nationalsozialismus und Revolution. Ursprung und Geschichte der NSDAP in Hamburg 1922-1933. Dokumente*, Frankfurt am Main 1963

Jüchen, Aurel von, 'Der Faschismus, eine Gefahr für das Christentum', *Zeitschrift für Religion und Sozialismus*, 1930, 299-311

Junker, D., *Die Deutsche Zentrumspartei und Hitler 1932/33. Ein Beitrag zur Problematik des politischen Katholizismus in Deutschland*, Stuttgart 1969

Kaas, L. (ed.), *Eugenio Pacelli. Erster Apostolischer Nuntius beim Deutschen Reich. Gesammelte Reden*, Berlin 1930

—, 'Der Konkordatstyp des faschistichen Italien', *Zeitschrift für ausländisches öffentliches Recht und Völkerrecht*, III.1, 1933, 488-522

Kaiser, M.U., *Deutscher Kirchenkampf und Schweizer Öffentlichkeit in den Jahren 1933 und 1934*, Zurich 1972

Kampffmeyer, K. (ed.), *Dein Wort ist Deiner Kirche Schutz. Predigten von der Kirche*, Göttingen 1934

— (ed.), *Widerstand und Solidarität der Christen in Deutschland 1933-1945. Eine Dokumentation zum Kirchenkampf aus den Papieren des D.Wilhelm Freiherrn von Pechmann*, Neustadt 1971

—, 'Generalsuperintendent D.Zoellner und der Herausgeber der *Allgemeinen Evangelisch-lutherischen Kirchenzeitung*. Ein Beitrag zur Kirchenkampfforschung', *Jahrbuch des Vereins für Westfälische Kirchengeschichte* 64, 1961, 134-68

—, 'Zeitwende. Zum Weg einer Kulturzeitschrift und ihre Münchner Redaktion im Dritten Reich', *Zeitschrift für bayerische Landesgeschichte* 37, 1974, 569-94

—, 'Kirchlich-theologischer Liberalismus und Kirchenkampf. Erwägungen zu einer Forschungsaufgabe', *Zeitschrift für Kirchengeschichte* 87, 1976, 298-320

Kappes, H., 'Der theologische Kampf der religiösen Sozialisten gegen das nationalsozialistische Christentum', in *Reich Gottes, Marxismus, Nationalsozialismus*, ed. G.Wünsch, Tübingen 1931, 90-116

Karwehl, R., 'Politisches Messiastum', *Zwischen den Zeiten* 9, 1931, 519-43

—, 'Was ich als lutherischer Prediger von Karl Barth gelernt habe', in *Antwort: Karl Barth zum 70. Geburtstag*, Zurich 1956, 897-905

Kater, H., *Die Deutsche Evangelische Kirche in den Jahren 1933 und 1934. Eine rechts- und verfassungsgeschichtliche Untersuchung*, Göttingen 1970

Kater, M.H., 'Zur Soziographie der frühen NSDAP', *Vierteljahrshefte für Zeitgeschichte* 19, 1971, 124-59

Kehrl, H., *Krisenmanager im Dritten Reich, 6 Jahre Frieden – 6 Jahre Krieg. Erinnerungen*, Düsseldorf 1973

Kessler, H., *Wilhelm Stapel als politischer Publizist. Ein Beitrag zur Geschichte des konservativen Nationalismus zwischen den beiden Weltkriegen*, Nuremberg 1967

Kinder, C., *Neue Beiträge zur Geschichte der evangelischen Kirche in Schleswig-Holstein und im Reich 1924-1945*, Flensburg 1966

Kirchliches Handbuch für das katholische Deutschland. Nebst Mitteilung der ämtlichen Zentralstelle für kirchliche Statistik, ed. H.A.Krose SJ, 9 (1919/20) – 16 (1928/29)

Kirchliches Jahrbuch für die evangelischen Landeskirche Deutschlands, ed. Johannes Schneider (from 1931 Hermann Sasse), 46-60, Gütersloh 1919-1933

Klepper, J., *Unter dem Schatten Deiner Flugel. Aus den Tagebüchern der Jahre 1932-1942*, Stuttgart 1956

Kloss, E. (ed.), *Reden des Führers. Politik und Propaganda Adolf Hitlers 1922-1945* Munich 1967

Klotz, L. (ed.), *Die Kirche und das Dritte Reich. Fragen und Forderung deutscher Theologen*, 2 vols, Gotha 1932

Klügel, E., *Die lutherische Landeskirche Hannovers und ihr Bischof 1933-1945*, 2 vols Berlin and Hamburg 1962, 1965

Kluke, P., 'Der Fall Potempa', *Vierteljahrshefte für Zeitgeschichte* 5, 1957, 279-97

Koch, H.W., *Geschichte der Hitlerjugend. Ihre Ursprünge und ihre Entwicklung 1922 1945*, Percha 1975

Koch, W., 'Wechselwirkungen zwischen Kirchenkampf und Theologie, beobachtet ai Karl Barth', in *Freispruch und Freiheit. Theologische Aufsätze für W.Kreck zun 65.Geburtstag*, ed. H.G.Geyer, Munich 1973, 272-93

Köhler, G., *Die Auswirkungen der Novemberrevolution von 1918 auf die altpreussisch Evangelische Landeskirche*, theological dissertation, Kirchliche Hochschule Berli 1967

Kolb, E., *Die Arbeiterräte in der deutschen Innenpolitik 1918-1919*, Düsseldorf 1962

— (ed.), *Vom Kaiserreich zur Weimarer Republik*, Cologne 1972

Kopp, W., *Die gegenwärtige Geisteslage und die dialektische Theologie*, Tübingen 1930

Koschorke, M. (ed.), *Geschichte der Bekennenden Kirche in Ostpreussen 1933-1945* Göttingen 1976

Kottje, R. and B.Moeller (eds.), *Ökumenische Kirchengeschichte* 3, 1974

Krause, R. (ed.), *Rede des Gauobmanns der Glaubensbewegung 'Deutsche Christen' i Gross-Berlin Dr Krause gehalten im Sportpalast am 13 November 1933 (nach doppelter stenographischen Bericht)*, pamphlet, no place or date, Verlag Unsere Volkskirche

Kremers, H., *Nationalsozialismus und Protestantismus*, Volksschriften des Evangelische Bundes 35, Berlin 1931

Kretschmar, G., 'Die Auseinandersetzung der Bekennenden Kirche mit den Deutsche Christen', in *Tutzinger Texte*, ed. P.Rieger and J.Strauss, Sonderband 1, *Kirche un Nationalsozialismus*, Munich 1969, 117-50

—(ed.), *Dokumente zur Kirchenpolitik des Dritten Reiches 1, Das Jahr 1933*, revised t C.Nicolaisen, Munich 1971

Krog, F., *Lagarde und der deutsche Staat. Eine Ubersicht über Lagardes Denken*, Munic 1930

Kruck, A., *Geschichte des Alldeutschen Verbands 1890-1939*, Wiesbaden 1954

Kübel, J., *Erinnerungen. Mensch und Christ, Theologe, Pfarrer und Kirchenman* privately printed by his daughter, Dr Martha Frommer, Villingen-Schwenningen 197. for the centenary of his death

Kühnl, R., *Die nationalsozialistischen Linke 1925-1930*, Marburg 1965

694

Künneth, W., W.Wilm and H.Schemm, *Was haben wir als evangelische Christen zum Rufe des Nationalsozialismus zu sagen?*, Dresden 1931

Künneth, W., and H.Schreiner, *Die Nation vor Gott. Zur Botschaft der Kirche im Dritten Reich*, Berlin ([1]1933) [3]1934

Kupisch, K., *Studenten entdecken die Bibel. Die Geschichte der Deutschen Christlichen Studenten-Vereinigung (DCSV)*, Hamburg 1964

—, 'Zur Genesis des Pfarrernotbundes', *Theologische Literaturzeitung* 91, 1966, 721-30

Kupper, A., 'Zur Geschichte des Reichskonkordats. Ein Beitrag zur Geschichte des Verhandlungsablaufs zwischen Ostern 1933 und der Ratifikation des Konkordats', *Stimmen der Zeit* 164, 1958/59, 278-302 and 354-75

—, 'Zur Geschichte des Reichskonkordats', *Stimmen der Zeit* 171, 1962/3, 25-50

—, *Staatliche Akten über die Reichskonkordatsverhandlungen 1933*, Mainz 1969

Lagarde, P.de, 'Über das Verhältnis des deutschen Staates zu Theologie, Kirche und Religion. Ein Versuch, Nicht-Theologen zu orientieren' (1873), in id., *Deutsche Schriften*, Munich 1924, 45-90

Lama, F. von, *Papst und Kurie in ihrer Politik nach dem Weltkrieg. Dargestellt unter besonderer Berücksichtigung des Verhältnisses zwischen dem Vatikan und Deutschland*, Illertissen 1925

Lamparter, E., *Evangelische Kirche und Judentum*, no place or date, privately published Stuttgart 1927. Reprinted in R.R.Geis and H.J.Kraus (eds), *Versuche des Verstehens. Dokumente jüdisch-christlicher Begegnung aus den Jahren 1918-1933*, Munich 1966, 256-302

—, *Das Judentum in seiner kultur- und religionsgeschichtlichen Erscheinung*, Gotha 1928

Lange, K., *Hitlers unbeachtete Maximen. Mein Kampf und die Öffentlichkeit*, Stuttgart, Berlin, Cologne and Mainz 1968

Lange, P., *Konkrete Theologie? Karl Barth und Friedrich Gogarten Zwischen den Zeiten (1922-1933). Eine theologisch-systematische Untersuchung im Blick auf die Praxis theologischen Verhaltens*, Zurich 1972

Die Lateran-Verträge zwischen dem Heiligen Stuhl und Italien vom 11. Februar 1929. Authorized edition with an introduction by the Papal Nuncio Eugenio Pacelli in Berlin, Freiburg 1929

Leber, A. (ed.), *Das Gewissen steht auf. 64 Lebensbilder aus dem deutschen Widerstand 1933-1945*, Berlin and Frankfurt 1954

Leffler, S., *Christus im Dritten Reich der Deutschen. Wesen, Weg und Ziele der Kirchenbewegung Deutsche Christen*, Weimar nd [1935]

Lehmann, H., *Pietismus und weltliche Ordnung in Württemberg*, Stuttgart, Berlin, Cologne and Mainz 1969

Lehr, S., *Antisemitismus – religiöse Motive im sozialen Vorurteil*, Munich 1974

Leiber, R., 'Die Lösung der römischen Frage durch die Lateranverträge', *Stimmen der Zeit* 59, 1929, 161-81

—, 'Pius XII', *Stimmen der Zeit* 163, 1958-59, 81-100

—, 'Reichskonkordat und Ende der Zentrumspartei', *Stimmen der Zeit* 167, 1960/61, 213-23

Lersner, D. von, *Die evangelische Jugendverbände Württembergs und die Hitler-Jugend 1933/34*, Göttingen 1958

Lewy, G., *Die Catholic Church and Nazi Germany*, New York 1964

Liebe, W., *Die Deutschnationale Volkspartei 1918-1924*, Düsseldorf 1956

Liermann, H., 'Staat und Kirche in den Lateranverträgen', *Archiv des öffentlichen Rechts* 57, NF 18, 1930, 379-410

—, 'Der evangelische Bischofsamt in Deutschland seit 1933', *Zeitschrift für evangelisches Kirchenrecht* 3, 1953/54, 1-29

Lill, R., 'Die deutsche Katholiken und die Juden in der Zeit von 1850 bis zur Machtübernahme Hitlers', in K.H.Rengstorf and S.von Kortzfleisch, *Kirche und Synagoge. Handbuch zur Geschichte von Christen und Juden* 2, Stuttgart 1970

Linck, H., *Der Kirchenkampf in Ostpreussen 1933-1945. Geschichte und Dokumentation*, Munich 1968

Lohalm, U. *Völkischer Radikalismus. Geschichte des Deutschvölkischen Schutz- und Trutzbundes 1919-23*, Hamburg 1970

Lortz, J. *Geschichte der Kirche in ideengeschichtlicher Betrachtung. Eine geschichtliche Sinndeutung der christliche Vergangenheit*, Münster [3]1933

—, *Katholischer Zugang zum Nationalsozialismus*, Reich und Kirche 2, Münster [2]1934

Ludendorff, E. *Vom Feldherrn zum Weltrevolutionär und Wegbereiter Deutscher Volksschöpfung, Lebenserinnerung von 1919 bis 1925*, Munich 1941

Lueken, W., *Kampf, Behauptung und Gestalt der Evangelischen Landeskirche Nassau-Hessen*, Göttingen 1963

Lulvès, J., 'Der Lateran-Vertrag zwischen dem Heiligen Stuhl und Italien', *Preussische Jahrbücher* 216, 1929, 61-76

Lutz, H. *Demokratie im Zwielicht. Der Weg der deutschen Katholiken aus dem Kaiserreich in die Republik 1914-1926*, Munich 1963

Maas, H., 'Friedrich Siegmund-Schultze. Ein Bahnbrecher christlicher Solidarität', in *Ökumenische Profile. Brückenbauer der einen Kirche*, ed. G.Gloede 1, Stuttgart 1961, 253-63

Maron, G., *Die römisch-katholische Kirche von 1870 bis 1970*, Göttingen 1972.

Mann, T., *Betrachtungen eines Unpolitischen*, Stockholmer Gesamtausgabe, Frankfurt 1956

Marquardt, F.-W. *Theologie und Sozialismus. Das Beispiel Karl Barths*, Munich and Mainz 1972

Marsch, W.-D., 'Gerechtigkeit im Tal des Todes. Christliche Glaube und politische Vernunft im Denken Karl Barths', in W.Dantine and K.Luthi (eds.), *Theologie zwischen Gestern und Morgen*, Munich 1968, 167-91

Maser, W., *Die Frühgeschichte der NSDAP. Hitlers Weg bis 1924*, Frankfurt and Bonn 1965

—, *Hitlers Briefe und Notizen. Sein Weltbild in handschriftlichen Dokumente*, Düsseldorf and Vienna 1973

Massing, P.W., *Vorgeschichte des politischen Antisemitismus*, Frankfurt am Main 1959

Materialdienst, published by the Landesgeschäftsstelle des Evangelischen Volksbundes für Württemberg 4, 1932; 5, 1933

Matthias, E., 'Die Sozialdemokratische Partei Deutschlands', in E.Matthias and R.Morsey (eds), *Das Ende der Parteien 1933*, Düsseldorf 1960, 101-278

Matthias, E., and R.Morsey (eds.), *Das Ende der Parteien 1933*, Düsseldorf 1960

Mehnert, G., *Evangelische Kirche und Politik 1917-1919. Die politischen Strömungen im deutschen Protestantismus von der Julikrise 1917 bis zum Herbst 1919*, Düsseldorf 1959

Meier, K., *Die Deutschen Christen. Das Bild einer Bewegung im Kirchenkampf des Dritten Reiches*, Halle 1964 (edition licensed for the Federal Republic, Göttingen 1964)

—, 'Die Religionspolitik der NSDAP in der Zeit der Weimarer Republik', in *Zur Geschichte des Kirchenkampfes*, Gesammelte Aufsätze 2, Göttingen 1971, 9-24

—, *Der evangelische Kirchenkampf. Gesamtdarstellung in drei Bände*, 1. *Der Kampf um die Reichskirche*, 2. *Gescheiterte Neuordnungsversuche im Zeichen staatliche Rechtshilfe*, Göttingen 1976

Meinertz, M., and H.Sacher, *Deutschland und der Katholizismus. Gedanken zur Neugestaltung des deutschen Geistes und Gesellschaftsleben*, two vols, Freiburg 1918

Merkle, S., 'Konfessionelle Vorurteile im alten Deutschland', *Suddeutsche Monatshefte*, December 1914, 390-406

696

Merton, R.K., 'Die Eigendynamik gesellschaftlicher Voraussagen', in E.Topitsch (ed.), *Logik der Sozialwissenschaften*, Cologne and Berlin 1971, 144-61

Merz, G., 'Die Begegnung Karl Barths mit der deutschen Theologie', *Kerygma und Dogma* 2, 1956, 157-75

Michel, O., *Vorwärts zu Christus! Fort mit Paulus! Deutsche Religion!*, Berlin ³1906

Milatz, A., *Wähler und Wahlen in der Weimarer Republik*, Bonn ²1968

Miller, S., *Burgfrieden und Klassenkampf. Die deutsche Sozialdemokratie im ersten Weltkrieg*, Düsseldorf 1974

Mohler, A., *Die konservative Revolution in Deutschland 1918- 1932. Ein Handbuch*, Darmstadt ²1972

Moltmann, J. (ed.), *Die Anfänge der dialektischen Theologie*, two parts, Munich 1962/63. For a partial ET see Robinson, James M., *The Beginnings of Dialectical Theology*

Morsey, R., 'Zur Vorgeschichte des Reichskonkordats aus den Jahren 1920 und 1921', *Zeitschrift der Savigny Stiftung für Rechtsgeschichte* 75, Kanonistische Abteilung 54, 1958, 237-67

—, 'Die Deutsche Zentrumspartei', in E.Matthias and R.Morsey (eds), *Das Ende der Parteien 1933*, Düsseldorf 1960, 281-453

—, 'Hitlers Verhandlungen mit dem Zentrumsführung am 30. Januar 1933', *Vierteljahrshefte für Zeitgeschichte* 9, 1961, 182-94

—, *Die Deutsche Zentrumspartei 1917-1923*, Düsseldorf 1966

— (ed.), *Die Protokolle der Reichstagsfraktion und des Fraktionsvorstands der Deutschen Zentrumspartei 1926-1933*, Mainz 1969

—, 'Die deutschen Katholiken und der Nationalstaat zwischen Kulturkampf und dem ersten Weltkrieg', *Historisches Jahrbuch der Görresgesellschaft* 90, 1970, 31-64

Mosse, W.E. (ed.), *Entscheidungsjahr 1932. Zur Judenfrage in der Endphase der Weimarer Republik*, Tübingen 1965

Motschmann, C., *Evangelische Kirche und preussischer Staat in den Anfängen der Weimarer Republik. Möglichkeiten und Grenzen ihrer Zusammenarbeit*, Lübeck and Hamburg 1969

Muckermann, F., *Im Kampf zwischen zwei Epochen. Lebenserinnerungen*, edited with an introduction by Nikolaus Junk, Mainz 1973

Müller, H., *Katholische Kirche und Nationalsozialismus. Dokumente 1930-1935*, Munich 1963

—, 'Der deutsche Katholizismus 1918/1919', *Geschichte in Wissenschaft und Unterricht* 17, 1966, 521-36

Mulert, H., 'Konfession und politische Parteistellung in Deutschland', *Zeitschrift für Politik* 21, 1932, 334-45

Murtorinne, E., *Erzbischof Eidem zum Deutschen Kirchenkampf 1933-1934*, Helsinki 1968

Der Nationalsozialismus und die deutschen Kaholiken, published by the Zentralstelle des Volksvereins für das Katholische Deutschland, München-Gladbach 1931

Neuhäusler, J., *Kreuz und Hakenkreuz. Der Kampf des Nationalsozialismus gegen die katholische Kirche und der kirchliche Widerstand*, Munich ²1946

Neumann, J., 'Zum Entwurf einer *Lex Fundamentalis Ecclesiae*. Gesetz-technische Anmerkungen', in M.Seckler et al., *Begegnung. Beiträge zu einer Hermeneutik des theologischen Gesprächs*, Graz, Vienna and Cologne 1971, 369-87

—, *Das Kirchenrecht – Chance und Versuchung*, Graz, Vienna and Cologne 1972

Neumann, P., *Die Jungreformatorische Bewegung*, Göttingen 1971

Neundörfer, K, 'Die Kirchenpolitik des italienischen Faschismus', *Hochland* 23 II, 1926, 369-71

Nicolaisen, C., 'Die Stellung der Deutschen Christen zum Alten Testament', in *Zur Geschichte des Kirchenkampfes* II, 197-220

Niemöller, M., *Vom U-Boot zur Kanzel*, Berlin 1934
Niemöller, W. *Bekennende Kirche im Westfalen*, Bielefeld 1952
—, 'Karl Barth's Mitwirkung im deutschen Kirchenkampf' (1954), in id., *Wort und Tat im Kirchenkampf*, Munich 1969, 59-79
—, *Die Evangelische Kirche im Dritten Reich. Handbuch des Kirchenkampfes*, Bielefeld 1956
— (ed.), *Texte zur Geschichte des Pfarrernotbundes*, Berlin 1958
—, 'Vor fünfundzwanzig Jahren (1933)' (1958), in id., *Wort und Tat im Kirchenkampf*, Munich 1969, 59-79
—, *Der Pfarrernotbund. Geschichte einer kämpfenden Bruderschaft*, Hamburg 1973
Niesel, W. (ed.), *Um Verkündigung und Ordnung der Kirche. Die Bekenntnissynoden der evangelischen Kirche der altpreussischen Union 1934-1943*, Bielefeld 1949
—, 'Kirche unter dem Wort. Die Entstehung und Entwicklung der Bekennenden Kirche der altpreussischen Union', in *Freispruch und Freiheit. Theologische Aufsätze für Walter Kreck*, Munich 1973, 348-62
Nötges, J., *Katholizismus und Kommunismus*, Cologne 1931
—, *Nationalsozialismus und Katholizismus*, Cologne 1931
Nolte, E., *Der Faschismus in seiner Epoche. Die Action française. Der italienische Faschismus. Der Nationalsozialismus*, Munich 1963
—, 'Eine frühe Quelle zu Hitlers Antisemitismus', *Historische Zeitschrift* 192, 1961, 584-606
Norden, G. van, *Kirche in der Krise. Die Stellung der evangelischen Kirche zum nationalsozialistischen Staat im Jahre 1933*, Düsseldorf 1963

Opitz, G., *Der Christlich-soziale Volksdienst. Versuch einer protestantischen Partei in der Weimarer Republik*, Düsseldorf 1969

Papen, F. von, *Der 12 November 1933 und die deutschen Katholiken*, Reich und Kirche 3, Münster 1934
Patemann, P., 'Der deutsche Episkopat und das preussische Wahlrechtsprobe, 1917-18', *Vierteljahrshefte für Zeitgeschichte* 13, 1965, 345-71
Pertiet, M., *Das Ringen um Wesen und Auftrag der Kirche in der nationalsozialistischen Zeit*, Göttingen 1968
Phelps, R.H., 'Before Hitler Came: Thule Society and Germanen Order', *The Journal of Modern History* 35, 1963
—, 'Hitler als Parteiredner im Jahre 1920', *Vierteljahrshefte für Zeitgeschichte* 11, 1963, 274-330
—, 'Hitlers grundlegende Rede über den Antisemitismus', *Vierteljahrshefte für Zeitgeschichte* 16, 1968, 390-420
Piechowski, P., *Proletarischer Glaube. Die religiöse Gedankenwelt der organisierten deutschen Arbeiterschaft nach sozialistischen und kommunistischen Selbstzeugnissen*, Berlin 1928
Pieper, J., *Noch wusste es niemand. Autobiographische Aufzeichnungen 1904-1943*, Munich 1976
Plewnia, M., *Auf dem Weg zu Hitler. Der völkische Publizist Dietrich Eckart*, Bremen 1970
Plum, G., *Gesellschaftsstruktur und politisches Bewusstsein in einer katholischen Region 1928-1933. Untersuchung am Beispiel des Regierungsbezirks Aachen*, Stuttgart 1972
Prater, G. (ed.), *Kämpfer wider Willen., Erinnerungen des Landesbischofs von Sachsen D. Hugo Hahn aus dem Kirchenkampf 1933-1945*, Metzingen 1969
Preuss, H., 'Luther und Hitler', *Allgemeine Evangelisch-Lutherische Kirchenzeitung* 55, 1933, 970-3, 994-9
Priebe, H., *Kirchliches Handbuch für die evangelische Gemeinde unter besonderer*

Berücksichtigung der Evangelischen Kirche der altpreussischen Union. Zugleich ein Beitrag zur Kirchenkunde der Gegenwart, Berlin ³1928

Priepke, M., *Die evangelische Jugend im Dritten Reich 1933-1936*, Hanover and Frankfurt 1960

Prokoph, W., 'Die politische Seite des Falles Dehn', *Wissenschaftliche Zeitschrift der Universitäts Halle* XVI, 1967, 249-71

Prophetien wider das Dritte Reich. Aus den Schriften des Dr Fritz Gerlich und des Paters Ingbert Nash, collected by Johannes Steiner, Munich 1946

Rathje, J., *Die Welt des freien Protestantismus. Ein Beitrag zur deutsch-evangelisch Geistesgeschichte. Dargestellt am Leben und Werk von Martin Rade*, Stuttgart 1952

Reese, H.-J., *Bekenntnis und Bekennen. Vom 19.Jahrhundert zum Kirchenkampf der nationalsozialistischen Zeit*, Göttingen 1974

Regensburger, M., and K.Scholder, *30 Jahre Deutschland und die Kirche*, Munich 1963

Regner, F., *Paulus und Jesus im 19.Jahrhundert. Beiträge zur Geschichte des Themas Paulus und Jesus in der neutestamentlichen Theologie von der Aufklärung bis zur Religionsgeschichtlichen Schule*, Protestant theological dissertation, Tübingen 1975 (ms)

Reichmann, E., *Die Flucht in den Hass. Die Ursachen der deutschen Judenkatastrophe*, Frankfurt nd

Reimers, K.F., *Lübeck im Kirchenkampf des Dritten Reiches. Nationalsozialistische Führerprinzip und evangelisch-lutherische Landeskirche vom 1933-1945*, Göttingen 1965

Rendtorff, H., *Das Wort Gottes über das Volk*, Schriftenreihe der Christlich-deutschen Bewegung 1, Küstrin 1931

Repgen, K., *Hitlers Machtergreifung und der deutsche Katholizismus. Versuch einer Bilanz* (1963), Saarbrücken 1967

—, 'Das Ende der Zentrumspartei und die Enstehung des Reichskonkordats', *Militärseelsorge* 2, 1970, 83-122

—, *Historische Klopfsignale für die Gegenwart*, Münster 1974

Riedel, H., *Kampf um die Jugend. Evangelische Jugendarbeit 1933-1945*, Munich 1976

Rieker, K., *Zur Neugestaltung der protestantischen Kirchenverfassung in Deutschland*, Leipzig und Erlangen 1919

Riemer, S., 'Zur Soziologie des Nationalsozialismus', *Die Arbeit* 9, 1932, 101-18

Riesenberger, D., *Die katholische Friedensbewegung in der Weimarer Republik*, Düsseldorf 1976

Rittberg, E.von, *Der preussische Kirchenvertrag von 1931. Seine Entstehung und seine Bedeutung für das Verhältnis von Staat und Kirche in der Weimarer Republik*, Bonn philosophical dissertation 1959, Bonn 1960

Robinson, J.M. (ed.), *The Beginnings of Dialectical Theology*, partial ET of J.Moltmann (ed.), *Die Anfänge der dialektischen Theologie*, Richmond, Va. 1968

Roon, G.van, *Neordnung im Widerstand. Der Kreisauer Kreis innerhalb der deutschen Widerstandsbewegung*, Munich 1967

—, *Protestants Nederland en Duitsland 1933-1941*, Utrecht and Antwerp 1973

Rosenberg, A., *Das Parteiprogramm. Wesen, Grundsätze und Ziele der NSDAP*, Munich (1922) ²⁷1943

—, *Der Mythus des 20.Jahrhunderts*, Munich (1930) ²³,²⁴1934

Rückert, H., *Das Wiedererwachen reformatorischer Frömmigkeit in der Gegenwart. Öffentliche Vorträge der Universität Tübingen Sommersemester 1933. Deutsche Gegenwart und ihre geschichtlichen Wurzeln*, Stuttgart 1933

Rühle, G., *Das Dritte Reich. Dokumentarische Darstellung des Aufbaus der Nation. Das erste Jahr 1933*, Berlin ²1934

699

Rüppel, E.G., *Die Gemeinschaftsbewegung im Dritten Reich. Ein Beitrag zur Geschichte des Kirchenkampfes*, Göttingen 1969

Rürup, R., *Emanzipation und Antisemitismus*, Göttingen 1975

Sandmann, F., *Die Haltung des Vatikans zum Nationalsozialismus im Spiegel des Osservatore Romano von 1929 bis zum Kreigsausbruch*, Mainz philosophical dissertation, Mainz 1965

Sauer, P., *Dokumente über die Verfolgung der jüdischen Bürger in Baden-Württemberg durch das nationalsozialistische Regime 1933-1945*, 1, Stuttgart 1966

Sebottendorff, R.von, *Bevor Hitler kam. Urkundliches aus der Frühzeit der nationalsozialistischen Bewegung*, Munich 1933

Seel, H., 'Die Erneuerung des Berufsbeamtentums', in *Das Recht der nationalen Revolution* 4, Berlin 1933

Senn, W.M., *Halt! Katholizismus und Nationalsozialismus. Meine zweite Rede an den deutschen Katholizismus und – nach Rom*, Franz Eher Verlag, Munich nd [1932]

Shannon P., 'The Code of Canon Law 1918-1967', *Concilium* 8.3, 1967, 26-30

Siegele-Wenschkewitz, L., *Nationalsozialismus und Kirchen. Religionspolitik von Partei und Staat bis 1935*, Düsseldorf 1974

Söhngen, O., *Die erste Phase des Kirchenkampfes (24.Juni bis einschliesslich 2.Juli 1933)*, privately printed 1972

Sontheimer, K., *Antidemokratisches Denken in der Weimarer Republik. Die politischen Ideen des deutschen Nationalismus zwischen 1918 und 1933*, Munich 1968

Spael, W., *Das katholische Deutschland im 20.Jahrhundert. Sein Pionier- und Krisenzeiten 1890-1945*, Würzburg 1964

Schäfer, G., *Die Evangelische Landeskirche in Württemberg unter Nationalsozialismus. Eine Dokumentation zum Kirchenkampf. 1. Um das politische Engagement der Kirche 1932-33; 2. Um eine deutsche Reichskirche 1933; 3. Der Einbruch des Reichsbischofs in die württembergische Landeskirche 1934*, Stuttgart 1972-74

Schafft, H., *Ein Lebenswerk*, ed. W.Kindt, Kassel 1960

Scharf, K., 'Der Pfarrernotbund', in *Bekennende Kirche. Martin Niemöller zum 60. Geburtstag*, Munich 1952, 136-41

—, *Für ein politisches Gewissen der Kirche. Aus Reden und Schriften 1932-1972*, ed. W.Erk, Stuttgart 1972

Schauff, J., *Das Wahlverhalten der deutschen Katholiken im Kaiserreich und in der Weimarer Republik. Untersuchungen aus dem Jahre 1928*, edited with an introduction by R.Morsey, Mainz 1975

Schellenberger, B., *Katholische Jugend und Drittes Reich. Eine Geschichte des Katholischen Jungmännerverbandes 1933-1939 unter besonderer Berücksichtigung der Rheinprovinz*, Mainz 1975

Hans Schemm spricht. Seine Reden und sein Werk, ed. G.Kahl-Furtmann, Bayreuth 1935

Schempp, P., 'Randglossen zum Barthianismus', *Zwischen den Zeiten* 6, 1928, 529-39

Schian, M., *Ecclesiam habemus. Ein Beitrag zur Auseinandersetzung zwischen Karl Barth und Otto Dibelius*, Berlin 1931

Schian, M., et al (ed.), *Die evangelische Kirche der Neuzeit in Deutschland und in den benachbarten Gebieten deutscher Sprache, besonders in der Schweiz und in Österreich*, Wiesbaden 1930

Schieder, T.H., *Rauschnings Gespräche mit Hitler als Geschichtsquelle*, Rheinland-Westfälische Akademie der Wissenschaften, Vorträge G 178, Opladen 1972

Schirach, B. von, *Ich glaubte an Hitler*, Hamburg 1967

Schirmacher, H., *Männer in der Kirche. Die evangelische Männerdienst-Bewegung*, Berlin 1931

Schjørring, J.H., 'Moralische Aufrüstung und westeuropäische Politik bis 1945', in *Zeitschrift für Kirchengeschichte* 87, 1976, 65-100

700

Schmaus, M., *Begegnungen zwischen katholischem Christentum und national-sozialistischer Weltanschauung*, Reich und Kirche 1, Münster 1933

Schmid, H., *Apokalyptisches Wetterleuchten. Ein Beitrag der Evangelischen Kirche zum Kampf im Dritten Reich*, Munich 1947

Schmidlin, J., *Papstgeschichte der neuesten Zeit* 3, *Pius X. und Benedikt XV. (1903-1922)*; 4. *Pius XI (1922-1939)*, Munich 1936/39

Schmidt, J., 'Studien zur Vorgeschichte des Pfarrernotbundes', *Zeitschrift für Kirchengeschichte* 79, 1968, 43-67

—, *Martin Niemöller im Kirchenkampf*, Hamburg 1971

Schmidt, K.D. (ed.), *Die Bekenntnisse und grundsätzlichen Äusserungen zur Kirchenfrage des Jahres 1933*, Göttingen 1934

—, 'Eine folgenreiche Episode. Der Staatskommissar für die Kirche in Mecklenburg', *Evangelische Theologie* 22, 1962, 379-92

Schmidtchen, G., *Protestanten und Katholiken. Soziologische Analyse konfesioneller Kultur*, Bern and Munich 1973

Schneider, B (ed.), *Die Briefe Pius' XII an die deutschen Bischöfe 1939-1944*, Mainz 1966

Schneider-Flume, G., *Die politische Theologie Emanuel Hirschs 1918-1933*, Bern and Frankfurt 1971

Schoen, P., *Das neue Verfassungsrecht der evangelischen Landeskirchen in Preussen*, Berlin 1929

Schoenberner, G (ed.), *Wir haben es gesehen. Augenzeugenberichte über Terror und Judenverfolgung im Dritten Reich*, Hamburg 1962

Scholder, K., 'Ideologie und Politik', in *Aus Politik und Zeitgeschichte, Beilage zur Wochenzeitung Das Parlament* 1962, 377-82

—, 'Neuere deutsche Geschichte und protestantische Theologie', *Evangelische Theologie* 23, 1963, ⁵1936

—, 'Die evangelische Kirche und das Jahr 1933', *Geschichte in Wissenschaft und Unterricht*, 1965, 700-14

—, 'Die evangelische Kirche in der Sicht der nationalsozialistischen Führung bis zum Kriegsausbruch', *Vierteljahrshefte für Zeitgeschichte* 16, 1968, 15-35

—, '1000 Jahre Württembergische Landessynode', in *Verhandlungen der 7. Württembergischer Landesynode*, Stuttgart 1969, 849-56

—, 'Die Kapitulation der evangelischen Kirche vor dem nationalsozialistischen Staat', *Zeitschrift für Kirchengeschichte* 81, 1970, 183-206

—, 'Paulus und die Aufklärung', in G.C.Berkouwer and H.A.Oberman (eds.), *De dertiende apostel en het elfde gebod. Paulus in de loop der eeuwen*, Kampen 1971, 124-34

—, 'Baden im Kirchenkampf des Dritten Reiches. Aspekte und Fragen', *Oberrheinische Studien* 2, ed. A.Schäfer, Karlsruhe 1973, 223-41

Schreiber, G., *Zwischen Demokratie und Diktatur. Persönliche Erinnerungen an die Politik und Kultur des Reiches (1919-1944)*, Münster 1949

—, 'Deutsche Kirchenpolitik nach dem ersten Weltkrieg. Gestalten und Geschehnisse der Novemberrevolution 1918 und der Weimarer Zeit', *Historisches Jahrbuch der Görresgesellschaft* 71, 1951, 296-333

Schreiner, H., *Die deutsch-evangelischen Einheitsbestrebungen am Beginn des 19.Jahrhunderts bis zur Gegenwart*, Berlin 1919

Schubert, H. von, *Unsere religiös-kirchliche Lage in ihrem geschichtlichen Zusammenhänge*, Tübingen 1920

Schutte, H.W., *Lagarde und Fichte. Die verborgenen spekulativen Voraussetzungen des Christentumsverständnisses Paul de Lagardes*, Gütersloh 1965

Schulz, G., *Zwischen Demokratie und Diktatur. Verfassungspolitik und Reichsreform in der Weimarer Republik. 1. Die Periode der Konsolidierung und der Revision des Bismarckschen Reichsaufbaus 1919-1930*, Berlin 1963

—, *Aufstieg des Nationalsozialismus. Krise und Revolution in Deutschland*, Frankfurt, Berlin and Vienna 1975

Schwaiger, G., *Geschichte der Päpste. Von den Anfängen bis zur Gegenwart*, Munich 1964

Schweitzer, C., *Das religiöse Deutschland der Gegenwart*, two vols., Berlin 1928/29

Schwengel, G., 'Wirkung der *Theologischen Existenz heute* in einem Pfarrhaus auf dem Lande', in *Antwort. Karl Barth zum 70.Geburtstag*, Zurich 1956

Speer, A., *Inside the Third Reich*, London and New York 1970

Stählin, W., *Die völkische Bewegung und unsere Verantwortung*, Buchverlag des Bundes Deutscher Jugendvereine, Solstedt nd [1924]

—, *Via Vitae. Lebenserinnerungen*, Kassel 1968

Stapel, W., 'Volk und Volkstum', in *Die neue Front*, ed. A.Moeller van den Bruck, H.von Geichen and H.Boehm, Berlin 1922

—, *Sechs Kapitel über Christentum und Nationalsozialismus*, Hamburg 51931

—, *Der christliche Staatsmann. Eine Theologie des Nationalismus*, Hamburg 1932

—, *Die Kirche Christi und der Staat Hitlers*, Hamburg 1933

—, *Volkskirche oder Sekte?*, Hamburg 1934

Stark, J., *Nationalsozialismus und katholische Kirche – mit einer Antwort auf Kundgebungen deutscher Bischöfe*, Munich (1931), 31931

Stasiewski, B., *Akten deutscher Bischöfe über die Lage der Kirche 1933-1945*, I, *1933-1934*, Mainz 1968

Statistik des Deutschen Reiches, NF 257, 335, Berlin 1913, 1925

Stegemann, J., 'Um Demokratie und Republik. Zur Diskussion im deutschen Katholizismus der Weimarer Zeit', *Jahrbuch des Instituts für Christliche Sozialwissenschaft* 10, 1969, 101-27

Steiger, A., *Der neudeutsche Heide im Kampf gegen Christen und Juden*, Verlag der Germania, Berlin 1924

Stoll, G.E., *Die evangelische Zeitschriftenpresse im Jahre 1933*, Witten 1963

Strathmann, H., *Nationalsozialistische Weltanschauung?*, Volksdienstverlag Nürnberg nd [1931], second enlarged edition 1932

Stutz, U., *Der Geist des* Codex iuris canonici, Stuttgart 1918

—, *Konkordat und Codex*, Sitzungsberichte der preussischen Akademie der Wissenschaften, Philosophisch-historische Klasse, Berlin 1930

Tagebuch eines Grossstadtpfarrers, see Jacobi, G.

Das Tagebuch im Spiegel der Presse. Pressestimmen zum Tagebuch eines Grosstandtpfarrers, collected and edited by Furche Verlag, Berlin 1930

Thadden, R.von, *Auf verlorenem Posten? Ein Laie erlebt den evangelichen Kirchenkampf in Hitlerdeutschland*, Tübingen 1948

Themel, K., *Der religiöse Gehalt der völkischen Bewegung und ihre Stellung zur Kirche*, Berlin 1926

Thomme, F. and E.Rolffs (ed.), *Revolution und Kirche. Zur Neuordnung des Kirchenwesens im deutschen Volksstaat*, Berlin 1919

Thimme, L.(ed.), *Im Kampf um die Kirche. Versuch einer Lösung der Spannungen zwischen Kirche, Theologie und Gemeinschaft*, Gotha 1930

Thyssen, K.-W., *Begegnung und Verantwortung. Der Weg der Theologie Friedrich Gogartens von den Anfängen bis zum Zweiten Weltkrieg*, Tübingen 1970

Tilgner, W., *Volksnomostheologie und Schöpfungsglaube. Ein Beitrag zur Geschichte des Kirchenkampfes*, Göttingen 1966

Tillich, P., *Gesammelte Werke*, 2. *Christentum und soziale Gestaltung. Frühe Schriften zum religiosen Sozialismus*; 7. *Der Protestantismus als kritisches und gestaltendes Prinzip*, Schriften zur Theologie I, Stuttgart 1958/66

702

Tischleder, P., *Der katholische Klerus und der deutsche Gegenwartsstaat*, Freiburg im Breisgau 1928

Trippen, N., *Das Domkapitel und die Erzbischofswählen in Köln 1821-1929*, Cologne and Vienna 1972

Troeltsch, E., *Spektator-Briefe. Aufsätze über die deutsche Revolution und die Weltpolitik 1918/22*, Tübingen 1924

Troschke, P., *Evangelische Kirchenstatistik Deutschlands* I-III, Berlin 1930/32

Trossmann, K., *Hitler und Rom*, Nuremberg 1931

Tschirschky, F.G., *Erinnerungen eines Hochverräters*, Stuttgart 1972

Tügel, F., *Unmögliche Existenz! Ein Wort wider Karl Barth*, Hamburg 1933

—, *Mein Weg 1888-1946. Erinnerungen eines Hamburger Bischofs*, ed. C.Nicolaisen, Hamburg 1972

Tyrell, A., *Führer befiehl...Selbstzeugnisse aus der 'Kampfzeit' der NSDAP. Dokumentation und Analyse*, Düsseldorf 1969

Ulmenried, W., *Hossenfelder*, Die Reihe der Deutschen Führer 6, Berlin 1933

Verhandlungen der verfassungsgebenden Deutschen Nationalversammlung 328, 329, 336, Berlin [1920]

Verhandlungen des (1.) Deutschen Evangelischen Kirchentages 1919, published by the Deutscher Evangelischer Kirchenausschuss, Berlin nd [1920]

Verhandlungen des (2.) Deutschen Evangelischen Kirchentages 1921. Stuttgart 11-15 September 1921, Berlin nd [1922]

Verhandlungen des zweiten Deutschen Evangelischen Kirchentages 1927, Königsberg im Preussen 7-21 Juni 1927, Berlin-Steglitz nd [1928]

Vogelsang, T., 'Hitlers Brief an Reichenau von 4. Dezember 1932', *Vierteljahrshefte für Zeitgeschichte* 7, 1959, 429-37

—, *Reichswehr, Staat und NSDAP. Beiträge zur deutschen Geschichte 1930-1932*, Stuttgart 1962

—, 'Zu den Anfängen der Verfolgung im Dritten Reich (Februar-April 1933)', in *Gutachten des Instituts für Zeitgeschichte* II, Stuttgart 1966

Volk, L., 'Päpstliche Laudatio auf Hitler', *Stimmen der Zeit* 173, 1963/4, 221-9

—, 'Zur Kundgebung des deutschen Episkopats vom 28. Marz 1933', *Stimmen der Zeit* 173, 1963/64, 431-56

—, *Der bayerische Episkopat und der Nationalsozialismus 1930-1934*, Mainz [2]1966

—, 'Kardinal Faulhabers Stellung zur Weimarer Republik und zum NS Staat', *Stimmen der Zeit* 177, 1966, 173-95

—, 'Die Fuldaer Bischofskonferenz von Hitlers Machtergreifung bis zur Enzyklika "Mit brennender Sorge"', *Stimmen der Zeit* 183, 1969, 10-31

—, *Kirchliche Akten über die Reichskonkordatsverhandlungen 1933*, Mainz 1969

—, *Das Reichskonkordat vom 20.Juli 1933. Von den Ansätzen in der Weimarer Republik bis zur Ratifizierung am 10.September 1933*, Mainz 1972

— (ed.), *Akten Kardinal Michael von Faulhabers 1917-1945*, I, Mainz 1975

Vollmer, A., *Die Neuwerkbewegung 1919-1935. Ein Beitrag zur Geschichte der Jugendbewegung, des religiösen Sozialismus und der Arbeiterbildung*, Stuttgart 1973

Vorländer, H., *Kirchenkampf in Elberfeld 1933-1945. Ein kritischer Beitrag zur Erforschung des Kirchenkampfes in Deutschland*, Göttingen 1968

—, *Aufbruch und Krise. Ein Beitrag zur Geschichte der deutschen Reformierten vor dem Kirchenkampf*, Neukirchen 1974

Weber, W. *Die deutschen Konkordate und Kirchenverträge der Gegenwart*, Göttingen 1962

Weinzierl-Fischer, E. *Die österreichischen Konkordate von 1855 und 1933*, Munich 1960

703

Wendland, H.-W., 'Sozialismus und Nationalismus. Fragen zur politischen Ethik der Gegenwart', *Neue Kirchliche Zeitschrift* 42, 1931

Wieneke, F., *Die Glaubensbewegung Deutsche Christen*, Schriftenreihe der Deutschen Christen No.2, Soldin ⁵1933

Wild, A., *Hitler und das Christentum*, Augsburg 1931

Wilhelmi, H., *Die Hamburger Kirche in der nationalsozialistischen Zeit, 1933-1945*, Göttingen 1968

Witte, K., 'Deutschtum und Christentum', in *Das religiöse Deutschland der Gegenwart* 1, Berlin 1928, 124-37

Witte, K., 'Der Tannenbergbund', in W.Künneth and H.Schreiner, *Die Nation vor Gott*, Berlin ³1934, 416-63

Wolf, E., 'Vom Problem des Gewissens in reformatorischer Sicht' (1942), in id., *Peregrinatio. Studien zur reformatorischen Theologie und zum Kirchenproblem*, Munich ²1962, 81-112

—, *Barmen. Kirche zwischen Versuchung und Gnade*, Munich (1957) ²1970

—, *Die evangelischen Kirchen und der Staat im Dritten Reich*, Zurich 1963

Wolff, W., *Die Verfassung der Evangelischen Kirche der Altpreussischen Union*, Berlin 1925

Wright, J.R.., 'Above Parties.' *The Political Attitudes of the German Protestant Church Leadership 1918-1933*, Oxford 1974. There is a revised and expanded German version, *'Über den Parteien.' Die politische Haltung der evangelischen Kirchenführer 1918-1933*, Göttingen 1977

Wünsch, G. (ed.), *Reich Gottes, Marxismus, Nationalsozialismus, Ein Bekenntnis religiöser Sozialisten*, Tübingen 1931

—, *Evangelische Ethik des Politischen*, Tübingen 1936

Wurm, T., *Erinnerungen aus meinem Leben*, Stuttgart 1953

Zahn-Harnack, A.von, *Adolf von Harnack*, Berlin ²1951

Zeiger, I., 'Das Reichskonkordat', *Stimmen der Zeit* 126, 1933/34, 1-7

Zimmermann, O., 'Revolutionäre Trennung von Kirche und Staat', *Stimmen der Zeit* 96, 1919, 345-59

Zimmermann, W.D. (ed.), *I Knew Dietrich Bonhoeffer*, London and New York 1966

Zipfel, F., *Kirchenkampf in Deutschland. Religionsverfolgung und Selbstbehauptung der Kirche in der nationalsozialistischen Zeit*, Berlin 1965

Zmarzlik, H.G., 'Der Sozialdarwinismus in Deutschland als geschichtliches Problem' (1962), in id., *Wieviel Zukunft hat unsere Vergangenheit?*, Munich 1970, 56-85

—, 'Der Antisemitismus im Kaiserreich von 1871' (1962), in id., *Wieviel Zukunft hat unsere Vergangenheit?*, 22-50

Zoellner, W., *Die Ökumenische Arbeit des deutschen Evangelischen Kirchenausschusses und die Kriegsschuldfrage*, Berlin 1931

—, *Die Kirche der Geschichte und die Kirche des Glaubens. Beiträge zum Neubau der Kirche*, Berlin 1933

Zscharnack, L., *Trennung von Staat und Kirche*, Volksschriften zum Aufbau, 1, Berlin 1919

Index of Persons

Adam, Karl, 427f., 430
Adenauer, Konrad, 220
Adler, Bruno, 360, 371, 621
Algermissen, Konrad, 252
Althaus, Paul, 100f, 103–5, 107, 111–13, 118f., 127, 136, 138, 143, 169f., 173, 199, 209, 270, 296, 347, 354, 418, 423–5, 485, 606, 615
Ammundsen, Valdemar, 486
Andersen, Friedrich, 117, 605
Arendsee, Fritz, 554
Aretin, Erwein von, 413
Arndt, Ernst Moritz, 100
Aselmann, Hans, 285, 338f., 477f., 636
Asmussen, Hants, 184–7, 295f., 312, 438
Aubin, Gustav, 174
August Wilhelm, Prince of Prussia, 199
Augustin, Aurelius 428

Bachem, Karl, 398, 628
Backhaus, Erich, 366f.
Bähr, D., 464f.
Bartels, Adolf, 117
Barth, Heinrich, 48
Barth, Karl, 40–51, 102, 105f., 111, 117, 121–6, 141, 143, 171f., 175–7, 185f., 220f., 233f., 295, 317, 321f., 423, 437–440, 448, 454, 457f., 494, 532–5, 537–541, 552–6, 580–2, 591f., 606f., 657f., 675
Baumgarten, Otto, 50, 109, 115f., 173
Baumgartner, Eugen, 155, 613
Becker, Carl Heinrich, 64, 66, 68, 70
Beckmann, Joachim, 455, 532f.
Bell, George, 486
Benedict XV., Pope, 12, 13, 54f., 57, 68, 585f.

Bergen, Diego von, 60, 66, 148f., 151, 242f., 247, 398, 499, 517
Bergmann, Ernst, 526
Bernewitz, Alexander, 331, 477
Berning, Wilhelm, 273, 307, 392f., 406, 408, 495, 504
Bertram, Adolf, 63f., 67, 133, 244, 251–3, 270f., 273, 382, 390f., 393, 402, 406, 409–11, 496–9, 504–6, 508, 514
Bethge, Eberhard, 456, 634
Bethmann Hollweg, Theobald von, 122
Beye, Wilhelm, 477, 666
Beyer, Hans, 187
Beyer, Hermann Wolfgang, 317, 339f., 417, 568, 573, 576, 579
Bierschwale, Alfred, 213, 287, 467, 546
Birnbaum, Walter, 521, 672, 676
Bismarck, Otto von, 56, 78, 122, 381
Bodelschwingh, Friedrich von, 325f., 328–33, 335, 337f., 340–50, 352–5, 363f., 366, 370f., 375, 382, 390, 393, 420, 422, 435, 454–6, 458f., 482f., 488, 553, 555, 578, 643, 680
Boelitz, Otto, 66
Bohm, Walter, 299–301
Bolz, Eugen, 398
Bonhoeffer, Dietrich, 188, 257, 266, 275–7, 341f., 440, 443f., 456, 458, 480–2, 486f., 491f., 535, 666, 674
Bonsen, Rudolf zur, 498
Bormann, Martin, 95f., 98, 450, 524
Bornewasser, Franz Rudolf, 405
Bornkamm, Heinrich, 199, 317, 417, 564
Bracher, Karl Dietrich, 244
Brauer, Max, 187
Braun, Otto, 71, 92
Breucker, Wilhelm, 92
Bronisch-Holtze, Ernst, 342

Brüning, Heinrich, 148, 150–6, 238f.,
    244–6, 248, 389f., 612, 651
Brunner, Emil, 48f.
Bry, C. C., 596f.
Buch, Walter, 96, 189
Buchberger, Michael, 157, 267, 273, 412
Buchmann, Frank, 530
Buchwieser, Ferdinand, 496
Buck, Hermann, 182
Bülow, Bernard von, 408, 487
Bückle, Josef, 314
Bultmann, Rudolf, 40, 48, 438, 440
Bunsen, Christian Karl Josias, 55
Burghart, Georg, 209f.
Buttmann, Rudolf, 94, 138, 191f., 402–4,
    406–9, 491, 495, 502f., 505, 508, 514f.,
    565f., 603, 650

Cadman, Parkes, 263
Chamberlain, Houston Stewart, 83, 90,
    117, 190, 600
Christiansen, Nikolaus, 284, 464
Class, Heinrich, 78
Coch, Friedrich, 342, 377, 477, 492, 537,
    564, 579
Conrad, Walter, 369, 402, 491, 544, 565
Cordier, Leopold, 176, 574

Dannenmann, Arnold, 576
Darré, Richard Walther, 299, 301
Dauser, Hans, 498
Dehn, Günther, 40, 48, 171–7, 341, 431,
    539, 555, 616, 675
Dessmann, Adolf, 17, 50
Delbrück, Richard, 62f., 67f., 596
Detten, Hermann, 498
Deuerlein, Ernst, 132, 614
Dibelius, Martin, 173
Dibelius, Otto, 10, 28, 33–5, 123, 125f.,
    209, 215, 226, 232–4, 236, 263, 268f.,
    275, 289f., 292, 321, 330f., 351, 359f.,
    448, 455, 462, 476, 555, 626, 663
Diehl, Wilhelm, 464, 477
Diels, Rudolf, 257, 262, 444, 631
Diem, Hermann, 48
Diestel, Max, 467
Dietrich, Ernst-Ludwig, 476, 521, 646
Dingfelder, Johannes, 84
Dinter, Artur, 76f., 83f., 89f., 92, 94–8,
    108, 115f., 119, 134f., 136, 164, 190–2,
    451, 519, 597f., 601–3
Dirks, Walter, 132, 243
Disraeli, Benjamin, 85

Dithmar, Theodor, 464
Doehring, Bruno, 107, 109, 199
Dörries, Hermann, 175f.
Dohnanyi, Hans von, 257
Drexler, Anton, 84
Dryander, Ernst von, 6, 122, 234
Duncan-Jones, A. S., 368

Ebert, Friedrich, 57, 105
Eckhart, Dietrich, 76f., 83, 89–91, 97,
    190, 597f., 601
Eckert, Erwin, 139, 170, 196, 615, 619
Eckert, Karl, 203, 205, 287, 358, 370,
    467, 472, 621
Eggersdorfer, France, 388, 390
Eidem, Erling, 475, 487
Eitel Friedrich, Prince of Prussia, 199
Elert, Werner, 485
Eltz-Rübenach, Paul von, 241
Erzberger, Matthias, 14f., 55, 57, 60f.,
    65, 122, 585f.
Eschweiler, Karl, 425–8, 430
Esser, Hermann, 94, 97, 246, 506

Fahrenhorst, Wilhelm, 109
Fassbender, Martin, 17
Faulhaber, Michael von, 3, 11, 14, 239,
    242f., 249, 251f., 259, 271f., 390f.,
    396f., 402, 406, 412, 504, 506f., 514,
    518, 624
Feder, Gottfried, 94, 141, 190
Fezer, Karl, 317–20, 323, 326, 328, 330,
    339, 344, 350, 353–5, 362, 373f., 377,
    416, 420, 459f., 463f., 475, 478, 485–7
    492, 528–30, 562–4
Fichte, Johann Gottlieb, 75, 82, 98, 100
    102, 104, 124, 190, 553
Fink, 476
Fischer, Pastor, 521
Fleisch, Paul, 283
Flor, Wilhelm, 578f.
Föhr, Ernst, 72, 149f., 154f., 388, 391
Forell, Birger, 487
Fort, Gertrud von le, 46
Fraenkel, Ernst, 308
Freisler, Roland, 256
Freitag, Albert, 313, 335, 338, 360, 467,
    621
Freitag, Kurt, 213
Frick, Robert, 296
Frick, Wilhelm, 94, 127, 189f., 240, 246f
    282, 288, 301, 304, 308, 345, 368f.,

372–4, 377f., 402, 461, 470, 526, 544, 625, 629f., 635
Friedrich, Hans Eberhard, 135
Friedrich II, King of Prussia, 55, 122
Friedrich Wilhelm III, King of Prussia, 55
Fritsch, Theodor, 76f., 79, 83, 85, 11f., 190, 598, 600
Fritz, Carl, 72, 154f.
Frühwirth, Andreas, 54
Fürle, Günther, 358, 360

Galen, Augustin, 19
Galen, Clemens August Graf., 239
Gasparri, Pietro, 54, 57, 59, 61, 68f., 72
Geiger, Theodor, 129f.
Geismar, Eduard, 103
Geist, Raymond H., 630
Gensichen, Gerhard, 205
Gerlich, Fritz, 134f.
Gerstein, Kurt, 577
Gerstenhauer, Max Robert, 75, 189
Geyer, Christian, 116
Giese, Adolf, 29
Gobineau, Joseph Arthur Graf, 73, 190
Goebbels, Joseph, 131, 200, 224f., 233, 246, 251, 261, 264f., 288, 370, 444, 603, 632
Göring, Hermann, 151, 212, 219f., 222, 238, 240, 254, 261, 269, 288, 307, 314, 357, 360f., 391, 470, 603, 624, 626
Görnandt, Werner, 226, 467
Goeters, Wilhelm, 296, 318, 323, 358
Goethe, Johann Wolfgang, 452
Gogarten, Friedrich 45–50, 100, 322, 418, 423–30, 439f., 564, 592, 656
Gollwitzer, Helmut, 435
Goltz, Graf Rüdiger von der, 523
Grabowsky, Adolf, 129f.
Granzow, Walter, 299–301
Graue, Dietrich, 109, 116
Greifenstein, Hans, 560
Grell, Johannes, 213, 467f.
Grevemeyer, Max, 358
Grimme, Adolf, 174, 177
Gröber, Conrad, 155, 239, 251, 271, 273, 384, 390–5, 398–402, 408, 410, 493, 495–8, 502, 504f., 508, 513–18, 575
Groener, Wilhelm, 178
Grossmann, Otto, 370
Gründler, Georg, 475
Grundmann, Walter, 571

Guardini, Romano, 162

Haack, Hans Georg, 35
Hackelsberger, Albert, 400
Haenchen, Ernst, 564
Haenisch, Konrad, 15–17, 59, 586
Haeuser, Phillip, 135
Hahn, Hugo, 342, 438, 536f, 557
Hahn, Traugott 342
Harder, Günther, 467
Harnack, Adolf von, 49f., 105, 117, 215, 229
Harnisch, Wilhelm, 670
Harrer, Karl, 84
Hartmann, Felix von, 59
Hase, Wilibald, 193
Hasselmann, Karl, 184, 295f.
Hauck, Jacobus von, 506
Hauck, Albert, 23
Hauer, Jakob Wilhelm, 428, 451–3, 455, 488, 526, 548
Heckel, Johannes, 311, 324, 331, 335, 373–8, 460, 475, 542, 568, 676
Heckel, Theodor, 485f.
Hegel, Georg Wilhelm Friedrich, 452
Heidenreich, Gustav, 529, 662
Heider, Otto, 372
Heim, Karl, 322, 418, 458
Heimann, Eduard, 139
Heinemann, Gustav W., 564
Heintze, Traugott von, 283
Helfferich, Karl, 41
Helldorf, Wolf Heinrich Graf, 288
Hempel, Johannes, 317
Henle, Franz Anton von, 3
Henrici, Ernst, 76
Henriod, Henri-Louis, 260
Herder, Johann Gottfried von, 100
Hermann, Rudolf, 467
Herrmann, Wilhelm, 37f., 44, 99, 103, 106, 124, 432
Hertling, Georg von, 59
Hess, Rudolf, 98, 223, 347, 450, 497, 525–7
Hessberger, Maria, 391
Hesse, Hermann Albert, 33, 302, 304f., 311, 328f., 348, 353, 356, 363, 372, 374, 590, 649
Heuss, Theodor, 50
Heuss-Knapp, Elly, 322
Heydrich, Reinhard, 396, 495, 505
Hierl, Konstantin, 621

Hildebrand, Fritz, 478
Hildebrandt, Franz, 480–2, 491, 674f.
Himmler, Heinrich, 98, 396f., 495, 519, 630
Hindenburg, Paul von, 78, 158, 220, 223, 225, 227, 244, 247, 347, 356, 367–9, 371f., 448, 555, 633
Hinderer, August, 358, 607, 609
Hinkel, Hans, 288
Hirsch, Emanuel, 100, 102–5, 113, 119, 127, 136, 141, 143, 169f, 173, 175–7, 199, 270, 317f., 323, 328, 334f., 337, 339, 347, 354, 362, 416–22, 424–6, 430f., 438f., 564, 606, 615
Hitler, Adolf, 49, 65, 67, 74f, 78–81, 84–99, 102, 107–9, 113, 119, 122, 127f., 129–36, 139f., 143f., 146, 150f., 153, 156–61, 164–7, 178, 180f., 184, 189f., 192f., 195, 197–202, 205f., 212f., 219–28, 230f., 237f., 240–6, 248–51, 254f., 257–62, 264, 273, 278f., 281f., 292f., 301, 303f., 306–10, 313, 320, 324, 327, 333–7, 339, 342, 346f., 357, 364–8, 373f., 377–93, 396–406, 417, 427, 441–3, 445–53, 461, 465f, 469f, 491, 453, 497, 499–503, 506f, 509f., 512f., 515f., 518–22, 524–6, 540f., 545f., 548–51, 554f, 560, 565–7, 575–8, 597, 599, 601, 603f., 606, 609, 621, 624f., 632, 662, 679
Hoefler, Konrad, 107–10, 604
Hölderlin, Friedrich, 452
Hoffmann, Adolf, 16f., 19f., 26, 28, 34, 303, 584, 586
Holl, Karl, 40, 106f., 418
Hollje, Ernst August, 315
Hosemann, Johannes, 267, 301f., 304f., 311, 324, 329, 346, 355, 363, 633, 640
Hossenfelder, Joachim, 204–7, 209–14, 216, 222, 231, 285–8, 291, 310, 313–16, 320, 327f., 331, 336–8, 343, 352, 357–60, 362f., 370f., 415f., 443, 448f., 461, 464, 467, 471–3, 475, 479, 489–91, 520, 525, 529f., 545, 547f., 551–5, 557, 559–65, 567–72, 574, 621, 636, 643, 659, 662, 665, 676f.
Hürth, Theodor, 396
Hugenberg, Alfred, 153, 220f., 240, 367, 606, 624
Humboldt, Wilhelm von, 55
Humburg, Paul, 448
Hundt, Ernst, 229, 356–7, 377

Hunzinger, Walter, 139

Ihmels, Ludwig, 235, 263, 371, 477
Immer, Karl, 533
Iwand, Hans Joachim, 467

Jacob, Günter, 455, 482
Jacobi, Gerhard, 121f., 172, 322, 370f., 373, 443f., 453, 455, 467–9, 482, 491f., 535f., 538, 540f., 553f., 678
Jäckel, Eberhard, 81
Jäger, August, 350–65, 367, 369, 371, 373f., 376–9, 405, 443, 445, 448, 452, 459–67, 470–7, 479f., 484f., 488–90, 526, 529, 542, 567f., 573, 579, 646, 662f., 680
Jakubski, Karl, 327f.
Jannasch, Wilhelm, 444
Jeep, Walter, 325
Jenetzky, Konrad, 621
Jensen, Julius, 339
Jirku, Anton, 317
John à Lasco, 534
Joos, Josef, 147, 248, 388, 401
Jüchen, Aurel von, 138

Kaas, Ludwig, 64f., 67, 71f., 146–50, 152–6, 166f., 238, 240–2, 244–50, 253, 306, 381–93, 395, 400–1, 403, 410, 496, 499, 503f., 514–16, 614, 639, 650f.
Kähler, Martin, 319
Kaftan, Julius, 5
Kahl, Wilhelm, 117
Kant, Immanuel, 44, 115, 452
Kapler, Hermann, 30, 120, 178, 210, 228, 246f., 252, 258, 263, 267, 269f., 277f., 282–4, 290, 292–5, 298, 301–5, 307–9, 311, 313, 318, 321, 328, 331, 343, 348f., 352f., 365, 382f., 462, 466, 629, 635, 650
Kappes, Georg, 139
Karnatz, Bernhard, 355, 377, 645
Karow, Emil, 362, 374
Karwehl, Richard, 141f., 555
Katzer, Ernst, 117
Kemnitz, Mathilde von, 91–3, 601
Kerenski, Alexander, 516
Kerrl, Hanns, 255, 288, 603
Kessel, Friedrich, 213, 215, 313, 467, 621
Kinder, Christian, 286, 358, 464, 571
Kirschbaum, Charlotte von, 435f., 675
Kirste, Gustav, 621
Kittel, Gerhard, 679

711

712

Sources of Illustrations

Photographs

Karl Barth Archiv, Basel, 24
Karl Barth Archiv, Basel/Peter Hemann, Basel, 72
Bildarchiv Preußischer Kulturbesitz, Berlin, 44
Bundesarchiv, Koblenz, 1, 7, 11, 16, 17, 18, 21, 27, 28, 29, 30, 32, 33, 34, 42, 46, 47, 48, 67, 88, 89, 90, 92
Evangelische Kirche in Deutschland/Archiv, Berlin, 14, 40, 51, 52, 53, 55, 84, 85
Evangelisch-Lutherischer Oberkirchenrat, Oldenburg, 62
Heinrich Hoffmann, Munich, 4, 5, 8
Landesbildstelle, Berlin, 59, 94
Niedersächsisches Hauptstaatsarchiv, Hanover, 9, 61
Gertrud Röhricht, Berlin, 74
Süddeutscher Verlag/Bilderdienst, Munich, 2, 6, 12, 13, 15, 35, 37, 39, 50, 56, 58, 60, 64, 66, 70, 71, 80, 81, 82, 83, 91, 93
Ullstein Bilderdienst, Berlin, 3, 19, 20, 22, 26, 31, 36, 43, 57, 65, 68, 69

Newspapers and books

Bildbericht für das deutsche Christenvolke, Supplement to *Evangelium im Dritten Reiche*, second week in September 1933, 77, 78
Busch, Eberhard, *Karl Barths Lebenslauf*, Munich ²1976 (Christian Kaiser Verlag), 23
Busch, Eberhard, *Karl Barths Lebenslauf*, Munich ²1976 (Christian Kaiser Verlag/ Peter Walter, Gelterkinder), 63
Christenkreuz und Hakenkreuz, November 1933, 87
Dehn, Günther, *Die alte Zeit, die vorigen Jahre*, Munich 1962 (Christian Kaiser Verlag), 25
Evangelium im Dritten Reich, 6 November 1932, 38
Ibid, 5 February 1933, 41
Ibid, 5 November 1933, 86
Ibid., Picture Supplement, last week in August 1933, 79
Mochalski, Herbert (ed.), *Der Mann in der Brandung*, Frankfurt/Main 1962 (Stimme Verlag), 75
Rühle, Gerd, *Das Dritte Reich, Dokumentarische Darstellung des Aufbaus der Nation. Das erste Jahr 1933*, Berlin ²1934, 45, 49
Schmidt, Jürgen, *Martin Niemöller im Kirchenkampf*, Hamburg 1971 (Leibniz Verlag), 76
Völkischer Beobachter, 22 February 1929, 10

0   100 miles

Kiel◆
Eutin◆
Lübeck◆
Mecklenburg-
Schwerin
Schwerin
Neustrelitz
Aurich◆
Hamburg
Oldenburg◆
Bremen◆
R. Elbe
S
Berlin
R. Ems
R. Oldenburg
Osnabrück
Bückeburg
Hannover◆
Wolfenbüttel
Münster
Detmold
S-L
Hildesheim
Magdeburg▲
Paderborn
Lippe
Brunswick
Dessau
Br.
Anhalt
R. Rhine
Arolsen◆
Kassel
Waldeck
Köln
Eisenach
Dre
Aachen
Thuringia
P
Limburg
Fulda
Greiz
Koblenz
Hessen
Saxo
Wiesbaden
Frankfurt◆
Trier
Mainz
Darmstadt
Birkenfeld◆
Bamburg
Saar-
gebiet
Palatinate
Würzburg
Speyer
Ansbach▲
Karlsruhe
Eichstätt
Regensb
Stuttgart◆
Württemberg
R. Isar
Pass
Rottenburg
Baden
Hohenzollern
Augsburg
Freising
R. Mosel
Freiburg
Munich◆
Bavaria

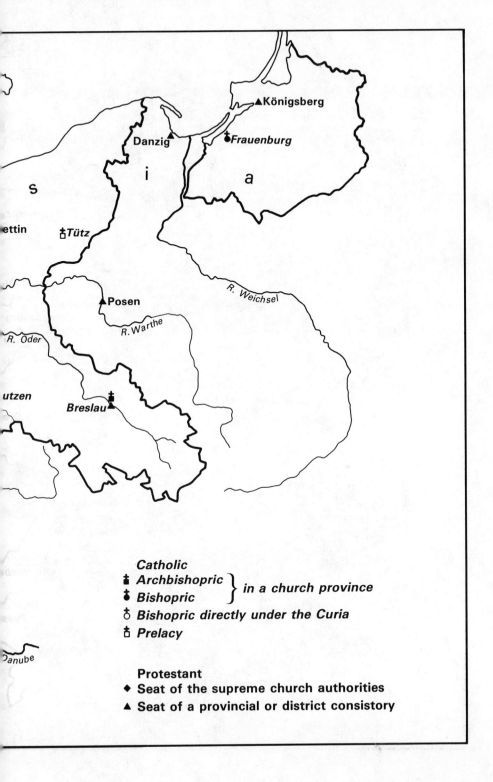

s

ettin

☩Tütz

▲Posen

Danzig ▲

i

▲Königsberg

☩Frauenburg

a

R. Weichsel

R. Warthe

R. Oder

utzen

Breslau ▲

Danube

Catholic
☩ **Archbishopric** ⎫
♙ **Bishopric** ⎬ *in a church province*
☩ **Bishopric directly under the Curia**
☩ **Prelacy**

Protestant
◆ **Seat of the supreme church authorities**
▲ **Seat of a provincial or district consistory**